Ward 1–Precinct 1

City of Boston

List of Residents 20 years of Age and Over

(Non-Citizens Indicated by Asterisk)

(Females Indicated by Dagger) as of January 1, 1943

Unknown

Alpha Editions

This edition published in 2020

ISBN : 9789354028953

Design and Setting By
Alpha Editions
email - alphaedis@gmail.com

Ward 1–Precinct 1

CITY OF BOSTON

LIST OF RESIDENTS
20 YEARS OF AGE AND OVER

(NON-CITIZENS INDICATED BY ASTERISK)
(FEMALES INDICATED BY DAGGER)

AS OF

JANUARY 1, 1943

JOSEPH F. TIMILTY, *Chairman*
FREDERIC E. DOWLING, *Secretary*
WILLIAM A. MOTLEY, JR.
FRANCIS B. McKINNEY
EVERETT R. PROUT

Listing Board.

CITY OF BOSTON PRINTING DEPARTMENT

1

Bennington Street

F	Laskaris Constantina †	11	housewife	25	21 Bennington
G	*Laskaris Leone	11	laborer	32	21 "
O	Schraffa Joseph J	19	U S N	41	here
P	Schraffa Louis E	19	physician	39	"
R	Schraffa Thomasina †	19	housewife	37	"
T	Ferrino Julia †	21	"	29	"
U	Ferrino Peter J	21	physician	29	"
V	*Bailey Elizabeth †	21	housewife	59	"
W	*Bailey Patrick	21	shoemaker	69	"
X	*Massa Antonio	23	physician	55	"
Y	Buccheri Mary †	23	housewife	31	47 Bennington
Z	Buccheri Paul	23	welder	31	47 "

2

B	Conlin Nellie E †	25	housekeeper	76	here
C	Higgins Joseph H	25	laborer	37	"
D	*Whalen Margaret †	25	housekeeper	75	"
E	Becker Ludivine †	25	housewife	52	"
F	McKenna Doris †	25	clerk	30	"
G	McKenna George	25	laborer	32	"
K	Ruggiero Filomena †	29A	housewife	44	"
L	Ruggiero Michael	29A	laborer	44	"
O	Hopkins Israel	35	"	53	"
P	Mennella Charles	35	jeweler	47	"
R	Mennella Edith †	35	housewife	42	"
S	Mennella James	35	laborer	20	"
T	Carney George F	35	U S M C	20	"
U	Carney John J	35	laborer	55	"
V	Carney John J, jr	35	U S A	28	"
W	Carney Margaret A †	35	housewife	54	"
X	Carney Rita M †	35	at home	22	"
Y	Carney William L	35	U S A	24	"
Z	Little Anna †	37	housewife	40	"

3

A	Little John	37	laborer	42	"
B	McGrath Margaret J †	37	housewife	69	"
C	McGrath William W	37	retired	79	"
D	Driscoll Hannah †	37	housewife	65	"
E	Driscoll Michael J	37	clerk	70	"
G	*Rose Adelaide †	41	housewife	63	"
H	Rose George	41	shoemaker	35	"

Bennington Street (Continued)

Letter	FULL NAME	Residence	Occupation	Age	Reported Residence
K	Rose Phoebe †	41	seamstress	32	here
L	Casaletto Joseph	41	musician	50	"
M	Casaletto Mary †	41	housewife	39	"
N	Rose Helen †	41	"	25	"
O	Rose William	41	foreman	24	"
R	LaMonica Concetta †	43	housewife	41	"
S	LaMonica Jean †	43	floorwoman	20	"
T	LaMonica Joseph	43	blacksmith	46	"
U	LaMonica Joseph D	43	U S A	21	"
W	Hickey Edward	45	ropemaker	27	208 Lexington
X	Hickey Mary †	45	housewife	27	342 Saratoga
Y	Gorva Francesco P	45	laborer	50	here
Z	*Gorva Mary †	45	housewife	44	"
4					
B	Matthews Alfred	47	janitor	39	6 Lexington pl
C	Matthews Catherine †	47	housewife	40	6 "
D	*Coetta Margaret †	47	"	48	here
E	Coetta Thomas	47	tanner	23	"
F	Maimone Carmen	47	laborer	20	"
G	Brogna Joseph	49	guard	33	5 Ardee
H	Brogna Rose †	49	housewife	26	5 "
K	Cachalino Pietro	49	laborer	54	here
L	Pizzoli Rocco G	49	blacksmith	42	"
M	Conti Ethel †	49	housewife	23	"
N	Conti Salvatore	49	laborer	25	"
O	Rose Albert	51	chauffeur	42	"
P	Rose Naomi †	51	housewife	41	"
S	Marotta Alfonso	53	baker	55	"
T	Marotta Frank	53	"	21	"
U	*Marotta Vincenza †	53	housewife	49	"
V	Landolfi Domenic	53	contractor	24	Revere
W	Landolfi Mary †	53	housewife	21	"
Y	Taurasi Frank	57	pipefitter	32	here
Z	Taurasi Stella †	57	housewife	30	"
5					
A	Emma Rose †	57	"	37	"
B	Emma Salvatore	57	shoemaker	40	"
C	Tracia Frederick	57	laborer	20	7 Chelsea pl
D	Tracia Mary †	57	housewife	21	221 Webster
E	Wall Elizabeth †	57	housekeeper	46	221 "
F	Minichello Anthony	59	foreman	32	here

5

Bennington Street Continued

G	Minichello Emily †	59	housewife	31	here	
H	Barberi Antonio	59	laborer	55	"	
K	De Benidetto Alfred	59	"	50	"	
L	De Benidetto Josephine †	59	housewife	54	"	
M	Fiantacca Ferdinando	59	cabinetmaker	67	"	
N	Celestra Angela †	59	stitcher	22	"	
O	Celestra Jean †	59	"	20	"	
P	*Papia Josephine †	59	housewife	50	"	
R	Papia Rosario	59	weaver	51	"	
S	Rondino Antonio	59	U S A	55	"	
T	Rondino Benedetto	59	U S N	21	"	
U	Rondino Vincenzo	59	tailor	55	"	
V	*Lunetta Anna †	61	housewife	52	"	
W	De Gregorio Antonette †	61	tailor	32	"	
X	De Gregorio Carmella †	61	housewife	58	"	
Y	De Gregorio Fiore A	61	U S A	21	"	
Z	DiCenso Costanza †	61	housewife	34	"	
	6					
A	DiCenso Ercole	61	operator	40	"	
B	*DiCenso Paul	61	retired	80	"	
C	Turco Anthony	67	laborer	47	"	
D	Turco John	67	U S A	20	"	
E	*Turco Mary †	67	housewife	48	"	
F	Turco Evelyn †	67	"	23	"	
G	Turco Rosario	67	engraver	23	"	
K	Pistone Fannie †	69	housewife	21	"	
L	Pistone Rosario	69	pedler	53	"	
M	MacDougal Elizabeth †	69	housewife	51	237 Trenton	
N	MacDougal Walter	69	machinist	20	237 "	
O	Cunha Mary †	71	at home	70	here	
P	*Gorgopulos Bertha †	71	housewife	44	"	
R	Gorgopulos Peter	71	storekeeper	44	"	
S	Gorgopulos Priscilla †	71	saleswoman	21	"	

Border Street

V	*Haddock Agnes †	65	housewife	35	Chelsea	
W	Haddock Walter	65	boilermaker	37	"	
Y	Lindstrom Dorothy †	67	housewife	36	here	
Z	Lindstrom Frederick	67	fisherman	44	"	

7

Border Street Continued

A	*Lindstrom Walter	67	fisherman	31	here
B	Martin Frank	67	machinist	50	"
C	*Martin Rose †	67	housewife	46	"
D	Petrakes Bessie †	67	at home	26	"
E	Petrakes Leo	67	U S A	20	"
F	Petrakes Nicholas	67	machinist	28	"
G	*Petrakes Pauline †	67	housewife	59	"
H	Petrakes Sotero	67	U S A	29	"
K	Manuel Francis	69	"	23	"
L	Leao Albertina †	69	at home	27	"
M	*Leao Docelina †	69	housewife	55	"
N	*Leao Luiz M	69	longshoreman	62	"
O	Leao Orlando A	69	fishcutter	26	"
P	Leao Piedade †	69	operator	23	"
R	Ruivo Maria †	69	"	21	Portugal
S	Remer Bessie †	71	housewife	59	here
T	Remer Edward	71	storekeeper	69	"
U	Rodriguez Anthony	75	guard	25	"
V	Rodriguez Mabel †	75	housewife	24	168 Marion
W	Rodriguez John	75	U S A	24	here
X	Rodriguez Mary †	75	at home	60	"
Y	*Franco John	75	spinner	46	"
Z	Ventresca Anthony	77	electrician	39	"

8

A	Ventresca Beatrice †	77	housewife	32	"
B	Diaz Joseph	77	fireman	56	"
C	Diaz Joseph	77	U S N	21	"
D	*Diaz Josephina †	77	housewife	45	"
E	*Maurici Angelena †	77	"	50	"
F	Maurici Placido	77	laborer	60	"
H	Curto Frank	79	musician	26	"
G	Curto Rosie †	79	proprietor	33	"

9

B	Willis Andrew	rear 148	watchman	46	"

10   Decatur Street

U	White Bernadette M †	20	housewife	31	here
V	White James V	20	rigger	34	"
W	Sbordoni Madeline †	20	housewife	34	"

5

Page	Letter	FULL NAME.	Residence, Jan. 1, 1943.	Occupation.	Supposed Age.	Reported Residence, Jan. 1, 1942. Street and Number.

Decatur Street Continued

	X	Sbordoni Ralph	20	shipfitter	33	here
	Y	Sbordoni Carmella †	20	housewife	63	"
	Z	Sbordoni Joan †	20	stitcher	25	"

11

	A	Sbordoni Joseph	20	laborer	69	"
	B	Sbordoni Nunzio	20	U S A	22	"
	C	Salsi Alfonso	22	laborer	58	"
	D	Saldi Angelina †	22	housewife	50	"
	E	*Materazzo Nunzia †	22	"	59	"
	F	*Materazzo Pasquale	22	laborer	63	"
	G	Greco Esther †	22	housewife	28	"
	H	Greco Joseph	22	carpenter	30	"
	K	Dell Orfano Michael	24	retired	71	"
	L	Dell Orfano Richard	24	eletrician	23	"
	M	Dell Orfano Rose †	24	housewife	26	"
	N	Dell Orfano Anthony	24	electrician	32	"
	O	Dell Orfano Mary †	24	housewife	31	"
	P	Caponigro Vincent	25	painter	25	"
	R	Fernandez Adolfo	25	engineer	26	"
	S	Fernandez Anita †	25	housewife	27	"
	U	Palermo Concetta †	26	"	27	"
	V	Palermo Dominick	26	painter	29	"
	W	*LoConte Filomena †	26	housewife	29	"
	X	LoConte Joseph	26	laborer	30	"
	Y	Rosetti Angelina †	26	housewife	33	"
	Z	Rosetti Stephen	26	laborer	34	"

12

	A	*Vitale Vincenza †	27	housewife	62	31 Decatur
	B	*Tirone Angelina †	27	"	48	here
	C	*Tirone Paul	27	foundryman	58	"
	D	Tirone Teresa †	27	stitcher	22	"
	F	*DiClerico Cesira †	28	housewife	44	"
	G	DiClerico Felice	28	woodcarver	70	"
	H	*DeVito Concetta †	28	housewife	64	"
	K	DeVito Frank	28	laborer	55	"
	L	Coronite Rose †	28	housewife	30	"
	M	*Coronite Samuel	28	tinsmith	44	"
	N	Penta John	29	retired	78	"
	O	Penta Joseph	29	foreman	40	"
	P	Penta Marguerite †	29	factoryhand	28	"
	R	Belt Laura †	29	at home	67	93 London

6

Decatur Street Continued

c	*Rizzo Carmella †	30	housewife	61	here
v	*Rizzo Thomas	30	retired	72	172 Cottage
w	*Amato Fannie †	30	stitcher	21	here
x	*Amato Felippa †	30	housewife	38	"
y	Noonan Mary †	30	at home	63	"
z	Lariviere Eugene	32	millhand	58	"

13

A	Lariviere Lydia †	32	housewife	51	"
B	*Allescia Angela †	32	"	54	"
C	*Allescia Peter	32	factoryhand	60	"
D	Natkiel Albertha †	32	housewife	41	216A Saratoga
E	Natkiel Benjamin	32	retired	44	216 "
F	Marley Annie E †	34	housewife	78	here
G	Marley Harry J	34	policeman	48	"
H	Marley Walter F	34	U S A	38	"
K	Marley Agnes L †	34	clerk	34	"
M	Bognanni Frank	36	storekeeper	56	"
N	Bognanni Gaetano	36	shoemaker	22	"
O	Bognanni Rose †	36	housewife	49	"
P	Saporito Fannie †	36	"	28	"
R	Saporito Ralph	36	mechanic	31	"
s	*Vella Angelina †	36	housewife	65	"
T	Bianchino Caroline †	38	"	24	"
U	Bianchino Ernest	38	machinist	30	"
V	Colantonio Lorenzo	38	laborer	55	"
W	*Colantonio Maria †	38	housewife	46	"
X	Turco Rose †	38	"	40	"
Y	Pericolo Eve †	40	"	27	"
Z	Pericolo Virginio	40	machinist	25	"

14

A	*Pisano Anna †	40	housewife	60	"
B	Pisano John	40	laborer	21	"

Grady Court

D	Paulson John A	1	U S N	39	N Hampshire
E	Paulson Laura R	1	housewife	39	"
G	Rose John E	1	rigger	32	Somerville
H	Rose Josephine †	1	housewife	27	"
K	Joslin Leslie H	1	U S N	30	Mississippi
L	Joslin Loretta †	1	housewife	26	Washington

Grady Court — Continued

	M	Sweeney C Marjorie †	1	housewife	31	Rhode Island
	N	Sweeney John P	1	instruments	32	"
	P	Quesenberry Jeanette †	1	housewife	26	Maine
	O	Quesenberry John	1	U S N	24	W Virginia
	S	Kantelis Delia †	1	housewife	21	17 Aberdeen
	T	Kantelis George J	1	shipwright	22	17 "
	U	Brinson Ernest	1	U S N	33	Connecticut
	V	Brinson Margaret †	1	housewife	25	"
	W	Powers Helen †	1	housekeeper	34	Somerville
	X	Snow Abraham	1	U S C G	28	Virginia
	Y	Snow Ellie †	1	housewife	27	"

15

	A	Gitner Samuel	1	coppersmith	22	46 Evelyn
	B	Gitner Sylvia †	1	housewife	20	46 "
	C	Runfola Bella †	17	"	30	California
	D	Runfola Joseph	17	U S N	40	"
	E	Leone Carrol	17	shipfitter	32	N Hampshire
	F	Leone Mary †	17	housewife	26	"
	G	Dutra Diana †	17	"	27	Fall River
	H	Dutra Norman	17	metalworker	32	"
	K	Ciarletta Daniel	17	U S N	37	Connecticut
	L	Ciarletta Mary †	17	housewife	34	"
	M	Proulx Hector	17	welder	25	N Hampshire
	N	Proulx Rita †	17	housewife	22	"
	O	Cheverie Catherine †	17	"	34	203 Saratoga
	P	Cheverie Percy	17	machinist	34	203 "
	R	Prophet Eleanor †	17	housewife	23	Natick
	S	Prophet Gail	17	U S N	28	"
	T	Foley Clara M †	17	housewife	42	Somerville
	U	Foley Thomas J	17	U S N	41	"
	W	Norman Lillian	17	housewife	29	N Hampshire
	X	Norman Lionel	17	welder	31	"
	Y	Nagle Anna †	17	housewife	22	152 Putnam
	Z	Nagle John F	17	watchman	26	152 "

16

	A	Sawin Josephine †	17	housewife	34	Andover
	B	Sawin Samuel R	17	tester	31	"
	C	Iver Hans	25	mechanic	34	Woburn
	D	Iver Meredith †	25	housewife	36	"
	E	Milliken Mary †	25	"	25	Somerville
	F	Milliken Paul	25	U S N	29	"

Grady Court Continued

H	Aulenbach Elwood	25	rigger	33	Pennsylvania
K	Aulenbach Marion †	25	housewife	22	"
L	Amiraunt Angelina †	25	"	43	98 Princeton
M	Amiraunt Edward	25	shipwright	42	98 "
N	Duke Forrest	25	"	26	N Hampshire
O	Duke Margaret †	25	housewife	26	"
R	Butterfield Edith †	25	"	23	California
S	Butterfield William E	25	machinist	23	"
T	Bradley Manassah E	25	U S N	42	43 W Eagle
U	Bradley Mary T †	25	housewife	40	43 "
V	Suski Helen †	25	"	23	Maryland
W	Suski John T	25	U S C G	35	"
Y	Serino Rocco	25	laborer	25	Holyoke
Z	Greer Jeanette †	41	housekeeper	42	Chelsea
	17				
A	Stevens Edith †	41	housewife	27	"
B	Stevens Roland	41	laborer	28	"
C	Marineau Gerard	41	welder	26	N Hampshire
D	Marineau Margaret †	41	housewife	22	"
E	Perrier Charles E	41	rigger	32	Somerville
F	Perrier Ida B †	41	housewife	31	"
G	Barry Glenda †	41	"	24	Milton
H	Barry Walter B	41	welder	29	"
K	Forestiere Adeline †	41	housewife	29	Medford
L	Forestiere Phillip J	41	molder	28	"
M	Gagnon Alphonse	41	welder	32	N Hampshire
N	Gagnon Marie N †	41	housewife	31	"
O	Lewis Mari †	41	"	26	Brookline
P	Lewis Robert E	41	operator	31	"
R	Furtado William	41	U S N	24	Arlington
S	Payne Arthur	41	laborer	35	Winthrop
T	Payne Eva †	41	housewife	37	"
U	Leary Ada †	41	"	29	Lakeville
V	Leary Edward J	41	machinist	46	"
W	Fitzgibbons John J	41	laborer	45	10 Haverford
X	Fitzgibbons Mary F †	41	housewife	37	10 "
Y	York Donald R	49	shipfitter	35	N Hampshire
Z	York Pearl S †	49	housewife	31	"
	18				
A	McDonough Bertha C †	49	"	28	73 Telegraph
B	McDonough Joseph	49	laborer	32	73 "

9

Grady Court Continued

C	McDonald Ann E †	49	housewife	27	Chelsea
D	McDonald Wilfred L	49	electrician	31	"
E	Engle Lee	49	mechanic	30	Pennsylvania
F	Engle Marion †	49	housewife	28	"
G	Hunt Gerald F	49	laborer	37	31 Decatur
H	Hunt Laura G †	49	housewife	27	31 "
K	Hollis Jean †	49	"	34	Rhode Island
L	Hollis Melvin C	49	U S N	39	"
M	Forrestall Gladys A †	49	housewife	38	Revere
N	Forrestall Wilfred J	49	storekeeper	38	"
O	Crocker Dorothy C †	49	housewife	23	Wash'n D C
P	Crocker Robert C	49	U S N	27	"
R	Cunio Catherine †	49	housekeeper	58	166 Leyden
S	Healy John R	49	salesman	44	166 "
T	Healy Sylvia †	49	housewife	37	166 "
U	Matz Adolph	49	inspector	38	Gloucester
V	Matz Eva †	49	housewife	40	"
W	Retzsch Margaret M †	49	"	22	Fall River
X	Retzsch Norton	49	U S M C	24	Ohio
Y	Toolin Margaret A †	49	housekeeper	64	Fall River
Z	Morano Mary †	49	housewife	21	11 Chelsea

19

A	Morano Richard	49	machinist	24	37 "
B	Green Ann N †	65	housewife	26	Maine
C	Green Bertine	65	signalman	26	"
D	Hewitt George S	65	rigger	42	Newton
E	Hewitt Lillian †	65	housewife	39	"
F	Kingery Martha †	65	"	28	N Carolina
G	Kingery Rhada L	65	U S C G	35	"
H	Scarpato Joseph	65	confectioner	39	7 Ashland
K	Scarpato Rose †	65	housewife	34	7 "
L	D'Addario Elda †	65	"	22	82 Chelsea
M	D'Addario Matteo	65	welder	25	82 "
O	Denisov Gabriel V	65	U S C G	36	Nantucket
P	Denisov Mary †	65	housewife	33	"
R	Hussey John J	65	laborer	49	7 Armstrong
S	*Hussey Nora †	65	housewife	43	7 "
T	Jarvis Eva †	65	"	28	265 Meridian
U	Jarvis Joseph T	65	U S N	28	265 "
V	Radzik Edward	65	U S A	27	367 Dorchester
W	Thompson Abraham D	65	chauffeur	33	367 "

Grady Court Continued

	x	Thompson Angela M †	65	housewife	33	367 Dorchester
	y	Duverger Orina †	65	operator	23	Fall River
	z	Pugliese Norman	65	U S N	44	Pennsylvania
20						
	a	Pugliese Ruby R †	65	housewife	27	"
	b	Olsen Andrew	65	shipfitter	54	Pittsfield
	c	Olsen Jennie †	65	housewife	54	"
	d	Olsen Thomas	65	U S C G	22	
	e	Johnson Hilding	66	inspector	31	Brookline
	f	Johnson Louise †	66	housewife	33	"
	g	Fowler Edwin	66	signalman	37	Wilmington
	h	Fowler Mary †	66	housewife	35	"
	k	Tousignant Florence †	66	"	35	N Hampshire
	l	Tousignant Leon	66	electrician	38	"
	m	Morrison Joseph D	66	foreman	28	109 Northampton
	n	Fabbri Joseph	66	machinist	31	Chelsea
	o	Fabbri Olympia †	66	housewife	25	"
	p	Conrad George D	66	electrician	33	Gloucester
	r	Conrad Grace †	66	housewife	32	"
	s	Parker Madeline †	66	"	28	94 Chelsea
	t	Parker Purlin	66	carpenter	48	94 "
	u	Skinner Gweneth †	66	clerk	20	32 Saratoga
	v	Thomason Helen †	66	housewife	20	Cambridge
	w	Thomason Henry	66	U S C G	23	"
	x	Sweeney Elsie M †	66	housewife	22	Gloucester
	y	Sweeney Walter A	66	U S N	28	"
	z	Watson Arthur J	66	shipwright	31	N Hampshire
21						
	a	Watson Marion E †	66	housewife	29	"
	c	Dichard Adelard	73	shipfitter	56	"
	d	Dichard Daisy †	73	housewife	49	"
	e	Marks Edna M †	73	"	29	Virginia
	f	Marks Elbert H	73	U S N	32	"
	g	Thomas Dorothy K †	73	housewife	35	Winthrop
	h	Thomas William J	73	U S N	44	"
	k	Stewart Ethelbert	73	"	33	Chelsea
	l	Stewart Gladys †	73	housewife	23	"
	m	Cogswell Alfred J	73	printer	28	48 Marion
	n	Cogswell Frances †	73	housewife	27	48 "
	o	Roe Lee S	73	U S C G	34	Virginia
	p	Roe Odessa †	73	housewife	30	"

11

Grady Court—Continued

R	Bowers Albert B	73	U S N	34	Maine
S	Bowers Mary M †	73	housewife	27	"
T	Splane Ann M †	73	"	26	Worcester
U	Splane John H	73	clerk	35	"
V	Duckworth Arthar F	73	U S A	24	Natick
W	Duckworth Arthur H	73	retired	67	"
X	Duckworth Mary E †	73	housewife	65	"
Y	Duckworth Mary H †	73	operator	21	"
Z	Christie Madeline †	73	housewife	28	Maine

22

A	Christie Milton	73	tester	30	"
B	Smith Samson H	73	guard	33	7 Dixfield
C	Smith Veronica A †	73	housewife	34	7 "
D	Rideout Christine †	73	packer	40	Revere
E	Katinas Frances †	74	housewife	25	Worcester
F	Katinas John	74	U S C G	30	"
G	Therberge Eva †	74	housewife	49	N Hampshire
H	Therberge Jeanette †	74	clerk	22	"
K	Therberge Ludgen	74	machinist	51	3 Trenton
L	Burke John F	74	retired	75	1053 Saratoga
M	O'Connor Gertrude C †	74	housewife	40	1053 "
N	O'Connor James T	74	U S N	21	1053 "
O	O'Connor Thomas J	74	insulator	44	1053 "
P	Cahill Elizabeth G †	74	housewife	30	Quincy
R	Cahill William J	74	shipfitter	47	"
S	Hayes Yvette †	74	housekeeper	34	18 Perrin
T	Olsen Roy	74	shipfitter	33	18 "
U	Dunn Charles	74	driller	29	159 Benningt'n
V	Dunn Margaret †	74	housewife	25	159 "
W	Rudinsky Marion L †	74	"	28	N Hampshire
X	Rudinsky Peter	74	shipfitter	32	"
Y	Fleming Gertrude †	74	housewife	30	Wilmington
Z	Fleming James	74	welder	32	"

23

A	Mathis Christabel †	74	housewife	28	Florida
B	Mathis James W	74	U S N	43	"
C	Hunt Alice †	74	housewife	47	Norwood
D	Hunt DeForest	74	mechanic	48	"
E	Adams John	74	driller	26	Chelsea
F	Adams Ruby †	74	housewife	24	"
G	Tuck Lillian M †	74	"	30	Somerville

Grady Court Continued

	u	Tuck Raymond H	74	U S C G	33	Somerville
	L	Munroe Mary A †	89	housewife	36	Reading
	M	Munroe William J	89	welder	39	"
	N	Griffin Lena E †	89	clerk	42	51 Joy
	o	Griffin Louise G †	89	"	44	29 Monument sq
	P	Griffin Mary F †	89	at home	48	51 Joy
	R	Clark Bernard	89	carpenter	38	Methuen
	s	Clark Rita †	89	housewife	37	"
	T	Wilson Ashley E	89	shipfitter	47	"
	U	Wilson Elizabeth A †	89	housewife	56	"
	W	Larson Dorothy †	89	"	24	Florida
	X	Larson James P	89	U S C G	24	"
	Y	Savoie Elizabeth D †	89	housewife	39	N Hampshire
	Z	Savoie George	89	electrician	42	"
24						
	A	Fitzemeyer Mabel F †	89	housewife	64	Revere
	B	Fitzemeyer Mabel F †	89	winder	28	"
	C	Hunt Emilia M †	89	housewife	36	N Hampshire
	D	Hunt Philip J	89	carpenter	41	"
	E	White Peter J	89	inspector	32	24 East
	F	White Rita M †	89	housewife	26	24 "
	H	Downie Helen †	90	"	26	Quincy
	K	Downie William	90	U S N	34	"
	L	Abbott Margaret K †	90	housewife	25	Virginia
	M	Abbott Wellington J	90	U S N	35	"
	N	Govostes Rose †	90	housewife	36	Woburn
	o	Govostes Theodore	90	chauffeur	34	"
	P	Davis Franklin	90	welder	29	N Hampshire
	R	Davis Julia †	90	housewife	25	"
	s	Buckley Gladys †	90	"	36	Virginia
	T	Buckley Michael D	90	U S N	39	"
	U	Wood Eugene W	90	"	29	25 Virginia
	V	Wood Martha M †	90	housewife	23	25 "
	X	Flores Frank	90	U S C G	25	8 Cheever ct
	Y	Macaluso Julia †	90	housewife	38	New York
	Z	Macaluso Samuel	90	chipper	41	"
25						
	A	Bassler Fred	90	plumber	29	Connecticut
	B	Bassler Helen †	90	housewife	28	"
	D	Lacoco Josephine †	90	clerk	28	Panama

Page	Letter	Full Name	Residence, Jan. 1, 1943.	Occupation	Supposed Age.	Reported Residence, Jan. 1, 1942. Street and Number.

Liverpool Avenue

	G	*Mazzola Salvatore	2	retired	73	here
	H	Toscano Frank	2	"	75	"
	K	Morgardo John	2	steamfitter	24	93 Liverpool
	L	*Morgardo Josephine †	2	housewife	59	93 "
	M	*McCormack William H	2	porter	75	here
	N	*Fagone Agrippina †	3	housewife	86	"
	O	*Amico Grace †	3	at home	86	"
	P	*Cordaro Francesca †	3	housewife	63	"
	R	Giovanniello Amelio	4	laborer	26	"
	S	*Giovanniello Marie †	4	housewife	48	"
	T	Giovanniello Michael	4	U S A	23	"
	U	Giovanniello Rocco	4	laborer	52	"
	V	*Merchilo Philemena †	4	at home	73	"
	W	Lauria Anthony	4	laborer	39	"
	Y	Caristinos Amelia †	6	housewife	28	"
	Z	Caristinos Michael	6	seaman	39	"

26

| | A | *Marshall Mary † | 6 | at home | 65 | " |

Liverpool Street

	B	Gregorio Josephine †	52	clerk	24	here
	C	Gregorio Ralph	52	U S A	21	"
	D	Gregorio Rudolph	52	U S C G	20	"
	E	*Gregorio Theresa †	52	housewife	48	"
	F	LaSalla Isabella †	52	"	27	338 Meridian
	G	LaSalla Joseph	52	machinist	25	143 London
	H	Palladino Anne †	52	housewife	45	here
	K	Palladino Ella †	52	saleswoman	24	"
	L	Nugent Eleanor †	53	at home	65	"
	M	*Amerault Edward J	53	seaman	42	"
	N	*Amerault Madeline †	53	housewife	40	"
	O	*Peckicalos Rose †	54	"	55	41 Sumner
	P	*Peckicalos Vasilio W	54	laborer	55	41 "
	R	*Sardino Asuncion †	54	housewife	53	here
	S	Sardino Marcelino	54	fireman	53	"
	T	Cicarello Joseph	56	storekeeper	57	39 Sumner
	U	*Cicarello Mary †	56	housewife	57	39 "
	V	*Paglucca Angelina †	56	typist	22	here
	W	Paglucca Julia †	56	attendant	22	"
	X	*Paglucca Marion †	56	housewife	49	"

Liverpool Street Continued

	Letter	FULL NAME	Residence	Occupation	Age	Reported Residence
	Y	Paglucca Michael	56	laborer	57	here
	Z	Paglucca Vincenza †	56	sorter	20	"
27						
	A	Marinos John	58	seaman	48	"
	B	Perry Clara †	58	housewife	48	"
	C	Catalanotto Leonardo	58	mason	45	"
	D*	Catalanotto Vicenza †	58	housewife	41	"
	E	Briana Charles	58	painter	31	57 Webster
	F	Briana Louise †	58	housewife	33	57 "
	G	Cuddi Anthony	60	mechanic	25	here
	H	Cuddi Josephine †	60	housewife	64	"
	K	Flaherty Evelyn †	60	"	37	"
	L	Flaherty John	60	electrician	31	"
	M	Cuddi Clementina †	60	clerk	26	"
	N	Cuddi Louis	60	mechanic	30	"
	O	Falzarano Rose †	62	stitcher	20	"
	P*	Falzarano Stephen	62	laborer	56	"
	R*	Falzarano Susan †	62	housewife	50	"
	S	Miraglia Nancy †	62	"	57	"
	T	Miraglia Salvatore	62	laborer	63	"
	U	Vella Frances †	62	housewife	29	"
	V	Vella Joseph	62	barber	34	"
	W	Rizzo Carmella †	62	factoryhand	35	"
	X	Rizzo Ernest	62	laborer	31	"
	Y	Rizzo Grace †	62	housewife	65	"
	Z	Rizzo Grace †	62	stitcher	22	"
28						
	A	Rizzo Mary †	62	boxmaker	24	"
	B	Rizzo Pellegrino	62	laborer	64	"
	C	Rizzo Philomena †	62	rubberworker	31	"
	D	Buccelli Edmond	62	U S A	26	"
	E	Buccelli Victoria †	62	florist	26	"
	F	LaMarco Ida B †	71	housewife	30	"
	G	LaMarco Orlando	71	shoemaker	34	"
	H	Fatalo Emilio	71	U S A	21	"
	K	Fatalo Grace †	71	housewife	60	"
	L	Fatalo Grace †	71	operator	21	"
	M	Fatalo Jennie †	71	"	29	"
	N	Fatalo Sylvia †	71		25	"
	O*	Brogna Angeline †	71	housewife	64	"
	P*	Brogna Pasquale	71	fireman	65	"

15

Liverpool Street Continued

R	Romano Louis	71	chauffeur	24	here
S	Romano Theresa †	71	housewife	23	"
T	Bruno Andrew	72	laborer	22	"
U*	Bruno Mary †	72	housewife	60	"
V	Lauria Anthony	72	U S A	23	"
W	Lauria Joseph	72	welder	21	"
X	Lauria Nellie †	72	housewife	26	"
Y*	Sala Geraldine †	72	"	64	"
Z	Sala Jerome	72	retired	67	"

29

A	Sala Josephine †	72	clerk	27	"
B	Sala Mary †	72	stitcher	33	"
C	Cusimano Casimero	73	barber	62	"
D	Cusimano James	73	U S A	22	"
E	Cusimano Joseph	73	"	22	"
F*	Cusimano Josephine †	73	housewife	61	"
G	Cusimano Teresa †	73	stitcher	31	"
H	Guarini Annette †	73	clerk	22	"
K	Guarini Calogera L	73	housewife	55	"
L	Guarini Richard	73	engineer	58	"
M	Tollis Angelo	73	operator	51	"
N	Tollis Flora †	73	housewife	47	"
O	Robinson Catherine †	74	"	28	"
P	Robinson John H	74	clerk	36	"
R	Chiampa Frederick	74	U S A	21	"
S	Chiampa Louisa †	74	at home	55	"
T	Chiampa Mary †	74	clerk	30	"
U	Chiampa Teresa †	74	"	23	"
V	Capone Carmen	74	chauffeur	37	"
W	Capone Frances †	74	housewife	37	"
X	Durante Adelaide †	75	"	30	"
Y	Durante Carlo	75	chauffeur	27	"
Z	Dorso Anglina †	75	housewife	58	"

30

A	Dorso Anthony	75	fisherman	22	"
B	Dorso Frank	75	"	33	"
C	Dorso Michael	75	rigger	34	"
F	Laiacona Florence †	85	housewife	32	"
G	Laiacona James	85	merchant	34	"
H*	Tucci Mary †	85	housewife	37	188 Maverick
K	Tucci Nickolas	85	radioman	40	188 "

Liverpool Street Continued

M	*Golisano Grace †	89	housewife	42	94 Summer
N	*Golisano Guy	89	clerk	51	94 "
O	Golisano Guy	89	chauffeur	20	94 "
P	Golisano Joseph	89	U S A	23	94 "
R	Aleo Alexander	89	retired	54	here
S	Aleo Alphonse	89	U S C G	21	"
T	*Aleo Dorothy †	89	operator	52	"
U	*Poccio Enrico	89	laborer	48	"
V	Poccio Peter	89	U S A	21	"
W	*Poccio Sebastiana †	89	housewife	47	"
Y	Greco Anthony	93	tailor	45	"
Z	Voci George	93	metalworker	24	"
31					
A	*Voci Gregorio	93	retired	60	"
B	*Voci Marie—†	93	housewife	60	"
C	Pisano Albert	93	rigger	30	"
D	Pisano Ann—†	93	at home	26	"
E	Pisano Carmine	93	laborer	57	"
F	*Pisano Christina †	93	housewife	55	"
G	Pisano Frederick	93	U S A	23	"
H	Gallo Mary—†	93	at home	33	"
K	Defino Concetta—†	93	stitcher	24	"
L	*Defino Josephine—†	93	housewife	48	New York
M	Defino Stefano	93	plasterer	52	here
S	Burke Helen L—†	97	housewife	44	"
T	Burke Thomas J	97	janitor	52	"
32					
A	Doucette Edna—†	103	housewife	34	"
B	Doucette George	103	fishcutter	34	"
C	*Caggiano Marciano	103	laborer	58	"
D	Recupero Paul	103	clerk	38	"
E	Recupero Rose †	103	housewife	32	"
F	Rota Phyllis—†	105	"	23	"
G	Rota Victor	105	meatcutter	23	"
H	Celestino Catino	105	shoeworker	59	"
K	Celestino Jennie—†	105	stitcher	21	"
L	Celestino Josephine †	105	clerk	25	"
M	*Celestino Rose—†	105	housewife	53	"
N	Caggiano Fiore	105	chauffeur	29	"
O	Caggiano Grace †	105	housewife	27	"
P	Masucci Gelsomina †	107	"	30	"

1—1   17

Liverpool Street—Continued

E	Masucci John	107	shipfitter	35	here
S	DeAngelis Anthony	107	laborer	58	"
T *DeAngelis Elvera †	107	housewife	53	"
U	DeAngelis Ralph	107	printer	21	"
W	Caponigro Andrew	109	laborer	23	"
X *Caponigro Angelina †	109	housewife	53	"
Y	Caponigro Serafino	109	laborer	55	"
Z	Caponigro Angelo	109	carpenter	32	"

33

A	Caponigro Rose †	109	housewife	28	"

London Street

H	Biaucucci Vincenzo	50	laborer	64	here
K	Belmonte Allesandro	50	lithographer	26	70 Havre
L	Belmonte Maria †	50	housewife	65	70 "
M	Belmonte Phyllis †	50	bowmaker	32	70 "
N	Lovering Leon	50	rigger	30	50 Chelsea
O	Lovering Mary †	50	housewife	26	50 "
P	Petrella Gaetano	52	mechanic	25	here
R	Petrella Saverio	52	U S A	31	"
S	Colombo Anthony	52	presser	65	"
T	Colombo Concetta †	52	stitcher	22	"
U	Colombo Gaetano	52	U S A	25	"
V *Colombo Marion †	52	housewife	58	"
W	Petrilla Concetta †	52	stitcher	24	"
X *Petrilla Rose †	52	housewife	56	"
Y	Petrilla Rose M †	52	stitcher	22	"
Z *Petrilla Saverio	52	retired	60	"

34

B	Fatalo Americo	54	shipfitter	31	"
C	Fatalo Ann †	54	housewife	29	"
D	Vitale Emilio	54	shoemaker	71	"
E	Vitale Letitzia †	54	housewife	65	"
F	Hanrahan Elizabeth †	56	housekeeper	66	"
G	Lyons Joseph	56	shipfitter	28	"
H	Lyons Patrick	56	longshoreman	60	"
K	Lanning Hannah †	56	housewife	60	186 Maverick
L	Lanning Julia †	56	maid	23	186 "
M	Cagnina Mary †	56	housewife	30	here
N *Cagnina Michael	56	shoemaker	38	"

18

Page.	Letter.	FULL NAME.	Residence, Jan. 1, 1943	Occupation.	Supposed Age.	Reported Residence, Jan. 1, 1942. Street and Number.

London Street Continued

o	Cagnina Nunzio	56	welder	48	here
p	Amico Joseph	58	U S N	20	"
r	Amico Pasquale	58	laborer	55	"
s	Bringola Carmella †	58	housewife	23	"
t	Bringola Thomas	58	shipfitter	38	"
u	Vella Joseph	58	laborer	45	"
v	*Vella Josephine †	58	housewife	35	"
w	*Doull Mary J †	60	at home	91	87 Homer
x	Locke Lillian F †	60	"	48	87 "
y	Chellemi Francesca †	60	stitcher	35	here
z	DiLorenzo Grover	60	machinist	32	190 Cottage

35

a	DiLorenzo Mickelena †	60	housewife	27	190 "
b	Joyce Annie †	62	"	73	here
c	Joyce Jeffrey	62	retired	74	"
d	Sousa Laura †	62	housewife	27	14 Bremen
e	Sousa William	62	presser	29	14 "
f	Meli Flora †	62	housewife	37	here
g	Meli Joseph P	62	welder	41	"
h	Vito Marco S	64	laborer	60	"
k	Fleming Hannah †	64	clerk	64	"
l	Jeffers John	64	retired	65	"
m	DiGirolamo Anthony	66	laborer	31	"
n	DiGirolamo Josephine †	66	housewife	26	"
o	Incrovato James	66	fishcutter	32	"
p	Incrovato Vivian †	66	housewife	32	"
s	Bannon Sarah G †	68	teacher	73	"
t	Jeffers Mary †	68	at home	74	"
u	Walsh William A	68	constable	50	"
v	Gallagher Margaret †	68	housekeeper	56	"
w	Anderson Peter	70	fisherman	53	"
x	*Dalton Richard	70	"	69	"
y	Murphy Michael	70	"	53	"
z	Colombo Ernest	70	agent	60	"

36

a	*Colombo Filomena †	70	housewife	59	"
b	Murphy Frances †	70	technician	68	"
c	Tiana Antonio	72	finisher	45	"
d	*Tiana Eleanor †	72	housewife	36	"
e	Poto Edward	72	manager	28	"
f	Poto Ida †	72	housewife	27	"

19

London Street—Continued

G	Scanapico Antonetta †	72	stitcher	22	here
H	*Scanapico Emelia †	72	housewife	53	"
K	*Scanapico John	72	retired	68	"
L	*Tiana Nicola	72	porter	51	"
N	*Melito Anna †	74	housewife	39	"
O	Melito Joseph	74	welder	44	"
P	Cirrone Justino	74	"	20	"
R	*Cirrone Margaret †	74	housewife	46	"
S	Caristo Albert	76	U S N	21	"
T	Caristo Maria †	76	operator	20	"
U	Caristo Riccardo	76	clerk	23	"
V	Caristo Rose †	76	housewife	54	"
W	*Lopes Elvira †	76	"	43	"
X	Lopes Frank	76	rigger	46	"
Y	*Anastos Caroline †	76	housewife	44	"
Z	Anastos Cleo †	76	operator	20	"

37

A	Anastos Georgia †	76	stitcher	24	"
B	Anastos Nicolas	76	retired	60	"
C	Ahern Alfred	78	laborer	57	6 Lexington pl
D	Ahern Rose †	78	packer	52	6 "
E	Sacramone Daniel	78	laborer	38	209 Saratoga
F	*Sacramone Josephine †	78	housewife	29	209 "
G	Aiesi Frank	78	laborer	55	here
H	*Aiesi Rosaria †	78	housewife	51	"
K	Salvaggio Josephine †	78	stitcher	25	"
L	Pistone Joseph	80	laborer	51	"
M	Pistone Maria †	80	housewife	43	"
N	Marino Nicolas	80	shipper	64	"
O	Marino William	80	electrician	36	"
P	Polia Joseph A	80	U S A	20	"
R	*Polia Maria J †	80	finisher	38	78 London
S	Polia Paolo	80	laborer	47	78 "
T	Smaldone Josephine †	80	at home	21	198 Salem
U	Kennedy Mary W †	82	"	57	here
V	Woodford William	82	welder	30	"
W	Pecorella Angela †	82	at home	34	133 Havre
X	Ferragamo Agnes †	82	housewife	31	here
Y	Ferragamo Christopher	82	laborer	32	"
Z	DeBonis Vincent	84	chipper	33	"

38

London Street Continued

A	DeBonis Virginia—†	84	housewife	27	here
B	Dello Iacono Lena—†	84	operator	21	"
C	Dello Iacono Pasquale	84	chairmaker	56	"
D	Dello Iacono Paceno	84	repairman	24	"
E	*Dello Iacono Virginia †	84	housewife	50	"
F	DiPalma Mary †	99	"	32	"
G	DiPalma Nicholas	99	mechanic	38	"
H	Miano Albert	99	grinder	35	"
K	Miano Elizabeth †	99	housewife	33	"
L	Chintos Florence †	99	"	40	175 Paris
M	Chintos Nicholas	99	seaman	48	175 "
N	*Russano Katherine †	101	housewife	51	184 London
O	Russano Thomas	101	laborer	51	184 "
P	Vasapolli Philip	101	U S A	22	184 "
R	*Camplese John	101	shoeworker	26	39 Everett
S	Camplese Margaret †	101	stitcher	24	here
T	Caponigro Andrew	101	U S A	23	"
U	Caponigro Armando	101	casketmaker	21	"
V	*Caponigro Madeline †	101	housewife	50	"
W	Siracusa Maria A—†	101	operator	36	"
X	*Vitale Maria G †	101	"	55	"
Y	Vitale Michael	101	shoeworker	59	"

39

A	Lauza Irene—†	102	manager	34	"
B	Lauza James †	102	manufacturer	34	"
C	Cioffi Anna †	102	stitcher	29	"
D	*Lauza Angelina †	102	housewife	57	"
E	Lauza Frank	102	presser	63	"
F	Miano Frank	102	U S A	22	"
G	Miano Louis	102	gardener	46	"
H	Miano Mary †	102	housewife	44	"
K	Romano Anthony	102	chauffeur	35	29 Havre
L	Romano Mary †	102	housewife	33	29 "
P	Belt Helen †	104	at home	32	here
R	Sasso Anthony	104	mechanic	31	"
S	Sasso Emelia †	104	housewife	28	"
T	Maurici Salvatore	104	presser	38	11 Decatur
U	Giacobbe Guiseppe	106	retired	73	here
V	Giacobbe Margaret †	106	operator	33	"

21

London Street Continued

w	Giacobbe Carmelo	106	engineer	35	here
x	Giacobbe Elizabeth A †	106	housewife	31	"
y	*Amengual Bartolome	106	rigger	47	"
z	*Amengual Maria †	106	housewife	50	"

40

B	Butaro Beatrice †	108	"	25	"
C	Butaro Nicola	108	clerk	25	"
D	Solvi Angelo	108	U S A	22	"
E	Solvi Antonetta †	108	housewife	44	"
F	Solvi Frank	108	laborer	51	"
G	Pucillo Albert	108	U S A	28	"
H	Pucillo Helen †	108	saleswoman	24	"
K	*Pucillo Nicola	108	meatcutter	64	"
L	*Pucillo Rosaria †	108	housewife	66	"
M	Pucillo Samuel	108	U S A	25	"
N	DiLavari Felice	110	retired	69	"
O	*DiLavari Rosaria †	110	housewife	68	"
P	Locke Alice G †	110	packer	33	57 Havre
R	Locke George S	110	machinist	54	4 Winthrop
S	Schifano Antonetta †	110	housewife	25	here
T	*Schifano Charles	110	presser	28	"
U	Altieri Filomena †	110	housewife	50	"
V	*Altieri Frank	110	merchant	46	"
W	Lamie David J	112	engineer	54	"
X	Lamie William	112	laborer	49	"
Y	LaCascia Anna †	112	student	21	"
Z	LaCascia Gaspar	112	baker	47	"

41

A	LaCascia Maria †	112	housewife	43	"
B	Little Frances †	112	"	22	Revere
C	Little Valentine, jr	112	distributor	28	"
D	DiLorenzo Maria S †	114	housewife	33	here
E	DiLorenzo William	114	plumber	35	"
F	DeSantis Anthony	114	musician	40	"
G	DeSantis Mary †	114	at home	58	"
H	DeSantis Rose †	114	housewife	33	"
K	Drakoalas Eltherios	114	salesman	46	"
L	Casato John J	114	tailor	37	"
M	Casato Madeline †	114	housewife	37	"
O	Leavitt Genevieve †	116	"	28	Pennsylvania
P	Leavitt Newton A	116	trafficman	34	"

Page.	Letter.	Full Name.	Residence Jan. 1, 1943.	Occupation.	Age.	Reported Residence, Jan. 1, 1942. Street and Number.

London Street Continued

	R	Rinelli Jean †	116	housewife	29	here
	S	Rinelli Vincent	116	inspector	28	"
	T	Spadorcia Fiore	116	retired	76	"
	U	Amoratos Michael	118	seaman	48	42 Maverick
	V	Dixon Anne T †	118	housewife	62	here
	W	Galloway Dorothea †	118	"	33	"
	X	Gose Martin	118	fisherman	42	"
	Y	Kelley Thomas	118	clerk	38	319 Havre
	Z	O'Rourke John	118	fisherman	38	here

42

	A	Partee Althea †	118	housewife	30	"
	B	Partee Henry	118	operator	34	"
	C	Schmall Gertrude †	118	housewife	34	Virginia
	D	Slyvan Joseph	118	millhand	40	here
	E	Vallee Anibale	118	"	45	"
	F	Hamilton Ralph P	120	operator	49	6 Central sq
	G	Oliver Anthony	120	salesman	55	here
	H	Rock Mary M †	120	housewife	63	"
	K	Rock Timothy J	120	retired	65	"
	L	Scorzello Rocco	120	mechanic	26	Revere
	M	Titis Herman	120	yardmaster	55	here
	N	Colbert Patrick J	122	laborer	58	"
	O	Dunn John J	122	fisherman	53	"
	P	Hoffman Elizabeth †	122	housewife	69	"
	R	Inana Giuseppe	122	barber	46	"
	S	Macdonald Robert H	122	retired	73	"
	T	Martin Patrick	122	fisherman	42	"
	U	Mitts Joseph	122	operator	55	"
	V	Murray John	122	rigger	50	Florida
	W	Norris George	122	shipworker	41	here
	X	Snow George	122	retired	76	"
	Y	Brady Dorothy †	124	clerk	36	"
	Z	Brady Edward	124	"	63	"

43

	A	Brady Margaret †	124	housewife	62	"
	B	Dioguardi George	124	chauffeur	25	"
	C	Dioguardi Nicolas	124	salesman	34	"
	D	Doyle Arthur	124	"	45	109 Meridian
	E	Fraser William	124	seaman	45	here
	F	Frechette Albert	124	foreman	45	"
	G	Lessy Thomas	124	clerk	28	Maine

23

London Street—Continued

		FULL NAME.	Res.	Occupation.	Age	Res.
H		Lyons Horace W	124	foreman	73	here
K		Powers John	124	watchman	64	"
L		Walsh Joseph	124	salesman	50	"
M		Shuck Chui Wah	128	laundryman	47	"
O		Bonfiglio Mary †	128	housewife	29	"
P		Edmands Hattie A †	128½	"	62	"
R*		Reitano Monica †	138	"	44	"
S		Reitano Robert J	138	U S C G	22	"
T*		Reitano Sylvester	138	wireworker	45	"
U		Barbanti Mary †	138	housewife	55	"
V		Barbanti Rose †	138	clerk	25	"
W		Lazzaro Joseph	140	foreman	31	"
X		Lazzaro Mary †	140	housewife	30	"
Y		Mongiello James	140	carpenter	53	"
Z*		Mongiello Philomena †	140	housewife	49	"

44

		FULL NAME.	Res.	Occupation.	Age	Res.
A		Ricciardelli Anthony	140	laborer	34	"
B*		Ricciardelli Bennedetto	140	retired	78	"
C*		Ricciardelli Josephine †	140	housewife	78	"
D		Ricciardelli Vera †	140	"	29	"
E		McCarthy Helen V †	142	tel operator	42	"
F		McGrane Helen B †	142	clerk	31	"
G		McGrane Mary E †	142	housewife	70	"
H		McGrane Thomas J	142	machinist	67	"
L		Pace Mary A †	144	housewife	29	"
M		Pace Salvatore	144	electrician	29	"
N		Tipping Joseph	144	longshoreman	28	"
O		Tipping Violet †	144	housewife	28	"
P		Miller Edward	144	janitor	31	"
R		Miller Emma †	144	housewife	74	"
S		Miller Louis C	144	janitor	81	"
T		Leonard Gilda †	146	housewife	23	"
U		Leonard James	146	longshoreman	25	"
V		Boisoneau George H	146	millhand	78	"
W		Boisoneau Harold	146	"	67	"
X		Boisoneau Mathilde M †	146	housewife	70	"
Y		Boisoneau Ralph C	146	engineer	48	"
Z		Kelly Agnes M †	146	housewife	49	"

45

		FULL NAME.	Res.	Occupation.	Age	Res.
A		Kelly Catherine T †	146	"	74	"
B		Kelly John F	146	salesman	40	"

London Street Continued

c	Ciampa Arthur	148	welder	26	42 Porter
d	Ciampa Rose †	148	housewife	25	42 "
e	Augusta Baige	148	foreman	31	here
f	Augusta Elena †	148	clerk	27	"
g*	Augusta Madeline †	148	housewife	58	"
h	Augusta Pasquale	148	laborer	61	"
k	Camarra Clement	148	machinist	26	72 Frankfort
l	Camarra Marie †	148	housewife	26	72 "
m	Augusta Anthony	150	chipper	37	here
n	Augusta Celia †	150	housewife	32	"
o	Nappa Carmen	150	merchant	61	"
p	Nappa Michale	150	U S A	30	"
r*	Nappa Petronilla †	150	housewife	65	"
s	Amico Josephine †	150	"	35	"
t	Amico Philip, jr	150	beautician	35	"
u	Penta Josephine †	152	housewife	25	"
v	Penta Salvatore	152	candymaker	28	"
w	Penta Arthur	152	U S A	24	"
x	Penta Sabina †	152	housewife	50	"
y	Penta Samuel	152	U S A	26	"
z	Penta Saverio	152	candymaker	53	"

46

a	Capozzi Carmella †	152	housewife	29	"
b*	Capozzi Peter	152	cook	32	"
c*	Rizzo Concetta †	158	housewife	51	"
d*	Rizzo Paul	158	salesman	60	"
e	Rizzo Salvatore	158	U S A	20	"
f	Marino Alphonse	158	clerk	23	"
g	Marino Cecilia †	158	packer	21	"
h	Marino Nicholas	158	laborer	56	"
k	Marino Raffalla †	158	housewife	42	"
l	Marino Theresa †	158	clerk	24	"
m*	DiDonato Negolatta †	158	housewife	54	"
n	DiDonato Vincent	158	merchant	19	"
o	Coggio Anna †	160	housewife	36	"
p	Coggio Jerome	160	janitor	36	"
r	Celata Frederick J	160	tailor	47	"
s	Celata Frederick J, jr	160	U S A	22	"
t	Celata Lena †	160	housewife	43	"
u*	Serima Frank	160	retired	69	"
v*	Serima Mary †	160	housewife	68	"

London Street—Continued

Y	Shea Mary A †	172	housewife	70	here	
Z	Shea Michael J	172	retired	75	"	
47						
A	Buckley Anna L †	172	housewife	68	"	
B	Buckley John H	172	inspector	72	"	
C	Harding Anne †	172	housewife	68	"	
D	Coughlin John J	174	fireman	65	"	
E	Nugent Mary A †	174	clerk	23	"	
F	Nugent Nellie M †	174	housewife	53	"	
G	Nugent Richard J	174	retired	64	"	
K	Donahue Mary †	174	housewife	61	"	
L	Luiz William	174	clerk	59	"	
M	Delisso Gaetano	180	pedler	49	"	
N	*Orlandino Edward	180	salesman	31	239 Havre	
O	Orlandino Margaret †	180	housewife	21	239 "	
P	Wessling Anne G †	180	"	61	here	
R	Wessling Herman F	180	painter	34	"	
S	Wessling John B	180	"	59	"	
T	McKenna Rose †	182	clerk	56	"	
U	*Lamonica Esther †	184	housewife	80	"	
V	Lamonica Samuel	184	mechanic	28	"	
W	Antonucci Corinna †	184	housewife	41	"	
X	Antonucci George	184	bricklayer	52	"	
Y	Caccamesi Charles	184	cobbler	32	"	
Z	Caccamesi Josephine †	184	housewife	32	"	
48						
A	Tamagna Anna †	186	"	39	"	
B	*Tamagna Dominic	186	salesman	44	"	
C	Chiampa Anthony	186	mechanic	43	"	
D	Chiampa Marion †	186	housewife	43	"	
E	Russo Joseph	186	brakeman	44	2A Lincoln	
F	Tamagna Andreana †	186	clerk	28	here	
G	Tamagna Angelina †	186	housewife	30	"	
H	*Tamagna Guy	186	foreman	42	"	
K	Tamagna Rose †	186	clerk	23	"	
L	Tamagna Victor S	186	U S A	31	"	
M	Tamagna Vincent	186	candymaker	38	"	
N	Sordillo Angelina †	188	clerk	23	"	
O	Sordillo Arthur	188	U S A	26	"	
P	Sordillo Carmella †	188	clerk	21	"	
R	Sordillo Julia †	188	housewife	46	"	
S	Sordillo Ralph	188	candymaker	54	"	

26

London Street Continued

T	Ramos Carlisto	190	millhand	44	here
U	*Ramos Ondina †	190	housewife	36	"
V	Fariole Edward	192	mechanic	22	"
W	Fariole Ella †	192	housewife	62	"
X	Fariole Robert	192	retired	62	"
Y	*Lottero Joseph	194	operator	64	"
Z	Lottero Joseph jr	194	draftsman	22	"

49

A	*Lottero Rose †	194	housewife	60	"
B	Lottero Albert	194	U S A	25	"
C	Lottero Evelyn M †	194	housewife	23	"
D	Lottero Michael	194	clerk	30	"
E	Shea Ambrose V	196	mechanic	54	"
F	Shea Mary †	196	housewife	48	"
G	DiBerto Mary †	198	"	28	"
H	DiBerto Romeo	198	butcher	31	"
K	Barnes Charles	198	machinist	30	"
L	Barnes Josephine †	198	housewife	57	"
M	Barnes William	198	U S A	24	"
N	Imprescia Joseph	198	electrician	27	"
O	Imprescia Phyllis †	198	housewife	24	"
P	*DiDonato Alphonso	200	retired	59	"
R	DiDonato Helen †	200	clerk	26	"
S	Laconte Yolanda †	200	housekeeper	33	"
T	DeChristoforo Amelia †	200	housewife	28	"
U	DeChristoforo Flaviano	200	mechanic	33	"
V	Vasapolli John	200	U S N	23	"
W	*Vasapolli Phillipa †	200	housewife	42	"
X	Vasapolli Sebastian	200	U S A	21	"
Y	Vasapolli Vincenzo	200	candymaker	54	"
Z	Bruttaniti Evelyn †	202	housewife	21	148 Havre

50

A	Bruttaniti Joseph	202	mechanic	22	149 Chelsea
B	Morello Ida †	202	clerk	28	here
C	Morello Salvatore	202	"	30	"
D	Cali Anthony	202	machinist	27	"
E	Cali Virginia †	202	housewife	26	"

Maverick Street

H	Goddard Floyd D	1	carpenter	40	Vermont
K	Goddard Leona M †	1	housewife	42	"

Maverick Street—Continued

L	Qualey Marie—†	1	housewife	28	Medford
M	Qualey Thomas	1	foreman	28	"
N	Marie Frank	1	fishcutter	36	55 W Eagle
O	Marie Helen—†	1	housewife	32	55 "
P	Martell Elizabeth †	1	"	34	6 Alvan ter
R	Martell Joseph M	1	pipefitter	33	6 "
S	Robinson Cora—†	1	housewife	32	California
T	Robinson Harry N	1	pipefitter	45	"
U	MacInnis Beulah M—†	1	housewife	32	Gloucester
V	MacInnis John W	1	painter	38	"
W	Coughlin F David	1	chipper	30	Saugus
X	Coughlin Florence—†	1	housewife	26	"
Y	Verune George	1	U S C G	45	Washington
Z	Verune Rose—†	1	housewife	35	"
	51				
A	Lynch Julia—†	1	"	40	153 W Second
B	Lynch Thomas	1	carpenter	44	153 "
C	McMullen Orral	1	U S N	43	Florida
D	McMullen Veronica †	1	housewife	29	"
E	Alimonti Mary—†	1	at home	38	54 Maverick
F	Cunningham Marjorie †	1	housewife	24	4 Trull
G	Cunningham William G	1	U S M C	27	4 "
H	O'Neil Frank	17	clerk	30	Somerville
K	O'Neil Marie †	17	housewife	26	"
L	Garrett Helen T †	17	"	32	California
M	Garrett Thomas S	17	U S N	36	"
N	Lyons Mary A †	17	"	33	N Hampshire
O	Lyons William	17	"	34	"
P	Doherty Edwin J	17	electrician	35	Reading
R	Doherty Elizabeth F †	17	housewife	39	"
S	Desrosier Kenneth A	17	blacksmith	22	Fall River
T	Desrosier Mary E †	17	housewife	23	"
U	Berry Albertine †	17	"	23	Waltham
V	Berry Louis	17	trackman	32	"
W	Cummings Florence †	17	housewife	30	Maine
X	Cummings Maxwell	17	welder	33	"
Y	Wynters John W	17	U S M C	39	37 St Edward rd
Z	Wynters Matilda †	17	housewife	39	37 "
	52				
A	Carter George W	17	U S N	26	Concord
B	Carter Mary W †	17	at home	61	"

28

Maverick Street Continued

	c	Giordano Ciro	17	inspector	47	Revere
	d	Giordano Judith †	17	housewife	43	"
	e	Silhary Beulah †	17		31	California
	f	Silhary Thomas	17	U S N	37	"
	g	Gilbert Anna †	17	housewife	28	Texas
	h	Gilbert Earl	17	U S N	33	"
	l	Apicco Angelina †	22	housewife	49	here
	m	Apicco James	22	shoeworker	48	"
	n	Apicco Michael	22	U S A	27	"
	o	McQuillan Catherine †	24	at home	65	"
	p	Hart Catherine †	24	"	50	"
	r	Mack James F	24	expressman	65	"
	s	Mack Mary †	24	housewife	62	"
	t	Colangelo Doris †	25		29	19 Chelsea
	u	Colangelo Frank	25	rigger	28	19 "
	v	Cottle George	25	machinist	49	Hyannis
	w	Cottle Mary †	25	housewife	47	"
	x	Desharnais Eva †	25	"	35	Lawrence
	y	Desharnais Walter	25	shipfitter	32	"
	z	Hoffman Margaret †	25	at home	66	Chelsea
53						
	a	Young Margaret M †	25	operator	36	"
	b	Venable Elmer	25	U S N	39	Virginia
	c	Venable Vera †	25	housewife	28	"
	d	Kelley Charles E	25	rigger	39	Revere
	e	Kelly Mary E †	25	housewife	37	"
	f	Bernard Arthur E	25	welder	27	New Bedford
	g	Bernard Exire S †	25	housewife	24	"
	h	Wallins Dorothy †	25	"	27	Rockport
	k	Wallis Toivo W	25	dyesetter	32	"
	l	Cordeau Arthur	25	guard	38	Lawrence
	m	Cordeau Pearl †	25	housewife	33	"
	n	Morris Frank	25	clerk	38	2 Brooks
	o	Morris Mary †	25	housewife	40	2 "
	p	LaHar Florence R †	25	"	35	Everett
	r	LaHar Norman F	25	machinist	36	"
	s	*Caruso Josephine †	26	housewife	38	here
	t	*Caruso Matteo	26	storekeeper	54	"
	u	*Damplo Antonette †	26	stenographer	21	"
	v	Mess Charles W	26	foreman	46	Chelsea
	w	Mess Helen †	26	housewife	48	"

29

Maverick Street—Continued

x	Bibbey Lillian J—†	28	inspector	32	here
z	Buckley Margaret F—†	28	housewife	40	Everett
y	Buckley William F	28	operator	47	"

54

A	D'Eramo Concetta—†	30	housewife	22	here
B	D'Eramo Robert V	30	machinist	30	"
c	Penta Anthony	30	"	50	"
D	Penta John C	30	operator	27	"
E	Penta Joseph C	30	U S A	23	"
F	Penta Mary L—†	30	housewife	48	"
G	Pope Charlotte M—†	30	at home	21	"
H	Cenoulos Alex	42	seaman	55	"
K	*Cenoulos Peter	42	"	49	"
L	*Mathiodakis George	42	"	58	"
M	Mavros Louis	42	"	60	"
N	Flaherty Rose—†	44	at home	70	"
O	*Pettipas Anna M—†	44	saleswoman	21	"
P	Pettipas Herbert	44	U S A	23	"
R	*Pettipas Marion—†	44	housewife	68	"
S	*Bongiovanni Giuseppe	46	laborer	55	"
T	*Bongiovanni Nancy—†	46	housewife	49	"
V	Lombardo Anna—†	46	"	39	"
W	Lombardo Joseph	48	carpenter	48	"
X	*Morello Angelo	48	retired	69	58 Liverpool
Y	*Morello Concetta—†	48	housewife	59	58 "
Z	Morello James	48	welder	22	58 "

55

A	Piazza Alexander	48	pipefitter	44	here
B	Piazza Rose—†	48	housewife	36	"
c	*Marsiglia Anthony	48	marblecutter	30	14 Cooper
D	Marsiglia Grace—†	48	housewife	25	58 Liverpool
F	*Cali Antonio	50	shoemaker	63	here
G	*Cali Mary—†	50	housewife	54	"
H	Michalis Dennis	50	watchman	56	79 Border
K	Michalis Sophia—†	50	housewife	48	79 "
L	Gualtieri Angelo	54	U S A	21	here
M	Gualtieri Carmella—†	54	seamstress	25	"
N	Gualtieri Domenic	54	laborer	52	"
O	*Gualtieri Louise—†	54	housewife	48	"
P	Mannetta Filomena—†	54	"	35	200 Marion
R	Mannetta Thomas	54	laborer	47	200 "

Maverick Street Continued

s	Filippone Leo	54	painter	44	25 Decatur
r	Filippone Mary †	54	housewife	34	25 "
t	Zichella Amedeo	58	shoeworker	31	here
v	Zichella Rose †	58	housewife	28	"
y	Naso Josephine †	60	packer	20	"
z	Naso Maria †	60	housewife	48	"

56

a	Naso Nicola	60	storekeeper	49	"
b	Logiudice Frances †	60	stenographer	20	"
c	Logiudice Rocco	60	carpenter	51	"
d	Logiudice Rose †	60	housewife	39	"

Meridian Street

g	Spolsino Anthony	86	mechanic	26	here
h	Spolsino Emily †	86	housewife	26	"
k	Avalone Nunzianto	86	barber	52	"
n	Lenoci Domenic	92	laborer	48	"
o	McNulty Concetta A †	92	housewife	25	"
p	McNulty Raymond L	92	U S A	25	"
r	Socci Antonio J	92	U S N	20	"
s	Socci Austin R	92	U S A	23	"
t	Socci Carmen	92	laborer	26	"
u	Socci Lucy †	92	housewife	55	"
v	Socci Stephen	92	laborer	56	"

57

b	Hollingsworth Mary C †	102A	housekeeper	54	271 Princeton
c	Hollingsworth Sadie M †	102A	waitress	62	271 "
d	Sheehan Elizabeth †	102A	housewife	57	here
e	Sheehan James	102A	watchman	57	"
f	Cohen Eva †	108	technician	32	"
g	Cohen Helen †	108	housewife	32	"
h	Cohen Louis	108	physician	43	"
k	Novakoff Goldie †	108	housewife	40	"
l	Novakoff Joseph	108	tailor	50	"
o	*Gillis Alexander	122	grinder	53	"
p	Gillis Laura †	122	housewife	42	"
r	Chase Margaret †	122	"	51	"
s	*Chase Roy	122	plumber	56	"
t	Hagerty Catherine †	122	housekeeper	63	"
w	Vallen Catherine †	126	housewife	37	"

31

Meridian Street—Continued

x	Vallen Daniel	126	guard	44	here
y	Deveau Margaret †	126	housewife	31	20 Paris
z	Deveau Patrick	126	carpenter	40	20 "

58

A*	Melanson Fannie †	126	housewife	49	here
B	Melanson Raymond	126	U S A	21	"
D	Bellavia Angelo	130	laborer	53	"
E	Bellavia Fannie †	130	operator	26	"
F	Bellavia Joseph	130	U S A	27	"
G*	Bellavia Theresa †	130	housewife	48	"
H	Centifanti Vincent	130	machinist	20	"
K	Iorio Clorinda †	130	housewife	40	"
L	Iorio John	130	carpenter	46	"
M	Testa Antonio	130	U S A	22	"
N	Testa Christina †	130	housewife	48	"
O	Testa Joseph	130	pressman	51	
R	Santangelo Angelo	134	laborer	30	33 Maverick sq
S	Santangelo Ida †	134	housewife	20	33 "
T*	Nigro Eupremio	134	laborer	51	here
U*	Nigro Filomena †	134	housewife	51	"
V	Nigro Madeline †	134	bookkeeper	23	"
W	Nigro Gilda †	134	housewife	25	"
X	Nigro Giro	134	salesman	27	
Z	Pendleton Alice †	138	operator	25	78 White

59

A	Pendleton Clarissa †	138	housewife	51	78 "
B*	Fingerman Joseph	138	tailor	45	here
C*	Fingerman Mary †	138	housewife	38	"
E	Farmer Elizabeth †	141	"	65	"
F	Farmer Mary †	141	boxmaker	46	"
G	Dwyer Andrew J	141	welder	35	"
H	Dwyer Lillian †	141	housewife	31	"
K	Joy Catherine †	143	"	61	"
L	Joy James	143	retired	67	"
M*	Bishop Bernard	143	watchman	52	"
N*	Bishop Maude †	143	housewife	49	"
O	Bishop Paul	143	U S N	22	"
P	Lawrence Helen †	143	housewife	21	"
R	Lawrence Leo R	143	U S A	24	464 Meridian
U	Bishop Aiden C	149	"	24	here
V*	Bishop Cecelia †	149	housewife	64	"

32

Meridian Street Continued

w	Bishop Geraldine M †	149	attendant	34	here
x	*Bishop Harold J	149	agent	29	"
y	Gaugh Mary B †	149	secretary	34	"
z	Critch Catherine †	149	clerk	21	"
60					
A	Dobbins Catherine †	149	housewife	55	"
B	Dobbins David	149	carpenter	67	"
C	McMillan Helen †	149	sorter	28	"
D	Maloney Catherine †	151	operator	23	103 Meridian
E	Maloney James	151	rigger	50	103 "
F	Maloney Sadie †	151	housewife	53	103 "
G	Chefero Helen †	151	housekeeper	27	28 Orleans
H	Vaccari Andrew	151	teamster	42	28 "
K	Vaccari Margaret †	151	housewife	29	28 "
L	Burge George J	157	laborer	33	here
M	Burge Josephine †	157	housewife	32	Bridgewater
N	Donovan Cornelius J	157	carpenter	57	here
O	Donovan Cornelius J, jr	157	contractor	35	"
P	Willis James A	157	bartender	56	"
R	*Willis Stella †	157	housewife	38	"
S	Ford Harry	157	U S A	21	"
T	Morey Robert	157	rigger	38	"
U	Perry Jennie †	157	housewife	39	"

New Street

Y	Lawrence Clare E	9	U S N	21	Michigan
z	Card Harold M	9	machinist	40	Rhode Island
61					
A	Card Helen V †	9	housewife	40	"
C	DeSousa Joseph	9	painter	41	19 Havre
D	DeSousa Mary †	9	housewife	33	19 "
E	Hutchins Claude	9	U S C G	23	Chelsea
F	Hutchins Marjorie †	9	housewife	21	"
G	Rethmel Fay †	9	"	29	Ohio
H	Rethmel Lester	9	U S N	28	"
K	Strehow Carol †	9	housewife	27	Iowa
L	Strehow Lyle	9	U S N	32	"
M	Lemos Arthur P	9	laborer	34	Plymouth
N	Lemos Louise †	9	housewife	30	"
P	MacKrell Jessie †	9	"	28	Pennsylvania

New Street—Continued

	R	MacKrell William	9	U S N	29	Pennsylvania
	T	Lundgren Doris—†	9	housewife	28	New York
	U	Lundgren Gustave	9	U S C G	36	"
	X	Cumby Geneva M—†	17	housewife	28	Texas
	Y	Cumby Roy T	17	U S C G	36	"
	Z	Remillard Cecilia E—†	17	housewife	27	Connecticut
62						
	A	Remillard Ullysses C	17	shipfitter	27	"
	B	Brueggeman Eileen—†	17	nurse	25	N Brookfield
	C	Coyne Elizabeth—†	17	housewife	58	"
	D	Coyne Thomas	17	U S N	56	"
	E	Coyne Thomas, jr	17	U S A	23	"
	F	Baker Corrine—†	17	housewife	28	Everett
	G	Baker Paul	17	chipper	32	"
	H	Menzies Edythe—†	17	housewife	24	Chelsea
	K	Menzies Norman M, jr	17	U S N	31	"
	L	Baldassare Frances—†	17	housewife	21	44 Jeffries
	M	Baldassare Pasquale	17	inspector	26	44 "
	N	Bradford Robert F	17	rigger	30	Illinois
	O	Bradford Theresa—†	17	housewife	32	"
	P	Sanborn Dorothy—†	17	"	21	Vermont
	R	Sanborn Erwin	17	welder	23	"
	S	Burns Herbert	17	U S N	41	California
	T	Burns Irene—†	17	housewife	37	"
	U	Hughes Victor	17	U S C G	32	Virginia
	V	Hughes Winifred—†	17	housewife	27	"
	W	Silver Lillian—†	17	"	27	Chelsea
	X	Silver Maurice	17	carpenter	28	"
	Y	Rudnicki Julian	17	U S N	31	105 Gainsboro
	Z	Rudnicki Stephania—†	17	housewife	26	105 "
63						
	D	Atkinson Nora—†	33	"	26	12 Lawnwood pl
	E	Atkinson William	33	boilermaker	39	12 "
	F	Leuchte Frances—†	33	housewife	25	Quincy
	G	Leuchte Paul	33	welder	28	"
	H	Watus David	33	U S N	22	65 Hemenw'y
	K	Watus Pauline—†	33	housewife	24	65 "
	L	Fiorillo Monica—†	33	"	35	80 Everett
	M	Fiorillo Salvatore	33	welder	32	80 "
	P	Peck Edson L	33	"	22	Haverhill
	R	Prevost Mary A—†	33	at home	42	29 Cross

New Street —Continued

s	Arvin Clara — †	33	housewife	33	Missouri	
t	Arvin Samuel	33	U S N	22	Virginia	
v	Healey Daniel F	33	inspector	64	Fitchburg	
w	Healey Mary E — †	33	housewife	53	"	
x	Downey Charles	33	U S N	23	23½ Lexington	
y	Downey Helen — †	33	housewife	42	23½ "	
z	Downey Joseph	33	machinist	43	23½ "	

64 Porter Street

x	Lazzaro Frances — †	22	housekeeper	28	here
o	Lazzaro Gaetano	22	meatcutter	60	"
p	Lazzaro Rosaria — †	22	housewife	53	"
r*	Minichiello Angelina — †	24	"	51	"
s	Minichiello Antonio	24	storekeeper	48	"
t	Minichiello Ralph	24	U S A	21	"
v	Caggiano Bernard	26	laborer	31	"
w	Caggiano John	26	"	58	"
x	DeVingo Edward J	26	leathercutter	34	"
y	DeVingo Josephine — †	26	housewife	25	"

65

a	Lozzi Joseph	28	tailor	43	"
b	Lozzi Theresa — †	28	housewife	37	"
c*	Ehler Anna — †	28	"	60	244 Meridian
d*	Dimubla Paul	30	bootblack	54	here
e	Santiano Anthony	30	chauffeur	31	"
f	Santiano Domenic	30	U S A	23	"
g	Santiano John	30	"	21	"
h*	Santiano Lena — †	30	housewife	65	"
k*	Santiano Luigi	30	retired	69	"
l	Caruso Phillane — †	30	housewife	33	"

Sumner Street

n	Hoskins Lena — †	34	housewife	32	Chelsea
o	Hoskins Raymond	34	foreman	38	"
p	Reese Ardis V — †	34	housewife	20	New York
r	Reese William A	34	U S N	24	"
s	Hughett Annie M — †	34	at home	50	Virginia
t	O'Berg George A	34	U S N	29	"
u	O'Berg Jewell M — †	34	housewife	21	"

Sumner Street Continued

	v	Peters J Miller	34	U S N	30	New York
	w	Peters Maxine †	34	housewife	28	"
	y	Chambless Fred H	34	U S N	27	Louisiana
	z	Chambless Helen †	34	housewife	27	"
66						
	a	Chambless Ida †	34	at home	53	"
	b	Carter Bruce	34	rigger	28	129 Chambers
	b	Carter Dorothy †	34	housewife	25	129 "
	c	Belanger Frances †	34	"	26	Worcester
	d	Belanger Lucien	34	U S C G	25	"
	e	Gooby John	34	rigger	26	14 Medford
	f	Sullo Johana †	34	at home	49	14 "
	g	Durkee Frances A †	34	housewife	33	Maryland
	h	Durkee Harold C	34	U S N	42	"
	k	James Arthur P	34	electrician	34	N Hampshire
	l	James Josephine E †	34	housewife	28	"
	m	Foresta Marie M †	34	"	23	Revere
	n	Foresta Victor A	34	clerk	23	"
	o	Duhamel George	42	U S N	35	Maine
	p	Duhamel Mildred †	42	housewife	35	"
	r	Fitch Edward	42	calker	54	Connecticut
	s	Fitch Ruby †	42	housewife	50	Rhode Island
	t	Rector Virginia †	42	"	26	Everett
	u	Rector William	42	boilermaker	33	"
	v	Wheeler Bertha V †	42	housewife	29	Weymouth
	w	Wheeler Stanley G	42	mechanic	37	"
	x	Casey Caroline †	42	housewife	33	130 Webster
	y	Casey Edwin F	42	shipfitter	26	197 Joy
	z	Maines Clayton	42	cutter	30	Winthrop
67						
	a	Maines Frances †	42	housewife	36	"
	c	Cibello Edith †	42	"	32	14 Paris
	d	Cibello Louis	42	operator	37	14 "
	e	Nelson Hilda †	42	housewife	48	Waltham
	f	Nelson John	42	metalworker	55	"
	g	Parker James T	42	U S N	28	Alabama
	h	Parker Margaret †	42	housewife	26	"
	k	Rowson Betty L †	42	"	23	Kansas
	l	Rowson Louis	42	U S N	25	"

Sumner Street Continued

M	Byrne Esther †	42	housewife	39	Everett
N	Byrne William J	42	metalworker	36	"

William J Kelly Square

O	*Ferrara Thomas	6	chef	67	here
P	Orlandi Pasquale	6	molder	53	"
R	*Pallazzo James	6	laborer	52	"
S	Palma Helen—†	6	housewife	32	48 Maverick sq
T	*Palma William	6	painter	36	48 "
U	*Pasquale Vincent	6	carpenter	50	here
V	Testa Vincent	6	"	60	"
W	Wilcox Benjamin	6	watchman	62	"
X	Wilcox Joseph	6	U S A	24	"
Y	Wilcox Marie—†	6	at home	25	"
Z	Bogdanowiz Frank	7	machinist	24	"

68

A	Bonner Bernard F	7	guard	43	"
B	Bonner Margaret F †	7	housewife	42	"
C	Bonner Margaret F †	7	cashier	21	"
D	Dietrich Ernest	7	asbestos worker	59	"
E	Riley Edward	7	insulator	24	"
F	Riley Mildred—†	7	housewife	23	"
L	Nevola Fred	13	machinist	29	"
M	Nevola Mary—†	13	housewife	24	"
N	Rizzo Angie †	13	"	49	"
O	Rizzo Michael	13	laborer	44	"
P	Carney John J	13	retired	80	"
R	Ciccarilla Caesar	13	U S A	43	"
T	D'Argenio Beatrice—†	14	at home	20	"
U	Ferreira Antonio	14	carder	49	"
V	Ferreira Antonio	14	seaman	26	"
W	*Ferreira Condida—†	14	housewife	51	"
X	Morelli Nieda—†	14	shoeworker	30	"
Y	Morelli Theodore	14	U S A	29	"
Z	Valiante Alfred	14	"	28	"

69

A	Valiante Edith—†	14	operator	30	"
B	Valiante Peter	14	machinist	37	"

Page.	Letter.	Full Name.	Residence, Jan. 1, 1943.	Occupation.	Supposed Age.	Reported Residence, Jan. 1, 1942. Street and Number.

William J Kelly Square—Continued

	c	Valiante Robert	14	U S A	26	here
	D	Valiante Rose—†	14	housewife	56	"
	F	Fazio Salvatore	17	barber	56	"
	G	Hannon Mildred—†	17	stitcher	26	"
	H	Pitseo Stamatios	17	chef	48	"
	K	Shiveree Mary—†	17	housekeeper	38	"
	L	Sprague Rodella M—†	17	at home	68	"
	N	Stanley Charles A	64	U S A	25	"
	O	Stanley Coralie W—†	64	student	20	"
	P	Stanley Jane E—†	64	housewife	51	"
	R	Stanley Martin K	64	operator	51	"
	S	Stanley Martin K, jr	64	U S A	28	"

Ward 1—Precinct 2

CITY OF BOSTON

LIST OF RESIDENTS
20 YEARS OF AGE AND OVER

(NON-CITIZENS INDICATED BY ASTERISK)
(FEMALES INDICATED BY DAGGER)

AS OF

JANUARY 1, 1943

JOSEPH F. TIMILTY, *Chairman*
FREDERIC E. DOWLING, *Secretary*
WILLIAM A. MOTLEY, JR.
FRANCIS B. McKINNEY
EVERETT R. PROUT

Listing Board.

CITY OF BOSTON PRINTING DEPARTMENT

200

Alna Place

	A	Hanlon Bernard	1	longshoreman	35	here
	B	Hanlon John	1	retired	71	"
	C	Snow Elizabeth V—†	1	at home	26	"

Brigham Street

	D	Menard Alfred	1	longshoreman	36	here
	E	Menard Emilia—†	1	housewife	33	"
	F	Hahn Elizabeth—†	1	"	72	"
	G*	Holley John	1	longshoreman	52	"
	H	Jones Thomas	1	bricklayer	69	"
	K	Cuninngham Lillian †	1	housekeeper	23	Connecticut
	L	Disario Angelina—†	1	housewife	52	here
	M	Disario Emilio	1	sculptor	54	"
	N*	Hill John	2	ironworker	55	"
	O	Hill Martha—†	2	clerk	20	"
	P*	Hill Olga—†	2	housewife	57	"
	R	Matson Adolph	2	seaman	31	"
	S	Matson Fred	2	operator	34	"
	T	Centeio Antonio	2	seaman	21	"
	U	Monteiro Anthony	2	"	29	"
	V	Monteiro Joseph	2	"	26	"
	W	Monteiro Louise—†	2	at home	28	"
	X	Monteiro Theodore	2	U S A	23	"
	Y	Monteiro William	2	seaman	25	"

201

	A	Rossi Girolamo	3	laborer	53	"
	D	McCarthy Patrick	4	fishcutter	32	271 Webster
	E	McCarthy Phyllis—†	4	housewife	27	271 "
	F	Ward John	4	watchman	26	14 Cottage
	G	Ward Rita—†	4	housewife	22	14 "
	M*	Ferrera Giobatta	6	laborer	66	here
	N	Ferrera John	6	U S A	26	"
	O	Ferrera Joseph	6	longshoreman	32	"
	P	Ferrera Louise †	6	cashier	36	"
	R	Ferrera Mary †	6	clerk	24	"
	S*	Ferrera Rosa †	6	housewife	61	"

202

	H	Interrante Carmella—†	10	"	27	"
	K*	Interrante Charles	10	laborer	45	"

2

Brigham Street Continued

L	Johnston Catherine †	10	marker	30	here
M	Johnston Margaret †	10	operator	23	"
N	*Johnston Nellie †	10	housewife	63	"
O	*Johnston William	10	longshoreman	64	"
P	Rocco Anthony	10	operator	45	"
R	Rocco Mary †	10	housewife	38	"
S	Iacona Gaspar	10	U S A	24	"
T	Iacona Lena †	10	seamstress	22	"
U	Stornaiuolo Carmine	10	mechanic	40	"
V	*Stornaiuolo Jennie †	10	housewife	46	"
W	McCarthy John J	18	longshoreman	34	"
X	*McCarthy Mabel M †	18	housewife	35	"
Y	Barone Amelia †	20	"	41	"
Z	*Barone Louis	20	spinner	51	"

203

A	McCarthy Alice †	21	housewife	33	"
B	McCarthy Daniel	21	U S A	29	"
C	McCarthy Joseph	21	pipefitter	36	"
D	Sweeney Annie †	22	housewife	71	"
E	*Sweeney William	22	fisherman	69	"

Cottage Street

H	Caruso Anthony	10	chauffeur	27	here
K	Caruso Edith †	10	housewife	28	"
L	*Cocchi Lena †	10	"	53	"
M	*Cocchi Paul	10	laborer	55	"
N	Chianca Josephine †	10	housewife	21	"
O	Chianca Louis	10	shipper	28	"
P	DeRosa Anna †	12	housewife	35	"
R	DeRosa Carmine	12	bricklayer	33	"
S	DiSimone Anthony	12	laborer	45	"
T	*DiSimone Mary †	12	candymaker	51	"
U	*Graziano Angelo	12	laborer	44	"
V	*Graziano Generosa †	12	seamstress	48	"
W	Falanga Clara †	14	housewife	27	"
X	Falanga Leo	14	shoeworker	27	"
Y	Giaquinto Andrew	14	longshoreman	34	"
Z	Giaquinto Theresa †	14	housewife	34	"

204

B	Ialuna Angelo	15	engineer	23	"

3

Cottage Street—Continued

c	Ialuna Concetta—†	15	housewife	24	here
d	*Conti Anthony	15	trackman	60	"
e	Conti Helen—†	15	stitcher	21	"
f	Conti Rose—†	15	housekeeper	25	"
g	Conti Sadie—†	15	laborer	27	"
h	Salvo Joseph	15	"	30	"
k	Salvo Theresa—†	15	housewife	29	"
l	Gravallese Antonio A	16	salesman	26	"
m	Gravallese Rose—†	16	housewife	25	"
n	Gravallese Josephine—†	16	"	28	"
o	Gravallese Michael	16	garageman	30	"
p	Gravallese Pasquale	16	shoeworker	45	"
r	McKenna Catherine †	17	housewife	21	70 Trenton
s	McKenna Edward	17	laborer	23	70 "
t	Siciliano Joseph	17	bartender	28	here
u	Siciliano Rose—†	17	housewife	27	"
v	McKenna Jeremiah	17	laborer	21	"
w	*McKenna Nora—†	17	housewife	62	"
x	*McKenna William	17	longshoreman	62	"
y	Benelli Columbia †	17	housewife	49	"
z	Benelli Mary—†	18	at home	29	"
	205				
a	Benelli Ubaldo	18	barber	52	"
b	Samms Catherine—†	18	housewife	21	422 Chelsea
c	Samms James	18	electrician	24	422 "
d	Testa Joseph, jr	18	machinist	26	here
e	Testa Linda—†	18	housewife	29	"
f	Camerlengo Lucy—†	31	housekeeper	48	"
g	*Laurina Michael	31	laborer	61	"
n	Bellio Mary—†	33	housewife	34	94 Webster
o	Bellio Silvio	33	painter	47	94 "
p	*Carini Adeline—†	33	housewife	57	242 "
r	*Carini Joseph	33	laborer	67	242 "
s	Carini Joseph, jr	33	painter	29	242 "
t	Carini Louise—†	33	dressmaker	25	242 "
u	Lombardi Ida †	34	housewife	35	here
v	Lombardi Jennie †	34	finisher	39	"
w	*Lombardi Mary †	34	housewife	84	"
x	Lombardi Michael J	34	ironworker	37	"
y	Stasio Amelia T †	34	housewife	39	"
z	Stasio John B	34	installer	44	"

4

206

Cottage Street Continued

A	Stasio Emilio	34	technician	39	here
B	Stasio Rose—†	34	housewife	36	"
D	Razza Josephine †	36	"	22	"
E	Razza Samuel	36	shipper	28	"
F	*DiFilippa Mary—†	36	housewife	54	"
G	*Mendolia Mary—†	36	candymaker	40	"
H	Malafronte Nicolo	36	clerk	56	307 Sumner
K	*Malafronte Olga †	36	housewife	53	307 "
L	Malafronte Theresa—†	36	clerk	21	here
O	Natalucci Rose—†	38	housewife	35	'
P	Natalucci Vincent	38	bartender	39	"
R	Zenkin Walter	38	upholsterer	43	"
S	Mazzotta Gregory	38	janitor	55	"
T	Mazzotta Marion—†	38	housewife	48	"
U	Bulger Mary—†	39	saleswoman	56	"
V	Pagliuca Michael	41	painter	44	"
W	Pagliuca Philomena—†	41	housewife	30	"
X	Malerba Anna—†	41	"	25	"
Y	Malerba Dominic	41	painter	28	"
Z	*Tripari Alfonsina—†	41	housewife	45	"

207

A	LuPorta Catherine—†	42	clerk	24	"
B	*LuPorta Ignazio	42	longshoreman	56	"
C	LuPorta Joseph	42	"	26	"
D	Amato Giovanni	42	laborer	55	6 Sumner pl
E	DiChiara Angelo	42	mason	26	here
F	DiChiara Dorothy—†	42	housewife	23	"
G	Abruzzese Generoso	42	laborer	29	1 Percival pl
H	Abruzzese Maria—†	42	housewife	29	1 "
K	*Ramo Conchetta—†	42	"	54	here
L	Ramo Mario	42	chauffeur	32	"
M	Ramo Turilli	42	laborer	59	"
N	*Figliolino Giuseppe	42A	storekeeper	50	"
P	*DiChiara Olga—†	43	housewife	43	"
R	DiChiara Ralph	43	ironworker	47	"
S	Guancial Anthony	43	welder	32	"
T	Guancial Mary—†	43	housewife	30	"
U	*Milo Lena—†	44	"	37	"
V	Milo Leonard	44	barber	43	"
W	Chin Danny	47	laundryworker	38	"

5

Cottage Street Continued

A	Ragusa Dorothy †	49	housewife	28	2 Webster av
Z	Ragusa James	49	U S A	32	2 "
	208				
A	Calabrese Fannie †	49	housewife	25	here
B	Calabrese Nello	49	mechanic	28	"
D	Martel Ernest	54	steamfitter	62	57 W Sixth
E	Martel Mary †	54	housewife	60	57 "
G	Carso Florence †	54	"	29	here
H	Carso Frank M	54	chauffeur	34	"
K	Vocino Imbriani D	54	welder	47	"

Cottage Street Place

L	Runney Arline †	2	matron	50	here
M	Runney Georgianna †	2	housewife	89	"
N	Chiarella Mildred †	2	"	28	"
O	Chiarella Vincent	2	laborer	27	"
P*	Mazzarini Anna †	2	housewife	31	"
R*	Mazzarini Giacomo	2	laborer	43	"
S	Amico Jennie †	2	candymaker	55	"
T	Amico Luciano	2	mason	60	"
U	Polignone Anthony	4	"	55	"
V	Polignone Josephine †	4	clerk	23	"
W*	Polignone Margaret †	4	housewife	50	"
X	Polignone Michael	4	U S N	21	"
Y	Carraggi Ida †	4	housewife	56	"
Z	Carraggi Joseph	4	laborer	56	"

209   Haynes Street

B	Mascis Frank	2	laborer	29	here
C	Mascis Ruby †	2	housewife	28	"
D	Toriso Antoinette †	2	"	20	"
E	Toriso Joseph	2	plasterer	58	"
F	Toriso Louis	2	laborer	21	"
G*	Toriso Sabina †	2	housewife	56	"
L	Baroni John	6	longshoreman	44	"
M	Capone Dominic	6	agent	21	"
N	Capone Jeremiah	6	U S A	21	"
O	Capone Josephine †	6	housekeeper	44	"
P	Forgione Antonio	6	U S A	22	"

Haynes Street Continued

	Letter	FULL NAME	Residence Jan. 1, 1943	Occupation	Supposed Age	Reported Residence Jan. 1, 1942 Street and Number
	R	Forgione Joseph	6	laborer	53	here
	S	Forgione Martin	6	U S A	21	"
	T	*Forgione Mary — †	6	housewife	47	"
	U	Cusizzioni Joseph	7	carpenter	46	"
	W	*Petrinelli Etta — †	7	housewife	38	"
	X	Petrinelli Frank	7	laborer	21	"
	Y	*Petrinelli Joseph	7	"	46	"
	Z	*Zagorella Lena — †	8	housewife	50	6 Haynes
210						
	A	Zagorella Rocco	8	laborer	52	6 "
	B	Cioffi Anthony	8	U S A	24	here
	C	Cioffi Benjamin	8	"	20	"
	D	Cioffi Enrico	8	tailor	53	"
	E	Cioffi Enrico, jr	8	U S N	22	"
	F	*Cioffi Jennie — †	8	housewife	52	"
	G	Cioffi Jennie — †	8	stitcher	22	"
	H	DePasquale Paris	9	laborer	66	
	K	Moran Margaret — †	9	at home	62	154 Chelsea
	L	Moran Thomas	9	laborer	25	154 "
	M	Powers Margaret — †	9	at home	23	154 "
	N	*Sorrentino Louis	9	laborer	47	here
	O	Sorrentino Virginia — †	9	housewife	35	"
	P	Bruno Ralph	10	clerk	30	"
	R	Bruno Virginia — †	10	packer	25	"
	S	DeGregorio Michael	10	laborer	66	"
	T	DeGregorio Phyllis — †	10	housewife	55	"
	U	Jameson Helen — †	11	at home	42	"
	V	Jameson John	11	laborer	39	"
	W	*DiVigo Anna — †	11	housewife	65	"
	X	*DiVigo Salvatore	11	laborer	67	"
	Y	Malola Anthony	11	packer	31	"
	Z	Malola Rose — †	11	housewife	26	"
211						
	A	*Rongo Giardano	12	retired	77	"
	B	*Rongo Josephine — †	12	housewife	77	"
	E	O'Leary Daniel	13	longshoreman	66	"
	F	O'Leary Margaret M — †	13	inspector	32	"
	G	O'Leary Mary M — †	13	housewife	67	"
	H	O'Leary William F	13	guard	28	"
	K	*Cullicci Michael	14	porter	28	"
	L	Memmolo Josephine — †	14	housewife	21	16 Haynes

7

Page.	Letter	FULL NAME.	Residence, Jan. 1, 1943.	Occupation.	Supposed Age.	Reported Residence, Jan. 1, 1942. Street and Number.

Haynes Street— Continued

	M	Memmolo Rocco	14	laborer	22	16 Haynes
	O	*Montalto Agrippino	14	"	61	here
	N	*Montalto Josephine—†	14	housewife	56	"
	P	Hanson John E	15	foreman	60	"
	R	Hanson Katherine A—†	15	housewife	64	"
	T	*Bellino Daisy—†	16	at home	66	"
	U	Driscoll Mary—†	16	"	80	"
	V	Enenrato Anna—†	16	housewife	52	"
	W	Enenrato Anna—†	16	packer	23	"
	X	Enenrato Louis	16	laborer	55	"
	Y	Malagrifa Theresa—†	17	at home	45	"
	Z	Barbetta Elizabeth S—†	18	stitcher	24	"
212						
	A	Barbetta Lillian F—†	18	"	21	"
	B	Barbetta Rose—†	18	housewife	56	"
	C	Barbetta Santo W	18	painter	26	"
	D	Sweeney Eleanor—†	18	housewife	31	"
	E	Sweeney William F	18	painter	35	"
	F	Sweeney Philomena—†	18	housewife	29	"
	G	Sweeney Ralph	18	painter	34	"
	H	*Kirby Catherine—†	19	housewife	65	"
	K	*Kirby James J	19	retired	68	"
	L	*Malerba Maria—†	20	housewife	58	"
	M	*Malerba Michael	20	laborer	64	"
	N	Prioio Michael R	20	"	24	"
	O	Petrillo Jennie—†	20	housewife	35	8 Haynes
	P	Petrillo Pasquale	20	janitor	47	8 "
	R	Fiorillo Arthur A	20	shipfitter	38	here
	S	Fiorillo Saveria S—†	20	housewife	25	"
	T	Peterson Albert E	21	manager	36	"
	U	Peterson Ruth—†	21	housewife	34	"
	W	*Stasio Anthony	22	retired	75	"
	X	*Stasio Lucy—†	22	at home	72	"
	Y	Bickford Charles	22	laborer	45	"
	Z	Bickford Victoria—†	22	housewife	38	"
213						
	A	Russo Marie—†	22	at home	47	98 Everett
	B	Barretta Anthony	23	welder	36	here
	C	Barretta Charlotte—†	23	housewife	32	"
	D	DuGuay Elizabeth—†	23	packer	34	Newton
	E	Modica Michael	24	watchman	30	here

8

Haynes Street Continued

F	Modica Rose—†	24	housewife	23	here
G	Modica Antonio	24	laborer	56	"
H	Modica Josephine †	24	housewife	53	"
K	Modica Nunzio	24	longshoreman	28	"
L	Cintolo Alec	24	"	27	"
M	Cintolo Ethel—†	24	housewife	22	"
N	Sullivan Catherine †	26	teacher	68	"
O	Cappucci Anthony	28	U S A	24	"
P	Cappucci Constantino	28	laborer	35	"
R	Cappucci Daniel	28	carpenter	64	"
S	Cappucci Daniel, jr	28	U S A	22	"
T	Cappucci Denuzio	28	marblesetter	33	"
U	Cappucci Louis	28	U S A	26	"
V	Cappucci Marion—†	28	housewife	54	"
W	Cappucci Robert	28	laborer	28	"
X	D'Avolio Rosaria M—†	30	housewife	52	87 Orleans
Y	Pagliuca Domenic	30	laborer	22	here
Z	Pagliuca Felix	30	retired	66	"
	214				
A	*Ancello Rosa—†	30	housewife	55	"
B	*Ancello Sebastiano	30	laborer	60	"
C	O'Neil Arthur F	31	"	30	"
D	O'Neil Lena—†	31	housewife	24	"
E	Cintolo Carmen	31	U S A	20	"
F	Cintolo Frank	31	butcher	38	"
G	Cintolo Margaret—†	31	stitcher	25	"
H	Cintolo Michael	31	retired	67	"
K	*Cintolo Susie—†	31	housewife	61	"
L	Fiorillo Mary—†	31	at home	39	"
M	Fiorillo Paul	31	laborer	41	"
N	Materazzo Armand	31	U S A	29	"
O	Materazzo Jennie—†	31	stitcher	26	"
P	Materazzo Letitia †	31	at home	27	"
R	Materazzo Marie C—†	31	bookbinder	31	"
S	Harnish Lottie—†	32	at home	49	"
T	McCashion Joseph	32	laborer	56	"
U	McCashion Sarah A—†	32	housewife	56	"
V	Costello Mary E—†	32	"	31	"
W	Costello William J	32	longshoreman	39	"
X	Porrazzo James V	32	chauffeur	35	"
Y	Porrazzo Mary—†	32	housewife	30	"

9

Haynes Street Continued

	z	Blumer Alice — †	33	housewife	27	Texas
215						
	A	Blumer Samuel, jr	33	U S N	29	"
	B	Sears Angelina — †	33	housewife	29	here
	C	Sears Luther H	33	U S N	31	"
	D*	Ciampa Antonio	33	laborer	63	"
	E	Ciampa Antonio	33	U S A	31	"
	F	Ciampa Carmella — †	33	packer	28	"
	G	Ciampa Carmen	33	U S N	21	"
	H	Ciampa Constance — †	33	at home	26	"
	K	Ciampa Elizabeth — †	33	saleswoman	23	"
	L*	Siracusa Anna — †	34	housewife	58	"
	M*	Siracusa Joseph	34	laborer	56	"
	N*	Nocera Angelo	34	cobbler	35	"
	O	Nocera Elvira — †	34	housewife	30	"
	P	Matanza Santa — †	34	"	33	"
	R	Matanza Sebastian	34	shipper	35	"
	S*	Pagluca Irene — †	35	housewife	60	"
	T	Pagluca Michael	35	laborer	64	"
	U*	Cardolla Charles	35	retired	69	45 Haynes
	V*	Renaldi Frank	35	laborer	42	here
	W	Renaldi Lucy — †	35	housewife	32	"
	X*	Montaldo Peter	36	retired	69	"
	Y	Nazzaro Ellen — †	36	at home	36	"
	Z	Oliveri Louis	36	painter	51	"
216						
	A	Oliveri Mario	36	laborer	27	"
	B	Oliveri Nancy — †	36	housewife	48	"
	C	Sega Romeo	37	laborer	53	"
	D*	Pagluica Maria — †	37	housewife	45	"
	E	Nordstrom Carl	37	U S C G	36	9 Haynes
	F	Nordstrom Santa — †	37	housewife	24	9 "
	G	Picardi Pasquale	39	laborer	36	here
	H	Voto Anthony	39	painter	59	"
	K*	Voto Antonette — †	39	housewife	57	"
	L*	LaRosa Jennie — †	39	"	33	"
	M	LaRosa Philip	39	laborer	38	"
	N*	Landrigan Nora — †	41	at home	61	"
	O	Guerreri Florence — †	41	packer	21	"

Haynes Street Continued

	P	*Guerreri Mary †	41	housewife	40	here
	R	Guerreri Salvatore	41	laborer	48	"
	S	*Bragioni Ernest	43	"	53	"
	U	Muise Dorothy C †	44	housewife	29	339 Chelsea
	V	Muise Vincent W	44	U S N	31	339 "
	W	*Giammatteo Andrew	45	laborer	61	here
	X	*Graziana Nicholas	45	"	68	73 Cottage
	Y	*Martina Antonio	45	"	36	here
	Z	Beatrice Ellen—†	47	stenographer	25	"

217

	A	Casey Hugh	47	retired	65	"
	B	Costello Nellie †	47	housewife	65	"
	C	McKenna Isabel M †	47	"	28	"
	D	McKenna Thomas E	47	longshoreman	28	"
	E	Cammarano Anthony	48	fireman	30	"
	F	Cammarano Ernestine †	48	housewife	30	"
	G	Cammarano Domenic	48	foreman	59	"
	H	*Cammarano Maria—†	48	housewife	58	"
	K	Cammarano Pasquale	48	U S A	25	"
	L	Cammarano Vincenzo	48	retired	58	"
	M	Gill Helen †	49	housewife	42	142 Marginal
	N	Gill Henry	49	longshoreman	52	142 "
	O	Callahan Charles L	49	accountant	30	here
	P	Callahan John B	49	U S N	33	"
	R	Callahan John J	49	laborer	61	"
	S	Callahan Mary—†	49	housewife	61	"
	T	Dennehy Helen †	49	cook	56	"
	U	Dorazzio Arline—†	49	housewife	29	"
	V	Dorazzio John J	49	U S A	28	"
	W	Shine Anna—†	49	cook	63	"
	X	Shine Mary P—†	49	nurse	25	"
	Y	Driscoll Julia E—†	52	at home	68	"
	Z	McCarthy Dennis	52	longshoreman	61	"

218

	A	*DeMori Anna—†	62	housewife	52	"
	B	DeMori Domenic	62	laborer	20	"
	C	DeMori Genoti	62	"	50	"
	D	DeMori Samuel	62	U S A	22	"
	E	O'Leary Harry	62	longshoreman	30	"

11

Page.	Letter.	Full Name.	Residence, Jan. 1, 1943.	Occupation.	Supposed Age.	Reported Residence, Jan. 1, 1942. Street and Number.

Haynes Street—Continued

	F	O'Leary Sadie—†	62	housewife	24	here
	G	Cogliano Jennie—†	62	"	27	"
	H	Cogliano Louis	62	laborer	28	"

Marginal Street

	M	Abell Louise—†	72	social worker	25	here
	N	Anderson Irene N—†	72	"	38	"
	O	Phelps Dorothy—†	72	"	36	N Hampshire
	P	Williams Mary F—†	72	"	22	New York
	U	Lanza Biagio	90	U S A	32	here
	V	Lanza Frank	90	clerk	27	"
	W*	Lanza Venera—†	90	housekeeper	62	"
	X	Davenport Loren	90	U S C G	21	Iowa
	Z	Santa Maria Pasqualina—†	91	housekeeper	72	here
219						
	A	Waters Antoinette—†	91	housewife	30	"
	B	Waters Edmund	91	rigger	33	"
	C	Bruno Jeremiah	92	laborer	28	559 E Second
	D	Bruno Stella J—†	92	housewife	25	559 "
	E	Bruno Eva—†	92	clerk	22	170 W Canton
	F	Perratta Louis	92	waiter	32	Worcester
	K	Gigliello Florence—†	100	housewife	26	here
	H	Gigliello Michael	100	carpenter	65	"
	L	Gigliello Nicholas	100	painter	30	"
	M	DiSpirito James	100	U S A	24	"
	N	Kirkorian Louise—†	100	stitcher	28	"
	O*	Mascis Frank	102	retired	70	"
	P	Mascis Louis	102	U S A	28	"
	R*	Mascis Michalina—†	102	housewife	58	"
	S	Marchi Mary—†	106	"	23	"
	T	Marchi Richard	106	chauffeur	27	"
	U	Voto Alma—†	106	housewife	33	"
	V	Voto Ralph	106	painter	35	"
	W	Manganelli Antonette—†	110	clerk	21	"
	X	Manganelli Frank	110	salesman	62	"
	Y	Manganelli Rose—†	110	housewife	53	"
	Z	Reidy Mary C—†	110	"	26	"
220						
	A	Reidy Michael	110	painter	29	"
	B	Smith Nathaniel	112	longshoreman	52	"

12

Marginal Street—Continued

c	Fahey Bridget †	112	housewife	67	here	
D	Fahey Catherine †	112	clerk	26	"	
F	Fahey David	112	longshoreman	70	"	
G	Fahey David F, jr	112	checker	38	"	
E	Fahey Leo D	112	U S N	27	"	
H	Fahey Mary M †	112	clerk	35	"	
K	O'Brien John T	112	checker	48	"	
M	Goodwin Beatrice †	116	housewife	29	"	
N	Goodwin James	116	U S N	37	"	
O	Kelly Mary †	116	at home	36	"	
P	Quilty Jessie †	116	housewife	48	"	
R	Quilty John	116	U S N	26	"	
S	Quilty Joseph	116	"	21	"	
T	Hanlon John	116	longshoreman	42	"	
U	Hanlon Rita †	116	housewife	35	"	
V	Chiango Carmen	118	roofer	28	"	
W	Chiango Grace †	118	housewife	24	"	
X	Chiango Frank	118	painter	33	"	
Y	Chiango Helen †	118	housewife	32	"	

221

A	*Aceto Beatrice †	126	"	64	"	
B	*Aceto Simone	126	laborer	63	"	
c	Whalen Elizabeth †	126	stitcher	59	18 Cottage	
D	Whalen Helen †	126	at home	63	18 "	
E	Whalen William J	126	shipper	57	18 "	
F	Crowley Catherine †	126	housewife	47	here	
G	Crowley Daniel J	126	longshoreman	48	"	
H	Aceto Antonio	128	laborer	28	"	
K	Aceto Lena †	128	housewife	25	"	
L	Schipani Mary †	128	"	34	"	
M	Schipani Thomas	128	shoemaker	40	"	
N	Kennedy Mary A †	128	housewife	27	"	
O	Kennedy William J	128	pipefitter	37	"	
P	Salvaggio Joseph	132	painter	25	"	
R	Salvaggio Mary †	132	housewife	25	"	
S	Lisci Hugo	132	driller	42	"	
T	Pearson James	132	pipefitter	25	Ohio	
U	*Terenzi Emelia †	132	housewife	49	here	
V	Terenzi Marino	132	U S A	20	"	
W	Terenzi Martha †	132	candymaker	24	"	
X	*Terenzi Osvaldo	132	tailor	55	"	

Page.	Letter.	FULL NAME.	Residence, Jan. 1, 1913.	Occupation.	Supposed Age.	Reported Residence, Jan. 1, 1942. Street and Number.

Marginal Street—Continued

	Y	Terenzi Thomas	132	driller	27	here
	Z	Gigliello John	136	painter	32	92 Marginal
222						
	A	Gigliello Theresa—†	136	housewife	31	92 "
	V	Vallen John	136	laborer	50	here
	C	Vallen Lillian—†	136	housewife	55	"
	D	Vallen Ruth—†	136	clerk	20	"
	E	Goggin Edward	136	longshoreman	36	"
	F	Goggin Mary—†	136	housekeeper	43	"
	G	Goggin Thomas	136	longshoreman	32	"
	H	Morcaldi Gabriel	138	chauffeur	20	"
	K	*Morcaldi Raffaele	138	retired	74	"
	L	Santagata Sylvester	138	U S A	24	"
	M	Costello Mary—†	138	housewife	35	44 Haynes
	N	Costello Michael	138	longshoreman	37	44 "
	O	Froio Mary—†	138	housewife	37	here
	P	Froio Salvatore	138	blacksmith	43	"
	S	Ratta Celia—†	140	housewife	39	"
	T	Ratta Onofrio	140	blacksmith	44	"
	U	Qualtieri Carmen	140	U S A	26	"
	V	*Qualtieri Christina †	140	housekeeper	54	"
	W	Qualtieri James	140	clerk	21	"
	Z	Lomanno Joseph	140	laborer	37	"
	X	*Lomanno Marie—†	140	at home	78	"
	Y	Lomanno Mary—†	140	housewife	31	"
223						
	A	Siciliano Antonio	142	bartender	51	"
	B	Siciliano Maria—†	142	housewife	48	"
	C	Siciliano Panteleone	142	welder	26	"
	D	Siracusa Giuseppe	142	laborer	20	34 Haynes
	F	Mastrangelo Angelo	184	"	49	here
	G	*Mastrangelo Antonetta †	184	housewife	44	"
	H	*Mastrangelo Michael	184	U S A	22	"
	K	*Cinelli Nancy †	184	housekeeper	59	"
	L	Grifoni Giaconda	188	laborer	51	"
	M	Girfoni Nancy—†	188	operator	24	"
	N	*Girfoni Virginia—†	188	housewife	46	"
	O	*Russo Aniello	188	laborer	49	"
	P	Russo Charlotte—†	188	housewife	26	"
	R	Lowry Ernest L	194	fireman	37	141 Webster
	S	Twitchell Gladys †	194	housewife	36	141 "

14

Marginal Street Continued

T	Twitchell James F	194	painter	37	141 Webster
U	O'Brien Alice †	194	housewife	22	here
V	O'Brien James	194	painter	28	"
W	Cadden Bernard	198	watchman	60	"
X	Cadden Bernard J, jr	198	U S A	20	"
Y	Cadden Bridget †	198	housewife	42	"
Z	Hagan Elizabeth M †	198	housekeeper	70	"

224

A	Hagan Henry J	198	janitor	39	"
B	DiFiore Gertrude †	210	stitcher	23	"
C	*DiFiore Michelina †	210	housewife	49	"
E	Leonard Edward	210	U S A	21	"
F	Leonard Mary E †	210	housewife	56	"
G	Leonard Michael	210	longshoreman	58	"
K	Cavagnaro Angelina † r	216	housewife	35	"
L	Cavagnaro Genaro "	216	shipfitter	35	"
M	Cavagnaro Alexander "	216	U S A	22	"
N	*Cavagnaro Frank "	216	laborer	64	"
O	*Cavagnaro Josephine † "	216	housekeeper	62	"
P	Cavagnaro Mildred † "	216	dressmaker	25	"

Murray Court

X	Coviello Anna †	1	stitcher	38	here
Y	Coviello Anthony	1	laborer	36	"
Z	Garafalo Carmella †	1	packer	23	"

225

A	Garafalo Frank	1	laborer	62	"
B	Garafalo Frank	1	U S A	21	"
C	Garafalo Josephine †	1	stitcher	24	"
D	*Garafalo Raffaella †	1	housewife	55	"
E	DeRocco Domenic	1	supervisor	44	"
F	DeRocco Grace †	1	packer	35	"
G	*Bozza Cesare	2	painter	57	"
H	Bozza Elenor †	2	housewife	40	"
K	*Bozza Emelio	2	barber	44	"
L	Indorato Albena †	2	housewife	20	256 Summer
M	*Indorato Anna †	2	at home	45	here
N	Indorato Joseph	2	laborer	25	"
O	Indorato Josephine †	2	packer	23	"

15

Murray Court Continued

P*Messina Christine—†	2	housewife	58	here
R Messina Dora—†	2	packer	22	"
S Messina Gloria—†	2	"	20	"
T Messina Silvester	2	laborer	62	"
U Cameron William H	3	"	50	"
V Cameron Winifred—†	3	housewife	49	"
W*McDonald Alice—†	3	"	68	"
X*McDonald John	3	laborer	36	"
Y*McDonald Richard	3	longshoreman	63	"
Z McDonald William	3	painter	34	"

226

A Campagnoni Frank	3	clerk	47	"
B Campagnoni Jennie—†	3	housewife	43	"
C Ciano Caroline—†	4	packer	21	"
D Ciano Michael	4	laborer	65	"
E Pedalino Charles J	4	chauffeur	48	"
F Pedalino Giovanna—†	4	examiner	28	"
G Pedalino Josephine—†	4	saleswoman	20	"
H Pedalino Mary—†	4	dressmaker	24	"
K Pedalino Rose—†	4	operator	27	"
L Pedalino Theresa—†	4	housewife	48	"
M DeAngelis Ernest	4	machinist	27	"
N DeAngelis Mildred—†	4	housewife	28	"
O*Farziale Pasquale	5	laborer	52	"
P Giello John	5	shipfitter	47	"
R Giello Michael	5	laborer	39	"
S*Giello Ralph	5	retired	86	"
T*Giello Rose—†	5	housewife	77	"
U Disario Celestina—†	9	operator	33	"
V Disario Maria—†	9	at home	75	"
W Limongiello Gabriel	9	machinist	44	"
X Limongiello Mary—†	9	housewife	38	"
Y Cardello Joseph	9	laborer	46	"
Z*Cardello Rose—†	9	housewife	36	"

227

D*Fagone Josephine—†	15	"	51	"
E Fagone Peter	15	laborer	52	"
F Parziale John	15	pipefitter	36	"
G Parziale Mary—†	15	housewife	30	"
H McDonald Leo	16	painter	40	15 Murray ct
K McDonald Ruth—†	16	housewife	29	15 "

16

Murray Court Continued

L	Ciano Carmella—†	17	housewife	27	here
M	Ciano Pasquale	17	plumber	30	"
N	Valerio Antonio	17	laborer	15	108 Orleans
O	*Valerio Nancy—†	17	housewife	33	108 "
P	Chiampa Albert	17	chauffeur	37	here
R	Chiampa Mary—†	17	housewife	30	"
S	Bona Emma—†	19	"	32	"
T	Bona Leo	19	laborer	32	"
U	Triulzi Edith—†	19	clerk	24	"
V	Triulzi Emelio	19	storekeeper	59	"
W	Triulzi James	19	"	35	"
X	*Triulzi Rose—†	19	housewife	59	"
Y	Chiampa James	19	storekeeper	35	"
Z	Repucci George	22	U S A	31	"

228

A	*Repucci Mary—†	22	housewife	65	"
B	Repucci Pellegrino	22	laborer	63	"
C	Repucci Philomeno—†	22	saleswoman	33	"
D	Iaconelli Mary—†	22	seamstress	31	"
E	Iaconelli Nicholas	22	laborer	30	"

Orleans Street

G	Scaramella Albert	39	undertaker	42	here
H	Scaramella Madeline—†	39	at home	85	"
K	Scaramella Rose—†	39	housewife	31	"
L	Scaramella Flora—†	39	"	43	"
M	Scaramella Flora—†	39	stitcher	21	"
N	Scaramella Rita—†	39	cashier	22	"
O	Scaramella Vincent	39	salesman	52	"
R	Tiso Anthony	41	machinist	29	"
S	Tiso Madeline—†	41	housewife	24	"
T	DiPietro Bessie—†	41	"	31	"
U	DiPietro Michael	41	plumber	34	"
V	Grugnale Mary—†	43	housewife	56	352 Princeton
W	Grugnale William	43	laborer	21	352 "
X	Caserta Anna—†	43	housewife	47	here
Y	Caserta Carmen	43	tinsmith	60	"
Z	Piccardi Grace—†	43	housewife	22	"

229

A	Simole Agrippino	43	laborer	60	"

Page.	Letter	FULL NAME.	Residence, Jan. 1, 1943.	Occupation.	Supposed Age.	Reported Residence Jan. 1, 1942. Street and Number.

Orleans Street—Continued

	B	Simole Joseph	43	U S N	21	here
	C	Simole Josephine—†	43	stitcher	23	"
	D*	Simole Mary—†	43	housewife	50	"
	E	Simole Mary—†	43	stitcher	30	"
	F	Larsen Edith—†	45	saleswoman	26	"
	G	Larsen James P	45	seaman	55	"
	H	Larsen Mary A—†	45	housewife	50	"
	K	Katz David	45	student	21	"
	L	Katz Louis M	45	U S A	24	"
	M	Katz Mollie—†	45	housewife	61	"
	N	Katz Samuel	45	clerk	60	"
	O	Milgram David	45	U S A	32	"
	P	Milgram Rose—†	45	housewife	26	"

Sumner Street

	S	Picardi Carmella—†	265	housewife	48	here
	T	Picardi Carmen	265	U S A	22	"
	U	Picardi Dominick	265	salesman	20	"
	V	Picardi Joseph	265	laborer	23	"
	W	Picardi Michael	265	storekeeper	49	"
	X	Andelacaro Antonetta—†	265	dressmaker	21	"
	Y	Andelacaro Sadie—†	265	housewife	27	"
	Z	Andelacaro Samuel	265	butcher	27	"

230

	A	Caliendo Anna—†	269	housewife	43	"
	B	Caliendo Raymond	269	barber	52	"
	C	Alesiani Henry	269	riveter	47	"
	D	Alesiani Margaret—†	269	housewife	38	"
	E	Martucci Augustino	269	salesman	27	73 Webster
	F	Martucci Marguerite—†	269	housewife	25	73 "
	H	Addivinola John	271	shoeworker	57	here
	K	Addivinola Lawrence	271	checker	21	"
	L	Addivinola Raffaela—†	271	housewife	47	"
	M	Addivinola Ulanda—†	271	dressmaker	20	"
	N	Addivinola Carmella—†	271	housewife	21	"
	O	Addivinola Joseph	271	welder	24	"
	P	Amato Patrick	273	clerk	20	130 Lovell
	R*	Corleto Mary—†	273	housewife	38	here
	S	Quartararo Catherine—†	273	dressmaker	20	5 Wilbur ct
	T	Quartararo Josephine—†	273	housewife	37	5 "

18

Page.	Letter.	Full Name	Residence, Jan. 1, 1943.	Occupation	Supposed Age.	Reported Residence, Jan. 1, 1942. Street and Number.

Sumner Street Continued

u	Abate Elvino	275	U S N	24	New York
v	Abate Rose—†	275	housewife	23	12 Paris
w	Simonelli Angelo	275	machinist	30	71 Frankfort
x	Simonelli Mary—†	275	housewife	27	142 Paris
y	Catena Frank	275	rigger	38	60 Frankfort
z	Catena Rose—†	275	housewife	35	60 "

231

A	*Gugliccello Gelasta—†	279	"	72	here
B	*Gugliccello Vito	279	retired	77	"
c	Cornetta John	279	laborer	48	"
D	Cornetta Mary R—†	279	housewife	39	"
E	*Cornetta Raffaela—†	279	"	83	"
F	Cornetta Phyllis—†	279	"	33	"
G	Cornetta Rosario	279	shoeworker	43	"
K	Panzini Dominick	281	laborer	42	"
L	*Panzini Mary—†	281	housewife	38	"
M	*Valestrini Luigi	281	retired	68	"
N	*Valestrini Sofia—†	281	housewife	64	"
O	*Mangiaratti Ida—†	281	"	52	"
P	Mangiaratti Josephine—†	281	laundress	22	"
R	Lupoli Nicolas	283	laborer	58	"
S	Lupoli Nicolas, jr	283	mechanic	20	"
T	*Lupoli Silvia—†	283	housewife	63	"
U	Infantino Joseph	283	laborer	58	269 Sumner
V	Infantino Josephine—†	283	housewife	22	269 "
W	*Infantino Rose—†	283	"	60	269 "
X	Infantino Salvatore	283	machinist	21	269 "
Y	Marannano Mario	283	engineer	33	269 "
Z	*Matarese Clara—†	283	housewife	40	here

232

A	Matarese James	283	pressman	42	"
B	*Matarese Vito	283	barber	44	"
c	Belsito Alfred	285	U S A	22	"
D	Belsito Gerardo	285	chuaffeur	49	"
E	Belsito Josephine—†	285	tailor	46	"
F	*Bruno Maria—†	285	housewife	83	"
G	*Desimone Minaca—†	287	"	60	"
H	Gulinello Anthony	287	U S A	21	"
K	*Gulinello Josephine—†	287	housewife	60	"
L	*Gulinello Salvatore	287	laborer	64	"
M	Enos Bessie—†	287	housewife	76	"

19

Sumner Street —Continued

N	Ladorella Antonio	289	coremaker	49	here
O	Ladorella Susie— †	289	housewife	43	"
P	Bardi Antonio	289	checker	21	"
R*	Bardi Conchetta— †	289	housewife	46	"
S	Bardi Luigi	289	welder	46	"
T	Pace Albert N	289	U S A	28	"
U	Pace Alfred G	289	"	23	"
V	Pace Edmund C	289	"	27	"
W	Pace Helen— †	289	tailor	25	"
X	Pace Pacifico	289	cobbler	54	"
Y	Pace Theresa — †	289	housewife	53	"

233

A	Russo Dominick	rear 289	retired	77	268 Sumner
D	Gaeta Adolph	291	U S A	20	here
E	Gaeta Anthony	291	shipper	27	"
F*	Gaeta Matteo	291	retired	62	"
G*	Gaeta Nicolina— †	291	housewife	50	"
H	Dalelio Dominick	rear 291	laborer	39	"
K*	Dalelio James	" 291	retired	69	"
L	Cappelletti Lucy — †	293	housewife	37	"
M	Cappelletti Toaldo	293	hairdresser	38	"
N	Targuinio Charles	293	manager	50	"
O*	Amiro James	293	fisherman	47	"
P*	Amiro Oscar	293	"	49	"
R	Belliveau Margaret †	293	waitress	24	"
S*	Belliveau Mary †	293	housewife	61	"
U	DeLisa Anthony	rear 293	laborer	20	"
V*	DeLisa Frank	" 293	"	52	"
W*	Gregario Eva †	" 293	houseworker	48	"
X	Jorgensen Esther — †	295	housewife	48	"
Y	Jorgensen George	295	oiler	25	"
Z	Jorgensen Jorgen P	295	steward	50	"

234

A	Serenci Joseph	295	chauffeur	25	198 Everett
B	Serenci Phyllis— †	295	housewife	25	198 "
C	Porcaro Alfred	295	painter	35	here
D	Porcaro Florence — †	295	housewife	33	"
E	Constantino Joseph	297	electrician	37	"
F	Constantino Rose †	297	housewife	31	"
G	Jenkins Julia †	297	"	62	"
H	Yoconn Ernest	297	retired	73	"

Sumner Street Continued

	K	Constantino George	297	retired	65	here
	L	Falanga Joseph	299	electrician	29	"
	M	Falanga Rose—†	299	housewife	28	"
	N	Bottaro Anthony	299	U S A	26	"
	O	Bottaro Mary—†	299	operator	25	"
	P	Doria Anna—†	299	housewife	28	"
	R	Doria Vito	299	shoeworker	32	"
	S	*Manzo Maria—†	299	housewife	64	"
	T	*Manzo Ralph	299	laborer	66	"
	U	Manzo Virginia—†	299	operator	22	"
	V	Giambroni Frank	299	U S A	24	"
	W	Giambroni Joseph	299	"	27	"
	X	Giambroni Michael	299	"	21	"
	Y	Marino Antonio	299	laborer	60	"
	Z	*Marino Frances—†	299	housewife	50	"
235						
	B	Todisco Emma—†	305	laborer	30	"
	C	Todisco Genoroso	305	U S A	25	"
	D	Todisco Louise—†	305	checker	31	"
	E	Todisco Mildred—†	305	housewife	52	"
	F	Todisco Vincent	305	shoeworker	63	"
	G	Granna Leonard	305	U S A	34	"
	H	Granna Mary—†	305	housewife	34	"
	K	Buono Guirino	305	machinist	35	"
	L	Buono Minnie D—†	305	housewife	29	"
	M	Gualtieri Catherine—†	307	"	38	"
	N	Gualtieri Salvatore	307	clerk	45	"
	O	Crocetti Alfred A	307	electrician	23	4501 Wash'n
	P	Crocetti Valrie—†	307	housewife	24	4501 "
	S	Melrzo Luigi	rear 309	manager	59	here
	T	Marano Vincent	" 309	tailor	44	"
	V	Russell Lillian—†	" 309	housewife	28	"
	W	Russell Roland	" 309	pinboy	34	"
	X	*Ventresca Joseph	" 309	waiter	62	"
	Y	Petrillo Frank	" 309	machinist	27	"
	Z	Petrillo Mary—†	" 309	housewife	23	"
236						
	A	*Scavo Antonio	315	baker	48	"
	B	*Scavo Josephine—†	315	housewife	44	"
	C	Dello Russo Constance—†	315	hairdresser	32	"
	D	Raffaele Eva—†	315	housewife	30	"

Sumner Street—Continued

E	Raffaele Samuel	315	laborer	35	here
F	Nardelli Pasquale	315	chauffeur	23	138 Porter
G	Nardelli Rose—†	315	housewife	23	138 "
H	Venuti Antonio	315	laborer	46	here
K*	Venuti Conchetta †	315	housewife	46	"
L	Ferraro Angelo	315	chipper	27	"
M	Ferraro Ida—†	315	housewife	24	"
N	Santasusso Rose—†	315	"	30	"
R*	DeBarros Antonio	317	laborer	42	"
S	DeBarros Linda—†	317	housewife	32	"
T	Guiffrida Joseph	317	operator	34	"
U	Guiffrida Mary—†	317	housewife	27	"
V	Fabella Americo	rear 317	shipfitter	21	"
W	Fabella Frank	" 317	U S A	27	"
X*	Fabella Henry	" 317	manager	60	"
Y	Fabella Louis	" 317	U S A	23	"
Z	Fabella Pelma—†	" 317	housewife	58	"
237					
A*	Abruzzese Adele—†	" 317	"	36	"
B*	Abruzzese Generoso	" 317	tailor	39	"
D*	Campo Angelina—†	319	housewife	46	"
E	Campo Paul	319	salesman	53	"
F	Campo Sarah—†	319	saleswoman	21	"
G	Scimone Gasper	319	chauffeur	26	"
H	Scimone Louise—†	319	housewife	26	"
K*	Masullo Madeline †	rear 319	"	75	"
L	DiPeitro Angelo	" 319	guard	46	"
M	DiPeitro Blanche—†	" 319	housewife	44	"
N	DiPeitro Joseph	" 319	U S N	44	"
O	Pelosi Agnes—†	" 319	housewife	30	"
P	Pelosi Michael	" 319	shoeworker	48	"
U	DePasquale Antonio	329	baker	28	"
V	DePasquale Theresa †	329	housewife	26	"
Z	St John Marie—†	341	"	44	"
238					
C	Albano Anna—†	345	"	56	"
D	Albano Anna—†	345	housekeeper	27	"
E	Albano Conchetta—†	345	storekeeper	20	"
F	Albano Fred	345	baker	38	"
G*	Albano Gaetano	345	storekeeper	36	"
H	Albano Joseph	345	baker	24	"

Sumner Street Continued

K	Connell John	347	counterman	58	here
L	Connell Mary †	347	housewife	58	"
M	Murphy Margaret †	347	"	62	"
N	Walsh Margaret †	349	"	65	8 Sumner pl
O	Walsh Patrick T	349	laborer	70	8 "
P	Ciampa Amando	349	patternmaker	23	74 Everett
R	Ciampa Lucy †	349	housewife	22	233 Trenton
S	Cecca Anthony	349	painter	24	358 Sumner
T	Cecca Arigo	349	laborer	51	358 "
U	*Cecca Carmella †	349	housewife	47	358 "
V	Cecca Luigi	349	clerk	22	358 "

Webster Avenue

X	*DiBlasi Lucy †	2	housekeeper	29	141 Webster
Y	DiBlasi Salvatore	2	pressman	46	141 "
Z	*Rozzi James	4	retired	78	here

239

A	*Rozzi Pietronella †	4	housewife	78	"
B	Rozzi Thomas	4	cook	38	"
C	Venuti Angela †	6	at home	32	"
D	Venuti Arthur	6	U S A	23	"
E	*Venuti Carmella †	6	housewife	55	"
F	Venuti Henry	6	U S N	20	"
G	Venuti John	6	laborer	58	"
H	Venuti Michael	6	U S A	24	"
K	DiGregorio Antonio	8	retired	70	"
L	DiGregorio Michael	8	shipfitter	30	"
M	DiGregorio Christopher	8	retired	39	"
N	DiGregorio Phyllis †	8	housekeeper	30	"
P	*Rosa Rose †	10	housewife	42	New York
R	Rosa Vincent	10	laborer	45	"
S	Orsini Albert	12	U S A	29	here
T	Orsini Angelina †	12	housewife	53	"
U	Orsini Daniel	12	electrician	30	"
V	Orsini Henry	12	shoeworker	53	"

Webster Street

X	*Baglio Carmella †	55	housewife	50	here
Y	Baglio Eugene	55	U S A	21	"

Page.	Letter.	FULL NAME.	Residence, Jan. 1, 1943.	Occupation.	Supposed Age.	Reported Residence, Jan. 1, 1942. Street and Number.

Webster Street - Continued

	z	*Baglio John	55	laborer	53	here
240						
	B	*DeFlorio Maria F—†	57	housewife	77	"
	C	DeFlorio Sarah —†	57	dressmaker	41	"
	D	Kimak Margaret E—†	57	factoryhand	23	"
	E	Schultz Anna—†	57	at home	43	"
	G	Styzynski Frances †	59	housewife	25	"
	H	Styzynski Stanley	59	chauffeur	30	"
	K	Lelli Americo	59	laborer	28	"
	L	Lelli Mary—†	59	housewife	25	"
	M	*Indorato Aggrippina †	59	"	47	"
	N	Indorato Octavio	59	laborer	26	"
	O	Indorato Salvatore	59	"	58	"
	P	Indorato Santina—†	59	factoryhand	21	"
	R	Indorato Sebastian	59	U S N	23	"
	S	Biancucco John	59	butcher	62	"
	T	Mirra Joseph	59	factoryhand	46	"
	U	Lanzilli Albert	60	chauffeur	36	"
	V	Lanzilli Cornelia—†	60	housewife	31	"
	W	Pizzano Andrew	60	mechanic	38	"
	X	Pizzano Mildred—†	60	housewife	31	"
	Y	*Liberatore Anna—†	60	"	44	"
	z	*Lineratore Mary—†	60	"	42	"
241						
	A	Liberatore Peter	60	candymaker	43	"
	B	Liberatore Stanley	60	baker	45	"
	D	*LaGambina Sarah —†	61	housewife	42	"
	E	LaGambina Sebastino	61	factoryhand	49	"
	H	Brisette Rhoda—†	62	housewife	28	8 Brigham
	K	Brisette William	62	mechanic	31	8 "
	L	DiGianvittorio Fiorindo	62	"	24	174 Cottage
	M	DiGianvittorio Helen —†	62	housewife	20	4 Lamson
	N	DiSavino Frances—†	62	"	40	here
	O	DiSavino Michael	62	laborer	51	"
	P	D'Agostino Angelo	63	baker	29	"
	R	D'Agostino Mary—†	63	housewife	27	"
	S	Franco Mafalda—†	63	"	24	494 Sumner
	T	Franco Vincent	63	welder	23	494 "
	U	Giordano Pasquale	63	laborer	26	here
	V	Giordano Theresa —†	63	housewife	25	"
	W	Goggin Florence —†	64	"	22	"

24

Webster Street Continued

x	Goggin James	64	laborer	37	here
y	Dimino Ignatius	64	factoryhand	23	"
z	Dimino Lillian—†	64	housewife	41	"
242					
A*	Dimino Salvatore	64	laborer	50	"
B*	Lombardo Anthony	65	fisherman	58	"
c*	Lombardo Sebastiana †	65	housewife	50	"
D	Giangrade Louis	65	laborer	46	"
E	Giangrade Rose—†	65	housewife	36	"
F*	Incagnoli Augusto G	65	shoemaker	61	"
G	Incagnoli Joseph	65	laborer	24	"
H	Incagnoli Mary—†	65	factoryhand	26	"
K*	Incagnoli Susy—†	65	housewife	60	"
L	Grana Maria—†	66	"	60	"
M	Grana Vincent	66	carpenter	67	"
N	Cugliano Elena—†	67	housewife	28	"
O	Cugliano Salvatore	67	mechanic	26	"
P	Montalto Jennie—†	67	housewife	30	"
R	Montalto Joseph	67	laborer	35	"
s	Bocino Joseph	67	mechanic	25	"
T	Bocino Martha—†	67	packer	22	"
U	Bocino Matteo	67	laborer	54	"
V	Bocino Remo	67	U S A	21	"
W	Bocino Theresa—†	67	housewife	52	"
X	Paguin Joseph	68	electrician	47	216 Marginal
Y*	Paguin Myrtle—†	68	housewife	32	216 "
z	Anderson Charles	68	mechanic	29	here
243					
A	Anderson Maria G—†	68	housewife	23	"
B	Tedesco Albert	68	U S A	24	"
c	Tedesco Jennie—†	68	housewife	46	"
D	DiDio Lucy—†	68	"	31	"
E	DiDio Salvatore	68	mechanic	50	"
F	Pelargonio Carmena—†	69	factoryhand	20	Watertown
G*	Pelargonio Susan—†	69	housewife	48	"
H	Romano Constantino	69	retired	69	here
K	Romano Virginia—†	69	housewife	65	"
L	Amico Joseph	69	laborer	40	"
M	Amico Mary C—†	69	housewife	33	"
N	Marione Phillip	70	laborer	49	"
O	Marione Sadie—†	70	housewife	37	"

Page.	Letter.	FULL NAME.	Residence, Jan. 1, 1943.	Occupation.	Supposed Age.	Reported Residence, Jan. 1, 1942. Street and Number.

Webster Street—Continued

	P	Giadone John	70	U S N	22	here
	R	Giadone Josephine—†	70	dressmaker	26	"
	S*	Giadone Lucy—†	70	housewife	50	"
	T	Giadone Phillip	70	laborer	58	"
	U*	Panarelli Fanny—†	70	housewife	46	267 Lexington
	V	Panarelli Joseph	70	laborer	58	267 "
	W	Panarelli Louis	70	welder	21	267 "
	X*	DiBello Elizabeth—†	71	housewife	79	here
	Y	DiBello John	71	welder	47	"
	Z*	Siracusa Frances—†	71	housewife	63	"

244

	A*	Siracusa Nicolo	71	laborer	59	"
	B	Formicola Frank	71	watchman	52	"
	C	Formicola Mary—†	71	factoryhand	25	"
	D	Formicola Michelina—†	71	housewife	47	"
	E	Salvo Anthony	73	shipper	24	Somerville
	F	Salvo Emma—†	73	housewife	20	"
	G	Carbone Jennie—†	73	"	27	here
	H	Carbone John	73	rigger	25	"
	K	Carbone Alfred	73	laborer	60	"
	L	Carbone Amelia—†	73	housewife	57	"
	M	Bertelino Frank	74	fisherman	35	"
	N	Bertelino Mary—†	74	housewife	21	"
	O	Mottola Fiorella	74	laborer	29	76 Webster
	P*	Mottola Stefana—†	74	housewife	65	76 "
	R*	Mottola Vincent	74	laborer	66	76 "
	S	Mottola Amato	74	carpenter	37	here
	T	Mottola Michelina—†	74	housewife	36	"
	U	Carbone Antonetta—†	75	"	34	"
	V	Carbone Vincent	75	laborer	34	"
	W	Cavignano Eleanor—†	75	factoryhand	22	"
	X*	Cavignano Filomena—†	75	housewife	51	"
	Y	Cavignano Gennaro	75	ironworker	53	"
	Z	Cavignano Joseph	75	laborer	24	"

245

	A	Cavignano Michael	75	U S A	28	"
	B	DiGirolamo Elvira—†	75	factoryhand	35	"
	C	Girolano Frank	75	laborer	67	"
	D	Girolano Frederick	75	U S A	22	"
	E*	Girolano Nicolina—†	75	housewife	65	"

Webster Street Continued

F	DelGrazio Maria †	76	housewife	47	92 Everett
G	Giordano Joseph	76	painter	25	89 Maverick
H	Giordano Rose †	76	housewife	21	8 Lexington av
K	*Mottola Margaret †	76	"	36	here
L	Mottola Michael	76	printer	38	"
M	*Mazzola Michelina †	77	housewife	42	"
N	Mazzola Phillip	77	U S N	24	"
O	Mazzola Sebastian	77	rubberworker	45	"
P	Mazzola Ciro	77	machinist	24	"
R	Mazzola Mary †	77	housewife	23	"
S	DiTomaso Domenic	77	cable splicer	39	"
T	DiTomaso Dora †	77	housewife	32	"
U	Giordano Cologero	79	clerk	52	89 Maverick
V	*Giordano Fannie †	79	housewife	43	89 "
W	Giordano Rose †	79	stitcher	22	89 "
X	Lightbody Carmela †	79	housewife	27	here
Y	Lightbody William	79	welder	27	"
Z	Rotando Letitia †	79	housewife	20	"
	246					
A	Rotando Salvatore	79	laborer	24	"
B	Bozza Sarah †	80	housewife	70	"
C	Bozza Zacria	80	storekeeper	81	"
D	Bozza Aurora †	80	clerk	30	"
E	Bozza Filomena †	80	housewife	50	"
F	Bozza Mary †	80	clerk	28	"
G	Bozza Sittimeo	80	barber	59	"
H	Bozza Albert	80	foreman	50	"
K	*Bozza Amelia †	80	housewife	34	"
M	*DeCicco Maria †	81	at home	70	"
N	Pagliuca James	81	shipper	38	"
O	Pagliuca Lucy †	81	housewife	33	"
P	*Vassallo Angelina †	81	"	36	"
R	Vassallo James	81	meatcutter	41	"
S	Nocito Antonetta †	82	housewife	24	"
T	Nocito Joseph	82	pipefitter	27	"
U	Nocito Carmella †	82	housewife	30	"
V	Nocito Michael	82	salesman	42	"
W	*Nocito Elizabeth †	82	housewife	49	"
X	Nocito Michael	82	laborer	21	"
Y	Nocito Rose †	82	clerk	23	"

27

Page.	Letter.	Full Name.	Residence, Jan. 1, 1943.	Occupation.	Supposed Age.	Reported Residence Jan. 1, 1942. Street and Number.

Webster Street—Continued

	z	Fabiano Julia—†	83	housewife	20	31 Cottage
247						
	A	Fabiano Nicholas T	83	longshoreman	30	31 "
	B	Mezzetti Frances—†	83	housewife	20	64 Webster
	C	Mezzetti Herbert	83	laborer	23	108 Cornell
	E	*DeBuzzio Angie—†	84	housewife	59	100 Cottage
	F	*DeBuzzio Nicholas	84	tailor	66	100 "
	G	Vaccaro Carmella—†	84	housewife	40	here
	H	Vaccaro John	84	laborer	52	"
	K	Ferrara Girolamo	84	"	70	"
	L	*Ferrara Victoria—†	84	housewife	61	"
	M	Rausco Filomina—†	85	"	47	"
	N	Rausco Geraldo	85	laborer	58	"
	O	Rausco Michael	85	metalworker	20	"
	P	Molea Nancy—†	85	housewife	34	"
	R	Molea Nicholas	85	rigger	40	"
	S	Mottola Frances—†	85	laundryworker	29	76 Webster
	T	Rossi Antonio	85	laborer	60	here
	U	Rossi Raffaela—†	85	at home	26	"
	V	Rossi Ralph	85	U S A	23	"
	W	Rossi William	85	laborer	21	"
	X	Christina Lillian—†	87	housewife	25	"
	Y	Christina Louis	87	machinist	27	"
	Z	Cotti Adelaide—†	87	boxmaker	20	"
248						
	A	*Cotti Michelina—†	87	housewife	49	"
	B	Cotti Ralph	87	janitor	64	"
	C	Cotti Nunncio	87	laborer	28	"
	D	Cotti Olga—†	87	housewife	27	"
	E	Pisiello George	88	laborer	37	"
	F	Pisiello Mary—†	88	housewife	35	"
	G	DeAngelis Archangelo	88	laborer	60	"
	H	DeAngelis Mary—†	88	housewife	66	"
	K	Scire Trusiana—†	88	"	37	"
	L	Marmorle Anthony	88	laborer	47	"
	M	Marmorle Caroline—†	88	housewife	39	"
	N	Marotta Louise—†	89	"	33	"
	O	Marotta Phillip	89	longshoreman	33	"
	P	Zeoli Josephine—†	89	housewife	48	"
	R	Zeoli Nicholas	89	baker	24	"
	S	Zeoli Phyllis—†	89	stitcher	22	"

Webster Street Continued

T	Prisco Joseph	89	pipefitter	38	176 Gove
U	Prisco Quinta †	89	housewife	32	176 "
V	*Hagstrom Amelia †	90	"	60	here
W	Hagstrom Olga †	90	stitcher	36	"
X	*Hagstrom Otto	90	laborer	69	"
Y	Forte John	90	candymaker	44	"
Z	Forte Margaret †	90	housewife	41	"

249

A	*Fiore Fortunato	90	fisherman	39	50 Maverick
B	Fiore Lillian †	90	housewife	31	50 "
C	Cleary Helen †	91	cleaner	52	here
D	Moore Joseph A	91	U S A	27	"
E	O'Hare John F	91	seaman	43	"
F	*D'Christoforo Domenic	91A	carpenter	66	"
G	*D'Christoforo Palma †	91A	housewife	64	"
H	Pessia Alvira †	91A	"	55	"
K	Pessia Aurelio	91A	laborer	25	"
L	Pessia Gilda †	91A	stitcher	20	"
M	Pessia Mary †	91A	at home	22	"
N	Lutanno Luigi	92	laborer	49	"
O	Lutanno Rose †	92	operator	50	"
P	Criscoli Anthony	92	laborer	53	"
R	Criscoli Jennie †	92	housewife	43	"
S	Esposito Gaetano	92	laborer	51	"
T	Esposito Josephine †	92	housewife	46	"
U	Peroni John	92	laborer	64	"
W	Pasco Margaret †	93A	housewife	37	210 Everett
X	Pasco Nicholas	93A	carpenter	43	210 "
Y	*DiGiacomo Isadore	93A	retired	76	here
Z	Sistillio Antonetta †	93A	housewife	43	"

250

A	Sistillio Florence †	93A	saleswoman	20	"
B	Sistillio Frank	93A	tinsmith	54	"
C	Sistillio Frederick	93A	shoeworker	29	"
D	Astuccio James	94	laborer	24	20 Haynes
E	Astuccio Lucy †	94	factoryhand	20	20 "
F	*Astuccio Mary †	94	housewife	50	20 "
G	*Astuccio Michael	94	laborer	52	20 "
H	*Vacirca Felix	94	shoemaker	53	here
K	Vacirca Joseph	94	laborer	27	"
L	*Vacirca Josephine †	94	housewife	47	"

Page.	Letter.	FULL NAME.	Residence, Jan. 1, 1943.	Occupation	Supposed Age.	Reported Residence, Jan. 1, 1942. Street and Number.

Webster Street Continued

	M	Vacirca Mary—†	94	clerk	21	here
	N	Persson Henry	94	U S N	21	"
	O	Persson Peter	94	longshoreman	67	"
	P	Christoforo Charles	95	chauffeur	46	"
	R	Christoforo Marie—†	95	candyworker	30	"
	S	Christoforo Maurice	95	U S A	30	"
	T	Piccardi Hugo	96	pipefitter	46	"
	U	Piccardi Theresa—†	96	housewife	38	"
	V	Gasvarone Daniel	96	mechanic	43	45 Decatur
	W	Gasvarone Louise—†	96	housewife	31	45 "
	X	*Squadrito Jerome	96	laborer	48	6 Everett
	Y	*Squadrito Martha—†	96	housewife	36	6 "
	Z	Distaso Joseph	97	U S A	23	here

251

	A	*Distaso Maria—†	97	housewife	54	"
	B	Distaso Santo	97	typist	26	"
	C	Cesero Angela—†	97	stitcher	21	"
	D	Cesero Lucy—†	97	housewife	40	"
	E	Cesero Oreste	97	fish handler	46	"
	F	DeAngelis Julius	98	packer	27	"
	G	DeAngelis Lucy—†	98	housewife	30	"
	H	Grallo Joseph	98	shipper	28	168 Cottage
	K	Grallo Mary—†	98	housewife	26	168 "
	L	*Bruno Louise—†	98	"	42	here
	M	Bruno Michael	98	laborer	50	"
	N	Rougone Alfred	99	engineer	38	"
	O	Rougone Susan—†	99	housewife	35	"
	P	Roach Allen	100	chauffeur	43	"
	R	Roach Margaret—†	100	housewife	43	"
	S	Gagliardi Anthony	100	U S A	21	"
	T	*Gagliardi Rose—†	100	housewife	46	"
	U	Gagliardi Sabino	100	laborer	46	"
	V	DiBello Anne—†	100	clerk	26	"
	W	*DiBello Josephine—†	100	housewife	73	"
	X	*Costello Bridget—†	101	at home	62	"
	Y	Costello Michael	101	laborer	37	"
	Z	Forgione Mildred—†	101	stitcher	33	"

252

	A	*Walsh William	101	longshoreman	56	Chelsea
	B	Kennedy Albert M	101	U S N	24	here
	C	Kennedy David J	101	retired	70	"

Webster Street Continued

	Letter	FULL NAME	Residence	Occupation	Age	Reported Residence
	D	Kennedy Elizabeth A †	101	at home	38	here
	E	Kennedy Ernest E	101	longshoreman	25	"
	F	Kennedy Mary M †	101	housewife	34	"
	G	Kennedy Robert W	101	U S N	26	"
	H	DiBello Joseph	102	musician	51	"
	K	DiBello Josephine †	102	housewife	40	"
	L	DiBello Salvatore	102	U S A	22	"
	M	Altri John	102	longshoreman	34	248 Maverick
	N	Altri Laura †	102	housewife	31	248 "
	O	Warner Laura †	102	"	68	248 "
	P	Whiting Joseph	102	chauffeur	39	248 "
	R*	Pantano Nancy †	102	housewife	45	here
	S	Pantano Rose †	102	clerk	20	"
	T	Pantano Santo	102	laborer	48	"
	U	DiRago Pasquale	rear 102	"	58	"
	V	Giello Florence †	103	typist	35	"
	W	Giello Joseph	103	retired	76	"
	X	Giello Lillian †	103	typist	22	"
	Y	Giello Rose †	103	housewife	65	"
	Z	Simione Joseph	106	salesman	38	102 Webster
253						
	A	Simione Mary †	106	housewife	43	102 "
	B	Danna Benjamin	108	chauffeur	24	here
	C	Danna Lillian †	108	housewife	22	"
	D	Karavas May †	108	"	49	"
	E	Karavas Nicholas	108	fireman	61	"
	F	Magliano Antonetta †	110	housewife	27	"
	G	Magliano John	110	mechanic	28	"
	H	Cravotta Charles	110	machinist	23	116 Gladstone
	K	Cravotta Josephine †	110	housewife	21	116 "
	L	Morgan Edward	112	laborer	37	6 Jeffries
	M	Morgan Helen †	112	housewife	36	6 "
	N	Lemire William	112	mechanic	53	here
	O	Lemire William J	112	laborer	23	"
	S	Coggin Helen †	115	housewife	29	"
	T	Coggin Joseph	115	chauffeur	34	"
	U	Coggin John	115	retired	70	"
	V	Coggin Josephine †	115	housewife	74	"
	W	Gillon James	116	longshoreman	45	"
	X	Gillon Margaret †	116	clerk	28	"
	Y	Gillon May †	116	at home	39	"

31

Page	Letter	Full Name.	Residence, Jan. 1, 1943.	Occupation.	Supposed Age.	Reported Residence, Jan. 1, 1942. Street and Number.

Webster Street Continued

	z	DiBello James	116	B F D	37	470 Sumner
254						
	A	DiBello Jennie †	116	housewife	36	470 "
	B	*Piscatelli Angelina †	116	"	43	here
	C	Piscatelli Joseph	116	laborer	42	"
	D	Mortimer John	117	retired	68	"
	E	O'Leary Jessie A †	117	housewife	33	"
	F	O'Leary John J	117	longshoreman	34	"
	G	Sheehan Mary †	117	at home	59	"
	H	Bergquist Elmer E	117	maint'n'ceman	47	"
	K	Johnson Andrew	117	"	65	"
	L	Salome Domenic	117	salesman	60	"
	M	Albano Carmen	118	chauffeur	30	"
	N	Albano Mary †	118	housewife	28	"
	O	Rauseo Domenic	118	pressman	29	"
	P	Rauseo Mary †	118	clerk	20	"
	R	*Rauseo Michelina †	118	housewife	52	"
	S	Rauseo Rocco	118	factoryhand	30	"
	T	Rauseo Vito	118	U S A	26	"
	U	Albano James	118	laborer	34	"
	V	Albano Theresa †	118	housewife	32	"
	W	Fulgeniti Frank	118	laborer	33	"
	X	Coggin Catherine †	119	housewife	38	"
	Y	Coggin Richard	119	foreman	38	"
	Z	*LaPenna Frances †	119	at home	80	"
255						
	A	Rausco Anthony	119	U S A	20	"
	B	Rausco Ella †	119	housewife	53	"
	C	Rausco Rocco	119	laborer	58	"
	D	Bagnera Anthony	119	shipfitter	33	"
	E	Bagnera Viola †	119	housewife	27	"
	G	Ranese Antonetta †	120	"	33	11 Haynes
	H	Ranese Joseph	120	laborer	52	11 "
	K	Covalucci Filomena †	120	factoryhand	23	here
	L	Covalucci Joseph	120	ironworker	58	"
	M	Covalucci Joseph	120	laborer	28	"
	N	DeAngelis Anthony	120	"	50	"
	O	*DeAngelis Margaret †	120	housewife	53	"
	P	DeAngelis Mary †	120	stitcher	20	"
	R	Uccello Concetto	122	storekeeper	53	"
	S	*Uccello Filomena †	122	housewife	47	"

Webster Street — Continued

T	Uccello Rose †	122	factoryhand	21	here
U	Adamo Concetta †	122	housewife	26	"
V	Adamo Frank	122	operator	26	"
W	Marciano Anthony	123	painter	29	"
X	*Marciano Grace †	123	housewife	54	"
Y	Marciano Joseph	123	storekeeper	53	"
Z	Faiia Anna †	123	housewife	57	"
	256				
A	Faiia Mary A †	123	typist	28	"
B	Faiia Raffaele	123	janitor	67	"
C	Morgante Albert	123	laborer	52	125 Cottage
D	*Morgante Felisa †	123	housewife	49	125 "
E	Morgante Pasquale	123	machinist	20	125 "
G	Barrasso Carmella †	125	housewife	26	here
H	Barrasso Jeremiah	125	laborer	33	"
K	Henebury Ellen †	125	housewife	26	13 Haynes
L	Henebury John	125	fishcutter	30	241 Lexington
M	Walsh Ann †	125	housewife	37	158 Webster
N	Walsh Mary J †	125	"	67	here
O	Walsh William J	125	retired	66	"
P	*Picardi Esther †	126	housewife	43	"
R	Picardi Ralph	126	laborer	46	"
S	*Ambrosino Michele	126	"	77	"
T	Ambrosino Rose †	126	operator	33	"
U	Salucco Carmen	126	chauffeur	40	"
V	Salucco Josephine †	126	housewife	38	"
W	Bowman Jane A †	127	at home	75	"
X	Bowman Jane A †	127	clerk	40	"
Y	Parise Alvina †	127	housewife	24	33 Chelsea
Z	Parise Anthony	127	cobbler	28	33 "
	257				
A	*Parise Michael	127	"	64	33 "
B	Crocetti Carl	127	storekeeper	55	here
C	Crocetti Doris †	127	at home	25	"
D	Crocetti Jennie †	127	housewife	45	"
E	Zirpolo Angelina †	128	"	39	"
F	Zirpolo Michael	128	longshoreman	47	"
G	D'Olympia Filomena †	128	housewife	35	"
H	Chiuchiolo John	128	laborer	28	"
K	*Chiuchiolo Joseph	128	candymaker	58	"
L	Chiuchiolo Louise †	128	operator	21	"

4—2

33

Page.	Letter	FULL NAME.	Residence, Jan. 1, 1943	Occupation.	Supposed Age.	Reported Residence, Jan. 1. 1942. Street and Number.

Webster Street—Continued

	Letter	FULL NAME.	Res.	Occupation.	Age	Reported Residence
	M	Chiuchiolo Rose—†	128	at home	23	here
	N	Racana John	129	retired	65	"
	O	Racana Louise—†	129	housewife	57	"
	P	Racana Olga—†	129	candymaker	24	"
	R	Iannarone Agnes—†	129	housewife	31	"
	S	Iannarone Leonard	129	metalworker	31	"
	T	Racana Lena—†	129	housewife	23	"
	U	Racana Rocco	129	chauffeur	29	"
	V	Cirilli Umberto	130	tailor	47	"
	W	Curze Giovanni	130	laborer	39	"
	X	Gallo Elvira—†	130	factoryhand	24	"
	Y	Varone Grace—†	130	housewife	31	"
	Z	Varone Salvatore	130	mechanic	32	"
258						
	A	DiBiasio Angelina—†	130	housewife	34	"
	B	DiBiasio Emilio	130	shipper	34	"
	C	Rigano Margaret—†	130	operator	50	"
	D	Liberti Ettore	131	laborer	56	"
	E	Liberti Ferminia—†	131	stenographer	31	"
	F	*Liberti Prasside—†	131	housewife	55	"
	G	Liberti Sebastino	131	driller	30	"
	H	Liberti Ugo	131	U S A	21	"
	K	Liberti Vira—†	131	hairdresser	25	"
	L	Buonopane Angelo	135	driller	45	"
	M	Buonopane Nancy—†	135	housewife	40	"
	N	Buonopane Ralph	135	U S A	21	"
	O	*Tosi Helen—†	136	housewife	45	"
	P	DiGiovanni Joseph	136	laborer	40	"
	R	DiGiovanni Raffaella—†	136	housewife	37	"
	S	*Elia Anthony	136	laborer	73	
	T	Hibbard Harry	136	seaman	25	4 Paris ct
	U	Hibbard Mary—†	136	housewife	25	4 "
	V	Ciampa Frances—†	136	"	25	here
	W	Ciampa Samuel	136	painter	25	"
	X	Digan Anna W—†	137	at home	58	"
	Y	Digan Arthur E	137	attorney	54	"
	Z	Digan Carrie L—†	137	saleswoman	56	"
259						
	A	Digan Lucy E—†	137	at home	52	"
	B	Barbere Anthony	138	engineer	24	508 Sumner
	C	*Marotta Emilia—†	138	housewife	53	here

Webster Street Continued

D	Marotta Enrico	138	painter	49	here	
E	Marotta Esther †	138	operator	22	"	
F	Neri Angelo	138	chauffeur	35	"	
G	Neri Lena—†	138	housewife	33	"	
H	Velardo John	138	mechanic	30	"	
K	Velardo Nicolette †	138	housewife	26	"	
S	Petrillo Anthony	147	laborer	53	"	
T	*Petrillo Carmella—†	147	housewife	54	"	
U	Petrillo Peter	147	U S N	21	"	
V	Varone Mario	147	shipfitter	21	"	
W	Varone Ruggiero	147	U S A	23	"	
X	Varone Severo	147	boilermaker	58	"	
Y	DiRenzo Anna †	147	housewife	68	"	
Z	DiRenzo Gaetano	147	retired	71	"	

260

A	Andriotti George	149	U S N	22	"	
B	*Andriotti Mary—†	149	at home	62	"	
C	Andriotti Yolanda—†	149	stitcher	25	"	
D	*Ciampa Aurora—†	149	housewife	37	"	
E	Ciampa Nicholas	149	shipper	36	"	
F	Musi Evelyn—†	149	housewife	39	"	
G	Musi Michael	149	engineer	38	"	
H	Rotigliano Michael	155	shoemaker	65	"	
K	Rotigliano Michael	155	machinist	23	"	
L	Aronson Aaron	155	storekeeper	45	"	
M	Aronson Goldie—†	155	housewife	43	"	
N	Rotigliano Joseph	155	machinist	28	"	
O	Rotigliano Mary—†	155	housewife	26	"	
P	Howe Frances C—†	177	"	38	1181 Saratoga	
R	Howe Lawrence P	177	social worker	37	1181 "	
S	Beveridge Dorothy G—†	179	housewife	35	Vermont	
T	Beveridge Eliot P	179	social worker	35	"	
U	*Serino Angelina—†	181	housewife	49	here	
V	*Serino Domenic	181	cobbler	51	"	
W	Serino Nancy—†	181	leatherworker	21	"	
X	Pelosi Achille	181	presser	48	"	
Y	Pelosi Mary—†	181	housewife	40	"	
Z	Cerullo Louis	181	chauffeur	42	"	

261

A	Cerullo Mary—†	181	housewife	40	"	
B	Vardaro Anthony	181	candyworker	37	"	

Page.	Letter.	FULL NAME.	Residence, Jan. 1, 1943.	Occupation.	Supposed Age.	Reported Residence, Jan. 1, 1942. Street and Number.

Webster Street—Continued

	C	Vardaro Domenic	181	U S A	42	here
	D	*Vardaro Mary—†	181	at home	73	"
	F	Gregorio Joseph	183	baker	29	36 Gove
	G	Gregorio Mary—†	183	housewife	27	36 "
	H	Marriano Joseph	183	U S A	22	here
	K	Marriano Louis	183	laborer	48	"
	L	Marriano Olympia—†	183	housewife	49	"
	M	Santilli Angelina—†	183	"	33	191 Webster
	N	Santilli Pasquale	183	chauffeur	28	191 "
	P	LaMarca Catherine—†	185	at home	56	here
	R	LaMarca Catherine—†	185	tailor	36	"
	S	LaMarca Josephine—†	185	"	27	"
	U	Manzo Marie—†	185	housewife	29	"
	T	Manzo Peter	185	shipper	38	"
	V	Frasca Mary—†	185	housekeeper	32	"
	W	Pierce James E	187	bookkeeper	36	"
	X	Pierce James F	187	janitor	61	"
	Y	Pierce Mary A—†	187	housewife	57	"
	Z	Pierce Mary G—†	187	clerk	24	"

262

	A	Pierce William J	187	U S A	33	"
	B	Davis Elizabeth D—†	187	housewife	38	"
	C	Davis Joseph F	187	salesman	42	"
	D	Anderson Anise A—†	189	teacher	57	"
	E	Anderson Mary E—†	189	secretary	24	"
	F	Watt Helen E—†	189	at home	65	"
	G	MacLean Grace—†	189	"	55	"
	H	Cretara Anthony	191	photographer	39	"
	K	Cretara Carmella—†	191	housewife	35	"
	L	Clay Bernard	191	U S M C	23	35 Ferrin
	M	Melito Domenic	191	U S A	20	110 Everett
	N	Melito Palmina—†	191	housewife	39	110 "
	O	Melito Vito	191	laborer	39	110 "
	P	Healy William C	193	retired	69	here
	R	Leonard Elizabeth F—†	193	housekeeper	61	"
	S	Leonard William L	193	clerk	57	"
	T	Marotta Celia—†	195	hairdresser	33	"
	U	Dalton Margaret A—†	195	housewife	37	"
	V	Dalton Walter	195	foreman	34	"
	W	Reidy John E	195	laborer	27	"
	Y	King Edward N	rear 195	U S A	24	210 Marginal

Webster Street Continued

z	Porter Irene H—†	rear 195	at home	26	210 Marginal	
263						
A	Porter Joseph R	" 195	fireman	44	210 "	
B	Porter Margaret I—†	" 195	housewife	50	210 "	
C	Gigli Leonilda—†	" 195	"	61	here	
D	Gigli Lydia—†	" 195	dressmaker	32	"	
E	Gigli Nicola	" 195	laborer	65	"	
G	Barry William J	199	clergyman	70	"	
H	Burke Ellen—†	199	cook	67	"	
K	Sweeney George V	199	clergyman	32	"	
L	Matarazzo Alfred	201	brushmaker	30	"	
M	Matarazzo Susan—†	201	housewife	31	"	
N	*Tringali Carmello	201	retired	75	"	
O	Tringali Domenic	201	boatbuilder	28	"	
P	Tringali Domenica—†	201	at home	31	"	
R	Siriani Jennie—†	201	housewife	40	"	
S	Siriani Rose—†	201	stitcher	21	"	
T	*Torti Louise—†	205	housewife	42	"	
U	Torti Zeno	205	tailor	44	"	
V	Manganiello Joseph	205	printer	52	"	
W	Pollini Domenic	205	stonecutter	57	"	
X	Pollini Frances—†	205	housewife	54	"	
Y	Dowd Mary A—†	207	at home	70	"	
Z	Dowd Mary C—†	207	secretary	41	"	
264						
A	Finn Sarah G—†	207	clerk	55	"	
B	Usseglio Aurelia—†	211	at home	68	"	
C	Usseglio Mary—†	211	clerk	45	"	
D	Muldoon Joseph J	211	fireman	52	"	
E	Muldoon Mary A—†	211	housewife	47	"	
F	Muldoon Mary M—†	211	saleswoman	21	"	
G	Usseglio Charles	213	pipefitter	37	"	
H	Usseglio Helen J—†	213	housewife	33	"	
K	Blake Andrew	213	pipefitter	46	"	
L	Blake Anna—†	213	housewife	43	"	
M	Faiello Anna—†	215	"	29	"	
N	Ventresca Anna—†	215	packer	20	"	
O	Ventresca Delia—†	215	nurse	26	"	
P	Ventresca Lino	215	U S A	22	"	
R	Ventresca Liveo	215	laborer	24	"	
S	*Ventresca Mary—†	215	housewife	48	"	

Page.	Letter.	FULL NAME.	Residence, Jan. 1, 1943	Occupation.	Supposed Age.	Reported Residence, Jan. 1, 1942. Street and Number.

Webster Street — Continued

T	Ventresca Viola — †	215	inspector	21	here
U	Amore Ciriaco	215	operator	31	"
V	Amore Lucy — †	215	housewife	29	"
W*	Paoluccelli Emma — †	217	"	56	11 Henchman
X	Paoluccelli John	217	cook	21	11 "
Y	Paoluccelli Rose — †	217	factoryhand	31	11 "
Z	Vardaro Julia — †	217	housewife	34	183 Webster

265

A	Vardaro Louis	217	shoeworker	39	183 "
B	Munofo Ida — †	217	housewife	35	here
C	Munofo Ignazio	217	laborer	45	"
G	Crowley Mary — †	223	at home	80	"
H	Knowles Catherine — †	223	"	25	"
K	Knowles Catherine M — †	223	"	52	"
L	Knowles James E	223	operator	54	"
M	Gay Ernest W	223	janitor	55	"
N	Gay Ernest W, jr	223	U S A	23	"
O	Gay Francis R	223	"	21	"
P	Gay Veronica E — †	223	housewife	47	"
R	Burke Mary — †	225	at home	63	"
S	Leahy Helen — †	225	clerk	37	"
T	Knowles Inez — †	225	housewife	25	346 Sumner
U	Knowles James E, jr	225	clerk	29	223 Webster
V	Kelley Annie F — †	225	housewife	36	here
W	Kelley Jerome T	225	cook	41	"
X	Blake Lillian — †	227	laundress	42	"
Y	Smiddy Joseph	227	longshoreman	53	"
Z*	Smiddy Mary E — †	227	at home	83	"

266

A	Pfeifer Helen — †	227	housewife	38	"
B	Pfeifer John	227	rigger	35	"
C	Duane Mary — †	227	at home	79	"
D	Lambert Alexander P	227	steamfitter	70	"

Wilbur Court

E*	Rehn John	1	pipefitter	50	here
F*	Rehn Manda — †	1	housewife	56	"
G	Carapezza Joseph	1	electrician	30	"
H	Carapezza Sarah — †	1	housewife	30	"
K	Donacelli Lucrezia — †	2	"	30	"

Wilbur Court Continued

L	Donacelli Luigi	2	laborer	26	here
M	Lopes Caesar	2	checker	40	"
N	Lopes Dorothy †	2	housewife	23	"
P	Evangelista John	3	laborer	37	"
R	*Evangelista Theresa †	3	housewife	35	"
S	Agusta Louise †	3	secretary	33	"
T	*Agusta Rose †	3	housewife	74	"
V	D'Ambrosio Ernest	3	laborer	26	"
U	D'Ambrosio Mildred †	3	housewife	25	"
W	Sartori John	4	shipper	38	"
X	Sartori Mollie †	4	housewife	32	"
Z	Martella Henry	4	longshoreman	36	"

267

A	Martella Lena †	4	housewife	36	"
E	Gigliello Frank A	6	buffer	29	"
F	*Gigliello Mary †	6	housewife	20	"
G	Donolfo Vincent	6	salesman	59	"
H	Drago Joseph	6	"	60	"
K	*Marignetti Antonio	6	laborer	48	"
L	*Marignetti Olympia †	6	housewife	45	"

Ward 1–Precinct 3

CITY OF BOSTON

LIST OF RESIDENTS
20 YEARS OF AGE AND OVER

(NON-CITIZENS INDICATED BY ASTERISK)
(FEMALES INDICATED BY DAGGER)

AS OF

JANUARY 1, 1943

JOSEPH F. TIMILTY, *Chairman*
FREDERIC E. DOWLING, *Secretary*
WILLIAM A. MOTLEY, Jr.
FRANCIS B. McKINNEY
EVERETT R. PROUT

Listing Board.

CITY OF BOSTON PRINTING DEPARTMENT

Page.	Letter	FULL NAME.	Residence. Jan. 1, 1943.	Occupation.	Supposed Age.	Reported Residence. Jan. 1, 1942. Street and Number.

300

Airport Street

	M	Fletcher Pearl —†	3	at home	28	119 Alexander
	O	Ambrosino John	5	U S A	37	here
	P	Merrullo Angelo	5	laborer	49	"
	R	Salemi Joseph	5	"	50	"
	S	Salemi Mary —†	5	housewife	50	"

Ardee Street

	T	Ciulla Joan —†	1	housewife	35	here
	U	Ciulla Vincenzo	1	fisherman	39	"
	W	Mogauro Assunta —†	3	housewife	35	"
	X	Mogauro James	3	laborer	34	"
	Y	*Bonavista Caterina —†	3	housewife	58	"
	Z	Bonavista Rosina —†	3	stitcher	21	"

301

	A	*Bonavista Vincenzo	3	salesman	59	"
	B	Bruno Concetta †	4	housewife	56	"
	C	Bruno John	4	laborer	61	"
	D	Bruno Vincent	4	rubberworker	25	"
	E	Meninno Dorothy —†	5	housewife	35	"
	F	Meninno Robert	5	laborer	35	"
	H	Salemi Clara—†	5	housewife	20	"
	K	Salemi Joseph	5	welder	24	"
	L	*Salemi Josephine —†	5	housewife	52	"
	M	Salemi Sebastiano	5	operator	51	"
	N	Pagnini Gino	5	tailor	20	"
	O	Pagnini Ugo	5	laborer	50	"

Deer Island

	P	Black Frances †		housewife	58	here
	R	Black Frank		engineer	59	"
	S	Black June †		clerk	21	"
	T	Borden Cora E †		housewife	50	"
	U	Borden George E		engineer	56	"
	V	Connelly Joseph F		guard	51	"
	W	Cronin Fred J		"	46	"
	X	Devine Joseph A		"	49	"
	Y	Donahue Daniel F		engineer	65	"
	Z	Donahue Michael		"	68	"

2

302

Deer Island — Continued

A	Doyle John P	superintendent	44	here
B	Doyle Mary E †	housewife	36	"
C	Doyle Mary E †	"	71	"
D	Drewes Henry F	supervisor	47	"
E	Ford Daniel F	guard	48	"
F	Gallagher Francis W	"	49	"
G	Gallant Leo	clerk	54	"
H	Gilbert Clifford M	engineer	45	"
K	Gilbert Lela F †	housewife	30	"
L	Gilmore John P	clerk	41	"
M	King Charles E	engineer	68	"
N	Luciano Frank J	guard	40	"
O	Lucy Joseph R	"	49	"
P	Martin Coleman J	"	60	"
R	Maynard Annette C †	clerk	30	"
S	Maynard George A	engineer	62	"
T	Maynard Lillian C †	teacher	26	"
U	Maynard Robert W	U S N	24	"
V	Maynard Philomena V †	housewife	55	"
W	McCarthy Andrew H	guard	52	"
X	McCarthy Margaret A †	housewife	50	"
Y	McMullen Peter A	clerk	40	"
Z	Moylette William J	guard	54	"

303

A	O'Brien John J	"	58	"
B	O'Keefe Daniel J	"	47	"
C	O'Neil Francis P	machinist	73	"
D	O'Neil Helen M †	housewife	72	"
E	Reilly Joseph L	clergyman	33	"
F	Teevens Patrick H	guard	57	"
G	Tirrell Frederick W	proprietor	42	"

Everett Court

H	Trainor Catherine †	1	housewife	28	here
K	Trainor William	1	longshoreman	32	"
L	Lombardozzi Edith †	2	housewife	26	60 Liverpool
M	Kirby Catherine †	3	"	24	96 Cottage
N	Kirby Paul	3	freighthandler	27	96 "
O	McDonough Emily †	3	housewife	27	63 White

3

Everett Court Continued

P	McDonough George	3	fireman	27	63 White
R	LaPia Antonette †	4	stitcher	28	here
S	LaPia James	4	carpenter	55	"
T	LaPia Jennie †	4	housewife	48	"
U	LaPia Michael	4	U S A	27	"
V	Coviello Philomena †	4	housewife	36	"
W	Coviello Prisco	4	shoeworker	39	"
X	Sanelli Domenic	5	chauffeur	26	"
Y	Sanelli Eva †	5	housewife	24	"
Z	Costopoulos Anthony	5	U S N	21	"

304

A	Costopoulos Christofer	5	U S A	23	"
B*| Costopoulos John	5	dishwasher	53	"
C*| Costopoulos Olga †	5	housewife	44	"
D	Costopoulos Stefano	5	U S A	22	"
E*| Cinelli Bridget †	6	housewife	42	"
F	Cinelli James	6	U S A	21	"
G*| Cinelli Rocco	6	ironworker	52	"
H	Mancuso Joseph	6	chauffeur	23	"
K	Mancuso Olga †	6	housewife	21	"

Everett Place

L	Clex Charles	2	laborer	50	here
M	Mucci Anna †	4	housewife	31	"
N	Mucci Carmelo	4	U S A	33	"
O	Mucci John	4	laborer	67	"
P	Mucci Mary †	4	factoryhand	22	"
R	Mucci Susan †	4	stitcher	20	"
U	Todesco Rocco	7	mechanic	37	"
V	Todesco Violet †	7	housewife	26	"

Everett Street

X	Patti Pauline †	185	housewife	23	here
W*| Patti Mary †	185	"	38	"
Y	Patti Philip	185	pressman	43	"
Z	Cifuni Amelia †	187	laundress	26	"

305

A	Cifuni Charles	187	mechanic	33	"
B	Cifuni Edith †	187	tailor	22	"

Everett Street (Continued)

c	*Cifuni Genaro	187	carpenter	61	here	
d	*Cifuni Marie †	187	housewife	56	"	
E	Serenci Saverio	189	"	54	"	
F	Serenci Thomas	189	laborer	51	"	
H	Albanese Anthony	191	U S A	21	"	
K	*Albanese Josephine †	191	housewife	54	"	
L	Albanese Michael	191	laborer	65	"	
M	*Sarino John	191	carpenter	58	"	
N	Sarino Joseph	191	U S A	26	"	
O	*Sarino Lucy †	191	housewife	53	"	
P	Albanese Francis	191	shipfitter	23	"	
R	Albanese Madeline †	191	operator	23	"	
S	Patterson Alice †	192	housewife	51	"	
T	Sassa Carmella †	192	"	22	"	
U	Sassa Michael	192	chauffeur	22	"	
V	Legore Augustine	192	painter	21	"	
W	*Legore Frank	192	checker	63	"	
X	*Legore Josephine †	192	housewife	59	"	
Y	Legore Louis	192	U S A	23	"	
Z	Ravagno Angelo	193	coppersmith	28	"	

306

A	Ravagno Thomasina †	193	housewife	28	"	
B	Murphy Dennis W	193	letter carrier	46	"	
C	Hogan Anastasia †	193	housewife	52	"	
D	Hogan Thomas	193	cleanser	50	"	
E	Iuliano Rosario	195	metalworker	32	"	
F	Iuliano Rose †	195	housewife	29	"	
H	*Lauletta Angelina †	195	"	44	"	
G	*Lauletta Antonio	195	baker	49	"	
K	Cifuni Mary †	195	housewife	27	"	
L	Cifuni Salvatore	195	machinist	28	"	
M	Lacey Alice T †	196	stitcher	25	"	
N	Stenman Ulis W	196	retired	62	"	
O	Sullivan Nora D †	196	housewife	55	"	
P	Adamoviez Anna †	198	"	23	267 W Second	
R	Adamoviez Edward G	198	operator	23	267 "	
S	Small Annie †	198	housewife	56	500 Summer	
T	Downing Catherine M †	200	"	45	here	
V	Greenall Annie M †	200	housekeeper	63	"	
W	Festa Angelina †	206	housewife	27	"	
X	Festa Nicholas	206	laborer	34	"	

5

Everett Street Continued

z	Cook Claude	206	welder	30	228 Everett
307						
A	Cook Inez †	206	housewife	29	228 "
¹A	Prezioso Ovedio	206	machinist	27	228 "
B	Porzio Alphonzo	206	electrician	22	210 "
C	Cifelli Genaro	210	porter	52	30 Orleans
D	*Cifelli Rosaria †	210	housewife	58	30 "
E	Porzio Geano	210	machinist	20	585 Saratoga
F	Porzio Nora †	210	housewife	44	585 "
G	Potzio Nicola	210	pipefitter	47	585 "
H	*Licciardi Antonetta †	210	housewife	28	here
K	Licciardi Paul	210	machinist	34	"
L	Tedesco John	214	baker	46	"
M	Tedesco Marguerite †	214	housewife	45	"
N	Tedesco Phillip	214	U S A	21	"
O	D'Amato Fred	216	laborer	46	"
P	D'Amato Gerardo	216	U S A	21	"
R	Pulese Antonio	216	draftsman	55	"
S	Pulese Concetta †	216	housewife	47	"
T	Pulese Saverio	216	student	22	"
U	Ferranti Anthony	216	laborer	58	"
V	*Ferranti Carmella †	216	housewife	55	"
W	*Piazza Antonetta †	218	"	23	"
X	Piazza Benedetto	218	U S A	27	"
Y	Salemi Agripino	218	retired	71	"
Z	Salemi Marie †	218	housewife	80	"
308						
A	Marinelli Carmella †	218	"	33	"
B	Marinelli John	218	laborer	45	"
C	Cuzzi Isabella †	221	housewife	28	"
D	Cuzzi Luigi	221	manager	25	"
E	Masciulli Lucia †	221	housewife	58	"
F	Pepe Elena †	221	stitcher	26	"
G	Pellecchia Carlo	221	welder	29	194 Cottage
H	Pellecchia Elvira †	221	housewife	27	194 "
K	Aiello Gasper	222	laborer	52	here
L	Pasquariello James	222	carpenter	44	"
M	Pasquariello Theresa †	222	housewife	36	"
O	Prezioso Antonetta †	223	"	32	"
P	Prezioso Edward	223	welder	32	"
R	Perosino Genaro	223	tailor	50	"

Everett Street Continued

s	Perosino Ruffina †	223	housewife	48	here
t	Perosino Vincent	223	machinist	24	"
u	Squillacioti Alphonse	223	tinsmith	47	"
v	Squillacioti Victoria †	223	housewife	44	"
w	Tramonte Howard	224	longshoreman	20	11 Lamson ct
x	DelSette Anna †	224	housewife	60	here
y	DelSette Peter	224	retired	64	"
z	DeForti Filippa †	224	laundress	20	"

309

A	*DeForti Joseph	224	laborer	68	"
B	*DeForti Marie †	224	housewife	63	"
E	DiLorenzo Ethel †	225	"	27	5 Ardee
F	DiLorenzo Frank	225	carpenter	27	5 "
H	Macchia Alphonso	226	clerk	26	here
K	Macchia Ernestine †	226	packer	22	"
L	*Macchia Leo	226	shoeworker	63	"
M	*Macchia Mary †	226	housewife	59	"
N	Macchia Nellie †	226	"	30	Malden
O	Macchia Peter	226	checker	29	here
R	Salamone Josephine †	226	housewife	22	"
P	Salamone Rocco	226	mechanic	23	"
T	*Pereira Emma †	227	housewife	45	"
s	*DeMartino Emelia †	227	stitcher	45	225 Everett
V	Gravallesi Giuseppe	228	retired	73	here
W	Gravallesi Lucy †	228	housewife	73	"
X	Gerosa Frances †	228	"	42	"
Y	*Constanza Frances †	228	"	45	108 Summer
z	Constanza John	228	laborer	48	108 "

310

A	Sansone Antonio	229	"	32	here
B	Sansone Sarah †	229	housewife	30	"
c	DePalma Eileen †	229	"	24	"
D	DePalma Mario	229	shipfitter	25	"
E	Thibeau Cusha †	229	housewife	26	9 Jeffries
F	Thibeau George H	229	driller	33	9 "
G	Giggi Angelina †	230	housewife	54	here
H	Giggi Mary †	230	student	20	"
K	Giggi Thomas	230	plasterer	68	"
L	Grady Albert	233	brazier	33	"
M	Grady Ruth †	233	housewife	28	"
X	Todisco Ann †	234	stitcher	20	"

Everett Street Continued

o	Todisco Aurilla †	234	housewife	49	here
p	Todisco Carmen	234	tailor	52	"
r	Todisco Celeste †	234	stitcher	21	"
u*	Colannino Anthony	235	welder	28	"
v	Colannino Mary †	235	housewife	28	"
s	Tringale Antonio J	235	boatbuilder	46	"
t	Tringale Mary †	235	housewife	41	"
w	Burnside Mary E †	237	"	42	37 N Beacon
x	Donahue Hugh	237	boilermaker	33	here
y	Donahue Mary †	237	housewife	30	"
z	Zichello Alexander	237	U S A	23	"

311

a	Zichello Anthony	237	mechanic	22	"
b*	Zichello Michael	237	laborer	56	"
c	Zichello Nicholas	237	instructor	25	"
d*	Zichello Vincenza †	237	housewife	45	"
f*	Bevilacqua Jeana †	238	stitcher	50	"
g	Bevilacqua Libro	238	U S A	31	"
h	Todisco Albert	238	painter	26	"
k	Todisco Lena †	238	housewife	27	"
l	Carbone Jennie †	239	"	35	"
m	Carbone Ralph M	239	painter	36	"
n	Gioiosa Claire †	239	housewife	26	"
o	Gioiosa Edward J	239	machinist	28	"
p	Driscoll Daniel	239	U S A	35	"
r	Driscoll Marie †	239	housewife	34	"
s	Antillio Humbert	241	chauffeur	28	"
t	Antillio Mary †	241	housewife	26	"
t	Gesa Lena †	241	"	28	"
v	Gesa William V	241	manager	30	"
w*	Baldassare Carmella M †	241	housewife	54	"
x	Baldassare Giuseppe F	241	retired	61	"
y	DiSessa Charles	242	welder	29	"
z	DiSessa Samuel	242	barber	71	"

312

a	DiSessa Sarah †	242	housewife	64	"
b	Walker Daniel P	243	shipfitter	20	"
c	Bona Elizabeth †	243	housewife	47	"
d	Bona Helen †	243	clerk	26	"
f	Lavoie Beatrice †	244	housewife	33	"

Everett Street Continued

G	Lavoie George	244	shipper	42	here
H	Flanagan Andrew H	245	machinist	27	"
K	Flanagan Eleanor †	245	housewife	57	"
L	Fullerton Clarence	245	laborer	46	"
M	Fullerton Emma †	245	housewife	27	"
N	Larsen Clarence	245	U S A	24	"
O	Larsen Lillian †	245	housewife	23	"
P	Smith Thomas	245	carpenter	65	"
R	Stuffle Mildred †	246	housewife	27	"
S	Stuffle William	246	laborer	35	"
T	*Brogna Antonio	246	"	58	"
U	Brogna Domenic	246	dredger	31	"
V	Brogna Michael	246	painter	26	"
W	Milano Louis	247	U S A	30	230 Sumner
X	Milano Rosalie †	247	housewife	25	52 Jeffries
Y	*Carruso Anna †	247	"	48	here
Z	Carruso Anthony	247	shoemaker	51	"

313

A	Carruso Mary †	247	shoeworker	23	"
B	DiTomasso Anthony	247	U S A	25	"
C	DiTomasso Domenic	247	"	22	"
D	DiTomasso Frances †	247	operator	27	"
E	*DiTomasso Justino	247	laborer	63	"
F	*DiTomasso Mary †	247	housewife	53	"
G	DiTomasso Peter	247	U S A	20	"
H	DiTomasso Santo	247	mechanic	29	"
K	Bagnera Joseph	249	clerk	32	"
L	Bagnera Mary †	249	housewife	27	"
M	Amerena Anthony	249	candymaker	35	"
N	Amerena Frances †	249	housewife	32	"
O	*Piazza Angelina †	249	"	48	"
P	Piazza Bennetta †	249	operator	23	"
R	Piazza John L	249	U S A	25	"
T	Piazza Joseph	249	pressman	21	"
S	Piazza Luigi	249	laborer	59	"
U	Ollio Giuseppe	250	"	53	"
V	Rindone Anthony	250	U S A	24	"
W	Rindone Giuseppe	250	"	20	"
X	*Rindone Lena †	250	housewife	53	"
Y	Rindone Michael	250	U S A	22	"

Everett Street — Continued

z	*Rindone Vincenzo	250	retired		63	here
314						
B	Bell Julian	254	painter		35	"
C	Bell Ruth †	254	housewife		32	"
D	Nardone Giuseppe	255 257	retired		62	"
E	Nardone Joseph F	255 257	pedler		37	"
F	Nardone Pasqualina †255 257		housewife		61	"
G	*Coviello Geraldine †	256	"		32	"
H	Coviello John	256	laborer		29	"
K	Bickford Arthur	256	shipper		33	"
L	*Bickford Elvira T †	256	housewife		77	"
M	*Bickford Herbert	256	retired		74	"
N	Bona Dorothy M †	258	housewife		23	1 Ipswich pl
O	Bona Joseph H	258	rigger		23	1 "
P	Haasman Anna †	258	housewife		43	here
R	Haasman Philip	258	mechanic		45	"
S	Larsen Herbert	258	painter		29	"
U	Walker Daniel P	258	rigger		43	"
T	Walker Esther H †	258	housewife		40	"
V	Giannasoli Elvira †	259	"		24	291 Sumner
W	Giannasoli Ricardo	259	carpenter		27	261 Everett
X	Fay George	259	U S A		21	here
Y	Fay Helen G †	259	housewife		46	"
Z	Fay Herbert C	259	painter		38	"
315						
A	Fay Josephine †	259	housewife		38	"
B	Briggs Margaret M †	260	"		49	"
C	O'Leary Rita B †	260	clerk		26	"
D	Kornahrens Fred	260	U S N		23	S Carolina
E	Kornahrens Lillian †	260	housewife		22	here
G	O'Brion James W	260	U S C G		20	"
F	O'Brion Lillian †	260	housewife		46	"
H	Mucci Domenic	261	mechanic		25	"
K	Mucci Michelina †	261	housewife		26	"
L	Ascolillo Amerigo	261	shoeworker		39	"
M	Ascolillo Rose †	261	housewife		33	"
N	Cinelli Florinda †	261	"		36	"
O	Cinelli Joseph	261	operator		48	"
R	Bruno Frank	263	U S A		23	"
S	Bruno John	263	laborer		53	"
T	Bruno Lillian †	263	housewife		46	"

Everett Street Continued

c	Gaito Anthony	263	laborer	25	here
v	Gaito Mary †	263	housewife	25	"

Ipswich Place

x	Murphy James	1	U S A	23	here
y	*Murphy Patrick	1	retired	76	"
z	Volta Helen †	1	housewife	33	"

316

A	Volta Salvatore	1	shipper	35	"
B	Taromano Joseph	1	inspector	40	"
c	Taromano Louise †	1	housewife	33	"

Jeffries Street

K	Burrows Elizabeth †	4	at home	43	here
L	Meuse Daniel	4	laborer	37	"
M	*Meuse Lawrence	4	fishcutter	44	"
N	*Meuse Mary †	4	housewife	75	"
o	Larsen Arthur H	4	U S N	22	"
P	Larsen Charles J	4	painter	50	"
R	Larsen Charles J, jr	4	"	24	"
s	Larsen Clarence O	4	U S A	23	"
T	Larsen Francis	4	"	20	"
c	Larsen Mary B †	4	housewife	50	"
Y	Lombardi Jennie †	7	"	35	"
z	Lombardi Michael	7	laborer	35	"

317

A	Lombardi Nicholas	7	fishcutter	23	172 Maverick
B	Lombardi Vittoria †	7	housewife	20	172 "
D	Rock Gilbert	8	watchman	42	here
E	Rock Rose †	8	housewife	26	"
F	*Gonsalves Anthony	8	laborer	67	"
G	*Gonsalves Mary †	8	housewife	65	"
K	Dorato Carmen	9	U S A	22	"
L	Dorato Gennaro	9	candymaker	47	"
M	Dorato Vincenza †	9	housewife	37	"
N	Gregorio Agnes †	10	"	40	"
o	*Gregorio Cecil	10	weaver	55	"
P	Newbury Sadie †	10	at home	38	"
R	Spinney George A	10	welder	23	227 Everett

Jeffries Street Continued

s	Spinney Vincenza —†	10	housewife	20	227 Everett
u	Eisenburg Mary —†	12	stitcher	35	here
v	Eisenburg William C	12	U S N	42	"
w	Costa Alice—†	12	clerk	23	"
x	Costa Laura—†	12	"	34	"
y	Costa Margaret †	12	at home	36	"
z*	Costa Virginia —†	12	housewife	62	"

318

A	Jacobs Aagot —†	23	"	64	"
B	Jacobs John G	23	retired	66	"
c	Anderson George	25	U S N	25	"
D	Anderson Mary †	25	at home	23	"
E	Keohane James	25	riveter	21	72 Everett
F	Keohane Rita —†	25	clerk	23	72 "
G	Vitale Domenic	25	electrician	28	72 "
H	Vitale Joseph	25	bartender	52	here
K	Vitale Mary —†	25	housewife	25	72 Everett
L	Morrissey Helen E †	27	"	46	here
M	Morrissey Joseph P	27	laborer	45	"
N	Morrissey Joseph W	27	U S A	20	"
o	Heil Margaret †	27	housewife	32	"
P	Heil William J	27	painter	34	"
R	Fay Gerald	27	laborer	45	"
s	Fay Richard R	27	"	32	"
T	Fay William M	27	U S A	38	"
U	Montesanti Elizabeth †	29	housewife	32	"
V	Montesanti Frank	29	shipfitter	32	"
W	Spinney Charles	29	wrapper	28	"
X	Spinney Jane †	29	at home	65	"
Y	Nigrelli John	29	laborer	57	"
z	Nigrelli Maria †	29	housewife	51	"

319

B	DiStasio Anna †	40	proprietor	35	42 Jeffries
c	DiStasio Joseph	40	watchman	38	42 "
E	DeGregorio Eileen †	40	waitress	29	here
F	DeGregorio Robert	40	U S A	32	"
D	Rhoades Lillian †	40	at home	45	"
G*	Perriello Caroline †	42	"	60	"
H	Frazier Helen †	42	housewife	45	"
K	Frazier Joseph	42	fishcutter	54	"

Jeffries Street Continued

M	Nigrelli Cosimo	44	U S A	23	29 Jeffries
N	Nigrelli Maria †	44	weaver	23	Chelsea
O	Jackson Gilbert	44	weigher	44	here
P	Jackson Margaret †	44	housewife	39	"
R	Lingergren Elizabeth †	44	"	64	"
S	Lingergren Rudolph	44	longshoreman	59	"
T	Sheremeta Frances R †	45	clerk	25	"
U	Sheremeta Vladimir J	45	millhand	29	"
V	Shaughnessy Edward	45	U S A	24	"
W	White James	45	machinist	37	77 Morris
X	White Mary †	45	clerk	28	here
Y	Copeman Estelle †	45	housewife	35	"
Z	Copeman John W	45	checker	36	"

320

A	Hankard Esther †	46	stitcher	56	"
B	Hankard Ruth C †	46	stenographer	30	"
C	Pineo Stephen	46	proprietor	60	"
D	Innes Arthur H	46	printer	53	"
E	Innes Ruth L †	46	stitcher	52	"
F	MacDonald George A	46	aviator	41	"
G	MacDonald Hazel M †	46	housewife	29	"
H	Campbell Anna C †	46	"	60	"
K	Campbell Archibald D	46	electrician	65	"
L	Campbell Francis N	46	operator	39	"
N	Moran Clara B †	47	housewife	66	"
M	Moran Michael	47	retired	72	"
O	Dermody Margaret I †	47	clerk	23	"
P	Dermody Robert E	47	U S N	20	236 Webster
R	Moran Ethel B †	47	clerk	37	here
S	Moran Agnes †	47	housewife	30	"
T	Moran Francis W	47	draftsman	32	"
U	Capone Alfred	48	operator	27	502 Summer
V	Capone Mary †	48	clerk	23	312 "
W	Judge Christine †	48	housewife	41	here
X	Judge Frank	48	laborer	42	"
Z	Porcaro Francesco	49	retired	70	"

321

A*	Porcaro Rosina †	49	housewife	64	"
B	Porcaro Fiorello	49	painter	32	"
C	Porcaro John S	49	"	22	"

13

Jeffries Street Continued

D	*Pepe Maria D †	49	packer	40	here
F	Henton George	50	deckhand	44	"
G	Henton Julia †	50	housewife	40	"
H	Dudley Albert	50	welder	30	"
K	Dudley Beatrice S †	50	housewife	25	"
L	*Ciavola Allesandro	51	retired	69	"
M	Ciavola Nunzio	51	laborer	27	"
N	Swenson Emil R	51	guard	40	"
O	Swenson Genevieve †	51	housewife	40	"
P	Barron Leo	51	riveter	40	"
R	Barron Violet †	51	housewife	38	"
S	*Milano Antonetta †	52	"	56	"
T	Milano Luigi	52	retired	69	"
U	Milano James	52	U S N	21	"
V	Milano Riccardo	52	"	25	"
W	Milano Samuel	52	shipfitter	28	"
X	Masello Carmelo M	52	laborer	34	"
Y	Masello Christina †	52	housewife	30	"
Z	Riley Joseph	53	pipefitter	25	"

322

A	Riley Mafalda †	53	housewife	25	"
B	Tulepani Rosina †	53	at home	58	"
C	Tulepani Salvatore	53	guard	33	"
D	Tulepani Louis	53	clerk	39	"
E	Tulepani Nellie †	53	housewife	36	"
F	Correale James	54	laborer	24	"
G	Correale Josephine †	54	housewife	23	"
H	Giampietro John	54	laborer	50	"
K	*Giampietro Phyllis †	54	housewife	47	"
L	Gianfelice Gaetano	54	laborer	47	"
M	Gianfelice Teresa †	54	knitter	30	"
N	*Cuzzi Carmen	56	retired	59	551 Summer
O	Cuzzi Donato	56	shipper	23	here
P	*Cuzzi Maria †	56	at home	63	551 Summer
R	DellBene Caroline †	56	stitcher	23	here
S	DellBene Guilio	56	laborer	51	"
T	DellBene Mary †	56	stitcher	21	"
U	*DellBene Michelina †	56	housewife	56	"
V	Lombardi Paul	56	chemist	27	"
W	Lombardi Teresa †	56	housewife	24	"

Lamson Street

x	Powell Elizabeth †	1	housekeeper	51	here	
y	Powell Joseph M	1	retired	67	"	
z	Powell Sarah †	1	housekeeper	53	"	
	323					
a	McDonald Gertrude L †	1	housewife	49	"	
b	McDonald Warren F	1	clerk	49	"	
c	Walter Emma †	1	housekeeper	78	"	
d	Walter Mary R †	1	clerk	54	"	
e	Adams Nellie †	2	tel operator	27	"	
f	Riley Harriet †	2	housekeeper	74	"	
g	Riley Regina M †	2	clerk	50	"	
h	Curll Ellen M †	2	at home	75	"	
k	McLaughlin James A	2	retired	71	"	
l	Thompson Susie F †	2	housekeeper	65	"	
m	Storlazzi Alfred	3	inspector	31	"	
n	Storlazzi Gertrude †	3	housewife	31	"	
o	DiPietro Irene M †	3	"	29	"	
p	DiPietro Pasquale	3	machinist	36	"	
r	*Storlazzi Adolph	3	tailor	54	"	
s	Storlazzi Anna †	3	saleswoman	23	"	
t	Storlazzi Anthony	3	U S A	28	"	
u	*Storlazzi Caesira †	3	housewife	56	"	
v	Storlazzi Enis †	3	seamstress	33	"	
w	Storlazzi Ernani	3	U S N	29	"	
x	Storlazzi Gloria †	3	at home	20	"	
y	Cioffi Joseph	3	stitcher	27	"	
z	Cioffi Mary †	3	housewife	24	"	
	324					
a	Capraro Rose †	4	machinist	23	"	
b	D'Olympia Anthony	4	chauffeur	42	"	
c	*D'Olympia Lawrence	4	retired	72	"	
d	*D'Olympia Mary †	4	at home	73	"	
e	Novara Josephine †	4	housewife	36	"	
f	Novara Matthew	4	laborer	47	"	
g	Faugno Carmella †	4	housewife	40	"	
h	Faugno Michael	4	shoeworker	50	"	
k	*Greco Alphonso	5	laborer	47	"	
l	Greco James	5	U S A	35	"	
m	*Greco Philomena †	5	housekeeper	51	"	
n	Marino Frank	5	janitor	39	"	

Lamson Street Continued

o	Sinopoli Mary †	5	housewife	36	here
p	Sinopoli Michael	5	welder	42	"
R	Carlucci Carmella †	5	housewife	25	"
s*	Carlucci Joseph	5	retired	71	"
T	Carlucci Joseph, jr	5	bartender	34	"
U	Larsen George	5	longshoreman	45	"

Long Island

v	Bailey James		superintendent	52	here
w	Berry Katherine L †		nurse	46	"
x	Boyle Gertrude F †		attendant	40	"
y	Brady Christopher G		clerk	55	"
z	Broderick Margaret †		maid	65	"
	325				
A	Browne Ethel C †		teacher	37	"
B	Cahill Nora M †		nurse	53	"
c	Connelly Mary F †		housekeeper	38	"
D	Connors Elizabeth A †		dietitian	36	"
E	Croke Edmund W		clergyman	41	"
F	Curran James W		watchman	62	"
G	Dalton Margaret M †		laundress	36	"
H	Danley Ruth †		cook	45	"
K	Dodd Anna J †		attendant	56	"
L	Dodd Katherine I †		maid	64	"
M	Donnelly Frances †		technician	32	"
N	Donnelly Rita †		social worker	24	"
o	Dwyer Rose P †		laundress	57	"
P	Evans Margaret E †		maid	57	104 Pleasant av
R	Fawcett Alice B †		nurse	57	here
s	Greene Mabel B †		"	49	"
T	Hackett Mary †		laundress	48	"
U	Hickey Annie †		supervisor	40	"
v	Hughes Annie L †		"	37	"
w	Johnson Michael		laundryworker	40	"
x	Kingman Albert P		laborer	53	"
y	Long Edmund W		caretaker	54	"
	326				
B	MacGillivary Florence †		laundress	50	"
¹B	Magrath George I		technician	36	"
A	McFadden Daniel J		laborer	66	"

16

Long Island — Continued

c	McGraile Bartholomew		watchman	66	here
D	McGrath Mary A †		maid	45	"
E	McLean Christine †		housekeeper	47	"
G	McNamara Catherine L †		matron	58	"
F	Morrill Marion R †		"	60	"
H	Nutter Doris O †		nurse	33	"
K	O'Neil Theresa B †		seamstress	51	"
L	Scheeler Mary J †		housekeeper	49	"
M	Shaughnessy Patrick		laborer	47	82 Shepton
N	Smith Mary B †		attendant	41	here
O	Strain Margaret M †		technician	27	"
P	Stratton Mary E †		seamstress	46	"
R	Tobin Patrick F		laborer	67	"
S	Yarrow Alphonse G		clerk	30	245 Kennebec

Marginal Street

U	Moore Josephine †	286	housewife	42	here
V	Moore Raymond	286	painter	40	"
W	Rolfe Geraldine †	286	housewife	29	301 Belgrade av
X	Rolfe James	286	B F D	30	301 "
Y	Rolfe Arthur	286	laborer	34	here
Z	Rolfe Josephine †	286	housewife	27	"

327

A	MacCormick Charles	288	boilermaker	41	"
B	MacCormick Sadie †	288	housewife	40	"
C	Dalton Florence N †	288	"	33	276 Marginal
D	Dalton James J	288	longshoreman	36	276 "
E	Dalton Joseph L	288	U S A	24	276 "
F	McInnes Daniel B	288	boilermaker	70	here
G	McInnes Edith E †	288	stenographer	35	"
H	McInnes Ellen †	288	housewife	55	"
K	Pepe Alice †	290	"	38	"
L	Pepe Orazio	290	laborer	51	"
M	Smith Arthur J	290	chauffeur	35	"
N	Smith Catherine E †	290	housewife	31	"
S*	Belleveau Moses	292	retired	70	"
T	Eagle Veneta †	292	waitress	21	"
U	Guay Joseph	292	retired	73	"
V	Scolastico Angelina †	294	at home	78	"
W	Scolastico Gina †	294	housewife	36	"

1 3   17

Page	Letter	Full Name.	Residence, Jan. 1, 1943	Occupation.	Supposed Age.	Reported Residence, Jan. 1, 1942. Street and Number.

Marginal Street—Continued

	X	Scolastico Michael	294	laborer	43	here
	Y	DeFelice Cesidio	294	retired	83	"
	Z	DeFelice Domenic	294	laborer	49	"
328						
	A	DeFelice Rosalie †	294	housewife	80	"
	C	Hansjon Henry	300	retired	48	"
	D	Hansjon Henry N, jr	300	machinist	21	"
	E	Hansjon Nora †	300	housewife	43	"
	F	Otterson Anna †	300	"	68	"
	G	Otterson Harry	300	retired	70	"
	H	Buckley Beda †	300	housekeeper	58	"
	K	Buckley Edward L	300	painter	52	"
	L	Buckley Thelma †	300	clerk	27	"
	M	Neth Dorothy †	300	"	23	"

Maverick Street

	N	Annese Anthony	333	U S A	21	here
	O	Annese Domenic	333	laborer	47	"
	P*	Annese Mary †	333	housewife	39	"
	R	Annese Orlando	333	machinist	20	"
	S	Arena Salvatore	333	pressman	20	"
	T	Costanzo Concetta †	333	tailor	21	"
	U	Costanzo Leonardo	333	pressman	20	"
	V*	Costanzo Lucia †	333	tailor	40	"
	W	Costanzo Nicola	333	laborer	47	"
	X	Dzedulonus James	333	fishcutter	38	Chelsea
	Y	Dzedulonus Rose †	333	housewife	31	"
	Z	Dalimonte George F	335	laborer	31	7 Webster av
329						
	A	Dalimonte Rachel †	335	housewife	30	7 "
	B	Salamone Evelyn †	335	"	42	here
	C	Salamone Vincent	335	chauffeur	42	"
	D	Letteri Matilda †	335	housewife	29	"
	E	Letteri Samuel	335	bootblack	32	"
	F	Leccese Domenic	337	machinist	28	"
	G	Leccese Teresa †	337	housewife	26	"
	H	Scandone Albert	337	machinist	21	"
	K	Scandone Eleanor †	337	at home	26	"
	L	Scandone Elvira †	337	toolmaker	23	"
	N	Scandone Madeline †	337	at home	29	"

18

Maverick Street Continued

M	Scandone Nellie †	337	housewife	51	here
O	Scandone Peter A	337	musician	56	"
P	Manzo Anna †	337	housewife	40	"
S	Manzo Louis R	337	chauffeur	43	"
R	Manzo Mary J †	337	spinner	23	"
T	Durante Catherine †	343	housewife	26	"
U	Durante John	343	shipfitter	30	"
V *Bonavita Angelina †	343	housewife	57	"
W	Bonavita Anthony	343	welder	24	"
X	Bonavita Francesco	343	laborer	56	"
Y	Bonavita Mildred †	343	at home	26	"
Z	Bonavita Nicholas	343	U S A	28	"
	330					
A	Bonavita Sarafina †	343	clerk	21	"
B	Fagone Clara †	343	housewife	28	23 Murray et
C	Fagone Frank	343	shipfitter	23	23 "
D	Jones John	345	roofer	44	here
E	Jones Margaret †	345	housewife	35	"
F	DiRienzo Agostino	345	U S A	24	"
G	DiRienzo Anthony	345	shipfitter	23	"
H	DiRienzo Assunta †	345	leatherworker	26	"
K	DiRienzo Carmela †	345	"	29	"
L	DiRienzo Edith †	345	packer	21	"
M	DiRienzo Frank	345	U S A	40	"
N *DiRienzo Rosina †	345	housewife	61	"
O	Faiella Jennie †	345	"	27	"
P	Faiella Joseph	345	laborer	30	"
R	Rizzo Angelo J	347	clerk	33	"
S	Rizzo Edith †	347	housewife	32	"
T	Rizzo Catherine †	347	"	59	"
U	Rizzo Michael	347	laborer	60	"
V	Rizzo Marciano F	347	upholsterer	38	"
W	Rizzo Mary †	347	housewife	36	"
X	Lauletta Grace †	363	"	35	"
Y	Lauletta Vincent	363	laborer	42	"
Z *DellaCroci Vincenzo	363	retired	68	"
	231					
A	Liardi Anthony	363	operator	51	"
B *Liardi Josephine †	363	packer	32	"
C *Carabott Albert	367	chef	62	"
D *Carabott Anna †	367	housewife	59	"

19

Maverick Street Continued

E	Carabott Lucy †	367	inspector	22	here
F	Carabott Rose †	367	at home	23	"
G	Annese Domenic	367	laborer	60	"
H	Annese Lucy †	367	leatherworker	29	"
K*	Annese Teresa †	367	housewife	55	"
L	Cappezzi Vincenzo	367	retired	71	"
M	Ardito Anna C †	369	housewife	54	"
N	Ardito Carmen	369	bootblack	56	"
O	Small Eleanor †	369	housewife	26	"
P	Small Samuel L	369	welder	26	"
R	Emmet Helen C †	369	stitcher	54	"
S	Emmet Oliver R	369	deckhand	30	"
T	Hancock John H	369	welder	51	"
U	Lombardi Eleanor †	371	operator	25	"
V	Lombardi Jennie †	371	"	22	"
W	Lombardi Rose †	371	packer	28	"
Y	D'Eramo Dante	375	laborer	39	"
Z	D'Eramo Rose †	375	housewife	35	"

332

A*	Ventresca Dolores M †	375	at home	58	"
B	Ventresca Lucy †	375	stitcher	28	"
C*	Santi Genoveffa †	377	housewife	57	"
D	Santi Luigi	377	bricklayer	60	"
E	Santi Carmen	377	pressman	38	"
F	Santi Filippa †	377	knitter	35	"
G	Belmonte Allesandro	377	laborer	47	"
H	Belmonte Angelina †	377	dressmaker	36	"
K	Autilio Raffaele	379	laborer	25	"
L	Correale Frederick	379	"	20	"
M*	Correale O James	379	chauffeur	42	"
N*	Correale Rose †	379	housewife	39	"
O	Correale Vincent J	379	U S A	20	"
R	Grasso Josephine †	381	housewife	41	"
S	Grasso Nicola	381	laborer	47	"
U	Gaeto Domenic	381	U S A	22	"
T*	Gaeto Teresa †	381	at home	45	"
V	Nardone Charles S	383	engineer	30	"
W	Nardone Mary †	383	housewife	30	"
X	Goglia Amodeo	383	pedler	46	"
Y	Goglia Mary †	383	housewife	38	"
Z	Belmonte Agostino	383	laborer	49	56 Jeffries

333

Maverick Street (Continued)

A	Belmonte Agostino J jr	383	U S A	22	56 Jeffries
B	Belmonte Clorinda †	383	housewife	46	56 "
C	Belmonte Mary †	383	leatherworker	21	56 "
F	Poquette Arthur R	395	caretaker	58	here
G	Poquette Avis †	395	housewife	57	"

McCormick Square

H	Tranfaglia George	1	shoeworker	39	here
K	Tranfaglia Jennie †	1	housewife	27	"
M	Tranfaglia Leonora †	1	stitcher	22	"
L	Tranfaglia Orlando	1	shoeworker	36	"
N	Tranfaglia Orsela	1	housewife	59	"
O	Tranfaglia Pasquale	1	U S A	37	"
P	Angrisano Generosa †	1	housewife	38	"
R	Angrisano George	1	barber	38	"
S	Rowan Catherine †	3	housewife	54	"
T	Rowan Edward	3	repairman	52	"
U	Rowan John E	3	U S A	22	"
V	Ciampa Carmen	3	laborer	53	"
W	Ciampa Frederick	3	U S A	21	"
X	Ciampa John	3	chef	22	"
Y	*Ciampa Mary †	3	housewife	49	"
Z	Ciampa Ralph	3	U S A	21	"

334

A	Sharp Allan M	3	clerk	60	"
B	Sharp Mary †	3	housewife	58	"

Spectacle Island

C	Barnes Anna M †		housewife	30	173 W Fifth
D	Barnes John R		laborer	31	173 "
E	*Kalinsky Karol		janitor	70	here
F	*Leskewicz Michael		watchman	54	"
G	Lowther George P		"	62	"
H	Riell William W		clerk	68	"
K	Rudnicki Martin		laborer	68	"
L	*Strominski John		operator	58	"
M	Timmons Annie P †		housewife	53	"
N	Timmons Warren W		painter	54	"

Page	Letter	Full Name	Residence, Jan. 1, 1943.	Occupation.	Supposed Age	Reported Residence, Jan. 1, 1942. Street and Number.

Spectacle Island   Continued

	P	Wyatt Benjamin L		U S N	24	here
	O	Wyatt Elsie M †		housewife	50	"
	R	Wyatt Robert H		U S N	25	"
	S	Wyatt Roy E		mechanic	52	"

Sumner Street

	T	LaMar Carmella †	460	shoeworker	21	here
	U	Sarro Anthony	460	laborer	54	"
	V	Sarro Catherine †	460	at home	29	"
	W	Sarro Jennie †	460	housewife	49	"
	X	Sarro Josephine †	460	at home	28	"
	Y	*Arsenio Felix	461	laborer	60	2 Wilbur ct
	Z	*Arsenio Mary C †	461	housewife	56	2 "
335						
	A	Frazier Felice †	461	"	26	Chelsea
	B	Frazier William H	461	painter	26	"
	C	Mottola Adeline †	461	housewife	28	here
	D	Mottola Arthur	461	boxmaker	29	"
	E	Penta Concetta †	462	housewife	22	"
	F	Penta Edward L	462	artist	25	"
	G	Ambrosina Alfred	462	printer	37	"
	H	Ambrosina Carmella †	462	housewife	30	"
	K	Alabiso Angelo	462	barber	57	"
	L	*Alabiso Rosaria †	462	housewife	53	"
	M	Buchanan Mildred †	463	"	35	"
	N	Buchanan William E	463	chauffeur	36	"
	O	*DeLuca Lucia †	463	housewife	59	"
	P	DeLuca Romeo	463	machinist	32	"
	R	Bossi Charles	463	shipfitter	31	"
	S	Bossi Clara †	463	housewife	31	"
	T	*Porzio Carmella †	463	at home	72	"
	U	McLaughlin Edward	464	U S A	41	"
	V	Costello Harold	464	U S N	31	19 Marion
	W	Costello Mary †	464	housewife	30	19 "
	X	Scott William	464	freighthandler	28	here
	Y	Costello Albert	464	plumber	35	"
	Z	Costello Isabel †	464	housewife	32	"
336						
	A	Natale Nicholas	465	machinist	62	"
	B	*Natale Stella †	465	housewife	45	"

Sumner Street — Continued

	c	Duffy Emma †	465	operator	35	here
	D	Flood John H	466	laborer	51	"
	E	Smith S Catherine †	466	teacher	60	"
	F	McColgan John C	467	janitor	60	"
	G	McColgan Julia T †	467	housewife	57	"
	H	McColgan Mary E †	467	secretary	21	"
	K	McColgan Thomas J	467	U S N	22	"
	L	Murphy Charles J	468	assembler	27	"
	M	Murphy Margaret †	468	housewife	58	"
	N	Phelan Edward	468	U S N	21	"
	O	Phelan Mary †	468	housewife	55	"
	P	Phelan Michael J	468	guard	58	"
	R	Scarfo Celia †	469	housewife	28	"
	S	Scarfo Joseph	469	rubberworker	28	"
	T	Zambella Andrew	469	machinist	57	"
	U	Zambella Emma †	469	stitcher	27	"
	V	Zambella Lucia †	469	housewife	51	"
	W	Grillo Arthur	470	inspector	26	"
	X	Grillo Yolanda A †	470	housewife	23	"
	Y	*Sarpi Ambrose	470	laborer	49	"
	Z	Sarpi Antonetta †	470	saleswoman	25	"

337

	A	Sarpi Helen †	470	stitcher	24	"
	B	*Sarpi Josephine G †	470	housewife	46	"
	c	Giorgione Marie †	470	"	26	Wash'n D C
	D	Giorgione Sylvio	470	collector	27	"
	E	*LaPilato Ann †	472	housewife	51	here
	F	LaPilato Edith †	472	technician	27	"
	G	LaPilato James	472	proprietor	58	"
	K	Catania Santa †	472	housewife	26	"
	H	Catania William	472	operator	29	"
	M	Clark Annette †	472	housewife	30	"
	L	Clark Willam	472	clerk	36	"
	N	DeLuca Frederick	473	laborer	60	"
	O	DeLuca Gemma †	473	leatherworker	28	"
	R	*DeLuca Ingronata †	473	housewife	47	"
	P	DeLuca Maria †	473	leatherworker	26	"
	S	DellaCroce Anthony	473	mechanic	22	"
	T	DellaCroce Yolanda †	473	housewife	25	"
	U	Ford Theresa M †	474	maid	54	"
	V	Sherwin Albert	474	U S A	23	"

Page.	Letter	FULL NAME.	Residence, Jan. 1, 1943	Occupation.	Supposed Age.	Reported Residence, Jan. 1, 1942. Street and Number.

Sumner Street Continued

w	Sherwin Catherine †	474	housewife	55	here
x	Sherwin Francis	474	U S N	25	"
y	Sherwin James	474	"	29	"
z	Sherwin John	474	U S A	27	"

338

A	Sherwin Joseph	474	"	30	"
B	Foster Anna †	475	housewife	31	"
C	Foster John F	475	painter	41	"
D	Bussey John	475	retired	81	"
E	Bussey Mary †	475	housewife	68	"
F	*Grasso Mildred †	477	"	42	"
G	Grasso Ralph	477	shoeworker	51	"
H	Claudio Clementina †	477	housewife	28	"
K	Claudio Joseph	477	chauffeur	33	"
L	Lee Carl	477	machinist	51	"
M	Lee Christine †	477	housewife	52	"
N	DeMarco Alfred	477	chauffeur	27	"
O	DeMarco Virginia †	477	housewife	30	"
P	*Zambella Bruna †	479	"	40	"
R	Zambella Vincent	479	barber	50	"
S	Pettiniachio Louis	479	laborer	49	"
T	Pettiniachio Mary †	479	housewife	50	"
U	*Corrente Angelo	479	tailor	46	"
V	*Corrente Jennie †	479	housewife	41	"
W	LaRosa Bianca †	481	"	22	483 Sumner
X	LaRosa Frederick	481	U S A	21	here
Y	LaRosa Frederick	481	carpenter	54	"
Z	*LaRosa Gaetana †	481	housewife	55	"

339

A	Zecchino Frank	481	U S A	23	"
B	Zecchino Ida †	481	shoeworker	21	"
C	*Zecchino Mary †	481	housewife	46	"
D	Zecchino Ralph	481	shoeworker	46	"
E	DeBerti Amelia †	483	housewife	47	"
F	DeBerti Edward	483	tailor	50	"
G	Barbere Frank	483	engineer	49	"
H	Barbere Theresa †	483	housewife	46	"
K	Barbere Alfred	483	mechanic	20	204 Bremen
L	Kenney Alice C †	488	domestic	57	here
M	*Melanson Priscilla †	488	leatherworker	62	"
N	Fravold Clarence	488	U S A	33	64 Falcon

24

Sumner Street Continued

o	Fravold Edna †	488	shipper	24	64 Falcon
p	Fravold Margaret †	488	winder	35	64 "
R	Fravold Olivia †	488	at home	64	64 "
s*	Wesad Herman	488	seaman	59	64 "
T	Harkins Mary E †	490	clerk	48	here
u	Long Margaret A †	490	operator	42	"
v	Long William	490	laborer	47	"
w	Kilduff Ellen T †	490	matron	44	"
x	Chiochetti Edmond	492	leatherworker	44	"
y	Chiochetti Theresa †	492	housewife	42	"
z	Penta John F	492	machinist	20	"

340

A	Penta Mary †	492	housewife	43	"
B	Penta Michael C	492	agent	43	"
c	Mercandante Elsie †	492	housewife	32	Revere
D	Mercandante Joseph	492	laborer	33	"
E*	Mercandante Raffaela †	492	housewife	67	here
F*	Mercandante Vincenzo	492	laborer	67	"
G	Petitto Ida †	494	housewife	25	Fitchburg
H	Petitto Samuel	494	welder	29	"
K	Bartolo Andrew	494	U S A	28	here
L	Bartolo Biagio	494	foreman	59	"
M	Bartolo Louise †	494	artist	20	"
N	Bartolo Mary C †	494	housewife	59	"
o	Griffiths Florence †	494	"	21	"
P	Griffiths Walter F	494	painter	61	273 Havre
R	Griffiths William J	494	fireman	25	here
s	Doherty Frank J	496	laborer	36	"
T	Doherty Rita J †	496	housewife	26	"
u	Sasso Anthony	496	laborer	24	40 Jeffries
v*	Sasso Isabel †	496	housewife	53	40 "
w	Sasso Joseph	496	U S N	26	40 "
x	DeAngelis Frances †	496	housewife	25	here
y	DeAngelis Joseph	496	machinist	29	"
z	Discenza Doris †	497	housewife	23	59 Forest Hills

341

A	Discenza Nicholas	497	laborer	32	59 "
B	Capone Concetta †	497	housewife	34	48 Jeffries
c	Capone John L	497	rigger	35	48 "
D	DellaRusso Raffaele	497	retired	83	48 "
E	Stoddard Anna M †	497	housewife	28	499 Sumner

Sumner Street Continued

F	Stoddard John G	497	foreman	29	499 Sumner
G	Humphrey Mary T—†	498	housewife	45	here
H	Humphrey Oliver L	498	longshoreman	51	"
K	Mahoney Marie—†	498	operator	22	"
L	Jacobs Arthur	498	foreman	31	"
M	Jacobs Helen †	498	housewife	31	"
N	Pezzella Angelina †	498	at home	30	"
O	Pezzella Henry	498	machinist	22	"
P	Mirasolo Frank	498	dairyman	29	Revere
R	Mirasolo Leona †	498	housewife	21	"
S	Saponaro Evelyn †	499	"	23	here
T	Saponaro Joseph A	499	clerk	25	"
U	Belmonte Anita †	499	housewife	30	"
V	Belmonte Salvatore	499	machinist	35	"
W	Woodside Edward A	499	painter	39	280 Marginal
X	Woodside Josephine †	499	housewife	37	280 "
Y	*Arcinoli Elvira †	500	"	59	here
Z	Arcinoli John	500	laborer	63	"

342

A	Arcinolo Joseph	500	U S A	23	"
B	Catalano Angelo	500	pedler	52	"
C	*Catalano Filomina †	500	housewife	39	"
E	Catalano Joseph	500	U S A	22	"
D	Catalano Mary †	500	stitcher	20	"
F	Valentine Ludie L	500	rigger	34	"
G	*Valentine Theresa †	500	housewife	30	"
H	*Capone Antonetta †	502	"	55	"
K	*Capone Ceriaco	502	laborer	59	"
L	Capone Grace †	502	candymaker	31	"
M	Capone Julia †	502	candyworker	21	"
N	Caprini Amelia †	502	housewife	24	"
O	Caprini Stanley	502	welder	27	345 Saratoga
P	*Marrazzo Agostino	502	painter	39	here
R	Marrazzo Rose †	502	housewife	28	"
S	Clark Caroline †	504	"	42	"
T	Clark Edward	504	U S A	21	"
U	Clark Margaret †	504	packer	20	"
V	Clark Thomas	504	longshoreman	43	"
W	Lafferty Edith †	504	housewife	76	229 Everett
X	Lafferty Margaret †	504	forewoman	39	229 "
Y	Lafferty Robert	504	retired	83	229 "

Page.	Letter	Full Name.	Residence, Jan. 1, 1943.	Occupation.	Supposed Age.	Reported Residence, Jan. 1, 1942. Street and Number.

Sumner Street Continued

	Z	Crocker Catherine †	504	housewife	38	107 St Andrew rd
343						
	A	Crocker George C	504	boilermaker	39	here
	B	Crocker Nellie †	504	housewife	65	"
	C	Hopp Edith †	504	typist	40	"
	D	*Mirasola Joseph	506	carpenter	55	"
	E	Mirasola Rose †	506	at home	20	"
	F	*DiPietro Marie †	506	"	65	"
	G	*DiPietro Pasquale	506	janitor	75	"
	H	*DiPietro Rocco	506	pressman	34	"
	K	Volpini Angelo	506	bookbinder	54	"
	L	Volpini Elvira †	506	stitcher	23	"
	M	Volpini Josephine †	506	housewife	50	"
	O	Casiello Elvira M †	508	"	30	"
	P	Casiello Joseph	508	laborer	36	"
	R	*Vernucci Josephine †	508	housewife	61	"
	S	*Vernucci Nicholas	508	tailor	60	"
	T	*Terenzio Ralph	510	retired	79	"
	U	Micciche Antonette †	510	housewife	37	"
	V	Micciche Joseph	510	laborer	42	"
	Y	Capone Anna †	512	at home	55	"
	Z	Capone Anthony	512	welder	26	"
344						
	A	*Carangillo Angelina †	512	housewife	55	"
	B	Carangillo Anthony	512	U S N	20	"
	C	Carangillo Cosimo	512	laborer	54	"
	D	Carangillo John	512	U S A	24	"
	E	Carangillo Vincenzo	512	"	21	"
	G	Penny Elizabeth †	514	at home	70	"
	H	Saponaro Anna †	514	housewife	44	"
	K	Saponaro Edith †	514	stitcher	24	"
	L	Saponaro Emma †	514	packer	20	"
	M	Saponaro William	514	U S N	22	"
	P	Venezia Anthony	516	rigger	41	"
	R	Venezia Mary †	516	housewife	41	"
	S	Woodside Viola †	516	"	32	10 Jeffries
	T	Woodside William	516	painter	37	10 "
	U	*Pingiaro Mary †	516	housewife	45	here
	V	*Pingiaro Severio	516	barber	54	"
	W	McCormick Anna F †	518	stenographer	29	"
	X	McCormick Annie †	518	at home	69	"

Sumner Street Continued

Y	Treiber Frederick	518	U S N	25	here
Z	Treiber Rita †	518	clerk	20	"

345

A	Treiber Rose †	518	housewife	59	"
B	Treiber Ruth †	518	operator	22	"
C	Antonellis James	518	leatherworker	53	"
D	Cioppa Joseph A	518	welder	39	"
E	Cioppa Louise †	518	housewife	34	"
F	Platt Ernest C	520	laborer	36	"
G	Platt Helen M †	520	housewife	32	"
H	Heil Elizabeth M †	520	"	39	"
K	Heil John F	520	painter	43	"
L	Reidy James J	520	at home	21	"
M	Jameson Isabelle †	520	operator	48	"
N	Jameson Walter	520	U S N	24	"
O	Visca Carlo	522	laborer	52	6 Everett pl
P*	Visca Valentino	522	"	56	6 "
R	Cilibrosi Charles	522	"	52	2 Jeffries
S*	Cilibrosi Josephine †	522	housewife	47	2 "
T	Angell Edward F	522	painter	36	here
U	Angell Harold	522	U S A	28	"
V*	Angell Helen †	522	housewife	60	"
W*	Catalano Antonetta †	524	"	45	"
X	Catalano Pasquale	524	bartender	52	"
Y	Trainor Dorothy M †	524	housewife	29	"
Z	Trainor Edward J	524	longshoreman	29	"

346

B	Smith Robert	535	steamfitter	55	"
C	Higginbotham Alice †	535	at home	70	"
D	Higginbotham John J	535	plumber	53	"
E	Clark Clara †	535	at home	42	Danvers
F	Clark Sarah †	535	leatherworker	50	here
G	Crowley Edward A	537	guard	58	176 Falcon
H	Crowley Elsie †	537	housewife	55	176 "
K	Togariello Carlo	537	U S A	22	here
M	Togariello Catherine †	537	leatherworker	20	"
L*	Togariello Isabelle †	537	housewife	46	"
N	Togariello Leonardo	537	laborer	53	"
O	Warner Alfonsine †	537	housewife	20	188 Webster
P	Warner Edward J	537	shipwright	21	here
R	Botting William J	539	freighthandler	63	280 Marginal

Page	Letter	FULL NAME	Residence, Jan. 1, 1943.	Occupation.	Supposed Age.	Reported Residence, Jan. 1, 1942. Street and Number.

Sumner Street Continued

	s	Fraser Albert	539	U S C G	70	here
	t	Fraser Theresa †	539	housewife	76	"
	u	Smith Anna L †	539	"	67	"
	v	Smith James	539	mechanic	57	"
	w	Fay Eleanor †	541	housewife	21	2 Webster av
	x	Fay Joseph	541	pipefitter	28	2 "
	y	DePalma Joseph	541	laborer	56	here
	z	*DePalma Olympia †	541	housewife	50	"

347

	a	Boy Catherine †	541	"	28	"
	b	Boy Domenic	541	printer	31	"
	c	*Popeo Esther †	545	housewife	42	"
	d	Popeo Vincent	545	agent	45	"
	e	*Correalle Minicela †	549	at home	76	"
	g	Fay Charles	549	U S A	30	"
	h	Fay Herbert	549	painter	25	"
	k	Fay Isabella E †	549	housewife	50	"
	l	Fay Joseph J	549	operator	51	"
	m	Bibo Ralph J	551	U S A	20	414 Sumner
	o	Pelusi Joseph F	551	clerk	23	here
	n	Pelusi Theresa †	551	housewife	22	"
	p	Pelusi Eleanor †	551	"	41	"
	r	Pelusi Frank	551	U S N	22	"
	s	Pelusi Luigi	551	laborer	50	"

Thompson's Island

	t	Albee Clifton E		director	36	here
	u	Baird Mark C		instructor	43	"
	v	Baird Zella M †		"	39	"
	w	Coffill Henrietta †		"	56	"
	x	Cook John B		"	62	New Jersey
	y	Cook Sadie B †		housewife	61	"
	z	Hunt Mary R †		instructor	50	here

348

	a	*Jardine James H		U S N	33	"
	b	Jones Jeanette A †		instructor	29	"
	d	Jones R Carroll		U S A	29	"
	c	Jones Ronald B		herdsman	31	"
	e	Kihlstrom Bror Y		instructor	59	"
	f	Kitching Robert R		"	59	"

Thompson's Island Continued

H	Mathewson Mary F †	instructor	55	here
K	Matteson Abijah	engineer	71	"
G	Meacham Rena M †	teacher	46	"
L	Meacham William M	"	46	"
M	Pickard Arthur H	U S A	26	"
N	Pickard Dorothy R †	teacher	22	Vermont
O	Stiles Carlton W	instructor	29	here
P	Stiles Isabel L †	bookkeeper	31	"
R	Thomas Raymond	supervisor	32	"
S	Thomas Wilhelmina B †	secretary	30	"
T	Wills Grovenor A	seaman	60	Buzzards Bay
U	Wills Harriet L †	instructor	52	Maine

Webster Place

V	Cicero Bartolo	1	laborer	50	here
W	Cicero Emma †	1	housewife	42	"

Webster Street

X	*Fazio Charles	208	barber	49	here
Y	Fazio Emilia †	208	housewife	33	"
Z	*Barrelli Antonetta †	208	"	50	"

349

A	Borrelli Michael	208	machinist	56	"
B	Hennessy James L	210	attorney	28	"
C	Hennessy Mary A †	210	housekeeper	57	"
D	Hennessy Maxine A †	210	bookkeeper	55	"
E	Stafford Charles A	212	retired	76	"
F	Stafford Mary E †	212	housewife	70	"
G	Welch Eleanor K †	212	"	33	"
H	Ruggiero Michael	216	inspector	27	36 Lamson
K	Ruggiero Theresa †	216	housewife	24	178 Webster
L	Dioguardi Alfred	216	U S N	21	here
M	Dioguardi Anna †	216	operator	25	"
N	Dioguardi Alvira †	216	housewife	53	"
O	Dioguardi Gilda †	216	factoryhand	23	"
P	Dioguardi Joseph	216	machinist	27	"
R	Dioguardi Vincenzo	216	shoeworker	57	"
S	*Catrone Jeanette †	218	housekeeper	72	"
T	Russo Margaret †	218	housewife	47	"

30

Webster Street Continued

U	Russo Modestino	218	machinist	53	here
V	Maioli Anthony	218	tailor	48	"
W	Maioli Jeanette †	218	housekeeper	20	"
X	Maioli Susie †	218	housewife	44	"
Z	Campanaro Donato	228	carpenter	47	"
350					
A	Campanaro Fiorentina †	228	dressmaker	42	"
B	Tancredi Anillo	228	student	24	"
C	Tancredi Giovanni	228	salesman	34	"
D*	Tancredi Maria R †	228	housewife	61	"
E	Tancredi Pasquale	228	retired	59	"
F	Marino Anthony	228	rigger	28	"
G	Marino Georgia †	228	housewife	25	"
H	Younie Beatrice †	233	"	41	"
K	Younie Edward	233	machinist	43	"
L	Younie William	233	retired	89	"
M	Murphy Anna A †	233	housekeeper	67	"
O	Leary Daniel	234	salesman	47	"
P	Leary Frances †	234	housewife	43	"
R	McIsaac Grace †	234	nurse	21	"
S	McIsaac John	234	U S A	44	"
T	McIsaac Marsha †	234	nurse	20	"
U	McIsaac Mary †	234	matron	42	"
V	Barry Elizabeth †	235	housewife	30	"
W	Barry Frank	235	machinist	33	"
X	Vargus Edmund	235	fishcutter	30	"
Y	Vargus Rose †	235	housewife	26	"
Z	Domegan James P	235	canner	31	"
351					
A	Domegan Mary C †	235	housewife	28	"
B	Murphy Lucy †	236	"	61	"
C	Dermody Anna †	236	"	39	"
D	Dermody George	236	steamfitter	42	"
E	Donavon Dorothy †	236	candymaker	31	"
F	Donavon Francis	236	longshoreman	45	"
G	Donavon Margaret †	236	operator	28	"
H	Donavon Mary K †	236	housewife	69	"
K	Brogna Achille	237	boilermaker	58	"
L	Brogna Anna †	237	housewife	50	"
M	Brogna Eleanor †	237	stitcher	21	"
N	Carroll Agatha †	237	housewife	25	"

Webster Street   Continued

o	Carroll Robert	237	U S N	25	here
p	Lombardi Ethel †	237	housewife	24	"
R	Lombardi Vincent	237	shipfitter	26	"
s*	Bosco Antonetta †	238	at home	78	"
T	Tarquinii Christina †	238	housewife	42	"
U	Tarquinii Ralph	238	laborer	45	"
V*	Marotta Charles	238	meatcutter	54	"
W*	Marotta Jamma †	238	housewife	43	"
X	Marotta Josephine †	238	dressmaker	23	"
Y	Marotta Mario	238	U S A	23	"
Z	Marotta Mary †	238	seamstress	21	"

352

A	DeLuca John	238	retired	74	"
C	Grana James M	238	repairman	31	"
B	Grana Marion E †	238	housewife	29	"
D	Sweeney Mary E †	239	housekeeper	55	"
E	Winchenbach Gertrude †	239	housewife	35	"
F	Winchenbach Lester F	239	U S A	38	"
G	Blasetti Angelo	239	machinist	35	"
H	Blasetti Yolanda †	239	housewife	30	"
K	McDonald Mary †	239	housekeeper	45	"
L	O'Keefe John	239	U S A	20	"
M	Barker Gilda †	241	housewife	25	245 Webster
N	Barker James	241	longshoreman	34	245 "
O	DiSalvo Anthony	241	painter	36	here
P	DiSalvo Frances †	241	housewife	33	"
R	DiSalvo Joseph	241	retired	72	"
S	DiSalvo Mildred †	241	housewife	67	"
T	DiSalvo Yolanda †	241	stitcher	22	"
U	DiTroia Mario	241	attorney	42	"
V	DiTroia Rose †	241	housewife	39	"
W	LaScalea Amedeo	241	clerk	27	"
X	DeBenidetto Augustino	242	springmaker	37	"
Y	DeBenidetto Mary †	242	housewife	35	"
Z*	Sacco Jerry	242	foundryman	58	"

353

A*	Sacco Josephine †	242	housewife	60	"
B	Sinagra Joseph	242	fireman	34	"
C*	Sinagra Luigi	242	retired	60	"
D	Sinagra Nancy †	242	housewife	33	"

Webster Street Continued

E	Zinna Agrippino	244	laborer	48	2 Power's ct
F	*Zinna Santa †	244	housewife	37	2 "
G	Garofolo Mary †	245	housekeeper	55	here
H	Puccia Natalie †	245	housewife	37	"
K	Puccia Philip	245	candymaker	43	"
L	DeLeonardis Umberto	245	pressman	62	"
M	DeLeonardis Vincenza †	245	housewife	53	"
O	Joy Mary †	246	"	29	"
P	Penney Joseph	246	U S A	21	"
R	Fagone Joseph	246	cutter	55	"
S	Fagone Josephine †	246	forewoman	26	"
U	Fagone Phillip	246	U S M C	22	"
V	Fagone Rose †	246	housewife	54	"
W	Millerick Elizabeth †	247	housekeeper	72	"
X	Millerick Elizabeth †	247	teacher	46	"
Y	Millerick Helen †	247	housewife	33	"
Z	Millerick Thomas J	247	laborer	32	"

354

A	*Jensen Arne	248	rigger	45	"
B	Nelsen Magdalene †	248	housekeeper	54	"
C	DeAngelis Ida †	249	at home	68	"
D	Mastrangelo Frank	249	laborer	47	"
E	Mastrangelo Michelena †	249	housewife	34	"
F	Fagoli Amarosa †	249	"	36	"
G	Fagoli Amerino	249	laborer	39	"
H	Coscia Anthony J	249	shipfitter	22	"
K	Coscia Carolina †	249	housewife	54	"
L	Coscia Michael	249	cobbler	55	"
M	Coscia Vincenza J †	249	secretary	31	"
N	Ranieri Anthony	250	U S A	20	"
O	Ranieri Donato	250	laborer	48	"
P	*Ranieri Elvira †	250	housewife	42	"
R	*Cirone Elisa †	250	"	48	"
S	Cirone Ricardo	250	bricklayer	57	"
T	Cirone Rita †	250	dressmaker	23	"
U	Paulicelli Cosimo	250	chef	28	"
V	Paulicelli Marien †	250	housewife	28	"
W	Stibolt Eugene	251	retired	70	"
X	Stibolt Mina J †	251	housewife	68	"
Y	Gilmore Emaline E †	251	housekeeper	46	"

Webster Street Continued

	z	Johnson Adolph	251	carpenter	32	here
355						
	A	Johnson Florence †	251	housewife	27	"
	B	Sharkey James P	252	clerk	72	"
	c	Sharkey Julia †	252	housekeeper	39	"
	D	Cappelluzzo Ida †	252	housewife	44	"
	E	Cappelluzzo Liberato	252	chauffeur	47	"
	F	Petrucelli Frank	254	machinist	24	"
	G	Petrucelli Jennie †	254	housewife	23	"
	H	Landolfi Dominick	254	tailor	49	"
	K*	Landolfi Virginia †	254	housewife	42	"
	L	Faiello Felix	254	machinist	25	"
	M	Faiello Olga †	254	housewife	20	"
	o*	Tipping Charles	255	longshoreman	56	"
	P	Tipping Helen F †	255	saleswoman	22	"
	R	Tipping Margaret †	255	"	22	"
	s*	Tipping Nettie †	255	housewife	56	"
	U	Ranieri Fredericko	256	blacksmith	53	"
	V	Ranieri Fulvio	256	U S N	21	"
	W*	Ranieri Natalina †	256	housewife	52	"
	X	Ranieri Anthony	256	machinist	24	158 Cottage
	Y	Ranieri Gladys †	256	housewife	23	158 "
	z	Palmeri Edward	256	barber	35	here
356						
	A	Palmeri Josephine †	256	seamstress	33	"
	B	Eskedahl Carl	257	fisherman	60	"
	c	Porzio Alfonso	257	operator	49	"
	D	Porzio Louis	257	U S A	22	"
	E	Porzio Rafaela †	257	housewife	42	"
	F*	Farren Frances †	257	"	41	"
	G	Farren James J	257	boilermaker	46	"
	H	Trapasso Anna †	258	housewife	26	"
	K	Trapasso Frank S	258	fireman	27	"
	L*	Coscia Nunziata †	258	housewife	40	"
	M	Coscia Pasquale	258	shoemaker	53	"
	N	Tringale Clara †	258	housewife	42	"
	o	Tringale Sebastian	258	boatbuilder	49	"
	P	Tringale Theodora †	258	chemist	20	"
	R	Crescenzo Antonetta †	259	operator	24	"
	s	Crescenzo Camino A	259	tailor	67	"
	T	Crescenzo Louis	259	U S A	41	"

Webster Street—Continued

	U	Crescenzo Rosa—†	259	housewife	61	here
	V	Ottosson Carl	259	rigger	45	"
	W	Ottosson Frances—†	259	housewife	37	"
	X	Gleason Elizabeth P—†	259	"	44	"
	Y	Gleason Joseph E	259	molder	46	"
	Z	Andriotti Anna—†	261	housewife	30	"
357						
	A	Andriotti Michael	261	engineer	31	"
	B	DiMaio Concetta—†	261	housekeeper	46	"
	C	DiMaio Eva—†	261	hairdresser	23	"
	D	DiMaio Mary—†	261	operator	24	"
	E	DiMaio William A	261	U S N	26	"
	F	Paolini Salvatore	261	shoemaker	61	"
	G	*Paolini Virginia—†	261	housewife	66	"
	H	Galvin Estelle A—†	263	"	53	"
	K	Galvin William F	263	printer	59	"
	L	Goodwin Carrie—†	263	housekeeper	49	"
	M	Morelli Margaret—†	263	housewife	36	"
	N	Morelli Nicholas	263	shoemaker	39	"
	O	Ferrara Alfred	263	U S A	28	"
	P	Ferrara Joseph	263	machinist	30	"
	R	Ferrara Nancy—†	263	housekeeper	66	"
	S	Laconca John	264	laborer	46	"
	T	Laconca Louise—†	264	housewife	42	"
	U	Laconca Vincent	264	U S A	20	"
	V	Iannarone Grace—†	264	housewife	56	"
	W	Iannarone Lillian—†	264	dressmaker	36	"
	X	Iannarone Olga—†	264	"	33	"
	Y	D'Amico Alphonso	264	laborer	30	167 Cottage
	Z	D'Amico Minnie—†	264	housewife	28	here
358						
	A	Pizzi Daniel	264	shoeworker	32	"
	B	Pizzi Rose—†	264	operator	22	"
	C	*Gallo Elizabeth—†	265	housekeeper	37	"
	D	Gallo Rose—†	265	dressmaker	21	"
	E	Tavella Eleanor—†	265	housewife	28	"
	F	Tavella Philip	265	U S A	30	227 Chelsea
	G	*Marino Louise—†	265	housekeeper	37	here
	H	DeMarco Frank	265	operator	46	"
	K	*DeMarco Jennie—†	265	housewife	46	"
	M	Aliprandi Domenic	269	storekeeper	66	"

Webster Street—Continued

		Full Name	Res.	Occupation	Age	Reported Residence
N	Aliprandi Frances— †	269	housewife	49	here
O	Aliprandi Louise— †	269	pianist	21	"
P	Carney Mary G— †	269	teacher	53	"
R	McNiel Albert	271	painter	34	"
S	McNiel Bridget— †	271	housewife	70	"
T	Kendrick Clifford	271	U S N	42	"
U	Kendrick Ellen— †	271	housewife	42	"
V	Nielson Beatrice— †	271	housekeeper	25	"
X	Sullivan Rose N— †	273	operator	39	"
Y	Sullivan Timothy F	273	retired	73	"
Z	Gallagher Edward	273	"	75	50 Jeffries

359

A	Gallagher Mary E— †	273	operator	34	50 "
B	McLaughlin Elizabeth— †	273	matron	44	here
C	McLaughlin Mary— †	273	clerk	40	"
D	Cashman Charlotte F— †	275	"	44	"
E	Cashman Eleanor— †	275		22	"
F	Cashman Mary P— †	275	typist	20	"
G	Simpson David P	275	longshoreman	65	"
H	Simpson Margaret— †	275	housewife	63	"
K	Stibolt Frank	275	rigger	36	251 Webster
L	Stibolt Mary— †	275	housewife	32	here
M	Maramaldi Federo	275	shipfitter	50	"
N	Maramaldi Raffaela— †	275	clerk	23	"
O	Maramaldi Theresa— †	275	housewife	43	"
P	Donahue Agnes F— †	277	housekeeper	67	"
R	Donahue Arthur J	277	operator	34	"
S	Donahue Margaret M— †	277	housewife	31	"
T	Barry Florence— †	277	clerk	24	"
U	Barry Mary— †	277	housewife	45	"
V	Travaglino Dominic	277	coremaker	56	"
W	Travaglino Dominick	277	U S A	26	"
X	Travaglino Giovana— †	277	housekeeper	78	"
Y	Travaglino Horace	277	U S A	27	"
Z	Travaglino Jane M— †	277	stenographer	22	"

360

A	Travaglino Matilda— †	277	housewife	52	"
B	Milledick Edward C	279	chauffeur	40	"
C	Milledick Inesha— †	279	housewife	34	"
D	Cullen Elizabeth— †	279	"	47	"
E	Cullen James	279	watchman	49	"

Webster Street Continued

	F	*Matera Dominick	279	barber	52	here
	G	*Matera Eugene	279	rubberworker	46	"
	H	*Matera Joseph	279	retired	83	"
	K	Matera Joseph	279	U S N	21	"
	L	*Matera Margaret †	279	housekeeper	42	"
	M	Long Annie T †	281	at home	83	"
	N	Connell James H	281	freighthandler	33	"
	O	Connell Margaret †	281	housekeeper	72	"
	P	Connell Mary L †	281	"	37	"
	R	Flanagan Rose M †	281	housewife	29	"
	S	Flanagan William J	281	shipper	31	"
	T	DeNictolis Anna †	283	housewife	32	"
	U	DeNictolis Vincent	283	clerk	35	"
	V	Moran Charles L	283	"	42	"
	W	Moran Margaret I †	283	housewife	28	"
	X	Voto Lydia †	283	"	29	"
	Y	Voto Salvatore	283	guard	30	"
	Z	DiDonato Lucy †	285	operator	35	"

361

	A	DiDonato Phillip	285	salesman	29	30 Lubec
	B	*Cundari Mary †	285	housekeeper	60	here
	C	Florentine Dorothy †	285	housewife	25	"
	D	Florentine Frank	285	laborer	27	"
	E	McLaughlin Elizabeth T †	285	housekeeper	48	"
	F	Howland Catherine †	291	maid	33	"
	G	Howland James	291	freighthandler	70	"
	H	Howland Margaret †	291	stitcher	35	"
	K	Heil Joseph	291	fireman	42	"
	L	Heil Otto	291	painter	49	"
	M	Heil Rita †	291	housewife	42	"
	N	McDonough Helen †	291	"	27	"
	O	McDonough Thomas	291	bartender	31	"
	P	Wingard Caroline †	293	housewife	60	"
	R	Wingard Olaf	293	stevedore	61	"
	S	Finn Evelyn †	293	housewife	41	"
	T	O'Brien Mary J †	293	"	61	"
	U	O'Brien Patrick J	293	rigger	56	"
	V	Sorensen Lars	295	"	56	"
	W	Sorensen Nancy †	295	housewife	54	"

37

Ward 1–Precinct 4

CITY OF BOSTON

LIST OF RESIDENTS
20 YEARS OF AGE AND OVER

(NON-CITIZENS INDICATED BY ASTERISK)
(FEMALES INDICATED BY DAGGER)

AS OF

JANUARY 1, 1943

JOSEPH F. TIMILTY, *Chairman*
FREDERIC E. DOWLING, *Secretary*
WILLIAM A. MOTLEY, Jr.
FRANCIS B. McKINNEY
EVERETT R. PROUT

Listing Board.

CITY OF BOSTON PRINTING DEPARTMENT

Page.	Letter	FULL NAME.	Residence. Jan. 1, 1943.	Occupation.	Supposed Age.	Reported Residence. Jan. 1, 1942. Street and Number.

400

Bremen Place

	A	Zanfani Domenica —†	4	shoeworker	22	here
	B	*Monterro Joseph	4	baker	68	"
	C	*Vasques Anna —†	4	housewife	43	"
	D	Vasques Sebastiano	4	mason	46	"

Bremen Street

	E	*Luke Frederick B	6	laborer	47	here
	F	*Luke Olive A —†	6	housewife	48	"
	G	Hasson Joseph	8	fireman	49	"
	H	Hasson Mary E —†	8	housewife	60	"
	K	Messina Marie —†	8	"	58	"
	L	Messina Mary T †	8	factoryhand	20	"
	O	Minichiello Angelo	12	retired	77	"
	P	Minichiello Anthony	12	chef	22	"
	R	Russo Adeline —†	12	housewife	35	289 Sumner
	S	Russo Anthony	12	laborer	35	289 "
	T	Minichiello Frank	12	musician	38	here
	U	Minichiello Josephine †	12	housewife	34	"
	V	Ciampa Generoso	14	chauffeur	28	2 Percival pl
	W	Ciampa Rosaria —†	14	housewife	24	2 "
	X	DeSimone Angelina —†	14	"	41	here
	Y	DeSimone Emelio	14	laborer	40	"
	Z	D'Argenio Alfred	16	U S A	25	"

401

	A	D'Argenio Anthony	16	conductor	49	"
	B	Giordano Antonette —†	16½	housewife	20	158 Cottage
	C	Giordano Italo	16½	chauffeur	25	26 Parmenter
	D	Mirata Aggrippino	16½	laborer	37	here
	E	*Mirata Giovannina †	16½	housewife	63	"
	F	D'Argenio Mary †	16½	"	45	158 Cottage
	G	D'Argenio Rose †	16½	factoryhand	23	158 "
	H	Antonelli Frank	16½	tailor	67	here
	K	Vitelli Anthony	18	electrician	26	"
	L	Vitelli Theresa †	18	housewife	23	"
	M	Rizzuti Dorothy †	18	"	35	"
	N	Rizzuti John	18	shipfitter	36	"
	O	Loverro John	18	butcher	52	"
	P	Loverro Mary J —†	18	housewife	43	"
	R	Loverro Tina †	18	dressmaker	21	"

2

Bremen Street—Continued

	s	*Ippolito Maria †	20	housewife	76	here
	t	*Ippolito Thomas	20	retired	75	"
	u	Sacco Concetta †	20	housewife	25	"
	v	Sacco Joseph	20	pipefitter	34	"
	w	Costa Filippo	20	retired	67	"
	x	Costa Nunzia—†	20	housewife	67	"
	y	Mastrogiovanni Josephine—†	22	"	24	21 Maverick sq
	z	Mastrogiovanni Silvio	22	metalworker	25	21 "
402						
	a	DeFranzo Anthony	22	riveter	27	89 Everett
	b	DeFranzo Josephine—†	22	housewife	23	89 "
	c	Azzatto Emma †	22	housekeeper	36	368 Summer
	d	DeFranzo John F	22	U S N	29	here
	e	*DeFranzo Maria C—†	22	housewife	60	"
	f	Grandolfi Giorgio	24	retired	70	93 Orleans
	g	*Grandolfi Jennie—†	24	housewife	66	93 "
	h	*Fradistefano Domenic	24	retired	74	here
	k	Fradistefano Domenic	24	artist	42	"
	l	Fradistefano Henry	24	U S N	27	"
	m	Giglio John	24	U S A	22	"
	n	*Giglio Josephine —†	24	housewife	51	"
	o	*Giglio Mario	24	laborer	52	"
	p	Daveau David	26	retired	80	"
	r	Daveau Millie —†	26	housewife	74	"
	s	Acquaviva Caroline—†	26	"	48	180 Maverick
	t	Acquaviva Rose —†	26	diamond cutter	20	180 "
	u	*Cianci Annie—†	26	housewife	52	here
	v	*Cianci James	26	laborer	59	"
	x	*Amare Theresa †	28	housewife	70	"
	y	*Franco Angelina —†	28	housekeeper	40	"
403						
	a	Ciampa Fioravante	28	mechanic	39	"
	b	Ciampa Mary—†	28	housewife	28	"
	c	Masalli Domenic	30	retired	68	11 Emmons
	d	Spano Anna—†	30	housewife	33	401 Meridian
	e	Spano Patrick	30	laborer	51	401 "
	f	Malcaso Philomena —†	30	packer	22	here
	g	Malcaso Rose—†	30	operator	25	"
	h	Surette Arthur	32	riveter	21	36 Lamson
	k	Surette Theresa —†	32	housewife	21	here
	l	Cataruzolo Antonio	32	electrician	27	"

Page.	Letter	FULL NAME.	Residence, Jan. 1, 1943.	Occupation.	Supposed Age.	Reported Residence, Jan. 1, 1942. Street and Number.

Bremen Street — Continued

	M	Cataruzolo Mildred †	32	housewife	25	here
	N*	Gentile Maria †	32	"	58	"
	O	Murphy Francis J	34	laborer	59	"
	P	Murphy Helen E †	34	housewife	56	"
	R	Pizzano Julia †	34	"	48	"
	S	Coleman Patrick	34	teamster	70	"
	T	Gutchi John	36	laborer	61	"
	U	Antillio Frederico	36	shoeworker	61	"
	V	Antillio Ralph	36	painter	25	"
	W*	Profecto Amilio	36	tailor	63	"
	X*	Tedesco Angelo	38	laborer	59	"
	Y*	Tedesco Nellie A †	38	housewife	59	"
	Z*	Anello Ezio	38	fireman	32	"

404

	A*	Anello Giuseppe	38	retired	70	"
	B*	Anello Mary †	38	housewife	56	"
	C	Montana Rose †	38	"	61	125 St Andrew rd

Decatur Street

	D	Latorella Annie †	35	housewife	69	48 Maverick
	E	Latorella Camilla	35	retired	74	48 "
	F*	DiDio Angelo	37	"	75	here
	G*	DiDio Josephine †	37	housewife	64	"
	H	Giordano Catherine †	37	"	23	"
	K	Giordano Domenic	37	stripper	24	31 Billerica
	M	Gallo Daniel	37	U S A	21	Chelsea
	N	Cammarata Charles	37	shipper	26	here
	O	Cammarata Sarah †	37	housewife	23	"
	P	Guerra Joseph	37	welder	33	315 Saratoga
	R	Guerra Teresa †	37	housewife	26	315 "
	T	Paci Domenic	39	laborer	49	here
	U	Paci Mary †	39	housewife	36	"
	V	Vitale James	39	machinist	34	"
	W*	Vitale Sarah †	39	housewife	34	"
	X*	Cammarata Catherine †	39	"	46	"
	Y	Cammarata Catherine †	39	cutler	22	"

405

| | A* | Italiano Benedetto | 41 | plumber | 57 | " |
| | B* | Italiano Maria † | 41 | housewife | 57 | " |

Decatur Street Continued

c	Ferranti Angelina—†	41	stitcher	22	here
d	Ferranti Anthony	41	U S A	20	"
e	Ferranti Joseph	41	barber	48	"
f	Ferranti Mary—†	41	housewife	30	"
g	Italiano Peter	41	U S A	25	"
l	DeMarco Mary—†	43	stitcher	21	"
m	*DeMarco Salvatore	43	retired	69	"
n	Cardosi Edith—†	43	housewife	50	"
o	Cardosi Joseph	43	buyer	51	"
r	Kelley Maria L—†	45	housewife	26	133 Orleans
s	*Kelley Richard	45	inspector	22	133 "
t	Gutro Elizabeth—†	45	at home	55	here
u	Gutro Rita—†	45	factoryhand	20	"

Grady Court

w	Levasseur Lillian—†	2	housewife	22	New York
x	Levasseur Norman	2	rigger	26	"
y	Storey Lena—†	2	housewife	32	408 Benningt'n
z	Storey Walter	2	steelworker	37	408 "
	406				
a	Gagnon Charles E	2	U S N	25	Salem
b	Gagnon Edith J—†	2	housewife	22	"
c	Trainor Bertha—†	2	"	29	Whitman
d	Trainor Percy B	2	instructor	45	"
h	Adamo Olga—†	2	housewife	29	Florida
k	Adamo Sebastian	2	welder	30	"
l	Russell Hardy	2	mechanic	49	Reading
m	Russell Lena—†	2	housewife	43	"
n	Blair Charles H	2	U S N	20	Michigan
o	Blair Dorothy—†	2	housewife	24	Lynn
r	Hoyle Claire R	2	U S M C	27	California
s	Hoyle Ruth S—†	2	housewife	22	Natick
t	Grainger Everett	2	machinist	30	Fitchburg
u	Grainger Helen M—†	2	housewife	30	"
v	Motley Helen F—†	2	housekeeper	65	Brookline
w	Young Mabel—†	18	housewife	29	Brockton
x	Young Malcolm	18	pipefitter	31	"
y	Gravelese Carmella—†	18	housewife	34	221 Leyden
z	Gravelese John	18	machinist	35	221 "

407

Grady Court—Continued

A	Reidy Margaret—†	18	housewife	36	346 Chelsea
B	Reidy Patrick J	18	porter	40	346 "
C	Pascole Helena—†	18	housewife	25	Methuen
D	Pascole William	18	mechanic	30	"
E	Guebin Clara—†	18	housewife	42	N Hampshire
F	Guebin Ernest	18	pipefitter	41	"
G	Bernier Joseph R	18	U S N	30	Bedford
H	Bernier Mary L—†	18	housewife	30	"
K	Horn Arthur	18	longshoreman	38	17 Havre
L	Horn Isabel—†	18	housewife	37	17 "
N	Moores Anne—†	18	"	33	522 Sumner
O	Moores John C	18	machinist	43	522 "
P	Land Catherine—†	18	housewife	35	N Carolina
R	Land John G	18	U S M C	35	"
S	French Bessie—†	18	housewife	49	Methuen
T	French Raymond C	18	machinist	51	"
U	Libby Gertrude—†	18	housewife	32	Connecticut
V	Libby Luther	18	U S N	32	"
W	Williamson Marietta—†	26	housewife	20	Mississippi
X	Williamson Theodore	26	carpenter	24	"
Z	Frye James E	26	U S C G	34	152 Lexington

408

A	Frye Winifred—†	26	housewife	33	152 "
B	Brogie Elizabeth—†	26	at home	65	167 King
C	Rounds Harriet—†	26	waitress	38	167 "
D	Dickson James D	26	U S M C	49	Sheffield
E	Dickson Lois H—†	26	housewife	35	"
G	Cohen Ann—†	26	"	26	1420 Blue Hill av
H	Cohen Charles	26	mechanic	31	1420 "
K	Simard Alfred A	26	shipfitter	29	Salem
L	Simard Helen M—†	26	housewife	25	"
M	Kennedy Catherine—†	26	"	31	Gloucester
N	Kennedy Charles	26	U S N	42	"
O	Guevin Antoine E	26	electrician	44	366 Meridian
P	Guevin Claire F—†	26	stenographer	21	N Hampshire
R	Guevin Edesse D—†	26	housewife	39	"
S	*Lavigne Nathalie M—†	26	at home	64	"
T	Lynch Betty E—†	26	housewife	30	Virginia
U	Lynch Francis K	26	U S N	31	"

Havre Street

w	Carlson Hjalmar	3	oiler	50	here
x	Bergin Daniel J	3	salesman	74	"
y	Hill Edna — †	3	housewife	28	"
z	SanFillippo Charles	3	machinist	32	"

409

A	DeZenzo Arthur	5	carpenter	30	"
B	DeZenzo Mary — †	5	housewife	25	"
c	Coutinho Emelia — †	5	"	60	"
D	Coutinho Manuel	5	seaman	59	"
E	Silva Alice — †	5	housewife	43	"
F	Silva Anselmo	5	engineer	41	"
G	Piazza Louis	7	tailor	29	"
H	Piazza Mary — †	7	housewife	23	"
K	*Celeste Fillippo	7	factoryhand	57	"
L	*Celeste Josephine — †	7	housewife	47	"
N	McArdle Albert A	9	policeman	46	"
o	McArdle Margaret A — †	9	housewife	43	"
P	Vecchione Vincent	9	machinist	21	96 Lexington
R	McArdle Monica — †	9	factoryhand	21	here
s	Reno Catherine — †	9	housewife	21	"
T	DeCola Joseph	10	rigger	31	Oxford
U	DeCola Mary — †	10	housewife	30	"
V	Landrey Edgar	10	pipefitter	40	105 Falcon
W	Landrey Mary — †	10	housewife	30	105 "
X	Keith Donald	10	machinist	32	74 London
Y	Keith Kathleen — †	10	housewife	28	74 "
z	Maloney Louise — †	10	"	21	103 Meridian

410

A	Maloney Roland	10	machinist	22	103 "
B	Bozzi John A	10	pipefitter	34	255 Paris
c	Bozzi Rose M — †	10	housewife	31	255 "
D	Hennington Hazel — †	10	"	29	291 Chelsea
E	Hennington Richard J	10	U S N	32	291 "
G	Burttinwood Marcelle — †	10	housewife	23	Methuen
H	Burttinwood Raymond	10	clerk	28	"
K	Collaruso Antonina †	10	housewife	27	2 Jeffries
L	Collaruso Fioranto	10	chauffeur	32	2 "
M	Bowers Aubrey	10	U S N	31	N Carolina
N	Bowers Lavender — †	10	housewife	26	"
R	Murray Annie E — †	11	"	69	here

7

Page.	Letter.	FULL NAME.	Residence, Jan. 1, 1943	Occupation.	Supposed Age.	Reported Residence, Jan. 1, 1942. Street and Number.

Havre Street—Continued

	s	Murray John J	11	fisherman	36	here
	T	Villa Joseph	11	machinist	29	"
	U	Villa Julia —†	11	housewife	27	"
	V	Villa Jesus	11	seaman	57	"
	w	*Villa Mary—†	11	housewife	57	"
	X	Limbo Adeline —†	13	"	34	"
	Y	Limbo Genaro	13	ironworker	33	"
	Z	Sforza John	13	retired	70	"
411						
	A	Limbo Anthony	13	brazier	24	"
	B	Limbo Carmella—†	13	dressmaker	28	"
	c	*Limbo Catherine —†	13	housewife	64	"
	D	*Limbo Filomena—†	13	"	63	"
	E	*Limbo Michael	13	dairyman	63	"
	F	Limbo Nancy—†	13	stitcher	26	"
	G	Limbo Peter	13	factoryhand	64	"
	H	Rotundo Blanche—†	15	housewife	53	"
	K	Limbo Carmine	15	retired	51	"
	L	*Limbo Rose —†	15	housewife	80	"
	M	Cavallaro Alexander	15	electrician	26	"
	N	Cavallaro Angelina —†	15	housewife	24	"
	O	Carnevale Concetta †	15	"	21	273 Sumner
	P	Carnevale Frank	15	factoryhand	23	here
	R	Carnevale Joseph	15	laborer	45	"
	s	Carnevale Madeline —†	15	housewife	36	"
	U	*Mauriello Angela †	17	"	54	"
	V	Mauriello Connie †	17	stitcher	26	"
	W	Mauriello Joseph	17	retired	53	"
	X	Mauriello Louis	17	U S N	22	"
	Y	Mauriello Mildred †	17	bookkeeper	20	"
	Z	Mauriello Pasquale	17	U S A	24	"
412						
	A	Tamburro Anthony G	17	tailor	42	16 Paris
	B	*Tamburro Julia †	17	housewife	67	here
	c	Iacono Francis M	17	operator	26	"
	D	*Iacono Josephine †	17	housewife	61	"
	E	Iacono Pia E †	17	clerk	28	"
	F	Leader Estelle †	18	waitress	37	Chelsea
	G	Pardy Claire †	18	housewife	30	4789 Wash'n
	H	Pardy John E	18	machinist	33	4789 "
	K	Brooks Gertrude †	18	housewife	42	Pennsylvania

8

Havre Street — Continued

L	Brooks Joseph H	18	mechanic	42	Pennsylvania
M	Brooks Lorraine — †	18	operator	21	"
N	DiCarlo Mary — †	18	housewife	30	Somerville
O	DiCarlo Thomas	18	attendant	33	"
R	Nazzaro Carl	18	barber	33	127 Cottage
S	Nazzaro Grace — †	18	housewife	33	127 "
T	Hollcomb Dorothy — †	18	"	33	Maine
U	Hollcomb Mark C	18	U S N	43	"
V	Amerault Frances — †	18	housewife	42	Haverhill
W	Amerault Peter H	18	carpenter	43	"
X	Renaud Alice — †	18	housewife	28	Rhode Island
Y	Renaud Arthur	18	U S N	35	"
Z	Collins Phyllis — †	18	housewife	34	Georgia
	413				
A	Collins Russell	18	U S A	40	"
B	DeMarzo Anita — †	18	housewife	33	492 Commerc'l
C	DeMarzo Salvatore	18	laborer	35	492 "
E	Moscillo Frank	19	electrician	23	here
F	Moscillo Lillian — †	19	shoeworker	23	"
G	Belmonte Angelina — †	19	housewife	33	"
H	Belmonte John	19	pressman	37	"
K	Amato Emilio	19	laborer	44	"
L	*Paterno Angelina — †	19	housewife	46	"
N	Coyle Marjory — †	21	stitcher	50	"
O	Angel Catherine — †	21	housewife	75	"
P	Cordeau Catherine — †	21	"	58	"
R	Cordeau Walter	21	laborer	59	"
S	Anderson Anton	23	rigger	67	"
T	*Anderson Olga — †	23	housewife	56	"
U	Anderson Edith — †	23	teacher	28	"
V	*Ward William	23	longshoreman	71	"
W	Paolillo Carmen	27	laborer	55	"
X	Paolillo Jennie — †	27	housewife	44	"
Y	Paolillo Jennie — †	27	stitcher	21	"
Z	Benevento Anna — †	27	"	23	"
	414				
A	*Benevento Antonina — †	27	housewife	48	"
B	Benevento Antonio	27	U S N	21	"
C	*Benevento Nunzio	27	fisherman	58	"
D	Cicchetti August	27	factoryhand	41	"
E	Cicchetti Edith — †	27	housewife	31	Revere

9

Page.	Letter	FULL NAME.	Residence, Jan. 1, 1943.	Occupation.	Supposed Age.	Reported Residence, Jan. 1, 1942. Street and Number.

Havre Street — Continued

	F	Romano Anthony	29	chauffeur	35	here
	G	Romano Mary — †	29	housewife	32	"
	H	Galente Gaetano	29	carpenter	45	"
	K	Galente Gregorio	29	machinist	21	"
	L	Galente Josephine — †	29	housewife	44	"
	M	Brogna Albert	31	driller	30	"
	N	Brogna Angela — †	31	housewife	27	"
	O	Spattarro Filomena — †	31	"	29	"
	P	Spattarro Salvatore	31	foreman	29	"
	R	Giangregorio Antonia — †	31	housewife	61	"
	S	Giangregorio Antonio	31	retired	81	"
	T	Giangregorio Enrico	31	U S A	22	"
	U	Giangregorio Louis	31	shipfitter	39	"
	V	Meola Antonio	33	driller	28	"
	W	Meola Fannie — †	33	housewife	28	"
	X	Meola John	33	blacksmith	70	"
	Y	Meola Lucia — †	33	housewife	61	"
	Z	*Marks Beatrice — †	33	"	50	31 Chelsea

415

	A	*Marks John	33	chef	52	31 "
	B	Meola Americo	33	U S A	20	here
	C	Meola Carlo	33	"	22	"
	D	Moliga Antonio	33	retired	71	"
	E	Muro Beatrice †	34	at home	50	22 Bremen
	F	Doran Mary J †	34	"	44	4 Haviland
	H	Killjack Aftin †	34	housewife	20	Cambridge
	K	Killjack Val	34	U S C G	22	"
	L	Pothier Ann †	34	housewife	39	22 Trenton
	M	Pothier Laurine A	34	seaman	42	22 "
	O	Heatley Albert F	34	guard	52	118 High
	P	Heatley Eva M †	34	housewife	50	118 "
	V	Jenkins Ethel †	34	"	29	Quincy
	W	Jenkins William G	34	U S C G	26	"
	X	Ardagna Baldasari	35	laborer	43	here
	Y	*Ardagna Gandolfa †	35	housewife	38	"
	Z	Ferrario Aldo	35	guard	29	"

416

	A	Ferrario Rose †	35	housewife	26	"
	B	*Fresco Grace †	35	"	61	"
	C	Fresco Pasquale	35	U S N	28	"
	D	Cincotti Jennie †	37	housewife	31	"

10

Havre Street — Continued

E	Cincotti Phillip	37	U S A	37	Belmont
F	DiNatale Joseph	37	"	23	here
G	*DiNatale Josephine—†	37	housewife	62	"
H	*DiNatale Vincenzo	37	barber	66	"
K	Carvotta Joseph	37	laborer	48	"
L	Carvotta Rose—†	37	housewife	32	"
M	Moscillo Mary—†	51	"	55	"
N	Pasqualino Angelina—†	51		24	31 Spring
O	Pasqualino Salvatore	51	presser	22	137 Havre
P	Powers James	51	laborer	58	here
R	Powers James, jr	51	shipfitter	26	"
S	Powers Loretta—†	51	millhand	31	"
T	Powers William	51	laborer	33	"
U	*Mazzola Sebastiana—†	53	at home	70	"
V	*DellaPola Joseph	53	rigger	54	"
W	Gaeta Anthony M	53	carpenter	58	"
X	Gaeta Lucy—†	53	housewife	49	"
Y	DiMartino Giovanna—†	53	at home	74	"
Z	DiMartino Margaret—†	53	factoryhand	32	"
	417				
A	Marino Margaret—†	55	housewife	28	22 Princeton
B	Marino Peter	55	laborer	32	22 "
C	*Colatrella Anna—†	55	housewife	54	93 London
D	Colatrella John	55	U S N	21	here
E	*Croce Domenic	55	storekeeper	52	"
F	DeSimone Alfred	55	painter	24	93 London
G	DeSimone Rose—†	55	at home	25	93 "
H	Barry Rita—†	56	teacher	25	Salem
K	Bergazzi Mary—†	56	"	29	Lawrence
L	Carson Anna—†	56	housekeeper	58	here
M	Crowley Mary—†	56	teacher	42	"
N	*Curtin Catherine—†	56	housekeeper	73	"
O	Dailey Mary—†	56	teacher	27	"
P	Devine Helen—†	56	"	50	2214 Dor av
R	Devlin Margaret—†	56	"	59	here
S	Donovan Mary—†	56	"	33	"
T	Ferren Mary—†	56	"	22	"
U	Haban Mary—†	56	"	25	207 E
V	Heukamp Edith—†	56	"	42	here
W	Kennedy Marion—†	56	"	32	"
X	Lamond Teresa—†	56	"	30	207 E

11

Havre Street—Continued

	Y	Lynch Margaret—†	56	teacher	47	Waltham
	z	Moriarty Anna—†	56	"	33	here
418						
	A	*Morrissey Mary—†	56	housekeeper	63	"
	B	*Myrick Rita—†	56	teacher	23	Salem
	c	O'Brien Teresa—†	56	"	35	here
	D	Quinn Helen—†	56	"	33	"
	E	Reid Esther—†	56	"	47	"
	F	Scannell Alice—†	56	"	30	Lawrence
	G	Scollard Mary—†	56	"	43	here
	H	Sexton Helen—†	56	"	22	"
	K	Shea Geraldine—†	56	"	36	"
	L	Timmy Mary—†	56	"	48	"
	M	Welch Mary—†	56	"	52	"
	N	DeSpirito Edward	57	U S A	26	"
	O	DeSpirito Mary—†	57	housewife	45	"
	P	Powers Grace—†	57	clerk	36	"
	R	Powers John	57	policeman	51	"
	S	Powers Patrick	57	guard	55	"
	T	Reichart Anna—†	57	at home	46	"
	U	*O'Brien Cyril	57	laborer	32	"
	V	*O'Brien Frances—†	57	cutter	22	"
	W	*O'Brien Katherine—†	57	housewife	53	"
	X	*O'Brien Marguerite—†	57	cutter	20	"
	Y	*O'Brien Mary—†	57	"	26	"
	Z	*O'Brien Patrick	57	laborer	55	"
419						
	A	*Iacomino Antonetta—†	59	housewife	35	143 Webster
	B	*Iacomino John	59	painter	45	143 "
	c	DiNubla Mary—†	61	housewife	49	here
	D	DiNubla Rocco	61	mixer	54	"
	E	DiGregorio Andrew A	61	U S A	32	"
	F	DiGregorio Michael A	61	"	34	"
	G	DiGregorio Paul	61	laborer	60	"
	H	DiGregorio Pauline—†	61	at home	30	"
	K	DiGregorio Salvatore E	61	U S A	21	"
	L	Rapa Joseph	63	shoeworker	61	"
	M	*Murphy Anna—†	63	laundryman	54	"
	N	Murphy Bridget—†	63	checker	60	"
	O	Murphy Elizabeth—†	63	clerk	68	"
	P	*Fidalgo John	76	baker	37	102 Orleans

12

Havre Street—Continued

		FULL NAME.	Residence, Jan. 1, 1943.	Occupation.	Supposed Age.	Reported Residence, Jan. 1, 1942. Street and Number.
R	*Fidalgo Regina—†	76	housewife	29	102 Orleans
S	Luiso Angelina—†	76	"	50	here
T	Luiso Angelo	76	laborer	60	"
U	*Cardinale Anna—†	76	housewife	42	"
V	Cardinale Frank	76	fisherman	52	"
W	Cardinale Louis	76	"	20	"
X	Volta Joseph	78	repairman	35	"
Y	Volta Rose—†	78	housewife	32	"
Z	Meola Carmen	78	painter	32	"
	420				
A	Meola Marion—†	78	housewife	32	"
B	Volta Anna—†	78	clerk	27	"
C	Volta Elizabeth—†	78	seamstress	22	"
D	Volta Mary—†	78	leatherworker	24	"
E	Volta Minnie—†	78	at home	37	"
F	Lesser Dorothy—†	80	housewife	35	"
G	Lesser Louis	80	storekeeper	33	"
H	Casoletto Frank	80	plumber	37	"
K	Casoletto Lena—†	80	housewife	33	"
L	Buontempo Michael	80	carpenter	46	"
M	Buontempo Rose—†	80	housewife	42	"
N	Iacobucci Angelina—†	82	at home	46	"
O	Iacobucci Leo	82	painter	25	"
P	*DePaolo Frances—†	82	at home	58	"
R	DePaolo John	82	painter	20	"
S	DePaolo Louise—†	82	housewife	22	"
T	Ardagna Bert	82	painter	45	"
U	Ardagna Carmella—†	82	housewife	29	"
V	Spinetti Lucy—†	84	"	28	"
W	Spinetti Rudolph	84	diver	28	"
X	Terilli Albert	84	U S A	23	"
Y	Terilli Angelina—†	84	inspector	22	"
Z	Terilli Mary—†	84	housekeeper	20	"
	421				
A	Terilli Raymond	84	mover	57	"
B	*Farro Lena—†	84	housewife	31	105 Addison
C	*Farro Michael	84	operator	37	105 "
D	DelBianco Alphonso	86	retired	73	106 Orleans
E	*DelBianco Rosa—†	86	housewife	72	106 "
F	Rotundo Orazio	86	baker	44	here
G	*Rotundo Rose—†	86	housewife	43	"

13

Havre Street—Continued

H	Santarpio Arnold	86	salesman	30	here
K	Santarpio Theresa—†	86	housewife	28	"
L	Faretra Antonio	88	laborer	21	"
M	Faretra Caroline—†	88	dressmaker	27	"
N	Faretra Charles	88	laborer	24	"
O	Faretra Ida—†	88	housewife	24	"
P	Faretra Mary—†	88	"	54	"
R	Faretra Pasquale	88	carpenter	69	"
S	Faretra Pasquale	88	U S A	20	"
T	DiDonato Joseph	88	welder	44	"
U	Caso Elena—†	88	housewife	22	177 Cottage
V	Caso Thomas J	88	welder	24	177 "
W	Semino Carmella—†	90	housewife	30	here
X	LaMonica Joseph	90	student	20	"
Y	LaMonica Michelina—†	90	operator	25	"
Z	LaMonica Philip	90	retired	76	"
	422				
A*	LaMonica Rosa—†	90	housewife	76	"
B	LaMonica Carmella—†	90	operator	21	"
C	LaMonica Gaetano	90	retired	69	"
D	LaMonica James	90	laborer	23	"
E	LaMonica John	90	machinist	24	"
F*	LaMonica Josephine—†	90	housewife	52	"
G	LaMonica Rosario	90	laborer	22	"

Henry Street

R*	Anderson Olaf	11	cook	57	New York
S	Arvidson John H	11	superintendent	35	Maine
T*	Clausen Carl A	11	machinist	30	here
U	Coboy John	11	seaman	30	Illinois
V	Falstad Alfred	11	"	42	"
W	Fletcher Elliott	11	"	42	Michigan
X	Fradua Christopher	11	engineer	52	52 White
Y	Golen Alfred	11	seaman	28	New Bedford
Z	Hamot Eugene	11	"	30	"
	423				
A*	Henrickson Henry	11	"	28	Norway
B	Hjerpe Adele E—†	11	teacher	24	here
C	Hjerpe Theodore A	11	clergyman	56	"
D	Johnson Eric	11	seaman	45	Illinois

11

Page.	Letter.	FULL NAME.	Residence, Jan. 1, 1943.	Occupation.	Supposed Age.	Reported Residence, Jan. 1, 1942. Street and Number.

Henry Street—Continued

	E	Johnston Charles H	11	seaman	30	Illinois
	F	Kass John	11	"	51	"
	G	Kitchell George W	11	retired	90	here
	H	Lamrock Harold	11	seaman	45	Michigan
	K	Larson Oscar E	11	machinist	55	here
	L	Leslie Joseph A	11	seaman	48	Illinois
	M	Manski Clifford	11	"	33	"
	N	Matuniewicy Clement E	11	"	28	Wisconsin
	O	McNamara John	11	"	42	Illinois
	P	Olafson Hjalmar	11	"	38	"
	R	Peterson John M	11	U S C G	27	Rhode Island
	S	Piazik John P	11	seaman	32	here
	T	Post Edgar M	11	U S C G	25	Maine
	U	Rogers Benjamin B	11	seaman	38	Illinois
	V	Romano Charles J	11	laborer	30	Somerville
	W	Russell Abraham L	11	retired	67	195 Sumner
	X	*Simonsen Harold	11	seaman	32	here
	Y	Swanson Martin S	11	"	50	Illinois
	Z	Greco Isabella—†	12	housewife	33	10 Henry

424

	A	Greco Pasquale	12	bricklayer	37	10 "
	B	Sinatra Concetta—†	12	housewife	45	10 "
	C	Sinatra Paul	12	painter	46	10 "
	D	*Viola Antonio	12	weaver	43	here
	E	Viola Costanza—†	12	housewife	48	"
	F	Viola Joseph	12	laborer	27	"
	G	*Carabello Agrippino	12	retired	62	10 Henry
	H	Carabello Concetta—†	12	factoryhand	25	10 "
	K	*Carabello Louise—†	12	housewife	55	10 "
	L	Carabello Nancy—†	12	factoryhand	29	10 "
	M	Carabello Angelo	12	machinist	23	10 "
	N	*Ingravardo Anna—†	12	housewife	69	here
	O	Mariello Eleanor—†	12	"	26	"
	P	Rinaldi Sylvesta	12	laborer	45	"
	R	DeFillippo Elvira—†	16	factoryhand	22	"
	S	*DeFillippo Luigi	16	tinsmith	52	"
	T	*DeFillippo Rosina—†	16	housewife	48	"
	U	DeFillippo Theresa—†	16	stitcher	27	"
	V	Petitto Joseph	16	factoryhand	38	"
	W	Petitto Mary—†	16	housewife	35	"
	X	Bradley Annette—†	16	"	28	"

15

Page.	Letter.	FULL NAME.	Residence Jan. 1, 1943.	Occupation.	Supposed Age.	Reported Residence, Jan. 1, 1942. Street and Number.

Henry Street Continued

	Y	Bradley Walter	16	shipworker	28	here
	Z	Capizzi Isabelle †	16	stitcher	32	"
425						
	A*	Capizzi Josephine †	16	housewife	73	"

Lewis Street

	B	Juliano John	3	rigger	44	here
	C	Juliano Philomena †	3	housewife	42	"
	D	Juliano Rosario	3	U S N	21	"
	E	Carmer Jacob	3	retired	72	"
	F*	Lynch Frederick	3	"	77	"
	G	Lynch Frederick F	3	U S C G	32	"
	H	Lynch Ida M †	3	bookkeeper	37	"
	K	Lynch John P	3	U S C G	20	"
	L*	Lynch Margaret †	3	housewife	63	"
	M	Furlong William	7	retired	60	"
	N	Kelly John	7	"	60	"
	O*	Kramp Jacob	7	"	68	"
	P	LaGrosso Antonio	7	laborer	60	"
	R	Murphy Joseph	7	chauffeur	58	"
	S	Pallusso Enrice	7	pedler	49	"

426   London Street

	B	Bayers Sydney H	65	clergyman	35	here
	C	Kaveny Catherine †	65	cook	48	Haverhill
	D	McMahon John J	65	clergyman	57	here
	E	Seckel Theodore	65	"	37	"
	F	Keith Lulu †	75	housewife	37	"
	G	Keith Ralph	75	attendant	35	"
	K	Zagarella Frances †	75	packer	26	"
	L	Zagarella Josephine †	75	operator	22	"
	M*	Zagarella Mary †	75	at home	65	"
	N*	Zagarella Peter	75	retired	67	"
	O	Carvotta Andrew	77	roofer	40	"
	P*	Carvotta Josephine †	77	at home	75	"
	R	Callari Louise †	77	weaver	30	2 Lexington av
	S	Caraganis Anna †	77	stringer	39	here
	T	Caraganis Demetris	77	fireman	49	"
	U	Micciche Frank	77	U S A	24	"

London Street Continued

	v*	Micciche Joseph	77	laundryman	63	here
	w*	Micciche Stella—†	77	housewife	61	"
	x	Micciche Stella T †	77	packer	34	"
	y	Micciche Vincenzo	77	U S A	20	"
427						
	a	Gibbons Helen L †	79	at home	31	"
	b	Gibbons William	79	retired	63	"
	c	Gibbons William H	79	pipefitter	38	"
	d	Bevilacqua Giuseppe	81	laborer	46	"
	e*	Bevilacqua Vincenza †	81	housewife	41	"
	f	DiSalv Dieg	81	machinist	25	"
	g	DiSalv Mary †	81	housewife	24	"
	h	Tortorice Angelo	81	cobbler	59	"
	k	Tortorice Josephine—†	81	stitcher	20	"
	l	Tortorice Rosalia—†	81	housewife	48	"
	m*	Stocco Concetta—†	83	at home	71	"
	n	Stocco Frank	83	assembler	42	"
	o*	Sclafani Emanuela—†	83	at home	38	"
	p	Trippi Giacomo	83	candyworker	42	"
	r*	Trippi Vincenza †	83	housewife	38	"
	s*	Costa Maria V †	85	"	59	"
	t*	Costa Salvatore	85	retired	62	"
	u	Lanovara Rose—†	85	housewife	27	"
	v	Lanovara Stephen	85	chipper	28	"
	w	DiPerri John	85	brazier	29	"
	x	DiPerri Lucy †	85	housewife	26	"
	y*	Salerno Carmela—†	87	"	55	"
	z*	Salerno Michael	87	retired	70	"
428						
	a	DiBenedictis Edward	87	operator	29	"
	b	DiBenedictis Maria—†	87	housewife	34	"
	c	Salerno Elizabeth—†	87	"	30	"
	d	Salerno Joseph	87	draftsman	32	"
	e	Colacchio Anthony	89	welder	39	"
	f	Colacchio Josephine †	89	housewife	33	"
	g*	Ferrara Francesca—†	89	at home	53	"
	h	Ferrara Joseph	89	U S A	26	"
	k	Ferrara Josephine †	89	stitcher	20	"
	l	Walsh John J	89	toolmaker	27	"
	m	Walsh Leonilda †	89	housewife	27	"
	n*	Scifano Anthony	91	retired	63	"

1—4

London Street— Continued

o	Scifano Josephine—†	91	tailor	22	here
p	*Scifano Maria—†	91	housewife	56	"
r	Amico Catherine—†	91	stitcher	33	"
s	*Amico Grace—†	91	at home	55	"
t	Amico Peter	91	U S A	28	"
u	Joy Austin J	91	U S N	26	180 Paris
v	Joy Filomena †	91	housewife	27	180 "
x	Cavalieri Vita †	93	"	21	244 Havre
y	Caporelli John	93	U S A	20	here
z	Caporelli Joseph	93	laborer	42	"

429

a	Caporelli Julia †	93	housewife	36	"
b	LoPilato Joseph	93	rubberworker	30	"
c	LoPilato Vittoria †	93	housewife	27	"
d	*Pasqualetto Caterina †	95	"	44	"
e	Pasqualetto Gaspare	95	pressman	53	"
f	Pasqualetto Josephine—†	95	dressmaker	20	"
g	Martello Rose †	95	at home	22	"
h	Martello Vincenzo	95	buffer	60	"

Maverick Square

t	Rago Charles	3	pressman	32	here
u	Rago Josephine †	3	housewife	28	"
x	Campbell Daniel J	3	operator	52	"
o	Campbell Elizabeth E †	3	housewife	67	"
p	Frazier Thomas A	3	retired	70	"
r	Ippolito Frederick	3	"	61	8 Winthrop
s	McArthur Angus	3	machinist	70	here
t	Wise John P	3	retired	70	"
y	Thompson George	7	guard	47	94 Everett
z	Thompson Josephine †	7	housewife	42	94 "

430

a	Sullivan John	7	laborer	60	62 Bremen
b	Sullivan Mary F †	7	housewife	55	62 "
f	Barry Bridget †	11	"	52	190 Summer
g	Barry John J	11	longshoreman	62	190 "
h	Barry Raymond J	11	U S A	23	190 "
k	Morgan Dennis	11	retired	69	here
l	White Emma †	11	housewife	71	"
m	White Ernest	11	laborer	29	"

18

Page.	Letter.	Full Name.	Residence, Jan. 1, 1943	Occupation.	Supposed Age.	Reported Residence, Jan. 1, 1942. Street and Number.

Maverick Square Continued

R	Rosario Francis	15	clerk	21	here
S	Selos Margaret †	15	housewife	42	"
T	Bellevue Anna J †	15	at home	75	"
U	Bellevue Mary F †	15	housewife	70	"
Z	DelloRusso Fred	21	florist	32	32 Bremen
431
A	DelloRusso Genevieve †	21	housewife	31	32 "
B	*Francis Joseph	21	longshoreman	46	here
C	*Francis Rose †	21	housewife	38	"
D	*Restina Concetta †	21	"	58	"
E	Restina Jennie †	21	clerk	21	"
F	Restina Joseph	21	laborer	58	"
G	DelloRusso Joseph	21	florist	33	"
H	DelloRusso Mary †	21	housewife	32	"
M	Carrozza Americo	27	U S A	30	"
N	Carrozza David	27	bricklayer	64	"
O	Carrozza Francis	27	housewife	56	"
P	Carrozza John	27	dairyman	35	"
R	Carrozza Leo	27	U S A	26	"
S	Carrozza Lisantrina †	27	factoryhand	32	"
T	Carrozza Mildred †	27	"	22	"
U	Carrozza Ralph	27	U S A	23	"
V	Carrozza Themistocles	27	mason	37	"
W	Barressi Anthony	27	U S A	28	"
X	Barressi Carlo	27	welder	20	"
Y	Barressi Ernest	27	U S N	23	"
Z	Barressi Joseph	27	"	29	"
432
A	Barressi Josephine †	27	factoryhand	37	"
B	Barressi Virginia †	27	housewife	58	"
C	Barressi Virginia †	27	factoryhand	26	"
D	Giaquinto Angelo	27	proprietor	53	"
E	Giaquinto Jennie †	27	housewife	38	"
F	*DiCicco Anna †	29	"	48	"
G	DiCicco Anthony	29	laborer	23	"
H	DiCicco Pasquale	29	plasterer	51	"
K	*Hlabanis Filomena †	29	housewife	42	"
L	Hlabanis George	29	carpenter	43	"
M	Lopez Albert	29	student	22	"
N	Riccio Domenic	29	laborer	52	35 Lubec
O	*Riccio Lena †	29	housewife	47	35 "

19

Maverick Square—Continued

P	Riccio Mary —†	29	dressmaker	24	55 Lubec
R	Riccio Nicholas	29	laborer	22	55 "
U	Frazier Lawrence	33	carpenter	63	here
V	Clark John	33	longshoreman	25	"
W	Clark William	33	shipworker	27	"
X	*Walsh John	33	longshoreman	61	"
Y	Walsh John, jr	33	U S A	26	"
Z	Walsh Marie —†	33	housewife	58	"

433

A	Walsh Mary M —†	33	operator	24	"
B	Cyr Eva —†	33	housewife	48	193 Sumner
C	Cyr Joseph	33	fisherman	57	193 "
D	Foley Catherine —†	33	housewife	53	here
K	Bertelino Antonio	39	fisherman	21	"
L	*Bertelino Carmella †	39	housewife	44	"
M	*Bertelino Petro	39	fisherman	46	"
O	Fiore Filomena —†	41	housewife	61	"
W	Trevisonne Clementina —†	47	"	43	"
X	Trevisonne Luigi	47	shipfitter	61	"
Y	Trevisonne Olivio	47	factoryhand	21	"
Z	Cimino Emma †	47	housewife	39	"

434

A	Cimino Joseph	47	proprietor	48	"
C	Stott Gertrude †	51	housewife	38	"
D	Shippard Jane †	51	packer	25	"
E	Young Alexander	51	fisherman	48	"
F	Young Celia †	51	housewife	50	"
H	*Lomas Louis	55	shoeworker	49	"
K	Bocchetti Carmillo	55	barber	52	"
L	Bocchetti Concetta —†	55	stitcher	26	"
M	Bocchetti Eleanor †	55	counter girl	21	"
N	Bocchetti Louise †	55	housewife	47	"
O	Marrone Lucy †	55	trimmer	20	"
R	*LaFratta Frances †	59	housewife	55	"
S	LaFratta Frank J	59	U S N	22	"
T	La Fratta John	59	clerk	57	"
U	*LaFratta Joseph	59	retired	59	"
W	Palmera Edward	59	welder	22	"
X	Palmera George	59	machinist	25	"
Y	*Palmera Joseph	59	retired	60	"
Z	*Palmera Mary †	59	housewife	60	"

435
Maverick Square—Continued

F	Carlson Frances—†	67	housewife	54	here
G	Carlson Olaf	67	retired	70	"
H	Sparvieri Michael	67	laborer	60	"
K	DeStefano Arthur	67	clerk	28	"
L	DeStefano Louise—†	67	housewife	65	"
M	DeStefano Peter	67	clerk	67	"
N	Vernacchio Mildred—†	67	housewife	39	"
O	Vernacchio Philip	67	mechanic	39	"
P	Cardinale Anna—†	67	factoryhand	25	"
R	Cardinale Benedetto	67	U S A	26	"
S	Cardinale Cosimo	67	U S C G	21	"
T	Cardinale Domenic	67	fisherman	57	"
U	Cardinale Josephine—†	67	housewife	48	"
X	Salvatore Angie—†	73	"	49	"
Y	Salvatore Anna—†	73	clerk	24	"
Z	Salvatore Louis	73	secretary	53	"

436   Maverick Street

G	Crowell Raymond	rear 49	agent	38	31 Fulton
H	Crowell Ruth—†	" 49	housewife	37	31 "
L	Florence Marie—†	" 49	at home	20	151 Leverett
M	Sasso Caroline—†	" 49	housewife	39	151 "
N	Sasso John	" 49	rigger	40	151 "
O	Ward John J	65	machinist	32	Waltham
P	Ward Mary C—†	65	housewife	32	"
R	Blades Edith—†	65	"	39	Stoneham
S	Blades Mary—†	65	packer	20	"
T	Blades William	65	pipefitter	41	"
U	Blades Margaret—†	65	housewife	25	Scituate
V	Blades Russell	65	machinist	28	"
W	Vieira Frank	65	packer	56	43 Soley
X	Vieira Mary R—†	65	housewife	34	43 "
Y	Laliberte Louise—†	65	"	29	N Hampshire
Z	Laliberte Noel	65	welder	34	"
	437					
A	Monahan Alphonsus G	65	painter	43	33 Mascot
B	Monahan Mary R—†	65	housewife	37	33 "
C	Menz George	65	inspector	33	128 School
D	Menz Marion—†	65	housewife	26	128 "

Page.	Letter	FULL NAME.	Residence, Jan. 1, 1943	Occupation.	Supposed Age.	Reported Residence, Jan. 1, 1942. Street and Number.

Maverick Street — Continued

E	Garofalo Concetta—†	65	housewife	28		15 Gavin way
F	Garofalo Domenic	65	U S C G	32		15 "
G	Ippolito Antonio	65	retired	67		326 Bremen
H	Magaldi Florence—†	65	housewife	32		137 London
K	Magaldi Samuel	65	machinist	34		137 "
M	Corbett Emily—†	65	at home	24		188 Cottage
N	Sullivan Ethel—†	65	housewife	29		198 Everett
O	Sullivan John M	65	janitor	30		198 "
P	Overlan Josephine—†	73	housewife	28		Connecticut
R	Overlan Peter	73	machinist	29		"
S	Barney Elmer O	73	"	39		Vermont
T	Barney Evelyn M—†	73	housewife	28		"
U	Donenech Dolores—†	73	"	34		New York
V	Donenech Lauro	73	machinist	34		"
W	Devan Coralie—†	73	housewife	28		Chelsea
X	Devan George	73	metalworker	30		"
Y	Doody James A	73	clerk	34		Cambridge
Z	Doody Julia—†	73	housewife	35		"

438

A	Stowe Lillian—†	73	"	22		Revere
B	Stowe Ray	73	U S N	26		Michigan
C	Hamilton Helen R—†	73	at home	55		79 Wrentham
D	Hildreth John E	73	guard	37		Reading
E	Hildreth Marion I—†	73	housewife	35		"
F	Stanley Albert R	73	welder	33		Topsfield
G	Stanley Margaret M—†	73	housewife	32		"
H	Carrozza Marie—†	73	"	27		91 Maverick
K	Carrozza Mario	73	foreman	33		91 "
L	McColgan Beatrice—†	73	housewife	28		Revere
M	McColgan Elmer	73	electrician	29		"
O	Schmidt Edward	73	clerk	25		Watertown
P	Schmidt Louise—†	73	housewife	25		"
R	Light Harry	81	brazier	29		Missouri
S	Light Mary—†	81	housewife	24		"
T	Santagati Ethel F—†	81	"	28		284 Old Colony av
U	Santagati Joseph J	81	calker	29		284 "
V	Matthews Clarence	81	rigger	38		11 Chelsea
W	Matthews Evelyn—†	81	housewife	26		11 "
X	McMullin Barbara—†	81	"	35		Newton
Y	McMullin Philip	81	machinist	36		"
Z	Sawyer Bernard G	81	"	33		Worcester

22

Page.	Letter.	FULL NAME.	Residence, Jan. 1, 1943.	Occupation.	Supposed Age.	Reported Residence, Jan. 1, 1942. Street and Number.

439
Maverick Street—Continued

	Letter	FULL NAME	Res.	Occupation	Age	Reported Residence
	A	Sawyer Susan L—†	81	housewife	34	Worcester
	B	Quinlan Ruth—†	81	at home	35	13 Roach
	C	Carozza Joseph	81	machinist	25	Revere
	D	Carozza Margaret—†	81	housewife	25	"
	E	David Anna—†	81	"	40	Haverhill
	F	David Oliver	81	welder	40	"
	G	Bailey Helen—†	81	housewife	37	Somerville
	H	Bailey Niles	81	U S C G	45	"
	K	Grabowski Helen—†	81	housewife	35	13 James
	L	Grabowski Joseph L	81	machinist	36	13 "
	M	Rahilly Joseph P	81	guard	30	Revere
	N	Rahilly Virginia K—†	81	housewife	26	"
	O	Cabaleri Joseph	81	laborer	53	54 Maverick
	P	*Cabaleri Mary—†	81	housewife	39	54 "
	S	*Ruggiero Mary—†	86	at home	64	here
	T	Scopa Angelina—†	86	housewife	25	"
	U	Scopa Pasquale	86	shipfitter	28	"
	V	Gallo Baldassare	86	shoeworker	49	"
	W	Gallo Benedetta—†	86	housewife	33	"
	X	*Buck Patrick	88	longshoreman	76	126 Meridian
	Y	*Capezutto Beatrice—†	88	housewife	28	here
	Z	*Crowley John	88	fisherman	55	"

440

	Letter	FULL NAME	Res.	Occupation	Age	Reported Residence
	A	Dill Alwyth—†	88	at home	23	"
	B	Mahoney Richard	88	retired	68	"
	C	Poirier Edward	89	U S A	22	Maine
	D	*Poirier Onesine—†	89	housewife	59	"
	E	Poirier Palma—†	89	waitress	25	"
	F	Poirier Rita—†	89	"	20	"
	G	*Poirier Rosario	89	carpenter	57	"
	H	Poirier Viola—†	89	waitress	23	"
	K	Armstrong Clifford	89	U S M C	23	here
	L	Armstrong James	89	retired	76	Wilmington
	M	O'Brien Harry	89	machinist	56	here
	N	O'Brien Laura—†	89	housewife	44	"
	R	Fatalo Joseph	91	retired	76	"
	S	Fatalo Rosa—†	91	housewife	70	"
	T	Ruggiero Anthony	91	assembler	35	"
	U	Ruggiero Julia—†	91	housewife	35	"
	V	Salamone Jennie—†	91	"	46	210 Maverick

23

Maverick Street—Continued

	w	Salamone Joseph	91	electrician	48	210 Maverick
	x	*Scaffeo Alfonso	92	retired	79	here
	y	Bonasoro John	92	mechanic	28	"
	z	Bonasoro Josephine—†	92	housewife	23	"
441						
	a	DeFronzo Alfonso	92	inspector	27	"
	b	DeFronzo Josephine—†	92	housewife	28	"
	c	Riley John J	95	watchman	58	"
	d	Riley Lillian—†	95	housewife	58	"
	e	Gregory Anthony	95	finisher	45	"
	f	Gregory Rose—†	95	housewife	35	"
	g	*Mangiafico Lena—†	95	"	38	"
	h	Mangiafico Paul	95	laborer	42	"
	l	Dunn Edith—†	97	housewife	28	"
	m	McDonald Rose—†	97	"	50	"
	n	McDonald Thomas F	97	laborer	41	"
	o	Tribuna Antonetta—†	97	at home	73	"
	p	Tribuna Joseph	97	fishcutter	34	"
	r	Bonta Carmello	97	pressman	39	"
	s	Bonta Rosaria—†	97	housewife	36	"
	t	Barletta Grace—†	98	"	27	"
	u	Barletta James	98	shipfitter	30	"
	v	Celona Lena—†	98	housewife	33	89 Webster
	w	Celona Nicholas	98	shipfitter	32	89 "
	y	Zaltsberg Irving	100	student	22	here
	z	Zaltsberg Samuel	100	proprietor	58	"
442						
	a	Zaltsberg Sarah—†	100	housewife	52	"
	b	*Goldenberg Nellie—†	100	at home	75	"
	c	Goldenberg Ruth—†	100	dressmaker	23	"
	d	*Goldenberg Sarah—†	100	housewife	47	"
	e	Goldenberg William	100	grocer	47	"
	f	Latour Nellie—†	101	housewife	62	"
	g	Latour William F	101	inspector	66	"
	h	Harris Grace E—†	101	housewife	32	"
	k	Harris James E	101	U S N	33	"
	l	Mosko Leo	101	laborer	29	103 Maverick
	n	Bollard Stephen M	103	rigger	46	here
	o	Catino Albert R	103	mechanic	23	Rhode Island
	p	Cimino Orlando	103	salesman	23	3 Paris pl
	r	Drolet Charles	103	carpenter	42	Maine

24

Maverick Street—Continued

s	Forini Anthony	103	shoemaker	48	here
T	Jeffery Allie M—†	103	housekeeper	60	"
U	Macri John	103	carpenter	63	"
V	McNamara Mary—†	103	packer	59	"
X	Cady Clara—†	106	at home	47	"
Y	*Nardo Antonio	106	retired	62	"
Z	*Olitsky Louis	106	junk dealer	60	8 Winthrop

443

A	Kirk Karl	106	laborer	60	here
C	Chin Chung Shaw	108	laundryman	61	"
D	Chin Quan Shee—†	108	at home	51	"
E	*Bakerman Peter	109	fisherman	46	"
F	Colburne Andrew	109	deckhand	58	"
G	Delespro Michael	109	plumber	30	"
H	DiCicco Henry	109	carpenter	46	"
K	Donovan Peter	109	letter carrier	49	"
L	Garvin Isabella—†	109	housekeeper	67	"
M	*Keough James	109	ironworker	54	256 Lexington
N	*O'Shaughnessy Augustine	109	fisherman	38	Chelsea
O	*McCloud Sadie—†	111	at home	70	here
P	*Wheaton Annie—†	111	"	66	"
R	Wheaton Charles E	111	deckhand	43	"
S	Miller Bridget—†	111	at home	77	"
U	Laurino Rocco M	117	tailor	56	"
V	Onessimo Erminia—†	117	housewife	54	"
W	Onessimo Patrick	117	plumber	58	"
X	DiLorenzo Beatrice—†	117	candyworker	29	"
Y	Palladino Jennie—†	117	housewife	37	"
Z	Palladino Joseph	117	salesman	44	"

444

B	DelPrato Nicholas	119	shoeworker	48	"
C	Gasbaro James	119	machinist	39	"
D	Leonardi Angelo	119	laborer	46	"
H	Gueli John	125	U S A	21	"
K	Gueli Rocco	125	proprietor	52	"
L	Gueli Teresa—†	125	housewife	42	"
M	Ligiero Fiore	125	clerk	21	"
N	*Ligiero Michaelina—†	125	at home	55	"
O	*Girozola Teresa—†	125	"	70	"
P	Corey Nellie—†	127	housekeeper	70	"
R	Olders Frank	127	longshoreman	52	"

Maverick Street—Continued

	U	*Saracino Anna—†	147	housewife	37	here
	V	Saracino Emilio	147	shoemaker	39	"
	X	Lombardi Joseph	149	laborer	26	"
	Y	Lombardi Josephine—†	149	housewife	25	"
	Z	DiMarzo Michael	149	laborer	36	"
445						
	A	DiMarzo Rose—†	149	clerk	63	"
	B	Terlino Eleanor—†	151	housewife	20	225 Marion
	C	Terlino Vincent	151	machinist	20	228 Havre
	D	*Puzzo Maria—†	151	housewife	60	13 Chelsea
	E	*Puzzo Salvatore	151	retired	64	13 "
	F	Puzzo Vito	151	operator	39	13 "
	G	Christina Albert	153	musician	36	here
	H	*Christina Santa—†	153	dressmaker	62	"
	K	Poto Nicholas	153	chauffeur	53	139 Condor
	L	Poto Susan—†	153	housewife	48	20 Frankfort
	N	*Giannoccaro Almina—†	157	"	57	here
	O	Giannoccaro Anthony	157	laborer	24	"
	P	Giannoccaro Florence—†	157	checker	26	"
	R	Spano Leo	157	lather	45	"
	S	Spano Theresa—†	157	housewife	40	"

Meridian Street

	Z	Gorman James L	62	retired	65	Chelsea
446						
	A	Sheffield William	62	calker	66	here
	B	Panteleeff Nicholas	62	millhand	66	"
	C	Meaney Edward	62	ironworker	55	"
	F	Sullivan William J	66	mortician	40	"
	P	*Bitto Grace—†	78	housekeeper	55	Revere
	R	DeBenedictis Elvira—†	78	"	66	here

Orleans Street

	T	Citron Joseph H	28	clerk	62	here
	U	Citron Rose I—†	28	housewife	54	"
	V	DeAngelis Eleanora—†	28	clerk	21	40 Webster
	W	DeAngelis Harry	28	musician	34	40 "
	X	*DeAngelis Nicoletta—†	28	housewife	52	40 "
	Y	*Telesparo Carmine	30	laborer	64	151 Sumner

Orleans Street — Continued

	z	Telesparo Maria—†	30	operator	36	61 Webster
447						
	A	Vacirca Michael	30	laborer	25	here
	B	Vacirca Stella—†	30	housewife	25	"
	c	*Petrizzi Maria—†	30	"	63	"
	D	*Petrizzi Nicola	30	retired	76	"
	E	*Briana Frank	32	"	73	"
	F	*Briana Mary—†	32	housewife	67	"
	G	Petrilli Alfred	32	mechanic	49	"
	H	Petrilli Anna—†	32	dressmaker	45	"
	K	Briana Florence—†	32	housewife	32	30 Haynes
	L	Briana James	32	guard	39	here

Paris Street

	M	Bringola Lucia—†	6	at home	68	here
	N	Dorso Margaret—†	6	"	61	"
	o	*Antico Domenic	6	candymaker	46	"
	P	*Cook Harry I	8	retired	69	"
	R	Cook Helen A—†	8	housewife	64	"
	s	Cook Wallace W	8	watchman	20	"
	T	*DiSousa Manuel	8	fireman	48	"
	U	Scorzella Alfred	8	"	24	"
	V	Scorzella Rose—†	8	housewife	22	"
	W	Smallcomb Stephen	8	fisherman	63	"
	X	Borrows Margaret—†	10	housewife	44	"
	Y	Borrows Robert	10	clerk	62	"
448						
	A	*DeCicco Dionizia—†	11	housewife	46	166 Sumner
	B	*DeCicco Joseph	11	plasterer	46	166 "
	c	*Sharaffa Mary—†	11	housewife	36	30 Bremen
	D	Venturelli Josephine—†	11	"	20	30 "
	E	Iarossi George	11	U S A	23	234 Bolton
	F	Iarossi Phyllis—†	11	housewife	21	234 "
	G	Melchionda Gaetano	12	laborer	31	here
	H	Melchionda Jennie—†	12	housewife	30	"
	K	DiPerri Calogero	12	laborer	55	"
	L	DiPerri John	12	cutter	27	"
	M	*DiPerri Vincenza—†	12	housewife	45	"
	N	*DiPerri Filippa—†	12	"	54	"
	o	DiPerri Joseph	12	laborer	61	"

Page.	Letter	FULL NAME.	Residence, Jan. 1, 1943.	Occupation.	Supposed Age.	Reported Residence, Jan. 1, 1942.
						Street and Number.

Paris Street — Continued

P	Cibello Anthony	14	shoeworker	38	Cambridge
R	Cibello Isabelle —†	14	housewife	28	"
S*	Perillo Elizabeth—†	14	"	38	here
T	Perillo Gustave	14	shoecutter	42	"
U*	Cibello Mary—†	14	at home	67	"
V*	Imbrici Raffaela —†	16	housewife	66	63 Lubec
W	Imbrici Rose—†	16	clerk	30	here
X	Imbrici Sabino	16	retired	67	63 Lubec
Y	Imbrici Salvatore	16	U S A	20	63 "
Z*	Degna Sabino	16	at home	56	175 Chelsea

449

A*	Degna Vingenza —†	16	housewife	55	175 "
B	Tribuna Angelo	16	floorman	38	18 Hartland
C	Tribuna Edith—†	16	housewife	33	18 "
D*	Anderson Albert	18	fisherman	50	11 Henry
E	Anderson Hans	18	"	50	here
F*	Anello Ezio	18	trainman	40	38 Bremen
G	Brown Harvey	18	deckhand	50	here
H*	Davidson Herman	18	chef	64	"
K	DiPaola Raeffaele	18	mason	60	"
L	Holmberg Emma —†	18	housekeeper	65	"
M*	Holmberg Gustav	18	painter	55	"
N*	Ippolito Salvatore	18	electrician	50	"
O	Iversen Bjarne	18	machinist	64	Reading
P	Jacobsen Oskar	18	seaman	49	South America
R	Kofoed Wiggo	18	retired	62	here
S	Barsalow James	20	seaman	35	New Jersey
T	Bussey James	20	retired	84	here
U	Dinan James	20	freighthandler	55	"
V	Francis Fred	20	retired	70	"
W	Marchand Peter	20	"	79	"
X*	O'Brien James	20	fisherman	65	"
Y	Rice Fred	20	laborer	67	"
Z	Stanton Frank	20	retired	68	"

450

A*	Turnbull Amy †	20	housewife	22	120 London
B	Turnbull Grant	20	fishcutter	32	120 "
C	Anderson Catherine †	22	housewife	60	here
D	Anderson Hans P	22	watchman	57	"
E	Anderson Lillian †	22	stenographer	22	"
F	Anderson Mary †	22	"	27	"

28

Paris Street — Continued

G	Anderson Paul	22	operator	25	here
H	Anderson William	22	U S A	26	"
K	Fitzgerald Mary — †	22	at home	62	"
L	Frydenlund Valdemar	22	fisherman	60	"
M	Haase Max	24	seaman	64	"
N	Lanning Cornelius	24	U S A	32	"
O	Lanning Ellen — †	24	housewife	65	"
P	Lanning Ellen M — †	24	stenographer	24	"
R	Lanning Julia A — †	24	"	28	"
S	Lanning Michael C	24	retired	73	"
T	Obit Anton	24	deckhand	50	"
W	Betts Emma S — †	32	housewife	60	"
X	Betts George L	32	laundryman	55	"
Y	Fleming Jeanette — †	32	operator	20	"
z	*Beliveau Gus	34	calker	60	"

451

A	Careau Richard	34	millhand	63	"
B	Cronin William	34	retired	65	"
C	Flynn Harry	34	welder	58	"
D	McArdle Thomas	34	retired	56	"
E	Meers John	34	chef	50	"
F	Owens Fred	34	retired	68	"
G	Rubino Michael	34	longshoreman	50	"
H	Story George	34	retired	78	"
K	Penta Ernest	36	rigger	34	"
L	Penta Margaret — †	36	housewife	33	"
M	Mecrones Mary — †	36	"	37	"
N	Mecrones Spero	36	chef	44	"
P	Cleary Ethel — †	38	packer	38	242 E Eagle
R	Crandall Harold F	38	longshoreman	48	here
S	Dooley Elizabeth — †	38	factoryhand	34	48 Maverick sq
T	Fay Andrew E	38	machinist	45	111 Walk Hill
U	Graf Killian	38	retired	70	here
V	*Hirtle Frank	38	carpenter	49	118 Falcon
W	Murphy Marie — †	38	saleswoman	25	62 "
X	*Perry Joseph	38	fisherman	63	157 Meridian
Y	Willis Andrew	38	longshoreman	57	here
Z	Cone Birthday	46	retired	84	"

452

A	Diaz Leocardo	46	mechanic	23	"
B	Diaz Mary — †	46	seamstress	59	"

Page.	Letter.	FULL NAME.	Residence, Jan. 1, 1943	Occupation.	Supposed Age.	Reported Residence, Jan. 1, 1942. Street and Number.

Paris Street — Continued

	c	*Diaz Virginia —†	46	housewife	25	Costa Rica
	d	*Rosato Rachel —†	48	"	57	here
	e	*Rosato Thomas A	48	plasterer	59	"
	f	Lapelato Louis	48	clerk	36	"
	g	Lapelato Mary —†	48	housewife	35	"

Sumner Street

	l	Cotreau Caleb A	66	coppersmith	47	130 Putnam
	m	Cotreau Lennie M —†	66	housewife	45	130 "
	o	Pigeon A Standish	66	clerk	34	Provincetown
	p	Pigeon Mary B —†	66	housewife	34	"
	r	Kaczmarczk Edith G †	66	"	30	New Bedford
	s	Kaczmarczk Martin J	66	pipefitter	37	Connecticut
	t	Daily Rose M —†	66	housewife	26	128 Florida
	u	Daily William R	66	metalworker	29	128 "
	v	Dickard James	66	carpenter	22	N Hampshire
	w	Dickard Margaret †	66	housewife	21	"
	x	Holder Elsie —†	66	"	37	Palmer
	y	Holder Nelson	66	draftsman	37	"
	z	Cormany Gladys V †	66	housewife	21	Ohio

453

	a	Cormany Lowell W	66	U S N	24	"
	b	Peterson Albert E	66	U S C G	65	Lowell
	c	Peterson Amanda E †	66	housewife	56	"
	d	Peterson Arline E †	66	packer	21	"
	e	Forgue Emile	66	shipfitter	33	N Hampshire
	f	Forgue Gertrude †	66	housewife	27	"
	g	Johnson Frank E	66	U S N	31	New York
	h	Johnson Luella I †	66	housewife	30	"
	k	Frongello Dorothy E †	66	"	27	51 Bennington
	l	Frongello John	66	coppersmith	23	11 Everett
	m	Huggard Ann B †	74	housewife	27	Woburn
	n	Huggard Gordon B	74	electrician	33	"
	p	Sanders Alius C	74	machinist	46	18 Mystic
	r	Sanders Christine L †	74	housewife	43	18 "
	s	Harris Genevieve †	74	"	40	Everett
	t	Harris Harold L	74	U S N	41	"
	u	Daffin Louise K †	74	clerk	36	New York
	v	King Mary M †	74	at home	65	37 Jenkins
	w	Lowney Helen F †	74	housewife	44	58 Monument

30

Page.	Letter.	FULL NAME.	Residence, Jan. 1, 1943	Occupation.	Supposed Age.	Reported Residence, Jan. 1, 1942. Street and Number.

Sumner Street Continued

	x	Lowney Herbert J	74	operator	43	58 Monument
	y	Asselin Louis	74	electrician	28	Southbridge
454						
	a	Relyea Lita —†	74	housewife	36	Missouri
	c	Carrignan Agnes M —†	74	"	25	Rhode Island
	d	Carrignan Henry J	74	painter	29	"
	e	Bettano Doris O —†	74	housewife	38	196 Maverick
	f	Bettano Joseph R	74	shipper	44	196 "
	g	Bettano Roy J	74	U S N	20	196 "
	h	Begin Bella —†	90	housewife	30	Salem
	k	Begin Henry J	90	pipefitter	32	"
	n	Courter Albert F	90	U S C G	22	12 Hancock
	o	Courter Edith M —†	90	housewife	20	12 "
	r	Barrows Helen—†	90	"	23	Virginia
	s	Barrows Robert	90	U S N	25	"
	u	Taber William	90	operator	22	Wash D C
	w	Elder Ethel M—†	90	housewife	28	Somerville
	x	Elder Warren D	90	U S N	30	"
	z	Creselious Earl E	90	laborer	25	Florida
455						
	a	Bachelder Albert E	98	U S N	40	N Hampshire
	b	Bachelder Doris M —†	98	housewife	40	"
	c	Shilinsky Charles	98	U S N	25	Somerville
	d	Shilinsky Grace—†	98	housewife	27	"
	e	Holden Violet E †	98	clerk	24	New Bedford
	f	Luce Arthur R	98	electrician	48	"
	g	Luce Mary—†	98	housewife	49	"
	h	Warden John H	98	U S N	46	Illinois
	k	Warden Velma †	98	housewife	44	"
	l	Capobianco Angelo	98	machinist	30	14 Haynes
	m	Capobianco Erica—†	98	housewife	26	14 "
	n	Sheffield Thomas	98	laborer	49	Lowell
	o	Bissett Mary †	98	housewife	35	Saugus
	p	Bissett Robert A	98	U S N	45	"
	s	Bailey Evelyn †	98	housewife	31	Chicopee Falls
	t	Bailey Gerald R	98	U S N	33	"
	u	Walsh Julia M— †	98	housewife	40	Framingham
	v	Walsh Michael J	98	carpenter	47	"
	w	Sell Henrietta —†	98	housewife	34	Connecticut
	x	Sell Robert	98	U S N	38	"
	y	Hart Charlotte R—†	98	housewife	25	Florida

31

Sumner Street Continued

	z	Hart Joseph M	98	U S N	37	Florida
456						
	c	Santaniello John	122	chauffeur	43	New York
	d	Santaniello Rose —†	122	housewife	34	"
	e	Premont Archie	122	machinist	26	Stoneham
	f	Premont Esther—†	122	housewife	21	"
	g	Myers Hazel—†	122	"	29	New York
	h	Myers Robert	122	electrician	31	"
	l	Brownlow Charlotte—†	122	housewife	31	Texas
	m	Brownlow Eugene	122	U S N	28	"
	n	Coppell Carmella D—†	122	housewife	24	379 Geneva av
	o	Coppell William A	122	machinist	29	379 "
	p	St. Francis Ernest	122	electrician	34	N Hampshire
	r	St. Francis Madeline †	122	housewife	30	"
	t	Burke Henry J	122	clerk	39	Newton
	u	Burke Jolane M †	122	housewife	27	"
	v	Valcourt Bernard D	122	mechanic	27	Delaware
	w	Valcourt Helen —†	122	housewife	29	"
	x	Bennett Mary J—†	122	at home	65	38 Surrey
	y	Filoso Anthony	130	laborer	29	Somerville
	z	Filoso Palma †	130	housewife	26	"
457						
	b	Paris Charles	130	polisher	28	Chelsea
	c	Paris Frances †	130	housewife	25	"
	e	Jeskey Anthony J	130	shipfitter	26	437 Meridian
	f	Jeskey Edna M †	130	housewife	26	437 "
	g	DeAngelis Amelia †	130	"	30	212 Chelsea
	h	DeAngelis Nicholas	130	baker	34	212 "
	k	Burke Evelyn †	130	housewife	21	Chelsea
	l	Burke Joseph F	130	clerk	21	"
	m	Cann Victor	130	radioman	25	Saugus
	n	Cann Ruth †	130	housewife	24	"
	x	Ching Chung	154	laundryman	62	here
	z	DelloRusso Louis	154½	laborer	37	"
	y	DelloRusso Louise —†	154½	housewife	35	"
458						
	a	Merchant Catherine—†	154½	"	50	S Bremen
	c	Boudrean Steven	158	laborer	41	here
	d	Cleary John	158	retired	76	"
	e	Cleary John P, jr	158	longshoreman	42	"
	f*	Flynn Benjamin	158	fireman	61	"

Sumner Street —Continued

G	Forrey Lillian R —†	158	housewife	42	here
H	Forrey Patrick L	158	proprietor	43	"
K	*French Silas	158	retired	75	"
L	*George Axel	158	longshoreman	63	"
M	Hart George	158	retired	68	"
N	*Leary Thomas	158	fireman	63	"
O	Silvia Frank	158	rigger	54	"
P	Boyle John	160	retired	66	"
R	Kingsbury Harold	160	fisherman	48	"
S	Miller Elizabeth—†	160	housewife	58	"
T	Miller James W	160	retired	63	"
U	Riley Matthew	160	laborer	55	"

459

A	Angelides Peter	168	fireman	51	126 Marion
B	Doherty Edward	168	retired	67	here
C	*Franciscos Irene—†	168	housekeeper	43	"
D	Garvey Joseph	168	shipfitter	41	"
E	Garvey Margaret—†	168	housewife	38	"
F	*Papafotiou Alex	168	chef	28	"
G	Theodore Michelina—†	168	housewife	30	126 Marion
H	Theodore Nicholas	168	seaman	48	126 "
K	*Chacos George	172	painter	68	here
L	*Pantilas Dimitrios	172	retired	59	"
M	Tsolakis Anastasia	172	fireman	44	"
N	Cornetta Mary—†	172	clerk	47	"
S	Alexanderson Alex	184	fireman	44	255 Webster
T	*DiGianvittorio Cesar	184	carpenter	63	here
U	Heino Fred	184	ironworker	49	"
V	Johnson Astrid—†	184	clerk	39	"
W	Lavano Nicholas	184	fireman	59	"
X	Margiotti Antonio	184	retired	74	11 Emmons
Y	Milani Peter	184	longshoreman	70	here
Z	*Nelson Armand	184	retired	72	"

460

A	*Petti Joseph	184	chef	60	"
B	Swanson Eric	184	machinist	49	Topsfield
C	*Youngquist Elizabeth—†	184	housewife	70	here
D	Cameron John	184½	retired	67	193 Summer
E	*Corcoran Thomas	184½	"	74	here
F	Quinn Bridget—†	184½	housekeeper	64	"
G	Quinn Hugh	184½	clerk	43	"

1—4   33

Page.	Letter.	Full Name.	Residence, Jan. 1, 1943.	Occupation.	Supposed Age.	Reported Residence, Jan. 1, 1942. Street and Number.

Sumner Street Continued

	H	*Vitale Pasquale	184½	mason	58	115 Saratoga
	K	*Walsh James	184½	laborer	65	here
	O	Carlson Elsie †	190½	housewife	38	"
	P	Carlson Ingvald	190½	painter	43	"
	R	*Erickson Ernest	190½	fireman	62	"
	S	*Gilbert Theodore	190½	"	71	"
	T	Hansen Louis	190½	seaman	67	"
	U	*Iversen Nils	190½	"	42	"
	V	Arciero Angelina †	191	housewife	43	"
	W	Arciero Antonio	191	U S A	22	"
	X	Arciero Carlo	191	clerk	20	New York
	Y	Arciero Christopher	191	chauffeur	46	here

461

	A	Aldus Mary A †	193	housewife	41	"
	B	Curran Nicholas	193	retired	69	"
	C	Doherty James	193	"	66	"
	D	Kehoe William	193	"	80	"
	E	*Marafino Pasquale	193	plumber	40	"
	F	Murray John	193	retired	65	New York
	G	O'Connell Agnes †	193	housewife	48	109 Meridian
	H	O'Connell Richard	193	checker	60	109 "
	K	*Sampson Robert	193	fisherman	50	here
	L	*Santonio Julio	193	retired	70	"
	M	*Burke Patrick	195	fisherman	53	"
	N	Digan Joseph	195	laborer	54	184 Benningt'n
	O	Haynes Warren	195	"	50	182 London
	P	*Jensen Martin	195	seaman	46	here
	R	Lawlor Peter	195	laborer	68	"
	S	McAteer John	195	longshoreman	46	184½ Sumner
	T	*Pinsh Christopher	195	seaman	42	here
	U	*Sammarco Antonio	195	retired	60	"
	V	*Sheehan Timothy	195	fisherman	54	"

462

	F	Fontana Libera †	228	cigarmaker	20	"
	G	*Fontana Maria †	228	housewife	53	"
	H	Fontana Maria †	228	dressmaker	23	"
	K	*Fontana Michael	228	machinist	53	"
	L	*Chillemi Mary †	228	housewife	39	"
	M	Chillemi Tindaro	228	fisherman	46	"
	N	Joslin Santa †	230	housewife	29	"
	O	*Panto Bernardina †	230	"	52	"

Sumner Street Continued

	P	Panto Charles	230	fisherman	28	here
	R	Panto Frances †	230	operator	23	"
	S	Panto Frank	230	fisherman	21	"
	T	Panto Peter	230	bricklayer	61	"
	U	LeMarco Alphonse	230	retired	72	"
	V	LeMarco Anthony M	230	bartender	25	"
	W	LeMarco Gloria—†	230	housewife	62	"

Webster Street

	Z	McPhee George	40	longshoreman	48	here
463						
	A	McPhee Helen—†	40	housewife	47	"
	B	McPhee Joseph	40	seaman	22	"
	C	McPhee Thomas	40	U S A	24	"
	E	Riley Annie B—†	42	housewife	75	"

Winthrop Street

	H	Day James	4	waiter	35	Revere
	K	Grasiose Eugene	4	laborer	32	687 Benn9ngt'n
	L	Johnsen Harold	4	guard	50	Medford
	M	Kremer Carl	4	waiter	48	here
	N	Layhe Elizabeth—†	4	housewife	60	"
	O	Layhe George	4	clerk	32	"
	P	Lombardi Paul	4	painter	43	276 Lexington
	R	Olsen Hans	4	fisherman	56	here
	S	Belmonte Jennie †	6	housewife	53	"
	T	*Giangregorio Carmella †	6	"	66	"
	U	Giangregorio Raphaele	6	laborer	51	"
	V	Mercurio Carmella—†	6	housewife	27	"
	W	Belmonte Joseph	6	U S A	22	"
	X	Belmonte Phyllis—†	6	bookkeeper	25	"
	Y	Mercurio Pasquale	6	U S A	27	"
464						
	B	*Belmonte Ralph	8	painter	50	"
	C	*Bonder Thomas	8	millhand	50	"
	D	Ezekiel Michael	8	retired	70	"
	E	Frazier George	8	engineer	35	"
	F	Hallasy Harry	8	retired	70	"
	G	Pizzi Edwardo	8	"	68	132 Webster

Page.	Letter.	FULL NAME.	Residence, Jan. 1, 1943.	Occupation.	Supposed Age.	Reported Residence, Jan. 1, 1942. Street and Number.

Winthrop Street—Continued

	H	Sinclair Alice —†	8	at home	68	here
	K	Smith William	8	retired	71	"
	L	Handy Mary—†	9	at home	64	"
	M	Lambert Charles	9	painter	60	"
	N	Murray William	9	longshoreman	45	"
	O	Venta Elmer	9	laborer	45	"
	P	Weeks Elmer	9	waiter	47	"
	R*	Zambetti Amato	9	laborer	48	18 Paris
	T	Falzone Michael	10	electrician	47	here
	U	Falzone Santa— †	10	housewife	41	"
	V*	Salerno Phillip	10	retired	83	"
	W	Amico Charles	10	bricklayer	58	"
	X*	Amico Lena—†	10	housewife	52	"
	Y	Vasapolli Joseph	10	carpenter	26	"
	Z	Vasapolli Phyllis—†	10	housewife	21	"
465						
	A	Aleto Angelo	11	laborer	60	"
	B	Baker John C	11	steamfitter	50	Springfield
	C	Coty Patrick	11	laborer	35	Chelsea
	D	DiStefano Albert	11	plumber	33	24 Bremen
	E	Habberley Josephine E—†	11	at home	75	here
	F	Hurley Dorothy— †	11	cashier	25	35 Central sq
	G	Jones Adeline †	11	waitress	39	Worcester
	H*	Luongo Pasquale	11	retired	80	here
	K	Paine Frank	11	"	68	"
	L	Bellboy Angelo	13	seaman	45	"
	M	Fleming George	13	retired	52	"
	N	Martini Nicholas	13	laborer	45	"
	O	Notz Grace †	13	at home	33	"
	P	Pimento Paul	13	millhand	38	"
	R	Verpocki John	13	chauffeur	28	"
	S	Webber Ella M †	13	housewife	62	"

Ward 1–Precinct 5

CITY OF BOSTON

LIST OF RESIDENTS
20 YEARS OF AGE AND OVER

(NON-CITIZENS INDICATED BY ASTERISK)
(FEMALES INDICATED BY DAGGER)

AS OF

JANUARY 1, 1943

JOSEPH F. TIMILTY, *Chairman*
FREDERIC E. DOWLING, *Secretary*
WILLIAM A. MOTLEY, Jr.
FRANCIS B. McKINNEY
EVERETT R. PROUT

Listing Board.

CITY OF BOSTON PRINTING DEPARTMENT

Page.	Letter	FULL NAME.	Residence, Jan. 1, 1943	Occupation.	Supposed Age.	Reported Residence, Jan. 1, 1942. Street and Number.

500

Bremen Street

	Letter	FULL NAME.	Res.	Occupation	Age	Residence
	B	Cardinale Domenic	54	laborer	21	here
	C	Cardinale Joseph	54	longshoreman	50	"
	D	Chisari Antonetta—†	56	clerk	20	"
	E	*Piscetti Nunzia—†	56	housewife	60	"
	F	Montalto Joseph P	56	mechanic	43	"
	G	Montalto Josephine—†	56	housewife	36	"
	H	DelloRusso Arthur	58	florist	30	"
	K	DelloRusso Carlo	58	"	66	"
	L	DelloRusso Rose—†	58	housekeeper	28	"
	M	*Fasano John	60	retired	75	"
	N	*Palumbo Antonetta—†	60	housewife	49	"
	O	Palumbo Marie—†	60	shoeworker	22	"
	P	Palumbo Palmarino	60	U S A	21	"
	R	*Palumbo Pasquale	60	retired	55	"
	S	*Sullivan James	62	longshoreman	52	50 Chelsea
	T	*Sullivan Margaret—†	62	housewife	39	50 "
	U	Montecano Josephine—†	62	"	30	107 Orleans
	V	Porcaro Antonette—†	64	"	30	here
	W	Porcaro Emilio	64	finisher	28	"
	X	Porcaro Agnes—†	64	inspector	25	"
	Y	Porcaro George	64	barber	57	"
	Z	*Porcaro Marie—†	64	housewife	51	"

501

	Letter	FULL NAME.	Res.	Occupation	Age	Residence
	A	Porcaro Rose—†	64	packer	29	"
	B	Spitaleri Frank	64	chauffeur	31	"
	C	Spitaleri Nancy—†	64	housewife	25	"
	D	Grosso Mary—†	66	dressmaker	42	"
	E	Grosso Samuel	66	laborer	42	"
	F	Gallagher Helen—†	66	candymaker	34	"
	G	Gallagher Mary—†	66	operator	60	"
	H	Daly Andrew	66	clerk	55	"
	K	McMullen George J	66	stevedore	46	"
	L	McMullen Marie J—†	66	housewife	45	"
	O	*Leto Biagi—†	82	"	62	57 Chelsea
	P	Leto Joseph	82	U S A	20	here
	R	Rossi Concetta—†	82	housewife	44	"
	S	Rossi Elvera—†	82	housekeeper	20	"
	T	Rossi Giuseppe	82	laborer	54	"
	U	*Costanzo Frank	82	retired	74	"
	V	Spinazzolo Marie—†	84	housewife	26	"

2

Bremen Street Continued

w	Spinazzolo Pasquale	84	laborer	28	here
x	Conti Blanche †	84	housewife	49	"
y	Conti Carmelo	84	contractor	49	"
z	Balzano Adeline †	84	housewife	38	"
	502				
A	Simione George	86	chauffeur	20	"
B	Simione Mary †	86	operator	22	"
c	Simione Nicola	86	retired	73	"
D	Leone Leo	86	chauffeur	38	"
E	Leone Mildred †	86	housewife	33	"
F	Grieco Carmella †	86	housekeeper	54	"
G	Portrait Alice †	86	housewife	31	"
H	Portrait George	86	operator	29	"
K	Collorne Angelo	88	shoeworker	27	"
L	Collorne Lillian †	88	housewife	28	"
M	Ferullo Alfred	88	shipper	33	"
X	Ferullo Elizabeth †	88	housewife	30	"
o	Charlone Stella †	88	"	70	107 Orleans
P	Collins Mary J †	90	"	65	here
s	Farro Evelyn †	92	"	23	58 Bremen
T	Farro Frank	92	custodian	26	96 Chelsea
U	Sammarco Carmelo	92	laborer	31	here
V	Sammarco Mary †	92	housewife	29	"
w	*Fabio Frank	92	retired	74	"
X	Poltrone Vincenzo	92	laborer	60	"
Y	*Sammarco Rose †	92	housewife	74	"

Chelsea Place

z	Correle Alfonso	5	laborer	49	here
	503				
A	*Correle Concetta †	5	housewife	52	"
B	Ippolito Antonette †	5	stitcher	29	90 Chelsea
c	Ippolito Frances †	5	"	23	90 "
D	Ippolito Rose †	5	dietitian	26	90 "
E	*Cucugliata Rosario	5	laborer	62	here
G	Fiore Filomena †	6	at home	71	"
H	Ferrara Joseph	6	laborer	39	"
K	Ferrara Margaret †	6	housewife	35	"
L	*Tracia Louise †	7	at home	60	"
M	*Gobbi Carmella †	7	housewife	37	128 Chelsea

3

Page.	Letter	FULL NAME.	Residence, Jan. 1, 1943.	Occupation.	Supposed Age.	Reported Residence, Jan. 1, 1942. Street and Number.

Chelsea Place Continued

N	*Gobbi Frank	7	laborer	53	128 Chelsea
O	Melchionna Louis	7	"	49	8 Chelsea pl
P	Melchionna Nancy †	7	housewife	34	8 "
T	Severino Arthur	8	buffer	33	here
U	Severino Concetta †	8	housewife	30	"
V	Genovese Carmella †	10	"	67	"
W	Genovese Donato	10	laborer	65	"
X	Genovese Joseph	10	"	32	"
Y	DiNoto Andrew	10	"	48	"
Z	DiNoto Angelina †	10	dressmaker	20	"

504

A	DiNoto Fred	10	U S A	24	"
B	*DiNoto Mary †	10	housewife	48	"
C	Paino Alfred	10	operator	21	"
D	Paino Felix	10	shoeworker	49	"
E	Paino Mary †	10	housewife	43	"

Chelsea Street

N	Calsimetto Paul	5	hairdresser	27	here
O	Calsimetto Phillis †	5	housewife	28	"
P	Presti Frank	5	metalworker	31	"
R	Presti Lena †	5	housewife	29	"
S	Aprea Gilda †	5	"	33	"
T	Aprea Orlando	5	ironworker	37	"
U	Opidre Joseph	6	machinist	40	"
V	*Opidre Mary †	6	housewife	37	"
W	Turieri Angelo	6	laborer	48	60 Gove
X	Turieri Mary †	6	housewife	49	60 "

505

A	*Iacuzzio Jennie †	7	"	30	here
B	Iacuzzio Nicholas	7	baker	31	"
C	Renna Angelina †	7	housewife	27	"
D	Renna Joseph	7	chauffeur	28	"
E	Pastore Mary †	7	housewife	38	"
F	Pastore Michael	7	storekeeper	32	94 Cottage
G	Ierossi Joseph	8	plumber	40	57 Chelsea
H	*Ierossi Lawrence	8	carpenter	63	57 "
K	*Ierossi Rose †	8	housewife	35	57 "
L	*Ierossi Vivian †	8	"	63	57 "
M	*Appignani Celeste †	8	"	56	here

Chelsea Street — Continued

N	Appignani Frank	8	cabinetmaker	66	here
R	Rapino Margaret —†	9	housewife	48	"
S	Rapino Mary —†	9	at home	22	"
T	Rapino Patsy	9	mortician	53	"
V	Clark Rufus	10	aviator	50	"
W	Cunningham Benjamin	10	shipfitter	50	"
X	Cunningham Theresa —†	10	housekeeper	48	"
Y	Gibbons Frank G	10	machinist	46	"
Z	Gibbons George	10	clerk	45	"

506

A	Altieri Adeline —†	10	housewife	38	"
B	Altieri Carlo	10	upholsterer	42	"
C	Bonito Edith —†	11	stitcher	22	"
D	*Bonito Leah —†	11	housewife	52	"
E	Sica Eleanor —†	11	at home	21	Malden
F	*Caliguri Elizabeth —†	11	housewife	44	here
G	Caliguri Sadie —†	11	operator	24	"
H	Narbonne J Adrian	11	machinist	28	58 Chelsea
K	Narbonne Rose —†	11	housewife	20	58 "
M	DeMarzo Domenic	12	metalworker	27	here
N	DeMarzo Lena —†	12	housewife	27	"
O	DeMarzo Catherine —†	12	"	34	"
P	DeMarzo Romolo	12	shoeworker	38	"
S	Caggiano Louis P	13	salesman	34	"
T	Guarini Evelyn G —†	13	housewife	31	"
U	Guarini Peter R	13	engineer	34	"
V	Pittella Joseph	13	operator	47	139 Havre
W	*Pittella Mary —†	13	housewife	42	139 "
Y	Milano Peter	14	chauffeur	46	here
Z	Milano Phyllis —†	14	housewife	39	"

507

A	Milano Antonette —†	14	at home	31	"
B	Milano Daniel	14	operator	35	"
C	Milano Joseph	14	laborer	40	"
D	Milano Patrick A	14	operator	49	"
E	Morello Anthony	14	chauffeur	44	"
F	*Luise Filomena —†	15	housewife	66	"
G	Luise Pasquale	15	retired	69	"
H	Marino Andrew	15	carpenter	42	"
K	*Marino Maria —†	15	housewife	33	"
L	Magaletta Anthony	15	leatherworker	30	"

5

Chelsea Street Continued

M	*Magaletta Mary—†	15	housewife	72	here
O	Polvere Alexander	16	foreman	29	"
P	Polvere Maria—†	16	housewife	28	"
R	*Rosetti Florence—†	16	"	47	"
S	Rosetti Joseph	16	shoeworker	52	"
T	Brignolo Frederick	16	laborer	47	"
U	Brignolo Josephine—†	16	housewife	41	"
X	Nargi Rachel—†	18	at home	39	"
Y	Aiello Helen—†	19	housewife	27	"
Z	Aiello Leonard	19	shipfitter	30	"

508

A	Trapeno Charles	19	barber	31	"
B	Trapeno Mary—†	19	housewife	27	"
C	Speciale Emily—†	19	"	25	"
D	Speciale James	19	shipper	25	"
E	*Speciale Ida—†	19	housewife	60	"
F	Speciale Virginia—†	19	operator	23	"
H	Beninati Blanche—†	20	housewife	36	"
K	Beninati Frank	20	pipefitter	36	"
L	Laurano Catherine—†	20	at home	78	"
M	Laurano Frank	20	U S N	41	"
N	Laurano Michael	20	"	26	"
O	Pisano Domenic	20	tailor	59	"
P	*Pisano John	20	"	24	"
R	*Pisano Pasqualina—†	20	housewife	49	"
S	Laurano Emilio	20	chauffeur	38	"
T	Laurano Florence—†	20	housewife	29	"
U	Davis Howard	21	machinist	39	"
V	Davis Libra—†	21	housewife	31	"
W	DiCorato Frances—†	21	"	32	"
X	DiCorato Rocco	21	barber	32	"
Y	Bellone Gaetano	21	pipefitter	28	"
Z	Bellone Ida—†	21	housewife	29	"

509

A	Vigliaroli Jennie—†	21	"	25	"
B	Vigliaroli Michael	21	shipfitter	26	"
D	Cardillo Carmella—†	22	at home	68	"
E	Tango Ida—†	22	housewife	32	13 Chelsea
F	Tango James	22	chauffeur	34	13 "
G	Raphanelli Adeline—†	22	operator	36	here
H	Raphanelli Joseph	22	machinist	38	"

6

Chelsea Street Continued

K	Picardi Carmino F	22	salesman	37	here
L	Picardi Emma †	22	housewife	34	"
M	Covalucci Amando	23	laborer	26	120 Webster
N	Covalucci Anna †	23	housewife	23	here
O*	Pantano Michaelina †	23	"	47	"
P	Pantano Santi	23	salesman	54	"
R	Chiampa Henry	23	machinist	27	"
S	Chiampa Marie †	23	housewife	26	"
T	Laurano Lillian †	23	"	24	"
U	Laurano Michael, jr	23	U S N	26	"
W*	Esposito Mary †	24	housewife	32	"
X	Esposito William	24	plumber	32	"
Y	Termina Lena †	24	stitcher	24	"
Z	Termina Louis	24	U S N	32	"

510

A	Spampinato Carmella †	24	candymaker	45	"
B	Spampinato Rosario	24	laborer	45	"
C*	Bernardinelli Joseph	25	retired	60	"
D	Bernardinelli Peter	25	U S A	42	"
E	Bernardinelli Salvatore M	25	laborer	30	"
F	Fiumara Frances †	25	at home	28	"
G*	Fiumara Josephine †	25	housewife	50	"
H	Fiumara Mary †	25	clerk	22	"
K*	Fiumara Salvatore	25	merchant	63	"
L	D'Amore Frank	25	draftsman	23	"
M*	D'Amore Lucy †	25	housewife	63	"
N	D'Amore Mary †	25	"	23	5 Seaver
O	Ciampi Louis	25	storekeeper	35	here
P	Ciampi Susie †	25	housewife	30	"
S	Diaz Jose	26	rigger	40	"
T	Diaz Virginia †	26	housewife	39	"
U	DeVito Angela †	26	"	20	"
V	DeVito Anthony	26	woodworker	24	Revere
W	DeVito Elvira †	26	housewife	53	here
X	DeVito Joseph	26	machinist	22	"
Y	DeVito Salvatore	26	watchman	52	"
Z*	Falco Ralph	27	laborer	50	"

511

A	Perrotti Anthony	27	machinist	22	"
B*	Perrotti Domenic	27	laborer	60	"
C	Perrotti Giaconda †	27	factoryhand	24	"

7

Chelsea Street—Continued

D	Perrotti Rita—†	27	at home	20	here
E	Perrotti Salvatore	27	technician	27	"
F	*Perrotti Vera—†	27	housewife	46	"
G	Brunco Esther—†	27	"	35	"
H	Brunco Joseph	27	electrician	46	"
L	Nicosia Grace—†	28	housewife	32	"
M	Nicosia Salvatore	28	baker	43	"
N	*Umbro Elizabeth—†	28	housewife	39	"
O	Umbro Joseph	28	laborer	50	"
P	Rosetti Augustine	28	clerk	31	61 Maverick sq
R	*Rosetti Fred	28	machinist	54	61 "
S	Rosetti Louise—†	28	at home	20	61 "
T	Rosetti Marie—†	28	"	27	61 "
U	Rosetti Philip	28	painter	29	61 "
V	*Rosetti Theresa—†	28	housewife	49	61 "
W	Rosetti Virginia—†	28	operator	26	61 "
X	Maranza Rocco	29	chef	33	63 Gove
Y	Bragoglia Vincenzo	29	laborer	55	100 Bremen
Z	Giglielli Melina—†	29	factoryhand	22	here

512

A	*Grani Josephine—†	29	housewife	56	"
C	*Ingalla Michaelina—†	31	"	40	188 Cottage
D	*Ingalla Phillip	31	retired	47	188 "
E	Calafato Mary—†	31	housewife	61	here
F	Spinelli Frank G	31	rigger	36	Revere
H	*Messina Antonio	31	fisherman	64	342 North
K	*Messina Grace—†	31	housewife	51	342 "
L	Scoffi Alfonse	33	electrician	31	here
M	*Scoffi Mary—†	33	housewife	33	"
N	LaMarco Armando	33	boilermaker	29	"
O	LaMarco Viola—†	33	shoeworker	27	"
P	D'Avolio Flora—†	33	at home	23	"
R	D'Avolio Michael	33	painter	50	"
S	D'Avolio Michael, jr	33	riveter	21	"
T	*Lanciotti Cesira—†	33	dressmaker	60	283 Princeton
U	*Lanciotti Victor	33	presser	24	283 "
V	Basilio Alexander	35	laborer	52	here
W	Basilio Gregory	35	"	21	"
X	*Basilio Rose—†	35	housewife	47	"
Z	*Giampapa Charles	35	painter	51	"
Y	*Giampapa Connie—†	35	housewife	44	"

S

513

Chelsea Street Continued

A	Giampapa Josephine—†	35	operator	22	here
c*	Federico Albert	35	laborer	51	"
D*	Federico Jennie—†	35	housewife	47	"
F	DiFilippo Joseph	37	clerk	62	"
G	Ruggiero Laura—†	37	housewife	39	"
H	Ruggiero Raphaele	37	painter	40	"
K	Morano Anna—†	37	housewife	33	"
L	Morano Joseph	37	electrician	34	"
M	Morano Anthony	37	machinist	20	"
N*	Morano Catherine—†	37	housewife	58	"
O	Morano Mary—†	37	saleswoman	21	"
P	Morano Rocco	37	retired	65	
R	Esposito Antonio	39	factoryhand	20	159 Havre
s*	Esposito Frances—†	39	housewife	58	159 "
T*	Esposito Frank	39	retired	59	159 "
U	Esposito Lucy—†	39	factoryhand	22	159 "
V	Esposito Anna—†	39	housewife	24	here
W	Esposito Thomas	39	carpenter	29	"
X	Russo Lucy—†	39	housewife	57	92 Bremen
Y	Meola Helen—†	39	millhand	26	here
Z	Dabrenger Herman	40	fireman	75	"

514

A	Lizine Amelia—†	40	housewife	38	"
B	Lizine Edgar	40	fireman	40	"
C	D'Amico Albert	40	mortician	24	"
D	D'Amico Annette—†	40	at home	23	"
E*	D'Amico Fiore	40	baker	62	"
F	D'Amico Michelina—†	40	housewife	20	"
G*	D'Amico Peter	40	clerk	65	"
H	D'Amico Ugo	40	chauffeur	22	199 Lexington
K	Galante Silvio	40	bartender	57	here
L*	Femino Nunzia—†	40	housewife	65	"
M	Femino Santo	40	retired	68	"
N	Femino Stella—†	40	seamstress	28	"
O	Femino Theresa—†	40	"	36	"
P	Palladino Emily—†	41	housewife	26	"
R	Palladino Salvatore	41	laborer	29	"
S	Pratola Antonio	41	shoeworker	44	"
T	Pratola Mary—†	41	housewife	37	"
U	Peazza Alphonse	41	shoemaker	55	193 Chelsea

Chelsea Street— Continued

	v	*Morelli Anthony	41	retired	68	here
	w	DeFranzo Isabel—†	42	housewife	38	"
	x	DeFranzo Michael	42	collector	40	"
	y	Femino Andrew	42	shoeworker	43	"
	z	Femino Margaret—†	42	housewife	41	"
		515				
	A	*Lazzaro Anna—†	42	"	47	122 Saratoga
	B	Lazzaro Phillip	42	laborer	52	122 "
	c	Rotondo Samuel	42	chauffeur	46	122 "
	D	Bertillino Anthony	43	fisherman	28	here
	E	Bertillino Jennie—†	43	housewife	26	"
	F	Rigione Anna—†	43	"	38	"
	G	Rigione Domenic	43	laborer	50	"
	H	*Vitagliano Angela—†	43	housewife	78	"
	K	*Vitagliano Paul	43	printer	65	"
	M	Marruzzo Angelo	43	laborer	28	"
	L	*Marruzzo Joseph	43	retired	50	"
	N	Bauschetto Andrew W	45	laborer	34	"
	O	*Caliendo Amelia—†	45	housewife	53	"
	P	Caliendo Carlo	45	barber	54	"
	R	Caliendo Frank	45	U S A	27	"
	S	Cammerano Angelo	45	carpenter	22	138 St Botolph
	T	Cammerano Frances—†	45	housewife	20	here
	U	Tutela Anthony	45	machinist	21	"
	V	*Tutela Pasqualina—†	45	housewife	50	"
	w	Iacuzio Jerry	46	bartender	30	"
	x	Iacuzio Mary—†	46	housewife	30	"
	z	Modica Mario	46	shoeworker	56	"
	Y	*Modica Mary—†	46	housewife	49	"
		516				
	A	Siracusa Albert	46	U S N	22	"
	B	Siracusa Angelina—†	46	housewife	20	"
	C	Torrone Josephine—†	46	stitcher	20	"
	D	*Torrone Mary—†	46	housewife	49	"
	E	Torrone Nicola	46	laborer	54	"
	F	Torrone Stella—†	46	stitcher	22	"
	G	Porovecchio Giovanni	47	retired	73	"
	H	Simonelli Concetta—†	47	housewife	34	"
	K	Simonelli Giuseppe	47	tailor	36	"
	L	LaConte Nicholas	47	laborer	57	"
	M	LaConte Rose—†	47	housewife	34	"

Chelsea Street (Continued)

	N*	Boncore Salvatore	47	laborer	46	here
	O	LaBella Domenic	48	welder	34	"
	P	LaBella Esther—†	48	housewife	32	"
	R	Langone Augusta G—†	48	shoeworker	21	"
	S	Langone Florence M—†	48	housewife	43	"
	T	Langone James F	48	laborer	46	"
	U	Angelo Joseph	48	tailor	51	"
	V	Angelo Mary—†	48	housewife	47	"
	W	Angelo Salvatore	48	machinist	20	"
	X*	Camuso Elizabeth—†	49	housewife	52	6 Everett
	Y*	Camuso Louis	49	laborer	53	6 "
	Z	Casey Marie—†	49	housewife	20	Salem

517

	A	Mazzio Antonio	49	laborer	48	here
	B	Mazzio Josephine—†	49	housewife	49	"
	C*	DeSciscio Angelo	49	shoeworker	38	"
	D	DeSciscio Yolanda—†	49	housewife	36	"
	E	D'Ambrosio Elsie—†	49	dressmaker	23	"
	F	D'Ambrosio Ernest	49	laborer	63	"
	G	D'Ambrosio Filomena—†	49	factoryhand	29	"
	H	D'Ambrosio Frank	49	laborer	20	"
	K	D'Ambrosio Mary—†	49	housewife	61	"
	L	D'Ambrosio Rose—†	49	dressmaker	28	"
	M*	Beaulieu Joseph	50	weaver	52	93 Neptune rd
	N*	Lava Anthony	50	shoeworker	58	here
	O	Mazzola Catherine—†	50	housewife	48	"
	P	Mazzola Phillip	50	laborer	58	"
	R	Coppney Charles	50	"	30	"
	S	Coppney Jennie—†	50	housewife	30	"
	T	Annunziata Frank	51	U S A	28	"
	U	Annunziata Santa—†	51	housewife	29	"
	V*	Paglierone Josephine—†	51	"	46	"
	W	Paglierone Julio	51	millhand	46	"
	X*	Amarose Rosaria—†	51	housewife	49	"
	Z	Pisello Elizabeth—†	52	"	45	"

518

	A	Pisello Joseph	52	roofer	44	"
	B	Capone Mary—†	52	housewife	25	161 Cottage
	C	Capone Pellegrine	52	laborer	26	161 "
	D	Simione James	52	chauffeur	35	here
	E	Simione Minnie—†	52	housewife	37	"

11

Chelsea Street—Continued

F	Gentile Alvera—†	53	housewife	32	here
G	Gentile Francis	53	artist	38	"
H	Gentile Domenic	53	retired	71	"
K	Gentile Marshall	53	salesman	27	"
L	*Amaroso Jennie—†	53	housewife	56	"
M	Damiano Mary—†	53	"	34	"
O	Festa Henry	53	operator	47	"
N	Festa Jennie—†	53	housewife	42	"
P	Repici Anna—†	53	"	35	"
R	Repici Charles	53	baker	41	"
S	*Verrazani Josephine—†	53	housewife	39	"
T	Verrazani Lawrence	53	factoryhand	44	"
W	*Perrone Antonetta—†	54	housewife	41	"
X	Perrone Frank	54	carpenter	42	"
Y	Oliva Leo	54	U S N	23	"
Z	Oliva Mary—†	54	stitcher	20	"
	519				
A	*Oliva Vincenza—†	54	housewife	52	"
B	Farina Irene—†	56	"	31	"
C	Farina Joseph J	56	painter	30	"
D	*DeMondi Elvira—†	58	housewife	49	101 Maverick
E	DeMondi Matteo	58	U S A	20	101 "
F	*DeMondi Raffaele	58	laborer	54	101 "
G	Quattrocchi Rose M—†	58	housewife	35	here
H	DiTomasso Francesco	58	laborer	53	N Hampshire
K	Tanzo Michael	58	painter	51	here
L	Macaluso Biaggio J	58	musician	23	"
M	*Macaluso Mary—†	58	housewife	69	"
N	Barbetta Dorothy—†	60	"	23	"
O	Barbetta Michael L	60	painter	33	18 Haynes
P	Fiorino Emanuel	60	pressman	57	here
R	*Fiorino Mary—†	60	housewife	47	"
S	Fiorino Salvatore	60	U S A	25	"
T	*Forgione Antonette—†	60	housewife	36	"
U	Forgione Salvatore	60	laborer	45	"
V	Bruccato Pietro	62	retired	80	534 E Third
W	Bruccato Vincenza—†	62	housewife	71	534 "
X	LaCort Pietro	62	clerk	63	here
Y	LaMonica Joseph	64	laborer	31	"
Z	LaMonica Rose—†	64	housewife	28	"

520
Chelsea Street Continued

A	Paradiso Alesandro	64	pressman	39	here
B	*Paradiso Vincenza — †	64	housewife	34	"
C	LaMonica Mildred — †	64	"	40	"
D	LaMonica Salvatore	64	chauffeur	39	"
E	Gneco Giuseppina — †	66	at home	74	"
F	*LaMonica Cologera †	66	housewife	57	85 Liverpool
G	LaMonica Orlando	66	U S A	20	85 "
H	LaMonica Rosario	66	"	25	85 "
K	LaMonica Santo	66	laborer	62	85 "
L	Salvo Vita — †	66	housewife	40	here
M	Salvo Vito	66	shoeworker	49	"
N	DiFiore Fred	68	"	49	383 Maverick
O	DiFiore Fred, jr	68	U S A	20	383 "
P	DiFiore Pauline — †	68	housewife	35	383 "
R	*Martello Mary — †	68	"	43	here
S	Martello Nicola	68	tailor	45	"
T	*Paradiso Julia — †	68	housewife	69	"
U	Paradiso Luigi	68	laborer	69	"
V	*Colangelo Giovannina — †	68	housewife	43	"
W	*Colangelo Guerino	68	laborer	46	"
X	Varallo Assunta — †	68	housewife	47	"
Y	Varallo Humbert	68	carpenter	50	"
Z	Barrasso Americo	70	printer	28	45 Chelsea

521

A	*Barrasso Julia — †	70	at home	66	45 "
B	Barrasso Mary — †	70	housewife	27	144 "
C	DeMondi Angelo	70	laborer	53	here
D	*DeMondi Rose — †	70	housewife	41	"
E	Sarro Frank	70	chauffeur	42	226 Lexington
F	Sarro Josephine — †	70	housewife	42	226 "
H	Zambello Anna — †	72	"	25	here
K	Zambello Frank	72	butcher	25	"
L	*Galindo Benjamin	72	laborer	45	"
M	Galindo Theresa — †	72	housewife	46	"
N	Lauria Henry	72	upholsterer	33	"
O	Lauria Josephine — †	72	housewife	25	"
P	Iarossi Nettie — †	74	"	20	"
R	Iarossi Pasquale	74	pipefitter	31	"
S	Astuccio Frances — †	74	operator	34	"

13

Page.	Letter	FULL NAME.	Residence, Jan. 1, 1943.	Occupation.	Supposed Age.	Reported Residence, Jan. 1, 1942. Street and Number.

Chelsea Street — Continued

	T	Indorato Lena—†	74	housewife	51	here
	U	Indorato Mario	74	tailor	54	"
	V	Albano Anthony	74	painter	23	345 Sumner
	W	Olivolo Antonio	74	laborer	25	2 Appian pl
	X	Olivolo Emma—†	74	housewife	20	2 "
	Y	Indorato Salvatore	74	tailor	31	here
	Z	Indorato Viola—†	74	housewife	29	"
522						
	A	Basillio Concetta—†	76	"	25	"
	B	Basillio Gregory	76	rigger	27	"
	C*	Ciarcia Antonetta—†	76	housewife	42	"
	D	Ciarcia Eleanor—†	76	clerk	21	"
	E*	Ciarcia Paolo	76	tailor	50	"
	F*	Odice Vincenza—†	76	at home	63	"
	G*	Baldini Assunta—†	76	"	57	"
	H	Baldini Carlo	76	machinist	28	"
	K	Baldini Clara—†	76	dressmaker	23	"
	L	Magnifico Anna—†	78	housewife	54	85 Chelsea
	M	Magnifico John	78	barber	57	85 "
	N	Magnifico Joseph	78	clerk	31	85 "
	O	Magnifico Philip	78	U S A	25	85 "
	S	Gluffing Frances—†	78	housewife	30	here
	P	Hurley Catherine V—†	78	secretary	34	"
	R	Hurley Margaret M—†	78	housewife	32	"
	T	Puzzo Lena—†	78	stitcher	32	178 Havre
	U	Puzzo Salvatore	78	carpenter	42	178 "
	V	Scudieri Frank	80	U S A	21	here
	W*	Scudieri Louise—†	80	housewife	56	"
	X*	Scudieri Vincenzo	80	retired	62	"
	Y*	Mondovano Rose—†	80	at home	54	"
	Z	Faldetta Carmela—†	80	housewife	45	"
523						
	A	Faldetta Eleanor—†	80	operator	22	"
	B	Faldetta Mary—†	80	bookkeeper	24	"
	C	Faldetta Salvatore	80	carpenter	50	"
	E	D'Addario Carmela—†	82	dressmaker	24	"
	F	D'Addario Carmen	82	U S A	21	"
	G*	D'Addario Julia—†	82	housewife	47	"
	H	D'Addario Salvatore	82	retired	54	"
	K	D'Addario Vincent	82	butcher	22	"
	L	Bertolini Anthony	82	U S A	21	28 Chelsea

11

Chelsea Street Continued

M	Bertolini Carlo	82	laborer	59	28 Chelsea
N	Bertolini Catherine—†	82	housewife	57	28 "
O	Bertolini Paul	82	U S A	31	28 "
R	Leonard Annie—†	84	housewife	49	Malden
S	Leonard Charles	84	laborer	51	"
T	Leonard Charles, jr	84	florist	21	"
U	Paone Aida J—†	84	housewife	26	here
V	Paone Armando H	84	merchant	26	"
W	*Vanni Aniceto S	84	plasterer	67	"
X	*Vanni Mary D—†	84	housewife	60	"
Y	Vanni Rennet M	84	U S A	20	"
Z	Vanni Walter E	84	plasterer	23	"
	524				
A	Volo Giacomo	84	presser	24	"
B	Volo Gilda—†	84	housewife	23	"
C	Grillo Giuseppe	86	retired	72	"
D	Maggio Marion—†	86	housewife	23	"
E	*Maggio Salvatore	86	barber	32	"
F	Schillaci Catherine—†	86	stitcher	27	"
G	Schillaci Giuseppina—†	86	"	20	"
H	Schillaci Maria—†	86	"	23	"
K	Schillaci Salvatore	86	welder	23	"
L	Schillaci Stefana—†	86	housewife	54	"
M	Schillaci Vincenzo	86	cabinetmaker	55	"
N	LaGrassa Lena—†	86	housewife	40	"
O	LaGrassa Vincenzo	86	laborer	51	"
R	Aloi Catino	88	machinist	29	7 Emmons
S	*Aloi Maria—†	88	housewife	55	here
T	*Samprone Catherine—†	88	"	45	"
U	*Samprone Frank	88	laborer	56	"
V	Samprone Joseph	88	U S A	22	"
W	Samprone Virginia—†	88	stitcher	21	"
X	Ippolito Josephine—†	88	housewife	24	"
Y	Ippolito Rocco	88	laborer	33	"
Z	Censeruli Ella—†	90	housewife	39	"
	525				
A	Censeruli Vincent	90	pipefitter	45	"
B	Basillio Anibale	90	bartender	58	"
C	Basillio Carmen	90	U S A	21	"
D	Basillio Josephine—†	90	housewife	48	"
E	Pugliese Mary—†	90	"	22	"

15

Page.	Letter.	FULL NAME.	Residence, Jan. 1, 1943.	Occupation.	Supposed Age.	Reported Residence, Jan. 1, 1942. Street and Number.

Chelsea Street—Continued

	F	Pugliese Sabatino	90	welder	24	here
	G	LaMattina James	92	U S N	20	11 Hanover av
	H	LaMattina Mary —†	92	stitcher	21	11 "
	K	LaMattina Rocco	92	laborer	59	11 "
	L*	LaMattina Vita —†	92	housewife	48	11 "
	M*	Pistone Maria —†	92	"	59	here
	N	Pistone Paul	92	retired	62	"
	O	Rosa Filomena—†	92	housewife	29	"
	P	Rosa Mario E	92	welder	32	"
	R	Nicolantonio Concenzio	94	laborer	62	"
	S	Nicolantonio Geneva—†	94	stitcher	25	"
	T	Nicolantonio Mary—†	94	"	21	"
	U	Nicolantonio Ralph	94	U S A	29	"
	V	Nicolantonio Romeo	94	"	23	"
	W	Parziale Carmen	94	metalworker	39	10 Lamson
	X*	Parziale Maria—†	94	housewife	35	10 "
	Y*	Fiorino Josephine—†	94	"	39	here
	Z	Fiorino Vincenzo	94	baker	44	"

526

	A*	DiPrimio Annie—†	96	housewife	53	"
	B	DiPrimio Antonio	96	laborer	50	"
	C	DiPrimio Dino	96	U S A	22	"
	D	DiPrimio Elvira—†	96	stitcher	20	"
	E*	Abbate Frances—†	96	housewife	42	"
	F	Abbate Louis	96	bricklayer	49	"
	G	Famiglietti Genaro P	96	mason	46	6 Chelsea pl
	H	Famiglietti Joseph	96	"	24	6 "
	K	Curzi Biagio	98	laborer	49	here
	L	Curzi Emilio	98	machinist	20	"
	M	Curzi Santa —†	98	housewife	43	"
	N	Oliva Carmen	98	salesman	50	"
	O*	Oliva Inez —†	98	housewife	33	"
	P	Oliva Vincent	98	metalworker	22	"
	R	DiMarino Josephine —†	102	housewife	29	"
	S	DiMarino Philip	102	electrician	30	"
	T*	Sena John	102	retired	74	"
	U*	Freni Mary—†	102	housewife	48	"
	V	Freni Pauline —†	102	stenographer	22	"
	W	Saia Mary —†	102	housewife	24	New Jersey
	X	Saia Michael A	102	chemist	29	"
	Y	Capuzzo Inez —†	102	housewife	34	here

16

Chelsea Street Continued

z	*Capuzzo Ubaldo	102	painter	39	here
527						
A	Cravotta Giuseppe	102	laborer	54	"
B	*Cravotta Maria †	102	housewife	42	"
C	Cravotta Phillip	102	U S A	20	"
D	*Melino Concetta †	102	housewife	52	"
E	*Melino Frank	102	laborer	58	"
F	Pisapia Caroline †	104	at home	21	"
G	*Pisapia Grace †	104	housewife	44	"
H	Pisapia Luigi	104	baker	48	"
K	Pisapia Ray	104	U S N	20	"
L	*Rodrigues Alice †	104	housewife	35	"
M	*Rodrigues Jose	104	engineer	39	"
N	Gomes Anthony	104	laborer	26	"
O	Gomes Julia †	104	housewife	24	"
P	Ricciardi James	104	chauffeur	34	"
R	Ricciardi Palma †	104	housewife	25	"
S	*Piazza Catherine †	104	"	42	"
T	Piazza Catherine †	104	at home	21	"
U	Piazza Joseph	104	laborer	49	"
V	Sforza Antonio	104	plumber	38	"
W	Sforza Elvira †	104	housewife	31	"
X	Minichiello Generoso	106	laborer	62	"
Y	*Minichiello Melia †	106	housewife	57	"
528						
A	Bartolo Concetta †	106	"	26	"
B	Bartolo Frank	106	laborer	25	"
C	*DiStolfo Antonetta †	106	at home	69	"
D	DiStolfo Jennie †	106	housewife	47	"
E	DiStolfo Leonard	106	laborer	49	"
F	Celesti Angelina †	106	housewife	24	"
G	Celesti Gaetano	106	tailor	28	"
H	*Torsi Adele †	106	housewife	72	"
K	Torsi John	106	machinist	37	"
L	Torsi Maria †	106	stitcher	33	"
M	*Torsi Peter	106	carpenter	69	"
N	Cardinale Calogera †	106	housewife	25	"
O	Cardinale Joseph	106	laborer	28	"
P	Vella Lucy †	108	housewife	25	"
R	Vella Salvatore	108	electrician	27	"
S	Saldi Margaret †	108	housewife	22	58 Chelsea

1—5

Chelsea Street—Continued

T	Saldi Salvatore	108	U S A	20	22 Decatur
U	LoDuca Alfonse	108	porter	33	here
V	LoDuca Lillian—†	108	housewife	37	"
W	*Balba Agripina—†	108	at home	55	"
X	*Balba Santa—†	108	stitcher	23	"
Y	Barone Christopher	108	painter	43	"
Z	Barone Mary—†	108	housewife	37	"

529

B	*Siciliano Filipa—†	110	"	53	10 Cheever ct
C	*Siciliano Rocco	110	retired	63	10 "
D	Latorroca Domenic	110	marbleworker	45	here
E	*Latorroca Enrichetta—†	110	housewife	45	"

Drake Place

H	*Addario Antonetta—†	1	housewife	63	here
K	Addario Margaret—†	1	clerk	21	"
L	Addario Nicolas	1	laborer	65	"
M	Serima Frank	1	tailor	29	"
N	Serima Helen—†	1	housewife	24	"
O	Capozzi Antonio	1	guard	56	"
R	Capozzi Concetta—†	1	housewife	54	"
P	Capozzi Pasquale	1	U S N	22	"
S	*Galati Catherine—†	1	housewife	58	"
T	*Galati Giuseppe	1	brakeman	53	"
U	*Jardin Julia—†	1	housewife	43	"
V	*Jardin Julio	1	weaver	42	"
W	*Lopilato Anthony	2	retired	83	"
X	Lopilato Emanuel	2	U S A	27	"
Y	*Lopilato Lena—†	2	housewife	57	"
Z	Lopilato Sebastian	2	laborer	62	"

530

A	Mirabella Emilio	2	"	41	"
B	Maggio Josephine—†	3	housewife	38	"
C	Maggio Nicholas	3	shipfitter	38	"
D	Avola Colegro	4	laborer	63	"
E	Avola Rose—†	4	housewife	46	"
F	Albanese Angelina—†	4	"	46	"
G	Albanese Guy	4	U S A	23	"
H	Albanese Joseph	4	U S C G	20	"
K	Albanese Mary C—†	4	stitcher	22	"

Page.	Letter.	FULL NAME.	Residence, Jan. 1, 1943.	Occupation.	Supposed Age.	Reported Residence, Jan. 1, 1942. Street and Number.

Drake Place—Continued

	L	Albanese Severino	4	laborer	48	here
	M	Dalosio Alfred	5	U S A	30	110 Benningt'n
	N	*Dalosio Angelina — †	5	housewife	62	110 "
	O	Dalosio Ernest	5	U S A	24	110 "
	P	Dalosio Gino	5	electrician	21	110 "
	R	*Dalosio Ralph	5	laborer	59	110 "
	S	Riccio Liugi	5	clerk	38	here
	T	Riccio Marie — †	5	housewife	30	"
	U	*DaLiusio Marie — †	6	"	57	"
	V	Barletta Ferdinand	6	laborer	42	"
	W	Barletta Rose — †	6	housewife	36	"
	X	Marzzola Anna — †	7	"	25	Revere
	Y	Marzzola Anthony	7	laborer	30	"
	Z	DeRuosi Angelo	7	salesman	22	here

531

	A	*DeRuosi Domenica — †	7	housewife	23	"
	B	DeRuosi Sylvester	7	brazier	47	"
	C	DiSousa Joseph	8	laborer	28	"
	D	*Grasso Emilio	8	"	53	"
	E	*Grasso Frabonia — †	8	housewife	53	"

Elbow Street

	F	*Salamone Lorenzo	2	retired	80	here
	G	*Salamone Maria C — †	2	housewife	76	"
	H	DeMarco Vincent	2	longshoreman	47	"
	K	Zeelen Helen A — †	2	housewife	26	389 Meridian
	L	Zeelen Robert L	2	longshoreman	29	389 "
	M	Bianchi Angelo	4	U S A	20	here
	N	*Bianchi Fidelia — †	4	housewife	49	"
	O	Bianchi Frank	4	U S A	21	"
	P	*Bianchi Michael	4	florist	60	"
	R	Buonopane Anthony	4	rigger	30	60 London
	S	Buonopane Margaret — †	4	housewife	27	60 "
	T	Iacobacci Peter	4	laborer	47	here
	U	*Iacobacci Winifred — †	4	housewife	47	"

Emmons Street

| | V | D'Agostino Anthony | 1 | tailor | 48 | here |
| | W | D'Agostino Virginia — † | 1 | housewife | 40 | " |

19

Emmons Street—Continued

Y*	Ianotti Pellegrino	3	compositor	50	here
X	Imperato Louis	3	salesman	33	"
Z	Visconte Michael J	5	painter	41	41 Orleans
532					
A	Visconte Mildred—†	5	housewife	38	41 "
B*	DePietro Elizabeth—†	7	at home	65	here
C	DePietro John	7	machinist	29	"
D	Gilleo Frances B—†	8	housewife	24	"
E	Gilleo Joseph F	8	fireman	25	"
F	Bucci Anna—†	8	housewife	58	"
G	Bucci James	8	pipefitter	57	"
H	Bucci Vincent	8	seaman	22	"
K	Sgroi John	8	laborer	35	"
L	Sgroi Rose—†	8	housewife	34	"
M	Williams Earl C	8	brazier	24	Beverly
N	Williams Mary—†	8	housewife	20	here
O	Angelo Frances—†	9	seamstress	24	14 Haynes
P	Angelo Gaetana—†	9	"	28	14 "
R*	Angelo James	9	retired	69	14 "
S*	Angelo Sara—†	9	housewife	59	14 "
T	Calabrese Alfred	9	clerk	38	here
U	Rosato Anthony	10	pipefitter	30	"
V	Rosato Josephine—†	10	housewife	29	"
W	Wilson Joseph	10	machinist	53	67 Chelsea
X	Wilson Lena—†	10	housewife	34	67 "
Y	Thirens Edith—†	10	"	37	here
Z	Thirens George	10	painter	47	"
533					
A	Messina Emma—†	10	supervisor	24	"
B	Messina Lucy—†	10	housewife	48	"
C	Messina Nicholas	10	janitor	51	"
D	Famigletti Anthony	11	U S A	20	"
E	Famigletti John	11	laborer	48	"
F	Famigletti Mary—†	11	housewife	37	"
G	Gallo Vincent	11	machinist	23	103 Porter
H*	Perez Carmela—†	11	housewife	50	103 "
K	Perez Manuel	11	longshoreman	50	103 "
L	Sorrentino Anthony	12	barber	26	here
M	Sorrentino Rose—†	12	housewife	24	"
N	Scanlon Anna—†	12	"	24	Winthrop
O	Scanlon James E	12	pipefitter	30	"

Emmons Street Continued

P	Scopa Albert	12	machinist	30	here
R	*Scopa Mary — †	12	housewife	30	"
S	Maggio Andrew	12	bartender	43	"
T	*Maggio Angelina †	12	housewife	77	"
U	*Liuzza Frances — †	12	"	41	"
V	Liuzza Leonardo	12	laborer	48	"
W	Liuzza Mary — †	12	clerk	24	"
X	*Liuzza Michael	12	shoeworker	62	"
Y	*Liuzza Sarah — †	12	housewife	56	"
Z	Nazzaro Anthony	12	U S A	28	"

534

A	Schraffa Vito	12	rigger	30	"
B	Tartaglini Mildred — †	12	packer	33	"
D	Vozzella Mary — †	12	housewife	39	"
C	Vozzella Ralph	12	printer	37	"
E	*Carnabuci Josie — †	13	at home	57	"
F	Carnabuci Joseph	13	barber	50	"
G	Carnabuci Josephine — †	13	housewife	35	"

Gove Street

K	*Carrillo Domenic	11	retired	65	here
L	*Carrillo Veneranda — †	11	housewife	50	"
O	*Cannatella Mary — †	21	"	54	"
P	*Cannatella Salvatore	21	pedler	53	"
R	Boudreau Antonetta †	21	housewife	27	"
S	Boudreau Herbert	21	laborer	30	"
T	*Ferrario John	25	baker	53	12 Henry
U	*Ferrario Louise — †	25	housewife	53	12 "
V	Disisto Anthony J	25	guard	51	here
W	*Disisto Jennie †	25	housewife	43	"
X	Columbo Frederick	25	mechanic	55	"
Y	*Columbo Rose †	25	housewife	50	"

535

A	DiDonato Albert	36	U S A	24	"
B	*DiDonato Carmella — †	36	housewife	57	"
C	DiDonato Joseph	36	painter	57	"
D	DiDonato Lucy — †	36	at home	22	"
E	DiDonato Margaret — †	36	saleswoman	23	"
F	Cioffi Esther †	36	housewife	31	127 Paris
G	Cioffi John	36	baker	29	127 "

Page.	Letter.	Full Name.	Residence, Jan. 1, 1943.	Occupation.	Supposed Age.	Reported Residence, Jan. 1, 1942. Street and Number.

Gove Street—Continued

	H	Mottola Agnes —†	36	housewife	31	56 Webster
	K	Mottola Joseph	36	painter	31	56 "
	L	Simmons Palmina—†	38	housewife	28	here
	M	*Bellino Antonietta—†	38	"	49	"
	N	*Bellino Paul	38	mason	69	"
	O	Bellino Salvatore M	38	chauffeur	28	"
	P	Degloria Joseph	38	mechanic	29	133 Orleans
	R	Degloria Margaret—†	38	housewife	24	133 "
	S	Capobianco Anthony	40	janitor	35	here
	T	Capobianco Josephine—†	40	housewife	32	"
	U	*Simonelli Jessie—†	40	"	32	"
	V	Simonelli Salvatore	40	shipfitter	32	"
	W	*Capobianco Jessie—†	40	housewife	58	"
	X	Capobianco Joseph	40	U S A	22	"
	Y	Capobianco Patsy	40	laborer	61	"
	Z	Capobianco Rose—†	40	at home	20	"

536

	B	Madden Joseph	42	pipefitter	38	"
	C	Madden Josephine —†	42	housewife	30	"
	D	Geralomo Josephine—†	42	"	33	"
	E	Geralomo Pasquale	42	chauffeur	36	"
	F	Anzalone Eleanor —†	43	attendant	27	74 Cottage
	G	Anzalone Pasquale	43	chauffeur	27	74 "
	H	Tutello Mary †	43	at home	64	74 "
	K	*Fuccillo Anne †	43	housewife	45	here
	L	Fuccillo Florence—†	43	clerk	20	"
	M	Fuccillo Lillian —†	43	stitcher	24	"
	N	Fuccillo Massimino	43	laborer	50	"
	O	Fuccillo Olympia R—†	43	entertainer	23	"
	P	D'apice Carmen	43	mechanic	40	"
	R	D'apice Edith †	43	stitcher	37	"
	S	Collura Rosario	44	laborer	68	"
	T	Collura Grace †	44	shoeworker	35	"
	U	Collura Vincent	44	painter	35	"
	V	Biancucci Anthony	44	laborer	30	"
	W	Biancucci Pauline—†	44	housewife	25	"
	X	*Rabba Concerta †	59	"	64	46 Cottage
	Y	*Rabba Mike	59	retired	75	46 "
	Z	*Waddingham Arthur	59	carpenter	37	83 Webster

537

	A	Waddingham Sadie—†	59	housewife	49	83 "

22

Gove Street Continued

B	Moscuzzo Josephine—†	59	housewife	30	here
C	*Giacinto Adriana—†	61	"	67	"
D	*Giacinto Manuel	61	fireman	50	"
E	Spinazzola Mary—†	61	stitcher	29	"
F	Spinazzola Patsy	61	barber	35	"
G	Salamoni Angelo	61	laborer	53	"
H	Salamoni Stella—†	61	stitcher	24	"
K	Salamoni Vincenza—†	61	housewife	50	"
M	Maienza Rocco	63	laborer	30	"
L	*Provenzona Joseph	63	"	49	"
N	Rizza Angela—†	63	housewife	67	"
O	Rizza Salvatore	63	laborer	67	"
P	Gimilaro Alice—†	63	housewife	41	"
R	*Gimilaro Peter	63	laborer	54	"
T	Drago Anna M—†	65	housewife	25	"
U	Drago William V	65	metalworker	25	"
V	DiMarzo Antonetta—†	65	housewife	28	"
W	DiMarzo Raymond	65	machinist	30	"

Havre Street

X	*Messina Jennie—†	110	housewife	42	here
Y	Messina Mariano	110	storekeeper	52	"
Z	*Petronio Catherine—†	112	housewife	72	"
538					
A	*Petronio Gregorio	112	shoemaker	78	"
B	DeLuca Anthony	112	chauffeur	29	77 Chelsea
C	DeLuca Dorothy—†	112	housewife	27	77 "
D	Antelmi Frances—†	112	"	31	here
E	Antelmi Frederick	112	salesman	31	"
F	Nigri Arminio	113	laborer	49	"
G	Nigri Carmella—†	113	housewife	44	"
H	Nigri Concetta—†	113	clerk	21	"
K	Giordano Angelo	113	shoemaker	32	227 Chelsea
L	Giordano Josephine—†	113	housewife	28	227 "
M	Lacorazza Carmella—†	113	"	25	here
N	Lacorazza Daniel	113	mechanic	26	"
O	Terlino Constantino	rear 113	"	29	"
P	Terlino Mary—†	" 113	housewife	27	"
R	*DeLorenzo Frank	" 113	laborer	39	"
S	DeLorenzo Sarah—†	" 113	housewife	34	"

Havre Street Continued

	Letter	Full Name	Res.	Occupation	Age	Reported Residence
	T	Lussier Nora A—†	114	clerk	34	here
	U	Wellings Francis J	114	dispenser	73	"
	V	Wellings Nora A—†	114	housewife	73	"
	W	MacDonald James S	115	carpenter	64	"
	X	*Tomasello Josephine—†	115	housewife	50	"
	Y	Tomasello Luigi	115	laborer	58	"
	Z	Tomasello Sarah—†	115	dressmaker	25	"
539						
	A	Lalicata Angelo	115	laborer	54	"
	B	*Lalicata Concetta—†	115	housewife	56	"
	C	Lalicata Gaetano	115	U S A	21	"
	D	*Palermo Mary—† 1st r	115	housewife	41	"
	E	*Palermo Salvatore 1st "	115	laborer	53	"
	F	Testa Mary—† 1st "	115	housewife	48	"
	G	Tasca Calogero 1st "	115	laborer	47	"
	H	Tasca Maria—† 1st "	115	factoryhand	26	"
	K	Tasca Nancy—† 1st "	115	housewife	59	"
	L	*Rindone Maria—† 2d "	115	"	80	"
	M	DiMarzo Joseph 2d "	115	shipper	30	"
	N	DiMarzo Margaret—† 2d "	115	housewife	27	"
	O	Melio Andrew 2d "	115	laborer	57	"
	P	*Melio Carmella—† 2d "	115	housewife	47	"
	R	Lynch Jessie B—†	116	"	56	"
	S	Lynch Robert M	116	mechanic	20	"
	T	Lynch William C	116	U S A	24	"
	U	Murphy Frederick J	116	laborer	50	"
	V	Giordano Caroline—†	117	housewife	69	"
	W	Giordano Phillip	117	retired	74	"
	X	Caprera Grace—†	117	factoryhand	20	"
	Y	Caprera Josephine—†	117	"	21	"
	Z	*Caprera Mario	117	laborer	51	"
540						
	A	*Caprera Mary—†	117	housewife	40	"
	B	Lalicata Salvatore F	117	salesman	26	"
	C	Lalicata Santa—†	117	housewife	29	"
	D	*Renda Angela—†	117	"	59	"
	E	Miles Frederick E	118	chauffeur	42	"
	F	Miles Josephine—†	118	housewife	37	"
	G	Miles Stephen	118	retired	77	"
	H	Miles Stephen H	118	laborer	51	"
	K	Sorrento Frank	119	"	20	347 Border

Havre Street — Continued

	L	Sorrento Fred	119	laborer	57	347 Border
	M	*Sorrento Gaetana —†	119	housewife	45	347 "
	N	Bruno Mary —†	119	"	51	here
	O	Bruno Netta —†	119	clerk	31	"
	P	Bruno Nicholas	119	candymaker	57	"
	R	Bruno Michael	119	retired	65	"
	S	Bruno Rose —†	119	clerk	35	"
	T	Pargoli Michael	120	storekeeper	49	"
	U	Camerlengo Alphonse	120	mechanic	38	"
	V	Camerlengo Clementina—†	120	housewife	36	"
	W	Dicarolis Amato	120	laborer	60	"
	X	Dicarolis Ralph	120	U S A	20	"
	Y	Pastore Anna—†	120	housewife	27	"
	Z	Freda Margaret—†	121	"	25	82 Bremen
541						
	A	Freda Pasquale	121	laborer	27	82 "
	B	Stocco Charles	121	electrician	41	here
	C	Stocco Concetta—†	121	housewife	35	"
	D	Acone Mary—†	121	"	22	"
	E	Acone Modestino	121	U S N	21	88 Webster
	F	*Camerlengo Angela—†	121	housewife	63	here
	G	Camerlengo Arthur	121	U S N	20	"
	H	Camerlengo Benjamin	121	longshoreman	42	"
	K	Delsie Clara—†	122	operator	23	"
	L	Fera Lucy—†	122	housewife	30	"
	M	Fera Martin	122	laborer	31	"
	N	Hanafin Mildred—†	122	housewife	24	40 Decatur
	O	Hanafin William	122	laborer	39	40 "
	P	*Petagna Romualdo	122	"	37	40 "
	R	DiPerri Louise—†	122	housewife	21	347 Princeton
	S	DiPerri Salvatore	122	presser	23	21 Battery
	T	*Giordano Antonio	126	laborer	58	here
	U	Giordano Pasquale	126	U S A	21	"
	V	Giordano Victoria—†	126	housewife	22	Everett
	W	Gambardella Theresa—†	126	"	30	114 Cottage
	X	Gambardella Vincent	126	laborer	31	114 "
	Y	Puglia Albert	126	U S A	29	209 London
	Z	Puglia Barbarino	126	laborer	59	209 "
542						
	A	*Puglia Louise—†	126	housewife	57	209 "
	B	Puglia Mario	126	musician	30	209 "

Havre Street—Continued

c	Puglia Santa—†	126	clerk	23	209 London
E	Lopresti Adeline—†	128	housewife	28	here
F	Lopresti Anthony	128	podiatrist	29	"
G	LaMonica Clara—†	128	housewife	24	54 Porter
H	LaMonica Phillip	128	laborer	29	54 "
K	*Lopresti Frances—†	128	housewife	53	here
L	Lopresti Frank	128	barber	67	"
M	Lopresti Lillian—†	128	dressmaker	33	"
N	*Motica Angelina—†	131	housewife	83	"
O	*Motica Joseph	131	laborer	65	"
P	Motica Ella—†	131	housewife	34	"
R	Motica Joseph	131	painter	40	"
S	*Langone Annetta—†	131	housewife	66	154 Bremen
T	Langone Gerardo	131	laborer	24	154 "
U	Seracusa Alice—†	132	housewife	27	here
V	Seracusa Joseph	132	laborer	27	"
W	Spina Luciano	132	welder	22	134 Havre
X	Spina Maria R—†	132	housewife	22	312 Princeton
Y	Pasucci Anthony	132	U S A	21	here
Z	Pasucci Joseph	132	laborer	46	"

543

A	*Pasucci Olimpia—†	132	housewife	46	"
B	DeRuosi Joseph	133	clerk	27	1 Saratoga pl
C	DeRuosi Mary—†	133	housewife	26	1 "
D	Barber Maria—†	133	"	36	here
E	*Caruso Catherine—†	133	"	50	"
F	*Caruso Natale	133	laborer	55	"
G	Caruso Rose—†	133	clerk	21	"
H	DeCarlo Elizabeth—†	134	housewife	47	"
K	Bard Sylvia—†	134	"	24	"
L	Bard Thomas D	134	longshoreman	27	"
M	Spina Angelo	134	U S A	25	"
N	Spina Caroline—†	134	housewife	49	"
O	Spina Gaetano	134	salesman	53	"
P	Scarpelli Henry	135	clerk	22	"
R	Scarpelli Mary—†	135	housewife	42	"
S	Lewis Alice—†	135	factoryhand	22	"
T	Lewis Arthur	135	cook	44	"
U	Lewis Josephine—†	135	housewife	43	"
X	*DiPerri Palma—†	135	"	60	230 Havre
Y	*DiPerri Salvatore	135	laborer	62	230 "

Havre Street— Continued

	w	DiPerri Salvatore	135	U S A	28	230 Havre
	y	Mancuso Concetta—†	136	housewife	21	here
	z	Mancuso Frederick	136	laborer	23	"
544						
	A	Mancusso Anthony	136	U S C G	20	"
	B	Mancuso Gabriel	136	U S A	24	"
	c	Mancuso Mary—†	136	housewife	43	"
	D	Mancuso Salvatore	136	shoemaker	54	"
	E	Marciello Domenic	136	laborer	27	35 Decatur
	F	Marciello Grace—†	136	housewife	24	35 "
	G	Arcara Nellie—†	137	"	39	here
	H	Arcara Pasquale	137	tailor	49	"
	K	Pasqualino Angelo	137	laborer	57	"
	L	*Pasqualino Frances—†	137	housewife	50	"
	M	*Salaggo Filippa—†	137	"	78	"
	N	Salaggo Leo	137	candymaker	43	"
	o	Tedesco Amalia—†	138	housewife	33	"
	P	Tedesco Anthony	138	shoemaker	42	"
	R	*Tedesco Joseph	138	laborer	65	"
	s	Kanelakos Arthur	138	storekeeper	54	"
	T	Kanelakos George	138	"	52	"
	U	DeAngelo Margaret—†	138	housewife	24	"
	v	DeAngelo Pasquale	138	shoemaker	29	"
	w	Uva Helen—†	139	housewife	25	119 Trenton
	x	Uva Peter	139	shoemaker	25	119 "
	y	*Chiango Augustino	139	laborer	67	here
	z	Chiango Augustino	139	factoryhand	24	"
545						
	A	Chiango Helen—†	139	housewife	20	Chelsea
	B	*Chiango Jennie—†	139	"	67	here
	c	Mulcahy Albert B	139	carpenter	28	2 Savage ct
	D	Mulcahy Mary—†	139	housewife	23	2 "
	E	Iacovino Frank	140	mechanic	43	here
	F	Iacovino Josephine—†	140	housewife	35	"
	G	Scorzello Joseph	140	laborer	27	107 Lexington
	H	Scorzello Maria—†	140	housewife	22	145 Chelsea
	K	Pitari Agrippina—†	141	"	48	here
	L	Pitari Agrippino	141	clerk	50	"
	M	Cavagnaro Joseph	141	welder	33	"
	N	Cavagnaro Maria—†	141	housewife	26	"
	o	Scaduto Agrippina—†	141	"	29	"

Page.	Letter.	Full Name.	Residence, Jan. 1, 1943.	Occupation.	Supposed Age.	Reported Residence, Jan. 1, 1942. Street and Number.

Havre Street—Continued

	P	Scaduto Salvatore	141	rigger	33	here
	R	*DelVento Incoronata—†	142	housewife	42	"
	S	DelVento Nicola	142	laborer	52	"
	T	*Grasso Angelina—†	142	housewife	47	"
	U	Grasso Carmen	142	laborer	20	"
	V	*Grasso Felix	142	barber	58	"
	W	Valiante George	143	laborer	34	"
	X	Valiante Nina—†	143	housewife	29	"
	Y	Velloni Ernest	143	shipper	40	"
	Z	Velloni Mary—†	143	housewife	35	"

546

	A	*Giannino Lucy—†	143	stitcher	38	"
	B	*Prato Mary—†	143	"	51	"
	C	*Cataldo Mary—†	144	housewife	59	"
	D	Norcia May—†	144	stitcher	30	"
	E	Norcia Ralph	144	mechanic	49	"
	F	Norcia Sylvio	144	laborer	41	"
	G	Coco Joseph	145	shoemaker	57	"
	H	Coco Mary—†	145	housewife	35	"
	K	DeSimone Josephine—†	145	"	27	"
	L	DeSimone Paul	145	welder	29	"
	M	Coco Helen—†	145	factoryhand	25	"
	N	Coco Mary—†	145	at home	22	"
	O	Coco Salvatore	145	U S N	20	"
	P	Saldi Angelo	147	rigger	22	"
	R	Saldi Mary—†	147	housewife	21	"
	S	*LaRosa Anthony	147	factoryhand	45	"
	T	*LaRosa Grace—†	147	housewife	32	"
	U	*Cali Rose—†	147	"	42	"
	V	Cali Vincent	147	dishwasher	45	"
	W	Carrafiello Mary—†	148	housewife	47	Everett
	X	Briana Caroline—†	148	"	47	here
	Y	Briana William	148	operator	50	"
	Z	Recupero Carmen	149	laborer	21	"

547

	A	*Recupero Frank	149	"	56	"
	B	*Recupero Lora—†	149	housewife	59	"
	C	Recupero Matilda—†	149	"	22	"
	D	*Bando Antonetta—†	149	"	58	"
	E	Bando Frank T	149	shoemaker	45	"
	F	Miccio Antonetta—†	149	housewife	50	"

28

Havre Street Continued

G	Miscio Filomena †	149	factoryhand	28	here
H	*Miscio Michael	149	laborer	56	"
K	Storniacolo Louise †	153	housewife	24	"
L	Storniacolo Pasquale	153	foreman	28	"
M	*Cucinotta Mary †	153	housewife	58	11 Winthrop
N	MacDougall Sally †	153	"	29	11 "
O	Iozzo Joseph	153	laborer	28	here
P	Iozzo Mary †	153	housewife	23	"
R	Meloni Fred	155	mechanic	30	"
S	Meloni Phyllis †	155	housewife	32	"
T	Santora Arthur	155	chauffeur	29	"
U	Santora Gilda †	155	housewife	31	"
V	Capone Anthony	155	chauffeur	37	"
W	Capone Mary †	155	housewife	38	"
X	Ferraro Jennie †	157	"	22	128 Chelsea
Y	Ferraro Nunzio	157	carpenter	28	128 "
Z	*Volletta Frank	157	laborer	54	here

548

A	*Volletta Maria †	157	housewife	55	"
B	*Pucillo Vincenzo	157	laborer	57	"
C	*Zaccaria Maria G †	157	housewife	53	"
D	Bremner Jennie †	159	"	22	"
E	Bremner William	159	merchant	22	"
G	DeStefano Joseph	159	mechanic	54	"
H	*DeStefano Leboria †	159	housewife	44	"
K	Villani Anna †	161	"	24	87 Everett
L	Villani Domenic	161	pipefitter	35	87 "
M	Villani Maria †	161	housewife	54	87 "
N	Bucchera Angelo	161	U S A	22	here
O	Gallo Pauline †	161	housewife	48	"
P	Gallo Sebastiano	161	mason	49	"
R	Viola Joseph	161	candymaker	35	"
S	Viola Phyllis †	161	housewife	29	"

London Street

U	Burk Gladys †	119	clerk	38	here
V	Burk Irving	119	salesman	39	"
W	Golden Edward	119	electrician	46	"
X	Golden Estelle †	119	housewife	42	"
Y	Baudanza Emanuel	119	chef	57	"

Page.	Letter	FULL NAME.	Residence, Jan. 1, 1943	Occupation.	Supposed Age.	Reported Residence, Jan. 1, 1942.
						Street and Number.

London Street—Continued

z	Baudanza Mary—†	119	housewife	31	here	
549						
c	Montalto Camille	125	machinist	31	"	
d	Montalto Jennie—†	125	operator	25	"	
e	Donnelly Julia—†	125	housewife	50	"	
f	Donnelly William	125	engineer	60	"	
g	Monaco Americo	125	seaman	28	"	
h	Monaco Frances—†	125	housewife	30	"	
k	*Frank Ada—†	127	at home	67	"	
l	*Frank Harry	127	retired	75	"	
m	Frank Marion—†	127	secretary	26	"	
n	Frank David	127	salesman	45	"	
o	Frank Lena—†	127	housewife	40	"	
p	Carnabuci Dora—†	127	"	24	381 Meridian	
r	Carnabuci Leo	127	clerk	25	381 "	
t	DeRocco Concetta—†	131	housewife	37	here	
u	DeRocco Gaetano	131	foreman	41	"	
v	DeRocco Mary—†	131	housewife	39	"	
w	DeRocco Peter	131	carpenter	43	"	
y	Martinelli Henry	131	clerk	47	101 Meridian	
x	Martinelli Joseph	131	U S A	20	101 "	
z	*Martinelli Margaret—†	131	housewife	45	101 "	
550						
a	Field Ellen A—†	133	at home	75	here	
b	Doyle Susan—†	133	housekeeper	55	"	
c	McGrane Thomas J. jr	133	pipefitter	48	"	
d	Zuffante Anna—†	133	housewife	20	"	
e	Scott Agnes—†	133	"	38	"	
f	Scott Rufus W	133	chauffeur	51	"	
g	Scott William J	133	U S A	22	"	
h	Callahan Laura—†	135	candyworker	65	"	
k	Dooley Catherine L—†	135	at home	73	"	
m	McDonough Catherine—†	135	"	77	"	
l	Morris Annie—†	135	"	77	"	
n	White Ellen C—†	135	housewife	34	"	
o	White John T	135	bookkeeper	33	"	
p	Ramirez Lillian—†	137	dressmaker	48	"	
r	Ramirez Mary—†	137	at home	26	"	
s	Ramirez Rosario	137	finisher	56	"	
u	*Reitano Jennie—†	137	at home	75	"	
t	Reitano Pauline—†	137	bookkeeper	34	"	

London Street – Continued

v	Bourgoin Arthur	137	seaman	39	here
w	*Bourgoin Emma — †	137	housewife	44	"
x	DePaolo Margaret — †	137	"	28	"
y	DePaolo Pasquale	137	shipfitter	30	"
z	Livolsi Andrew J	139	barber	47	"

551

A	Livolsi Frances — †	139	examiner	20	"
F	Livolsi Josephine — †	139	housewife	43	"
B	Anastasio Anna — †	139	at home	23	"
C	Anastasio Theresa — †	139	dressmaker	45	"
D	Anastasio Vincent	139	laborer	46	"
E	*Anastasio Sebastiana — †	139	at home	71	"
G	DePaula Joseph	139	chauffeur	43	"
H	DePaula Mary — †	139	finisher	39	"
K	McCarthy Catherine — †	141	housewife	62	"
M	McCarthy Richard	141	U S A	34	"
L	McCarthy Simon	141	retired	71	"
N	Troy Rose H — †	141	matron	66	"
O	Maloney Ella — †	141	housewife	75	"
P	Maloney John	141	retired	74	"
R	*LaSala Bridget — †	143	shoeworker	22	"
S	LaSala Louis	143	waiter	52	"
T	*Cennamo Gaetana — †	143	at home	50	"
U	Cennamo Ida — †	143	shoeworker	22	"
V	Cennamo Mary — †	143	"	26	"
W	*Cennamo Salvatore	143	"	57	"
X	Iannaccone Mary — †	143	housewife	39	"
Y	Iannaccone Michael	143	candymaker	47	"

552   Maverick Street

G	Amato Peter	146	carpenter	44	here
H	Freeze Harry	146	mechanic	45	"
K	Napolitano Achilles	146	shoemaker	44	"
L	Ratti Ugo	146	chef	45	"
N	Previte Catherine — †	148	beautician	22	"
O	*Previte Grazia — †	148	housewife	49	"
P	Previte Jeanette — †	148	stenographer	20	"
R	Previte John J	148	storekeeper	53	"
S	Previte Joseph J	148	U S A	25	"
T	Previte Matthew	148	accountant	27	"

Meridian Street

X	Packard Elma A—†	1A	proprietor	67	here	
W	Tubin Bessie—†	1A	storekeeper	50	"	

553

K	Graves John F	11	mortician	53	"
L	Wright Christina—†	11	housewife	52	"
M	Wright Christina—†	11	at home	23	"
N	Wright John F	11	clerk	54	"
O	Beaton Lillian—†	11	housewife	24	"
P	Beaton Melvin	11	U S A	25	"
R*	Curran Katherine—†	11	factoryhand	52	"
T	Raimo Anthony	13A	clerk	56	"
U	Raimo Anthony, jr	13A	baker	20	"
V	Raimo Mary—†	13A	housewife	50	"
W	Fiscione Jerry	13A	butcher	22	"
X	Fiscione Josephine—†	13A	housewife	26	"

554

A	Samuels Philip	20	attorney	61	"
F*	Forrest Jennie—†	49	housewife	74	"
G	Forrest John J	49	retired	83	"
H	Sullivan Mary C—†	49	operator	42	"
K	Dumas Godfrey	49	factoryhand	40	"
M	Morin Joseph F	49	shipfitter	49	"
L	Morin Vitalina—†	49	waitress	47	"
W	Sullivan John P	65	engineer	52	"
X*	Sullivan Mary—†	65	housekeeper	42	"
Y	Akerberg Chester E	65	clerk	34	"
Z*	Akerberg Mary—†	65	housewife	35	"

555

B	Kokoska Anthony	67	mechanic	24	"
C	Kokoska Mary—†	67	housewife	21	"
E	Honsepian Harry	71	laborer	42	"
F	O'Neil Olive M—†	71	housewife	41	"
K	O'Leary Daniel V	77	painter	24	"
L	O'Leary Hanna—†	77	domestic	57	"
M	O'Leary Mildred R—†	77	housewife	20	449 Frankfort
N	O'Leary Timothy F	77	U S A	22	here
O	Maher Ann—†	77	housewife	62	"
P	Maher Daniel J	77	fisherman	59	"
R	Maher William F	77	U S A	23	"
T	Trocano Domenic	77	laborer	44	51 Saratoga
S*	Trocano Grace—†	77	housewife	45	51 "

556

Meridian Street Continued

A	Powers James	95	laborer	59	51 Havre
B	Powers Loretta—†	95	housekeeper	30	51 "
C	Powers William	95	clerk	32	51 "
D	*Rodgers John	95	longshoreman	66	here
E	Rodgers Michael	95	"	29	"
F	Fracasso Frank	97	tailor	40	"
G	Howard Fred	97	chef	63	"
H	*Hunter James	97	retired	66	"
K	Mothola Antonio	97	laborer	25	113 Orleans
L	Piveth Gennaro	97	"	36	Chelsea
P	Hogan Daniel	103	longshoreman	49	51 Havre
R	Maloney Margaret—†	103	housekeeper	43	here
S	Maloney Thomas H	103	carpenter	51	"
U	Riley Melvin	107	riveter	28	26 Paris
V	*Thibeau Paul	107	retired	74	26 "
X	Allen Fred	109	chef	56	11 Addison
Y	Amirault Reuben	109	cutter	56	here
Z	Cave Frances—†	109	housewife	22	Louisiana

557

A	Cave Thomas	109	machinist	32	"
B	Cunningham John J	109	laborer	53	here
C	Giamposa Alphonso	109	shoeworker	40	5 Winthrop
D	Jensen Carl	109	machinist	40	124 London
E	McPhee John	109	pipefitter	44	371 Meridian
F	Miller Richard	109	machinist	56	11 Addison
G	Newell Frank	109	pipefitter	46	116 Havre
H	Pepe Antonio	109	laborer	62	19 Saratoga
L	*Maloney Christina M—†	111	housewife	33	here
M	Maloney Patrick M	111	fisherman	31	"
N	Witter Andrew E	111	baker	30	"
O	Witter Nellie—†	111	housewife	27	"
P	Usher David N	111	engineer	41	Georgia
R	Usher Hazel G—†	111	housewife	36	"

Model Place

V	*Guaracino Vincent	3	laborer	64	here
Y	*Ventresca Domenic	4	"	65	Somerville
X	Hitchcock John	4	"	49	230 Havre
Z	*Woodger Susan—†	4	at home	49	230 "

1—5   33

Page.	Letter.	FULL NAME.	Residence, Jan. 1, 1943.	Occupation.	Supposed Age.	Reported Residence, Jan. 1, 1942. Street and Number.

558

Paris Court

	A	Dodge Marguerite—†	2	housewife	48	here
	B	Sawyer Marie—†	2	"	39	"
	C	Sawyer Walter	2	clerk	40	"
	D	*Bracali Vincenzo	4	retired	91	"

Paris Place

	H	*Barile Biagio	1	retired	63	here
	G	*Farago Antonio	1	laborer	44	"
	K	Pimento Mary—†	1	seamstress	65	"
	N	Goodwin Eva—†	3	housewife	57	"
	O	Kennedy Anna—†	3	"	21	"
	P	Young Jennie—†	3	"	62	"
	R	Young Robert	3	U S A	20	"
	S	Cangiamila Calogero	5	retired	74	4 Model pl
	T	D'India Angelo	5	machinist	33	7 Paris pl
	U	D'India Mildred—†	5	housewife	30	7 "
	V	Platt Mary M—†	5	at home	64	here
	W	Lunetta Salvatore	6	retired	76	"
	X	*Gulino Salvatore	6	"	80	"
	Y	*Foschi Anna—†	6	at home	60	"
	Z	Molfesis Constantino	6	machinist	44	"

559

	A	Feolo Charlotte—†	7	housewife	46	"
	B	*Feolo Frank	7	retired	66	"
	C	*Shephard Robert	7	carpenter	62	"
	D	Usher Mary—†	7	at home	44	Middleboro

Paris Street

	G	Perez Clara—†	78	housewife	23	here
	H	Perez Donald R	78	longshoreman	23	"
	K	Allotti Angelina—†	78	housewife	52	"
	L	Allotti Joseph	78	storekeeper	65	"
	R	Ciampa Alfonse	83	welder	28	"
	S	Ciampa Lucy—†	83	housewife	26	"
	T	*DeStefano Angelina—†	83	"	50	"
	U	*DeStefano John	83	laborer	49	"
	V	DeStefano Louise—†	83	inspector	22	"
	W	DeStefano Tino	83	U S A	20	"

Page.	Letter.	FULL NAME.	Residence, Jan. 1, 1943.	Occupation.	Supposed Age.	Reported Residence, Jan. 1, 1942. Street and Number.

Paris Street—Continued

x	*DeFazio Antonette—†	83	housewife	41	here	
y	Napoleon Nicholas	84	painter	51	42 Maverick	
z	*DeCrescenzio Mary—†	84	housewife	42	158 Chelsea	
560						
A	DeCrescenzio Saverio	84	laborer	58	158 "	
B	Twersky Naomi—†	85	housewife	28	here	
C	Twersky Samuel	85	clergyman	31	"	
E	Faldetta Gerlando	87	welder	21		
F	Faldetta Palma—†	87	housewife	20	230 Havre	
G	Faldetta Edwardo	87	oiler	56	here	
H	Faldetta Grace—†	87	stitcher	23	"	
K	*Faldetta Maria—†	87	housewife	49	"	
L	Riley Mary A—†	87	candymaker	66	"	
M	Bernardinelli Nellie—†	98	housewife	39	"	
N	Bernardinelli Pasquale	98	machinist	43	"	
O	Reppucci Angelina—†	98	housewife	61	"	
P	Reppucci Herbert	98	U S A	28	"	
R	Reppucci Joseph	98	candymaker	62	"	
S	Reppucci Lydia—†	98	at home	89	"	
T	Reppucci Lydia—†	98	teacher	30	"	
U	Reppucci Michael	98	candymaker	60	"	
V	Russo Lena—†	98	housewife	34	"	
W	Russo Sebastian	98	chauffeur	37	"	
X	Catinazzo Adelaide—†	100	stitcher	23	"	
Y	Catinazzo Josephine—†	100	shoeworker	28	"	
Z	Catinazzo Mafalda—†	100	at home	21	"	
561						
A	*Catinazzo Nicholas	100	laborer	58	"	
B	Perra Frances—†	100	housewife	33	108 Paris	
C	Perra John	100	proprietor	40	108 "	
D	Fewer James J	100	machinist	55	here	
E	Fewer Mary—†	100	housewife	50	"	
F	Barrasso Anthony	102	U S A	20	"	
G	Barrasso Frank	102	cleaner	53	"	
H	Barrasso Manuela—†	102	housewife	48	"	
K	Barrasso Michael	102	cleaner	22	"	
L	Barrasso Rosario	102	shipper	24	"	
M	Ciaburri Carmella—†	102	stitcher	47	"	
N	Ciaburri Mary—†	102	dressmaker	24	"	
O	Ciaburri Ralph	102	glazier	50	"	
P	Ciaburri Rose—†	102	dressmaker	22	"	

Paris Street—Continued

		FULL NAME.	Res.	Occupation.	Age	Reported Residence
	R	*Bellone Fannie—†	102	housewife	48	here
	S	Bellone Fannie—†	102	stitcher	21	"
	T	Bellone Joseph	102	laborer	57	"
	U	Savoia Frank	104	shipfitter	37	"
	V	Savoia Miranda—†	104	housewife	33	"
	W	Dell'Orfano Luigi	104	blacksmith	60	"
	X	Dell'Orfano Maria—†	104	housewife	58	"
	Y	Petzke Henry	104	carpenter	30	54 Neptune rd
	Z	Petzke Hilda—†	104	housewife	29	54 "
562						
	A	*Vozella Nancy—†	106	saleswoman	25	137A Paris
	B	Vozella Theodore	106	carpenter	26	here
	C	Minichello Antonette—†	106	housewife	46	"
	D	Minichello Nunziato	106	longshoreman	52	"
	E	Vozella Anthony	106	U S N	20	"
	F	Vozella Joseph	106	"	24	"
	G	Zappulla Salvatore	106	printer	29	"
	H	Zappulla Viola—†	106	housewife	26	"
	K	Bisieglia Albert	108	U S A	29	54 Neptune rd
	L	Bisieglia Eva—†	108	manicurist	24	54 "
	M	Dell'Orfano Evelyn—†	108	stitcher	29	54 "
	N	Abbate Albert	108	shoemaker	28	here
	O	Abbate Enes—†	108	stitcher	20	"
	P	*Abbate Esther—†	108	housewife	52	"
	R	Abbate Fred	108	U S A	23	"
	S	Abbate Ida—†	108	stitcher	25	"
	T	*Abbate Joseph	108	barber	59	"
	U	Ferrante Charles	108	retired	47	"
	V	Ferrante Filomena—†	108	housewife	39	"
	W	Ferrante Marie—†	108	operator	21	"
	X	*Finocchio Anna—†	110	housewife	50	"
	Y	Finocchio Anthony	110	rigger	27	"
	Z	Finocchio Assunta—†	110	stitcher	21	"
563						
	A	Morabito Domenic	110	cutter	53	"
	B	Morabito Matilda—†	110	typist	23	"
	C	Morabito Michael	110	U S A	21	"
	D	Morabito Rose—†	110	housewife	47	"
	E	Morabito Sadie—†	110	at home	28	"
	F	Covino Anthony	110	painter	37	"
	G	Covino Rose—†	110	housewife	31	"

Paris Street Continued

k	Amato Mary †	127	housewife	30	here
l	Amato Salvatore	127	letter carrier	46	"
m	Marino Rose †	127	houseworker	39	"
n	Morelli Antonio	127	laborer	50	187 Princeton
o	*Rizzo Gaspar	127	butcher	45	86 Meridian
p	Gagnon Josephine †	127	saleswoman	26	here
r	Rotondo Concetta †	127		29	"
u	Rotondo Francesco	127	U S A	24	"
v	Rotondo Mary †	127	housewife	56	"
s	Rotondo Philip	127	chauffeur	59	"
t	Rotondo Philip A	127	U S A	22	"
w	Rotondo Salvatore	127	laborer	31	"
x	*Loduca Charles	rear 127	plasterer	64	"
y	Loduca Giuseppe	" 127	"	29	"
z	Amato Albina †	" 127	housewife	44	"
	564				
a	Amato Andrew	" 127	bookbinder	49	"
c	Gravallese Ida †	132	housewife	26	"
d	Gravallese John	132	chauffeur	28	"
e	Barrasso Eleanor †	132	dressmaker	24	"
f	Barrasso Louise C †	132	ropemaker	25	"
g	Barrasso Lucy †	132	housewife	53	"
h	Barrasso Mary †	132	dressmaker	25	"
k	Barrasso Thomas	132	shoeworker	54	"
l	Phillips Bessie †	132	housewife	52	"
m	Phillips Stanley D	132	salesman	21	"
n	Giordano Concetta †	133	housewife	21	"
o	Giordano Salvatore	133	shipfitter	25	"
p	Giordano Charles	133	laborer	55	"
r	Giordano Jennie †	133	packer	27	"
s	*Giordano Mary †	133	housewife	50	"
u	Megna Joseph	133	chauffeur	28	"
v	Megna Rose †	133	housewife	27	"
t	Bottilieri Mary †	133	finisher	58	"
w	Rotondo Caroline †	134	housewife	32	"
x	Rotondo Michael	134	barber	33	"
y	Guarino Louis	134	laborer	22	"
z	Guarino Maria †	134	housewife	58	"
	565				
a	Guarino Nicola †	134	"	67	"
b	Dana James	134	laborer	31	"

37

Page.	Letter.	FULL NAME.	Residence, Jan. 1, 1943.	Occupation.	Supposed Age.	Reported Residence, Jan. 1, 1942. Street and Number.

Paris Street Continued

	c	Dana Josephine—†	134	housewife	25	here
	D	Martorana John	135	cutter	26	"
	E	Martorana Susie—†	135	housewife	23	"
	F	Megna John	135	chauffeur	36	"
	G	Megna Lena—†	135	housewife	34	"
	H	Megna Anthony	135	U S M C	21	"
	K	Megna Antonio	135	barber	54	"
	L	Megna Mildred—†	135	housewife	34	"
	M	Vella Giuseppe	136	retired	71	85 Chelsea
	N	Vella Giuseppa—†	136	housewife	58	85 "
	O	Vella Joseph	136	U S A	32	85 "
	P	Vella Louis	136	shipworker	30	85 "
	R	Umbrello Domenic	136	laborer	48	here
	S	Umbrello Emma—†	136	housewife	41	"
	T	Antonucci Aladino	136	operator	25	"
	U	Antonucci Giacomo	136	tailor	48	"
	V	*Antonucci Louisa—†	136	"	46	"
	W	Chiarini Anna—†	136	at home	22	"
	X	LaSala Henry	137	barber	41	"
	Y	LaSala Mary—†	137	housewife	40	"
	Z	Spitaleri Concetta—†	137	packer	26	"

566

	A	*Spitaleri Nancy—†	137	at home	62	"
	B	*Barrasso Mary—†	137	"	43	"
	C	Barrasso Nicholas	137	U S A	20	"
	D	Barrasso Rose—†	137	dressmaker	21	"
	E	*DePalmo Theresa—†	137A	at home	76	"
	F	Vasapolli Joseph	137A	mattressmaker	50	"
	G	*Vasapolli Mary—†	137A	housewife	39	"
	H	*Zappulla Rose—†	137A	candymaker	35	"
	K	*Zappulla Vincent	137A	cleaner	45	"
	L	*Dannolfo Carlo	138	tailor	38	"
	M	Dannolfo Theresa—†	138	housewife	38	"
	N	Lavogna Anthony	138	chauffeur	31	"
	O	*Lavogna Maria—†	138	at home	61	"
	P	Montuori Aniello	138	builder	49	"
	R	Montuori Rose—†	138	clerk	35	"
	S	Ardagna Bartolomeo	138	shoemaker	47	"
	T	*Ardagna Giuseppina—†	138	at home	76	"
	U	Ardagna Josephine—†	138	stitcher	39	"
	V	Bianco Michael	139	laborer	46	"

Paris Street — Continued

Page.	Letter.	FULL NAME.	Residence, Jan. 1 1943.	Occupation.	Supposed Age.	Reported Residence Jan. 1, 1942. Street and Number.
	w	*Capobianco Josephine—†	139	at home	74	here
	x	Anzalone Anthony	139	U S C G	29	108 Orleans
	y	*Anzalone Josephine—†	139	housewife	36	108 "
	z	*Grasso Beatrice—†	139	"	52	here
567						
	A	Grasso Mary—†	139	stitcher	23	"
	B	Grasso Nicola	139	laborer	53	"
	c	Grasso Peter	139	U S A	21	"
	D	Petruzzillo Anthony	140	tailor	44	"
	E	*Petruzzillo Marie—†	140	housewife	70	"
	F	*Petruzzillo Pasquale	140	retired	73	"
	H	Pargola Filippo	140	carpenter	55	"
	G	Pargola Petrina—†	140	housewife	46	"
	K	Pettruzzeli Annie—†	140	"	37	"
	L	Pettruzzeli Lawrence	140	candymaker	42	"
	M	Puopolo Alfred	141	U S A	21	"
	N	Puopolo Angela—†	141	laborer	63	"
	o	*Puopolo Carmella—†	141	housewife	60	"
	P	Puopolo Carmen	141	U S A	30	"
	R	DeFeo Constance—†	141	at home	49	"
	s	DeFeo Gennaro	141	candymaker	21	"
	T	DeFeo Sue—†	141	supervisor	23	Somerville
	u	Capprini Josephine—†	142	housewife	25	here
	v	Capprini Leo	142	welder	28	"
	w	Petruccelli Daniel	142	shoeworker	40	"
	x	Petruccelli Joseph	142	retired	65	"
	y	Agresta Gaetano	142	machinist	26	22 Haynes
	z	*Agresta Louis	142	retired	68	22 "
568						
	A	Agresta Mary—†	142	housewife	27	22 "
	B	DeVingo Filomena—†	143	at home	53	here
	c	DeVingo Joseph	143	U S A	22	"
	D	Zirpolo Angelina—†	143	housewife	33	"
	E	Zirpolo John	143	painter	39	"
	F	Russo James	143	brewer	29	"
	G	Russo Josephine—†	143	stitcher	27	"
	H	Marcotullio Albert	144	tailor	33	"
	K	*Marcotullio Beatrice M †	144	housewife	32	"
	L	Micciche Giuseppe	144	shoeworker	70	"
	M	Micciche Giuseppe	144	U S A	32	"
	N	Micciche Josephine—†	144	housewife	62	"

39

Page.	Letter	FULL NAME.	Residence, Jan. 1, 1943.	Occupation.	Supposed Age.	Reported Residence, Jan. 1. 1942. Street and Number.

Paris Street—Continued

	o	Vitale Mary—†	144	housewife	40	here
	p	Vitale Rocco	144	shoeworker	45	"
	R	Carrabino Angelina L—†	146	housewife	37	"
	s	Carrabino Angelo F	146	clerk	35	"
	T	Scozzella Angelina—†	146	housewife	68	"
	u	Scozzella Giuseppe	146	retired	74	"
	v	Aste Florence—†	146	housewife	23	194 Falcon
	w	Aste Giacomo J	146	rigger	27	194 "
	x	Conti Joseph	149	laborer	55	here
	y	Conti Rose—†	149	housewife	59	"
	z	*Todisco Celeste—†	149	at home	83	"

569

	A	Todisco Joseph	149	constable	54	"
	B	Todisco Mary—†	149	housewife	45	"
	c	Todisco Michael	149	storekeeper	60	"
	D	Todisco Virginio J	149	U S A	22	"
	E	Parla Carmello	149	blacksmith	36	537 Sumner
	F	Warner Josephine—†	149	housekeeper	57	537 "
	H	*Beggelman Abram	153	stripper	63	here
	K	Beggelman Eva—†	153	bookkeeper	32	"
	L	Beggelman Israel	153	U S A	23	"
	M	Beggelman Rose—†	153	housewife	25	Chelsea
	N	Beggelman Ruby	153	U S A	27	here
	o	Beggelman Samuel	153	metalworker	29	Chelsea
	P	*Beggelman Sarah—†	153	housewife	58	here

Porter Street

	R	*Sorrentini Erminia—†	87	housewife	55	here
	U	DiNapoli Anthony	87	tailor	22	"
	s	DiNapoli Archangela—†	87	housewife	57	"
	T	DiNapoli Joseph	87	retired	64	"
	v	DiNapoli Mary—†	87	factoryhand	29	"
	x	Borisowsky Abraham C	103	U S A	39	"
	y	Borisowsky Israel	103	retired	69	"
	z	Borisowsky Lena—†	103	housewife	71	"

570

	A	Borisowsky Samuel	103	U S A	36	"
	B	*Rotundo Angelina—†	103	housewife	48	55 Webster
	c	Rotundo Anthony	103	laborer	55	55 "
	D	Rotundo William	103	U S A	21	55 "

40

Porter Street Continued

H	Caruso Samuel	109	laborer	54	here	
K	*Forte Josephine †	109	waitress	30	Chelsea	
L	Beatrice Salvatore	111	laborer	53	here	
M	*Memmolo Pasquale	111	"	49	"	
N	*Memmolo Peter	111	"	49	"	
P	*Mason Fannie T †	115	housewife	76	"	
R	Nicolette Alice M †	115	"	36	"	
S	Nicolette Savatore S	115	laborer	38	"	
T	*Nicolette Barbara †	115A	housewife	64	"	
U	Nicolette Phillip	115A	laborer	73	"	
V	Ferrera Leonard	117	watchman	23	"	
W	Ferrera Leonera †	117	housewife	24	"	
Y	Tuberosi Anthony	117	U S A	24	"	
X	Tuberosi Catherine †	117	housewife	59	"	
Z	Tuberosi Salvatore	117	laborer	60	"	

571

B	Giannasoli Jessie †	117	housewife	22	32 Wall	
A	Giannasoli Santino	117	rigger	23	32 "	

Ward 1–Precinct 6

CITY OF BOSTON

LIST OF RESIDENTS
20 YEARS OF AGE AND OVER

(NON-CITIZENS INDICATED BY ASTERISK)
(FEMALES INDICATED BY DAGGER)

AS OF

JANUARY 1, 1943

JOSEPH F. TIMILTY, *Chairman*
FREDERIC E. DOWLING, *Secretary*
WILLIAM A. MOTLEY, JR.
FRANCIS B. McKINNEY
EVERETT R. PROUT

Listing Board.

CITY OF BOSTON PRINTING DEPARTMENT

600

Bennington Street

H	*Cohen Esther —†	34	housewife	58	here
K	Cohen Ethel —†	34	clerk	34	"
L	*Cohen Max	34	proprietor	58	"
M	Salovsky Jacob	34	electrician	27	Michigan
U	Brown Ann B —†	56	housewife	37	here
V	Brown Cecelia B —†	56	at home	72	"
W	Brown Joseph C	56	metalworker	36	"
X	Gardas Catherine —†	56	housewife	49	"
Y	Gardas William H	56	fireman	50	"
Z	Gardas William H, jr	56	U S N	20	Virginia

601

A	Pero Henry	56	U S A	32	here
B	Hall Alma F —†	56	bookkeeper	25	"
C	Hall Bertha F —†	56	cook	50	"
D	Hewitt Fannie M —†	56	housewife	70	"
E	*McShane Thomas	56	shoeworker	55	"
F	DiPietro Attilio	58	sprayer	37	"
G	DiPietro Josephine —†	58	housewife	37	"
H	*Nicosia Josephine —†	58	"	58	"
K	Nicosia Rose —†	58	at home	38	"
L	Nicosia Charles	58	electrician	33	"
M	Dagenais Alfred	60	guard	32	158 Benningt'n
N	Dagenais Carmella —†	60	housewife	51	158 "
O	Santanello Armando	60	laborer	23	158 "
P	Schiff Bessie —†	60	housewife	60	here
R	Schiff Jacob	60	retired	65	"
S	Shipley James M	62	carpenter	57	60 Bennington
T	Shipley Julia M —†	62	housewife	41	60 "
U	DiGregorio Anthony	62	laborer	49	here
V	DiGregorio Criciffisa —†	62	housewife	39	"
W	Giordano Louis	62	driller	22	198 Benningt'n
X	Scala Angelina —†	64	housewife	58	here
Y	Scala Anthony	64	technician	25	"
Z	Scala John	64	tailor	67	"

602

A	Scala John, jr	64	U S A	27	"
B	Goshgarian Ardemis —†	64	housewife	41	"
C	Goshgarian Serop	64	factoryhand	52	"
F	Joe Goon	68	laundryman	38	"
G	Deglia Angelli Luigi	70	proprietor	50	

2

Page.	Letter.	FULL NAME.	Residence. Jan. 1. 1943	Occupation.	Supposed Age.	Reported Residence, Jan. 1, 1942. Street and Number

Bennington Street—Continued

	H	Marrotta Charles	70	U S N	34	here
	K	Marotta Domenic	70	retired	67	"
	L	Marotta Gilda —†	70	clerk	23	"
	M	Marotta Michael	70	tailor	32	"
	N	Marotta Phyllis —†	70	stitcher	28	"
	O	Marotta Rose —†	70	"	21	"
	P	Marotta Salvatore	70	clerk	27	"
	R	Preshong Albert W	70	watchman	70	"
	T	Preshong Joseph S	70	seaman	33	"
	S	Preshong Josephine —†	70	housewife	60	"
	U	Preshong Marie —†	70	at home	30	"
	W	Carolan Elizabeth †	72	factoryhand	32	Chelsea
	X	Hogan Joseph	72	U S A	24	here
	Y	Hogan Sarah —†	72	housewife	64	"
	Z	Hogan Thomas	72	carpenter	66	"
603						
	A	Keating Charlotte —†	72	housewife	69	"
	B	Keating Florence L †	72	saleswoman	52	"
	C	Keating Michael E	72	retired	69	"
	D	Bonice Mary—†	74	clerk	35	"
	E	Bonice Michael	74	fisherman	38	"
	F	Joyce Margaret A —†	74	housewife	82	25 Bennington
	G	Joyce Melvin	74	printer	44	25 "
	H	Rizzo Charles	74	laborer	29	here
	K	Rizzo Constance —†	74	housewife	27	"
	L	Fratto Eleanor †	76	stitcher	23	"
	M	Fratto Thomas	76	retired	72	"
	N	Rodriques Josephine L †	76	housewife	26	"
	O	Rodriques William J	76	stitcher	32	"
	P	Botta Carmen	76	fishcutter	31	"
	R	Botta Mary —†	76	housewife	31	"
	T	Merigan Catherine —†	78	at home	56	"
	W*	Festa Armanlinda †	80	housewife	56	"
	X	Festa Arthur	80	manager	26	"
	Y	Festa Augustine	80	butcher	64	"
	Z	Festa Ernest	80	U S A	24	"
604						
	A*	Enos Joseph	80	retired	74	"
	B*	Rezendes Mary L —†	80	housekeeper	48	"
	C	Burge Tina —†	82	housewife	22	"
	D	Burge Walter	82	U S N	24	"

Bennington Street — Continued

E	Plante Lucy—†	82	housewife	39	here
F	Plante Wilfred	82	tester	44	"

Border Street

H	Stearns Benjamin	219	watchman	75	here
K	Bruno Antonio	219	laborer	55	"
L	*Bruno Esther—†	219	housewife	54	"
M	Iannelli Anna—†	221	"	23	3 Lewis
N	Iannelli Ugo	221	bartender	25	22 Falcon
O	Buccheri Attilia—†	221	housewife	24	here
P	Buccheri Paul	221	laborer	63	"
R	Buccheri Samuel	221	"	26	"
S	Buccheri Joseph	221	plumber	29	"
T	Buccheri Mildred—†	221	factoryhand	24	"
U	*Buccheri Paula—†	221	housewife	50	"
V	Buccheri Santa—†	221	U S A	23	"
W	Buccheri Victor	221	"	26	"
X	Donnarumma Anthony	223	laborer	23	"
Y	Donnarumma Bessie—†	223	housewife	21	"
Z	Fortini Jennie—†	223	factoryhand	28	"
	605				
A	Fortini Joseph	223	laborer	55	"
B	*Fortini Mary—†	223	housewife	53	"
C	Stewart Leo	223	U S A	38	"
D	Stewart Rose—†	223	housewife	30	"
E	Falzarono Christopher	225	laborer	29	"
F	Falzarono Margaret—†	225	housewife	22	"
G	Fortini Antonette—†	225	"	23	"
H	Fortini Salvatore	225	laborer	23	"
K	Volo James	225	operator	29	"
L	Volo Michelina—†	225	housewife	28	"
M	LaRosa Alfonso	227	laborer	30	148 Saratoga
N	LaRosa Lillian—†	227	housewife	29	148 "
O	Letteriello Adolph	227	machinist	31	here
P	Letteriello Louise—†	227	housewife	34	"
R	Mondello Elizabeth—†	227	"	27	"
S	Mondello John	227	machinist	34	"
T	Mondello Natale	227	"	48	"
U	Barrett James	255	laborer	42	"

4

Border Street—Continued

v	McPhee Elizabeth—†	255	housekeeper	71	here	
w	Mulkurn Mary—†	255	factoryhand	20	"	
x	Whalen Mary—†	255	at home	68	"	
y	Wilkie Helen—†	255	factoryhand	24	"	
z	Wilkie Norma †	255	saleswoman	21	"	
606						
A	Gallo Battisto	257	U S A	38	"	
B	*Gallo Philomena—†	257	housewife	69	"	
c	Bradley Mary—†	257	housekeeper	50	"	
D	Gallo Mary—†	257	housewife	33	"	
E	Gallo Michael	257	laborer	36	"	
F	Fendo Florence—†	259	housewife	22	Revere	
G	Fendo Peter	259	laborer	22	here	
H	*DiPietro Filippa—†	259	housekeeper	65	"	
K	*Fendo Angelina—†	259	housewife	42	"	
L	*Fendo Vincenzo	259	laborer	51	"	
M	DiLoreto Constance—†	259	housewife	24	"	
N	DiLoreto Guido	259	laborer	25	"	
o	McVey James	261	machinist	36	76 Havre	
P	McVey Margaret—†	261	housewife	29	76 "	
R	McVey Mary—†	261	housekeeper	61	76 "	
s	*Buttiglieri Mary—†	261	housewife	42	here	
T	Buttiglieri Rocco	261	laborer	50	"	
U	DiGirolamo Antonette—†	261	housewife	25	"	
V	DiGirolamo Joseph	261	laborer	28	"	
w	Bagley Mary M—†	263	housewife	32	"	
x	Bagley Robert J	263	plumber	36	"	
Y	Golisano Salvatore	263	U S A	26	"	
z	Spada Leonardo	263	laborer	52	"	
607						
A	Spada Tina †	263	housewife	44	"	
B	Winer Anna †	263	"	33	"	
c	Winer James	263	laborer	38	"	
D	O'Donnell Arthur J	265	"	47	"	
E	O'Donnell Arthur J	265	U S N	20	"	
F	O'Donnell James	265	U S A	23	"	
G	O'Donnell Mary—†	265	housewife	47	"	
H	Verbanas Jane †	265	"	20	"	
K	Verbanas Juilio	265	laborer	22	"	
L	Cassara Peter	265	machinist	33	"	
M	Cassara Tina—†	265	housewife	28	"	

5

Page.	Letter.	FULL NAME.	Residence, Jan. 1, 1943.	Occupation.	Supposed Age.	Reported Residence, Jan. 1, 1942. Street and Number.

Brooks Street

N	Pisano Angela—†	100	housewife	35	206 Marion
O	Pisano Nicholas J	100	shoeworker	35	206 "
P	DiPietro Claude	100	U S A	22	117 Eutaw
R	DiPietro Lucy—†	100	housewife	59	117 "
S	DiPietro Rinaldo	100	U S A	24	117 "
T	DiPietro Rocco	100	proprietor	60	117 "
U	DiPietro William	100	chauffeur	26	117 "
V	Rose Emily—†	102	at home	73	here
W	Rose George	102	machinist	21	"
X	Rose Mary—†	102	at home	40	"
Y	Bavaro Anthony	104	U S A	25	224 Princeton

608

A	*Bavaro John	104	laborer	55	224 "
B	*Bavaro Josephine—†	104	housewife	50	224 "
C	*McCormick Anna—†	104	"	54	here
D	*McCormick John	104	ironworker	56	"
E	McCormick Leonard	104	U S A	31	"
F	McCormick Loretta—†	104	inspector	20	"
G	*Kelly Helen †	106	housewife	52	"
H	Kelly Helen †	106	examiner	21	"
K	Kelly John	106	fisherman	57	"
L	Muse Anthony	106	laborer	47	"
M	Muse Marion †	106	housewife	42	"
N	Joyce Harriet †	106	"	51	"
O	Joyce Joseph	106	fireman	57	"
R	Cali Phyllis †	108	housewife	29	"
S	Cali Rocco	108	salesman	35	"
T	*DiFilippo Maria †	108	housewife	53	"
U	DiFilippo Michael	108	laborer	60	"

Lexington Avenue

V	McGray Charles	1	fireman	53	here
W	McGray Dorcas †	1	housewife	47	"
X	Callari Joseph	1	millhand	30	"
Y	*Callari Josephine †	1	housewife	52	"
Z	Callari Phillip	1	laborer	56	"

609

A	Callari Phillip, jr	1	U S A	26	"
B	Fontana Nunzio	2	electrician	26	"
C	Fontana Rose †	2	housewife	22	"

6

Lexington Avenue — Continued

D	McEachern James W	2	U S A	24	here
E	McEachern John F	2	"	22	"
F	McEachern Joseph A	2	painter	54	"
G	McEachern Joseph A, jr	2	U S A	29	"
H	McEachern Leonard M	2	"	21	"
K	McEachern Rita—†	2	housewife	46	"
M	*Silva Gertrude—†	3	"	46	"
N	Silva Juliet—†	3	clerk	21	"
O	Silva Manuel	3	retired	65	"
P	Fothergell Mary—†	4	housewife	54	"
R	*McMillen Allan	4	laborer	64	"
T	Brennan Catherine—†	4	housewife	38	"
S	Brennan Fred	4	laborer	41	"
U	Zavarelli Antonio	5	retired	67	"
V	Zavarelli Frank	5	U S N	29	"
W	Zavarelli Panfilo	5	laborer	20	"
X	DiPerri Charles	5	millworker	26	"
Y	DiPerri Lorenzo	5	laborer	61	"
Z	DiPerri Louis	5	U S A	28	"

610

A	*DiPerri Maria—†	5	housewife	48	"
B	DiPerri Michael	5	U S A	21	"
C	DiPerri Salvatore	5	"	24	"
D	Brennan Mary—†	6	housewife	38	"
E	Brennan William	6	electrician	38	"
F	Brennan Albert	6	laborer	27	"
G	Brennan Blanche—†	6	housewife	66	"
H	Avola Adeline—†	7	"	28	"
K	Avola Francis	7	shoeworker	27	"
L	Casso Louis	7	mechanic	37	"
M	*Casso Philomena—†	7	housewife	48	"
N	Pericolo Mario	7	U S A	21	"
O	Pericolo Peter	7	laborer	24	"
P	*Crowell Ernest	8	fireman	56	"
R	Crowell Lottie—†	8	clerk	68	"
S	*Baglio Lillian—†	8	housewife	42	"
T	Baglio Louis	8	tailor	46	"
U	Preshong Mabel—†	9	laundress	53	"
V	Polito Devigia—†	9	housewife	38	"
W	Polito Gabriel	9	boilermaker	38	"
X	Polito Joseph	9	U S A	40	"

7

Page.	Letter.	FULL NAME.	Residence, Jan. 1, 1943.	Occupation.	Supposed Age.	Reported Residence, Jan. 1, 1942. Street and Number.

Lexington Avenue—Continued

	Y	Sirava Enrico	9	U S N	33	here
	Z	Coco Anthony J	10	shipfitter	26	"
611						
	A	Coco Phyllis—†	10	housewife	23	"
	B	*Cara Maria—†	10	at home	72	"
	C	Vitale John	10	laborer	47	"
	D	*Vitale Mary—†	10	housewife	40	"

Lexington Place

	E	Adams Pleasant A	1	U S N	32	here
	F	Collins Mary E—†	1	housewife	60	"
	G	Collins William	1	engineer	63	"
	H	Collins William G	1	"	21	"
	K	Symons Arthur A	1	U S A	25	"
	L	Mason James	1	guard	55	"
	M	Murphy Amelia—†	1	housewife	26	127 Meridian
	N	Murphy Raymond	1	milkman	36	301 Maverick
	O	Minichello Angelo	2	watchman	35	here
	P	Minichello Etta—†	2	housewife	34	"
	R	*Minichello Michael	2	mason	63	"
	S	Vitale Lena—†	2	cutter	35	"
	T	Balbere Susie—†	2	"	25	"
	U	Vitale Mary—†	2	housewife	31	"
	V	Vitale Michael	2	boilermaker	42	"
	W	*Barrett Mildred—†	3	housewife	50	"
	X	Barrett Peter	3	painter	63	"
	Y	Littlefield Harold	3	cook	56	"
	Z	Burke Thomas J	3	seaman	38	"
612						
	A	Lighthody Charles A	3	U S C G	56	"
	B	Lighthody Edith—†	3	housewife	53	"
	C	Mulligan Bertha—†	3	"	23	Quincy
	D	Mikkelsen Mary—†	4	"	29	here
	E	Mikkelsen Sverre	4	engineer	29	"
	F	Peterson George F	4	U S N	30	35 Princeton
	G	Peterson Mary—†	4	housewife	24	35 "
	H	LaBlanc James	4	operator	56	here
	K	Ryan Alfred	4	blacksmith	51	Maine
	L	Ryan Mildred—†	4	housewife	51	"
	N	Moore Madeline F—†	5	at home	36	here

S

Lexington Place – Continued

o	Noon Helen—†	5	housewife	35	here	
p	Noon John T	5	chauffeur	39	"	
s	DeSantis Louise—†	6	welder	24	94 Everett	
t	Lightbody Charles T	6	fireman	30	here	
u	Lightbody Mary—†	6	housewife	32	"	
v	Johnson Herbert	6	guard	42	98 Trenton	
w	Johnson Louise—†	6	housewife	38	98 "	
x	Parsons Albert	7	U S A	24	here	
y	Parsons Margaret—†	7	housewife	20	"	

613

a	D'Aregnio Anthony	7	operator	23	"	
b	D'Argenio Edward	7	U S M C	21	"	
c	*D'Aregnio Sally—†	7	housewife	59	"	
d	*Gerollo Vincent	7	barber	65	"	

Lexington Street

e	Rumney Sarah—†	21	at home	80	here	
f	Tyler John	21	retired	64	"	
g	Alfama Anthony F	21	chef	58	385 Meridian	
1g	Alfama Mary S—†	21	housewife	50	385 "	
h	Beacham Ernest E	21	shipfitter	20	here	
k	Beacham Helen G—†	21	housewife	44	"	
m	Amico Joseph	23	machinist	23	"	
n	Amico Phillip	23	retired	65	"	
o	Swett Charles W	23	machinist	73	"	
p	Swett Elizabeth M—†	23	housewife	59	"	
r	*Surette John	23	deckhand	22	145 Trenton	
t	Pepe Michael	27	machinist	23	here	
u	Pepe Nicolina—†	27	housewife	24	"	
v	Caruso Frederick	27	cutter	52	"	
w	Caruso Mary—†	27	housewife	43	"	
x	Cinelli Catherine—†	27	stitcher	23	"	
y	Lomas Harold, jr	27	toolmaker	20	"	
z	Lomas Josephine—†	27	housewife	20	"	

614

a	*Scioscia Camille—†	27	stitcher	31	"	
b	Vozzella Mario	27	pressman	38	Pennsylvania	
c	Hemenway Nahum	29	retired	78	625 Saratoga	
d	*Grant Mary—†	29	housewife	40	here	
e	Grant Nathan S	29	chauffeur	37	"	

9

Page.	Letter.	FULL NAME.	Residence, Jan. 1. 1943	Occupation.	Supposed Age.	Reported Residence, Jan. 1. 1942. Street and Number.

Lexington Street—Continued

F	Sharp Hugh	29	laborer	65	here
G	Sharp Hugh, jr	29	mechanic	35	"
H	Avery Joseph M	31	fisherman	44	30 Lexington
K	DeCoste Henry	31	deckhand	42	here
L	Donaldson Ernest	31	salesman	29	"
M	Dubie Ludger	31	welder	44	Waltham
N	Ezekiel Theresa—†	31	at home	68	here
¹N	Fitzgerald William H	31	cooper	69	"
O	Hancock Deborah—†	31	housewife	55	"
P	Hancock Joseph	31	carpenter	61	"
R	Hancock Mary—†	31	operator	29	"
S	LaMarca Gaetano	31	retired	67	110 Brooks
T*	Martell Leo	31	brushmaker	60	here
U	McComisky Emmy—†	31	housewife	58	1 Monmouth
V	McComisky William	31	machinist	59	1 "
W	Nolan John F	31	printer	55	here
X	Nolan Victoria—†	31	housewife	54	"
Y	O'Neil Henry	31	electrician	26	"
Z	Perry Everett	31	carpenter	60	Mississippi

615

A	Regan James J	31	machinist	37	Somerville
B	Regan Margaret—†	31	bookkeeper	30	here
C*	Verkoski Victor	31	tailor	65	Chelsea
D	Grana John	33	electrician	28	Burlington
E	Grana Matilda—†	33	housewife	26	"
F	Faraci Joseph	33	painter	27	here
G	Faraci Violet—†	33	housewife	26	"
H	Peri Pasquale	33	retired	67	"
K	Riccobene Angelo	45	"	70	"
L	Riccobene Concetta—†	45	housewife	59	"
M	Mirabella Joseph	45	laborer	55	"
N*	Mirabella Santa—†	45	housewife	51	"
O	Consalvi Angelina—†	45	"	24	"
P	Consalvi Joseph	45	operator	25	"
R*	Lotti Deofrasio	47	chauffeur	21	"
S	Russo Ciriaco	47	barber	72	"
T*	Russo Rachel—†	47	housewife	58	"
U	Fiorita Leonardo	47	laborer	45	"
V	Fiorita Philomena—†	47	housewife	38	"
W*	Parsons Robert W	49	rigger	52	"
X*	Parsons Violet—†	49	housewife	46	"

10

Lexington Street Continued

	Y	DiNunzio Evelyn—†	49	housewife	33	here
	Z	DiNunzio Joseph	49	shoe worker	38	"
616						
	A	Almeida Passantonio	49	U S A	46	285 Meridian
	B	*Costa Pauline—†	49	weaver	56	285 "
	C	Kelly Helen—†	51	housewife	22	here
	D	Kelly Mark	51	clerk	28	"
	E	Cunha Joseph	51	machinist	30	"
	F	*Cunha Octavia—†	51	housewife	35	"
	G	Cunha Alfred	51	machinist	35	"
	H	Cunha Mary—†	51	housewife	65	"
	K	Hardy James	53	chef	60	"
	L	Hardy Virginia—†	53	housewife	45	"
	M	Jones Frederick	53	electrician	36	"
	N	Jones Ruth—†	53	housewife	30	"
	O	Salerno Dorothy—†	53	"	25	"
	P	Salerno Michael	53	chauffeur	27	"
	R	Scarfo Pearl—†	61	housewife	20	"
	S	Scarfo Phillip	61	cutter	26	"
	T	Codagnone Edith—†	61	forewoman	25	"
	U	Codagnone Joseph	61	chef	53	"
	V	Codagnone Robert	61	U S A	28	"
	W	Codagnone Sylvia—†	61	housewife	44	"
	X	Zaccaria Anthony	61	salesman	53	"
	Y	Zaccaria Leo	61	chemist	22	"
	Z	Zaccaria Mary—†	61	housewife	46	"
617						
	A	Cheffi Celia—†	63	"	25	11 Gove
	B	Cheffi Saverio	63	welder	28	11 "
	C	Gordon Clifford C	63	engineer	48	here
	D	Gordon Elizabeth—†	63	housewife	45	"
	E	Psihogios Mary—†	63	"	46	"
	F	Psihogios Peter	63	salesman	52	"
	O	Magnasco Anna—†	65	housewife	28	"
	P	Magnasco Gismondo	65	operator	36	"
	G	Mannetta Carlo	65	laborer	61	"
	H	Mannetta George	65	machinist	26	"
	K	Mannetta John	65	salesman	30	"
	L	Manetta Lena—†	65	housewife	58	"
	M	Mannetta Olympia—†	65	hairdresser	23	"
	R	Casiello Samuel	67	painter	39	"

11

Lexington Street—Continued

s	*Casiello Louise—†	67	housewife	39	here
t	DiNatale Emma—†	67	"	31	"
u	DiNatale Michael	67	clerk	34	"
v	Covino Angelo	67	barber	43	155 Marion
w	Covino Carmella—†	67	housewife	41	159 "
x	MacDonald Daniel	69	operator	52	here
y	MacDonald Eugenia—†	69	typist	21	"
z	MacDonald Mary—†	69	housewife	48	"

618

a	MacDonald Steven A	69	carpenter	49	"
b	Ferreira Cleo—†	71	housewife	34	68 Marion
c	Ferreira John	71	engineer	36	68 "

Marion Street

e	Giordano Antonette—†	103	housewife	29	here
f	Giordano Wilfred	103	shipjoiner	30	"
g	Leavitt David	103	proprietor	54	"
h	Leavitt Sadie—†	103	housewife	50	"
k	Mingoia Filippa—†	103	"	52	"
l	Mingoia Joseph	103	at home	53	"
m	Tuberosa Ernest	105	painter	26	8 Drake pl
n	Tuberosa Rafaella—†	105	housewife	24	8 "
o	Chieppo Antonio	105	carpenter	61	here
p	Chieppo Teresa—†	105	housewife	57	"
r	Savino Charles	105	welder	35	"
s	Savino Rose—†	105	housewife	29	"
t	Bozzi Helen—†	107	"	27	"
u	Bozzi John	107	tailor	31	"
v	Kelly Agnes—†	107	housewife	55	"
w	Kelly Lawrence	107	U S A	22	"
x	Murphy Thomas	107	fireman	65	"
y	Iantosca Consolata—†	107	housewife	42	"
z	Iantosca Felice	107	U S A	43	"

619

a	Iantosca Philip	107	laborer	59	"
c	Tabbi Charles	126	reporter	28	"
b	Tabbi Frank	126	U S A	25	"
d	Tabbi Mary—†	126	tailor	32	"
e	*Tabbi Rosaria—†	126	housewife	59	"

12

Marion Street — Continued

	Letter	Full Name	Residence	Occupation	Age	Reported Residence
	F	Tabbi Rosaria —†	126	tailor	29	here
	G	Tabbi Salvatore	126	laborer	67	"
	H	Tabbi Salvatore	126	U S A	23	"
	K	Pinto Maria —†	126	housewife	25	3 Everett ct
	L	Pinto Nicholas	126	laborer	28	3 "
	N	Amirault Leslie A	130	U S A	31	here
	O*	Amirault Tessie —†	130	housewife	27	"
	P*	LeBlanc Margaret —†	130	"	33	"
	R*	LeBlanc Simon	130	fisherman	39	"
	S	Deveau Agnes —†	130	clerk	23	"
	T	Deveau Isaie	130	shipwright	56	"
	U	Deveau Mary —†	130	housewife	45	"
	V	Deveau Walter	130	machinist	21	"
	W	Lombard Rosalie —†	130	clerk	21	Connecticut
	X*	Deveau Daisy —†	130	factoryhand	40	here
	Y	Deveau Edward	130	U S A	22	"
	Z	Deveau Frank L	130	carpenter	47	"
620						
	A	Elwell James H	132	laborer	38	75 Saratoga
	B	Elwell Josephine A —†	132	housewife	40	75 "
	C	Passoriello Carmen	132	electrician	23	here
	D*	Passoriello Concerta —†	132	housewife	52	"
	E*	Passoriello Emilio	132	laborer	52	"
	F	Passoriello Salvatore	132	U S A	21	"
	G	Barros Henry	132	cook	52	"
	H	Barros Zulmira —†	132	housewife	42	"
	K	Driscoll Agnes C —†	134	"	30	"
	L	Driscoll Julia M —†	134	clerk	38	"
	M	Driscoll Lillian —†	134	"	33	"
	N	Driscoll Margaret J —†	134	"	37	"
	O	Tirone Carl	134	U S A	22	"
	P*	Tirone Giacinto —†	134	housewife	47	"
	R	Tirone John	134	U S A	27	"
	S	Tirone Louis	134	"	20	"
	T	Tirone Marco	134	factoryhand	54	"
	U	Tirone Margaret —†	134	at home	24	"
	V	Contino Michael	134	pipecoverer	20	198 Trenton
	W	Comeau Joseph	149	carpenter	63	2 Eutaw pl
	X	Comeau Joseph S	149	"	52	2 "
	Y*	Ahearn Michael	149	fisherman	32	here
	Z*	Boland Violet —†	149	housewife	38	"

621

Marion Street—Continued

	Letter	FULL NAME	Residence 1943	Occupation	Age	Reported Residence 1942
	A	Steph Ethel—†	149	housewife	36	here
	B	Lombardi Mary—†	151	waitress	41	"
	C	Taylor Ida—†	151	factoryhand	37	"
	E	Sciarappa Jane—†	151	housewife	24	5 Lexington pl
	F	Sciarappa John	151	guard	36	5 "
	G	Salerno Francis	153	U S A	28	46 Saratoga
	H	Salerno Helen M—†	153	housewife	24	here
	K	Silva Albert	153	garageman	54	"
	L	*Silva Anne—†	153	housewife	50	"
	O	MacMillan Charles	153	U S A	27	"
	M	Scofield Charles	153	"	21	"
	N	Scofield Margaret—†	153	housewife	45	"
	P	Block John	153	baker	67	"
	R	Block Mary—†	153	housewife	52	"
	S	Vicini Anthony	155	machinist	27	"
	T	*Vicini Frances—†	155	housewife	68	"
	U	Vicini Guy	155	U S A	29	"
	V	Vicini Henry	155	retired	69	"
	W	Cogliona Michael	155	laborer	45	"
	X	Penta Michael	155	retired	72	"
	Y	Penta Rose—†	155	housewife	65	"
	Z	*Mascis Antonio	155	retired	72	

622

	Letter	FULL NAME	Residence 1943	Occupation	Age	Reported Residence 1942
	A	*Mascis Margaret—†	155	housewife	73	"
	B	Mascis Michael	155	laborer	27	"
	C	Critch Charles W	157	chauffeur	27	39A Greenwich
	D	Critch Josephine—†	157	housewife	26	39A "
	E	Catalano Fiorino	157	salesman	21	here
	F	*Catalano Geraldine—†	157	housewife	67	"
	G	*Ciambrone Cristina M—†	157	"	39	"
	H	*Ciambrone Joseph A	157	machinist	49	"
	K	Bruno Jennie—†	159	housewife	28	32 Bremen
	L	Bruno Vincent	159	welder	29	32 "
	M	Zerola Aida—†	159	bookkeeper	22	here
	N	Zerola Antonio	159	shoeworker	54	"
	O	Zerola Frank	159	U S N	21	"
	P	Zerola Mafalda—†	159	dressmaker	24	"
	R	Zerola Mary—†	159	housewife	52	"
	S	Ferrara Joseph	159	factoryhand	34	129 Putnam
	T	Ferrara Sarah—†	159	housewife	29	129 "

14

Meridian Street

	v	Boudreau Anna—†	234	housewife	63	here
	w	Boudreau William	234	laborer	65	"
	x	Chiccinello Frank	234	U S A	24	"
	y	*Salerno Clara—†	234	housewife	40	"
	z	Salerno Edward	234	carpenter	33	"
623						
	A	Bell Frank	236	proprietor	64	"
	B	Bell Gertrude E—†	236	housewife	49	"
	c	Aitken Florence E—†	236	"	68	"
	D	Aitken Harold	236	operator	34	"
	E	Aitken Joseph	236	chauffeur	34	"
	K	Grant Alice—†	242	housekeeper	38	27 Wm J Kelly Sq
	L	Guey Lee	244	laundryman	65	here
	M	Lee William	244	operator	20	"
	N	*Wong Kim Hay—†	244	housewife	45	"
	o	Butts Vincent	244	physician	62	"
	P	Cappucci Vincenzo M	244	barber	59	"
	R	O'Brien Dennis J	244	lumberman	42	Weymouth
	s	O'Brien Marie L—†	244	housewife	41	"
	v	Coffin Margaret—†	249	housekeeper	51	here
	x	Gurevich Gertrude—†	251	housewife	55	"
	y	Gurevich Harry	251	proprietor	64	"
	z	Schatz Charles	251	laborer	29	"
624						
	A	Schatz Ida—†	251	housewife	29	"
	D	Mariani Peter	257	boilermaker	53	"
	c	Mariani Philomena—†	257	housewife	42	"
	E	Panzera Frank	257	retired	73	"
	F	Ferrara Antoinetta—†	257	packer	29	"
	G	Ferrara Mary—†	257	dressmaker	22	"
	H	Ferrara Peter	257	longshoreman	24	"
	K	Monaco Antonio	257	laborer	46	"
	L	Monaco Biago W	257	U S A	21	"
	M	Monaco Concetta F—†	257	housewife	41	"
	N	Monaco Mary G—†	257	clerk	20	"
	o	*Cantara George	259	spinner	55	"
	P	*Cantara Phoebeana—†	259	housewife	53	"
	R	Capodilupo Antonio	259	proprietor	38	"
	s	Capodilupo Concetta—†	259	housewife	28	"
	T	*Caporeale Angelo	259	retired	68	"
	U	*Caporeale Carmella—†	259	housewife	64	"

15

Page.	Letter.	Full Name.	Residence, Jan. 1, 1943.	Occupation.	Supposed Age.	Reported Residence, Jan. 1, 1942. Street and Number.

Meridian Street—Continued

	v	*Lococo Louis	259	carpenter	63	85 Liverpool
	w	Pinkham Edward R	259	mechanic	64	here
	x	Pinkham Helen J—†	259	housewife	58	"
	y	Sabio Domenic	259	U S A	29	New York

625

	c	Barcellos Edward	265	retired	63	here
	d	*Bolands Jeremiah	265	fisherman	47	Chelsea
	e	Myers Edward G	265	diver	60	56 Bennington
	f	Myers George L	265	U S M C	23	56 "
	g	Myers Georgianna —†	265	housewife	60	56 "
	h	Myers William R	265	U S A	22	56 "
	k	*Nicoletti Angelo	265	retired	77	here
	l	Rowe Elizabeth—†	265	housewife	37	36 Princeton
	m	Rowe Henry	265	fisherman	40	36 "
	n	Waldron Lucy—†	265	at home	82	here
	r	Donovan Helen L —†	269	housekeeper	38	"
	s	Nickerson Clara —†	269	"	63	"
	w	Greenwood Edna N —†	274	housewife	70	"
	x	Greenwood Lester	274	seaman	35	"
	y	Greenwood Reginald	274	engineer	41	"
	z	Greenwood Valetta B —†	274	at home	40	"

626

	a	Swimm Marguerite C —†	274	decorator	40	"
	b	Nickerson Alberta —†	274	packer	31	"
	c	Nickerson Benjamin L	274	splicer	62	"
	d	Nickerson Elsie M —†	274	decorator	33	"
	e	Nickerson Rose A —†	274	housewife	63	"
	f	Payne Frederick	274	mechanic	30	"
	g	Payne Mildred —†	274	housewife	28	"
	m	Owens Charles W	281	retired	69	111 Meridian
	n	Turnesky Florence —†	281	housewife	50	111 "
	o	Turnesky Fred	281	janitor	45	111 "
	r	Baker William	284	laborer	26	Chelsea
	s	Brooks Herbert S	284	watchman	65	here
	t	Brown Frank E	284	undertaker	63	"
	u	Penney Eileen —†	284	housewife	23	Chelsea
	v	*Penney William E	284	steamfitter	26	"
	w	Synotte John	284	retired	83	52 White
	x	Synotte William	284	mason	45	52 "
	y	Walsh Jennie —†	284	dishwasher	52	here
	z	Bryce Gertrude —†	285	housewife	25	118 Falcon

16

627
Meridian Street Continued

A	Bryce Wyman	285	machinist	30	118 Falcon
B	Clark Florence M †	285	presser	32	228 Benningt'n
C	Curtin John	285	seaman	52	228 "
D	Curtin Michael J	285	fireman	54	228 "
E	Cerbare Angeline †	285	stitcher	20	Pennsylvania
F	Mastrolia Rose †	285	housewife	31	here
G	Mastrolia Vito	285	U S A	31	"
L	Bertolino Angelo	287A	U S N	22	"
M	*Bertolino Antoinetta †	287A	housewife	54	"
N	Bertolino Antonio	287A	U S A	28	"
O	*Bertolino Baldassare	287A	fisherman	61	"
P	Bertolino Lawrence	287A	U S A	27	"
R	Bertolino Pauline †	287A	at home	24	"
S	Dean Benjamin	288	welder	32	"
T	Dean Mildred †	288	housewife	30	"
U	Driscoll Evelyn †	288	at home	28	"
V	*Burke Mary †	288	clerk	40	"
W	*Curtis Frank	288	laborer	43	"
X	*Poirier Francis	288	"	35	"
Y	*Poirier Georgina †	288	housekeeper	71	"
Z	Poirier Hubert	288	U S A	33	"

628

A	Dean Edith M †	288	housewife	47	"
B	Dean Joseph R	288	inspector	49	"
C	Gibbs Nellie A †	289	housekeeper	82	"
E	Marciel Ellen †	290	at home	87	"
F	Goldberg Harry	291	operator	45	18 Trenton
G	Pierce Joseph	291	janitor	73	here
H	Sanford Earl W	291	engineer	48	60 White
K	Smith Sarah A †	291	housekeeper	66	here
L	*Toddy Lillian †	291	at home	72	1 Monmouth
O	*Armen Irzean †	293	housekeeper	57	here
P	Armen Richard	293	proprietor	38	"
R	Giffin Charles	293	tailor	49	"
S	Vitale Louis	293	bartender	47	"
T	Zona Helen †	293	housekeeper	36	"
U	Gruditta Frank	294	shoemaker	50	"
V	Gruditta Mary †	294	housewife	45	"
W	Barnes Blanche B †	294	"	72	"
X	Barnes George H	294	retired	73	"

1—6   17

Meridian Street—Continued

z	Gannon Catherine—†	296	tel operator	39	here

629

A	Gannon Mary N—†	296	housewife	75	"
B	Gannon Timothy H	296	florist	77	"
C	Quinn Isabella—†	296	at home	80	"
E	Brown Ray	297	chauffeur	37	"
F	Dane John	297	clerk	21	27 Eutaw
G	Dane William	297	foreman	52	27 "
H	Desmond Theodore	297	proprietor	50	here
L	Dattler James	298	laborer	54	"
M	Dattler Lillian—†	298	housewife	47	"
N	Duffy Frank	298	clerk	48	"
O	Newnan Dorothy—†	298	housewife	31	"
P	Newnan William	298	laborer	36	"
R	*Martin Moses	299	carpenter	65	101 Benningt'n
S	*Martin Sarah—†	299	housewife	59	101 "
T	Pompeo Aida—†	299	clerk	22	here
U	Pompeo Frank	299	musician	49	"
V	*Pompeo Matilda—†	299	housewife	54	"
X	Rollins Emma C—†	300	housekeeper	75	"
Y	Jansen Lillian M—†	300	"	42	"
Z	Kerrigan Patrick	300	seaman	60	"

630

A	Murphy Charles G	300	machinist	59	"

Morton Place

B	*Muise John Z	1	retired	79	here
C	Muise Lucien R	1	laborer	42	"
D	Davis Catherine—†	1	at home	75	"
E	*Edmonds Sadie—†	2	housewife	50	"
F	*Edmonds William	2	laborer	56	"
G	Carey Ellen M—†	2	housewife	62	"
H	Carey Norman P	2	U S A	24	"
K	Carey Peter J	2	machinist	52	"
L	Peterson Mary—†	3	at home	72	Lynn
M	Francis Mary—†	3	"	76	here

Princeton Street

N	Hicks Sabina—†	4	matron	59	here
O	Harloff Nellie—†	4	housewife	37	"

18

Princeton Street Continued

	P	Harloff William	4	fisherman	32	here
	R	Comeau Arthur	7	laborer	41	Canada
	S	McCluskey Harry	7	"	30	269 Meridian
	T	Robicheau Alphonse E	7	mechanic	33	Chelsea
	U	Robicheau Maria C—†	7	at home	29	here
	V	Robicheau Marion—†	7	welder	22	"
	W	Bona Simon	9	rigger	58	"
	X	Doyle Robert	9	longshoreman	60	"
	Y	Driscoll Frances †	9	housewife	35	"
	Z	Driscoll John	9	longshoreman	39	"
631						
	A	Sullivan James J	9	factoryhand	35	Somerville
	B	Townsend James	9	mechanic	59	here
	C	Burke John	10	retired	74	"
	D	Burke Sabina—†	10	housewife	72	"
	E	Flanagan Agnes †	10	clerk	20	"
	F	Flanagan Helen—†	10	"	24	"
	G	Courier Edward	10	painter	35	"
	H	Courier Elizabeth—†	10	housewife	33	"
	K	Mullane Helen—†	11	"	30	63 Condor
	L	Mullane Thomas	11	laborer	29	63 "
	M	Gowdy George	11	U S A	39	here
	N	Gowdy Sarah †	11	housewife	59	"
	O	Dalton Eleanor †	12	"	28	"
	P	Dalton Mark	12	longshoreman	30	"
	R	Crumley Anna M—†	12	housewife	51	"
	S	Crumley Francis J	12	painter	20	"
	T	Crumley Leonard R	12	U S A	22	"
	U	Clancy Edward A	12	longshoreman	36	"
	V	Clancy Helen R †	12	housewife	31	"
	W	Barker Emily M †	13	"	69	"
	X	Waters Jennie R—†	13	"	70	"
	Y	Iovanna Carmen W	14	U S A	20	49 Lexington
	Z	Iovanna Charles	14	machinist	51	49 "
632						
	A	Walker Charles	14	musician	34	here
	B	Walker Margaret—†	14	housewife	38	"
	C	Richard Ethel—†	14	"	30	"
	D	Richard Harold	14	welder	31	"
	E	Banks Joseph L	15	engineer	28	Maine
	F	Banks Virginia—†	15	housewife	24	4 Saratoga pl
	L	McMullen Margaret †	15	"	53	here

Princeton Street— Continued

G	Muccio John	15	U S A	21	here
H	*Muccio Lena—†	15	housewife	59	"
K	Muccio Salvatore	15	laborer	66	"
M	Cox John E	16	inspector	40	"
N	*Parsons William I	16	retired	81	"
O	Parsons William S	16	machinist	51	"
P	Goggin Adele—†	16	housewife	34	"
R	McCarthy Frances E—†	16	"	47	"
S	Tait William	17	retired	86	"
T	Tait Winifred—†	17	housewife	71	"
U	Ambrose Olive C—†	17	"	58	"
V	Barnacle Edward A	17	mechanic	46	"
W	Barnacle Henry A	17	musician	37	"
X	Barnacle Thomas J	17	mechanic	48	"
Y	Coffey Thomas	17	"	48	284 Meridian
Z	Lavoye John	17	laborer	59	234 "

633

A	Sullivan John S	17	reporter	60	here
B	Wood Mary E—†	17	housewife	81	"
C	Dwyer James J	19	longshoreman	39	13 Wordsworth
D	Dwyer Madeline—†	19	housewife	37	13 "
E	Schwartz Anna—†	19	"	73	here
F	Schwartz George H	19	physician	51	"
G	McLaughlin Evangeline A—†	19	tel operator	38	"
H	O'Keefe Mary—†	19	housewife	35	"
K	O'Keefe Maurice J	19	policeman	42	"
L	*Fitzpatrick Peter	19	rigger	50	"
M	Hines Ashton S	19	fisherman	50	"
N	Hines Evangeline—†	19	housewife	40	"
O	Nickerson Florence G—†	19	"	60	"
P	Fagan Benjamin	19A	fisherman	61	"
R	St Croix Andrew	19A	"	57	"
S	*St Croix Elizabeth—†	19A	housewife	57	"
T	Campbell Evelyn M—†	19A	"	46	"
U	Campbell John W	19A	policeman	51	"
V	Campbell John W	19A	U S A	27	"
W	*Bennett Henry	19A	laborer	48	"
X	Ford Daniel	19A	carpenter	53	"
Y	Ford Joseph L	19A	U S A	23	"
Z	*Ford Mary E—†	19A	housewife	55	"

634
Princeton Street—Continued

A	Powers Maurice	20	shipfitter	41	here
B	Walker Arthur J	20	carpenter	61	"
C	Walker Emily—†	20	housewife	64	"
D	Ewing Harriet—†	20	"	29	"
E	Ewing Ronald	20	rigger	29	"
F	*Avila Camillo	21	tailor	47	"
G	Avila Ida—†	21	saleswoman	21	"
H	Avila Isabella—†	21	housewife	21	"
K	Avila Rose—†	21	"	43	"
L	Avila Rose—†	21	clerk	24	"
M	Avila Samuel	21	U S A	22	"
N	Campagna Alfred	21	clerk	28	"
O	Campagna Maria—†	21	housewife	25	"
P	*Briand Joseph	22	fishcutter	58	"
R	Briand Loretta—†	22	housewife	49	"
S	Doherty Joseph	22	retired	71	"
T	Drake Albert J	22	laborer	58	"
U	*Drake Annie M—†	22	housewife	54	"
V	Drake Phillip J	22	seaman	23	"
W	Monihan Hanna—†	22	housewife	84	"
X	Pepe Helen—†	22	"	30	New Jersey
Y	Pepe Joseph	22	chauffeur	30	"
Z	Santirocio Domenic	22	laborer	54	217 E Eagle

635

A	*Clouter George	23	retired	72	here
B	Conway Phillip	23	longshoreman	68	"
D	Frye Elizabeth—†	23	housewife	62	"
E	Frye James	23	carpenter	53	"
F	Frye Mary E—†	23	housewife	42	"
G	Hogan William	23	laborer	60	N Hampshire
H	Iverson Roy	23	"	31	Reading
C	Francis Leon	23	welder	45	Lawrence
K	Rose Jessie—†	23	housewife	21	Florida
L	Rose Thomas	23	U S N	24	"
M	Whalen Joseph	23	foreman	45	Somerville
N	Cheverie Margaret—†	24	housewife	32	Chelsea
O	Cogliano Alphonse	24	laborer	46	13 Central sq
P	Danforth Frederick E	24	foreman	40	Franklin
R	Lopez Manuel	24	welder	40	9 Princeton

21

			Residence, Jan. 1, 1943.		Supposed Age.	Reported Residence, Jan. 1, 1942.
Page.	Letter	FULL NAME.		Occupation.		Street and Number.

Princeton Street—Continued

s	Maupas John	24	foreman	35	119 Princeton
T	Maupas Phyllis †	24	housewife	28	119 "
U	Richards Lewis	24	seaman	30	Chelsea
V *Sinyard Michael	24	welder	33	119 Saratoga
W *Smart Thomas	24	engineer	40	here
X *Swan Edward A	24	laborer	60	34 Lexington
Y Delaney Elizabeth J †	25	factoryhand	22	here
Z Delaney Frank L	25	U S A	20	"

636

A	Gardner Edward	25	chauffeur	37	"
B	Gardner Jane †	25	housewife	79	"
C	Gardner Jefferson	25	laborer	48	"
D	Gardner John G	25	steamfitter	46	"
E	Cann Joseph	25	steward	59	"
F	Cann Sarepta †	25	housewife	63	"
G	DellaGrotte Albert	26	policeman	25	"
H *DellaGrotte Josephine †	26	housewife	71	"
K	Condakes George	26	U S A	20	"
L	Condakes John	26	student	22	"
M *Condakes Nicholas	26	proprietor	56	"
N	Condakes Pauline †	26	bookkeeper	21	"
O	Condakes Peter	26	salesman	62	"
P	Condakes Stella †	26	housewife	48	"
R	Mazzareno Francesca †	26	"	52	"
S	Mazzareno Joseph	26	musician	29	"
T	Mazzareno Pasquale	26	presser	56	"
U *Beninati Antonetta †	27	housewife	44	236 Maverick
V	Beninati Joseph	27	laborer	56	236 "
W	Beninati Mary †	27	factoryhand	21	236 "
X	DeGloria Mildred †	27	housewife	33	207 London
Y	Cleary James	27	janitor	58	here
Z	Cleary Sadie †	27	housewife	66	"

637

A *Amero Lena †	28	"	35	"
B	Amero William	28	carpenter	46	"
C	Connors Mary †	28	housewife	40	"
D	Connors Stephen F	28	chauffeur	43	"
E	Morabito William	28	machinist	25	110 Paris
F	Frizzell Helen †	29	housewife	54	here
G	Celona Nunzio	29	laborer	58	"
H *Armstrong Helen †	29	housewife	37	"

22

Princeton Street Continued

K	*Armstrong William	29	rigger	40	here
L	Ferrera Eleanor —†	30	housewife	26	"
M	Ferrera Frank	30	carpenter	30	"
N	*Indingaro Mary —†	20	housewife	58	"
O	*Indingaro Samuel	30	proprietor	57	"
P	White Everett	31	carpenter	37	"
R	White Rose —†	31	housewife	26	"
S	Boudreau Harold T	31	bridgetender	24	158 Princeton
T	Boudreau Mary R —†	31	housewife	22	here
U	Doucette Bertha L —†	31	"	52	"
V	Doucette Dorothy A —†	31	forewoman	21	"
W	Doucette Frederick M	31	carpenter	52	"
X	Doucette Frederick M	31	U S A	25	"
Y	*Beninati Mary —†	32	housewife	33	"
Z	Beninati Rocco	32	tailor	47	"

638

A	DeGruttola Elizabeth—†	32	housewife	47	"
B	DeGruttola Joseph	32	laborer	43	"
C	DeGruttola Rose—†	32	saleswoman	20	"
D	Ferrara Angelina—†	32	housewife	42	15 Princeton
E	Ferrara Vincent	32	glazier	43	15 "
F	Caruso Adam E	33	mechanic	50	here
G	Caruso Margaret T—†	33	manager	44	"
K	Munstraberg Elizabeth—†	33	social worker	27	108 White
H	Terhune Margaret—†	33	"	25	108 "
L	Andrews Thomas	33	chef	64	here
M	*Dobrakhosoff Nicholas	33	baker	46	"
N	Durocker Albert	33	mechanic	28	Woburn
O	Tacelli Benjamin	33	retired	69	here
P	Crescenzi Adam, jr	34	inspector	27	"
R	Crescenzi Rose—†	34	housewife	22	"
S	Leo Martin	34	rigger	42	"
T	Leo Mary E—†	34	housewife	39	"
U	Anthony Elizabeth—†	35	"	38	593 Saratoga
V	Anthony John	35	fisherman	43	593 "
W	Askins Leo E	35	carpenter	64	Medford
X	Askins Margaret J—†	35	housewife	64	"
Y	Bean Clifford W	35	engineer	54	Quincy
Z	Beaulieu Raymond	35	machinist	52	Cambridge

639

A	*Clark Mary—†	35	housewife	68	259 Meridian

23

Page.	Letter.	FULL NAME.	Residence, Jan. 1, 1943.	Occupation.	Supposed Age.	Reported Residence, Jan. 1, 1942. Street and Number.

Princeton Street—Continued

		FULL NAME	Res.	Occupation	Age	Reported Residence
	B	*Clark Stella †	35	housewife	66	259 Meridian
	B	DeMasellis Josephine †	35	stitcher	54	43 Orleans
	C	DeMasellis Vincent	35	tailor	52	43 "
	D	Kirby John J	35	engineer	42	Wakefield
	E	Leary Thomas	35	laborer	45	here
	F	Lelander Ellen—†	35	at home	43	Vermont
	G	Lelander Lea †	35	housewife	45	"
	H	Lelander Oscar	35	welder	45	here
	K	Francey Anna M—†	36	housewife	34	5 Hawthorne
	L	Francey Carlton R	36	engineer	36	5 "
	M	Gill Mary—†	36	housewife	32	143 Webster
	N	Gill William H	36	longshoreman	33	143 "
	O	Coombs Alexander	36	U S A	31	here
	P	*Coombs Mary—†	36	cashier	20	"
	R	Braff Jacob	37	merchant	57	"
	S	Farwell Phoebe J †	37	housewife	82	"
	T	Hewey Leon N	37	mechanic	58	"
	U	Hewey Mildred H—†	37	housewife	53	"
	V	Swimm Amaryllis N—†	37	"	41	"
	W	Swimm Herbert J	37	foreman	52	"
	X	Corado Emelia—†	38	housewife	40	"
	Y	Corado John	38	laborer	46	"
	Z	Beranger Angeline—†	38	packer	28	62 Bennington
		640				
	A	Beranger Charles	38	chef	68	62 "
	B	*Beranger Millie—†	38	housewife	64	62 "
	C	Goodwin Maude L †	39	"	78	here
	D	Robertson Ellen †	39	"	69	"
	E	Davidson Alma E †	40	"	27	49A Saratoga
	F	Davisdon John J	40	pipefitter	36	49A "
	G	Spagnuolo Constantine	40	candymaker	48	here
	H	Spagnuolo Olympia †	40	housewife	50	"
	K	Spagnuolo Quirino	40	U S A	23	"
	L	Spagnuolo Carmen	40	carpenter	29	"
	M	Spagnuolo Louise †	40	housewife	26	"
	N	Stevenson Helen †	41	at home	66	"
	O	Stevenson Stella †	41	"	65	
	P	Brown Stanley A	44	machinist	25	733 South
	R	Donaldson Albert L	44	mover	35	here
	S	Donaldson Mary A †	44	housewife	32	"
	T	Madison Edward R	44	rigger	34	"

24

Princeton Street Continued

u	Parsons Charles S	44	retired	70	Revere
v	Green Thomas	46	fisherman	37	11 Maverick sq
w	Karaglanes Nicholas	46	shipfitter	50	here
x	Lyons Reginald S	46	chef	45	Marblehead
y	Gallagher Emma †	48	housewife	47	here
z	Gallagher Francis	48	shipfitter	46	"
	641				
A	Indigaro Michael	48	carpenter	28	"
B	Indigaro Vera †	48	housewife	26	"
C	Thompson Ruth †	48	stenographer	46	"
D	Bradley Emily M †	50	housewife	43	"
E	Bradley Frederick V	50	laborer	43	"
F	Guarente Nerina †	50	housewife	22	Medford
G	Guarente Orlando	50	laborer	28	126 Havre
H	Wilson Dorothy †	50	tel operator	36	here
K*	Barrett Dennis	54	laborer	53	"
L	Crowell Arnold	54	deckhand	42	"
M	Crowell Mary †	54	housewife	49	"
N	Healey Thomas	54	deckhand	47	"
O	Hodson May †	54	housewife	21	New Jersey
P	Hodson Robert	54	U S C G	23	"
R	Mayes Agnes †	54	housewife	29	here
S	Mayes Clyde	54	U S C G	32	Texas
T	Stevens Charles	54	rigger	53	here
U	Bergstrom Annie †	56	housewife	56	"
V	Bergstrom Harold	56	electrician	40	"
W	Bergstrom Regina †	56	wrapper	36	"
X	Haggard Paul	56	fisherman	50	"
Y	Nichols Earl	56	laborer	50	"
Z	Soldram Nicholas	56	fisherman	48	"
	642				
A	Marino Albert	58	fishcutter	23	"
B*	Marino Mary †	58	housewife	67	"
C	Ruddock Clarence P	58	mechanic	36	"
D	Ruddock Lena †	58	housewife	31	"
E	Arnoldson Madeline †	60	nurse	30	"
F	Cavanaugh Elizabeth †	60	housewife	57	"
G*	Cavanaugh Patrick	60	ironworker	59	"
H	Connors Anna †	60	nurse	40	"
K*	Lee Thomas	60	fishcutter	62	"
L	Sharker Salvatore	60	chauffeur	27	"

Princeton Street — Continued

		FULL NAME.	Residence, Jan. 1, 1943.	Occupation.	Supposed Age.	Reported Residence, Jan. 1, 1942. Street and Number.
	M	Cordiner Annie—†	62	hairdresser	65	74 Bennington
	N	Faraci Charles	62	tailor	27	here
	O	Faraci Josephine—†	62	housewife	25	"
	P	*Faraci Angelina—†	62	"	51	"
	R	Faraci Joseph	62	barber	52	"
	S	*Caristo Assunta—†	77	housewife	70	"
	T	Caristo Rocco V	77	U S A	30	"
	U	Schraffa Joseph H	77	mechanic	35	"
	V	Schraffa Rose—†	77	housewife	35	"
	W	*Theriault Joseph	79	carpenter	37	"
	X	*Theriault Lena—†	79	housewife	36	"
	Y	*Giangrande Jennie—†	81	"	23	273 Lexington
	Z	Giangrande Nicholas	81	chauffeur	28	273 "
643						
	A	*Pasquarello Adelaide—†	81	housewife	55	here
	B	Agostino Margaret—†	81	"	40	"
	C	*Agostino Nicholas	81	tailor	48	"
	D	Matheson Anna M—†	83	housewife	27	"
	E	Matheson Neil E	83	teacher	37	"
	F	*Impreba Immaculata—†	83	housewife	42	"
	G	Impreba John	83	laborer	45	"
	H	Precopio Catherine—†	87	at home	20	"
	K	Precopio Concetta—†	87	factoryhand	34	"
	L	*Precopio Leo	87	retired	69	"
	M	Precopio Mario	87	electrician	36	"
	N	Precopio Natale	87	foreman	27	"
	O	Precopio Phyllis—†	87	factoryhand	36	"
	P	Precopio Rocco	87	U S A	24	"
	R	Precopio Vito	87	"	20	"
	S	*Langone Jennie—†	89	housewife	33	"
	T	Langone John	89	welder	32	"
	U	Lynch Gerard	89	chauffeur	32	"
	V	Lynch Phyllis—†	89	housewife	34	"
	W	Scarfo Eugene	89	factoryhand	23	"
	X	Scarfo Geraldine—†	89	housewife	44	"
	Y	Scarfo Nicholas	89	tailor	53	"
	Z	Giansiracusa Joseph	91	shoemaker	54	"
644						
	A	Giansiracusa Nicola	91	blacksmith	45	"
	B	*Giansiracusa Pauline—†	91	housewife	83	"
	C	Britten Henry	93	fireman	64	"

26

Princeton Street Continued

D	Poirier Mary B †	93	housewife	61	here
E	Poirier Wallace	93	rigger	65	"
F	Pignato David	93	laborer	62	"
G	*Pignato Josephine —†	93	housewife	52	"
H	DeRosa James	93	laborer	26	"
K	DeRosa Susan—†	93	housewife	26	"
L	Pignato Margaret—† rear	93	"	31	"
M	Pignato Pasquale "	93	clerk	30	"
O	Cionti Frank	95	U S A	28	179 Princeton
P	*Cionti Josephine —†	95	housewife	52	179 "
R	*Sicuranza Angela—†	95	"	74	here
S	*Sicuranza Carmella—†	95	hairdresser	33	"
T	Roberto Pietro	97	laborer	36	"
U	*Fendo Julia— †	97	housewife	34	"
V	Fendo Samuel	97	laborer	48	"
W	Aiello Ignazio	101	chef	48	"
X	*Benvissuto Theresa—†	101	housewife	73	"
Y	Benvissuto Viola—†	101	"	27	"
Z	Benvissuto William	101	mechanic	29	"
	645				
A	Pesaturo Amando	103	U S A	20	"
B	*Pesaturo Angie †	103	housewife	48	"
C	Pesaturo Anna †	103	dressmaker	28	"
D	Pesaturo John	103	shoemaker	50	"
E	Taurasi Agnes—†	103	factoryhand	30	"
F	*Taurasi Assunta—†	103	housewife	64	"
G	Taurasi Elvira— †	103	factoryhand	29	"
H	Beath James A	105	mechanic	50	"
K	Willis Andrew	105	clerk	35	"
L	Willis Christine —†	105	housewife	34	"
M	Brown Beverly J —†	105	typist	20	"
N	Brown Ethel M—†	105	housewife	50	"
O	Brown Harold R	105	mariner	55	"
P	Brown Harold R	105	U S A	25	"
R	Tacelli Arthur	107	clerk	38	"
S	Tacelli Grace —†	107	housewife	26	"
T	Tacelli Stacia —†	107	"	38	"
U	Tacelli William	107	clerk	37	"
V	Tacelli Albert	107	teacher	35	"
W	*Tacelli Carmella—†	107	housewife	75	"
X	Tacelli Edith— †	107	dressmaker	32	"

Princeton Street—Continued

	y	Tacelli Joseph	107	mechanic	73	here
	z	Butler Alice—†	109	housewife	23	"
646						
	a	Butler Margaret—†	109	"	64	"
	b	Butler Marguerite Y—†	109	factoryhand	22	"
	c	Carney William	109	laborer	52	"
	d	Harrington Mary—†	109	housewife	89	"
	e	*Jackman Gerald	109	fisherman	41	"
	f	*Sampson William	109	"	41	"
	g	*Toomey Gregory	109	"	41	120 London
	h	Serra Joseph P	111	carpenter	29	here
	k	Serra Mary—†	111	housewife	31	"
	l	Preziosi Alphonse	111	U S A	27	"
	m	Preziosi Americo	111	meatcutter	23	"
	n	Preziosi Andrew	111	butcher	29	"
	o	Preziosi Angelo	111	"	55	"
	p	*Preziosi Columbia—†	111	housewife	39	"
	r	Preziosi John	111	U S A	26	"
	s	Barranco Agostino	113	laborer	61	"
	t	Barranco Armando	113	pipefitter	28	"
	u	Barranco Charles	113	U S N	25	"
	v	*Barranco Sadie—†	113	housewife	53	"
	w	Barranco Samuel	113	laborer	23	"
	x	Barranco Frank	113	U S N	30	"
	y	Barranco Mary—†	113	housewife	31	237 Princeton
	z	DeSantis Ida—†	113	teacher	35	here
647						
	a	DeSantis Vito	113	laborer	67	"
	b	Carrozza George	115	"	23	"
	c	Carrozza James	115	mechanic	20	"
	d	Carrozza Josephine—†	115	saleswoman	27	"
	e	Carrozza Phillip	115	mason	53	"
	f	*Carrozza Philomena—†	115	housewife	52	"
	g	Nastri Carlo	115	inspector	40	"
	h	Nastri Ralph	115	U S A	32	"
	k	Nastri Stella—†	115	housewife	39	"
	l	Hunter Lettie—†	117	"	55	"
	m	Delto Domenic	117	laborer	30	374 Frankfort
	n	Delto Rose—†	117	housewife	29	374 "
	o	Delto Samuel	117	clerk	28	374 "
	p	Bickley Alma—†	117	housewife	48	here

28

Page.	Letter.	FULL NAME.	Residence, Jan. 1, 1943.	Occupation.	Supposed Age.	Reported Residence, Jan. 1, 1942. Street and Number.

Princeton Street—Continued

	Letter	FULL NAME	Residence	Occupation	Age	Reported Residence
	R	Bickley Joseph W	117	engineer	43	here
	s	Goglia Anna—†	119	housewife	21	118 Brooks
	T	Goglia Julian	119	U S N	21	42 Falcon
	U	Ventre Mary—†	119	housewife	39	here
	V	Ventre Rocco	119	foreman	39	"
	W	Pelrine Agnes T—†	121	housewife	52	120 Everett
	X	Pelrine Alice—†	121	"	24	8 Ringgold
	Y	Pelrine Edwin A	121	laborer	57	120 Everett
	Z	Pelrine Eleanor R—†	121	factoryhand	22	120 "
648						
	A	Pelrine John G	121	U S A	24	120 "
	B	Pelrine Theresa M—†	121	factoryhand	20	120 "
	C	Delahanty Anna—†	121	housewife	75	here
	D	Delahanty Catherine—†	121	at home	52	"
	E	Delahanty John J	121	laborer	50	"
	F	Delahanty Joseph	121	U S A	42	"
	G	Frevold Eleanor—†	123	housewife	28	108 Princeton
	H	Frevold Stanley	123	painter	28	108 "
	L	Maglio Erminia—†	123	housewife	49	here
	M	Maglio Frank	123	shoemaker	47	"
	N	Maglio Maria C—†	123	bookkeeper	22	"
	O	Maglio Michael	123	U S A	21	"
	K	Paglialonga Domenic	123	laborer	48	"
	P	Rotondo Anna—†	125	factoryhand	41	"
	R*	Rotondo Calogera—†	125	housewife	67	"
	S	Rotondo Nellie—†	125	factoryhand	36	"
	T	Rotondo Rosario	125	retired	72	"
	U	Scandura John	125	factoryhand	50	"
	V	Scandura Mary—†	125	housewife	46	"
	W	Cestone Florence—†	125	"	23	231A Saratoga
	X	Cestone John	125	U S A	25	245 Lexington
	Y	Patti Andrew	125	"	22	231A Saratoga
	Z*	Patti Rose—†	125	housewife	45	231A "
649						
	A	Driscoll Patrick J	127	laborer	67	here
	B*	Rubbico Anthony	127	shoemaker	58	"
	C	Rubbico Antonetta—†	127	factoryhand	22	"
	D	Rubbico Mary—†	127	"	24	"
	E	Rubbico Silvio	127	laborer	26	"
	F	Rubbico Theresa—†	127	housewife	53	"
	G	Rubbico William	127	U S N	20	"

Princeton Street Continued

	Letter	Full Name	Residence	Occupation	Age	Reported Residence
	K	Heeck Margaret †	127	housewife	69	here
	H	Schroider Mary †	127	"	68	"
	L	Moore Jennie †	131	"	66	"
	M	Delcore Bart	131	U S A	29	"
	N*	Delcore Bettina †	131	housewife	53	"
	O	Delcore Elsie †	131	nurse	27	"
	P	Murray James F	133	retired	79	"
	R	Murray Mary A †	133	housewife	76	"
	S	DeDeo Gemma †	133	factoryhand	32	"
	T	DeDeo Leonardo	133	retired	68	"
	U	DeDeo Rudolph	133	U S A	37	"
	V	DeDeo Violetta †	133	secretary	38	"

Saratoga Place

	Letter	Full Name	Residence	Occupation	Age	Reported Residence
	X	Contestabile Eleanor †	1	housewife	28	110 Benningt'n
	Y	Contestabile Louis	1	chauffeur	33	150 Webster
	Z*	Sousa Louis F	1	casketmaker	38	22 Princeton
650						
	A*	Sousa Mary H †	1	housewife	26	22 "
	B	Moni Germano	2	laborer	51	1 Saratoga pl
	C*	D'Errico Constance †	2	housewife	30	here
	D	D'Errico Michele	2	welder	29	"
	E	Passananti Anthony	2	foundryman	38	"
	F	Passananti Carmen	2	chauffeur	54	3 Emmons
	G	Passananti Marcella †	2	housewife	37	here
	H	Walker Samuel	3	retired	61	"
	L	Wright Frances †	3	winder	27	4 Saratoga pl
	M*	Hickey Patrick	4	laborer	72	here
	N	Gilmore Margaret †	4	at home	37	1 Eutaw pl
	O*	Miner Olive †	4	"	67	1 "
	P	Miner Robert	4	seaman	30	1 "
	R	Insley Aphra	4	mariner	61	here
	S	Insley Leonard	4	blacksmith	22	"
	T	Insley Lessie †	4	housewife	52	"
	U	Jackson Nettie †	4	waitress	30	Virginia
	V	Hickey Daniel	5	retired	66	here
	W	Hickey John	5	"	68	"
	X*	Sullivan Annie †	5	cleaner	60	"
	Y	Sullivan Eugene J	5	baker	31	"
	Z	McCormick William H	5	shipfitter	34	111 Eutaw

651

Saratoga Street

A	Malone Helen J—†	9	housewife	35	here
B	Malone Thomas J	9	operator	44	"
C	Carter Samuel	9	janitor	64	"
D	Day Charles F	9	mason	70	"
E	Day Edith—†	9	secretary	22	"
F	Day Jennie—†	9	housewife	56	"
G	Sarro Edward	9	chauffeur	37	7 Chelsea
H	Sarro Jennie—†	9	housewife	38	7 "
K	Maxwell William H	11	printer	76	here
L	Noble Mary J—†	11	housekeeper	55	"
M	Noble Thomas S	11	galvanizer	33	"
N	Barry Adelaide—†	13	housewife	41	"
O	Barry Joseph	13	welder	47	"
P	Bois Beatrice—†	13	housewife	42	"
R	Bois John	13	janitor	45	"
S	Crochictiere Alice—†	13	at home	68	"
T	Ritchie Arline—†	15	operator	42	"
U	Ritchie Harry L	15	retired	54	"
V	Goff Edward	15	U S A	29	"
W	Goff Jane E—†	15	housewife	50	"
X	Goff Leo	15	cashier	50	"
Y	Goff Leo, jr	15	shipworker	26	"
Z	Ferriani Dante	17	operator	32	"

652

A	Ferriani Eva—†	17	housewife	31	"
B	Ricci Anna—†	17	packer	27	"
C	Ricci Anthony	17	laborer	55	"
D	*Ricci Josephine—†	17	housewife	50	"
E	Ricci Mary—†	17	hairdresser	22	"
F	Ricci Michael	17	U S A	25	"
G	Langone Joseph	19	mechanic	29	116 Bremen
H	Langone Margaret—†	19	housewife	28	116 "
K	DiCocco Adelcho	19	welder	25	144 Saratoga
L	DiCocco Angelina—†	19	inspector	21	144 "
M	DiCocco Anthony	19	laborer	22	144 "
N	DiCocco Joseph	19	chipper	55	144 "
O	DiCocco Loretta—†	19	shoeworker	27	144 "
P	DiCocco Rita—†	19	housewife	45	144 "
V	White Helen—†	20	clerk	55	here
R	*Burke Georgia—†	20	housewife	42	"

31

Page.	Letter.	FULL NAME.	Residence, Jan. 1, 1943.	Occupation.	Supposed Age.	Reported Residence, Jan. 1, 1942. Street and Number.

Saratoga Street—Continued

	s	Burke James D	20	laborer	45	here
	T	Deering Emily †	20	at home	56	"
	U	Deering Mary †	20	secretary	20	"
	W	Fahey Gladys †	21	housewife	35	"
	X	Fahey James F	21	shipfitter	35	"
	Y	*Lovetere John	21	laborer	49	"
	Z	*Lovetere Josephine †	21	packer	35	"
653						
	A	Iverstrom Freda †	22	housewife	64	"
	B	Iverstrom Frithjof C	22	engineer	73	"
	C	Alexander Maud M †	22	at home	68	"
	D	Keough Julia †	22	clerk	27	"
	E	*Keough William	22	checker	27	"
	F	Boland Evelyn I †	25	housewife	32	"
	G	Boland Thomas J	25	laundryman	33	"
	H	Lowell Alice M †	25	tel operator	36	"
	K	Lowell Bridget A †	25	housewife	64	"
	L	Lowell Harold J	25	U S A	23	"
	M	Lowell James R	25	"	38	"
	N	Cardullo Domenic	26	manager	38	"
	O	*Cardullo Margaret †	26	housewife	35	"
	P	Marino Adele †	26	clerk	26	"
	R	*Marino Amedee	26	painter	61	"
	S	Marino Americo	26	metalworker	24	"
	T	Marino Antonio	26	U S A	31	"
	U	*Marino Giovanina †	26	housewife	63	"
	V	Marino Josephine †	26	"	23	"
	Y	Corrado Carl	27	bartender	30	"
	X	Corrado Elena †	27	housewife	30	"
	Z	Boffetta John	28	superintendent	52	Sagamore
654						
	A	Bowers Arthur L	28	machinist	54	here
	B	Gannon Joseph	28	ropemaker	25	240 Lexington
	C	Gannon Mary †	28	housewife	23	220 "
	D	Keough Edward W	28	U S A	32	here
	E	Keough Helen G †	28	housewife	52	"
	F	Kraytenberg George	28	porter	50	56 Princeton
	G	Pederzonni Charles V	28	laborer	40	Sagamore
	H	Romocher Douglas W	28	pipefitter	34	Taunton
	K	Volkman Berthold	28	carpenter	54	here
	L	Winston James F	28	U S A	50	"

Page.	Letter.	FULL NAME.	Residence, Jan. 1, 1943	Occupation.	Supposed Age.	Reported Residence, Jan. 1, 1942. Street and Number.

Saratoga Street Continued

M	Guarino Frederick	30	machinist	33	here
N	Guarino Vincenza †	30	clerk	28	"
O	Ferro Anthony	20	U S A	23	"
P	Ferro Carmela M †	30	housewife	42	"
R	Ferro Carmela M †	30	at home	21	"
S	Ferro Frances †	30	stitcher	26	"
T	Ferro John	30	laborer	48	"
U	Ferro Nancy †	30	at home	22	"
V	Lasco Anna †	31	housewife	33	"
W	Lasco Joseph	31	barber	35	"
X	Barnard Verna †	32	housewife	50	"
Y	Barnard William	32	laborer	42	"
Z	Jensen Ivar	32	foreman	60	"

655

A	McFarran Annie †	32	at home	79	"
B	Morse John	32	laborer	30	865 Saratoga
C	Thomas William	32	retired	80	here
D	Tekulsky Anna H †	34	stenographer	33	"
E	Tekulsky Jacob	34	agent	37	"
G	Bolan Lawrence	36	seaman	26	"
H	Holm Marie †	38	at home	57	"
K	Graves Mabel F †	41	"	50	23 W Eagle
L	Richard Emily S †	41	housewife	65	here
M	Richard Ernest W	41	vulcanizer	43	"
N	Richard Noel A	41	laborer	74	"
O	Carleton Ruth †	42	social worker	24	Connecticut
P*	McLean Christie †	42	"	28	here
R	Bickford Edwin	43	custodian	67	"
S	Bickford Lillian A †	43	at home	60	"
T	Bickford Mabel †	43	"	52	"
U	Cerrone Antonio	43	laborer	57	"
V*	Cerrone Frances †	43	housewife	56	"
W	Cerrone Joseph	43	clerk	27	"
X	Cerrone Mary †	43	operator	25	"
Y	Cerrone Phyllis †	43	clerk	22	"
Z	Cerrone Prudence †	43	at home	29	"

656

A	Sinibaldi Albert	43	operator	27	"
B	Sinibaldi Bertine †	43	housewife	25	"
C	McCarthy Ellen L † rear	43	at home	73	"
D	Sullivan Mary T † "	43	housekeeper	60	"

1 6   33

Page.	Letter.	FULL NAME.	Residence, Jan. 1, 1943.	Occupation.	Supposed Age.	Reported Residence, Jan. 1, 1942. Street and Number.

Saratoga Street — Continued

	E	McGrath Mabel F † rear	43	housewife	50	here
	F	McGrath Wilfred E "	43	metalworker	43	"
	G	Mullen Frances R † "	43	shipfitter	24	"
	H	Salerno Ferdinand	44	retired	76	"
	K	Salerno Louis F	44	physician	49	"
	L	Salerno Pasqualina †	44	housewife	73	"
	M	Ackerman Florence R †	44	"	21	"
	N	Ackerman John M	44	seaman	28	"
	O	Martel Philomena †	44	at home	77	45 Saratoga
	P	Martel Florence J †	44	housewife	48	here
	R	Martel Howard D	44	watchman	52	"
	S	McDonald Victor	44	retired	76	"
	T	D'India Albert	45	machinist	27	267 Lexington
	U	D'India Margaret †	45	housewife	24	267 "
	V	*Muise Joseph R	45	chef	42	here
	W	*Muise Margaret †	45	housewife	38	"
	X	Staropoli Joseph	45	shoemaker	49	"
	Y	*Staropoli Josephine †	45	housewife	39	"
	Z	Staropoli Michael	45	electrician	20	"
		657				
	A	Nicastro Mary †	46	housewife	53	"
	B	Nicastro Michael	46	machinist	57	"
	C	Nicastro Rocco	46	U S A	25	"
	D	Nicastro Saverio	46	machinist	22	"
	E	*Dota Rosaria †	46	at home	59	255 Princeton
	F	Jones Clara †	46	cook	54	here
	G	Jones Thomas	46	U S A	26	"
	H	Orton Evelyn †	47	housewife	20	87 Trenton
	K	Orton Raymond	47	U S N	24	87 "
	L	Whitten Gladys †	47	saleswoman	25	87 "
	M	Catizone Alfred	47	millworker	25	here
	N	Catizone Jennie †	47	housewife	21	"
	O	Principe Albert	47	operator	52	"
	P	*Principe Celia †	47	housewife	45	"
	R	Principe Edith †	47	cutter	23	"
	S	Boland Celia †	48	housewife	52	"
	T	Boland John	48	laborer	58	"
	U	Boland John	48	U S A	22	"
	V	Boland Stephen	48	"	25	"
	W	Hern Ronald	48	"	39	"
	X	McGurn Harold	48	boilermaker	59	35 Falcon

Saratoga Street—Continued

Y	Dolaher Albert	49	attendant	31	here
Z	Hedrington Eleanor —†	49	saleswoman	35	"
658						
B	D'Entremont Alvinie	49A	rigger	42	"
A	D'Eon Pauline †	49A	electrician	27	Randolph
C	Mallett Jeremiah	49A	carpenter	58	here
D	Mallett Josephine †	49A	housewife	61	"
E	Mallett Robert	49A	carpenter	36	"
F	Alves Jesse J	49A	chauffeur	46	"
G	Alves John J	49A	U S A	26	"
H	Burke Elizabeth —†	51	housewife	37	20 Saratoga
K	Burke George R	51	laborer	40	20 "
L	Rompon John	51	operator	31	180 Chelsea
M	Rompon Lydia —†	51	housewife	23	180 "
N	Santoro Sadie F —†	52	cleaner	54	here
P	Ciampa Joseph	52	springmaker	34	"
O	Ciampa Philomena —†	52	housewife	34	"
R	Miller Catherine —†	56	"	54	"
S	Miller Dorothea —†	56	stenographer	25	"
T	Miller Eileen —†	56	clerk	22	"
U	Miller Harry	56	longhoreman	56	"
V	Miller Lorraine —†	56	mechanic	20	"
W	Miller Phyllis—†	56	clerk	23	"
X	*Gonis Peter G	56	proprietor	44	"
Y	*Gonis Rose —†	56	clerk	38	"
Z	Famiglietti Alfred	56	U S A	26	"
659						
A	Famiglietti Antonetta †	56	clerk	53	"
B	Famiglietti Mary—†	56	stenographer	28	"
C	Famiglietti Raffaele	56	proprietor	62	"
D	Murphy John F	57	fisherman	36	109 Maverick
E	Murphy Rita J —†	57	housewife	50	82 London
F	*Luongo Concetta —†	57	"	55	here
G	Luongo Michael	57	laborer	54	"
H	Luongo Pasquale	57	shipworker	24	"
K	Nason Margaret—†	59	cleaner	59	"
L	*Italiano Ida—†	59	housewife	26	"
M	Italiano Salvatore	59	pipefitter	27	"
N	Pearson Alfred E	59	policeman	52	"
O	Pearson Edward J	59	metalworker	25	"
P	Pearson Josephine—†	59	housewife	47	"

35

Page.	Letter.	FULL NAME.	Residence. Jan. 1, 1943.	Occupation.	Supposed Age.	Reported Residence Jan. 1, 1942. Street and Number.

Saratoga Street—Continued

	R	Restaino Helen—†	61	housewife	22	91 Woodcliff
	s	Restaino Joseph A	61	cutter	22	91 "
	T	Giangregorio Carmella—†	61	housewife	51	here
	U	Giangregorio Dante	61	broker	62	"
	V	Giangregorio Lawrence	61	clerk	30	"
	W	Manning Alice—†	63	shoeworker	26	"
	X	Manning Blanche—†	63	inspector	46	"
	Y	Hickey John	65	retired	79	"
	Z	Hickey Mary—†	65	housewife	68	"
660						
	A	Reddy Joanna—†	65	at home	70	"
	¹A	Blake Nora A—†	67	housewife	62	27 Saratoga
	B	Martin Edward	67	seaman	22	here
	C	Martin Estelle—†	67	bookkeeper	23	"
	D*	Martin Mary A—†	67	housewife	59	"
	E	Martin Mary A—†	67	stenographer	25	"
	F*	Martin Thomas	67	engineer	62	"
	G	Apenas Christopher	69	repairman	45	"
	H	Hewes Nettie—†	69	housekeeper	68	"
	K	Hogan Eugene	69	retired	69	"
	L	Irving William W	69	"	64	Chelsea
	M*	King Annabelle—†	69	at home	95	here
	N*	King Sarah—†	69	"	59	"
	O	Leonard George	69	operator	40	"
	P	McKenna Harriet—†	69	housekeeper	68	"
	R	San John	69	millworker	44	"
	S	Walsh John	69	retired	68	"
	T	Williams Walter	69	shipworker	40	"
	U	Coro Angelina—†	71	packer	27	"
	V	Coro Peter	71	bartender	29	"
	W	Carnevale Alberto	71	U S A	42	"
	X	Carnevale Emma—†	71	candymaker	33	"
	Y*	Carnevale Frank	71	barber	36	"
	Z*	Carnevale Salvatore	71	retired	52	"
661						
	A	Mazzi Anthony	71	shoeworker	47	"
	B	Mazzi Elena—†	71	at home	20	"
	C*	Mazzi Rose—†	71	housewife	47	"
	D	Cannon Sadie—†	75	at home	54	316 Princeton
	E	Hoey Albert	75	chipper	32	300 Paris
	F	Hoey Evelyn—†	75	housewife	33	300 "

36

Page.	Letter	FULL NAME.	Residence, Jan. 1, 1943.	Occupation.	Supposed Age.	Reported Residence, Jan. 1, 1942. Street and Number.

Saratoga Street Continued

	L	Hughes Grace —†	102	waitress	43	here
	M	Hughes Kathleen —†	102	clerk	23	"
	N	Hughes Ruth —†	102	"	20	"
	O	Hughes Thomas	102	deckhand	45	"
	P	Burke Clarence W	102	retired	41	"
	R	Burke Elmer	102	U S A	32	"
	S	Burke Florence E †	102	at home	24	"
	T	*Burke Isabel—†	102	housewife	65	"
	U	Burke Marion E—†	102	packer	29	"
	V	Burke Paul	102	U S A	25	"
	W	Burke William R	102	retired	73	"
	X	Burke William R	102	"	46	"
	Y	Derome Anna G—†	104	housewife	49	"
	Z	Derome Arthur L	104	painter	49	"
662						
	A	Derome Arthur P	104	laborer	24	"
	B	Derome George E	104	cutter	22	"
	C	Picco Cecelia —†	106	housewife	27	Everett
	D	Picco Harold	106	fisherman	40	"
	E	*Walsh Patrick J	106	U S A	27	23 Monmouth
	F	Bremer Adelia J —†	106	manager	51	here
	G	Mann Gertrude C—†	106	at home	67	"
	H	Schaneck Johannah M †	106	"	82	"
	K	*Morrissey Catherine—†	110	"	36	"
	L	Moriarty Edward	110	longshoreman	62	"
	M	Moriarty Gertrude —†	110	operator	21	"
	N	Moriarty Julia †	110	"	26	"
	O	Moriarty Mary †	110	housewife	55	"
	P	Moriarty William	110	U S N	25	"
	R	Brennan Katherine A †	114	housekeeper	69	"
	S	Greenbaum Joseph G	114	watertender	48	"
	T	Jackson William	114	meatcutter	61	"
	U	Miglionico Joseph	114	longshoreman	36	"
	V	Shea James J	114	shipfitter	44	166 Princeton
	W	Smith Louis F	114	chauffeur	38	here
	X	Smith Mary C †	114	housewife	36	103 Saratoga
	Y	Greenwood Anna E †	116	"	42	here
	Z	Greenwood John W	116	metalworker	42	"
663						
	A	Mann Elizabeth L †	116	teller	35	"
	B	Mann Henry C	116	proprietor	73	"

37

Saratoga Street—Continued

c	Mann Minna G—†	116	housewife	71	here
d	Cardinale James	120	baker	36	"
e	Cardinale Maria—†	120	housewife	34	"
f	Leventhal Jacob	120	salesman	54	"
g	*Leventhal Sarah—†	120	housewife	52	"
h	*Doucette Edith—†	122	candymaker	30	28 Princeton
k	*Doucette Fred	122	laborer	32	28 "
l	Halloran Ambrose	122	longshoreman	59	28 "
m	Halloran Mary—†	122	housewife	59	28 "
n	Levelle Anna J—†	122	rubberworker	32	28 "
o	Bruno Marlin—†	126	housewife	28	here
p	Bruno Phillip	126	accountant	29	"
r	Matson Gustaf	126	ironworker	68	"
s	Matson Mary—†	126	housewife	67	"
u	Vietri Michael	130	laborer	36	"
v	*Bodkins Gertrude—†	130	at home	71	"
w	Paolini Anthony	134	rubberworker	34	"
x	Paolini Mildred—†	134	housewife	26	"
y	Placet Adeline—†	134	laundryworker	35	"
z	Placet Armand	134	ironworker	35	"

664

b	Mendolia Christine—†	134	housewife	21	"
a	Mendolia Joseph	134	U S A	21	"
c	Tacardo Anthony	134	packer	25	"
d	*Tacardo Joseph	134	laborer	56	"
e	*Guisti Giovanina †	136	housewife	42	"
f	Guisti Jennie—†	136	at home	21	"
g	Guisti Joseph	136	salesman	48	"
h	Harris Frances—†	136	housewife	42	"
k	Harris Timothy	136	manufacturer	41	"
l	Lerro Annie—†	136	housewife	51	"
m	Lerro Josephine †	136	stenographer	29	"
n	Lerro Vito	136	carpenter	49	"
o	Russo Gaetano	140	barber	61	"
p	Russo Jennie—†	140	clerk	31	"
r	*Russo Stephanie—†	140	housewife	61	"
s	Martorano Ernest	140	plumber	35	"
t	Martorano Gladys V—†	140	housewife	28	"
u	Lino Frances—†	140	"	26	229 Princeton
v	Lino Louis	140	mechanic	28	229 "
w	Giannario Gabriel	144	chef	38	here

Page.	Letter.	FULL NAME.	Residence, Jan. 1, 1943.	Occupation.	Supposed Age.	Reported Residence, Jan. 1, 1942. Street and Number.

Saratoga Street — Continued

	X	Giannario Mary — †	144	housewife	32	here
	Y	Dantona Francis	144	shipper	36	"
	Z	Dantona Mary — †	144	housewife	34	"
665						
	A*	Dantona Maria — †	144	at home	67	"
	B	Abate Cesare	146	salesman	27	166 Leyden
	C	Abate Phyllis — †	146	housewife	25	166 "
	D*	Abate Grace — †	146	"	51	here
	E*	Abate John	146	shoeworker	56	"
	F	Abate Rosina — †	146	stitcher	21	"
	G	Abate Vincenza — †	146	"	24	"
	H	Dugas Concetta — †	146	packer	40	"
	K	Dugas Walter	146	shipfitter	44	"
	L	Marmiani Angelina — †	148	housewife	28	165 Cottage
	M	Marmiani Antonio	148	shipfitter	30	165 "
	N	LaRosa Frank	148	U S A	24	here
	O*	LaRosa Maria — †	148	housewife	57	"
	P	LaRosa Rosario	148	retired	68	"
	S	MacDonald Eleanor — †	152	housewife	31	"
	T	MacDonald John E	152	machinist	29	"
	U	MacDanald Edward	154	calker	59	"
	V	Albanese Betty — †	156	at home	32	"
	W	Davenport Carmella — †	156	housewife	22	Chelsea
	X	Davenport William	156	U S N	26	"
	Y	Deep Jennie — †	156	at home	24	"
	Z	Rubino Mary — †	156	stitcher	26	"
666						
	A*	Moggi Umberto	156	laborer	63	here
	B	Tontodonato Camille — †	158	housewife	55	"
	C	Tontodonato Luigi	158	tilesetter	59	"
	D	Tontodonato Anthony	158	clerk	29	"
	F	Tontodonato Maria — †	158	stenographer	24	"
	E	Tontodonato Philomena — †	158	clerk	22	"
	G	Cannon Cornelius S	160	chauffeur	55	"
	H	Cannon John J	160	manager	59	"
	K	Cannon Mary E — †	160	at home	67	"
	L*	Brobecker Helen — †	162	"	64	"
	M	Gatis Joseph	162	meatcutter	23	199 Westville
	N	Gatis Mary — †	162	clerk	25	here
	O	Tracey Agnes — †	162	examiner	46	"
	R	Sanders Alta E — †	174	housewife	63	"

39

Page	Letter	Full Name.	Residence, Jan. 1, 1943	Occupation.	Supposed Age.	Reported Residence, Jan. 1, 1942. Street and Number.

Saratoga Street—Continued

s	Sanders Ernest L	174	retired	69	here
t	Celona Frank J	174	mariner	25	29 Princeton
u	Cobb Mabel—†	174	clerk	60	here

667   William J Kelly Square

a	Flynn Helen—†	27	housewife	39	10 Border
b	Flynn Helen W—†	27	factoryhand	20	10 "
c	Flynn William W	27	U S A	21	10 "
d	McCormack Winifred—†	27	housewife	70	10 "
f	Deering Catherine—†	27	"	69	here
g	Deering Michael	27	chauffeur	30	"
h	McKay Harold	27	laborer	46	10 Border
k	McKay Mary—†	27	factoryhand	46	10 "
r	Ahearn Lillian †	35	at home	78	here
s	*Carroll Joseph	35	laborer	56	107 Meridian
t	Gardner Anna—†	35	housewife	45	here
u	Gardner Edward F	35	shipfitter	51	"
v	*Good Lemuel R	35	fireman	65	9 Winthrop
w	*Hall John	35	weaver	50	here
x	Irvin Mary—†	35	at home	67	9 Winthrop
y	Lawlor Edward	35	chauffeur	34	9 Saratoga
z	Mackey William	35	U S N	45	38 Paris

668

a	Morgan Helen †	35	housewife	41	157 Condor
b	Nazzaro James	35	rigger	37	here
c	*Nicolaisen Carl	35	seaman	30	"
d	White Thomas	35	chef	35	157 Condor
h	Bernaspanni Ethel M—†	40	housekeeper	46	here
k	Stevens Ida M—†	40	at home	65	"
l	Stevens William H	40	watchman	71	"
m	Vitale Anthony A	40	proprietor	50	"

Ward 1–Precinct 7

CITY OF BOSTON

LIST OF RESIDENTS
20 YEARS OF AGE AND OVER

(NON-CITIZENS INDICATED BY ASTERISK)
(FEMALES INDICATED BY DAGGER)

AS OF

JANUARY 1, 1943

JOSEPH F. TIMILTY, *Chairman*
FREDERIC E. DOWLING, *Secretary*
WILLIAM A. MOTLEY, Jr.
FRANCIS B. McKINNEY
EVERETT R. PROUT

Listing Board.

CITY OF BOSTON PRINTING DEPARTMENT

Page	Letter	FULL NAME.	Residence, Jan. 1, 1943.	Occupation.	Supposed Age.	Reported Residence, Jan. 1, 1942. Street and Number.

700

Border Street

A	*Souza Mary—†	275	housewife	42	8 Lexington
B	Souza Peter	275	laborer	48	8 "
c	Aia Alfred	275	U S A	20	here
D	Aia Mary—†	275	housewife	46	"
E	Aia Michael	275	pipefitter	55	"
F	Dickinson John E	305	machinist	56	"
G	Paradis Mildred—†	319	housewife	30	243 Everett
H	Berry George E	319	metalworker	27	here
K	Berry Ida—†	319	housewife	50	"
M	Adams Dorothy—†	321	at home	26	Cambridge
N	Adams Gerald	321	U S A	28	"
O	Oxley Edith—†	321	housewife	49	225 Saratoga
P	Oxley Lloyd	321	U S A	25	225 "
R	Oxley Marie—†	321	clerk	20	225 "
S	Oxley Ralph A	321	engineer	54	225 "
T	Autuori Andriana—†	321	housewife	52	here
U	Autuori Carmela—†	321	stitcher	26	"
V	Autuori Domenic	321	U S A	28	"
W	Autuori Francesco	321	fisherman	55	"
X	*Imparato Ciro	321	baker	50	84 Everett
Y	*Imparato Mary—†	321	housewife	41	84 "

701

A	Duffy Frank	323	U S A	20	here
B	Duffy Maud—†	323	housewife	47	"
c	Duffy William	323	pipefitter	49	"
D	Duffy William P	323	U S A	24	"
E	Burns Gerald F	323	operator	45	"
F	Burns Lillian—†	323	housewife	44	"
G	Burns Marion—†	323	saleswoman	20	"

Brooks Street

H	Carmen Israel	116	storekeeper	49	here
K	Carmen Sarah—†	116	housewife	44	"
L	Sheehan Anna L—†	116	"	58	"
M	Sheehan Daniel J	116	operator	58	"
N	DiDonato Mary—†	118	housewife	45	"
O	DiDonato Otto	118	U S A	20	"
P	DiDonato Rose—†	118	clerk	23	"
R	*Cappozzi Vincenzo	120	retired	79	"

2

Brooks Street Continued

	s	DePesa Gerard	120	laborer	59	here
	t	DePesa Jennie †	120	operator	30	"
	u	*DePesa Nicoletta †	120	housewife	55	"
	v	Hulke Benjamin, jr	122	policeman	46	"
	w	Hulke Florence K—†	122	housewife	40	"
	x	Powers Marjorie I—†	122	"	22	"
	y	Campbell Clinton D	126	seaman	52	"
	z	Campbell Savilla †	126	waitress	50	"
702						
	a	Keane Mary F—†	127	housewife	60	"
	b	Keane Walter P	127	U S N	22	"
	c	McDonnell Alphonso	127	undertaker	39	"
	d	McDonnell Mary H—†	127	housewife	35	"
	e	Peterson Marion—†	127	saleswoman	45	"
	f	Splaine John	128	janitor	54	"
	g	Splaine Mary †	128	housewife	55	"
	h	Doherty Mary—†	128	"	67	"
	k	Doherty Philip	128	retired	67	"
	l	Sorensen Andrew	129	laborer	53	"
	m	Sorensen Arthur	129	salesman	21	"
	n	Sorensen Bernard	129	U S A	22	"
	o	Sorensen Stanley	129	"	23	"
	p	Murphy Elizabeth E †	130	housekeeper	76	"
	s	DeYoung Louise—†	131	"	75	"
	t	Trippi Giuseppe	131	laborer	48	"
	u	*Trippi Philipe—†	131	housewife	38	"
	v	Trippi Phyllis—†	131	inspector	20	"
	w	Domega Catherine †	131	housewife	24	125 Meridian
	x	Domega Richard	131	laborer	25	125 "
	y	DiGirolamo Dorothy—†	133	dressmaker	27	here
	z	*DiGirolamo Erminio	133	tailor	55	"
703						
	a	*DiGirolamo Mary—†	133	housewife	64	"
	b	LaMotta Leonard	133	stevedore	42	"
	c	LaMotta Michael	133	"	44	"
	d	Mogan Violet †	133	secretary	34	"
	e	Johnston Arthur D	135	chauffeur	44	"
	f	Johnston Marion T †	135	housewife	44	"
	g	Fogg Lena C—†	135	at home	89	"
	h	Garvey Carrie—†	137	housewife	27	"
	k	Garvey William	137	laborer	32	"

3

Page.	Letter.	FULL NAME.	Residence, Jan. 1, 1943.	Occupation.	Supposed Age.	Reported Residence, Jan. 1, 1942. Street and Number.

Brooks Street—Continued

	Letter	FULL NAME	Res.	Occupation	Age	Reported Residence
	L	Rabasco Ann— †	137	saleswoman	21	here
	M	Rabasco Josephine— †	137	housewife	42	"
	N	Rabasco Pasquale	137	machinist	53	"
	O	Faber John A	139	carpenter	26	"
	P	Faber John T	139	machinist	58	"
	R	Faber Mary E— †	139	housewife	58	"
	S	Bonzey Charles M	140	baker	47	"
	T	Bonzey Charles M, jr	140	student	24	"
	U	Bonzey Theresa M— †	140	housewife	45	"
	V	Swansburg Dwight	140	carpenter	57	"
	W	Huggan Mary R— †	144	housekeeper	52	"
	X	Ryder Grace M— †	144	"	55	"
	Y	Swett Lillian A— †	144	housewife	50	"
	Z	Swett Robert	144	salesman	61	"
704						
	A	Correnti John	146	machinist	28	5 Holden ct
	B	Correnti Sabina— †	146	housewife	23	Chelsea
	C	Sirignano Arthur	146	U S A	21	here
	D	Sirignano Frances— †	146	housewife	21	"
	E	*Vitale Joseph	146	barber	54	"
	F	*Vitale Rose— †	146	candymaker	43	"
	G	Keough Anita— †	146	housewife	20	86 Eutaw
	H	Keough Charles, jr	146	machinist	23	303 Lexington
	K	Hyslop Caroline A— †	147	housewife	46	here
	L	Hyslop Harold J	147	laborer	48	"
	M	Hyslop James	147	watchman	72	"
	N	*Hyslop Serean— †	147	storekeeper	70	"
	O	Thibodeau Lorraine— †	147	housewife	21	128 Lexington
	P	Thibodeau Paul	147	U S A	24	198 Falcon
	R	Bergh Axel A	148	clergyman	69	here
	S	Bergh Inga— †	148	housewife	65	"
	U	Driscoll Catherine— †	149	housekeeper	76	"
	V	Hodgens Francis W	149	welder	29	"
	W	Hodgens Mary K— †	149	housewife	33	"
	X	*Chapman Fannie— †	151	storekeeper	46	"
	Y	Freda Carmino C	151	chauffeur	29	"
	Z	Freda Ethel— †	151	housewife	29	"
705						
	A	Smith Angus	153	retired	72	"
	B	Smith Cecelia M— †	153	housewife	50	"

Page.	Letter.	FULL NAME.	Residence, Jan. 1. 1943.	Occupation	Supposed Age.	Reported Residence, Jan. 1, 1942. Street and Number.

Brooks Street—Continued

	c	Smith Cecelia M —†	153	housekeeper	20	here
	d	Smith Hugh A	153	foreman	48	"

Eutaw Street

	E	Lyons Arnold	19	electrician	33	here
	F	*Lyons Evanell †	19	housewife	34	"
	G	Newell Hazel †	19	"	37	"
	H	Newell Sylvester	19	laborer	43	"
	K	*Doucette Edward	19	"	48	"
	L	Ellis Mary †	19	operator	42	"
	M	*Barrett Mary C—†	21	housekeeper	58	11 Maverick sq
	N	Czerwinski Joseph A	21	laborer	34	23 White
	O	Czerwinski Mary E —†	21	housewife	35	23 "
	P	Kincaid William R	21	U S A	22	23 "
	R	Tarr Augusta †	21	storekeeper	29	here
	S	Tarr Jennie †	21	"	60	"
	T	Pearson Alfred W	23	shipfitter	29	"
	U	Pearson Alice †	23	housewife	28	"
	V	Rossetti Albert	23	foreman	40	"
	W	Rossetti Rose †	23	housewife	40	"
	X	Conti Frank	23	shipwright	41	"
	Y	Conti Mary †	23	housewife	38	"
	Z	Leary James G	25	fireman	30	"

706

	A	Leary Margaret †	25	housewife	28	"
	B	Siraco Anthony	25	U S A	24	"
	C	Siraco Dominic	25	inspector	21	"
	D	Siraco John	25	tilesetter	52	"
	E	Siraco Lucy †	25	housewife	49	"
	F	Siraco Mary—†	25	housekeeper	31	"
	G	Siraco Vincenzia †	25	marker	26	"
	H	Siraco Anthony	25	coppersmith	60	"
	K	Siraco Carmello	25	mechanic	25	"
	L	Siraco Vincenzia †	25	housewife	58	"
	M	Pitts Charlotte †	27	"	30	45 Benningt'n
	N	Pitts Frank J	27	rigger	37	45 "
	O	Carino Joseph A	27	tailor	57	here
	P	Carino Margaret —†	27	housewife	42	"
	R	Carino Reynold A	27	U S A	23	"

Page	Letter	FULL NAME.	Residence, Jan. 1, 1943.	Occupation.	Supposed Age.	Reported Residence, Jan. 1, 1942. Street and Number.

Eutaw Street—Continued

	Letter	FULL NAME.	Res.	Occupation.	Age	Reported Residence
	s	Carino Walter	27	U S A	23	here
	t	Pierro Angelo	29	meatcutter	26	"
	u	Pierro Constance	29	housewife	24	"
	v	*Fiore Antonio	29	laborer	53	"
	w	Fiore Lena—†	29	housewife	41	"
	x	Fiore Mary—†	29	seamstress	22	"
	y	Pierro Albert	29	stenographer	24	"
	z	*Pierro Carmino	29	meatcutter	50	"

707

	Letter	FULL NAME.	Res.	Occupation.	Age	Reported Residence
	a	Pierro Elvira T—†	29	factoryhand	21	"
	b	*Pierro Marie E—†	29	housewife	45	"
	c	Indresano Albert	31	chauffeur	36	"
	d	Indresano Leonora—†	31	housewife	33	"
	e	*Indresano Thomasina—†	31	"	60	"
	f	Foster Adeline—†	33	housekeeper	42	341 Border
	g	Abramovitch Basil	33	millwright	57	here
	h	Abramovitch Margaret—†	33	housewife	53	"
	k	DeBay Mary—†	33	"	24	"
	l	DeBay Philip	33	laborer	33	"
	m	Zelinich Anany	33	"	48	"
	n	Fitzgerald Ann A—†	35	clerk	28	"
	o	Fitzgerald Bridget—†	35	housewife	70	"
	p	Donahue Ellen—†	35	"	54	"
	r	Donahue Irene—†	35	"	25	4 Everett pl
	s	Donahue John	35	foreman	29	here
	t	Gawlinsky Grace—†	35	stenographer	21	"
	u	Bevilaqua Dorothea—†	37	housewife	25	246 Maverick
	v	Bevilaqua James E	37	shoeworker	25	246 "
	w	Facchino Angelo	37	presser	54	here
	x	Facchino Mary—†	37	housewife	49	"
	y	Bevilaqua Anthony	37	operator	28	"
	z	*Bevilaqua Rose—†	37	housewife	23	"

708   Lexington Street

	Letter	FULL NAME.	Res.	Occupation.	Age	Reported Residence
	c	Welch Frank H	20	retired	72	here
	d	*Ennis Annie—†	26	housewife	70	"
	e	Ling Bernard	26	retired	66	"
	f	*Sullivan Catherine—†	26	at home	42	"
	g	Nardine Emilio	28	laborer	48	259 Everett
	h	Granese Adeline—†	28	factoryhand	21	104 Marion

Lexington Street —Continued

K	Granese Mary †	28	housewife	54	104 Marion
L	Hannon Rose—†	28	factoryhand	20	104 "
M	Foster Alice M †	30	housewife	54	here
N	Foster Mary M †	30	at home	80	"
O*	Foster Melvin	30	seaman	54	"
P	Brown Albert	30	painter	35	193 Sumner
R	Fothergill John	30	guard	60	here
S	Green John	30	retired	70	87 Meridian
T*	Kelley James	30	counterman	40	43 Decatur
U	Olson Frank	30	seaman	58	Sharon
V	Sutherland Daniel	30	retired	70	Arlington
W	Thompson John	30	"	62	here
X	Fullerton Doris †	34	housewife	30	65 W Eagle
Y	Fullerton Frederick D	34	fisherman	36	65 "
Z	George Albert	34	seaman	32	here
	709				
A	Swan Arthur H	34	"	26	"
B	Swan Catherine †	34	housewife	26	"
C	Swan Edwin A, jr	34	chauffeur	34	"
D	Swan Willard	34	U S N	23	65 W Eagle
E	Ciampa Joseph	36	shoeworker	48	here
F	Ciampa Louise †	36	housewife	37	"
G	Rizza Ralph	36	millhand	62	"
H	Tirone Caroline †	36	seamstress	28	"
K	Troiano Columba †	36	dressmaker	52	"
L	Troiano Theresa †	36	seamstress	21	"
M	Vozzella Guisippe	36	laborer	62	"
N	Anderson Andrew	38	draftsman	27	"
O	Anderson Mary †	38	housewife	53	"
R	Brimfield Jennie †	40	"	60	"
S	Brimfield John	40	operator	52	"
T	Roche Charles	40	shipper	38	"
U	Roche Frank A	40	supervisor	58	"
V	Roche Gertrude †	40	housewife	58	"
W	Parker Gladys M †	42	"	31	Maine
X	Parker Perry P	42	engineer	35	"
Y	Keenan Harry	42	electrician	62	here
Z	Cuccinota Flavia †	42	housewife	65	"
	710				
A	Beebe Lauretta †	44	cook	39	"
B*	Brugione Frank	44	"	46	"

7

Page.	Letter.	FULL NAME.	Residence Jan. 1, 1943.	Occupation.	Supposed Age.	Reported Residence, Jan. 1, 1942. Street and Number.

Lexington Street—Continued

	c	Chase Nellie—†	44	at home	83	here
	d	Dempsey Helen—†	44	"	46	"
	e*	Lynch Michael	44	fisherman	45	"
	f	McDonough Dorothy—†	44	housewife	30	303 Princeton
	g	McDonough Walter A	44	electrician	39	303 "
	h	McFarrell Gertrude—†	44	waitress	24	46 "
	k	McFarrell James	44	foundryman	26	46 "
	l*	Rider William	44	retired	70	here
	m	Sanders Herman	44	laborer	67	"
	n	Stewart Annie—†	44	housewife	43	"
	o	Wilson Alfreda—†	44	clerk	23	"
	p	Buonopane Delores—†	46	housewife	37	"
	r	Buonopane Ralph	46	clerk	41	"
	s	Buonopane John	46	"	37	"
	t	Buonopane Mary—†	46	housewife	33	"
	u*	Buonopane Pasqualina—†	46	"	69	"
	v	Buonopane Phyllis—†	46	factoryhand	32	"
	x	Testa Amadio	70	machinist	32	"
	y	Testa Jennie—†	70	housewife	27	"
	z	Testa Eugenio	70	burner	30	"

711

	a	Testa Josephine—†	70	housewife	29	"
	b	Testa Anna—†	70	candymaker	27	"
	c	Testa Assunta—†	70	housewife	66	"
	d	Testa Carmen	70	salesman	39	"
	e	Testa Felice	70	candymaker	67	"
	f	Serpone Frank	72	stitcher	28	36 Marshfield
	g	Serpone Lena—†	72	housewife	29	242 Saratoga
	h	Belino John	72	barber	40	here
	k	Belino Mary—†	72	housewife	34	"
	l	Belino Agrapino	72	millhand	65	"
	m*	Belino Jennie—†	72	housewife	61	"
	n	Surette Adolf	74	counterman	40	72 Lexington
	o	Surette James	74	retired	67	72 "
	p	Surette Louise—†	74	housewife	45	72 "
	s	Beach E Darwin	78	porter	59	here
	t	Hagar Elson K	78	fisherman	52	"
	u	McLeash Charlotte—†	78	housewife	56	"
	v	Lee Joseph	78	clerk	39	"
	w	Lee Thelma—†	78	housewife	29	"
	x	Ducette Annette—†	78	stitcher	34	"

8

Lexington Street—Continued

Y	Carrigan Daisy—†	78	housewife	44	here	
Z	Carrigan Richard	78	clerk	42	"	
	712					
A	McCall Jean—†	78	saleswoman	22	"	
B	Lindell Elina—†	78	at home	51	Connecticut	
C	Lindell John M	78	machinist	58	Maine	
E	Alanzo Nicolo	81	laborer	42	here	
F	Comeau Albert B	81	carpenter	52	"	
G	Comeau Mary—†	81	housewife	59	"	
H	*Crowell Ivan	81	fisherman	40	"	
K	Dutemple Rose—†	81	housewife	53	103 Meridian	
L	Dutemple Williard	81	clerk	54	103 "	
M	Flumari Ralph	81	laborer	29	here	
N	Jeddry Edward	81	carpenter	65	7 Central sq	
R	Kenney Wxeyford	81	watchman	54	here	
O	Madais Luigi	81	clerk	67	"	
P	Vencenzo John	81	retired	65	Illinois	
S	DeBeccaro Edith—†	83	housewife	23	here	
T	DeBeccaro Frank	83	salesman	27	"	
U	*Pastore Anthony	83	carpenter	46	"	
V	Pastore Rose—†	83	housewife	37	"	
W	Bouchie Maria—†	85	at home	77	Somerville	
X	*McLellan Anne E—†	85	housewife	64	42 Lexington	
Y	McLellan William	85	laundryman	60	42 "	
Z	Daley Edward	85	U S A	37	Watertown	
	713					
A	Daley Mary—†	85	clerk	36	here	
B	Monson Albertine—†	85	bookkeeper	40	"	
C	Monson Henry L	85	rigger	48	"	
D	Roy Armandine—†	85	housewife	48	"	
E	Roy Elias	85	cook	73	"	
H	Saunier Anna V—†	88	housewife	48	"	
K	Saunier Daniel	88	U S A	22	"	
L	Saunier Melvin	88	retired	49	"	
M	Doherty Constance—†	88	nurse	20	"	
N	Doherty Mary—†	88	"	21	"	
O	Doherty Nora—†	88	housewife	51	6 Eutaw	
P	Swindell Jane—†	88	"	48	here	
R	Swindell Samuel	88	mechanic	63	"	
S	Molloy Sadie—†	89	housewife	44	"	
T	Molloy Thomas	89	clerk	45	"	

9

Page	Letter	Full Name.	Residence, Jan. 1, 1943.	Occupation.	Supposed Age.	Reported Residence, Jan. 1, 1942. Street and Number.

Lexington Street — Continued

	Letter	Full Name.	Residence	Occupation.	Age	Reported Residence
	U	Arcari Anthony	89	electrician	43	here
	V	Arcari Christine †	89	housewife	32	"
	W	Lanni Angelo	89	shoemaker	51	"
	X	Lanni Mary †	89	clerk	21	"
	Y*	Lanni Nancy †	89	housewife	51	"
	Z	Fabiano Anna †	90	"	38	"

714

	Letter	Full Name.	Residence	Occupation.	Age	Reported Residence
	A	Fabiano Joseph	90	counterman	38	"
	B	Cerundolo Mary †	90	housewife	41	"
	C	Cerundolo Salvatore	90	laborer	47	"
	D	Therrault Eva †	90	shoemaker	33	"
	E	Cardinelli Andrew	92	painter	27	"
	F	Cardinelle Josephine †	92	housewife	23	"
	G	Giglio Edith †	92	"	26	"
	H	Giglio Joseph	92	counterman	25	"
	K	Mento Charles	92	chauffeur	35	"
	L	Mento Michelina †	92	housewife	32	"
	M	Lofgren Frederick W	93	clerk	47	"
	N	Lofgren Gladys T †	93	housewife	35	"
	O	Pierce Ernest	93	engineer	54	122 London
	P	Iapicca Esther †	93	housewife	28	here
	R	Iapicca Felix	93	U S A	24	697 Benningt'n
	S*	Paolini Anselmo	93	laborer	58	here
	T	Paolini Emma †	93	clerk	33	"
	U	Paolini Linda †	93	"	23	"
	V*	Paolini Lucia †	93	housewife	58	"
	W	Paolini Mario	93	U S N	20	"
	X	Paolini Renato	93	seaman	21	"
	Y	Carter Clarence A	94	machinist	42	60 Trenton
	Z	Carter Rose †	94	housewife	24	60 "

715

	Letter	Full Name.	Residence	Occupation.	Age	Reported Residence
	A	Kruger Lena †	94	"	35	here
	B	Martucci Anthony	94	painter	45	"
	C*	Cuozzo Anthony	94	shoeworker	30	"
	D	Cuozzo Florence †	94	housewife	29	"
	E	Foster Henry B	95	clerk	33	"
	F	Foster Natalie R †	95	housewife	31	"
	G	Olson Bonoria †	95	"	63	"
	H*	Hansen Fritz	95	machinist	56	87 Trenton
	K	Whitten Irene †	95	housewife	33	87 "
	L	Whitten Woodrow W	95	chauffeur	30	87 "

Lexington Street — Continued

M	Lynch James	96	retired	76	here
N	Morgan Anna †	96	housewife	74	"
O	O'Hara Ronald	96	chauffeur	25	"
P	Amiro Andrew J	96	seaman	30	"
R*	Amiro Landry D	96	"	64	"
S	Amiro Roger J	96	engineer	47	6 Eutaw
T	Borich Frances J †	96	housewife	50	here
U	French John J	96	retired	76	"
V	Lang Edward	96	boilermaker	60	"
W	Lang Edward F	96	U S A	23	"
X	Liacho Pandy	96	storekeeper	48	"
Y	Vecchione Elvira L †	96	teacher	36	"
Z	Gross Calvin S	97	messenger	47	"

716

A	McGloan Freda †	97	student	20	"
B	McGloan Frederick A	97	retired	72	"
C	McGloan Martha J †	97	housewife	55	"
D	Foster Avis †	97	at home	32	"
E	Foster Hattie L †	97	housewife	57	"
F	Foster Thomas E	97	clerk	28	"
G	Foster William L	97	fireman	58	"
H	Puzzo Anna †	98	housewife	38	"
K	Puzzo Samuel	98	laborer	45	"
L	Licari Giacomina †	98	housewife	40	"
M	Reed Gertrude E †	99	at home	68	"
N	Guerriero Jennie †	100	housewife	47	"
O	Guerriero Ralph	100	chauffeur	51	"
P	Guerriero Sarah †	100	factoryhand	22	"
R	Nickerson Frank J	103	student	20	"
S	Nickerson Gardner H	103	mechanic	49	"
T	Nickerson Marion A †	103	housewife	49	"
U	Pizzerto Frank L	105	clergyman	46	"
W	Pizzerto Santina †	105	housewife	33	"
Y	Benner George F	107	retired	83	291 Meridian
Z*	Comuso Joseph	107	tailor	26	here

717

A	Dingley Albert F	107	seaman	55	"
B	Hunt Herbert L	107	retired	69	"
C	Hunt Rosamond J †	107	housekeeper	69	"
D	Rebboli James A	107	guard	68	Worcester
E	O'Brien Edward J	108	retired	79	here

Lexington Street— Continued

F	O'Brien Francis J	108	salesman	48	here
G	O'Brien Julia M —†	108	housewife	82	"
H	O'Brien Mary F —†	108	stenographer	51	"
K	Boman Carl V	109	U S A	40	109 Lexington
L	Gage Gertrude —†	109	housekeeper	69	here
M	Melanson Philip	109	storekeeper	58	"
N	Roberts Venchard L	109	retired	70	"
O	McCoy Helen R —†	110	stenographer	21	"
P	McCoy Mary M —†	110	housewife	47	"
R	McGuire Thomas B	110	fireman	54	"
S	MacDonald Murdock	111	retired	84	"
T	McAlpern Effie —†	111	at home	77	"
U	White Walter S	111	cook	45	"
V	Yeaton Clinton G	111	U S N	24	"
W	Yeaton Josephine —†	111	housewife	54	"
X	Penny Martha E —†	114	"	40	"
Y	Penny Vincent	114	welder	42	"
Z	Crozier Charlotte M —†	116	teacher	33	"

718

A	Crozier Grace —†	116	housewife	59	"
B	DeSimone Angelina —†	117	stitcher	25	"
C	DeSimone Joseph	117	seaman	29	"
D*	DeSimone Pasqualina —†	117	housewife	53	"
E	DeSimone Sadie —†	117	clerk	22	"
F	DeSimone Sophie —†	117	stitcher	23	"
G	Monaco Anthony	117	laborer	33	"
H	Monaco Marie —†	117	housewife	28	"
K	Warren Elsie —†	117	saleswoman	48	"
L	Warren Gladys —†	117	inspector	23	"
M	Warren Harold	117	boilermaker	49	"
N	Nichols Emma J —†	118	housewife	69	"
O	Thibodeau Annie —†	119	"	67	"
P	Thibodeau Charles	119	carpenter	38	"
R	Thibodeau Elizabeth —†	119	finisher	30	"
S*	Thibodeau Henry	119	carpenter	65	"
T	Thibodeau Hilda —†	119	at home	24	"
U	Comeau Eva —†	119	housewife	40	"
V	Comeau Leo	119	boatbuilder	38	"
W	Cote Dorothy —†	119	housewife	34	"
X	Cote Paul	119	chef	37	"
Y	Crouse Charles	119	carpenter	65	"

Lexington Street — Continued

z	Royster Angelina †	119	housewife	30	200 Brooks
719						
A	Royster Eugene	119	bartender	30	200 "
B	Raab Blanche †	119	housewife	22	60 Bennington
C	Raab Paul J	119	U S N	30	60 "
D	Magnano Gertrude †	119	at home	46	here
E	Staples George F	123	retired	81	"
F	Walsh Joseph J	123	"	62	"
G	Woods Fred E	123	"	77	"
H	Woods Isabel M †	123	housewife	70	"
K	Hargrave Cora M †	124	at home	70	"
L	McCallum Malcolm L	124	secretary	36	"
M	McCallum Minnie B †	124	at home	76	"
N	Small Henrietta †	124	"	77	"
O	d'Entremont Anna †	125	housewife	43	"
P	d'Entremont Edward	125	accountant	50	"
R*	Amirault Annie A †	125	housekeeper	44	"
S	Glass Evelena F †	125	at home	81	"
T	Nutter Caroline E †	125	"	81	"
U	Alves Mary M †	126	"	75	"
V	Forster Barbara D †	126	supervisor	52	"
W	Forster Gertrude L †	126	housewife	46	"
X	Forster Mary A †	126	at home	76	"
Y	Forster Mary Z †	126	clerk	20	"
Z	Forster Rita G †	126	"	26	"
720						
A	Forster William J	126	fireman	49	"
B	Hannigan John	126	U S C G	24	"
C	Hannigan Ruth †	126	secretary	22	"
D	DeCicco Elizabeth †	127	housewife	20	169 Brooks
E	DeCicco Robert	127	welder	24	26 Frankfort
F	Surrette Augustine	127	"	33	1318 Com av
G	Surrette Ina †	127	housewife	31	1318 "
H	Boudreau Simon A	128	retired	65	here
K	Edmunds Alvin E	128	shipfitter	42	"
L	Edmunds Marie H †	128	housewife	37	"
M	Lee Delores L †	128	"	40	"
N	Lee Robert J	128	engineer	53	"
O	Lee Robert J, jr	128	U S N	21	"
P	Richard Charles P	128	fisherman	54	39 Hemenway
R	Hondius Mary S †	129	at home	55	here

Lexington Street — Continued

	Letter	FULL NAME.	Residence	Occupation	Age	Reported Residence
	s	Hughes Anna †	129	operator	23	here
	t	Hughes Mary †	129	housewife	49	"
	u	Hughes Thomas A	129	pipefitter	50	"
	v	Hughes Dorothy †	129	housewife	25	"
	w	Hughes Thomas J	129	carpenter	27	"
	x	Gueranti Donald	136	U S A	28	"
	y	Gueranti Enrico	136	U S N	20	"
	z	*Gueranti Florence †	136	housewife	53	"

721

	Letter	FULL NAME.	Residence	Occupation	Age	Reported Residence
	A	*Gueranti Henry	136	storekeeper	58	"
	B	Gueranti Margaret †	136	stitcher	22	"
	C	McDonald Anslem	136	carpenter	50	"
	D	McDonald Sadie †	136	housewife	40	"
	E	Amico Annie †	138	"	48	"
	F	Amico Pietro	138	laborer	63	"
	G	Impeduglia Laurence	138	operator	32	"
	H	Impeduglia Lillian †	138	housewife	28	"
	K	Fagone Joseph	138	pipefitter	30	"
	L	Fagone Phyllis †	138	housewife	28	"
	M	*Fitzgerald Lottie †	140	"	28	100 Marion
	N	*Surette Clifford	140	fishcutter	34	here
	O	*Surette Margaret †	140	housewife	30	"
	P	Letterie Anna †	140	at home	20	3 Davis ct
	R	Letterie Frank	140	molder	20	99 Trenton
	S	Ristino Grace †	141	housewife	28	here
	T	Ristino Patrick	141	inspector	29	"
	U	Collins Dennis A	141	salesman	37	113 Trenton
	V	Gavaghan Frank J	141	chauffeur	45	here
	W	Gavaghan Julia †	141	housewife	39	"
	Y	Coscia Ferdinand	142	operator	28	"
	X	Coscia Yolanda †	142	housewife	21	"
	Z	Minichiello Antonio	142	operator	65	"

722

	Letter	FULL NAME.	Residence	Occupation	Age	Reported Residence
	A	Minichiello Elizabeth †	142	stitcher	21	"
	B	Minichiello Rosalie †	142	housewife	63	"
	C	Gallinaro Salvatore	142	machinist	30	"
	D	Gallinaro Sylvia †	142	housewife	29	"
	E	*Letteriello Anna †	143	"	51	"
	F	Letteriello Joseph	143	barber	56	"
	G	Letteriello Nora †	143	seamstress	25	"
	H	*Digiacomo Santo	143	cook	58	"

14

Lexington Street Continued

K	Falzone Helen †	144	housewife	26	here
L	Falzone Salvatore	144	laborer	28	"
M	Marino Catherine †	144	housewife	22	32A Leverett
N	Marino Leo	144	brakeman	24	85 Gladstone
O	DiGianvittorio Dano	144	musician	25	here
P	DiGianvittorio Jennie †	144	housewife	26	"
R	Laura Domenic	145	welder	39	"
S	Laura Emma †	145	housewife	39	"
T	Mantia Josephine †	145	at home	42	"
U	*Maurano Caroline †	145	housewife	76	"
V	Maurano Peter	145	machinist	37	"
W	*Bartalo Tina †	145	at home	57	"
X	Fennell Martha E †	145	"	65	"
Y	Leslie Jennie V †	145	waitress	48	"
Z	Carney Francis	146	chauffeur	22	40 Perkins

723

A	*Clark Thomas W	146	laborer	37	150 Lexington
B	*Lambert Margaret †	146	housewife	43	150 "
C	Page Gladys †	146	"	25	here
D	Page Laurence	146	laborer	30	"
E	*Nardile Luigi	147	retired	77	"
F	*Nardile Marie †	147	housewife	72	"
G	Schiapa Joseph A	147	bartender	53	"
H	Jones Edmund	148	welder	48	"
K	Jones Elsie †	148	housewife	41	"
L	Jones George	148	welder	35	"
M	Jones Rose †	148	housewife	35	"
N	Jones Mary †	148	"	60	"
O	Jones William	148	chauffeur	22	"
P	*Zeuli Adolfo	149	barber	52	"
R	*Zeuli Filomena †	149	housewife	52	"
S	DeFeo Anna †	149	"	56	"
T	DeFeo Arnold	149	laborer	59	"
U	DeFeo Ruth †	149	packer	22	"
V	*VanBuskirk Albert G	150	meatcutter	50	569 Benningt'n
W	*VanBuskirk Elizabeth †	150	housewife	53	569 "
X	*Holden Blanche †	150	"	30	here
Y	Holden Frederick	150	factoryhand	43	"
Z	Schroffer Florence †	150	housewife	35	"

724

A	Schroffer Thomas C	150	retired	35	"

15

Lexington Street— Continued

c	Eriksen Irene †	152	housewife	41	here
d	Eriksen Roy	152	millwright	43	"
e	Eriksen Virginia †	152	at home	21	"
f	Ohlson Christine †	153	"	50	"
g	Ponzio-Vaglia Alfred	153	clerk	55	"
h	Picardi Mary †	154	housewife	33	"
k	Picardi Massamino	154	photographer	35	"
l	Nunes Alfred J	154	laborer	39	13 Condor
m	Ward Rose †	154	operator	38	here
n	Nichols George W	154	retired	73	"
o	Nichols Mary E †	154	housewife	68	"
p	Giorgio Domenic	156	electrician	29	"
r	Giorgio Marie †	156	housewife	27	"
s	Anderson Alice C †	156	"	49	"
t	Anderson Oscar C	156	carpenter	49	"
u	Gammon George A	156	U S N	23	"
v	O'Meara Hattie †	156	housewife	45	"
w	O'Meara Michael	156	pipefitter	44	"
x	Rollins Charles A	156	retired	80	"
y	Fitzpatrick James F rear	156	"	68	"
z	DiBartolo Giuseppe	157	tailor	43	146 Maverick

725

a	Mulcahy Francis E	157	machinist	21	here
b	*Mulcahy Mary E †	157	housewife	61	"
c	*Pellegrini Mary †	157	seamstress	29	Cambridge
d	Sorenson Christian	157	engineer	51	here
e	*Basil Leo	158	painter	58	"
f	Basil Sylvia †	158	housewife	48	"
g	*Ramirez Lena †	158	"	66	"
h	Ramirez Leo	158	floorlayer	65	"
k	Ramirez Sally †	158	clerk	38	"
l	Ramirez Salvatore J	158	draftsman	33	"
m	Ramirez Teresa †	158	housewife	32	"
n	DeSimone Joseph	159	electrician	50	"
o	DeSimone Mary †	159	housewife	50	"
p	Duane Arthur	162	painter	31	"
r	Duane Marie †	162	housewife	28	"
s	Pignotti John	162	tailor	52	"
t	Pignotti Olimpia †	162	housewife	44	"
u	Bozza Josephine †	162	"	35	"
v	Bozza Michael	162	barber	40	"

Lexington Street—Continued

w	Nota Angelo	163	laborer	54	here
x	Nota Anne—†	163	seamstress	26	"
y	*Nota Josephine—†	163	housewife	49	"
z	Nota Peter	163	U S A	23	"
	726				
a	Nota Thomas	163	clerk	21	"
b	*d'Entremont Elie	163	fishcutter	44	"
c	*d'Entremont Exilda—†	163	housewife	39	"
d	Doucette Jeanette—†	163	"	33	"
e	Doucette Joseph	163	carpenter	31	"
f	Larkin Helen—†	164	housewife	45	"
g	Bosco Edith—†	164	"	38	"
h	Bosco Lincoln	164	pipefitter	20	"
k	DiSisto Joseph	164	factoryhand	29	"
l	Pavone Emilio	164	seaman	22	"
m	*Pavone Prisco	164	factoryhand	58	"
n	*Pavone Rose—†	164	housewife	55	"
o	Brown Edna M—†	165	stenographer	39	"
p	Brown Sabina—†	165	housewife	71	"
r	Oxley Emma L—†	165	at home	66	"
t	*Ricci May—†	167	housewife	48	"
u	Ricci Theodore	167	laborer	46	"
v	Ricci Theodore J	167	clerk	22	"
w	Selvati Joseph	167	U S A	20	"
x	*Selvati Leo	167	shoemaker	64	"
y	*Selvati Rose—†	167	housewife	54	"
z	Piro Joseph	170	chauffeur	38	"
	727				
a	Piro Mary—†	170	housewife	28	"
b	Ferrara Anthony—†	170	electrician	40	"
c	*Ferrara Rosena—†	170	housewife	70	"
d	Ferrara Anna—†	170	"	31	"
e	Ferrara Benjamin	170	clerk	38	"
f	Sullivan Edward	170	guard	41	"
g	Sullivan Rose—†	170	housewife	31	"
h	Lightbody Frederick F	170	seaman	24	"
k	Lightbody Mary—†	170	housewife	22	"
l	Buckley Dennis	171	clerk	68	"
m	Buckley John L	171	machinist	30	"
n	O'Connell James J	171	clerk	40	"
o	O'Connell Margaret M—†	171	housewife	36	"

17

Lexington Street Continued

	P	Howard Edna †	173	housewife	22	30 Cumberland
	R	Howard William	173	chauffeur	28	30 "
	S	Mirabello Anthony	173	salesman	56	here
	T	Mirabello Anthony	173	"	27	"
	U	*Mirabello Gasparina †	173	housewife	48	"
	V	Mirabello Grace †	173	at home	26	"
	W	Anthes Naomi A †	174	housewife	41	"
	X	Anthes Philip E	174	clergyman	43	"
	Y	Spack David	174	storekeeper	57	"
	Z	Spack Harold	174	U S A	24	"

728

	A	Spack Ida †	174	clerk	52	"
	B	Spack Rea †	174	stenographer	23	Malden
	C	Lopardi Angelina †	174	housewife	37	here
	D	Lopardi Anthony	174	painter	43	"
	E	Ayres Evelyn †	176	waitress	28	"
	F	Hamilton Charles	176	rigger	24	"
	G	Hamilton Edith †	176	housewife	54	"
	H	Hamilton Robert	176	stevedore	54	"
	K	Smith William C	177	banker	65	"
	L	Hansen Henry	178	student	21	"
	M	Hansen Neils A	178	guard	62	"
	N	Hansen Olga †	178	housewife	50	"
	O	Iannuzzi Grace †	179	"	31	"
	P	Iannuzzi John	179	candymaker	32	"
	R	Beamish Florence †	179	clerk	35	"
	S	Murphy Bertha †	179	housewife	62	"
	T	Murphy George F	179	retired	72	"
	U	Laurano Eleanor †	179	at home	21	"
	V	Laurano Rita †	179	housewife	48	"
	W	Frisco Joseph	180	U S A	20	"
	X	*Frisco Mary †	180	housewife	51	"
	Y	Frisco Mary †	180	factoryhand	22	"
	Z	O'Donnell Catherine E †	182	housewife	31	"

729

	A	O'Donnell William J	182	electrician	33	"
	B	*Trahan Angelina †	184	housewife	48	"
	C	Trahan John	184	shipwright	43	"
	D	*Trahan Maria †	184	attendant	37	"
	E	Hagen Evelyn †	185	housewife	25	416 Bremen
	F	Hagen Everett	185	fishcutter	26	416 "

Lexington Street — Continued

G	Melchionda Angelo	185	leathercutter	52	here
H	Melchionda John	185	U S A	22	"
K	Melchionda Louise †	185	housewife	46	"
L	Spina Anthony D	186	U S C G	24	134 Havre
M	Spina Margaret †	186	housewife	21	95 Trenton
N	Scimone Ann †	186	clerk	23	here
O*	Scimone Camela †	186	housewife	54	"
P	Scimone Frank	186	U S N	30	"
R	Scimone Jos	186	U S C G	20	"
S	Scimone Joseph	186	foundryman	59	"
T	Hoffman John M	187	engineer	56	"
U	Swansburg Dora G †	187	at home	60	"
V	Swansburg Edna J †	187	clerk	48	"
W	Swansburg James M	187	custodian	44	"
X	Frati James	188	electrician	26	90 Marion
Y	Frati Philomena †	188	housewife	24	90 "
Z	Peraino Margaret †	188	at home	55	here
	730				
A	Sozio Josephine †	188	housewife	35	"
B	Sozio Louis	188	printer	40	"
E	Vega Antoinetta †	190	housewife	48	"
F	Vega Clarinda †	190	secretary	21	"
G	Vega Pasquale	190	laborer	52	"
H	Massio Dolores †	191	nurse	37	"
K	Massucci Amadeo	191	laborer	28	"
L	Massucci Frances †	191	at home	70	"
M	Massucci Guido	191	cutter	38	"
N	Massucci Leonita †	191	stitcher	34	"
O	Stefano Ethel †	191	housewife	29	85 Chelsea
P	Stefano Frederick	191	clerk	33	85 "
S	Carlo Emma †	192	stitcher	21	here
T	Carlo Nicholas	192	pipefitter	43	"
U	Carlo Rose †	192	housewife	36	"
W*	Tusa Francesco	193	retired	68	"
X*	Tusa Rosaria †	193	housewife	65	"
Y	Tusa Victor	193	operator	33	"
Z	Paladino Gene	193	tailor	44	"
	731				
A	Paladino Victoria †	193	beautician	42	"
B	Finamorra Antonetta †	194	housewife	42	"
C	Finamorra Donald	194	U S A	20	"

Lexington Street—Continued

D	Finamorra Gaetano	194	laborer	51	here	
E	Luciano Antonio	194	tailor	46	"	
F	Luciano Helen—†	194	housewife	42	"	

Marion Street

L	D'Amato Gaetano	53	laborer	65	here	
M	D'Amato Josephine—†	53	housewife	67	"	
O	George Manuel P	55	laborer	69	"	
P	Faretra Anne—†	55	housewife	28	"	
R	Faretra Armando	55	metalworker	31	"	
S	Terry Anna—†	55	housewife	35	"	
T	Terry Seraphin	55	foreman	35	"	
U	Merlino Mary C—†	57	housewife	42	"	
V	*Arnone Joseph	57	carpenter	60	"	
W	Arnone Josephine—†	57	factoryhand	28	"	
X	*Arnone Latzia—†	57	housewife	58	"	
Y	Arnone Paul	57	chauffeur	30	"	
Z	*Rispoli Angelina—†	57	housewife	64	"	

732

A	Morton Annie—†	59	"	28	"	
B	Morton Archibald	59	shipper	28	"	
C	Canney Helen—†	59	housewife	31	"	
D	Canney John F	59	U S C G	48	"	
E	*Reinberg Hjalmar	59	longshoreman	62	"	
F	Reinberg John D	59	U S A	24	"	
G	Reinberg Lillian—†	59	clerk	21	"	
H	Reinberg Margaret—†	59	factoryhand	23	"	
K	*Reinberg Olga M—†	59	housewife	62	"	
M	McWeeny Ella E—†	61	"	67	"	
N	Powers Walter	61	fisherman	45	"	
O	*Riley Thomas J	61	"	54	"	
P	Brown Margaret—†	63	housewife	73	"	
R	Brown William H	63	laborer	70	"	
S	DeJacimor Louis	63	U S N	21	"	
T	Maffeo Anthony	63	laborer	67	"	
U	Maffeo Mary—†	63	housewife	57	"	
V	Doherty Kathleen A—†	63	operator	33	"	
W	Flynn Annie F—†	65	housewife	69	13 Monmouth	
X	Flynn William H	65	mechanic	33	13 "	
Y	*Calla Diana—†	65	housewife	59	here	

Page.	Letter.	Full Name.	Residence, Jan. 1, 1943.	Occupation.	Supposed Age.	Reported Residence, Jan. 1, 1942. Street and Number.

Marion Street—Continued

	z	Calla Domenic	65	salesman	25	here
733						
	A	Calla Ernest	65	mechanic	31	"
	B	Calla Phyllis—†	65	housewife	30	"
	c	Loy Gladys—†	67	"	35	18 Trenton
	D	Loy Raymond	67	cook	38	18 "
	E	Cormo Adeline J—†	67	housewife	35	here
	F	Cormo Edward J	67	mechanic	37	"
	G	Cormo Robert E	67	U S A	35	"
	H	Carabello Louis	67	U S N	22	10 Henry
	K	Carabello Mary—†	67	wrapper	25	296 Paris
	L	DePalma Salvatore	69	seaman	35	here
	M*	Porcelli Elizabeth—†	69	housewife	40	"
	N	Porcelli John	69	U S A	22	"
	o*	Porcelli Joseph	69	laborer	46	"
	P	Salerno Anna—†	69	housewife	41	"
	R	Salerno Emilio	69	mechanic	52	"
	s	Salerno John	69	"	21	"
	T*	Celeste Annie—†	69	housewife	45	"
	U	Celeste Marian—†	69	teacher	25	"
	v*	Celeste Pasquale	69	shoemaker	64	"
	w	Celeste Rita—†	69	clerk	23	"
	x	Boudreau Adeline C—†	71	housewife	31	60 Trenton
	Y	Boudreau John R	71	mechanic	34	60 "
	z	McMillian Edith E—†	71	housewife	36	Winthrop
734						
	A	Ferraro Carmine	71	storekeeper	48	here
	B*	Ferraro Lucia—†	71	housewife	42	"
	c	Walsh Annie M—†	75	at home	79	"
	D	Walsh Mary A—†	75	"	72	"
	E	Walsh William F	75	mechanic	37	"
	F	Creamer Jeremiah	75	chauffeur	46	"
	G	Creamer Mary—†	75	housewife	39	"
	H	Lawrence Emily—†	77	"	74	"
	K	Lawrence Louise V—†	77	dressmaker	49	"
	L	Martin Catherine—†	77	at home	65	"
	M	Martin Mary—†	77	"	69	"
	N	Bailey Mildred O—†	79	secretary	25	"
	o	McGinness Dorothy E—†	79	housewife	28	"
	P	McGinness Mason F	79	clergyman	27	"
	R	Cacciatore Grace—†	80	housewife	24	122 Falcon

21

Marion Street—Continued

s	Cacciatore Stephen	80	millwright	29	122 Falcon
t	Thornton Henry	80	mechanic	46	153 Maverick
u	Thornton Mary— †	80	housewife	41	153 "
v	Candeliere Lillian— †	82	"	37	here
w	Candeliere Pasquale A	82	chauffeur	38	"
x	Sorrells Thomas C	82	U S C G	22	Georgia
y	Candeliere Arthur	82	mechanic	34	here
z	Candeliere Ettore	82	"	25	"

735

A	Candeliere Sarah— †	82	housewife	60	"
c	Calla Albert	87	salesman	33	"
D	*Calla Angelina— †	87	housewife	57	"
E	Calla Emma— †	87	manager	35	"
F	*Calla John	87	retired	73	"
G	*Landry Edna †	90	stitcher	45	"
H	*Landry Peter	90	painter	51	
K	Macrina Frank	90	seaman	24	277 Princeton
L	Macrina Mary †	90	housewife	21	277 "
M	Osterle Bertha †	98	"	64	here
N	Osterle Frank	98	carpenter	66	"
O	Halliday Ida— †	98	at home	66	"
P	Crouse Sophie E †	100	housewife	85	Chelsea
R	Moritz Elsie †	100	"	32	here
S	Moritz Robert	100	presser	35	"
T	*Cohen Rose †	100	housewife	69	"
U	*Allen Mary †	102	at home	72	1 Wilbur ct
V	Femino Celia †	102	housewife	24	here
W	Femino Charles	102	U S A	28	"
X	*Torrone Angelina †	102	housewife	52	"
Y	Torrone Luigi	102	laborer	52	"
Z	Censullo Angelo	104	U S A	27	"

736

A	Censullo Joseph	104	laborer	23	"
B	Censullo Peter	104	U S A	21	"
C	Censullo Rose †	104	housewife	52	"
D	Parry John	104	electrician	32	"
E	Parry Julia †	104	housewife	52	"
F	Censullo Dorothy †	104	"	21	133 Saratoga
G	Censullo Frank	104	mechanic	25	133 "
H	DeRose Mary †	106	housewife	36	232 Havre
K	DeRose Rocco	106	foreman	38	232 "

Page.	Letter.	FULL NAME.	Residence, Jan. 1, 1943.	Occupation.	Supposed Age.	Reported Residence, Jan. 1, 1942. Street and Number.

Marion Street—Continued

	L	McArdle Elizabeth M — †	110	housewife	48	here
	M	McArdle James	110	clerk	50	"
	N	DeCristoforo Adeline—†	110	housewife	29	"
	O	DeCristoforo Americo	110	shipper	31	"
	P	Fitzpatrick Phyllis—†	110	housewife	23	247 Saratoga
	R	Fitzpatrick William	110	U S A	26	247 "
	S	Murray Arthur J	112	mechanic	28	here
	T	Murray Hannah A—†	112	housewife	63	"
	U	Murray John J	112	painter	69	"
	V	Murray John L	112	U S A	39	"
	W	Quinn James F	112	laborer	56	"
	X	Damelgo Francis L	112	clerk	34	"
	Y	Damelgo Josephine — †	112	housewife	51	"
	Z	Shelley Henry J	112	janitor	57	"

737

| | A | Goldberg Frank | 112 | realtor | 45 | " |
| | B | *Goldberg Sarah — † | 112 | housewife | 52 | " |

Meridian Street

	D	Amato Sebastian	306	tailor	48	here
	E	Anderson Paul	306	laborer	40	"
	F	Babbin Benjamin	306	retired	74	"
	G	Carlson Charles	306	"	76	"
	H	Davenport Emery	306	laborer	59	188 Lexington
	K	*Griffin Etta — †	306	dressmaker	73	here
	L	Griffin Olivia — †	306	housekeeper	65	"
	M	Guthrie Edward S	306	retired	83	"
	N	Iverson Thomas	306	seaman	30	"
	O	Melanson John	306	"	52	"
	P	Morrison Edward	306	laborer	45	"
	R	Peacock William	306	"	55	"
	S	Aitkins Herbert	308	boilermaker	35	"
	T	Surette Leo	308	fisherman	40	"
	U	Walker Helen †	308	housewife	40	"
	V	Walker John J	308	shipbuilder	59	"
	X	Ferri Ernest	309A	plumber	43	"
	Y	Ferri Jennie — †	309A	housewife	44	"
	Z	Ferri Richard	309A	U S N	21	"

738

| | A | *Repucci Concetta — † | 309A | housekeeper | 66 | " |

23

Meridian Street—Continued

B	Reppucci George	309A	U S A	34	here
C	Reppucci Helena—†	309A	shoeworker	24	"
D	Martino Florence—†	310	housewife	20	53 Falcon
E	Martino William	310	laborer	21	81 Gladstone
F	Magnasco Ann—†	310	housewife	29	here
G	Magnasco Emil	310	riveter	30	"
H	Rogers Dorothy—†	310	housewife	25	"
K	Rogers William	310	longshoreman	33	"
L	Feeley Alfred	311	fisherman	36	"
M	Feeley Caroline P—†	311	housewife	73	"
N	Feeley Elizabeth C—†	311	at home	32	"
O	Feeley James P	311	retired	75	"
P	Doran Frank	312	engineer	31	117 Eutaw
R	Doran Rose—†	312	housewife	32	117 "
S	Tronoloni Mary—†	312	clerk	34	New York
U	Lovett Eva F—†	313A	at home	49	here
V	Lovett Sarah—†	313A	"	81	"
W	McLaughlin James	313A	meatcutter	47	"
X	Campbell Susan—†	314	housekeeper	62	Chelsea
Y	George Catherine M—†	314	housewife	35	here
Z	George John P	314	seaman	30	"
	739				
A	Lacourtiglia Francis	314	fireman	23	"
B	Lacourtiglia Gertrude—†	314	housewife	21	"
C	Donahue Edward F	315	at home	42	"
D	Donahue Ruth †	315	housewife	41	"
F	Fife Frances R †	317	"	59	"
G	Fife John W	317	guard	60	"
H	McKillop Catherine—†	319	housekeeper	69	"
K	McKillop William	319	clerk	44	"
M*	Garron Austin	323	fisherman	55	
N	Laracy William	323	shipper	34	55 Maverick sq
O	Sampson Catherine †	323	housewife	41	here
P	Sampson Clarence	323	rigger	49	"
R	Palumbo Millie †	326	factoryhand	30	"
S	Tino Dominic	326	cook	26	"
W	Tino Frank	326	laborer	60	"
X*	Tino Mary †	326	housewife	64	"
Y	Tino Anthony	326	cook	35	"
Z	Tino Virginia —†	326	housewife	35	"

740

Meridian Street—Continued

A	Leonard Gertrude—†	328	bookbinder	29	here
B	Leonard Mary—†	328	housewife	60	"
C	*Burrage Emma—†	328	"	65	"
D	*Burrage Henry	328	carpenter	71	
E	Gallagher Clara—†	328	housekeeper	28	Cambridge
F	Palermo Josephine—†	328	housewife	26	here
G	Palermo Victor	328	guard	27	"
H	Joyce Sophia—†	330	waitress	50	"
K	Marsh James	330	electrician	51	Chelsea
L	Marsh Sarah—†	330	housewife	49	"
M	*Cameron David E	330	laborer	36	here
N	*Cameron John W	330	"	39	"
O	Ford Percy	330	cook	45	"
P	Sinclair Susan—†	330	housewife	67	"
R	Sinclair Whit	330	retired	79	"
S	Longmoore Stella—†	330	housewife	30	Vermont
T	Longmoore Stephen	330	electrician	32	"
U	D'Errico Anna—†	332	housewife	20	5 Saratoga pl
V	D'Errico Vincent	332	laborer	24	5 "
W	Muise Lillian—†	332	housekeeper	55	here
X	Censullo Jennie—†	332	housewife	44	"
Y	Censullo Peter	332	chauffeur	55	"
Z	Censullo Vincent	332	U S A	20	"

741

A	Coombs Edward V	332	laborer	27	148 Saratoga
B	Coombs Elena—†	332	housewife	22	148 "
C	Murphy John F	333	U S A	34	here
D	Simonian Agnes—†	333	housekeeper	58	"
E	Simonian Kane	333	investigator	30	"
¹E	Simonian Mabel—†	333	stenographer	23	"
F	Simonian Wynott	333	U S A	32	"
G	Muise Dorothy—†	334	housewife	31	"
H	Muise Lester	334	fireman	40	"
K	Bois Dorothy—†	334	factoryhand	20	"
L	Bois Eugene	334	machinist	50	"
M	Bois Margaret—†	334	housewife	57	"
N	Porras Perfecto	334	laborer	54	"
O	Porras Rafaele	334	U S A	21	"
P	Rizzuto Marguerita—†	334	housekeeper	76	"

Meridian Street—Continued

R	Almeida Francis T	335	laborer	29	here
s	Martino Frank	335	"	37	"
T	Spencer Gertrude—†	335	housekeeper	53	"
U	Simpson Concetta—†	335	housewife	48	"
V	Simpson Matthew K	335	laborer	49	"
W	Krafve Genevieve—†	336	housewife	31	"
X	Krafve William	336	machinist	40	"
Y	Robicheau Anna—†	336	housewife	58	"
Z	Robicheau Zacharie	336	laborer	61	"

742

A	Moore Helen—†	336	housewife	42	"
B	Moore John R	336	rigger	45	"
C	Nunes Emery	336	barber	22	"
D	Nunes Frank	336	U S N	30	"
E	*Nunes Minnie—†	336	housewife	58	"
F	Warchol Edward	336	U S N	21	New Jersey
G	Bogosian Armen	337	U S A	33	here
H	Bogosian Lillian—†	337	clerk	31	"
K	Bogosian Mary—†	337	housewife	55	"
L	Bogosian Paul	337	tailor	66	"
M	Marcella James	338	blacksmith	35	"
N	Marcella Theresa—†	338	housewife	36	"
O	Domegan James	338	laborer	44	"
P	Domegan Mary—†	338	housewife	38	"
R	Domegan Patrick	338	laborer	60	"
S	Domegan Thomas	338	"	41	"
T	Domegan Winifred—†	338	housewife	55	"
U	McDonald Andrew	338	U S A	32	"
V	McDonald Luke	338	laborer	30	"
W	McDonald Mary—†	338	housewife	53	"
X	Ranahan Alice—†	339	"	45	"
Y	Ranahan William	339	checker	45	"
Z	McCormick Anna M—†	339	housewife	43	"

743

A	McCormick Joseph M	339	laborer	53	"
B	Layhe Francis	340	mechanic	36	"
C	Layhe Sarah—†	340	housewife	30	"
D	Mombourquette Anna—†	340	"	39	"
E	Mombourquette Charles	340	fisherman	42	"
F	*Fawcett Irene—†	340	housewife	35	238 Princeton
G	Fawcett Peter	340	carpenter	36	238 "

26

Page.	Letter	FULL NAME.	Residence, Jan. 1, 1943	Occupation.	Supposed Age.	Reported Residence, Jan. 1, 1942. Street and Number.

Meridian Street—Continued

H	*LeBlanc Edward	340	fishcutter	45	238 Princeton
L	Forti James	342	laborer	31	here
M	*Forti Jennie †	342	housekeeper	67	"
N	Forti Michael	342	U S A	27	"
O	Forti Santa †	342	factoryhand	24	"
P	Delehanty James M	342	chauffeur	48	"
R	Delehanty Theresa L †	342	housewife	45	"
S	Bryant Gertrude R †	342	"	31	"
T	Bryant William C	342	operator	33	"
U	McCluskey Malcolm	342	U S A	20	"
W	Peterson Carl	345	coppersmith	40	"
X	Peterson Sarah †	345	housewife	38	"
Y	Botchie Anna †	347	"	30	"
Z	Botchie Paul	347	U S N	35	"

744

A	Cavalieri Frank	347	printer	24	"
B	*Cavalieri Joseph	347	laborer	54	"
C	Cavalieri Rose †	347	housewife	42	"
D	Cavalieri Rose †	347	clerk	21	"
E	Charello Anna †	347	housewife	58	"
F	Charello Guy	347	laundryman	22	"
G	Charello Peter	347	laborer	63	"
H	Lavangie Charles A	349	shipper	56	"
K	Lavangie Mary H †	349	housewife	60	"
L	Loomer Dorothy †	349	clerk	38	"
M	Magnusson Ellen †	349	stenographer	21	"
N	Magnusson William	349	U S A	23	"
O	Clericuzio Carmella †	349½	clerk	23	"
P	*Clericuzio Florino	349½	shoeworker	53	"
R	Clericuzio Joseph	349½	U S A	21	"
S	*Clericuzio Maria †	349½	housewife	49	"
T	Teta Anthony	349½	machinist	22	26 Bremen
U	Teta Antonetta †	349½	housewife	40	26 "
V	Teta Carmen	349½	machinist	20	26 "
W	Teta Ralph	349½	U S N	20	26 "
X	Teta Stefano	349½	molder	47	26 "
Y	Cresey Catherine †	351	housewife	32	here
Z	Cresey Herbert	351	seaman	40	"

745

A	Campbell Helen †	351	housewife	39	"
B	Campbell Robert	351	locksmith	46	"

27

Princeton Street

D	Eld Marie—†	80	maid	67	here
E	Morrison Jean E—†	80	houseworker	54	"
F	Graff Edward	90	seaman	45	"
G	Graff Mary—†	90	housewife	37	"
H	Cashman Laura E—†	94	milliner	60	"
K	Tedford Minnie E—†	96	housewife	65	"
L	Ciarcian Anna—†	98	"	29	205 Saratoga
M	Ciarcian Antonio	98	shipfitter	29	205 "
N	Turner George	98	pipefitter	54	Acton
O	Turner Ruth—†	98	housewife	51	"
S	Fossett John	102	operator	26	here
T	Fossett Marion—†	102	housewife	24	"
U	Loperfido Manuel	102	mechanic	22	"
V	Serrapica Celia—†	102	housewife	49	"
W	*Serrapica Sebastian	102	baker	59	"
X	*Balestriere Antonina—†	104	housewife	75	81 Princeton
Y	D'Anca Frank	104	barber	40	81 "
Z	*D'Anca Santina—†	104	housewife	36	81 "

746

A	Asci Filippo	104	laborer	43	here
B	Asci Vincenza—†	104	housewife	43	"
C	*Caravella Lorenza—†	104	"	87	"
D	Coelho John	104	laborer	30	"
E	Coelho Lucille—†	104	housewife	27	"
F	McCaul Dorothy M—†	106	"	37	120 Princeton
G	McCaul William J	106	laborer	37	120 "
H	Pesaturo Marietta—†	106	housewife	26	here
K	Pesaturo Salvatore	106	printer	26	"
L	Emmons Anna—†	108	housewife	28	54 London
M	Emmons Howard J	108	electrician	26	7 Condor
N	DiSalvo Lydia—†	108	housewife	22	here
O	DiSalvo Victor	108	painter	28	"
P	Vitale Mildred—†	108	housewife	30	"
R	Asci Diomira—†	110	"	41	"
S	Asci Gaetano	110	engineer	50	"
T	Castrucci Biagio	110	machinist	51	"
U	DelCora Louis	110	laborer	54	"
X	Catina Conzenzo	110	"	46	42 Frankfort
V	*DiAndrew Andrew	110	"	49	here
W	*DiAndrew Olympia—†	110	housewife	47	"
Y	Sofia Louis	110	laborer	26	"

28

Princeton Street— Continued

z		Nickerson Cecil	112	U S A	23	126 Falcon
747						
A	*Nickerson Eva—†	112	housewife	43	126 "
B	Nickerson Louise—†	112	laundress	40	126 "
c	Nickerson Melvin	112	U S A	21	126 "
D	*Nickerson Wallace	112	cooper	56	126 "
E	Harding Gertrude—†	112	housewife	31	here
F	Harding Gustave J	112	rigger	32	"
G	Bassett Arthur	114	U S N	24	"
H	Bassett Florence M—†	114	housewife	56	"
K	Bassett Herbert A	114	clerk	58	"
L	Bassett Merrill E	114	U S A	27	"
M	Hannon Edmund	116	"	25	"
N	Hannon Thelma—†	116	housewife	25	"
O	Hannon Douglas	116	U S A	22	"
P	Hannon Edward T	116	stevedore	48	"
R	Hannon Gertrude—†	116	housewife	48	"
S	Hannon Robert J	116	longshoreman	23	"
T	Hannon Ruth—†	116	housewife	24	"
U	Nardo Annette—†	118	"	32	"
V	Nardo Frank	118	machinist	36	"
W	*Vlogiave Fannie—†	118	housewife	49	"
X	*Vlogiave George	118	millhand	50	"
Y	Vlogiave Joan—†	118	leatherworker	27	"
Z	DeSanctis Wilson	118	manager	25	62 Webster
748						
A	Antonelli Guiseppi	120	janitor	45	142 Putnam
B	O'Brion Inez J—†	124	housewife	28	here
c	O'Brion William F	124	rigger	30	"
D	Quindley Andrew	124	engineer	43	"
E	Quindley Marion—†	124	housewife	43	"
F	Tritto Frank	126	operator	53	"
G	*Tritto Mary—†	126	housewife	42	"
H	Tritto Rena—†	126	stitcher	20	"
K	Tramonte Antonio	126	laborer	20	"
L	Tramonte Leonard	126	barber	43	"
M	Tremonte Mary—†	126	housewife	31	"
N	Lane Elizabeth—†	128	"	62	"
O	Lane Joseph	128	retired	77	89 Falcon
P	Lane Mary—†	128	houseworker	41	here
R	Powell Robert H	128	retired	78	"

Princeton Street Continued

s	Powell Stephen R	128	shipfitter	50	here
t	Hunt James	128	painter	63	15 Wait
u	Chevaire Dominick	130	laborer	23	here
v*	Chevaire Grace †	130	housewife	25	"
w	Zucco Julia †	130	"	60	"
x	Ciampi Amelio	130	U S A	25	"
y*	Ciampi Fred	130	hairdresser	54	"
z	Ciampi Louis	130	U S N	23	"

749

a*	Ciampi Mary †	130	housewife	49	"
b	Ciampi Mildred †	130	operator	23	"
e	Gushue Bridget †	142	housewife	50	"
f	Gushue Eleanor †	142	stenographer	20	"
g	Gushue Gerald	142	mechanic	25	"
h	Gushue Madeline †	142	packer	22	"
k	Landry Irene †	144	housewife	38	"
l	Landry Wilfred	144	engineer	40	"
m	Boudreau Joseph B	146	shipfitter	44	"
n	Boudreau Mary A †	146	housewife	40	"
o	Sampson Edith B †	146	"	43	"
p	Sampson Leo W	146	machinist	52	"
r	Sampson Leo W	146	U S A	20	"
s	Sampson Louise B †	146	splicer	22	"
t	Driscoll John J	148	retired	65	"
u	Driscoll Margaret E †	148	houseworker	53	"
v	Russo Anna †	150	housewife	28	426 Chelsea
w	Russo James	150	millhand	60	426 "
x	Russo Thomas	150	electrician	30	426 "
y	Giannattasio Angelina †	150	housewife	47	here
z	Giannattasio Antonio	150	upholsterer	52	"

750

a*	Pettinicchio Emilio	150	bartender	47	13 Central sq
b	Bosco Caroline †	154	housewife	36	here
c	Bosco John	154	machinist	42	"
d	DePippo Tina †	154	housewife	27	"
e	DePippo William	154	mechanic	30	"
f	Maskell Catherine L †	154	housewife	29	15A Norwell
g	Maskell Edward F	154	oiler	28	15A "
h	Castelluccio Michael	158	chauffeur	43	173 Paris
k	Castelluccio Rose †	158	housewife	47	173 "
l	Boudreau Anna †	158	wrapper	38	here

Princeton Street — Continued

M	Boudreau Blanche †	158	wrapper	23	here	
N*	Boudreau Emma †	158	housewife	73	"	
O	Bluhm Minnie †	160	"	71	"	
P	Bluhm Morris	160	metalworker	68	"	
R	Poirier Jane †	160	housewife	80	"	
S	Poirier Sabine †	160	"	57	"	
T	Poirier Wilfred	160	buyer	57	"	
U*	Chievers Helen †	166	stenographer	25	"	
V	Chievers Margaret †	166	housewife	72	"	
W	Chievers Nicolas	166	retired	73	"	
X	Bennett Mary †	166	housewife	50	"	
Y	Bennett Peter	166	engineer	61	"	
Z	Distasio John	166	welder	50	14 Hanover	
	751					
A	Moynihan Catherine †	166	housewife	23	84 W Eagle	
B	Moynihan Gerald	166	U S N	23	Newton	
C	Lochiatto Alphonzo	168	laborer	37	here	
D	Lochiatto Eleanor †	168	housewife	32	"	
E	Sampson Alfred	168	engineer	68	"	
F	Sampson Francis	168	machinist	20	"	
G	Sampson Mary †	168	housewife	55	"	
H	Bage Frederick	168	cutter	31	"	
K	Bage Thora †	168	housewife	27	"	
L	Ekman Carl	172	fisherman	48	"	
M	Erskine Harry T	172	bookkeeper	23	"	
N	Erskine Walter T	172	engineer	54	"	
O	Guimont Camille	172	operator	43	19 Saratoga	
P	Hemenway Annie †	172	"	52	here	
R*	Magnuson John	172	fisherman	49	"	
S	Ward Harry H	172	machinist	51	New York	
T	Wright Gilbert A	174	rigger	35	here	
U	Wright Winifred †	174	housewife	23	"	
V	Raeke Charles J	174	starter	43	"	
W	Raeke John F	174	truckman	45	"	
X	Driver Anna †	176	housewife	24	"	
Y	Driver John	176	seaman	30	"	
Z	Bompane Amando	176	U S A	25	"	
	752					
A	Bompane Bruno	176	"	29	"	
B	Bompane Rita †	176	presser	23	"	
C*	Bompane Viola †	176	packer	32	"	

31

Princeton Street—Continued

	D	Ventola Arthur	176	electrician	26	24 Eutaw
	E	DeNunzio Amelia—†	178	housewife	28	here
	F	DeNunzio Clement	178	laborer	29	"
	G	Blasi Angelina—†	178	housewife	74	"
	H	Blasi Michael	178	retired	75	"
	K	Nappi Amando	178	welder	38	"
	L	Nappi Marie—†	178	housewife	37	"
	M	Katz Albert	180	merchant	29	"
	N*	Katz Annie—†	180	housewife	64	"
	O	Katz Irving	180	U S N	35	"
	P	Katz Lillian—†	180	stenographer	32	"
	R	Katz Max	180	paperhanger	65	"
	S	Katz Sally—†	180	clerk	26	"
	T	Rindone John	180	operator	34	"
	U	Rindone Rose—†	180	housewife	32	"
	V	DiFilippo Joseph	182	stonecutter	46	"
	W	DiFilippo Rita—†	182	housewife	42	"
	X	Alei Joseph	182	laborer	24	"
	Y	Alei Mary—†	182	housewife	20	"
	Z	Cipriano Carmella—†	184	"	31	"

753

	A	Cipriano Pasquale	184	electrician	35	"
	B	Sabza Concordia—†	184	housewife	55	"
	C	Sabza John A	184	U S A	26	"
	D	Sabza Louis	184	"	24	"
	E	Sabza Nicola	184	laborer	61	"
	F	Sabza Ponzy	184	U S A	21	"
	G*	Boudreau Mary—†	186	housewife	67	"
	H	Babine Margaret—†	190	"	33	"
	K	Babine Robert G	190	chauffeur	34	"
	L*	Babine Samuel R	190	shipper	32	"
	M	Boudreau Mary E—†	190	stenographer	36	"
	N	Caplan Abraham N	190	physician	40	"

Putnam Street

	O	Melanson Georgina—†	87	housewife	33	here
	P	Melanson Joseph	87	diver	39	"
	R*	Melanson Marion—†	87	at home	72	"
	S*	Melanson Thomas	87	retired	76	"
	T	Fernandes Helen—†	87	clerk	23	"
	U	Fernandes John	87	retired	63	"

Putnam Street — Continued

	v	*Fernandes Marie †	87	housewife	60	here
	w	Portella Anthony	87	molder	48	"
	x	Portella Mary †	87	housewife	36	"
	y	Flot Lillian †	87	"	47	162 Falcon
	z	Flot Louis	87	welder	43	162 "
754						
	A	Robicheau David	87	U S A	37	162 "
	B	Fernandes John	89	machinist	30	here
	c	*Fernandes Lucy †	89	housewife	28	"
	D	Monkewicz Ruth M †	89	"	28	"
	E	Salerno Albert	89	clerk	39	"
	F	Salerno Frank	89	retired	78	"
	G	*Salerno Mary †	89	housewife	74	"
	H	Fox Gertrude †	91	at home	68	Brockton
	K	Giardina Michelina †	91	housewife	38	here
	L	Giardina Vincent	91	laborer	51	"
	M	Sozio George	107	machinist	28	263 Princeton
	N	Sozio Letitia †	107	housewife	22	263 "
	O	Banks Ellen P †	107	at home	78	here
	P	Banks Ellen V †	107	clerk	53	"
	R	Duca Ida †	109	housewife	35	"
	s	Duca Joseph	109	painter	35	"
	T	*Carlson Mary †	111	housekeeper	62	106 Putnam
	U	Denehy Alice †	111	housewife	35	here
	V	Denehy Henry J	111	machinist	37	"

Trenton Street

	w	LaVertue August A	3	foreman	26	N Hampshire
	x	LaVertue Fernand P	3	laborer	20	"
	y	LaVertue George A	3	shipfitter	55	"
	z	LaVertue Matilda †	3	housewife	46	"
755						
	A	Lanzone Camella †	4	laundress	24	here
	B	*Lanzone Caroline †	4	housewife	59	"
	c	*Lanzone Joseph	4	laborer	59	"
	D	Lanzone Lucy †	4	clerk	21	"
	E	*Drew Ora M †	4	at home	52	"
	F	Grecco James	4	mason	65	"
	G	Materese Anthony	4	presser	21	"
	H	Materese James	4	U S A	23	"

1—7

Page.	Letter.	FULL NAME.	Residence, Jan. 1, 1943.	Occupation.	Supposed Age.	Reported Residence, Jan. 1, 1942. Street and Number.

Trenton Street—Continued

	Letter.	FULL NAME.	Res.	Occupation.	Age.	Reported Residence
	K	*Materese Jennie —†	4	housewife	50	here
	L	Materese Michael	4	laborer	61	"
	M	Santiano Grace—†	6	housewife	37	"
	N	Santiano Joseph	6	printer	40	"
	O	Cuzzi Anthony N	6	cutter	33	"
	P	Cuzzi Lucy —†	6	housewife	33	"
	R	Rizzo Adele—†	6	"	27	"
	S	Rizzo George	6	plumber	32	"
	T	Mosco Joseph A	7	melter	32	"
	U	Mosco Maria —†	7	housewife	32	"
	V	Coombs Bridget M —†	7	"	65	"
	W	Coombs Eli F	7	retired	71	"
	X	Coombs William J	7	laborer	27	"
	Y	Costigan Bernard	7	longshoreman	52	"
	Z	*Costigan Mary —†	7	housewife	47	"

756

	Letter.	FULL NAME.	Res.	Occupation.	Age.	Reported Residence
	A	Rizzuto Joseph J	9	laborer	33	"
	B	*Rizzuto Mafalda —†	9	housewife	34	"
	C	Irvin Edmund J	9	seaman	40	"
	D	Saunders Albert W	9	electrician	35	"
	E	Saunders Alice G —†	9	housewife	33	"
	F	Ahern James	9	laundryworker	30	27 Princeton
	G	St John James F	9	rigger	49	27 "
	H	St John Mary —†	9	housewife	52	27 "
	K	Moore Charles V	11	painter	32	here
	L	Moore Ruth M †	11	housewife	28	"
	M	Muise Ignatius	11	chef	44	"
	N	*Muise Loretta —†	11	housewife	45	"
	O	Fawcett Dorothy —†	12	"	31	"
	P	Fawcett Elizabeth †	12	"	65	"
	R	Fawcett John	12	chipper	38	"
	S	Fawcett Patrick A	12	mechanic	28	"
	T	Fawcett Richard W	12	retired	68	"
	U	Partridge Lena †	14	waitress	53	"
	V	Fortenberry Charlotte †	14	housewife	23	943 Harris'n av
	W	Fortenberry Walter I	14	pharmacist	24	943 "
	X	Mortimer John	14	pipefitter	37	35 Central sq
	Y	Mortimer Mary †	14	housewife	29	35 "
	Z	Simms Mary E †	15	at home	48	here

757

	Letter.	FULL NAME.	Res.	Occupation.	Age.	Reported Residence
	A	Fougere Grace †	15	"	32	"

Trenton Street Continued

B	Bailey Elizabeth—†	17	housewife	63	here
C	Bailey Harry C	17	clerk	65	"
G	Constantino Joseph	19	carpenter	29	"
H	Constantino Mildred—†	19	housewife	25	"
K	Bowden Anna—†	19	"	48	"
L	Bowden Edward L	19	installer	55	"
M	Lovett John W	19	seaman	59	"
N	Whitten Louise—†	19	at home	68	314 Meridian
O	Winer Frances—†	20	housewife	30	here
P	Winer George	20	welder	32	"
R	Kirby Helen—†	20	housewife	31	"
S	Kirby James	20	metalworker	34	"
T	*D'Errico Antonetta—†	20	housewife	42	"
U	D'Errico Celesta—†	20	dressmaker	20	"
V	D'Errico Susie—†	20	presser	22	"
W	D'Errico Tobia	20	plasterer	60	"
X	Carino Rose—†	21	housewife	31	"
Y	Carino William R	21	U S A	27	"
Z	Nicholas James	21	"	30	"

758

A	Constantino Concetta—†	21	housewife	58	"
B	Constantino Frank	21	retired	62	"
C	Constantino John	21	U S A	23	"
D	Constantino Matthew	21	"	27	"
F	DeSisto Edward	22	"	25	"
G	DeSisto Josephine—†	22	candy packer	25	"
H	*Imbriano Lena—†	22	housewife	57	"
K	Imbriano Margaret—†	22	candy packer	34	"
L	Imbriano Helen—†	22	housewife	25	"
M	Imbriano Ralph	22	machinist	25	"
N	Nickerson Harriett—†	24	assembler	32	"
O	Nickerson Ralph	24	fishcutter	31	"
P	Nickerson Violet—†	24	housewife	31	"
R	Capodilupo Angelina—†	24	"	33	"
S	Capodilupo Anthony	24	chef	39	"
T	Ciampolillo John	24	machinist	49	"
U	Ciampolillo Sarah—†	24	storekeeper	40	"
V	Picciuolo Louis	26	carpenter	29	"
W	Picciuolo Mildred—†	26	housewife	28	"
Y	Ballen Concetta—†	26	at home	31	"
Z	Doble Henry	28	electrician	49	"

35

759

Trenton Street Continued

	A	Doble Paul	28	electrician	22	here
	B	Schepici Rose †	28	housewife	26	"
	C	Schepici Salvatore	28	clerk	30	"
	D	Howe Emma †	28	housewife	56	"
	E	Howe Harry	28	blacksmith	57	"
	G	Coppola Peter	30	machinist	36	"
	H	Coppola Philomena †	30	housewife	34	"
	K	DiMauro Joseph	30	barber	37	"
	L	DiMauro Santa †	30	housewife	32	"
	M	Gifford Mary E †	32	at home	74	"
	N*	Guarino Anna †	32	housewife	44	"
	O	Guarino Giuseppe	32	operator	48	"
	P	Guarino Jacqueline †	32	clerk	21	"
	R	Guarino Michelina †	32	dressmaker	20	"
	S	O'Hearn Malachi	34	rigger	35	"
	T	O'Hearn Rose †	34	housewife	35	"
	U	Powers Austin	34	director	42	"
	V	Lorizio Anthony	34	U S A	31	"
	W	Lorizio Edith †	34	clerk	27	"
	X*	Lorizio Emma †	34	housewife	55	"
	Y	Lorizio Joseph	34	U S A	25	"
	Z	Lorizio Vincent	34	storekeeper	55	"

760

	A	Lorizio Vito	34	bartender	32	"
	B	Lorizio Marion †	34	housewife	29	"
	C	Lorizio Pasquale	34	chauffeur	31	"
	D	Petre Alphonse	36	laborer	65	"
	E	Petre Fred	36	barber	25	"
	F	Petre Mary †	36	housewife	22	"
	G	Petre Rose †	36	"	57	"
	H	D'Eon Albert	36	painter	40	"
	K	D'Eon Ida †	36	housewife	28	"
	M	Della-Grotta Milanda †	57	"	57	"
	N	Della-Grotto Peter	57	laborer	48	"
	O	Santoro Carmella †	57	housewife	64	"
	P	Santoro John	57	attorney	42	"
	R	Santoro Joseph	57	retired	70	"
	S	Santoro Tomasina †	57	teacher	39	"
	T	Picardi Amorino	61	welder	40	"
	U	Picardi Eva †	61	housewife	38	"

36

Trenton Street Continued

v	Parziole James	61	bricklayer	42	here
w	Parziole Josephine †	61	at home	69	"
x	Parziole Lillian †	61	"	40	"

761

A	Richard Goldie †	75	housewife	50	"
B	Richard Maurice	75	grocer	53	"
c	Richard Stanley	75	U S A	26	"
D	Moore Esther C †	77	housewife	25	174 Brooks
E	Moore William E	77	rigger	26	174 "
F*	Thibodeau Edward	77	retired	72	here
G	Thibodeau Joseph	77	fishcutter	32	"
H	Thibodeau Lillian †	77	nurse	30	"
K*	Thibodeau Nellie †	77	housewife	72	"
L	Beattie Margaret O †	77	at home	73	"
M*	Levenson Dora †	81	housewife	65	"
N	Levenson Ethel †	81	clerk	25	"
o	Levenson Henry	81	U S A	23	"
P*	Levenson Joseph	81	retired	72	"
R	Cadigan Anna M †	85	housewife	36	"
s	Cadigan John F	85	operator	44	"
T*	Cole Anna †	85	at home	61	Chelsea
U*	Cole John	85	fisherman	56	"
v	Yetman Mary †	85	housewife	52	"
w	Yetman Robert	85	retired	60	"
x	Bellino Agrippino	85	"	75	here
Y	Bellino Lucia †	85	housewife	68	"
z	Giarratano John	85	tailor	43	"

762

A	Giarratano Josephine †	85	housewife	43	"
B	DeLucia Amedio	87	metalworker	52	"
c	DeLucia Eleanor †	87	clerk	22	"
D	DeLucia Grace †	87	housewife	51	"
E	DeLucia Josephine †	87	candyworker	26	"
F	DeLucia Mary †	87	"	28	"
G	Tibbetts Arlando	87	clergyman	28	Newton
H	Tibbetts Phyllis †	87	housewife	27	"
K	Nicosia Susan †	87	at home	30	58 Bennington
L	McCully James I	89	retired	87	here
M	McCully Sarah M †	89	housewife	86	"
N	Spada Bartholomew	89	U S A	25	78 Chelsea
o*	Spada Catherine †	89	housewife	51	78 "

37

Page	Letter	Full Name.	Residence, Jan. 1, 1943.	Occupation.	Supposed Age.	Reported Residence, Jan. 1, 1942. Street and Number.

Trenton Street—Continued

	P	Spada Frank	89	laborer	51	78 Chelsea
	R	Spada Leo	89	U S A	21	78 "
	S	Spada Sergio	89	"	26	78 "
	T	Dunn Medora C—†	89	at home	75	here
	U*	Thibodeau Augustine	91	painter	41	"
	V*	Thibodeau Mary—†	91	housewife	41	"
	W	Crowley Agnes E—†	91	at home	43	326 Bremen
	X	Barletta Rose—†	91	stitcher	25	463 Meridian
	Y	DeGiorgio Mildred—†	91	housewife	23	85 Brooks
	Z	DeGiorgio Vitale	91	machinist	24	85 "

763

	A	Flynn Katherine—†	93	clerk	58	here
	C	Greer Alice H—†	93	housewife	55	"
	B	Greer Frank B	93	guard	60	"
	E	Larkin Cecil	95	fisherman	41	123 Eutaw
	F	Nickerson Bradford	95	fishcutter	37	123 "
	G	Nickerson Mary—†	95	saleswoman	31	123 "
	H	McEachern Allen	95	retired	25	here
	K	McEachern Elizabeth—†	95	housewife	50	"
	L	McEachern Ronald	95	B F D	51	"
	M	Ingersoll John	97	ironworker	26	4 Shelby
	N	Ingersoll Lorraine—†	97	housewife	24	4 "
	O	Connolly Phyllis—†	97	"	35	here
	P	Connolly Thomas	97	machinist	35	"
	R	Wellings Agnes G—†	97	operator	54	"
	S	Aiello Generosa—†	99	housewife	30	"
	T	Aiello Peter	99	salesman	32	"
	U*	Letterie Florence—†	99	housewife	46	"
	V	Letterie Vencenzo	99	laborer	54	"
	W	Szymanski Nora—†	99	at home	26	268 Paris
	X	Giorino Anna—†	101	housewife	31	here
	Y	Giorino Edward	101	plumber	36	"
	Z	Repucci Philomena—†	101	at home	36	"

764

	A	Luvaris Charles	101	welder	30	"
	B	Luvaris Rose—†	101	housewife	28	"
	C*	Giovino Concetta—†	103	"	29	"
	D	Giovino Edmund	103	musician	31	"
	E	Pagliaro Anthony	103	shoeworker	35	"
	F*	Pagliaro Carmella—†	103	retired	72	"
	G*	Pagliaro Rose—†	103	housewife	63	"

Trenton Street — Continued

		FULL NAME.	Residence, Jan. 1, 1943.	Occupation.	Supposed Age	Reported Residence, Jan. 1, 1942. Street and Number.
H	*	Vadala Fortunata —†	103	at home	41	here
K		DiPietro Josephine —†	103	stitcher	38	"
L		DiPietro Vincent J	103	tailor	44	"
N		Lewis Evelyn —†	107	stenographer	28	"
O		Lewis George A	107	salesman	59	"
P		Lewis Gertrude M —†	107	housewife	54	"
R		Lewis Sidney L	107	U S A	20	"
S		Slofsky Catherine —†	107	housewife	26	49 Bennington
T		Slofsky Samuel	107	rigger	30	49 "
U		Viola Anthony	109	welder	31	here
V		Viola Louise —†	109	housewife	29	"
W		Viola Calogera —†	109	"	60	"
X		Viola Frank	109	U S M C	20	"
Y		Viola Joseph	109	retired	61	"
Z		Viola Mary —†	109	packer	22	"

765

		FULL NAME.	Residence, Jan. 1, 1943.	Occupation.	Supposed Age	Reported Residence
A		McCallum Dorothy A —†	111	clerk	21	"
B		McCallum John E	111	painter	47	"
C		McCallum Josephine —†	111	housewife	44	"
D		Logan Annie —†	111	at home	68	"
E		Logan Julia A —†	111	"	72	"
H		Palermo Jennie —†	115	stitcher	22	"
K		Palermo Joseph	115	laborer	52	"
L	*	Palermo Josephine —†	115	housewife	47	"
M		Palermo Paul	115	clerk	21	"
N		Analoro Joseph	115	baker	52	"
O		Analoro Lena —†	115	stitcher	24	"
P		Analoro Theresa —†	115	housewife	44	"
R	*	Pino Concetta —†	115	"	42	"
S		Pino Gaetano	115	factoryhand	47	"
T	*	Pino Mary —†	115	housewife	40	"
U		Pino Stephen	115	butcher	49	"
V		Meuse John	117	fishcutter	35	"
W		Meuse Loretta —†	117	housewife	42	"
X	*	Babin Esther —†	117	"	35	"
Y		Babin Linus	117	fishcutter	38	"
Z		Davidson Ellen M —†	117	housewife	40	"

766

		FULL NAME.	Residence, Jan. 1, 1943.	Occupation.	Supposed Age	Reported Residence
A		Davidson Joseph J	117	metalworker	36	"
B		Davidson Mary I —†	117	student	20	"
C		O'Meara Thomas H	117	clerk	35	"

39

Trenton Street Continued

D	*Uva Anna —†	119	housewife	58	here
E	Uva Carmella —†	119	clerk	27	"
F	Uva Michael	119	laborer	57	"
G	Chaffee Della —†	119	housewife	68	"
H	Chaffee Dora L—†	119	at home	40	"
K	Chaffee Frederick W	119	retired	69	"
L	Capasso Maria L —†	119	housewife	40	"
M	Capasso Vincent	119	lettercarrier	49	"
N	*McLaughlin George	121	carpenter	58	"
O	McLaughlin Theresa —†	121	housewife	40	"
P	*LeBlanc Euphemia —†	121	saleswoman	25	"
R	*LeBlanc Eve P— †	121	carpenter	59	"
S	*LeBlanc Flora —†	121	at home	20	"
T	*LeBlanc Naomie —†	121	housewife	59	"
U	King Estelle †	121	"	43	"
V	King James F	121	fisherman	51	"
W	Mullins Bridget †	121	packer	23	New Bedford
X	*Murray Anna †	121	at home	72	here
Y	Ferrante Frank	123	entertainer	46	"
Z	Ferrante Justina †	123	housewife	42	"

767

A	Ferri Alvertine †	123	"	24	"
B	Ferri Carl	123	welder	34	"
C	*Fioravanti Elizabeth †	123	housewife	65	"
D	Fioravanti Fera	123	clerk	65	"
E	Palano Joseph	125	chauffeur	22	881 Harris'n av
F	Figliolini Frank	125	cutter	23	12 Monmouth
G	Figliolini Maria †	125	housewife	23	12 "
H	Consolo Felice	125	mechanic	27	here
K	Consolo Rose †	125	housewife	24	"
L	McGray Herbert B	129	engineer	31	"
M	McGray Isaline V †	129	housewife	26	"
N	White Isabel †	129	"	33	"
O	White Terrence	129	fishhandler	34	"
P	Hurley Helena †	129	housewife	28	"
R	Hurley John	129	printer	36	"
S	Tanner Margaret †	131	housewife	22	"
T	Tanner William E	131	U S N	23	"
U	Turco Michael	131	coppersmith	23	Everett
V	*Cerrulo Mary †	131	housewife	65	104 Princeton
W	Cerrulo Mary †	131	candy packer	27	104 "

Trenton Street Continued

x	Cerrulo Nicholas	131	retired	66	104 Princeton
y	*Surette Jane E —†	133	housewife	37	here
z	Surette Sylvester	133	machinist	36	"

768

b	*Ventre Carmella —†	139	housewife	63	"
c	Ventre Charles	139	sorter	39	"
d	Ventre Lillian —†	139	housewife	34	"
e	*Ventre Massino	139	retired	69	"
f	Ventre Peter	139	inspector	30	"
g	Chillamei John	139	tailor	38	"
h	Chillamei Josephine—†	139	stitcher	36	"
k	Russo Joseph	141	chauffeur	43	"
l	Russo Mary—†	141	housewife	35	"
m	Taurase Katherine—†	141	"	38	"
n	Taurase Peter	141	laborer	45	"
o	Connor Frank	141	foreman	55	"
p	Connor Palmina—†	141	housewife	37	"
r	Myett Frank	143	machinist	38	"
s	Myett Margaret —†	143	housewife	37	"
t	Sheffield Catherine—†	143	saleswoman	55	"
u	Sheffield James	143	laborer	58	"
v	Sheffield Pauline—†	143	operator	36	"
w	Dow Nettie—†	143	housewife	78	"
x	Dow Winthrop	143	machinist	40	"
y	Surette Leslie J	145	watchman	49	"
z	Mackey Elizabeth —†	145	housewife	44	"

769

a	Mackey Richard	145	rigger	48	"
b	Mackey Rita †	145	clerk	22	"
c	Mackey Thomas	145	U S A	21	"
d	*Vitale Josephine †	145	housewife	48	"
e	Vitale Peter	145	storekeeper	21	"
f	Vitale Philip	145	pedler	56	"
g	*Daly Bridget †	147	at home	77	"
h	*Senior Charles	147	fisherman	35	"
k	*Senior Loretta †	147	housewife	34	"
l	Vars Clara—†	147A	clerk	28	284 Meridian
m	Vars Harold	147A	U S N	31	284 "
n	Sheffield Emma †	147A	housekeeper	58	here
o	Sheffield James	147A	retired	89	"
u	*DeGrace Jean †	149	clerk	35	"

Trenton Street—Continued

p	*DiBicarri Albert	149	shoemaker	59	here
r	DiBicarri Eva—†	149	clerk	26	"
s	*DiBicarri Leonora †	149	housewife	55	"
t	DiBicarri Lillian—†	149	packer	22	"
v	*D'Entremont Edgar	151	fishcutter	39	"
w	*D'Entremont George	151	retired	75	"
x	Deon Clayton	151	U S A	35	"
y	Surett Damien	151	laborer	47	"
z	*Surett Rose—†	151	housewife	43	"

770

a	Orlando Carmella †	151	at home	54	"
b	Orlando Domenic	151	retired	50	"
c	*Abreau Anna—†	151	housewife	76	"
d	*Abreau John	151	retired	69	"
e	*Abreau John	151	spinner	37	"
f	Linehan Elizabeth †	153	at home	68	11 Hendry
g	Mealey Madeline †	153	housewife	29	here
h	Mealey Thomas	153	cashier	37	"
k	Sacco Mary †	153	housewife	30	344 Chelsea
l	Sacco Peter	153	welder	33	344 "
m	Piacenza Carlo	153	plumber	53	here
n	*Piacenza Josephine †	153	housewife	47	"
o	*D'Entremont Edmund	155	ironworker	55	"
p	*D'Entremont Rose †	155	housewife	54	"
r	Romano Pauline †	155	"	28	"
s	Romano Principio	155	barber	31	"
t	Spinazzola Carrie †	155	at home	29	"
u	*Spinazzola Josephine †	155	housewife	62	"
v	Spinazzola Pasquale	155	laborer	64	"
w	Festa Benjamin	157	U S A	26	"
x	Festa William	157	"	22	"
y	Marinella Albert	157	laborer	74	"
z	Marinella Columba †	157	housewife	55	"

771

a	*Cataldo Camella †	157	"	54	"
b	Cataldo Ernest	157	butcher	58	"
c	Cataldo John	157	U S A	31	"
d	Carino Alfred	157	manager	37	"
e	Carino Marino	157	butcher	29	"
f	Figliolini Rose †	157A	housewife	27	"
g	Figliolini Salvatore	157A	laborer	30	"

Ward 1–Precinct 8

CITY OF BOSTON

LIST OF RESIDENTS
20 YEARS OF AGE AND OVER

(NON-CITIZENS INDICATED BY ASTERISK)
(FEMALES INDICATED BY DAGGER)

AS OF

JANUARY 1, 1943

JOSEPH F. TIMILTY, *Chairman*
FREDERIC E. DOWLING, *Secretary*
WILLIAM A. MOTLEY, JR.
FRANCIS B. McKINNEY
EVERETT R. PROUT

Listing Board.

CITY OF BOSTON PRINTING DEPARTMENT

Page.	Letter.	Full Name.	Residence. Jan. 1, 1943.	Occupation.	Supposed Age.	Reported Residence. Jan. 1, 1942. Street and Number.

800

Border Street

	F	*Mascis Catherine — †	325	housewife	45	here
	G	Mascis Domenic	325	barber	46	"
	H	Mascis Margaret — †	325	factoryhand	23	"
	K	Morrison Herbert	325	operator	27	172 Border
	L	Preble John	325	seaman	21	172 "
	M	Preble Susan E — †	325	housewife	21	172 "
	N	Smith Josephine — †	325	"	56	here
	O	Smith Urben	325	seaman	57	"
	P	Gambine Joseph	327	pipefitter	41	"
	R	Gambine Pauline †	327	housewife	32	"
	S	Caruso Enis — †	329	"	32	"
	T	*Caruso Maria — †	329	housekeeper	68	"
	U	Caruso Steven	329	mechanic	31	"
	V	Cappanelli George	329	welder	29	"
	W	Cappanelli Mary †	329	housewife	27	"
	X	Caruso Jacqueline — †	329	"	29	"
	Y	Caruso Joseph	329	salesman	30	"

801

	B	Hamilton Christina — †	339	housekeeper	74	"
	C	Hamilton James	339	busboy	45	"
	D	Doyle Nora M †	339	waitress	40	"
	E	Thornell Blanche †	339	housewife	39	"
	F	Thornell James J	339	tel worker	41	"
	H	Landers John F	341	deckhand	48	"
	K	Landers Nora †	341	housewife	50	"
	L	Clark George	341	janitor	61	165 Putnam
	M	Clark Mabel †	341	housewife	43	165 "
	N	Monaco Frances †	343	"	25	here
	O	Monaco Ralph	343	blacksmith	24	"
	P	Morani Thomas	343	plumber	56	"
	R	Averill Louis	343	retired	74	"
	S	Culken Agnes †	343	housewife	27	"
	T	Culken Joseph	343	laborer	38	"
	U	Garron Clayton J	343	"	52	"
	V	Meyers Agnes †	345	housewife	35	"
	W	Meyers Edward	345	shipfitter	32	"
	X	King Anne F †	345	weaver	54	"
	Y	King Gertrude †	345	housewife	60	"
	Z	MacCallum Elizabeth †	345	at home	21	"

802

Border Street Continued

	A	Morani Marion E †	345	housewife	23	here
	B	Morani Thomas L	345	grinder	28	"
	C	Caizzi Antonetta †	347	housewife	25	"
	D	Caizzi Attilio	347	laborer	24	"
	E	Dente Christopher	347	"	28	"
	F	Dente Joseph	347	stripper	50	"
	G	Dente Madeline †	347	stitcher	20	"
	H	*Dente Mary †	347	housewife	46	"
	K	Dente Nicholas	347	factoryhand	22	"
	L	Femiano Joseph	347	baker	35	127 White
	M	Femiano Minnie †	347	housewife	35	127 "
	W	Grifone James	366	laundryworker	44	here
	X	Grifone Lulu—†	366	housewife	54	"
	Y	Oliver Charlotte—†	366	"	27	"
	Z	Oliver Clifford	366	seaman	30	"

803

	A	Oliver Stanley	366	brazier	33	"
	B	Minnescali Anthony	366	janitor	62	"
	C	Minnescali Margaret †	366	housewife	56	"
	D	Nash Lillian †	367	housekeeper	51	"
	E	Pedro Manuel	367	laborer	38	"
	F	Richards Hanna †	367	housewife	78	"
	G	Golding Frank T	367	ironworker	35	"
	H	Smith Velma—†	367	housewife	37	"
	N	Nelson Charlotte †	369	"	40	"
	O	Nelson Henry	369	laborer	48	"
	P	Whippen Marion †	369	housewife	25	364 Border
	R	Whippen William	369	grinder	29	364 "
	S	Cotreau Adeline †	369	housewife	38	364 "
	T	Cotreau Charles	369	brazier	42	364 "
	U	Cresey Edna †	370	seamstress	50	here
	V	Cresey Lottie †	370	at home	80	"
	W	McAuley Bertha †	370	housewife	43	"
	X	McAuley Lawrence	370	guard	43	"

804

	A	Zimmer Albert	373	laborer	35	"
	B	Zimmer Chester	373	U S A	21	"
	C	Zimmer Elmer	373	laborer	25	"
	D	Zimmer Ernest	373	"	27	"

3

Border Street Continued

E	Zimmer George	373	plater	33	here
F	Zimmer George W	373	guard	60	"
G	Zimmer Harold	373	U S C G	23	New York
H	Zimmer Sarah — †	373	housewife	58	here

Brooks Street

R	Conners Harold	166	laborer	51	7 Mt Pleasant av
S	Conners Irene — †	166	housewife	35	here
T	Conners Joseph	166	laborer	42	"
U	Jarvis Charles	166	U S C G	62	"
V	Dellaria John	168	welder	33	"
W	Dellaria Rita — †	168	housewife	28	"
X	Morrison Edna — †	168	"	59	"
Y	Morrison William	168	finisher	63	"
Z	Ratti Mary — †	168	at home	88	"
	805				
A	Buonopane Nicholas	169	operator	44	"
B	Buonopane Philomena †	169	housewife	36	"
C	Doucette Loretta — †	169	housekeeper	37	"
D	Pellegrini Armand	169	U S M C	23	75 Putnam
E	Pellegrini Carmen	169	"	24	75 "
F	Pellegrini Edward	169	U S N	20	75 "
G	*Pellegrini Leondina — †	169	housewife	45	75 "
H	Pellegrini Ralph	169	tailor	54	75 "
K	Messina John	170	machinist	34	here
L	Messina Nancy †	170	housewife	30	"
M	Raddin Everett	170	longshoreman	53	"
N	Raddin Lillian M †	170	housewife	46	"
O	Staffier Domenic J	171	upholsterer	31	"
P	Staffier Jennie †	171	housewife	22	215 Princeton
R	Staffier Emilio	171	tailor	52	here
S	*Staffier Louise †	171	housewife	50	"
T	Ciandella Eleanora †	171	housekeeper	56	178 Lexington
V	DuMoulin Harold F	174	inspector	30	here
W	DuMoulin Margaret †	174	housewife	37	"
X	Battaglia John	174	welder	27	Chelsea
Y	Battaglia Lucy †	174	housewife	20	33 Lexington
Z	Ferraro Carmen	174	operator	20	here
	806				
A	Ferraro Frank	174	proprietor	46	"

Brooks Street Continued

B	*Ferraro Pellegrini †	174	housewife	47	here
D	Cooper Morris A	176	steamfitter	29	54 Porter
E	Cooper Philomena †	176	housewife	23	54 "
F	Giorgio Anthony	176	U S A	20	here
G	Giorgio Carmen	176	machinist	22	"
H	Giorgio Joseph	176	U S A	28	"
K	*Giorgio Maria †	176	housewife	50	"
L	Giorgio Mildred †	176	clerk	23	"
M	Giorgio Ralph	176	laborer	60	"
N	Ohlson James H	176	fireman	40	2 Lexington pl
O	Ohlson Margaret †	176	housewife	34	2 "
R	Nickerson Frances †	178	"	25	140 Falcon
S	Nickerson Lester	178	seaman	31	140 "
T	*Belliveau Frances †	178	housewife	37	here
U	Belliveau Frank	178	foreman	37	"
V	Tagariello Joseph	178	finisher	56	"
W	Tagariello Mary †	178	housewife	44	"
X	Welch Edward R	188	teacher	35	"
Y	Welch Loretta J †	188	housewife	36	"
Z	Burgess Katherine †	190	housekeeper	65	"
	807				
A	Chapman Samuel	190	machinist	40	Chelsea
B	Pomeroy Andrew	190	shipper	34	here
C	Pomeroy Arthur	190	laborer	22	"
D	Pomeroy Bridget M †	190	housewife	64	"
E	Mulieri Alfred	192	U S N	25	"
F	Mulieri Ernest	192	machinist	24	"
G	Mulieri Ida †	192	housewife	21	"
H	Meuse Antoinette †	192	"	38	"
K	Meuse John S	192	chauffeur	46	"
L	Phelan George R	192	rigger	35	"
M	Phelan Josephine M †	192	housewife	28	"
O	*Bonito Anita †	194	"	60	"
P	Bonito Paolo	194	retired	70	"
R	Limbo Mary †	194	housewife	32	"
S	Limbo Michael	194	laborer	45	"
T	Balliro Joseph	196	chipper	25	"
U	Balliro Vincenza †	196	housewife	25	"
V	Catoggio Antonetta †	196	"	32	"
W	Catoggio Nicholas	196	shoecutter	38	"
X	Catoggio Mary †	196	housekeeper	56	"

Brooks Street Continued

Y	Lanieri Carl	198	physician	30	here
z	Lanieri Phyllis †	198	housewife	25	"

808

A	Ceruolo Angelina †	198	"	36	"
B	Hopkins Katherine †	198	housekeeper	60	Virginia
C	Bennett Eugene	198	shoeworker	60	here
D	Bennett Margaret †	198	housekeeper	50	"
E	Bennett William	198	shoeworker	64	"
F	Diorio Domenic	200	painter	55	"
G	Diorio Susie †	200	housewife	55	"
H	McKee John	200	manager	36	"
K	McKee Pauline †	200	housewife	23	"
L	Kehoe Louise †	200	housekeeper	43	277 Chelsea

Eutaw Place

M	Crouse James E	1	carpenter	61	Wilmington
N	Crouse Lillian G †	1	housewife	65	"
O	Crouse Thomas A	1	floorlayer	33	"
R	Fortier Eliza †	2	housewife	81	here
S	Fabiano Angela †	3	"	26	"
T	Fabiano Joseph	3	metalworker	36	"
U	Grasso Josephine †	3	at home	27	"
V	Grasso Louis	3	U S A	25	"
W	*Violetto Concetta †	3	housewife	54	"
X	Violetto Joseph	3	inspector	23	"
Y	Violetto Mary †	3	saleswoman	22	"
Z	*Pisano Antonio	3	factoryhand	49	"

809

A	*Pisano Leonard	3	pedler	29	"
B	Pisano Louis	3	brazier	25	"
C	*Pisano Marie †	3	housewife	53	"
D	Pisano Mary †	3	packer	23	"
E	Norcott Gans	4	fishcutter	39	Chelsea
F	Norcott Maude †	4	housewife	29	"
G	Pickles Mary E †	5	"	50	15 Condor
H	Stella Charles	5	U S A	32	here
K	Stella John	5	laborer	61	"
L	*Stella Lucy †	5	housewife	48	"
M	Stella Rose †	5	stitcher	20	"
N	Mattina Margaret †	6	housewife	24	"

Eutaw Place Continued

o	Mattina Peter	6	welder	26	here
p	Mattina Fannie †	6	housekeeper	26	"
r*	Mattina John	6	laborer	55	"
s	Gallagher Joseph	7	"	50	
t	Frevold Elizabeth †	7	housewife	25	88 Eutaw
u	Frevold William R	7	painter	29	88 "
v	Barry Augustine W	7	retired	77	here
w	Lewis Alfred	8	salesman	39	"
x	Lewis Anna †	8	housewife	33	"

Eutaw Street

y*	LeBlanc Ely	6	carpenter	47	393 Meridian
z*	LeBlanc Julia †	6	housewife	47	393 "
810					
a	Rose Joseph	6	proprietor	65	here
b	Wilkie William	6	mechanic	46	"
c	Beck Dorothy †	20	bookkeeper	37	"
d	Beck Nathan	20	retired	69	"
e	Beck Rosalind E †	20	clerk	23	"
f	Beck Rose †	20	housewife	59	"
g*	Kenney Everett	20	boatbuilder	20	"
h*	Kenney Geneva †	20	housewife	52	"
k*	Kenney Minard	20	boatbuilder	57	"
l*	Kenney Minnie †	20	inspector	23	"
m	Brown Amy E †	20	housewife	36	"
n	Brown Edward C	20	U S A	31	"
o	Brown George A	20	"	23	"
p	Brown Helen H †	20	tel operator	29	"
r	Brown Robert R	20	clerk	21	"
s	Keefe Lillian †	24	inspector	47	"
t	Corbett George	24	fisherman	50	"
u*	DeRoaches Charles	24	"	34	"
v	DeRoaches Mildred †	24	housewife	28	"
w	Dunbar Charles	24	U S A	20	"
x	Dunbar Mary †	24	housewife	49	"
y	Hegner Dora †	24	"	21	347 Meridian
z	Scaperotti Edith †	24	chauffeur	30	here
811					
a*	Ventola Nicholas	24	barber	57	466½ Commercial
b	Ciulla Margaret †	26	housewife	21	here

Eutaw Street — Continued

	c	Ciulla Stephen	26	fish handler	21	here
	D	Grover Harold L	26	painter	39	"
	E	Grover Josephine B †	26	housewife	42	"
	F	Madison Herbert W	26	U S A	29	28 Eutaw
	G	Madison Hilda †	26	at home	64	28 "
	H*	Gentile Armando	26	shoeworker	49	here
	K	Gentile Grace †	26	housewife	42	"
	L	Murphy Frederick J	28	foreman	37	21 Lexington
	M	Perry George	28	retired	70	21 "
	N	Perry George, jr	28	U S A	21	21 "
	O	Perry Margaret †	28	housewife	58	21 "
	P	Boehner Emma †	30	"	29	here
	R	Boehner Gordon W	30	leatherworker	56	112 Princeton
	S	Boehner Wilfred	30	chauffeur	31	here
	T	Miller Charles D	30	forger	35	Taunton
	U	Miller Mildred †	30	housewife	28	"
	V	Tedesco Anna †	32	"	27	33 Eutaw
	W	Tedesco Anthony	32	chauffeur	29	33 "
	X	Cerrato Elizabeth †	34	housewife	49	here
	Y	Cerrato Francis	34	shipper	26	"
	Z*	Cerrato Pasquale	34	shoeworker	53	"

812

	A	Cuccinotta Anthony	34	operator	29	Revere
	B	Cuccinotta Theresa †	34	candyworker	28	here
	C	Harrigan Edwin C	34	millhand	56	Westford
	D	Harrigan Harriet †	34	at home	79	here
	E	Marchesi Felix	36	chauffeur	50	"
	F	Marchesi Margaret †	36	housewife	45	"
	G*	Maggio Angelina †	38	"	67	"
	H*	Maggio Michael	38	laborer	60	"
	K	Marchesi Domenic	38	foreman	45	"
	L	Marchesi Ella †	38	housewife	38	Revere
	M	Dunbar Myron	40	laborer	44	191 Sumner
	N	Dunbar Thelma †	40	housewife	40	191 "
	O	Harmon Barbara †	40	nurse	20	191 "
	R	LaVoie Alice †	44	housewife	48	32 Eutaw
	S	LaVoie Alice M †	44	operator	20	32 "
	T	LaVoie Frances G †	44	inspector	32	32 "
	U	LaVoie Mary G †	44	housewife	21	451 Meridian
	W	LaVoie Norbert J	44	machinist	45	32 Eutaw
	Y	LaVoie Norbert L	44	brazier	24	451 Meridian

8

Eutaw Street Continued

		FULL NAME.	Residence, Jan. 1, 1943	Occupation.	Age	Reported Residence
	y	Winsor Frank M	48	carpenter	66	here
	z	Winsor Rebecca †	48	housewife	56	"
813						
	a	Gillogly Mildred B †	49	"	43	"
	b	Gillogly William C	49	electrician	50	"
	c	McDonnell Edward A	49	policeman	47	"
	d	McDonnell Richard	49	retired	74	"
	e	Piretti Elizabeth G †	49	housewife	36	"
	f	Piretti Raymond	49	painter	38	"
	g	DiIeso Ellen †	49	housewife	24	"
	h	DiIeso Paul	49	electrician	27	"
	i	Hunter James	50	machinist	26	"
	k	Hunter Jean †	50	housewife	73	"
	m	Keenan Margaret †	50	"	60	"
	n	Keenan Walter F	50	electrician	62	"
	o	Keenan Walter F	50	U S N	22	"
	p	O'Brien Agnes G †	50	at home	71	"
	r	Crotty Andrew J	51	tel worker	44	"
	s	Crotty Evelyn †	51	housewife	42	"
	t	Crotty Evelyn M †	51	secretary	20	"
	u	Salerno Antonetta †	52	stitcher	21	"
	v	*Salerno Florinda †	52	housewife	56	"
	w	Salerno Nicolas	52	calker	55	"
	x	Salerno Samuel	52	seaman	22	"
	y	Mancini Alma M †	52	housewife	29	83 Eutaw
	z	Mancini Armando J	52	painter	26	83 "
814						
	b	Salerno Madeline †	54	housewife	33	here
	c	Salerno Michael	54	painter	29	"
	d	Magnell Hilma C †	56	housewife	44	"
	e	Magnell Joseph	56	U S N	21	"
	f	Magnell Joseph	56	printer	44	"
	g	Bianco Catherine †	58	housewife	53	"
	h	Bianco Katherine †	58	clerk	27	"
	k	Bianco Olive †	58	"	22	Everett
	l	Walsh Joseph B	58	laborer	36	here
	m	Walsh Mary †	58	housewife	34	"
	n	Staretz Leah †	60	"	36	"
	o	Staretz Samuel	60	plumber	37	"
	p	Adelman Max H	60	carpenter	63	"
	r	Adelman Sarah D †	60	housewife	56	"

9

Eutaw Street—Continued

s	Rogers Anna †	60	shoeworker	45	here
t	Jacobs Jacob	62	tailor	66	"
u	Jacobs Miriam †	62	at home	34	"
v	D'Amato Accurzia †	62	housewife	26	"
w	D'Amato Alfred W	62	chauffeur	36	"
x	D'Amato Vincent	62	machinist	29	"
y	DePaulis Alexander	62	proprietor	23	"
z	DePaulis Catherine †	62	operator	20	"

815

A	*DePaulis Lena †	62	housewife	54	"
B	DePaulis Ugo	62	proprietor	50	"
C	Bailey Dorothea G †	64	housewife	60	"
D	Bailey John P	64	laborer	53	"
E	Preston Charles	64	packer	23	"
F	Preston Edith †	64	housewife	21	"
G	Cimo Jennie †	64A	"	56	"
H	Cimo Samuel	64A	laborer	52	"
K	Tarquinio Mario	64A	"	25	"
L	Latson Mary O †	66	clerk	23	66 Trenton
M	Latson Timothy C	66	U S A	23	66 "
N	DeLoretti Pasquale	66	laborer	42	here
O	Machado Justine	66	machinist	50	"
P	Re Angela †	66	at home	33	"
R	Re Celso †	66	bartender	64	"
S	Re Elvira †	66	operator	36	"
T	*Re Mary †	66	housewife	60	"
U	Alexander Marie J †	68	teacher	50	"
V	Alexander Robert	68	superintendent	47	"
W	Alexander Robert R. jr	68	boilermaker	25	"
X	*Contini Jennie †	70	housewife	54	"
Y	Contini Louis	70	pipefitter	24	"
Z	Contini Michael	70	carpenter	63	"

816

A	Christofore Ann †	70	housewife	33	"
B	Christofore John	70	musician	32	"
C	Contini Eleanor †	70	housewife	37	"
D	Contini Paul	70	printer	37	"
E	*Sousa Anthony	71	laborer	62	"
F	Sousa John	71	U S A	25	"
G	Sousa Joseph R	71	"	20	"
H	Sousa Mary †	71	housewife	57	"

Eutaw Street Continued

K	Pedro Albert	71	U S C G	24	here
L	*Pedro Anna †	71	housewife	58	"
M	Pedro Anna M †	71	"	26	"
N	*Pedro Antonio F	71	laborer	86	"
P	Pedro Joseph A	71	woolhandler	28	"
O	Pedro Louise †	71	factoryhand	22	"
R	Iantosca Angelo	72	U S A	32	Connecticut
S	Iantosca Marietta †	72	housewife	31	"
T	LoVetere Rosina †	72	"	59	here
U	Brigandi Gaetano	72	laborer	37	"
V	Brigandi Josephine †	72	housewife	34	"
W	Crotty Anna J †	73	clerk	34	"
X	Crotty Mary E †	73	housewife	70	"
Y	Crotty Mary H †	73	teacher	36	"
Z	Nihen Margaret †	73	dressmaker	72	"

817

A	Bellitti Gasparo	74	welder	24	"
B	Bellitti Rose †	74	housewife	22	"
C	Barranco Angelina †	74	stitcher	34	"
D	*Barranco Angelo	74	retired	79	"
E	*Barranco Josephine †	74	housewife	73	"
F	Barranco Salvatore	74	painter	38	"
H	Neilson Charles	75	dairyman	24	280 Havre
K	Neilson Matilda †	75	housewife	23	280 "
L	Cotecchia Rose †	75	"	28	289 "
M	Cotecchia Warren	75	machinist	25	289 "
N	Froio Jean †	75	housewife	30	289 "
O	Froio John	75	guard	31	289 "
P	Bernardi Alfred	75	laborer	35	289 "
R	Bernardi Mary †	75	housewife	34	289 "
S	Dame Abbie L †	76	at home	75	here
T	Dame Della F †	76	"	59	"
U	Field Ada M †	76	"	70	"
V	Crawford Myron E	77	operator	46	"
W	Crawford Ralph M	77	U S A	21	Newfoundland
X	Crawford Ruth †	77	housewife	45	here
Y	Rubino Angelina †	77	at home	28	"
Z	*Rubino Jennie †	77	housewife	55	"

818

A	Rubino Louis	77	U S A	24	"
B	Rubino Luigi	77	clerk	55	"

H

Eutaw Street— Continued

c	Rubino Mary †	77	saleswoman	30	here
d*	Kelly Bertha †	79	housewife	44	"
E	Kelly James L	79	U S C G	38	"
F	Levy Ruby H †	79	at home	23	"
G	Levy William H	79	U S N	20	"
K	Curcio Carmella †	79	housewife	48	"
L	Curcio Catherine †	79	clerk	20	"
H	Curcio Emilio	79	engineer	46	"
M	Curcio Emilio	79	laborer	52	"
N	DiMartino Catherine †	79	housewife	33	"
O	DiMartino Joseph	79	machinist	39	"
P	Ciampa Joseph	80	painter	26	"
R	Ciampa Mary †	80	housewife	26	"
S	Clifford Virginia †	80	"	21	210 Bremen
T	Clifford Warren	80	U S A	21	156 Falcon
U	Johnson Mary †	80	housewife	24	285 Webster
V	Johnson William	80	longshoreman	28	285 "
W	Myers Edith †	80	housewife	22	284 Sumner
X	Myers Merle D	80	U S N	25	Iowa
Y	Regan Anne S †	81	housewife	34	here
Z	Regan Daniel J	81	factoryhand	34	"
	819				
A	Orlando Lillian †	81	"	24	155 Trenton
B	Snowdon Emma M †	81	waitress	56	here
C	Snowdon Wallace E	81	sexton	66	"
D	Snowdon Wallace E. jr	81	chauffeur	29	"
E	Tango Domenic	81	painter	24	344 Saratoga
F	Elkins Eva †	82	housewife	46	here
G	Berrigan Leo	83	rigger	34	280 Lexington
H	Berrigan Rita †	83	housewife	26	280 "
K	Albino Edith †	83	at home	40	here
L	Albino George	83	shoemaker	50	"
M	Clare John	83	fishcutter	55	"
N	Moore Catherine †	84	leatherworker	54	"
O	Marshall Alfred	84	brazier	30	236 Princeton
P	Marshall Alfred H	84	carpenter	57	236 "
R	Marshall Anna †	84	housewife	23	236 "
S	Orlando John P	84	printer	32	here
T	Orlando Victoria A †	84	housewife	32	"
U	Atkinson Olive †	85	housekeeper	37	"
V	Isaacs Thomas	85	fisherman	44	"

Eutaw Street Continued

	w	*Cacciatore Angelina †	85	housewife	48	here
	x	Cacciatore Angelo	85	U S A	23	"
	y	Cacciatore Raymond	85	millhand	60	"
	z	Stasio Mary A †	86	housewife	49	"
820						
	a	Stasio Ralph A	86	foreman	53	"
	b	DeSantis John	86	carpenter	39	"
	c	*DeSantis Michelina †	86	housewife	38	"
	e	Markis Charles	86	laborer	46	"
	d	Markis May †	86	housewife	40	"
	f	*Nardi Agazio	87	factoryhand	56	"
	g	*Nardi Mary †	87	housewife	46	"
	h	Nardi Victor	87	U S A	23	N Carolina
	k	Bickford Edward	87	clerk	43	here
	l	Bickford Mildred †	87	housewife	38	"
	m	Pacella Frank	87	barber	30	"
	n	*Pacella Marie †	87	housewife	60	"
	o	Pacella Marie †	87	at home	33	"
	p	*Pacella Rocco	87	laborer	58	"
	r	Russo Domenico	88	porter	60	202 Benningt'n
	s	Russo Sarah †	88	housewife	60	202 "
	t	Marotta Albert	88	barber	43	here
	u	Marotta Mary †	88	housewife	33	"
	v	Russo Margaret †	88	candyworker	28	"
	w	Santoro Eleanor †	90	housewife	28	"
	x	Santoro Salvatore	90	machinist	28	"
	y	Day Louise H †	90	housewife	28	"
	z	Day Walter I	90	chauffeur	31	"
821						
	a	Alba Andrew	90	laborer	64	57 Bennington
	b	Alba Marie †	90	boxmaker	22	57 "
	c	Alba Mary †	90	housewife	55	57 "
	d	Christiansen Carl G	92	machinist	41	here
	e	Christiansen Harold J	92	painter	38	"
	f	Christiansen Sophia †	92	housewife	74	"
	g	MacDonald Catherine †	96	"	58	"
	h	MacDonald Davis T	96	electrician	24	"
	l	Zavarelli Frances †	105	housewife	31	5 Lexington pl
	m	Zavarelli Phillip	105	laborer	29	5 "
	n	*Doucette Grace †	105	housewife	46	140 Lexington
	o	*Doucette Norman	105	calker	44	140 "

13

Eutaw Street—Continued

P	Pusatere James	105	chauffeur	27	124 Eutaw
R	Pusatere Lola—†	105	housewife	20	124 "
S	Abbott Clarence	107	baker	25	here
T	Abbott Irene—†	107	housewife	22	"
U	Scattino Antonetta—†	107	"	47	6 Jeffries
V	Scattino Michael	107	shoemaker	51	6 "
W	Ford George E	107	longshoreman	34	133 Eutaw
X	Ford Thetla—†	107	housewife	31	133 "
Y	Slaney John	109	rigger	37	here
Z	Slaney Mary—†	109	housewife	24	"

822

A	DePalma Albert	109	seaman	23	"
B	DePalma Luigi	109	carpenter	50	"
C*	DePalma Maria—†	109	housewife	51	"
D	DePalma Virginia—†	109	rubberworker	20	"
E	DeLaria Mary—†	109	housewife	26	"
F	DeLaria Vincent J	109	operator	25	"
G	Gentuso Ignazio	111	rubberworker	62	"
H	Gentuso Rose—†	111	housewife	57	"
K	Hopp Alfred	111	electrician	42	Reading
L	Giuliano Joseph	111	machinist	22	here
M	Giuliano Maria—†	111	housewife	42	"
N*	Vella Maria—†	111	at home	60	"
O	Grasso Joan—†	111	housewife	27	123 Princeton
P	Grasso Joseph	111	foreman	27	123 "
R	Macrina Louise—†	111	operator	20	123 "
S	Caristo Ottavina—†	113	housewife	30	here
T	Caristo Salvatore	113	tailor	37	"
U	Camelengo Louise—†	113	housewife	49	"
V	Camelengo Philip	113	assessor	50	"
W	Camelengo Rita—†	113	stitcher	21	"
X	Daley John	113	bookbinder	48	"
Y	Daley Mary—†	113	housewife	50	"
Z	Chadwick Milton R	115	galvanizer	24	Medford

823

A	Chadwick Nancy G—†	115	housewife	23	198 Chelsea
B	Dolan Margaret E—†	115	at home	70	here
C	Gallagher Sarah A—†	115	"	78	"
D	O'Brien Fred L	115	probat'n officer	56	"
E	Ingala Charles	117	toolmaker	24	175 Marion
F	Ingala Frances—†	117	housewife	22	106 White

14

Eutaw Street Continued

Page.	Letter.	FULL NAME.	Residence, Jan. 1, 1943.	Occupation.	Supposed Age.	Reported Residence, Jan. 1, 1942. Street and Number
	G	*D'Errico Antonetta †	117	housewife	50	here
	H	D'Errico Louise †	117	rubberworker	20	"
	K	D'Errico Savino	117	laborer	59	"
	L	Lalli Joseph	117	"	50	140 Lexington
	M	Lalli Josephine †	117	housewife	37	140 "
	N	D'Errico Christine †	119	"	28	192 "
	O	D'Errico Michael	119	welder	29	192 "
	P	*Cochrane Catherine †	119	housewife	46	here
	R	*Cochrane Frank	119	laborer	41	"
	S	Donegan Dorothy †	119	housewife	34	"
	T	Donegan John	119	agent	30	"
	U	Lagammo Joseph	121	shoeworker	35	"
	V	Lagammo Theresa †	121	housewife	32	"
	W	Miraglia Ida †	121	at home	22	"
	X	Miraglia Mary †	121	packer	21	"
	Y	Miraglia Vincent	121	tailor	54	"
	Z	Tavano Antonio	121	shoeworker	52	"
824						
	A	Tavano Daniel R	121	machinist	22	"
	B	Tavano Josephine †	121	housewife	49	"
	C	Tavano Michelina †	121	stitcher	26	"
	D	Tavano Rose †	121	at home	24	"
	E	Accomando Michael	123	pipefitter	23	27 Brooks
	F	Accomando Veronica †	123	housewife	23	27 "
	G	Clancy Gladys †	123	"	28	319 Border
	H	Clancy Peter J	123	welder	30	319 "
	K	Iozza Joseph	123	laborer	50	here
	L	*Vega Caroline †	125	housewife	42	"
	M	Vega Domenic	125	retired	48	"
	N	Butchard Joseph H	125	chef	29	"
	O	Butchard Virginia †	125	housewife	26	"
	P	*Comunale Antonetta †	125	"	40	"
	R	Comunale Joseph	125	millhand	48	"
	S	Comunale Vincent	125	draftsman	20	"
	T	*Comunale Rose †	127	housewife	69	"
	U	*Comunale Vincenzo	127	shoemaker	68	"
	W	DiFiore Nicholas	127	artist	28	"
	X	DiFiore Vincenza †	127	housewife	27	"
	Y	Martins James	129	laborer	23	"
825						
	A	Martins Joseph	129	guard	26	"

15

Eutaw Street Continued

B	*Martins Mary †	129	housewife	48	here	
C	*Martins Mary J †	129	at home	84	"	
D	Kehoe Mary A †	129	housewife	34	"	
E	Barbare James	129	laborer	35	"	
F	Barbare Theresa †	129	housewife	31	"	
G	Amoroso Bernice †	131	"	32	"	
H	Amoroso Joseph	131	blacksmith	53	"	
K	Amoroso Joseph, jr	131	U S A	21	"	
L	Manucci Cosimo	131	barber	63	302 Paris	
M	*Manucci Maria †	131	housewife	67	302 "	
N	Orlando Attilio	131	waiter	22	92 G	
O	Taurasi Anthony	133	U S A	21	here	
R	Taurasi Salvatore	133	bootblack	61	"	
P	Taurasi Virginia †	133	housewife	51	"	
S	Warner Leonard	133	cutter	26	"	
T	Warner Mildred †	133	housewife	28	"	
U	Marks Lester W	133	shipworker	26	Revere	
V	Marks Margaret †	133	housewife	33	"	
W	*Perrisco Anna †	135	"	49	here	
X	*Perrisco Michael	135	laborer	49	"	
Y	Battaglia Frank	135	"	66	"	
Z	*Battaglia Grace †	135	housewife	69	"	

826

A	Battaglia Samuel	135	broker	30	"	
B	Waters Joseph	135	pedler	47	"	
C	Waters Mary †	135	housewife	37	"	
D	Vila John	137	fireman	47	"	
E	Vila Rita †	137	housewife	33	"	
F	Votta Antonio	137	guard	58	"	
G	*Votta Rose †	137	housewife	47	"	
H	Magaletta Albert	137	chauffeur	23	"	
K	Magaletta Ida †	137	housewife	23	"	
L	McDonald Helen †	139	"	27	"	
M	McDonald John	139	fireman	50	"	
N	McDonald William J	139	letter carrier	26	"	
O	*Smith Albert R	141	fishcutter	55	"	
P	Smith Augusta †	141	manager	31	"	
R	*Smith Gladys †	141	housewife	50	"	
S	Smith Randal M	141	rigger	37	"	
T	Scofli John	143	storekeeper	52	"	
U	*Scofli Louise †	143	housewife	46	"	

Eutaw Street Continued

	v	Scotti Salvatore	143	electrician	28	here
	w	Blasi Anna †	145	housewife	44	"
	x	Blasi Olindo C	145	investigator	46	"

827   Marion Street

	A	Brown Frederick E	3	storekeeper	41	here
	B	Brown Sophia †	3	housewife	40	"
	c	*McLean Jeanette †	5	"	31	"
	D	*McLean John	5	chauffeur	39	"
	E	Cotreau Anne R †	5	housewife	34	"
	F	Cotreau Frederick A	5	laborer	39	"
	G	*Smith Edward	5	salesman	39	"
	H	*Smith Ethel †	5	housewife	39	"
	K	Flaherty Lavinia †	9	"	54	"
	L	Flaherty William H	9	mason	60	"
	M	Grace Gerald A	11	mechanic	44	29 Falcon
	N	Grace Mildred P †	11	housewife	39	29 "
	o	Verdy Charlesina †	11	"	63	here
	P	Verdy Edward	11	guard	62	"
	R	Verdy George	11	U S A	33	"
	s	Cox Joseph	12	baker	62	"
	T	Cox Vincenza †	12	housewife	53	"
	U	Anderson Marian L †	12	"	22	9 Marion
	V	Anderson William J	12	checker	31	9 "
	W	Leighton Arthur L	13	laborer	46	here
	X	Leighton Grace A †	13	housewife	75	"
	Y	Driscoll John E	14	baker	70	"
	z	Fariole Clara †	14	housewife	54	"

828

	A	Fariole William H	14	chauffeur	36	"
	B	Moriarty Elizabeth †	14	at home	68	"
	c	Brown Eileen L †	15	housewife	20	"
	D	Brown Raymond H	15	U S C G	21	Florida
	E	Turco Jennie †	16	housewife	34	here
	F	Turco Morris	16	presser	47	"
	G	Cotter Orma †	16	housewife	27	"
	H	Cotter Thomas B	16	U S A	32	219 Lexington
	K	Webb Grace †	16	accountant	24	here
	L	Webb Maria †	16	housewife	50	"
	M	Webb Patrick	16	cook	61	"

18   17

Marion Street—Continued

	N	Doran John	17	rigger	34	here
	O	Doran Julia—†	17	housewife	33	"
	P	Joyce George P	17	oiler	37	"
	R	Joyce Maria A—†	17	housewife	32	"
	S	LeBlanc Blanche—†	17	"	52	"
	T	LeBlanc Louis C	17	chef	59	"
	U	LeBlanc Ralph	17	student	20	"
	V	*Gray David	18	manager	69	"
	W	Smith Edith—†	18	housewife	40	"
	X	Smith Paul	18	optometrist	48	"
	Y	Pearson Rita—†	19	housewife	24	"
	Z	Pearson Walter	19	mechanic	28	"
829						
	A	Harney Phyllis—†	19	factoryhand	21	71 Falcon
	B	*Smith Louis	19	mechanic	26	75 Eutaw
	C	Smith Regina—†	19	housewife	21	75 "
	D	*White Helen—†	19	"	56	3 Lexington av
	E	*White James	19	laborer	60	4 Lexington pl
	F	Morris Ernest H	20	manager	31	here
	G	Morris Florence L—†	20	housewife	37	"
	H	Loverro Felix	20	welder	25	"
	K	Loverro Margaret—†	20	housewife	25	"
	L	Ruggiero Annie—†	20	"	28	371 Meridian
	M	Ruggiero Anthony	20	U S A	30	371 "
	N	Melanson Daniel J	21	carpenter	50	165 Trenton
	O	*Melanson Rebecca—†	21	housewife	54	165 "
	P	Richards Charles	21	U S N	28	here
	R	Richards Mary—†	21	housewife	21	"
	S	DeNaro Constance—†	21	"	30	"
	T	DeNaro Michael	21	rigger	30	"
	U	Keyes Edith M—†	22	housewife	48	"
	V	Nicholson Doris M—†	22	winder	23	"
	W	Nicholson Edith E—†	22	packer	25	"
	X	Nicholson Frederick M	22	U S A	39	"
	Y	Nicholson Marian E—†	22	housewife	49	"
	Z	Nicholson William G	22	mechanic	51	
830						
	A	Keyes Bertha—†	22	housewife	76	"
	B	Keyes Chester A	22	engineer	51	"
	C	Tracostaro Joseph	24	laborer	55	437 Meridian
	D	*Tracostaro Matilda—†	24	housewife	49	437 "

18

Marion Street—Continued

E	Gannon Augustine S	26	policeman	47	here
F	Gannon Helen E †	26	housewife	43	"
G	Holland Jennie G—†	37	"	64	53 Marion
H	McCluskey Charles W	37	laborer	58	53 "
K	O'Brien Catherine—†	39	housewife	53	here
L	Sullivan William J	39	shipper	58	"
M	*Montello Frances—†	40	housewife	52	"
N	Montello Frank	40	laborer	49	"
O	Rose Mary—†	40	housewife	30	"
P	Gardiello Fannie—†	40	"	50	"
R	Gardiello Roger	40	U S C G	22	"
S	Gardiello Michael	40	tailor	51	"
T	McDonald Margaret D †	41	housewife	71	"
U	Lewis Frederick	43	pressman	64	"
V	Lewis Mary C—†	43	housewife	52	"
W	O'Hara Margaret—†	43	typist	21	"
X	Lantini Louise—†	44	housewife	36	"
Y	Lantini Samuel	44	mechanic	42	"
Z	Dichiare Alphonso	44	U S A	22	"

831

A	Dichiare Nicholas	44	laborer	52	"
B	*DiPaola Mary—†	44	housewife	41	"
C	DiPaola Nicholas	44	laborer	45	"
D	*Carbonari Joseph	48	carpenter	58	78 London
E	*Carbonari Santa—†	48	housewife	58	78 "
F	*Capocci Ernest	48	chef	34	119 Eutaw
G	*Capocci Mary—†	48	housewife	28	119 "
H	*DiChiara Delores—†	48	"	47	here
K	DiChiara Emma—†	48	dressmaker	20	"
L	DiChiara Mildred—†	48	"	23	"
M	*DiChiara Ralph	48	laborer	52	"
N	Gagone John	52	clerk	27	60 White
O	*Gagone Marcella †	52	housewife	26	60 "
P	*Grifone Anthony	52	butcher	42	here
R	Grifone Lucy—†	52	housewife	36	"
S	Delia Anthony	52	mechanic	20	"
T	Delia Michael	52	laborer	46	"
U	*Delia Philomena †	52	housewife	41	"
V	*Frederico Frank	52A	presser	65	"
W	Frederico Mary—†	52A	housewife	36	Worcester
X	*Frederico Vita †	52A	"	54	here

19

Page.	Letter	FULL NAME.	Residence, Jan. 1, 1943.	Occupation.	Supposed Age.	Reported Residence, Jan. 1, 1942. Street and Number.

Marion Street—Continued

	Y	Frederico William R	52A	mechanic	32	Worcester
	z	Frederico James	52A	cook	35	here
832						
	A	Frederico Mildred—†	52A	housewife	34	"
	B	Dexter Evelyn—†	54	"	75	"
	c	Dexter Myrtle—†	54	at home	50	"
	D	Coffin Ellen—†	56	housewife	71	"
	E	Coffin James	56	retired	77	"
	F	Crawford Margaret—†	56	housewife	32	"
	G	Mangone Albert	58	carpenter	33	146 Saratoga
	H	Mangone Anna—†	58	housewife	35	146 "
	K*	Maffie Alphonse	58	retired	77	here
	L	Maffie John	58	U S A	20	"
	M	Maffie Joseph L	58	"	24	"
	N	Maffie Mildred—†	58	housewife	50	"
	O	Maffie Mildred—†	58	clerk	22	"
	P	Maffie Peter	58	laborer	51	"
	R	Repucci Carlo	60	barber	56	"
	s*	Repucci Maria—†	60	housewife	57	"
	T	Repucci Anthony	60	laborer	26	"
	U	Repucci Carmella—†	60	clerk	23	"
	V	Repucci John	60	U S A	22	"
	W	Repucci Lucy—†	60	factoryhand	20	"
	X	Bonney Frances—†	68	housewife	60	"
	Y	Cook Florence—†	68	at home	27	"
	z	Worth Gladys—†	68	clerk	27	"

833   Meridian Street

	D	Benziger Irene—†	358	housewife	34	New York
	G	Cook Claude	358	machinist	60	here
	H	Cook George	358	U S A	32	"
	K	Cook Julia—†	358	housewife	60	"
	E	Oldanie Anthony J	358	U S N	40	"
	F	Oldanie Cecelia—†	358	housewife	36	"
	L	Ross Edna M—†	358	clerk	21	"
	M	Ross Howard M	358	packer	55	"
	N	Ross Myrtle C—†	358	housewife	48	"
	O	Donohue John H	358	plumber	38	"
	P	Donohue Madeline—†	358	housewife	37	"
	s	Roche Catherine T—†	359A	"	58	"

Page.	Letter.	FULL NAME.	Residence, Jan. 1, 1943.	Occupation.	Supposed Age.	Reported Residence, Jan. 1, 1942. Street and Number.

Meridian Street—Continued

T	Roche Charles A	359A	laborer	24	here
U	Roche Thomas A	359A	retired	75	"
V	Hackett Johanna †	359A	housewife	78	"
W	Garron Florence †	359A	packer	37	"
X	Garron Gertrude †	359A	houseworker	24	"
Y	Garron Ida—†	359A	housewife	60	"
Z	Garron Kenneth	359A	operator	34	"

834

A	Garron Walter	359A	chauffeur	28	"
C	Cole Jennie—†	361	housewife	78	"
D*	Winer Celia—†	361	"	59	"
E*	Winer Myer	361	retired	69	"
F	Guppy Laura †	361	housewife	56	"
G*	Huey Mary—†	361	"	80	"
H	Nolan Florence—†	362	"	26	"
K	Nolan Francis	362	machinist	28	"
L	Wilson John H	362	shipper	37	"
M	Wilson John R	362	retired	72	"
N	Wilson Suzan—†	362	housewife	65	"
O	Gunning Laurence J	362	U S M C	20	"
P	Gunning Margaret R †	362	housewife	42	"
R	Gunning Robert J	362	deckhand	44	"
S	Gunning Walter E	362	printer	22	"
T	Smith Mary †	362	housewife	36	"
U	Smith Raymond R	362	engineer	36	"
V	Newhall James A	363	retired	83	"
W	Scott Annie L—†	363	housewife	79	"
X	Huey Murray	363	painter	45	"
Y	Huey Victoria †	363	housewife	29	"
Z	Sullivan Ethel †	363	"	24	Chelsea

835

A	Sullivan Robert	363	deckhand	25	"
B	Wamness William	363	"	22	"
C	MacDonald Daniel W	364	ironworker	58	here
D	Preble Elisabeth †	364	housewife	75	"
E	Porreca Anna †	364	"	49	"
F	Porreca Elide †	364	operator	23	"
G	Porreca John	364	retired	54	"
H	Aiello Antonetta †	364	clerk	21	"
K	Aiello Catherina †	364	saleswoman	24	"
L	Aiello Frances †	364	housewife	58	"

21

Page	Letter	FULL NAME.	Residence, Jan. 1, 1943.	Occupation.	Supposed Age.	Reported Residence, Jan. 1, 1942. Street and Number.

Meridian Street—Continued

M	Aiello Lorenzo	364	pressman	57	here
N	Amerina Maud—†	365	housewife	49	"
O	Amerina Vincent J	365	clerk	46	"
P	McCoy Agnes—†	365	housewife	54	"
R	McCoy John E	365	U S N	30	"
S	McCoy Laurence D	365	machinist	27	"
T	McCoy Rose—†	365	typist	21	"
U	McCoy Thomas E	365	U S N	25	"
V	Maiolino Florence—†	365	housewife	48	"
W	Maiolino Joseph	365	U S A	21	"
X	Maiolino Mary—†	365	welder	24	"
Y	Masoli Salvatore	365	shoeworker	59	"
Z	Donahue David	366	bartender	68	"

836

A	Stephen David	366	clerk	45	"
B	Malfy Frederick	366A	conductor	56	"
C	Malfy Frederick, jr	366A	U S A	25	"
D	Malfy Mabel E—†	366A	housewife	50	"
E	Almond Jennie—†	366A	"	53	"
F	Almond Norma—†	366A	operator	26	"
G	Almond Peter	366A	blacksmith	63	"
H	Rock Helen B—†	368	housewife	35	"
K	Rock Timothy J, jr	368	painter	37	"
L	Lurvey Albert	368A	millhand	25	"
M	Lurvey Ellen—†	368A	housewife	50	"
N	Lurvey Helen—†	368A	bookkeeper	21	"
O	Lurvey John	368A	mechanic	23	"
P	Lurvey Mary—†	368A	housewife	28	"
R	Lurvey Reginald	368A	engineer	53	"
S	McCarthy Ruth—†	368A	housewife	34	"
T	Christopher Dorothy †	368A	"	26	"
U	Christopher Joseph	368A	bartender	30	"
V	*Rose Elisabeth †	368A	housewife	64	"
W	Rose Harold	368A	U S N	21	"
X	Rose Patrick	368A	laborer	64	"
Y	Rose William	368A	clerk	33	"
Z	Enos Barbara †	369	hairdresser	25	"

837

A	Enos John	369	boxmaker	56	"
B	Enos John, jr	369	messenger	21	"
C	Enos Mary †	369	housewife	54	"

22

Meridian Street — Continued

D	Denning June — †	369	housewife	54	here
E	Denning Thomas D	369	longshoreman	62	"
G	Deering Annie C — †	370	teacher	63	"
H	*Attwood Angus K	370	retired	80	"
K	*Attwood Nancy — †	370	housewife	76	"
L	*Bethel Hilton	370	deckhand	60	"
M	Quandt Mary — †	370	housewife	68	"
N	Quandt William	370	printer	67	"
O	Shea Reta — †	370	candymaker	28	Pennsylvania
P	Smith Georgie M — †	370	shoeworker	64	here
R	Tallman Daniel	370	laborer	68	26 White
S	Cameron Alice H — †	370	housekeeper	60	here
T	Cameron Ruth E — †	370	secretary	38	"
U	Hunter Cora E — †	370	housewife	60	"
V	Nocito Clara — †	371	"	41	"
W	Nocito Joseph	371	rigger	47	"
X	Aia John	371	machinist	22	183 Webster
Y	McCormack Elizabeth — †	372	housewife	57	here
Z	McCormack John J	372	shipfitter	57	"

838

A	McCormack John J, jr	372	mechanic	24	"
B	McCormack Mary E — †	372	houseworker	22	"
C	McCormack Thomas A	372	U S N	22	"
D	Clauss Mary L — †	372	housewife	30	"
E	Clauss Paul E	372	lithographer	33	"
F	Cunningham Helen N — †	372	housewife	40	Cambridge
G	Cunningham Helen P — †	372	clerk	26	here
H	Cunningham Thomas H	372	"	48	"
K	Olsen Carl	373	asbestos work'r	59	"
L	Olsen Elsie — †	373	housewife	40	"
M	*King Annie L — †	379	"	62	"
N	King Helen E — †	379	waitress	27	"
O	*King James R	379	fisherman	66	"
P	*King John J	379	"	37	"
R	Shaw Clarence	379	retired	68	"
S	Shaw Delia — †	379	housewife	70	"
T	DiBenedetto Mary L — †	379	"	29	"
U	DiBenedetto Vincent	379	chef	48	"
V	DiBenedetto Corina — †	379	laundress	23	"
W	DiBenedetto Mary — †	379	housewife	44	"
X	*DiBenedetto Ralph	379	tailor	50	"

23

Page.	Letter.	FULL NAME.	Residence, Jan. 1, 1943	Occupation.	Supposed Age.	Reported Residence, Jan. 1, 1942. Street and Number.

Meridian Street—Continued

	Y	Parma Antonio	379	U S A	21	here
	z	Parma John	379	laborer	49	"
839						
	A*	Parma Mary—†	379	housewife	49	"
	B	Parma Mary—†	379	student	22	"
	F*	Catinazzo Louis	383	laborer	36	"
	G	Catinazzo Margaret †	383	housewife	41	"
	H	Blasi Anthony	383	machinist	26	"
	K	Blasi Mildred—†	383	housewife	25	"
	L	Hoy Helen—†	383	housekeeper	29	"
	M	Hoy John	383	electrician	30	"
	N	McCoy Alberta †	385	housewife	20	"
	O	McCoy Joseph W	385	boilermaker	23	"
	P	Browne John B	385	storekeeper	39	"
	R	Browne Mary T †	385	housewife	34	"
	T	Zazzeretti Joseph	387	brakeman	29	"
	U	Zazzeretti Petrina †	387	housewife	29	"
	V	Fazio Aurelio	387	shoeworker	57	"
	W	Fazio Josephine †	387	housewife	50	"
	X	Fazio Josephine †	387	stenographer	20	"
	Y*	Perna Josephine †	387	housewife	52	"
	Z	Perna Nicola	387	plasterer	55	"
840						
	A	Graves Janet H †	388	secretary	45	"
	B	Graves Jennie H †	388	housewife	68	"
	C	Kieling John	388	secretary	66	"
	D	Kieling Lillian E †	388	housewife	59	"
	F	McGinnis Hazel †	389	"	34	"
	G	McGinnis John	389	guard	48	"
	H	Goldenberg Edward B	389	salesman	53	"
	K	Goldenberg Lillian †	389	housewife	52	"
	L	Goldenberg Regina †	389	clerk	22	"
	M	Dillon John	389	printer	26	97 Lawn
	N	Dillon Josephine F †	389	housewife	24	97 "
	O	Wellington Alfred E	390	banker	76	here
	P	Boudreau Daniel	391	carpenter	50	"
	R	Greene Edward P	391	retired	70	"
	S	Greene Margaret †	391	houseworker	25	"
	T	Hynes Florence †	391	housewife	30	"
	U	Merchant Agnes †	391	"	38	"
	V	Merchant Edward C	391	collector	46	"

24

Page.	Letter	FULL NAME.	Residence, Jan. 1, 1943	Occupation.	Supposed Age.	Reported Residence, Jan. 1, 1942. Street and Number.

Meridian Street Continued

x	Horne Marie — †	393A	housewife	38	145 Saratoga
y	Horne Walter	393A	boilermaker	40	145 "
z	*Almond Jennie — †	393A	housewife	57	here
841					
A	Almond Richard	393A	storekeeper	38	"
B	Zoner Helen — †	393A	housewife	36	"
C	Frongello Louis	393A	electrician	39	"
D	Safrin Annie M — †	393A	housewife	58	"
E	Safrin Francis A	393A	decorator	62	"
F	Safrin Francis E	393A	boilermaker	41	"
G	Benoit Arthur	394	rigger	37	"
H	Benoit Victoria — †	394	housewife	29	"
K	DePlacido Frank	394	cableman	58	"
L	DePlacido Mary — †	394	houseworker	33	"
M	Flynn Ethel B — †	394	housewife	54	"
N	Flynn Grace M — †	394	secretary	24	"
O	Geo Jennie M — †	394	housekeeper	64	"
P	Boudreau Ernest	395	fireman	31	"
R	*Boudreau Peter A	395	fisherman	50	"
S	Porter Clarence	395	seaman	31	"
T	*Porter Elisabeth — †	395	housewife	59	"
U	Porter Margaret — †	395	packer	24	"
V	*Muise Natalie — †	395	housewife	40	"
W	Hunt John	395	seaman	21	11 Princeton
X	Hunt Lulu — †	395	housewife	21	11 "
Y	*Smith Bessie — †	395	"	48	Canada
Z	Hardigan Richard	396	retired	72	here
842					
A	*Sloane Ann — †	396	housewife	70	"
B	Sloane Margaret A — †	396	clerk	62	"
C	Stokes Ellen T — †	396	housewife	40	50 Monmouth
E	Stokes Walter A	396	electrician	36	50 "
D	Stokes Jennie — †	396	housewife	70	314 Princeton
F	Brown Bertha O — †	398	"	74	here
G	Brown Willis S	398	engineer	80	"
H	McElman Arabel — †	398	housewife	29	"
K	McElman John A	398	welder	29	"
L	Davis Lucy J — †	398	housewife	56	"
M	Davis Sumner C	398	druggist	55	"
N	*Celozzi Dora — †	401	housewife	42	300 Maverick
O	Celozzi Lee — †	401	dressmaker	22	300 "

Meridian Street—Continued

	P	Porcaro Edward	401	barber	55	447 Meridian
	R	*Porcaro Florence †	401	housewife	49	447 "
	S	Porcaro Frances †	401	tailor	27	447 "
	T	Porcaro Helen †	401	"	24	447 "
	U	Porcaro Henry	401	U S A	22	447 "
	V	Porcaro Hilda †	401	housewife	20	447 "
	X	Porcaro Mary †	401	tailor	28	447 "
	W	Porcaro Minnie †	401	"	26	447 "
	Y	Porcaro Viola †	401	shoeworker	24	447 "
	Z	Barbarisi Antonetta †	401	tailor	23	447 "
843						
	A	Barbarisi Emelio	401	U S A	24	447 "
	B	Barbarisi Robert	401	"	22	447 "
	C	Bordonaro Constance †	402	factoryhand	22	here
	D	Bordonaro Felicia †	402	housewife	51	"
	E	Bordonaro Joseph	402	mechanic	57	"
	F	Bordonaro Peter	402	U S A	27	"
	G	Bordonaro Tina †	402	wrapper	29	"
	H	Siracusa Palma †	402	houseworker	32	"
	K	Siracusa Nicolas	402	cobbler	32	"
	L	Zagarella Joseph L	402	machinist	24	"
	M	Zagarella Marion †	402	housewife	23	"
	N	Trodella Anthony	402	electrician	24	"
	O	Trodella Phyllis †	402	housewife	25	"
	P	Belmonte Frank C	402	machinist	33	"
	R	Belmonte Helen D †	402	housewife	31	"
	T	Vitello Joseph	403A	presser	57	"
	U	*Vitello Mary †	403A	housewife	53	"
	V	Montesando Joseph	403A	U S A	25	30 W Eagle
	W	Montesando Rose †	403A	housewife	25	30 "
	X	Gray LeForest	404	retired	77	Winthrop
	Y	McLaren Charlotte †	404	housewife	46	"
	Z	McLaren Felton C	404	musician	47	"
844						
	A	*Allen Edward J	404	fishcutter	59	here
	B	Allen Olive L †	404	housewife	43	"
	C	Santaniello Concetta †	404	"	44	"
	D	Santaniello Michael	404	butcher	52	"
	E	Lipinsky Fannie †	404	housewife	52	82 White
	F	Lipinsky Samuel	404	conductor	57	82 "
	G	Wenesky Herbert	404	U S A	44	82 "

26

Meridian Street Continued

H	Kergald Alice †	404	houseworker	24	here
K	Kergald George	404	electrician	56	"
L	Silva Anthony	404	clerk	39	"
M	Silva Julia †	404	housewife	33	"
P	Orr Marie E †	406	"	60	Winthrop
R	Orr Mary C †	406	social worker	31	"
S	*Abrie Grace †	407	housewife	34	here
T	*Abrie Louis	407	manager	40	"
U	Sullivan Irving	407	deckhand	41	"

Monmouth Square

X	Walsh Helen †	1	nurse	30	here

Monmouth Street

Y	Gunning Catherine †	1	housewife	60	here
Z	Gunning Robert W	1	engineer	64	"

845

A	DeSisto Angelina †	1	rubberworker	23	101 Leyden
B	DeSisto Anthony	1	machinist	24	101 "
C	*DeSisto Lena †	1	housewife	53	101 "
D	*DeSisto Thomas	1	operator	47	101 "
E	Bennett Mary †	1	at home	70	here
F	Chamberland Shirley †	1	housewife	23	154 Trenton
G	Chamberland Warren	1	machinist	20	56 Alexander
H	Farrell John P	3	fireman	27	here
K	Farrell Phyllis †	3	housewife	26	"
L	Smith Dorothy M †	3	"	26	"
M	Smith Elwyn	3	chemist	28	"
N	Leman Arthur A	3	manufacturer	72	"
O	Leman Maude L †	3	housewife	62	"
P	*Berinato Anna †	5	"	55	"
R	*Berinato Anthony	5	finisher	65	"
S	Berinato Anthony, jr	5	printer	28	"
T	Berinato Carrie †	5	stitcher	22	"
U	Drane Helen †	5	at home	32	Melrose
V	Johnson Dorothy †	5	seamstress	28	here
W	*Johnson Jennie †	5	housewife	60	"
X	Marshall Ruth †	5	clerk	21	"
Y	Quirk James W	7	retired	70	426 Meridian

27

Page.	Letter.	FULL NAME.	Residence, Jan. 1, 1943.	Occupation.	Supposed Age.	Reported Residence, Jan. 1, 1942. Street and Number.

Monmouth Street—Continued

	z	Quirk Mary E—†	7	housewife	73	426 Meridian
846						
	A	Lawless Agnes G—†	7	"	58	here
	B	Lawless John J	7	mover	52	"
	c*	Viga Nicholas	8	barber	59	"
	D*	Viga Rose—†	8	housewife	57	"
	E	Carbon Dorothy—†	8	"	32	"
	F	Carbon Warren	8	clerk	34	"
	G	Parmenter Charles R	9	retired	65	"
	H	Crosby Effie G—†	9	at home	65	"
	K	McMahon Helen—†	9	maid	44	"
	L	Martell Helen—†	10	housekeeper	65	"
	M	Martell William	10	laborer	34	"
	N	Bertucelli George	10	baker	35	"
	O	Bertucelli Mary—†	10	housewife	40	"
	P	McDonald Mary—†	10	housekeeper	68	63 Homer
	R*	Hopp Richard	11	tailor	65	178 Brooks
	S	Surette John	11	operator	37	178 "
	T	Surette Lillian—†	11	housewife	29	178 "
	U	Cotillo Adeline—†	11	"	51	here
	V	Cotillo Olga—†	11	clerk	20	"
	W	Cotillo Ralph	11	barber	52	"
	X	DeAngelis Jennie—†	11	housewife	26	"
	Y	Natola Eleanor—†	11	rubberworker	24	"
	Z	Finney Charles B	11	foreman	64	"
847						
	A	Finney Clarinda—†	11	housewife	68	"
	c	Melisi Bridget—†	12	"	37	"
	D	Melisi Thomas	12	machinist	40	"
	E*	Klinko Peter	13	chef	45	Sagamore
	F	Klinko Selma C—†	13	waitress	36	"
	G*	Olsson Julia—†	13	at home	68	"
	H	Greenwood Margaret—†	13	"	57	here
	K	Jeffrey Dwight	13	shipfitter	43	"
	L	Jeffrey Inez—†	13	housewife	39	"
	M	Freni Louis	14	pressman	26	396 Meridian
	N	Freni Mary—†	14	housewife	28	396 "
	O	Gillis Peter	14	glazier	62	here
	P	McCormick Alexander R	14	roofer	45	"
	R	McCormick Florence G—†	14	housewife	35	"
	S	McQuade Catherine—†	15	"	78	"

Page.	Letter.	FULL NAME.	Residence, Jan. 1, 1943.	Occupation.	Supposed Age.	Reported Residence, Jan. 1, 1942. Street and Number.

Monmouth Street Continued

T	McQuade Henry	15	retired	73	here
U	Ingalls Bernard	15	"	61	"
V	Ingalls Margaret †	15	housewife	61	"
W	*Kenney Earl E	15	chauffeur	40	"
X	*Kenney Marie B †	15	housewife	39	"
Y	*Melanson Rose †	15	at home	35	131 Trenton
Z	Reed Annie B †	17	housewife	68	here
848						
A	Reed Gilbert C	17	engineer	70	"
B	Bolan Catherine †	17	housewife	55	36 Saratoga
C	Bolan Lawrence	17	rigger	22	36 "
D	Bolan Lawrence J	17	fisherman	56	36 "
E	Dean George R	17	U S A	27	36 "
F	Dean Rita †	17	at home	27	36 "
G	Cogswell Frank	21	shipworker	25	here
H	Cogswell Mary †	21	candymaker	23	"
K	Gurney Alton	21	machinist	34	30 Lexington
L	Gurney Olive †	21	housewife	26	30 "
M	Zaino Albert	21	U S A	22	here
N	*Zaino Angela †	21	housewife	60	"
O	Zaino Arthur	21	shipworker	21	"
P	Zaino Frank	21	laborer	62	"
R	D'Addieco Louis	22	pressman	29	"
S	D'Addieco Mary †	22	housewife	27	"
T	Cucchiaro Gaetano	22	presser	61	"
U	Cucchiaro Paul	22	U S A	31	"
V	Cucchiaro Rose †	22	housewife	53	"
W	*Buontempo Anna †	23	"	37	"
X	Buontempo Patrick	23	guard	40	"
Y	*Cassaro Diego	23	laborer	60	"
Z	Cassaro Josephine †	23	saleswoman	26	"
849						
A	Cassaro Liberus †	23	at home	27	"
B	Cassaro Michael J	23	U S A	30	"
C	*Cassaro Rose †	23	housewife	50	"
D	*Dunn Anna †	23	at home	20	"
E	Walsh Frances †	23	inspector	23	"
F	*Walsh Margaret †	23	at home	45	"
G	Stone Frederick	25	U S A	43	"
H	Stone Margaret W †	25	at home	76	"
K	Sullivan Frank	26	retired	62	"

Monmouth Street— Continued

	L	Hamilton Linwood S	26	mariner	58	here
	M	Hamilton Mary J—†	26	housewife	57	"
	N	O'Brien Elizabeth—†	27	"	42	"
	O	O'Brien Francis F	27	U S N	21	"
	P	O'Brien Thomas F	27	garageman	44	"
	R	*Maggio Mary—†	28	housewife	47	"
	S	*Maggio Michael	28	carpenter	53	"
	T	Kamin Edward O	28	engineer	45	"
	U	Kamin Mary G—†	28	housewife	44	"
	V	Sullivan Francis	28	seaman	43	"
	W	Sullivan Violet—†	28	housewife	32	"
	X	Miller Elizabeth—†	29	saleswoman	30	"
	Y	Miller John	29	shipfitter	57	"
	Z	Miller Priscilla—†	29	housewife	64	"
850						
	A	Miller Sarah I—†	29	clerk	28	"
	B	Coffin Seymour	29	retired	77	"
	C	Coffin Susanna—†	29	housewife	72	"
	D	Comeau George R	30	shipfitter	31	"
	E	Comeau Verna—†	30	housewife	29	"
	F	Nostro Frank	30	clerk	42	"
	G	Nostro Josephine—†	30	housewife	35	"
	H	Sherzi James	30	contractor	50	"
	K	Sherzi Mary—†	30	housewife	43	"
	L	Sherzi Mary H—†	30	clerk	20	"
	M	*Ryan Renee—†	31	housewife	39	"
	N	Ryan Thomas	31	longshoreman	37	"
	O	*LePeron Henrietta—†	31	at home	65	"
	P	Lawler Harold	32	leatherworker	28	"
	R	Lawler Marion—†	32	housewife	22	"
	S	*Scopa Filomena—†	32	"	63	"
	T	Scopa Joseph	32	laborer	62	"
	U	Scopa Joseph, jr	32	U S A	37	"
	V	Scopa Lucy—†	32	factoryhand	29	"
	W	Scopa Margaret—†	32	housekeeper	27	"
	X	Scopa Michael	32	U S A	21	"
	Y	Ballam Gertrude L—†	33	machinist	30	"
	Z	Ballam Mary G—†	33	at home	69	"
851						
	A	Nazzalo Jennie—†	34	winder	36	"
	B	Nazzalo Josephine—†	34	candymaker	26	"

Monmouth Street — Continued

c	*Prisco Claire— †	34	housewife	53	here
d	Prisco Elizabeth— †	34	stitcher	24	"
e	Prisco Frank	34	waiter	63	"
f	Guarnera Carmella— †	36	stitcher	27	"
g	Guarnera Carmello	36	retired	62	"
h	Guarnera Catherine— †	36	housewife	60	"
k	Guarnera Elene— †	36	stitcher	25	"
l	Guarnera Guy	36	operator	32	"
m	Guarnera Josephine— †	36	housewife	26	"
n	Fox Constance— †	36	"	30	New York
o	Fox Edward	36	U S A	37	"
p	Wessling Frank A	37	laborer	47	here
r	Wessling Margaret— †	37	housewife	49	"
s	*Kennedy Annie— †	37	"	71	"
t	*Kennedy Bernard	37	retired	73	"
u	Bulens Harry	38	machinist	39	"
v	Bulens Nellie K— †	38	housewife	35	"
w	Chase Mary L— †	38	at home	77	"
x	*Harnish Leona— †	38	housewife	40	"
y	*Harnish Madeline— †	38	teacher	21	"
z	Harnish Robert	38	rigger	48	"

852

a	Francis Blanche— † rear	38	housekeeper	29	Taunton
b	Francis John "	38	seaman	23	here
c	Francis Joseph "	38	drillmaker	22	"
d	*Francis Manuel "	38	cabinetmaker	56	"
e	Francis Manuel, jr "	38	"	20	"
f	Francis Mary— † "	38	operator	25	"
g	*Amerault Elise— †	39	housewife	40	"
h	Amerault Leslie	39	engineer	42	"
k	*Crowley Mary Y— †	39	operator	22	"
l	*Doucette Genevieve— †	39	saleswoman	24	"
m	*Doucette Margaret— †	39	housewife	47	"
n	*Doucette Phillip	39	laborer	50	"
o	Maginn Edward	39	machinist	70	"
p	Pascucci Mario	40	builder	30	"
r	Pascucci Mary— †	40	housewife	31	"
s	Pascucci Edward	40	U S N	26	"
t	Pascucci Madelyn— †	40	operator	20	"
u	Pascucci Marino	40	U S N	22	"
v	*Pascucci Nicoletta— †	40	housewife	58	"

Monmouth Street— Continued

w	Pascucci Sabino	40	retired	61	here
x	Lane Anthony	41	operator	36	89 Falcon
y	Lane Rose— †	41	housewife	36	89 "
z	Boland Julia— †	41	"	45	here

853

A	Boland Vincent	41	seaman	42	"
B*	Penney Bridget— †	41	at home	77	Canada
D	Maginn Charles H	42	mechanic	64	here
E	McCarthy Bessie— †	43	housewife	42	"
F	McCarthy James B	43	engineer	45	"
G	Burr Elizabeth K— †	43	electrolysist	67	"
H	Tracy Ethel V— †	44	nurse	33	"
K	Tracy May E— †	44	housewife	56	"
L	Tracy Paul D	44	machinist	64	"
N	Crocker Carlton W	45	druggist	69	"
M	Crocker Caroline— †	45	at home	27	"
O	Crocker Eliza— †	45	housewife	68	"
P	Crocker Harvey J	45	physician	25	"
R	Crocker Kimball T	45	clerk	24	"
S	Lister Jean E— †	45	at home	27	"
T	Murphy Edward	45	machinist	53	"
U	McCarthy Edward J	46	teacher	50	"
V	McCarthy Mary— †	46	housekeeper	76	"
W	McCarthy William E	46	teacher	37	"
X	Ingalls Mary— †	47	housewife	34	"
Y	Ingalls Reginald	47	laborer	48	"
Z	Gallagher Elizabeth— †	47	at home	55	"

854

A	Gallagher Mary M— †	47	clerk	21	"
B	Indingaro Anthony	47	collector	30	"
C	Indingaro Louise— †	47	housewife	29	"
D	Furness Catherine— †	48	bookkeeper	71	"
E	Hart Gertrude— †	48	stenographer	34	"
F	Power Lillian— †	48	waitress	38	"
G	Power Mabel— †	48	clerk	35	"
H	Power Susan— †	48	housewife	64	"
K	Power Stephen	48	retired	68	"
L	Campbell Joseph A	49	fireman	44	"
M	Campbell Margaret A— †	49	housewife	44	"
N	Campbell Norman J	49	student	20	"
O	Thivierge Virginia— †	49	at home	78	"

Monmouth Street Continued

	Letter	FULL NAME	Residence	Occupation	Age	Reported Residence
	P	Thivierge William	49	painter	51	here
	R	Lombard Arlene †	50	housewife	27	"
	S	Lombard Robert	50	attorney	26	"
	T	Cestoni Anthony	50	metalworker	28	112 Leyden
	U	Cestoni Josephine †	50	housewife	26	112 "
	V	Ferris Anton L	50	guard	64	here
	W	Lombard Frances †	50	housekeeper	46	"
	X	Forrest Elizabeth †	51	at home	74	"
	Y	Forrest Maude †	51	bowmaker	44	"
	Z	Clohesy Thomas	51	U S A	23	"

855

	Letter	FULL NAME	Residence	Occupation	Age	Reported Residence
	A	Nazzaro Elizabeth †	51	housewife	42	"
	B	Nazzaro Robert	51	electrician	41	"
	D	Narroway Rose †	52	at home	82	"
	E	Strong James H	52	physician	68	"
	F	O'Brien Alice †	53	stenographer	34	"
	G	O'Brien Annie M †	53	at home	76	"
	H	Sorensen George	55	U S N	28	"
	K	Sorensen Olive †	55	housewife	53	"
	L	Sorensen Theodore	55	machinist	54	"
	M	Sorensen Walter	55	U S A	22	"
	N	Sullivan Thomas C	57	retired	63	"
	O	Wellings John S	57	policeman	49	"
	P	Wellings Loretta M †	57	teacher	29	"
	R	Wellings Mary A †	57	housewife	48	"
	S	Warren Fred L	59	artist	47	"
	T	Warren George W	59	clergyman	83	"
	U	Warren Marjorie C †	59	social worker	49	"
	V	Guide Mildred †	61	housewife	28	Pennsylvania
	W	Guide Thomas	61	clerk	28	"
	X	LaMotta Grace †	61	housewife	36	here
	Y	LaMotta Harold A	61	inspector	35	"
	Z	Guide Joseph	61	barber	31	"

856

	Letter	FULL NAME	Residence	Occupation	Age	Reported Residence
	A	Guide Rose †	61	stenographer	33	"
	B	Pisello Carmen	63	builder	46	"
	C	Pisello Marie †	63	housewife	38	"
	D	Repucci Edith †	63	candymaker	27	"
	E	Repucci Edmund	63	wrapper	33	"
	F	*Repucci Joseph	63	retired	75	"
	G	Repucci Alfred	63	custodian	43	"

1 8   33

Page.	Letter.	FULL NAME.	Residence. Jan. 1, 1943.	Occupation.	Supposed Age.	Reported Residence. Jan. 1, 1942. Street and Number.

Monmouth Street—Continued

	H	Repucci Caroline —†	63	housewife	39	here
	K	Repucci John	63	chauffeur	46	"
	L	Repucci Rose —†	63	housewife	34	"

Putnam Street

	O	*Morella Marino	65	retired	76	here
	M	Morella Anthony C	65	undertaker	38	"
	N	Morella Laura —†	65	housewife	35	"
	P	LePore Anthony	67	shoeworker	47	"
	R	*LePore Concetta —†	67	housewife	32	"
	S	LePore Geraldine —†	67	stitcher	20	"
	T	Fitzgerald Catherine M†	67	housewife	40	"
	U	Fitzgerald Francis L	67	U S N	20	"
	V	*Maienza Frank	69	salesman	30	"
	W	Maienza Mary —†	69	housewife	26	"
	X	Moreschi Lena —†	69	"	48	"
	Y	Moreschi Ralph	69	molder	52	"
	Z	Iapicca Marion —†	69	housewife	26	697 Benningt'n

857

	A	Iapicca Rocco	69	operator	26	697 "
	B	Gallo Joseph	71	laborer	39	Needham
	C	Gallo Mary —†	71	housewife	31	103 Lexington
	D	Caparelli Amelia †	71	"	43	here
	E	Caparelli Frank	71	U S A	21	"
	F	Caparelli Thomas	71	manufacturer	44	"
	G	Young Mary —†	71	at home	33	"
	H	Maxwell Effie D †	73	"	73	"
	K	*Wyman Della M †	73	"	63	"
	L	Bertino Anthony	75	fruit	24	"
	M	*Bertino Antonetta —†	75	housewife	51	"
	N	Bertino Carmen	75	milkman	22	"
	O	Bertino Mary †	75	housewife	24	"

Trenton Street

	R	*Druken Patrick	56	fisherman	46	here
	S	Powers Augustus	56	"	38	"
	T	Shanahan Adeline B †	56	clerk	21	"
	U	Shanahan Rose —†	56	housekeeper	50	"
	V	Barros Anna —†	56	housewife	40	"

34

Trenton Street — Continued

w	*Barros Antonio	56	millhand	55	here	
x	Barros Mary †	56	"	23	"	
y	Barros Teofilo	56	cook	50	"	
z	Cronin Catherine †	58	housewife	38	"	

858

A	Cronin James F	58	policeman	38	"
B	Sullivan Margaret †	58	clerk	36	"
C	Giovino Alfred	58	plumber	28	"
D	*Giovino Carmen	58	retired	73	"
E	*Giovino Jennie †	58	housewife	67	"
F	Giovino Louis	58	U S A	32	"
G	Faldetta John	60	machinist	27	Chelsea
H	Impemba Concetta †	60	housewife	23	161 Benningt'n
K	Impemba Martin	60	millhand	26	161 "
L	Ferrino Antonetta †	60	stitcher	22	here
M	Ferrino Enrico	60	laborer	58	"
N	Ferrino Josephine †	60	housewife	56	"
O	Alves Caroline †	62	"	28	"
P	Alves Napoleon	62	steward	30	"
R	Stacey Bessie †	62	housewife	48	"
S	Stacey Hubbard	62	machinist	56	"
T	Colatrella Carmen	62	shoeworker	51	"
U	Colatrella Jennie †	62	housewife	46	"
V	Colatrella Josephine †	62	at home	20	"
W	Colatrella Marie †	62	clerk	22	"
X	Robicheau Lucy †	rear 62	housewife	37	"
Y	Robicheau Wilbourn	" 62	shipwright	42	"
Z	Penney Mary †	64	housewife	68	37 Eutaw

859

A	Penney William	64	fisherman	65	37 "
B	Campagna Adelaide †	64	clerk	48	here
C	Iocco Joseph	64	U S A	21	"
D	Iocco Rocco	64	laborer	49	"
E	*Iocco Theresa †	64	housewife	52	"
F	*Costa Theresa †	66	housekeeper	58	"
G	Neves Anna †	66	housewife	45	"
H	Neves Lawrence	66	seaman	55	"
K	Vasapolle Josephine †	68	housewife	22	"
L	Vasapolle Salvatore	68	painter	28	"
M	Tortora Anna †	68	housewife	42	"
N	Tortora Francesco	68	painter	56	"

Page.	Letter.	FULL NAME.	Residence, Jan. 1, 1943.	Occupation.	Supposed Age.	Reported Residence, Jan. 1, 1942. Street and Number.

Trenton Street—Continued

o	Tortora Leo	68	U S N	21	here
p	Guida Giacomo	68	retired	62	"
R	Guida Leo	68	"	67	"
s	Iavicoli George	70	welder	33	286 Chelsea
T	Iavicoli Rose—†	70	housewife	27	286 "
u	DiNicola Albert	70	U S A	26	here
v	Marinani Carina—†	70	housewife	48	"
w	Marinani Domenic	70	U S A	31	"
x	Marinani Sabatino	70	laborer	63	"
y	Spera Catherine—†	72	housewife	32	"
z	Spera Louis	72	boilermaker	33	"
	860				
A	LaBella Charles	72	salesman	34	"
B	LaBella Margaret †	72	housewife	27	"
c	Bellabona Joseph	74	carpenter	31	"
D	Bellabona Olympia †	74	housewife	29	"
E	Saggese Anthony	74	barber	33	"
F	Saggese Sistina †	74	housewife	31	"
G	Catania Alberta †	74	"	30	"
H	Catania Joseph L	74	machinist	27	"
K	LaBella Gerardo	76	fireman	28	"
L	LaBella Marie †	76	housewife	27	"
M	D'Avolio Carmen	76	shipfitter	47	"
N	D'Avolio Eugene	76	U S A	21	"
o	D'Avolio Margaret †	76	housewife	45	"
P	Staffier Anthony J	78	welder	24	"
R	Staffier Mary—†	78	housewife	22	"
s	Saggese Helen †	78	"	25	275 Chelsea
T	Saggese Lawrence	78	blacksmith	25	275 "
u	McBride Julia †	80	housewife	77	here
v	McBride William	80	retired	82	"
w	Harrison Anna †	80	housewife	67	"
x	Harrison John	80	laborer	67	"
y	Riggs Anna †	80	waitress	38	"
z	Scott Anthony L	82	seaman	46	"
	861				
A	Scott Anthony L, jr	82	U S A	21	"
B	Scott Marie †	82	housewife	39	"
c	Scott Walter E	82	U S M C	20	"
D*	Muise Cecelia †	82	housewife	37	"
E*	Muise Peter	82	retired	43	"

36

Trenton Street—Continued

	F	Fermicolo Lucy †	82	clerk	23	here
	G	*Fermicolo Mary †	82	housekeeper	53	"
	H	Ducey Catherine †	86	housewife	39	"
	K	Ducey Thomas	86	carpenter	47	"
	L	Martino Angela †	86	housewife	38	"
	M	Martino Peter	86	barber	44	"
	N	*DiBilio Gaetano	86	laborer	50	"
	O	*DiBilio Maria †	86	housewife	49	"
	P	Rasetta Luigi	88	engineer	47	"
	R	Rasetta Mary †	88	housewife	43	"
	S	LaBella Antonio	88	barber	59	"
	T	LaBella Erminia †	88	housewife	59	"
	U	LaBella Laura †	88	stitcher	20	"
	V	Marchand Francis	90	laborer	41	"
	W	Marchand Maude †	90	housewife	41	"
	X	Buono Antonio	90	laborer	48	"
	Y	Buono Mary †	90	housewife	45	"
	Z	Baccardax Juanita †	92	housekeeper	43	"

862

	A	*Lombardi Mary †	92	housewife	51	"
	B	Lombardi Nicholas	92	U S A	23	"
	C	Lombardi Philip	92	laborer	58	"
	D	Lombardi Ralph	92	U S A	21	"
	E	Puorro Antonio	94	shoemaker	48	"
	F	Puorro Filomena †	94	housewife	42	"
	G	Govoni Carmella †	94	"	42	"
	H	Govoni John	94	fireman	47	"
	K	Nappa Augusto	94	laborer	38	"
	L	Nappa Michalena †	94	housewife	28	"
	N	Severo Carlo C	96	metalworker	29	39 Lamson
	O	Severo Vincenza L †	96	housewife	22	39 "
	P	Drigotas Rose †	96	"	27	91 Putnam
	R	Drigotas Stanley	96	deckhand	24	91 "
	S	Grasso Consolino †	96	instructor	28	here
	T	Grasso Mary †	96	housewife	26	"
	U	Hardy Charles O	98	plater	49	"
	V	Hardy Lillian V †	98	housewife	46	"
	W	Thompson Anne L †	100	housekeeper	65	"
	X	Thompson Helen I †	100	teacher	33	"
	Y	Ford John C	102	garageman	48	"
	Z	Micciche Blanche †	102	housewife	21	"

Page.	Letter.	FULL NAME.	Residence. Jan. 1, 1943.	Occupation.	Supposed Age.	Reported Residence, Jan. 1, 1942. Street and Number.

863

Trenton Street—Continued

	A	Micciche Michael	102	U S A	20	116 Trenton
	B	Wennerberg Emil F	102	retired	75	here
	E	Trainor Georgiana—†	110	housewife	46	"
	F	Trainor John J	110	shipfitter	56	"
	G	Trainor John L	110	U S A	23	"
	H	Trainor Robert F	110	"	21	"
	L	*Purello Philip	112	laborer	78	"
	M	Elvey Estelle †	112	housewife	42	"
	N	Elvey Milton	112	secretary	45	"
	O	Bruno Florence—†	112	housewife	26	"
	P	Bruno George	112	laborer	26	"
	R	Petrillo Joseph	114	"	25	Chelsea
	S	Petrillo Sarah—†	114	housewife	21	"
	T	Pugliese Albert	114	U S A	21	here
	U	*Pugliese Andrew	114	carpenter	64	"
	V	Pugliese John	114	U S A	25	"
	W	Pugliese Joseph	114	carpenter	60	"
	X	*Pugliese Julia—†	114	housewife	54	"
	Y	Pugliese Josephine †	114	clerk	23	"
	Z	Benvesuto Alfred	116	shipfitter	36	140 Putnam

864

	A	Benvesuto Serafina †	116	housewife	32	140 "
	B	*Connors David	116	fisherman	34	here
	C	*Connors Lucy—†	116	housewife	31	"
	D	*Whelan Alexander	116	retired	69	"
	E	Lewis Gordon	116	fisherman	31	1 White
	F	Lewis Mary—†	116	housewife	31	1 "
	G	D'Avolio Helen—†	118	"	24	223 Saratoga
	H	D'Avolio Michael	118	driller	25	223 "
	K	St Croix Henry	118	rigger	27	here
	L	St Croix Ruth †	118	housewife	25	"
	M	French Angelina †	118	"	27	"
	N	French Roy	118	inspector	32	"
	O	LaBella Giro P	120	welder	31	"
	P	LaBella Louise †	120	housewife	29	"
	R	Morgan Daniel J	120	shipfitter	45	"
	S	Morgan Gertrude †	120	clerk	46	"
	T	Ristaino Antonio	120	freighthandler	50	"
	U	Ristaino Carmella †	120	housewife	47	"
	V	Ristaino Clementina †	120	stitcher	20	"

38

Trenton Street — Continued

w	McEwen Allen W	122	cooper	78	here	
x	McEwen Mary E †	122	housewife	63	"	
y	Whiteway Arthur	122	retired	74	"	
z	Whiteway Martha †	122	housewife	73	"	

865

A	French Harold	124	clerk	20	220 Saratoga	
B	French Jennie †	124	housekeeper	65	220 "	
D	Santangelo Savino	124	retired	70	here	
C	Santangelo Victoria †	124	housewife	65	"	
E	Driver Arthur	124	laborer	29	"	
F	Driver Mildred †	124	housewife	26	"	
G	*Stoico Anthony	126	barber	30	"	
H	Stoico Theresa †	126	housewife	33	"	
K	*Muise Bertha †	126	"	41	"	
L	*Muise George E	126	fishcutter	41	"	
M	Gall Charles	126	laborer	47	"	
N	*Gall Olga †	126	housewife	55	"	
O	Scimone Angelina †	128	"	42	"	
P	Scimone Domenic	128	presser	50	"	
R	Scimone Jennie †	128	stitcher	20	"	
T	D'Antona Grace †	128	housewife	43	"	
U	D'Antona Joseph	128	candymaker	50	"	
S	D'Antona Leo R	128	U S N	21	"	
V	Murray Isabella E †	128	housewife	45	"	
W	Murray John F	128	boilermaker	47	"	
X	Murray Lillian M †	128	clerk	23	"	
Y	Enos Mary C †	130	boxmaker	50	"	
Z	Enos Paulmeda M †	130	"	46	"	

866

A	Enos Virginia C †	130	housekeeper	75	"	
B	Enos William L jr	130	electrician	37	"	
C	McGillivray Alexander	130	laborer	60	"	
D	McGillivray Stella †	130	housekeeper	60	"	
E	Ward Bertha †	130	housewife	58	"	
F	Ward John	130	forger	60	"	
G	O'Connell Josephine †	132	housewife	28	"	
H	O'Connell Thomas	132	freighthandler	33	"	
K	Musto Angelo	132	social worker	25	"	
L	Musto Delores †	132	housewife	24	"	
M	Basile Anna †	132	"	30	"	
N	Basile Salvatore	132	clerk	29	"	

Trenton Street — Continued

		FULL NAME.	Residence	Occupation.	Age	Reported Residence
	o	Perry Ernest	134	laborer	20	210 Paris
	p	Capolupo Emanuela †	134	housewife	42	here
	R	Capolupo Vincent	134	shoeworker	44	"
	s	Hawes Anna †	134	housekeeper	63	"
	T	McNamee Elizabeth †	134	clerk	68	"
	U	Sauchello Asunta †	136	at home	33	"
	V	Sauchello Pasqualina †	136	housekeeper	68	"
	W	Sauchello Paul	136	at home	32	"
	X	Amenta Lucy †	136	shoeworker	28	"
	Y	Amenta Mary †	136	"	21	"
	Z*	Amenta Michalena †	136	housekeeper	66	"
867						
	A	Caputo Josephine †	136	housewife	29	"
	B	Caputo Paul	136	welder	33	"
	C	Moralis John	138	mason	55	"
	D	Moralis Sebastiana †	138	housewife	56	"
	E	Battaglia Joseph	138	laborer	35	"
	F	Battaglia Julia †	138	housewife	31	"
	G	Bertino Andrew	138	storekeeper	28	"
	H	Bertino Mary †	138	housewife	25	"
	K*	DeMauro Antonetta †	140	"	63	"
	L	DeMauro Sebastiano	140	laborer	66	"
	M	Cadotte Margaret †	140	housewife	27	Connecticut
	X*	Dwyer Mary †	140	housekeeper	53	here
	o	Dwyer Raymond	140	seaman	22	"
	R	Angelina Mary †	142	housekeeper	39	"
	s	Susan Robert	142	laborer	60	"
	T	Dunning Agnes F †	142	housewife	27	"
	U	Dunning Harry	142	chauffeur	34	"
	V	Francis Esther C †	142	housewife	64	"
	W	Francis Joseph A	142	retired	66	"
	X	Susan Leo	142	salesman	64	"
	Y	Susan Samuel	142	glazier	62	"
	Z	Hayden Nellie †	144	housewife	36	"
868						
	A	Hayden Richard	144	foreman	37	"
	B	Bertino Florence †	144	housewife	26	"
	C	Bertino Frank	144	laborer	28	Revere
	D	Florentino Angelo	144	"	46	here
	E	Florentino Mary †	144	housewife	42	"
	F	Deveau Edward	146	carpenter	22	"

40

Trenton Street Continued

G	*Deveau Fannie †	146	housekeeper	53	here
H	Deveau Mary A †	146	cardmaker	20	"
K	Gillen Martin	146	longshoreman	35	"
L	Gillen Mary †	146	housewife	33	"
M	Casetta Anthony	146	laborer	28	"
N	Casetta Mildred †	146	housewife	21	"
O	LaBlanc George	148	calker	58	"
P	LaBlanc J Everett	148	U S A	28	"
R	LaBlanc James	148	"	24	"
S	LaBlanc Mary †	148	housewife	51	"
T	LaBlanc Melvin	148	U S A	23	"
U	Godbold Caroline A †	150	secretary	71	"
V	Smith Harold K	150	proofreader	36	"
W	*Gonsolves John	152	laborer	45	"
X	Silva Manuel J	152	"	48	"
Y	*Silva Mary †	152	housewife	44	"
Z	Testa Myrtle †	154	"	46	"

869

A	Testa Robert	154	storekeeper	53	"
B	Testa Phyllis †	154	housewife	22	"
C	Testa Robert, jr	154	clerk	27	"
D	Lake Harry	156	engineer	56	"
E	Lake Marion G †	156	housekeeper	44	"

White Street

G	Voltero Fannie †	1	housewife	28	403 Meridian
H	Voltero John	1	presser	28	403 "
K	Hipwell Gertrude †	1	housewife	42	here
L	Hipwell Joseph	1	foreman	41	"
M	Trott Albert	1	retired	75	"
N	Costigan John	1	longshoreman	65	"
O	Fitzpatrick Thomas M	17	clerk	57	"
P	Herman Helen F †	17	housekeeper	67	"
R	Brannen Amy †	17	housewife	37	"
S	Brannen Winston C	17	chef	42	"
T	Bartolo Marie †	19	housewife	20	"
U	Bartolo Michael	19	clerk	24	"
V	LeBlanc Cora M †	19	housewife	29	"
W	LeBlanc Joseph A	19	seaman	32	"
X	Peterson Alfred O	19	clerk	32	"

1—8   41

Page.	Letter	FULL NAME.	Residence, Jan. 1, 1943.	Occupation.	Supposed Age.	Reported Residence, Jan. 1, 1942. Street and Number.

White Street—Continued

	Letter	FULL NAME	Res. 1943	Occupation	Age	Reported Residence
	Y	Peterson Veronica—†	19	housewife	30	here
	z	Swim Harriet—†	21	at home	38	65 Condor
870						
	A	Chalmers Catherine—†	21	housewife	75	here
	B	Chalmers William	21	retired	76	"
	C	Foster Emma—†	21	at home	39	"
	D	Evans Liston C	23	chef	46	Chelsea
	E	Barnett James	23	electrician	33	here
	F	Barnett Lillian—†	23	housewife	26	"
	G	Boci Betty—†	23	sitcher	25	"
	H	*Schipani Angelina—†	23	housewife	34	"
	K	Schipani Anthony	23	machinist	43	"
	L	Pickles Carol—†	25	housewife	22	"
	M	Pickles Elmer	25	chauffeur	25	"
	N	Joyce Charles H	25	rigger	29	"
	O	Joyce Frederick J	25	engineer	56	"
	P	Joyce Mathilda—†	25	housewife	52	"
	R	McGrath John F	25	U S A	23	"
	S	McGrath Marion G—†	25	housewife	22	"
	T	Ducharme Elric	27	laborer	54	"
	U	Ducharme Leo	27	metalworker	27	"
	V	Grace Elizabeth—†	27	housewife	59	"
	W	Grace George	27	shipfitter	37	"
	X	Grace Joseph	27	U S A	27	"
	Y	Grace William	27	"	33	"
	z	*McComiskey Bernard	29	maint'n'ceman	22	"
871						
	A	McComiskey Goldie—†	29	housewife	23	"
	B	Waltman Blanche—†	29	"	45	"
	C	Waltman Carl E	29	machinist	41	"
	D	Boudreau Arthur C	29	fisherman	37	"
	E	Boudreau Rose—†	29	housewife	31	"
	F	Shea James F	31	retired	66	"
	G	Shea Jeremiah L	31	agent	56	"
	H	Shea Thomas J	31	retired	62	"
	K	*Dooley Margaret—†	33	housewife	20	172 Border
	L	Dooley Michael	33	longshoreman	27	172 "
	M	McCarthy Margaret—†	33	housewife	21	here
	N	McCarthy Paul J	33	ropemaker	25	"
	O	Stones Amanda—†	33	housewife	51	"
	P	Stones Henry S	33	machinist	51	"

White Street Continued

R	O'Connell Cornelius	35	bartender	34	here	
S	O'Connell Marjorie †	35	housewife	31	"	
T	Coyle Florence M †	35	"	35	"	
U	Coyle Frances †	35	inspector	22	"	
V	Coyle Joseph A	35	retired	71	"	
W	Coyle Joseph A, jr	35	machinist	33	"	
X	Coyle Mary E †	35	housewife	61	"	
Y	Cayon Angelina †	37	clerk	21	"	
Z	Cayon Roy G	37	chef	58	"	

872

A	Cayon Rosealia †	37	housewife	51	"	
B	Lemery Mary E †	39	at home	69	"	
C	McLaughlin Rose G †	39	"	55	"	
D	Lehtola Armas	41	pipefitter	35	"	
E	Polm Susanna †	41	at home	63	"	
F	Salonen Arthur	41	laborer	33	"	
G	Davis David	41	shoemaker	61	"	
H	*Davis Rose †	41	housewife	61	"	
K	Healey John	41	retired	75	"	
M	*Carnevale Esther †	87	housewife	51	"	
N	Carnevale Zefferino	87	tailor	50	"	
O	Carneval Walter	87	U S A	20	"	
P	Carnevale William	87	"	20	"	
R	Anzalone Philomena †	89	housewife	42	"	
S	*Piccarello Costable	89	retired	77	"	
T	Vincola Rose †	89	clerk	24	"	
U	Morelli Anne †	91	housewife	38	"	
V	Morelli Joseph	91	longshoreman	42	"	

Ward 1–Precinct 9

CITY OF BOSTON

LIST OF RESIDENTS
20 YEARS OF AGE AND OVER

(NON-CITIZENS INDICATED BY ASTERISK)
(FEMALES INDICATED BY DAGGER)

AS OF

JANUARY 1, 1943

JOSEPH F. TIMILTY, *Chairman*
FREDERIC E. DOWLING, *Secretary*
WILLIAM A. MOTLEY, JR.
FRANCIS B. McKINNEY
EVERETT R. PROUT

Listing Board.

CITY OF BOSTON PRINTING DEPARTMENT

Page.	Letter.	FULL NAME.	Residence, Jan. 1, 1943.	Occupation.	Supposed Age.	Reported Residence, Jan. 1, 1942. Street and Number.

900

Bennet Place

A	Caton Bertha—†	1	housewife	62	here
B	Caton Frances—†	1	inspector	24	"
C	Caton Manuel	1	laborer	33	"
D	Morrisson John R	1	toolmaker	39	"
E	Morrisson Helen—†	1	housekeeper	40	"
F	Hodgkins Carrie—†	2	housewife	32	"
G	Hodgkins Rupert	2	operator	39	"
H	Scott Mary—†	3	housewife	40	"
K	Ford Daniel	4	fireman	28	"
L	Kennedy Alphonsus	4	rigger	58	"
M	Kennedy Catherine—†	4	housewife	60	"

Brooks Street

U	*Costigan Nora †	185	housewife	44	here
V	*Costigan Patrick F	185	fisherman	45	"
W	Surette John	187	shipper	27	2 Savage ct
X	Surette Louise †	187	housewife	21	2 "
Z	Murray Edward H	189	ironworker	61	here

901

A	Murray Helen E †	189	housewife	45	"
B	Gates Anna G †	189	at home	31	122 Meridian
C	Gates Edward P	189	cook	61	122 "
D	McGuire Alice †	191	housewife	79	here
E	McGuire William J	191	retired	85	"
F	Basile Mary †	191	housewife	25	"
G	Basile Peter	191	shipper	27	"
H	Costanza Anna †	193	clerk	64	"
K	Sousa Manuel	193	meatcutter	65	"
L	DiGiovanni Anthony	195	chauffeur	41	"
M	DiGiovanni Mary †	195	housewife	41	"
N	Sousa John	195	fireman	29	"
O	Sousa Mary †	195	housewife	25	"
P	Baker Josephine †	195	clerk	52	"
R	Mooney Arthur J	195	electrician	37	"
S	Mooney Claire †	195	housewife	33	"
T	Gonzales Frank L	214	engineer	53	"
U	Lopez Carmen †	214	housewife	46	"
V	Lopez Frank	214	U S C G	21	"
W	Lopez Josephine †	214	stitcher	24	"

2

Brooks Street—Continued

	x	Lopez Lillian—†	214	stitcher	23	here
	y	Otiro John	214	engineer	50	"
	z	Lavieri Antonette—†	214	stitcher	54	"

902

	a	Lavieri Jane—†	214	at home	30	"
	b	Lavieri Joan—†	214	stitcher	24	"
	c	Lavieri Rinaldo	214	upholsterer	54	"
	d	Bruno John	214	foreman	51	125 Princeton
	e	Bruno Louise—†	214	packer	28	125 "
	f	*Bruno Victoria—†	214	housewife	51	125 "
	g	Greeley Elizabeth—†	214	"	21	125 "
	h	Greeley Thomas	214	U S A	24	Lynn
	k	Annese Anthony	216	merchant	36	here
	l	Annese Cecilia—†	216	housewife	37	"
	m	Forgione Frank	216	shipper	35	"
	n	Forgione Mary—†	216	housewife	39	"
	o	Safrin Diana L—†	218	at home	52	218 Webster
	p	Thibodeau Alcide	218	carpenter	50	140 Benningt'n
	r	Silva Edith—†	218	housewife	35	here
	s	Silva Joseph H	218	agent	40	"
	t	Loracy Frederick J	220	pipefitter	42	"
	u	Loracy Mary F—†	220	housewife	42	"
	v	Connolly Mary A—†	220	at home	64	"
	w	Connolly Mary A—†	220	teacher	24	"
	x	Connolly Patrick J	220	clerk	34	"
	y	Capolupo Anthony	220	shoemaker	50	"
	z	Capolupo Philomena—†	220	housewife	41	"

903

	a	Whynott George	224	at home	77	"
	b	Whynott Jane—†	224	housewife	72	"
	c	Hill Amanda—†	224	houseworker	48	"
	d	Hill Frederick	224	U S A	26	"
	e	*Selin Hulda—†	rear 224	housewife	54	"
	f	*Selin Richard	" 224	ironworker	53	"

Condor Street

	g	Leville Annie T—†	5	at home	62	here
	m	Boudreau Albert	5	electrician	31	"
	h	*Boudreau Elias	5	retired	70	"
	n	Boudreau Ethel—†	5	packer	31	"

Condor Street—Continued

K	Boudreau Evelyn—†	5	rubberworker	23	here
L	*Boudreau Virginia—†	5	housewife	65	"
O	Gallagher Katherine—†	5	at home	70	"
P	Tedford Althea—†	5	housewife	40	"
R	Tedford George	5	machinist	40	"
S	Magee Florence—†	7	at home	68	"
T	Riley William	7	clerk	62	"
U	Emmons Frederick J	7	salesman	53	"
V	Emmons Muriel J—†	7	housewife	43	"
W	Emmons Ruth—†	7	operator	22	"
X	Channess Ambrosine—†	9	waitress	45	"
Y	Garcia Ambrosine—†	9	at home	75	"
Z	Finn Lawrence	11	welder	24	"

904

A	Finn Maryba—†	11	at home	53	"
B	Finn William P	11	U S A	28	"
C	Losco Mary—†	13	housewife	42	"
D	Losco William	13	chauffeur	45	"
E	Hoy James	13	custodian	56	"
F	Hoy Margaret—†	13	housewife	52	"
G	Tallman Ethel F—†	13	"	53	"
H	Tallman Harry T	13	salesman	58	"
K	Simons Alexander D	15	retired	79	155 Condor
L	Simons Robert	15	"	42	155 "
M	Simons Rosella—†	15	housewife	78	155 "
N	Heeck Cornelius R	15	printer	70	here
O	Heeck Florence L—†	15	housewife	59	"
P	Kelleher Cornelius J	15	plumber	56	"
R	Kelleher Lawrence	15	machinist	26	"
S	Kelleher Margaret—†	15	housewife	56	"
T	Whitehead James E	21	U S N	42	"
U	Whitehead Rose—†	21	clerk	38	"
W	Mahoney Julia M—†	30	housewife	38	"
X	Mahoney Timothy J	30	laborer	46	"
Y	Murphy Daniel F	30	retired	78	"
Z	Murphy Mary—†	30	housewife	70	"

905

A	Murphy Antonina—†	32	"	45	"
B	Murphy William F	32	chauffeur	44	"
C	Burke John	33	carpenter	63	"
D	Coogan Lawrence	33	machinist	63	"

4

Page.	Letter.	FULL NAME.	Residence, Jan. 1, 1943.	Occupation.	Supposed Age.	Reported Residence, Jan. 1, 1942. Street and Number.

Condor Street Continued

E	Coogan Mary †	33	housewife	60	here
F	Kane Emma E †	33	"	45	"
G	Kane Joseph A	33	engineer	44	"
H	Leary Florence E †	33	housewife	54	"
K	Leary Lewis B	33	painter	55	"
L	McGillivary Arlene P †	33	clerk	27	"
M	McGillivary William B	33	U S N	27	Lynn
N	Scandone Joseph	34	ironworker	43	here
O	Scandone Lillian †	34	housewife	51	"
P	Smith Ernest	34	U S A	20	"
R	Fortier Charles	36	laborer	23	"
S	Fortier Martha †	36	housewife	25	"
T	Johnson Harold	36	U S A	29	"
U	Melville Hazel A †	37	housewife	55	"
V	Melville James A	37	machinist	55	"
W	Ellis Frank A	37	clerk	52	"
X	Ellis Marion †	37	librarian	47	"
Y	Smith Ella †	37	at home	74	"
Z	Smith Nema V †	37	maid	48	"
	906				
A	Hickey Frederick	38	welder	28	"
B	Hickey Mary C †	38	at home	46	"
C	Hickey Peter	38	U S N	22	"
D	Hickey Richard	38	shipfitter	25	"
E	Siraco Joseph	40	shipper	30	"
F	Siraco Rose †	40	rubberworker	30	"
G	Rizzo Michael	41	shipper	43	"
H	Rizzo Rita †	41	housewife	29	"
K	Cataldo Enrico	41	laborer	46	"
L	Cataldo Tina †	41	housewife	36	"
M	Rizzo Emma †	41	at home	30	"
N	*Rizzo Gennaro	41	retired	74	"
O	Rizzo Louise †	41	packer	32	"
P	Rizzo Mary †	41	clerk	29	"
R	Thornton Charles R	42	U S A	22	"
S	Thornton Elizabeth †	42	housewife	65	"
T	Thornton James	42	fireman	67	"
V	Groome Helena †	46	housewife	39	"
W	Groome Robert J	46	agent	51	"
X	Hulke William A	46	machinist	51	"
Z	Bruce Harold	47A	painter	34	"

Page	Letter	Full Name	Residence, Jan. 1, 1943.	Occupation.	Supposed Age.	Reported Residence, Jan. 1, 1942. Street and Number.

907
Condor Street - Continued

	Letter	Full Name	Residence	Occupation	Age	Reported Residence
	A	Bruce Mary O †	47A	housewife	44	here
	B	Cunningham Franklin D	47A	U S M C	21	"
	C	Cunningham Henry D	47A	U S A	22	"
	D	Cunningham Walter A	47A	U S N	24	"
	E*	Melanson Emily †	47B	housewife	38	"
	F*	Melanson John	47B	machinist	43	"
	G	Thornton Patrick	48	engineer	41	"
	H	Toft Henry	49	fishcutter	39	"
	K	Toft Irene †	49	housewife	31	"
	L	Sanford Grace †	51	"	51	"
	M	Sanford William	51	maint'n'eeman	60	"
	N	DeVito Edna L †	57	housewife	25	"
	O	DeVito Thomas	57	U S A	25	Revere
	P	Hall Edward	57	retired	63	here
	R	Hall Olivia F †	57	housewife	56	"
	S	O'Keefe Lawrence	57	U S N	22	Chelsea
	T	O'Keefe Mary †	57	housewife	22	here
	U	Ryan Bridget †	61	at home	70	22 Falcon
	V	Grady Alice †	61	attendant	21	here
	W	Grady Daniel	61	finisher	68	"
	X	Grady Jessie †	61	housewife	51	"
	Y	Grady Katherine †	61	clerk	25	"
	Z	Whitmarsh Frederick	61	machinist	59	133 Condor

908

	Letter	Full Name	Residence	Occupation	Age	Reported Residence
	A	Whitmarsh Mabel †	61	housewife	56	133 "
	B	Recupero Rosalie †	63	"	28	here
	C*	Johnson William	63	fisherman	61	"
	G	Napier Rita †	65	at home	25	63 Condor
	H	Hoy Bertha †	65	housewife	27	here
	K	Hoy Charles	65	attorney	26	47 Perkins
	L	Egan Helen J †	65	housewife	49	here
	M	Egan James J	65	shipfitter	51	"
	N	Amirault Eleanor †	67	housewife	26	"
	O	Amirault Frank	67	millhand	21	"
	P*	Surette Ernest P	67	repairman	34	"
	R	Surette Marion L †	67	housewife	32	"
	S	Dowd Hazel †	67	forewoman	65	"
	T	Peterson Doris †	75	stenographer	21	Winchester

Condor Street— Continued

U	Peterson Emma L †	75	housewife	68	here
V	Peterson John T	75	repairman	70	"
W	Peterson Alice F— †	77	housewife	31	"
X	Peterson John F	77	machinist	33	"
Y	Hagerty Edith— †	79	housewife	55	"
Z	Haggerty Edward J	79	expressman	62	"
	909				
A	Laine Margaret— †	79	domestic	27	36 Princeton
E	*Silva Alice— †	81	housewife	38	here
F	*Silva Manuel	81	laborer	49	"
G	Clark Frank L	81	clerk	63	"
H	Napier Paul E	81	fishcutter	23	61 Condor
K	Napier Rita A— †	81	at home	28	here
L	West Cynthia— †	81	clerk	20	"
M	West James H	81	engineer	52	"
N	West Katherine E— †	81	housewife	53	"
P	Whalen John	85	seaman	22	"
R	Whalen John J	85	electrician	58	"
S	Whalen Mary J— †	85	housewife	48	"
T	McDermott John F	87	retired	71	"
U	McDermott Mary A †	87	housewife	64	"
V	Corbett George	89	fishcutter	60	"
W	Corbett George T	89	carpenter	35	"
X	Corbett Mary H— †	89	housewife	45	"
Y	Corbett William	89	U S A	25	"
Z	Johnson Richard P	89	retired	62	"
	910				
A	DiPola Carmelo	91	"	89	"
B	Lucido Angelina— †	91	at home	44	"
C	Lucido Angelina M †	91	packer	27	"
D	Flammia Michael	91	machinist	45	"
E	Flammia Virginia— †	91	housewife	43	"
F	DeFeo Caroline— †	93	"	41	"
G	DeFeo Pasquale	93	laborer	48	"
H	DeLucas Matteo	97	chauffeur	38	"
K	DeLucas Pauline †	97	housewife	26	"
L	*McKay Anna— †	97	at home	15	"
M	*McKay Jean †	97	operator	22	"
N	*McKay Melvin T	97	U S A	27	"

Page.	Letter.	FULL NAME.	Residence, Jan. 1, 1943.	Occupation.	Supposed Age.	Reported Residence, Jan. 1, 1942. Street and Number.

Eutaw Street

	P	Froio Louis	104	mechanic	25	here
	R	Froio Vita—†	104	clerk	28	"
	s*	Froio John	106	finisher	56	"
	T*	Froio Rose—†	106	housewife	57	"
	U	Froio Theresa—†	106	clerk	28	"
	v	LaBrie Georgina—†	108	housewife	62	"
	w	McLean Catherine—†	108	dressmaker	64	"
	x	McNeil Emily †	108	houseworker	54	"
	y	Cordaw Ada—†	110	housewife	36	57 Saratoga
	z	Cordaw Arthur	110	ironworker	43	57 "

911

	A	McLaughlin Aloysius	112	letter carrier	48	here
	B	McLaughlin Margaret—†	112	housewife	48	"
	c	McLaughlin Mary A—†	112	floorwoman	52	"
	D	Shea Ellen—†	112	housewife	50	"
	E	Shea Helen—†	112	boxmaker	46	"
	F	Shea Timothy	112	watchman	45	"
	G	Donahue Bridget—†	116	at home	75	"
	K	Stacy Evelyn—†	120	housewife	27	"
	L	Stacy Roland	120	clerk	26	"
	M	Fallavollita Angelina—†	120	at home	51	"
	N	Fallavollita Antonio	120	electrician	30	"
	O	Fallavollita Arcangela—†	120	seamstress	22	"
	P	Buonagurio Julia—†	122	housewife	64	"
	R*	Buonagurio Sabino	122	retired	69	"
	s	Buonagurio Stanislaus	122	laborer	21	"
	T	Barry Florence—†	124	housewife	40	138 Orleans

Falcon Street

	U	Bragdon Clifford B	5	retired	73	here
	v	Bragdon Sarah R †	5	housewife	68	"
	w	Gibbon John F	5	merchant	30	"
	x	Gibbon Mary C †	5	housewife	26	"
	y	D'Entremont Charles J	7	fish handler	44	"
	z*	D'Entremont Domitille—†	7	housewife	43	"

912

	A	McIntyre Clarence T	9	metalworker	41	"
	B	McIntyre Eva M †	9	housewife	41	"
	D	King Anna—†	14	"	66	"
	F	Lang Beatrice B †	14	"	44	"

8

Falcon Street Continued

F	Lang Edward P	14	inspector	48	here
G	Moran Florence J †	14	housewife	44	"
H	Moran James F	14	manager	49	"
K	Innalli Charles	22	U S A	33	"
L	Innalli Evelyn †	22	housewife	31	"
M	Innalli James	22	salesman	35	"
N	Innalli John	22	U S A	21	"
O	Innalli Louise †	22	housewife	54	"
P	Innalli Sylvia †	22	barber	58	"
R	Banks Arthur F	22	mechanic	25	Winthrop
S	Banks Elizabeth †	22	housewife	28	"
T	Danner Edward J	22	fireman	55	here
U	Danner Joseph	22	U S N	24	"
V	Danner Nina M †	22	housewife	42	"
W	Danner William J	22	U S N	23	"
X	*Grifone Anibal	24	retired	76	"
Y	Grifone Carlo	24	pressman	34	"
Z	Grifone Emma †	24	forewoman	39	"

913

A	Grifone Jennie †	24	stitcher	41	"
B	*Grifone Madeline †	24	housewife	27	"
C	McPhee Charles D	25	operator	53	"
D	McPhee Mary J †	25	at home	52	"
E	McPhee Melvin J	25	milkman	30	"
F	Ryan Margaret †	25	at home	70	"
G	Healey Monica †	25	housewife	36	118 Eutaw
H	Healey Philip J	25	ironworker	42	118 "
K	Gallagher Frances R †	25	stenographer	25	here
L	Gallagher Mary L †	25	at home	59	"
M	McKinnon Herbert	26	U S A	21	"
N	McKinnon Lena †	26	at home	28	"
O	*McKinnon Mary K †	26	housewife	63	"
P	*McKinnon Stephen	26	fisherman	61	"
R	LaBohn Catherine M †	27	at home	86	"
S	LaBohn Willard J	27	dredger	52	"
T	Sforzo Angela R †	27	housewife	51	"
U	Sforzo Anna †	27	shoeworker	22	"
V	Sforzo Charles	27	laborer	60	"
W	Sforzo Frank	27	U S A	25	"
X	Sforzo Helen †	27	spinner	32	"
Y	Sforzo Marino	27	U S N	20	"

Page.	Letter.	FULL NAME.	Residence, Jan. 1, 1943.	Occupation.	Supposed Age.	Reported Residence, Jan. 1, 1942. Street and Number.

Falcon Street — Continued

	Z	Donahue Coleman B	27	chauffeur	34	Chelsea
914						
	A	Donahue Helen E — †	27	housewife	33	here
	B	Nelson August E	27	clerk	58	"
	C	Nelson Helen — †	27	housewife	58	"
	D	Nelson Robert A	27	U S N	20	"
	E	Nelson Warren F	27	U S A	27	Illinois
	F	Cutcliffe Charles R	28	machinist	43	here
	G	Cutcliffe Mary — †	28	housewife	37	"
	H	*Hansen Barbara — †	28	"	56	"
	K	Hansen Hoken N	28	radios	28	"
	L	Hansen John C	28	painter	62	"
	M	Hansen Ruth B — †	28	bookkeeper	27	"
	N	Fanaro Anthony	29	bartender	25	95 Trenton
	O	Fanaro Carmella — †	29	housewife	21	95 "
	P	Delcore Elvira — †	29	"	32	here
	R	Delcore John	29	meatcutter	37	"
	S	Johnson Theresa — †	30	clerk	40	"
	T	Shea Dorothy — †	30	housewife	32	"
	U	Shea John	30	foreman	36	"
	V	Parker Charles	30	retired	70	"
	W	Parker Grace — †	30	housewife	66	"
	X	Litchfield Catherine — †	31	nurse	54	"
	Y	Litchfield Lawrence	31	painter	30	"
	Z	Litchfield Muriel — †	31	housewife	25	"
915						
	A	*McBournie John W	31	watchman	75	"
	B	*McBournie Margaret — †	31	housewife	75	"
	C	McBournie Walter S	31	U S A	40	"
	D	McRae Ira	31	millhand	50	"
	E	McRae Jessie M — †	31	housewife	42	"
	F	DeRienzo Angelo	32	U S A	21	"
	G	DeRienzo Frank	32	laborer	42	"
	H	DeRienzo Rose — †	32	housewife	42	"
	K	*Guarene Elizabeth — †	32	at home	84	"
	L	Clark Christine — †	33	housewife	35	"
	M	Clark George	33	welder	36	"
	N	McCormack Ella W — †	33	housewife	57	"
	O	McCormack Helen M — †	33	teacher	31	"
	P	McCormack Norma E — †	33	"	26	"
	R	McCormack Wilton M	33	U S A	22	"

10

Page.	Letter.	FULL NAME.	Residence, Jan. 1, 1943.	Occupation.	Supposed Age.	Reported Residence, Jan. 1, 1942. Street and Number.

Falcon Street Continued

	s	Elliott Jennie †	33	housewife	50	here
	T	Elliott Robert A	33	operator	53	"
	U	Wall Amy †	34	clerk	26	"
	V	Wall Constance †	34	housewife	62	"
	W	Wall Mary †	34	clerk	35	"
	X	Cooper Daniel A	34	mariner	60	"
	Y	Cooper Jessie H †	34	housewife	61	"
	Z	Morse Mabel M †	34	at home	54	"
916						
	A	Morse Richard	34	shipfitter	23	"
	B	Bonner Edward L	35	gatetender	56	"
	C	Bonner Ella A †	35	housewife	52	"
	D	Corcoran Helen R †	35	clerk	28	"
	E	Corcoran John J	35	"	29	90 High
	F	Sullivan John J	35	oiler	63	here
	G	Bonner Anna T †	35	housewife	48	"
	H	Bonner George J	35	carpenter	45	"
	K	Bozzi Helen F †	36	housewife	33	"
	L	Bozzi Vincent	36	tailor	27	"
	M	Johnson Clara †	36	at home	68	"
	N	Johnson Harry E	36	laborer	48	"
	O	Sullivan Helen †	36	clerk	22	"
	P	Sullivan Joseph H	36	mariner	48	"
	R	Sullivan Stella †	36	housewife	42	"
	T	Noyes Vera L †	37	"	45	"
	U	McElman Allen	37	mechanic	61	"
	V	McElman Ellen †	37	housewife	59	"
	W	McElman James	37	machinist	23	"
	X	Gage Laura L †	38	bookkeeper	52	"
	Y	Gage Winthrop H	38	salesman	50	"
	Z	Logan Blanche E †	38	clerk	50	"
917						
	A	Logan Julia M †	38	housewife	44	"
	B	Logan Leslie D	38	grocer	50	"
	C	Denehy Alice E †	39	at home	36	"
	D	Denehy Edward J	39	fish handler	33	"
	E	Denehy Louise M †	39	housekeeper	42	"
	F	*D'Entremont Albert	40	fishcutter	36	"
	G	*D'Entremont Margaret †	40	housewife	33	"
	H	Kane Addie L †	40	"	55	"
	K	Kane Thomas	40	watchman	59	"

11

Falcon Street—Continued

	Letter	FULL NAME.	Residence	Occupation	Age	Reported Residence
	L	*Scopa Jennie—†	40	at home	58	here
	M	Parker Agnes—†	41	housewife	37	"
	N	Parker Donald	41	mechanic	40	"
	O	Clemens Edward J	41	ironworker	44	"
	P	Clemens Helen F †	41	housewife	37	"
	R	*Fitzgerald Anastasia—†	41	at home	69	"
	S	Alves Anthony	42	retired	81	"
	T	Alves Leo	42	operator	40	"
	U	Alves Mary †	42	housewife	80	"
	V	Finney Arthur	42	blacksmith	61	220 E Eagle
	W	Finney Ethel M †	42	housewife	60	220 "
	X	Finney Warren	42	shipfitter	34	220 "
	Y	Finney William A	42	painter	41	220 "
	Z	McCue Helen E †	42	housewife	24	305 "
918						
	A	McCue Henry J	42	fisherman	31	305 "
	B	Russo Edward D	44	laborer	31	here
	C	Russo Lena D †	44	clerk	25	"
	D	LeMoure Abigail †	44	housewife	52	"
	E	LeMoure Edward R	44	U S N	23	"
	F	LeMoure Francis X	44	U S A	28	"
	G	LeMoure Joseph A	44	"	30	"
	H	LeMoure Richard	44	"	20	"
	K	LeMoure Thomas J	44	scaler	27	"
	L	Eldridge Arthur S	44	operator	27	105 Union Park
	M	Eldridge Mary F †	44	housewife	24	105 "
	N	Gallagher Rose H †	44	matron	46	101 "
	O	Morini Alice †	47	housewife	42	here
	P	Morino John	47	machinist	55	"
	R	Morini John	47	U S A	21	"
	S	Morini Ralph	47	U S N	23	"
	T	*Nickerson Catherine M †	48	housewife	41	"
	U	Nickerson Ivan F	48	packer	42	"
	V	*Nickerson Mary E †	48	at home	65	"
	W	Nickerson Nellie M †	48	clerk	33	"
	X	Crosby Dedrick C	48	retired	72	"
	Y	Crosby Lillian M †	48	housewife	75	"
	Z	Guerino Angelo	48	shoeworker	42	"
919						
	A	Guerino Mary †	48	housewife	37	"
	B	Fobert Jennie †	49	at home	53	"

12

Page	Letter	Full Name.	Residence, Jan. 1, 1943.	Occupation.	Supposed Age.	Reported Residence, Jan. 1, 1942. Street and Number.

Falcon Street Continued

	C	Fobert Victoria †	49	clerk	24	here
	D	O'Connor Daniel	49	U S A	33	Pennsylvania
	E	O'Connor Josephine †	49	housewife	27	here
	F	Chase Fred E	50	dispatcher	63	"
	G	Chase Josephine I †	50	housewife	62	"
	H	Dacey Walter W	50	steamfitter	36	"
	K	Baptista Adeline †	50	housewife	48	"
	L	Baptista Adeline †	50	clerk	26	"
	M	Baptista John	50	janitor	52	"
	N	O'Connell Alfred	51	foreman	37	"
	O	O'Connell Nellie †	51	housewife	38	"
	P	Trainor Florence †	51	"	42	"
	R	Trainor William	51	bartender	45	"
	S	*O'Leary Cecelia †	52	housewife	52	"
	T	O'Leary Gerard	52	laborer	22	"
	U	O'Leary Gertrude †	52	operator	24	"
	V	*O'Leary Richard J	52	longshoreman	53	"
	W	DeMattia Alfred	53	U S A	24	"
	X	*DeMattia Anna †	53	operator	44	"
	Y	DeMattia Stanley	53	clerk	22	"
	Z	Costa Vivian †	53	at home	70	"

920

	A	Stapleton Edna G †	54	housewife	37	"
	B	Stapleton Leo J	54	gasman	42	"
	C	Curran Julia E †	55	at home	82	"
	D	Holstead Charles A	55	guard	45	"
	E	Holstead Edith J †	55	housewife	44	"
	F	Holstead Etta M †	55	seamstress	23	"
	G	Halstead Bertha †	55	housewife	68	"
	H	Halstead William F	55	seaman	75	"
	K	Virginio Leo	56	electrician	52	"
	L	Virginio Philomena †	56	housewife	53	"
	M	Macaulay Franklin	57	U S N	39	"
	N	Macaulay Rosalie †	57	operator	20	"
	O	Macaulay Verna †	57	housewife	39	"
	P	Hamel Angie V †	57	"	42	"
	R	Hamel Donald T	57	mechanic	42	"
	S	Gubitose Guy	58	bookbinder	34	"
	T	Gubitose Theresa †	58	housewife	31	"
	U	Scopa Ralph	60	machinist	27	"
	V	Scopa Stella †	60	housewife	25	"

15

Page.	Letter.	FULL NAME.	Residence, Jan. 1, 1943.	Occupation.	Supposed Age.	Reported Residence, Jan. 1, 1942. Street and Number.

Falcon Street—Continued

w	Addy John	60	U S C G	20	here
x	Addy Veronica—†	60	housewife	20	"
y	Calsimitto Louise—†	60	at home	59	"
z	LaVita Anthony	60	pipecoverer	38	"

921

A	LaVita Mary †	60	housewife	36	"
B	Laskey Daisy—†	60	"	25	"
C	Laskey Herbert	60	chauffeur	28	"
D	*Verbanas Caroline—†	60	at home	39	"
E	St John Catherine—†	62	housewife	21	12 Jeffries
F	St John Walter	62	repairman	24	12 "
G	Dalton Elizabeth G—†	62	attendant	60	here
H	Heffron Elizabeth C—†	62	inspector	23	"
K	Heffron Fredrick L	62	tollman	58	"
L	Heffron Margaret E †	62	housewife	57	"
M	Heffron Margaret J †	62	manicurist	23	"
N	Heffron Margaret M—†	62	bookkeeper	21	"
O	Heffron William	62	laborer	67	"
P	Heffron William A	62	storekeeper	24	"
R	Preston Blanche L †	63	housewife	29	"
S	Preston Michael J	63	timekeeper	33	"
T	Preston Frances A †	63	housewife	26	"
U	Preston John F	63	policeman	27	"
V	Preston Mary E—†	63	at home	52	"
W	Ryan Charles J	63	chauffeur	40	"
X	Ryan Rose A †	63	housewife	40	"
Y	Duncan Richard	64	laborer	60	"
Z	Tobin Michael	64	"	60	"

922

A	Tobin Nora †	64	housewife	58	"
B	Eldridge Alice A †	64	"	52	103 Union Park
C	Eldridge John A	64	pressman	54	103 "
D	O'Keefe Eugene J	64	operator	34	103 "
E	O'Keefe Sarah †	64	housewife	29	103 "
F	DeAngelo Frank	66	sawyer	24	126 Webster
G	DeAngelo Margaret †	66	housewife	21	126 "
H	Merchant Albert	66	painter	43	here
K	Merchant Helen—†	66	housewife	30	"
L	Merchant James H	66	machinst	32	"
M	Pagano Charles	66	laborer	33	"
N	Pagano Esther—†	66	housewife	29	"

14

Falcon Street— Continued

	o	Mangone Augusta	68	salesman	31	here
	p	Mangone Benjamin	68	retired	66	"
	r*	Mangone Frances †	68	housewife	73	"
	s	Viscio Mary †	68	"	25	"
	t	Viscio Michael	68	painter	28	"
	u	Cerrone Angela †	68	housewife	35	"
	v	Cerrone Carlo	68	laborer	28	"
	w	Hicks Alice †	69	housewife	32	"
	x	Hicks James	69	millwright	35	"
	y	Patz Clara †	69	housewife	45	"
	z	Patz George J	69	U S A	22	"
923						
	a	Patz John J	69	mason	50	"
	b	Hodgkins Louise M †	69	housewife	45	"
	c	Hodgkins Paul A	69	U S A	22	"
	d	Hodgkins Robert W	69	"	21	"
	e	Hodgkins William F	69	engineer	51	"
	f	Hodgkins Wilma M †	69	operator	25	"
	h*	Maceiras Felice †	71	housewife	48	"
	k	Maceiras Juan	71	engineer	47	"
	l	Noguerol Joseph	71	carpenter	49	"
	m	Nigro Angelina †	71	housewife	44	"
	n	Nigro Giro	71	U S A	21	"
	o	Nigro Joseph	71	laborer	53	"
	p	Cleary Christopher	71	"	41	"
	r	Cleary Jeanette †	71	housewife	37	"
	s	Whitten Louise †	71	at home	40	"
	t	Whitten Margaret †	71	"	68	"
	u	Kristofferson Agnes †	74	housewife	55	"
	v	Kristofferson Mathias	74	laborer	60	"
	w	Murphy John	74	"	24	Chelsea
	x	Osborn George	74	"	39	here
	y	LeGallo Helen †	77	housewife	36	"
	z	LeGallo Joseph	77	painter	36	"
924						
	a	Rideout Jane †	77	housewife	63	"
	b	Blowers Anna †	77	"	31	"
	c	Blowers Reginald	77	machinist	40	"
	d	Malacasso Charles	77	pipefitter	24	238 Chelsea
	e	Malacasso Mary †	77	housewife	21	238 "
	f*	Atkins Anne †	78	"	75	here

15

Falcon Street—Continued

G	Atkins Harry	78	seaman	40	here
H	*Atkins James A	78	retired	76	"
K	Johnson Vernon	78	agent	24	Minneapolis
L	Butler Leslie I	78	guard	43	here
M	Butler Viola—†	78	housewife	47	"
N	D'Addieco Ida—†	79	clerk	24	"
O	D'Addieco Michael	79	pressman	58	"
P	D'Addieco Susie—†	79	housewife	50	"
R	Millar Nellie—†	79	at home	57	"
S	Millar Thomas P	79	shipfitter	28	"
T	Millar William J	79	fish handler	23	"
U	Foley James J	81	engineer	23	"
V	Rafuse Gertrude M—†	81	housewife	21	"
W	Rafuse Robert M	81	machinist	25	"
X	*Favrizzio Margaret—†	87	at home	85	"
Y	*Iandoli Edward	87	storekeeper	51	"
Z	Iandoli Esther—†	87	clerk	25	"

925

A	Iandoli Ettore	87	U S A	22	"
B	Iandoli Stanley	87	at home	24	"
C	*Iandoli Susie—†	87	housewife	47	"
D	Duke James	87	fisherman	55	"
E	Duke Mary—†	87	housewife	50	"
F	*LaTorre Filippa—†	87	at home	75	"
G	LaTorre Josephine—†	87	housewife	38	"
H	LaTorre Salvatore	87	baker	45	"
K	Cianciarulo Gerardo	89	teacher	42	"
L	Cianciarulo Mary—†	89	housewife	41	"
M	Cianciarulo Raffaela—†	89	"	63	"
N	Repetto Florence—†	89	"	25	223 Brooks
O	Repetto Nicholas	89	B F D	29	223 "
P	*Borghero Frank	89	retired	68	here
R	Repetto Batista	89	"	57	"
S	Repetto Salvatore	89	machinist	20	"
T	Maher Elsie—†	93	housewife	33	"
U	Maher Michael	93	rigger	37	"
V	Doherty Grace—†	93	clerk	32	"
W	Ryan John	93	U S N	29	"
X	Ryan Margaret—†	93	tel operator	28	"
Y	Thibidore Mabel—†	93	at home	55	"
Z	Meyer Frances M—†	95	housewife	32	"

926

Falcon Street—Continued

A	Meyer Paul H	95	painter	34	here
B	Irving Herbert E	95A	laborer	68	"
C	Irving Viola P—†	95A	housewife	67	"
D	Bailey Benjamin	97	machinist	59	"
E	Bailey Benjamin A	97	clerk	32	"
F	Bailey Elizabeth C—†	97	housewife	55	"
G	Bailey Lawrence C	97	clerk	29	"
H	Curry George L	97	U S A	42	"
K	Curry Mary M—†	97	tel operator	44	"
L	McBournie Ina—†	99	housewife	47	"
M	McBournie William	99	clerk	46	"
N	Robicheau Edith—†	99	housewife	30	61 Monmouth
O	Robicheau Joseph	99	shipwright	37	61 "
P	McCabe Bernard	101	chauffeur	31	here
R	McCabe Dorothy—†	101	housewife	29	"
S	Mills Lawrence	101	U S A	22	"
T	Long Alice—†	101	housewife	60	"
U	Long Thomas G	101	U S A	26	"
V	Long William	101	operator	55	"
W	Long William F	101	U S N	29	"
X	Collins Frances—†	103	matron	63	1065 Bennington
Y	McAuliffe Dennis	103	retired	77	1065 "
Z	O'Rourke Ellen—†	103	operator	24	1065 "

927

A	Turpin Ella J—†	103	housewife	52	here
B	Turpin John E	103	engineer	55	"
C	Grady Alice P—†	103	at home	45	"
D	Grady Pauline—†	103	operator	24	"
E	Grady William F	103	metalworker	52	"
F	Broussard James E	105	salesman	39	"
G	Broussard Mary E—†	105	housewife	38	"
H	Keough Annie F—†	105	"	65	"
K	Keough William A	105	watchman	65	"
M	Martinez Domingo	107	machinist	57	"
N*	Martinez Manuela—†	107	housewife	46	"
O	Fernandez America—†	107	nurse	21	"
P	Fernandez Jose	107	machinist	56	"
R	Fernandez Virginia—†	107	housewife	50	"
S	Amico Luciano	109	rigger	32	"
T	Amico Theresa—†	109	housewife	29	"

Page.	Letter.	FULL NAME.	Residence, Jan. 1, 1943.	Occupation.	Supposed Age.	Reported Residence, Jan. 1, 1942. Street and Number.

Falcon Street — Continued

	U	Renzi Costantino	109	laborer	31	here
	V	Renzi Diamond E —†	109	housewife	32	"
	W	Nolan Esther H —†	111	"	44	451 Meridian
	X	Nolan John E	111	optician	52	451 "
	Y	Sullivan John J	111	B F D	46	here
	Z	Sullivan Mary J —†	111	at home	68	451 Meridian
928						
	A	Sullivan Ruth —†	111	housewife	42	here
	B	Benson Charles	111	retired	79	"
	C	Benson Herbert B	111	carpenter	45	"
	D	Benson Signe R —†	111	housewife	37	"
	E	Borglei Abbie —†	117	"	48	"
	F	Borglei Harold A	117	pipefitter	22	"
	G	Borglei Raymond	117	"	50	"
	H	Allen Kathleen —†	117	housewife	21	"
	K	Enos Diolda —†	117	"	42	"
	L	Enos Isabel —†	117	at home	70	Provincetown
	M	Enos John	117	fireman	46	here
	N	Fiore Lillian —†	117	housewife	23	"
	O	Fiore Mario	117	machinist	24	"
	P	Mitchell Lillian —†	117	housewife	42	"
	R	Mitchell Percy	117	metalworker	47	"
	S	Kimball Ann —†	119	housewife	26	"
	T	Kimball Arthur	119	laborer	34	"
	U	Berry Dorothy —†	119	housewife	32	Somerville
	V	Berry Thomas	119	clerk	36	"
	W	*Doucette Francis A	119	engineer	56	here
	X	Doucette James W	119	machinist	21	"
	Y	*Doucette Mary H —†	119	housewife	51	"
929						
	A	Garofano Frank	121	chauffeur	44	"
	B	Garofano Mary —†	121	housewife	36	"
	C	Fulginiti Christine —†	121	"	42	"
	D	Fulginiti James D	121	plasterer	52	"
	E	Page Emil G	121	U S A	26	"
	F	Pagliarulo Adelaide —†	121	housewife	62	"
	G	Pagliarulo Anthony	121	retired	69	"
	H	Pagliarulo Evelyn —†	121	housewife	39	"
	K	Pagliarulo Henry	121	engineer	21	"
	L	Pagliarulo John	121	U S A	24	"
	M	Pagliarulo Joseph G	121	engineer	40	"

18

Falcon Street Continued

N	Pagliarulo Michael	121	U S A	27	here
O	McGinn Frederick D	129	retired	50	"
P	McGinn Frederick J	129	U S A	22	"
R	McGinn Josephine M †	129	housewife	49	"
S	Sweeney Michael	129	retired	79	"
T	*Molloy Clara †	129A	housewife	41	"
U	Molloy George J	129A	rigger	41	"
V	Gray Joseph	131	retired	71	"
W	Norris Bridget A †	131	housewife	41	"
X	Norris Michael J	131	longshoreman	40	"
Y	Norcott Lorna †	131A	housewife	25	"
Z	*Norcott Peter	131A	rigger	32	"

930

A	*McLaughlin Alice †	133	housewife	43	"
B	*McLaughlin Charles E	133	pedler	52	"
C	Copithorn Charlotte †	133A	housewife	38	"
D	Copithorn Richard	133A	chauffeur	42	"
E	Boyer Francis J	135	rigger	37	"
F	Boyer Mary †	135	housewife	32	"
G	Deveau Edward	135A	U S A	21	"
H	*Deveau Irenee E	135A	carpenter	51	"
K	*Deveau Lucy †	135A	housewife	44	"

Meridian Street

L	Dorazio John J	414	chipper	48	61 Maverick sq
M	Dorazio Phyllis †	414	bookkeeper	21	61 "
N	Dorazio Rose †	414	housewife	48	61 "
O	Dorazio Victor F	414	U S N	24	61 "
P	Hardy William	414	machinist	26	98 Trenton
R	Murphy Florence †	414	factoryhand	36	418 Meridian
S	Murphy James	414	U S N	39	418 "
T	*DiRoto Ettore	416	carpenter	60	here
U	DiRoto Lydia †	416	waitress	20	"
V	*DiRoto Rachel †	416	housewife	53	"
W	DiRoto Ralph	416	U S N	22	"
X	DiRoto Victoria †	416	factoryhand	24	"
Y	Pastore James	416	bartender	31	72 Gladstone
Z	Pastore Sarah †	416	housewife	25	72 "

931

A	Kovacev Anthony	416	meatcutter	29	here

19

Meridian Street—Continued

B	Kovacev Maria †	416	housewife	27	here
C	Nicastro Cosimo D	417	attorney	47	104 Lexington
D	Nicastro Esther F †	417	housewife	42	104 "
E	Maggio Antonio	418	welder	36	96 Princeton
F	Maggio Arlene †	418	housewife	33	96 "
G	Orr Donald L	418	shipper	41	here
H	Orr Irene V †	418	housewife	39	"
K	Persson Edith V †	418	"	64	"
L	Persson Nils E	418	detective	64	"
M	Reed Frank	418	machinist	35	"
N	Marcucella Anthony	419	carpenter	29	"
O	Marcucella Joseph	419	proprietor	66	"
P	Marcucella Theresa †	419	at home	25	"
R	Marcucella Clara †	419	housewife	25	"
S	Marcucella Vincent J	419	bartender	30	"
T	O'Rourke Catherine †	421	at home	47	"
U	O'Rourke Mary E †	421	housekeeper	53	"
V	O'Rourke Patrick J	421	policeman	47	"
W	Pastore John	421	shipwright	37	"
X	Pastore Yolanda †	421	housewife	33	"
Y	Pastore Carmen	421	chipper	39	"
Z	Pastore Frank	421	retired	68	"
	932				
A	Pastore Helen †	421	at home	39	"
B	Pastore Julia †	421	housewife	69	"
C	Singer Angelina †	421	at home	29	"
D	*Kovacev Angelina †	422	housekeeper	53	"
E	Kovacev John	422	clerk	22	"
F	Kovacev Natale	422	meatcutter	27	"
G	Kovacev Patricia †	422	housewife	25	"
H	D'Angelo Amedio	422	laborer	50	396 Meridian
K	D'Angelo Mary †	422	housewife	27	396 "
L	Bracciotti Anello	422	clerk	31	here
M	*Bracciotti Anna †	422	housewife	71	"
N	Bracciotti Lombardo	422	retired	76	"
O	Goodwin Douglas	423	machinist	26	"
P	Goodwin Katherine †	423	housewife	24	"
R	*Goodwin Thomas	423	retired	76	"
S	*Maragioglio Gasparina	†423	housewife	52	"
T	Maragioglio Stefano	423	laborer	59	"
U	Gislason Caroline E †	423	housewife	30	"

Meridian Street Continued

v	Gislason Oscar	423	fisherman	40	here
w	Youngberg George	423	U S N	40	"
y	Campbell Cecil J	425	welder	25	326 Meridian
z	Campbell John F	425	cabinetmaker	53	326 "

933

A	Grey Mary C—†	425	at home	23	326 "
B	McNear Georgiana N †	425	dressmaker	64	here
C	Farrar Ross	426	U S A	36	"
D	Panasese John	426	laborer	48	"
E	Panasese Mary — †	426	housewife	36	"
F	Gallant Cyrus E	426	carpenter	48	61 Saratoga
G	Gallant Helen—†	426	housewife	46	61 "
H	McArthur Edgar	426	shipfitter	42	298 Paris
K	Sherman Loretta—†	426	housewife	30	158 Webster
L	Sherman Norman	426	laborer	30	Everett
M	Cuccolillo Domenic	427	retired	80	here
N	Day Emma F—†	427	at home	70	"
O	Moon Mary E—†	427	"	66	"
P	Ryan Edward L	427	deckhand	58	"
R	McInnis Beatrice — †	427	inspector	26	"
S	McInnis Gertrude—†	427	"	21	"
T	McInnis Helen —†	427	housekeeper	53	"
U	McInnis Helen—†	427	inspector	20	"
V	McInnis Lillian—†	427	operator	30	"
W	Riley Emily—†	427	at home	70	"
X	Curran Emma M — †	427	housewife	56	"
Y	Curran Henry P	427	repairman	58	"
Z	Smith Lillian M—†	428	teacher	53	"

934

A	Libby Caroline M — †	428	tel operator	40	"
B	Libby Mary—†	428	operator	50	"
C	Hoffman Barbara †	428	stamper	15	"
D	Hoffman Christie †	428	housekeeper	76	"
E	Hoffman Donald	428	brazier	40	"
F	Hoffman Lucy †	428	housekeeper	33	"
G	Hoffman Sadie — †	428	operator	37	"
H	MacDonald Christie †	428	timekeeper	47	"
K	Grant Margaret B—†	430	housekeeper	54	"
L	Keough Henry G	430	laborer	34	Lynn
M	Kerr Catherine L —†	430	housekeeper	84	here
N	Kerr Mary L—†	430	clerk	52	"

Meridian Street—Continued

o	Riley Elizabeth A—†	432	housewife	52	here
p	Riley Frederick A	432	policeman	54	"
R	McKeough Cecelia—†	432	at home	83	"
s	McKeough Josephine—†	432	tel operator	46	"
T	McKeough Margaret—†	432	at home	48	"
v	Bass Esther—†	434	operator	29	"
w	Donohue Thomas	434	retired	74	"
x	Kincaid Francis	434	U S A	21	"
y	Kincaid Frank	434	retired	59	"
z	Kincaid Sarah C—†	434	housewife	50	"

935

A	Sheridan Jane—†	434	matron	72	"
B	Bostrom Ambia—†	436	housewife	59	"
c	Bostrom Helen—†	436	bookkeeper	20	"
D	Olsson Charles	436	technician	46	"
E	Olsson Ruth—†	436	housewife	25	"
F	Barrett John E	436	machinist	44	"
G	*Barrett Margaret—†	436	housewife	69	"
H	Barrett Margaret J—†	436	bookkeeper	29	"
K	*Barrett Robert	436	retired	71	"
L	Johnson Lillian—†	437	clerk	21	"
M	Phillips Daniel A	437	policeman	45	"
N	Phillips Ethel C—†	437	housewife	41	"
o	Payne Catherine—†	437	operator	23	"
P	Payne Charles H	437	foreman	48	"
R	Memmolo Helen—†	437	housewife	24	183 Chelsea
s	Memmolo Pasquale	437	steamfitter	26	183 "
T	DeAngelis Amelia—†	438	housewife	45	here
U	DeAngelis Florence—†	438	tel operator	21	"
V	DeAngelis Henry	438	shoecutter	48	"
w	DeAngelis Joseph H	438	U S N	22	"
x	Mulone Anna—†	438	housewife	26	"
Y	Mulone Antonio	438	chemist	25	"
z	Colantuono Edith G—†	438	stitcher	38	"

936

A	O'Connor Cyril	439	steelworker	26	"
B	O'Connor Ellen M—†	439	at home	68	"
c	Mullane Daniel F	439	U S A	25	"
D	Mullane Jeremiah	439	"	27	"
E	Mullane Michael J	439	fisherman	31	"
F	*Mullane Thomas	439	retired	68	"

Meridian Street—Continued

	H	Cranitch George L	440	letter carrier	54	here
	K	Cranitch Helen L—†	440	housekeeper	52	"
	L	May Mary E—†	440	housewife	62	"
	M	May William J	440	machinist	69	"
	N	Tooma George	440	mechanic	22	California
	O	Lipson William	440	polisher	43	here
	P	McCarthy Charles J	440	clerk	60	"
	R	McCarthy Mabel C—†	440	housewife	61	"
	S	Freethy Isabelle C—†	440	"	48	"
	T	Freethy Roy H	440	engineer	56	"
	U	Hunter Virginia L—†	440	housewife	25	"
	V	Hunter William S	440	clerk	25	"
	W	Mottola Lena—†	441	shoeworker	25	133 Orleans
	X	Tufo Anthony	441	U S A	22	16½ Bremen
	Y	Tufo Edward	441	laborer	24	16½ "
	Z*	Tufo Josephine—†	441	housewife	41	16½ "
937						
	A	Tufo Umberto	441	barber	45	16½ "
	B	Mascetta Ambrose	441	machinist	23	here
	C	Mascetta Elizabeth—†	441	tailor	25	"
	D	Mascetta Ferdinand	441	trimmer	60	"
	E	Tufo Filomena—†	441	tailor	31	"
	F	Tufo Josephine—†	441	housewife	27	"
	G	Tufo Remigio	441	cutter	27	"
	H	Mascetta Romilda—†	441	housewife	57	"
	K	Mascetta Thomasina—†	441	tailor	29	"
	L	DeFrancesco Frances—†	441	winder	25	"
	M	DeFrancesco Joseph	441	millhand	61	"
	N	DeFrancesco Stephen	441	U S A	20	"
	O*	DeFrancesco Theresa—†	441	housewife	56	"
	P	DeFrancesco Thomas	441	U S A	20	"
	S	Moore Arthur E	443	"	34	"
	T	Moore Charles V	443	retired	72	"
	U	Moore Lillian E—†	443	at home	71	"
	V*	Comeau Leo	443	laborer	63	"
	W*	Comeau Leone—†	443	housewife	73	"
	X	Richard Pius	443	fisherman	34	"
	Y	Flaherty Bertha—†	445	tel operator	39	"
	Z	Flaherty Frank	445	foreman	43	"
938						
	A	Tierney Irene—†	445	housekeeper	41	"

23

Meridian Street—Continued

	B	Tierney William	445	fireman	49	here
	C	Woods Esther—†	445	at home	65	"
	D	Mann Bertha L—†	445	housewife	66	"
	E	Mann Diedrick H	445	grocer	69	"
	F	Wiegand Frieda B—†	445	at home	63	"
	G	Wiegand Louise A—†	445	clerk	53	"
	H	Cooney William L	445	operator	48	"
	K	Dolaker Frederick F	445	fireman	58	"
	L	Dolaker Jennie F—†	445	housewife	59	"
	M	Gallo Annie—†	447	"	51	"
	N	Gallo Jennie—†	447	clerk	21	"
	O	Gallo Ralph	447	proprietor	51	"
	P	Veje Andrew H	447	seaman	45	184 Summer
	R	Veje Evelyn—†	447	housewife	44	184 "
	S	DiAngelis John	451	pharmacist	29	here
	T	DiAngelis Margaret—†	451	housewife	24	"
	U	Coffey Edna A—†	451	"	36	473 Meridian
	V	Coffey James S	451	executive	43	here
	W	Coffey Joseph L	451	driller	35	473 Meridian
	X	Coffey Mary A—†	451	at home	70	473 "
	Y	Coffey Mary G—†	451	"	42	here
	Z	Coffey Thomas F	451	retired	72	473 Meridian

939

	A	Locke William A	451	salesman	46	473 "
	B*	McKenna Annie—†	451	housewife	63	here
	C	McKenna Catherine—†	451	operator	20	"
	D	McKenna Edward	451	longshoreman	56	"
	E	McKenna John F	451	seaman	25	"
	F	O'Brien Helen—†	451	operator	22	"
	G	Parmenter Charles J	452	retired	75	"
	H	Parmenter Fannie R—†	452	housewife	75	"
	K	Keyes Clement	453	motorman	48	"
	L	Keyes Dorothy—†	453	saleswoman	28	"
	M	Keyes Melvin	453	U S A	23	"
	N	Keyes Winifred—†	453	housewife	46	"
	O	Ranelli Antoinette—†	453	chemist	29	"
	P	Ranelli Dominic	453	U S A	22	"
	R*	Ranelli Eliza—†	453	housewife	58	"
	S	Ranelli Enrico	453	proprietor	61	"
	T	Ranelli Theresa—†	453	stitcher	20	"
	U	Crosby Francis M	453	printer	51	"

Meridian Street—Continued

v	Crosby Josephine A— †	453	housewife	45	here
w	Crosby Rita A †	453	cashier	21	"
x	Kincade Richard F	453	clerk	27	"
y	Sennett Arthur J	453	printer	52	123 St Andrew rd
z	Lang Joseph	454	plumber	40	here
	940					
A	Lang Patrick A	454	"	75	"
B	Weeks Frederick	455	engineer	83	"
C	Weeks Margaret M— †	455	housewife	56	"
D	Weeks Robert T	455	U S C G	28	"
E	Weeks Ruby— †	455	clerk	26	"
F	McGrath John J	455	rigger	49	"
G	McGrath Joseph D	455	U S A	21	"
H	McGrath Theresa M— †	455	housewife	46	"
K	Bartolo Julia— †	456	"	26	"
L	Bartolo Michael	456	machinist	29	"
M	Butler Frank	456	clerk	28	"
N	Butler Margaret— †	456	housewife	70	"
O	Butler Robert	456	retired	73	"
P	Cannon Gertrude— †	456	nurse	45	"
R	Culkeen Joseph L	458	shipfitter	26	25 Breed
S	Culkeen Mary E— †	458	nurse	24	43 W Eagle
T	Palmieri Anthony	458	decorator	50	here
U	Palmieri Celia— †	458	student	22	"
v*	Palmieri Louise— †	458	housewife	47	"
w	Dean Matilda— †	459	"	50	"
x	Dean Norman	459	chauffeur	52	"
y	Trevor Edward J	459	buyer	41	119 Falcon
z	Trevor Margaret— †	459	housewife	41	119 "
	941					
A	Burke Catherine— †	459	"	50	87 Putnam
B	Burke Joseph	459	pipefitter	48	87 "
C	Burke Joseph P	459	U S A	24	87 "
D	Butler Mary— †	459	stitcher	22	87 "
E	Butler Raymond	459	electrician	21	87 "
F	Worthy Alice M †	460	housewife	29	here
G	Worthy Edward S	460	inspector	33	"
H	Mitchell Joseph E	460	rigger	50	"
K	Mitchell Mary C— †	460	housewife	46	"
L	Perry Hattie B— †	460	rubberworker	49	"
M	Perry Ivan M	460	fireman	42	"

25

Meridian Street—Continued

	N	*Muise Eugene J	462	chauffeur	31	63 Marion
	O	Muise Mae—†	462	stitcher	30	63 "
	P	Smith Dorothy E—†	462	housewife	26	here
	R	Smith Lawrence O	462	electrician	26	"
	S	Hoy Mary—†	462	housewife	27	"
	T	Hoy Walter	462	mechanic	28	"
	U	Powers Catherine A—†	463	nurse	22	"
	V	Powers Edward	463	operator	27	"
	W	Powers Loretta R—†	463	stenographer	24	"
	X	Powers Nicholas L	463	instructor	47	"
	Y	Powers Rose A—†	463	housewife	48	"
	Z	Powers Rosemarie—†	463	clerk	21	"

942

	A	Randal Anna M—†	463	housekeeper	52	"
	B	Zagarella Louise—†	463	stitcher	35	"
	C	Zagarella Peter	463	presser	37	"
	D	Lane Evelyn—†	464	housewife	23	9 Havre
	E	Lane Maxwell	464	agent	22	475 Meridian
	F	Cooke Clarence D	464	metalworker	51	here
	G	Cooke Olivetta E—†	464	housewife	50	"
	H	Doucette Frank	464	welder	24	172 Border
	K	Doucette Lydia—†	464	housewife	23	172 "
	L	Foote Charles	465	seaman	49	here
	M	*Fraser Maud—†	465	at home	63	"
	N	Fraser William	465	seaman	41	"
	O	Buontempo Grace—†	465	housewife	25	"
	P	Buontempo Edward	465	chauffeur	27	"
	S	Flynn Ellen—†	469	housewife	58	"
	T	Flynn Joseph B	469	repairman	24	"
	U	Flynn Joseph P	469	brazier	63	"
	V	Flynn Rose—†	469	housewife	21	"
	W	Waldron Michael	469	repairman	59	"
	X	Dwyer John J	469	fireman	51	"
	Y	Dwyer Maud—†	469	housewife	53	"
	Z	Dwyer Thomas	469	policeman	23	"

943

	A	Dwyer Viola—†	469	housewife	21	"
	B	Ferry Beatrice—†	469	floorman	28	"
	C	Gangemi Anthony	469	laborer	50	"
	D	Gangemi Elizabeth—†	469	housewife	45	"
	E	Gangemi Joseph A	469	U S N	20	"

Meridian Street—Continued

F	DelTorto Anthony	471	carpenter	46	Wilmington
G	DelTorto Edwina —†	471	housewife	42	"
H	DelTorto Francis	471	U S A	23	"
K	DelTorto Helen —†	471	housewife	22	"
L	DelTorto Joseph	471	U S C G	22	"
M	Abbott John	471	fireman	31	198 Falcon
N	Abbott Josephine —†	471	housewife	28	198 "
O	McInnis Edward F	473	electrician	30	427 Meridian
P	McInnis Dorothy L —†	473	housewife	22	Medford
R	Hayden Alice —†	473	cook	64	here
S	Hayden Patrick	473	repairman	65	"
T	*Kelly Mary A —†	473	at home	59	"
U	Lane Albert	475	machinist	26	"
V	Lane Florence —†	475	housewife	24	"
W	Lane Anna —†	475	waitress	23	"
X	Lane Helen —†	475	cook	50	"
Y	Lane Samuel	475	U S A	20	"
Z	Hunt Daniel	477	watchman	50	"

944

A	Hunt Daniel J	477	U S A	22	"
B	Hunt Ethel —†	477	housewife	44	"
C	Gallagher William	477	watchman	42	137 Condor
D	Kinder Ethel —†	477	housewife	36	137 "
E	Connolly Catherine —†	477	"	48	here
F	Connolly John	477	engineer	50	"

West Eagle Street

O	McIver James P	2	retired	73	here
P	Newbury Etta —†	2	housekeeper	67	"
R	Coffin Anna M —†	2	stenographer	21	"
S	Coffin Beatrice A —†	2	housewife	48	"
T	Coffin William M	2	shipfitter	48	"
U	Shipp George M	4	pipefitter	30	"
V	Shipp Minnie W —†	4	housekeeper	67	"
W	Capobianco Jennie —†	4	seamstress	40	"
X	Capobianco Thomas	4	laborer	45	"
Y	*Jacobsen John	6	rigger	58	"
Z	LaCroix Thelma —†	6	housewife	23	"

945

A	Pedersen Elizabeth —†	6	"	48	"

27

West Eagle Street Continued

B	Pedersen Thomas	6	machinist	54	here
C	Buontempa Albert	6	chauffeur	30	"
D	Buontempa Mary—†	6	housewife	26	"
E	Scali Dante	6	timekeeper	20	"
F	Scali Joseph	6	tailor	55	"
G	*Scali Theresa—†	6	housewife	44	"
H	Jewkes Anna L—†	8	"	31	"
K	Jewkes Benjamin F	8	accountant	32	"
L	Kelly Earl B	8	engineer	55	"
M	Kelly Hilda C—†	8	housewife	56	"
N	Sullivan Helen C—†	8	clerk	22	"
O	Sullivan Leo	8	"	28	268 Bremen
P	Marshall Cornelius B	23	baggageman	67	here
R	Marshall Ena M—†	23	operator	23	"
S	Marshall Gertrude E—†	23	"	39	"
T	Alfamo Carlotta—†	23	secretary	21	441 Meridian
U	Alfamo Florence—†	23	seamstress	23	441 "
V	*Alfamo Mary—†	23	housewife	54	441 "
W	Morrisroe Bertha—†	26	organist	55	here
X	Stewart James H	26	supervisor	50	"
Y	Stewart Kathleen—†	26	housewife	44	"
Z	Begley Edward	27	longshoreman	46	"
	946				
A	Begley Elizabeth—†	27	housewife	74	"
B	Begley Michael F	27	seaman	44	"
C	Begley Thomas	27	U S N	48	"
D	Quigley Antoinette—†	28	housewife	30	"
E	Quigley William	28	laborer	34	"
F	Corochio Louis	28	U S A	40	"
G	Corochio Louise—†	28	stenographer	40	"
H	Quigley Mary—†	28	housekeeper	70	"
K	Quigley Mary—†	28	inspector	37	"
L	Quigley Thomas	28	retired	76	"
M	Tanner George A	29	operator	22	"
N	Tanner Hattie E—†	29	housewife	54	"
O	Tanner Louis A	29	machinist	58	"
P	Tanner Louis A, jr	29	U S A	27	"
R	Tanner Mildred E—†	29	stenographer	24	"
S	Cadigan Mary G—†	30	clerk	52	"
T	Collins John J	30	splicer	43	"
U	Collins Lillian A—†	30	housewife	39	"

West Eagle Street—Continued

v	Sanchez Mary R—†	30	housewife	57	here
w	Sanchez Frank G	30	engineer	58	"
x	Sanchez Frank T	30	U S A	22	"
y	Dolan Mary—†	31	tel operator	27	"
z	Lang Anna G—†	31	housewife	50	"

947

A	Lang Fred	31	meatcutter	47	"
B	McEachern Eleanor—†	31	inspector	23	"
C	Dingwell Chester	31	expressman	46	"
D	Dingwell Mary—†	31	housewife	37	"
E	Rizzo John	32	chauffeur	38	"
F	Rizzo Theresa—†	32	housewife	36	"
G	Bonanno Louise—†	32	shoeworker	35	"
H	Cannariato Anna—†	32	housewife	43	"
K	Cannariato George	32	shoeworker	45	"
L	Cannariato Josephine—†	32	housekeeper	53	"
M	Cannariato Lawrence	32	salesman	25	"
N	Baptista Alice—†	33	housewife	30	"
O	Baptista Manuel	33	cook	45	"
P	Morgera Domenic A	33	locksmith	28	"
R	Morgera Mary—†	33	housewife	28	"
S	Ciampa Armando	34	welder	34	"
T	Ciampa Benjamin	34	"	36	"
U	Ciampa Ersillia—†	34	clerk	32	"
V	Manetta Angelo	34	candymaker	63	"
W	Manetta Evelyn—†	34	housewife	26	"
X	Manetta Richard	34	painter	29	"
Y	Lottero Louis	34	foreman	28	194 London
Z	Lottero Vincenza—†	34	housewife	24	here

948

A	Massaro Henry	34	electrician	36	"
B	Massaro Louise—†	34	housewife	31	"
C	Denehy Daniel A	35	woodworker	47	"
D	Denehy Josephine M—†	35	housewife	43	"
E	Denehy Mary L—†	35	stenographer	22	"
F	Hines Albert L	35	seaman	61	"
G	Hines Albert L	35	U S A	32	"
H	Hines Annie B—†	35	housewife	58	"
K	Hines Arnold L	35	clerk	37	"
L	Hines Wilfred H	35	U S C G	35	"
M	Maguire Jennie A—†	35	operator	29	"

West Eagle Street—Continued

Page.	Letter.	FULL NAME.	Residence, Jan. 1, 1943.	Occupation.	Supposed Age.	Reported Residence, Jan. 1, 1942. Street and Number.
	N	Gibbons Catherine—†	35	housewife	76	here
	O	Gibbons Hazel M—†	35	tel operator	50	"
	P	Gibbons John J	35	shipfitter	51	"
	R	*Gibbons Morgan	35	retired	80	"
	S	Massaro Carmella—†	36	housewife	31	"
	T	Massaro Herman J	36	repairman	36	"
	U	DeStefano Josephine—†	36	housewife	38	"
	V	DeStefano Ralph	36	barber	42	"
	W	Festa Dora—†	36	housewife	31	"
	X	Festa Louis	36	welder	31	"
	Y	*Bruno Marie—†	37	housewife	51	"
	Z	*Bruno Peter	37	laborer	52	"
949						
	A	Powers Harold	37	longshoreman	52	"
	B	Powers Herbert	37	U S N	20	"
	C	Powers John	37	U S A	22	"
	D	Powers Mary—†	37	housewife	51	"
	E	Hegner Andrew G	37	laborer	56	"
	F	Hegner Francis L	37	policeman	25	343 Meridian
	G	Hegner Ruth—†	37	operator	21	here
	H	Hegner Sarah J—†	37	housewife	53	"
	K	Cotreau Andrew	37	U S C G	26	"
	L	*Cotreau Andrew L	37	carpenter	54	"
	M	Cotreau Edward	38	seaman	22	"
	N	*Cotreau Lucy—†	38	housewife	57	"
	O	Cotreau Paul	38	U S N	20	"
	P	McClellan Annie—†	38	housekeeper	72	"
	R	McClellan Joseph	38	shipfitter	32	"
	S	*O'Hanley Agnes—†	39	housewife	39	"
	T	O'Hanley Roy F	39	brazier	35	"
	U	Johnson Albert	39	rubberworker	24	"
	V	Johnson Mary—†	39	housewife	48	"
	W	Johnson Norman	39	U S A	20	"
	X	Sousa John P	39	assembler	20	"
	Y	Sousa Joseph J	39	machinist	34	"
	Z	Sousa Lillian—†	39	clerk	22	"
950						
	A	Sousa Mary T—†	39	housekeeper	53	"
	B	Sousa Matilda E—†	39	clerk	30	"
	C	Barbarossa John	40	U S N	26	"
	D	Barbarossa Louis	40	retired	73	"

Page	Letter	Full Name.	Residence, Jan. 1, 1943	Occupation.	Supposed Age.	Reported Residence, Jan. 1, 1942. Street and Number.

West Eagle Street Continued

	Letter	Full Name.	Residence	Occupation	Age	Reported Residence
	E	Barbarossa Louis, jr	40	mechanic	37	here
	F	Barbarossa Madeline †	40	housewife	59	"
	G	Barbarossa Mary †	40	packer	23	"
	H	Barbarossa Theodore	40	U S A	38	"
	K	Barranco Delphine †	40	housewife	32	34 White
	L	Barranco John	40	foreman	32	34 "
	M	DeChristoforo Celia †	40	housewife	39	here
	N	DeChristoforo Paul	40	teacher	36	"
	O*	McNeil Mabel †	41	housewife	36	"
	P	McNeil Milton	41	laundryman	38	"
	R	Wyse David	41	rigger	53	"
	S*	Wyse Elizabeth †	41	housewife	48	"
	T	Tedesco Frances †	41	"	62	"
	U	Tedesco Joseph	41	carpenter	65	"
	V	Tedesco Santa	41	tailor	62	"
	W	Austin Marion †	42	tel operator	21	"
	X	Forbes Arthur H	42	chauffeur	48	"
	Y	Forbes Mary J †	42	housewife	50	"
	Z	Tanner Ernest	42	pipefitter	35	"

951

	Letter	Full Name.	Residence	Occupation	Age	Reported Residence
	A*	Tanner Rita †	42	housewife	31	"
	C	White James	43	B F D	42	37 Falcon
	D	White Margaret †	43	housewife	37	37 "
	E	McArdle Andrew P	43	inspector	45	here
	F	McArdle Helen M †	43	clerk	21	"
	G	McArdle Irene G †	43	housewife	43	"
	H	Barbarossa Eleanor †	44	"	24	42 W Eagle
	K	Barbarossa Lionel	44	woodworker	30	42 "
	L	Nickerson Douglas	44	machinist	23	here
	M*	Nickerson Meredith †	44	housewife	21	"
	N	Hembrough Evelyn †	44	"	31	"
	O	Hembrough Frederick	44	electrician	28	"
	P	Hopkins Effie †	49	at home	35	"
	R	Snow Leonard	49	engineer	50	"
	S*	Snow Mildred †	49	housewife	45	"
	T	Roche Anna †	49	"	79	"
	U	Roche Helen †	49	stitcher	44	"
	V	Roche James	49	calker	47	"
	W	Danielson Esther †	49	clerk	24	"
	X	Danielson George	49	grocer	66	"
	Y	Danielson Helen †	49	clerk	28	"

Page	Letter	FULL NAME.	Residence, Jan. 1, 1943.	Occupation.	Supposed Age.	Reported Residence, Jan. 1, 1942. Street and Number.

West Eagle Street—Continued

	z	Danielson John	49	architect	32	here
952						
	A	Danielson Yeranooki—†	49	housewife	50	"
	B	*Nalbandian Bagdassar	49	grocer	72	"
	C	Cafano Alice—†	51	stenographer	31	"
	D	Cafano Mildred—†	51	housewife	24	"
	E	Veggiano Carmella—†	51	"	62	"
	F	Veggiano Joseph	51	retired	72	"
	G	Stevens Ernest	51	instructor	35	"
	H	Stevens Rose M—†	51	housewife	35	"
	K	Buccafusca Frank	51	boxmaker	47	"
	L	Buccafusca Jennie—†	51	housewife	41	"
	M	Bona Daniel	52	rigger	43	"
	N	Bona Mildred—†	52	housewife	40	"
	O	McDonald Edward L	52A	engineer	64	"
	P	Obdens Benjamin	52A	shipper	33	"
	R	Obdens Marie—†	52A	housewife	25	"
	S	Austin Emily—†	52A	"	22	"
	T	Austin Esther—†	52A	"	45	"
	U	Austin Thomas M	52A	loom fixer	23	"
	V	Austin William J	52A	clerk	54	"
	W	Austin William J, jr	52A	machinist	26	"
	X	*Cruppi Angelina—†	53	domestic	63	"
	Y	Scarcella Antonio	53	retired	65	"
	Z	Blowers Eliza—†	53	housewife	74	"
953						
	A	Blowers James E	53	U S A	33	"
	B	Lasky Charles	53	fireman	25	"
	C	Lasky Helen—†	53	housewife	27	"
	D	Munroe Fred M	54	laborer	43	"
	E	*Munroe Margaret A—†	54	housewife	42	"
	F	O'Neill Abraham J	54A	seaman	33	"
	G	O'Neill Arthur J	54A	U S A	27	"
	H	O'Neill Mary A—†	54A	housewife	55	"
	K	O'Neill Rita V—†	54A	welder	21	"
	L	O'Neill William P	54A	trainman	66	"
	M	Botto Mary—†	54A	housewife	51	"
	O	Dunbar Florence—†	55	"	27	"
	P	Dunbar Ralph	55	chauffeur	28	"
	R	Hagen Alvah	55	millhand	48	"
	S	Hagen Earl	55	U S A	21	"

West Eagle Street Continued

F	Hagen Mary E †	55	housewife		51	here
U	Doyle Lucy †	56	"		33	481 Summer
V	Doyle Martin	56	stevedore		37	481 "
W	McRae Mary L †	56	housewife		52	here
X	McRae William D	56	mechanic		54	"
Y	Dalasta Marie P †	56	housewife		44	"
Z	DaCosta Paulino	56	storekeeper		57	"

954

B	*Giambusco Frank	57	mechanic		50	"
C	*Giambusso Sarah †	57	housewife		48	"
D	Costa Margaret †	57	"		25	331 E Eagle
E	Costa Rocco	57	painter		26	331 "
F	Menezes John	58	U S A		21	here
G	*Menezes Lorenzia †	58	housewife		45	"
H	*Menezes Louis	58	longshoreman		59	"
K	Romano Assunta †	58	housewife		34	"
L	*Romano Giacomo	58	fishcutter		38	"
M	Cabrault Filomena †	58	housewife		25	"
N	Cabrault James	58	millhand		43	"
O	Rodriguez Juanita †	59	housewife		34	"
P	DelVecchio Flora †	59	"		34	"
R	DelVecchio Joseph	59	welder		46	"
S	Amari Alba †	59	dressmaker		20	"
T	Amari Guiseppe	59	freighthandler		53	"
U	Amari Mary †	59	dressmaker		22	"
V	*Amari Peter	59	retired		86	"
W	*Amari Rose †	59	housewife		49	"
X	Luzinski Frank P	60	policeman		44	"
Y	Luzinski Henrietta †	60	housewife		39	"
Z	Murphy Francis	61	watchman		24	"

955

A	Murphy Mildred †	61	housewife		22	"
B	Meyer Melvin	61	laborer		28	"
C	Meyer Rachel †	61	housewife		29	"
D	Leno Henry	61	machinist		34	"
E	Leno Mary †	61	housewife		36	"
F	Clifford Sadie †	62	"		78	"
G	Sennington Charles	62	mechanic		37	"
H	Stoddard Florence †	63	housewife		28	"
K	*Stoddard Reginald	63	mechanic		32	"
L	Morrison Doris A †	63	housewife		38	"

1—9

Page.	Letter.	Full Name.	Residence. Jan. 1, 1943.	Occupation.	Supposed Age.	Reported Residence. Jan. 1, 1942. Street and Number.

West Eagle Street Continued

M	Morrison William W	63	pipefitter	32	here
N	Andrade Gabriel	63	millhand	44	"
O*	Andrade Helen †	63	housewife	41	"
P	Visco Dominica †	64	"	42	"
R	Visco Frank	64	tailor	56	"
S	Carney Mary †	64	housewife	42	Canada
T*	Visco Carmello †	64	"	75	here
U	Visco Rose †	64	stitcher	37	"
V	Rich John J	65	packer	32	91 Moore
W	Rich Peter	65	retired	56	91 "
X	Zagarella Anna †	65	housewife	28	here
Y	Zagarella James	65	presser	30	"
Z	Dantona Frances †	65	housewife	46	"

956

A	Dantona Leo R	65	U S A	26	"
B	Dantona Liborio	65	tailor	52	"
C	D'Eon Bernard	66	carpenter	35	"
D*	D'Eon Emmeline †	66	housewife	70	"
E	D'Eon Irene †	66	"	35	"
F*	Costantino Alice †	66	"	53	"
G	Costantino Edward	66	U S N	21	"
H	Costantino Pasquale	66	shipper	53	"
K	Munn Ada L †	66	housewife	36	"
L	Munn George E	66	chauffeur	40	"
M*	Ross Charles	67	watchman	42	"
N*	Ross Emma †	67	housewife	42	"
O	Hamel Mary †	67	"	25	"
P	Hamel Roland	67	operator	25	"
R	McLoughlin Hilda †	67	housewife	24	Maine
S	Burrone Charles	67	carpenter	58	here
T	Burrone Iolanda †	67	operator	21	"
U	Burrone Josephine †	67	housewife	53	"
V	Burrone Salvatore	67	seaman	29	"
W	Sousa Mary †	67	domestic	28	"
X	Parson Marion †	69	housewife	20	112 Trenton
Y*	Parson Robert	69	deckhand	21	112 "

957

A	Carusone John	69	retired	68	here
B	Carusone John, jr	69	mechanic	21	"
C	Carusone Josephine †	69	housewife	53	"
D	Winn Doris †	69	"	28	"

West Eagle Street Continued

E	Winn Harold	69	shipfitter	34	here
F	Aitken Catherine †	70	housewife	39	"
G	Aitken Francis	70	machinist	41	"
H *Poirier Ina †	70	housewife	47	"
K	DesJardins Joseph	70	fireman	50	77 Warren
L	DesJardins Nellie †	70	housewife	35	here
M	DesJardins Oscar	70	fireman	43	"
N	Clements Marie C †	71	housewife	51	"
O	Clements Raymond A	71	U S A	22	"
P	Clements Richard W	71	"	27	"
R	Clements Robert L	71	"	26	"
S	Clements William	71	operator	65	"
T	Vitello Francis	72	painter	38	"
U	Vitello Theresa †	72	housewife	34	"
V	Leville Frederick J	72	U S A	23	"
W	Leville Mary †	72	housewife	54	"
X	Leville Paul B	72	U S C G	21	"
Y	Leville William H	72	dyesetter	55	"
Z	Jaakola Arthur	72	mechanic	49	"

958

A	Jaakola Elvira †	72	housewife	51	"
B	Iaderosa Mary †	73	"	45	"
C	Morante Anna †	73	cashier	30	"
D	Boyle Margaret †	74	cook	56	"
E	Powers Margaret L †	74	housewife	45	"
F	Powers Marie L †	74	clerk	20	"
G	Powers Robert E	74	machinist	22	"
H	Powers Robert J	75	retired	45	"
K	Crooks Charlotte †	75	domestic	52	38 Eutaw
L	Crooks Robert	75	U S A	21	38 "
M	Crooks Woodrow	75	"	27	38 "
N	McIntyre Daniel	75	carpenter	41	here
O	McIntyre Edgar F	75	dispatcher	36	"
P	McIntyre Herbert	75	operator	39	"
R	McIntyre Mary E †	75	factoryhand	26	"
S	McIntyre Rhoda †	75	housewife	33	"
T	Shapiro Anna †	76	"	41	"
U	Shapiro Joseph	76	chauffeur	44	"
V	*Cowzo John	77	fireman	48	103 Porter
W	Diaz Ann †	77	housewife	26	126 Marginal
X	Diaz Richard	77	machinist	29	126 "

West Eagle Street—Continued

	y	Veglione Anthony	77	machinist	36	173 Lexington
	z	Veglione Josephine †	77	housewife	28	173 "
959						
	A	LaRaia Annie †	77	"	54	here
	B	LaRaia Isabelle †	77	waitress	22	"
	C	LaRaia Joseph	77	U S A	23	"
	D	LaRaia Nicolas	77	U S C G	20	"
	E	Nolan Louis F	81	caretaker	50	"
	F	Nolan Mary C †	81	housewife	55	"
	G	Hardy Elizabeth †	81	"	87	"
	H	Hardy Howard	81	retired	85	"
	K	Hemeon Calvin H	81	U S A	20	"
	L	Hemeon Edith H †	81	housewife	57	"
	M	Hemeon Edward B	81	fisherman	60	"
	N	Matera James	82	engineer	31	"
	O	Matera Livia †	82	housewife	35	"
	P*	Tonon Pasqua †	82	"	63	"
	R	Keenan Edna †	82	"	51	"
	S	Keenan William	82	B F D	51	"
	T	Oak Walter	84	machinist	23	"
	U	Whittendale Ruth L †	84	housewife	84	"
	V	Whittendale Walter	84	laborer	54	"
	W*	Walker Catherine †	84	housewife	55	"
	X*	Walker John T	84	carpenter	54	"
	Y	Walker Mark	84	letter carrier	26	"
	Z	Carlry Mary †	84	housewife	30	"
969						
	B	Nickerson John A	86	teller	38	"
	C	Nickerson Mildred †	86	housewife	38	"
	D*	Amirault Edgar	86	fishcutter	41	77 W Eagle
	E*	Amirault Mary †	86	housewife	40	77 "

White Street

	G	Boretta Esther †	24	housewife	46	here
	H	Boretta Leonard	24	estimator	53	"
	K	Boretta Winifred †	24	finisher	23	"
	L	Goldberg Bertha †	24	housewife	49	"
	M	Goldberg Joseph	24	physician	52	"
	N	Goldberg Ruth †	24	technician	27	"
	O	Goldberg Sophie †	24	secretary	23	"

White Street Continued

P	Costigan Albert	26	fishcutter	26	here
R	Costigan James	26	longshoreman	56	"
S	*Costigan Margaret †	26	housewife	50	"
T	Bernard Catherine †	26	laundress	43	132 Marion
U	Bernard Mary †	26	factoryhand	20	132 "
V	Hudson Eva †	26	laundress	32	Chelsea
W	LeBlanc Frank	28	fish handler	35	here
X	*LeBlanc Regina †	28	housewife	30	"
Y	O'Driscoll Edward T	28	U S A	30	"
Z	O'Driscoll George	28	"	22	"

961

A	O'Driscoll James M	28	clerk	38	"
B	O'Driscoll Mary †	28	housewife	62	"
C	O'Driscoll Mary E †	28	inspector	40	"
D	O'Driscoll Thomas	28	U S A	29	"
E	Stubbs Anna †	28	housewife	36	Connecticut
F	Larson Isabel †	32	"	27	here
G	Larson William	32	machinist	29	"
H	Comeau Joseph E	32	clerk	35	"
K	*Comeau Leander	32	carpenter	68	"
L	Comeau Marie L †	32	housewife	26	"
M	*Comeau Philomena †	32	"	69	"
N	Doyle Marion †	32	"	25	12 Marion
O	Doyle Ralph	32	molder	29	12 "
P	D'Entremont Joseph R	34	rigger	38	here
R	D'Entremont Theresa †	34	housewife	38	"
C	*Hansen Anna †	34	housekeeper	75	404 Meridian
S	Mullen Arthur R	34	chauffeur	34	404 "
T	Mullen Sadie H †	34	housewife	35	404 "
V	Vaccaro Angelina †	34	"	45	here
W	Vaccaro Francisco	34	bricklayer	54	"
X	Vaccaro Nellie F †	34	factoryhand	20	"
Y	Cahalane Helen †	36	housewife	31	"
Z	Cahalane Robert	36	chauffeur	36	"

962

A	Cahalane Catherine †	36	housewife	72	"
B	*Morrow Nina †	38	housekeeper	60	"
C	Carson Clara †	38	"	52	"
D	Carson Dorothy †	38	housewife	23	"
E	Carson Robert	38	clerk	29	"
G	Panzine Barbara †	42	housewife	36	"

37

Page.	Letter.	FULL NAME.	Residence, Jan. 1, 1943.	Occupation.	Supposed Age.	Reported Residence, Jan. 1, 1942. Street and Number.

White Street — Continued

	H	Panzine John	42	candymaker	40	here
	K	Grasso John	42	U S A	23	"
	L	*Grasso Martin	42	laborer	67	"
	M	*Grasso Sophie †	42	housewife	56	"
	N	*Cardone Emilie †	44	"	43	"
	O	Cardone Gabriel	44	laborer	43	"
	P	Soriano Rosina †	44	operator	20	"
	R	Vaccaro Luigi	44	laborer	52	"
	S	*Vaccaro Nicolena †	44	housewife	50	"
	T	Donnelly Dorothy †	44	clerk	39	"
	U	Murray Homer	46	U S C G	39	"
	V	*Murray Marguerite M †	46	housewife	31	"
	W	Russi Anthony	46	U S A	24	133 Eutaw
	X	Russi Joseph	46	clerk	22	133 "
	Y	*Russi Theresa †	46	housewife	47	133 "
	Z	*Babine Gertrude †	46	"	33	here

963

	A	Harvey Albert	46	machinist	26	35 Princeton
	B	*Pipi Antoinetta †	48	housewife	52	here
	C	Pipi Catherine †	48	"	25	548 Benningt'n
	D	Pipi John	48	clerk	22	here
	E	Pipi Joseph	48	insulator	31	"
	F	Pipi Michael	48	retired	54	"
	G	Marmaud Emma †	48	housewife	27	"
	H	Marmaud Joseph	48	longshoreman	32	"
	K	Basile Anthony	48	U S A	31	"
	L	Basile Carmela †	48	housewife	58	"
	M	Basile Vincent	48	laborer	62	"
	N	Basile Vincent	48	U S M C	22	"
	O	Rauseo Mary †	48	housewife	26	"
	P	Falla John	52	laborer	46	Somerville
	R	Gorman Frank	52	driller	61	here
	S	Joyce Marcella †	52	housewife	45	"
	T	Joyce Wilfred P	52	caretaker	49	"
	U	Kehoe James	52	machinist	42	"
	V	McAuliff Dennis	52	clerk	43	"
	W	Melanson George	52	calker	51	"
	X	Sheridan Frank	52	guard	48	"
	Y	Stearns Ina †	52	housewife	43	N Hampshire
	Z	Stearns James J	52	builder	51	"

964

White Street Continued

A	Hegner Agnes †	53	packer	63	here
B	Hegner Annie †	53	housewife	53	"
C	Hegner Arthur	53	checker	21	"
D	Hegner Joseph	53	U S A	24	"
E	Hegner Walter	53	garageman	52	"
F	Mazzarino Adeline †	53	seamstress	26	"
G	Mazzarino Joseph	53	welder	25	"
H	*Mazzarino Rosalie †	53	housekeeper	51	"
K	Pingiaro Anna †	53	seamstress	22	"
L	Pingiaro John	53	welder	22	516 Sumner
M	*German Hermeline †	53	housewife	48	26 Trenton
N	*German Thomas	53	laborer	50	26 "
O	Cordes Doris †	55	housewife	23	569 Benningt'n
P	Cordes Joseph	55	U S C G	25	569 "
R	Grant Edith F †	55	housekeeper	52	here
S	Winn Lester E	55	driller	56	"
T	*Standrick Julia †	55	baker	48	"
U	Garcia Eugenia †	57	housewife	30	"
V	*Garcia John	57	fireman	38	"
W	Barros John	57	"	54	"
X	Barros Mary †	57	factoryhand	40	"
Y	Samchez Jose	57	U S A	39	"
Z	*Sousa Maria †	57	housekeeper	60	"

965

A	Pigeon Elizabeth N †	58	housewife	65	"
B	Pigeon Fred L	58	merchant	67	"
C	Sandquist Dorothy F †	59	housewife	27	"
D	Sandquist Eric J	59	pressman	29	"
E	Dutchie Bessie †	59	housekeeper	78	"
F	Sandquist Catherine L †	59	housewife	49	"
G	Sandquist Eric T	59	clerk	52	"
H	Cohane John	60	finisher	27	175 Benningt'n
K	Cohane Mary †	60	housewife	25	175 "
L	Tanner Grace †	60	operator	24	here
M	Tanner Harriet †	60	housekeeper	84	"
N	Tanner Marie †	60	saleswoman	21	"
O	Blanciforte Frank	60	clerk	22	"
P	Carney Eleanor †	60	operator	24	"
R	*Vetri Anna †	60	housewife	51	"

White Street — Continued

s	Fagone Angelina †	60	housewife	28	here
t	Fagone Charles	60	chauffeur	33	"
u	McInnis Donald R	61	painter	42	"
v	McInnis Violet M †	61	housewife	43	"
w	Preshong Louise †	61	waitress	61	"
x	Scott Charlotte M †	63	laundress	59	3 Lexington pl
y	Woolley Catherine A †	63	waitress	41	3 "
z	Alves Imelda †	63	clerk	21	here

966

a	Hawes Margaret †	63	housewife	42	"
b	Hawes Stephen	63	laborer	46	"
c	Gill Albert	63	carpenter	38	"
d	Dalton Grace M †	68	clerk	59	"
e	Dalton Joseph H	68	U S A	36	"
f	Corrado Alphonse	68	painter	27	"
g	*Corrado Pasqualina †	68	housewife	61	"
h	Corrado Anna †	68	housekeeper	37	"
k	*Fenton Ellen †	68	"	76	"
m	Cresta Rose †	75	factoryhand	21	"
n	Giancristiano Doris †	75	operator	23	"
o	*Giancristiano Ida †	75	housewife	46	"
p	Giancristiano Michael	75	machinist	53	"
r	Worthy Doris †	75	stenographer	30	"
s	Worthy Ella †	75	housekeeper	52	"
t	Martin Sophie †	76	stenographer	21	"
u	*Monkewicz Antonina †	76	housewife	52	"
v	*Monkewicz Konstanty	76	meatcutter	63	"
w	Covino Joseph	76	U S A	22	"
x	Grosso Vincenzo	76	shoemaker	66	"
y	Zollo Fedele	76	laborer	45	"
z	Zollo Malvina †	76	laundryworker	43	"

967

a	*Hughes Willa †	76	housewife	35	"
b	Hughes William	76	machinist	36	"
c	Pagliccia Emidio	77	laborer	48	"
d	Podmostko Veronica †	77	stenographer	28	"
e	Casella Frances †	78	housewife	34	1004 Bennington
f	Casella Joseph	78	chauffeur	36	1004 "
g	Flaherty Hannah †	79	housekeeper	72	here
h	Kelleher Mary †	79	"	73	"
k	D'Alessandro Biago	79	presser	42	256 Lexington

White Street Continued

L	D'Alessandro Elena †	79	housewife	42	256 Lexington	
M	Cappucci Ann †	80	"	24	262 Havre	
N	Cappucci Thomas A	80	laborer	27	262 "	
O	Troiano Joseph	80	foreman	38	Watertown	
P	Troiano Rachele †	80	housewife	29	"	
R	O'Brien Elizabeth †	81	"	83	here	
S	O'Brien Patrick D	81	carpenter	65	"	
U	Flynn Elizabeth †	82	housewife	20	Chelsea	
V	Flynn William E	82	toolmaker	22	"	
W	Gaeta Anna †	82	housewife	36	147 Cottage	
X	Gaeta Dante	82	blacksmith	45	147 "	
Y	Eaton Marion A †	82	housewife	25	here	
Z	Eaton Walter	82	chauffeur	30	"	

968

A	Severino Allessandra †	82	housekeeper	76	"	
B	Severino Erminia †	82	tailor	33	"	
D	Lukman Fergus	85	supervisor	43	"	
E	*Mario Antoinetta †	85	housewife	37	"	
F	*Mario Carmen	85	baker	38	"	

White Street Place

G	Surette Basil	1	carpenter	49	here	
H	*Surette Lena †	1	housewife	43	"	
K	Deveau Alphie	2	U S A	23	"	
L	Deveau Enos	2	retired	67	"	
M	Deveau Honore †	2	housewife	24	New York	
N	Deveau Joseph D	2	welder	25	here	
O	*Doucette Annie E †	4	housewife	63	"	
P	*Doucette Arthur	4	carpenter	79	"	
R	Doucette Clara M †	4	operator	24	"	
S	Doucette Joseph E	4	U S A	21	"	

Ward 1–Precinct 10

CITY OF BOSTON

LIST OF RESIDENTS
20 YEARS OF AGE AND OVER

(NON-CITIZENS INDICATED BY ASTERISK)
(FEMALES INDICATED BY DAGGER)

AS OF

JANUARY 1, 1943

JOSEPH F. TIMILTY, *Chairman*
FREDERIC E. DOWLING, *Secretary*
WILLIAM A. MOTLEY, JR.
FRANCIS B. McKINNEY
EVERETT R. PROUT

Listing Board.

CITY OF BOSTON PRINTING DEPARTMENT

1000

Brooks Street

B	Salmi Arnil	223	longshoreman	47	here
C	Salmi Ida—†	223	housewife	45	"
D	Towlson James	225	laundryman	54	Chelsea
E	Towlson Mary E—†	225	housewife	47	"
F	Towlson Charles	225	salesman	58	here
G	Towlson Stella M—†	225	housewife	47	"
H	Eccleston Laura—†	227	waitress	49	"
K	*Nickerson Forman	227	retired	68	"
L	Batson Edward M	227	laborer	52	"
M	Batson Lena—†	227	housewife	49	"
N	Heffron Catherine—†	227	at home	65	Everett

Condor Street

S	Knig Margaret—†	121	housewife	38	here
T	Knig Mary F—†	121	"	64	"
U	Knig William C	121	machinist	41	"
V	Knig William T	121	lithographer	63	"
X	Jordan Bernice—†	133	housewife	27	62 C
Y	Jordan Gordon D	133	machinist	30	62 "
Z	Gillis John	133A	"	38	here

1001

A	Gillis Lillian—†	133A	housewife	32	"
B	Gillis Margaret—†	133A	at home	74	"
C	McCarthy James H	133A	U S N	21	"
D	McCarthy John F	133A	ropemaker	22	"
E	McCarthy Patrick J	133A	B F D	49	"
F	Engley Mary F—†	135	at home	63	"
G	Wainwright Lottie—†	135A	"	63	"
H	Smith Herbert	135A	machinist	38	"
K	Orr Alfred J	137	"	37	Ohio
L	Orr Mabel—†	137	housewife	36	"
M	*Sturrock Jessie—†	137A	"	50	here
N	*Sturrock Martin	137A	machinist	52	"
O	*Duffy Annie—†	137A	housewife	43	"
P	*Duffy Patrick	137A	driller	50	"
R	Brown Alice M—†	139	housewife	64	Winthrop
S	Brown Arthur R	139	U S N	21	"
T	Grube Evelyn—†	139	at home	24	174 Saratoga
U	Merrigan Mary T—†	139A	housewife	27	here

2

Condor Street Continued

v	Merrigan Thomas F	139A	reporter	31	here
w	Holt Richard	139A	mechanic	28	288 Princeton
y	Lally Frances E †	155	at home	23	here
z	Lally Frank J	155	watchman	46	"

1002

A	Lally Mary A †	155	housewife	43	"
B	Moore Albertina †	157	at home	64	"
D	*Bateman Laura †	163	housewife	32	"
F	*Boudreau Clayton	167	rigger	38	"
G	*Boudreau Gladys †	167	housewife	30	"
H	Nolfo Giuseppe	169	laborer	60	"
K	*Nolfo Josephine †	169	housewife	58	"
L	Marshall Henry	171	carpenter	43	"
M	Marshall Julia †	171	housewife	47	"
N	*Albergo Angela †	173	"	55	"
O	*Albergo Filippo	173	pedler	62	"
P	Riley Helen V †	175	tel operator	42	"
R	Leone Anthony	177	laborer	55	"
S	Leone Jennie †	177	rubberworker	22	"
T	Leone Lena †	177	housewife	44	"
U	Leone Matteo	177	U S N	20	"
V	*Veader Marie †	179	housewife	42	"
W	Veader Perry	179	fireman	42	"
X	MacNeill Francis	181	clerk	34	"
Y	MacNeill Margaret R †	181	housewife	34	"
Z	Phillips Mary F †	181	clerk	36	"

1003

C	Rawlings Earle R	195	laborer	33	"
D	Rawlings Hazel †	195	housewife	29	"
E	Correia Matilda †	195	"	63	"
F	Adams Albert	197	machinist	41	"
G	Adams Alice †	197	housewife	34	"
K	Goodwin Burns I	203	clerk	60	"
L	Goodwin Lillian †	203	housewife	55	"
M	Anderson Andrew	203	retired	67	"
N	Anderson Jennie C †	203	housewife	67	"
P	DeFeo Gaetano	213	pipefitter	22	"
R	DeFeo Sarah †	213	housewife	20	"
S	*Margiotti Carmela †	213	"	68	"
T	*Margiotti Frank	213	refiner	52	"
U	*Margiotti Rosina †	213	at home	73	"

3

Page.	Letter.	Full Name.	Residence, Jan. 1, 1943.	Occupation.	Supposed Age.	Reported Residence, Jan. 1, 1942. Street and Number.

Condor Street—Continued

	w	Flammia A William	225	machinist	33	here
	x	Flammia Antonio	225	dealer	37	"
	y	Flammia Frances—†	225	housewife	34	"
	z	Flammia Michael A	225	retired	71	"
1004						
	a	Flammia Teresa—†	225	inspector	30	"
	g	Brutas Adolph	237	carpenter	60	"
	h	Brutas Anna—†	237	housewife	60	"
	k	Fraser Mary—†	237	at home	58	"
	l	Pitts Charlotte B—†	237	"	55	"
	m	Sullivan James M	237	machinist	35	"
	n	*Candido Ignazia—†	243	housewife	63	"
	o	*Candido Salvatore	243	manufacturer	58	"
	p	Pizzi Daniel	243	clerk	31	"
	r	Pizzi Grace—†	243	housewife	23	"

East Eagle Street

	v	*Runstein Louis	200	proprietor	67	here
	w	Cleary George	202	repairman	46	"
	x	Tuttle Anna—†	202	at home	42	"
	y	Tuttle Harold	202	painter	52	"
	z	Roselli Etta—†	204	housewife	29	"
1005						
	a	Roselli Louis	204	painter	33	"
	b	Piretti Louis	204	maint'n'ceman	35	"
	c	Piretti Mary—†	204	housewife	34	"
	d	Catanese Domenic	204	painter	28	"
	e	Catanese Mary—†	204	housewife	29	"
	f	Mazzone Anthony	205	salesman	25	161 Havre
	g	Mazzone Josephine—†	205	housewife	26	161 "
	h	Melchionda Alfred	205	welder	25	318 Summer
	k	Melchionda Lillian—†	205	housewife	25	318 "
	l	Melchionda Ida—†	205	"	27	here
	m	Melchionda William	205	laborer	28	"
	n	Marolda Daniel	206	machinist	34	"
	o	Marolda Rose—†	206	housewife	34	"
	p	*DiLorenzo Fredericko	206	carpenter	56	"
	r	DiLorenzo Gerald	206	pressman	20	"
	s	DiLorenzo Jennie—†	206	shoeworker	27	"
	t	DiLorenzo Joseph	206	"	30	"

4

East Eagle Street—Continued

	U	DiLorenzo Recco	206	U S A	24	here
	V	*DiLorenzo Yola †	206	housewife	56	"
	W	Cucinotta Anthony	206	U S A	22	"
	X	*Cucinotta Celia †	206	housewife	45	"
	Y	*Cucinotta Joseph	206	salesman	53	"
	Z	Cucinotta Sadie †	206	stitcher	26	"

1006

	A	Marracco John	207	clerk	25	"
	B	Marracco Marie †	207	"	25	"
	C	Marracco Marie †	207	stitcher	23	"
	D	*Marracco Mary †	207	housewife	56	"
	E	Marracco Vincent	207	laborer	49	"
	F	Maniacci Mary †	207	housewife	26	"
	G	Maniacci Salvatore	207	baker	30	"
	H	Berardi Angelina †	207	housewife	32	"
	K	Berardi Frank	207	rubberworker	38	"
	L	*Berardi Mary †	207	at home	59	"
	M	*McCormack Ellen B †	208	housewife	50	"
	N	McCormack Patrick	208	pile driver	46	"
	S	Vinesky Patricia †	208	operator	31	"
	O	Zeringis Alice †	208	housewife	32	"
	P	Zeringis Anthony	208	engineer	30	"
	R	Zeringis Peter	208	retired	63	"
	T	Canty Frederick	208	"	45	"
	U	Casucci Augusto	208	machinist	31	"
	V	Casucci Louise †	208	housewife	26	"
	W	Casucci Albert A	210	U S A	21	185 Lexington
	X	Casucci Ceasar	210	carpenter	55	185 "
	Y	*Casucci Rose †	210	housewife	52	185 "

1007

	A	MacDonald Dorothy †	210	operator	24	here
	B	MacDonald Margaret †	210	at home	58	"
	C	MacDonald William	210	U S A	28	"
	D	Zeuli Henry	211	barber	47	"
	E	*Zeuli Rose M †	211	housewife	34	"
	F	McCormack Anna †	211	at home	53	"
	G	McCormack James	211	U S A	28	"
	H	Gallagher Ruth †	212	inspector	24	"
	K	Milroy Bertram	212	operator	57	"
	L	Milroy Marguerite †	212	housewife	47	"
	M	Walsh Mildred †	212	at home	29	"

East Eagle Street Continued

N	*Surette Alice †	212	housewife	32	here	
O	*Surette Roger	212	fishcutter	33	"	
P	*Surette Rose †	212	at home	54	"	
R	King Elmer, jr	212	guard	23	"	
S	King Elmer A	212	chauffeur	50	"	
T	King Grace M †	212	housewife	49	"	
U	Phillips Margaret A †	212	"	24	Revere	
V	Phillips Stephen	212	U S N	23	"	
W	Frongillo Nicholas	213	tailor	36	8 Prescott	
X	Staff Anna †	213	housewife	33	8 "	
Y	Staff Leonard	213	chauffeur	33	8 "	
Z	DeLuca Ettore	213	tailor	58	here	
	1008					
A	DeLuca Lucy †	213	housewife	51	"	
B	Cameron Dorothy †	214	waitress	22	"	
C	Cameron Eustace	214	U S A	24	"	
D	Cameron Florence †	214	housewife	48	"	
E	Cameron Roderick	214	carpenter	62	"	
F	Fay Marie †	214	rubberworker	20	"	
H	Goodwin Dexter	214	laborer	36	"	
K	Goodwin Gladys †	214	housewife	29	"	
M	Clee Gertrude †	216	"	26	"	
N	*Riggillo Alice †	216	"	38	"	
O	Riggillo Joseph	216	welder	41	"	
P	Lugrin Bertrand	217	machinist	68	"	
R	Lugrin Elizabeth †	217	housewife	68	"	
S	Lugrin Frederick W	217	retired	46	"	
T	Santirocco George	217	engineer	49	"	
U	Santirocco Theresa †	217	housewife	27	"	
V	*Breda Joseph	217	proprietor	63	"	
W	Breda Mary	217	housewife	60	"	
X	Giancristiano Lillian †	218	"	47	"	
Y	Giancristiano Nicholas	218	retired	47	"	
Z	Primavera Frances †	218	housewife	40	"	
	1009					
A	Primavera Pasquale	218	tailor	57	"	
B	Bordieri Concetta †	218	at home	52	"	
D	Chiulli Elizabeth †	220	clerk	27	"	
E	Chiulli Liberato	220	retired	60	"	
F	*DeSanctis Asunta †	220	housewife	52	"	

Page	Letter	Full Name	Residence, Jan. 1, 1943	Occupation	Supposed Age	Reported Residence, Jan. 1, 1942. Street and Number.

East Eagle Street Continued

G	DeSanctis Frank	220	mason	54	here
H	DeSanctis Louis	220	U S N	28	"
K	DeSanctis Vera †	220	clerk	30	"
L	Bevere Marion †	221	candymaker	32	"
M	Melchiano Alphonse	221	chauffeur	39	"
N	Melchiano Fannie	221	housewife	38	"
O	Fuccillo Louis	221	retired	73	"
P	Renzi Palmina †	221	housewife	40	"
R	Renzi Phillip	221	adjuster	39	"
S	Renzi Ralph	221	clerk	21	"
T	DeStefano Margaret †	221	housewife	28	"
U	DeStefano Peter	221	carpet layer	30	"
V	Anzalone Edward	222	carpenter	33	"
W*	Anzalone Philomena †	222	at home	57	"
X	Anzalone Rose †	222	housewife	32	"
Y	Anzalone Ernestine †	222	"	29	209 Prescott
Z	Anzalone Joseph	222	agent	35	209 "
1010					
A	DeLellis Amelia †	222	clerk	22	here
B*	DeLellis Michael	222	pressman	52	"
C	Marasca Anthony	223	U S A	29	"
D*	Marasca Christine	223	housewife	67	"
E	Marasca Ferdinand	223	machinist	36	"
F	Mercurio Adelaide †	223	housewife	41	"
G	Mercurio Mary †	223	operator	21	"
H	Mercurio Michael †	223	boilermaker	44	"
K	Marasca Louis	223	diemaker	43	"
L	Marasca Margaret †	223	housewife	34	"
M	Pastore Angelina †	224	"	36	"
N	Pastore Lorenzo	224	reamer	51	"
O*	Saccardo Adeline †	224	housewife	63	"
P	Saccardo Anthony	224	laborer	32	"
R	Saccardo Felix	224	"	30	"
S	Saccardo Theresa †	224	stitcher	33	"
T	Geer Alden L	224	mechanic	42	"
U*	Geer Anna †	224	housewife	36	"
V*	Roberts Mary †	224	at home	54	"
W	DiBilio Carmello	225	longshoreman	37	"
X	DiBilio Mary †	225	housewife	36	"
Y	DiBilio Mary †	225	"	35	"

7

Page.	Letter	FULL NAME.	Residence, Jan. 1, 1943.	Occupation.	Supposed Age.	Reported Residence, Jan. 1, 1942. Street and Number.

East Eagle Street—Continued

z	DiBilio Phillip	225	longshoreman	39	here

1011

A	Pergola Lena—†	225	housewife	23	"
B	Pergola Michael	225	upholsterer	25	"
C	DeSanctis Frank	230	tailor	48	"
D	DeSanctis Santina—†	230	housewife	48	"
E	Mazzone Eugene	235	molder	55	254 E Eagle
F	Mazzone Mary—†	235	housewife	53	254 "
G	Mazzone Theodore	235	U S A	23	254 "
H	Vena Constance †	235	housewife	32	here
K	Vena Louis	235	at home	34	"
L	Viscione Frank	235	merchant	24	"
M	Viscione Nicolina †	235	housewife	24	"
N	Mastercusio Joseph	242	waiter	42	Concord
O	Mastercusio Margaret—†	242	housewife	35	
P	Veccio Frank	242	tailor	40	here
R	Veccio Geraldine †	242	stitcher	39	"
S	Johnson Mary S—†	242	housewife	47	N Hampshire
T	Johnson Nels O	242	pipefitter	45	here
U	Johnson Walter G	242	fishcutter	36	"
V	DiCesare Emily †	250	housewife	36	"
W	DiCesare Henry	250	laborer	38	"
X	Healy Henry	250	shipfitter	43	"
Y	Healy Henry, jr	250	U S A	20	"
Z	Healy Sarah C †	250	housewife	44	"

1012

A	Moore Christine L †	252	teacher	31	90 Putnam
B	Moore Herbert W	252	embalmer	38	90 "
C	Cunha Alice †	252	maid	24	here
D	Cunha George	252	U S M C	20	"
E*	Cunha Mary †	252	housekeeper	55	"
F	Murphy Anna †	252	housewife	29	"
G	Murphy Paul J	252	chauffeur	30	"
H	Magaletta Albert Y	254	retired	46	"
K	Magaletta Mary R †	254	typist	20	"
L	Magaletta Rosina †	254	housewife	45	"
M	Gill Frances †	254	"	34	49 Walford way
N	Gill Francis W	254	accountant	37	49 "
O	Madden Mary A †	254	at home	59	49 "
P	Chiarenza Charles	254	pressman	28	42 Union av
R	Chiarenza Maria †	254	at home	55	42 "

East Eagle Street Continued

s	Ricupero Irene †	258	housewife	27	here
t	Ricupero Richard	258	salesman	29	"
u	Milano Joseph	258	U S A	21	"
v	Vasquez Alphonse	258	electrician	29	"
w	Vasquez Augusta †	258	housewife	27	"
x	Deraedt Edmund R	258	fireman	34	5 Drake pl
y	Deraedt Rose M †	258	housewife	28	5 "
z	Mozzetta Albert	262	painter	42	here

1013

A*	Mozzetta Dena †	262	housewife	36	"
B	Consolo Mary †	262	"	26	"
C	Consolo Phillip	262	baker	27	"
D*	Cianfrocca Assunta †	262	housewife	44	"
E*	Cianfrocca Emilio	262	tailor	51	"
F	Cianfrocca Gilda †	262	dressmaker	21	"
G	Cianfrocca Joseph	262	laborer	23	"
H	Jones Lillian †	264	at home	53	"
K	Jones Thomas	264	chauffeur	55	"
L	Cashman Catherine †	266	shoeworker	29	"
M	Cashman Michael	266	seaman	30	"
N	Cashman Michael J	266	electrician	58	"
O	Cashman Richard J	266	U S A	28	"
P	Downing Rita L †	266	housewife	28	"
R	Gilbrook Marion †	268	"	23	"
S	Gilbrook Ralph	268	U S N	24	"
T	Lauber William	268	laborer	48	"
U	Butler Lillian †	270	clerk	54	"
V	Butler Mary F †	270	at home	60	"
W	Favale Giuseppe	272	carpenter	60	"
X	Favale Joseph V	272	plumber	21	"
Y	Favale Rosina †	272	housewife	48	"
Z	LoConte John	272	chauffeur	34	"

1014

A	LoConte Lena †	272	housewife	34	"
B*	Consolo Fedela †	272	"	48	"
C*	Consolo Joseph	272	barber	53	"
D	DePerri Richard	274	U S A	24	"
E	DeFerri Rosalie †	274	housewife	22	"
F	Sciortino Rosina †	274	housekeeper	43	"
G	Sciortino Joseph, jr	274	waiter	29	"
H	Sciortino Mary †	274	housewife	26	"

Page	Letter	FULL NAME.	Residence, Jan. 1, 1943.	Occupation.	Supposed Age	Reported Residence, Jan. 1, 1942. Street and Number.

East Eagle Street—Continued

K	DeFeo John	274	U S C G	21	91 Condor
L	DeFeo Vincenza †	274	clerk	20	91 "
M	Sciortino Christine †	274	housewife	45	here
N	Sciortino Gaetano	274	waiter	55	"
O	Sciortino Giuseppe	274	retired	73	"
P	Spencer Joseph E	278	leatherworker	29	"
R	Spencer Martha †	278	housewife	27	"
S	Buttiglieri Millie †	278	"	35	106 Paris
T	Buttiglieri Rocco	278	machinist	40	106 "
U	Melchionda Josephine †	278	housewife	25	here
V	Melchionda Michael	278	welder	29	"
W	Sampson Dorothy †	280	housewife	31	"
X	Sampson William	280	fisherman	33	"
Y	Canha Frank	280	laborer	48	"
Z	Canha Mary †	280	housewife	45	"
	1015				
A	Manfredonia Grace †	280	"	29	"
B	Manfredonia Ralph	280	machinist	31	"
C	Magner Emily F †	291	housewife	52	"
D	Magner John	291	tel worker	52	"
E	*Elo John	291	retired	53	"
F	*Elo Rosa †	291	housewife	50	"
G	McCormack Allen J	291	retired	76	"
H	McCormack Flora †	291	housewife	67	"
K	McCormack Sarah †	291	candyworker	38	"
L	DeAnglis Margaret †	297	housewife	34	"
M	Quilty Evelyn †	297	"	29	"
N	Quilty George	297	machinist	30	"
O	Beech Jabez	297	retired	65	"
P	*Crowell Susan †	297	housekeeper	59	"
R	Boyle Patrick J	301	laborer	35	"
S	Sodergren Anna †	303	housewife	58	"
T	Sodergren Catherine †	303	"	35	"
U	Sodergren Henry E	303	shipfitter	37	"
V	Sodergren John	303	retired	65	"
W	Mahoney Ann J †	305	housewife	71	"
X	Mahoney Michael F	305	retired	69	"
Y	Morgner Francis	305	U S N	30	Winthrop
Z	Morgner Rita †	305	housewife	28	"
	1016				
A	*Grandi Ernestina †	307	"	41	here

10

East Eagle Street (Continued)

B	Grandi Ralph	307	engineer	47	here
C	Scuppituoli Carmen	309	laborer	40	"
D	Scuppituoli Josephine †	309	housewife	34	"
E	*Uva Theresa †	309	housekeeper	53	"
L	Day Winfield S	315	machinist	61	Connecticut
M	Simonson Cecelia †	315	housekeeper	68	here
N	Doren Elizabeth R †	317	housewife	41	"
O	Doren William J	317	laborer	52	"
P	McGlinchey Catherine †	317	housewife	70	"
R	McGlinchey William F	317	machinist	36	"

Falcon Street

T	Goodwin George G	84	U S A	25	203 Condor
U	Goodwin Irene †	84	saleswoman	22	here
V	Hayden Charles F	84	machinist	55	"
W	Hayden Clifford W	84	U S A	25	"
X	Hayden John F	84	"	29	"
Y	Hayden Lillian †	84	housewife	57	"
Z	Ewing Edna †	84	"	48	"

1017

A	Ewing Keith R	84	U S N	23	"
B	Ewing Robert P	84	engineer	50	"
C	Meuse Ruben	84	fireman	72	"
D	Korsvak Hans	86	engineer	55	"
E	Korsvak Ludvik	86	metalworker	53	Connecticut
F	Korsvak Signe †	86	housewife	52	here
G	Midgett Cecil A	86A	machinist	53	"
H	Midgett Gladys B †	86A	housewife	48	"
K	Midgett John R	86A	U S N	20	"
L	*Catone Clara †	88	housewife	45	"
M	Catone Elda †	88	stitcher	23	"
N	Catone Gaetano	88	laborer	55	"
O	Catone Gaetano, jr	88	U S A	21	"
P	Catone Michael	88	"	27	"
R	Catone Orlando	88	"	22	"
S	*Fraytis Frank S	88A	candymaker	56	"
T	Knox Albert C	88A	printer	47	"
U	Knox Margaret C †	88A	housewife	45	"
V	Knox Margaret F †	88A	operator	24	"
W	*Garcia Evelyn N †	90	housewife	48	"

11

Page	Letter	Full Name	Residence, Jan. 1, 1943.	Occupation.	Supposed Age.	Reported Residence, Jan. 1, 1942. Street and Number.

Falcon Street Continued

	X	Garcia John W	90	electrician	43	here
	Y	Nelson Francis	90½	U S A	28	"
	Z	Nelson John	90½	"	24	"
1018						
	A	Nelson Joseph A	90½	B F D	55	"
	B	Nelson Margaret †	90½	nurse	20	"
	C	Nelson Mary †	90½	housewife	55	"
	D	Moraitopoulos George	92	waiter	49	"
	E	Moraitopoulos Lavonia †	92	housewife	40	"
	F	Whitman Margaret †	92	at home	62	"
	K*	DeMeo Florence †	92A	"	61	"
	G	Fringuelli Arpino	92A	barber	30	"
	H	Fringuelli Mary †	92A	housewife	26	"
	L	Smith Enos C	94	machinist	42	"
	M	Smith Lelia †	94	housewife	39	"
	N	Hollohan Michael	94	machinist	48	"
	O	Hollohan Monica †	94	housewife	42	"
	P	Connell Dennis	96	checker	46	"
	R	Connell Sarah †	96	housewife	28	"
	S	Snowden Clarence M	96	watchman	64	"
	T	Dotoli Louise A †	96	cashier	44	"
	U	Dotoli Ralph W	96	engineer	43	"
	V	Richards John J	96	U S N	20	"
	W	Riley Marjorie M †	98	at home	22	"
	X	Riley Mary C †	98	stenographer	20	"
	Y	Riley Thomas J	98	clerk	53	"
	Z	Crowley Gertrude G †	98	packer	44	"
1019						
	A	Crowley Gertrude G †	98	stenographer	23	"
	B	Crowley John J	98	U S A	25	"
	C	White William H	98	drawtender	53	"
	D	Allen Dorothy †	102	clerk	25	"
	E	Fariole Alfred	104	laborer	35	"
	F	Fariole Louise †	104	housewife	39	"
	G	Sozio Carl	104	machinist	30	"
	H	Sozio Santa †	104	housewife	28	"
	K	Manganiello Catherine †	104	at home	21	"
	L*	Sozio Anna †	104	housewife	59	"
	M	Sozio Jerry	104	candymaker	62	"
	N	Bonner Joseph W	106	laborer	39	"
	O	Bonner Joseph W, jr	106	U S A	21	"

12

Falcon Street Continued

P	Bonner Louise †	106	housewife	44	here
R	Possehl Fred W	108	machinist	49	"
S	Possehl Vivian E †	108	housewife	43	"
T	Possehl William F	108	U S A	22	"
U	Rogers William E	108	chef	65	"
V	DeChico Angelo †	112	patternmaker	55	"
W	Mattson Gertrude E †	112	housewife	37	"
X	Mattson John P	112	patternmaker	41	"
Y	Mattson Mary M †	112	at home	62	"
Z	*Goglia Julian	112	candymaker	50	"

1020

A	Goglia Louise †	112	housewife	49	"
B	Marino Augustine	112	U S C G	23	"
C	Marino Josephine †	112	stitcher	26	"
D	Marino Nicholas	112	welder	21	"
E	Marino Rose †	112	at home	31	"
F	Gioiosa Domenic	114	laborer	50	"
G	Gioiosa Maria— †	114	housewife	45	"
H	McKenzie Collin	114	carpenter	57	"
K	McKenzie Susan †	114	housewife	54	"
L	Joy Anne— †	114	"	60	"
M	Joy William	114	machinist	63	"
N	Amodeo Emelia †	116	housewife	55	"
O	Amodeo Miranda †	116	clerk	29	"
P	Amodeo Nicholas	116	barber	55	"
R	Colarossi Nicholas	116	letter carrier	45	"
S	*Colarossi Vanda †	116	housewife	44	"
T	Occhipinti Alba †	116	at home	24	"
U	*Occhipinti Joseph	116	carpenter	58	"
V	*Occhipinti Mildred †	116	housewife	54	"
W	Galia Anna †	118	"	37	"
X	Galia Frank	118	laborer	48	"
Y	Ciliberto Anthony	118	driller	30	93 Webster
Z	Ciliberto Frank	118	U S A	21	93 "

1021

A	Ciliberto Frederick	118	"	23	93 "
B	Ciliberto Henrietta †	118	at home	37	93 "
C	Cupiraggi James	118	barber	56	93 "
D	Sinopoli Jerry	118	shipworker	46	93 "
E	Gaffney Mildred M †	120	clerk	25	here
F	Gaffney Robert A	120	U S A	30	"

Falcon Street — Continued

	Letter	FULL NAME	Residence	Occupation	Age	Reported Residence
	G	Hudson Jack M	120	U S A	44	here
	H	Hudson Lillian †	120	housewife	48	"
	K	Melling Margaret L †	120	clerk	32	"
	L	Cruise William A	120	retired	73	"
	M	Miller Ellen J †	120	at home	72	"
	N	Miller Gladys K †	120	clerk	33	"
	O	Barrett Benjamin F	122	seaman	32	9 Decatur
	P	Barrett Helen E †	122	housewife	27	9 "
	R	Ferris Doris N †	122	clerk	21	here
	S	Ferris Hugh	122	welder	30	"
	T	Ferris Nellie †	122	at home	59	"
	U	Tedeschi Gaetano	124	carpenter	29	"
	V	Tedeschi Helen †	124	housewife	26	"
	W	Marasca Albert	124	machinist	27	"
	X	Marasca Marie †	124	housewife	22	"
	Y	Parilla Anthony	124	shoeworker	37	"
	Z	Parilla Emily †	124	housewife	34	"

1022

	Letter	FULL NAME	Residence	Occupation	Age	Reported Residence
	A	*Brazzo Charles	126	ironworker	45	205 Marion
	B	*Brazzo Fannie †	126	housewife	35	205 "
	C	*Banks Esmeralda †	126	"	39	123 Eutaw
	D	*Banks James	126	fishcutter	40	123 "
	D	Boudreau Edward	128	shipfitter	32	141 Trenton
	E	Boudreau Hattie †	128	housewife	31	141 "
	F	Todd John W	128	fishcutter	60	here
	G	Todd Mary †	128	housewife	55	"
	H	Costa Domenic	128	U S N	21	"
	K	Costa Joseph	128	cutter	56	"
	L	Costa Martha †	128	housewife	46	"
	M	Costa Nicholas	128	U S N	29	"
	N	Murphy Mary E †	130	housewife	54	65 Neptune rd
	O	Murphy Michael	130	laborer	58	65 "
	P	Murphy Rita M †	130	inspector	22	65 "
	R	Caristo Mary D †	130	housewife	37	here
	S	Caristo Salvatore	130	shoeworker	40	"
	T	Keating Ruth †	134	at home	25	"
	U	Breen Andrew J	134	clerk	32	"
	V	Breen Hilda J †	134	housewife	34	"
	W	Butler Philip H	136	packer	50	Winthrop
	X	Butler Raymond	136	U S N	21	"
	Y	Folger Ethel M †	136	at home	60	here

14

Page.	Letter	Full Name.	Residence Jan. 1, 1943.	Occupation.	Supposed Age	Reported Residence Jan. 1, 1942. Street and Number.

Falcon Street Continued

	z	Folger Gladys C †	136	at home	50	here
1023						
	A	Folger Edmund A	136	clerk	66	"
	B	Folger Esther M †	136	housewife	52	"
	C	Sturrock Doris †	137	"	24	"
	D*	Sturrock Peter	137	machinist	24	"
	E	Baxter Mary †	137	at home	79	"
	F	Sciortino Elizabeth †	137	housewife	42	"
	G	Sciortino Guy	137	rubberworker	44	"
	H	Daisy Clara †	138	forewoman	53	"
	K	Bostrom Walter N	138	brazier	22	321 Border
	L	Anderson Annie †	139	housewife	32	here
	M	Anderson Arthur	139	letter carrier	41	"
	N	Anderson Alfred	139	retired	77	"
	O	Anderson Alfred H	139	packer	32	"
	P*	McLaughlin Charles	140	laborer	63	"
	R*	McLaughlin Evelyn †	140	housewife	59	"
	S	McInnis John J	140	electrician	32	"
	T	McInnis Mary L †	140	housewife	31	"
	U	Bentilla Hilda †	140	"	53	"
	V	Bentilla Isaac	140	boilermaker	56	"
	W	Reekast August	140	laborer	47	"
	X	Reekast Grace L †	140	housewife	47	"
	Y	Bielaksewicz Anthony	141	laborer	29	"
	Z	Bielaksewicz Helen †	141	housewife	25	"
1024						
	A	Anderson Ellen V †	141	"	53	"
	B	Anderson John N	141	laborer	54	"
	C	Driver George R	142	pressman	32	"
	D	Driver Sylvia H †	142	housewife	27	"
	E	Houlihan Edna †	142	"	34	"
	F	Houlihan Thomas J	142	pilot	42	"
	G	Heino Impi M †	142	at home	47	"
	H	Lynch Martha †	142	saleswoman	24	"
	K	Marks Arthur S	143	machinist	34	"
	L	Marks Frances O †	143	matron	61	"
	M	Teevens Eugene F	144	salesman	45	"
	N	Teevens Margaret L †	144	housewife	42	"
	O	Mangin Ernest	144	manager	50	"
	P	Mangin Mary †	144	housewife	51	"
	R	Moore Albert	144	salesman	32	"

Falcon Street—Continued

s	Moore Veronica †	144	at home	22	here	
t	Hartman Eliza †	145	housewife	54	755 Saratoga	
u	Hartman James F	145	proprietor	71	755 "	
v	Powell Ardelia †	145	at home	86	755 "	
w	Smithson Samuel	145	clerk	57	755 "	
x	*Bielakiewicz Mary †	145	housewife	52	here	
y	*Bielakiewicz Stanley	145	painter	59	"	
z	*Elixson Gusti	145	carpenter	60	"	

1025

A	*Elixson Mandy †	145	housewife	54	"	
B	Hope Margaret †	146	"	63	"	
C	Hope Walter J	146	painter	64	"	
D	*Ivany Althea †	146	housewife	58	"	
E	Ivany Gladys †	146	clerk	20	"	
F	Ivany Harry	146	builder	58	"	
G	Ivany Jessie †	146	packer	25	"	
H	Murphy Maurice	148	clerk	39	"	
K	Murphy Mildred †	148	housekeeper	40	"	
L	Stanton William	148	laborer	55	"	
M	Maguire John	148	"	66	"	
N	Maguire Susan †	148	housewife	56	"	
O	Mastrogiovani Carmen	149	laborer	65	"	
P	Mastrogiovani Margaret †	149	housewife	58	"	
R	McAdams Charles	150	metalworker	40	"	
S	McAdams Elizabeth †	150	housewife	35	"	
T	McAdams Emma †	150	at home	78	"	
U	McAdams Thomas	150	dairyman	38	"	
V	*Vrankin Impie †	151	housewife	52	"	
W	*Vrankin John F	151	chef	50	"	
X	Loconte Ellen †	152	clerk	22	"	
Y	Loconte Luigi	152	laborer	50	"	
Z	Loconte Mary †	152	clerk	26	"	

1026

A	Loconte Philomena †	152	housewife	45	"	
B	Tarentino Ambrose	152	carpenter	29	116 Falcon	
C	Tarentino Ida †	152	housewife	28	116 "	
D	Balboni William F	153	laborer	41	here	
E	Lopez Evelyn †	153	housewife	22	"	
F	Lopez Thomas R	153	fireman	25	"	
G	Iacoviello Marie †	153	housewife	33	"	
H	Iacoviello Nicholas	153	laborer	38	"	

16

Falcon Street Continued

K *O'Brien Catherine †	154	housewife	56	147A Trenton
L O'Brien Catherine †	154	waitress	24	147A "
M O'Brien Mary †	154	"	23	147A "
N *O'Brien Michael J	154	fisherman	57	147A "
O O'Brien Thomas	154	U S A	21	147A "
P O'Brien William	154	"	21	147A "
R Brennan Lawrence	154	fireman	42	here
S *Brennan Ragnhild †	154	housewife	44	"
T Laurano Felicia †	154	clerk	36	"
U Sannella Ralph	154	laborer	53	"
V Sannella Thomassa †	154	housewife	39	"
W Jedrey Elias H	156	pilot	48	41 Saratoga
X McClellan Rosena †	156	waitress	40	41 "
Y Clifford Mazie †	156	housekeeper	33	here
Z Clifford Warren J	156	U S A	21	"
1027				
A Bowie Samuel	156	plumber	56	"
B McWilliams Richard	156	laborer	43	"
C Giles George	158	machinist	45	"
D Giles Margaret †	158	housewife	43	"
E Denetolis Carmela †	158	"	35	"
F Denetolis Nicholas	158	plumber	38	"
G Bithell Evelyn †	159	housewife	35	"
H Bithell William	159	plasterer	46	"
K Bithell William G	159	machinist	32	"
L O'Brien John F	160	"	21	Watertown
M O'Brien Ruth I †	160	housewife	21	"
R McGray Avard	160	seaman	27	here
N McGray Mary L †	160	housewife	27	"
O O'Brien Edward J	160	guard	49	"
P O'Brien James F	160	retired	65	"
S Trahan Anna †	162	housewife	29	"
T Trahan Clarence	162	seaman	31	"
U DelSardo Anna †	163	at home	25	"
V *DelSardo Antonio	163	retired	65	"
W *DelSardo Jelsomina †	163	housewife	58	"
X DelSardo Josephine †	163	candyworker	23	"
Y *Roderiques Antonio	163A	deckhand	39	"
Z *Roderiques Mary †	163A	housewife	33	"
1028				
A *Lopes Jean †	163A	"	49	"

Falcon Street — Continued

B	Hancock George E	164	chauffeur	37	here
C	Hancock Helen—†	164	housewife	35	"
D	Keller Catherine—†	164	clerk	30	"
E	Keller Eugene	164	U S N	34	"
F	Perry Elizabeth †	166	housewife	60	58 Marion
G	Perry Oliver	166	mechanic	68	here
H	*D'Amico Nunziata—†	167	housewife	60	"
K	*D'Amico Sebastiano	167	retired	66	"
L	D'Amico Angie—†	167A	housewife	33	"
M	D'Amico Charles	167A	metalworker	34	"
N	Masciulli Josephine—†	167A	housewife	37	"
O	Masciulli Nunzio	167A	laborer	31	"
P	Banks John	168	U S A	21	324 Border
R	Banks Virginia—†	168	waitress	20	here
S	Hammond Lottie—†	168	housekeeper	55	"
T	Perry Bessie—†	168	housewife	38	"
U	*Hudson Elizabeth A—†	170	"	67	"
V	*Hudson William P	170	rigger	70	"
W	Deon Adelbert	171	inspector	36	"
X	*Deon Lora—†	171	housewife	37	"
Y	Cole Florence †	171A	"	26	"
Z	Cole John	171A	clerk	30	"

1029

A	Joyce Stewart	171A	rigger	70	"
B	Page Helen—†	171A	at home	47	"
C	Hamilton Charlotte †	171A	"	22	"
D	Harney Edward	171A	painter	45	"
E	Harney Edward	171A	U S A	24	"
F	Harney Elizabeth †	171A	housewife	44	"
G	Gallagher Irene—†	172	"	34	"
H	Gallagher James F	172	ironworker	32	"
K	Gallagher John A	172	guard	35	"
L	Gallagher Margaret †	172	at home	69	"
M	Gallagher Rita C †	172	housewife	30	"
N	Lewis Herbert H	174	retired	48	"
O	Lewis Margaret S †	174	housekeeper	79	"
P	Walker George V	174	U S N	23	"
R	Walker Harry B	174	bricklayer	52	"
S	Walker Ida A †	174	housewife	52	"
U	D'Entremont Arthur	175	seaman	40	"
T	D'Entremont Mildred †	175	forewoman	38	"

18

Falcon Street Continued

v	McCusker Catherine †	175A	at home	70	here
w	Murphy Marie †	175A	clerk	21	"
x	Murphy Wilhelmina †	175A	at home	40	"
y	Faria Mary †	175A	housewife	31	"
z	Faria Stephen	175A	engineer	32	"

1030

A	Williams Anna P †	176	housewife	44	"
B	Williams Charles	176	fireman	49	"
C	Williams Charles, jr	176	student	20	"
D	DeGregorio Anthony	178	fireman	49	"
E	DeGregorio Dorothea †	178	secretary	20	"
F	DeGregorio Mary E †	178	housewife	39	"
G	Stapleton Nellie †	180	"	62	"
H	Whitman Agnes †	180	"	39	"
K	Whitman Ernest	180	pile driver	42	"
L	Santos Carmelita †	182	housewife	50	"
M*	Santos Joseph	182	laborer	51	"
N	Rose Domenica †	182	housewife	41	"
O	Rose Frank	182	boilermaker	40	"
P	Conway Emily †	188	housewife	21	Somerville
R	Conway Frederick	188	pipefitter	24	"
S	DeNuccio Francis	188	U S A	26	75 Byron
T	DeNuccio Violanda †	188	packer	20	75 "
U	Nickinello Anthony	188	pipefitter	27	here
V	Nickinello Mary †	188	housewife	26	"
W	Ciampi Catherine †	188	"	26	91 Putnam
X	Ciampi Charles	188	chauffeur	29	91 "
Y	Bergh Alice †	191	housewife	28	here
Z	Bergh Herbert	191	welder	30	"

1031

A	Tammick Agnes †	191	factoryhand	23	"
B	Dove Lempi	191	housewife	39	"
C	Dove Matti	191	ironworker	52	"
E*	Edison Dorothy †	192	housewife	37	144 Princeton
F	Edison Thomas	192	chauffeur	40	144 "
G	Aitken Alice G †	192	housewife	44	139 Condor
H	Aitken William B	192	chauffeur	43	139 "
K	Keating Dorothy M †	194	factoryhand	23	here
L	Keating Thomas W	194	clerk	25	134 Falcon
M	McLaughlin Charles M	194	shipper	50	here
N	McLaughlin Louise M †	194	housewife	46	"

19

Falcon Street Continued

o	Enos Eleanor †	194	factoryhand	20	here	
p	Enos Mario	194	"	53	"	
R	Enos Virginia †	194	housewife	42	"	
s	O'Hanley Cyril	194	welder	30	160 Falcon	
T	O'Hanley Margaret †	194	housewife	31	160 "	
U	Boyle Mary A †	195	"	69	here	
v	Thornton George D	196	clerk	43	"	
w	Thornton Margaret †	196	housewife	40	"	
x	Muldoon Edward	196	machinist	27	"	
y	Muldoon Joseph	196	U S A	29	"	
z	Muldoon Lawrence	196	"	31	"	

1032

A	Muldoon Mary †	196	housewife	52	"	
B	Sullivan Catherine †	196	waitress	42	"	
c	Curtin John	197	longshoreman	58	"	
D	Driscoll Florence †	197	laborer	63	"	
E	Driscoll Mary †	197	housewife	59	"	
F	Thibodeau Edith †	198	"	44	"	
G	Thibodeau Joseph W	198	carpenter	46	"	
H	Thibodeau Warren	198	draftsman	21		
K	Healy Doris †	198	stenographer	20	205 E Eagle	
L	Healy Laura †	198	housewife	47	205 "	
M	Healy Lawrence	198	U S A	22	205 "	
N	Healy Matthew	198	rigger	52	205 "	
o	Leonard Catherine †	199	housewife	42	here	
p	Leonard John	199	inspector	52	"	
R	McCarthy Margaret †	199	packer	30	"	
T	Magnanelli Marie †	200	clerk	27	"	
U	Magnanelli Peter	200	retired	78	"	
v	McDonald Annie †	201	operator	22	"	
w	McDonald Duncan	201	motorman	42	"	
x	McDonald Margaret A †	201	housewife	38	"	
y	Keleher Albert F	202	printer	27	"	
z	Keleher Marie †	202	housewife	23		

1033

A	Keleher Edwin M	202	electrician	33	"	
B	Keleher Lawrence M	202	seaman	39	"	
c	Keleher Susan †	202	housewife	68	"	
D	McCabe Francis P	202	janitor	35	"	
E	McCabe Loretta C †	202	housewife	35	"	
F	*Gillis William	203	packer	20	300 Princeton	

20

Falcon Street Continued

G	Tinao Helen †	203	housewife	28	here
H	Tinao John	203	shipper	32	"
L	Powell Clarence E	204	electrician	34	"
M	Powell Mary E †	205	housewife	32	"
N	O'Brien Catherine L †	205	"	39	"
O	O'Brien John J	205	policeman	42	"
P	Gould Arthur H	206	storekeeper	74	"
R	Gould Edith L †	206	housewife	60	"
S	Tobe Esther †	206	"	58	"
T	Tobe Lydia †	206	secretary	23	"
U	Tobe Samuel	206	caretaker	58	"
V	Bryan Doris †	206	housewife	20	"
W	Bryan Garvis	206	U S N	25	"
X	Olsen Margaret †	206	housewife	61	"
Y	Olsen Ole	206	watchman	60	"
Z	Ahern Marie B †	207	housewife	47	"

1034

A	Ahern William H	207	letter carrier	58	"
B	Healy Mary E †	207	at home	80	"

Glendon Street

C	Foster Clarence W	6	engineer	58	here
D	Smith Bertha †	6	housekeeper	51	"
E	Smith Mary †	6	at home	82	"
F	DeSanctis Emma †	6	housewife	22	230 E Eagle
G	DeSanctis Joseph	6	cutter	25	230 "
H	O'Keefe Mary †	6	housewife	65	here
K	O'Keefe Mary L †	6	bookbinder	29	"
L	Preston Michael J	6	laborer	35	"
M	Cohan Virginia R †	24	housewife	26	"
N	Cohan William M	24	welder	26	"
O	Cohan Margaret †	24	housewife	52	"
P	Cohan Maurice	24	foreman	52	"
R	Flannigan John	24	clerk	45	456 Bennington
S	Boczkowski Lydia †	28	secretary	25	here
T	Boczkowski Marie †	28	housewife	53	"
U	Boczkowski Stanley	28	machinist	58	"
V	Kearney James	28	molder	51	"
W	Kearney Josephine †	28	housewife	47	"

21

Page.	Letter.	FULL NAME.	Residence, Jan. 1, 1943.	Occupation.	Supposed Age.	Reported Residence, Jan. 1, 1942. Street and Number.

Lexington Square

X	O'Neil Catherine †	1	housewife	55	here
Y	O'Neil Daniel J	1	clerk	63	"
Z	O'Neil Pauline †	1	secretary	24	"

1035

A	O'Neil Robert E	1	student	21	"
B	Walker Henry W	2	U S N	27	Everett
C	Walker Martha L †	2	housewife	22	"
D	Wagner Albert F	2	policeman	45	109 Princeton

Lexington Street

E	O'Brien Ella M †	198	housewife	47	222 Lexington
F	O'Brien Jeremiah	198	fisherman	47	222 "
H	DeFelice Guy	200	laborer	32	here
K	DeFelice Margaret †	200	housewife	28	"
L	*Belmonte Agatina †	200	"	50	"
M	Belmonte Crecenzio	200	U S A	22	"
N	Belmonte Frank	200	shoemaker	49	"
O	Caprio Frances †	200	housewife	24	74 Chelsea
P	Caprio John A, jr	200	mechanic	24	74 "
R	Ellis Edith V †	202	housekeeper	43	here
S	Ellis John J, jr	202	U S A	23	"
T	Melanson Mary †	202	housewife	32	"
U	*Melanson William	202	machinist	41	"
V	McManus Alice †	202	housewife	62	"
W	McManus Alice †	202	operator	20	"
X	McManus Thomas	202	warehouseman	65	"
Y	Sheehan Francis	202	U S A	28	"
Z	Thibeau Lena †	204	housekeeper	68	218 Brooks

1036

A	Manning Charles	204	U S A	35	here
B	Manning Isabel †	204	housewife	48	"
C	Forti Paul	204	painter	34	"
D	Forti Theresa †	204	housewife	22	"
E	Rudd Matilda †	206	housekeeper	71	"
F	Bowen Martha †	206	"	65	"
G	Scott John	206	laborer	67	"
H	*Perrullo Louis	208	"	52	"
K	*Perrullo Mary †	208	housewife	48	"
L	Hickey Charles F	208	chauffeur	60	"
M	Hickey George B	208	machinist	22	"

22

Lexington Street Continued

N	Hickey Mary †	208	housewife	60	here
O	Scapetta Angelina †	208	clerk	20	"
P	Scapetta Antonio	208	laborer	25	"
R	*Scapetta Michael	208	retired	63	"
S	*Scapetta Saveria †	208	housewife	55	"
T	*Amirault Augustine	210	U S A	38	"
U	*Amirault Gertrude †	210	housewife	40	"
V	*Amirault Rose †	210	housekeeper	68	"
W	Amirault William	210	machinist	43	"
X	Alves George H	210	leatherworker	74	"
Y	Alves Sarah R †	210	housewife	74	"
Z	O'Brien Joseph	210	busboy	33	198 Lexington
	1037					
A	O'Brien Mabel	210	housewife	31	198 "
B	Scharaffa Elvira †	212	"	23	here
C	Scharaffa Frank	212	machinist	23	"
D	Corvi Eduino	212	cabinetmaker	64	"
E	Corvi Emma †	212	dressmaker	26	"
F	Corvi Iris †	212	"	29	"
G	Corvi Ivano	212	U S A	25	"
H	Corvi Madaline †	212	housewife	55	"
K	Kaplan Anna †	218	"	45	"
L	Kaplan Harry	218	storekeeper	48	"
M	McCarthy Dorothy †	218	clerk	22	"
N	McCarthy Sarah F †	218	housewife	60	"
O	Haberlin James	218	machinist	23	"
P	Haberlin John T	218	sexton	57	"
R	Haberlin Rita J †	218	housekeeper	25	"
S	Marino Antonio	220	painter	29	"
T	Marino Augustina †	220	housewife	25	"
U	Tosto Celia †	220	"	40	"
V	Tosto Martin	220	machinist	43	"
W	Daddario Emilia †	220	housekeeper	24	"
X	Daddario Matthew	220	machinist	23	"
Y	Daddario Nicholas	220	"	50	"
Z	Rondilone Lucy †	220	housewife	48	"
	1038					
A	Rondilone Savino	220	laborer	48	"
B	Lightbody John E	222	engineer	31	86 Lexington
C	Lightbody Rosanna E †	222	housewife	36	86 "
D	Capasi Eugene	222	laborer	11	86 "

23

Lexington Street—Continued

E	Capasi Rose †	222	housewife	34	86 Lexington
F	Juliano Carlo	222	picture framer	30	here
G*	Juliano Concetta †	222	housewife	54	"
H*	Juliano Joseph	222	laborer	63	"
K	Juliano Salvatore	222	U S N	21	"
L	Forti Cecelia †	224	housewife	26	190 Benningt'n
M	Forti Ottavio	224	salesman	27	190 "
N	Lopilato Anthony	224	laborer	30	here
O	Lopilato Mary G †	224	housewife	30	"
P	Silver Israel	224	U S C G	28	"
R	Silver Jessie †	224	nurse	22	"
S	Silver Mollie †	224	housekeeper	49	"
T	Banks Elsie †	226	housewife	48	172 Border
U	Banks Oran	226	watchman	58	172 "
V	Hancock Anna †	226	housewife	34	here
W	Hancock Ruben	226	boilermaker	36	"
X	Young Margaret †	226	housewife	43	346 Saratoga
Y	Young Stanley P	226	janitor	56	346 "
Z	McIntyre Wilfred	226	laborer	45	346 "

1039

A	Young Elizabeth †	226	millhand	20	346 "
B	Young Wilfred	226	U S A	22	346 "
D*	Doucette Clarise † rear	228	housewife	62	here
E	Doucette Clifford "	228	metalworker	37	"
F	Doucette Lucy † "	228	housewife	28	"
G	Lombardi Helen †	230	"	21	"
H	Lombardi Henry, jr	230	machinist	25	"
K	Pray Delia †	230	housewife	68	"
L	Pray Frank	230	retired	76	"
N	Denicola Anna †	232	housewife	42	"
O	Denicola Clementina †	232	candyworker	21	"
P	Denicola Louis	232	laborer	45	"
R	Denicola Mary C †	232	candymaker	24	"
S	Sequeira Benedetta †	232	housewife	23	191 Marion
T	Sequeira Emilio	232	welder	25	191 "
V	Donaruma Benjamin	234	laborer	48	here
W	Donaruma Ralph	234	musician	20	"
X	Donaruma Victoria †	234	housewife	30	"
Y	Carlson Natale †	234	"	27	"
Z	Carlson Walter	234	brazier	29	"

1040
Lexington Street Continued

A	*Fulchino Antonio	236	shoeworker	49	here
B	*Fulchino Margaret †	236	housewife	41	"
C	Fulchino Oltino	236	U S A	21	"
D	Fulchino Rose †	236	boxmaker	20	"
E	Carbone Marion †	236	seamstress	26	"
F	*Carbone Rose †	236	housewife	48	"
G	Carbone Sabato	236	mason	53	"
H	Gasbaro Adeline †	236	housewife	27	"
K	Gasbaro Jesse	236	cook	30	"
L	Balange Matteo	238	mason	46	"
M	*Balange Theresa †	238	housewife	34	"
N	DeCosta Anna †	238	"	30	85 Green
O	DeCosta Mario	238	seaman	50	85 "
P	Curcio Anna †	240	housewife	43	here
R	Curcio Ettore	240	mechanic	39	"
S	Curcio Linda †	240	at home	27	"
T	White Fergus	240	boilermaker	55	"
U	White John	240	seaman	30	"
V	White Margaret †	240	housewife	26	"
W	Gannon Ellen †	240	"	56	"
X	Gannon Michael	240	laborer	57	"
Y	Keller Agnes E †	242	housewife	48	"
Z	Keller James B	242	carpenter	53	"

1041

B	Loring Benjamin	242	laborer	60	"
A	Loring Ethel †	242	housewife	40	"
C	Todisco Mario	244	chauffeur	30	Revere
D	Todisco Phyllis	244	housewife	26	"
E	DeMeo Domenic	244	U S A	26	here
F	DeMeo Frances †	244	housewife	31	"
G	DeMeo George	244	laborer	23	"
H	DeMeo Ralph	244	chauffeur	32	"
K	*DeMeo Rose †	244	housekeeper	62	"
M	Meuse Frank	246	laborer	30	"
L	Meuse Pauline †	246	housewife	26	"
N	Ventresca Antonio	246	salesman	30	"
O	Ventresca Dorothy †	246	clerk	24	"
P	*Ventresca Mary †	246	housewife	67	"
R	Ventresca Nellie †	246	seamstress	27	"

Page.	Letter.	FULL NAME.	Residence, Jan. 1, 1943.	Occupation.	Supposed Age.	Reported Residence, Jan. 1, 1942. Street and Number.

Lexington Street Continued

s*	Ventresca Philip	246	at home	71	here
U*	Miniscalco Anna †	250	housewife	46	"
V*	Miniscalco Vincent	250	laborer	62	"
W	Venuti Angela †	250	housewife	28	"
X	Venuti Stellario	250	printer	28	"
Y	Antonelli Anthony	250	manufacturer	35	"
Z	Antonelli Louise †	250	housewife	33	"

1042

B	McPhee Mary †	256	"	25	"
C	McPhee Robert	256	rigger	27	"
D	D'Allesandro Anna †	256	housewife	40	"
E	D'Allesandro Benjamin	256	tailor	45	"
F	Ferrara Margaret †	256	housewife	32	"
G	Ferrara Rocco	256	chauffeur	35	"
H	Costa Anthony	258	machinist	62	"
K	Costa Vincent	258	shoemaker	58	"
L	Capolupo Gloria †	258	housewife	20	"
M	Capolupo Michael	258	laborer	23	"
N	Pelusi John	260	U S A	21	"
O*	Pelusi Theresa †	260	housewife	39	"
P	Pelusi Torindo	260	tailor	42	"
R	Pelusi Anthony	260	shoeworker	46	"
S*	Pelusi Julia †	260	housewife	41	"
T	Lawrence Ernest	262	engineer	50	"
U	Lawrence Margaret †	262	housewife	48	"
V	Welch Alice L †	264	"	61	"
W	Welch John W	264	printer	59	"
X	Fitzgerald Ethel †	266	housewife	28	"
Y	Fitzgerald Herbert P	266	laborer	35	"
Z	LoChiatto Angelo	266	"	40	"

1043

A	LoChiatto Marie †	266	housewife	35	"
B	Bickford John H	266	laborer	51	"
C	Walters Amy †	266	housewife	57	"
D	Walters James	266	calker	70	"
E	Cullen Arthur B	270	U S A	25	"
F	Cullen Helen C †	270	housewife	23	"
G	McInnis Sadie †	270	cook	54	"
H	McPherson Mary E †	270	clerk	52	"
K	Melcher Florence E †	270	"	50	"
L	Deveau Fred	274	fishcutter	62	"

26

Lexington Street Continued

m	Deveau Grace †	274	nurse	40	here	
n	Shiras Bertha †	274	seamstress	24	"	
o	Shiras Daniel	274	baker	27	"	
p*	Shiras George	274	retired	67	"	
r*	Shiras Helen †	274	housewife	45	"	
s	Shiras Olga †	274	clerk	21	"	
t	Shiras Peter	274	U S A	23	"	
u	Shiras Socrates	274	"	24	"	
v	Gilbrook Ida M †	276	housewife	62	"	
w	Gilbrook Joseph W	276	inspector	59	"	
x	Earl Everett	276	retired	77	"	
y	Nickerson Cecelia †	276	housewife	21	"	
z	Roome Anne E †	276	"	48	"	

1044

a	Roome Everett G	276	U S A	22	"	
b	Roome Frank G	276	machinist	61	"	
c	Surette Dorothy †	278	housewife	33	"	
d	Surette James R	278	carpenter	36	"	
e	Baker Clarence T	278	watchman	58	"	
f	Baker Flora †	278	housewife	27	"	
g	McDonald Mary A †	278	secretary	43	"	
h	Hulke Lawrence E	280	U S A	20	122 Brooks	
k	Coulombe Albert	280	spinner	34	here	
l	Coulombe Eugene J	280	"	46	"	
m*	Coulombe Josephine †	280	operator	49	"	
n*	Coulombe Mary A †	280	at home	81	"	
o	Daimi Aino	280	ironworker	51	"	
p*	Daimi Hilda †	280	housewife	56	"	
r	Tiano Joseph	282	retired	68	"	
s	Tiano Maria †	282	housewife	66	"	
t	Felice Dorothy †	282	"	23	"	
u	Felice Frank	282	stockman	23	"	
v	Nunes Anna †	282	housewife	49	"	
w	Nunes Joseph	282	at home	49	"	
x	Nunes Joseph E	282	U S N	21	"	
y	Nunes Ruth †	282	operator	20	"	
z	Pellegrino Frances †	282	housewife	38	"	

1045

a	Pellegrino Joseph	282	bricklayer	38	"	
b	Bellino James M	282A	baker	30	"	
c	Bellino Laura †	282A	housewife	29	"	

Lexington Street — Continued

D	*LaRosa Jennie †	282A	housewife	45	here
E	LaRosa Joseph	282A	presser	47	"
F	Maranda Arthur A	282A	U S N	21	"
G	Maranda Rose M †	282A	housewife	21	"
H	Burke John J	282A	millhand	47	"
K	Burke Mary O †	282A	housewife	44	"
L	McCormack Ann R †	282A	packer	38	"
M	DeFeo Frank	284	shipper	21	"
N	DeFeo Fred	284	driller	47	"
O	Thornton Fred G	284	letter carrier	46	"
P	Thornton Helen G †	284	housekeeper	51	"
R	Abrahams Dorothy †	284	housewife	20	"
S	Gleason Edmund	284	chauffeur	43	"
T	Gleason Ina †	284	housewife	38	"
U	Trott Andrew	284	lumberman	34	"
V	Fiore Angelina †	286	housewife	52	"
W	Fiore Antonio	286	laborer	23	"
X	Fiore Carmella †	286	at home	24	"
Y	Carmella James	286	U S A	21	"
Z	Carmella Vincent	286	watchman	58	"

1046

A	Paiva Frank T	286	salesman	39	"
B	Paiva Mary †	286	housekeeper	76	"
C	Paiva Violet †	286	housewife	39	"
D	Ferriani Henry	286	assembler	25	"
E	*Ferriani Luigi	286	grinder	63	"
F	*Ferriani Mary †	286	housewife	55	"
G	Hanlon Albert	288	operator	52	"
H	Hanlon Albert A	288	U S A	25	"
K	Hanlon Mary †	288	housewife	51	"
L	Hanlon Mary V †	288	stenographer	23	"
M	Hanlon Paul C	288	U S M C	21	"
N	Dalton John	290	machinist	48	"
O	Flavin Susan †	292	housekeeper	48	"
P	Marmand Frank B	292	watchman	48	"
R	Marmand Frederick	292	retired	81	"
S	Marmand Marjorie R †	292	housewife	70	"
T	Costello Howard	294	clerk	27	"
U	Costello Rita †	294	housewife	28	"
V	Maylor Clyde †	294	chauffeur	35	"
W	O'Connor Hannah †	296	housekeeper	65	"

Lexington Street Continued

x	Hawes Maude †	296	housewife	32	here
y	Hawes William	296	guard	39	Connecticut
z	Muscatelli Felicia †	298	housewife	49	here

1047

A	Muscatelli Laura †	298	operator	25	"
B	Muscatelli Michael	298	laborer	53	"
C	Muscatelli Rita †	298	candyworker	20	"
D	Muscatelli Rose †	298	"	24	"
E	*Malloy Catherine †	300	housewife	31	28 Saratoga
F	*Malloy Rupert J	300	rigger	30	28 "
G	Ridge Anna— †	302	at home	21	here
H	Ridge Coleman T	302	seaman	30	"
K	Ridge John P	302	surveyor	22	"
L	Ridge Mary M— †	302	housewife	63	"
M	Ridge Michael J	302	U S N	25	"
N	Ridge Thomas A	302	laborer	72	"
O	Ridge Thomas F	302	U S N	27	"
P	Werner Elizabeth †	306	housewife	56	"
R	Werner John	306	laborer	66	"
S	Almeida Anthony J	306	sorter	53	"
T	Almeida Rhoda— †	306	housewife	47	"
U	Almeida Roderick J	306	clerk	27	"
V	McLeod John R	306	retired	79	"
W	Morrison Margaret †	306	housewife	35	"
X	Morrison Robert H	306	chipper	37	"

Prescott Street

z	Sheehan Catherine †	3	clerk	38	here

1048

A	Kennedy Catherine A †	3	housewife	49	"
B	Neal William	3	U S A	26	"
C	Regan Patrick	3	electrician	37	"
D	Cusenza Anna— †	5	housewife	26	"
E	Cusenza Joseph	5	pipefitter	38	"
F	Cappuccio Mario	5	student	22	"
G	Cappuccio Mary †	5	housewife	47	"
H	Velona Anna— †	5	shoeworker	28	"
L	*Dell'Aria Charles	6	"	44	"
M	*Dell'Aria Sadie †	6	housewife	45	"
N	Zuccala Anna †	6	"	37	"

Prescott Street — Continued

o	Zuccala Giacomo	6	mattressmaker	39	here
p	Wilcox Guy	6	assembler	61	"
R	Zimmer Albert W	6	machinist	28	"
s	Zimmer Lillian †	6	housewife	64	"
T	DiGirolamo Elena †	7	"	42	"
U	DiGirolamo Joseph	7	tilesetter	43	"
V	Gerome Stephen	7	U S A	20	"
W	Valenti Antonio	7	candymaker	52	"
X	Valenti George	7	"	21	"
Y	Valenti Helen †	7	operator	26	"
Z	Valenti Margarita †	7	housewife	46	"

1049

A	Valenti Teresa †	7	operator	30	"
B	Good Joseph	8	"	31	Somerville
C	Good Rose †	8	housewife	31	"
D	Luongo Alice †	8	"	30	here
E	Luongo Silvio	8	salesman	31	"
F	DeFrancisco Eleanor †	8	housewife	32	"
G	DeFrancisco Joseph	8	pedler	34	"
K	Garchinsky Joseph	10	machinist	25	"
L	Garchinsky Mary †	10	housewife	21	"
M	Silva Joseph	10	weaver	44	"
N	Silva Philomena †	10	housewife	31	"
O	Costigliola Josephine †	10	"	30	"
P	Costigliola Peter	10	pressman	32	"

Putnam Street

R	Frasier Mary E †	2	at home	72	here
S	Purcell Mary †	2	housewife	47	"
T	Purcell Thomas J	2	retired	53	"
U	Purcell Winifred †	2	operator	21	"
V *D'Entremont Catherine †		7	housewife	31	7 Falcon
W	D'Entremont Elmer C	7	machinist	33	7 "
X	Beard Curtis A	7	electrician	42	here
Y *Beard Verna F †		7	housewife	35	"
Z *Crowell Lottie E †		7	"	52	"

1050

A	Crowell Murray A	7	trimmer	54	"
B	Anderson Susan †	8	at home	70	220 Lexington
C	Ikka Kosti	8	laborer	52	Michigan

Putnam Street Continued

	D	Mastrogiovanni Anthony	10	foreman	30	here
	E	Mastrogiovanni Lena †	10	at home	28	"
	F	Adractas Elvira A †	10	operator	32	"
	G	Adractas George D	10	chef	43	"
	H	Alberghini Attilio	47	machinist	52	"
	K	Alberghini Mary †	47	housewife	50	"
	L	Zuccaro Frank	48	painter	34	"
	M	Zuccaro Rose †	48	housewife	32	"
	N	Gagnon Emma †	48	"	54	1055 Saratoga
	O	Gagnon Joseph	48	textileworker	58	1055 "
	P	Scala Edward	48	shoeworker	39	here
	R	Scala Inez –†	48	housewife	34	"
	T	Lopilato George	49	chauffeur	50	"
	U	Lopilato Lillian †	49	housewife	39	"
	V	*Vaccaro Charles	50	weaver	32	"
	W	Vaccaro Jennie †	50	housewife	26	"
	X	*DePaola Carmela †	50	at home	53	"
	Y	Olga Gabriel T	50	U S A	30	"
	Z	Asci Catherine †	50	housewife	32	"

1051

	A	Asci Ernest	50	laborer	36	"
	B	Brown Mary †	51	at home	49	"
	C	Sordillo Angelo	52	mechanic	29	"
	D	Sordillo Elizabeth †	52	housewife	27	"
	E	Romano Albert	52	rigger	26	"
	F	Romano Minnie †	52	housewife	27	"
	G	Blasi Concetta †	52	stitcher	22	"
	H	Blasi James	52	finisher	56	"
	K	*Blasi Jennie †	52	housewife	58	"
	L	Patterson Florence †	53	"	28	"
	M	Patterson Robert	53	repairman	30	48 Putnam
	N	George Aubrey	53	galvanizer	31	128 Princeton
	O	George Grace †	53	housewife	23	128 "
	P	McInnes Angus	53	electrician	70	here
	R	Patterson Catherine †	53	at home	62	"
	S	Patterson Jean †	53	mechanic	28	"
	T	McCormick Dorothy †	54	housewife	34	"
	U	McCormick Edward	54	carpenter	37	"
	V	Law Elizabeth †	54	housewife	32	"
	W	Law John	54	clerk	41	"
	X	Curcio Fannie †	54	housewife	40	192 Falcon

31

Page.	Letter.	FULL NAME.	Residence, Jan. 1, 1943	Occupation.	Supposed Age.	Reported Residence, Jan. 1, 1942. Street and Number.

Putnam Street Continued

	Y	Curcio John	54	tailor	46	192 Falcon
		1052				
	A	Sorrento Joseph	56	"	21	187 Brooks
	B	Sorrento Santina †	56	housewife	26	207 Lexington
	C	Rizzari Giacomo	56	tailor	49	here
	D	Rizzari Michelina †	56	housewife	38	"
	E	Silva Alice †	56	"	23	"
	F	Silva Richard	56	mechanic	25	"
	G	Barry Catherine †	58	at home	62	"
	H	Barry Gertrude †	58	technician	23	"
	K	Barry Josephine †	58	clerk	25	"
	L	Barry Mary †	58	"	30	"
	M	Barry Thomas	58	U S N	33	"
	N	Lidback George	60	custodian	42	"
	O	Lidback Isabel †	60	housewife	31	"
	P	Stamm Mary †	61	at home	59	"
	R	Chetwynd Ida †	61	cook	28	136 Falcon
	S*	Chetwynd Samuel	61	seaman	53	136 "
	T*	Goodwin Mildred †	61	domestic	42	136 "
	U	Burden Florence †	62	saleswoman	35	here
	V	Burke Catherine A †	62	at home	63	"
	W	Garrity Lillian †	63	"	68	"
	X	Garrity Thomas	63	laborer	44	"
	Y	Ryan James	63	retired	57	"
	Z	Doran Helen †	63	housewife	66	"
		1053				
	A	Doran William	63	locksmith	62	"
	C	DiFranza Louis	86	shipfitter	28	"
	D	DiFranza Virginia †	86	housewife	24	"
	E*	Falsini Amelia †	86	"	53	372 Lovell
	F	Falsini Louis	86	chef	55	372 "
	G	Falsini Arthur	86	painter	30	here
	H	Falsini Margaret †	86	housewife	27	"
	K	Beraldo John	88	butcher	21	"
	L*	DeMarco Angelina †	88	at home	61	"
	M	DeRosa Armando	88	bartender	30	"
	N*	DeGruttola Carmella †	88	at home	70	"
	O	DeGruttola Frank	88	bartender	34	"
	P	DeGruttola Joseph	88	U S A	37	"
	R	DeGruttola Matilda †	88	stitcher	23	"
	S	Colluccini John	88	U S N	20	"

Putnam Street Continued

	r	Colluccini Josephine †	88	packer	38	here
	u	Colluccini Pasquale	88	candymaker	48	"
	v	Kaeneman Mary L †	90	housewife	39	26 White
	w	Kaeneman Robert H	90	engineer	42	26 "
	x	Hurley Blanche †	92	housewife	37	here
	y	*Hurley Sylvester	92	laundryman	34	"

1054 Trenton Street

	a	Cipriano Elsie †	159	housewife	25	here
	b	Cipriano Joseph	159	machinist	28	"
	c	*Cipriano Mary †	159	housewife	67	"
	d	Joyce James P	159	longshoreman	53	"
	e	Joyce Josephine †	159	housewife	43	"
	f	Joyce William	159	U S A	24	"
	g	Petroni Dorothy †	159	housewife	23	"
	h	Petroni Lawrence	159	chauffeur	24	"
	k	*Fiorito Concetta †	161	housewife	72	"
	m	*Altobelli Carolina †	161	"	47	"
	n	Altobelli Natale	161	machinist	51	"
	o	Altobelli Primo	161	U S N	20	"
	p	Kavin Catherine †	163	housewife	62	34 O'Meara ct
	r	Kavin William J	163	chauffeur	33	34 "
	s	Campbell Alice †	163	librarian	30	here
	t	Campbell Joseph	163	operator	31	"
	u	Guerreiro Marie †	163	housewife	21	216 Bremen
	v	Guerreiro Nicholas	163	machinist	23	216 "
	w	Lombardi Henry	165	cutter	52	here
	x	Lombardi Margaret †	165	dressmaker	23	"
	y	*Lombardi Mary †	165	housewife	49	"
	z	Lombardi Sarah †	165	operator	29	"
1055						
	a	Busheme Anna †	165	housewife	27	299 Lexington
	b	Busheme Paul	165	bricklayer	29	299 "
	c	Lombardi Albert	165	cutter	26	here
	d	Lombardi Bessie †	165	housewife	24	"
	e	Anderson Edwin N	167	chauffeur	43	205 Florence
	f	Anderson Helen D †	167	housewife	38	205 "
	h	Connolly Michael	169	chauffeur	42	here
	k	Connolly Theresa †	169	housewife	37	"
	l	Viglione Adelaide †	169	tailoress	39	"

I 10   33

Trenton Street—Continued

	M*	Viglione Angelo	169	tailor	72	here
	N	Viglione Edmund	169	U S A	32	"
	O*	Viglione Julia—†	169	housewife	61	"
	P	Viglione Lillian—†	169	at home	34	"
	R	Potito Alfio	169	U S A	27	"
	S*	Potito Epifanio	169	tailor	57	"
	T*	Potito Margaret—†	169	housewife	57	"
	V*	Grinkawich Michael	171	mechanic	57	"
	W	Grinkawich Victoria †	171	housewife	42	"
	X	Costello Annie—†	171	"	54	"
	Y	Costello Mary C †	171	student	20	"
	Z	Costello Michael	171	repairman	55	"
1056						
	A	Reed Charles H	171	rigger	65	"
	B	Reed Charles W	171	"	33	Maine
	C	Reed Clarabelle †	171	housewife	57	here
	D	Richardson Ada †	171	at home	59	"
	E	DiMargio Antonio	173	clerk	53	"
	F	DiMargio Assunta †	173	housewife	37	"
	G	DeLucci Antonia—†	173	"	24	"
	H	DeLucci Benjamin	173	welder	29	"
	K	Landano Gerald	173	shoeworker	34	131 Eutaw
	L	Landano Sophie †	173	housewife	20	131 "
	M	Polimeno Lena †	175	"	33	173 Trenton
	N	Polimeno Matteo	175	tailor	45	173 "
	O	Trainito Gaetana †	175	dressmaker	22	here
	P	Trainito Gaspero	175	U S A	20	"
	R	Trainito Rose †	175	housewife	40	"
	S	Trainito Stefano	175	machinist	52	"
	T	Trainito Calogero	175	plumber	43	"
	U*	Trainito Gaspero	175	retired	85	"
	V*	Trainito Maria †	175	housewife	30	"
	W*	Fox Carmela †	179	"	31	"
	X	Fox Ernest	179	chauffeur	34	"
	Y	Luongo Angelina †	179	housewife	52	"
	Z	Luongo Filomena †	179	dressmaker	24	"
1057						
	A	Luongo Louisa †	179	"	26	"
	B	Luongo Phillip	179	laborer	52	"
	C	DeMattia Anna—†	179	packer	38	"
	D*	DeMattia Joseph	179	painter	43	"

34

Trenton Street Continued

E	Aliberti Alimino	189	toolmaker	22	here
F	*Aliberti Angelina †	189	housewife	52	"
G	Aliberti Edna †	189	dressmaker	25	"
H	Aliberti James V	189	U S A	24	"
K	Aliberti Jennie †	189	dressmaker	29	"
L	Aliberti Luigi	189	U S A	20	"
M	*Aliberti Rocco	189	laborer	60	"
N	Perella Carmella †	189	housewife	25	201 Chelsea
O	Perella John	189	sprayer	28	here
P	*Avilla Joseph	189	retired	69	"
R	Contino Rose †	189	operator	21	"
S	Siciliano Louis	189	proprietor	52	"
T	Siciliano Mary †	189	housewife	43	"
U	Daddario Albert	191	chauffeur	24	"
V	Daddario Guerino	191	merchant	56	"
W	*Daddario Maria †	191	housewife	57	"
X	Rubbico Joseph	191	salesman	32	"
Y	Rubbico Rose †	191	housewife	31	"
Z	DeLuca Carmella †	193	"	24	213 E Eagle

1058

A	DeLuca Ignatius	193	pharmacist	31	213 "
B	*Mancini Santino	193	tailor	56	here
C	*Santini Alice †	193	bookkeeper	27	"
D	Santini Lillian †	193	beautician	25	"
E	*Santini Palmi †	193	housewife	54	"
F	Christopher Carmella †	195	"	22	"
G	Christopher Frank	195	shipfitter	26	"
H	Lawson George	195	carpenter	53	"
K	Lawson Howard	195	U S A	22	"
L	Lawson Pearl †	195	housewife	43	"
M	Lawson Ralph	195	manager	24	"
N	Kanall A Paul	196	chauffeur	23	"
O	Kanall Agnes †	196	housewife	52	"
P	Kanall Marion A †	196	agent	22	"
R	Kanall Paul	196	pedler	52	"
S	Kelley Ina M †	196	saleswoman	45	"
T	Capolupo John	196	barber	18	"
U	*Capolupo Mary †	196	housewife	35	"
V	Graziano Josephine †	196	proprietor	25	"
W	Graziano Thomas	196	welder	29	"
X	Giordano Angelo	197	shipfitter	26	"

Page.	Letter.	FULL NAME.	Residence, Jan. 1, 1943.	Occupation.	Supposed Age.	Reported Residence, Jan. 1, 1942. Street and Number.

Trenton Street Continued

	Y	Giordano Cristine †	197	housewife	24	here
	Z	Golden Helen †	197	"	37	"
1059						
	A	Golden Mitchell	197	carpenter	39	"
	B	Young Catherine †	197	housewife	63	"
	C	Young Irving	197	guard	63	"
	D	Champa Francis	198	mechanic	35	"
	E	Champa Rose †	198	housewife	32	"
	F	Thomas Edgar W	198	mariner	40	"
	G	*Thomas Effie †	198	housewife	38	"
	H	Tarquinio Amedeo	199	retired	63	"
	K	Tarquinio Frank	199	shipfitter	32	"
	L	Tarquinio Jean	199	packer	28	"
	M	Tyman James E	199	checker	36	"
	N	Tyman Mary M †	199	housewife	35	"
	O	Flaherty Anita †	199	"	33	"
	P	Flaherty William L	199	U S C G	37	"
	R	McDonald Joseph, jr	207	electrician	32	"
	S	McDonald Madeline †	207	housewife	27	"
	T	McDonald George	207	electrician	31	"
	U	McDonald Hannah †	207	housewife	68	"
	V	McDonald Joseph	207	retired	75	"
	W	Jollimore Alma E †	209	housewife	31	"
	X	Emmons Harold K	209	chemist	23	"
	Y	Emmons Hazel M †	209	housewife	22	"
	Z	Fenton Loretta †	209	"	42	"
1060						
	A	Fenton Michael E	209	clerk	43	"
	B	Burroughs Adeline †	211	housewife	25	421 Saratoga
	C	*DellAria Salvatore	211	shoeworker	47	here
	D	DellAria Salvatore	211	U S A	24	"
	E	Barletta Alfonso	211	"	30	"
	F	*Barletta Gerardo	211	retired	62	"
	G	Ruggiero Domenic	211	carpenter	30	"
	H	Ruggiero Helen †	211	housewife	24	"
	K	Galluccio Gabriel	213	U S A	21	"
	L	*Wiscione Antonio	213	butcher	47	"
	M	*Wiscione Jennie †	213	housewife	46	"
	N	Deane Charles	213	retired	45	"
	O	Deane Grace †	213	housewife	43	"
	S	Park Catherine †	217	"	51	"

Trenton Street   Continued

T	Park George C	217	baker	52	here
U	Park James W	217	U S A	24	"
V	McNeil Edmund L	217	"	45	"
W	McNeil Edmund L, jr	217	"	21	"
X	McNeil Viola †	217	housewife	43	"

1061

A	Bright Albert	219	oiler	24	"
B	Bright Sarah †	219	egg candler	48	"
C	Bright Thomas	219	U S N	21	"
D	O'Brien Matthew	219	operator	48	"
E	Balboni Gladys †	221	housewife	44	"
F	Balboni Joseph	221	laborer	38	"
G	DeAngelis Achille	221	clerk	32	"
H	DeAngelis Salvatrica †	221	housewife	29	"
K	McCarthy Lena †	221	"	23	"
L	McCarthy Nicholas	221	shipfitter	36	"
M	Rivers Isabel †	223	housewife	30	N Hampshire
N	Rivers Thomas	223	mechanic	26	"
O	O'Brien Mary A †	223	housekeeper	47	here
P	*Favola Angelina †	227	housewife	53	"
R	Favola Mary †	227	dressmaker	27	"
S	Favola Michael	227	operator	56	"
T	Scorzello Mary †	227	housewife	20	66 Byron
U	Scorzello Michael	227	manager	28	66 "
W	Potenza Antonetta †	233	housewife	38	here
X	Potenza Peter	233	laborer	48	"

1062

B	Delahanty Elizabeth †	235	housewife	28	"
C	Delahanty James	235	U S A	31	"
D	Flood Mary †	237	housewife	71	"
E	Lanetin John	237	machinist	29	312 Princeton
F	Lanetin Marie †	237	housewife	27	312 "
G	LaCedra Barbara †	237	"	28	4 Shelby
H	LaCedra Patrick	237	printer	33	4 "
K	Palmer Annie †	239	at home	74	here
L	Held Alfred D	239	U S A	21	"
M	Held Jessica †	239	housewife	44	"
N	*Bianchino Florindo	239	laborer	50	"
O	*Bianchino Jennie †	239	housewife	60	"
P	Nelson Pearl †	241	shoeworker	28	"
R	McDonald Mildred †	241	housewife	27	"

Trenton Street — Continued

s	Dobbins Frank	241	mechanic	27	here
t	Dobbins Ruth— †	241	housewife	25	"
u	Murphy Arthur	243	retired	40	"
v	Murphy Bridget— †	243	housewife	36	"
w	Marino Albert	243	instructor	26	"
x	Marino Teresa— †	243	housewife	24	"
y	Corkum Frances— †	243	"	44	"
z	Corkum Lester	243	rigger	48	"

1063

a	Daley Mary— †	247	housewife	40	526 Saratoga
b	Daley Timothy	247	laborer	45	526 "
c	Seppa John O	247	accountant	23	here
d	Seppa Oscar	247	engineer	55	"
e	Seppa Rica— †	247	housewife	58	"
f	Cullinane Helen G— †	247	clerk	28	"
g	Cullinane Jennie M— †	247	housewife	55	"
h	Cullinane William J	247	clerk	55	"

White Street

k	Ohlson Alice— †	88	clerk	20	here
l	Ohlson Cristina— †	88	saleswoman	45	"
m	Ohlson Frank A	88	engineer	45	"
n	Cooper Mary E— †	rear 88	at home	82	"
o	Langley Capitola— †	" 88	"	75	"
p	*Saulnier Bertha †	90	saleswoman	20	"
r	*Saulnier Edmond	90	laborer	53	"
s	*Saulnier Lavinia— †	90	housewife	45	"
t	Saulnier Richard	90	laborer	21	"
u	Bonugli Frank R	90	metalworker	42	"
v	Bonugli Margaret †	90	housewife	38	"
w	Williams Edward H	90	shipfitter	31	"
x	Williams James F	90	retired	83	"
y	Williams James J	90	seaman	42	"
z	Amiro Harold	92	engineer	45	"

1064

a	Amiro Julia— †	92	housewife	41	"
b	Saggese Alfred	92	tailor	34	"
c	Saggese Dorothy †	92	milliner	32	"
d	Saggese Margaret †	92	teacher	41	"

White Street Continued

E	Saggese Mary †	92	housewife	70	here
F	Saggese Michael	92	mechanic	49	"
G	Saggese Nicholas	92	millhand	52	"
H	Saggese Victoria †	92	teacher	38	"
K	Dalton Mary †	102	at home	29	"
L	*Nugent Margaret †	102	housewife	59	"
M	Nugent Terrance	102	U S A	21	"
N	*Nugent William	102	carpenter	63	"
O	Marani Annette †	104	housewife	26	"
P	Marani Joseph	104	machinist	28	"
R	Pizzano Helen †	104	operator	24	325 Saratoga
S	Nazzaro Antonio C	104	janitor	47	here
T	Nazzaro Carmella †	104	housewife	40	"
U	*Fucillo Antonetta †	106	operator	20	"
V	Fucillo Carlo	106	"	55	"
W	*Fucillo Carmella †	106	at home	78	"
X	Fucillo Linda E †	106	tailor	22	"
Y	Fucillo Mary †	106	housewife	47	"
Z	Salierno Josephine †	106	operator	21	"

1065

A	Salierno Louise †	106	housewife	46	"
B	Salierno Savino	106	mechanic	52	"
E	Nelson Samuel M	110	social worker	53	"
F	*Pontrandolfo Frank	112	barber	55	"
G	*Pontrandolfo Rose †	112	housewife	55	"
H	Pitts Florence †	112	"	38	"
K	Pitts George D	112	engineer	42	"
L	Bradley Dennis	112	chauffeur	42	"
M	Bradley Louise H †	112	housewife	36	"
N	Ippolito John	114	chauffeur	34	"
O	Ippolito Rose †	114	housewife	28	"
P	Clemente Angelo	114	repairman	45	"
R	*Clemente Lena †	114	housewife	40	"
S	Corvi Libero	114	salesman	31	"
T	Corvi Nina †	114	housewife	25	"
U	Nugent Ann †	116	at home	42	"
V	Matera Francis V	116	attorney	29	"
W	Matera Nanda †	116	housewife	25	"
X	DiLeonardo Rosina †	116	"	54	"
Y	DiLeonardo Salvatore	116	guard	56	"

Page.	Letter.	Full Name.	Residence, Jan. 1, 1943.	Occupation.	Supposed Age.	Reported Residence, Jan. 1, 1942. Street and Number.

White Street—Continued

	z	Ferrante Agostino	116	operator	42	here
1066						
	A	Sacco Annette †	118	hairdresser	39	"
	B	Sacco August	118	plumber	41	"
	c	*Sacco Biagio	118	laborer	65	"
	D	Sacco Charles	118	retired	36	"
	E	Sacco Helen †	118	hairdresser	24	"
	F	*Sacco Marie †	118	housewife	61	"
	G	Guerra Helen †	118	"	33	176 Brooks
	H	Guerra Victor	118	cleaner	31	here

Ward 1–Precinct 11

CITY OF BOSTON

LIST OF RESIDENTS
20 YEARS OF AGE AND OVER

(NON-CITIZENS INDICATED BY ASTERISK)
(FEMALES INDICATED BY DAGGER)

AS OF

JANUARY 1, 1943

JOSEPH F. TIMILTY, *Chairman*
FREDERIC E. DOWLING, *Secretary*
WILLIAM A. MOTLEY, JR.
FRANCIS B. McKINNEY
EVERETT R. PROUT

Listing Board.

CITY OF BOSTON PRINTING DEPARTMENT

Page.	Letter.	FULL NAME.	Residence, Jan. 1, 1943.	Occupation.	Supposed Age.	Reported Residence, Jan. 1, 1942. Street and Number.

1100

Bennington Street

	A	Bernstein Louis	194	U S C G	40	here
	B	Pisani Matthew	194	chauffeur	23	Cambridge
	C	Pisani Pauline — †	194	housewife	21	"
	D	Trocano Flora — †	194	"	33	here
	E	Trocano Pasquale	194	shipper	37	"
	G	Albanese Michael	196	laborer	63	"
	H	Amodeo Giacchino	196	electrician	37	"
	K	Amodeo Sarah — †	196	housewife	36	"
	L	Bossone Saveno	196	blacksmith	58	
	O	Dixon Herbert R	198	engineer	37	83 Brooks
	P	Dixon Vernice J †	198	housewife	37	83 "
	R	Mello Agnes — †	198	operator	22	204 "
	S	Mello Charles	198	carpenter	50	204 "
	T*	Mello Ethel — †	198	housewife	49	204 "
	U	Mello James	198	U S A	25	204 "
	W*	Scire Carmelo	202	proprietor	57	here
	X	Scire Frank	202	U S A	25	"
	Y*	Scire Mary — †	202	housewife	55	"
	Z	DiLorenzo Anna †	202	"	26	"

1101

	A	DiLorenzo Salvatore	202	carpenter	25	"
	B	Scheaffa Pasquale	204	retired	67	"
	C	Surette Joseph S	204	fishcutter	40	"
	D	Surette Margaret H †	204	housewife	37	"
	E	Vargus Harold A	204	laborer	23	"
	F	Vargus Helen — †	204	housewife	21	"
	H	Filosa Antonio	206	laborer	63	172 Princeton
	K	Caggiano Jennie †	206	saleswoman	21	103 Liverpool
	L	Caggiano Mary — †	206	housewife	58	103 "
	M	Scansillo Luigi	206	laborer	54	here
	N*	Scansillo Maria — †	206	housewife	43	"
	O	Brancucci Mary †	208	operator	32	"
	P	Grieco Elizabeth †	208	housewife	29	27 Decatur
	R*	Grieco Vincenzo	208	shoemaker	33	27 "
	S	Capone Antonia †	208	operator	29	160 Cottage
	T	Capone Benjamin	208	cleaner	46	160 "
	U	Imbimbo Viola †	208	operator	23	160 "
	V	Cappello Chester	210	chipper	27	205 London
	W	Cappello Frances †	210	housewife	27	205 "
	X	Faretra Eva †	210	"	32	here

2

Bennington Street Continued

Y	Faretra Richard	210	laborer	30	here
Z	Canto Angelo †	210	housewife	34	"
1102						
A	Canto Guy	210	laborer	30	"
B	Smith Dennis J	212	plumber	50	"
C	Smith Mary J †	212	housewife	48	"
D	Murnane Mary J †	212	saleswoman	53	"
E	Smith Joseph D	212	U S A	21	"
F	Incerto Lena †	214	housewife	29	"
G	Incerto Virgilio	214	salesman	34	"
H	Hogan Anna †	214	nurse	34	"
K	McCaffrey Arthur	214	electrician	27	"
L	McCaffrey Lillian †	214	housewife	30	"
M	Riley Daniel F	214	guard	51	"
N	Riley Mary †	214	housewife	54	"
O	Moran Francis A	215	driller	37	"
P	Moran Irene G †	215	housewife	33	"
R	Puopolo Allessio	215	driller	43	"
S	Puopolo Emilio	215	laborer	21	"
T	McCormick Leo J	215	ironworker	27	"
U	McCormick Winifred M †	215	housewife	25	"
V	Ferranti Elvira †	216	"	23	"
W	Ferranti Walter	216	welder	25	"
X	Podeia Frank	216	foundryworker	49	"
Y	Podeia Lena	216	operator	21	"
Z*	Podeia Mary †	216	housewife	44	"
1103						
A	Coady Harold	216	machinist	36	"
B*	Coady Mary †	216	housewife	32	"
C	Ranieri Anthony	217	operator	25	"
D	Ranieri Concetta †	217	housewife	20	"
E	Rubino Alfred	217	chauffeur	26	127 Webster
F	Rubino Phyllis †	217	housewife	24	127 "
G	Zevolo Anthony	217	laborer	21	here
H	Zevolo James	217	plumber	21	"
K	Zevolo Pasquale	217	laborer	50	"
L	Zevolo Rose †	217	packer	27	"
M	Zevolo Thomasina †	217	housewife	47	"
N	Hollohan Catherine †	219	"	47	"
O	Hollohan Thomas	219	carpenter	52	"
P*	Mahony Sadie †	219	dishwasher	42	265 Princeton

		Full Name.	Residence, Jan. 1, 1943.	Occupation.	Supposed Age.	Reported Residence, Jan. 1, 1942. Street and Number.

Bennington Street — Continued

		Full Name	Res.	Occupation	Age	Residence
R	*	Judge Agnes —†	219	housekeeper	87	here
S		McCarthy Frances G —†	219	"	59	"
T		McCarthy Frederick T	219	fireman	67	"
V		DeMatteo Anthony	221	chauffeur	28	Medford
W		DeMatteo Margaret —†	221	housewife	28	"
X		Guinta Jennie —†	221	stitcher	23	159 Marion
Y		Guinta Luciano	221	laborer	53	159 "
Z		Guinta Mary —†	211	housewife	48	159 "

1104

A		Guinta Phyllis —†	221	seamstress	26	159 "
B		Blandino Carmella —†	221	housekeeper	22	233 Saratoga
C		Blandino Filippa —†	221	housewife	49	233 "
D		Blandino Frank	221	finisher	53	233 "
E		Blandino James	221	musician	24	233 "
F		Blandino Salvatore	221	entertainer	21	233 "
G		Loscocco Louis	223	rigger	22	here
H	*	Loscocco Manuel	223	laborer	54	"
K	*	Loscocco Philomena —†	223	housewife	48	"
L		Calicchio Agnes —†	223	"	50	"
M		Calicchio Joseph	223	barber	28	"
N		Calicchio Mildred —†	223	saleswoman	20	"
O		Calicchio Nicholas	223	barber	64	"
P		Pacella Anna —†	223	buffer	34	"
R		Pacella Antonio	223	barber	50	"
S		Pacella Michael	223	salesman	20	"
T	*	Guiffrida Mary —†	225	housewife	41	"
U		Guiffrida Phillip	225	salesman	20	"
V		Guiffrida Sebastian	225	candymaker	43	"
W	*	D'Amico Concetta —†	225	housewife	69	"
X		D'Amico Concetta —†	225	seamstress	25	"
Y	*	D'Amico Felix	225	retired	73	"
Z		D'Amico Felix	225	U S N	21	"

1105

A	*	D'Amico Josephine —†	225	housewife	44	"
B		D'Amico Peter	225	floorlayer	47	"
C		D'Amico Sarah —†	225	housekeeper	23	"
D		Zona Anthony	225	U S N	21	"
E		Zona Joseph	225	operator	47	"
F		Zona Theresa —†	225	housewife	43	"
G		Burdett Mary —†	226	operator	47	"
H		Carroll Albert	226	laborer	40	"

4

Bennington Street Continued

K	Carroll Edward	226	machinist	45	here
L	Carroll Sarah —†	226	housekeeper	72	"
M	Neil Hannah —†	226	housewife	43	"
N	Neil Joseph	226	fisherman	45	"
O	Dove Walter F	228	clerk	39	Dover
P	Barrett Emma—†	228	housekeeper	53	here
R	Barrett Florence V —†	228	clerk	32	"
S	Barrett Mary V —†	228	"	35	"
T	Grillo Francesca — †	229	housewife	65	"
U	Grillo John	229	retired	65	"
V	Mastrangelo Carmella—†	229	housewife	24	207 Princeton
W	Mastrangelo Domenic J	229	pipefitter	35	109 Benningt'n
X	Ruggiero Bella A—†	229	housewife	27	68 Faywood av
Y	Ruggiero Daniel	229	brazier	30	68 "
	1106					
A	Shlager Anna —†	230	housewife	45	here
B	Shlager Charles	230	merchant	45	"
C	Campisano Michael	231	butcher	35	"
D	Campisano Rose—†	231	housewife	29	"
E	Frongillo Grace—†	231	bowmaker	40	"
F	Frongillo Henry	231	machinist	42	"
G	Frongillo Louis	231	"	20	"
H	Vitolo Louis	231	retired	70	"
K	Vitolo Mary — †	231	bowmaker	42	"
L	*Mastorcola Frank	231	candymaker	56	"
M	*Mastorcola Rose—†	231	housewife	49	"
N	Moynihan Frederick F	232	salesman	34	"
O	Moynihan Loretta —†	232	housewife	34	"
P	Berry George F	232	weigher	33	"
R	Berry Mary—†	232	housewife	34	"
S	Haggett Alice L —†	232	"	36	"
T	Haggett Reginald L	232	rigger	35	"
U	Ambersino Anthony	233	laborer	50	"
V	Ambersino Mary—†	233	candypacker	49	"
W	Driscoll Hannah A —†	233	housekeeper	65	"
X	Willis Frances †	233	waitress	63	"
Y	Bowden Doris †	233	nurse	23	"
Z	Delahanty Mary —†	233	operator	43	"
	1107					
A	Maguire John	233	retired	78	"
B	Thorne Eileen †	233	nurse	23	"

Bennington Street—Continued

	c	Cogswell Annie—†	234	housekeeper	63	120 Benningt'n
	d	Souza Ann—†	234	housewife	24	120 "
	e	Souza George	234	operator	23	120 "
	f	Manetta Eugene	234	shipfitter	30	65 Lexington
	g	Manetta Philomena—†	234	housewife	29	65 "
	h	Mulholland Peter J	235	janitor	60	here
	k	Mulholland Sarah C—†	235	housewife	48	"
	l	Shaw John C	235	carpenter	60	"
	m	Skane George	235	U S C G	21	"
	n	Skane Gertrude—†	235	housewife	50	"
	o	Skane Gertrude—†	235	stenographer	25	"
	p	Skane John	235	U S A	28	"
	r	Skane Richard	235	laborer	50	"
	s	Skane Richard	235	seaman	29	"
	t	Coolin Edward J	236	laborer	57	"
	u	Coolin Sophia—†	236	housekeeper	92	"
	v	McPhee Helen—†	236	candymaker	43	"
	w	Goglia Edward	236	U S A	24	"
	x	Goglia Ernest	236	physician	29	"
	y	Goglia Lucy—†	236	housewife	57	"
	z	Goglia Nicholas	236	porter	60	"
1108						
	a	Long Mary—†	236	social worker	31	"
	b	Puzzanghera Josephine—†	236	housewife	24	151 Benningt'n
	c	Puzzanghera Salvatore	236	machinist	25	151 "
	d	Lauricella Antonio	237	barber	65	here
	e	*Lauricella Francesca—†	237	housewife	57	"
	f	Lauricella Salvatore	237	U S A	22	"
	g	Tringale Frances—†	237	seamstress	27	"
	h	DeFelice Domenic	237	U S A	25	"
	k	*DeFelice Leo	237	retired	73	"
	l	*DeFelice Lucy—†	237	housewife	59	"
	m	DeFelice Michael	237	U S A	29	"
	n	Ricioli Domenic	237	hairdresser	45	"
	o	Ricioli Mary—†	237	dressmaker	36	"
	p	Carroll Emma—†	239	housekeeper	75	"
	r	Rich Annie—†	239	housewife	75	"
	s	Rich Margaret T—†	239	"	43	"
	t	Rich Webster A	239	boatbuilder	40	"
	u	Keyes Milton	247	laborer	33	146 Lexington
	v	Keyes Rita—†	247	housewife	27	146 "

6

Bennington Street Continued

w	Gordon Lawrence	247	laborer	37	107 Meridian
x	*Gordon Michael	247	"	65	here
y	Portrait Catherine †	247	housewife	30	"
z	Diaz Mary—†	247	clerk	27	"

1109

a	Larkin Helen—†	249	housewife	44	"
b	Larkin William	249	chauffeur	46	"
c	*Mastascusa Filomena †	249	housewife	61	"
d	Mastascusa Frank	249	barber	56	"
e	O'Keefe Cornelius H	249	longshoreman	49	"
f	Shephard Elmer	249	U S A	23	"
g	Shephard James	249	"	25	"
h	Shephard Mary E †	249	housewife	51	"
k	Vilkas Cecilia—†	251	"	30	"
l	Vilkas John	251	laborer	29	"
m	Cuozzo Guy	251	molder	29	"
n	Cuozzo Phyllis—†	251	housewife	34	"
o	DellaRusso Carmen	251	butcher	48	"
p	*DellaRusso Matilda—†	251	housewife	49	"
r	DellaRusso Ralph	251	seaman	21	"
s	Pitts James	253	sprayer	37	214 E Eagle
t	Scarpa Joseph	253	upholsterer	22	here
u	*Scarpa Rosario	253	laborer	48	"
v	*Scarpa Rosina †	253	housewife	48	"
w	Bellardino Carmella—†	253	packer	22	"
x	*Bellardino Concetta †	253	housewife	59	"
y	Bellardino James	253	laborer	30	"
z	*Bellardino John	253	"	65	"

1110

a	Cocozza Charles	255	shipper	27	"
b	Cocozza Theresa †	255	housewife	27	"
c	Cirillo Anthony	255	at home	24	"
d	Cirillo Emma—†	255	housekeeper	22	"
e	*Cirillo Mary †	255	housewife	44	"
f	*Antignano Josephine †	255	"	44	"
g	*Antignano Luigi	255	laborer	51	"
h	*Milligan Annie †	257	housekeeper	74	"
k	Milligan Fred	257	U S C G	48	"
l	Silva Arthur	257	U S A	29	"
m	Silva Harold R	257	operator	20	"
n	Silva Madeline—†	257	"	28	"

7

Bennington Street—Continued

o	Silva Manuel J	257	longshoreman	59	here
p	Silva Sarah—†	257	housewife	56	"
R	*Baucher Louis	257	retired	76	"
s	Ingersoll James	257	mechanic	33	"
T	Ingersoll Sarah J—†	257	housewife	50	"

Bremen Street

w	Sebatini Anthony	326	chauffeur	25	here
x	Sebatini Frances—†	326	clerk	21	"
y	Botticelli Grace—†	326	housewife	24	"
z	Botticelli Ralph	326	painter	25	"
	1111				
A	Disario Emma—†	326	housewife	46	401 Saratoga
B	Disario Gabriel	326	plasterer	51	401 "
c	Disario Gabriel	326	U S A	21	401 "
D	Disario George	326	"	22	401 "
E	Kelly John J	344	chauffeur	52	here
F	Ranahan John J	344	longshoreman	35	"
G	Ranahan Mary A—†	344	cleaner	64	"
H	Wilson Mona—†	344	bookkeeper	25	"
K	Chiampa James	350	machinist	35	23 Chelsea
L	Chiampa Margaret—†	350	housewife	30	23 "
M	DeRosa Catherine—†	350	"	26	Chelsea
N	DeRosa Patsy	350	painter	27	"
o	Lanney Frank	352	U S A	23	here
P	Lanney Josephine—†	352	housewife	46	"
R	Lanney Michael	352	U S A	20	"
s	Lanney Nicholas	352	oil dealer	56	"

Chelsea Street

T	Deprospo Lawrence J	303	laborer	35	here
U	Deprospo Malvine—†	303	housewife	35	"
V	Ciardo Jennie—†	303	"	37	"
w	Ciardo Peter	303	guard	47	"
x	*Guardalascio Assunta—†	303	housewife	71	"
y	Venuti Carmella—†	303	winder	21	"
z	Venuti Louise—†	303	packer	42	"
	1112				
A	Littlejohn Arthur L	305	machinist	31	"

8

Chelsea Street Continued

B	Littlejohn Margaret A—†	305	housewife	29	here
C	Latorella Anthony	305	retired	67	"
D	Latorella Mary—†	305	housewife	66	"
E	Petella Josephine—†	305	"	45	"
F	Petella Leo	305	U S A	23	"
G	Petella Stephen	305	trackman	56	"
H	Cardullo Antonetta—†	307	housewife	60	"
K	Cardullo Salvatore	307	machinist	21	"
L	Genovitch Frank	307	seaman	21	"
M	Genovitch John	307	U S A	27	"
N	*Genovitch Mary—†	307	housewife	60	"
O	*Genovitch Stephen	307	retired	64	"
P	Speranza John	307	U S A	21	"
R	*Speranza Josephine—†	307	housewife	45	"
S	Speranza Santo	307	cleaner	55	"
T	Brown Joseph F	309	clerk	38	"
U	Brown Louise F—†	309	housewife	38	"
V	McGunigle Agnes J—†	309	operator	42	"
W	McGunigle Mary J—†	309	housewife	75	"
X	McGunigle Ethel—†	309	"	34	"
Y	McGunigle Hilary J	309	policeman	34	"
Z	Drago Guy	311	candymaker	30	"
	1113				
A	Drago Pauline—†	311	housewife	29	"
B	*Bonafini Frank	311	retired	65	"
C	*Bonafini Rosaria—†	311	housewife	67	"
D	Simili Joseph	311	clerk	23	"
E	Simili Lorenzo	311	laborer	56	"
F	*Simili Marie—†	311	housewife	50	"
G	Simili Mary—†	311	wrapper	25	"
H	Maffeo Christy	313	cobbler	39	"
K	Maffeo Helen—†	313	housewife	34	"
L	Consolo Concetta—†	313	"	35	"
M	Consolo Filippo	313	shoeworker	39	"
N	*Consolo Josephine—†	313	housewife	65	"
O	*Simoli Anna—†	313	"	49	"
P	*Simoli Mario	313	laborer	57	"
R	Simoli Mary—†	313	clerk	23	"
V	Giarle Louis	320	builder	25	"
W	Giarle Violet—†	320	housewife	25	"
X	Pezzella Carmen	320	laborer	57	"

Chelsea Street Continued

	Y	Nuttoli Harry	320	repairman	56	here
	Z	Nuttoli Harry	320	U S A	21	"
1114						
	A	Nuttoli Lucy—†	320	housewife	53	"
	B	Nuttoli Roccina—†	320	shoeworker	23	"
	C	Colangelo Michael	320	pipefitter	29	"
	D	Colangelo Sarah—†	320	housewife	29	"
	E	Cannella Charles	322	ropemaker	30	"
	F	Cannella Domenica—†	322	housewife	28	"
	G	*Giambussi Catherine—†	322	"	58	"
	H	*Giambussi Joseph	322	retired	66	"
	K	Weeker Jennie—†	322	housewife	29	"
	L	Weeker Julian A	322	electrician	32	"
	M	*Cappello Annarose—†	324	housewife	74	"
	N	Velona Anna—†	324	"	89	"
	O	Velona Anna—†	324	leatherworker	29	"
	P	Velona Antonetta—†	324	shoeworker	24	"
	R	Velona Bruno	324	U S A	30	"
	S	Velona Domenic	324	carpenter	56	"
	T	Velona Maria—†	324	housewife	53	"
	U	Caruso Albert	324	U S N	20	"
	V	Caruso Alfred	324	"	23	"
	W	Caruso Domenic	324	U S A	29	"
	X	Caruso Eleanor—†	324	secretary	25	"
	Y	*Caruso Mary—†	324	housewife	52	"
	Z	Caruso Rose—†	324	packer	31	"
1115						
	A	*Vincent Bertha—†	326	housewife	55	"
	B	Vincent William	326	shipcalker	65	"
	C	*Fagone Ida—†	326	housewife	43	"
	D	Fagone Josephine—†	326	clerk	20	"
	E	Fagone Sebastian	326	barber	49	"
	F	*Mangino Filomena—†	326	housewife	70	"
	G	Mangino Louis	326	retired	73	"
	H	LoDuco Cosimo	326	printer	30	"
	K	*LoDuco Mary—†	326	housewife	75	"
	L	LoDuco Mary C—†	326	stitcher	33	"
	M	DiMarino Anthony	328	machinist	34	"
	N	DiMarino Theresa—†	328	housewife	30	"
	O	Coriani Amelio	328	porter	34	"
	P	Coriani Catherine—†	328	housewife	29	"

Chelsea Street Continued

R	*DiMarino Antonetta †	328	housewife	68	here
S	DiMarino Costanzo	328	retired	72	"
T	Fagone Joseph	328	pipefitter	30	"
U	Fagone Mary — †	328	housewife	33	"
V	McGraham Lillian — †	330	tester	39	"
W	McGraham Richard	330	steelworker	46	"
X	Fagone Georgia †	330	housewife	32	"
Y	Fagone Louis	330	meter reader	36	"
Z	Fagone Frank	330	retired	66	"

1116

A	Fagone Josephine — †	330	inspector	25	"
B	*Mazza Mary — †	330	stitcher	48	"
D	Cioffi Frank	331	U S M C	21	"
E	Cioffi Joseph	331	baker	54	"
F	Cioffi Rose — †	331	housewife	52	"
G	Cioffi Sigismondo	331	U S A	26	"
H	*Fox Emma — †	332	housewife	70	"
K	Fielding Annie J — †	332	housekeeper	54	"
L	Fielding Esther T — †	332	factoryhand	46	"
M	Ormond Elizabeth A — †	332	housewife	66	"
N	Sullivan Frances J — †	332	"	63	"
O	Sullivan Mary J — †	332	clerk	25	"
P	Sullivan William L	332	laborer	63	"
R	Sacco Daniel	333	baker	54	"
S	Sacco Viola — †	333	housewife	34	"
T	*Masciola Mary — †	333	"	65	"
U	Barron Helen — †	334	"	30	"
V	Barron Jacob	334	manager	40	"
W	Barron Bessie — †	334	packer	30	"
X	*Barron Fannie — †	334	housewife	66	"
Y	Marino Nelson	334	laborer	38	"
Z	Marino Rita — †	334	housewife	37	"

1117

A	DiAngelo Rose — †	335	"	73	"
B	Meyer Julian	335	bartender	32	"
C	Meyer Rose — †	335	housewife	32	"
D	Reilly Gertrude — †	337	forewoman	42	"
F	Minichello Anna — †	339	entertainer	22	219 Trenton
G	Minichello Elvira — †	339	housewife	44	219 "
H	Minichello Nicholas	339	electrician	24	219 "
K	Collins Arthur H	339	chauffeur	33	here

11

Page.	Letter.	FULL NAME.	Residence, Jan. 1, 1943.	Occupation.	Supposed Age.	Reported Residence, Jan. 1, 1942. Street and Number.

Chelsea Street—Continued

	L	Collins Margaret H—†	339	housewife	70	here
	M	Collins William C	339	policeman	42	"
	N	Levee Minnie—†	339	housewife	69	"
	O	Coughlin Catherine F—†	339	"	74	"
	P	Coughlin Matthew J	339	machinist	47	"
	R	LaBlanc Albert S	341	chef	57	"
	S	LaBlanc Maud A—†	341	housewife	53	"
	T	Young Eleanor M—†	341	"	44	"
	U	Young Elmer H	341	riveter	46	"
	V	Cioffi Orlando	342	assembler	27	"
	W	Cioffi Theresa—†	342	housewife	27	"
	X	Santosuosso Eleanor—†	342	"	24	"
	Y	Santosuosso Nicholas	342	packer	25	"
	Z	Dedulonus Frank	342	custodian	28	Revere

1118

	A	Dedulonus Phyllis—†	342	housewife	29	"
	B	Samms Cecile—†	344	"	52	here
	C	Samms James	344	fishcutter	49	"
	D	Devella Margaret—†	344	housewife	57	"
	E	Devella Mario	344	U S A	21	"
	F	Devella Pasquale	344	laborer	57	"
	G	Candelora Frank	344	"	24	37 Havre
	H	Candelora Lucy—†	344	housewife	24	37 "
	K	Dorso John	346	welder	35	here
	L	Dorso Leona—†	346	housewife	43	"
	M	DiChiara Ella—†	346	"	34	New York
	N	DiChiara Felix	346	rigger	44	Revere
	O	Carberry Irene H—†	346	housewife	39	New York
	P	Doyle Mary L—†	346	"	35	here
	R	Doyle Paul F	346	operator	38	"
	S	Jacobs William R	346	U S A	37	"
	T	*Barletta Alice—†	352	housewife	63	3 Wash'n av
	V	*Barletta John	352	finisher	66	3 "
	W	Barletta Lawrence	352	stockman	30	3 "
	X	*DiNatale Catherine—†	352	housewife	33	here
	Y	Romano Louis	352	chauffeur	31	139 Leyden
	Z	Romano Mary—†	352	housewife	26	139 "

1119

	A	Santosuosso Generino	354	fireman	36	here
	B	Santosuosso Josephine—†	354	housewife	34	"
	C	Ruggiero Angelo	354	laborer	23	"

12

Chelsea Street Continued

	D	Ruggiero Anthony	354	laborer	54	here
	E	Ruggiero Jerry	354	U S A	20	"
	F	Ruggiero Rose †	354	housewife	52	"
	G	Pagliaro Alice †	354	"	24	"
	H	Pagliaro Santo	354	machinist	25	"
	K	Mortimer Catherine †	356	housewife	44	434 Chelsea
	L	DeMarco Annie †	356	"	48	here
	M	DeMarco Frank	356	student	21	"
	N	DeMarco Pasquale	356	candymaker	49	"
	O	Watts Herbert	356	U S N	21	Illinois
	P	Watts Mary †	356	housewife	25	249 Benning'n
	R	Ducette Doris †	358	"	32	75 Border
	S	Ducette William	358	fishcutter	32	75 "
	T	*Theotokake Pauline †	358	teacher	49	here

Lexington Street

	W	*Marotta Charles	195	pressman	41	here
	X	*Marotta Mary †	195	housewife	31	"
	Y	Barbaro Catherine †	195	"	50	"
	Z	Barbaro John	195	butcher	56	"
1120						
	A	*Young Wing Yep	197	laundryman	43	45 Curve
	B	Tusa Domenic	197	carpenter	30	here
	C	Tusa Patrina †	197	housewife	31	"
	D	Zambello Joseph	197	operator	25	"
	E	*Zambello Josephine †	197	housewife	20	"
	F	*Raimondi Mary †	199	"	38	"
	G	Raimondi Tancredi	199	bricklayer	41	"
	H	Riccardelli Antonio	199	laborer	51	"
	K	Riccardelli Mary †	199	housewife	47	"
	L	*Riccardelli Rachael †	199	housekeeper	34	Tewksbury
	M	Powers Mary E †	201	at home	73	here
	N	Bernard Elizabeth †	203	housewife	22	Vermont
	O	Bernard Irene †	203	"	42	"
	P	Bernard Joseph I	203	shipfitter	43	"
	R	Bernard Louis L	203	laborer	21	"
	S	Amato Frank	203	machinist	23	380 Lovell
	T	Amato Mary †	203	housewife	21	239 Lexington
	U	D'Amelio Emma †	205	"	30	here
	V	D'Amelio Eugene	205	boilermaker	32	"

13

Page.	Letter.	FULL NAME.	Residence, Jan. 1, 1943.	Occupation.	Supposed Age.	Reported Residence, Jan. 1, 1942. Street and Number.

Lexington Street— Continued

	w	*Fonte Joseph	207	candymaker	42	here
	x	*Fonte Vincenza—†	207	housewife	33	"
	y	Giangreco Anthony	207	student	24	"
	z	*Giangreco Josephine—†	207	operator	28	"
1121						
	A	*Giangreco Viega—†	207	housekeeper	54	"
	B	Capezuto Charles	207	tailor	43	"
	c	Capezuto Helen—†	207	housewife	38	"
	D	*Capezuto Maria—†	207	housekeeper	68	"
	E	*Surette Celina—†	209	housewife	48	"
	F	Surette Gertrude—†	209	artist	20	"
	G	Surette William	209	rigger	48	"
	H	Giacchetta Ignacio	209	driller	36	"
	K	Giacchetta Thomasina—†	209	housewife	32	"
	L	Ciasullo Eugene	211	rigger	41	"
	M	Ciasullo Ida—†	211	housewife	31	"
	N	Pagliarulo Angelo	211	operator	25	"
	O	Pagliarulo Euplio	211	retired	67	"
	P	Barravechio Angelo	213	laborer	36	"
	R	*Barravechio Jennie—†	213	housewife	76	"
	S	*Barravechio Joseph	213	retired	84	"
	T	Camuso Aurora—†	213	packer	22	"
	V	Camuso Olga—†	213	housewife	58	"
	V	Camuso Pasquale	213	tailor	58	"
	W	Hutchinson Margaret—†	213A	housewife	29	"
	X	Hutchinson Richard J	213A	chemist	29	"
	Y	Mercadante Antoinette—†	215	saleswoman	20	"
	z	Mercadante Michael	215	foreman	41	"
1122						
	A	Mercadante Theresa—†	215	housewife	39	"
	B	Mercadante Antonetta—†	215	"	64	"
	c	Mercadante Antonio	215	laborer	65	"
	D	Mercadante Gaetano	215	"	26	"
	E	Mercadante Mary—†	215	operator	29	"
	F	Courtoglous Anne E—†	215	housewife	49	"
	G	Courtoglous Theodore	215	chef	51	"
	H	*D'Agostino Grace—†	217	housewife	64	"
	K	D'Agostino Rosario	217	laborer	30	"
	L	D'Agostino Salvatore	217	retired	74	"
	M	D'Agostino Josephine—†	217	housewife	35	"
	X	D'Agostino Salvatore, jr	217	plumber	36	"

14

Page.	Letter.	FULL NAME.	Residence, Jan. 1, 1943.	Occupation.	Supposed Age.	Reported Residence, Jan. 1, 1942. Street and Number

Lexington Street—Continued

	o	Bonasera Joseph	217	pressman	48	here
	p	Bonasera Theresa †	217	housewife	38	"
	r	Trainor Anna G †	219	"	39	"
	s	Trainor James E	219	longshoreman	43	"
	t	Trainor James E, jr	219	U S N	20	"
	u	Cotter Frederick E	219	machinist	67	"
	v	Cotter Mary J †	219	housewife	64	"
	x	Burke Felix	221	laborer	46	"
	y	Burke Helen †	221	housewife	41	"
	z	Brown Lawrence	221	welder	37	"

1123

	a	*Doucette Simon	221	retired	88	"
	b	Geddry Frank V	221	"	70	"
	c	*Geddry Sarah †	221	housewife	61	"
	d	Preshong Elizabeth †	221	supervisor	27	"
	e	Preshong Zetha †	221	housewife	54	"
	f	Thorne Pauline †	223	"	32	"
	g	Thorne Richard C	223	clerk	33	"
	h	Callahan Catherine †	223	housekeeper	54	"
	k	Callahan Isabel M †	223	secretary	52	"
	l	Letteriello Louis	225	laborer	33	"
	m	Letteriello Rose †	225	clerk	28	"
	n	Douchi Anita †	225	packer	27	"
	o	*Douchi Julia †	225	housewife	57	"
	p	Douchi Ugo	225	pressman	55	"
	r	*Ferrari Fidalma †	225	at home	78	"
	s	Corbett Elizabeth F †	225	housewife	57	"
	t	Corbett Henry D	225	painter	54	"
	u	Corbett Robert D	225	U S A	28	"
	v	Delmont Henry	225	"	20	"
	w	DeGregorio Helga †	227	housewife	35	"
	x	DeGregorio Mario	227	shipfitter	35	"
	y	*Maravas Bessie †	227	housewife	44	"
	z	Maravas Ethel †	227	packer	24	"

1124

	a	Maravas Richard	227	laborer	55	"
	b	Maravas Stella †	227	weaver	22	"
	c	Romano Columbus	235	U S A	20	"
	d	Romano John	235	retired	65	"
	e	*Romano Nancy †	235	housewife	60	"
	f	Oricchio Domenic	235	U S A	24	"

15

Lexington Street—Continued

G	Oricchio Enrico	235	laborer	50	here
H	*Oricchio Lena—†	235	housewife	45	"
K	Oricchio Nicholas	235	U S A	20	"
L	Barrett Catherine—†	237	matron	54	"
M	Perez Alice—†	237	at home	54	"
N	Perez Francis L	237	machinist	20	"
O	Perez Joseph	237	U S A	22	"
P	Perez Rose—†	237	clerk	26	"
R	King Genevieve F—†	237	housewife	25	"
S	King Horace W	237	shipfitter	28	"
T	*Mercuri Lucy—†	237	at home	55	"
U	Mercuri Mary—†	237	forewoman	21	"
V	Butare Louis	239	shipfitter	30	"
W	Butare Mary—†	239	housewife	26	"
X	*Butare John	239	retired	64	"
Y	*Butare Mary—†	239	housewife	53	"
Z	Mattera Josephine—†	239	"	26	"

1125

A	Mattera Salvadore	239	longshoreman	30	"
B	Beresford Ellen—†	241	housewife	57	"
C	Beresford Joseph	241	carpenter	63	"
D	Beresford Joseph	241	U S A	27	"
E	Beresford Vincent	241	laborer	29	"
F	Perry Frank A	241	shipwright	42	"
G	Perry Helen A—†	241	housewife	35	"
H	Butare Angelo	241	shipfitter	33	"
K	Butare Anna—†	241	housewife	28	"
L	Gangi Jean—†	243	clerk	30	"
M	Gangi Samuel	243	laborer	31	"
N	Berardino Emilio	243	welder	26	"
O	Berardino Francesca—†	243	clerk	28	"
P	DiGregorio Esther—†	243	saleswoman	23	"
R	Ricciardelli Antonio	243	tailor	42	"
S	Ricciardelli Jennie—†	243	housewife	26	"
T	Tennerina J Edmond	243½	welder	24	"
U	*Tennerina Joseph	243½	boilermaker	56	"
V	Tennerina Louise—†	243½	packer	24	"
W	*Tennerina Mary—†	243½	housewife	52	"
X	Paterno Anthony	243½	U S A	28	"
Y	Paterno Theresa—†	243½	housewife	26	"
Z	Cestone Mafalda—†	245	stitcher	21	"

16

1126

Lexington Street Continued

A	Cestone Pasquale	245	operator	52	here
B	*Cestone Pauline †	245	housewife	50	"
C	Borden Albert	245	ironworker	27	"
D	Borden Celia †	245	instructor	27	"
E	Montalto Mary †	245	housewife	23	"
F	Montalto Vincent J	245	laborer	22	"
G	D'Addio Gennaro	247	barber	44	"
H	D'Addio Rose †	247	housewife	36	"
K	Ventresca Concetta †	247	"	24	"
L	Ventresca Frank	247	shipper	27	"
M	*D'Addio Josephine †	247	housewife	34	"
N	D'Addio Louis	247	laborer	48	"
O	Dalton Michael L	249	"	36	"
P	Dalton Phyllis C †	249	housewife	26	"
R	Rios Alfred	249	rigger	25	"
S	Rios Beatrice †	249	housewife	26	"
T	Muratore Savina †	249	"	29	"
U	Muratore William	249	machinist	30	"
V	Gifun Grace †	251	clerk	47	"
W	Caruccio Angela †	251	housewife	45	"
X	Caruccio Frank	251	bartender	49	"
Y	Caruccio Michael	251	U S A	21	"
Z	Ferris Albert	253	butcher	38	"

1127

A	Ferris Jennie †	253	packer	38	"
B	*Correia Catherine †	253	housewife	46	"
C	*Correia Jordan	253	laborer	41	"
D	Correia Jordan, jr	253	U S N	21	"
E	Correia Manuel	253	"	20	"
F	Centracchio Domenic	253	retired	76	"
G	Centracchio Jennie †	253	housewife	50	"
H	*Cerniglio Gesualdo	253	retired	80	"
K	Furtado Concetta †	263	housewife	24	131 Eutaw
L	Furtado Frank	263	laborer	59	412 Saratoga
M	Furtado Frank	263	shipbuilder	25	131 Eutaw
N	*Furtado Mary †	263	housewife	60	412 Saratoga
O	Bertulli Alfred	263	packer	33	here
P	Bertulli Edith †	263	housewife	30	"
R	Misiano Anthony	263	U S A	21	"
S	Misiano John	263	laborer	50	"
T	Misiano Mary †	263	housewife	46	"

1—11

Lexington Street—Continued

u	Clark Harriet— †	265	at home	27	38 White
v	Sheets Ervis	265	machinist	32	38 "
w	Smith Katherine— †	265	housewife	25	362 Princeton
x	Smith Robert W	265	metalworker	27	362 "
y	Maylor Clyde	265	attorney	38	here
z	*Maylor Hilda— †	265	housewife	29	"

1128

A	Cavagnaro Josephine †	267	clerk	30	57 Trenton
B	Alio Alexander	267	U S A	20	273 Lexington
C	Alio Joseph	267	barber	46	273 "
D	Alio Josephine— †	267	stitcher	42	273 "
E	Alio Peter	267	U S A	22	273 "
F	LaSala James	267	welder	43	here
G	LaSala Mary— †	267	housewife	40	"
H	Gallucio Amelia— †	269	"	40	"
K	Gallucio Egidio	269	laborer	46	"
L	Colantuone Ida— †	269	housewife	33	"
M	Colantuone Samuel	269	candymaker	36	"
N	Gallagan Victoria— †	269	clerk	45	"
O	Gallagan William	269	waiter	50	"
R	Durgin Carrie †	271	at home	68	"
S	Gatchell Hazel— †	271	forewoman	22	"
T	Crowley Catherine L †	271	housewife	24	"
U	Crowley John F	271	B F D	27	"
V	Danilchuk Joseph	273	U S A	22	283 Lexington
W	Danilchuk Laura A †	273	at home	42	283 "
X	Danilchuk Peter	273	U S A	20	283 "
Y	*Hilton Catherine †	273	at home	85	here
Z	*Shanahan Anastasia †	273	"	77	"

1129

A	Amerena Anna †	273	housewife	32	"
B	Amerena Frank J	273	shipper	35	"
C	Wood Charles J	275	inspector	45	"
D	Wood Ethel M †	275	housewife	40	"
E	Nickerson Elmer J	275	chauffeur	43	"
F	*Nickerson John	275	retired	70	"
G	Nickerson Mary A †	275	housewife	39	"
H	Silva Americo F	275	foreman	35	"
K	Silva Mary H †	275	housewife	31	"
L	Porter Mildred †	279	"	42	"
M	*Porter Racine	279	fisherman	58	"

18

Lexington Street Continued

N	Bordieri Anna †	279	stitcher	23	here	
O	Bordieri Paul	279	mason	53	"	
P	Busheme Frank	279	U S A	26	"	
R	Busheme Josephine †	279	housewife	26	"	
S	Poto Annette †	279	"	27	"	
T	Poto John	279	manager	40	"	
U	Pelosi Angelo J	281	electrician	23	260 Lexington	
V	Pelosi Catherine A †	281	housewife	20	260 "	
W	Santosuosso Albert	281	chauffeur	29	2 Brooks	
X	Santosuosso Theresa †	281	housewife	28	2 "	
Y	*McCue John P	281	fishcutter	47	here	
Z	*McCue Mary †	281	housewife	39	"	

1130

A	Cotter James	283	mechanic	23	"	
B	Francis Marguerite †	283	at home	43	"	
C	Hilton Frank	283	shipfitter	24	235 Trenton	
D	Hilton Grace †	283	housewife	22	235 "	
E	Neal Charles M	285	fishcutter	38	here	
F	Neal Mary †	285	housewife	34	"	
G	Reed Earle C	285	rigger	31	235 Trenton	
H	Reed Olga C †	285	housewife	28	235 "	
K	Henderson Daniel	285	U S A	27	512 Benningt'n	
L	Henderson Martha †	285	housewife	27	Revere	
M	Machado John	287	retired	35	here	
N	Machado Mary L †	287	housewife	61	"	
O	Machado Rose S †	287	clerk	31	"	
P	Machado Zeferino	287	retired	78	"	
R	Muccidelli Anthony	289	laborer	56	"	
S	*Muccidelli Mary †	289	housewife	46	"	
T	Materazzo Mary †	291	"	21	"	
U	Materazzo Ralph	291	painter	25	"	
V	Cristallo Ciriaco	291	laborer	39	167A Falcon	
W	Cristallo Lucy †	291	housewife	34	167A "	
X	O'Keefe Anna E †	293	"	47	here	
Y	O'Keefe David	293	laborer	49	"	

1131

B	Fiore Anthony	295	rigger	28	"	
C	Fiore Irene †	295	housewife	28	"	
D	Scandurra Jeanette †	295	"	25	290 Chelsea	
E	Scandurra Vincent	295	shipfitter	23	93 Homer	
F	Gallo Eugene	295	pressman	47	here	

Lexington Street—Continued

G	Gallo Mary—†	295	finisher	21	here	
H	*Gallo Rose—†	295	housewife	47	"	
K	Santoro Grace—†	295	operator	29	"	
L	Inacio Flora—†	297	housewife	31	"	
M	Inacio John S	297	chauffeur	42	"	
N	Mazzone Clara—†	297	housewife	30	"	
O	Mazzone Onofrio	297	laborer	33	"	
P	*Polito Filomena—†	297	housewife	53	"	
R	Polito Gennaro	297	U S A	29	"	
S	Polito Joseph	297	laborer	53	"	
T	Polito Peter	297	U S A	21	"	
U	Ledoux Angelina †	299	housewife	29	"	
V	*Ledoux Rosario	299	operator	37	"	
W	Goulet Leo P	299	welder	24	"	
X	Goulet Mary—†	299	housewife	22	"	
Y	*Fahey Margaret—†	299	"	62	"	
Z	Fahey Phillip	299	retired	73	"	

1132

A	Mietzner Olga S—†	301	housewife	36	"	
B	Mietzner William A	301	electrician	40	"	
C	Palmunen Maria L—†	301	housewife	71	"	
D	Palmunen Otto N	301	bridgetender	62	"	
E	Coady James T	301	laborer	58	"	
F	Coady Mary L—†	301	housewife	64	"	
G	Keough Charles F	303	serviceman	47	"	
H	Keough Donald P	303	U S N	20	"	
K	Keough Marie C—†	303	housewife	43	"	
L	McClellan Claire M—†	303	at home	24	"	
M	Greeley Marion—†	305	stitcher	37	"	
N	Ghelfi Alfred	307	U S A	29	Rhode Island	
O	*Ghelfi Aristide	307	merchant	65	here	
P	*Ghelfi Claudia †	307	housewife	59	"	
R	Ghelfi Naomi—†	307	student	20	"	
S	Ghelfi Sophia—†	307	"	23	"	
T	Murray Jennie †	307	egg candler	61	"	
U	Rothwell Henry	307	laborer	53	"	
V	Oliveri Catherine—†	307	housewife	24	"	
W	Oliveri Joseph	307	tailor	28	"	
X	Baker Donald	309	machinist	23	"	
Y	Baker Florence †	309	clerk	23	"	

Lexington Street Continued

	z	Malone Adeline—†	309	housewife	29	210 E Eagle
1133						
	A	Malone Francis	309	chauffeur	39	210 "
	B	Langford Catherine—†	309	waitress	47	175 Benningt'n
	c	McGlew Mary E—†	309	housewife	52	175 "
	D	McGlew William H	309	longshoreman	48	175 "
	E	Spencer Ruth I—†	309	stenographer	27	175 "
	F	Kelsen Anna—†	311	at home	61	here
	G	Kelsen Donald G	311	U S C G	22	"
	H	Russo Louis L	311	laborer	33	78 Brooks
	K	Russo Margaret—†	311	housewife	28	78 "
	L	Sleeper Alice J—†	311	"	51	here
	M	Sleeper Frederick W	311	salesman	56	"
	N	Britt Mary E—†	311	housewife	47	"
	o	Britt Michael F	311	laborer	49	"
	P	Arena Anthony	313	U S N	21	329 E Eagle
	R	Arena Josephine—†	313	at home	53	329 "
	s	Matt Caroline—†	313	housewife	28	here
	T	Matt Michael	313	machinist	30	"
	U	Scarpa Innocenza—†	313	housewife	39	"
	V	Scarpa Ralph X	313	operator	46	"

Prescott Street

	w	Caruso Carmen	31	janitor	54	here
	x	Caruso Frances—†	31	stitcher	21	"
	Y	Caruso Ignazio	31	engineer	29	"
	z*	Caruso Lillian—†	31	housewife	47	"
1134						
	A	Caruso Silvia—†	31	"	24	"
	B	Diaz Frank R	33	chauffeur	52	35 Prescott
	c	Meads Julia—†	33	housewife	47	here
	D	Meads Manuel	33	engineer	48	"
	E	Silva Alfred	35	machinist	29	"
	F	Silva Constance—†	35	housewife	25	217 Benningt'n
	G*	Silva Mary—†	35	housekeeper	59	here
	H	Kerrigan Louis A	35	chauffeur	52	"
	K	Kerrigan Mary A—†	35	housewife	48	"
	L	Brazil Gertrude—†	37	housekeeper	39	226 Lexington
	M	Johannessen Christian	37	machinist	50	here

21

Prescott Street — Continued

N	Johannessen Henrietta— †	37	housewife	46	here
O	Corduro Peter	47	retired	68	"
P	Costa Manuel	47	"	50	"
R	Fielding Joseph	47	printer	50	"
T	McCarthy Daniel	47	laborer	68	Cambridge
S	Oliver George F	47	retired	74	here
U	Wilson Elizabeth— †	47	housewife	60	"
V	Wilson Archie	47	shipfitter	55	"
W	Murray Anna —†	49	housewife	50	"
X	Murray Arthur	49	longshoreman	55	"
Z	*Stoumbelis Catherine— †	77	housewife	29	"

1135

A	Stoumbelis Nicholas E	77	proprietor	39	"
D	Carroll Agnes— †	79	housekeeper	67	"
E	Mitchell Anna— †	79	"	74	"
H	Caruti Agnes—†	93	laundress	34	"
K	Lamborghini Arthur	93	U S N	20	"
L	Lamborghini Mary— †	93	housekeeper	54	"
M	Lamborghini Robert	93	U S A	22	"
N	Mondello Ethel — †	95	housewife	43	"
O	Mondello Frank	95	coremaker	50	"
P	Mondello James	95	U S A	25	"
R	Cerbone Anthony	97	"	32	"
S	*Cerbone Rose— †	97	housekeeper	48	"
T	Lamborghini Dora —†	97	housewife	22	237 Chelsea
U	Lamborghini Ernest	97	machinist	24	237 "
V	Fucci Josephine — †	97	housewife	51	here
W	Fucci Josephine — †	97	checker	21	"
X	Fucci Michael	97	cooper	53	"

Princeton Place

Y	Guglincciello Anna †	1	teacher	28	here
Z	Guglinceiello Jessie †	1	cleanser	42	"

1136

A	Guglinceiello Mary J—†	1	bookkeeper	30	"
B	*Guglinceiello Sabato	1	bootblack	74	"

Princeton Street

D	Balzotti Charles	200	manager	31	here
E	Balzotti Nancy M †	200	housewife	32	"

Princeton Street Continued

F	Jackson Prudence †	200	housewife	30	here
G	Jackson Thomas C	200	pipefitter	28	"
H	*Cotreau Adrian S	201	fisherman	49	"
K	Cotreau Bernard J	201	U S A	43	"
L	Cotreau George S	201	fisherman	47	"
M	*Cotreau Mark A	201	"	52	"
N	*Cotreau Mary M †	201	housekeeper	75	"
O	*Cotreau Rock H	201	fishcutter	39	"
P	Livingstone Duncan	201	millwright	56	"
R	Livingstone Frank	201	U S A	22	"
S	Livingstone George	201	U S M C	20	"
T	Livingstone John	201	laborer	25	"
U	Livingstone Lawrence	201	U S A	23	"
V	Livingstone Mary †	201	housewife	56	"
W	Livingstone Mary †	201	saleswoman	31	"
X	Polcari Anthony	201	bridgetender	44	"
Y	Polcari Louis	201	laborer	39	"
Z	*Polcari Maria †	201	housekeeper	69	"

1137

A	Barletta Angelo	202	U S A	24	"
B	*Ruggiero Carmen	202	laborer	42	"
C	*Ruggiero Raffaela †	202	housewife	35	"
D	Barletta Ciriaco	202	carpenter	26	"
E	Barletta Evelyn †	202	housewife	22	"
F	Principato Henrietta †	203	"	49	"
G	Principato Josephine †	203	clerk	20	"
H	Principato Joseph	203	plumber	45	"
K	Flaschner Caroline M †	203	housewife	40	"
L	Flaschner Laura L †	203	"	20	"
M	Flaschner Leo H	203	chauffeur	43	"
N	Flaschner Leo R	203	"	20	"
O	Giovino Patrick	203	pipefitter	38	"
P	Giovino Rose †	203	housewife	31	"
R	Serra Carlo	204	electrician	38	"
S	Serra Rose †	204	housewife	35	"
T	Cleary Dorothy K †	204	packer	30	"
U	Cleary Herbert C	204	U S A	21	"
V	Cleary Sarah L †	204	at home	61	"
W	Lombard Edward P	204	accountant	31	"
X	Rossetti Andrew	204	U S A	21	"
Y	Rossetti Antonetta †	204	housewife	44	"
Z	Rossetti Pasquale	204	laborer	49	"

1138

Princeton Street—Continued

A	D'Entremont Caroline †	205	housewife	46	here	
B	D'Entremont Joseph	205	fishcutter	51	"	
C	Norcott Mary—†	205	housewife	25	"	
D	Norcott Ronald	205	fisherman	32	"	
E	Caci Anne—†	205	stitcher	25	"	
F	Caci Benjamin	205	laborer	60	"	
G	Caci Joseph	205	U S A	29	"	
H	*Caci Louise—†	205	housewife	59	"	
K	Cornacchia Antonio	206	shipper	24	"	
L	Cornacchia Esther—†	206	housewife	25	"	
M	Clark Nellie—†	206	at home	50	"	
N	LaTorre Liborio	206	laborer	58	"	
O	LaTorre Mary—†	206	housewife	51	"	
P	Inserra Angie—†	207	"	55	"	
R	Inserra Jennie—†	207	clerk	25	"	
S	Inserra Louis	207	laborer	59	"	
T	Inserra Vito	207	U S A	24	"	
U	*Canata Mary—†	207	housewife	50	"	
V	*Canata Rosario	207	plasterer	56	"	
W	LaMonica Jennie—†	207	housewife	22	"	
X	LaMonica Joseph	207	electrician	25	497 Hanover	
Y	*Guisti Augusta—†	207	housewife	63	here	
Z	Guisti Hugo	207	laborer	24	"	

1139

A	Guisti Joseph	207	retired	68	"	
B	Guisti Maria—†	207	housewife	21	"	
C	Connolly Elsie—†	208	"	21	"	
D	Connolly Lawrence	208	fish handler	24	"	
E	Connelly Emilie—†	208	housewife	41	"	
F	Connelly Martin J	208	teamster	46	"	
G	Connelly Mary A—†	208	maid	61	"	
H	Cohen George M	208	U S A	24	"	
K	Cohen Virginia—†	208	housewife	20	"	
L	*Simons Louis	208	tailor	65	"	
M	*Simons Pearl—†	208	housewife	56	"	
N	Ribaudo Concetta—†	211	at home	20	"	
O	Ribaudo Maria—†	211	housekeeper	43	"	
P	Ribaudo Vincent	211	U S A	21	"	
R	Trunfio Anthony	211	student	21	"	
S	Trunfio Etta—†	211	at home	26	"	
T	Trunfio Filomena—†	211	housewife	45	"	

24

Princeton Street Continued

u	Trunfio Marie †	211	clerk	24	here
v	Trunfio Paul	211	finisher	50	"
w	*Scopa Carmella †	211	housewife	66	"
x	Scopa Elvira †	211	operator	26	"
y	Scopa Paul	211	laborer	62	"
z	Ventresca Josephine †	211	operator	25	"

1140

A	Matthews Catherine †	212	housewife	43	"
B	Matthews Wallace	212	mechanic	43	"
C	Bickford Leslie	212	chauffeur	44	"
D	Bickford Loretta †	212	housewife	28	"
E	Lutanno Mary †	213	"	24	"
F	Lutanno Michael	213	baker	27	"
G	Rocco Rose †	213	housewife	45	"
H	Rocco Salvatore	213	candymaker	46	"
K	Curry Isabelle †	213	housewife	45	"
L	Curry James L	213	foreman	46	"
M	Hemenway Gerald	214	mechanic	24	188 Falcon
N	Hemenway Seraphine †	214	housewife	24	188 "
O	Graziano Anna †	214	shoeworker	31	here
P	Graziano Generoso	214	mechanic	30	"
S	*Graziano Josephine †	214	housewife	55	"
T	Graziano Mildred †	214	at home	20	"
R	*Graziano Ottino	214	laborer	55	"
U	*Gallanti Giustina †	214	housewife	60	"
V	Gallanti Paulina †	214	candyworker	22	"
W	Gallanti Tito	214	blacksmith	59	"
X	Paldo Carolina †	215	clerk	24	"
Y	Paldo Domenic	215	laborer	60	"
Z	Paldo Florence †	215	housewife	58	"

1141

A	Coffin Bertha M †	215	stitcher	20	"
B	Coffin Kenneth N	215	welder	23	"
C	Coffin Lucy †	215	housewife	53	"
D	Coffin Melbourne	215	welder	46	"
E	Complici Frances †	215	housewife	23	"
F	*Complici Hugo	215	shoeworker	27	"
G	*Saporito Concetta †	215	housewife	50	"
H	Saporito Rocco	215	laborer	54	"
K	Castagnia Enrico	216	barber	47	"
L	Leno Albert J	216	operator	20	"

25

Page	Letter	FULL NAME.	Residence, Jan. 1, 1943.	Occupation.	Supposed Age.	Reported Residence, Jan. 1, 1942. Street and Number.

Princeton Street—Continued

	M	Leno Mary —†	216	housewife	54	here
	N	Tusini Alphonse	216	shipper	30	"
	O	Tusini Rose—†	216	housewife	29	"
	P	*Garofolini Leonilda—†	216	"	41	"
	R	*Garofolini Louis	216	painter	48	"
	S	*Vincentori Adelino	216	carpenter	52	"
	T	Lynch David	217	laborer	43	"
	U	Lynch Marjorie—†	217	housewife	40	"
	V	Cassetta Anthony	217	student	22	"
	W	Cassetta Palma—†	217	housewife	42	"
	X	Cassetta Salvatore	217	inspector	46	"
	Y	Pastore Frederick G	217	student	23	142 Porter
	Z	Ellis Alexander	217	tailor	60	here
1142						
	A	Ellis Eva —†	217	secretary	24	"
	B	Ellis Sarah—†	217	housewife	54	"
	C	Butare Joseph	218	welder	26	"
	D	Butare Louise —†	218	housewife	22	"
	E	Hatch Jennie —†	218	"	28	"
	F	Hatch Linwood R	218	clerk	31	"
	G	McCallum Archie	218	U S N	24	Nebraska
	H	McCallum Rosalie —†	218	housewife	22	New York
	K	Barker James F	221	watchman	60	here
	L	Fitzgerald Agnes M —†	221	housewife	36	"
	M	Fitzgerald John R	221	longshoreman	40	"
	N	*DiBattista Giuseppe	222	laborer	49	"
	O	DiBattista Helen —†	222	candyworker	20	"
	P	*DiBattista Maria —†	222	housewife	47	"
	R	*Mosca Carmella —†	222	"	46	"
	S	Mosca Nicholas	222	laborer	21	"
	T	*Mosca Peter	222	foreman	50	"
	U	Hawes Alice —†	223	housewife	42	"
	V	Hawes Richard	223	packer	41	"
	W	LaRizza Lillian —† rear	223	housewife	44	"
	X	LaRizza Rudolph "	223	coppersmith	49	"
	Y	*Bellabona Clementina—† 2d r	223	housewife	54	"
	Z	Bellabona Genneroso 2d "	223	carpenter	53	"
1143						
	A	Bellabona Michelina—† 2d "	223	dressmaker	23	"
	B	Bellabona Theresa—† 2d "	223	operator	21	"
	D	Ciampa Anna—†	226	housewife	22	"

Princeton Street Continued

E	Ciampa John	226	electrician	27	here
F	Scarfo Adolfo	226	laborer	26	"
G*	Scarfo Angelina †	226	housewife	58	"
H	Gallo John	226	shipfitter	29	32 Decatur
K	Gallo Michelina †	226	housewife	27	32 "
L	Lessa Adelaide †	227	"	60	here
M	Lessa Charles	227	shoeworker	60	"
N	Lessa Charles	227	U S A	21	"
O	Lessa Josephine †	227	typist	25	"
P	Lessa Mary †	227	embroiderer	28	"
R	Lessa Michael	227	laborer	23	"
S	Lessa Vera †	227	stenographer	27	"
T	Hurley Clara †	227	housewife	28	"
U	Hurley James	227	B F D	30	"
V	Dibicarri Arline †	227	housewife	25	"
W	Dibicarri Louis	227	laborer	27	"
X	Burke Norma †	228	housewife	23	271 Princeton
Y	Burke William	228	electrician	23	271 "
Z	Bonano Anthony	228	U S A	21	here
	1144				
A	Bonano Carmella †	228	housewife	48	"
B	Bonano Salvatore	228	rubberworker	59	"
C*	Geraci Santa †	228	at home	85	"
D	Smaldone Emelio	228	ship joiner	38	"
E	Smaldone Florence †	228	housewife	36	"
F	Marinelli Frank	229	laborer	47	"
G*	Marinelli Mary †	229	housewife	42	"
H	Faretra Alfonso	229	laborer	24	"
K	Faretra Carmine	229	"	26	"
L	Faretra Joseph	229	"	58	"
M	Faretra Lillian †	229	operator	22	"
N	Faretra Mary †	229	housewife	52	"
P	Kinnear George E	231	expressman	65	"
R	Kinnear Sarah †	231	housewife	63	"
S	Rogers John	233	at home	72	"
T	Rogers Joseph	233	U S A	30	"
U	Rogers Mary †	233	housewife	67	"
V	Miles Louise †	234	dressmaker	28	"
W	Miles Margaret †	234	housekeeper	45	"
X	Miles Michael J	234	attorney	48	"
Y	Miles William	234	painter	56	"

Princeton Street— Continued

z	Doherty James	234	mechanic	65	here

1145

A	LoConte Anthony	236	welder	24	238 Bremen
B	LoConte Helen— †	236	housewife	26	320 Chelsea
C	Coluccino John	236	chauffeur	27	here
D	Coluccino Theresa— †	236	housewife	23	"
E	Farrand John E	236	foreman	32	"
F	*Farrand Margaret M— †	236	housewife	29	"
G	Sarno Anna— †	237	"	25	"
H	Sarno Carmine	237	painter	28	"
K	*Sarno Angelina— †	237	housewife	50	"
L	Sarno Joseph	237	U S M C	20	"
M	Sarno Onofrio	237	finisher	56	"
N	Sarno Susan— †	237	operator	24	"
O	Centofanti Alfred	238	machinist	23	"
P	Miller Henry P	238	shipfitter	43	"
R	Miller Mildred C— †	238	housewife	35	"
S	Miller Thomas S	238	machinist	45	New York
T	*Geraci Agostino	238	painter	52	here
U	Geraci Anthony	238	U S A	24	"
V	*Geraci Jennie— †	238	housewife	49	"
W	Shulz Gladys— †	rear 238	"	23	58 London
Y	Marley Alice R— †	239	"	39	here
¹Y	Marley Frederick	239	B F D	39	"
Z	Bossi Fiore	240	machinist	20	"

1146

A	Bossi Joseph	240	retired	61	"
B	*Bossi Pauline— †	240	housewife	56	"
C	Beekman Dorothy— †	240	"	23	Cambridge
D	Beekman Myles J	240	rigger	30	"
E	Bossi Domenic	240	laborer	27	here
F	Bossi Ida— †	240	housewife	27	"
G	Viscione Charles	241	laborer	26	"
K	Viscione Mary— †	241	housewife	26	"
H	Viscione Frank	241	candymaker	26	"
L	Viscione Mildred— †	241	housewife	25	"
O	Jones Emma— †	242	"	41	"
P	Jones James D	242	painter	40	"
M	Jesus Alfred	242	millworker	43	"
N	*Jesus Mary— †	242	housewife	41	"
R	Butare John	243	shipper	24	"

28

Princeton Street Continued

s	Butare Mary †	243	housewife	23	here
t	Roach Herbert	243	laborer	27	"
u	Roach Lawrence	243	salesman	37	"
v	Roach Mary G †	243	at home	37	"
w	Roach Sarah †	243	housekeeper	59	"
x	Babine Edmond	244	fishcutter	71	"
y	Babine Elizabeth †	244	housewife	62	"
z	Babine Louis E	244	U S A	32	"

1147

a	Babine Peter P	244	fishcutter	27	"
b	Babine Nellie †	244	housewife	41	"
c	Babine Simon	244	fishcutter	43	"
f	Sarno Antonio	246	plumber	23	"
g	Sarno Christina †	246	housewife	25	"
h	O'Donnell Ethel †	247	housekeeper	42	"
k	O'Donnell Henry	247	laborer	68	"
l	August Bernadette M †	247	clerk	21	"
m	August Irving J	247	U S M C	25	"
n	August Manuel F	247	finisher	59	"
o	August Sarah F †	247	housewife	59	"
p	Burnham Earl	247	letter carrier	60	"
r	Burnham Grace †	247	housewife	53	"
s	Despony Paul L	248	clergyman	66	"
t	*Veiga Mary B †	248	housekeeper	52	"
u	Kelley Henry L	249	B F D	46	"
v	Kelley Marie M †	249	housewife	37	"
w	Pumphret Alice L †	249	teacher	35	"
x	Pumphret Michael J	249	retired	78	"
y	McInnis George	250	boilermaker	44	"
z	August Albina †	250	housewife	47	42 Falcon

1148

a	August Anna †	250	operator	23	42 "
b	August Joseph F	250	accountant	25	42 "
c	August William	250	laborer	20	42 "
d	Hennessey John L	250	U S N	20	42 Soley
e	Peterson Marion †	250	stenographer	21	here
f	Peterson Mary †	250	housewife	48	"
g	Peterson Sigurd	250	engineer	53	"
h	Owen Aloyse †	251	teacher	60	"
k	Anderson Mary †	252	clerk	47	"
l	Anderson Thomas G	252	U S N	20	"

Princeton Street—Continued

M	Stevenson Annie—†	252	at home	70	here
N	Neal Charles W	252	retired	71	"
O	Neal Frances A—†	252	shoeworker	22	"
P	Neal Mary E—†	252	housewife	61	"
R	Neal Mona M—†	252	chemist	20	"
S	Neal Regina—†	252	factoryhand	24	"
T	Shannon Edward	252	U S A	44	"
U	Shannon Frederick L	252	mechanic	37	"
V	Shannon Mary—†	252	at home	75	"
W	Swadel Charles	253	clerk	23	"
X	Swadel June—†	253	housewife	22	"
Y	Mangioratti Filomena—†	253	"	32	"
Z	Mangioratti Joseph	253	electrician	33	"

1149

A	Lacorazza Anthony	253	plater	32	"
B	Lacorazza Lena—†	253	housewife	27	"
C	Riccardi Fannie—†	255	"	25	"
D	Riccardi Joseph	255	U S A	28	"
E	DiFranza Americo	255	artist	24	"
F	DiFranza Antonio	255	laborer	62	"
G	DiFranza Joseph	255	U S A	26	"
H	*DiFranza Saveria—†	255	housewife	59	"
K	Malgioglio Joseph	255	presser	36	"
L	*Malgioglio Marie T—†	255	housewife	34	"
N	Borgess Henry B	262	laborer	26	Lowell
P	Borgess Henry L	262	woodworker	56	90 Eutaw
O	Borgess Louise—†	262	housewife	53	90 "
R	Palange Antonio	262	retired	59	here
S	Palange Josephine—†	262	housewife	57	"
T	Corrino Joseph	262	rubberworker	20	2 Wash'n av
U	Corrino Marita—†	262	housewife	22	2 "
V	*Gomes Manuel	262	retired	55	2 "
W	*Gomes Mary—†	262	housewife	50	2 "
X	Vena Ella—†	266	"	38	here
Y	Vena John	266	chipper	38	"
Z	*Vena Antonetta—†	266	housewife	59	"

1150

A	*Vena Pelegrino	266	bootblack	64	"
B	Kelley John	266	chauffeur	50	"
C	Kelley Margaret—†	266	housewife	48	"
D	Irwin Edward	268	clerk	39	"

20

Princeton Street Continued

E	Irwin Kathleen †	268	housewife	36	here
F	*Petralia Frances †	268	"	49	"
G	Petralia Sebastiano	268	carpenter	68	"
H	Dumas Eugene	268	millworker	38	368 Princeton
K	*Dumas Simone †	268	housewife	31	368 "
L	Toscano Angelo	270	retired	65	here
M	Toscano Carmella †	270	at home	22	"
N	Toscano Domenic	270	plumber	26	"
O	Buontempo John	270	musician	65	"
P	*Buontempo Julia †	270	housewife	67	"
R	Nazzaro Caroline †	270	"	30	143 Putnam
S	Nazzaro Joseph	270	welder	31	143 "
T	*DiFuria Angelina †	272	housewife	54	here
U	DiFuria Carmello	272	laborer	58	"
V	DiFuria Julio	272	U S N	24	"
W	DiFuria Lucy †	272	at home	28	"
X	DiFuria Maria D †	272	millworker	22	"
Y	Coutreau Albany	272	bartender	47	"
Z	Pothier George	272	engineer	32	"

1151

A	Pothier Isadore	272	seaman	63	"
B	Pothier Madeline †	272	housewife	34	"
C	Barrasso Armando	272	cobbler	38	"
D	Barrasso Margaret †	272	housewife	35	"
E	Nalen Anthony W	274	clerk	39	"
F	Nalen Gertrude M †	274	housewife	32	"
H	Rubico Amelia †	274	"	34	"
K	Rubico Jerome	274	cobbler	31	"
L	Saggese Adelina †	276	housewife	57	"
M	Saggese Giuseppe	276	laborer	64	"
N	Chalmers Fred W	276	fireman	44	"
O	Chalmers Fred W, jr	276	U S A	20	"
P	Chalmers Mary A †	276	housewife	44	"
R	*Mitchell Elizabeth †	276	"	35	"
S	Mitchell Frederick	276	fisherman	34	"
T	*Scanlon Elizabeth †	276	at home	69	"
U	*Antello Carl	278	mechanic	45	"
V	Stenberg Anna †	278	at home	75	"
W	Lee Evelyn †	rear 278	housewife	33	10 Shelby
X	Lee Karl B	" 278	machinist	32	10 "
Y	Bordieri Jennie †	284	housewife	27	here

31

Princeton Street — Continued

z	Bordieri Salvatore	284	welder	25	here

1152

A*	Capo Angelina †	284	housewife	64	"
B	Capo John	284	millhand	63	"
C	Messenger Mary †	286	at home	80	"
D	Baldassaro Louis	286	tailor	28	"
E	Baldassaro Santina †	286	housewife	28	"
F	Sinclair Margaret †	288	"	33	13 Wadsworth
G	Sinclair William	288	longshoreman	39	13 "
H	Shanahan Leo	288	"	39	here
K	Shanahan Lillian †	288	housewife	38	"
L	Shanahan Patrick	288	longshoreman	50	"
M	Genzale Angelina †	288	housewife	30	"
N	Genzale Anthony	288	painter	30	"
O	Alexander Ellen †	292	housewife	44	"
P	Dean Gertrude †	294	"	40	"
R	Dean Ralph	294	B F D	42	"
S	Donnelly Frances †	294	at home	78	"
T	Alexander Victor	296	laborer	42	"
U	Alexander Winifred †	296	housewife	37	"
V	Peterson Ernest	298	brazier	24	"
W	Peterson Irene †	298	housewife	27	"
X	Smith Mary †	298	at home	64	"
Y*	Rossi Louis	300	laborer	59	"
Z*	Rossi Rose †	300	at home	55	"

1153

A	Driscoll Catherine †	310	housewife	24	"
B	Driscoll Paul	310	electrician	26	"
C	Walsh Charles	310	machinist	28	"
D	Walsh Doris †	310	housewife	28	"
E	Lavender Marie †	310	at home	65	"
F	O'Neil Delia †	310	housewife	60	"
G	O'Neil John J	310	laborer	24	"
L	Salimbene Elsie †	312	housewife	22	"
M	Salimbene Frank	312	machinist	24	"
N	Fabiano Rocco	312	shipfitter	25	"
O	Fabiano Rose †	312	housewife	49	"
P*	Vitalli Dorothy †	312	at home	75	"
R	Vitalli Emilio	312	laborer	40	"
S	Vitalli Mary †	312	housewife	35	"
T	Saviano Phillip	314	machinist	31	"

Princeton Street Continued

	U	Saviano Phyllis †	314	housewife	28	here
	V	Simione Alfred	314	laborer	29	"
	W	*Simione Jennie †	314	housewife	36	"
	X	Albanese Domenic	314	retired	62	"
	Y	Albanese Madeline †	314	housewife	54	"
	Z	Albanese Thomas	314	shipfitter	24	"

1154

	A	Gill Joseph P	316	laborer	33	"
	B	Gill Phyllis †	316	housewife	35	"
	C	St Croix Jean †	316	"	21	399 Chelsea
	D	St Croix Joseph E	316	shipfitter	22	320 Saratoga
	E	Gill Joseph P	316	retired	63	320 "
	F	Gill Manuel	316	machinist	23	here
	G	*Gill Wilmina P †	316	housewife	58	"
	H	Orlando Frank	318	carpenter	53	"
	K	Orlando Helen †	318	housewife	24	"
	L	Orlanda John	318	carpenter	31	"
	M	Szkolt Frank	318	busboy	34	Springfield
	N	Siraco Domenic	318	retired	69	here
	O	Siraco Frank	318	mattressmaker	42	"
	P	*Siraco Mary †	318	housewife	69	"
	R	*Tasso Mary †	318	"	37	"
	S	Tasso Samuel	318	weaver	47	"
	T	Mirabello Emilia †	320	housewife	39	"
	U	Mirabello Joseph	320	boilermaker	45	"
	V	Siraco Joseph	320	tinsmith	39	"
	W	Siraco Mary †	320	housewife	35	"
	X	Walker Margaret †	320	"	22	Beachmont
	Y	Walker Ralph P	320	machinist	27	"
	Z	Campbell Florence †	322	housekeeper	63	here

1155

	D	Regan Harriett †	324	housewife	37	"
	E	Regan James M	324	laborer	32	"
	F	Garnache Carl	324	U S A	25	"
	G	Garnache Stella †	324	housewife	21	"

Putnam Street

	H	Harris Elizabeth †	106	housewife	71	Cambridge
	K	Harris George C	106	chef	71	"
	L	*Colantino Leo	106	candymaker	63	here

Putnam Street—Continued

	M	*Colantino Mary †	106	housewife	54	here
	N	Gleason John B	106	U S A	38	"
	O	Wyse Catherine †	106	housewife	62	"
	P	Wyse John	106	laborer	39	"
	R	Cerrate Carmella †	108	housewife	34	"
	S	Cerrate Louis	108	laborer	39	"
	T	Frizoli Carmela †	108	clerk	20	"
	U	Frizoli Domenic	108	laborer	55	"
	V	Frizoli Gilda †	108	housewife	44	"
	W	Benvissuto John	108	barber	50	"
	X	Benvissuto Mary †	108	housewife	42	"
	Y	*Hallander Emil	110	ironworker	54	"
	Z	*Hallander Hilma †	110	housewife	63	"

1156

	A	Amundsen Andrew	112	foreman	57	"
	B	Jensen Annie M †	112	housewife	56	"
	C	Jensen Anton	112	carpenter	62	"
	D	Jensen Ethel †	112	cashier	22	"
	E	Peterson Pauline †	112	housewife	82	"
	F	Amoroso Joseph	126	laborer	53	"
	G	Amoroso Rose †	126	housewife	46	"
	H	Amoroso Samuel	126	U S N	22	"
	K	Blunda Frances †	126	housewife	67	"
	L	Blunda Frank	126	laborer	69	"
	M	Blunda Josephine †	126	bookkeeper	29	"
	N	Blunda Mary †	126	"	31	"
	O	*Interbartolo Joseph	126	retired	80	"
	P	Matthews Joseph	126	mechanic	37	"
	R	Matthews Mary †	126	housewife	35	"
	S	*Caruso Frank	128	laborer	60	"
	T	Ruotola Angelo	128	student	23	"
	U	Ruotola Fank	128	laborer	59	"
	V	*Ruotola Mary †	128	housewife	61	"
	W	Ruotola Louis	128	steamfitter	33	"
	X	Ruotola Rose †	128	housewife	30	"
	Y	Ruotola Girardo	128	electrician	36	"
	Z	Ruotola Helen †	128	housewife	35	"

1157

	A	Caci Angelo	130	laborer	27	306 Saratoga
	B	Caci Betrina †	130	housewife	25	306 "
	C	LaMonica Josephine †	130	"	48	194 Benningt'n

Putnam Street   Continued

D	La Monica Santo	130	barber	49	194 Benningt'n
E	Nolan Catherine M †	130	clerk	29	here
F	Nolan James	130	"	53	"
G	Nolan Mary M †	130	housewife	48	"
K	Catinezzo Norma †	140	"	23	38 Paris
L	Catinezzo Vincent	140	laborer	26	38 "
M	Silano Ralph	140	"	73	here
N	Silano Rose †	140	housewife	60	"
O	Tranquilano Anthony	140	laborer	42	"
P	Powers Cecil	141	"	42	"
R	Powers Lillian †	141	housewife	31	"
S	Staffier Anthony F	141	draftsman	21	"
T	Staffier Christina †	141	orator	23	"
U	Staffier Frank J	141	butcher	52	"
V	Staffier Anthony	141	barber	47	"
W	Staffier Domenic T	141	printer	23	"
X	*Staffier Mary †	141	housewife	47	"
Y	Staffier Thomasine †	141	at home	26	"

1158

A	*Ardita Anthony	142	laborer	64	"
B	*Ardita Maria †	142	housewife	45	"
C	Ardita Michael	142	U S A	21	"
D	*Ciampa Nicola M	142	laborer	77	"
E	Santoro Alesio	143	U S A	27	"
F	Santoro Angelo	143	coppersmith	22	"
G	*Santoro Frances †	143	housewife	52	"
H	Santoro Margaret †	143	factoryhand	24	"
K	*Laurano Maria G †	143	housewife	43	38 Bremen
L	Calvano Antonetta †	143	"	44	here
M	Calvano Giovanni	143	laborer	54	"
N	Visconte Vincenzo	143	"	81	"
O	Lamb Hannah †	144	housewife	72	"
P	McLellan Johanna †	144	"	69	"
R	Regan Daniel	144	mechanic	27	"
S	Regan Ellen †	144	clerk	30	"
T	Puopolo John	145	mechanic	33	"
U	Puopolo Josephine †	145	at home	23	"
V	Puopolo Nicola	145	retired	76	"
W	Flammia Angelina †	145	housewife	36	"
X	Flammia Joseph	145	driller	40	"
Y	Lodise Christine †	145	housewife	39	"

25

Putnam Street — Continued

z	Lodise Joseph	145	driller	43	here
1159						
A	Bonim Emmie — †	146	housewife	74	277 Meridian
B	Ricciardelli Joseph F	146	metal polisher	26	here
C	*Ricciardelli Mary — †	146	housewife	26	"
D	Saia Arthur	146	U S A	29	4 Elbow
E	Saia Rita — †	146	housewife	58	4 "
F	Saia Romeo	146	shipper	25	4 "
G	Saia Valerio	146	retired	70	4 "
H	Chianca Rose — †	146	housewife	26	here
K	Chianca Vincent	146	laborer	28	"
L	Simmons Joan — †	146	housewife	20	"
M	Puopolo Jennie — †	147	"	31	"
N	Puopolo Ralph	147	proprietor	35	"
O	McCarthy Jane E — †	147	housewife	48	"
P	Generson Mary — †	148	"	70	"
R	Antonuccia Rose — †	148	"	54	"
S	Antonuccia Salvatore	148	laborer	56	"
T	*Bartolo Joseph	148	mechanic	37	"
U	Bartolo Lucy †	148	housewife	30	"
V	Schraffa Angela M — †	149	"	62	"
W	Schraffa Francis P	149	U S A	30	"
X	Schraffa Rocco J	149	tailor	34	"
Y	Grasso Angelo	149	mechanic	42	"
Z	Grasso Josephine †	149	housewife	41	"
1160						
B	Joyce Andrew M	150A	U S A	30	"
C	Joyce Elizabeth C — †	150A	housewife	67	"
D	Joyce Lawrence P	150A	laborer	38	"
E	Joyce Mary A — †	150A	saleswoman	33	"
F	Joyce Peter F	150A	mechanic	42	"
G	DiFlumeri Antonetta †	150A	housewife	30	"
H	DiFlumeri Patrick	150A	mechanic	31	"
K	Goveia Joseph	151	clerk	20	"
L	*Goveia Mary — †	151	housewife	37	"
M	*Delario Jenny — †	151	"	59	"
N	Delario John	151	laborer	63	"
O	Gomes Aurelia — †	151	housewife	49	"
P	Gomes Eugene	151	laborer	49	"
R	*Iannuzzi Thomasina †	152	stitcher	48	653 Benningt'n
S	Smaldone John	152	mechanic	37	here

Putnam Street Continued

T	Smaldone Mildred †	152	housewife	36	here	
U	Vetano Salvatore	152	candymaker	18	"	
V	Vetano Theresa †	152	housewife	37	"	
X	*Abate John	153	proprietor	58	"	
Y	*Abate Rose †	153	housewife	57	"	
Z	Lane Leo J	153	checker	44	"	

1161

A	*Lane Sarah T †	153	housewife	42	"	
B	DeDeo Anthony	154	laborer	44	"	
C	DeDeo Jeanette †	154	housewife	41	"	
D	Montecalvo Marciano	154	mechanic	34	"	
E	Montecalvo Selma †	154	housewife	31	"	
F	*Ceraso Camillo	154	laborer	60	"	
G	Ceraso Joseph	154	U S A	22	"	
H	*Ceraso Josephine †	154	housewife	49	"	
K	Viera Arthur	156	attendant	23	437 Bennington	
L	Viera Elvira †	156	housewife	23	437 "	
M	Flaherty Agnes T †	156	secretary	27	here	
N	Flaherty Lawrence J	156	U S N	22	"	
O	Flaherty Nellie †	156	housewife	59	"	
P	Salvo Domenic	156	laborer	48	"	
R	*Salvo Rose †	156	housewife	44	"	
S	*Nickerson Alston	158	foreman	29	"	
T	Nickerson Maria †	158	housewife	29	"	
U	Iodice Nicholas	158	shoemaker	37	"	
V	Iodice Rose †	158	housewife	33	"	
W	Vitello Anna †	158	factoryhand	30	"	
X	Vitello Concetta †	158	housewife	57	"	
Y	Vitello Pasquale	158	laborer	59	"	
Z	Vella Alice †	160	housewife	28	"	

1162

A	Vella Salvatore	160	spinner	31	"	
B	*Coscia Alphonse	160	baker	48	"	
C	Coscia Carmella †	160	housewife	38	"	
D	*Gramaldo Philomena †	160	"	83	"	
E	*Masci Angelina †	160	"	44	"	
F	Masci Anthony	160	candymaker	47	"	
G	Grande Christopher	162	fishcutter	29	"	
H	Grande Emily †	162	housewife	27	"	
K	Corvino Josephine †	162	"	26	"	
L	Corvino Vincent	162	fishcutter	31	"	

Page.	Letter.	FULL NAME.	Residence. Jan. 1, 1943.	Occupation.	Supposed Age.	Reported Residence. Jan. 1, 1942. Street and Number.

Putnam Street—Continued

M	Agave Minnie—†	162	housewife	44	here
N	Agave Umberto	162	baker	50	"
O	Bonito Daniel	164	U S A	38	"
P	Bonito Effie—†	164	housewife	35	"
R	*Picinisco Frances—†	164	"	66	"
S	Picinisco John	164	laborer	64	"
T	Picinisco John	164	U S A	38	"
U	Scanzillo Louis	164	pipefitter	26	"
V	Scanzillo Susan—†	164	housewife	26	"
W	Colagiovanni Anna—†	166	"	20	12 Webster av
X	Colagiovanni Donato	166	mechanic	20	255 Marion
Y	Carpinelli Lucy—†	166	housewife	32	here
Z	Carpinelli Nicholas	166	mechanic	31	"

1163

A	*Cornetta Angelo	166	retired	74	"
B	Cornetta Angelo	166	butcher	20	"
C	Cornetta John	166	welder	40	"
D	*Cornetta Rose—†	166	housewife	75	"
E	Cornetta Rose—†	166	"	36	"
F	Blundo Josephine—†	168	"	23	"
G	Blundo Nicholas	168	welder	24	"
H	Oliver Albert	168	mechanic	31	"
K	*Oliver Mary—†	168	housewife	30	"
L	*Interbartolo Antonetta—†	168	"	36	"
M	Interbartolo Charles	168	chauffeur	38	"
N	Frusciante Anthony	170	laborer	35	"
O	Frusciante Carmella—†	170	housewife	30	"
P	Frusciante Joseph	170	laborer	30	"
R	Curallo Angela—†	170	housewife	56	"
S	Curallo Luciano	170	laborer	67	"
T	Curallo Rosario	170	welder	23	"
U	Beaupre Alfred	170	"	36	"
V	Beaupre Caroline—†	170	housewife	29	"
X	*Brass Elizabeth—†	172	saleswoman	32	"
Y	*Brass Minnie—†	172	"	35	"
Z	Miller David	172	proprietor	61	"

1164

A	Miller Sarah—†	172	housewife	61	"
B	Marinelli Domenic	172	mechanic	31	166 Putnam
C	Marinelli Minnie—†	172	housewife	26	166 "
F	Bennett Earl	198	laborer	21	111 Brooks

28

Putnam Street — Continued

G	Bennett Nolia †	198	housewife	67	111 Brooks
H	Balliro Joseph	198	laborer	57	here

Saratoga Street

K	McLaughlin Mary †	251	at home	67	here
L	Murphy Mary M †	251	"	72	75 Eutaw
M	Murphy Neil M	251	U S A	42	75 "
N	Sullivan Mary †	251	housewife	32	here
O	Sullivan William	251	chauffeur	33	"
P	Indingaro Charles	253	fishcutter	47	243 Chelsea
R	Indingaro Frances †	253	housewife	31	243 "
S	Ciampi Charles	253	driller	26	here
T	Ciampi Mildred †	253	housewife	27	"
U	*Manganella Louise †	253	at home	64	"
V	Ciampi Caroline †	253	packer	23	"
W	*Ciampi Filomena †	253	housewife	48	"
X	Ciampi Luigi	253	candyworker	56	"
Y	Guardabasso Frank	255	driller	30	"
Z	Guardabasso Margaret †	255	housewife	28	"

1465

A	Nobile G Rudolph	255	attorney	38	"
B	Nobile Raffaella †	255	housewife	34	"
C	Guardabasso Antonio	255	laborer	32	"
D	Guardabasso John	255	"	56	"
E	Guardabasso Lena †	255	housewife	60	"
F	Russo Angelina †	257	"	22	"
G	Russo Louis	257	barber	24	"
K	Bossi Carmen	257	laborer	60	"
H	Bossi Caroline †	257	optical worker	21	"
L	Bossi Genevieve †	257	"	26	"
M	*Bossi Teresa †	257	housewife	56	"
N	Bossi Yolanda †	257	florist	24	"
O	DiCrescenzo Mary †	257	housewife	28	"
P	DiCrescenzo Michael	257	reamer	31	"
R	Indingaro Arthur	259	inspector	32	"
S	Indingaro Caroline †	259	housewife	30	"
T	Scramazzino Anthony	259	keyman	24	"
U	Scramazzino Esther †	259	housewife	25	"
X	Sambrone Mary †	301A	stitcher	36	"
Y	Sambrone Rosario	301A	musician	46	"

Saratoga Street— Continued

z	Gambino Benjamin J	301A	U S A	28	here	

1166

A	Gambino Nellie—†	301A	at home	48	"	
B	*Crescenzo Albina—†	302	housewife	38	"	
C	Crescenzo Vincenzo	302	joiner	41	"	
D	Panzina Benjamin	302	painter	35	34 N Russell	
E	Panzina Grace—†	302	housewife	36	34 "	
F	*Asgrizzi Gelsomina —†	303	"	56	here	
G	Asgrizzi Salvatore	303	retired	62	"	
H	Clarke Julia—†	303	nurse	45	"	
K	Crumley Grace—†	303	at home	62	"	
L	Surette Elizabeth—†	303	housewife	31	"	
M	Surette William	303	machinist	35	"	
N	Mastrogiovanni Carlo	304	clerk	27	"	
O	Mastrogiovanni Helen —†	304	housewife	24	"	
P	Zambuto Carmela—†	304	"	45	"	
R	Zambuto Giuseppe	304	rubberworker	51	"	
S	Gullifa Grace—†	304	housewife	38	"	
T	*Gullifa Ludo	304	chauffeur	40	"	
U	*Natale Maria—†	305	housewife	67	"	
V	Natale Rocco	305	U S A	21	"	
W	*Natale Salvatore	305	retired	80	"	
X	*Puzzo Rocca—†	305	packer	47	"	
Y	Puzzo Vitale	305	laborer	48	"	
Z	Barletta Agnes—†	305	at home	47	"	

1167

A	Barletta Anthony	305	U S A	22	"	
B	Callahan Ann—†	306	housewife	22	"	
C	Callahan John	306	policeman	25	"	
D	Lombardo Carmen	306	manager	24	"	
E	Lombardo Mary—†	306	housewife	22	"	
F	Lombardo Florence—†	306	"	42	"	
G	Lombardo Florence—†	306	tailoress	25	"	
H	Lombardo Phillip	306	chef	58	"	
K	Lepore Natalie—†	306	housewife	21	"	
L	Lepore Peter	306	rigger	22	266 Lexington	
M	Peatfield Mary—†	307	housewife	28	here	
N	Peatfield Wilbur E	307	electrician	36	"	
O	*Amirault Mary—†	307	housewife	33	"	
P	*Amirault Ray	307	fishcutter	39	"	
R	*DeAngelis Carmela—†	307	housewife	63	"	

40

Saratoga Street Continued

s	DeAngelis Carmen	307	laborer	23	here
T*	DeAngelis Massamino	307	"	62	"
U	DeAngelis Michael	307	"	33	"
V	DeAngelis Pasquale	307	U S A	22	"
W	DeAngelis Vincenzo	307	laborer	29	"
X	Staffier Mary A †	308	housewife	45	"
Y*	Staffier Phyllis †	308	at home	74	"
Z	Staffier Rocco	308	merchant	41	"

1168

A	Nazzaro Joseph	308	shoeworker	48	"
B	Nazzaro Mary E †	308	housewife	49	"
C	Staffier Agnes E †	308	"	52	"
D	Staffier Angelo A	308	shoeworker	54	"
E	Staffier Eleanor †	308	clerk	21	"
F	Staffier Rocco A	308	U S A	24	"
G	Mancusi Frances †	309	at home	25	365 Sumner
H	Telespro Joseph	309	retired	65	here
K*	Telespro Manuella †	309	housewife	75	"
L	Telespro Pasquale	309	messenger	42	"
M	Volpe Marie †	309	housewife	23	"
N	Volpe Peter	309	supervisor	26	"
O*	Bossi Antonette †	310	housewife	34	"
P	Bossi Joseph	310	painter	34	"
R	Alfano Antonio	310	splicer	57	"
S	Alfano Domenico	310	U S A	26	"
T	Alfano Generoso	310	"	22	"
U	Alfano Giovannina †	310	housewife	52	"
V	Alfano Jennie †	310	stitcher	20	"
W	Alfano Vincenzo	310	U S A	23	"
X	Riggillo Rocco	310	foreman	37	"
Y	Riggillo Yolanda †	310	housewife	26	"
Z	Manfredonia Florence †	311	"	29	"

1169

A	Manfredonia Joseph	311	trainman	28	"
B	Grande Anastasia †	311	housewife	53	"
C	Pierro Antonetta †	311	"	29	"
D	Pierro Joseph	311	printer	31	"
E*	Cerullo Adelina †	312	housewife	28	112 Saratoga
F	Cerullo William G	312	welder	26	151 Trenton
G	Collins Ellen †	312	at home	80	here
H	Collins Thomas	312	plumber	38	"

H

Page.	Letter.	FULL NAME.	Residence, Jan. 1, 1943.	Occupation.	Supposed Age.	Reported Residence, Jan. 1, 1942. Street and Number.

Saratoga Street—Continued

	K	Colucci Carl	312	shipfitter	27	here
	L	Colucci Genovina—†	312	housewife	59	"
	M	Colucci Gerardo	312	barber	60	"
	N	Coleman Ida E—†	313	at home	62	"
	O*	DeFeo Angelina—†	313	housewife	53	"
	P*	DeFeo Antonio	313	blacksmith	60	"
	R	DeFeo Guido	313	U S A	21	"
	S	DeFeo William	313	"	31	"
	T*	Babine Helen—†	314	housewife	40	"
	U*	Babine James	314	fisherman	53	"
	V	Ferrara Nancy—†	314	dressmaker	21	"
	W	Ferrara Nellie—†	314	housewife	42	"
	X	Ferrara Nicholas	314	barber	55	"
	Y	Ferrara Placido	314	cleaner	22	"
	Z*	Waldron Beatrice—†	314	waitress	36	"

1170

	B	Converse James	315	laborer	28	Florida
	C	Shea Anna G—†	315	housewife	51	here
	D	Shea Richard F	315	retired	66	"
	E	Toomey George H	315	"	59	"
	F	Viscay Frances—†	315	housewife	25	212 Saratoga
	G	Viscay Joseph	315	sealer	33	212 "
	H	Gallo Jennie—†	316	stitcher	43	here
	K	Gallo John	316	painter	49	"
	L	Schleich Mary F—†	316	inspector	33	Pennsylvania
	M	Aloise Peter	316	U S N	21	320 Princeton
	N*	DeMeo Carmella—†	316	housewife	45	320 "
	O	DeMeo Cesare	316	barber	44	320 "
	P	Hender Frederick J	316	laborer	20	here
	R	Hender Mary E—†	316	housewife	50	"
	S	Hender Walter J	316	shipfitter	57	"
	T	Hender Walter J, jr	316	U S A	22	"
	U*	McDonnell Daniel	316	retired	86	"
	V	Ruotolo Joseph	317	laborer	63	"
	W	Stella Mary—†	317	housewife	30	76 Frankfort
	X	Stella Rinaldo	317	plumber	25	76 "
	Y	LeBlanc Josephine—†	317	housewife	27	here
	Z	LeBlanc Lawrence	317	fishcutter	24	"

1171

| | A | DelVecchio Antonetta—† | 317 | housewife | 60 | " |
| | B | DelVecchio Ottavio | 317 | candymaker | 58 | " |

42

Saratoga Street Continued

c	Laquaglia Antonio	319	tailor	62	here
d*	Laquaglia Rose †	319	housewife	59	"
e	Laquaglia Margaret †	319	dressmaker	30	"
f	Laquaglia Santo	319	packer	20	"
g	Laquaglia Teresa †	319	tailoress	31	"
h	Laquaglia Charles	319	U S N	29	"
k	Laquaglia Frank	319	U S A	25	"
l	Laquaglia George	319	"	21	"
m	Laquaglia Rocco	319	"	27	"
n*	St Croix Charlotte †	320	housewife	56	"
o*	St Croix William	320	fisherman	62	"
p	Bruno Frank P	320	librarian	28	"
r	Bruno Lucia †	320	housewife	58	"
s	Bruno Nicholas	320	typist	26	"
t	Bruno Ralph	320	U S A	24	"
u	Bruno Riccardo	320	joiner	56	"
v	Bruno Riccardo, jr	320	U S A	20	"
w	Bruno Rose †	320	clerk	29	"
x	Abbruzze Giovanina †	320	at home	26	"
y*	Abbruzze Maria †	320	"	56	"
z	Abbruzze Marian †	320	stitcher	28	"

1172

a	Abbruzze Pasquale	320	U S A	25	"
b	Abbruzze Vincenzo	320	operator	22	"
c	Leonard Alice †	321	housewife	30	103 Falcon
d	Leonard Frank	321	chauffeur	31	103 "
e	Banks Gertrude †	322	housewife	31	here
f	Banks John R	322	metalworker	38	"
g	Jackson Florence †	322	housewife	28	220 Chelsea
h	Jackson William	322	brazier	29	220 "
k	Pucciarello Elizabeth †	322	stenographer	25	here
l	Pucciarello Lawrence	322	U S A	22	"
m	Pucciarello Mary †	322	housewife	48	"
n	Pucciarello Pasquale	322	foreman	49	"
o	Jeffrey Florence R †	323	housewife	45	"
p	Jeffrey William J	323	U S C G	46	"
r	Caggiano Adeline †	324	clerk	20	"
s	Caggiano Antonetta †	324	dressmaker	24	"
t	Caggiano Antonio	324	retired	60	"
u	Caggiano Concetta †	324	stenographer	25	"
v*	Caggiano Francesca †	324	housewife	60	"

43

Saratoga Street — Continued

w	Caggiano Teresa—†	324	clerk	32	here
x	Caggiano Nunziata—†	324	housewife	25	128 Putnam
y	Caggiano Saverio	324	agent	31	here
z	Cagnina Anthony	324	U S A	28	Woburn

1173

A	Cagnina Elizabeth—†	324	clerk	25	Pennsylvania
B	DeDominico Secondino	324	retired	65	215 Saratoga
C	Scarparetto Gabriello	324	laborer	55	here
E	Pizzano Antonio rear	325	retired	70	"
D	Pizzano Assunta † "	325	operator	35	"
F*	Pizzano Elvira—† "	325	housewife	61	"
G	Pizzano John "	325	U S A	21	"
H	Pizzano Vincenzo J "	325	"	22	"
K	Iannello Pasquale	326	mechanic	40	277 Havre
L	Iannello Santa—†	326	stitcher	36	277 "
N	Jeffrey John E	329	U S A	42	here
O	Jeffrey Joseph H	329	retired	77	"
P	Jeffrey Mary—†	329	at home	50	"
R	Jeffrey Walter J	329	U S A	40	"
S	Dwyer Margaret L †	330	bookkeeper	48	"
T	Ahern James J	330	longshoreman	45	"
U	Ahern William F	330	policeman	49	"
V	Bly Catherine A—†	330	at home	66	"
W	Donovan George A	330	U S A	36	"
X	Grant Josephine M †	330	housewife	51	"
Y	Grant Patrick J	330	policeman	54	"
Z	Parker Frederick R	330	U S A	40	"

1174

B	Keenan Henry T	331	"	24	"
C	Keenan Jane F †	331	tel operator	38	"
D	Keenan John E	331	machinist	36	"
E	Keenan John T	331	retired	70	"
F	Keenan Katherine M †	331	bookkeeper	30	"
G	Keenan Katherine W †	331	housewife	69	"
H	Keenan Leo B	331	clerk	28	"
K	Jardine Gladys †	333	millworker	21	"
L*	Vieira Louisa—†	333	housewife	49	"
M	Vieira Manuel	333	machinist	42	"
O	Amico Frances—†	340	housewife	24	156 Putnam
P	Amico Michael	340	brushmaker	31	156 "
R	Calliri Joseph	340	barber	52	here

44

Saratoga Street Continued

s	Calliri Lucy †	340	housewife	50	here
t	Calliri Rosalie †	340	stenographer	21	"
u	Natale Carmella †	340	housewife	44	"
v	Natale Frances †	340	secretary	23	"
w	Natale Joseph	340	rubberworker	49	"
x	Rossi Angeline †	342	millworker	21	"
y	Rossi Josephine †	342	bookkeeper	33	"
z	Rossi Stella †	342	housewife	55	"

1175

a	Rossi Vito	342	barber	57	"
b	Puopolo Angelina †	342	tailoress	25	"
c	Puopolo Antonetta †	342	housewife	44	"
d	Puopolo John	342	student	20	"
e	Puopolo Joseph	342	U S M C	24	"
f	Puopolo Rocco	342	retired	52	"
g	Marino Angelina †	344	housewife	32	"
h	Marino James	344	painter	34	"
k	*Zampitella Margaret †	344	cook	57	"
l	Alpha Georgia †	344	cashier	25	"
m	*Alpha Harriet †	344	housewife	47	"
n	*Alpha Louis	344	retired	52	"
o	Alpha Mary †	344	baker	23	"
p	Alpha Sophie †	344	rubberworker	20	"
r	Marino Anthony	344	painter	32	"
s	Marino Maria †	344	housewife	28	"
t	*Paraskepoulos George	344	cook	53	"
u	*Sinatra Gertrude †	346	housewife	36	302 Saratoga
v	Sinatra Vincent	346	shipper	40	302 "
w	Miller Eleanor J †	346	nurse	22	710 Mass av
x	Miller Florence †	346	housewife	47	here
y	Miller Gladys C †	346	clerk	21	"
z	Miller James E	346	boilermaker	48	"

1176

a	Whynot Abbie †	346	at home	71	"
b	Whynot Beulah †	346	packer	38	"
c	Whynot Elsie †	346	"	28	"
d	Whynot Mae †	346	"	31	"
e	DeVeau Joseph C	348	metalworker	43	"
f	Saulnier Laurence S	348	shipwright	47	"
g	Saulnier Mary E †	348	housewife	39	"
h	Prudente Anna †	348	operator	35	"

15

Saratoga Street — Continued

	K	Prudente Antonio	348	retired	73	here
	L	*Prudente Fiorinda †	348	housewife	70	"
	M	Prudente Giulia —†	348	operator	34	"
	N	Prudente Josephine —†	348	stenographer	32	"
	O	Prudente William	348	U S A	29	"
	P	Marotta Pasquale	348		27	"
	R	Marotta Ruth —†	348	at home	23	65 Condor
	S	*Romano Angelina †	348	stitcher	35	here
	T	Romano Salvatore	348	porter	50	"
	V	Anderson Henry T	400	U S A	22	Chelsea
	W	DeFrietas John J	400	janitor	65	here
	X	DeFrietas Julia —†	400	housewife	45	"
	Y	Nichols Agnes —†	400	at home	45	404 Meridian
	Z	*Ferrette Perine †	400	"	40	835 Saratoga

1177

	B	*Cimmino Louis	400	presser	43	here
	C	Cimmino Rose —†	400	housewife	35	"

Shelby Street

	D	Scarofare Gennaro	5	spinner	47	here
	E	Scarofare Margaret †	5	housewife	38	"
	F	Daviaux Elizabeth †	5	"	21	"
	G	Daviaux Robert	5	shipper	21	"
	H	Mercurio Josephine —†	5	stitcher	42	"
	K	Costello Arthur	5	longshoreman	28	"
	L	Costello Frances †	5	housewife	27	"
	M	Olsen John	5	U S A	25	"

Ward 1–Precinct 12

CITY OF BOSTON

LIST OF RESIDENTS
20 YEARS OF AGE AND OVER

(NON-CITIZENS INDICATED BY ASTERISK)
(FEMALES INDICATED BY DAGGER)

AS OF

JANUARY 1, 1943

JOSEPH F. TIMILTY, *Chairman*
FREDERIC E. DOWLING, *Secretary*
WILLIAM A. MOTLEY, JR.
FRANCIS B. McKINNEY
EVERETT R. PROUT

Listing Board.

CITY OF BOSTON PRINTING DEPARTMENT

Page.	Letter.	FULL NAME.	Residence, Jan. 1, 1943.	Occupation.	Supposed Age.	Reported Residence, Jan. 1, 1942. Street and Number.

1200

Bennington Street

A	Gianetti Benjamin	149	U S N	21	here
B	Stoppolone Giuseppe	149	proprietor	53	"
c	*Stoppolone Mary—†	149	housewife	47	"
D	Graziano Antonette—†	149	"	31	"
E	Graziano Paul	149	machinist	29	"
F	Tortora Antonio	149	finisher	65	"
G	*Tortora Josephine—†	149	housewife	64	"
K	Flodin Anna—†	151	at home	75	"
L	Flodin Carl	151	machinist	55	"
N	Tisi Filomena—†	151	housewife	67	"
M	Tisi Joseph	151	retired	72	271 Paris
R	*Walsh Mary—†	153	housewife	44	here
s	Walsh Michael	153	shoemaker	44	"
T	Pepe Antonette—†	153	housewife	54	"
U	Pepe Carmella—†	153	stenographer	25	"
X	Pepe Filomena—†	153	clerk	27	"
V	Pepe Mary—†	153	"	20	"
W	Pepe Pellegrino	153	pipefitter	33	"
Z	Romano Frances—†	154	stitcher	22	"

1201

A	*Romano Jennie—†	154	housewife	46	"
B	Romano Phillip N	154	laborer	48	"
c	Romano Rocco	154	U S A	22	"
D	Saulnier Alvin	154	carpenter	48	33 Lexington
E	Saulnier Grace—†	154	housewife	44	33 "
F	Saulnier Leonard	154	welder	20	33 "
G	Ferrara Charles	154	physician	24	here
H	*Ferrara Grace—†	154	housewife	52	"
K	*Ferrara Ignazio	154	retired	56	"
L	Pinella Joseph	155	plumber	39	"
M	Pinella Mary—†	155	housewife	35	"
N	Pinella Samuel	155	U S A	29	"
O	Cashman Eleanor—†	155	housewife	49	"
P	Cashman Frank	155	laborer	54	"
s	*Ruggiero Anne—†	156	at home	48	"
T	*Rizzo Carmen	156	laborer	61	"
U	*Rizzo Rose—†	156	housewife	53	"
V	Falzarano Joseph	156	merchant	25	"
W	Falzarano Olga—†	156	housewife	23	"
X	Giangrieco Anthony	157	painter	46	"

2

Bennington Street Continued

	Y	Giangrieco Louise †	157	housewife	52	here
	Z	Luongo Edna †	157	"	26	"
1202						
	A	Luongo Phillip	157	pressman	27	"
	C	Pellegrino Bernardino	158	shoeworker	45	"
	D	Pellegrino Francesca †	158	housewife	47	"
	E	Pellegrino Joseph	158	shoeworker	22	"
	H	Johnson Frank	159	laborer	50	"
	K	Johnson Frederick	159	"	56	"
	L	Johnson Winthrop	159	"	48	"
	O	Marino Antonio	160	jeweler	38	"
	P	Marino Kathleen †	160	housewife	30	"
	R	Picariello Jennie †	160	"	33	"
	S	Picariello Joseph	160	painter	33	"
	T	Pepe Amelia †	160	housekeeper	59	"
	U	Pepe Enrico	160	student	25	"
	W	Impemba Anthony	161	shoemaker	60	"
	X	Impemba Assunta †	161	housewife	52	"
	Y	Brown Howard	161	U S A	21	Malden
	Z	Brown Lena †	161	housewife	23	here
1203						
	A	Imperioso Annette †	161	"	29	57 W Eagle
	B	Imperioso Joseph	161	laborer	27	57 "
	C	Hoey Frederick	162	U S A	30	67 St Andrew rd
	D	Hoey Ruth E †	162	collector	29	here
	E	Moynihan Bridget G †	162	at home	55	"
	F	Moynihan Lillian G †	162	clerk	30	"
	G	Moynihan Maurice E	162	U S N	38	"
	H	DiGregorio Michael	163	porter	50	409 Chelsea
	K	DiBacco Giustino	163	laborer	47	here
	L	DiBacco Lucy †	163	housewife	41	"
	M	Auger Leo	163	weaver	27	"
	N	Massano Georginna †	164	at home	68	"
	O	King Louis	164	machinist	42	188 Marion
	P	King Violet †	164	housewife	33	188 "
	R	Nicosia Arthur	164	shoeworker	23	88 Eutaw
	S	Nicosia Dorothy †	164	housewife	22	313 Border
	T	Sciacca Frank	164	machinist	24	231 Benningt'n
	U	Sciacca Mary †	164	housewife	23	231 "
	V*	Marro Antonette †	165	at home	54	here
	W	DeCalogero Jennie †	165	housewife	58	"

3

Bennington Street—Continued

Letter	FULL NAME	Residence, Jan. 1, 1943	Occupation	Supposed Age	Reported Residence Jan. 1, 1942
x	DeCalogero Salvatore	165	musician	25	here
y	*Maglio Domenic	165	laborer	48	"
z	*Maglio Raffaela †	165	housewife	47	"
1204					
A	Devine Helen †	166	"	29	"
B	Devine Louis	166	machinist	33	"
C	*Pagliarullo John	166	laborer	65	"
D	*Pagliarullo Josephine †	166	housewife	60	"
E	Pagliarullo Mary †	166	clerk	22	"
F	Alteri Frank	166	laborer	36	"
G	Alteri Rose †	166	housewife	31	"
H	*Gusto Giuseppe	167	retired	83	"
K	Imperioso Arthur	167	seaman	22	"
L	Imperioso Eramo	167	machinist	20	"
M	*Imperioso Maria †	167	housekeeper	46	"
N	Imperioso Priscilla †	167	clerk	24	"
O	Minolla Ciriaco	167	custodian	67	"
P	Minolla Palmina †	167	housewife	49	"
R	Paldo Lena †	167	"	23	"
S	Paldo Liberato J	167	U S A	28	"
T	*Reilly Catherine †	168	at home	47	"
U	Reilly James J	168	retired	76	"
V	Reilly Lorraine †	168	at home	24	"
W	Farrell Minnie †	168	"	48	Hamilton
X	McMullen Hugh A	168	retired	61	here
Y	McMullen Joseph J	168	houseman	52	"
Z	McMullen Ruth E †	168	machinist	22	"
1205					
A	Bartlett Elizabeth M †	169	nurse	55	"
B	Hogan Annie J †	169	at home	75	"
C	LeBlanc Alphonse	169	machinist	42	Haverhill
D	LeBlanc Theresa †	169	housewife	42	"
E	Crawford Mary †	170	typist	62	here
F	Hearn Helen †	170	housewife	35	"
G	Hearn John	170	rigger	38	"
H	Silva Anastasia †	170	housewife	45	"
K	Silva Anthony	170	clerk	57	"
L	Silva Anthony, jr	170	U S N	22	"
M	Greene Muriel †	173	housewife	37	127 London
N	Greene Walter	173	electrician	43	127 "
O	Coriani Louis	173	welder	35	here

4

Page.	Letter.	Full Name.	Residence Jan. 1, 1913.	Occupation.	Supposed Age.	Reported Residence Jan. 1, 1912. Street and Number.

Bennington Street Continued

	P	Coriani Raffaela †	173	housewife	37	here
	R	Sulprizo George	173	plumber	42	"
	S	Murray Dora A †	174	housewife	57	"
	T	Murray Walter	174	chauffeur	59	"
	U	Murray Walter, jr	174	"	28	"
	V	Pitts John E	174	watchman	48	45 Bennington
	W	Barry Catherine †	174	housekeeper	71	here
	X	Barry Hannah F †	174	"	73	"
	Y	Corkery Louise A †	174	"	35	"
	Z	Donovan Timothy F	174	retired	71	"

1206

	A	*Castagnio Concetta †	175	housewife	43	63 Morris
	B	*Castagnio Frank	175	barber	53	63 "
	C	McGuire James	175	letter carrier	27	113 Bunker Hill
	D	McGuire Jennie †	175	housewife	27	113 "
	E	Nolan Aaron	177	fisherman	42	here
	F	*Nolan Anna †	177	housewife	42	"
	H	Curran Bridget †	178	at home	72	"
	K	Curran Catherine †	178	housewife	36	"
	L	Curran Charles L	178	machinist	37	"
	M	Curran Edward	178	boilermaker	31	"
	N	Curran Ethel †	178	at home	35	"
	O	Curran Leo F	178	painter	39	"
	P	Curran William H	178	pipefitter	40	"
	R	Cunha Joseph	178	molder	45	184 Benningt'n
	S	Cunha Lordes †	178	housewife	41	184 "
	T	Paolini Americo	180	U S A	25	77 Lexington
	U	Paolini Edith †	180	clerk	22	here
	V	Zambella Antonio	180	laborer	61	"
	W	*Zambella Concetta †	180	housewife	58	"
	X	Zambella Michael	180	U S A	20	"
	Z	Albano Angelina †	180	housewife	56	"

1207

	A	Albano Anthony	180	laborer	26	"
	B	Albano Lucy †	180	at home	24	"
	C	Albano Philomena †	180	candymaker	32	"
	D	DeFalco Ella †	180	stitcher	28	"
	E	*Tortora Gerardo	180	tailor	57	"
	F	Silva Marion †	181	at home	46	"
	G	Falzone Fannie †	182	stitcher	20	"
	H	Falzone Mary †	182	at home	23	"

5

Bennington Street — Continued

к	Falzone Michael	182	welder	47	here
L	*Falzone Phyllis †	182	housewife	44	"
м	Mattera Cesare	182	longshoreman	56	"
N	Mattera Eva †	182	clerk	21	"
o	Mattera Hennie †	182	"	26	"
P	Mattera Joseph	182	machinist	24	"
R	*Mattera Josephine †	182	housewife	55	"
s	Mattera Louise †	182	clerk	22	"
T	Mattera Mary †	182	"	34	"
U	Mattera Michael	182	U S N	30	"
v	Ferriero Angelo	182	fireman	44	"
w	Ferriero Mario	182	U S A	20	"
x	Ferriero Mary †	182	housewife	45	"
y	Ferriero Mary †	182	clerk	21	"
z	Erwin Haskell	184	U S N	29	N Carolina

1208

A	Erwin Mildred †	184	housewife	24	127 Paris
B	*Lema Antone	184	weaver	49	101 Orleans
c	*Lema Mary †	184	housewife	48	101 "
D	*Grieco Emanual	184	presser	55	223 Marion
E	Grieco John	184	U S N	22	223 "
F	*Grieco Margaret †	184	housewife	46	223 "
G	Spaulding Lloyd	184	U S A	23	23 Lynde
H	Spaulding Mary †	184	housewife	23	23 "
L	Colucci Arthur	185	laborer	25	196 Benningt'n
м	Colucci Edward	185	chauffeur	20	312 Saratoga
N	*Colucci Santa †	185	housewife	21	196 Benningt'n
o	Vargus Vincenza †	185	"	22	here
P	Vargus William	185	fishcutter	28	"
s	Lee Joseph	186	U S A	20	188 Benningt'n
T	*Lee Mary †	186	housewife	54	188 "
U	Graziano Carmello	186	U S A	24	here
V	*Raimondi Mary †	186	housewife	48	"
w	Raimondi Peter	186	boilermaker	61	"
z	Sullivan Joseph	187	inspector	32	"

1209

A	Sullivan Leah †	187	at home	33	"
B	*Rossetti Theresa †	187	"	55	"
F	*LeBlanc Alphee	188	laborer	45	"
G	*LeBlanc Elizabeth †	188	housewife	35	"
H	Accommando Enrico	190	electrician	21	27 Brook

Bennington Street Continued

K	*Accommando Mary †	190	at home	59	27 Brooks
L	Accommando Nicholas	190	baker	23	27 "
M	DiMinico Louise †	190	housewife	22	here
N	DiMinico Nicholas	190	chauffeur	22	"
O	Politano Joseph	190	laborer	46	"
P	Politano Josephine †	190	housewife	48	"
R	O'Connor Lawrence	190	laborer	54	"
S	O'Connor Nora †	190	housewife	52	"
T	Russell Helen †	190	inspector	25	"
U	Peddle Mary †	192	at home	50	"
V	Peddle Patrick	192	fisherman	42	"
W	Gianino Lena †	192	housewife	27	"
X	Gianino Ralph	192	laborer	29	"
Y	*Malvey Timothy	192	seaman	45	New York

1210 Bremen Street

B	Cardarelli Grace †	236	housewife	35	here
C	Cardarelli Ralph	236	contractor	35	"
D	Forgione Joseph	236	chauffeur	41	"
E	Forgione Rose †	236	housewife	38	"
F	*Gianquito Vincent	236	retired	82	106 Orleans
G	*Genzale Carmella †	236	housewife	53	134 Chelsea
H	Genzale Carmello	236	mechanic	23	134 "
K	Genzale Michael	236	welder	21	134 "
L	Genzale Rose †	236	stitcher	25	134 "
M	Sollazzo Antonio	238	at home	73	here
N	*Sollazzo Emma †	238	housewife	62	"
O	Celeste Joseph	238	carpenter	30	"
P	Celeste Julia †	238	housewife	28	"
R	Loconte Dora †	238	operator	25	"
S	Loconte John	238	longshoreman	53	"
T	Loconte John	238	U S A	23	"
U	Loconte Lena †	238	housewife	47	"
V	Loconte Marion †	238	seamstress	21	"
X	Pepi Anna †	240	housewife	60	"
Y	Pepi Anthony	240	U S A	20	"
W	Pepi Augustine	240	laborer	65	"
Z	Cutrona Jennie †	240	housewife	32	"

1211

A	Cutrona Peter	240	tailor	36	"

Page.	Letter.	FULL NAME.	Residence, Jan. 1, 1943.	Occupation.	Supposed Age.	Reported Residence, Jan. 1, 1942. Street and Number.

Bremen Street—Continued

	B	*Costa Stephen	240	laborer	65	here
	C	Palermo Agrippino	240	shipwright	32	192 Bremen
	D	Palermo Santina —†	240	housewife	32	192 "
	E	Caprerella Florence—†	242	"	23	here
	F	Caprerella Gerald	242	operator	25	"
	G	Terramagra Alice —†	242	"	26	"
	H	Terramagra Angelina †	242	"	21	"
	K	*Terramagra Estelle—†	242	housewife	53	"
	L	*Terramagra Luigi	242	laborer	58	"
	M	Terramagra Mary †	242	operator	23	"
	N	Terramagra Rose —†	242	"	25	"
	O	Izzo Mary—†	242	housewife	39	"
	P	Izzo Paul	242	laborer	47	"
	R	*Ialuna Josephine —†	244	housewife	55	"
	S	Ialuna Nazzareno	244	laborer	55	"
	T	Blangiardi Agrippino	244	"	46	"
	U	*Blangiardi Grace —†	244	housewife	40	"
	V	Seracuso Antonio	244	laborer	48	"
	W	*Seracuso Joseph	244	operator	29	"
	X	*Seracuso Josephine —†	244	housewife	46	"
	Y	*Cutrona Joseph	246	retired	75	"
	Z	*Cutrona Marion —†	246	housewife	69	"

1212

	A	Luongo Charles	246	clerk	48	"
	B	Silva Edmund	246	mechanic	32	"
	C	Silva Marie —†	246	housewife	29	"
	D	*Bellitti Frances —†	246	"	51	"
	E	Bellitti Josephine †	246	typist	28	"
	F	Bellitti Leo	246	U S N	22	"
	G	Bellitti Vito	246	retired	58	"
	K	Fucillo Angelo	252	painter	27	"
	L	Fucillo Emanuella †	252	housewife	25	"
	M	DeVita James	252	cashier	34	"
	N	DeVita Rose †	252	housewife	35	"
	O	Tamasco John	252	U S A	21	"
	P	Tamasco Michael	252	"	20	"
	R	*Tamasco Nicholas	252	weaver	45	"
	S	*Tamasco Sylvia —†	252	housewife	40	"
	T	Raffaele James	254	machinist	37	"
	U	Raffaele Jean —†	254	housewife	32	"
	V	Carco Constantino	254	laborer	45	"

8

Bremen Street Continued

w	Carco Francesco	254	shoeworker	43	here
x	Carco Mary †	254	housewife	36	"
y	Massaro Carlo	254	retired	55	"
z*	Massaro Mary †	254	housewife	54	"

1213

A	Massaro Peter	254	brazier	25	"
D	Lopilato Arthur	264	U S A	26	"
E	Lopilato George	264	"	33	"
F	Lopilato Lucy †	264	housewife	66	"
G	Lopilato Massimo	264	printer	41	"
H	Lopilato Rose †	264	clerk	37	"
K	Lopilato Vincent	264	retired	70	"
L	Cali Frank	266	salesman	33	"
M	Cali Teresa †	266	housewife	32	"
N*	Joy Anna †	268	at home	80	"
O	Joy Joseph	268	retired	83	"
P	Sullivan Alice †	268	housewife	52	"
R	Sullivan Anna R †	268	buyer	21	"
S	Sullivan Daniel F	268	laborer	58	"
V	Familiare Augustina †	284	housewife	58	"
W	Familiare Inez †	284	teacher	35	"
X	Rogers Anthony A	284	laborer	55	"
Y	Rogers Mary †	284	seamstress	59	"
Z	Brady Catherine †	286	operator	24	"

1214

A	Brady Mary †	286	housewife	51	"
B	O'Neil John J	286	weaver	42	"
C	Zeoli Anthony	286	factoryhand	42	Lynn
D*	Zeoli Mary †	286	housewife	39	"
F	Tremonte Albert	290	fishcutter	26	here
G	Tremonte Yolanda †	290	housewife	21	"
H*	Nazzaro Eugene	290	barber	53	"
K*	Nazzaro Mary †	290	housewife	46	"
L*	Donnaruma John	292	weaver	51	"
M*	Donnaruma Rose †	292	housewife	45	"
N	Donnaruma Vincent J	292	U S N	21	"
O	Schraffa Angelo	294	laborer	28	"
P	Schraffa Mary †	294	housewife	28	"
R	Tremonte Constance †	294	"	21	240 Bremen
S	Tremonte William	294	U S A	23	192 Havre
T	Hollander Catherine †	294	operator	22	734 Bennington

Page	Letter	FULL NAME.	Residence, Jan. 1, 1943.	Occupation.	Supposed Age.	Reported Residence, Jan. 1, 1942. Street and Number.

Bremen Street — Continued

	U	Hollander William	294	operator	26	734 Benningt'n
	V	Brigante Augustine	294	U S M C	21	here
	W	Brigante Joseph	294	carpenter	63	"
	X	Carco Dora—†	294	housewife	24	"
	Y	Carco Louis	294	laborer	33	"
	Z	Carco Agrippina—†	294	housewife	52	"

1215

	A	Carco Emanuel	294	retired	61	"
	B	Carco John	294	laborer	22	"
	C	Carco Mary—†	294	saleswoman	21	"
	D	Leifari Constance—†	294	housewife	29	94 Orient av
	H	Simington Arthur	310	laborer	49	here
	K	Simington Edith—†	310	housewife	48	"
	L	Clark Edna—†	310	"	50	"
	M	Clark Herbert W	310	coppersmith	22	"
	N	Marks Anthony	310	laborer	47	206 Saratoga
	O	Marks Frank	310	operator	47	206 "
	P	*Marks Mary G †	310	housewife	43	206 "
	R	Powers Anna—†	312	boxmaker	33	here
	S	*Powers Eva—†	312	housewife	68	"
	T	Powers John	312	shipfitter	32	"
	U	Lombardo Arthur	312	U S A	22	"
	V	Lombardo Louis	312	ironworker	30	N Hampshire
	W	Powers Anna C—†	312	housewife	37	here
	X	*Powers Michael	312	operator	38	"
	Y	Powers Joseph	312	"	35	"
	Z	Powers Josephine †	312	"	33	"

1216   **Brooks Street**

	B	Finno Concetta †	2	housewife	34	151 Marion
	C	Finno Luigi	2	driller	38	151 "
	D	*Festa Gaetano	2	laborer	65	here
	E	Festa Jennie †	2	saleswoman	23	"
	G	*Orancio Edward	4	laborer	61	"
	H	*Orancio Margaret—†	4	housewife	50	"
	K	Cloro Jennie—†	4	"	47	"
	L	Cloro Rosario	4	laborer	48	"
	M	Boncore Alma—†	6	housewife	22	"
	N	Boncore Angelo	6	welder	23	"
	O	Boncore Catherine—†	6	stitcher	30	"

10

Brooks Street Continued

	Letter	Full Name	Res.	Occupation	Age	Reported Residence
	P	Boncore Charles	6	presser	52	here
	R	Boncore Louisa †	6	stitcher	43	"
	S	Boncore Louisa †	6	"	24	"
	T	Boncore Mary †	6	"	20	"
	U	Walsh Edward	6	metalworker	22	"
	V	Walsh Phyllis †	6	housewife	20	"

1217

	Letter	Full Name	Res.	Occupation	Age	Reported Residence
	B	Cappuccio Matilda †	20	"	45	"
	C	Cappuccio Nicholas	20	mason	50	"
	D	Dobbins Mary †	20	at home	20	"
	E	Minichello Carmella †	20	stitcher	21	"
	F	Minichello Crescenzio	20	U S N	20	"
	G	Minichello John	20	laborer	27	"
	H	Minichello Margaret †	20	operator	24	"
	K	*Minichello Raffaelo	20	laborer	65	"
	L	*Minichello Rose †	20	housewife	56	"
	M	Anzalone Ernest	21	electrician	33	"
	N	Anazlone Jennie †	21	housewife	33	"
	O	Anzalone Rose †	21	"	67	"
	P	D'Avolio Esther †	21	packer	31	"
	R	Manzo Alphonso	21	candymaker	61	"
	S	Manzo Jean †	21	inspector	22	"
	T	*Manzo Jennie †	21	housewife	52	"
	U	Manzo Salvatore	21	toolkeeper	28	"
	V	Manzo Theresa †	21	inspector	20	"
	W	*Markovitz Charles	22	proprietor	48	"
	X	*Markovitz Eva †	22	housewife	48	"
	Y	Markovitz Sarah †	22	clerk	22	"
	Z	DeStefano Giuseppe	22	baker	47	"

1218

	Letter	Full Name	Res.	Occupation	Age	Reported Residence
	A	*DeStefano Marianna †	22	housewife	43	"
	B	*Marrone Mary †	22	at home	77	"
	C	*Falzone Anna †	22	housewife	33	"
	D	Falzone Rosario	22	presser	49	"
	E	Falzone Salvatore	22	U S A	20	"
	F	Ferullo Joseph	23	welder	29	"
	G	Ferullo Leda †	23	housewife	26	"
	H	Kushner Anna †	23	at home	70	"
	K	Kushner Max	23	U S A	29	"
	L	Richmond Sally †	23	housewife	25	"
	M	Richmond Theodore	23	proprietor	27	"

11

Page.	Letter	FULL NAME.	Residence, Jan. 1, 1943.	Occupation.	Supposed Age.	Reported Residence, Jan. 1, 1942. Street and Number.

Brooks Street—Continued

x	Driver Harold	23	engineer	34	here
o	Driver Stella —†	23	housewife	28	"
p	Crowley Albert	25	guard	66	"
r	Crowley Henry R	25	seaman	30	153 Marion
s	Crowley Margaret J —†	25	housewife	60	here
t	*Sandler Eva —†	25	"	57	"
u	Sandler Morris	25	pedler	57	"
v	Sandler Tillie —†	25	typist	25	"
w	Gioia John C	25	painter	32	"
x	Gioia Josephine —†	25	housewife	31	"
y	Donohue Helen F —†	26	"	41	"
z	Donohue James E	26	clerk	43	"

1219

a	McDonald Margaret E —†	26	housewife	44	"
b	McDonald Thomas H	26	checker	50	"
c	Mogan Joseph	26	guard	48	"
d	Palumbo Loreen —†	27	housewife	46	171 Chelsea
e	Palumbo Michael	27	baker	55	171 "
f	Mastone Angelo	27	clerk	41	here
g	Mastone Rose —†	27	housewife	34	"
h	Collins Margaret —†	28	packer	23	"
k	Collins Marion —†	28	housekeeper	58	"
l	Palin Mary A —†	28	at home	83	Billerica
o	Donahue Charles A	35	clergyman	53	here
p	Fitzgerald Mary —†	35	cook	53	"
r	Gallagher Genevieve —†	35	domestic	44	"
s	Kearney Phillip	35	clergyman	35	"
t	McCabe Martin N	35	"	34	"
u	O'Donnell Walter	35	"	36	"
v	Correale Bartolo	44	laborer	39	"
w	Correale Rose —†	44	housewife	36	"
x	Recupero Nicola	44	foreman	57	"
z	*Gugliciello Paul	46	retired	80	"

1220

a	*Gugliciello Rosaria —†	46	housewife	77	"
b	*Porcelini Carmella —†	46	"	47	"
c	*Porcelini Joseph	46	buyer	52	"
d	*Villari Concetta —†	46	housewife	45	"
e	Villari James	46	U S A	20	"
f	*Villari Nunzio	46	barber	47	"

12

Brooks Street Continued

G	Zirilli Domenic	46	U S A	28	here
H	*Santosusso Louis	48	janitor	52	"
K	*Santosusso Theresa †	48	housewife	62	"
L	Ceraso Josephine †	48	"	39	"
M	Ceraso Julio	48	expressman	49	"
N	Lepore John	48	candymaker	33	"
O	Lepore Philomina †	48	housewife	31	"
P	*Cosentino Angelina †	57	"	61	"
R	*Cosentino James †	57	laborer	61	"
S	Frustaglia Antonio	57	plater	50	"
T	Frustaglia Elizabeth †	57	stitcher	39	"
U	Femia Mary †	57	housewife	29	"
V	Preshong Ephraim	59	painter	45	"
W	Preshong Helen †	59	housewife	35	"
Y	*Kerogas Mary †	59	"	71	"
X	Kurgan Anthony	59	shipworker	31	"
Z	Karish Alfred	59	machinist	43	"
	1221				
A	Karish Mary †	59	housewife	40	"
B	D Amico Louis	61	machinist	26	174 Cottage
C	D'Amico Mary †	61	housewife	24	184 Webster
D	Moscillo James	61	tailor	39	here
E	Moscillo Mary †	61	housewife	38	"
F	Panzini Josephine †	61	"	43	"
G	Panzini Pasquale	61	U S A	22	"
H	Panzini Rocco	61	chauffeur	45	"
K	Bruno Charles	63	shoeworker	51	"
L	*Bruno Helen †	63	housewife	40	"
M	DiNapoli Alfred	63	machinist	33	"
N	DiNapoli Esther †	63	housewife	31	"
O	*Pepe Angelina †	63	at home	72	"
P	Baldassare Angela M †	63	inspector	47	"
R	Baldassare Anthony G	63	student	20	"
S	Baldassare Joseph A	63	"	22	"
T	Baldassare Marcello	63	cleaner	53	"
U	Baldassare Pasquale J	63	U S A	25	"
V	Barrasso Andrew	65	porter	39	"
W	Barrasso Nicoletta †	65	housewife	35	"
X	*Barrasso Raffaela †	65	at home	64	"
Y	Sirianni Pasquale	65	salesman	36	"

Page.	Letter.	FULL NAME.	Residence, Jan. 1, 1943.	Occupation.	Supposed Age.	Reported Residence, Jan. 1, 1942. Street and Number.

Brooks Street—Continued

	z	Sirianni Thomasina †	65	housewife	32	here
1222						
	B*	Cosato Crescenzio	77	barber	56	"
	C*	Cosato Lucia †	77	housewife	54	"
	D*	Doucette Elizabeth †	77	"	64	"
	E	Doucette Joseph	77	fisherman	66	"
	F	Doucette Vincent	77	U S A	23	"
	G*	Russo Bernice †	79	at home	63	78 Brooks
	H*	Russo Prisco	79	laborer	63	78 "
	K*	Ippolito Frank	79	"	54	here
	L*	Ippolito Grace †	79	housewife	50	"
	M*	D'Agostino Jennie †	79	"	56	"
	N	D'Agostino Nancy †	79	inspector	29	"
	O	D'Agostino Pasquale	79	packer	24	"
	P	Vertuccio Emilio	81	plater	23	"
	R	Vertuccio Josephine †	81	housewife	22	"
	S	Bellone Amelia †	81	stitcher	37	"
	T	Bellone Ciro	81	shoeworker	55	"
	U	Lombardi Anthony	81	laborer	27	264 Summer
	V	Lombardi Sabina †	81	housewife	23	264 "
	W	Filippone Henry F	83	U S M C	27	here
	X	Filippone Margaret †	83	housewife	29	"
	Y	Frati Augustine	83	chauffeur	45	370 Princeton
	Z	Frati Margaret †	83	housewife	34	370 "
1223						
	A	Fiorentino Anna †	83	"	39	198 Benningt'n
	B	Fiorentino Charles	83	shipfitter	46	198 "
	C*	Marciano John	85	janitor	58	here
	D	Pastore Philip	85	chipper	24	76 Brooks
	E	Pastore Rose †	85	housewife	48	76 "
	F	Pastore Vito N	85	hairdresser	54	76 "
	G	Indingaro Louise †	85	housewife	29	109 Porter
	H	Indingaro Thomas	85	laborer	29	109 "
	K	Carpenito Anthony	87	proprietor	38	here
	L	Carpenito Mary †	87	housewife	35	"
	O	Cooley Francis T	101	baker	27	98 Lexington
	P*	Duffy Annie †	101	housewife	62	98 "
	R	Duffy Thomas F	101	retired	70	98 "
	S	Pupke Augustus H	101	"	50	here
	T	Caggiano James	103	packer	27	"
	U	Caggiano Rose †	103	housewife	28	"

14

Brooks Street Continued

v	Ceresi Angelo	103	presser	57	here
w	Ceresi Justine †	103	housewife	48	"
x	Ceresi Laura E †	103	typist	22	"
y	Regan Catherine †	107	housewife	37	"
z	Regan Herbert	107	tester	38	"

1224

A	Siracusa Anthony	107	U S A	26	"
B	*Siracusa Antonette †	107	housewife	50	"
c	Siracusa Frank	107	fishcutter	24	"
D	Siracusa Rosario	107	U S A	23	"
E	Siracusa Salvatore	107	"	30	"
F	Siracusa Sarah †	107	stitcher	21	"
G	Limole Helen †	107	housewife	31	"
K	Genualdo Arthur	111	rigger	29	108 Brooks
L	Genualdo Rose †	111	housewife	27	108 "
M	Paolucci Luigi	111	upholsterer	55	here
N	Glennon Joseph H	113	clerk	55	"

Chelsea Street

o	Tiano Florence †	194	clerk	32	here
P	*Tiano Jennie †	194	housewife	68	"
R	Tiano Samuel	194	engineer	29	"
s	*Salembene Antonia †	194	housewife	52	"
T	*Salembene Sebastiano	194	shoeworker	52	"
u	Amico Bernice †	194	housewife	26	"
v	Amico Joseph	194	receiver	30	"
w	Fumicello Jennie †	196	wrapper	36	"
x	Fumicello Joseph	196	presser	43	"
y	Aleo Mary †	196	housewife	24	"
z	Aleo Phillip	196	mechanic	27	"

1225

A	*Piermattei Panfilo	196	retired	64	"
B	*Rizzo Frank	196	"	89	"
c	Rizzo John	196	proprietor	59	"
D	Rizzo Stella †	196	housewife	56	"
E	Gagliolo Alfonso	197	operator	65	"
F	Gagliolo Mary †	197	housewife	58	"
G	*Murano Alba †	197	at home	42	"
H	Murano Raymond	197	laborer	20	"
K	Alviti Albina †	197	housewife	34	"

15

Page	Letter	Full Name	Residence, Jan. 1, 1943.	Occupation.	Supposed Age.	Reported Residence, Jan. 1, 1942. Street and Number.

Chelsea Street—Continued

	L	Alviti Americo	197	photographer	36	here
	N	Guerra Louis	198	retired	67	"
	O	Guerra William	198	U S N	22	California
	P	Serra Mary †	198	housewife	29	here
	R	Serra Thomas	198	operator	33	"
	S	Cormier Gerald	198	"	31	"
	T	Cormier Rose †	198	housewife	32	"
	U	Calabria Annette †	199	"	24	"
	V	Calabria Peter V	199	welder	25	"
	W	Lopilato Antonette †	199	stitcher	20	"
	X	Lopilato Frank	199	U S N	21	"
	Y	Lopilato Nellie †	199	housewife	49	"
	Z	Lopilato Salvatore	199	laborer	49	"

1226

	A	Salvatora Catherine †	199	housewife	39	"
	B	Salvatora John	199	butcher	48	"
	C	Morse Bernard	200	splicer	28	"
	D	Morse Mary †	200	housewife	23	"
	E	Walsh Mary †	200	operator	20	"
	F	Walsh Patrick	200	laborer	55	"
	G	Walsh Theresa †	200	housewife	52	"
	H	Angelo Michael	200	marbleworker	50	"
	K	Pasquantonio Angelo	200	operator	43	"
	L	Pasquantonio Margaret †	200	housewife	40	"
	M	Parrella Pelegrino	201	laborer	62	"
	N	Parrella Rubina †	201	housewife	58	"
	O	Doucette Peter	201	machinist	29	"
	P	Doucette Ruby †	201	housewife	22	"
	R	Zaffiro Margaret †	201	"	36	"
	S	Zaffiro Salvatore	201	machinist	38	"
	T	DeWart Antone	202	fishcutter	41	"
	U	DeWart Mary F †	202	housewife	41	"
	V	*Cohen Dora †	202	"	54	"
	W	*Cohen Max	202	cooper	60	"
	X	Muscarelli Angelina †	202	cashier	21	"
	Y	*Muscarelli Frances †	202	housewife	45	"
	Z	*Muscarelli Salvatore	202	presser	48	"

1227

	A	DiGiorgio Domenic	203	laborer	55	"
	B	DiGiorgio Maria †	203	housewife	47	"
	C	*Salemi Angelina †	203	"	59	"

16

Chelsea Street Continued

D	Salemi Santo	203	laborer	66	here
E	LaCascia Joseph	203	electrician	39	"
F	LaCascia Sadie †	203	housewife	35	"
G	Delli Priscole Geraldine †	204	operator	24	"
H	Delli Priscole Gerardo	204	laborer	53	"
K	Delli Priscole Mary G †	204	operator	22	"
L	Delli Priscole Virginia †	204	housewife	48	"
M	Palazzolo Anthony J	204	printer	28	"
N	Palazzolo Mary †	204	housewife	26	"
O	Yellin Abraham	204	storekeeper	52	"
P	Yellin Lillian †	204	bookkeeper	20	"
R	Yellin Rose †	204	operator	46	"
S	*Marchetti Jennie †	205	housewife	40	"
T	*Marchetti John	205	cutter	43	"
U	*Chianca Antonio	205	laborer	59	"
V	Chianca Arthur	205	retired	26	"
W	*Chianca Carmella †	205	housewife	56	"
X	Polizzi Angelo	205	U S A	20	"
Y	*Polizzi Josephine †	205	housewife	43	"
Z	Polizzi Philip	205	rigger	47	"

1228

A	*Cutrone Antonina †	206	housewife	72	"
B	Cutrone Orazio	206	retired	72	"
C	Caprio Louise †	206	housewife	35	"
D	Caprio Nicholas	206	clerk	48	"
E	*Lampiarni Josephine †	206	at home	62	"
F	*Saia Maria †	206	"	65	"
G	Amarosi Angelo, jr	207	operator	30	"
H	Amarosi Mary †	207	housewife	26	"
K	Caprigno Louise †	207	"	28	"
L	*Rosata Mary †	207	"	54	"
M	Rosata Viola †	207	stitcher	25	"
N	Amarosi Americo	207	tailor	21	"
O	*Amarosi Angelo	207	"	55	"
P	Amarosi Carmella †	207	stitcher	22	"
R	Amarosi Rose †	207	housewife	54	"
S	*Losco Maria †	208	at home	65	"
T	*Renda Agostino	208	retired	60	"
U	*Renda Agrippina †	208	housewife	60	"
V	Wahlquist Eva †	208	"	29	"
W	*Wahlquist Nils	208	engineer	44	"

Chelsea Street—Continued

x	Miranda Carmella—†	209	housewife	25	here
y	Miranda Peter	209	barber	27	"
z	Torra Catherine—†	209	housewife	32	"

1229

A	Torra Frank W	209	upholsterer	31	"
B	Mugnano Annette—†	209	housewife	31	"
C	Mugnano Charles	209	rigger	34	"
D	Mugnano Joseph	209	laborer	64	"
E*	Mugnano Josephine—†	209	housewife	60	"
F	Barrone Ciano	210	watchman	48	"
G	Hassett Agnes—†	210	housewife	44	"
H	Hassett Robert J	210	guard	45	"
L	Dell Orfano Liberata—†	211	housewife	32	58 Lubec
M	Dell Orfgano Pasquale	211	laborer	34	58 "
N	Miranda Americo	211	operator	34	58 "
O	Miranda Emma—†	211	candyworker	22	58 "
P	Cangiano Lucy—†	211	operator	35	here
R	Cangiano Michelina †	211	housewife	63	"
S	Cangiano Pasquale	211	carpenter	30	"
T	Cangiano Rose—†	211	trimmer	29	"
U	Marrocco Camella—†	211	housewife	38	"
V	Ferrara Joseph	211	retired	72	"
W	Ferrara Josephine—†	211	housewife	57	"
X	Ferrara Peter	211	operator	23	"
Y	Ferrara Rosalie—†	211	milliner	29	"

1230

B	Mancuso Grace—†	212	packer	26	"
D	Mancuso Marion †	212	housewife	50	"
E	Mancuso Peter	212	laborer	61	"
C	Mancuso Sabina—†	212	clerk	20	"
F	Logiudici Antonio	213	carpenter	57	75 Saratoga
G	Logiudici Frank	213	U S A	23	75 "
H	Logiudici Mary †	213	housewife	46	75 "
K	Logiudici Yolanda—†	213	stitcher	21	75 "
L	Fiandaca Joseph	213	clerk	20	214 Chelsea
M	Fiandaca Josephine †	213	housewife	60	214 "
N	Fiandaca Lauretta †	213	operator	30	214 "
O*	Radosta Josephine—†	213	at home	87	214 "
R	Sarro Edward	214	painter	22	here
S	Sarro Jennie—†	214	housewife	21	"
T	Harney Genevieve †	214	"	34	52 Marion

18

Page.	Letter	FULL NAME.	Residence, Jan. 1, 1943.	Occupation.	Supposed Age.	Reported Residence, Jan. 1, 1942. Street and Number.

Chelsea Street Continued

U	Harney John F	214	painter	39	52 Marion
V	Zecchino Anthony	214	laborer	46	here
W	Zecchino Raffaela †	214	housewife	44	"
Y	Ferrante Joseph	215	hatter	42	"
Z	Ferrante Phyllis †	215	housewife	32	"

1231

A	Ferrante Concetta †	215	candyworker	34	"
B	*Ferrante Florence †	215	at home	65	"
C	Ferrante John	215	waiter	31	"
D	Ferrante Rose †	215	candyworker	39	"
E	Brunassini Charles	215	barber	40	"
F	Brunassini Josephine †	215	housewife	41	"
G	Santosuosso Angelo	216	proprietor	41	"
H	*Santosuosso Frances †	216	housewife	39	"
K	Cacariello Eleanor †	216	"	23	"
L	Cacariello Joseph	216	dredger	23	"
M	Cacariello Thomas	216	tailor	65	"
O	Zarrella Generoso	217	clerk	44	"
P	Zarrella Natalie †	217	housewife	35	"
R	Phillips Abraham	217	chauffeur	40	"
S	Phillips Sophie †	217	housewife	40	"
T	Martucci Augustine	217	machinist	33	"
U	Martucci Lena †	217	housewife	33	"
V	Cuono Allesandra †	218	"	50	"
W	Cuono Concetta †	218	operator	24	"
X	Cuono John	218	U S N	22	"
Y	Cuono Luigi	218	dairyman	53	"
Z	Morgera Angelina †	218	housewife	38	154 Falcon

1232

A	Morgera Charles	218	locksmith	55	154 "
B	Caprera Antonio	218	laborer	46	29 Maverick sq
C	*Caprera Francesca †	218	housewife	36	29 "
E	Messina Antonette †	219	"	27	here
F	Messina Frank	219	welder	28	"
G	D'Agostino Filomena †	219	housewife	35	"
H	D'Agostino Pasquale	219	machinist	35	217 Lexington
K	Ferullo Concetta †	219	stitcher	33	here
L	*Ferullo Emilio	219	laborer	63	"
M	Ferullo Lena †	219	stitcher	31	"
N	Ferullo Ralph	219	receiver	36	"
O	Ferullo Elvira †	219	housewife	32	"

19

Page.	Letter.	FULL NAME.	Residence, Jan. 1, 1943.	Occupation.	Supposed Age.	Reported Residence, Jan. 1, 1942. Street and Number.

Chelsea Street—Continued

	P	Ferullo Louis	219	chauffeur	32	here
	*R	Brunaccini Mary—†	220	housewife	44	245 Roxbury
	T	Carmosino Angelina—†	221	"	28	here
	U	Carmosino Anthony	221	salesman	29	"
	V	Pisscitelli Angelina—†	221	housewife	34	"
	W	*Pisscitelli Lucia—†	221	at home	72	"
	X	Pisscitelli Pasquale	221	barber	36	"
	Y	Freda Angelina—†	221	operator	32	"
	Z	Freda Zerpoldo	221	U S A	34	"

1233

	A	*Longo Nicoletta—†	221	housewife	67	"
	B	Longo Potito	221	laborer	54	"
	C	Correia Charles	223	mechanic	31	"
	D	Correia Jennie—†	223	housewife	28	"
	E	Crusco Antonio	223	rubberworker	46	"
	F	*Crusco Mary J—†	223	housewife	44	"
	G	Grella Frank	223	chipper	43	"
	H	Grella Susan—†	223	housewife	40	"
	K	Vaiarella Italia—†	224	"	21	51 Morris
	L	Vaiarella Salvatore	224	fisherman	21	51 "
	M	*DeBenedictis Blanche—†	224	housewife	49	here
	N	DeBenedictis Daniel	224	U S A	25	"
	O	DeBenedictis Eugenia—†	224	stitcher	21	"
	P	DeBenedictis Louis	224	U S A	27	"
	R	*DeBenedictis Vincent	224	tailor	59	"
	S	Baldini Girio	224	electrician	29	"
	T	Baldini Palmina—†	224	housewife	26	"
	U	Ciaremalla Angelina—†	225	stitcher	29	"
	V	Marotta Annette—†	225	housewife	28	"
	W	Marotta Joseph	225	shipfitter	32	"
	X	Trabucco Anthony	225	mason	52	"
	Y	Trabucco Elena—†	225	teacher	23	"
	Z	*Trabucco Theresa—†	225	housewife	52	"

1234

	A	Mustone Angelina—†	225	"	49	"
	B	Mustone Antonette—†	225	stitcher	24	"
	C	Mustone Nicholas	225	laborer	50	"
	D	Mustone Pasquale	225	U S A	27	"
	E	Dalton Anne—†	226	housewife	25	"
	F	Dalton James	226	guard	29	"
	G	Minichino Ida—†	226	housewife	22	"

20

Page.	Letter.	FULL NAME.	Residence, Jan. 1, 1943.	Occupation.	Supposed Age.	Reported Residence, Jan. 1, 1942. Street and Number.

Chelsea Street — Continued

H	Minichino Michael	226	assembler	23	here
K	*DiMauro Grace—†	226	housewife	37	"
L	DiMauro John	226	metalworker	39	"
M	Tavella Mary—†	227	stitcher	23	"
N	Tavella Rose—†	227	"	25	"
O	*Tavella Rosina—†	227	housewife	46	"
P	*Ciccia Amelia †	227	laborer	24	"
R	Albanese Delizia—†	227	housewife	35	Webster
S	*Albanese Michael	227	shoeworker	39	"
T	Mirabile Benjamin	228	machinist	63	here
U	Mirabile Rocco	228	clerk	38	193 Summer
V	Mirabile Rose—†	228	operator	31	here
W	DiNucci Ferdinand	228	chauffeur	29	"
X	*DiNucci Nancy—†	228	housewife	29	"
Y	Pilato Angelo	229	clerk	39	"
Z	Pilato Josephine—†	229	housewife	36	"

1235

A	Micciche Andrina—†	229	"	38	"
B	Micciche Rocco	229	operator	39	"
C	Micciche Esther—†	229	candyworker	40	"
D	*Micciche Grace—†	229	at home	65	"
E	*Micciche Pasquale	229	retired	79	"
F	Micciche Pasquale	229	student	20	"
G	Micciche Samuel	229	shoeworker	44	"
H	Vertuccio Margaret—†	231	housewife	35	"
K	Vertuccio Nicholas	231	shipfitter	38	"
L	Desio Benjamin	231	laborer	48	"
M	*Desio Mary—†	231	housewife	41	"
N	Denisi Filomena †	231	"	50	"
O	Denisi Nicholas	231	U S A	30	"
P	Denisi Vincent	231	tailor	57	"
R	Denisi Vincent, jr	231	machinist	20	"
S	Minichino Celia †	232	operator	20	"
T	Minichino Domenic	232	laborer	60	"
U	Minichino Filomina—†	232	housewife	60	"
V	DePlacido Elizabeth—†	232	"	36	"
W	DePlacido Peter	232	tailor	40	"
X	*DeVingo Florence—†	232	at home	69	"
Z	Casaletto Eva †	233	housewife	33	"

1236

A	Casaletto Joseph	233	rubberworker	36	"

21

Chelsea Street—Continued

	Letter	FULL NAME	Residence	Occupation	Age	Reported Residence
	B	Casaletto Helen—†	233	housewife	26	here
	C	Casaletto Jerry	233	springmaker	31	"
	D*	Casaletto Grace—†	233	housewife	45	"
	E	Casaletto John	233	plumber	56	"
	G	Calistro Ralph F	235	electrician	27	"
	H	Calistro Rose—†	235	housewife	24	"
	K	Fiandaca Margaret—†	235	"	26	"
	L	Fiandaca Nunzio	235	laborer	28	"
	M*	Calistro Angelina—†	235	housewife	49	"
	N	Calistro Anna—†	235	stitcher	29	"
	O	Calistro Bruno	235	proprietor	60	"
	R	Cardinale Joseph	237	laborer	27	187 Chelsea
	S	Cardinale Josephine—†	237	housewife	27	187 "
	T*	Daley Clement	237	fisherman	36	here
	U*	Daley Gertrude—†	237	housewife	38	"
	V	Carrozza Lena—†	237	hairdresser	29	41 Maverick sq
	W	Schifano Anna—†	237	stitcher	20	41 "
	X*	Schifano Antonio	237	watchman	59	41 "
	Y*	Schifano Gaetana—†	237	housewife	49	41 "
1237						
	A	D'Alfonso Joseph	239	laborer	62	here
	B	D'Alfonso Josephine—†	239	operator	21	"
	C*	D'Alfonso Palma—†	239	housewife	58	"
	D	D'Alfonso Salvatore	239	U S A	25	"
	E	Goldberg Jeanette—†	239	housewife	22	"
	F*	Reifel Israel	239	manufacturer	56	"
	G*	Reifel Lena—†	239	housewife	50	"
	K	Shuel Christine—†	241	"	37	"
	L	Shuel James H	241	laborer	37	"
	M	Kutkowitz George	243	machinist	20	"
	N*	Kutkowitz Pauline—†	243	housewife	53	"
	O	Kutkowitz Sonia—†	243	clerk	23	"
	T	LaPusata Alexander	243	laborer	55	"
	U*	LaPusata Angelina—†	243	housewife	47	"
	V	LaPusata Louis	243	laborer	20	"
	P*	DeStefano Geraldo	243	"	57	"
	R*	DeStefano Vincenza—†	243	housewife	56	"
	W	Pezzullo Luigi	245	laborer	48	"
	X	Pezzullo Virginia—†	245	housewife	34	"
	Y	Bozzi Adeline—†	245	"	52	"
	Z*	Bozzi Louis	245	tailor	54	

22

Page.	Letter.	FULL NAME.	Residence, Jan. 1, 1943	Occupation.	Supposed Age.	Reported Residence, Jan. 1, 1942. Street and Number.

1238

Chelsea Street Continued

A	Bozzi Louis, jr	245	U S A	28	here
B	Urban Barbara — †	245	at home	26	"
C	Connolly Rose — †	245	housewife	24	"
D	Connolly Thomas	245	cutter	27	"
E	Nappa John	247	U S A	22	"
F	*Nappa Mary — †	247	housewife	55	"
G	Nappa Ralph	247	laborer	63	"
H	Vertuccio Pauline T — †	247	housewife	27	"
K	Vertuccio Ralph P	247	operator	26	"
L	Martori Edith — †	247	housewife	34	"
M	Martori Joseph	247	machinist	35	"
N	Tarentino Angelina — †	249	housewife	22	"
O	Tarentino Frank	249	machinist	24	"
P	*Graziano Antonetta — †	249	housewife	52	"
R	Graziano Joseph	249	laborer	43	"
S	Gubitose Anna — †	249	housewife	31	"
T	Gubitose Samuel	249	bookbinder	30	"
U	Olivieri Alfred	249	laborer	23	19 Allen
V	Olivieri James	249	"	26	here
W	*Perry Manuel	251	retired	69	"
X	Perry Natalie — †	251	operator	25	"
Y	*Cianculli Marie C — †	251	housewife	43	"
Z	Cianculli Nicholas	251	baker	43	"

1239

A	*Capobianco Angelina — †	251	housewife	52	"
B	Capobianco Anna — †	251	stitcher	21	"
C	*Capobianco Antonio	251	laborer	57	"
D	Capobianco Fred	251	U S A	27	"
E	Capobianco Rocco	251	shipfitter	22	"
F	Montiero Anthony P	253	retired	70	"
G	Spinazola Guy H	253	candymaker	30	"
H	Spinazola Mary — †	253	housewife	29	"
K	*Bettencourt Manuel	253	retired	70	"
L	*Bettencourt Olympia — †	253	housewife	52	"
M	Dunbar Anna J — †	253	"	41	"
N	Dunbar George A	253	painter	46	"
O	*Young Thomas	253	retired	82	"
P	*Pemintel John S	255	painter	52	"
R	Pemintel John S, jr	255	U S A	31	"
S	*Pemintel Mary — †	255	housewife	51	"

23

Page.	Letter.	FULL NAME.	Residence. Jan. 1. 1943.	Occupation.	Supposed Age.	Reported Residence, Jan. 1. 1942. Street and Number.

Chelsea Street—Continued

T	Falzone Concetta—†	255	candyworker	24	here
U	Falzone Josephine—†	255	stitcher	22	"
V	Falzone Phillip	255	painter	26	"
W	Falzone Salvatore	255	welder	21	"
X*	Falzone Theresa—†	255	housewife	55	"
Y	Brennan Emily T—†	255	"	64	"
Z	Brennan James N	255	retired	76	"
	1240				
A	Brennan Lillian A—†	255	clerk	38	"
B	Finelli Domenico	257	laborer	50	"
C*	Finelli Maria—†	257	housewife	45	"
D	Venezia Albert	257	laborer	27	"
E	Venezia Rose—†	257	housewife	28	"
F	Pepe John A	257	B F D	31	"
G	Pepe Margaret—†	257	housewife	27	"
H	Albanese Anthony	259	cutter	60	"
K	Albanese Maria—†	259	housewife	46	"
L	Albanese John	259	U S A	25	"
M	Albanese Michael	259	"	28	"
N	Albanese Raymond	259	"	32	"
O	Albanese Richard	259	U S N	20	"
P	Maguire Andrew	259	laundryworker	32	"
R	Maguire Dolphine—†	259	housewife	30	"
S	Vieira Joseph	261	U S A	40	"
T	Vieira Maria—†	261	at home	68	"
V	Vieira Florence—†	261	housewife	38	"
W	Vieira John	261	mechanic	43	"
Y	Provinzano Joseph	263	laborer	36	"
Z*	Provinzano Rosalie—†	263	housewife	31	
	1241				
A	Doble Angelo	263	cook	42	"
B*	Doble Antonetta—†	263	housewife	33	"
D	Rothwell Alice—†	271	at home	59	"
E	Rothwell Mitchell	271	assembler	32	"
F	Pungitore John	271	laborer	49	"
G*	Terrazano Michael	271	retired	69	"
H	Tango John	271	welder	28	"
K	Tango Margaret—†	271	housewife	26	"
L	Rich Alice—†	273	"	23	718 Saratoga
M	Rich Robert	273	machinist	27	718 "
N	Kent Florence—†	273	housewife	23	Georgetown

24

Chelsea Street Continued

o	Kent Matthew	273	welder	30	Georgetown
p	Albanese Joseph	273	laborer	62	here
r	*Albanese Maria—†	273	housewife	29	"
s	Bruno Erminegilda—†	274	teacher	27	"
t	Bruno Evelyn—†	274	clerk	20	"
u	*Bruno Maria—†	274	housewife	54	"
v	Bruno Michael	274	barber	53	"
w	Giarla Anthony	274	chauffeur	24	"
x	Giarla Josephine—†	274	housewife	25	"
y	Giarla Margaret—†	274	"	50	"
z	Giarla Pasquale	274	carpenter	50	"

1242

a	*Terrone Ann M—†	275	housewife	25	"
b	Terrone Anthony	275	tailor	27	"
c	Colella Filomena—†	275	housewife	44	N Hampshire
d	*Barbinti Frank	275	pressman	58	here
e	*Barbinti Mary—†	275	housewife	71	"
f	*Cotreau Albertini—†	276	"	52	"
g	*Cotreau Roy	276	fishcutter	53	"
k	Carco Agrippino	276	U S A	23	"
h	Carco Antonio	276	welder	20	"
l	Carco Caruso	276	machinist	39	73 Chelsea
m	Carco Girolama—†	276	packer	30	73 "
n	Carco John	276	U S A	25	Georgia
o	Carco Joseph	276	retired	71	73 Chelsea
p	*Carco Josephine—†	276	housewife	63	73 "
r	Carco Paul	276	laborer	28	73 "
s	Costa Lawrence C	276	U S N	24	Everett
t	Costa Victoria M—†	276	housewife	24	"
u	Mastrangelo Albert	276	U S A	28	here
v	Mastrangelo Anthony	276	U S N	25	"
w	Mastrangelo Carmela—†	276	factoryhand	24	"
x	Mastrangelo John	276	laborer	66	"
y	Mastrangelo Mary—†	276	housewife	58	"
z	Mastrangelo Mary—†	276	factoryhand	22	"

1243

a	Mastrangelo Ralph	276	U S A	33	"
b	O'Hara Hugh	277	electrician	23	43 Marion
c	*Carvalho Manuel	277	laborer	52	here
d	Carvalho Tina—†	277	at home	23	"
f	Veglia John	278	laborer	27	"

Chelsea Street—Continued

G	Pirrello Joseph	278	retired	52	here	
H	*Pirrello Josephine—†	278	housewife	40	"	
K	Pirrello Phillip	278	machinist	20	"	
L	Ingaciola Anthony	278	U S A	23	"	
M	Ingaciola Beatrice—†	278	at home	25	"	
N	Ingaciola Nicholas	278	U S A	21	"	
O	*Ingaciola Pasquale	278	retired	66	"	
P	*Ingaciola Theresa—†	278	housewife	58	"	
R	Gandreau John C	279	retired	75	"	
S	Gandreau Mary A—†	279	housewife	78	"	
T	Santaniello Alice—†	279	"	27	"	
U	Santaniello Michael	279	electrician	32	"	
W	Gallo Grace—†	280	factoryhand	20	"	
X	Gallo Mary—†	280	housewife	40	"	
Y	Gallo Pasquale	280	factoryhand	45	"	
Z	*DeStefano Mary—†	280	housewife	36	"	

1244

A	DeStefano Ralph	280	laborer	35	"	
B	Saccardi Annetta—†	280	seamstress	30	186 Paris	
C	*Saccardi Joseph	280	retired	70	186 "	
D	*Saccardi Maria—†	280	housewife	62	186 "	
F	*Rogowicz Amelia—†	281	"	45	here	
G	*Rogowicz John	281	baker	53	"	
H	Rogowicz Julia—†	281	inspector	22	"	
K	Mangino Frank	281	toolkeeper	27	"	
L	Mangino Stella—†	281	housewife	24	"	
M	Vasconcellos Annie L—†	282	"	66	"	
N	Vasconcellos Anthony	282	draftsman	38	"	
O	Vasconcellos Mary A—†	282	housewife	35	"	
P	Oliver James	282	salesman	31	"	
R	Oliver Vera—†	282	housewife	28	"	
S	*Sonn Catherine—†	283	"	76	"	
T	Sonn Joseph	283	U S A	29	England	
U	Boehner Minnie—†	283	clerk	44	here	
V	Mangino Anna—†	283	housewife	25	"	
W	Mangino John	283	mechanic	25	"	
X	Poirier Anthony	284	rigger	27	"	
Y	Poirier Lena—†	284	housewife	25	"	
Z	*Martin Gloria—†	284	"	64	"	

1245

A	Martin Jesse	284	factoryhand	23	"	

Chelsea Street Continued

Page	Letter	FULL NAME.	Residence	Occupation	Age	Reported Residence
	B	Companaro Frank	284	laborer	47	here
	C	Companaro Mary — †	284	housewife	46	"
	D	Ricciardi Alexandria — †	285	factoryhand	22	"
	E	Ricciardi Concetta — †	285	housewife	48	"
	F	Ricciardi Frank	285	laborer	53	"
	G	Sacco Rose — †	285	housewife	33	"
	H	Sacco Salvatore J	285	boilermaker	43	"
	K	Guazzerotti Lucy — †	285	factoryhand	20	"
	L	Guazzerotti Mary — †	285	housewife	39	203 Falcon
	M	Mirabile Mary — †	286	"	26	here
	N	Mirabile Pasquale	286	rigger	28	"
	O	*Mauro Amelia — †	286	housewife	49	"
	P	Mauro Pellegrino	286	tailor	52	64 Gove
	R	*Pisano Philip	286	shoemaker	29	here
	S	*Pisano Phyllis — †	286	housewife	26	"
	T	*Traiger Esther — †	287	at home	65	"
	U	Traiger Frances — †	287	housewife	31	"
	V	Traiger Louis	287	factoryhand	34	"
	W	Malafronte Angelo	287	laborer	23	40 Morris
	X	Malafronte Theresa — †	287	housewife	46	40 "
	Y	Angelo Catherine — †	288	"	44	here
	Z	Angelo Pasquale	288	laborer	53	"
1246						
	A	*Barletto Carmen	288	"	46	"
	B	Barletto Gaetano	288	"	50	"
	C	*Barletto Susan — †	288	housewife	55	"
	D	Colluccini Florence — †	288	stitcher	31	"
	E	Terranova Joseph	288	tilesetter	50	"
	F	Terrnaova Josephine — †	288	housewife	41	"
	G	Longo John	289	mechanic	28	"
	H	Longo Mary — †	289	housewife	25	"
	K	Adelman Bernard H	289	U S A	23	"
	L	Adelman Jacob	289	carpenter	60	"
	M	Adelman Milton	289	U S A	21	"
	N	Adelman Sadie — †	289	housewife	44	"
	O	Cotreau John	289	cutter	37	"
	P	*Cotreau Mary D — †	289	housewife	37	"
	R	Lachia Fannie — †	290	"	24	"
	S	Lachia Peter	290	salesman	30	"
	T	Amerina Alma — †	290	housewife	35	"
	U	Amerina John	290	chauffeur	38	"

Chelsea Street—Continued

	v	Mucci Celia—†	290	housewife	30	here
	w	Mucci Dominic	290	candymaker	32	"
	x	Sheehan Daniel	291	inspector	41	"
	y	Sheehan Mary—†	291	housewife	39	"
	z	Jackson Frederick	291	U S A	22	"
1247						
	A	Jackson Rita—†	291	housewife	23	"
	B	Muse Gladys—†	291	factoryhand	21	"
	c	Muse John W	291	carpenter	66	"
	D*	Muse Mary—†	291	housewife	48	"
	E	Velardo Lena—†	292	"	21	"
	F	Velardo Victor	292	U S A	24	23 Ashley
	G	Napolitano Frances—†	292	housewife	43	here
	H	Napolitano Pasquale	292	chauffeur	45	"
	K*	Grasso Marie—†	292	housewife	74	356 Chelsea
	L	Ruggiero Angelo	292	U S N	21	here
	M	Ruggiero Augustine	292	shoeworker	49	"
	N	Ruggiero Margaret—†	292	housewife	48	"
	O	Gauthier Homer	293	retired	34	"
	P	Gauthier John	293	longshoreman	32	"
	R	Gauthier Nellie—†	293	housewife	70	"
	S	LaCortiglia Catherine—†	294	"	40	"
	T	LaCortiglia Domenic	294	driller	42	"
	U	Frede Carmella—†	294	housewife	57	"
	V	Frede Pelegrino	294	laborer	56	"
	W	Guarnaccia Ida—†	294	housewife	42	"
	X	Guarnaccia Philip	294	rubberworker	46	"
	Y*	Pelozoto Benjamin	296	retired	86	"
	Z*	Pelozoto Gaetana—†	296	housewife	78	"
1248						
	A	Tangusso Lillian—†	296	"	42	"
	B	Tangusso Mario	296	shoeworker	47	"
	C	Tangusso Mary—†	296	rubberworker	20	"
	D	Murphy Edward G	296	U S A	25	940 Hyde Park av
	E	Murphy Evelyn—†	296	housewife	25	940 "
	F	Silva William P	298	retired	79	here
	G*	DiFuria Lorenzo	298	chauffeur	50	56 Putnam
	H*	DiFuria Margaret—†	298	housewife	37	56 "
	K	Fisher Anna—†	298	stitcher	25	here
	L	Fisher Gaetana—†	298	inspector	21	"
	M*	Rinaldi Florence—†	298	housewife	49	"

Chelsea Street—Continued

	N	*Rinaldi Frank	298	baker	50	here
	O	Locigno Louise—†	300	housewife	25	"
	P	Locigno Rocco	300	chauffeur	24	"
	R	Grillo Angeline—†	300	housewife	24	101 Chelsea
	S	Grillo Samuel	300	operator	30	101 "
	T	DeFronzo Clara—†	300	housewife	32	3 Wilbur ct
	U	DeFronzo James	300	painter	33	3 "
	V	Genualdo Josephine—†	302	housewife	31	here
	W	Genualdo Michael	302	painter	31	"
	X	Grieco Felix	302	salesman	59	"
	Y	Grieco Filomena—†	302	housewife	59	"
	Z	Grieco Anna—†	302	stitcher	24	"
1249						
	A	Grieco Margaret—†	302	"	26	"
	B	Grieco Vincent	302	U S A	23	"
	D	Russo Nicholas	304	"	23	"
	E	Russo Sophia—†	304	housewife	21	"
	F	*Fasano Josephine—†	304	"	33	"
	G	Fasano Michael	304	laborer	44	"
	H	*Sarmento Fernando	306	retired	76	"
	K	Rose Evelyn—†	306	housewife	31	"
	L	Rose Lillian B—†	306	folder	27	"
	M	Rose Mary A—†	306	housewife	58	"
	N	Rose Otto J	306	carpenter	59	"
	O	Bartello Josephine—†	306	housewife	39	"
	P	Bartello Lena—†	306	operator	20	"
	R	Bartello Mary—†	306	clerk	20	"
	S	*Foti Lena—†	306	housewife	66	1054 Bennington
	T	Ardita Frank	308	U S A	34	here
	U	Ardita Theresa—†	308	housewife	29	"
	V	Incerto Anthony	308	U S A	25	"
	W	*Incerto Josephine—†	308	housewife	54	"
	X	Incerto Mary—†	308	packer	28	"
	Y	Incerto Rose—†	308	hairdresser	22	"
	Z	Incerto Vincenzo	308	candymaker	62	"
1250						
	A	Cammorata Andrew	308	U S A	26	"
	B	*Cammorata Anna—†	308	housewife	50	"
	C	Cammorata Biagio	308	U S A	22	"
	D	Cammorata Gaetano	308	rubberworker	61	"
	E	Cammorata Pasquale	308	U S A	24	"

Chelsea Street—Continued

	F	Oliver Emily—†	310	housewife	23	here
	G	Oliver George E	310	machinist	23	181 Princeton
	H	Mirisola Angelina—†	310	housewife	40	here
	K	Mirisola Peter	310	laborer	45	"
	N	Mirisola Filomina—†	310	housewife	30	"
	L*	Mirisola Giuseppina—†	310	"	75	"
	M	Mirisola James	310	welder	32	"
	O	Bohanan Delia—†	312	housewife	65	177 Paris
	R	Flynn Helena—†	312	housekeeper	46	here
	S	Harrison Fred	314	seaman	55	"
	T	Harrison Winifred M—†	314	housewife	36	"
	U	Raia Anna—†	314	clerk	22	"
	V	Raia Edith—†	314	operator	20	"
	W	Raia Josephine I—†	314	"	23	"
	X*	Raia Mary—†	314	housewife	42	"
	Y	Raia Mildred—†	314	packer	29	"

1251   Marion Street

	B	Micele Anna—†	230	shoeworker	21	here
	C	Micele John	230	"	45	"
	D	Micele Minnie—†	230	housewife	40	"
	E	Micele Mary—†	230	shoeworker	20	"
	F*	Albanese Cecelia—†	230	housewife	44	"
	G	Albanese Consolata—†	230	stitcher	21	"
	H	Albanese Pasquale	230	U S A	20	"
	K	Albanese Salvatore	230	laborer	47	"
	M	Matarazza Enis A—†	232	housewife	26	"
	N	Matarazza Florence—†	232	cashier	24	"
	O	Matarazza Gabriel	232	candymaker	66	"
	P	Matarazza Joseph	232	U S A	33	"
	R	Matarazza Michael	232	foreman	28	"
	S*	Matarazza Rose—†	232	housewife	63	"
	T	DeAngelis Alfred R	232	salesman	45	"
	U	DeAngelis Mollie L—†	232	housewife	37	"
	V	Schepici Carmella—†	234	"	26	"
	W	Schepici Mario	234	painter	28	"
	X*	Adragna Filippa—†	234	housewife	38	"
	Y*	Adragna John	234	laborer	51	"
	Z	Adragna Rosario	234	shoeworker	42	238 Havre

Page.	Letter.	FULL NAME.	Residence, Jan. 1, 1943.	Occupation.	Supposed Age.	Reported Residence, Jan. 1, 1942. Street and Number.

1252

Marion Street—Continued

	A	Sinatra Joseph	234	painter	20	here
	B	Sinatra Sarah — †	234	housewife	39	"
	C	*Reynolds Catherine †	236	"	30	"
	D	*Reynolds Thomas	236	fisherman	36	"
	E	*Hayes James	236	cutter	23	"
	F	*Hayes Mary — †	236	housewife	62	"
	G	*Hayes William	236	fisherman	61	"
	H	*Rotondo Alice — †	236	housewife	50	"
	K	Rotondo Orazio	236	watchman	60	"
	L	Fallica John	238	storekeeper	52	"
	M	Fallica Sadie — †	238	trimmer	21	"
	N	Micciche Domiana — †	238	housewife	45	"
	O	Micciche Guiseppe	238	mason	46	"
	R	Bartolo Charles	252	laborer	36	"
	S	Bartolo Helen — †	252	housewife	30	"
	T	*Gambino Angelo	252	operator	44	"
	U	Gambino Anna — †	252	stitcher	21	"
	V	Gambino Eva — †	252	housewife	38	"
	W	Forgiona Angelo	252	packer	38	"
	X	Forgiona Baptista	252	seaman	60	"
	Y	Forgiona Christina — †	252	housewife	35	"
	Z	Chiello Angela — †	254	clerk	20	"

1253

	A	Chiello Joseph	254	porter	54	"
	B	Chiello Marie A — †	254	clerk	21	"
	C	Pisano Frank	254	finisher	49	"
	D	Pisano Palma †	254	housewife	44	"
	E	Burke Joseph J	254	U S N	22	"
	F	Burke Mary — †	254	candymaker	38	"
	G	*Chiello Angelo	256	retired	77	"
	H	*Chiello Marie A †	256	housewife	78	"
	K	Costa Angelo	256	U S A	20	"
	L	*Costa Rose — †	256	housewife	52	"
	M	Costa Salvatore	256	U S A	21	"
	N	*Costa Vincent	256	laborer	53	"
	O	*Cobino Amelia — †	256	housewife	38	"
	P	*Cobino Angelo	256	laborer	47	"
	R	*Walsh James	258	"	64	120 Benningt'n
	S	Walsh James, jr	258	chauffeur	31	here
	T	*Walsh John	258	cutter	27	120 Benningt'n

31

Page.	Letter.	FULL NAME.	Residence, Jan. 1, 1943.	Occupation.	Supposed Age.	Reported Residence, Jan. 1, 1942. Street and Number.

Marion Street Continued

		FULL NAME		Occupation	Age	Residence
c	*	Walsh Nellie †	258	housewife	65	120 Benningt'n
v		DiGirolamo Eugene	258	U S A	24	here
w	*	DiGirolamo Joseph	258	laborer	54	"
x		DiGirolamo Luigi	258	U S N	21	"
y	*	DiGirolamo Margaret †	258	housewife	53	"
z		DiGirolamo Mary †	258	"	24	"

1254

a		DiGirolamo Nicola	258	U S A	23	"
b		Sacks Edward	258	"	26	"
c	*	Sacks Louis	258	retired	66	"
d		Sacks Morris	258	salesman	30	"
e	*	Sacks Rachel †	258	housewife	65	"

Morris Street

g		Scirro Frances †	5	housewife	39	here
h		Scirro Ralph	5	mechanic	40	"
k		Catanese Anthony	5	laborer	33	"
l		Catanese Lena †	5	housewife	30	"
m	*	Chiuve Julia †	5	"	45	"
n		Chiuve Mario	5	laborer	52	"
o		Chiuve Martha †	5	factoryhand	21	"
p		Chiuve Michael M	5	U S A	23	"
r	*	Singarella Mario	5	retired	70	"
s		Mazzarella Anthony	7	laborer	37	"
t		Mazzarella Mary †	7	housewife	34	"
u		Capezzuto James	7	metalworker	26	"
v		Capezzuto Mary †	7	housewife	23	"
w		Capezzuto Grace †	7	"	27	"
x		Capezzuto Nicholas	7	metalworker	28	"
y		DiCicco Maria †	13	housewife	23	"
z		DiCicco Nicandro	13	laborer	38	"

1255

a	*	Giusto Filippa †	13	housewife	54	"
b		Giusto Josephine †	13	factoryhand	24	"
c		Giusto Salvatore	13	U S N	21	"
d	*	Rudica Carmello	13	shoemaker	49	"
e	*	Rudica Theresa † †	13	housewife	39	"
g		Salvati Dominic	15	laborer	26	"
f		Salvati Frank	15	"	57	"
h	*	Salvati Mary †	15	housewife	50	"

Morris Street Continued

K	Yancovitz Alice †	15	factoryhand	22	here
L	Yancovitz Charlotte—†	15	"	29	"
M	*Yancovitz Dominic	15	laborer	57	"
N	Yancovitz Frank	15	U S N	20	"
O	Yancovitz Joseph	15	U S A	34	"
P	*Yancovitz Monica—†	15	housewife	54	"
R	*Casaccio Angelo	15	storekeeper	66	"
S	*Casaccio Josephine — †	15	housewife	51	"
T	*Nesti Lena — †	17	"	50	"
U	Nesta Louis	17	laborer	51	"
V	Nesti Salvatore	17	"	20	"
W	Ottana Catherine †	17	factoryhand	21	"
X	Ottana Joseph	17	laborer	56	"
Y	Ottana Mary—†	17	housewife	44	"
Z	Schena Salvario	17	laborer	47	"

1256

A	Schena Theresa—†	17	housewife	41	"
B	Schena Thomas	17	U S A	21	"
C	Indorato Filadelfio	19	laborer	25	"
D	Indorato Filippa—†	19	housewife	23	"
E	*Indorato Julia—†	19	"	45	"
F	Indorato Sebastino	19	retired	59	"
G	Indorato Vincenzo	19	U S M C	20	"
H	*Montalto Mary †	19	housewife	37	"
K	Montalto Nicholas	19	laborer	47	"
L	*Fumicello Concetta—†	20	housewife	34	"
M	Fumicello Michael	20	chauffeur	36	"
N	*Celeste Anna †	21	housewife	53	75 Morris
O	Celeste Charles	21	U S A	31	75 "
P	Celeste Salvatore	21	tailor	20	75 "
R	*Fumicello Josephine—†	21	housewife	38	23 "
S	Fumicello Paul	21	plumber	47	23 "
T	Milano Mary †	21	housewife	47	here
U	Milano Philip	21	metalworker	47	"
V	Zarba William	21	artist	26	"
W	White George	22	rigger	44	"
X	*White Philomena †	22	housewife	38	"
Y	*Picariello Alicia †	22	"	62	"
Z	Picariello Salvatore	22	cobbler	62	"

1257

A	*Fumicello Filippa—†	23	housewife	76	"

1—12

Page.	Letter.	FULL NAME.	Residence, Jan. 1, 1943.	Occupation.	Supposed Age.	Reported Residence, Jan. 1, 1942. Street and Number.

Morris Street—Continued

	B	Lento Guy	23	clerk	31	21 Morris
	C	Lento Jane—†	23	housewife	25	21 "
	D*	Milano Laboria—†	23	"	49	here
	E	Milano Vincent	23	laborer	59	"
	F	Benedetti Alfred	24	cutter	36	"
	G	Benedetti Phyllis—†	24	housewife	35	"
	H	Flammia Angelo	24	electrician	22	"
	K	Flammia Anthony	24	laborer	46	"
	L*	Flammia Lucy—†	24	housewife	45	"
	M	Morris Elizabeth—†	25	"	37	"
	N	Morris James	25	shoemaker	35	"
	P	LaPlaca Clara—†	25	housewife	39	"
	R	LaPlaca John	25	laborer	49	"
	S	LaPlaca Mario	25	welder	22	"
	T	Cady Mary—†	26	packer	21	"
	U	Hickey Helen—†	26	housewife	26	"
	V	Hickey Thomas	26	laborer	28	"
	W*	Meloni Enrico	27	"	82	"
	X*	Meloni Mary—†	27	housewife	72	"
	Y*	Meloni Amelia—†	27	at home	40	"
	Z	Meloni John	27	laborer	33	"

1258

	A	Miranda Mary—†	27	housewife	37	"
	B	Miranda Salvatore	27	laborer	40	"
	C	LaMarca Alfred	28	electrician	31	"
	D	LaMarca Mary—†	28	housewife	29	"
	E	Parisse Alesio	28	shoemaker	42	"
	F	Parisse Mary A—†	28	housewife	35	"
	G	Mazza Antonetta—†	28	"	33	"
	H	Mazza John	28	laborer	38	"
	K	Pizzella Frank	30	"	49	"
	L*	Pizzella Philomena—†	30	housewife	46	"
	M	Casazza Theodore	30	mechanic	38	"
	N	Casazza Victoria—†	30	housewife	38	"
	O	Constantine Henry	30	rigger	31	"
	P	Constantine Louise—†	30	housewife	31	"
	R	O'Brien Mary—†	32	"	47	445 Saratoga
	S	O'Brien William F	32	laborer	54	445 "
	T	Dishinsky Annie—†	32	housewife	64	here
	U	Dishinsky Louis	32	tailor	72	"
	V	Gioioso Joseph	32	laborer	32	"

34

Page.	Letter.	FULL NAME.	Residence, Jan. 1, 1943.	Occupation	Supposed Age.	Reported Residence, Jan. 1, 1942. Street and Number.

Morris Street — Continued

	w	Gioioso Josephine †	32	housewife	27	here
	x	Pascarella Joseph	33	laborer	28	"
	y	Pascarella Theresa †	33	housewife	26	"
	z	Taurone Angelo	33	mechanic	46	"
1259						
	A	Pittella Joseph	33	laborer	45	"
	B	*Pittella Victoria †	33	housewife	36	"
	D	*Gomes Benvinda †	34	"	44	"
	E	*Gomes Manuel	34	laborer	48	"
	F	Colarusso John F	34	U S A	22	"
	G	Lemmo Joseph	34	foreman	38	"
	H	Lemmo Phyllis †	34	housewife	31	"
	K	Senese Michael	36	welder	31	"
	L	Senese Phyllis †	36	housewife	33	"
	M	Mello James	36	painter	41	"
	N	Mello Josephine †	36	housewife	40	"
	O	Muldoon Thomas P	36	mechanic	47	"
	P	Muldoon Victoria †	36	housewife	46	"
	R	Pellegrine Rose †	37	"	23	"
	S	Pellegrine Salverino	37	laborer	22	"
	T	Santaniello Augustine	37	"	25	"
	U	Santaniello Josephine †	37	housewife	25	"
	V	*Cagnina Anna †	37	"	52	"
	W	Cagnina Joseph	37	laborer	53	"
	X	*Bandini Antonetta †	38	housewife	77	"
	Y	*Bandini Paul	38	laborer	72	"
	Z	*Pimentel John	38	painter	39	"
1260						
	A	Pimentel Mary †	38	housewife	39	"
	B	Manfra Anna †	38	"	25	391 Chelsea
	C	Manfra Joseph	38	carpenter	22	391 "
	D	*Pasquantonio Anthony	40	laborer	72	here
	E	*Pasquantonio Jennie †	40	housewife	65	"
	G	DePari Vito	40	laborer	63	"
	H	Paghiso Alphonse	40	U S A	25	Chelsea
	K	Paghiso Anna †	40	housewife	22	here
	L	*Barone Carmella †	41	"	54	"
	M	Barone Vito	41	laborer	64	"
	N	*Polito Theresa †	42	housewife	75	"
	O	*Casteluccio Sadie †	42	"	38	"
	P	Casteluccio Samuel	42	mechanic	45	"

35

Morris Street—Continued

R	Pardi Frank	42	laborer	49	here
S	*Pardi Maria—†	42	housewife	48	"
T	LaMonica Lawrence	43	mechanic	31	"
U	LaMonica Lucy—†	43	housewife	31	"
V	Russo Angelo	43	U S A	33	"
W	Russo Gabriella—†	43	operator	26	"
X	*Russo Loretta—†	43	housewife	63	"
Y	Russo Madeleine †	43	typist	20	"
Z	Russo Mary—†	43	candymaker	39	"

1261

A	Russo Thomas	43	mechanic	29	"
B	Laurie Gene	44	chauffeur	24	25 Morris
C	Torname Angie—†	44	factoryhand	24	25 "
D	*Torname Joseph	44	laborer	68	25 "
E	Torname Louis	44	U S A	21	25 "
F	*Torname Mary—†	44	housewife	57	25 "
G	Torname Salvatore	44	chauffeur	25	25 "
H	*Incerto Antonio	44	laborer	65	here
K	Incerto Florence—†	44	packer	21	"
L	Incerto Jennie—†	44	"	24	"
M	*DiPlicido Bernard	44	laborer	52	"
N	DiPlicido Mary—†	44	housewife	45	"
O	Cassia Joseph	45	laborer	45	"
P	Cassia Joseph	45	mechanic	21	"
R	*Cassia Mary—†	45	housewife	39	"
S	Marino Frank	45	mechanic	46	"
T	*Aliano Concetta—†	45	housewife	64	"
U	Aliano Santo	45	laborer	39	"
V	Selvitella Ralph	46	"	47	"
W	Selvitella Virginia †	46	housewife	46	"
X	Vella Josephine—†	46	"	30	"
Y	Vella Rosario	46	shoemaker	34	"
Z	O'Connell Thomas	46	shipfitter	45	"

1262

B	Gubitosi Filomenia †	51	housewife	32	"
C	Gubitosi Joseph	51	bookbinder	32	"
D	Perrone Domenic	51	laborer	52	"
E	Perrone Jessie †	51	housewife	47	"
F	*Perrone Susan †	51	"	77	"
G	Manguso Charles	51	laborer	49	"
H	*Manguso Jennie—†	51	housewife	38	"

Page.	Letter.	Full Name.	Residence, Jan. 1, 1943.	Occupation.	Supposed Age.	Reported Residence, Jan. 1, 1942. Street and Number.

Morris Street—Continued

K	*Cali Catherine—†	63	housewife	56	80 Porter
L	Cali Joseph	63	laborer	29	80 "
M	Cali Michael	63	U S A	24	80 "
N	Cali Salvatore	63	"	26	80 "
O	Salimbene Charles	65	mechanic	29	here
P	Salimbene Palmira—†	65	housewife	24	"
R	Cello Adamo	65	U S A	23	"
S	Cello Anthony	65	mechanic	32	"
T	Cello Elizabeth—†	65	housewife	32	"
U	*Cello Ferdinando	65	laborer	66	"
V	*Guarino Lena—†	65	housewife	43	"
W	Saggese Amado	67	chauffeur	31	"
X	Saggese Ellen—†	67	housewife	28	"
Y	Ruggiero Fortunato	67	fireman	48	"
Z	Ruggiero Jennie—†	67	housewife	48	"

1263

A	Ruggiero Lillian—†	67	clerk	20	"
B	Penta Ernest	67	mechanic	29	"
C	Penta Helen—†	67	housewife	26	"
D	DeCristoforo Anthony	69	mechanic	31	"
E	DeCristoforo Fannie—†	69	housewife	29	"
F	*Lavine Louis	69	tailor	46	"
G	Lavine Robert	69	student	23	"
H	*Lavine Sarah—†	69	housewife	47	"
K	Columbus Angie—†	69	"	33	"
L	Columbus Frank	69	U S A	40	"
M	Graziano Louise—†	69	housewife	51	"
O	Olivieri Mario	71	U S A	21	"
P	Olivieri Mary—†	71	housewife	23	182 Cottage
R	Doucette Charles	71	clerk	35	here
S	Doucette Josephine—†	71	housewife	30	"
T	Olivieri John	71	laborer	44	"
U	*Olivieri Maria—†	71	housewife	44	"
V	Fratto Peter	73	laborer	35	"
W	Fratto Rose—†	73	housewife	34	"
X	Cardoza Ferdinand	73	foreman	44	"
Y	Cardoza Helen—†	73	housewife	38	"
Z	Johnson Ada D—†	73	factoryhand	23	"

1264

A	Johnson Joseph B	73	mechanic	48	"
B	Johnson Marion F—†	73	clerk	25	"

37

Morris Street—Continued

	c	Johnson Theresa—†	73	housewife	46	here
	d	Sousa Meda—†	75	"	42	"
	e	*Molino Carmen	75	laborer	56	"
	f	*Molino Rose—†	75	housewife	47	"
	g	Molino Theresa—†	75	factoryhand	23	"
	h	*Lattiere Joseph	75	laborer	54	210 Chelsea
	k	*Lattiere Josephine—†	75	housewife	53	210 "
	l	Lattiere Rosario	75	U S A	22	210 "
	m	*Delsie Antonetta—†	77	housewife	58	here
	n	Delsie John	77	U S A	22	"
	o	*Delsie Phillip	77	laborer	56	"
	p	Orso Anthony	77	tailor	24	"
	r	Orso Rose—†	77	factoryhand	22	"
	s	Sarro Angelina—†	77	"	27	"
	t	Sarro Anthony	77	U S A	23	"
	u	Sarro Carmella—†	77	clerk	28	"
	v	Sarro Elizabeth—†	77	factoryhand	20	"
	w	Sarro Theresa—†	77	housewife	49	"
	x	White Catherine—†	77	"	73	"
	y	White George F	77	laborer	39	"
	z	Cocozza Dominic	79	"	62	"
1265						
	a	Cocozza Julia—†	79	factoryhand	23	"
	b	McGuire Catherine—†	79	housewife	53	"
	c	McGuire James W	79	mechanic	55	"
	d	Cardosi Henry	79	inspector	42	"
	e	Cardosi Jennie—†	79	housewife	43	"
	f	Agri Anthony	81	laborer	67	"
	g	*Agri Frances—†	81	housewife	66	"
	h	Bartolomeo Helen—†	81	"	27	"
	k	Bartolomeo Lawrence	81	laborer	27	"
	l	*Farrulla Catherine—†	81	housewife	38	"
	m	Farrulla Vincent	81	laborer	47	"
	n	O'Connell Anna—†	83	housewife	25	"
	o	O'Connell Paul	83	laborer	25	"
	p	Shapiro Anna—†	83	clerk	20	"
	r	Shapiro Minnie—†	83	"	25	"
	s	Shapiro Samuel	83	pedler	64	"
	t	Chiaino Josephine—†	83	housewife	26	356 Chelsea
	u	*Pappalardo Mary—†	83	"	45	here
	v	Pappalardo Vincent	83	laborer	54	"

38

Page.	Letter.	FULL NAME.	Residence. Jan. 1. 1943.	Occupation.	Supposed Age.	Reported Residence, Jan. 1. 1942. Street and Number.

Morris Street — Continued

	w	Indingaro Edmund	87	U S A	23	here
	x	Indingaro Isabel †	87	housewife	62	"
	y	Indingaro Lawrence	87	manager	33	"
	z	Russo Alma †	87	housewife	37	"

1266

	a	Russo Anthony	87	manager	37	"
	b	Napolitano Clemente	89	laborer	37	Revere
	c	Napolitano Ida †	89	housewife	34	"
	d	Barone John	89	laborer	34	here
	e	Barone Rose †	89	housewife	30	"
	f	Lombardo Helen †	89	spinner	26	"
	g	Lombardo Joseph	89	mechanic	33	"
	h	Serra Alba †	89	housewife	31	"
	k	Serra Patrick	89	electrician	34	"
	l	Ruggiero Diega †	90	housewife	25	"
	m	Ruggiero Joseph	90	laborer	23	"
	n	Bratt Gustaf L	90	engineer	72	"
	o	Hennessy Anna †	90	housewife	34	"
	p	Scarpa Carmen	90	laborer	25	"
	r	Scarpa Margaret †	90	housewife	23	"
	t	Ferrante Graziano	91	retired	72	"
	u	LaCortiglia Harry	91	mechanic	36	"
	v	LaCortiglia Louise †	91	housewife	34	"
	w	Genova Anthony	99	U S A	27	"
	x	Genova Florence †	99	at home	22	"
	y	Genova Pasquale	99	porter	63	"
	z*	Genova Pasqualine †	99	housewife	62	"

1267

	a	Najaryan Elena †	99	"	21	153 Saratoga
	b*	Najaryan Peter	99	shipper	27	Cambridge
	c*	Barbanti Alfreda †	101	housewife	28	here
	d	Barbanti John	101	manager	34	"
	e	Mandella Helen †	101	housewife	43	"
	f*	Mandella Patrick	101	cabinetmaker	61	"
	g	Barbanti Antonio	101	retired	77	"
	h	Barbanti Josephine †	101	housewife	71	"
	l	Lanagan Elizabeth †	103	"	42	"
	m	Lanagan Henry J	103	laborer	48	"
	n	Napolitano Catherine †	103	housewife	31	"
	o	Napolitano Michael	103	laborer	47	"
	p	Francis Elizabeth †	103	housewife	59	"

Page.	Letter.	FULL NAME.	Residence, Jan. 1, 1943.	Occupation.	Supposed Age.	Reported Residence, Jan. 1, 1942. Street and Number.

Morris Street — Continued

	R	Francis John L	103	laborer	70	here
	S	Rizzuti Catherine—†	103	housewife	20	"
	T	Rizzuti Pasquale	103	U S A	24	114 Cottage
	U	Porter Christian	106	laborer	27	here
	V	Porter Grace—†	106	housewife	25	"
	W	Fine Anna—†	106	clerk	32	"
	X	Fine Harry	106	pedler	45	"
	Y	Fine Isabella—†	106	at home	31	"
	Z	Fine Morris	106	laborer	28	"
1268						
	A	Sarro Joseph	106	"	40	"
	B	Sarro Mary—†	106	housewife	38	"

Paris Street

	D	Pasquantonio Phyllis—†	253	housewife	27	here
	E	Pasquantonio William	253	laborer	31	"
	F	Lamonica Antonio	253	rubberworker	50	"
	G*	Lamonica Mary—†	253	housewife	40	"
	H*	DeMatteo Carmella—†	253	"	50	"
	K	DeMatteo John	253	painter	23	"
	L	Riccio Angelina—†	255	housewife	35	"
	M	Riccio Carmen	255	laborer	45	"
	N*	Cardone Esther—†	255	weaver	35	358 Chelsea
	O*	Cardone Rocco	255	laborer	46	358 "
	P	Luciano Joseph	255	"	25	256 Paris
	R	Luciano Michael	255	U S N	20	256 "
	S	Luciano Theresa—†	255	housewife	45	256 "
	T	Corrozza Carmela—†	257	"	38	here
	U	Corrozza Gerard	257	pipefitter	37	"
	V	Casamassima Amelia—†	257	cook	32	"
	W	Casamassima Domenic	257	shoemaker	39	"
	X*	Casamassima Gaetana—†	257	housewife	69	"
	Y	Casamassima Michael	257	retired	69	"
	Z	Casamassima Rocco	257	U S M C	23	"
1269						
	A*	Lauletta Catherine—†	257	at home	63	"
	B	Miraglia Vincenza—†	257	"	83	"
	C*	Albanese Carmela—†	259	here	54	"
	D	Albanese Fred	259	U S A	32	"

Paris Street Continued

E	Albanese John	259	laborer	28	here	
F	Albanese Luigi	259	U S A	30	"	
G	Siraco Antonio	259	retired	65	"	
H	*Siraco Dolorosa †	259	housewife	62	"	
K	Siraco Domenic	259	U S A	22	"	
L	Cedrone Anthony	259	U S N	21	"	
M	Cedrone Domenic	259	laborer	56	"	
N	*Cedrone Maria—†	259	housewife	53	"	
O	Orlandino Ettore	261	laborer	26	Somerville	
P	Orlandino Nicolina †	261	housewife	23	"	
R	Pazzanese Anna L—†	261	"	24	here	
S	Pazzanese Frank	261	welder	26	"	
T	Sorrentino Henry	261	electrician	37	13 Snow Hill	
U	Sorrentino Josephine—†	261	housewife	35	13 "	
V	Festa Alfred	263	meatcutter	31	here	
W	Festa Julia—†	263	housewife	32	"	
X	Capezzuto Charles	263	laborer	32	"	
Y	Capezzuto John	263	retired	54	"	
Z	*Capezzuto Theresa—†	263	at home	90	"	

1270

A	*Pazzanese Carmen	263	retired	56	"	
B	*Pazzanese Florence †	263	housewife	49	"	
C	Pazzanese Joseph	263	welder	20	"	
D	Ventullo Anthony	265	rigger	38	"	
E	Ventullo Margaret †	265	housewife	36	"	
G	O'Brien James	265	chauffeur	48	"	
H	O'Brien Mary A †	265	at home	70	"	
K	Alterisio Alexander	267	technician	38	"	
L	Alterisio Mary—†	267	housewife	38	"	
M	Guarino Anthony	267	student	21	"	
N	Guarino Carmela †	267	clerk	23	"	
O	*Guarino Ciriaco	267	retired	65	"	
P	*Guarino Mary—†	267	housewife	52	"	
R	Guarino Salvatore	267	U S N	27	"	
S	Zakarian Narsup	267	retired	66	136 Benningt'n	
T	*Zakarian Vartan †	267	at home	53	here	
U	Erickson Francis E	269	pipefitter	29	"	
V	Erickson Louise—†	269	housewife	25	"	
W	*Bove Christina —†	269	"	65	"	
X	*Bove Joseph	269	retired	70	"	
Z	Yarobino Luigi	271	laborer	44	"	

H

1271

Paris Street—Continued

A	Yarobino Pasqualina—†	271	housewife	38	here
B	Caucci Marion—†	271	"	47	266 Paris
C	Caucci Thomas	271	laborer	51	266 "
D	Caucci William	271	"	25	266 "
E	Panzini Minnie—†	271	housewife	26	110 Chelsea
F	Panzini Thomas	271	ropemaker	28	110 "
H	Spadorcia Domenic	273	laborer	31	here
K	Spadorcia Palminia—†	273	housewife	31	"
L*	Matarazzo Clementina—†	273	at home	47	"
M	Cannon Joseph	275	laborer	28	"
N	Cannon Mary—†	275	housewife	27	"
O	Cannon Annie—†	275	"	57	"
P	Cannon Thomas L	275	chauffeur	57	"
R	DeAcetis Angelina—†	275	housewife	24	"
S	DeAcetis Gene	275	welder	22	"
T	Ricciardi Antonetta—†	277	housewife	25	"
U	Ricciardi James	277	engineer	26	"
V	Gioioso Frances—†	277	housewife	31	32 Morris
W	Gioioso Patrick	277	clerk	33	32 "
X	Mercuri Joseph	277	musician	29	here
Y	Mercuri Nellie—†	277	housewife	27	"
Z	Dillon Catherine—†	279	at home	69	"

1272

A	Dillon Francis	279	chauffeur	30	"
B	Dillon Olga—†	279	housewife	29	"
D	Scopa Henry	292	ironworker	36	"
E	Scopa Philomena—†	292	housewife	32	"
F*	DeRosa Mary—†	292	"	53	"
G	DeRosa Pasquale	292	laborer	59	"
H	Walbourne Lena—†	292	housewife	28	"
K	Walbourne Leonard	292	U S A	24	"
L*	Gillespie Eileen—†	292	housewife	45	"
M	Gillespie Joseph	292	laborer	39	"
N	Collins Anna C—†	294	housewife	56	"
O	Collins William F	294	laborer	56	"
P	Curran John J	294	riveter	46	"
R	McKenna Elizabeth—†	294	housewife	41	"
S	McKenna Henry F	294	U S N	20	"
T	McMahon Frederick	294	salesman	29	38 Lexington
U	McMahon Richard	294	watchman	57	38 "

42

Page.	Letter.	Full Name.	Residence. Jan. 1, 1943.	Occupation.	Supposed Age.	Reported Residence, Jan. 1, 1942. Street and Number.

Paris Street Continued

	v	Todd Alice †	294	housewife	25	here
	w	Todd Stanley	294	rigger	29	"
	y	Melody Alonzo	296	machinist	50	300 Paris
	z	Willneff Annie †	296	at home	63	300 "
1273						
	b	Shephard Robert M	296	sexton	35	here
	a*	Shephard Sadie †	296	housewife	40	"
	d	Stella Charles	298	laborer	60	110 Bremen
	e	Stella Domenic	298	U S A	22	110 "
	f*	Stella Maria †	298	housewife	64	110 "
	g	Stella Maria †	298	clerk	27	110 "
	k	Cassidy Julia A †	300	housewife	65	here
	l	Cassidy Thomas A	300	retired	74	"
	o*	DeVincentis Frank	302	painter	39	15 Ashland
	p	DeVincentis Philomena—†	302	housewife	29	15 "
	r	Capozzoli Marie—†	302	"	34	here
	s	Capozzoli Robert	302	machinist	39	"
	t	Dicks Elizabeth—†	302	housewife	40	"
	u	Dicks Francis	302	U S N	38	"
	v	Connolly Mary A—†	303	teacher	27	New York
	w	Crowley Julia †	303	"	46	here
	x	Dickerson Thelma—†	303	housekeeper	30	Watertown
	y	Foley Margaret F—†	303	teacher	39	here
	z	Ford Marion †	303	"	33	"
1274						
	a	Hanrahan Catherine M—†	303	"	45	New York
	b	Hogan Lucina †	303	"	34	"
	c	Hughes Kathryn—†	303	"	48	325 Bunker Hill
	d	Hynes Ann—†	303	"	53	Watertown
	e	Keefe Ellen †	303	"	48	here
	f	Lafayette Mary J †	303	"	42	"
	g	Meehan Helen—†	303	"	52	"
	h	Murphy Catherine E—†	303	"	32	New York
	k	Murray Catherine—†	303	"	38	here
	l	O'Brien Mary F—†	303	"	53	Lynn
	m	Richards Mary J—†	303	"	40	here
	n	Scott Mary F †	303	"	65	"
	o	Sullivan Viola—†	303	"	40	"
	p	Trant Elizabeth R—†	303	"	39	Watertown
	r	Walsh Mary J—†	303	"	57	"
	s	Hagan Mary—†	306	at home	39	here

Page.	Letter	FULL NAME.	Residence, Jan. 1, 1943.	Occupation.	Supposed Age.	Reported Residence, Jan. 1, 1942. Street and Number.

Paris Street—Continued

	T	*Pedrazzi Enrica—†	306	at home	63	here
	U	Pedrazzi Henry	306	machinist	32	"
	V	Pedrazzi Louis	306	U S A	35	"
	W	*Ruo Carmella—†	308	housewife	68	186 Paris
	X	Ruo Michael	308	retired	68	186 "
	Y	*Aquino Annie—†	308	housewife	41	here
	Z	Aquino Carmen	308	laborer	42	"
1275						
	A	Hodson Harry R	310	U S A	43	"
	B	Doucette Evelyn—†	310	clerk	23	"
	C	Doucette Mary—†	310	housewife	49	"
	D	Doucette Stanley	310	electrician	50	"
	E	Hodson Clara L—†	312	at home	75	"
	F	Hodson Henry N	312	retired	80	"
	G	Hodson Margaret—†	312	housewife	43	"
	H	Hodson William	312	retired	50	"
	K	Baker Albert	315	custodian	46	"
	M	Baker John P	315	foreman	42	"
	L	*Baker Mary—†	315	housewife	38	"
	N	Aptekar Rebecca B—†	315	at home	70	"
	O	Doyle Annie T—†	315	"	77	"
	P	Gillar Rose—†	315	"	43	"
	R	MacKay Hilma—†	317	housewife	27	"
	S	MacKay James J	317	machinist	26	"
	T	Donovan Helena—†	317	housewife	28	130 Saratoga
	U	Donovan Sylvester	317	welder	28	130 "
	V	Ducey Katherine—†	317	housewife	21	here
	W	Ducey Samuel A	317	foreman	29	424 Saratoga
	X	Corumbo Catherine—†	319	operator	41	here
	Y	D'Angelico Flora—†	319	housewife	36	224 Paris
	Z	D'Angelico Michael	319	mechanic	47	224 "
1276						
	A	*Campanella Jennie—†	319	leatherworker	24	here
	B	Campanella Josephine—†	319	stitcher	20	"
	C	*Campanella Mary—†	319	"	22	"
	D	*Campanella Rocco	319	laborer	52	"
	E	*Campanella Rose—†	319	housewife	46	"
	F	Daye Ruth—†	321	"	26	"
	G	*Daye Wilfred	321	mechanic	42	"
	H	Ricciardi Joseph	321	carpenter	59	"
	K	Ricciardi Mary—†	321	housewife	42	"

44

Paris Street Continued

	L	Ricciardi Michelina— †	321	operator	21	here
	M	Stone Daniel	325	chauffeur	27	166 Marion
	N	Stone Edna— †	325	housewife	30	166 "
	O	St Croix John W	325	calker	34	here
	P	St Croix Mary E— †	325	housewife	34	"
	R	Griffin Helen E— †	325	"	43	"
	S	Griffin Mary E— †	325	saleswoman	20	"
	T	Griffin Michael F	325	laborer	45	"
	U	*D'Adamo Anthony	325	painter	52	"
	V	George Betty— †	325	factoryhand	53	"
	W	Grant George D	325	U S A	42	"
	X	Oliver Mary — †	325	at home	50	"
	Y	Oliver Rosemary— †	325	stitcher	25	"
	Z	Tarentino Hilda— †	325	housewife	21	"

1277

	A	Tarentino Joseph	325	U S N	22	249 Chelsea
	D	Charotas Mary— †	327	housewife	64	here
	E	*Charotas Stephen	327	laborer	62	"
	F	Parson John	327	mechanic	36	"
	G	Laurens Julia— †	327	at home	58	"
	H	Amico Angelina — †	327	housewife	52	"
	K	Amico Calogero	327	shoemaker	56	"
	L	Indelicato Anna— †	327	housewife	27	"
	M	Renoui Nicholas	327	U S A	21	"
	N	Renoui Philip	327	operator	37	"
	O	*Renoui Vincenza— †	327	housewife	54	"
	P	*Renoui Vincenzo	327	retired	64	"
	R	Gubitosi Charles	329	tailor	58	"
	S	*Gubitosi Maria— †	329	housewife	58	"
	T	Avola Joseph W	329	U S A	21	"
	U	*Avola Michael	329	shoemaker	53	"
	V	*Avola Ola — †	329	housewife	53	"
	W	Stuppia John	329	U S A	31	"
	X	*Stuppia Mary— †	329	housewife	50	"
	Y	Stuppia Michael	329	laborer	61	"
	Z	Whitehead Belle— †	331	at home	72	"

1278

	A	DeRosa Mary †	331	clerk	22	103 Beacon
	B	DeRosa Stephen	331	U S A	21	103 "
	C	Legotti Beatrice— †	331	clerk	20	here
	D	Legotti Charles	331	lawyer	24	"

45

Paris Street—Continued

E	*Legotti Ida—†	331	housewife	52	here	
F	Legotti John	331	clerk	26	"	
G	Morrison Ann—†	333	at home	73	"	
H	*Buono Elvira—†	333	"	57	"	
K	*Buono Gabriel	333	shoeworker	31	"	
L	Buono Margaret—†	333	checker	20	"	
M	Buono Ralph	333	U S A	24	"	
N	Buono Mildred—†	333	housewife	30	"	
O	Buono Pasquale	333	bartender	34	"	
P	Silva Edward	335	U S N	21	62 Bennington	
R	Silva Pauline—†	335	housewife	21	62 "	
S	*Grasso Frank	335	butcher	35	here	
T	*Grasso Rose—†	335	housewife	36	"	

Princeton Street

V	Ciampa Mary—†	137	housewife	47	here	
W	Ciampa Nicholas	137	bricklayer	51	"	
X	Ciampa William S	137	U S A	20	"	
Y	Interratto Louis	137	"	24	"	
Z	Interratto Mary—†	137	housewife	22	"	
1279						
A	D'Entremont Joseph A	139	carpenter	62	"	
B	D'Entremont Lester	139	U S A	23	"	
C	D'Entremont Mary H—†	139	housewife	58	"	
D	D'Entremont Philip	139	U S A	25	"	
E	Carlson Madeline—†	139	operator	31	"	
F	Godin Elizabeth—†	139	housewife	21	"	
G	Godin Henry	139	U S M C	24	"	
H	Penney Elizabeth—†	141	housewife	66	250 Princeton	
K	Penney John C	141	U S A	34	250 "	
L	Penney Joseph E	141	seaman	35	250 "	
M	*Nazzaro Rose—†	141	housekeeper	74	here	
N	Fiorillo Christina—†	141	housewife	38	"	
O	Fiorillo Vincent	141	laborer	45	"	
P	DeProspo Jennie—†	143	housewife	31	"	
R	DeProspo Michael	143	chauffeur	33	"	
S	Boudreau Evangeline—†	143	housewife	34	"	
T	Boudreau George	143	rigger	40	"	
U	Goyetch Emma—†	143	operator	35	"	
V	DelCore Arthur	143	"	33	"	

46

Page.	Letter.	FULL NAME.	Residence, Jan. 1, 1943.	Occupation.	Supposed Age.	Reported Residence Jan. 1, 1942 Street and Number.

Princeton Street—Continued

	W	DelCore Gertrude—†	143	housewife	32	here
	X	Lacarro Gesimina—†	145	housekeeper	42	"
	Y	Adinolfi Josephine—†	145	housewife	39	"
	Z	Adinolfi Nicola	145	upholsterer	46	"
1280						
	A	*Jannis Mary—†	147	housewife	40	"
	B	*Gangi Carmella—†	147	"	42	"
	C	Gangi John	147	U S A	21	"
	D	*Gangi Manuel	147	finisher	52	"
	E	Dispensiero Charles	149	musician	30	"
	F	Dispensiero Emalinda—†	149	housewife	29	"
	G	Sirrocco Daniel F	149	storekeeper	58	"
	H	*Sirrocco Romana—†	149	housewife	52	"
	K	Tontodonato Anna—†	149	"	33	"
	L	Tontodonato Nicholas	149	welder	35	"
	M	Ceccarossa Charles	151	laborer	43	"
	N	Ceccarossa Madalena—†	151	housewife	42	"
	O	Tontodonato Antonia—†	151	"	29	"
	P	Tontodonato John	151	laborer	30	"
	R	Flaherty Ernest	151	welder	29	"
	S	George Edward	151	shipfitter	34	"
	T	George Lillian—†	151	housewife	30	"
	U	Munn Edith—†	151	baker	34	185 Brooks
	V	Leville Alice C—†	153	housewife	34	here
	W	Leville William T	153	laborer	34	"
	X	Venedam Charles	153	shipwright	30	"
	Y	Venedam Rose—†	153	housewife	25	"
	Z	Silvy Pauline—†	153	"	31	"
1281						
	A	Silvy William	153	metalworker	36	"
	B	Giardini Dante	157	machinist	51	"
	C	Giardini Dante, jr	157	U S A	21	"
	D	Giardini Emilia—†	157	housewife	51	"
	E	Pesci Salvatore	157	U S A	22	"
	F	Gaeta Fiore	157	messenger	53	"
	G	Gaeta Lucy—†	157	housewife	53	"
	K	*Francis Augusta—†	157	"	50	"
	H	Francis Edwin	157	U S A	25	"
	L	Francis John	157	rigger	59	"
	M	Pignato James	159	salesman	31	"
	N	Pignato Theresa—†	159	housewife	30	"

17

Princeton Street— Continued

O	Sarravia Anthony	159	watchman	55	here
P	*Perrotta Gaetano	159	laborer	48	"
R	*Perrotta Olympia — †	159	housewife	43	"
S	Fortunato Anna — †	159	"	25	"
T	Fortunato Dario	159	U S A	26	Somerville
U	Picceo Anne — †	159	housekeeper	48	here
V	Picceo Barbara — †	159	saleswoman	23	"
W	Picceo Margaret — †	159	floorwoman	28	"
X	Moore Ellen — †	165	housewife	37	"
Y	Moore Henry A	165	cutter	40	"
Z	Barron Mary — †	165	housewife	39	"

1282

A	Barron Thomas	165	fisherman	40	"
B	Sandquist Kathleen — †	165	housewife	27	"
C	Sandquist William O	165	guard	26	"
D	Cuoco Alvira — †	167	housewife	38	"
E	Cuoco John	167	laborer	46	"
F	Muscatelli Olga — †	167	housewife	37	"
G	Muscatelli Savino	167	laborer	40	"
H	Barnabei Michael	167	plater	32	"
K	Barnabei Mildred — †	167	housewife	22	"
L	Mercadante Ethel — †	169	"	28	"
M	Mercadante Pasquale	169	inspector	30	"
N	Zuccarino Carpenella — †	169	stitcher	22	"
O	Zuccarino Rocco	169	laborer	44	"
P	*Zuccarino Tomasina — †	169	housewife	46	"
R	Zaffiro Anthony	169	machinist	39	"
S	Zaffiro Carmella — †	169	housewife	29	"
T	Nagle Edmund H	171	retired	73	"
U	Nagle Gertrude — †	171	housewife	73	"
V	Nagle Doris L — †	171	"	34	"
W	Nagle Edmund H, jr	171	U S N	36	"
X	Zafarana Alfonsina — †	173	housewife	50	"
Y	Zafarana Giacomo	173	retired	65	"
Z	Zafarana Giacomo	173	lawyer	29	"

1283

A	Petralia Joseph	173	tailor	25	"
B	Petralia Josephine — †	173	housewife	28	"
C	*Petralia Rosalie — †	173	at home	52	"
D	Kehoe Eugene	173	engineer	64	"
E	Kehoe Mary — †	173	housewife	66	"

48

Princeton Street Continued

F	Boyan John J	175	supervisor	51	here
G	Boyan Mary A †	175	housekeeper	71	"
H	Morrissey Elizabeth N †	175	at home	84	"
K	Malone Harry	175	U S A	35	"
L	Malone Herbert	175	machinist	62	"
M	Malone Lydia †	175	housewife	54	"
N	Malone Minnie †	175	clerk	22	"
O	Seggese Angelina †	179	housewife	23	205 E Eagle
P	Seggese Phillip	179	carpenter	23	205 "
R	DeBarco Filomena †	179	housewife	38	here
S	DeBarco Mario	179	laborer	50	"
T	Vaccaro Antonio	179	U S A	42	"
U	Vaccaro Carmella †	179	dressmaker	26	"
V	*Vaccaro Joseph	179	retired	70	"
W	Vaccaro Mary †	179	dressmaker	33	"
X	Vaccaro Phillip	179	student	21	"
Y	Casaletto Augustine	181	plumber	28	"
Z	Casaletto Mary †	181	housewife	26	"
	1284				
A	LaPorta Antonette †	181	spinner	22	"
B	*LaPorta Augustino	181	retired	55	"
C	*LaPorta Filomena †	181	housewife	50	"
D	LaPorta Frank	181	U S A	27	"
E	LaPorta Helen †	181	packer	24	"
F	DeMeo Frank	181	chauffeur	29	"
G	DeMeo Mary †	181	housewife	24	"
H	Poncia Gino	181	U S A	24	"
K	Poncia Mary †	181	housewife	23	"
L	Tuberosa Joseph	183	laborer	30	"
M	Tuberosa Margaret †	183	housewife	26	"
N	Cucchiello Frank	183	laborer	34	"
O	Cucchiello Margaret †	183	housewife	33	"
P	Beiras Jose	185	machinist	48	"
R	Beiras Pasqualina †	185	housewife	33	"
S	Ciampa Albert	185	U S A	20	"
T	Ciampa Caroline †	185	operator	24	"
U	Ciampa Marie T †	185	housewife	43	"
V	Milino Francisco	187	laborer	50	"
W	*Milino Maria †	187	housewife	53	"
X	Ferrara Anna †	187	"	29	181 Marion
Y	Ferrara Joseph	187	laborer	30	181 "

1—12   49

Page.	Letter.	FULL NAME.	Residence, Jan. 1, 1943.	Occupation.	Supposed Age.	Reported Residence, Jan. 1, 1942. Street and Number.

Princeton Street—Continued

	z	Giorgioni Anna—†	189	housewife	60	here
1285						
	A	Giorgioni Anna—†	189	social worker	35	"
	B	Giorgioni Lawrence	189	baker	74	"
	C	Allessi Josephine—†	189	housewife	33	"
	D	Allessi Vico	189	social worker	38	"

Putnam Street

	G	Giordano Albert	125	operator	34	131 Neptune rd
	H	Giordano Sarah—†	125	housewife	32	131 "
	K	Pannesi Angie—†	125	clerk	20	here
	L	Pannesi Anna—†	125	factoryhand	29	"
	M	Pannesi Anthony	125	electrician	32	"
	N	Pannesi David	125	clerk	25	"
	O	*Pannesi Mary—†	125	housewife	54	"
	P	*Bruno Albert	127	contractor	33	"
	R	Bruno Albina—†	127	housewife	31	"
	S	*DeMattio Mary †	127	"	73	"
	T	Timoli Agreppino	127	laborer	58	"
	U	Timoli Ambrosina—†	127	housewife	56	"
	V	Nastasi Anthony	127	salesman	31	"
	W	Nastasi Theresa—†	127	housewife	34	"
	X	*Danigella Florence—†	129	"	55	154 Benningt'n
	Y	*Danigella Joseph	129	baker	55	154 "
	Z	DeMattia Angelo	129	chauffeur	47	here
1286						
	A	*DeMattia Grace †	129	housewife	46	"
	B	Sullo John	129	mechanic	35	"
	C	Sullo Louise—†	129	housewife	27	"
	D	Centracchio Nicholas	131	clerk	40	"
	E	Callahan Ann—†	131	housewife	21	306 Saratoga
	F	Callahan John	131	policeman	25	306 "
	G	Acconando Josephine †	131	housewife	32	here
	H	Redosta John	131	laborer	64	"
	K	Redosta Josephine—†	131	housewife	54	"
	L	Redosta Mary—†	131	saleswoman	24	"
	M	Redosta Rocco	131	U S A	23	"
	O	Peraino Gemma—†	133	housewife	31	"
	P	Peraino John	133	mechanic	34	"
	R	Pagano John	133	butcher	48	"

Page.	Letter	FULL NAME.	Residence, Jan. 1, 1943.	Occupation.	Supposed Age.	Reported Residence, Jan. 1, 1942. Street and Number.

Putnam Street Continued

	S	Pagano Lena — †	133	housewife	39	here
	U	LaMonica Josephine — †	163	"	22	283 Chelsea
	V	LaMonica Vincent	163	chauffeur	22	283 "
	W	Columbo Christopher	163	"	25	here
	X	*Columbo Rose — †	163	housewife	52	"
	Y	Columbo Salvatore	163	shoemaker	50	"
	Z	Freni Anthony	163	U S A	23	"
1287						
	A	Freni Basilio	163	laborer	63	"
	B	*Freni Domenica — †	163	housewife	51	"
	C	Lalicata Joseph	165	machinist	25	"
	D	Lalicata Philomena — †	165	housewife	24	"
	E	Rossetti Mary — †	165	"	36	"
	F	Rossetti Ralph	165	mechanic	37	"
	G	*Cambria Joseph	165	laborer	54	76 Brooks
	H	Cambria Joseph	165	U S A	21	76 "
	K	Cambria Josephine — †	165	factoryhand	30	76 "
	L	*Cambria Lillian — †	165	housewife	44	76 "
	M	*Concolo Bruno	165	painter	47	76 "
	N	*Cassaro Theresa — †	167	housewife	38	here
	O	Cassaro Vincent	167	salesman	39	"
	P	Caggiano Anthony	167	mechanic	35	"
	R	Caggiano Mary — †	167	housewife	32	"
	S	Schena Jerry	167	U S A	22	"
	T	Schena Lena — †	167	stitcher	21	"
	U	Schena Michael	167	laborer	48	"
	V	*Schena Vincenza — †	167	housewife	46	"
	W	Costa Carlos	177	retired	72	"
	X	*Dettore Concetta — †	177	housewife	49	"
	Y	Dettore John	177	laborer	53	"
	Z	Cunningham Clara — †	177	housewife	35	"
1288						
	A	Cunningham Clifford	177	mechanic	38	"
	B	DeFrancisco Frank	179	"	28	Somerville
	C	DeFrancisco Mary — †	179	housewife	22	"
	D	Baglio Joseph	179	baker	26	here
	E	Baglio Mary — †	179	housewife	26	"
	F	DellOrfano Joseph	179	welder	42	"
	G	DellOrfano Mary — †	179	housewife	37	"
	H	Vernacchio Concetta — †	195	"	26	"
	K	Vernacchio Gerald	195	printer	26	"

51

Putnam Street—Continued

L	Ferrara Anna —†	195	factoryhand	23	here
M	*Ferrara Enrico	195	shoemaker	60	"
N	Ferrara Michael	195	U S A	21	"
O	*Ferrara Rose—†	195	housewife	53	"
P	Colangelo Anthony	195	mason	50	"
R	Colangelo Pauline —†	195	housewife	42	"
S	Ruggiero Frank	197	laborer	25	"
T	Ruggiero Helena —†	197	housewife	23	"
U	Nolan Beatrice —†	197	"	32	"
V	Nolan Herbert	197	laborer	28	"
W	*Russo Rose—†	197	housewife	31	226 Princeton
X	Currie Harriet †	199	"	26	here
Y	Currie Lawrence	199	boilermaker	26	"
Z	*DeLuca Hilda †	199	housewife	38	"

1289

A	DeLuca John	199	watchman	40	"
B	Silva Delphine V —†	199	housewife	62	"
C	Silva John F	199	laborer	42	"
D	Silva John G	199	"	63	"

Saratoga Street

F	Puzzanthera Maria —†	201	housewife	50	here
G	Puzzanthera Salvatore	201	tailor	55	"
H	Cerullo Margaret —†	201	housewife	29	"
K	Cerullo Marino	201	supervisor	29	"
L	Kehoe Lawrence J	201	operator	39	"
M	Kehoe Margaret —†	201	housewife	38	"
N	Donovan Robert	202	laborer	20	Vermont
O	Leddy Francis	202	watchman	40	here
P	Leddy Laura—†	202	housewife	42	"
R	*Smith Freeland	202	fisherman	53	425 Meridian
S	Surette Anna —†	202	factoryhand	21	here
T	Surette James	202	U S N	23	"
U	*Surette Laura—†	202	housewife	57	425 Meridian
V	McCormick John M	203	U S C G	48	here
W	McCormick Mary V —†	203	housewife	46	"
X	Poli Christine †	203	"	31	97 Polk
Y	Poli Raymond	203	operator	31	97 "
Z	Todisco Mildred —†	203	housewife	36	here

1290

Saratoga Street Continued

A	Todisco Pasquale	203	painter	36	here
B	Winston Thomas	203	chauffeur	30	"
C	DiGiorgio Christina †	204	housewife	35	"
D	DiGiorgio Leonard	204	electrician	40	"
E	Bellabona Flora †	204	housewife	27	"
F	Bellabona Leo	204	chauffeur	27	"
G	DeFilipio Mary †	204	housewife	33	"
H	DeFilipio Nicholas	204	candymaker	38	"
K	McGuire Elizabeth †	205	housewife	39	175 Trenton
L	*Hurley Daniel J	205	longshoreman	48	110 "
M	*Hurley Laura M †	205	housewife	46	110 "
N	Alfama Asa	205	machinist	26	18 "
O	Alfama Elvira †	205	housewife	26	18 "
P	Robinson Charles	206	printer	31	27 Lynde
R	Robinson Frances †	206	housewife	25	27 "
S	DelVisco Antonio	206	laborer	57	here
T	*DelVisco Maria †	206	housewife	60	"
U	Corbosiero Louis	206	shoeworker	40	"
V	Corbosiero Rose †	206	housewife	35	"
W	DeLucia Antonio	207	U S A	23	"
X	DeLucia Jennie †	207	factoryhand	29	"
Y	*DeLucia Rosa †	207	housewife	53	"
Z	DeLucia Thomas	207	laborer	57	"

1291

A	Vigliotta Anna †	207	housewife	32	"
B	Vigliotta Biagio	207	laborer	42	"
C	Gaeta Carmen	207	packer	23	291 Summer
D	Gaeta Mary †	207	housewife	21	345 "
E	*Fronduto John	208	shoeworker	59	here
F	*Fronduto Rose †	208	housewife	59	"
G	Sacco Marcus	208	laborer	39	"
H	Sacco Margaret †	208	housewife	33	"
L	Tutella Jennie †	209	"	35	"
M	Tutella Richard	209	pipefitter	37	"
N	Laffey Doris M †	209	housewife	28	25 Union
O	Laffey Raymond P	209	chauffeur	30	25 "
P	Tartoloni Anthony	209	shipper	29	here
R	Tartoloni Lucy †	209	housewife	28	"
S	Marley Frank	210	electrician	44	"
T	Marley Margaret †	210	housewife	45	"

Page.	Letter	FULL NAME.	Residence, Jan. 1, 1943.	Occupation.	Supposed Age.	Reported Residence, Jan. 1, 1942. Street and Number.

Saratoga Street—Continued

	U	Carey Helen—†	210	housewife	37	here
	V	Carey William H	210	clerk	39	"
	W	O'Connell Margaret M—†	210	housewife	63	"
	X	O'Connell Peter H	210	laborer	65	"
	Y	McNeil George E	210	U S A	22	"
	Z	McNeil James	210	usher	27	"
1292						
	A	McNeil Joseph L	210	carpenter	24	"
	B	*McNeil Lillian—†	210	housewife	65	"
	C	*Bombaci Rose—†	211	"	65	"
	D	Papsidoro Mary—†	211	factoryhand	33	"
	E	Mirra Alice—†	211	dressmaker	39	"
	F	Mirra Anthony	211	tailor	45	"
	G	*Agrala Frank	212	operator	56	"
	H	*Agrala Rosa—†	212	housewife	55	"
	K	Colantonio Constantino	212	blacksmith	34	18 Trenton
	L	Colantonio Filomena—†	212	housewife	32	here
	M	Urresti Alfred	212	U S A	24	"
	N	*Urresti Antonia—†	212	housewife	61	"
	O	Ferullo Clara—†	214	"	33	"
	P	Ferullo Michael	214	laborer	33	"
	R	Dore Antonette—†	214	housewife	45	"
	S	Dore John	214	mechanic	52	"
	U	DeDominices Alfred	215	printer	34	"
	V	DeDominices Helen E—†	215	housewife	31	"
	W	Eriksen Helen—†	215	"	44	"
	X	Missett Helen—†	215	"	21	"
	Y	Waters Gertrude—†	215	factoryhand	21	"
	Z	Whitten William	215	watchman	69	"
1293						
	A	Silva Blanche—†	216	housewife	29	"
	B	Silva John	216	painter	29	"
	C	*DiBonis Jennie—†	216	housewife	49	"
	D	*DiBonis Joseph	216	laborer	60	"
	E	Martucchi Anthony	216A	"	23	Revere
	F	Phillips Blanche—†	216A	mechanic	38	149 Brooks
	G	Phillips Louise—†	216A	clerk	20	63 White
	H	Abbatessa Anthony	217	welder	35	here
	K	Abbatessa Catherine—†	217	housewife	32	"
	L	Rowe Frederick	217	fisherman	34	"
	M	Rowe Mary H—†	217	housewife	31	"

54

Saratoga Street—Continued

Letter	FULL NAME	Residence	Occupation	Age	Reported Residence
N	Timbone Angelina—†	217	stitcher	24	here
O	Timbone Anna—†	217	housewife	44	"
P	Timbone Eugenia—†	217	clerk	22	"
R	Timbone John	217	U S C G	20	"
S	Timbone Vincent	217	cutter	53	"
T	Vitello Albert	218	shoeworker	28	"
U	Vitello Stella—†	218	housewife	26	"
V	DeBonis Frank	218	pipefitter	30	"
W	DeBonis Mary—†	218	housewife	26	"
X	Pagliarulo Antonette—†	218	"	29	"
Y	Pagliarulo Severio	218	laborer	29	"
	1294				
D	Petrucci Angelo	220	"	53	"
E	Petrucci Anna—†	220	shoeworker	21	"
F	Petrucci Rose—†	220	housewife	43	"
G	Holden George	220	factoryhand	28	"
H	Holden Julia—†	220	housewife	24	"
M	Diaz Francesco	223	U S A	25	"
N	Diaz Josephine—†	223	housewife	20	247 Havre
O	Viola Francisco	223	finisher	45	here
P	*Viola Mary—†	223	housewife	47	"
R	*Cordovano Jennie—†	223	"	65	"
S	Cordovano Salvatore	223	musicain	26	"
T	Cannizzaro Lucy—†	225	housewife	28	"
U	Cannizzaro Santo	225	barber	28	"
V	*Costigan Margaret—†	225	housewife	41	95 Princeton
W	*Costigan Thomas	225	fisherman	45	95 "
X	*Gushen Mary E—†	225	at home	51	200 Falcon
Y	Nealon Leo	225	machinist	36	120 Benningt'n
Z	Nealon Mildred—†	225	housewife	35	120 "
	1295				
A	*Halstead Mary—†	226	"	70	here
B	*Hyder Emily—†	226	operator	50	"
C	*Coilty Matilda—†	226	housewife	62	"
D	Coilty William	226	welder	26	"
E	Thompson Frederick	226	U S A	39	"
F	Thompson Gertrude—†	226	housewife	35	"
G	Aleo Alice—†	227	at home	34	"
H	*Aleo Stella—†	227	housewife	63	"
K	LoConte Angelo	227	chauffeur	22	"
L	LoConte Anthony	227	dealer	52	"

Saratoga Street — Continued

Letter	FULL NAME.	Residence Jan. 1, 1943.	Occupation.	Supposed Age.	Reported Residence Jan. 1, 1942.
M	LoConte Marion —†	227	housewife	55	here
N	Cambria Lena —†	227	"	28	"
O	Cambria Pasquale	227	laborer	28	"
P*	Siracusa Joseph	228	mattressmaker	35	"
R	Siracusa Rose —†	228	housewife	34	"
S	Antonelli Esther —†	228	"	30	"
T	Antonelli William	228	operator	30	"
U	Vernacchio Jennie —†	228	housewife	64	"
V	Vernacchio Louis	228	U S A	25	"
W	Vernacchio Mary—†	228	factoryhand	27	"
X	Vernacchio Pasquale	228	operator	65	"
Y	Gubitosi Henry	229	"	27	409 Frankfort
Z	Gubitosi Phyllis —†	229	housewife	23	409 "
1296					
A*	Marmo Sabato	229	retired	67	here
B	Rossi Teresa—†	229	housewife	44	"
C	Picarello Joseph	230	chauffeur	38	"
D	Picarello Josephine †	230	housewife	37	"
E	Palazzolo Jaqueline —†	230	factoryhand	30	270 Princeton
F*	Palazzolo Jennie— †	230	housewife	52	here
G	Palazzolo John T	230	U S A	20	270 Princeton
H	Palazzolo Joseph	230	candymaker	32	270 "
K	Palazzolo Josephine †	230	factoryhand	24	270 "
L	Palazzolo Paul	230	pedler	56	270 "
M*	Olitsky Abraham	230	"	58	here
N	Olitsky Henry	230	electrician	33	"
O*	Olitsky Minnie †	230	housewife	58	"
P	Verro Louise †	231	"	29	"
R	Verro Pasquale	231	shoeworker	29	"
S*	Birimbeau John	231A	U S A	22	"
T	Silva Anthony	231A	operator	23	"
U*	Silva Conceicoa †	231A	housewife	44	"
V*	Silva Ernest	231A	U S A	20	"
W*	Silva Manuel C	231A	weaver	45	"
X	Viscio Domenic	231A	painter	60	"
Y	Viscio Elvira †	231A	stitcher	23	"
Z	Viscio Louisa †	231A	housewife	58	"
1297					
A*	DiChiara Antoinetto †	232	"	52	"
B	DiChiara Camilla †	232	tailoress	23	"
C	DiChiara Joseph	232	repairman	54	"

Saratoga Street Continued

D	DiChiara Mary— †	232	tailoress	26	here
E	*Aronson Dora †	232	housewife	67	"
F	Denehy John	232	longshoreman	38	"
G	Denehy Mary— †	232	housewife	40	"
H	Wheeler Phyllis †	232	operator	21	"
K	Moreno Joseph	233	machinist	20	"
L	Coppola Mary— †	233	housewife	43	"
M	Coppola Pasquale	233	bricklayer	43	"
N	Coppola Ralph	233	machinist	21	"
O	Goveia Augustino	233	electrician	25	Lynn
P	Goveia Sarah— †	233	housewife	24	"
R	Pasquale John	234	chauffeur	30	184 Benningt'n
S	Pasquale Josephine †	234	housewife	31	184 "
T	*Fisher Esther— †	234	"	59	here
W	Fisher Samuel	234	retired	60	"
U	Fisher Harold	234	painter	40	"
V	Fisher Ida— †	234	housewife	33	"
X	Carroll Agnes— †	235	"	33	"
Y	Carroll Joseph	235	chauffeur	35	"
Z	*Alfano Anna— †	235	housewife	48	"

1298

A	Alfano Dominick	235	laborer	23	"
B	Alfano Joseph	235	"	52	"
C	*Favorito Angelina †	235	housewife	56	"
D	Favorito Emilio	235	operator	46	"
E	Favorito Jerry	235	U S A	22	"
F	*Favorito Mary †	235	housewife	22	"
G	Favorito Phillip	235	dye mixer	25	"
H	*Corrao Frank	236	operator	43	"
K	Corrao Jennie— †	236	housewife	37	"
L	Figliolini Antonette †	236	"	53	"
M	Figliolini Dominick	236	factoryhand	22	"
N	Figliolini Pasquale	236	tailor	51	"
O	Rideout Dorothy— †	236	housewife	25	288 Princeton
P	Rideout Wallace	236	factoryhand	33	288 "
R	LoConte Dominick	238	shipfitter	38	here
S	LoConte Mae— †	238	housewife	38	"
T	Interbartolo Charles	238	florist	44	"
V	Interbartolo Ida — †	238	housewife	28	"
W	Interbartolo Michael	238	electrician	34	"
U	Interbartolo Charles	238	U S A	21	"

1—12

Page	Letter	FULL NAME.	Residence, Jan. 1, 1943.	Occupation.	Supposed Age.	Reported Residence, Jan. 1, 1942. Street and Number.

Saratoga Street—Continued

	Letter	FULL NAME.	Residence	Occupation	Age	Reported Residence
	X	Interbartolo Peter	238	operator	20	here
	Y	*Interbartolo Rosario	238	factoryhand	56	"
	Z	Cordovano Charles	242	U S A	23	223 Saratoga
1299						
	A	Cordovano Yolanda —†	242	housewife	21	157 Benningt'n
	B	Alabiso Angelo	242	editor	22	here
	C	Alabiso Millie —†	242	saleswoman	20	"
	D	Alabiso Nora—†	242	housewife	41	"
	E	Alabiso Vincenzo	242	pressman	51	"
	G	D'Amico Alexandro	242	laborer	50	"
	F	D'Amico Antonette —†	242	housewife	21	"
	H	*D'Amico Jovanina —†	242	"	51	"
	K	D'Amico Laurence	242	U S A	21	"
	L	Ricci Carmella—†	243	housewife	47	"
	M	Ricci Eleanor—†	243	factoryhand	24	"
	N	Ricci Florence —†	243	stitcher	21	"
	O	Ricci Frances —†	243	clerk	22	"
	P	Ricci Frank	243	machinist	49	"
	R	Foster Camella —†	244	housewife	35	"
	S	Foster Joseph R	244	chauffeur	37	"
	T	*Palladino Constance—†	244	housewife	68	"
	U	Palladino Gerard	244	retired	80	"
	V	Palladino Victor	244	factoryhand	33	"
	W	Shannon John B	244	shipfitter	43	"
	X	Shannon Teresa —†	244	housewife	39	"
	Y	Coggio Charles	245	oiler	66	"
	Z	Coggio Thomas	245	U S A	24	"
1299A						
	A	LaPlaca Caroline —†	245	housewife	28	"
	B	*LaPlaca Mario	245	cutter	31	"
	C	*Cinardo Carmen	246	retired	67	"
	D	*Cinardo Crocifissa †	246	housewife	58	"
	E	Genaro David	246	U S N	23	"
	F	Genaro Elizabeth †	246	stitcher	30	"
	H	Framontozzi Antonio	246	machinist	31	"
	K	Framontozzi Concetta —†	246	housewife	31	"
	L	Liebman Mary—†	247	storekeeper	40	"
	M	Brown Gorley W	248	baker	60	"
	N	*Brown Sadie G —†	248	housewife	60	"
	O	*Ginardo Florence —†	248	"	27	"
	P	Ginardo Pasquale	248	cutter	28	"

58

Saratoga Street Continued

R	Schroffa Margaret —†	248	housewife	27	here
S	Schroffa Victor	248	blacksmith	25	"
T	Serra Anthony	249	coremaker	24	"
U	Serra Antonetta —†	249	at home	23	"
V	Serra Frank	249	laborer	62	"
W	Serra Frank, jr	249	U S A	21	"
X	Serra John	249	"	32	"
Y	Powers John	250	checker	35	"
Z	Powers Mary —†	250	housewife	25	"

1299B

A	*Costa John	250	laborer	54	"
B	*Costa Josephine —†	250	housewife	49	"
D	*Mello Mary —†	250	factoryhand	55	"
C	Lynch Maria —†	250	at home	67	"
E	Mercurio Agnes —†	252	"	80	"
F	Mercurio Annie —†	252	housewife	44	"
G	Mercurio James	252	inspector	48	"
H	DiNapoli Carmella —†	252	saleswoman	22	"
K	DiNapoli Catherine —†	252	housewife	44	"
L	DiNapoli Pasquale	252	machinist	49	"
M	Stasio Henry R	254	pipefitter	30	"
N	Stasio Lillian T —†	254	housewife	30	"
O	Silverman Gertrude —†	254	"	45	"
P	Silverman Robert	254	laborer	62	"
R	*Correia James F	254	spinner	37	"

Ward 1--Precinct 13

CITY OF BOSTON

LIST OF RESIDENTS
20 YEARS OF AGE AND OVER

(NON-CITIZENS INDICATED BY ASTERISK)
(FEMALES INDICATED BY DAGGER)

AS OF

JANUARY 1, 1943

JOSEPH F. TIMILTY, *Chairman*
FREDERIC E. DOWLING, *Secretary*
WILLIAM A. MOTLEY, Jr.
FRANCIS B. McKINNEY
EVERETT R. PROUT
Listing Board.

CITY OF BOSTON PRINTING DEPARTMENT

1300

Bennington Street

1	A	Nagle Catherine J —†	256	at home	82	here
	B	O'Keefe Margaret —†	256	housewife	49	178 Benningt'n
	C	O'Keefe William E	256	machinist	51	178 "
	E	Marshall Anna V —†	260	at home	52	here
	F	*DeViller Ada —†	260	"	59	"
	G	Lowe Patrick	260	seaman	37	"
	H	Muise John	260	laborer	26	"
	K	Deeran Josephine —†	262	housewife	20	106 Morris
	L	Deeran Martin	262	U S A	27	here
	M	Deeran Sarkis	262	mechanic	31	"
	N	Deeran Tavriz —†	262	at home	55	"
	P	McAllister Thomas	266	rigger	45	14 Monmouth
	R	*Nunes Lucille—†	266	at home	38	14 "
	Z	Quigley Augustine J	290	clerk	54	here

1301

	A	Quigley Ellen J —†	290	storekeeper	55	"
	B	Quigley Margaret M —†	290	housekeeper	57	"
	E	Bonzagni Leo A	292	proprietor	49	24 Marion
	F	Machado Frank W	292	painter	35	here
	G	Marshall Elizabeth A —†	292	housewife	55	"
	H	Marshall Frank J	292	painter	56	"
	K	Thornton Abigail —†	293	at home	30	"
	L	Thornton Gwendolyn —†	293	"	20	"
	M	Thornton John	293	seaman	64	"
	N	Thornton Thomas	293	U S A	28	"
	O	Thornton Virginia —†	293	tel operator	26	"
	P	Taylor Gertrude —†	293	housewife	35	"
	R	Taylor William	293	mechanic	35	"
	V	Tonelli Alice R —†	297	binderyworker	37	"
	W	Tonelli Angelo F	297	mechanic	29	"
	X	Tonelli Frederick J	297	laborer	33	"
	Y	*Tonelli Lawrence	297	retired	67	"
	Z	Tonelli Lawrence J	297	U S A	32	"

1302

	A	Pace Margaret —†	297	clerk	20	"
	B	Pace Mildred —†	297	housewife	28	"
	C	Pace William S	297	shipfitter	45	"
	D	Tassinari Horace V	301	chauffeur	34	95 Cowper
	E	Tassinari Marie A —†	301	housewife	29	95 "
	F	Covino Carmen	301	dairyworker	25	373 Chelsea

2

Bennington Street Continued

G	Covino Concetta †	301	housewife	26	373 Chelsea
H	DeWitt Herman W	301	metalworker	68	here
K	Dolan Margaret A †	301	laundress	43	"
L	Trayers Kathryn †	301	nurse	23	6 Brighton
N	Lepore John	305	shoeworker	26	here
O	Lepore Viola †	305	housewife	24	"
S	Austin Catherine †	315	"	63	"
T	Austin Michael	315	guard	55	"
U	Austin Michael, jr	315	U S A	22	"
V	Vaccoro Ralph	315	bartender	29	Revere
W	Vaccoro Ruth †	315	housewife	25	"
Y	*DeAngelo Carmela †	319	"	70	here
Z	*DeAngelo Michael	319	retired	67	"
1303					
A	Lonzetta Gennaro	319	U S A	38	"
B	Carco Maria E †	319	housewife	25	75 Montmorenci av
C	Carco Sebastian	319	grocer	25	75 "
F	Alessandroni Angelina †	360	housewife	41	here
G	Alessandroni Joseph	360	retired	72	"
H	Alessandroni Nino	360	interpreter	49	"

Bremen Street

K	Greenberg Celia †	364	operator	55	here
L	Weker Lottie G †	364	housewife	64	"
M	Weker Max	364	retired	70	"
N	Weker Meyer	364	lawyer	36	"
O	Weker Simon L	364	U S A	29	"
H	Wolfson Ida †	364	clerk	37	"
R	Benson Selma †	364A	saleswoman	40	"
S	Benson Sven	364A	retired	72	"
T	Gallagher Bernice †	364A	factoryhand	25	"
U	Gallagher Edward A	364A	U S N	27	"
V	Lynch Bridget †	364A	housewife	56	"
W	Lynch Leonard	364A	plasterer	22	"
X	Greene Theresa †	364A	housewife	62	"
Y	Greene William J	364A	tailor	63	"
Z	Scarpone Anna †	366	housewife	46	"
1304					
A	Scarpone Nicholas	366	laborer	42	"
B	LaMonica Charles	368	brazier	23	"

3

Bremen Street— Continued

c	LaMonica Joseph	368	weaver	48	here
d	LaMonica Samuel	368	laborer	28	"
e	Gennaco Joseph	374	chauffeur	30	"
f	Gennaco Pauline †	374	housewife	27	"
g	Rizzo Fannie †	374	"	40	"
h	Rizzo Joseph	374	factoryhand	44	"
k	*Rizzo Pauline †	374	at home	80	"
l	Merchant Edward	376	retired	79	"
m	Merchant Mary †	376	housewife	69	"
n	Caggiano Frank	376	engineer	33	"
o	Caggiano Rose †	376	housewife	32	"
p	Russell James E	398	factoryhand	60	"
r	Russell James E, jr	398	U S A	23	"
s	Russell Rose C †	398	housewife	53	"
t	Smith John	398	longshoreman	51	"
u	Ferriani Lillian †	400	housewife	31	"
v	Ferriani William	400	machinist	29	"
w	Amerene Joseph	400	cutter	58	421 Saratoga
x	Amerene Mary †	400	housewife	57	421 "
y	Amerene Robert	400	U S N	20	here
z	Corzo Anna †	400	housewife	37	421 Saratoga

1305

a	Colangelo Mary †	400	"	50	187 Princeton
b	Colangelo Otto	400	student	21	187 "
c	*Amodeo Ann †	408	housewife	38	here
d	Amodeo Edward	408	barber	54	"
e	Kelley Cornelius J	412	laborer	52	"
f	Kelley John C	412	U S A	23	"
g	Kelley Mary C †	412	housewife	49	"
k	Fairchild Bessie †	416	at home	83	"
l	Fairchild Charles	416	factoryhand	50	"
m	D'Eboli Mary †	452	at home	61	"

Chelsea Street

p	Stella John	345	chauffeur	30	here
r	Stella Josephine †	345	housewife	26	"
v	*Viola Theresa †	351	"	43	119 Benningt'n
w	McGinness Mary E †	351	"	33	here
x	McGinness William	351	leatherworker	33	"
y	Mora Angela †	353	housewife	23	"

Chelsea Street Continued

z	Mora Walter	353	laborer	26	here	
1306						
A	Grillo Frank	353	painter	48	"	
B	Grillo Mary — †	353	housewife	39	"	
c	Taschetta Joseph	353	presser	27	"	
D	Taschetta Vita — †	353	housewife	46	"	
F	Puopolo Alfred	355	checker	31	"	
G	Puopolo Josephine — †	355	housewife	30	"	
H*	Puopolo Carmella — †	355	"	49	"	
K	Puopolo Ida — †	355	"	26	"	
L	Puopolo John	355	machinist	29	"	
M	Puopolo Pasquale	355	laborer	53	"	
N	Manzelli Alfred	357	U S A	21	51 Prescott	
O	Manzelli Concetta — †	357	finisher	22	51 "	
P*	Manzelli Mary — †	357	housewife	53	51 "	
R	Manzelli Vincent	357	finisher	57	51 "	
S*	MacDonald Aylmer	357	bricklayer	33	Everett	
T	MacDonald Edith — †	357	housewife	29	"	
X	Mason Edward F	367	chauffeur	24	136 Paris	
Y	Mason Pearl — †	367	housewife	44	136 "	
Z	Silva Florence — †	367	candymaker	24	208 Saratoga	
1307						
A	Silva Joseph	367	machinist	22	208 "	
B*	Silva Rose — †	367	housewife	54	208 "	
c*	Maneri Fannie — †	369	"	60	here	
D*	Maneri Leonard	369	retired	65	"	
E	Marashka John	369	laborer	31	"	
F	Marashka Josephine — †	369	housewife	31	"	
H	Vadala Joseph	373	machinist	32	36 Paris	
K	Vadala Lena — †	373	housewife	26	36 "	
L	Smith James J	373	laborer	44	here	
M	Smith Julia †	373	housewife	42	"	
O	Van Dall Grace — †	376	packer	42	"	
P	Van Dall John	376	rigger	38	"	
R	Forshner Alma — †	376	housewife	40	21 Neptune rd	
S	Forshner Edward J	376	U S A	21	21 "	
T	Forshner Harold	376	tinsmith	50	21 "	
V	Bloom Abraham	378	caretaker	50	here	
W*	Bloom Lizzie — †	378	at home	81	"	
X	Shore Esther — †	378	housewife	39	"	
Y	Shore Samuel	378	merchant	45	"	

1308

Chelsea Street — Continued

A	Doherty Agnes C—†	380	operator	23	here
B	Doherty Catherine T—†	380	housewife	48	"
C	Doherty William F	380	laborer	49	"
D	Doherty William G	380	bricklayer	26	"
E	Fogone Catherine—†	380	at home	21	"
F	*Fucalaro Rose—†	380	housewife	39	"
G	*Fucalaro Victor	380	butcher	45	"
K	Kirk Rubina—†	382	housewife	35	"
O	Terranova Frances—†	390A	at home	23	"
P	*Terranova Michelina—†	390A	housewife	48	"
R	Fossett Freda H—†	390A	"	50	"
S	Fossett John R	390A	machinist	50	"
T	Dunn Robert	391	bartender	43	Lynn
U	Jevoli Leah—†	391	housewife	32	here
V	Jevoli Louis	391	bartender	36	"
W	Jevoli Pasquale	391	restaurateur	65	"
X	*Inza Mary—†	391	housewife	40	131 Eutaw
Y	Bowan Mary—†	391	waitress	40	42 Staniford
Z	Cincotta Phillip	391	laborer	22	42 "

1309

A	Papa Beatrice—†	391	packer	40	28 Prince
B	*Papa Benjamin	391	printer	42	28 "
C	Papa Thomas	391	engraver	20	28 "
D	Henderson Edith—†	392	housewife	38	here
E	Henderson Roderick	392	laundryman	38	"
F	Megna Frank	392	chauffeur	30	"
G	Megna Grace—†	392	housewife	34	"
H	Clee Hazel E—†	392	bookkeeper	31	"
K	Clee Jennie E—†	392	clerk	55	"
L	Clee Walter R	392	U S A	25	"
N	Florentino Elmer	397	shipfitter	42	"
O	Florentino Ernestine—†	397	housewife	40	"
P	Florentino Joseph	397	U S A	20	"
R	Murphy Agnes—†	397	tel operator	58	"
S	O'Rourke Florence M—†	397	at home	55	"
T	*Riccioli Frances—†	399	housewife	57	"
U	Riccioli Fred	399	barber	67	"
V	Riccioli Margaret—†	399	clerk	21	"
W	Rowe Lucille—†	399	entertainer	24	"
X	*Staffier Carmen	399	tailor	42	"

6

Chelsea Street Continued

Y	*Staflier Marie †	399	stitcher	41	here
Z	Manoli Charles	399	carpenter	50	"

1310

A	Manoli Sarah †	399	housewife	46	"
B	Cunningham Elizabeth †	401	at home	80	"
C	Cunningham Frederick J	401	clerk	40	"
D	Adams Anna †	401	cook	50	"
E	D'Addio Irene †	403	housewife	29	"
F	D'Addio Vincent	403	mechanic	33	"
H	Scarfo Dominic M	403	finisher	31	"
K	Scarfo Ida †	403	housewife	31	"
M	Rotondi Antonio	405	storekeeper	60	"
N	Rotondi Clara †	405	waitress	24	"
O	*Rotondi Maria †	405	housewife	60	"
R	Burns William	407	U S A	42	"
S	Sweeney Margaret †	407	operator	46	"
T	Sweeney Paul	407	U S N	20	"
U	DeRosa Alphonsina †	407	housewife	49	"
V	DeRosa Antoinette †	407	inspector	23	"
W	DeRosa Elena †	407	"	25	"
X	DeRosa Raymond	407	laborer	59	"
Y	Lightbody Anna E †	407	inspector	41	"
Z	Lightbody Catherine †	407	housewife	67	"

1311

A	Lightbody Frederick H	407	compositor	39	"
C	Gillespie Dennis	409	retired	73	"
D	Gillespie Francis	409	shipworker	36	"
E	Gillespie James	409	U S A	28	"
F	Gillespie Margaret †	409	housewife	73	"
G	Gallo Bernard	409	inspector	46	"
M	O'Regan Joanna †	413	at home	70	"
N	O'Regan Mary A †	413	"	78	"
P	Nastari Anna †	415	housewife	42	"
R	Nastari Gennaro	415	laborer	50	"
S	Nastari Rose †	415	clerk	23	"
U	Connelly Josephine †	417	housewife	29	47 McClellan H'way
V	Connelly Lawrence	417	guard	32	47 "
W	Moran Helen †	417	at home	38	here
X	Moran Joseph E	417	salesman	47	"
Y	Cirrone Mary †	420	housewife	24	"
Z	Cirrone Santo	420	laborer	26	"

Page.	Letter	FULL NAME.	Residence, Jan. 1, 1943.	Occupation.	Supposed Age.	Reported Residence, Jan. 1, 1942. Street and Number.

1312

Chelsea Street—Continued

A	Arbia Anthony	420	foreman	53	here
B	Arbia Bella—†	420	operator	25	"
C	Arbia Ernest	420	U S A	20	"
D	Arbia Joseph	420	"	23	"
E	Arbia Pasquale	420	"	25	"
F	Palumbo Anthony	420	machinist	28	"
G	Palumbo Jennie—†	420	housewife	27	"
H	Gordon Ellen P—†	422	attendant	25	"
K	Lucius Manuel	422	mechanic	40	"
L	*Lucius Margaret—†	422	housewife	38	"
M	DeModena Frances—†	422	"	36	"
N	DeModena Leo	422	machinist	43	"
O	Romolo Johanna—†	422	housewife	28	106 Princeton
P	Romolo John J	422	clergyman	59	106 "
S	DiGiovanni Amideo	424	watchman	51	here
T	DiGiovanni Joseph	424	machinist	21	"
U	DiGiovanni Mary—†	424	housewife	48	"
V	Doucette Joseph G	426	rigger	34	"
W	Doucette Mildred—†	426	housewife	32	"
X	Flynn John P	426	chauffeur	39	"
Z	*Consolante Leonina—†	428	housewife	42	"

1313

A	Consolante Peter	428	mechanic	46	"
B	DiCesare Concetta—†	428	housewife	35	"
C	DiCesare Fortunato	428	operator	40	"
D	DiCesare Munziata—†	428	housewife	69	"
E	DiCesare Pasquale	428	retired	72	"
F	Milano Biagio	428	woodworker	28	"
G	Milano Rose—†	428	housewife	32	"
H	Driscoll John M	430	ironworker	34	"
K	Driscoll Lawrence P	430	U S A	26	"
L	Driscoll Nellie—†	430	housewife	28	"
M	Toomey Alice—†	430	clerk	21	"
N	Toomey John A	430	asbestos worker	63	"
O	Gagliardi Maria—†	430	housewife	45	"
P	Gagliardi Michael	430	laborer	47	"
R	Gagliardi Theresa—†	430	at home	21	"
S	*Fucillo Filomena—†	432	"	69	"
T	Censebella Mary—†	432	operator	52	51 Spring
U	DeSisto Joseph	rear 432	"	26	here

8

Chelsea Street Continued

v	DeSisto Lillian †	rear 432	housewife	25	here
w	Aronson Muriel †	434	cleaner	32	"
x	Aronson Robert	434	retired	73	"
y	Tango Phyllis †	434	housewife	52	"
z	*Kilmartin Bridget †	434	"	64	"

1314

A	*Kilmartin Michael	434	retired	76	"

Cleveland Street

c	Monaco Agostino	3	laborer	46	here
D	Monaco Lena †	3	housewife	39	"

Eagle Square

F	*Sabbatini Carmella †	4	housewife	57	here
G	Sabbatini Ettore	4	manufacturer	59	"
H	Sabbatini Frances †	4	factoryhand	25	"
K	Sabbatini Pasquale	4	mechanic	27	"

East Eagle Street

L	Ivaldi Charles G	325	clerk	27	here
M	Ivaldi Joan †	325	housewife	25	"
N	Pecora Nickolas	325	laborer	25	313 Lexington
O	Pecora Rosalie †	325	housewife	25	313 "
P	McCormack Mary †	325	"	25	92 Trenton
R	McCormack Vincent	325	laborer	25	92 "
S	Venuti Jennie †	327	housewife	29	here
T	Venuti Joseph	327	pipefitter	29	"
U	DeMarino Marie †	327	shoeworker	27	"
V	Polito Charles	327	U S A	25	"
W	Polito Josephine †	327	factoryhand	23	"
X	Polito Peter	327	shoeworker	56	"
Y	*Polito Teresa †	327	housewife	56	"
Z	Lauria Assunta †	327	"	24	"

1315

A	Lauria Peter	327	barber	29	"
B	Aloise Domenic	329	blacksmith	30	128 Bremen
C	Aloise Rose †	329	housewife	26	128 "
D	*Romano Antonio	329	laborer	56	here

9

East Eagle Street — Continued

E	*Romano Assunta —†	329	housewife	54	here
F	Romano Gaetano	329	U S A	33	"
G	Romano Sophie —†	329	factoryhand	29	"
H	*Cuilla Accursia —†	329	housekeeper	79	"
K	Miraldi Anna —†	329	housewife	36	"
L	Arena Edith C —†	331	"	32	"
M	Arena Joseph	331	laborer	32	"
N	DellaSala Attilio	331	clerk	42	325 E Eagle
O	DellaSala Gabriella —†	331	housewife	42	325 "
P	Mainiero Carmella —†	331	"	40	here
R	Mainiero Michael	331	barber	42	"
S	Pope William P	333	cook	23	223 Trenton
T	Walsh Celia —†	333	housewife	27	here
U	*Walsh Patrick	333	fishcutter	29	"
V	Dutra Adelaide —†	333	clerk	23	"
W	Dutra Eleanor —†	333	housewife	39	"
X	Dutra Eleanor M —†	333	clerk	24	"
Y	Dutra John	333	machinist	49	"
Z	Dutra John L	333	"	21	"

1316

A	Maglitta Fred	335	laborer	40	"
B	Maglitta Mary —†	335	housewife	34	"
C	*Ciello Lena —†	335	housekeeper	40	"
D	DeStefano Edith —†	335	packer	28	"
E	DeStefano John	335	barber	65	"
F	DeStefano John	335	welder	32	"
G	DeStefano Josephine —†	335	housewife	61	"
H	Malzone Concetta —†	337	typist	23	"
K	Malzone Yolanda —†	337	student	22	"
L	Malzone Jennie —†	337	housewife	42	"
M	Malzone John	337	machinist	52	"
N	Critch Jennie —†	337	housewife	23	"
O	Critch Richard	337	machinist	26	"
P	Santelmo Anna —†	341	housewife	44	"
R	Santelmo Frank	341	welder	48	"
S	Martucci Antonio	341	operator	31	292 Chelsea
T	Martucci Mildred —†	341	housewife	33	292 "
U	Grande Joseph	341	machinist	43	here
V	Grande Pauline —†	341	housewife	42	"
W	Balboni Barbara C —†	345	"	46	"
X	Balboni John J	345	shipfitter	51	"

East Eagle Street Continued

y	Balboni Romano	345	retired	86	here
z	Balboni William M	345	U S A	24	"

1317

a	*Cerutti Angelina †	345	housewife	28	"
b	Cerutti Charles	345	laborer	45	"
c	Carroll Florence †	347	housewife	34	"
d	Carroll John	347	foreman	34	"

Frankfort Street

e	*Faccadio Peter	373	mechanic	42	here
f	*Faccadio Savino	373	retired	74	"
g	Puopolo Angelo	373	driller	36	536 Benningt'n
h	Puopolo Mabel †	373	housewife	40	here
k	Caprio Nicholas	373	chauffeur	36	"
l	Caprio Philomena †	373	housewife	38	"
m	Cardone Phillip	375	rigger	37	"
n	Cardone Virginia †	375	housewife	31	"
o	Silva Joseph	375	longshoreman	43	"
p	Silva Philomena †	375	housewife	42	"
r	Marino Armand	375	shoeworker	41	"
s	Marino Louise †	375	housewife	39	"
t	Aragona Frederick	377	U S N	33	"
u	Aragona Marion †	377	housewife	34	"
v	Dolimount Dorothy †	377	"	30	"
w	Dolimount George	377	welder	30	"
x	Rose Albert	377	longshoreman	22	"
y	Rose Dorothy †	377	housewife	44	"
z	Rose James	377	longshoreman	42	"

1318

a	Natale James	379	chauffeur	39	"
b	Natale Linda †	379	housewife	38	"
c	Scanzello Mary †	379	"	53	"
d	Scanzello Michael	379	tailor	56	"
e	Shea Brendan	379	fishcutter	34	"
f	Shea Hilda †	379	housewife	30	"
g	Donovan Anna L †	381	"	27	84 Brooks
h	Donovan James H	381	driller	30	84 "
k	Oliveri Anthony	381	finisher	37	here
l	Oliveri Arduina †	381	housewife	28	"

11

Page.	Letter.	Full Name.	Residence Jan. 1, 1943.	Occupation.	Supposed Age.	Reported Residence Jan. 1, 1942. Street and Number.

Frankfort Street—Continued

	Letter.	Full Name.	Residence	Occupation.	Age.	Street and Number.
	M	Filosa Albert	381	pipecoverer	35	here
	N	Filosa Elsie—†	381	housewife	34	"
	O*	Luongo Theresa—†	383	at home	62	"
	P	Minichino Louis	383	mechanic	33	"
	R	Minichino Margaret—†	383	housewife	31	"
	S	DeStefano Clementina—†	383	at home	75	"
	T	DeStefano Rose—†	383	"	47	"
	U	Porzio Constantino	383	machinist	35	"
	V	Porzio Margaret—†	383	housewife	34	"
	W	Doucette Alice M—†	385	"	53	"
	X	Doucette Henry A	385	rigger	48	"
	Y	Calello Angelina—†	385	housewife	40	"
	Z	Calello Gerald	385	collector	47	"
1319						
	A	Polino Carmella—†	385	at home	83	"
	B	Oliviero Domenic	385	merchant	44	"
	C	Oliviero Margaret—†	385	housewife	34	"

Lawson Place

	Letter.	Full Name.	Residence	Occupation.	Age.	Street and Number.
	D	Allie Nellie—†	1	housewife	36	here
	E	Allie William	1	laborer	35	"
	F	Alexander Dorothy—†	2	stenographer	38	"
	G	Alexander Rose L—†	2	housekeeper	68	"
	H	Eldridge Celia—†	3	housewife	30	"
	K	Eldridge Daniel	3	foreman	31	"
	L	Lopes Joseph	4	laborer	57	"
	M*	Lopes Lucinda—†	4	housewife	47	"
	N	Noble Annie—†	5	housekeeper	67	"
	O	Noble Florence—†	5	typist	44	"
	P	Goodrow Margaret—†	5	housewife	58	"
	R	Goodrow Thomas	5	retired	69	"
	S	Leary Catherine—†	5	factoryhand	55	"
	T	Frazier Annie J—†	6	housekeeper	77	"
	U	Johnson Ellen—†	6	clerk	43	"
	V	Johnson Evelyn—†	6	"	21	"
	W	Frazier Mary E—†	7	housewife	45	"
	X	Frazier Peter L	7	motorman	51	"

Page.	Letter.	FULL NAME.	Residence, Jan. 1, 1943	Occupation.	Supposed Age.	Reported Residence, Jan. 1, 1942. Street and Number.

Lexington Street

	z	Garchinsky Charles	317	fireman	29	here
1320						
	A	Garchinsky Loretta †	317	housewife	26	"
	B	Garchinsky Anna †	317	housekeeper	66	"
	C	Garchinsky Michael	317	U S A	23	"
	D	Garchinsky Walter F	317	chauffeur	38	"
	E	Gillespie Mildred †	317	housewife	23	"
	F	Gillespie William	317	U S A	26	"
	G	Holt Elizabeth †	317	housewife	52	"
	H	Holt Robert	317	fireman	63	"

Lovell Street

	K	Cammarano Angelina †	371	housewife	47	here
	L	Cammarano Vito	371	candymaker	47	"
	M	Berkhardt Ida †	371	housewife	35	"
	N	Berkhardt Morris	371	storekeeper	35	"
	O	Duncan Mae †	371	nurse	57	"
	P	Panetta Caroline †	371	housewife	34	"
	R	*Panetta Nicodemo	371	furrier	42	"
	S	Burke Eleanor †	372	housewife	33	"
	T	Burke Fred	372	longshoreman	34	"
	U	Giella Savina †	372	housekeeper	73	"
	V	Nugent Florence †	372	housewife	21	116 White
	W	Nugent William	372	operator	21	116 "
	X	Geronini Bruno	372	laborer	32	here
	Y	*Geronini Mary †	372	housekeeper	58	"
	Z	Lloyd Edith †	372	operator	23	"
1321						
	A	DeSimone Theresa †	373	housewife	23	"
	B	DeSimone William G	373	candymaker	30	"
	C	DeFronzo Louis	373	chauffeur	48	"
	D	DeFronzo Mary †	373	housewife	39	"
	E	Pasquale Angelo	373	shipfitter	37	"
	F	Saggese Elizabeth †	373	inspector	32	"
	G	*Saggese Minnie †	373	housekeeper	54	"
	H	Saggese Margaret †	373	cutter	21	"
	K	Saggese Nickola	373	retired	64	"
	L	Saggese Victoria †	373	inspector	23	"

13

Page	Letter	FULL NAME.	Residence, Jan. 1, 1943.	Occupation.	Supposed Age.	Reported Residence, Jan. 1, 1942. Street and Number.

Lovell Street— Continued

	Letter	FULL NAME.	Residence	Occupation.	Age	Reported Residence
	M	Jeffrey Bertha—†	374	housewife	46	here
	N	Jeffrey Joseph H	374	chauffeur	53	"
	O	Trunfio Helen—†	374	housewife	34	"
	P	Trunfio Michael	374	laborer	50	"
	R	Kelley Esther A—†	374	housewife	36	"
	S	Kelley James J	374	guard	38	"
	T	Sartori Brunetta—†	375	housewife	31	259 Princeton
	U	Sartori James	375	shipfitter	33	259 "
	V	Amato Frank	375	laborer	47	here
	W	*Amato Vincenza—†	375	housewife	41	"
	X	*Luongo Antoinetta—†	375	"	50	"
	Y	*Luongo Domenic	375	operator	54	"
	Z	Gallerini Albert	376	printer	43	"
	¹Z	Gallerini James	376	shoeworker	34	"
1322						
	A	*Gallerini Louis	376	retired	78	"
	B	DeCristoforo Anthony	376	investigator	35	"
	C	DeCristoforo Mary—†	376	housewife	32	"
	D	Lumia Joseph	376	welder	23	Malden
	E	Lumia Lucy—†	376	housewife	22	"
	F	DeStefano Margaret—†	377	"	26	here
	G	DeStefano Vincent	377	chauffeur	29	"
	H	Donovan John	377	carpenter	62	185 Benningt'n
	K	Donovan Sarah—†	377	housewife	63	185 "
	L	Bettini Flora—†	377	"	34	here
	M	Bettini Nicholas	377	shoeworker	36	"
	N	Salerno Anthony	378	salesman	33	"
	O	Salerno Marion—†	378	housewife	34	"
	P	Salerno Joseph	378	shipfitter	31	"
	R	*Salerno Mary—†	378	housewife	60	"
	S	Salerno Peter	378	retired	62	"
	T	Amato Albert	378	U S A	23	"
	U	Amato Frances—†	378	housekeeper	50	"
	V	Amato John	378	mechanic	29	"
	W	Amato Patrick	378	U S A	25	"
	X	Finn Bernard J	379	"	35	"
	Y	Finn Rita—†	379	housewife	28	"
	Z	Keough Nellie—†	379	"	63	"
1323						
	A	Sbordoni Phyllis—†	379	"	35	150 Princeton
	B	Sbordoni Saverio	379	shipfitter	36	150 "

14

Lovell Street — Continued

c	Moreira Luiz M	379	laborer	45	here
D*	Moreira Mary †	379	housewife	49	"
E	DeBerto Emio	380	U S A	25	"
F	DeBerto Gertrude †	380	housewife	24	"
G	Fatch Catherine †	380	"	27	"
H	Fatch Michael	380	U S A	25	"
K	McConnell Edward	380	"	22	"
L	McConnell Nora †	380	housewife	52	"
M	Amato Angelina †	380	housekeeper	49	"
N	Amato Catherine †	380	stitcher	24	"
O	Martocchio Angelo	380	chauffeur	30	"
P	Martocchio Ella †	380	housewife	27	"
R	Dulong Joseph A	381	operator	36	"
S	Dulong Pauline M †	381	housewife	33	"
T	Gallo Charles	381	driller	27	474 Saratoga
U	Gallo Eva †	381	housewife	27	283 Princeton
V*	Orlando Josephine †	381	housekeeper	57	126 Chelsea
W	Verposkey Albert	381	waiter	30	126 "
X	Verposkey Anna †	381	seamstress	35	126 "
Y	Kennedy Edward A	382	drawtender	56	here
Z	Kennedy Mary E †	382	housewife	53	"

1324

A	Kennedy Miriam F †	382	packer	26	here
B	Kennedy Richard M	382	U S A	23	"
C	DeStefano Carmen	382	shoecutter	54	"
D	DeStefano Frances †	382	housewife	52	"
E	Ottiano James	382	shipfitter	47	"
F	Ghelfi Louis	382	chauffeur	31	377 Lovell
G	Ghelfi Madeline †	382	housewife	28	377 "
H	Hedstrom Eleanor L †	383	"	28	here
K	Hedstrom Ernest G	383	machinist	43	"
L	Hedstrom Ida M †	383	housekeeper	80	"
M	Fuccillo Carmen	383	tailor	48	"
N	Fuccillo Carmen A	383	student	20	"
O	Fuccillo Isabella †	383	housewife	46	"
P	Fuccillo Pasquale C	383	U S C G	21	"
R	Fuccillo Agata †	383	housewife	40	"
S	Fuccillo Albert	383	retired	46	"
T	Fuccillo Celia †	383	packer	40	"
U*	Fuccillo Matilda M †	383	housekeeper	73	"
V	Conner James T	384	U S C G	27	83 Homer

15

Lovell Street—Continued

w	Conner Martha M †	384	housewife	28	83 Homer	
x	Searle Bertha M †	384	"	47	here	
y	Searle Edwin R	384	clerk	46	"	
z	Morse Annie M †	384	housewife	62	"	
1325						
A	Morse James	384	carpenter	52	"	

Neptune Road

B	Greene Annie †	15	housewife	69	Revere	
c	Guidora Adeline †	15	"	53	here	
D	Guidora Orlando	15	welder	25	"	
E	Guidora Paul	15	retired	63	"	
F	Hockbaum Esther †	15	housewife	52	"	
G	Hockbaum Morris	15	storekeeper	53	"	
H	Hockbaum Rae †	15	clerk	26	"	
K	Hockbaum Rose †	15	saleswoman	24	"	
L	Costello Bridget †	17	housewife	68	"	
M	Costello Frederick J	17	laborer	29	"	
N	Costello Martin J	17	retired	68	"	
O	Costello Nicolas	17	longshoreman	33	"	
P	Greene Elmer J	17	welder	41	"	
R	Greene Mary T †	17	housewife	39	"	
s	McDonough Elizabeth †	17	"	76	"	
T	Moynihan Cornelius J	17	U S A	21	"	
U	Moynihan Florence E †	17	housewife	50	"	
v	Moynihan Francis W	17	U S A	20	"	
w	Young Anna T †	17	housewife	53	384 Lovell	
x	Dempsey Raymond J	19	B F D	40	here	
y	Dempsey Sophie W †	19	housewife	29	"	
z	Toohig Warren A	19	B F D	45	"	
1326						
A	O'Neil Patrick J	19	baggageman	67	"	
B	Schrage Catherine †	19	housewife	27	"	
c	Schrage James R	19	laborer	38	"	
D	Avellar John	19	"	38	"	
E	Avellar Marie †	19	housewife	39	"	
F	Lewis Caroline †	19	houseworker	29	"	
G	Cotter Charles	21	inspector	26	15 Neptune rd	
H*	Cotter Marjorie †	21	housewife	25	15 "	
K	Kelley William P	21	porter	51	here	

Neptune Road Continued

L	Layne Ethel P †	21	clerk	54	here
M	Leveroni Blanche D †	21	tel operator	42	"
N	Leveroni Evelyn T †	21	stenographer	28	"
O	Leveroni Frank J	21	guard	41	"
P	Leveroni Fred J	21	U S A	33	"
R	Leveroni Helena G †	21	housewife	69	"
S	Leveroni Rose B †	21	houseworker	35	"
T	Ryan Eugene	23	pipefitter	40	"
U	Ryan Rose †	23	clerk	36	"
V	Vieira Georgiana †	23	houseworker	70	"
W	Camara Alexander L	23	welder	34	265 Lexington
X	Camara Evelyn L †	23	housewife	27	265 "
Y	Serenei Josephine †	23	"	25	142 Everett
Z	Serenei Salvatore	23	U S A	25	142 "
1327					
A	Fallon Julia †	25	housewife	49	here
B	Fallon Mildred †	25	houseworker	26	"
C	McClaren John	25	machinist	76	"
D	Murphy Johanna C †	25	housewife	82	"
E	Murphy Thomas	25	retired	85	"
F	Cardinal Caroline †	25	housewife	45	"
G	Cardinal William	25	meatcutter	51	"
H	Cardinal William E	25	U S A	22	"
K	Knudsen Anna C †	27	housewife	82	"
L	Knudsen Anna R †	27	operator	43	"
M	Currie John E	27	rigger	58	"
N	Currie Mary E †	27	housewife	61	"
O	Kayander Hilda †	27	"	52	"
P	Kayander John D	27	machinist	55	"
R	Kayander Tavio	27	"	27	"
S	Fougere Evelyn †	33	housewife	37	"
T	Fougere Napoleon A	33	bartender	37	"
U	Corriea Antonio	33	fireman	50	"
V*	Corriea Delphina †	33	housewife	38	"
W*	Luciano Eugena †	33	"	62	"
X	Perdigao Manuel R	33	rigger	38	"
Y	Perdigao Mary C †	33	housewife	31	"
Z	Vieire Manuel	35	laborer	40	"
1328					
A	Vieire Mary †	35	housewife	38	"
B	Henry Emil	35	lithographer	58	"

I 13   17

Neptune Road—Continued

c	Popp Raymond W	35	U S A	21	here
D	Popp Richard E	35	draftsman	23	"
E	Popp Virginia—†	35	housewife	56	"
F	Vieira Mary A—†	35	"	40	"
G	Vieira Mathew	35	laborer	38	"
H	Crowley Catherine F—†	37	housewife	64	"
K	Crowley Claire M—†	37	stenographer	32	"
L	Crowley Eileen G—†	37	"	30	"
M	Crowley Joseph D	37	U S A	21	"
N	Stasio Carlo J	37	salesman	40	"
O	Stasio Phyllis—†	37	housewife	37	"
P	Gaeta Alphonse	37	U S A	33	"
R	Gaeta Emily—†	37	operator	26	"
S	Gaeta Michael	37	sorter	29	"
T	Gaeta Theresa—†	37	housewife	58	"
U	*Maglio Irene—†	37	"	74	"
V	DeRosa Archie	39	tailor	49	"
W	DeRosa Edward	39	agent	25	"
X	DeRosa John	39	machinist	24	"
Y	DeRosa Margaret—†	39	housewife	46	"
Z	Acunzo Salvatore	39	messenger	60	"

1329

A	Mascetta Lydia—†	39	operator	24	"
B	Mascetta Mabel—†	39	stitcher	26	"
C	Mascetta Nicholas	39	pressman	54	"
D	*Mascetta Renata—†	39	housewife	53	"
E	Mascetta Rose—†	39	houseworker	22	"
F	Vitale Frances T—†	39	housewife	48	"
G	Vitale Joseph A	39	operator	49	"
H	Vitale Ralph J	39	engineer	22	"
K	Lumia Beatrice—†	41	housewife	27	375 Lovell
L	Lumia James	41	welder	30	375 "
M	Johnson Annie—†	41	housewife	40	here
N	Johnson James	41	repairman	47	"
O	Kennedy Annie—†	41	housewife	82	"
P	Cardarelli Arthur	41	U S N	21	"
R	Cardarelli Inez—†	41	finisher	29	"
S	Cardarelli Joseph	41	welder	22	"
T	Cardarelli Lawrence	41	shoeworker	49	"
U	Cardarelli Michael	41	U S A	27	"
V	Cardarelli Vincenza—†	41	housewife	44	"

18

Page.	Letter.	FULL NAME	Residence, Jan. 1, 1943	Occupation.	Supposed Age	Reported Residence, Jan. 1, 1942. Street and Number.

Neptune Road Continued

	X	Miraglia Anthony	45	retired	65	here
	Y	Miraglia Arthur	45	mechanic	37	"
	Z	Miraglia Eleanor †	45	houseworker	25	"
1330						
	A	Miraglia Francis	45	U S A	34	"
	B	Miraglia Grace †	45	housewife	37	"
	C	Miraglia James	45	lawyer	39	"
	D	Miraglia Josephine †	45	stenographer	30	"
	E	Miraglia Lorraine †	45	stitcher	23	"
	F	LaBlanc Mary L †	47	housewife	52	"
	G	LaBlanc Roy	47	fisherman	47	"
	H	Nicoletti Jean †	47	housewife	22	242 Bremen
	K	Nicoletti Philip	47	chauffeur	22	Medford
	L	Villane Ida †	47	housewife	21	242 Bremen
	M	Shea Bridget †	47	"	58	here
	N	Shea Catherine †	47	secretary	23	"
	O	Shea Irene †	47	"	35	"
	P	Shea Patrick	47	U S A	30	"
	R	Shea Raymond	47	freighthandler	25	"
	S	Granara Ann †	49	stenographer	24	"
	T	Granara Helena G †	49	housewife	44	"
	U	Granara William J	49	machinist	50	"
	V	Oliver Frank R	49	retired	59	"
	W	Oliver John F	49	machinist	23	"
	X	Oliver Maria C †	49	housewife	60	"
	Y	Oliver Paul G	49	U S C G	21	"
	Z	Teixeira Philomena †	49	packer	54	"
1331						
	A	Benson Helen †	49	tel operator	26	"
	B	Dafilo Manuel	49	engineer	63	"
	C	Dafilo Sarah †	49	housewife	62	"
	D	Walker John	51	salesman	31	"
	E	Walker Mary T †	51	housewife	28	"
	F	McWhinnie James R	51	blacksmith	34	"
	G	McWhinnie Mary P †	51	housewife	32	"
	H	Acres Charles J	51	painter	34	"
	K	Acres Julia A †	51	housewife	28	"
	L	Gomes Charlotte J †	53	"	39	"
	M	Gomes George L	53	chauffeur	47	"
	N*	Landrigan Mary E †	53	housewife	55	"
	O	Landrigan Russell F	53	clerk	27	"

19

Neptune Road — Continued

Letter	FULL NAME	Residence	Occupation	Age	Reported Residence
P	Landrigan William R	53	retired	60	here
R	Quinlan Harvey	53	engineer	36	"
S	Quinlan Nora — †	53	housewife	33	"
T	*Cantalupo Carmen	55	candymaker	56	"
U	*Cantalupo Gabrielle — †	55	housewife	52	"
V	Cantalupo Lucy — †	55	clerk	25	"
W	Knox Mary A — †	55	housewife	53	"
X	Knox Raymond J	55	seaman	23	"
Y	Knox Sylvester J	55	printer	53	"
Z	Pigott Marie A — †	55	clerk	25	"

1332

Letter	FULL NAME	Residence	Occupation	Age	Reported Residence
A	Pigott William J	55	U S A	25	"
B	*Johnson Madeline — †	55	housewife	61	"
C	Ryan Ellen S — †	55	"	31	"
D	Ryan John G	55	painter	32	"
E	Ryan Catherine — †	57	houseworker	63	"
F	Ryan Nellie M — †	57	housewife	66	"
G	Olson Elvira C — †	57	bookkeeper	45	"
H	Olson Frank W	57	machinist	48	"
K	Olson Octavius	57	retired	86	"
L	Olson Victoria E — †	57	stenographer	42	"
M	Telles Arthur W	57	salesman	32	"
N	Telles Rose G — †	57	housewife	27	"
O	Pelham Helen J — †	63	"	36	"
P	Pelham Ivan S	63	cook	44	"
R	*Silva Carolina — †	63	housewife	65	"
S	*Amico Lena I — †	63	"	23	"
T	Amico Salvatore	63	chemist	30	"
U	Kelly Angela J — †	65	operator	38	"
V	Kelly Richard T	65	retired	85	76 Faywood av
W	Pedro Alfred A	65	finisher	45	here
X	*Pedro Jeremina — †	65	housewife	40	"
Y	Andrade Manuel	65	seaman	42	"
Z	*Andrade Mary — †	65	housewife	38	"

1333

Letter	FULL NAME	Residence	Occupation	Age	Reported Residence
A	*Gonsalves Mary N — †	65	tailor	24	"
B	Butler Helen T — †	67	housewife	31	"
C	Butler William E	67	checker	37	"
D	Ahearn Edgar M	67	chauffeur	47	400 Benningt'n
E	Ahearn Lawrence H	67	U S N	25	400 "
F	Ahearn Louise — †	67	stenographer	27	400 "

Neptune Road Continued

G	*Bettini Peter	67	retired	76	here
H	Bettini Sebastian	67	printer	31	"
K	Dulong Helena B †	67	housewife	26	"
L	Cameron Agnes †	69	"	66	"
M	Coffin Ruth †	69	"	27	"
N	Coffin William	69	shipfitter	26	2 W Eagle
O	Conway Helen M †	69	housewife	45	here
P	Conway John J	69	carrier	49	"
R	Lynch Anna A †	69	housewife	36	"
S	Lynch Edward T	69	B F D	40	"
T	Johnson Charles J	75	carpenter	53	"
U	Johnson Maude †	75	housewife	51	"
V	Peterson Carrie †	75	"	30	"
W	Peterson Oscar	75	brazier	32	"
X	Rossano Frank	75	contractor	27	"
Y	Rossano Hazel †	75	housewife	27	"
Z	Stevens Josephine †	93	"	26	Braintree

1334

A	Stevens Theodore L	93	shipfitter	25	"
B	Pascucci Margaret †	93	packer	22	here
C	Pascucci Mary †	93	housewife	52	"
D	Pascucci Rocco	93	laborer	53	"
E	Goulet Camille †	93	housewife	30	"
F	Goulet Orise	93	chipper	33	"
G	Cianci Anthony M	111	buyer	51	"
H	Cianci Margaret †	111	housewife	47	"
K	Loschi Charles A	111	merchant	44	"
L	Loschi Harriette B †	111	housewife	44	"
M	Loschi John	111	retired	65	"
N	Loschi John A	111	lawyer	57	"
O	Loschi Mary A †	111	teacher	49	"
P	Loschi Victor	111	musician	54	"
R	Tassinari Agnes †	115	operator	21	"
S	Tassinari Anna †	115	"	29	"
T	Tassinari Augustus	115	driller	37	"
U	*Tassinari Joseph	115	retired	67	"
V	*Tassinari Josephine †	115	housewife	61	"
W	Tassinari William	115	welder	27	"
X	Sexton Richard J	115	policeman	43	"
Y	Sexton Ruth †	115	housewife	42	"
Z	Giggi Henry	115	bricklayer	39	"

1335

Neptune Road Continued

	Letter	Full Name	Res.	Occupation	Age	Reported Residence
	A	Giggi Louise †	115	housewife	31	here
	D	*Casterina Sarah †	131	"	32	"
	B	Mariotti Basco	131	laborer	59	"
	C	*Mariotti Carmella †	131	housewife	57	"
	E	Humphrey Annie †	131	"	71	"
	F	Humphrey Harry H	131	retired	74	"
	G	Miller Sarah †	131	housewife	94	"
	H	Humphrey Maude †	131	"	51	"
	K	Humphrey William L	131	shipper	52	"
	L	Mahoney John H	131	U S A	31	"

Prescott Street

	Letter	Full Name	Res.	Occupation	Age	Reported Residence
	O	Finn Ruth †	50	waitress	29	265 Lexington
	P	Halley Herbert	50	U S A	23	265 "
	R	Halley Mary †	50	saleswoman	22	265 "
	S	Cavanagh Edward J	50	electrician	37	Hawaii
	T	Cavanagh Margaret †	50	housewife	35	"
	U	*Monahan Annie †	50	cook	58	here
	V	Monahan Mary †	50	housewife	22	Malden
	W	Monahan Patrick	50	U S A	33	here
	X	Cain Eileen †	50	housewife	37	"
	Y	Cain John G	50	salesman	40	"
	Z	Vecchio Costanzo	62	chauffeur	53	"

1336

	Letter	Full Name	Res.	Occupation	Age	Reported Residence
	A	Vecchio Filomena †	62	housewife	42	"
	B	Souza Edward	62A	carpenter	21	242 Saratoga
	C	Souza Helen †	62A	housewife	21	242 "
	D	*Jackson Agnes †	68	"	54	here
	E	Jackson Albert E	68	machinist	56	"
	F	Jackson Albert P	68	clerk	25	"
	G	Parsons George A	70	fisherman	40	"
	H	*Parsons Magdalene †	70	housewife	30	"
	K	Viglione Americo	72	tailor	38	"
	L	Viglione Jennie †	72	housewife	33	"
	M	*Viglione Rosalie †	72	at home	71	"
	N	Bolino Gustaf	72	machinist	20	"
	O	Bolino Nicholas	72	cook	42	"
	P	Bolino Rose †	72	housewife	39	"

Prescott Street (Continued)

R	Bolino Rose †	72	stitcher	21	here
S	Dodge Emma †	72	housewife	36	"
T	Dodge Howard T	72	engineer	40	"
U	Brooks Lillian †	74	housewife	58	"
V	Brooks Robert W	74	seaman	62	"
W	Brooks William	74	grocer	39	"
X	Curtis Ethel R †	74	factoryhand	29	"
Y	Lupu Celia †	74	housewife	60	"
Z	O'Niell Jean †	74	saleswoman	35	"
1337						
A	O'Neill Paul W	74	U S A	30	Chelsea
B	Swadel Hannah †	74	housewife	59	here
C	Swadel Isabel †	74	laundress	64	"
D	Riley Edith †	90	housewife	58	"
E	Riley James	90	fireman	62	"
F	Riley Janet †	90	clerk	33	"
G	Cone Carl	94	painter	40	"
H	Cone Louise †	94	housewife	36	"
K	Higgins Eileen D †	181	factoryhand	21	"
L	Higgins Joseph H	181	U S A	25	"
M	Higgins Thomas H	181	inspector	53	"
N	Higgins Walter E	181	U S A	23	"
O	Higgins Zita M †	181	housewife	49	"
P	Duggan John A	181	foreman	54	"
R	Duggan John A, jr	181	U S A	24	"
S	Duggan Ralph E	181	"	22	"
T	Duggan Sophia B †	181	housewife	49	"
U	Murphy Angela J †	209	"	22	416 Meridian
V	Murphy Ralph W	209	cutter	25	416 "
W	Tucci Angelo M	209	bricklayer	37	here
X	Tucci Antonette M †	209	housewife	37	"
Y	Ciampa Anthony	249	U S A	23	Florida
Z	Ciampa Carmella †	249	clerk	39	here
1338						
A	Ciampa Celia †	249	housewife	59	"
B	Ciampa Ignatius J	249	clerk	39	"
C	Ciampa Lena †	249	stenographer	21	"
D	Ciampa Ralph	249	laborer	66	"
E	*Nalli Adolph	249	baker	55	"
F	Nalli Anthony	249	U S A	26	"

23

Prescott Street—Continued

	G	Nalli Elizabeth †	249	dressmaker	24	here
	H	Nalli Louis	249	U S A	21	"
	K	*Nalli Mary—†	249	housewife	52	"
	L	Nalli Pasquale	249	laborer	27	"
	M	*DellaPiana Eliza—†	249	housewife	51	"
	N	DellaPiana Leandro	249	laborer	57	"
	O	DellaPiana Pasquale	249	U S A	25	"
	P	DellaPiana Ralph	249	"	22	"
	R	DellaPiana Rita—†	249	dressmaker	24	"
	S	DellaPiana Rose—†	249	stitcher	20	"
	T	Poto Joseph D	259	shoecutter	55	"
	U	Tecci Anna—†	259	housewife	29	"
	V	Tecci Salvatore	259	carpenter	32	"
	W	Carvito Rose—†	259	housewife	30	44 Ashley
	X	DiFlumeri Joseph	259	welder	34	here
	Y	DiFlumeri Luigi	259	janitor	60	"
	Z	*DiFlumeri Mary—†	259	housewife	58	"
1339						
	A	Tecci Joseph	259	printer	32	"
	B	Harkins Anna C—†	260	housewife	32	"
	C	Harkins William H	260	laborer	32	"
	D	Bruno James	260	U S N	20	"
	E	Bruno John	260	weigher	24	"
	F	Bruno Lena—†	260	clerk	25	"
	G	Bruno Margaret—†	260	"	27	"
	H	MacKay Daniel	260	tel worker	51	"
	K	MacKay Louise—†	260	factoryhand	21	"
	L	MacKay Rebecca—†	260	housewife	50	"
	M	Boland Eleanor P—†	261	"	22	"
	N	Boland Stephen J	261	U S A	24	40 Saratoga
	O	Higgins Ellen W—†	261	housewife	61	here
	P	Higgins Joseph P	261	laborer	57	"
	R	Cowan James J	261	retired	77	"
	S	Cowan Mary J—†	261	housewife	64	"
	T	McIntyre John J	276	longshoreman	28	"
	U	McIntyre Nora G—†	276	housekeeper	51	"
	V	Packard Frederick M	276	printer	52	"
	W	Packard Mary F—†	276	housekeeper	72	"
	X	Hanson John J	276	U S N	33	"
	Y	Hanson Rose C—†	276	housewife	31	"

1340

Princeton Street

A	Lawton Catherine —†	257	housewife	62	here
B	Lawton James F	257	clerk	23	"
C	Lawton Katherine T †	257	inspector	24	"
D	Lawton Mary E —†	257	student	20	"
E	Lawton Patrick	257	retired	67	"
F	Pascone Charlotte —†	257	housewife	32	"
G	Pascone George	257	laborer	36	"
K	McDonald Katherine —†	259	housewife	31	282 Lexington
L	Ahern Bertha —†	259	boxmaker	37	here
M	Ahern Catherine —†	259	housekeeper	73	"
N	Ahern Catherine —†	259	at home	41	"
O	Ahern William J	259	laborer	35	"
P	DeFuria Domenic	259	chauffeur	25	21 White
R	DeFuria Margaret —†	259	housewife	22	21 "
S	Joyce Edith L—†	261	"	74	here
T	Joyce George W	261	builder	74	"
U	Joyce William L	261	U S A	37	"
V	Follo Anna—†	263	housewife	26	"
W	Follo Salvatore	263	machinist	32	"
X	*Sozio Assunta—†	263	housewife	51	"
Y	*Sozio Joseph	263	retired	60	"
Z	Sozio Louise—†	263	clerk	24	"

1341

A	Sozio Pasquale	263	U S M C	21	"
B	Corby Alberta—†	263	housewife	46	"
C	Corby Frederick	263	B F D	49	"
D	Cann Rita L—†	265	stenographer	29	"
E	*Clements Martha E—†	265	nurse	65	165 Princeton
F	MacDonald Jessie —†	265	housekeeper	88	here
G	MacLaren Jessie M †	265	"	65	"
H	Thibeault Martha A—†	265	waitress	23	165 Princeton
K	*Tosto John	267	laborer	40	here
L	Tosto Lena—†	267	housewife	36	"
M	DiPaolo Jane—†	269	"	22	188 Falcon
N	DiPaolo Mario	269	supervisor	23	188 "
O	Rothwell Anne—†	269	housekeeper	60	8 Shelby
P	Rothwell James	269	shipfitter	26	8 "
R	Vellante Giustino	269	chipper	49	here
S	Vellante Joseph	269	U S N	22	"

Princeton Street—Continued

T	*Vellante Theresa †	269	housewife	45	here	
U	Howe Marie E—†	271	"	48	Worcester	
V	Howe Walter F	271	machinist	54	"	
W	Patridge Kay †	271	housewife	42	Virginia	
X	Patridge William F	271	U S N	45	"	
Y	Blakley Perry	271	laborer	57	New York	
Z	Gerardell Harry	271	"	40	Florida	

1342

A	Gerardell Mary—†	271	housewife	35	"	
B	Lewis David	271	machinist	26	119 Lexington	
C	Lewis Kay—†	271	housewife	22	119 "	
D	Newbury Charles C	271	laborer	45	New York	
E	Pumphrey Ethel †	271	operator	48	here	
F	Keeley Joseph	273	laborer	42	"	
G	Keeley Rosalie—†	273	housewife	35	"	
H	Bahrs Annie M †	273	"	48	"	
K	Bahrs John H	273	laborer	70	"	
L	Kitis Helen—†	273	housewife	23	"	
M	Kitis Nicholas	273	U S N	35	"	
N	Kruse Carl W	273	laborer	46	"	
P	Valliani Constantino	277	"	50	"	
R	Valliani Lena †	277	housewife	42	"	
S	Mitchell Albion E	277	assembler	63	"	
T	Mitchell Ida †	277	housewife	59	"	
U	Nealon Harold	279	laborer	34	"	
V	Nealon Hazel †	279	housewife	30	"	
W	MacDonald Domenic A	279	carpenter	58	"	
X	MacDonald Mary J—†	279	at home	60	"	
Y	Schifano Joseph	279	presser	34	"	
Z	Schifano Vincenza A—†	279	housewife	31	"	

1343

A	Wheaton Lorenzo	281	chauffeur	40	"	
B	Wheaton Viola—†	281	housewife	38	"	
C	Huskins Arnold	281	timekeeper	24	"	
E	Huskins Joseph A	281	shipper	56	"	
D	Huskins Lloyd	281	laborer	21	"	
F	Huskins Margaret E—†	281	housewife	53	"	
G	Hendrickson Ruth—†	281	"	36	"	
H	Hendrickson Thomas W	281	laborer	38	"	
K	Carney Esther—†	283	housewife	29	95 Homer	
L	Carney William F	283	laborer	33	95 "	

Princeton Street Continued

M	Newman John H	283	U S A	31	95 Homer	
N	Saveriano Agnes †	283	housewife	52	here	
O	Saveriano Alfred	283	student	22	"	
P	Saveriano Aniello	283	foreman	56	"	
R	Saveriano Carmen	283	U S A	24	"	
S	Saveriano Mary †	283	dressmaker	23	"	
T	Galasi Antonio	283	machinist	35	"	
U*	Galasi Grace †	283	housewife	58	"	
V	Galasi Guarino	283	laborer	33	"	
W	Galasi Nicola	283	"	58	"	
X	Gray Cecil M	285	printer	48	"	
Y	Gray James	285	U S A	21	"	
Z	Gray Paul	285	"	22	"	

1344

A	Blanco Stalario	285	machinist	55	"	
B	Ruotolo Christofore	285	welder	24	"	
C	Ruotolo Rose †	285	housewife	22	"	
D	Ruotolo Lucy †	285	"	28	"	
E	Ruotolo Rocco	285	printer	29	"	
F	Faretra Joseph	301	glazier	35	"	
G	Faretra Matilda †	301	housewife	34	"	
H	Bonito Anne †	301	housekeeper	54	"	
K	Bonito Joseph	301	machinist	25	"	
L	Bonito Louis	301	clerk	32	"	
M	Bonito Mary †	301	bookkeeper	35	"	
N	Smith George	303	U S A	21	341 E Eagle	
O	Salerno Americo	303	welder	29	here	
P	Salerno Mary †	303	housewife	27	"	
R	Volpa Arthur	303	laborer	21	"	
S	Volpa Speranza †	303	housekeeper	58	"	
T*	Johnson Alma L †	305	housewife	64	"	
U*	Johnson Toivo	305	ironworker	55	"	
V	Gallagher Jennie †	305	housewife	32	"	
W	Gallagher Joseph	305	laborer	35	"	
X	King Max L	305	pharmacist	48	"	
Y	King Sima †	305	housewife	48	"	
Z	Brazzell Walter	336	retired	62	"	

1345

A	Laville Ada †	336	housekeeper	64	"	
B	Laville Joseph	336	longshoreman	33	"	
C	King Donald E	342	U S A	26	"	

Princeton Street—Continued

D	Vargus John	342	letter carrier	44	here
E	*Vargus Rose—†	342	housewife	49	"
F	Symanski Benjamin	342	packer	30	196 Paris
G	Symanski Elvira—†	342	housewife	31	196 "
H	Matt Elizabeth—† rear	342	"	26	here
K	Matt Nickolas "	342	laborer	32	"
L	Puleo Angelina † "	342	housewife	31	"
M	Puleo Charles "	342	driller	37	"
N	*Caprini Adele—†	345	housewife	53	"
O	Caprini Generoso	345	retired	63	"
P	Caprini Nancy †	345	operator	21	"
S	Crowley Anne—† rear	345	housewife	33	"
T	Crowley George "	345	laborer	36	"
U	Haskins Arthur	347	"	32	"
V	Haskins Jean—†	347	housewife	30	"
W	*Ciampa Lena—†	347	"	46	"
X	Ciampa Michael	347	laborer	52	"
Y	Salvaggio Philip	347	machinist	30	"
Z	Salvaggio Phyllis †	347	housewife	26	"

1346

A	Marzocchi Josephine †	349	operator	25	"
B	Marzocchi Louise—†	349	at home	23	"
C	*Marzocchi Mary—†	349	housewife	42	"
D	*Marzocchi Samuel	349	painter	47	"
E	Carvotta Catherine—†	352	student	21	88 Lexington
F	Carvotta Rose—†	352	housekeeper	42	88 "
K	Arena Cosimo C	356	painter	39	here
L	Arena Rose †	356	housewife	38	"
M	Gill Edward	356	foreman	35	"
N	Gill Lillian †	356	housewife	30	"
O	Carusso Ignazio	356	brazier	34	"
P	Carusso Maria †	356	housewife	26	"
R	DiBartolomeo Antoinette—†	357	clerk	25	"
S	DiBartolomeo Grace—†	357	housewife	45	"
T	DiBartolomeo Leonora †	357	clerk	20	"
U	DiBartolomeo Luciano	357	U S A	22	"
V	DiBartolomeo Nicolo	357	laborer	49	"
W	DiBartolomeo Rose—†	357	clerk	23	"
X	Moynihan William	357	guard	65	"
Y	Visco Jennie—†	358	housewife	40	"
Z	Visco Joseph	358	plumber	44	"

1347

Princeton Street Continued

A	Puopolo Mary †	358	housekeeper	35	here
B	Visco Carmella †	358	stenographer	21	"
C	Visco Rose †	358	housekeeper	46	"
D	Grasso Linda †	359	housewife	41	"
E	Grasso Thomas	359	machinist	44	"
F	DeBonis Caroline †	360	housewife	36	"
G	DeBonis Olivio	360	laborer	46	"
H	Heino Aina †	360	housekeeper	48	"
K	Heino Aune †	360	teacher	22	"
I	Heino Reino	360	machinist	24	"
M	Ilmonen Charles E	360	U S N	22	"
N	Ilmonen Helmi †	360	housekeeper	46	"
O	Bossi Orlando	361	chauffeur	30	"
P	Bossi Theresa †	361	housewife	28	"
R*	Blundo Carmella †	361	"	49	"
S	Blundo Joseph	361	laborer	55	"
T	Blundo Lawrence	361	U S A	22	"
U	LaMarco Anna †	362	housewife	29	14 Cottage
V	LaMarco Charles	362	rigger	36	14 "
W*	Miraldi Bridget †	362	housekeeper	82	here
X	Miraldi John	362	laborer	37	"
Y	Grandolfi Ciro	362	carpenter	32	"
Z	Grandolfi Mary †	362	housewife	30	"

1348

A	Love Alice †	366	housekeeper	55	"
B	Love Clarence	366	seaman	23	"
C	Love Margaret †	366	operator	28	"
D	Rich Elizabeth M †	366	housewife	55	310 Bremen
E	Rich George	366	U S A	31	310 "
F	Rich Herbert A	366	machinist	26	310 "
G	Rich Julius	366	molder	58	310 "
H	Luongo Alfred	368	inspector	28	370 Princeton
K	Luongo Mary J †	368	housewife	23	370 "
L	Gavin Frank J	368	clerk	52	here
M	Gavin Mary J †	368	housewife	34	"
N	Gillis Frances †	370	forewoman	25	"
O*	Gillis Mary †	370	housewife	57	"
P	Gillis William	370	watchman	54	"
R	Rich Mary †	370	housewife	32	"
S	Rich Peter	370	laborer	32	"

29

Saratoga Street

u	Cohen Minnie †	401	clerk	22	here
v	Cohen Morris	401	"	33	"
w	Cohen Rose †	401	storekeeper	55	"
x	Cohen Samuel	401	U S A	30	"
y	Bertulli Arthur	401A	mechanic	30	"
z	Bertulli Catherine †	401A	housewife	29	"

1349

A	Harding Walter	401A	cook	45	44 Maverick
B	Roy Elizabeth F †	401A	housewife	42	192 Falcon
C	Roy Thomas G	401A	fireman	42	192 "
D	Goodwin Albert W	402	operator	59	here
E	*Normandeau Elizabeth †	402	housekeeper	42	"
F	*Nappa Domenica †	402	operator	62	"
G	Nappa Joseph	402	shoeworker	64	"
H	Marshall Gertrude †	402	housewife	33	"
K	Marshall William H	402	stockman	33	"
L	Petrozzelli Angelo	403	machinist	40	"
M	Petrozzelli Antonetta †	403	finisher	38	"
N	Quinn Lillian †	404	at home	51	"
O	Walraven Edith †	404	housewife	55	"
P	Walraven Marinus	404	laborer	49	"
R	Mullen Elizabeth †	404	housewife	42	"
S	Mullen James	404	fireman	44	"
T	Petrozelli Antonio	405	carpenter	28	"
U	Petrozelli Ida †	405	housewife	27	"
V	Luti Frank	406	metalworker	28	"
W	Luti Jennie †	406	housewife	27	"
X	*Tsolakis Louis	406	cook	56	"
Y	Zambunos Hannah †	406	packer	44	"
Z	Zambunos William	406	fireman	65	"

1350

A	Sparaco Frank	406	clerk	25	"
B	Sparaco Mary †	406	housewife	23	"
C	Leone Ancleto	407	carpenter	29	"
D	*Leone Luisa †	407	at home	62	4 Linwood
E	Leone Mary †	407	housewife	25	here
F	Crockett Emily †	407	clerk	45	"
G	Souza Laura †	407	packer	23	"
H	Souza Mary †	407	housewife	48	"
K	Souza Victor	407	carpenter	53	"
L	Fernandez Manuel	408	seaman	45	"

Saratoga Street Continued

M	Lopez Eleanor †	408	housewife	23	here
N	Lopez Manuel	408	retired	38	"
O	DeBenedictis Claudia †	408	housewife	25	"
P	DeBenedictis Richard	408	grinder	27	"
R	Ricciordelli Frederick W	408	U S N	24	Chelsea
S	Ricciordelli Teresa †	408	student	20	"
T	Rose Isabel †	409	technician	23	here
U	Rose Marie †	409	clerk	22	"
V	Rose Thomas J	409	machinist	51	"
W	Rose Valentina †	409	housewife	46	"
X	Hansford James	409	U S N	21	"
Y	Hansford Mary †	409	cleaner	52	"
Z	Trainor Bessie †	409	housewife	48	"

1351

A	Trainor James H	409	U S A	29	"
B	Trainor James P	409	laborer	52	"
C	Trainor Raymond	409	"	26	"
D	McCarthy Edward	410	retired	36	"
E	McCarthy Johanna †	410	cleaner	69	"
F	McCarthy Lawrence	410	fireman	34	"
G	Gregory Benjamin	410	boilermaker	30	"
H	Gregory Margaret †	410	housewife	30	"
K	Mongello Frances †	410	"	24	"
L	Mongello John	410	metalworker	24	"
M	DeCosta Mary †	411	housewife	32	"
N	DeCosta Richard	411	candyworker	35	"
O	*Pecora Barbara †	411	at home	52	"
P	Pecora Francis	411	presser	27	"
R	Pecora Joseph	411	U S A	23	"
S	Pecora Rose †	411	finisher	21	"
T	DeCristoforo Alfred	411	U S A	20	"
U	DeCristoforo Angelina †	411	at home	59	"
V	DeCristoforo Angelina †	411	waitress	27	"
W	DeCristoforo Emanuel	411	U S A	37	"
X	DeCristoforo Joseph	411	packer	25	"
Y	Operacz Alice †	412	housewife	26	Cambridge
Z	Operacz Frank	412	U S N	26	"

1352

A	Montiero Anthony	412	U S M C	24	here
B	*Montiero Frank	412	painter	52	"
C	*Montiero Frank, jr	412	"	28	"

31

Saratoga Street—Continued

D	Montiero Joseph	412	painter	23	here
E	*Montiero Mary—†	412	housewife	51	"
G	Kibler Clarence J	413	inspector	58	"
H	Kibler Joseph M	413	U S A	26	"
K	Kibler Margaret L †	413	clerk	21	"
L	Kibler Nora E—†	413	housewife	54	"
M	Kibler Ruth N—†	413	clerk	24	"
N	*Oliveira Maria R—†	413	at home	67	"
O	*Tisi Maria—†	413	housewife	32	"
P	Tisi Pasquale	413	assembler	34	"
R	Green Catherine N—†	413	at home	83	"
S	Veiga Maria—†	414	housewife	25	"
T	Veiga Paul	414	blacksmith	28	"
U	Forrest Edward	414	U S A	23	"
V	Sampson Walter G	414	freighthandler	50	"
W	Stone Beatrice—†	414	at home	48	"
X	Tiblett Edith—†	414	operator	24	"
Y	Tibbett Willard	414	U S A	24	Oklahoma
Z	*Veiga Domingos	414	custodian	55	here
	1353				
A	Veiga Edward	414	laborer	21	"
B	*Veiga Maria—†	414	housewife	50	"
C	Veiga William	414	U S A	25	"
D	O'Brien George M	416	mechanic	42	"
E	O'Brien Mary M—†	416	housewife	27	"
F	Mantica Leo	416	machinist	29	"
G	Mantica Mary †	416	housewife	30	"
H	Picardi Albert	416	U S A	28	"
K	Picardi Louis	416	chauffeur	26	"
L	Picardi Margaret †	416	at home	32	"
M	Picardi Ralph	416	laborer	59	"
N	Pieretti Ottino	416	painter	60	"
O	Ferrara Louis	420	roofer	45	"
P	Ferrara Margaret—†	420	housewife	42	"
R	Cascieri Archangelo	420	sculptor	40	"
S	*Cascieri Corrado	420	retired	80	"
T	*Cascieri Maria †	420	at home	76	"
U	Cascieri Maria D—†	420	dressmaker	34	"
V	Reardon Frances—†	420	at home	49	"
W	Reardon Thomas E	420	U S N	22	"
X	*Costra John	421	weaver	53	"

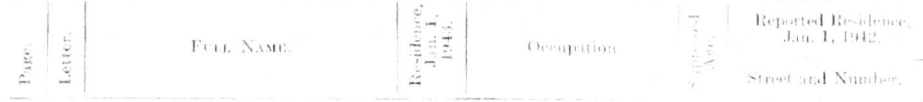

Saratoga Street Continued

y	Costra John, jr	421	operator	23	here
z	Travers Alice †	421	packer	21	"
	1354					
A*	Travers Manuel	421	janitor	56	"
B*	Travers Mary †	421	tailor	34	"
c	Hanton Bernadette †	421	clerk	33	516 Sumner
D	Hanton Elizabeth †	421	at home	72	516 "
E	Hanton John R	421	clerk	29	516 "
F	Quartarone John	422	woodworker	33	279 Chelsea
G	Quartarone Teresa †	422	housewife	32	279 "
H	DeLucia Frank	422	laborer	66	here
K	DeLucia Joseph	422	U S A	35	"
L*	DeLucia Maria †	422	housewife	65	"
M	Turco Alexander	422	machinist	45	"
N	Turco Angelina †	422	housewife	40	"
O	Hamilton Anna E †	423	"	37	"
P	Hamilton Peter C	423	chauffeur	39	"
R	Briana John H	423	machinist	20	"
s	Briana Mary E †	423	housewife	43	"
T	Briana Teresa H †	423	stenographer	21	"
U	Briana Thomas	423	laborer	45	"
V	Briana Thomas F	423	U S A	22	"
W	Collins Alice F †	423	housewife	55	"
X	Collins James J	423	guard	28	"
Y	Collins John J	423	laborer	54	"
Z	Collins Lawrence F	423	U S A	26	"
	1355					
B	Ferrioli Salvatore	424	clerk	31	"
c	Ferrioli Susan †	424	housewife	24	"
D*	Belgiorno Concetta †	424	"	56	"
E	Belgiorno Ermanno	424	laborer	28	"
F	Belgiorno Louis	424	U S A	25	"
G	Belgiorno Margaret †	424	housewife	25	129 Lexington
H	Belgiorno Pasquale	424	tailor	57	here
K	Coyle John F	425	U S A	26	"
L	Coyle John J	425	laborer	60	"
M	Coyle Thomas E	425	U S A	22	"
N	Hamilton Barbara C †	425	inspector	27	"
O	Hamilton William J	425	U S A	28	402 Savin Hill av
P*	Gaik Anna †	425	spinner	48	here
R*	Gaik John T	425	laborer	52	"

Saratoga Street—Continued

s	Gaik Regina †	425	typist	20	here
T	Gaik Stella †	425	tel operator	30	"
U	Giardella Devina †	425	housewife	36	"
V	Giardella Joseph	425	carpenter	40	"
W	King Angelina †	426	housewife	21	"
X	King Charles W	426	rigger	24	"
Y	*Moschella Maria †	426	housewife	51	"
Z	*Moschella Stanley F	426	contractor	56	"

1356

A	Sullivan Margaret † rear	426	at home	80	"
B	Sullivan Michael B "	426	laborer	42	"
C	Mosher Mary A † "	426	at home	60	"
D	Mosher Mary F † "	426	buffer	20	"
E	McGloan Catherine †	427	secretary	38	"
F	McGloan Mary E †	427	at home	68	"
G	O'Connell Daniel J	427	retired	71	"
H	Reardon Alice J †	427	clerk	60	"
K	Sennott Margaret G †	427	"	36	"
L	Battaglia Nettie †	427A	operator	31	Revere
M	Lerro Ernest	427A	clerk	24	277 Princeton
N	Lerro Stella †	427A	housewife	22	277 "
O	Long Margaret †	427A	at home	51	here
P	Veno Irving	427A	U S A	24	Long Island
R	Veno Madeline †	427A	clerk	24	here
S	Romano Paul	428	shoeworker	40	198 Havre
T	*Romano Sebatiana †	428	housewife	36	198 "
U	Stapleton Lillian W †	428	at home	43	here
V	Stapleton Mary C †	428	tel operator	44	"
W	Stapleton Patrick	428	retired	77	"
X	Petrucci Grace †	428	operator	26	"
Y	Petrucci Salvatore	428	U S A	30	"
Z	Provenzano John	428	laborer	63	"

1357

A	*Provenzano Maria †	428	candyworker	58	"
B	Hulke Benjamin	429	retired	75	"
C	Nickerson Lillian B †	429	secretary	47	"
D	*Ducey Agnes †	429A	operator	45	"
E	*Ducey Bridget †	429A	at home	73	"
F	*Ducey Nicholas	429A	laborer	32	"
G	Sexton Annie H †	431	at home	85	"
H	Sexton Mary T †	431	"	43	"

Saratoga Street Continued

	K	Sexton Robert E	431	inspector	62	here
	L	Sexton John	431A	machinist	40	"
	M	Sexton Sarah E †	431A	housewife	65	"
	N	Sexton William H	431A	engineer	64	"
	O	DiNicolautonio Frank	432	bricklayer	36	"
	P	DiNicolautonio Mary †	432	housewife	30	"
	R	Tarquinio Americo	432	U S A	24	"
	S	*Tarquinio Anthony	432	laborer	69	"
	T	*Tarquinio Beatrice †	432	housewife	70	"
	U	LaCortigha Charles	432	U S N	22	"
	V	*LaCortigha Peter	432	retired	65	"
	W	*LaCortigha Rose †	432	housewife	63	"
	X	Mastascusa John	432	laborer	37	"
	Y	Sansone Catherine †	432	stitcher	33	"
	Z	DeCosta Joseph	433	laborer	29	"
1358						
	A	DeCosta Lucy †	433	tailor	60	"
	B	Vieira Adelaide †	433	housewife	43	"
	C	Vieira Anthony J	433	welder	45	"
	D	Berardi Dora †	433	clerk	20	"
	E	Berardi Joseph	433	watchman	59	"
	F	Berardi Panfilo	433	U S A	30	"
	G	Beradri Tulio	433	"	22	"
	H	Anthony Edward J	433A	longshoreman	59	"
	K	Anthony Edward J, jr	433A	U S A	25	"
	L	Anthony Lawrence L	433A	"	21	"
	M	Anthony Mary E †	433A	housewife	53	"
	N	Ottone Angelo	440	laborer	57	"
	O	*Ottone Antonia †	440	housewife	67	"
	P	Ottone Michael	440	laborer	32	"
	R	Almedia Fred	440	policeman	45	"
	S	Almedia Isabel †	440	housewife	42	"
	T	Almedia Walter F	440	U S A	22	"
	U	Trabucco Carina †	440	housewife	54	"
	V	Trabucco Elizabeth †	440	stenographer	25	"
	W	Trabucco Gennaro	440	laborer	59	"
	X	Trabucco Mary †	440	at home	27	"
	Y	Pettipas Eva †	442	clerk	38	"
	Z	Pettipas James	442	fish handler	44	"
1359						
	A	Argenzio Carmella †	442	shoeworker	35	"

Saratoga Street Continued

B	Argenzio Emelia †	442	at home	68	here
C	Argenzio Joseph	442	shoeworker	37	"
D	Caponigro Andrew	442	"	67	"
E	Caponigro Fiore	442	linoleum layer	25	"
F*	Caponigro Maria †	442	housewife	59	"
G	Caponigro Teresa †	442	"	26	"
H	Caponigro Vincenzo	442	U S A	23	"
K	DiPaolo Albert	442	boxmaker	34	"
L	DiPaolo Mary †	442	housewife	26	"
M	Fougere Eva †	443	"	48	"
N	Fougere Jeanette †	443	at home	20	"
O	Fougere Leo	443	machinist	44	"
P	Brazil Bernard J	443	longshoreman	40	78 Trenton
R	Brazil Mary †	443	housewife	36	78 "
S	Maloney Teresa †	443	operator	34	78 "
T*	Eleftherion Elias	445	cook	44	here
U	Teris Mary †	445	housewife	44	"
V	Teris Michael	445	bartender	46	"
W	Saari Paul	445	laborer	51	"
X	Saari Saima †	445	housewife	55	"
Y	Richards Annie †	445½	at home	69	"
Z	Dinn John F	447	laborer	42	"

1360

A	Dinn Mary †	447	housewife	41	"
B	VanDyke Mary †	447½	at home	75	"
C	Surette Alma †	447½	factoryhand	26	"
D	Thibeau Elizabeth †	447½	housewife	33	"
E	Thibeau James	447½	factoryhand	39	"
F	Riccabeno Ada †	449	at home	35	"
G	Miraglia Mary †	449	housewife	21	390 Chelsea
H	Miraglia Richard J	449	electrician	28	45 Neptune rd
K*	Bordonaro Guiseppina †	449	tailor	54	here
L	Bordonaro Innocenzo	449	clerk	61	"
M	Cornetta Mary †	451	housewife	44	"
N	Cornetta Pasquale	451	inspector	45	"
O	Ricciardi Domenick	451	electrician	31	"
P	Ricciardi Jennie †	451	housewife	32	"
R	Venuti Anthony	451	cashier	38	"
S	Venuti Margaret †	451	operator	36	"
T*	D'Amato Alfonso	454	retired	87	"
U	D'Amato Alfonso, jr	454	chipper	41	"

36

Saratoga Street Continued

A	D'Amato Josephine †	454	housewife	35	here
W	Chafitz Hyman B	454	U S A	28	"
X	Chafitz Jacob	454	tailor	55	"
Y	Chafitz Mary— †	454	housewife	55	"
Z	Polito Anthony	454	shoeworker	61	"

1361

A	Polito Filomena— †	454	dressmaker	54	"
B	Polito Joseph	454	shoeworker	33	"
C	Polito Louise— †	454	housewife	29	"
D	Polito Mary— †	454	saleswoman	31	"
E	Russo Rose— †	454	dressmaker	28	"
F	Russo Salvatore	454	U S A	25	210 Havre
G	Mancini John	456	shoeworker	43	here
H*	Mancini Maria— †	456	tailor	40	"
K	Caton Edward J, jr	456	U S N	26	"
L	Caton John	456	machinist	23	"
M	Connolly Andrew	456	"	47	"
N	Connolly Edward	456	"	41	"
O	Connolly Sarah— †	456	at home	75	"
P	Guido James	456	laborer	60	"
R	Guido Louis	456	machinist	30	"
S	DeMarco Anna— †	458	housekeeper	39	"
T	DeMarco John	458	shipfitter	22	"
U	Privitero Lucy— †	458	housewife	36	"
V	Privitero Samuel	458	janitor	44	"
W	Scarpa Catherine— †	458	housewife	35	"
X	Scarpa Rosario	458	carpenter	52	"
Y	Connelly John J	458	boilermaker	51	"
Z	Gayne Barbara M †	458	housekeeper	57	"

1362

A	Scanlan Albert A	458	technician	23	"
B	Scanlan John L	458	brakeman	30	"
C	Scanlan Marie A †	458	housewife	30	"
D*	Lento Angelina †	460	"	24	"
E*	Lento Antonio	460	laborer	61	"
F	Lento Louise †	460	factoryhand	23	"
G	Scanlan Mary— †	460	"	25	"
H	Lento Nicholas	460	U S A	21	"
K	Caffrey Charles F	460	chauffeur	62	"
L	Faretra Joseph	460	laborer	49	"
M	Faretra Rose †	460	housewife	50	"

Saratoga Street — Continued

N	Cuozzo Peter	460	shoemaker	39	here
O	Cuozzo Rose †	460	housewife	30	"
P	DeGruttola Ettore	462	toolmaker	39	"
R	DeGruttola Ida †	462	housewife	36	"
S	Vanadia Calogiro	462	laborer	58	"
T *Vanadia Mary †	462	housewife	47	"
U	Pastor Carl	462	bartender	32	"
V *Pisaturo Pasqualina †	462	housekeeper	65	"
W	Banks Anna L †	464	housewife	39	"
X	Banks Martin R	464	machinist	41	"
Y	Pizzolante Dominic	464	laborer	48	"
Z	Pizzolante Mary E †	464	housewife	38	"

1363

A	Pizzolante Mary †	464	"	43	"
B	Pizzolante Vincent	464	fireman	53	"
C	Kirk Elizabeth J †	466	housekeeper	46	"
D	Kirk Nickolas J	466	U S A	21	"
E	Hancock John W	466	shipfitter	32	"
F	Hancock Julia E †	466	housewife	56	"
G	Hancock Reuben J	466	boilermaker	62	"
H	DeRosa Louise †	466	housewife	34	163 Putnam
K	DeRosa Pasquale	466	laborer	37	163 "
L *Siltanen Amos	468	machinist	51	here
M	Siltanen Amos L	468	U S A	22	"
N *Siltanen Fannie †	468	housewife	46	"
O	Donahue Bridget F †	468	"	52	"
P	Donahue John S	468	constable	52	"
R	Sacco Joseph	468	painter	40	"
S	Brinnan Catherine †	468	housewife	63	"
T	Brinnan Joseph	468	boilermaker	65	"
U	McGee Catherine †	468	housekeeper	44	"
V	DeAngelli Fiorindo	472	shoemaker	55	"
W *DeAngelli Theresa †	472	housewife	44	"
X *Vertuccio Felicia †	472	housekeeper	75	"
Y	Allegra Anthony	472	engineer	40	"
Z	Allegra Josephine A †	472	housewife	36	"

1364

B	Gallo Joseph A	474	U S A	26	"
C	Gallo Louise C †	474	student	23	"
D	Gallo Madeline †	474	housewife	63	"
E	Gallo Madeline R †	474	secretary	36	"

38

Saratoga Street Continued

	F	Gallo Mary A †	474	clerk	42	here
	G	Gallo Pasquale	474	retired	74	"
	H	Gallo Rose L †	474	clerk	34	"
	K	Gallo Virginia A †	474	"	20	"
	L	Messer Charles C	474	U S A	35	"
	M	Messer Regina †	474	housewife	31	"
	N	Biagi Frances †	474	"	21	"
	O	Biagi Mario	474	welder	22	"
	P	Russo Anna †	476	housewife	31	"
	R	Russo Charles	476	mechanic	37	"
	S	Gallo Agnes †	476	housewife	39	"
	T	Gallo Michael	476	machinist	44	"
	U	Riggi Liborio	476	laborer	55	"
	V	Riggi Rafaelle	476	U S A	24	"
	W	Riggi Salvatore	476	"	23	"
	X	*Riggi Theresa †	476	housewife	49	"
	Y	Fanale Angelina †	476	"	36	"
	Z	Fanale Anthony	476	proprietor	39	"

1365

	A	Caponigro Guido	478	laborer	24	"
	B	Caponigro Josephine †	478	housewife	22	"
	C	*Fusco Ralph	478	storekeeper	53	"
	D	*Capenigro Ada †	478	housekeeper	35	"
	E	Capenigro Enrico	478	U S A	30	"
	F	Capenigro Joseph	478	bartender	44	"
	G	Capenigro Liberto	478	"	28	"
	H	Capenigro Salvatore	478	artist	24	"
	K	Siraco Michael	480	buffer	40	"
	L	Siraco Philomena †	480	housewife	35	"
	M	Siraco Frank	480	electrician	28	"
	N	Siraco Salvatrica †	480	housekeeper	68	"
	O	Siraco Stephen	480	laborer	33	"
	P	Payne George W	480	"	56	"

Shelby Street

	S	DeLuca Anna †	4	housewife	38	129 Orleans
	T	DeLuca Carmen	4	janitor	52	129 "
	U	Scozzella Angela †	4	housewife	29	139 Havre
	V	Scozzella Louis	4	pipefitter	34	139 "

Shelby Street — Continued

w	Rella Angeline †	4	housewife	40	9 Trenton
x	Rella Sabino	4	bricklayer	51	9 "
y	Farrell Harold	6	U S N	35	here
z	Farrell Sophia †	6	housewife	32	"

1366

A	*Vertullo Carmen	6	retired	66	"
B	*Vertullo Gilorma †	6	housewife	59	"
c	Vertullo Mary †	6	shoeworker	33	"
D	Vertullo Pasquale	6	U S A	24	"
E	Vertullo Rose †	6	spinner	32	"
F	Lang Camilla †	6	housewife	27	"
G	Lang Vincent	6	upholsterer	32	"
H	Sacco Salvatore	8	shipfitter	42	"
K	Lee Carl	8	painter	32	"
L	Lee Edith †	8	housewife	32	"
M	Moriello Domenick	8	painter	29	49 Chelsea
N	Moriello Mary †	8	housewife	25	49 "
O	Pascucci Alfonso	8	laborer	60	49 "
P	Schiappa Anna †	10	housewife	27	Medford
R	Schiappa Guido	10	chauffeur	28	"
s	Pimentel Anthony	10	laborer	33	here
T	Pimentel Lena †	10	housewife	32	"
U	Pacifico Salvatore	10	laborer	60	"
V	Pacifico Theresa †	10	housewife	53	"
w	McGee Sara †	12	housekeeper	76	"
Y	*Rodophele Jennie †	12	"	59	"
z	Rodophele Joseph	12	pipefitter	22	"

1367

A	Johnston Charles	14	plumber	31	"
B	Johnston Lucy †	14	housewife	30	"
c	*Coombs Celia †	14	"	42	"
D	Coombs Henry	14	painter	44	"
E	Coombs Eli	14	machinist	35	"
F	Coombs Mary I †	14	housewife	29	"
G	Coviello Nicholas	16	laborer	33	"
H	Coviello Phyllis †	16	housewife	32	"
K	Giardullo Frances †	16	"	39	"
L	*Giardullo Maria †	16	housekeeper	71	"
M	Giardullo Nazario	16	operator	43	"
N	Corvi Margaret †	16	housewife	30	"
O	Corvi Spartico	16	laborer	35	"

Shelby Street Continued

P	Pugliese Rose †	16	stitcher	26		54 Neptune rd
R	*Saviano Aniello	18	retired	65		here
S	Saviano Joseph	18	U S A	26		"
T	Saviano Louis	18	storekeeper	20		"
U	*Saviano Sophia †	18	housewife	55		"
V	Saviano Victor	18	U S A	23		"
W	Saviano Angeline †	18	housewife	28		"
X	Saviano Stephen	18	laborer	34		"

1368

A	Lunetta Mary †	24	housewife	31		"
B	Lunetta Michael	24	manager	33		"
C	Rizzo Carmella †	24	stitcher	22		"
D	*Rizzo Elizabeth †	24	housewife	41		"
E	Rizzo Martin	24	laborer	44		"
F	Cefaioli Frank	26	baker	28		"
G	Cefaioli Helen †	26	housewife	23		"
K	Corso Ignatius	26	laborer	29		"
H	*Corso Ignazio	26	retired	76		"
L	Corso Katherine †	26	tailor	29		"
M	Zuccala Josephine †	26	"	58		"
N	Festa Louis	26	"	38		"
O	Festa Mary †	26	"	37		"
R	Bianco Margaret †	32	spinner	40		"
S	Umana Anna †	32	housewife	53		"
T	Umana Samuel	32	salesman	57		"
U	Luongo Anthony	32	constable	46		"
V	*Luongo Nellie †	32	housewife	41		"
X	Regan Dorothy †	34	"	30		350 Princeton
W	Regan Fred	34	boxmaker	30		350 "
Y	Costa Joseph	34	laborer	28		here
Z	Costa Margaret †	34	housewife	27		"

1369

A	*Valdo Anna †	34	"	46		"
B	Valdo Pasquale	34	laborer	56		"

Shrimpton Street

C	Silva Frances †	21	housewife	38		here
D	Silva Henry	21	packer	47		"
E	Silva Henry, jr	21	U S N	20		"
F	Pope Annie †	21	housekeeper	60		"

1—13   41

Page	Letter	Full Name	Residence, Jan. 1, 1943.	Occupation.	Supposed Age.	Reported Residence, Jan. 1, 1942. Street and Number.

Shrimpton Street—Continued

	Letter	Full Name	Residence	Occupation	Age	Reported Residence
	G	*Voni John B	22	machinist	62	here
	H	*Voni Norma — †	22	housewife	58	"
	K	Voni Rose — †	22	clerk	22	"
	L	Usseglio John J	24	painter	44	"
	M	Usseglio Theresa V — †	24	housewife	37	"
	N	Cavanaro Francis P	24	laborer	47	"
	O	Merullo John	24	blacksmith	29	45 Byron
	P	Merullo Mary E — †	24	housewife	29	here
	R	Marden Edwin M	24	shipper	59	"
	S	Marden Lillian R — †	24	housewife	59	"

Ward 1—Precinct 14

CITY OF BOSTON

LIST OF RESIDENTS
20 YEARS OF AGE AND OVER

(NON-CITIZENS INDICATED BY ASTERISK)
(FEMALES INDICATED BY DAGGER)

AS OF

JANUARY 1, 1943

JOSEPH F. TIMILTY, *Chairman*
FREDERIC E. DOWLING, *Secretary*
WILLIAM A. MOTLEY, JR.
FRANCIS B. McKINNEY
EVERETT R. PROUT

Listing Board.

CITY OF BOSTON PRINTING DEPARTMENT

1400

Bennington Street

	D	*Cashin Ellen — †	387	housewife	69	here
	E	Cashin Martina — †	387	clerk	29	"
	F	Cashin Richard	387	watchman	45	"
	G	LaTorre Joseph	387	baker	35	"
	H	LaTorre Mary — †	387	housewife	26	"
	K	*Velona Antonette †	387	stitcher	25	"
	L	Velona Celeste — †	387	shoeworker	29	"
	M	*Velona Cesira — †	387	housewife	60	"
	N	Velona Rocco	387	laborer	63	"
	O	Scarafone Domenic	394	shoemaker	66	"
	P	*Santoro Pasquale	394	laborer	53	"
	R	DiForte Carmela — †	396	housewife	29	"
	S	DiForte Salvatore	396	leatherworker	34	"
	U	Devezia Edward	398	welder	31	"
	V	Devezia Helen †	398	housewife	34	"
	W	Crump Anna — †	398	"	30	"
	X	Crump Willard	398	welder	34	"
	Y	Famolane James	400	chauffeur	26	"
	Z	Famolane Olivia †	400	housewife	26	"

1401

	A	Finneran Bridget †	400	at home	76	"
	B	Coffin Susan — †	402	"	70	"
	C	Burke Rosamond — †	402	housewife	29	"
	D	Burke William	402	electrician	34	"
	F	Nesbitt Clement B	407	operator	29	"
	G	Nesbitt Marie C — †	407	housewife	25	"
	H	DePanfilis Christopher	407	carpenter	20	"
	K	DePanfilis James	407	finisher	54	"
	L	DePanfilis Mary †	407	housewife	44	"
	M	Dumphy James	408	U S A	38	36 Prescott
	N	Dumphy John L	408	"	30	36 "
	O	*Dumphy Sarah †	408	at home	65	36 "
	P	*Bednaska Mary †	408	"	50	here
	R	Forlenza Clara †	408	housewife	36	"
	S	Forlenza Mario	408	pedler	38	"
	T	Flanagan Herbert	412	U S M C	24	"
	U	Flanagan Luke	412	newspaperman	46	"
	W	DeMartinis Anna †	420	housewife	32	"
	X	DeMartinis Salvatore	420	storekeeper	46	"
	Y	Mazzone Alice †	420	housewife	52	"

2

Bennington Street Continued

z	Mazzone James	420	retired	60	here
1402						
A	Brothers Arthur	423	plater	34	"
B	*Brothers Mary †	423	at home	70	"
C	Brothers Michael	423	laborer	50	"
D	Granara Louis A	423	chauffeur	45	"
E	Stevenson Doris R †	423	clerk	22	"
F	Stevenson Francis J	423	chauffeur	44	"
G	Stevenson Marguerite †	423	housewife	43	"
H	*Diorio Emily †	423	"	35	"
K	Diorio Nicholas	423	attendant	36	"
L	Collins Dorothy †	425	housewife	28	"
M	Collins John H	425	pharmacist	32	"
N	O'Shea Evelyn G †	425	housewife	41	"
O	O'Shea Patrick J	425	printer	51	"
P	Timmons Louis	425	chauffeur	46	"
R	McClellan Anna J †	430	housewife	48	"
S	McClellan Joseph A	430	clerk	48	"
T	Balboni James J	430	U S N	36	"
U	Balboni Mary E †	430	housewife	29	"
V	Reed John T	430	rigger	23	232 Lexington
W	Reed Rita †	430	housewife	23	232 "
X	Collins George	431	machinist	22	here
Y	Collins Margaret J †	431	housewife	47	"
Z	Messina Jennie †	431	"	51	"
1403						
A	Messina Santo	431	painter	54	"
B	Dellazoppa Anthony	431	fisherman	38	"
C	*Dellazoppa Louis	431	retired	69	"
D	Dellazoppa Margaret †	431	candyworker	28	"
E	Dellazoppa Mary †	431	"	34	"
F	*Dellazoppa Nora †	431	housewife	72	"
G	Knox Mary H †	432	"	24	"
H	Knox Sylvester J, jr	432	floorman	28	"
K	O'Shea Andrew J	432	printer	49	"
L	*O'Shea Bridget †	432	at home	80	"
M	O'Shea Nora G †	432	operator	45	"
N	Busquets Antonio	433	machinist	60	"
O	Busquets Catalina †	433	housewife	43	"
P	Busquets Isabelle †	433	clerk	21	"
R	Cabral Dorothy A †	433	"	22	"

3

Page.	Letter.	FULL NAME.	Residence, Jan. 1, 1943.	Occupation.	Supposed Age.	Reported Residence, Jan. 1, 1942. Street and Number.

Bennington Street — Continued

	s	Cabral Mary T †	433	clerk	24	here
	T	Cabral Rose C †	433	"	27	"
	U	Malinowski Anthony	433	laborer	51	4 Bellflower
	V	*Wolochka Mary †	433	housewife	44	4 "
	W	Wolochka Morris	433	machinist	22	4 "
	X	Suade Ernest	437	U S C G	21	here
	Y	*Suade Manuel V	437	longshoreman	64	"
	Z	Graham Francis Q	437	beautician	45	"
1404						
	A	Graham Muriel A †	437	clerk	43	"
	B	Maher Estelle C †	437	packer	39	"
	C	DiCicco Anna †	437	housewife	35	"
	D	DiCicco Rose †	437	stitcher	33	"
	E	Coyle Charles F	439	clerk	56	"
	F	Coyle Helen †	439	housewife	50	"
	G	Murphy Thomas	439	bridgetender	49	"
	H	Kelly Nora †	439	clerk	54	"
	K	Kidney Ellen †	439	at home	72	"
	L	*Kidney Mary †	439	"	74	"
	M	McCarthy Annie †	439	"	62	"
	N	Twomey Mary F †	441	"	55	"
	O	Twomey Joseph L	441	collector	43	"
	P	Twomey Monica M †	441	housewife	38	"
	R	Cashin Mary †	445	at home	71	Malden
	S	Colbert Edward	445	engineer	27	433 Frankfort
	T	Colbert Ellen †	445	housewife	27	433 "
	U	McGregor Catherine †	445	"	39	here
	V	McGregor John	445	pressman	41	"
	W	McNulty Bridget †	447	clerk	56	"
	X	Twomey Catherine W †	447	"	54	"
	Y	Shea Dennis F	447	retired	52	"
	Z	Shea Patrick	447	"	82	"
1405						
	A	Shea Patrick F	447	laborer	50	"
	B	Shea Thomas J	447	tel worker	53	"
	C	Hickey Anna †	449	housewife	47	"
	D	Hickey James	449	machinist	48	"
	E	Conlin Esther †	449	at home	42	"
	F	Coughlin Elizabeth †	449	"	73	"
	G	Coughlin Patrick	449	retired	72	"
	H	Coughlin Thomas	449	attendant	33	"

4

Bennington Street Continued

K	LeBlanc Alma †	451	housewife	47	here
L	LeBlanc Charles L	451	engineer	45	"
M	Barretto William	451	engraver	52	"
N	Brosnan Ruth E—†	451	housewife	30	"
O	Kepple Maude E—†	451	"	53	"
P	Kepple William F	451	blacksmith	45	"
S	Day Julia F—†	456	housewife	47	"
T	Flanagan Agnes E—†	456	clerk	41	"
U	Flanagan Grace J—†	456	stenographer	36	"
V	Flanagan John A	456	clerk	45	"
W	Flanagan William A	456	"	48	"
Y	Dennehy James F	460	"	61	"
Z	Dennehy Sarah A—†	460	housewife	65	"

1406

A	Colbert Edward T	460	retired	67	"
B	Colbert Josephine A—†	460	at home	52	"
C	Williams Isabella M—†	460	housewife	41	"
D	Williams William J	460	watchman	45	"
E	*Roncini Diomira—†	490	at home	57	"
F	Roncini Santino	490	carpenter	32	"
G	Maloney Mary J—†	496	housewife	36	"
H	Maloney Theodore W	496	storekeeper	37	"
K	Hickens George E	496	repairman	50	"
L	Hickens Gertrude M—†	496	secretary	21	"
M	Hickens Laura I—†	496	housewife	42	"
N	Murray Bertha B—†	498	"	53	"
O	Murray Henry B	498	retired	60	"
P	Petrillo Josephine †	498	housewife	42	"
R	Petrillo Louis	498	metalworker	42	"
S	Petrillo Louis C	498	machinist	21	"
T	Hallahan Charles D	504	U S C G	20	"
U	Hallahan James J	504	engineer	64	"
V	Hallahan Margaret A †	504	housewife	57	"
W	Maher Bridget—†	506	at home	65	"
X	Doyle Mary A †	506	instructor	46	"
Y	Paris Christi	508	operator	50	1022 Bennington
Z	Paris Margaret E—†	508	housewife	46	1022 "

1407

A	Callahan Francis C	508	U S A	24	here
B	Callahan John T	508	guard	59	"
C	Callahan Joseph T	508	instructor	26	"

5

Bennington Street — Continued

D	Callahan Mary J — †	508	housewife	53	here
E	Callahan Robert W	508	U S A	20	"
F	Powers Helen M — †	510	at home	44	"
G	Powers John E	510	metalworker	24	"
H	Henderson Cornelius	512	coppersmith	39	"
K	Henderson John E	512	retired	71	"
L	Henderson Josephine M — †	512	housewife	68	"
M	Henderson Mary J — †	512	clerk	30	"
N	Henderson Neil J	512	U S A	43	"
O	Vieira Genevieve J — †	512	clerk	35	"
P	Murphy Joseph H	516	metalworker	44	"
R	Murphy Madeline — †	516	housewife	45	"
S	Arone Arena — †	524	"	23	357 Chelsea
T	Arone John	524	mechanic	25	357 "
U	Memmolo Anthony	524	executive	29	here
V	Memmolo Carmela — †	524	at home	31	"
W	*Memmolo Maria — †	524	housewife	61	"
X	Memmolo Angelo	524	solicitor	38	"
Y	*Memmolo Phyllis — †	524	housewife	35	"
Z	Hickey Catherine — †	528	"	28	"
1408					
A	Hickey Joseph F	528	timekeeper	28	"
B	Volpini Augusto	528	tilesetter	40	"
C	*Volpini Osvalda — †	528	housewife	34	"
D	Mullaley Agnes — †	530	"	35	"
E	Mullaley Daniel	530	clerk	38	"
F	Mullaley Julia — †	530	at home	64	"
G	Avola Alex	532	finisher	34	"
H	Avola Jean — †	532	housewife	31	"
K	Giliberto Anna — †	532	"	22	"
L	Giliberto Augustino	532	receiver	24	"
M	Kondrasky Andrew	534	laborer	49	"
N	*Kondrasky Anna — †	534	housewife	48	"
O	Frazier Edmund W	534	U S A	42	"
P	Frazier Fred	534	retired	81	"
R	Frazier George F	534	electrician	38	"
S	Frazier Sarah J — †	534	at home	75	"
T	Burke Lillian M — †	534	"	73	"
U	Rutledge Elmira H — †	534	housewife	67	"
V	Rutledge Harold B	534	clerk	45	"
W	Gulla Rosario	536	painter	29	"

Bennington Street Continued

x	Gulla Vera †	536	housewife	32	here
y	Gaudino Anna †	536	"	21	"
z	Gaudino Joseph	536	electrician	24	"

1409

a	Carbone Gabriel	536	broker	37	"
b	Carbone Mary †	536	housewife	29	"
d	Butler James L	540	merchant	32	"
e	Butler Theresa †	540	housewife	31	"
f	Dinarello Joseph V	540	mechanic	29	336 Maverick
g	Dinarello Mary †	540	at home	51	244 Leyden
h	Dinarello Rena †	540	housewife	29	336 Maverick
k	Cataldo Charles	540	grocer	41	here
l	Cataldo Concetta †	540	housewife	41	"
m	Cantalupo Edna †	544	"	21	147 Cambridge
n	Cantalupo Gaetano	544	U S A	21	546 Benningt'n
o*	Cantalupo Maria †	544	at home	71	here
p	LaCortiglia Anthony	546	mechanic	33	"
r	LaCortiglia Theresa †	546	housewife	29	"
s	Cantalupo Flora †	546	"	38	"
t	Cantalupo Mary J †	546	clerk	20	"
u	Cantalupo Ottavio	546	weaver	48	"
v	Mezzocchi Alfred	546	chauffeur	33	"
w	Mezzocchi Anna †	546	housewife	29	"
x	Barrasso Lucy †	548	"	25	277 Paris
y	Barrasso Orazio R	548	chauffeur	27	277 "
z	Tarquinio Clement	548	laborer	40	here

1410

a	Tarquinio Pasqualina †	548	housewife	33	"
b*	Ferrari Barbara †	548	"	49	"
c	Ferrari Mario	548	marblecutter	58	"

Chaucer Street

f	Olsen Mary †	3	housewife	38	here
g	Olsen William	3	cashier	39	"
h	Conway James J	3	U S A	34	"
k	Conway Patrick J	3	retired	70	"
l	Conway Thomas G	3	U S A	35	"
m	Ahearn Catherine E †	3	clerk	31	"
n	Ahearn Mary E †	3	housewife	70	"
o	Ahearn Mary E †	3	tel operator	41	"

Chaucer Street—Continued

P	Weagle Elizabeth †	5	housewife	50	here
R*	Nowosielski Bolislawa †	5	"	47	45 Milton
S	Nowosielski Lucyna †	5	stenographer	21	45 "
T	Nowosielski Walery	5	loom fixer	51	45 "
U	Mierzykowski Joseph	5	"	49	here
U	Mierzykowski Kazimierz	5	U S A	21	"
W	Mierzykowski Mary †	5	housewife	46	"
X	Mierzykowski Zdzislaw A	5	U S A	25	"
Y	Bissette Margaret †	9	clerk	47	"
Z	Gowdy Blanche †	9	seamstress	50	"

1411

A	Gowdy Frank	9	pipefitter	61	"
B	Keyes Annie J †	9	housewife	73	"
C	Curran Celia E †	9	operator	43	"
D	Curran John J	9	ironworker	48	"
E*	Curran Mary A †	9	housewife	76	"
F*	Duffey Mary †	17	"	85	"
G	Duffey Thomas J	17	painter	54	"
H	Spear Louisa P †	17	housewife	57	"
K*	Direvia Edmund	19	finisher	31	"
L*	Direvia Mary †	19	housewife	57	"
M*	Direvia Mary †	19	"	29	"
N	Flannigan Beatrice W †	25	clerk	22	"
O	Flannigan Catherine M †	25	"	24	"
P	Flannigan Delia †	25	housewife	50	"
R	Flannigan Nicholas	25	shipper	60	"
S	Sullivan John	25	engineer	58	"
T	Sullivan Paul	25	retired	36	"
U	Mazza Teresa †	25	storekeeper	47	"
V	McCarthy William W	25	steamfitter	27	"
W	McLaughlin Gertrude †	25	at home	24	"
X	McLaughlin Hugh J	25	U S N	27	"
Y	Murphy Emma †	25	housewife	69	"
Z	Gill Helen T †	27	"	33	"

1412

A	Gill Joseph F	27	policeman	40	"
B	Gill Richard	27	retired	73	"
C	Laville Annie J †	27	cook	52	"
D	Murphy Mary F †	27	nurse	33	"
E	Murphy Warren W	27	manager	34	"
F	Hayes Michael J	31	fisherman	41	190 Sumner

S

Page.	Letter.	Full Name.	Residence, Jan. 1, 1943.	Occupation.	Supposed Age.	Reported Residence, Jan. 1, 1942. Street and Number.

Chaucer Street Continued

	G	Hayes Ruth C †	31	housewife	22	190 Summer
	H	Sandmo Beryl †	31	"	38	here
	K	Sandmo Karsten	31	fisherman	37	"
	L	Ferris Opal †	31	housewife	31	"
	M	Ferris Peter	31	supervisor	43	"
	N	Clingen Mildred † rear	35	clerk	30	"
	O	Clingen Robert E "	35	watchman	65	"
	P	Clingen Sadie † "	35	housewife	52	"
	R	Gay Frederick "	35	plumber	46	"
	S	Donovan Dennis F "	35	clerk	65	"
	T	Donovan Sarah † "	35	at home	54	"
	U	Almeida Frank	37	shipjoiner	56	"
	V	Almeida Josephine †	37	housewife	54	"
	W	Furlong Mary †	39	at home	86	"
	X	Jensen Susan †	39	clerk	40	"
	Y	Thibeault Gertrude †	39	housewife	45	"
	Z	Gannon Catherine †	39	bookkeeepr	27	"
1413						
	A	Gannon John	39	engineer	59	"
	B	Gannon Mary †	39	housewife	55	"
	C	Lavelle Michael	39	fireman	55	"
	D	Valardo Frances †	43	housewife	61	"
	E	Valardo Guy	43	U S A	30	"
	F	Valardo Joseph	43	painter	27	"
	G	Werner Harold	47	policeman	44	"
	H	Werner Harold E	47	clerk	23	"
	K	Werner Margaret T †	47	housewife	46	"
	L	Werner Mary V †	47	clerk	20	"
	M	Dunn Harry E	49	electrician	31	"
	N	Dunn Ruth A †	49	housewife	29	"
	O	Scannell Daniel P	49	seaman	42	"
	P	Scannell Elsie †	49	housewife	43	"
	R	Scannell Margaret †	49	laborer	22	"
	S	Hurley Daniel F	49	lumberman	60	"
	T	Hurley Mary A †	49	housewife	66	"
	U	Hurley William J	49	laborer	27	"
	V	Martin Edith L †	53	housewife	49	"
	W	Martin Ellsworth J	53	clerk	52	"
	X	DiChristoforo John	55	boilermaker	25	"
	Y	DiChristoforo Mary †	55	housewife	26	"
	Z	DiFezio Anthony	55	U S A	22	"

Page.	Letter	FULL NAME.	Residence, Jan. 1, 1943.	Occupation.	Supposed Age.	Reported Residence, Jan. 1, 1942.
						Street and Number.

1414

Chaucer Street Continued

	A	*DiFezio Camilla †	55	housewife	45	here
	B	DiFezio Camillo	55	contractor	45	"

Chelsea Street

	C	Busby Ella †	429	housewife	67	here
	D	Busby Ella F †	429	operator	40	"
	E	Busby John W	429	retired	77	"
	F	Powers Mary M †	429	rubberworker	20	"
	G	*Powers Mary S †	429	housewife	45	"
	H	*Powers Nicholas J	429	fish handler	50	"
	K	Semington Margaret †	429	clerk	21	"
	L	Semington Odina †	429	housewife	46	"
	M	Semington Robert	429	doorman	57	"
	N	Tucker Irene †	429	matron	43	Maine
	O	Dryden Cora B †	431	housewife	72	here
	P	McCormick William A	431	retired	78	"
	R	Ryan Peter J	431	laborer	45	"
	S	Riccioli Grace †	435	housewife	28	65 Joy
	T	Riccioli Joseph	435	entertainer	29	65 "
	U	Cordinale Carmen	435	U S A	25	here
	V	Cordinale Frank	435	operator	33	"
	W	Cordinale Marie †	435	housewife	56	"
	X	Cordinale Vincenzo	435	retired	65	"
	Y	Scarpa Anna †	437	housewife	36	"
	Z	Scarpa Ralph	437	pipefitter	42	"

1415

	A	Scarpa Frances †	437	housewife	69	"
	B	Scarpa Louis	437	shipworker	32	"
	C	Capo Rose †	439	at home	64	"
	D	Scorsello Joseph	439	operator	23	"
	E	Sullo Angelina †	439	housewife	65	"
	F	Sullo Ann †	439	inspector	20	"
	G	Sullo Michael	439	U S A	23	"
	H	Sullo Nicola	439	carpenter	65	"
	K	Sullo Salvatore	439	U S A	25	"
	L	Sullo Vera †	439	at home	21	"

Curtis Street

	z	Maguire Florence E †	S	housewife	43	here
1416						
	A	Maguire William J	S	boilermaker	41	"
	B	Fagan Mary J †	S	housewife	52	"
	C	Fagan Mary M †	S	saleswoman	21	"
	D	Fagan Thomas F	S	retired	54	"
	E	MacIntyre Alfred R	S	weaver	37	"
	F	MacIntyre Annie †	S	housewife	62	"
	G	Gayheart Harry	11	supervisor	26	663 Saratoga
	H	Gayheart Helen †	11	housewife	22	663 "
	K	Venezia Florence †	11	"	25	663 "
	L	Venezia Michael	11	chauffeur	24	215 Webster

Frankfort Street

	M	Morris Mary †	404	housewife	40	here
	N	Morris Thomas	404	laborer	49	"
	O	McGovern Ann †	404	housewife	50	"
	P	McGovern Patrick	404	janitor	62	"
	R	Sheremeta Boleslawa †	404	hairdresser	26	"
	s*	Sheremeta Henry	404	loom fixer	57	"
	T*	Sheremeta Johanna †	404	housewife	50	"
	U	Pastore Eugene J	406	policeman	28	"
	V	Pastore Rita †	406	housewife	25	"
	W*	Pastore Angelo	406	laborer	60	"
	X	Pastore Armand	406	barber	34	"
	Y	Pastore Carmen	406	manager	30	"
	Z	Pastore James	406	butcher	32	"
1417						
	A	Pastore Mary †	406	at home	21	"
	B	Ronayne Eileen J †	406	housewife	46	"
	C	Ronayne Margaret †	406	social worker	22	"
	D	Ronayne Robert F	406	inspector	57	"
	E	Ronayne Robert F, jr	406	U S A	23	"
	F	Passaggio Alphonse	409	loom fixer	29	"
	G	Passaggio Nancy †	409	housewife	28	"
	H	D'Addio Alexander	409	retired	62	"
	K	D'Addio Francis A	409	laborer	26	"
	L	Capanelli Albert	409	"	20	"

H

Page.	Letter	FULL NAME.	Residence, Jan. 1, 1943.	Occupation.	Supposed Age.	Reported Residence, Jan. 1, 1942. Street and Number.

Frankfort Street — Continued

	Letter	FULL NAME.	Residence	Occupation	Age	Reported Residence
	M	*Capanelli Elvira †	409	housewife	54	here
	N	Capanelli Frederick	409	U S A	22	"
	P	Capenelli Gordon	409	"	26	"
	O	Capanelli Sestilio	409	laborer	58	"
	R	Mazzarella Ralph	411	porter	33	"
	S	Mazzarella Rose †	411	housewife	33	"
	T	Morgan Anna †	411	"	53	"
	U	Ranahan Thomas	411	retired	67	"
	V	Staff Gertrude †	411	housewife	36	"
	W	Staff John	411	welder	36	"
	X	Aiello Carmella †	411	housewife	46	"
	Y	Aiello Ignazio	411	pressman	48	"
	Z	Aiello Peter	411	cutter	23	"

1418

	Letter	FULL NAME.	Residence	Occupation	Age	Reported Residence
	A	Aiello Sarah — †	411	shoeworker	21	"
	B	Albano Antonette †	415	housewife	29	"
	C	Albano Joseph	415	presser	28	"
	D	Butler Rita — †	415	clerk	21	"
	E	Butler William F	415	laborer	58	"
	F	*Mazzarella Columbia †	415	housewife	57	"
	G	Mazzarella Gerardo	415	mechanic	27	"
	H	*Mazzarella James	415	retired	58	"
	K	Rubbico Philomena †	415	at home	32	"
	L	Gallo Anna — †	417	housewife	31	98 Cowper
	M	Gallo Cesare	417	driller	47	98 "
	N	Brown Mabel H †	417	housewife	30	here
	O	Brown William P	417	U S C G	28	"
	P	Cullen Mabel H †	417	packer	55	"
	R	Fairchild Bernard A	417	seaman	34	"
	S	Connelly James	417	welder	29	"
	T	Connelly Mary †	417	housewife	59	"
	U	Connelly Mary E †	417	at home	24	144 St Andrew rd
	V	Landry John C	417	U S A	22	561 Benningt'n
	W	Cyr Albert	420	millhand	56	here
	X	Cyr Elizabeth †	420	housewife	50	"
	Y	Cyr Paul J	420	U S C G	21	"
	Z	McGrath Mary E †	420	housewife	46	"

1419

	Letter	FULL NAME.	Residence	Occupation	Age	Reported Residence
	A	McGrath Paul D	420	B F D	51	"
	B	King John F	420	shipper	44	"
	C	King Margaret †	420	housewife	41	"

12

Frankfort Street Continued

D	Campaglia Anthony	424	carpenter	54	here
E	Campaglia Giovanna †	424	housewife	44	"
F	Campaglia Marie †	424	bookkeeper	20	"
G	Ricci Anna †	424	housewife	64	"
H	Ricci Louis	424	retired	62	"
K	Gallidare Alfred	424	U S A	28	20 Neptune rd
L	*Callidare Michael	424	stonecutter	60	20 "
M	*Callidare Virginia †	424	housewife	49	20 "
N	*Lawrence Anthony	425	retired	72	here
O	Mosca Achilles, jr	426	chauffeur	34	"
P	Mosca Romilda †	426	housewife	29	"
R	*Mosca Achilles	426	retired	65	"
S	Mosca Concetta †	426	operator	29	"
T	*Mosca Louise †	426	housewife	68	"
U	Marranzini Carmella †	426	"	45	"
V	Marranzini Carmen	426	shoeworker	49	"
W	Marranzini Olga †	426	inspector	20	"
X	Cashin Elizabeth M †	427	housewife	33	"
Y	Cashin Leo F	427	molder	35	"
Z	Frati Giacomo	428	retired	70	"

1420

A	Frati Mary †	428	housewife	53	"
B	Surette Eloi J	428	storekeeper	45	"
C	*Surette Mary L †	428	housewife	39	"
D	McKurdy Alice †	428	"	30	"
E	McKurdy William	428	fireman	32	"
F	Manbucca Anthony	429	U S A	21	"
G	Manbucca Catherine †	429	clerk	31	"
H	Manbucca Francis	429	U S A	28	"
K	Manbucca James	429	laborer	52	"
L	Manbucca Marion †	429	inspector	23	"
M	Bolivar Helen †	430	housewife	45	"
N	Bolivar Herbert H	430	carpenter	40	"
O	Massa Girardo	431	welder	52	"
P	Massa Ida †	431	housewife	53	"
R	Massa Ralph	431	U S A	28	"
S	McClellan Henry P	431	mechanic	46	"
T	McClellan Henry P, jr	431	U S A	23	"
V	Belyea Jessica †	433	stitcher	59	40 Neptune rd
W	Pastore Carmen	433	meatcutter	25	here
X	Pastore Yolanda †	433	housewife	25	"

13

Frankfort Street — Continued

Y	Fariole Angelina — †	435	housewife	42	here
Z	Fariole Robert	435	shipper	42	"

1421

A	Petrillo Lena †	435	housewife	62	"
B*	Petrillo Vito	435	retired	68	"
C	Keating Albert	441	oiler	22	"
D	Keating Anna — †	441	housewife	56	"
E	Keating John	441	boatman	59	"
F	Murray Grace — †	441	inspector	27	"
G	Murray William J	441	U S C G	29	"
K	McGrath Dennis F	447	longshoreman	69	"
L	McGrath Dennis F, jr	447	"	36	"
M	McGrath Louise — †	447	tel operator	25	"
N	McGrath Margaret G — †	447	housewife	66	"
O	Thistle Charles	447	seaman	34	Cambridge
P	Thistle Mary — †	447	housewife	36	"
R	Liss Bessie — †	447	at home	22	here
S	Liss George	447	freighthandler	49	"
T	Liss Minnie — †	447	housewife	47	"
U	Keane Mary — †	449	"	27	"
V	Keane Matthew R	449	manager	29	"
W	Scopa James	453	shipfitter	42	"
X	Scopa Josephine — †	453	housewife	35	"
Y	Pepicelli Pasquale	453	shipjoiner	32	"
Z	Pepicelli Virginia †	453	housewife	30	"

1422

A	Pepicelli Antonio	453	shipwright	62	"
B	Pepicelli James	453	clerk	20	"
C*	Pepicelli Lucy — †	453	housewife	62	"
D	Pepicelli William	453	blacksmith	26	"
E*	Luccese Fannie †	455	housewife	64	"
F*	Luccese Luzzaro	455	shoeworker	62	"
G*	Sava Agata †	455	housewife	44	"
H	Sava John	455	storekeeper	44	"
K	DeCalogero Eleanor — †	455	housewife	23	157 Marion
L	DeCalogero James	455	presser	23	157 "

Lubec Street

M	LePage Elisabeth — †	428	housewife	53	here
N	LePage William G	428	shoeworker	58	"

Lubec Street Continued

o	DeFrancesco Charles	436	pipefitter	38	here	
p	DeFrancesco Emily — †	436	housewife	35	"	
r	Coleman Charles	437	carpenter	82	"	
s	Francis Mary— †	438	housekeeper	55	"	
t	Gibbons Ann M †	439	buyer	20	"	
u	Gibbons Edward F	439	U S C G	23	"	
v	Gibbons Fannie M †	439	housewife	49	"	
w	Gibbons Joseph P	439	U S N	25	"	
x	Gibbons Patrick J	439	janitor	56	"	
y	DeSimone Jennie †	440	housewife	29	"	
z	DeSimone John	440	janitor	39	"	

1423

A	*Clarke Ennis H	441	retired	82	"	
B	Clarke Gertrude †	441	housewife	69	"	
c	Clarke Robert W	441	mechanic	45	"	
D	Beatrice Annie—†	442	housewife	43	"	
E	Beatrice Marino	442	U S A	20	"	
F	Beatrice Salvatore	442	carpenter	45	"	
G	Carter Delia †	443	housekeeper	62	"	
H	Carter John	443	chauffeur	28	"	
k	Hazel Edward	443	retired	60	"	
L	Flynn Minnie †	443	housewife	29	64 Byron	
M	Flynn Roland	443	glazier	33	64 "	
N	Jones Earl F	446	roofer	35	here	
o	Jones Mary A †	446	housewife	67	"	
P	Jones Mildred †	446	saleswoman	28	"	
R	McArdle Charles J	446	boilermaker	31	"	
s	McArdle Dorothy A †	446	housewife	31	"	

Moore Street

t	Baker Cyril	30	boilermaker	36	9 Princeton	
u	Baker Theresa †	30	housewife	22	9 "	
v	*Cammarano Mary †	30	"	55	here	
w	*Cammarano Matteo	30	laborer	55	"	
x	Mosca Barbara †	30	housewife	27	"	
y	Mosca Thomas	30	laborer	32	"	
z	Donoghue Anna L †	36	operator	38	"	

1424

A	Donoghue Mae G †	36	at home	40	"	
B	Comeau Elizabeth †	36	cook	34	2 Chestnut	

15

Moore Street—Continued

c	Gaudet Clarence	36	machinist	39	here
d	Gaudet Emil	36	welder	52	"
e	Gaudet Mary — †	36	operator	42	"
g	Esposito Ellen — †	38	housewife	40	"
h	Esposito Peter	38	manager	47	"
k	Vecchio Ernestine — †	38	housewife	27	"
l	Vecchio Nicola	38	manager	39	"
m	Gleason Margaret — †	42	tel operator	48	"
n	Gleason Marguerite — †	42	clerk	21	"
o	Beck Anna — †	58	teacher	32	"
p	Casey Anna — †	58	"	65	"
r	Caulfield Margaret — †	58	"	32	"
s	Clifford Elizabeth — †	58	"	36	"
t	Conroy Margaret — †	58	domestic	51	"
u	Dolan Margaret — †	58	teacher	45	"
v	Dwyer Anna — †	58	"	27	"
w	Flanagan Mary — †	58	"	25	"
x	Fogg Carolyn — †	58	"	51	"
y	Griffin Dorothy — †	58	"	33	"
z	Johnson Eileen — †	58	"	25	"
	1425				
a	Lindsay Martha †	58	"	28	"
b	Shane Mary — †	58	"	34	"
c	Welch Helen — †	58	housekeeper	63	"

Neptune Road

d	Burns Edward F	4	U S A	22	here
e	Burns Edward J	4	welder	47	"
f	Burns Julia M — †	4	housewife	42	"
g	Mullen Bernard M	4	constable	62	"
h	Mullen Helena A — †	4	housewife	58	"
k	Mullen Herbert F	4	realtor	31	"
l	Greeley Anna — †	6	housekeeper	53	
m	Greeley Lloyd	6	dyesetter	26	
n	Tassinari Antenori	6	engineer	26	511 Saratoga
o	Tassinari Doris †	6	housewife	25	174 Falcon
p	Gleason John	6	U S A	21	here
r	Gleason Mary — †	6	housewife	49	"
s	Sampson Raymond	12	freighthandler	45	44 Neptune rd
t	Sampson Violet — †	12	housewife	37	44 "

16

Neptune Road—Continued

U	*Cariano Katherine—†	12	housewife	67	here	
V	Cariano Leo	12	watchman	69	"	
W	DeSimone Florence—†	12	housewife	28	"	
X	DeSimone Gabriel	12	dispatcher	27	"	
Y	Chaloner Mary—†	14	clerk	54	"	
Z	McIntosh Agnes L—†	14	housewife	48	"	
	1426					
A	McIntosh William J	14	motorman	49	"	
B	McIntosh William J	14	U S A	22	"	
C	Buono Joseph	14	marbleworker	47	"	
D	Buono Lavinia—†	14	housewife	47	"	
E	Schwamb Barbara—†	16	housekeeper	20	"	
F	Schwamb Gerald	16	U S A	21	"	
G	Schwamb Joseph	16	retired	37	"	
H	Schwamb Margaret—†	16	housewife	46	"	
K	Grace Annie—†	16	"	73	"	
L	Grace Clarence	16	timekeeper	37	"	
M	Grace Michael	16	retired	72	"	
N	Middleton Arthur	18	machinist	58	"	
O	Middleton Arthur	18	U S A	29	"	
P	Middleton Margaret—†	18	operator	21	"	
R	Middleton Mary—†	18	housewife	62	"	
S	Mattina Angelina—†	18	"	28	"	
T	Mattina Joseph	18	welder	28	"	
U	Picardi Florinda—†	18	housekeeper	72	"	
V	Fucillo Angelo	18	U S N	29	"	
W	Fucillo John	18	operator	48	"	
X	Fucillo John F	18	machinist	22	"	
Y	Fucillo Julia—†	18	housewife	45	"	
Z	Parziale Louis	20	engineer	28	976 Benningt'n	
	1427					
A	Parziale Phyllis—†	20	housewife	25	976 "	
B	Benincasa Alphonso	20	tailor	52	here	
C	Benincasa Philomena—†	20	housewife	43	"	
D	Benincasa Sarah—†	20	stitcher	21	"	
E	*Garufo Anna—†	20	housewife	47	"	
F	*Garufo Joseph	20	presser	54	"	
G	*Garufo Philomena—†	20	clerk	20	"	
H	Tassinari Archetta—†	22	housewife	27	242 E Eagle	
K	Tassinari Max M	22	welder	31	242 "	
L	LeFave Angelo	22	barber	33	here	

I—14   17

Neptune Road– Continued

M	*LeFave Pauline—†	22	housekeeper	60	here
N	*Serenci Josephine—†	22	housewife	38	"
O	Serenci William D	22	tailor	43	"
P	Marascia Concetta—†	24	housewife	23	159 Marion
R	Marascia John	24	sailmaker	25	159 "
S	Dykstra Harry M	24	rigger	58	here
T	Dykstra Margaret L †	24	housewife	52	"
U	Struzziro Alexander	24	manager	25	"
V	Struzziro Erminio	24	machinist	55	"
W	Struzziro Ernest	24	welder	26	"
X	Struzziro Esther †	24	housewife	55	"
Y	Struzziro Mary—†	24	secretary	23	"

1428

A	*Nartarano Esther †	30	clerk	32	"
B	Nartarano John	30	shoemaker	55	"
C	Nartarano Louis	30	U S N	24	"
D	*Nartarno Mary—†	30	housewife	54	"
E	Vecchio Carmela †	30	"	41	"
F	Vecchio Jerry	30	guard	47	"
G	Vecchio Louise—†	30	operator	34	"
H	Vecchio Rudolph	30	shoeworker	44	"
K	Massaro Anthony	32	tilesetter	40	"
L	Massaro Anthony	32	housewife	39	"
M	Picardi Celia—†	32	"	60	"
N	Picardi Emma—†	32	stitcher	30	"
O	Picardi Fred	32	shipfitter	28	"
P	Picardi Julia—†	32	stitcher	37	"
R	Picardi Michael	32	retired	70	"
S	Picardi Olivia—†	32	stitcher	35	"
T	Picardi Samuel	32	welder	31	"
U	Murphy Charles	32	U S A	30	"
V	Wirth Mary—†	32	housewife	63	"
W	Wirth William	32	longshoreman	67	"
X	*August Rose—†	34	operator	38	"
Y	*August William	34	clerk	56	"
Z	D'Addario Josephine †	34	housewife	36	"

1429

A	D'Addario Louis	34	salesman	30	"
B	Toscano Marion †	34	clerk	20	"
C	LaMarca Jennie †	34	stitcher	28	"
D	LaMarca Joseph	34	welder	34	"

18

Neptune Road—Continued

E	Traveis Ida †	36	clerk	25	637 Saratoga
F	Traveis Joseph F	36	shipper	25	823 "
G	O'Brien Alice M—†	36	housewife	44	here
H	O'Brien John F	36	pipefitter	24	"
K	O'Brien Richard T	36	steamfitter	48	"
L	Bulgaris Arthur C	36	accountant	30	"
M	Bulgaris Christy A	36	laborer	52	"
N	Bulgaris Evangeline—†	36	housewife	49	"
O	Bulgaris Lambrine—†	36	operator	24	"
P	Bulgaris Nicholas	36	U S A	20	"
R	Howard Charles C	38	clerk	55	"
S	Howard Margaret L—†	38	housewife	46	"
T*	Scheel Anna—†	38	"	47	71 Putnam
U	Scheel Carl	38	rigger	55	71 "
V	Lomas Harry	38	policeman	45	here
W	Lomas Mildred †	38	housewife	42	"
X	Natalucci Josephine—†	44	"	32	505 Orleans
Y	Natalucci Philip	44	rubberworker	33	505 "
Z*	DiNublia Frank	44	retired	61	here
	1430				
A	DiNublia John	44	U S A	24	"
B	DiNublia Mary—†	44	clerk	34	"
C*	DiNublia Minnie—†	44	houseworker	37	"
D	DiNublia Rose—†	44	clerk	30	"
E	Powers Elizabeth—†	44	housewife	42	"
F	Powers Harold O	44	shipfitter	46	"
G	Villani Dorothy—†	46	housewife	24	"
H	Villani Michael	46	machinist	34	"
K	Terranova Frank	46	laborer	46	"
L	Terranova Phyllis—†	46	housewife	32	"
M	Collins Charles H	46	clerk	28	"
N	Collins Dennis J	46	laborer	67	"
O	Collins Helen F †	46	clerk	30	"
P	Collins Joseph F	46	U S A	23	"
R	Collins Mary—†	46	housewife	58	"
S	Collins Mary I—†	46	secretary	25	"
T	Marshall Isabelle C—†	48	bookkeeper	37	"
U	Marshall John	48	retired	72	"
V	Fleming Julia M—†	48	housewife	64	"
W	Fleming Michael J	48	engineer	69	"
X	Terry Frank	48	policeman	45	"

Page.	Letter.	FULL NAME.	Residence, Jan. 1, 1943.	Occupation.	Supposed Age.	Reported Residence, Jan. 1, 1942.
						Street and Number.

Neptune Road—Continued

Y	Terry Mary—†	48	clerk	24	here
Z	Gallison Ann—†	50	housewife	34	"
1431					
A	Gallison Charles H	50	painter	38	"
B	Venti Rose—†	50	housewife	30	"
C	Venti Vincent	50	checker	34	"
D	Venti Amelia—†	50	stenographer	28	"
E	Venti Americo	50	U S A	30	"
F	Venti Biagio	50	laborer	55	"
G	Venti Eugenia—†	50	waitress	23	"
H	Venti Dino	50	machinist	22	"
K	Venti Nicolina—†	50	housewife	57	"
L	Wandra John A	52	clerk	28	32 Ashley
M	Wandra Rita M—†	52	housewife	27	32 "
N	Domenico Anceli	52	chauffeur	45	206 Havre
O	Domenico Rose—†	52	housewife	35	206 "
P	Musco Frances—†	52	"	45	here
R	Musco Joseph	52	salesman	21	"
S	Musco Michael	52	U S A	29	"
T	Musco Salvatore	52	salesman	55	"
U	Colagiovanni Frank	54	machinist	24	255 Marion
V	Colagiovanni Olga—†	54	housewife	21	938 Parker
W	Cardarelli Caroline—†	54	"	41	here
X	Cardarelli Gino	54	welder	41	"
Y	Iandoli Guy	54	jeweler	37	258 E Eagle
Z	Iandoli Josephine—†	54	housewife	38	258 "
1432					
A	Murray Catherine C—†	56	"	29	here
B	Murray Harold	56	checker	36	"
C	Doherty Margaret R—†	56	laundress	49	"
D	Hunter John A	56	superintendent	48	"
E	Hunter Mary A—†	56	housewife	48	"
F	Forgione Angelina—†	56	"	38	"
G	Forgione Ernest	56	U S N	20	"
H	Forgione Salvatore	56	U S A	22	"
K	Forgione Vincent	56	stevedore	46	"
L	MacGrath Adelaide—†	60	housewife	46	"
M	MacGrath Elinor—†	60	clerk	21	"
N	MacGrath Kathleen—†	60	trimmer	22	"
O	Miranda Emaculata—†	62	clerk	29	"
P	Miranda Ersilia—†	62	housewife	66	"

Page.	Letter.	FULL NAME.	Residence, Jan. 1, 1943.	Occupation.	Supposed Age.	Reported Residence, Jan. 1, 1942. Street and Number.

Neptune Road—Continued

	R	Miranda Michael	62	retired	64	here
	S	Butler Francis M	62	chauffeur	35	415 Frankfort
	T	Butler Mary D—†	62	housewife	33	415 "

Orleans Street

	V	Fiatarone Edith—†	505	housewife	23	432 Chelsea
	W	Fiatarone John V	505	toolmaker	23	432 "
	X	Fiatarone Anna—†	505	buffer	27	here
	Y	Fiatarone Margaret—†	505	housewife	47	"
	Z	Fiaratone Vincent	505	machinist	53	"

1433

	A	Vaccaro Annie—†	505	housewife	48	"
	B	Vaccaro Nicholas	505	salesman	51	"
	C	Smith Edward E	507	nurse	31	"
	D	Smith Margaret M—†	507	housewife	29	"
	E	Cullen Gertrude B—†	507	matron	50	"
	F	Cullen Mary E—†	507	housewife	65	"
	G	Cullen Thomas H	507	laborer	66	"
	H	*Borgosano Carmela—†	507	housewife	55	"
	K	Borgosano Gaetano	507	U S A	29	"
	L	Borgosano Lillian—†	507	operator	30	"
	M	Fouhy Charles J	509	U S A	58	31 Chaucer
	N	Fouhy Mabel C—†	509	housewife	42	31 "
	O	Ducey Anthony L	511	carpenter	42	here
	P	Ducey Rita—†	511	housewife	26	"
	R	Centracchio Cecelia—†	511	"	39	"
	S	Centracchio John	511	timekeeper	45	"
	T	Mazzone Pauline—†	511	housewife	22	"
	U	Mazzone Vincent	511	meatcutter	28	"
	V	*Baldenelli Angelina—†	513	housewife	53	34 W Cottage
	X	Collins Francis L	517	U S A	24	here
	Y	Collins James J	517	retired	78	"
	Z	Collins James J	517	electrician	32	"

1434

	A	Collins Mary A—†	517	housewife	70	"
	B	Collins Walter E	517	U S A	29	"
	C	Horne Elizabeth—†	517	housekeeper	37	25 Rockland
	D	Horne Ernest	517	retired	81	25 "
	E	Moran Lawrence	517	boilermaker	42	25 "

Page.	Letter.	FULL NAME.	Residence, Jan. 1, 1943.	Occupation.	Supposed Age.	Reported Residence, Jan. 1, 1942. Street and Number.

Saratoga Street

	Letter	FULL NAME	Res.	Occupation	Age	Reported Residence
	H	Elixon Margaret—†	514	housewife	29	here
	K	Elixon Toivo	514	boilermaker	29	"
	L	Marsh Margaret—†	514	housewife	65	"
	M*	Maguire Alice L—†	515	housekeeper	44	"
	N	Maguire Alice M—†	515	at home	20	"
	O	Maguire George	515	U S A	22	"
	P	Maguire John J	515	"	25	"
	R	Stock George V	515	retired	72	"
	S	Paull Charles E	515	clerk	59	"
	T	Paull Margaret L—†	515	housewife	45	"
	U	Farmer Rose—†	516	factoryhand	26	"
	V	Farmer Thomas	516	U S N	26	"
	W	Scanzello Florio	516	mechanic	30	"
	X	Scanzello Madeline—†	516	housewife	27	"
	Y	Coon Catherine—†	516	"	42	"
	Z	Coon James B	516	carpenter	50	"
1435						
	A*	Sartini Carolina—†	518	housewife	63	524 Saratoga
	B*	Grazziano Felicia—†	518	"	55	here
	C	Grazziano Nicholantonio	518	laborer	53	"
	E	McKenney Frances—†	520	housewife	30	"
	F	Fenton Bridget—†	520	"	66	"
	G	Albano Florence—†	520	"	26	"
	H	Albano Genario	520	chauffeur	29	"
	K	Herrick Charlotte M—†	522	housewife	63	"
	L	Herrick Joseph G	522	weigher	70	"
	M	O'Donnell Mary A—†	522	clerk	25	"
	N	O'Donnell Mary M—†	522	housewife	52	"
	O	Wignot John	522	baker	51	"
	P*	Bondi Elvira—†	524	housewife	42	"
	R*	Bondi Gino	524	painter	48	"
	S	Giannattasio Mary—†	524	housewife	27	"
	T	Giannattasio Michael	524	upholsterer	30	"
	U	Lucisano Angeline—†	524	housewife	30	319 Benningt'n
	V	Lucisano Nicholas	524	foreman	31	319 "
	W	Dooley Elizabeth—†	526	housewife	73	146 Chelsea
	X	Dooley Daniel	526	retired	78	146 "
	Y	Dare John P	526	laborer	35	here
	Z	Doherty Bernard	526	rigger	40	27 Green
1436						
	A	Doherty Margaret—†	526	housewife	33	27 "

22

Saratoga Street — Continued

Page.	Letter.	Full Name	Residence Jan. 1, 1943	Occupation	Age	Reported Residence Jan. 1, 1942
	B	Magas Mary—†	526	housewife	30	here
	C	Magas Peter	526	ironworker	33	"
	D	Henderson James	534	pipecoverer	41	"
	E	Henderson Laura—†	534	housewife	38	"
	F	Sentner Henry	534	laborer	30	"
	G	Sentner Margaret—†	534	housewife	30	"
	H	Martin Frank	534	laborer	26	"
	K	Martin Margaret—†	534	housewife	22	"
	M	*Marano Louis	538	barber	38	"
	N	Marano Rose—†	538	housewife	38	"
	O	Mancino Alfred	540	U S C G	20	"
	P	Mancino Carmen	540	factoryhand	55	"
	R	Mancino Joseph	540	U S N	25	"
	S	*Mancino Mary—†	540	housewife	50	"
	T	Randazzo Frank	540	storekeeper	32	"
	U	Randazzo Marie—†	540	housewife	29	"
	V	Lawson Edith—†	540	factoryhand	48	"
	W	Lawson Michael	540	retired	48	"
	X	Canty John A	542	maint'n'ceman	49	"
	Y	Canty Oliver F	542	pipecoverer	43	"
	Z	Canty Augustus T	542	U S A	39	"
1437						
	A	Canty Florence L—†	542	bookkeeper	35	"
	B	Canty Margaret E—†	542	housewife	73	"
	C	Canty Chester D	542	inspector	50	"
	D	Canty Genevieve—†	542	housewife	40	"
	E	McHugh Andrew	544	fisherman	48	"
	F	McHugh Margaret—†	544	housewife	46	"
	G	McBournie Mary—†	544	"	24	"
	H	McBournie William	544	machinist	25	"
	K	Visco Alfonse	544	clerk	25	"
	L	*Visco Assunta—†	544	housewife	45	"
	M	Visco Filomeno	544	weaver	49	"
	N	Visco Florence—†	544	stitcher	20	"
	O	Condon Alice M—†	546	housewife	26	"
	P	Condon John R	546	inspector	31	"
	R	Daley John P	551	U S A	32	"
	S	Granara Eleanor R—†	551	folder	25	"
	T	Granara Eugene J	551	U S A	22	"
	U	Granara Joseph E	551	chauffeur	47	"
	V	Granara Joseph E, jr	551	U S N	24	"

23

Page.	Letter.	Full Name.	Residence, Jan. 1, 1943	Occupation.	Supposed Age.	Reported Residence, Jan. 1, 1942. Street and Number.

Saratoga Street—Continued

	w	Granara Nora M—†	551	housewife	42	here
	x	Cody Dorothy—†	553	"	22	"
	y	Cody Herbert	553	U S A	22	"
	z	Flynn Mary—†	553	housewife	88	"
1438						
	b	Treanor Catherine G—†	559	"	46	78 Peterboro
	c	Treanor George F	559	chauffeur	52	here
	d	Hall Elizabeth—†	559	at home	77	"
	e	Hall Frederick	559	guard	49	"
	f	Walsh William P	561	machinist	48	"
	g	Baracchini Charles W	561	coppersmith	39	"
	h	Baracchini Charlotte—†	561	housewife	73	"
	k	Treanor Helen—†	561	"	28	"
	l	Treanor Louis	561	laborer	39	"
	m	Laquaglia Agnes R—†	563	housewife	31	"
	n	Laquaglia Joseph J	563	laborer	30	"
	o	Hansen Anna E—†	563	housewife	41	"
	p	Hansen Rangwell A	563	printer	42	"
	r	Kenney George H	563	"	20	"
	s	Seward Mary L—†	563	operator	31	"
	t	Comunale Frank P	567	toolkeeper	40	"
	u	Comunale Mary T—†	567	housewife	37	"
	v	*Ricci Ippolita—†	567	at home	79	"
	w	Ricci John	567	salesman	40	"
	x	*Ricci Mary—†	567	housewife	37	"
	y	Carino Ernest	567	butcher	34	"
	z	Carino Phyllis—†	567	housewife	28	"
1439						
	a	Prova Nicholas	567	butcher	22	"
	b	Sheehan John L	579	chauffeur	39	"
	c	Sheehan Mary M—†	579	housewife	38	"
	d	Church Ernestine—†	579	"	49	"
	e	Church James V	579	fireman	47	"
	f	Brems Elizabeth E—†	579	operator	22	"
	g	Brems Joseph F	579	machinist	20	"
	h	Brems Lillian E—†	579	at home	56	"
	k	Brems Philip E	579	U S C G	24	"
	l	Cicatelli Mary—†	585	housewife	45	"
	m	Cicatelli Nicholas	585	U S A	21	"
	n	Cicatelli Phyllis—†	585	stitcher	23	"
	o	Cicatelli Vincent	585	shoemaker	51	"

Page.	Letter	Full Name.	Residence, Jan. 1, 1943.	Occupation.	Supposed Age.	Reported Residence, Jan. 1, 1942. Street and Number

Saratoga Street—Continued

P	Migna Frederick	585	printer	43	47 Eutaw
R	Migna Marie—†	585	housewife	40	47 "
s*	Glatis Anna—†	585	"	40	here
T	Glatis William D	585	manager	47	"
U	Quagliati Angelina—†	587	packer	21	"
V	Quagliati Nicola	587	laborer	53	"
W	Quagliati Sophia—†	587	housewife	42	"
X	Manoli Martin	587	salesman	27	"
Y	Manoli Raffaela—†	587	housewife	26	"
Z	Kane Edward	589	laborer	52	597 Saratoga
	1440				
A	Kane William	589	U S N	24	597 "
B	Foster Evelyn A—†	589	housewife	26	here
C	Foster George F	589	rigger	25	"
D	McInnis James J	591	chauffeur	36	"
E	McInnis Mary G—†	591	housewife	36	"
F	Hogan Bridget J—†	591	"	59	"
G	Hogan Henry	591	clerk	31	"
H	Hogan Hugh J	591	electrician	26	"
K	Hogan Patrick	591	longshoreman	64	"
L	Landry Florence—†	593	at home	25	"
M	Landry Sarah—†	593	"	58	"
N	Thomas Beatrice—†	593	housewife	26	"
O	Thomas Joseph W	593	rigger	29	"
P*	Palma Frank	594	storekeeper	58	"
R*	Palma Rose—†	594	housewife	57	"
S	Abbot Helen H—†	595	operator	28	163 Byron
S	Abbott William H	595	electrician	32	163 "
T	Blaikie Doris I—†	595	housewife	20	678 Saratoga
U	Blaikie George W	595	shipfitter	20	678 "
V	Melillo Charles	596	laborer	32	here
W*	Melillo Frances—†	596	housewife	62	"
X	Melillo Mary—†	596	"	28	"
Y	Bua Angelo	596	electrician	29	"
Z	Bua Stella—†	596	housewife	22	"
	1441				
A	Moscone Leona—†	597	"	39	119 Maverick
B	Moscone Peter	597	mason	48	119 "
C*	Belfiglio Ersilia—†	600	housewife	43	here
D	Belfiglio Pierino	600	paint mixer	49	"
E	Armenia Dagnes	602	factoryhand	30	"

25

Page.	Letter.	FULL NAME.	Residence, Jan. 1, 1943	Occupation.	Supposed Age.	Reported Residence, Jan. 1, 1942. Street and Number.

Saratoga Street—Continued

F	Kenny William	602	laborer	64	here
G	*Keohane Arthur	604	retired	64	"
H	*Keohane Ellen—†	604	housewife	50	"
K	Weldes Winslow A	604	factoryhand	34	52 Sullivan
L	Lino Catherine—†	606	housewife	29	here
M	Lino John	606	U S N	29	"
N	Impemba Alfonse	608	shoemaker	64	"
O	Impemba Eleanor—†	608	factoryhand	24	"
P	Impemba Victoria—†	608	housewife	54	"
R	Impemba Victorio	608	painter	20	"
S	Sanchez Joseph	610	pipefitter	24	"
T	Sanchez Sarah—†	610	housewife	27	"
U	Morante Ralph	612	telegrapher	37	"
V	Morante Rose—†	612	housewife	39	"
W	*Marry Catherine—†	614	"	42	"
X	O'Hearn John	614	fisherman	46	"
Z	*Malgeri Carmela—†	616	housewife	43	"
	1442				
A	Malgeri Rocco	616	U S A	22	"
B	Malgeri Vincenzo	616	laborer	48	"
C	Turner Elizabeth—†	618	housewife	44	"
D	Turner Michael	618	fisherman	55	"
E	Lepore Henry J	619	electrician	28	"
F	Lepore Julia A—†	619	housewife	59	"
G	Lepore Peter A	619	machinist	59	"
H	Grady Leana M—†	619	housekeeper	57	"
K	Grady William	619	U S N	20	"
M	Wessling Henry B	619	blockmaker	48	"
L	Wessling Herman	619	machinist	55	"
N	*Gentile Daliano	620	cabinetmaker	45	"
O	Gentile Nancy—†	620	housewife	37	"
R	Velardo Alice—†	624	"	32	"
S	Velardo Domenick	624	painter	34	"
T	Sortini Catherine—†	625	housewife	25	Chelsea
U	Sortini Edmund	625	salesman	25	here
V	*Caveliere Camella—†	625	at home	92	"
W	Sortini Adam	625	watchman	21	"
X	*Sortini Lena—†	625	at home	42	"
Y	Titman Catherine—†	625	"	64	"
Z	Dewson Catherine E—†	626–628	clerk	43	"

1443

Saratoga Street — Continued

A	King Edward	626–628	starter	50	here
B	King Helen V — †	626–628	housewife	47	"
C	Micarelli Joseph	629	U S C G	20	"
D	Micarelli Louis	629	U S A	22	"
E	Micarelli Maria — †	629	housewife	51	"
F	Micarelli Mario	629	U S A	25	"
G	Micarelli Nicholas	629	storekeeper	56	"
H	Micarelli Phyllis — †	629	packer	25	84 N Margin
K	Cohan Laura — †	630	housewife	34	here
L	Cohan William M	630	foreman	34	"
M	Micarelli Catherine — †	631	housewife	37	"
N	Micarelli James	631	manager	30	"
O	DePaolo Adeline — †	631	housewife	23	"
P	DePaolo James	631	painter	25	"
R	Ryan Sarah — †	632	housewife	42	"
S	Ryan Thomas J	632	operator	50	"
T	DeWolfe Frank	634	laborer	50	"
U	DeWolfe May — †	634	housewife	46	"
V	DeWolfe William E	634	U S C G	21	"
W	Fitzgerald Annie — †	634	housewife	69	"
X	Fitzgerald Laurence	634	retired	79	"
Y	O'Regan Anna — †	635	housewife	47	"
Z	O'Regan John	635	electrician	50	"

1444

A	Dundon Mary — †	635	clerk	50	"
B	O'Donnell Agnes — †	636	housewife	41	"
C	O'Donnell Charles	636	longshoreman	37	"
D	DiGenio Annabile	636	pressman	57	"
E	DiGenio Antonetta — †	636	housewife	44	"
F	DiGenio Joseph	636	U S N	21	"
G	Marinelli Anthony	637	U S A	23	"
H	*Marinelli Joseph	637	retired	63	"
K	*Marinelli Josephine — †	637	housewife	53	"
L	Marinelli Rose — †	637	at home	26	"
M	Marinelli Severino	637	butcher	24	"
N	*DiFronzo Carmella — †	638	housewife	45	"
O	*DiFronzo Concetta — †	638	at home	86	391 Chelsea
P	DiFronzo Connie — †	638	secretary	22	391 "
R	DiFronzo Nicholas	638	U S A	21	391 "

Saratoga Street— Continued

s	DiFronzo Peter	638	storekeeper	48	391 Chelsea
t	Ambrogne Edward	638	chauffeur	52	here
u	Ambrogne Rose A—†	638	housewife	48	"
v	*DiOrio Vincenza—†	638	at home	82	"
w	Green Ella—†	639	bookkeeper	54	"
x	Green Mary L—†	639	at home	56	"
y	Martin Ann—†	639	nurse	46	"
z	Conte Grace W—†	641	housewife	48	"
	1445				
a	Conte Guilo	641	laborer	40	"
f	*Petrillo Carmen	645	chauffeur	32	"
g	Petrillo Nancy—†	645	housewife	25	"
h	*King Delia—†	647	at home	59	682 Benningt'n
k	King Hubert H	647	operator	20	682 "
l	*Lombardo Carmelia—†	647	housewife	38	here
m	Lombardo Nunzio	647	operator	50	"
n	Sanfilippo Salvatore	647	laborer	52	310 Chelsea
o	Sanfilippo Tina—†	647	housewife	39	310 "
p	*Daley Lillian—†	648	"	31	643 Saratoga
r	Daley Michael	648	shipper	38	643 "
s	Dutra Jerome J	648	cigarmaker	56	here
t	Dutra Mary A—†	648	housewife	59	"
u	Collins Alma E—†	648	storekeeper	22	"
v	Collins George E	648	U S A	26	"
w	Jones Herman W	648	shipper	50	"
x	Jones Rose M—†	648	housewife	53	"
y	Leonard John F	650	timekeeper	43	"
z	Leonard Teresa—†	650	housewife	42	"
	1446				
a	Hogan Alexander J	650	printer	42	"
b	Hogan Josephine M—†	650	housewife	42	"
c	Kirby John F	650	welder	36	"
d	Kirby Mary A—†	650	housewife	36	"
e	*McMullen Philomena—†	650	at home	92	"
f	Cronin Annie E—†	650	housewife	68	"
g	Dwelley Arthur F	652	foreman	37	"
h	Dwelley Josephine M—†	652	housewife	31	"
k	Dwelley Arthur G	652	electrician	62	"
l	Dwelley Donatella J—†	652	packer	26	"
m	Dwelley Elizabeth F—†	652	housewife	58	"
n	Dwelley George W	652	clerk	29	"

Saratoga Street—Continued

o	Herlihy James J	652	U S A	21	Revere
p	Kane Jennie—†	652	housewife	49	here
r	Kane Michael F	652	boilermaker	48	"
s	Kane Mildred M—†	652	clerk	22	"
t	*Medeiros Anthony	653	chauffeur	43	661 Saratoga
u	Medeiros Edward	653	laborer	24	661 "
v	*Medeiros Mary—†	653	housewife	41	661 "
w	Gioiosa Margaret—†	653		26	here
x	Gioiosa Michael	653	tester	29	"
y	Scarafone Anthony	653	U S A	24	"
z	Scarafone Domenick	653	"	27	"

1447

a	Scarafone Joseph	653	mechanic	32	"
b	Scarafone Romeo	653	U S A	22	"
c	*Joyce Anna S—†	rear 653	housewife	70	"
d	Joyce Patrick J	" 653	retired	84	"
e	Joyce William	" 653	engraver	42	"
f	Ward Florence R—†	" 653	at home	68	14 Grovenor rd
g	Denvro Lorraine—†	654	housewife	21	here
h	Denvro Paul	654	brazier	32	"
k	Foley Helen—†	654	inspector	27	658 Saratoga
l	Sullo Carolina—†	654	housewife	29	here
m	Sullo Marco	654	printer	29	"
n	Mambuca Mary—†	654	housewife	32	647 Saratoga
o	Mambuca Nicholas	654	shoeworker	29	647 "
r	Ward Katherine G—†	656	housewife	20	here
s	Ward Richard N	656	blacksmith	28	"
t	McCarthy Catherine—†	656	housewife	46	"
u	McCarthy Patrick	656	longshoreman	46	"
v	Morse Charles	656	U S N	21	"
w	Tierney Bridget A—†	656	housewife	52	"
x	Tierney Francis J	656	fireman	56	"
y	Wilkes Frederick C	658	driller	26	653 Saratoga
z	Wilkes Helen M—†	658	housewife	22	653 "

1448

a	DeNapoli Martin	658	painter	28	here
b	DeNapoli Ruth—†	658	housewife	25	"
c	Bonito Eugene	658	laborer	36	78 Meridian
d	Bonito Mary—†	658	housewife	31	78 "
e	Kinder Cecil F	658	laborer	41	324 Saratoga
f	Pupa Angelina—†	658	housewife	37	643 "

Page.	Letter.	FULL NAME.	Residence, Jan. 1, 1943.	Occupation.	Supposed Age.	Reported Residence, Jan. 1, 1942. Street and Number.

Saratoga Street—Continued

	G	Pupa Angelo	658	rigger	34	643 Saratoga
	H	Candla Emma—†	660	housewife	50	here
	K	Candla John	660	guard	52	"
	L	Ruggiero Carmen	660	laborer	50	"
	M	*Ruggiero Louisa—†	660	housewife	51	"
	N	Ruggiero Mary—†	660	at home	22	"
	O	Ruggiero Barbara—†	660	housewife	35	"
	P	Ruggiero Gennaro	660	chauffeur	38	"
	S	Kennedy Ruth M—†	661	at home	28	37 Wordsworth
	V	Sasso Joseph	663	electrician	54	here
	W	Sasso Mary A—†	663	at home	30	"
	X	Burnett Mary I—†	664	laundress	59	"
	Y	DeMark Mary—†	664	at home	65	"
	Z	Facey Harriet M—†	664	"	56	"

1449

	A	*Tsandaris Nicholas	664	laborer	60	"
	B	Ward Grace—†	664	operator	24	Winthrop
	D	Coleman Clara—†	665	storekeeper	68	437 Lubec
	E	Gomes Braz	666	seaman	38	254 Saratoga
	F	*Santos Frank F	666	laborer	50	254 "
	G	Benson John A	666	retired	69	here
	H	Benson Mary N—†	666	housewife	66	"
	K	Farmer Beatrice—†	666	"	41	"
	L	Farmer Edward H	666	pressman	41	"
	M	*White Dorothy M—†	667	waitress	23	"
	N	*White Ellen—†	667	housewife	49	"
	O	*White William	667	laborer	57	"
	P	DeLeo Alfred V	669	waiter	23	597 Benningt'n
	R	DeLeo Anna—†	669	housewife	23	597 "
	S	Sulkey Evelyn B—†	669	"	40	101 Decatur
	T	Sulkey William M	669	welder	44	101 "
	U	O'Regan Frederick B	670	physician	47	here
	V	O'Regan Lucille—†	670	housewife	28	Winthrop
	W	O'Regan William L	670	dentist	52	here
	X	Blaquiere Francis P	671	mechanic	33	"
	Y	Blaquiere Lillian M—†	671	housewife	26	"
	Z	Blaquiere Mary A—†	671	at home	67	"

1450

	A	Gallagher James A	671	welder	25	837 Saratoga
	B	Gallagher Julia M—†	671	housewife	21	519 Benningt'n
	C	Boudrot Delphine—†	673	at home	68	here

Saratoga Street — Continued

D	Dawler Joseph M	673	shipbuilder	43	here
E	Snow Arthur C	673	cook	61	"
F	Snow Sabina C—†	673	housewife	61	"
G	Cavaliere Nicholas	674	laborer	66	"
H	Cavaliere Rose—†	674	housewife	67	"
K	Cavaliere Frank O	674	carpenter	40	"
L	Cavaliere Josephine—†	674	housewife	36	"
M	Cavaliere Samuel O	674	painter	37	"
N	Nuzza Elizabeth—†	675	housewife	32	"
O	Nuzza Frank	675	rigger	37	"
P	Nuzza Marie—†	675	at home	72	"
R	Sturniolo Charles	675	laborer	45	"
S	Sturniolo James	675	U S A	23	"
T	Sturniolo Mary—†	675	housewife	44	"
U	Sturniolo Rose—†	675	operator	21	"
V	DeMeo Josephine—†	675	housewife	42	"
W	DeMeo Michael A	675	manager	46	"
X	DeMeo Michael B	675	U S A	23	"
Y	DeNapoli Frank	676	laborer	65	"
Z	DeNapoli Nicholas	676	chauffeur	24	"

1451

A	*DeNapoli Rose—†	676	housewife	67	"
B	Powers Anna—†	676	"	30	"
C	*Powers David	676	printer	29	"
D	Ruggiero Angelo J	677	laborer	20	"
E	Ruggiero Jennie—†	677	at home	51	"
F	Stefano Angelina—†	677	operator	29	"
G	Stefano Joseph	677	chef	31	"
H	Zitano James	677	laborer	43	"
K	Joyce Marion E—†	678	housewife	26	"
L	Joyce Thomas A	678	foreman	25	"
M	Salamone Alvira—†	678	clerk	22	"
N	*Salamone Joseph	678	barber	64	"
O	Salamone Lawrence	678	U S A	24	"
P	*Salamone Lillian—†	678	housewife	50	"
R	Salamone Virgil	678	machinist	21	"
S	Payne Anne M—†	678	at home	28	Winthrop
T	Vargus Ethel—†	679	housewife	25	643 Saratoga
U	Vargus James	679	assembler	25	643 "
V	Laundry Catherine L †	679	housewife	22	330 Meridian
W	Laundry George S	679	driller	24	330 "

31

Page	Letter	FULL NAME.	Residence, Jan. 1, 1943.	Occupation.	Supposed Age.	Reported Residence, Jan. 1, 1942. Street and Number.

Saratoga Street—Continued

	X	DeGrazia Martin	679	machinist	23	72 Edgewood
	Y	DeGrazia Rose—†	679	housewife	22	72 "
	Z	Giaraffa Gaetano	680	electrician	29	19 Pitts
1452						
	A	Giaraffa Mary—†	680	housewife	27	here
	B	Melkunas John	680	cook	30	"
	C	Melkunas Rita—†	680	housewife	26	"
	D	Smith Josephine—†	680	"	28	"
	E	Smith Wilfred	680	welder	34	"
	F	Nazzaro Carlo	681	counterman	25	"
	G	Nazzaro Louise—†	681	housewife	22	"
	H	Saviano Frank	681	shipfitter	32	"
	K	Saviano Isabelle—†	681	housewife	26	"
	L	Raymond Barbara—†	681	packer	37	"
	M	Raymond John	681	laborer	42	"
	N	Menninno Carmella—†	682	housewife	46	"
	O	Menninno Domenic	682	retired	50	"
	R	Beatrice Annie—†	687	at home	45	"
	S	Viveros Margaret—†	687	"	33	497 Sumner
	T	Newhook Hesta—†	689	"	76	here
	U	Newhook Mary—†	689	housewife	32	"
	V	Newhook Robert J	689	brazier	34	"
	W	Riley Edwin J	690	policeman	42	"
	X	Riley Florence J—†	690	housewife	42	"
	Y	Turner Margaret—†	691	"	56	"
	Z	Turner Robert C	691	mechanic	58	"
1453						
	A	Turner Jean—†	691	packer	51	"
	B	Turner Jean L—†	691	stenographer	21	"
	C	Watson Agnes L—†	691	saleswoman	47	"
	D	Turner Mary D—†	692	housewife	53	"
	E	Turner Rose E—†	692	at home	87	"
	F	Turner William L	692	engineer	58	"
	G	Butt Mae N—†	694	at home	60	"
	H	Turner Edwin J	694	U S A	33	"
	K	Turner Flora A—†	694	at home	67	"
	L	Turner Florence M—†	694	stenographer	32	"
	M	Turner Mae V—†	694	"	36	"
	N	Fife Mary A—†	696	auditor	65	"
	O	DeAngelis Grace—†	696	at home	34	"
	P	DeAngelis Joseph	696	optician	40	"

Saratoga Street Continued

R	Knudson Evelyn †	696	clerk	36	here	
S	Kelley Anna †	702	at home	45	"	
T	Kelley Dorothy †	702	operator	25	"	
U	Kelley Edmund	702	U S N	23	"	
V	Zinna Anthony	704	U S A	22	"	
W	Zinna Connie †	704	bookbinder	27	"	
X	Zinna Frances †	704	operator	30	"	
Y*	Zinna Nunzio	704	candyworker	60	"	
Z	Zinna Vincent	704	U S A	25	"	

1454

B	Thompson Amelia N †	710	housewife	43	"	
C	Thompson Newell L	710	chauffeur	43	"	

William F. McClellan Highway

F	Forster Gertrude †	47	clerk	24	47 Saratoga	
G	Forster William J	47	U S A	24	126 Lexington	
H	Keenan Edward	47	machinist	52	here	
K	Keenan Mary J †	47	housewife	42	"	
L	McGilvery Anna †	47	"	21	"	
M	McGilvery Earl	47	machinist	26	"	
N	Driscoll Bridget †	49	at home	77	"	
O	Colarusso Enrico	49	laborer	33	"	
P	Colarusso Phyllis †	49	secretary	30	"	
R	Pereira Joaquim B	49	weaver	39	"	
S	Pereira Marie B †	49	housewife	25	"	
T	Puopolo Domenick	51	tailor	33	"	
U	Puopolo Mary †	51	housewife	29	"	
V	Laffey Eileen †	51	"	29	"	
W	Laffey John	51	boilermaker	33	"	
X*	Santos Albert T	51	laborer	38	"	
Y*	Santos John F	51	fisherman	63	"	
Z*	Santos Mary T †	51	housewife	58	"	

1455

A	Granara Anna E †	53	"	40	"	
B	Granara Richard L	53	chauffeur	41	"	
C	DelBianco Ernest A	53	U S N	30	"	
D	DelBianco Kathryn †	53	clerk	30	"	
E	Reilly Catherine E †	53	housewife	31	"	
F	Reilly James J	53	salesman	35	"	
G	Altieri Edith †	55	housewife	26	"	

J—14

William F. McClellan Highway—Continued

	H	Altieri Ferdinand	55	chauffeur	26	here
	K	Monz Joseph	55	machinist	48	"
	L	Paolucci Louis	55	laborer	73	"
	M	*Paolucci Mary—†	55	housewife	70	"
	N	O'Connell Anna M—†	55	"	48	"
	O	O'Connell Edward F	55	calker	47	"
	P	O'Connell Edward F, jr	55	clerk	24	"
	R	O'Connell John J	55	agent	20	"
	S	Henneberry Edward F	57	U S N	23	"
	T	Henneberry Florence N—†	57	housewife	48	"
	U	Henneberry John T	57	policeman	49	"
	V	Henneberry Madeline N—†	57	inspector	21	"
	W	Conroy Barbara—†	57	housewife	61	"
	X	Conroy Bernadette A—†	57	clerk	24	"
	Y	Conroy Helen B—†	57	"	29	"
	Z	Conroy Joseph M	57	U S A	31	"
1456						
	A	Conroy Mary N—†	57	clerk	34	"
	B	Puleo Blanche—†	57	housewife	36	"
	C	Puleo Robert	57	electrician	36	"
	D	Campbell Annie—†	59	housewife	47	"
	E	Zaverson Anna—†	59	domestic	42	"
	F	Zaverson John J	59	mechanic	40	"
	G	Gallagher William F	59	laborer	78	"
	H	Gallagher William F, jr	59	shipfitter	41	"
	K	Smith Catherine—†	59	housekeeper	45	"
	L	Smith Ethel—†	59	stenographer	26	"

Ward 1—Precinct 15

CITY OF BOSTON

LIST OF RESIDENTS
20 YEARS OF AGE AND OVER

(NON-CITIZENS INDICATED BY ASTERISK)
(FEMALES INDICATED BY DAGGER)

AS OF

JANUARY 1, 1943

JOSEPH F. TIMILTY, *Chairman*
FREDERIC E. DOWLING, *Secretary*
WILLIAM A. MOTLEY, JR.
FRANCIS B. McKINNEY
EVERETT R. PROUT

Listing Board.

CITY OF BOSTON PRINTING DEPARTMENT

Page.	Letter	FULL NAME.	Residence, Jan. 1, 1943.	Occupation.	Supposed Age.	Reported Residence, Jan. 1, 1942. Street and Number.

1500

Bennington Street

B	Carty Mary — †	519	housewife	48	here
C	Carty Stephen J	519	machinist	51	"
D	Micarelli Anthony	521	presser	23	629 Saratoga
E	Micarelli Antoinetta — †	521	housewife	23	629 "
F	Rothwell Ethel M — †	521	clerk	43	here
G	Scaramella Christina — †	523	inspector	33	"
H	Scaramella Dominica — †	523	housewife	67	"
L	Marmo Anthony	527	rigger	25	"
M	Marmo Fred	527	grinder	23	"
N	Marmo Jane — †	527	inspector	48	"
O	Marmo Nicholas	527	loom fixer	53	"
P	Traina Angelo	527	clerk	21	"
R	Traina Annie — †	527	housewife	42	"
S	Traina Joseph	527	U S A	20	"
T	Traina Salvatore	527	physician	24	"
U	Long Bridget — †	527	housewife	53	"
V	Long Patrick J	527	rigger	60	"
W	Carideo Amelia — †	529	housewife	28	91 London
X	Carideo Frank	529	checker	30	91 "
Y	Alterisio Angelina — †	529	housewife	67	here
Z	Alterisio Antonio	529	laborer	67	"

1501

A	Alterisio James	529	at home	24	"
B	Alterisio Maria — †	529	candymaker	44	"
C	Caranfo Christina — †	529	housewife	24	"
D	Caranfo Dominic	529	finisher	59	"
E	Caranfo Ginevro	529	"	32	"
F	*Caranfo Umberto	529	"	23	"
G	Carino George	531	clerk	32	955 Saratoga
H	Carino Goldie — †	531	housewife	26	955 "
K	Gay Anna M — †	531	operator	20	here
L	Gay John J	531	U S A	21	"
M	Gay John W	531	chauffeur	49	"
N	Gay Theresa — †	531	housewife	49	"
O	Gay Thomas W	531	U S A	22	"
P	Tierney Annie — †	531	millhand	46	"
R	Clemente Caroline — †	531	at home	22	"
S	Clemente Louis	531	welder	30	"
T	Clemente Martha — †	531	housewife	30	"
U	O'Brien Helen — †	533	"	26	"

2

Bennington Street—Continued

v	*O'Brien William	533	clerk	29	here
w	Winston Alma P —†	533	stenographer	23	"
x	Winston Edward F	533	shipfitter	58	"
y	Winston Edward F, jr	533	student	21	"
z	Winston Sadie A —†	533	housewife	51	"
	1502				
a	Winston Thomas A	533	letter carrier	57	"
b	Holden Gertrude —†	533	packer	30	"
c	Holden Michael	533	repairman	25	"
d	Holden William	533	operator	23	"
e	*Morse Mary E—†	533	housewife	53	"
f	Morse William	533	chauffeur	46	"
g	Sands James	537	mechanic	51	"
h	Sands Mary B—†	537	housewife	56	"
k	Lewis Miriam C—†	537	packer	28	"
l	Lewis Miriam E—†	537	housewife	51	"
m	Lewis William A	537	inspector	53	"
n	Gundersen Dorothy S—†	537	housewife	38	"
o	Gundersen Tallman H	537	rigger	44	"
p	Visconti Anna—†	549	housewife	36	"
r	Visconti Anthony	549	plumber	36	"
s	Guerra Frank	549	laborer	47	"
t	Guerra Mary—†	549	housewife	43	"
u	Guerra Mary L—†	549	stitcher	21	"
v	Lazzaro Helen —†	549	housewife	24	"
w	*Lazzaro Maria—†	549	at home	60	"
x	Lazzaro Nicholas	549	plumber	26	"
y	Previte Frank	551	chauffeur	51	"
z	Previte Irene —†	551	housewife	44	"
	1503				
a	Brady Joseph P	553	yardman	27	"
b	Brady Margaret —†	553	housewife	28	"
c	Hankard Margaret E —†	553	"	37	35 S Munroe ter
d	Hankard Walter J	553	policeman	37	35 "
e	Hyland Emma I —†	555	housewife	55	here
f	Hyland Francis W	555	U S N	24	"
g	Hyland Frederick D	555	designer	52	"
h	Hyland William	555	retired	77	"
l	Newby Thomas H	557	"	93	"
m	Gilgan Harriet A —†	557	housewife	60	"
n	Gilgan James E	557	retired	65	"

3

Page.	Letter	FULL NAME.	Residence, Jan. 1, 1943.	Occupation.	Supposed Age.	Reported Residence, Jan. 1, 1942. Street and Number.

Bennington Street Continued

	o	Cook Georgianna M—†	559	teacher	35	here
	p	Scott George T	559	retired	64	"
	r	Budd Emily—†	559	at home	82	"
	s	Budd Emily E—†	559	millhand	55	"
	t	Budd Violet R—†	559	clerk	42	"
	u	McLaughlin Elizabeth—†	561	houseworker	41	"
	v	McLaughlin Joseph	561	shipper	41	"
	w	Laundry George S	561	printer	51	"
	x	Laundry Gladys—†	561	packer	26	"
	y	Laundry Helen—†	561	housewife	49	"
	z	Laundry Mabel—†	561	laborer	21	"
		1504				
	A	Donovan James R	563	shipfitter	22	"
	B	Donovan Margaret G—†	563	housewife	49	"
	c	Donovan Richard D	563	U S A	24	"
	D	Donovan Richard J	563	machinist	51	"
	E	Donovan Rita M—†	563	secretary	26	"
	F	Farmer Hannah T—†	563	at home	51	"
	K	Clark Martha—†	569	housekeeper	55	"
	L	McCulpa John H	569	retired	71	"
	M	Hyde Letitia—†	569	at home	61	513 Orleans
	N	McDonough Catherine—†	569	housewife	36	687 Saratoga
	o	McDonough Miles	569	fireman	36	687 "
	P	*Fernandez Anthony	571	millhand	50	here
	R	*Fernandez Clementina—†	571	factoryhand	45	"
	s	Barry Ellen M—†	571	housewife	32	"
	T	Barry Lawrence J	571	clerk	35	"
	u	Warner Ernest C	571	U S A	34	"
	v	Lyons Gerald	573	U S N	36	"
	w	Lyons Ruth L—†	573	housewife	34	"
	x	Mortimer Catherine G—†	573	"	39	"
	y	Mortimer Catherine M—†	573	bookkeeper	22	"
	z	Mortimer John	573	pipefitter	38	"
		1505				
	A	Mortimer Mary A—†	573	housewife	72	"
	B	Mortimer Peter	573	U S A	31	"
	c	Burns John J	575	boilermaker	34	148 Coleridge
	D	Burns Mary R—†	575	housewife	29	148 "
	E	Coletta Antonio	577	cabinetmaker	50	91 Trenton
	F	Coletta Joseph	577	U S A	23	91 "

4

Bennington Street Continued

		FULL NAME.	Residence, Jan. 1, 1943.	Occupation	Supposed Age.	Reported Residence, Jan. 1, 1942. Street and Number
	G	Coletta Nicholas	577	factoryhand	22	91 Trenton
	H	Coletta Rudolph	577	student	20	91 "
	K	Coletta Theresa —†	577	housewife	51	91 "
	L	Ashton Daisy —†	579	spinner	51	here
	M	Rossano Frank	579	contractor	58	"
	N	Rossano Louis	579	U S A	23	"
	O*	Rossano Madeline —†	579	housewife	57	"
	P	Ambrose Joseph	583	painter	22	"
	R	Ambrose Josephine —†	583	housewife	39	"
	S	Sullivan Ellen C —†	585	clerk	34	"
	T	Sullivan John J	585	retired	64	"
	U	Sullivan Mary E —†	585	housewife	60	"
	V	McCauley John	587	U S A	42	"
	W*	McCauley Mary —†	587	housewife	75	"
	X	McCauley Mary —†	587	operator	38	"
	Y	Maples Elva —†	589	housewife	36	"
	Z	Maples Joseph	589	operator	41	"

1506

		FULL NAME.	Residence, Jan. 1, 1943.	Occupation	Supposed Age.	Reported Residence, Jan. 1, 1942. Street and Number
	A	Hamilton Elizabeth D—†	591	housewife	40	"
	B	Hamilton John A	591	salesman	40	"
	C	Smith Mary —†	593	housewife	58	"
	D	Smith Michael	593	engineer	60	"
	E	Leoshena Alexander	595	factoryhand	27	"
	F	Leoshena Ann —†	595	housewife	28	"
	G	Cassetina Catherine —†	595	"	66	100 Paris
	H	Cassetina Joseph	595	retired	73	here
	K	Gannon Frances R —†	595	housewife	36	"
	L	Gannon Mark L	595	storekeeper	45	"
	M	Allegra Joseph	597	millwright	25	"
	N	Allegra Mary —†	597	housewife	25	"
	O	Marcella Benedict	597	laborer	31	"
	P	Marcella Frances —†	597	housewife	27	"
	R	Connolly Mary —†	599	"	78	"
	S	Curtin Thomas W	599	retired	70	"
	T	Sanderson Mary —†	599	clerk	53	"
	U	McLean Grace E —†	601	housewife	34	"
	V	McLean William A	601	policeman	37	"
	W	Gormley Catherine —†	601	saleswoman	45	"
	X	Gormley James F	601	fireman	48	"
	Y	Gormley Mary —†	601	housewife	80	"

Bennington Street— Continued

z	Miles Helen F—†	603	at home	35	Revere
1507						
A	O'Neil Margaret—†	603	"	72	here
B	Wood Laura B—†	603	housewife	47	"
C	Wood Randall E	603	painter	47	"
D	McGee Catherine A—†	603	clerk	37	575 Benningt'n
E	McGee Mary A—†	603	housewife	41	575 "
F	Dorso Angelina—†	605	"	29	here
G	Dorso Anthony	605	longshoreman	34	"
H	Schieb Margaret—†	605	housewife	43	"
K	Schieb William	605	electrician	43	"
L	White George	605	U S A	28	"
M	*White Henrietta—†	605	housewife	55	"
N	White Loretta—†	605	at home	23	"
O	White Rose—†	605	clerk	21	"
R	*Pennampede Anna—†	607	housewife	43	"
S	Pennampede Fabio	607	machinist	47	"
P	Ripandelli Giralamo	607	"	46	"
T	Tannone Andrew	607	U S A	26	260 Paris
U	Tannone Phyllis—†	607	housewife	28	260 "
V	Caprio Mary—†	609	"	29	here
W	Caprio Walter	609	factoryhand	29	"
X	Carresi Catherine—†	611	housewife	38	"
Y	Carresi Nora—†	611	electrician	20	"
Z	Carresi Pasquale	611	shipfitter	38	"
1508						
A	Smith Christina—†	613	housewife	26	101 Saratoga
B	Smith William H	613	U S N	30	here
C	Hill Mary—†	613	housekeeper	67	"
D	Mackey Joseph	615	machinist	27	"
E	Mackey Rita—†	615	housewife	25	"
F	Bois Henry	615	ropemaker	42	"
G	Bois Madeline M—†	615	housewife	42	"
H	Doyle Dorothy M—†	615	"	37	"
K	Doyle Leo F	615	typist	39	"
L	Howard Joseph	617	clerk	63	"
M	Howard William	617	retired	56	"
N	Melanson Adeline—†	617	operator	41	"
O	Melanson Melvin J	617	chauffeur	43	"
P	Murray Kathleen—†	617	librarian	39	"
R	Silva Mary A—†	617	at home	69	"

Bennington Street Continued

s	Murphy Edward J	617A	clerk	61	here
t	Galzerano Adeline —†	619	"	26	"
u	Galzerano Giuseppi	619	laborer	61	"
v	Galzerano Nancy —†	619	clerk	21	"
w	Galzerano Samuel	619	U S A	23	"
x	Galzerano Viola —†	619	housewife	29	"
y	Zocco Nellie —†	619	"	41	"
z	Zocco Thomas	619	meatcutter	45	"

1509

A	Treanor Charles H	619	undertaker	42	"
B	Treanor Louise G —†	619	housewife	42	"
c	Treanor Louise L —†	619	clerk	20	"
E	Lewis Frank	633	grinder	35	N Hampshire
F	Lewis Marion —†	633	housewife	30	"
H	Smith Sarah G —†	635	"	68	here
K	Smith William G	635	retired	69	"
L	D'Ambrosio Antonio	641	mechanic	33	"
M	D'Ambrosio Jennie —†	641	housewife	32	"
N	D'Ambrosio Alice —†	641A	millhand	30	"
o*	D'Ambrosio Amelia —†	641A	housewife	64	"
P	D'Ambrosio Carmen	641A	chauffeur	65	"
R	D'Ambrosio Leo	641A	foreman	60	"
s	D'Ambrosio Nancy —†	641A	millhand	24	"
T	D'Ambrosio Susan —†	641A	clerk	27	"
U	Molino Ettore	641A	tailor	47	"
V	Molino Nino	641A	student	21	"
W	Molino Rose —†	641A	housewife	45	"
X	DiGregorio Albert A	643	laborer	32	"
Y	DiGregorio Carmela —†	643	housewife	67	"
z	DiGregorio Natalina V —†	643	"	27	"

1510

A	DiGregorio Vincenzo	643	foreman	71	"
B	Picardi Amelia —†	643	at home	25	"
c	Picardi George	643	foreman	31	"
D*	Picardi Giacomo	643	retired	79	"
E*	Picardi Lucy —†	643	housewife	70	"
F*	Santosuosso Elizabeth —†	643	at home	88	"
G	Santosuosso Evelyn L —†	643	"	47	"
H	Santosuosso Principio	643	editor	51	"
K	DiGregorio Irene M —†	645	clerk	20	"
L	DiGregorio Jerome C	645	operator	54	"

7

Bennington Street—Continued

	M	DiGregorio Rose—†	645	housewife	50	here
	N	Skane Margaret E—†	645	packer	22	"
	O	Skane Margaret M †	645	housewife	51	"
	P	Skane William	645	operator	51	"
	R	Skane William J, jr	645	U S A	21	"
	S	Thompson Delia A—†	645	housewife	51	"
	T	Thompson George H	645	custodian	51	"
	U	Bagley Hugh J	647	retired	73	"
	V	Cody Catherine †	647	housewife	34	"
	W	Cody Joseph	647	brazier	43	"
	X	Peterson Mary L—†	647	housekeeper	63	"
	Y	Swift Margaret A—†	651	housewife	56	94 Byron
	Z	Swift Robert	651	boilermaker	56	94 "
1511						
	A	*Minichiello Elizabeth †	651	housewife	33	here
	B	Minichiello Gaetano	651	laborer	45	"
	C	Souza Albert	651	machinist	29	Cambridge
	D	Souza Gabriel	651	housewife	29	"
	E	*Russell Ellen—†	653	"	60	27 Wordsworth
	F	Russell Thomas	653	fireman	59	27 "
	G	McDonough Alfred	653	longshoreman	33	here
	H	McDonough Virginia—†	653	housewife	30	"
	K	*DiMinico James	653	chauffeur	44	"
	L	*DiMinico Mary †	653	housewife	36	"
	M	Bagley Dorothy—†	673	storekeeper	34	"
	N	Briscoe Alfred	673	operator	66	"
	O	Briscoe Catherine †	673	housewife	67	"
	P	DePalma Dorothy †	675	"	30	"
	R	DePalma Nicholas	675	operator	30	"
	S	Hudson Isabelle A †	675	housewife	37	"
	T	Hudson Roy A	675	chauffeur	37	"
	U	Donatelli Fernando	675	U S A	27	"
	V	Donatelli Lydia †	675	housewife	50	"
	W	*Donatelli William	675	tailor	50	"
	X	Pascucci Emilio	677	plumber	41	"
	Y	Pascucci Grace—†	677	housewife	39	"
	Z	Sullivan James	677	seaman	36	Somerville
1512						
	A	Sullivan Lillian—†	677	housewife	35	"
	C	Castagnola Alfonse	681	storekeeper	43	here
	D	Castagnola Aurelia—†	681	housewife	43	"

8

Bennington Street Continued

E	Moe Christian C	683	clerk	23	here
F	Moe Rosa C — †	683	housewife	53	"
G	Sorensen Freda — †	683	"	56	"
H	Sorensen Herman W	683	clerk	33	"
K	Sorensen John W	683	manager	59	"
L	Sorensen Norman C	683	U S A	28	"
M	Pinkham Ella B — †	687	housewife	51	"
N	Pinkham Harold A	687	laborer	30	"
O	*Uliano Joseph	687	factoryhand	59	"
P	*Uliano Mary — †	687	housewife	52	"
R	Scotti Mary — †	691	"	30	"
S	Scotti Walter	691	machinist	29	"
T	*Gallo Filomena — †	691	at home	81	"
U	Sena Gioechina	691	laborer	54	"
V	Sena Pompelia — †	691	housewife	53	"
W	Cancellieri Blanche — †	691	"	31	"
X	Cancellieri Joseph	691	clerk	32	"
Y	Sanford Mary A — †	693	housewife	66	"
Z	Sanford Patrick F	693	engineer	67	"

1513

A	Murphy Jean — †	693	typist	34	"
B	Murphy Walter	693	laborer	63	"
C	Cancellieri Eleanor M — †	693	housewife	28	"
D	Cancellieri Romeo G	693	carpenter	27	35 Falcon
E	Joyce Florence — †	695	housewife	30	here
F	Joyce John A	695	manager	32	"
G	Boudreau Daniel J	695	U S A	28	"
H	Boudreau Mary E — †	695	housewife	64	"
K	Boudreau Mary M — †	695	librarian	30	"
L	Boudreau William P	695	B F D	66	"
M	Carbon Christine — †	695	housewife	45	"
N	Carbon Francis W	695	rigger	37	"
O	Mainiero Anna — †	697	housewife	26	"
P	Mainiero Arthur	697	salesman	27	"
R	Altavilla Gaetana — †	697	housewife	87	"
S	Iapicca Bernardine — †	697	clerk	27	"
T	Iapicca Felix	697	U S A	23	"
U	*Iapicca Rose — †	697	housewife	52	"
V	Iapicca Vincenzo	697	barber	52	"
W	Powers Louise B — †	697	housewife	54	"
X	Powers Patrick J	697	clerk	58	"

Page.	Letter.	FULL NAME.	Residence, Jan. 1, 1943.	Occupation.	Supposed Age.	Reported Residence, Jan. 1, 1942. Street and Number.

Bennington Street — Continued

	Y	Powers Richard	697	U S N	31	here
	z	Curtin Eileen A—†	699	housewife	60	"
1514						
	A	Curtin John J	699	coppersmith	60	"
	B	Boyle Rose M—†	699	clerk	50	"
	c	McCarthy Gerald J	699	lawyer	48	"
	D	Green Charles	699	U S A	22	"
	E	Green Charles E	699	retired	63	"
	F	Green Elizabeth—†	699	housewife	54	"
	G	Green Helen—†	699	factoryhand	21	"
	H	Green Rita—†	699	stenographer	27	"
	K	Rogers Helen C—†	701	housewife	43	"
	L	Rogers William J	701	operator	58	"
	M	Rogers Henry D	701	retired	66	"
	N	Rogers Thomas M	701	stenotypist	68	"
	O	Porter Helen J—†	701	operator	25	"
	P	Porter James P	701	U S A	38	"
	R	Porter Joseph M	701	clerk	38	"
	s	Porter Margaret E—†	701	operator	35	"
	T	Porter S Agnes—†	701	teacher	32	"
	U	*Lacascia Anna—†	703	housewife	71	"
	V	Lacascia Salvatore	703	baker	30	"
	W	Fitzpatrick Dorothy M—†	703	bookkeeper	32	"
	X	Fitzpatrick Edward L	703	factoryhand	22	"
	Y	Fitzpatrick Gertrude R—†	703	typist	28	"
	z	Fitzpatrick Julia T—†	703	housewife	62	"
1515						
	A	Chimpa Emilio	703	springmaker	34	"
	B	Chimpa Jennie—†	703	housewife	34	"
	c	Mirotta Rose—†	703	tailor	51	"
	D	Melino Angela—†	705	housewife	43	"
	E	Melino Anthony	705	barber	55	"
	F	Testa Anna—†	705	housewife	38	"
	G	Testa Frank	705	salesman	38	"
	H	*Vilardo Catherine—†	705	housewife	64	"
	K	Vilardo Stephen	705	retired	76	"
	L	Pomfret Jennie—†	705	housewife	33	"
	M	Pomfret Timothy	705	electrician	39	"
	N	Dillon Joseph P	707	letter carrier	34	"
	O	Dillon Mildred—†	707	housewife	33	"
	P	McKay Elizabeth—†	707	"	65	"

Page.	Letter.	FULL NAME.	Residence, Jan. 1, 1943.	Occupation	Supposed Age	Reported Residence, Jan. 1, 1942. Street and Number.

Bennington Street Continued

	R	McKay Henry F	707	U S N	41	here
	S	McKay Mathew W	707	manager	37	"
	T	McDonald Alma M †	707	housewife	40	"
	U	McDonald John P	707	laborer	42	"
	V	*Goss Briget — †	709	at home	77	"
	W	Whalen Mary — †	709	"	79	"
	X	Wickstrom Josephine — †	709	detective	44	"
	Y	Boudreau Helen M — †	709	housewife	43	"
	Z	Boudreau Richard W	709	U S A	23	"

1516

	A	Boudreau William T	709	policeman	43	"
	B	Boudreau William T. jr	709	U S N	21	"
	C	Calorusso Helena — †	709	housewife	44	"
	D	Calorusso Joseph	709	foreman	45	"
	E	Calorusso Joseph	709	laborer	21	"
	F	Calorusso Mary — †	709	clerk	24	"

Byron Street

	G	*Picciulo Amelia — †	146	housewife	61	here
	H	Picciulo Carmino	146	U S A	37	"
	K	Picciulo Isabella — †	146	floorwoman	24	"
	L	Picciulo Stefano	146	retired	71	"
	M	Sexton Albert J	150	clerk	53	"
	N	Sexton Frederick B	150	retired	43	"
	O	Sexton Mary J — †	150	housekeeper	64	"
	P	Cutlip Warren	163	machinist	21	14 Austin
	R	McPhee John J	163	shipfitter	44	here
	S	McPhee Joseph H	163	U S A	23	"
	T	McPhee Marcella — †	163	housewife	46	"
	U	Fahey Martha — †	163	"	33	187 Brooks
	V	Gleason John T	163	guard	50	187 "
	W	Sacco Angelo	165	printer	37	here
	X	Sacco Mary — †	165	housewife	29	"
	Y	Davis Isabelle — †	165	"	41	"
	Z	Davis Stephen	165	fisherman	49	"

1517

	A	Matera Fred	165	painter	42	"
	B	Matera Louise — †	165	housewife	42	"
	C	Gould Mary A — †	167	"	32	"
	D	Gould Stephen	167	seaman	34	"

11

Page.	Letter.	FULL NAME.	Residence, Jan. 1, 1943.	Occupation.	Supposed Age.	Reported Residence, Jan. 1, 1942. Street and Number.

Byron Street—Continued

	E	Anderson Edwin L	167A	inspector	29	163 Byron
	F	Anderson Ruth M—†	167A	"	29	163 "
	G	Elkins Charles F	167A	retired	58	Maine
	K	Murphy Joseph H	169A	driller	39	here
	L	Murphy Margaret A—†	169A	housewife	39	"
	M	Ryan Elizabeth—†	198	"	46	"
	N	Ryan Margaret A—†	198	stenographer	23	"
	O	Ryan Marian—†	198	operator	20	"
	P	Ryan Michael J	198	longshoreman	52	"
	R	Ryan Michael J, jr	198	U S A	21	"
	S	Norton James T	200	laborer	66	"
	T	Norton William F	200	buyer	52	"
	U	Norton Mary E—†	201	housewife	64	"
	V	Norton Mary E—†	201	teacher	29	"
	W	Norton Thomas M	201	retired	74	"
	X	Niland Anna M—†	202	at home	74	"
	Y	Niland Thomas A	202	realtor	69	Phillipston
	Z	Lyons Alice M—†	206	housewife	47	here

1518

	A	Lyons Charles F	206	electrician	45	"
	B	Cotter Lillian M—†	206	factoryhand	45	"
	C	Mendoza Bartholomew	206	laborer	70	"
	D	Mendoza John J	206	U S A	31	"
	E*	Mendoza Mary L—†	206	housewife	64	"
	F	Noonan Alice—†	206	clerk	55	"
	G	DiNuccio Caroline—†	210	housewife	43	"
	H	DiNuccio Harry	210	pipecoverer	53	"
	K	Cahill Herbert J	210	fireman	42	"
	L	Cahill Mary L—†	210	housewife	42	"

Coleridge Street

	N	Laskey Jerome	120	policeman	45	here
	O	Laskey Margaret—†	120	housewife	41	"
	P	Thompson Alice—†	124	inspector	22	"
	R	Thompson Mary—†	124	housewife	53	"
	S	Thompson Mary—†	124	packer	27	"
	T	Thompson Robert E	124	U S A	31	"
	U	Thompson Sarah C—†	124	teacher	28	"
	V	Thompson Winfield S	124	U S A	20	"
	W	Whalen Thomas J	124	"	25	"

Page.	Letter.	FULL NAME.	Residence, Jan. 1, 1943.	Occupation.	Supposed Age.	Reported Residence, Jan. 1, 1942. Street and Number.

Coleridge Street Continued

	Letter	FULL NAME	Residence	Occupation	Age	Reported Residence
	x	Whalen Winifred B—†	124	housewife	24	here
	y	Page Arthur J	126	retired	83	"
	z	Page Dorothy J †	126	teacher	37	"

1519

	Letter	FULL NAME	Residence	Occupation	Age	Reported Residence
	a	Page Muriel M †	126	"	34	"
	b	Page Sarah H †	126	housewife	75	"
	c	McNabb Hugh	130	policeman	44	"
	d	McNabb Madeline †	130	housewife	40	"
	e	O'Brien Edward A	134	retired	61	"
	f	O'Brien Herbert J	134	U S A	24	"
	g	O'Brien Nicholas E	134	U S C G	26	"
	h	Fairclough Agnes—†	134	housewife	69	"
	k	Roche Elizabeth M—†	136	"	47	"
	l	Roche Michael T	136	guard	55	"
	m	Roche William	136	draftsman	23	"
	n	Boyan Helen—†	138	housewife	22	73 Homer
	o	Boyan Joseph	138	mechanic	23	28 Tremlett
	p	Sloan Charles	138	laborer	54	here
	r	Sloan Rose L—†	138	housewife	51	"
	s	McCarthy Geraldine—†	148	"	20	96 Lexington
	t	McCarthy Paul J	148	clerk	27	218 "
	u	Mealey Ann B †	148	housewife	29	here
	v	Mealey Martin J	148	shipper	35	"
	w	Gardner Catherine—†	148	clerk	20	595 Benningt'n
	x	Gardner Lucy—†	148	housewife	42	595 "
	y	Scigliano Frances—†	149	"	30	here
	z	Scigliano Frank	149	manager	34	"

1520

	Letter	FULL NAME	Residence	Occupation	Age	Reported Residence
	c*	McGonigle Phillip	149	retired	65	"
	a	Scigliano Jean	149	laborer	28	"
	b	Scigliano Joseph	149	U S A	29	"
	d	Anderson John E	156	mechanic	56	"
	e	Anderson Lilly E †	156	housewife	49	"
	f	Barnard Charles	156	mechanic	27	252 E Eagle
	g	Barnard Chester	156	foreman	53	here
	h	Barnard Marion †	156	housewife	52	"
	k	Musil Andrew H	157	shipwright	63	"
	l	Musil Letitia †	157	housewife	56	"
	m	Musil Thomas H	157	U S A	28	"
	o	Leahy James H	163	electrician	44	"
	p	Norton Thomas P	163	retired	71	835 Saratoga

13

Coleridge Street—Continued

	R	Vallam Evelyn †	163	housewife	39	here
	S	Parker Catherine G †	163	"	46	"
	T	Nagle Harriett †	165	"	54	"
	U	Nagle Horace	165	shipper	61	"
	V	Nagle Mary †	165	clerk	32	"
	W	Cantwell Benjamin	167	retired	63	"
	X	Cantwell Rose †	167	housewife	63	"
	Y	Brown Carrie †	169	"	54	"
	Z	Brown Ernest	169	checker	55	"
1521						
	A	Scigliano Alfred T	171	lawyer	42	"
	B	Scigliano Anna E †	171	housewife	38	"
	C	Shelton Constance I †	173	student	31	"
	D	*Shelton Elizabeth †	173	housewife	73	"
	F	McGunigle John E	176	foreman	41	"
	G	McGunigle Robina †	176	housewife	36	"
	H	McIsaac Francis C	177	electrician	46	"
	K	McIsaac Loretta †	177	housewife	43	"
	L	Nelson William	177	U S A	22	"

Cowper Street

	O	Donahue Catherine †	93	housekeeper	34	here
	P	Donahue Charles	93	longshoreman	38	"
	R	Donahue Fred	93	U S A	23	"
	S	Donahue Mildred †	93	clerk	32	"
	T	Donahue Thomas F	93	watchman	69	"
	U	Fraters Rita D †	93	timekeeper	26	"
	V	Barron Edward W	93	U S N	20	"
	W	Barron Elizabeth A †	93	housekeeper	80	"
	X	Barron Ellen E †	93	clerk	25	"
	Y	Barron Ellen P †	93	housewife	52	"
	Z	Dileso Margaret †	94	"	37	"
1522						
	A	Dileso Nicola	94	laborer	48	"
	B	Roach George H	94	longshoreman	50	"
	C	Roach Richard W	94	radioman	23	"
	D	Roach William A	94	longshoreman	52	"
	E	Trunfio Conchetta †	94	housewife	35	"
	F	Trunfio Paul	94	laborer	46	"

Cowper Street Continued

	G	Balboni John	95	polisher	26	here
	H	Balboni Ruth—†	95	housewife	26	"
	K	Gagin Henry A	95	clerk	40	"
	L	Gagin Josephine—†	95	housewife	31	"
	M	Cooper Albert H	97	retired	57	"
	N	Cooper Eva A—†	97	housewife	52	"
	O	Fenton John R	97	retired	80	"
	P	Trautz Margaret C †	97	housewife	69	"
	R	Trautz John G	97	rigger	39	"
	S	Trautz Mary M—†	97	housewife	38	"
	T	Spadaro George	98	sorter	25	300 Chelsea
	U	Spadaro Louise—†	98	saleswoman	22	300 "
	V	Torredimare Adelaide—†	98	stitcher	43	here
	W	Torredimare Anthony	98	U S M C	21	"
	X	Torredimare Frank	98	barber	46	"
	Y	Torredimare Rose—†	98	teacher	26	"
	Z	McWilliams Mary A—†	99	housewife	75	"
1523						
	A	McWilliams Mary A—†	99	operator	39	"
	B	Doherty Anna M †	99	housewife	50	"
	C	Doherty Edward J	99	millhand	23	"
	D	Doherty John P	99	stevedore	59	"
	E	Doherty John W	99	millhand	25	"
	F	Doherty Mary M †	99	secretary	21	"
	G	Lowell Ella—†	99	housekeeper	83	"
	H	Scott Dorothy †	100	housewife	27	"
	K	Scott Herbert	100	millhand	29	"
	L	Pantos Mary—†	100	housewife	32	"
	M	Pantos Stephen	100	operator	43	"
	P	Francis Joseph L	104	carpenter	26	140 Wordsworth
	R	Francis Maria E †	104	housewife	26	140 "
	S	Williams Agnes M †	104	"	50	here
	T	Williams Ann M †	104	operator	21	"
	U	Williams John A	104	custodian	55	"
	V	Love Merton	106	retired	77	"
	W	Ray Tavia—†	106	housekeeper	65	"
	X	Fowler Edward J	110	U S A	24	"
	Y	Fowler Mary C †	110	housekeeper	48	"
	Z	Fowler William L, jr	110	clerk	25	"
1524						
	A	Forshner Mabel B †	114	housekeeper	58	"

15

Cowper Street—Continued

B	Osborne Dorothy †	114	housewife	34	here
C	Osborne Merrill E	114	clerk	42	"
D	DeCosta Josephine †	118	housekeeper	80	"
E	DeCosta Mary A †	118	"	62	"
F	Hubbard Josephine †	118	"	59	"
G	Bennett Clifford S	118	carpenter	45	"
H	Bennett Jessie I †	118	housewife	48	"
K	Morgan Edmund	151	inspector	42	"
L	Morgan Frances †	151	housewife	40	"
M	Gallagher Frederick	151	U S N	26	"
N	Gallagher Kathryn †	151	bookkeeper	34	"
O	Gallagher Thomas	151	U S A	35	"
P	Mahoney Marie †	151	housekeeper	30	"
R	McFarland Mary G †	155	operator	20	"
S	McLean Arthur J	155	seaman	24	"
T	McLean Harold H	155	U S A	22	"
U	McLean Mary M †	155	housewife	50	"
V	McLean Thomas W	155	custodian	56	"
W	Callahan John F	172	carpenter	35	"
X	Callahan Margaret T †	172	housewife	32	"
Y	DuWors Ellen E †	174	"	77	"
Z	DuWors Robert J	174	retired	77	"

1525

A	Bagley Henry S	174	porter	63	"
B	Bagley Sarah E †	174	housekeeper	73	"
C	Bagley Kathryn G †	176	"	65	"
D	Moriarty Clarence J	176	painter	29	"
E	Moriarty Kathryn G †	176	housewife	28	"
F	Bagley Richard W	176	foreman	40	"
G	Bagley Ruth F †	176	housewife	36	"
H	Banks Minnie A †	177	housekeeper	67	"
K	Hagemeister Fred	177	metalworker	55	"
L	Hagemeister James E	177	U S A	27	"
M	Hagemeister Josephine A †	177	housewife	49	"
N	Chase Annie R †	179	laundryworker	55	"
O	Chase Edward D	179	U S A	29	"
P	Chase George W	179	guard	55	"
R	Chase James H	179	U S N	23	"
S	Chase Robert H	179	laborer	21	"
T	Harrison James J	179	U S A	42	"
U	Shea Eva M †	181	housewife	36	"

16

Cowper Street Continued

v	Shea William M	181	draftsman	39	here
w	Gayton Clifford	181	carpenter	41	"
x	Gayton Nellie †	181	packer	40	"
y	Barry Margaret †	184	stitcher	65	61 Templeton
z	Moran Lawrence J	184	inspector	54	here

1526

A	Moran Mary E †	184	housewife	52	"
B	Moran Sheila †	184	operator	21	"
c	Lombardi George P	184	machinist	22	"
D	Lombardi Joseph D	184	U S N	24	"
E	Ryan Michael J	184	accountant	50	"

Homer Street

F	Shea Francis X	58	U S N	21	here
G	Shea John J	58	operator	51	"
H	Shea Marguerite E †	58	housewife	47	"
K	Rogan Abbie J †	58	"	70	"
L	Rogan Abbie J †	58	clerk	36	"
M	Rogan Mary A †	58	operator	34	"
N	Welch John F	63	brakeman	51	"
O	Welch Mary L †	63	housewife	41	"
P	Johnson Bernard F	63	investigator	46	"
R	Johnson Daniel	63	U S C G	20	"
s	Johnson James P	63	laborer	50	"
T	Johnson Margaret †	63	housewife	42	"
U	Kelly Charles J	63	chauffeur	42	"
v	Kelly Charles O	63	U S A	20	"
w	Kelly Ethel M †	63	housewife	39	"
x	Kelly Frank J	63	laborer	54	"
y	McLaughlin Edward J	64	mechanic	64	"
z	McLaughlin Lena †	64	operator	21	"

1527

A	McLaughlin Phillip	64	painter	61	"
B	*Thompson Mary J †	66	housewife	44	"
c	Thompson Richard T	66	B F D	49	"
D	Babin Clarence J	67	chauffeur	28	"
E	Babin Lillian †	67	housewife	28	"
F	Potter Alice M †	67	"	30	"
G	Potter Joseph E	67	cleaner	29	"
H	Mealey Francis	69	clerk	42	"

Homer Street — Continued

K	Mealey Mary—†	69	housewife	40	here
L	Mealey Mary—†	69	secretary	20	"
M	Curran Kevin	69	laborer	54	"
N	Foley Joseph	69	ropemaker	31	"
O	Foley Mary—†	69	housewife	62	"
P	Sabbagh Florence—†	69	"	32	"
R	Sabbagh George	69	maint'n'ceman	33	"
S	Purciello Augustine	70	shoemaker	43	"
T	Purciello Edith—†	70	student	20	"
U	Purciello Florence—†	70	housewife	40	"
V	Cooney Lawrence	71	salesman	34	"
W	Cooney Mary—†	71	housewife	33	"
X	Doherty Ethel—†	71	"	30	"
Y	Doherty Henry	71	repairman	37	"
Z	Norton Claire—†	71	clerk	22	"
	1528				
A	Norton Nellie C—†	71	housewife	64	"
B	Norton William F	71	guard	64	"
C	Bagley Blanche I—†	72	housewife	28	"
D	Bagley Walter S	72	superintendent	30	"
E	Hartery Andrew T	72	plumber	52	"
F	Hartery Andrew T, jr	72	U S A	23	"
G	Hartery Eleanor J—†	72	housewife	49	"
H	Hartery William J	72	U S A	21	"
K	O'Hanley Elizabeth—†	73	housewife	43	"
L	O'Hanley John W	73	weaver	43	"
M	Brown Sarah—†	73	matron	59	"
N	*Diskin Ellen—†	73	housewife	70	"
O	*Diskin Patrick	73	retired	76	"
P	Boyce Bridget—†	73	housewife	47	"
R	Boyce Joseph	73	weaver	47	"
S	Boyce Marcel	73	mechanic	20	"
T	McGloan Dorothy—†	74	housewife	26	"
U	McGloan Jeffrey	74	laborer	32	"
V	Miller Charles W	74	mechanic	48	"
W	Miller Mary J—†	74	housewife	45	"
X	Hughes Eleanor M—†	75	operator	27	"
Y	Hughes Ellen M—†	75	housewife	48	"
Z	Hughes John K	75	mechanic	23	"
	1529				
A	Hughes John W	75	pipefitter	49	"

Homer Street Continued

B	Wren Thomas	75	B F D	60	here
C	Elias Anna M †	76	housewife	34	"
D	Elias Michael	76	mechanic	34	"
E	Boutchia Jeanne †	76	housewife	27	"
F	Boutchia John	76	metalworker	36	"
G	Laskey Helen †	78	housewife	40	"
H	Laskey Lloyd	78	policeman	42	"
K	Hartery Elena C †	78	housewife	36	"
L	Hartery William J	78	mechanic	40	"
M	*Ricciardi Anna †	82	housewife	49	"
N	Ricciardi Antonio	82	laborer	47	"
O	Ricciardi Joseph	82	metalworker	21	"
P	Ricciardi Sam	82	laborer	64	"
R	Goullaud James G	82	milkman	30	553 Saratoga
S	Goullaud Martha P †	82	housewife	28	756 "
T	Picard Jeanne H †	82	"	54	756 "
U	McGurin John J	83	retired	68	Revere
V	Murphy James P	83	policeman	42	here
W	Murphy Sadie H †	83	housewife	41	"
X	Meuse Alberta †	83	packer	20	"
Y	*Meuse Estelle †	83	housewife	48	"
Z	Meuse Raymond	83	engineer	54	"
	1530				
A	Meuse Raymond	83	laborer	26	"
B	D'Avella Helen †	83	housewife	28	"
C	D'Avella Vincent	83	weaver	29	"
D	Ruggiero Elvira †	87	housewife	38	424 Frankfort
E	Ruggiero Florentino	87	clerk	47	424 "
F	Pomer Joseph	90	metalworker	45	here
G	Pomer Margaret †	90	secretary	20	"
H	Pomer Sadie †	90	housewife	40	"
K	Cambria Luigi	91	cabinetmaker	59	"
L	Cambria Mary †	91	housewife	51	"
M	Cambria Peter	91	clerk	33	"
N	Storin Bertha A †	91	stenographer	28	"
O	Storin Ellen †	91	housewife	53	"
P	Storin George	91	clerk	24	"
R	Scarnice Jennie †	92	housewife	46	"
S	Scarnice Phillip	92	investigator	48	"
T	*Scandurra Joseph	93	cabinetmaker	61	"
U	Scandurra Josephine †	93	housewife	60	"

Page.	Letter	FULL NAME.	Residence, Jan. 1, 1943.	Occupation.	Supposed Age.	Reported Residence. Jan. 1, 1942. Street and Number.

Homer Street—Continued

v	Scandurra Mary —†	93	housewife	27	here
w	Scandurra Peter J	93	barber	28	"
x	Hoff Karl A	94	laborer	37	"
y	Hoff Marguerite M—†	94	housewife	36	"
z	Ferry Manuel	94A	laborer	52	"

1531

A	Gibbs Anna —†	94A	housewife	42	"
B	Gibbs Ivy	94A	engineer	41	"
C	Piva Geraldine—†	95	housewife	28	186 Benningt'n
D	Piva Joseph	95	mechanic	41	186 "
E	Manfra Alfred	96	cabinetmaker	42	here
F	Manfra Philomena —†	96	housewife	33	"
G	Romano Anna —†	96A	"	28	"
H	Romano Edmund	96A	chauffeur	28	"
K	Harrington Charlotte —†	97	clerk	21	"
L	Harrington Sadie —†	97	housewife	56	"
M	Harrington William H	97	retired	71	"
N	McCormack Mary C —†	99	housewife	59	"
O	McCormack Raymond J	99	clerk	37	"
P	Rowe Frederick A	101	repairman	50	"
R	Leonard Esther J —†	103	housewife	60	"
S	Leonard Esther J —†	103	librarian	32	"
T	Leonard Joseph W	103	U S A	22	"
U	Leonard Mary M —†	103	clerk	26	"
V	Leonard Nicholas F	103	manager	61	"
W	Clayton Charles W	105	retired	70	"
X	Clayton Constance M —†	105	typist	32	"
Y	Clayton John J	105	laborer	37	"
Z	Clayton Nora M —†	105	housewife	68	"

1532

A	Regan John J	107	coppersmith	50	167 Byron
B	Regan John J, jr	107	pipefitter	24	167 "
C	McLean Harold T	107	U S N	34	here
D	Quirk Anna M —†	107	nurse	33	"
E	Riley Anna —†	107	housewife	74	"
F	Riley William J	107	retired	75	"

Horace Street

H	Quinn George	53	porter	70	here
K	Quinn Marjorie —†	53	operator	35	"

Page.	Letter.	FULL NAME.	Residence, Jan. 1, 1943.	Occupation.	Supposed Age.	Reported Residence, Jan. 1, 1942. Street and Number.

Horace Street — Continued

	L	Lane Dorothy — †	57	housewife	28	here
	M	Lane John	57	carpenter	63	"
	N	Lane Wilfred	57	molder	31	"
	O	Rogers George J	59	seaman	20	"
	P	Rogers Mary — †	59	housewife	40	"
	R	O'Connell Lloyd M	60	machinist	54	"
	S	O'Connell Lloyd M, jr	60	U S A	22	"
	T	O'Connell Matilda M — †	60	housewife	52	"
	U	O'Connell Mildred — †	60	inspector	24	"
	V	Smith Albert E	63	cook	62	"
	W	Smith Alice M — †	63	housewife	61	"
	X	Smith Harold E	63	U S A	22	"
	Y	Smith Helen E — †	63	inspector	22	"
	Z	Carey Catherine — †	63	nurse	48	"

1533

	A	Horrigan Michael	63	clerk	61	"
	B	Coughlin Joseph	64	plumber	32	"
	C	Coughlin Rena — †	64	housewife	29	"
	D	Gillespie Michael F	64	janitor	53	"
	E	McHugh James	64	seaman	24	"
	F	McHugh Margaret — †	64	clerk	22	"
	G	McHugh William	64	U S C G	20	"
	H	Coughlin Catherine G — †	65	housewife	64	"
	K	Coughlin Helen — †	65	housekeeper	40	"
	L	Coughlin Michael F	65	engineer	65	"
	M	Coughlin Frank J	65	clerk	43	"
	N	Coughlin Mary — †	65	cashier	27	"
	O	Gillespie Gertrude — †	65	"	41	"
	P	Fitzpatrick Anna L — †	67	housewife	48	"
	R	Fitzpatrick Anna L — †	67	secretary	21	"
	S	Fitzpatrick Evelyn N — †	67	stenographer	23	"
	T	Fitzpatrick Joseph H	67	metalworker	55	"
	U	Fitzpatrick Joseph H, jr	67	electrician	22	"
	V	Fitzpatrick Marie A — †	67	secretary	24	"
	X	Sullivan Francis J	70	electrician	32	"
	Y	Sullivan Mary A — †	70	housewife	32	"
	Z	Parkinson Beatrice — †	70	"	46	"

1534

	A	Parkinson John	70	U S A	22	"
	B	Parkinson Robert E	70	electrician	47	"
	C	Tierney Margaret — †	70	operator	40	"

21

Horace Street—Continued

E	Gleason Anna M—†	73	housewife	32	here
F	Gleason William D	73	rigger	30	"
G	Joyce Andrew	73	U S A	23	"
H	Joyce Annie M—†	73	housewife	73	"
K	Joyce John F	73	painter	46	"
L	Joyce John F, jr	73	clerk	24	"
M	McWilliams Mary—†	74	housewife	33	"
N	McWilliams Richard	74	sparmaker	40	"
O	Austin Mary M—†	74	housewife	55	"
P	Austin Richard J	74	guard	55	"
R	Smith Mary E—†	74	housekeeper	76	"
T	McWilliams John H	75	sparmaker	36	"
U	McWilliams Margaret—†	75	housewife	31	"
V	Sweeney Emily M—†	77	"	30	"
W	Sweeney Wilfred J	77	letter carrier	31	"
B	Beale Edward A	77	electrician	35	"
Y	Beale Mildred—†	77	housewife	32	"
Z	DiFranza John	78	operator	26	"

1535

A	DiFranza Vincenza—†	78	clerk	24	"
B	Festa Florence—†	78	housewife	42	"
C	Festa Jean—†	78	nurse	20	"
D	Festa Joseph	78	bricklayer	54	"
E	Sacco Jeremiah	78	retired	74	"
F	Mortimer Nellie A—†	79	housewife	59	"
G	McCarthy Josephine—†	79	clerk	26	"
H	O'Donnell Mary C—†	79	housekeeper	45	"
K	O'Donnell Rose E—†	79	"	75	"
L	Montone Edward	80	clerk	20	"
M	Montone Frank	80	presser	51	"
N	Montone Gerald	80	U S A	22	"
O	Montone Theresa—†	80	housewife	44	"
P	Moran John	80	laborer	60	"
R	Moran Joseph	80	"	57	"
S	Moran Mary—†	80	housewife	58	"
T	Flanagan Anna M—†	81	"	48	"
U	Flanagan John F	81	decorator	50	"
V	Travaglini Albert	81	tilesetter	38	658 Saratoga
W	Travaglini Margaret—†	81	housewife	33	658 "
X	Cunningham Eleanor—†	82	"	43	here
Y	Cunningham Eleanor M—†	82	clerk	20	"

Horace Street Continued

z	Doherty Margaret F †	82	housewife	84	here	

1536

A	Howard Bridget F †	84	"	54	"
B	Howard Frances M †	84	clerk	23	"
C	Howard John C	84	splicer	55	"
D	Thibeault Dorothy †	84	housewife	25	"
E	Kelly Beatrice †	87	"	47	"
F	Kelly Richard F	87	custodian	47	"
G	McMullen William C	87	clerk	57	110 Bayswater
H	*Colucci Helene †	87	housewife	52	here
K	Colucci Louis	87	tilesetter	52	"
L	Buchanan Solange †	87	housewife	28	"
M	Buchanan William	87	operator	32	"
N	McGurin Cecelia †	91	housewife	30	"
O	McGurin Charles	91	repairman	26	"
P	Lewis Eva †	91	housewife	42	"
R	Lewis Glen	91	operator	52	"
S	Ahearn Margaret †	95	housewife	45	"
T	Guglielmo Anthony	97	chauffeur	28	234 Lexington
U	Guglielmo Florence †	97	messenger	25	234 "
V	Rothwell Louis J	97	repairman	39	here
W	Rothwell Mary H †	97	housewife	38	"

Milton Street

X	Colosi Antonette †	30	housewife	40	here
Y	Colosi Salvatore	30	shipwright	47	"
Z	Contois Rose †	30	saleswoman	21	"

1537

A	Lafay Frederick	30	weaver	32	"
B	*Lafay Thomas	30	laundryman	57	"
C	Murphy Florence †	30	housewife	52	"
D	Wilbur Evelyn †	30	"	23	"
E	Wilbur Fred	30	groom	32	Florida
F	Robicheau Dorothy †	34	housewife	43	38 Milton
H	Robicheau Peter M	34	U S A	20	38 "
G	Robicheau Peter R	34	warehouseman	41	38 "
K	Marcella Charles B	38	painter	38	45 "
L	Marcella Charlotte †	38	housewife	36	45 "
N	Belinsky Madeline †	45	"	23	1102 Saratoga
O	Belinsky Mitchell	45	brewer	29	408 Benningt'n

Milton Street—Continued

R	Warrino Dominick	45	oiler	55	here
P	Warrino Emerise—†	45	candymaker	34	"
S	Anderson Lily—†	45	housewife	38	157 Coleridge
T	Anderson Martin F	45	longshoreman	40	157 "
U	Finch Richard H	45	janitor	72	Methuen
V	Finch Thomas	45	mechanic	44	157 Coleridge
W	Callahan Catherine—†	134	housekeeper	72	here
X	Flynn Mary A—†	134	weaver	40	"
Y	Sammon Christopher	137	machinist	46	"
Z	Sammon James	137	fireman	51	"

1538

A	Sammon Joseph	137	clerk	48	"
B	Sammon Mary F—†	137	housewife	74	"

Moore Street

C	Greenwood Mary B—†	73	housewife	41	here
D	Shannon Arthur C	73	engineer	34	"
E	Shannon Catherine A—†	73	housewife	72	"
F	Shannon Francis T	73	engineer	30	"
G	McCaffrey Annie G—†	75	at home	76	"
H	Rich Evelyn C—†	75	housewife	35	"
K	Rich Frank J	75	superintendent	40	"
L	Sheehan James H	75	U S A	42	"
M	Carlton Helen F—†	76	clerk	42	"
N	Sullivan Ann M—†	76	instructor	31	"
O	Sullivan Florance	76	pilot	63	"
P	Sullivan Florence M—†	76	bookkeeper	23	"
R	Sullivan Margaret H—†	76	clerk	32	"
S	Sullivan Mary A—†	76	housewife	40	"
T	Stott Jessie G—†	78	"	32	"
U	Stott John W	78	mechanic	36	"
W	Berry James J	84	laborer	35	"
X	Berry Mary A—†	84	housewife	33	"
Y	Stott Charlotte—†	84	"	42	"
Z	Stott Harry	84	mechanic	63	"

1539

A	Porter Elda—†	88	housewife	30	"
B	Porter William	88	mechanic	33	"
C	Caizza Anthony	91	weaver	22	32 St Edward rd
D	Caizza Theresa—†	91	housewife	21	111 Readville

Moore Street Continued

E	*Campbell Alice A †	91	housewife	43	here
F	*Campbell William W	91	shipper	45	"
G	Dimond Daniel	92	custodian	67	"
H	Dimond Margaret E †	92	housewife	66	"
K	Curran Edgar	92	janitor	56	"
L	Curran Mary M †	92	housewife	58	"
M	Censale Domenico	93	upholsterer	35	"
N	Censale Iolanda †	93	housewife	28	"
O	Carideo Agnes G †	96	"	34	"
P	Carideo Joseph	96	mechanic	37	"
R	Fougere Ethel †	98	housewife	41	"
S	Fougere Phillip	98	seaman	42	"
T	*Dunn James	106	retired	78	"
U	*Dunn Josephine †	106	housewife	66	"
V	Riley Helen T †	106	"	34	"
W	Riley Thomas A	106	mechanic	34	"
X	Costa Theresa †	107	housewife	23	84 Lawn
Y	Costa Vincent	107	guard	25	84 "
Z	Costa Agnes †	107	housewife	47	here

1540

A	Costa Francis	107	U S C G	21	"
B	Costa John	107	painter	57	"
C	Costa John	107	U S C G	27	"
D	Rizzo Lillian †	108	housewife	29	22 Chestnut
E	Rizzo Santo	108	rigger	28	22 "
F	Cotte Joseph	108	salesman	37	here
G	Cotte Julia †	108	housewife	37	"
H	Carroll Evelyn †	109	"	23	30 Moore
K	Carroll James	109	electrician	28	30 "
L	*Lovell Ivy †	109	housewife	42	here
M	Lovell Raymond	109	fisherman	40	"
N	Gillies Ann †	110	operator	48	"
O	Gillies Anthony	110	letter carrier	43	"
P	Carfagna Helen †	111	housewife	32	"
R	Carfanga Henry	111	chauffeur	32	"
S	Kennedy Annie †	111	housewife	32	"
T	Kennedy Howard	111	electrician	40	"
U	Currie Henry	112	B F D	45	"
V	Currie Mildred E †	112	housewife	42	"
W	Currie William J	112	mechanic	20	"
X	Hoitt Charles R	113	"	23	Lynn

1—45   25

Page	Letter	FULL NAME.	Residence, Jan. 1, 1943.	Occupation.	Supposed Age.	Reported Residence, Jan. 1, 1942. Street and Number.

Moore Street— Continued

	y	Hoitt Dorothy A— †	113	housewife	23	Lynn
	z	Boyd Elizabeth— †	113	"	44	here
1541						
	a	Edwards George	114	U S A	34	"
	b	Edwards Jessie— †	114	housewife	73	"
	c	O'Connell Lucy— †	114	"	27	"
	d	O'Connell William T	114	laborer	32	"
	e	Driscoll Nellie— †	115	housewife	65	"
	f	Driscoll Timothy J	115	clerk	65	"
	g	Hawco Angela— †	115	"	37	"
	h	Hawco Mary B — †	115	housewife	72	"
	k	Hawco Mary L— †	115	at home	32	"
	l	Hawco Thomas	115	fireman	68	"
	m	Green Mary— †	116	housewife	52	"
	n	Green William	116	laborer	54	"
	o	Green William	116	U S A	20	"
	p	Nickerson Harold	116	longshoreman	50	"
	r	Burns Edward	116	laborer	31	"
	s	Burns Thomas	116	"	25	"
	t	Moseley Lotta— †	118	housewife	38	"
	u	Moseley Thomas	118	salesman	40	"
	v	Moseley Thomas	118	U S A	22	"
	w	Vierra Amelio	118	laborer	67	"
	x	Vierra Emily— †	118	housewife	67	"
	y	MacDonald Irene †	118	"	31	"
	z	MacDonald John	118	chauffeur	34	"
1542						
	a	Sullivan Christopher D	120	painter	52	"
	b	Sullivan Elizabeth A †	120	housewife	51	"
	c	Terrio Agnes †	120	"	46	"
	d	Terrio Irene †	120	factoryhand	21	"
	e	Terrio John	120	operator	49	"
	f	Flammia Theresa †	120	mechanic	30	225 Condor

Short Street

	g	Niles Catherine A †	4	housewife	68	here
	h	Niles Ruth E †	4	nurse	30	"
	k	Niles Sylvester C	4	accountant	32	"
	l	Shattuck Lillian N— †	4	housewife	34	"

Wordsworth Street

M	Benoit Augustus L	125	chauffeur	28	here	
N	Benoit Mary M †	125	housewife	29	"	
O	Mottola Angelina †	125	bookkeeper	24	"	
P	Mottola Archangela †	125	housewife	52	"	
R	Mottola Citiacco	125	shoemaker	52	"	
S	Mottola Joseph	125	U S A	22	"	
T	Russo Frank	125	plasterer	48	"	
U	Russo Guy	125	U S N	21	"	
V	Russo Mary †	125	housewife	44	"	
W	Doyle Alfred	127	mechanic	22	"	
X	Doyle Anna †	127	at home	26	"	
Y	Doyle Eleanor †	127	housewife	21	"	
Z	Doyle Joseph	127	carpenter	30	"	

1543

A	Doyle Thomas	127	clerk	24	"	
B	Ulwick Greta †	127	operator	28	"	
C	Ulwick Walter	127	U S C G	32	Revere	
D	Gormley John J	128	rigger	39	here	
E	Gormley Mary †	128	housewife	38	"	
M	*DiStasio Lucy †	128	at home	72	"	
F	Lupi Adeline †	128	housewife	51	"	
G	Lupi Anthony	128	machinist	30	"	
H	Lupi Helen †	128	at home	21	"	
K	Lupi Henry	128	machinist	23	"	
L	Lupi Nicholas	128	shoecutter	54	"	
N	Rawson Mildred B †	130	housewife	45	"	
O	Rawson William J	130	chauffeur	54	"	
P	Higer Lottie †	130	housewife	57	"	
R	Higer Samuel	130	pedler	58	"	
S	Jenkinson Elizabeth †	140	housewife	22	2 Rockville pk	
T	Jenkinson John	140	laborer	35	2 "	
U	Gannon Austin	142	U S A	21	here	
V	Gannon Mary †	142	cleaner	46	"	
W	Madden John D	142	packer	26	971 Saratoga	
X	Madden Theresa †	142	housewife	26	971 "	
Y	Andrews Ernest	148	carpenter	59	here	
Z	Andrews Helen †	148	housewife	45	"	

1544

A	Andrews Helen †	148	secretary	20	"	
B	McCarthy Dennis C	148	laborer	71	"	
C	McCarthy Josephine †	148	housewife	73	"	

27

Wordsworth Street—Continued

D	Pearson Alice C †	154	housewife	43	here
E	Pearson Arthur A	154	bridgetender	44	"
F	O'Kane James	158	superintendent	69	"
G	O'Kane Mary †	158	housewife	65	"
H	Hagemeister Eleanor †	178	"	29	"
K	Hagemeister Frederick	178	maint'n'ceman	29	"
L	Nutile John R	178	chauffeur	32	"
M	Nutile Mary F †	178	housewife	31	"
N	Conry Henry L	182	laborer	49	"
O	Murphy Eugene R	182	U S N	22	"
P	Murphy Susan †	182	housewife	59	"
R	Murphy William W	182	shipper	59	"
S	Breault John R	185	pipefitter	34	"
T	Breault Phyllis †	185	housewife	29	"
U *	Maglio Ida †	185	"	54	"
V	Maglio Louis	185	barber	27	"
W	Maglio Michael	185	candymaker	54	"
X	Potter Edith E †	186	housewife	61	"
Y	Potter Hannah M †	186	at home	36	"
Z	Potter Joseph E	186	manager	59	"

1545

A	Potter William R	186	U S A	23	"
B	Kacos Carl	189	proprietor	39	"
C	Kacos Louise †	189	housewife	36	"
D	Gilleo Leo	189	chauffeur	39	"
E	Gilleo Leona †	189	housewife	38	"

Ward 1–Precinct 16

CITY OF BOSTON

LIST OF RESIDENTS
20 YEARS OF AGE AND OVER

(NON-CITIZENS INDICATED BY ASTERISK)
(FEMALES INDICATED BY DAGGER)

AS OF

JANUARY 1, 1943

JOSEPH F. TIMILTY, *Chairman*
FREDERIC E. DOWLING, *Secretary*
WILLIAM A. MOTLEY, JR.
FRANCIS B. McKINNEY
EVERETT R. PROUT

Listing Board.

CITY OF BOSTON PRINTING DEPARTMENT

Page.	Letter.	FULL NAME.	Residence, Jan. 1, 1943.	Occupation.	Supposed Age.	Reported Residence, Jan. 1, 1942. Street and Number.

1600

Addison Street

	Letter	FULL NAME	Residence	Occupation	Age	Reported Residence
	B	Mingotti Eugene	81	welder	36	here
	C	Mingotti Frances †	81	wrapper	27	"
	D	*Mingotti Giselda †	81	housewife	62	"
	E	Mingotti Mary †	81	wrapper	32	"
	F	*Mikus Emily †	95–97	weaver	57	"
	G	*Pontolilo Teofila †	95–97	housewife	74	7 Ford
	H	Cross Mary †	95–97	"	21	7 Ford
	K	Cross Richard	95–97	U S A	23	94 Brooks
	L	Geremonte Irene †	95–97	housewife	43	here
	M	Geremonte Joseph	95–97	guard	55	Stoneham
	N	Bisupek Edward	95–97	U S A	21	here
	O	*Bisupek Walter	95–97	shoeworker	52	"
	P	Bisupek Wanda †	95–97	hairdresser	25	"
	R	*Bisupek Wladia †	95–97	housewife	49	"
	S	Suozzo Angelina M †	95–97	"	38	7 Ford
	T	Suozzo Pasquale	95–97	chauffeur	42	7 "
	U	LaSaba Pasquale	95–97	salesman	39	355 Chelsea
	V	Meyer Edward	95–97	laundryworker	29	here
	W	Meyer Lillian †	95–97	housewife	25	"
	X	*Halle Mary †	95–97	"	50	"
	Y	Halle Michael	95–97	millhand	55	"
	Z	Kennedy Cecile †	95–97	housewife	34	"

1601

	Letter	FULL NAME	Residence	Occupation	Age	Reported Residence
	A	Kennedy David R	95–97	U S A	36	"
	B	Cataldo Albert	95–97	salesman	38	"
	C	Cataldo Dorothy R †	95–97	housewife	33	"
	D	King Charles R	95–97	operator	29	"
	E	King Dorothy †	95–97	housewife	25	"
	F	Controus Francis	95–97	U S A	24	Malden
	G	Controus Rose †	95–97	housewife	23	12 Milton
	H	*Zebniak Tekla †	95–97	"	37	here
	K	*Zebniak Wasel	95–97	millhand	46	"
	L	O'Connell Mary †	99	housewife	33	"
	M	O'Connell Peter	99	bartender	33	"
	N	Goodwin Lorraine M †	101	waitress	40	"
	O	Hargrave John W	101	pipefitter	56	"
	P	Waterman Ethel †	101	housewife	47	"
	R	Waterman Robert S	101	U S N	22	"
	S	DeMarco May †	103	housewife	37	"
	T	Souza John	105	millhand	27	Chelsea

2

Addison Street — Continued

u	Souza Josephine †	105	housewife	27	Chelsea
w	*Repetto John	117	retired	86	here
x	*Repetto Louise †	117	housewife	72	"
y	Repetto Peter C	117	U S A	34	"
z	Repetto William	117	custodian	46	"

1602

a	Frith Elizabeth E †	117	millhand	42	20 Dartmouth pl
b	*Frith Harry C	117	painter	37	20 "
c	Gauthier Andrew	117	weaver	59	here
d	*Gauthier Aurora †	117	housewife	49	"
e	Gaeta Evelyn †	117	waitress	41	"
f	Silva Edna †	121	saleswoman	24	"
g	Silva Harriet †	121	housewife	30	"
h	Silva William	121	shipfitter	36	"
k	Turpin Louise †	121	housewife	59	"
l	Gilleo Joseph	125	guard	50	"
m	Gilleo Mary M †	125	housewife	35	"
n	Condon Catherine J †	131	cashier	40	"
o	Condon Elizabeth M †	131	housewife	49	"
p	Condon Johanna †	131	cashier	44	"
r	Condon Mary †	131	housekeeper	61	"
s	Cox Estelle †	135	housewife	46	"
t	Cox George L	135	policeman	47	"
u	Cox Margaret T †	135	clerk	20	"

Bennington Street

x	Calhoun George	600	U S A	36	here
y	Calhoun Jean †	600	housewife	28	"
z	McCarthy Francis G	602	U S C G	21	"

1603

a	Milward Anna P †	602	clerk	24	"
b	Milward Edward M	602	merchant	51	"
c	Milward Marcella L †	602	housewife	61	"
d	Wille John	602	retired	77	"
e	*Cestroni Achille	604	carpenter	49	"
f	Cestroni Concetta †	604	housewife	39	"
g	Ferrari Antonio	604	mason	64	"
h	Costello Benjamin	606	longshoreman	38	"
k	Costello Mary †	606	housewife	32	"
l	Dalton Agnes †	606	"	30	"

3

Bennington Street—Continued

		Full Name.	Res.	Occupation.	Age	Street and Number
M		Dalton Edward	606	fishcutter	34	here
N		Sullivan Mary—†	606	at home	57	"
O		Ward Albert	606	chauffeur	25	"
P		Sullivan Patrick	610	foreman	56	"
R		McDonnell Agnes—†	610	housewife	60	"
S		McDonnell Thomas J	610	laborer	60	"
T		Vargas Celia—†	610	housewife	42	"
U		Vargas Joseph	610	mechanic	43	"
V		Cody Lorraine—†	614	housewife	24	"
W		Cody Walter L	614	foreman	26	"
X		Follo Carlo	614	shipwright	38	"
Y		Follo Carmella—†	614	housewife	32	"
Z	*Follo Marie—†	614	at home	67	"
	1604					
A		Tranchina Ida—†	614	weaver	33	"
B		Tranchina Joseph	614	machinist	38	"
F		Gately George L	624	physician	44	"
G		Hulke Almeda—†	624	housewife	49	"
H		Hulke Ruth—†	624	bookkeeper	22	"
K		McGinn Thelma—†	624	housewife	25	"
L		Pease Warren	624	retired	81	"
M		D'Amico Anna M—†	624	inspector	21	"
N		D'Amico Delia—†	624	housewife	45	"
O		D'Amico Pasquale	624	custodian	50	"
P		D'Amico Ralph	624	U S A	22	"
R		Dooley John J	626	retired	73	59 Havre
S		Dooley John J, jr	626	brazier	43	59 "
T		Dooley Mary—†	626	housewife	74	59 "
U		Healy John H	626	millwright	65	here
V		Healy Mabel M—†	626	housewife	56	"
W		Garden Manuel	626	welder	37	"
X		Garden Mary—†	626	housewife	26	"
Y		Levangie Joseph I	628	gardener	53	"
Z		Levangie Margaret—†	628	housewife	55	"
	1605					
A		Coggswell Charles	628	mechanic	34	"
B		Coggswell Mildred—†	628	housewife	33	"
C		McMillan Dorothy—†	628	millhand	33	Arlington
D		Lanzilli Frank	628	welder	32	139 Sydney
E		Lanzilli Lucy—†	628	housewife	27	139 "

4

Bennington Street Continued

F	Whalen Henry J	630	chauffeur	42	here
G	Whalen Louise B †	630	housewife	41	"
H	Souza Elizabeth †	630	"	23	"
K	Souza Frances K †	630	saleswoman	20	"
L	Souza George L	630	longshoreman	47	"
M	Souza Henry T	630	U S A	25	"
N	Souza Mary A †	630	housewife	46	"
O	Strangie Augustine	630	salesman	29	"
P	Strangie Margaret †	630	housewife	26	"
R	McHatton Alexander J	632	packer	58	"
S	McHatton Mary †	632	housewife	62	"
T	*Korsak Anna †	632	"	66	"
U	*Korsak Roman	632	tester	66	"
V	Statkum Josephine †	632	housewife	35	"
W	Tracia Charles	632	chauffeur	42	236 Bremen
X	Tracia Marcella †	632	housewife	41	236 "
Y	Keane Anna †	634	"	39	here
Z	Keane James	634	laborer	39	"

1606

A	Pastore Anthony	634	checker	29	"
B	Pastore Norma †	634	housewife	28	"
C	Livesey Hannah †	634	"	56	"
D	Livesey Robert	634	piano tuner	57	"
F	Hunter David W	656	clerk	38	"
G	Hunter Mary M †	656	housewife	38	"
H	Ferrera Joseph	656	fireman	52	184 Benningt'n
K	Ferrera Mary †	656	housewife	37	184 "
L	Berube Evelyn †	656	"	46	here
M	Berube Lionel	656	U S A	24	"
N	Berube Pierre	656	loom fixer	45	"
O	Kaminski Dolores †	656	housewife	22	"
P	Kaminski John	656	machinist	23	Chelsea
R	Mercurio Frederick	656	U S N	22	12 Emmons
S	Mercurio Simone †	656	housewife	20	12 "
T	Schleicher Carl	660	retired	74	here
U	Schleicher Charlotte †	660	clerk	50	"
V	Schleicher Therese †	660	housewife	73	"
W	Schleicher Henry	660	chauffeur	42	"
X	Schleicher Margaret †	660	housewife	31	"
Y	Moran Edmund F	664	physician	62	"

Bennington Street— Continued

z	Moran Edmund F. jr	664	U S N	26	here
1607						
A	Moran Grace S— †	664	housewife	50	"
B	Moran Mary B— †	664	student	22	"
C	Stapleton Mary B— †	664	at home	53	"
D*	Adamo Annie— †	666	housewife	50	"
E*	Adamo Carmello	666	retired	68	"
F	Adamo Marion— †	666	hairdresser	24	"
G	Adamo Peter	666	plumber	26	"
H	Ruotolo Adeline— †	668	housewife	30	"
K	Ruotolo Gerard	668	pipefitter	32	"
L	Santamaria Amelia— †	668	housewife	57	"
M	Santamaria Arthur	668	U S A	29	"
N	Santamaria Beatrice— †	668	inspector	21	"
O	Santamaria Michael	668	barber	65	"
P	Bagley Freda E— †	670	housewife	38	"
R	Bagley James E. jr	670	attorney	42	"
S	Gorman Barbara— †	670	saleswoman	34	"
T	Gorman Peter	670	retired	76	"
U	Cohntino Helen— †	678	housewife	29	"
V	Cohntino Ralph	678	painter	35	"
W	DeLeo Lena— †	678	housewife	53	"
X	DeLeo Pasquale	678	carpenter	55	"
Y	Frongillo Armando	678	laborer	30	"
Z	Mari Florence— †	678	housewife	24	"
1608						
A	Souza Julia— †	680	at home	56	"
B	Desautell Cecil	680	clerk	28	"
C	Desautell Rubie— †	680	housewife	28	"
D	Roach Elizabeth— †	690	at home	69	"
E	Roach George	680	carpenter	53	"
F	Currie Lillian— †	680	housewife	29	"
G	Currie William	680	retired	76	"
H	Currie William W	680	chauffeur	35	"
L	Edwards Catherine T— †	682	at home	62	"
M	O'Connell Mary F— †	682	"	65	"
N	Cain Bernard J	684	machinist	50	"
O	Cain Eileen— †	684	housewife	40	"
P	Western Edmund	686	carpenter	65	"
R	Western Lena— †	686	housewife	68	"
S	DeRosa Anthony	688	mechanic	32	"

Bennington Street Continued

T	DeRosa Evelyn †	688	housewife	30	here
U	Burke John J	690	mechanic	53	"
V	*Burke Nora †	690	nurse	48	"
W	*Burke Thomas J	690	laborer	42	"
X	Nichols Joseph L	690	chauffeur	49	"
Y	Nichols Kathleen J †	690	housewife	46	"
Z	Duff James	692	printer	52	"

1609

A	Duff Sarah J †	692	housewife	53	"

Byron Street

B	Maggiore Anthony, jr	45	U S A	23	here
C	Maggiore Antonio P	45	tailor	51	"
D	Maggiore Imprimo	45	U S A	26	"
E	Maggiore Marie B— †	45	teacher	27	"
F	Maggiore Nellie— †	45	housewife	51	"
G	Cataldo Charles J	48	physician	37	"
H	Cataldo Helene M— †	48	housewife	37	"
K	Pasqua Carmella— †	49	"	31	"
L	Pasqua John	49	welder	35	"
M	*Merullo Angelina— †	49	housewife	57	"
N	Merullo Carmine	49	laborer	58	"
O	Merullo Emanual	49	student	22	"
P	Merullo Jennie— †	49	operator	23	"
R	Brosnan Alice †	52	housewife	34	"
S	Brosnan Eugene	52	laborer	36	"
T	Crowley William	52	retired	73	"
U	*Cataldo Louis	52	"	76	"
V	Donahue Eliazbeth M— †	52	housewife	40	107 Moore
W	Donahue George T	52	oiler	42	107 "
X	*Cardarelli Giovannina †	53	at home	59	54 Neptune rd
Y	Giardullo Emma— †	53	housewife	29	here
Z	Giardullo Leo	53	agent	30	"

1610

A	Wilcox Agnes— †	55	housewife	61	"
B	Wilcox Gifford D	55	foreman	60	"
C	Wilcox Stella— †	55	at home	24	"
E	*Cornetta Mary— †	56	"	79	"
F	Mazza Francis	56	U S A	28	"
G	Mazza Marion— †	56	weaver	27	"

7

Page.	Letter.	FULL NAME.	Residence, Jan. 1, 1943.	Occupation.	Supposed Age.	Reported Residence Jan. 1, 1942. Street and Number.

Byron Street—Continued

	H	Mazza Mary—†	56	housewife	49	here
	K	Mazza Mary A—†	56	assembler	25	"
	L	Mazza Nellie J—†	56	operator	24	"
	M	Mazza Nicholas	56	U S A	22	"
	N	Mazza Rita—†	56	clerk	20	"
	O	Alleas John M	57	mechanic	66	"
	P	Alleas Rose—†	57	housewife	63	"
	R	Cahill Herbert C	59	guard	66	"
	S	Cahill Rita T—†	59	operator	20	"
	T	Cahill Sophie M—†	59	housewife	62	"
	U	Cahill Thomas L	59	machinist	27	"
	V	Cahill William J	59	U S N	22	"
	W	Geggis John A	60	U S A	21	"
	X	Geggis Mary J—†	60	housewife	49	"
	Y	Geggis William F	60	steamfitter	52	"
		1611				
	A	Merullo Leonard R	60	instructor	25	"
	¹A	Merullo Mary E—†	60	housewife	22	"
	B	Czarnetzki Anna F—†	60	laundryworker	45	"
	C	Czarnetzki Augustine J	60	U S A	43	"
	D	O'Donnell Frances—†	60	housewife	46	"
	E	O'Donnell George H	60	waiter	46	Florida
	F	Fennelly Ambrose	61	U S A	24	here
	G	Fennelly Dennis J	61	longshoreman	53	"
	H	*Fennelly Sarah A—†	61	housewife	48	"
	K	Joy Eileen—†	61	operator	21	"
	L	Joy Jerry	61	U S A	24	"
	M	*Reddy Esther—†	61	domestic	31	"
	N	Grillo Emily—†	64	housewife	23	"
	O	Grillo Gioccino	64	toolmaker	23	"
	P	Stoia Veronica—†	64	housewife	65	"
	R	Stoia Vincenzo	64	laborer	64	"
	S	Stoia William F	64	clerk	27	"
	T	Molino Anna—†	64	shoeworker	22	"
	U	Molino Frank	64	"	50	"
	V	Molino Ida—†	64	housewife	41	"
	W	Venezia Edna—†	66	at home	37	"
	X	Venezia Mary—†	66	operator	39	"
	Y	Venezia Michael	66	machinist	28	"
	Z	Venezia Nellie—†	66	stitcher	46	"

1612
Byron Street Continued

A	*Venezia Victoria †	66	at home	72	here
C	Wilke William	66	janitor	60	"
D	Wright Basil	66	welder	37	"
E	Wright Ruth †	66	housewife	30	"
F	*Marcantonio Dora †	67	"	56	"
G	Marcantonio Giustino	67	operator	24	"
H	Marcantonio Louis	67	barber	58	"
K	Dritto Dominic	67	U S N	22	"
L	Dritto Mary—†	67	shoeworker	23	"
M	*Dritto Rose—†	67	housewife	46	"
N	Pagliccia Dominic	67	laborer	49	"
O	Isasi Antonio	67	engineer	50	"
P	Isasi Paola—†	67	housewife	40	"
R	Morse Daniel	68	longshoreman	42	"
S	Morse Mary F †	68	housewife	46	"
T	Barker George	68	carrier	36	"
U	Barker Harry	68	retired	64	"
V	Barker Henry R	68	inspector	34	"
W	Barker Isabel R †	68	clerk	27	"
X	Barker Susan—†	68	housewife	56	"
Y	Wilcox Fannie—†	70	"	24	"
Z	Wilcox John H	70	repairman	31	"

1613

A	D'Agnelli Domenico	70	laborer	39	"
B	*D'Agnelli Mary †	70	housewife	43	"
C	DiOrio Maria †	70	at home	75	"
D	Iannone Domenico	70	laborer	48	"
E	Rutledge Arthur E	71	rigger	47	"
F	Rutledge Arthur E, jr	71	U S A	22	"
G	Rutledge Mildred N †	71	clerk	21	"
H	Rutledge Nora C †	71	housewife	45	"
K	Vecchio Josephine †	72	"	27	"
L	Vecchio Vincent	72	millhand	29	"
M	*Vecchio Antoinetta †	72	housewife	50	"
N	Vecchio Assunta †	72	operator	23	"
O	Vecchio John	72	candyworker	50	"
P	Vecchio Vito	72	U S A	21	"
R	McIntyre Anna W—†	74	housewife	32	"
S	McIntyre John A	74	shipfitter	32	"

9

Byron Street—Continued

T	*Jackson John	74	ironworker	67	here
U	*Jackson Mary—†	74	housewife	58	"
V	MacLean Arthur	74	shipper	32	"
W	MacLean Eileen M—†	74	housewife	30	"
X	Dorgan Anna L—†	76	"	58	"
Y	Flanigan Laura—†	76	at home	53	"
Z	Flanigan Anna A—†	76	housewife	48	"

1614

A	Flanigan Charles H	76	plumber	53	"
B	Flanigan Eleanor A—†	76	stenographer	22	"
C	Belange Anthony	77	plumber	50	"
D	Belange Joseph	77	U S N	22	"
E	Belange Lucy—†	77	housewife	50	"
F	Belange Mary—†	77	clerk	23	"
G	Belange John	77	millhand	43	"
H	Cardillo Joseph	77	electrician	40	"
K	Cardillo Lucy—†	77	housewife	40	"
L	Mario Rosalie—†	77	"	21	"
M	Mario Vincent	77	U S A	23	198 Marion
N	Necco Annette E—†	79	at home	54	here
O	Necco Claire E—†	79	housewife	24	"
P	Necco John, jr	79	shipfitter	29	"
R	McDuffie Catherine S—†	79	housewife	30	"
S	McDuffie Daniel B	79	electrician	36	"
T	Mazza Angelina—†	81	housewife	45	170 Chelsea
U	Mazza Joseph	81	mechanic	48	170 "
V	McCormack Catherine F—†	81	fitter	58	here
W	McCormack Mary M—†	81	stitcher	50	"
X	Connelly Anna G—†	83	housewife	41	"
Y	Connelly Thomas J	83	chauffeur	38	"
Z	Lane Frederick J	84	broker	48	"

1615

A	Lane Helen—†	84	student	23	"
B	Lane Dorothy E—†	84	stenographer	35	"
C	Lane Mary E—†	84	housewife	73	"
D	Lane Mary E—†	84	operator	33	"
E	Lane Thomas F	84	retired	78	"
F	Olsen Ellen G—†	84	housewife	33	Panama
G	McIntyre Ella E—†	85	"	37	here
H	McIntyre Frank C	85	chauffeur	37	"
K	Lahti Charles A	85	calker	40	"

Byron Street Continued

L	*Lahti Tiami — †	85	housewife	38	here
M	Bobrek Edward	87	U S A	29	90 Byron
N	*Bobrek John	87	laborer	61	90 "
O	Cronin Anna M — †	87	housewife	33	90 "
P	Cronin John W	87	laborer	35	90 "
R	Bois Ernest	89	pedler	43	here
S	Bois Sarah — †	89	housewife	34	"
T	Bois Louis	89	weaver	53	"
U	Bois Malvina — †	89	housewife	52	"
V	Gannon Mary — †	90	"	37	298 Paris
W	Gannon Robert	90	machinist	43	298 "
X	Clayton John J	93	seaman	38	here
Y	Clayton Mabel A — †	93	housewife	36	"
Z	Graves Lester	94	foreman	40	"

1616

A	Graves Mary I — †	94	housewife	38	"
B	Abrahams Joseph W	94	longshoreman	40	"
C	Abrahams Lillian — †	94	housewife	42	"
D	Halgren Christopher	94	baker	52	Long Island
E	Flynn Amy — †	94	housewife	34	here
F	Flynn James E	94	operator	41	"
G	Irons Emily G — †	95	housewife	42	"
H	Aiken Irene — †	96	"	37	"
K	Aiken Leo C	96	salesman	38	"
L	Griffin Mary — †	96	factoryhand	38	"
M	*Amirault Cyrus	96	repairman	48	"
N	*Amirault Gertrude — †	96	housewife	45	"
O	McNeil Anna R — †	96	laundress	47	"
P	Forrest L Frances — †	96	housewife	26	"
R	Powers Christine E — †	96	"	46	"
S	Powers Francis J	96	fishcutter	58	"
T	Powers Joseph L	96	machinist	21	"
U	Powers William E	96	U S A	28	"
V	Cuneo Alfred	97	soapmaker	44	795 Saratoga
W	Cuneo Alfred, jr	97	U S A	23	795 "
X	Cuneo Catherine — †	97	clerk	25	795 "
Y	Cuneo Helen — †	97	housewife	43	795 "
Z	Cuneo Joseph	97	laundryworker	20	795 "

1617

A	O'Donnell Catherine — †	104	at home	80	here
B	O'Donnell James F	104	mechanic	46	"

11

Byron Street—Continued

c	Prendergast Frances—†	104	housewife	43	here
d	Prendergast Patricia—†	104	student	20	"
e	Ciarlone Audrey—†	106	secretary	25	"
f	Ciarlone Emma—†	106	stitcher	26	"
g	Ciarlone Linda—†	106	housewife	55	"
h	Ciarlone William	106	U S A	32	"
k	*DeMarco Celia—†	106	at home	84	"
l	DeMarco Emma—†	106	stitcher	22	"
m	DeMarco Guido	106	U S A	47	"
n	Howard Catherine A—†	108	at home	72	"
o	Canavan Catherine—†	112	housewife	47	"
p	Canavan Joseph I	112	B F D	49	"
r	Canavan Joseph I, jr	112	U S N	23	"
s	Turner Charles E	112	checker	35	"
t	Turner Lillian T—†	112	housewife	32	"
u	Thornton Edwin J	114	clerk	47	"
v	Thornton Edwin J, jr	114	machinist	20	"
w	Thornton Margaret—†	114	housewife	45	"
x	Wholly Mary E—†	114	at home	75	"
y	Morse Mary J—†	114	"	69	"
z	Morse William P	114	welder	44	"

1618

a	Impeduglia Carmella—†	127	clerk	24	"
b	*Impeduglia Sebastiana—†	127	at home	65	"
c	Ciampa Eleanor—†	129	stenographer	32	"
d	*Ciampa Giovanina—†	129	housewife	62	"
e	Ciampa Julia—†	129	entertainer	21	"
f	Ciampa Rocco	129	retired	71	"
g	Ciampa Theresa—†	129	stitcher	29	"
h	Palozzi Anna—†	129	"	21	"
k	Palozzi Josephine—†	129	housewife	48	"
l	Palozzi Lena—†	129	saleswoman	20	"
m	Palozzi Ralph	129	millhand	52	"
n	Palozzi Victor R	129	U S A	24	"

Moore Street

o	*McDonald Alexander	1	laborer	64	here
p	*McDonald Emma—†	1	housewife	65	"
r	McDonald Emma T—†	1	clerk	33	"
s	McDonald Joseph R	1	steamfitter	36	"

12

Moore Street — Continued

T	Chase William	3	mechanic	40	here
U	Chase William J	3	cook	70	"
V	McNamara Mary †	3	clerk	34	"
W	Higgins George	5	laborer	38	"
X	Higgins Mary †	5	operator	42	"
Y	LeBlanc Doris †	5	housekeeper	22	138 Meridian
Z	LeBlanc Ethel †	5	"	23	138 "

1619

A	LeBlanc Harold	5	U S A	21	138 "
B	LeBlanc James	5	carpenter	53	138 "
C	*LeBlanc Mary †	5	housewife	49	138 "
D	Carroll Genevieve †	15	"	48	here
E	Carroll James P	15	engineer	55	"
F	Carroll John A	15	ironworker	59	"
G	Carroll Kenneth J	15	U S A	22	"
H	Carroll Walter R	15	metalworker	45	"
K	Gillespie John P	15	forger	57	Everett
L	Zaberson Loretta †	15	housekeeper	52	here
N	Lockwood Marie G †	19	clerk	48	"
O	Lockwood Ralph	19	retired	48	"
P	McMasters Harry	19	painter	53	"
R	O'Connor Anna †	21	operator	37	"
S	Sullivan Louise G †	21	"	43	"
T	Pike Cambell	25	seaman	42	518 Saratoga
U	*Pike Mary †	25	housewife	40	518 "
V	Cervizzi Pasquale A	25	attorney	35	here
W	Cervizzi Thelma †	25	housewife	29	"
X	Crowley Mary †	25	"	53	"
Y	Crowley Michael	25	policeman	53	"
Z	Flynn Alice C †	27	housewife	36	"

1620

A	Flynn David B	27	longshoreman	38	"
B	McGeney Anna E †	27	clerk	37	"
C	Crowley Anna †	27	housekeeper	59	"
D	Crowley Joseph A	27	U S N	28	"
E	Crowley Timothy	27	retired	70	"
F	Doyle Anna †	31	teacher	50	"
G	Doyle Frank	31	carpenter	47	"
H	Doyle Gertrude †	31	stenographer	48	"
K	Doyle Nora †	31	housekeeper	81	"
L	Carino Anna M †	31	housewife	28	"

13

Moore Street—Continued

	M	Carino Matthew J	31	pharmacist	28	here
	N	Ahearn Cristine—†	35	housewife	23	"
	O	Ahearn Edgar	35	mechanic	23	"
	P	DeLuca John	35	barber	50	"
	R	DeLuca Mario	35	U S A	20	"
	S*	DeLuca Sophie—†	35	housewife	50	"
	T	McCarthy Jennie—†	39	"	39	91 Morris
	U	McCarthy Timothy M	39	laborer	44	91 "
	V	Trocano Frances—†	39	housewife	50	40 Frankfort
	W	Trocano Peter	39	shoeworker	49	40 "
	X	Coakley Mark J	63	clergyman	36	here
	Y	Flynn Leo B	63	"	42	"
	Z	Haughey Anna †	63	housekeeper	37	"

1621

	A	McCarthy Patrick J	63	clergyman	61	"
	B	McDonough Delia †	63	cook	52	Gloucester

Saratoga Street

	D	Newhook Arthur F	716	engineer	41	here
	E	Newhook Winifred G †	716	housewife	35	"
	F	Keating Hattie †	716	"	59	"
	G	Keating James P	716	bartender	67	"
	H	Mulloy John J	718	meatcutter	64	"
	K	Mulloy Margaret †	718	housewife	56	"
	L	Bibber Caroline †	718	"	57	"
	M	Bibber Caroline †	718	operator	20	"
	N	Bibber James	718	U S A	25	"
	O	Bibber Walter	718	U S C G	21	"
	P	Wing Yee Shung	720	laundryman	37	"
	R	Ying Hoo Moy	720	"	31	"
	S	Fronduto Jennie †	722	housewife	31	"
	T	Fronduto Vincent	722	serviceman	35	"
	U	Stasio Annette †	722	housewife	42	"
	V	Stasio Arthur	722	salesman	43	"
	W	Stasio Albert	722	brazier	22	"
	X	Stasio Dominic	722	plumber	51	"
	Y	Stasio Lillian †	722	inspector	21	"
	Z	Stasio Mary †	722	operator	24	"

1622

	A	Stasio Robert	722	U S A	26	"

14

Page.	Letter	FULL NAME.	Residence, Jan. 1, 1943.	Occupation	Supposed Age.	Reported Residence, Jan. 1, 1942. Street and Number.

Saratoga Street Continued

B	Stasio Stella †	722	housewife	49	here
C	Hughes Catherine †	724	"	64	"
D	Hughes Charles E	724	U S A	30	"
E	Hughes John	724	millhand	23	"
F	Meehan Mary †	724	clerk	42	"
G	Vetale Emma †	724	housewife	28	"
H	Pedersen Louis	724	fireman	46	"
K	Pedersen Michelina †	724	housewife	33	"
L	Connelly Mary L †	724	inspector	41	"
M	Young Anna R †	724	housewife	40	"
N	Young Joseph P	724	shipfitter	45	"
P	Treanor Alice C †	728	housewife	47	"
R	Lubofsky Louise †	736	"	25	"
S	Lubofsky Robert	736	shipfitter	26	"
T	Howard Mildred M †	736	housewife	37	"
U	Howard Richard P	736	draftsman	41	"
V	Rago Oreste	736	machinist	22	"
W	Rago Patrick	736	U S N	26	"
X	Rago Rose †	736	housewife	52	"
Z	Kelly Joseph E	740	U S A	21	"
	1623				
A	Kelly Mary A †	740	student	20	"
B	Kelly Mary E †	740	housewife	51	"
C	Kelly Paul J	740	U S A	25	"
D	Kelly William C	740	U S N	23	"
E	Hogan Margaret C †	740	bookkeeper	23	"
F	Hogan Mary P †	740	typist	21	"
G	Hogan Mary T †	740	housewife	48	"
H	Hogan William T	740	B F D	49	"
K	O'Brien William L	740	steamfitter	42	"
L	Cohen Dorothy †	740	bookkeeper	40	"
M	Cohen Edna †	740	"	23	"
N	Cohen Theresa †	740	matron	45	"
O	Cohen William	740	policeman	47	"
P	Rauth Doris D †	741	bookkeeper	20	"
R	Rauth Florence D †	741	housewife	55	"
S	Rauth William H	741	machinist	58	"
T	Millwood Louis	742	guard	50	"
U	Millwood Margaret †	742	housewife	45	"
V	Millwood Philip	742	U S A	22	"
W	Millwood William	742	"	20	"

Saratoga Street—Continued

x	Eastwood Audrey L—†	745	writer	21	27 Lorette
y	Eastwood Girard	745	U S M C	23	27 "
z	Eastwood Harry	745	B F D	55	27 "
	1624				
a	Eastwood Mary G—†	745	housewife	55	27 "
b	Eastwood Raymond	745	U S M C	27	27 "
c	Riley Catherine—†	745	at home	86	27 "
d	Byrnes Arthur	745	laborer	43	here
e	Keenan Hannah—†	745	housewife	70	"
f	Keenan James H	745	retired	74	"
g	Maher Theresa—†	745	at home	65	"
h	*Cocia Genosa	746	laborer	72	"
k	*Cocia Roro—†	746	housewife	58	"
l	Jeffrie Josephine—†	746	"	25	"
m	Jeffrie Padrie	746	metalworker	25	"
n	Millis Theodore D	746	clerk	39	"
o	Delaney Elizabeth B—†	746	housewife	48	Woburn
p	Delaney Michael J	746	foreman	58	"
r	Young Benjamin J	746	painter	50	here
s	Young Mary E—†	746	housewife	54	"
t	Morrison Herbert L	746	policeman	52	"
u	Morrison Mildred E—†	746	housewife	42	"
v	McQueeney John V	749	retired	67	"
w	McQueeney John V, jr	749	clerk	30	"
y	McQueeney Margaret A—†	749	librarian	31	"
x	McQueeney Margaret B—†	749	housewife	60	"
z	Crosby Marie A—†	749	"	43	"
	1625				
a	Crosby Robert E	749	inspector	48	"
b	Crosby Catherine—†	749	teacher	44	"
c	McGee Margaret—†	749	housewife	40	"
d	McGee Michael J	749	checker	43	"
e	Hamilton Amy—†	750	housewife	60	"
f	Havey Edwina—†	750	"	30	366 Princeton
g	Havey Walter	750	instructor	34	366 "
h	Hoey Amy—†	750	housewife	32	here
k	Hoey Matthew	750	guard	34	"
l	Park Mary J—†	753	at home	64	"
m	Park Phyllis G—†	753	W A A C	40	"
n	Balboni Fred J	753	policeman	34	"
o	Balboni Margaret H—†	753	housewife	29	"

Saratoga Street Continued

P	Spillane Lena †	754	housewife	69	here
R	Pennell Marie †	754	"	43	"
S	Duffy Arthur J	754	foreman	61	"
T	Duffy Arthur J jr	754	U S A	27	"
U	Duffy Ellen †	754	housewife	54	"
V	Duffy James P	754	U S A	23	"
W	Duffy Laura E †	754	clerk	21	"
X	Nugent Celia †	755	housewife	26	138 Falcon
Y	Nugent Mansell	755	carpenter	25	138 "
Z	Welch Harold H	755	machinist	42	Revere

1626

A	Welch Marie †	755	housewife	40	"
B	Berry Anna J †	755	operator	32	here
C	Berry Bridget †	755	housewife	66	"
D	Berry Patrick J	755	laborer	64	"
E	Keough Mary C †	756	housewife	75	"
F	Crowell Alfred	756	U S A	25	"
G	Crowell Eileen †	756	inspector	26	"
H	*Crowell Merle	756	gardener	56	"
K	Crowell Murray	756	U S A	22	"
L	*Crowell Myrta †	756	housewife	52	"
M	*Sheehan Olive †	756	operator	28	"
N	Murphy Evelyn †	756	packer	65	"
O	Murphy Mary A †	756	housewife	67	"
P	Murphy May A †	756	operator	44	"
S	Guay Annie †	759	housewife	62	"
T	Guay Catherine E †	759	stenographer	28	"
U	Guay Henry	759	guard	62	"
V	Guay Joseph P	759	U S A	26	"
W	McRae George	784	clerk	35	"
X	McRae Margaret †	784	housewife	34	"
Y	Ruggiero Mary †	784	"	55	"
Z	Ruggiero Nicola	784	molder	51	"

1627

A	Duffy Mary †	784	housewife	62	"
B	Duffy Mary M †	784	millhand	36	"
C	Dini Angelo	786	porter	57	"
D	Dini Julia †	786	housewife	47	"
E	Chase Evelyn E †	786	supervisor	37	"
F	O'Keefe Irene †	786	housewife	47	"
G	O'Keefe William	786	shipfitter	47	"

1—16

17

Saratoga Street — Continued

	H	Keohane John J	786	U S A	32	here
	K	McCarthy Daniel	786	manager	26	"
	L	McCarthy Mildred—†	786	housewife	25	"
	M	Donahue Catherine M—†	788	stenographer	48	"
	N	Donahue Cornelius	788	foreman	62	"
	O	Donahue John F	788	U S A	36	"
	P	Donahue Joseph G	788	clerk	51	"
	R	Donahue Julia—†	788	housewife	86	"
	S	Donahue Mary T—†	788	houseworker	65	"
	T	Twomey Andrew J	788	letter carrier	62	"
	U	Twomey Andrew J, jr	788	U S A	22	"
	V	Twomey Eleanor G—†	788	teacher	28	"
	W	Twomey Raymond A	788	U S A	26	"
	X	Canino Charles W	789	"	21	"
	Y	Canino Susan—†	789	housewife	51	"
	Z*	Canino Thomas Q	789	shoeworker	51	"
1628						
	A	Silano Angelo	789	guard	67	"
	B*	Silano Assunta—†	789	housewife	62	"
	C	Silano John	789	chauffeur	52	"
	D	Terrelli John A	789	"	27	212 Chelsea
	E	Terrelli Mary—†	789	housewife	22	212 "
	F	Frazier John W	790	U S A	41	here
	G	Gillespie John J	790	decorator	41	"
	H	Gillespie Mary L—†	790	housewife	33	"
	K	Gorman James	790	repairman	50	"
	L	Gorman Louise H—†	790	housewife	57	"
	M	Howard John A	790	laborer	45	"
	N	Howard Margaret J—†	790	housewife	32	"
	O	Hesenius Alfreda—†	790	inspector	26	"
	P	O'Connell David	790	U S N	20	"
	R	O'Connell Dorothy—†	790	millhand	24	"
	S*	O'Connell Mary—†	790	housewife	68	"
	T	O'Connell Mary—†	790	saleswoman	33	"
	U	O'Connell Richard	790	U S A	36	"
	V	Osterhout Helen—†	790	operator	31	"
	X	Gately Antoinette—†	791	at home	27	Cambridge
	Z	Hourihan Annie—†	792	housewife	27	here
1629						
	A	Hourihan Joseph	792	meatcutter	29	"
	B	McLaughlin Dorothy—†	792	housewife	35	"

18

Page.	Letter.	FULL NAME.	Residence Jan. 1, 1943.	Occupation.	Supposed Age.	Reported Residence, Jan. 1, 1942. Street and Number.

Saratoga Street Continued

	c	McLaughlin Samuel	792	welder	40	here
	D	Garisto Helen I †	793	housewife	27	"
	E	Garisto Joseph F	793	draftsman	31	"
	F*	Powers Ellen †	793	housewife	34	"
	G	Powers Patrick	793	ironworker	32	"
	H	Finn Catherine G †	794	clerk	48	"
	K	Finn Margaret †	794	bookkeeper	50	"
	L	Necco Edward	795	shipper	24	353 Chelsea
	M	Necco Irene †	795	housewife	21	353 "
	N	Cuneo Eva †	795	at home	50	here
	O	Cuneo Frederick	795	clerk	58	"
	P	Cuneo Nellie †	795	housewife	52	"
	R	Canavan Anna L †	796	clerk	48	"
	S	Welsh Mary L †	796	housewife	52	"
	T	Welsh Walter J	796	meatcutter	56	"
	U*	Richardson Charles W	796	foreman	50	"
	V*	Richardson Hazel †	796	housewife	46	"
	W	Moran Margaret H †	797	seamstress	50	"
	X	Moran Mary L †	797	at home	52	"
	Y	Burke Eleanor †	797	"	42	"
	Z*	Rockliff Charles	797	retired	77	"
1630						
	B	Walsh Mary R †	799	housewife	34	"
	C	Walsh Timothy J	799	carpenter	38	"
	D	Cook Flora M †	799	millhand	68	"
	F	Phillips Ernest	801	operator	32	"
	G	Phillips Katherine †	801	boxmaker	52	"
	H	McLaughlin George W	801	bartender	46	"
	K	Morey Emma †	801	clerk	46	"
	L	Barker Edward J	801	chauffeur	58	"
	M	Barker Lillian G †	801	housewife	54	"
	O	Barry Mary †	803	clerk	50	"
	P	Welling Augustine D	803	painter	62	"
	R	Welling Augustine J	803	U S A	21	"
	S	Welling Emily A †	803	housewife	52	"
	T	Welling Emily T †	803	stenographer	23	"
	X*	Capogreco Anna †	809	housewife	45	"
	Y	Capogreco Nicodemo	809	carpenter	45	"
	Z*	Ciccia Angela †	809	housewife	49	"
1631						
	A*	Ciccia John	809	chipper	21	"

19

Saratoga Street Continued

B	Ciccia Nicodemo	809	tailor	53	here
C	Bruzzese Filibarto	809	retired	51	"
D	*Bruzzese Nunziata—†	809	housewife	42	"
E	Scotti Angelina †	810	"	42	"
F	Scotti John	810	painter	43	"
G	Vieira Doris—†	814	housewife	22	Woburn
H	Vieira Francis P	814	engraver	28	825 Saratoga
K	Juliano Joseph	814	rigger	33	here
L	Juliano Lena—†	814	housewife	24	"
M	Carrigan Margaret †	815	at home	61	"
N	Haynes Frank E	815	printer	51	"
O	Haynes Margaret M—†	815	housewife	50	"
P	Kiley Bernice †	815	at home	26	"
R	Iapicca Agostino	815	shoeworker	67	"
S	*Iapicca Nicoletta †	815	housewife	65	"
T	Iapicca Salvatore	815	barber	44	"
U	Iapicca Tancredi	815	U S A	33	"
V	Iapicca Rocco	815	shoeworker	42	"
W	Iapicca Theresa—†	815	housewife	39	"
X	O'Brien Catherine †	816	"	38	"
Y	O'Brien James H	816	foreman	48	"
Z	Rogers Anna—†	816	housewife	40	"

1632

A	Rogers Florence—†	816	clerk	27	"
B	Rogers Manuel	816	electrician	46	"
C	Cooper Edwin L	818	mechanic	25	"
D	Cooper Margaret †	818	housewife	24	"
E	Smith Margaret V †	818	"	52	"
F	Smith Robert C	818	assembler	48	"
G	*Serge Carmela †	819	seamstress	63	"
H	*Serge Guiseppa—†	819	at home	87	"
K	Serge Guiseppe	819	barber	60	"
L	Smith Charles E	819	machinist	29	32 Princeton
M	Smith Mildred †	819	housekeeper	29	32 "
N	Silvagni Alexander	819	electrician	41	here
O	Silvagni Celia †	819	stenographer	22	"
P	Silvagni Rose †	819	housewife	48	"
R	Doyle Helen †	820	"	52	"
S	Doyle James	820	guard	50	"
T	Belton Francis J	820	electrician	41	"
U	Gustowski Mary E—†	820	housewife	57	"

20

Saratoga Street Continued

v	Jacobson Elvina †	820	housewife	68	here
w	Jacobson Marie †	820	bookkeeper	31	"
x	Jacobson Walter	820	U S A	30	"
y	Amoroso Catherine L †	821	housewife	24	"
z	Amoroso Michael A	821	U S C G	26	"

1633

A	Pepe Anthony	821	barber	56	"
B	Pepe Frank	821	chiropodist	29	"
C	Pepe John F	821	U S A	32	"
D*	Pepe Sofia †	821	housewife	51	"
E	Pepe William	821	mortician	24	"
F	DeAngelis Carmela †	821	operator	20	"
G	DeAngelis Christina †	821	metalworker	22	"
H	DeAngelis Pasquale	821	chauffeur	49	"
K	DeAngelis Rosine †	821	housewife	45	"
L	Grenier Catherine †	822	"	47	"
M	Grenier Joseph L	822	loom fixer	53	"
N	LaCroix Amedee	822	machinist	53	"
O	LaCroix Eleanor †	822	inspector	26	"
P	LaCroix Rita †	822	"	24	"
R	LaCroix Stella †	822	housewife	48	"
S	LaCroix Thomas	822	U S N	20	"
T	Jacobson Frank E	822	chauffeur	40	"
U	Jacobson Rose M †	822	housewife	42	"
V	Doyle James	823	seaman	60	"
W	Landry Henry	823	machinist	38	"
X	Doyle Arthur	823	U S A	21	"
Y	Doyle Josephine †	823	housewife	48	"
Z	Traveis Florence †	823	"	49	"

1634

A	Traveis Joseph F	823	machinist	49	"
B	Traveis Ruth †	823	clerk	21	"
C	Burns Agnes †	825	housewife	56	632 Benningt'n
D	Burns Daniel P	825	operator	54	632 "
E	Byrne Angela †	825	clerk	27	632 "
F	Byrne Veronica †	825	student	21	35 Fruit
G	Vieira Ursula †	825	housekeeper	54	here
H	Vieira William A	825	U S A	26	"
K	Jasus Justin	825	"	40	"
L*	Jasus Ursula S †	825	at home	80	"
M	Stokes Madeline F †	827	housewife	40	"

21

Saratoga Street—Continued

	N	Stokes William W	827	electrotyper	43	here
	O	Dodd Patrick F	827	retired	71	"
	P	Stack Agnes J—†	827	milliner	60	"
	R	Spindler John C	827	barber	63	"
	S	Spindler M Barbara—†	827	teacher	32	"
	T	Spindler Marie—†	827	housewife	62	"
	U	Greeley Mary K—†	829	secretary	39	"
	V	Kelley Helen J—†	829	"	37	"
	W	Kelley Sarah A—†	829	at home	71	"
	X	McNabb Mary C—†	829	dressmaker	52	"
	Y	O'Hare Alice G—†	829	at home	52	"
	Z	Geer Mary—†	831	"	38	57 Bennington
1635						
	A	Batchelder Esther—†	831	cook	55	here
	B	McLaughlin John J	831	guard	66	"
	C	McLaughlin Mary M—†	831	housewife	62	"
	D	McLaughlin Regina E—†	831	stenographer	25	"
	E	Frechett Annie—†	833	stitcher	48	"
	F	Terrill Dorothy—†	833	clerk	23	"
	G	Terrill Henry	833	U S C G	21	Winthrop
	H	Cipoletta Mary—†	833	housewife	43	here
	K	Cipoletta Nicholas	833	operator	49	"
	L	Ferrante Adeline—†	833	clerk	24	"
	M	Ferrante Domenick	833	electrician	25	"
	N	Ferrante Edward	833	clerk	23	"
	O	*Ferrante Rosaria—†	833	housewife	49	"
	P	Parker Robert W	835	U S N	21	61 Putnam
	R	Parker Ruth—†	835	housewife	20	61 "
	S	Lupi John	835	laborer	26	here
	T	Lupi Louise—†	835	housewife	26	"
	U	Sabbag Salemme—†	835	weaver	49	"
	V	Sabbag Samuel	835	U S A	31	"
	W	Sateriale Gaetano	835	chauffeur	46	35 Leyden
	X	Sateriale Olympia—†	835	operator	41	35 "
	Y	Cross David J	837	janitor	62	here
	Z	Gallagher Benjamin F	837	shipfitter	50	"
1636						
	A	Gallagher Susan A—†	837	housewife	46	"
	B	Gallagher William	837	student	23	"
	C	Mullen Charles	837	chauffeur	35	"
	D	Mullen Mabel T—†	837	housewife	35	"

22

Page	Letter	Full Name	Residence, Jan. 1, 1943	Occupation	Supposed Age	Reported Residence, Jan. 1, 1942. Street and Number.

Saratoga Street Continued

	E	Coe Jeanette —†	837	at home	73	here
	F	Cossetti Leo	837	salesman	28	42 Linden
	G	Cossetti Virginia —†	837	housewife	28	42 "
	H	Hanlon Eva M —†	837	"	45	here
	K	Hanlon Leonard	837	welder	25	"
	L	Hanlon William H	837	salesman	50	"
	M	Ramsay David A	837	compositor	60	"
	N	Ramsay David J, jr	837	treasurer	33	"
	O	Ramsay George A	837	U S A	23	"
	P	Ramsay Lucy E —†	837	housewife	69	"
	R	Petipas Bartholomew	839	laborer	47	"
	S*	Petipas Melina —†	839	housewife	42	"
	T	Cooper Mary —†	839	"	56	"
	U	Cooper William E	839	brakeman	68	"
	V	Cooper William F, jr	839	laborer	33	"
	W	Veiga Charles	839	ropemaker	29	"
	X	Veiga Florence —†	839	housewife	30	"
	Y	Cullen Catherine A —†	849	"	53	"
	Z	Cullen Joseph	849	guard	62	"

1637

	A	Cullen Thomas H	849	mechanic	24	"
	B	Steiner Evelyn —†	849	machinist	24	"
	C	Steiner Francis	849	U S A	28	"
	D	Steiner Irene —†	849	at home	22	"
	E	Steiner Thomas	849	salesman	53	"
	F	Wessling Helen —†	849	housewife	33	"
	G	Wessling William	849	foreman	41	"
	H	Mirakian Mary —†	850	housewife	75	"
	K	Mirakian Stephen	850	retired	84	"
	L	Felzani Ernest	850	mechanic	29	"
	M	Felzani Lena —†	850	housewife	32	"
	N	DeSimone Annette —†	851	"	42	"
	O	DeSimone James	851	bartender	42	"
	R	Leone Annette —†	851	housewife	37	"
	P	Leone Basil	851	shoeworker	38	"
	S	Vozzela Joseph	851	shipper	44	"
	T	Vozzela Mary —†	851	housewife	37	"
	U	Mascia Elsie —†	852	"	39	"
	V	Mascia James	852	laborer	35	"
	W	Terry Marion —†	852	housewife	44	"
	X	Terry Rene	852	guard	42	"

23

Saratoga Street—Continued

Y	Case Anthony	853	assembler	37	here
Z	Case Antoinette †	853	housewife	33	"

1638

A	Cutlip Susie †	853	at home	75	"
B	Webber Carl	853	textile worker	35	"
C	D'Agosta Adeline †	853	housewife	40	"
D	D'Agosta Frank	853	electrician	40	"
E	Polcari Carmen	854	painter	29	"
F	Polcari Tina †	854	housewife	25	"
G	Duffy Edward	854	warehouseman	27	"
H	Duffy Margaret †	854	housewife	24	"
K	Sacco Louise †	855	"	31	"
L	Sacco Orlando	855	welder	37	"
M	Frattaroli Beatrice †	855	clerk	21	"
N	Frattaroli Evelyn †	855	housewife	43	"
O	Frattaroli Henry	855	bookkeeper	22	"
P	DiPietro Hilda †	855	stitcher	25	"
R	DiPietro Marion †	855	dressmaker	28	"
S	DiPietro Michelina †	855	housekeeper	50	"
T	Sullivan Agnes †	856	housewife	31	"
U	Sullivan Francis	856	fisherman	37	"
V	Venezia Antoinetta †	856	operator	20	"
W	Venezia John	856	laborer	52	"
X	Venezia Theresa †	856	housewife	42	"
Y	MacCormack Eugenia †	857	clerk	22	"
Z	Smiddy Rita †	857	housewife	26	"

1639

A	Smiddy William P, jr	857	longshoreman	23	"
B	MacCormack Catherine †	857	housewife	54	"
C	MacCormack Herbert	857	printer	56	879 Saratoga
D	MacCormack William H	857	U S N	22	here
E	MacCormack Daniel A	857	clerk	25	17 Kimball
F	MacCormack Margaret E †	857	housewife	23	17 "
G	*Riley Catherine †	858	"	35	here
H	Riley Henry	858	chauffeur	38	"
K	Rice John	858	retired	70	"
L	Rice Louise †	858	housewife	65	"
M	Rice William	858	clerk	30	"
N	Pacifico Adeline †	859	housewife	40	"
O	*Pacifico Joseph	859	baker	50	"
P	Santoro Alfred	859	machinist	36	"

24

Saratoga Street Continued

R	Santoro Clara †	859	housewife	31	here
S*	Santoro Domenic	859	laborer	72	"
T*	Santoro Theresa †	859	housewife	71	"
U	Dalton David	859	welder	31	400 Saratoga
V	Dalton Florence †	859	housewife	26	400 "
W	Piano Donato	860	laborer	54	here
X	Piano Josephine †	860	housewife	53	"
Y	McCarthy Callahan	860	chauffeur	47	"
Z	McCarthy Mabel †	860	housewife	52	"

1640

A	Panora Alfred	861	U S N	22	"
B	Panora Anna †	861	at home	43	"
D	Anselone Frank	861	steamfitter	45	"
C	Anselone Kathleen †	861	housewife	42	"
E	McNeil Frank	861	chauffeur	50	"
F	McNeil George	861	U S A	29	"
G	McNeil James	861	U S N	25	"
H	McNeil Nellie †	861	housewife	50	"
K	Oliver Angelo	862	laborer	50	"
L	Oliver Rose †	862	housewife	48	"
M	Peterson Albert	862	policeman	41	"
N	Peterson Helen †	862	housewife	28	"
O	Belmont Louis	863	machinist	34	"
P*	Belmont Theresa †	863	housewife	33	"
R	Gross Elizabeth †	863	"	27	825 Saratoga
S	Gross George	863	electrician	43	825 "
T*	Memmolo Grace †	863	housewife	36	here
U	Memmolo Thomas	863	chauffeur	36	"
V*	Sepe Salvatore	863	retired	71	"
W	Ross Earl	864	shipper	22	206 Everett
X	Ross Margaret †	864	housewife	26	206 "
Y*	Nucci Divina †	864	"	58	here
Z	Nucci Enos	864	fishcutter	29	"

1641

A	Nucci John	864	diestamper	21	"

William F. McClellan Highway

B	English Alice E †	119	housewife	32	here
C	English Kenneth	119	fish packer	36	"
D	Karas Frank	121	laborer	45	"

Page	Letter	Full Name	Residence, Jan. 1, 1943	Occupation	Supposed Age	Reported Residence, Jan. 1, 1942. Street and Number.

William F. McClellan Highway— Continued

	E	Karas Rose—†	121	housewife	26	here
	F	Gleason Francis	121	laborer	34	"
	G	Gleason Josephine E—†	121	housewife	34	"

Wordsworth Street

	H	Marotta John	7	confectioner	55	here
	K	Quinn Frank	7	laborer	30	"
	L	Quinn Mary—†	7	at home	55	"
	M	Mannix Dennis	7	carpenter	53	"
	N	Mannix James	7	U S A	29	"
	O	Mannix Mary—†	7	housewife	50	"
	P	Mannix Mary M—†	7	mechanic	20	"
	R	*O'Hara Henry	9	retired	70	"
	S	O'Hara John	9	weaver	60	"
	T	Casaccia Carmela—†	9	housewife	31	193 London
	U	Casaccia Joseph	9	clerk	32	193 "
	V	Eriksen Franklin J	9	welder	24	here
	W	Eriksen Grace—†	9	housewife	23	"
	X	Cerela Ann—†	9A	stitcher	29	"
	Y	Rubino Antonio	9A	laborer	59	"
	Z	*Rubino Filomena—†	9A	housewife	63	"

1642

	A	Rubino Josephine—†	9A	at home	20	"
	B	Pascucci Anna—†	9A	housewife	27	"
	C	Pascucci Henry	9A	machinist	28	"
	D	Foster Charles L	9A	fireman	24	"
	E	Foster Virginia—†	9A	housewife	25	"
	F	Corcoran Theresa—†	10	"	38	"
	G	Corcoran William J	10	checker	39	"
	H	Campbell Julia—†	10	at home	68	"
	K	Jewkes Theresa—†	10	"	65	"
	L	Tonello Evelyn—†	11	housewife	27	"
	M	Tonello Guido	11	diemaker	39	"
	N	Langone Lena—†	11	housewife	27	"
	O	Langone Patrick	11	optician	30	"
	P	Ferragamo Antonio	11	U S N	22	"
	R	Ferragamo Pasquale	11	laborer	45	"
	S	Ferragamo Rosaria—†	11	housewife	40	"
	T	Anderson Sarah—†	12	at home	43	"
	U	Layne Alice—†	12	secretary	23	"

26

Wordsworth Street (Continued)

	Letter	FULL NAME	Res.	Occupation	Age	Reported Residence
	v	Layne Jennie — †	12	housekeeper	49	here
	w	Layne Warren	12	U S A	21	"
	x	Branfiforte Philip, jr	12	chauffeur	29	"
	y	Branfiforte Ruth — †	12	housewife	29	"
	z	Thomas Mary — †	12	at home	83	"
1643						
	A	Schena Rocco J	13	ironworker	48	278 Princeton
	B	Schena Sadie — †	13	housewife	43	278 "
	C	Regan Helen — †	13	"	43	221 Benningt'n
	D	Regan William	13	steamfitter	46	221 "
	E*	Rebak Claudia — †	13	housewife	41	here
	F*	Rebak Edward	13	wool sorter	52	"
	G	Rebak Jennie — †	13	typist	21	"
	K	Companaro Clara — †	15	housewife	20	23 Everett
	L	Companaro Louis	15	rigger	20	23 "
	M	Tedeschi Emelio	15	tailor	47	here
	N	Tedeschi Fortuna — †	15	housewife	44	"
	O	Celian Sarah — †	15	"	35	Brockton
	P	Celian William	15	laborer	39	"
	R	Gatti Bruno	16	machinist	47	here
	S	Gatti Gina — †	16	housewife	40	"
	T	Travaglini Attilio	16	retired	67	"
	U	Travaglini John	16	ropemaker	33	"
	V*	Travaglini Lucy — †	16	housewife	67	"
	W	Camerano Filomena — †	17	"	57	"
	X	Camerano Francesco	17	retired	64	"
	Y	Camerano Phillip	17	welder	21	"
	Z	MacDonald Elizabeth — †	17	housewife	38	"
1644						
	A	MacDonald Melvin	17	inspector	48	"
	B	McKay Duncan	17	bookkeeper	63	"
	C	Interbartolo Joseph	17	clerk	29	"
	D	Interbartolo Rose — †	17	housewife	31	"
	E	Keenan James	18	retired	85	"
	F	Keenan Mary E — †	18	at home	76	"
	G	Martello Peter	19	merchant	57	62 London
	H	Martello Phyllis — †	19	housewife	34	62 "
	K	DeSimone Angelo	19	laborer	22	here
	L	DeSimone Filomena — †	19	at home	47	"
	M	Barnes Charlotte — †	19	"	56	"
	N	McGee George	19	clerk	35	"

Page.	Letter	FULL NAME.	Residence, Jan. 1, 1943.	Occupation.	Supposed Age.	Reported Residence, Jan. 1, 1942. Street and Number.

Wordsworth Street — Continued

	Letter	FULL NAME.	Res.	Occupation.	Age	Reported Residence
	o	Turner Frank L	20	U S N	33	here
	p	Turner Olga G — †	20	housewife	32	"
	r	Seaberg Augustine W	20	patternmaker	55	"
	s	Seaberg Doris E — †	20	secretary	21	"
	t	Seaberg Elfrieda M — †	20	housewife	59	"
	u	Chiccola Gaetano	21	barber	33	"
	v	Chiccola Mary — †	21	housewife	31	"
	w	Mancuso Frank	21	rubberworker	49	"
	x	Mancuso Mary — †	21	housewife	42	"
	y	*Turco Fillipo	21	millhand	53	"
	z	Turco Pasquale	21	draftsman	23	"

1645

	Letter	FULL NAME.	Res.	Occupation.	Age	Reported Residence
	a	*Turco Vincenza — †	21	housewife	49	"
	b	D'Avella Armando	22	U S A	20	"
	c	D'Avella Louis	22	"	28	"
	d	D'Avella Michelina — †	22	housewife	51	"
	e	D'Avella Nicholas	22	mechanic	52	"
	f	Gross Lavina — †	22	at home	41	"
	g	Fontina Antonio	23	fireman	53	"
	h	Fontina Edmund	23	U S A	22	"
	k	*Fontina Hannah — †	23	housewife	47	"
	l	*Moniz Emma — †	23	operator	34	"
	m	*Moniz John B	23	grinder	41	"
	n	Cannata Aurora — †	23	housewife	23	"
	o	Cannata Charles	23	cutter	24	"
	p	Bossi James	25	painter	40	"
	r	Bruno Eleanor — †	25	housewife	32	"
	s	Sweeney Edward J	25	painter	44	"
	t	Sweeney Esther — †	25	housewife	42	"
	u	Sweeney John E	25	U S N	21	"
	v	*Bruno Libera — †	25	housewife	36	"
	w	Bruno Pasquale	25	candymaker	37	"
	x	Keefe Esther — †	27	at home	56	"
	y	Keefe Thomas	27	U S A	26	"
	z	Storey Cora — †	27	inspector	32	"

1646

	Letter	FULL NAME.	Res.	Occupation.	Age	Reported Residence
	b	Ruggiero Helen — †	29	housewife	28	603 Benningt'n
	c	Ruggiero Joseph	29	B F D	29	603 "
	d	*DiGennaro Antonette — †	29	housewife	45	here
	e	DiGennaro Benjamin	29	machinist	23	"
	f	DiGennaro Peter	29	attendant	57	"

Wordsworth Street (Continued)

G	DiGennaro Peter	29	clerk	24	here
H	Radosta Jacqueline †	30	housewife	28	Revere
K	Radosta John	30	machinist	32	"
L	McCarthy Charles	30	fireman	25	607 Benningt'n
M	McCarthy Violet †	30	housewife	23	607 "
N	Adelizzi Eugene	31	maint'n'ceman	26	here
O	Adelizzi Florence †	31	clerk	20	"
P*	Adelizzi Jacqueline †	31	at home	83	"
R	Adelizzi Pasquale	31	shoeworker	57	"
S	McCormack Claudia †	33	assembler	24	"
T	McCormack Edgar	33	U S N	33	"
U	McCormack Genevieve †	33	stenographer	20	"
V	McCormack Margaret †	33	operator	23	"
W	McCormack Thomas	33	U S N	29	"
X	Nickley Agnes †	35	boxmaker	33	"
Y	Nickley Alice †	35	"	45	"
Z	Nickley Francis	35	seaman	31	"

1647

A	Nickley Joseph	35	clerk	38	"
B	Nickley Rose †	35	at home	35	"
E	Fleming Joseph P	39	foreman	32	"
F	Fleming Margaret †	39	housewife	28	"
G	Dolan Florence M †	39	cashier	20	"
H	Mahoney Christine F †	39	at home	49	"
K	Mitchell Mary G †	39	"	73	"
L	Smith Dorothy †	41	housewife	31	"
M	Smith Edward	41	printer	32	"
N	Puopolo Anthony J	41	operator	42	"
O	Puopolo Rose †	41	housewife	37	"
P	Allie Georgiana †	41	at home	64	"
R	Allie Mary †	41	clerk	32	"
S	Hansford Catherine †	42	housewife	23	"
T	Hansford Leonard	42	mechanic	25	"
U	Kennedy John	42	retired	72	"
V	Harrington Anna †	42	at home	50	"
W	Harrington John	42	U S N	22	"
X	Aiello Concetta †	43	housewife	36	"
Y	Aiello Joseph A	43	fireman	38	"
Z	Aiello Leonard	43	shipfitter	43	"

1648

A*	Aiello Margaret †	43	at home	75	"

Page.	Letter.	FULL NAME.	Residence, Jan. 1, 1943	Occupation.	Supposed Age.	Reported Residence, Jan. 1, 1942. Street and Number.

Wordsworth Street—Continued

	Letter	FULL NAME	Residence	Occupation	Age	Reported Residence
	B	LaClair Delia †	45	housewife	59	here
	C	LaClair Ferdinand	45	millhand	63	"
	D	Martell Anita—†	45	housewife	36	"
	E	Martel Arthur	45	barber	39	"
	F	Curry Jane E—†	46	housewife	43	"
	G	Curry Joseph P	46	drawtender	46	"
	H	Donohue Catherine—†	46	at home	26	"
	K	Donohue Cornelius	46	U S A	45	"
	L	Donohue Gerard	46	"	34	"
	M	Donohue William	46	pipefitter	37	"
	N	McKenna Catherine—†	48	housewife	32	"
	O	McKenna John	48	longshoreman	34	"
	P	Giammatteo Antony	48	retired	62	502 Summer
	R	Giammatteo Frank	48	U S A	21	502 "
	S	Giammatteo Mary—†	48	housewife	49	502 "
	T	Hanson Charles G	50	clerk	42	here
	U	Hanson Frances H—†	50	housewife	39	"
	V	Hanson Annie—†	50	at home	70	"
	W	Hanson William	50	policeman	47	"
	X	Pinkham Arthur E	51	assembler	38	"
	Y	Pinkham Hilda E—†	51	housewife	34	"
	Z	Thomas Beatrice H—†	51	clerk	29	"

1649

	Letter	FULL NAME	Residence	Occupation	Age	Reported Residence
	A	McInnis Alice—†	51	housewife	35	"
	B	McInnis Herman	51	metalworker	39	"
	C	Cody Hazel F—†	51	packer	20	"
	D	Cody Jennie I—†	51	housewife	45	"
	E	Cody Thomas H	51	shipper	47	"
	F	Houghton Edna F †	52	operator	49	"
	G	Sullivan Arthur J	52	electrician	39	"
	H	Sullivan Dennis B	52	retired	78	"
	K	Sullivan Mildred †	52	operator	43	"
	L	Cecchino Angelina †	53	housewife	29	"
	M	Cecchino Hector J	53	operator	31	"
	N	Amato Anthony	53	machinist	31	"
	O	Amato Gertrude †	53	housewife	27	"
	P	Andrade Anthony	53	merchant	50	"
	R	Andrade Rose †	53	housewife	42	"
	S	Burke John P	54	clerk	37	"
	T	Burke Mary †	54	housewife	35	"
	U	Bambrick Henry J	54	mechanic	40	"

Wordsworth Street Continued

v	Bambrick Marcella †	54	housewife	38	here
w	Butler Florence †	55	"	29	"
x	Butler John J	55	guard	30	"
y	Mullen Catherine J †	55	housewife	46	"
z	Mullen Edward F	55	clerk	20	"

1650

a	Mullen James A	55	laborer	48	"
b	Mullen James A	55	U S N	23	"
c	Brennan Francis J	56	laborer	58	"
d	Brennan Nellie †	56	housewife	63	"
e	Callaghan Katherine †	56	"	54	"
f	Callaghan Mary M †	56	clerk	23	"
g	Callaghan William	56	laborer	62	"
h	Munroe Helen M †	57	housewife	37	"
k	Munroe Joseph	57	U S N	39	"
l	Huyge Gustave	57	laborer	65	"
m	Huyge Jennie †	57	housewife	60	"
n	Bradley Peter	58	retired	80	"
o	Sullivan Clara R †	58	housewife	27	"
p	Sullivan Lawrence J	58	clerk	26	"
r	Bottelsen Olaf B	59	retired	67	"
s	Bottelsen Olaf, jr	59	operator	37	"
t	Jensen Agnes †	59	housewife	43	97 Addison
u	Jensen William	59	U S N	44	97 "
v	Barry Helen A †	59	housewife	57	here
w	Barry Helen F †	59	clerk	22	"
x	Barry Thomas F	59	foreman	64	"
y	Leville Charles	60	clerk	31	"
z	Leville Jennie †	60	housewife	25	"

1651

a	Wingard Alice †	60	housewife	31	"
b	Wingard William	60	mechanic	38	"
c	Mortimer Abraham P	61	U S A	32	"
d	Mortimer Agnes †	61	clerk	22	"
e	Mortimer Thomas J	61	laborer	66	"
f	Benoit James W	61	U S N	22	"
g	Benoit Joseph	61	operator	58	"
h	Benoit Mary E †	61	housewife	52	"
k	Langley Wildred L	61	rigger	35	"
l	Shelton Catherine †	62	housewife	40	"
m	Shelton Franklin	62	U S A	20	"

31

Wordsworth Street Continued

N	Shelton George	62	machinist	46	here	
O	*Benoit Annie— †	63	housewife	25	61 W Eagle	
P	Benoit Joseph, jr	63	mechanic	29	61 "	
R	Mambuca Domenic	63	laborer	25	666 Saratoga	
S	Mambuca Rose— †	63	housewife	24	666 "	
T	Ramsdell George F	65	chauffeur	49	here	
U	Ramsdell Winifred— †	65	housewife	48	"	
V	Pennell Addie— †	65	"	49	"	
W	Pennell John C	65	foreman	53	"	
X	Pennell John C, jr	65	U S A	24	"	
Y	Yeo Margaret— †	67	housewife	31	"	
Z	Yeo Warren	67	seaman	29	"	

1652

A	Crosby John J	67	clerk	20	"	
B	Crosby Mary R †	67	housewife	40	"	
C	Olsen Charles E	69	retired	53	"	
D	Olsen Florence D — †	69	housewife	45	"	
E	Olsen Florence D — †	69	clerk	21	"	
F	Olsen Rita—†	69	"	22	"	
G	Dunbar Frank B	69	U S C G	22	"	
H	Palazzolo Leo	70	candymaker	35	"	
K	Palazzolo Rose †	70	housewife	31	"	
L	*Piano Josephine— †	70	"	64	"	
M	*Piano Pasquale	70	candymaker	60	"	
N	Dorgan Florence †	70	housewife	31	"	
O	Dorgan James	70	packer	31	"	
P	Brindamour Dorothy — †	70	housewife	29	"	
R	Brindamour Francis	70	shipper	34	"	
S	Caturano Dorinda— †	71	housewife	30	"	
T	Caturano James	71	mechanic	29	"	
U	Hastings Catherine M — †	71	housewife	60	"	
V	Hastings James F	71	supervisor	37	"	
W	Hastings James H	71	retired	71	"	
X	Hastings John M	71	supervisor	38	"	
Y	*Gardullo Ida—†	72	housewife	59	"	
Z	*Gardullo Joseph	72	candymaker	62	"	

1653

A	*Molino Henry	72	shoeworker	40	"	
B	Molino Josephine — †	72	housewife	33	"	
C	Jameson Evelyn T †	72	"	35	14 Antrim	
D	Jameson Robert J	72	optician	43	14 "	

Wordsworth Street Continued

		FULL NAME	Res.	Occupation	Age	Reported Residence
E	Driscoll Mary — †	73	housewife	24	here
F	Driscoll Thomas	73	pipefitter	29	"
G	Purvitsky Alice — †	73	operator	36	Malden
H	Purvitsky John	73	U S A	36	"
K	Stack John E	73	foreman	31	86 Wordsworth
L	Stack Mary E — †	73	housewife	23	86 "
M	Cook Mary E — †	74	operator	45	here
N	Gooby Ingham J	74	cook	55	"
O	Sweeney Gerald	75	drawtender	43	"
P	Sweeney Susan — †	75	housewife	43	"
R	Reilly Dorothy — †	75	"	33	343 Benningt'n
S	Reilly Morris	75	mechanic	40	345 "
T	O'Keefe Edward	78	retired	81	here
U	O'Keefe Henry	78	boilermaker	39	"
V	O'Keefe Joseph	78	painter	44	"
W	DeSisto Helen — †	80	housewife	39	"
X	DeSisto Jerry	80	engineer	56	"
Y	Searle John	86	U S A	20	742 Benningt'n
Z	Searle Mary — †	86	operator	22	742 "
	1654				
A	Wilcox Gifford	88	inspector	34	here
B	Wilcox Mildred — †	88	housewife	28	"
C	Fennelly Anna M — †	90	"	55	"
D	Fennelly Canice J	90	policeman	51	"
E	Fennelly Cyril L	90	U S C G	22	"
F	Harvender William	92	clerk	26	"
G	Sullivan Agnes E — †	92	housewife	43	"
H	Sullivan Alexander	92	electrician	52	"
K	Kelsey Arlene — †	96	housewife	29	"
L	Kelsey Rosferd	96	engineer	33	"
M	McMahon Anne — †	96	at home	75	"
N	Dever George F	107	custodian	47	"
O	Dever Mary A — †	107	housewife	47	"
R	Chisholm Annie — †	109	at home	61	"
S	Bullock Rose — †	109	housewife	43	"
T	Bullock William J	109	clerk	43	"

Ward 1–Precinct 17

CITY OF BOSTON

LIST OF RESIDENTS
20 YEARS OF AGE AND OVER

(NON-CITIZENS INDICATED BY ASTERISK)
(FEMALES INDICATED BY DAGGER)

AS OF

JANUARY 1, 1943

JOSEPH F. TIMILTY, *Chairman*
FREDERIC E. DOWLING, *Secretary*
WILLIAM A. MOTLEY, JR.
FRANCIS B. McKINNEY
EVERETT R. PROUT
Listing Board.

CITY OF BOSTON PRINTING DEPARTMENT

Page.	Letter.	FULL NAME.	Residence. Jan. 1, 1943.	Occupation.	Supposed Age.	Reported Residence, Jan. 1, 1942. Street and Number.

1700

Ashley Street

A	*Carideo Angelina—†	19	housewife	55	here
B	Carideo Patrick	19	shipper	28	"
C	Merrigan William	19	salesman	31	"
D	Ryan John J	19	engineer	65	"
E	Ryan Margaret—†	19	housewife	51	"
F	Conley Florence—†	19	"	32	"
G	Conley Harry	19	salesman	30	"
H	*Puzzo Angelina—†	19A	housewife	74	"
K	Puzzo Michalina—†	19A	clerk	40	"
L	Puzzo Pasqualina—†	19A	"	34	"
M	Marcella Arthur	19A	shipfitter	33	
N	*Marcella Michalina—†	19A	housekeeper	67	274 Princeton
O	Marcella Rachel—†	19A	housewife	36	here
P	McDonald Ellen F—†	21	"	70	"
R	McDonald Florence—†	21	clerk	41	"
S	McDonald James W	21	operator	40	"
T	Varlado Anthony	21	machinist	28	23 Ashley
U	Varlado Mary A—†	21	housewife	22	15 Morris
V	*Censabella Carmella—†	21A	"	72	here
W	Censabella Dominick	21A	laborer	72	"
X	Rosa Anthony J	21A	machinist	22	1215 Bennington
Y	Rosa Henrietta—†	21A	housewife	22	1215 "
Z	*Varlado Frank	23	retired	66	here

1701

A	Varlado George	23	clerk	20	"
B	Varlado Joseph G	23	"	35	"
C	*Varlado Rose—†	23	housewife	59	"
E	Venezia Patrick	23A	electrician	35	"
F	Venezia Rose—†	23A	housewife	40	"
G	*DeSimone Catherine—†	23A	"	30	"
H	DeSimone Louis	23A	painter	31	"
K	Cassale Elizabeth—†	25	housewife	37	"
L	Cassale Richard S	25	metalworker	40	"
M	*Minichiello Antonetta—†	27	housewife	41	"
N	*Minichiello Ralph	27	longshoreman	54	"
O	Gemelli John	29	tailor	23	"
P	Gemelli Michael	29	mason	54	"
R	Gemelli Rachel—†	29	housewife	52	"
S	Cassaro Liboria—†	31	stitcher	24	"
T	Cassaro Mary—†	31	trimmer	22	"

2

Page.	Letter.	FULL NAME.	Residence, Jan. 1, 1943.	Occupation	Supposed Age.	Reported Residence, Jan. 1, 1942. Street and Number.

Ashley Street Continued

	U	Cassaro Michael	31	laborer	56	here
	V	*Cassaro Sadie — †	31	housewife	45	"
	X	Gregory Joseph A	35	chauffeur	44	139 Leyden
	Y	Gregory Theresa — †	35	housewife	39	139 "
	Z	*Giglio Caroline — †	39	dressmaker	46	here
1702						
	A	Giglio Domenic	39	boxmaker	44	"
	B	Craviotto Margaret — †	39	housewife	34	"
	C	Craviotto Silvio	39	plumber	35	"
	D	Bellio Angela — †	41	housewife	44	"
	E	Bellio Moses	41	mechanic	46	"
	F	Masone Pasqualina — †	41	housewife	53	"
	G	Masone Ralph	41	pipefitter	54	"
	H	Roberts John W	rear 41	laborer	39	"
	K	Roberts Mildred — †	" 41	housewife	37	"

Beachview Road

	L	Flaherty Martin J	9	B F D	54	296 Paris
	M	Meaney David M	9	policeman	40	here
	N	Meaney Theresa — †	9	housewife	37	"
	O	Meaney William	9	U S A	23	"
	P	Brignatti Eleanor — †	11	housewife	73	"
	R	Brignatti Lawrence	11	laborer	36	"
	S	Smith Charles H	15	printer	61	"
	T	Groppi Anacleto	23	laborer	37	"
	U	Groppi Mildred — †	23	housewife	24	"
	V	Andressano Margaret — †	23	"	41	"
	W	Andressano Victor	23	tailor	42	"
	X	Groppi Alfred	23	U S N	22	"
	Y	Groppi Erina — †	23	housewife	63	"
	Z	Groppi John	23	U S A	26	"
1703						
	A	Groppi Joseph	23	laborer	28	"
	B	Groppi Oresto	23	retired	72	"
	C	Sardina Ida — †	27	housewife	34	"
	D	Sardina John	27	welder	33	"
	E	Antonucci Ancilla — †	27	housewife	29	"
	F	Antonucci Frank	27	painter	30	"
	G	Giorni Gabriel	27	clerk	62	"
	H	Ford Arthur F	30-32	superintendent	59	"

3

Beachview Road—Continued

	K	Ford Jennie—†	30-32	housewife	60	here
	L	Ford Ruth H—†	30-32	teacher	26	"
	M	Carrigg Margaret—†	30-32	clerk	31	Lowell
	N	Ford Charles H	30-32	U S N	29	here
	O	Ford Mary H—†	30-32	housewife	25	"
	P*	Perricotti Cesira—†	31	"	76	"
	R	Perricotti John W	31	plumber	49	"
	S	Perricotti Peter J	31	laborer	38	345 Princeton
	T*	Rondelli Adolph	31	"	76	here
	U	Rando Antonio	36	machinist	55	"
	V	Rando Josephine—†	36	examiner	21	"
	W	Rando Margaret—†	36	clerk	26	"
	X	Rando Mary—†	36	housewife	53	"
	Y*	Rando Paul	36	retired	82	"
	Z	Velardo Antonio	36	barber	65	"

1704

	A	Velardo Josephine—†	36	housewife	57	"
	B	Velardo Margaret—†	36	clerk	21	"
	C	Velardo Natalie—†	36	attendant	25	"
	D	Ciampa Frank	36	manager	40	"
	E	Ciampa Laurie—†	36	housewife	35	"
	F	Pesce Angelo	47	painter	59	"
	G	Pesce Anna—†	47	clerk	20	"
	H	Pearson George	47	U S N	38	"
	K	Pearson Lillian—†	47	inspector	24	"
	L	Palladino Joseph	47	machinist	29	"
	M	Palladino Pauline—†	47	clerk	33	"
	N	Hoyt Irving	53	policeman	51	"
	O	Hoyt Philip	53	U S A	22	"
	P	Hoyt Violetta—†	53	housewife	44	"
	R	Pollard Leigh	53	U S A	29	"

Bennington Street

	S	Vendetti Celia—†	1144	housewife	54	here
	T	Vendetti Edward	1144	tailor	56	"
	U	Vendetti Loretta—†	1144	saleswoman	25	"
	V	Casaletto Alfred	1144	mason	36	"
	W	Casaletto Joseph	1144	clerk	34	"
	X	Casaletto Josephine—†	1144	at home	64	"
	Y	Casaletto Vincenza—†	1144	housewife	31	"

4

Bennington Street (Continued)

	z	Caselden Daniel	1144	policeman	46	here
1705						
	A	Caselden Daniel, jr	1144	machinist	20	"
	B	Caselden Margaret —†	1144	housewife	46	"
	C	Queenan Agnes —†	1148	"	39	"
	D	Queenan John	1148	accountant	37	"
	E	Griffin Doris M —†	1148	inspector	23	Winthrop
	F	Griffin Edward R	1148	welder	29	"
	G	Griffin Elizabeth C —†	1148	housewife	54	"
	H	Griffin John F	1148	cashier	55	"
	K	Calledare Anthony	1148	shipper	31	791 Saratoga
	L	Calledare Mary—†	1148	housewife	24	791 "
	M	Savasta Anthony	1150	coppersmith	21	here
	N	*Savasta Antonia —†	1150	housewife	55	"
	O	Savasta Mary —†	1150	clerk	31	"
	P	Lanfranchi Antonetta—†	1150	housewife	41	"
	R	Lanfranchi John	1150	metalworker	42	"
	S	Lanfranchi Joseph	1150	U S N	20	"
	T	Bonanno Leo	1150	carpenter	18	"
	U	*Bonanno Mary —†	1150	housewife	42	"
	V	*DiBella Frank	1150	retired	76	"

Breed Street

	W	*Ferrara Frank	29	contractor	63	here
	X	*Ferrara Maria —†	29	housewife	60	"
	Y	Ferrara Lucy —†	29	"	24	36 Ashley
	Z	Ferrara Salvatore	29	laborer	25	36 "
1706						
	A	Rando Agnes —†	31	housewife	50	here
	B	Rando Marie —†	31	at home	29	"
	C	Rando Pasquale	31	barber	52	"
	D	Silvano Marcelle —†	31	housewife	24	"
	E	Silvano Pasquale	31	butcher	30	"
	F	Mini Andrew	33	chauffeur	31	131 Putnam
	G	Mini Lena —†	33	housewife	27	131 "
	H	Smith Alfred H	33	retired	64	here
	K	Smith Alfred H, jr	33	U S N	31	"
	L	Smith Annie C —†	33	housewife	64	"
	M	Lial Josephine —†	35	at home	64	"
	N	Camacho Louis G	35	machinist	24	"
	O	Camacho Theresa—†	35	housewife	24	"

5

Page	Letter	FULL NAME.	Residence. Jan. 1, 1943.	Occupation.	Supposed Age.	Reported Residence, Jan. 1, 1942. Street and Number.

Faywood Avenue

	R	Labadini Alda—†	31	housewife	35	here
	S	Labadini Ernest	31	bartender	37	"
	T	DeSimone Eleanor C—†	31	secretary	39	"
	U	DeSimone Saveria—†	31	housewife	66	"
	V	Grasso Edmund A	31	laborer	26	"
	W	DeLorenzo George	31	machinist	23	"
	X	DeLorenzo Virginia—†	31	housewife	23	"
	Y	Leigh Amy—†	33	"	75	"
	Z	Leigh Dorothy M—†	33	stenographer	43	"

1707

	A	Leigh John	33	retired	74	"
	B	Moran Henry F	33	foreman	43	"
	C	Moran Mary J—†	33	housewife	37	"
	D	Brean Marie E—†	33	waitress	29	"
	E	Brean Mary E—†	33	housewife	63	"
	F	Brean Thaddeus	33	retired	72	"
	G	Muse Mary E—†	35	housewife	43	"
	H	Muse Wilfred F	35	seaman	49	"
	K	Sparaco John	35	laborer	44	"
	L	Sparaco Lillian—†	35	housewife	44	"
	M	Quinlan Catherine—†	35	"	51	"
	N	Quinlan John	35	fisherman	58	"
	O	Wood Fred S	37	pilot	54	"
	P	Wood Mary M—†	37	housewife	53	"
	R	Wood Robert S	37	U S A	20	"
	S	Butera Jennie—†	37	housewife	40	"
	T	Butera Mary—†	37	secretary	20	"
	U	Butera Rocco	37	hairdresser	43	"
	V	Butera Rosario	37	musician	22	"
	W	Pignato Anthony	37	instructor	24	"
	X	Pignato Eleanor—†	37	housewife	24	"
	Y	Pesce Edith—†	43	at home	40	"
	Z	Pesce Jennie—†	43	housewife	67	"

1708

	A	Pesce Louis	43	metalworker	42	"
	B	Hallahan Evelyn—†	45	housewife	26	"
	C	Hallahan John	45	U S A	27	"
	D	Kennedy Anna—†	45	housewife	50	"
	E	Kennedy John	45	inspector	52	"
	F	McGurn Beatrice—†	45	housewife	24	"

Faywood Avenue Continued

G	McGurn John	45	boilermaker	28	here
H	Dundon Cornelius L	48	guard	61	"
K	Dundon Mary L—†	48	housewife	62	"
L	Lemos Clarence	51	engraver	48	"
M	Lemos Margaret—†	51	housewife	44	"
N	Velardi Anthony	52	policeman	49	"
O	Velardi Mildred—†	52	housewife	39	"
P	Giordano Mary—†	52	"	59	"
R	Giordano Oscar	52	U S A	21	"
S	Giordano Salvatore	52	welder	27	"
T	Palladino Domenick	52	supervisor	31	"
U	Palladino Mafalda—†	52	housewife	28	"
V	Doherty Edward	55	salesman	42	"
W	Doherty Louise—†	55	housewife	42	"
X	Kelley George	56	shipwright	29	Newton
Y	Kelley Ruth—†	56	housewife	27	Hull
Z	Kenney Alice K—†	56	"	40	here

1709

A	Kenney Nicholas C	56	policeman	47	"
B	Vincent Catherine—†	60	housewife	33	"
C	Vincent Robert H	60	dentist	46	"
D	Lavery Agnes—†	64	teacher	39	"
E	Tyrell John	64	custodian	40	"
F	Tyrell Marguerite M—†	64	housewife	38	"
G	Stasio Anthony	67	toolmaker	28	"
H	Stasio Genevieve—†	67	housewife	24	"
K	DeLeo Gaetano	67	musician	50	"
L	Serigmano Charles	67	U S N	23	"
M	Serigmano Michael	67	grocer	54	"
N	Serigmano Nancy—†	67	housewife	43	"
O	Serigmano Nancy—†	67	student	21	"
P	Celia Joseph	68	bartender	48	295 Sumner
R*	Celia Josephine—†	68	housewife	48	295 "
S	Cappucci Enrico	69	clerk	29	18 Haynes
T	Cappucci Virginia—†	69	housewife	26	Milton
U	O'Malley Delia A—†	69	housekeeper	70	here
V	O'Malley Lillian E—†	69	bookkeeper	42	"
W	Warren Samuel A	73	inspector	49	"
X	Warren Winifred—†	73	housewife	48	"
Y	Oresteen Mary A—†	74	housekeeper	69	"

Page	Letter	FULL NAME.	Residence, Jan. 1, 1943.	Occupation.	Supposed Age.	Reported Residence, Jan. 1, 1942. Street and Number.

Faywood Avenue—Continued

	z	Wright Charles D	74	inspector	49	here
1710						
	A	Wright Margaret J †	74	housewife	45	"
	B	Gahen Catherine †	76	"	31	51 Maverick sq
	C	Gahen John B	76	machinist	41	1114 Bennington
	D	MacDonald Lena †	76	cashier	44	1148 "
	E	Moran Marie †	76	secretary	22	Wash'n D C
	F	Moran Thomas J	76	U S N	62	1124 Saratoga
	G	Moran Thomas J jr	76	U S A	23	1124 "
	H	Tammas Charles	76	metalworker	42	1148 Bennington
	K	Tammas Margaret †	76	housewife	40	1148 "
	L	Newbury Warren C	79	superintendent	49	here
	M	Williams Catherine †	79	clerk	40	"
	N	Cantillo Alice †	84	housewife	39	"
	O	Cantillo William	84	chauffeur	44	"
	P	Cotreau Delphis M	85	rigger	42	"
	R	Cotreau Julia †	85	housewife	40	"
	S	Telese Assunta †	85	"	38	"
	T	Telese Eugene	85	machinist	43	"
	W	Ferraro Frank	87	"	21	"
	U	Ferraro Henrietta †	87	housewife	40	"
	V	Ferraro Joseph	87	welder	41	"
	X	Ferri George	87	decorator	26	"
	Y	Swartz Albert	87	packer	42	"
	Z	Swartz Beatrice †	87	tel operator	37	"
1711						
	A	Swartz Catherine †	87	housewife	62	"
	B	Swartz George	87	clerk	45	"
	C	Faiella Anna †	88	housewife	54	"
	D	Faiella Felix	88	barber	58	"
	E	Faiella John	88	merchant	23	"
	F	Breault Edna †	88	housewife	30	"
	G	Breault Joseph	88	laborer	32	"
	H	Reynolds Michael	88	"	56	"
	K	Faiella Ralph	88	barber	31	"
	L	Faiella Theresa †	88	housewife	28	"
	O	Palladino Josephine †	92	housekeeper	51	"
	M	DeFelice Leo	92	printer	37	"
	N	DeFelice Millie †	92	housewife	37	"
	P	Crouse Edward C	93	U S N	45	"
	R	Crouse Melvin	93	"	32	"

Faywood Avenue Continued

s	Crouse Mildred †	93	housewife	32	here	
T	Baker Catherine R †	93	"	24	105 Falcon	
U	Baker Herbert F	93	electrician	35	105 "	
V	Eugene Leora †	93	at home	46	105 "	
W	Shaughnessy Margaret †	93	waitress	25	Belmont	
X	Sorzio Alfredo	95	printer	38	here	
Y	Sorzio Lucy †	95	housewife	35	"	
Z	Randi Genaro	95	barber	60	"	

1712

A	Randi Mantanella †	95	housewife	60	"	
B	Osganian George	100	butcher	48	"	
C	Osganian Rose †	100	housewife	38	"	
D	Gotgart Charles	103	machinist	23	"	
E	Gotgart Elizabeth V †	103	housewife	24	"	
F	Thibeault Edward F	103	seaman	55	"	
G	Thibeault Elizabeth A †	103	housewife	55	"	
H	Thibeault Mary H—†	103	nurse	31	"	
K	Morelli Caesar	108	machinist	42	23 Breed	
L	Morelli Grace—†	108	housewife	38	89 Orient av	
M	Tribuna Bartholomew	110	foreman	41	here	
N	Tribuna Marion—†	110	housewife	38	"	
O	Capillo Joseph	116	chauffeur	45	"	
P	Capillo Margaret—†	116	housewife	48	"	
R	Doherty Eleanor—†	116	saleswoman	22	"	
S	Doto Horace J	116	U S A	29	"	
T	Fournier Catherine L—†	124	housewife	29	35 Lawrence	
U	Fournier John L	124	policeman	32	35 "	
V	Gallo Angelina †	125	decorator	22	here	
W	Gallo Frank	125	U S A	21	"	
X	*Gallo Joseph	125	baker	54	"	
Y	Gallo Nicholas	125	"	20	"	
Z	*Gallo Thomasina †	125	housewife	44	"	

1713

A	*Grifoni Joseph	125	tailor	73	"	
B	Bianco Carmen	150	manager	30	"	
C	Bianco Ethel †	150	housewife	31	"	
D	Clarke Richard	150	laborer	70	"	
E	McNealey Edward	150	chauffeur	46	"	
F	Gillis Dorothy N †	154	housewife	46	"	
G	Gillis Frank J	154	mechanic	50	"	
H	Wilke William J	154	U S A	24	Panama	

9

Gladstone Street

k	Cutillo Mary †	1	housewife	40	here
l	Cutillo Pasquale	1	shoemaker	41	"
m	Ciampa Anthony	1	barber	27	"
n	Ciampa Genaro	1	retired	72	"
o	Ciampa Helen †	1	dressmaker	25	"
p*	Ciampa Lucy †	1	housewife	65	"
r	Ciampa Theresa †	1	stitcher	34	"
u	DeWitt Marguerite †	5	operator	46	"
v	Doyle Alice †	5	"	41	Winthrop
w	Grady Mary E †	5	at home	41	here
x	Stavredis Christopher	7	merchant	58	"
y	Stavredis Viola †	7	housewife	43	"
z	Monahan Daniel J	8	retired	70	Chelsea

1714

a	Norton Agnes V †	8	housewife	62	here
b	Norton William L	8	operator	63	"
c	Anderson Abbie M †	9	receptionist	40	"
d	Anderson Frank E	9	retired	71	"
e	Anderson Lillian J †	9	housewife	70	"
f	Perry Thomas J	9	fisherman	68	"
g	Goldstein Anna †	9	housewife	51	"
h	Goldstein Ruth F †	9	stenographer	24	"
k	Goldstein Samuel	9	merchant	57	"
l	Maffeo Consiglia †	10	housewife	59	"
m	Maffeo Elvira †	10	technician	23	"
n	Maffeo Henry H	10	U S M C	27	"
o	Maffeo Paul	10	retired	59	"
p	Maffeo Paul, jr	10	U S A	22	"
r	Maffeo Peter	10	interne	25	"
s	Maffeo Sylvia †	10	technician	28	"
t	Krebs John	12	salesman	41	"
u	Krebs Joseph	12	student	20	"
v	Krebs Victoria †	12	housewife	40	"
w	Lovett John	12	retired	73	"
x	Lovett Stella †	12	clerk	50	"
y	Marino Louise †	12	housewife	46	"
z	Marino Mary †	12	saleswoman	22	"

1715

a*	Marino Samuel	12	barber	48	"
b	Chiampa John	16	manager	49	"
c	Chiampa Mary †	16	housewife	48	"

Gladstone Street Continued

D	Calla Connie †	16	housewife	22	here
E	Calla Silvio	16	metalworker	28	"
F	Barboza Joseph	17	operator	60	"
G	Barboza Maria †	17	housewife	52	"
H	Barboza Maria †	17	operator	33	"
K	Nolle John	17	seaman	38	"
L	Bertolino Ann E—†	17	nurse	26	"
M	Bertolino Gertrude H †	17	assembler	24	"
N	Bertolino Helen †	17	housewife	49	"
O	Bertolino Nicholas P	17	U S A	29	"
P	Bertolino Thomas S	17	U S N	24	"
R	Dimico John	17	textileworker	46	"
S	Gilbrock John F	18	boilermaker	45	"
T	Gilbrock John F. jr	18	U S N	22	"
U	Gilbrock Mary—†	18	housewife	45	"
V	Gilbrock Ralph W	18	U S N	23	"
W	Gilbrock William F	18	U S M C	21	"
X	Berg Mabel E—†	18	housewife	50	"
Y	Berg Olaf D	18	painter	57	"
Z	Grimshaw Cecelia B—†	20	housewife	39	97 Horace
1716					
A	Grimshaw James B	20	chauffeur	42	97 "
B	DeSessa Alice—†	21	housewife	24	59 Moore
C	DeSessa Louis	21	policeman	50	960 Saratoga
D	DeSessa Mary †	21	housewife	48	960 "
E	DeSessa Peter	21	U S N	26	39 Moore
F	Pinardi Gloria †	21	saleswoman	23	Clinton
G	Pinardi Raymond A	21	laborer	25	"
H	*Pinardi Rose †	21	at home	49	"
K	Freeman Agnes L—†	22	housewife	72	here
L	Freeman James H	22	retired	78	"
M	Sullivan Alice M †	22	teacher	52	"
N	Sullivan Michael N	22	retired	84	"
O	Sullivan John J	24	reporter	46	"
P	Sullivan Margaret E—†	24	housewife	42	"
R	Boushell Margaret I—†	24	packer	41	"
S	Boushell William F	24	timekeeper	52	"
T	DeSimone Carl	25	engineer	41	871 Saratoga
U	DeSimone Michael	25	U S A	22	871 "
V	Pastore Marciano	25	mechanic	52	871 "
W	*Pastore Rose—†	25	housewife	50	871 "

11

Page.	Letter	FULL NAME.	Residence, Jan. 1, 1943	Occupation.	Supposed Age.	Reported Residence, Jan. 1, 1942. Street and Number.

Gladstone Street—Continued

x	Sacco Angelina †	25	housewife	28	871 Saratoga
y	Sacco Ernest E	25	chemist	36	871 "
z	Pastore Ausilio	25	laborer	55	280 Chelsea

1717

A*	Pastore Concetta †	25	housewife	55	280 "
B	Genzale Frances †	25	"	29	34 W Eagle
C	Genzale Ralph	25	shipfitter	27	34 "
D	Silvano Arthur	25	storekeeper	27	117 Gladstone
E	Silvano Mary †	25	housewife	27	117 "
F	Giarrusso Caroline C †	26	"	42	here
G	Giarrusso James	26	draftsman	46	"
H	Bianco Gennara	26	retired	74	"
K	Cataldo Angelina †	26	at home	64	"
L	Cataldo Lawrence	26	shipfitter	36	"
M	Cataldo Marie †	26	housewife	26	"
N	Butt Cecelia †	26	"	47	"
O	Butt Joseph S	26	metalworker	56	"
P*	Belli Angelina †	33	housewife	49	42 Breed
R*	Belli Gelda †	33	operator	21	42 "
S	Belli Louis	33	engineer	56	42 "
T	Paci Angelo	33	U S A	28	here
U	Paci Charles	33	welder	32	"
V	Paci Domenic	33	retired	67	"
W	Paci Domenica †	33	at home	26	"
X*	Paci Elizabeth †	33	housewife	61	"
Y	Paci Victor	33	shipfitter	24	"
Z*	Strangie Carmella †	33	at home	52	"

1718

A	Strangie Jennie †	33	packer	21	"
B	Strangie Pasquale	33	U S M C	21	"
C	DiGregorio Angela †	34	housewife	42	"
D	DiGregorio Richard	34	carpenter	47	"
E	Arsenault Adam A	37	engineer	43	"
F	Arsenault Mary M †	37	housewife	45	"
G	Thibeault Mary †	37	at home	58	"
H	Caputo Andrew	37	steelworker	27	"
K	Caputo Elizabeth †	37	housewife	53	"
L	Caputo Gladys †	37	stenographer	22	"
M	Caputo John	37	ironworker	55	"
N	DeFronzo Angelina †	37	housewife	29	46 Gladstone
O	DeFronzo Pasquale	37	printer	33	46 "

Gladstone Street (Continued)

P	Cardinale Mary †	44	stenographer	26	here
R	Cardinale Nicholas	44	U S N	27	"
S	Cardinale Raffaela—†	44	clerk	23	"
T*	Cardinale Rose—†	44	at home	53	"
U	Cardinale Vincent	44	U S A	21	"
V	Piscopo Guy	45	"	38	"
W	Piscopo Lillian—†	45	clerk	42	"
X	Piscopo Louise †	45	receptionist	36	"
Y	Piscopo Mary—†	45	housewife	39	"
Z	Piscopo John	45	retired	67	"

1719

A	Guerrini Olga †	46	stitcher	21	"
B	Guerrini Purifica—†	46	housewife	56	"
C	Guerrini Valente	46	retired	62	"
D	Guerrini Maria—†	46	forewoman	23	117 George
E	Guerrini Onofrio	46	electrician	23	here
F	Palladino Aldo	51	U S A	28	"
G	Palladino Amy—†	51	teacher	30	"
H	Palladino Mary—†	51	at home	66	"
K	Ekholm Charles F	52	retired	68	"
L	Ekholm Helena I †	52	housewife	62	"
M	McGinn Helen E †	52	"	37	"
N	McGinn Joseph G	52	manager	38	"
O	Cummings Catherine—†	56	housewife	32	"
P	Cummings William	56	clerk	40	"
R	Cummings Catherine—†	56	forewoman	50	"
S	Cummings Edward	56	mechanic	44	"
T	Cummings Ellen—†	56	housewife	72	"
U	Cummings Ethel †	56	lawyer	40	"
V	Cummings John	56	retired	85	"
W	Cummings Joseph	56	clerk	37	"
X	Cummings Thomas	56	"	48	"
Y	Larkin Mary L †	57	at home	57	"
Z	McDonald Elias	57	engineer	67	"

1720

A	McDonald Josephine—†	57	housewife	66	"
C	Bruno Eleanor †	60	"	27	"
D	Bruno James	60	storekeeper	25	"
E	Angrisano Anthony S	61	mechanic	25	"
F	Angrisano Josephine—†	61	housewife	24	"
H*	Bruno Joseph	62	storekeeper	58	"

13

Page	Letter	Full Name.	Residence, Jan. 1, 1943.	Occupation.	Supposed Age.	Reported Residence, Jan. 1, 1942. Street and Number.

Gladstone Street—Continued

K	*Bruno Julia †	62	housewife	48	here
L	Abruzese Gabriel	65	retired	65	4 Shelby
M	Abruzese Gertrude †	65	housewife	24	234 Saratoga
N	Abruzese James	65	driller	34	234 "
O	*Carosella Antonetta †	65	housewife	46	here
P	Carosella Pasquale	65	laborer	48	"
R	Farley Marie †	66	housewife	32	102 Barnes av
S	Farley Vincent	66	optician	37	102 "
T	Riley James	66	boilermaker	21	here
U	Riley Mary †	66	housewife	59	"
V	Riley Thomas H	66	merchant	59	"
W	Jennings Mildred †	69	stenographer	24	29 Beach
X	Luongo John, jr	69	ironworker	29	here
Y	Luongo Madeline †	69	housewife	26	"
Z	Marino Irene †	69	"	39	"

1721

A	Marino Joseph	69	mechanic	41	"
B	Bronzo Anthony	71	U S A	26	"
C	Bronzo Charles	71	designer	52	"
D	Bronzo Madeline †	71	housewife	47	"
E	Bronzo Martha †	71	operator	24	"
F	Bronzo Raymond	71	student	20	"
G	Famolare John	72	contractor	36	6 Ford
H	Famolare Ruth †	72	housewife	35	9 "
K	Guptill Louis H	72	motorman	66	here
L	Neff Margaret B †	72	housewife	29	"
M	Neff Robert L	72	manager	30	"
N	O'Hara Dorothy M †	72	housewife	21	"
O	O'Hara James E	72	chauffeur	22	"
P	Luongo Joseph	73	U S A	23	"
Q	Luongo Margaret †	73	housewife	55	"
S	Luongo Mary †	73	stenographer	20	"
T	Luongo Michael	73	student	25	"
U	Luongo Ralph	73	manager	55	"
V	Martino Alphonsia †	81	housewife	50	"
W	Martino Eliseo	81	storekeeper	53	"
X	Martino Gerardo	81	U S A	22	"
Y	Patterella Mary †	81	at home	56	"
Z	DeFreitas Clementine †	81	housewife	28	206 Princeton

1722

A	DeFreitas Thomas	81	shipfitter	30	206 "

Gladstone Street Continued

B	Indrisano Mary—†	82	hostess	34	here
C	Marino John	82	chauffeur	43	"
D	Marino Rose—†	82	housewife	40	"
E	*Vardaro Antonio	82	retired	68	"
F	Vardaro Angelo L	82	U S N	27	"
G	Vardaro Dea—†	82	at home	22	"
H	Marino Delma—†	82	housewife	33	"
K	Marino Frank	82	manager	34	"
L	*Marino Grace—†	82	at home	74	"
M	Marino Antonio	85	fireman	51	"
N	Marino Flavia—†	85	housewife	48	"
O	Marino Frances F—†	85	clerk	22	"
P	Pratt Arthur W	86	retired	66	"
R	Pratt Mary—†	86	housewife	68	"
S	Sacco Grace C—†	87	"	32	"
T	Sacco John	87	carpenter	36	"
U	Bird Mary—†	88	at home	75	"
V	Bird Sarah—†	88	"	79	"
W	Sampson Blanche E—†	89	"	59	"
X	DeFronzo Rosemarie—†	90	student	22	"
Y	Duscio Concetto	90	shipper	70	"
Z	*Duscio Mary—†	90	housewife	59	"

1723

A	Spina Jeannette—†	92	"	42	"
B	Spina Joseph	92	laborer	60	"
C	Breed Helen—†	93	housewife	29	"
D	Breed James E	93	printer	31	"
E	Eramo Frederick	93	U S A	34	"
F	Eramo George	93	U S N	36	"
G	Eramo Guido	93	chauffeur	33	"
H	Eramo John	93	operator	24	"
K	Eramo Mary—†	93	housewife	57	"
L	Eramo Vincent	93	retired	66	"
M	Eramo Viola—†	93	clerk	26	"
N	Granato Carmello	94	U S A	29	"
O	*Granato Fannie—†	94	housewife	54	"
P	Granato Joseph	94	candymaker	58	"
R	Granato Salvatore	94	U S A	23	"
S	Granato Theresa—†	94	operator	30	"
T	Orlandello Anthony	94	tailor	27	Revere
U	Orlandello Tina—†	94	housewife	27	here

Gladstone Street—Continued

	FULL NAME.	Res.	Occupation.	Age	Residence
v	Indingaro Anthony	98	welder	23	here
w	Indingaro Bertha †	98	stitcher	21	"
x	Indingaro Evelyn †	98	"	33	"
y	Indingaro Margaret †	98	at home	52	"
z	Indingaro Romeo	98	guard	29	"
	1724				
a	Merluzzi Carlo	99	manager	63	"
b	Merluzzi Gino	99	laborer	36	"
c	Merluzzi Ida †	99	housewife	61	"
d	Whelan Annie F †	101	"	70	"
e	Whelan John I	101	retired	74	"
f	Whelan Marion L †	101	secretary	38	"
g	Bertagna Euba †	111	nurse	28	"
h	Bertagna Mary †	111	at home	26	"
k	Bertagna Robert J	111	U S N	31	"
l	Bertagna Speranza †	111	at home	52	"
m	Console Earl	112	laborer	41	"
n	Console Lillian †	112	milliner	38	"
o	Santarpio Elizabeth †	112	housewife	30	298 Chelsea
p	Santarpio Vincent	112	operator	31	298 "
r	Skehan Alice W †	112	housewife	53	here
s	Skehan John J	112	B F D	53	"
t	Skehan John J, jr	112	clerk	32	"
u	Skehan Lawrence W	112	welder	27	"
v	Vozzella Albert	114	clerk	34	"
w	Vozzella Florindo	114	retired	72	"
x	Vozzella Mildred †	114	housewife	34	"
y	Sacco Frank	114	engineer	46	"
z	Sacco Mary †	114	housewife	43	"
	1725				
a	Menno Louis R	114	machinist	28	15 Catherine
b	Menno Mary J †	114	housewife	26	15 "
c	Grande Joseph	116	operator	28	here
d	Grande Pauline †	116	housewife	28	"
e	Santarpio Mary †	116	"	22	"
f	Santarpio Victor	116	welder	24	"
g	Viscone Connie †	116	housewife	22	Watertown
h	Viscone Raymond	116	clerk	27	"
k	Castleton Doris †	117	housewife	53	N Carolina
l	Castleton William T	117	U S A	56	"
m	Allescia Grace †	117	housewife	27	here

Gladstone Street Continued

x	Allescia Louis	117	machinist	30	here
o	Vadaio Henry	117	U S C G	36	"
p	Vadaio Theresa †	117	housewife	34	"
r	Adams Lawrence P	118	U S N	36	167A Byron
s	Adams Rose †	118	housewife	21	167A "
t	Minick Mary V †	118	stenographer	22	here
u	Silvia Manuel	118	painter	42	"
v	Silvia Shandra †	118	housewife	43	"
y	Faccini Charles	118	clerk	46	"
z	Faccini Ida †	118	"	21	"

1726

A*	Faccini Victoria †	118	housewife	46	"
1A	DeBenedictis Alfred	118	clerk	25	"
2A	DeBenedictis Emma †	118	housewife	27	"
B	Perrone Ida E †	120	"	29	"
c	Perrone John V	120	foreman	36	"
D	Silvia August	120	laborer	40	"
E	Silvia Mary †	120	housewife	42	"
F	Mirra Antonetta †	120	stitcher	34	"
G	Mirra Florence †	120	"	26	"
H	Mirra Paul	120	U S A	32	"
K	Mirra Vito	120	retired	71	"
L	Caponigro Gerolomo	120	"	94	"
M	LaRosa Macrina †	120	housewife	51	"
N	LaRosa Vincent	120	engineer	50	"
o	Velardo John B	122	mason	32	1109 Saratoga
P	Velardo Mae †	122	housewife	30	1109 "
R	Dicello Mary †	122	"	38	here
s	Dicello Raymond	122	laborer	42	"
u	Silipigini Ada †	124	housewife	25	"
v	Silipigini Leo	124	operator	26	"
w	Colucci Margaret †	124	housewife	30	"
x	Colucci Raymond	124	barber	36	"
y*	Olivieri Agrippine †	124	dressmaker	52	"
z	Olivieri Joseph	124	carpenter	61	"

1727

A	Nunes Joseph	124	barber	34	"
B	Nunes Phyllis †	124	housewife	33	"
c	Vitagliano Frank E	126	metalworker	26	"
D	Vitagliano Leo	126	machinist	53	"
E	Vitagliano Mary †	126	housewife	46	"

I 17   17

Gladstone Street—Continued

F	Vitagliano Sue †	126	operator	24	here
G	Richards Fred A	128	agent	29	"
H	Richards Grace †	128	housewife	28	"
K*	Savoia Francesca †	129	at home	48	"
L	Savoia Domenic	129	laborer	24	"
M	Savoia Phyllis †	129	clerk	22	"
N	Sacco Frances †	137	housewife	41	"
O	Sacco Henry	137	engineer	38	"
P*	Sacco Michael	137	retired	62	"
R	Sacco Michael, jr	137	chauffeur	34	"
S	Sacco Pasquale	137	laborer	36	"
T*	Sacco Susie †	137	at home	75	"

Leyden Street

W	Goldstein Benjamin	150	student	25	here
X	Goldstein Cecelia L †	150	clerk	23	"
Y	Goldstein Isaac	150	storekeeper	49	"
Z	Goldstein Minnie †	150	housewife	50	"

1728

A	Basso Neva †	150	"	40	"
B	Basso William D	150	cook	41	"
C	Natali Joseph	150	factoryhand	21	"
D	Testa Joseph	150	electrician	63	"
E*	Testa Mary †	150	housewife	57	"
F	Testa Robert	150	factoryhand	24	"
G*	Testa Salvatore	150	electrician	30	"
H	Ciampa Angelo	151	retired	67	225 Leyden
K	Ciampa Guy	151	clerk	23	225 "
L	Ciampa Judith †	151	stitcher	20	225 "
M*	Ciampa Mary †	151	housewife	51	225 "
N	Vincenti Jean †	151	clerk	20	here
O	Ciampa Enrico	151	"	24	61 Leyden
P	Ciampa Mary †	151	housewife	23	61 "
R	Montanori Elbina †	151	factoryhand	22	here
S	Montanori Elvira †	151	"	42	"
T	McCarthy Anna †	151	housewife	31	"
U	McCarthy John J	151	printer	33	"
V*	Iovanna Carmen C	152	U S A	20	664 Saratoga
W	Iovanna Frank	152	bartender	50	664 "
X	Iovanna Mary E †	152	housewife	52	664 "

18

Leyden Street Continued

	x	*Todesca Artemia †	152	housewife	42	here
	y	*Todesca Idello	152	U S A	20	"
	z	Todesca Joseph	152	cabinetmaker	43	"
1729						
	B	Cocchi Aldo	152	longshoreman	32	653 Saratoga
	c	Cocchi Alice †	152	housewife	30	653 "
	D	Wolinsky Ethel †	152	packer	32	653 "
	E	Langone Aurelia †	153	housewife	67	here
	F	Langone Frank J	153	mechanic	46	"
	G	Alioto Joseph	153	barber	52	"
	H	Alioto Marion †	153	hairdresser	21	"
	K	Alioto Mary †	153	housewife	48	"
	L	Alioto Anthony	153	chauffeur	43	"
	M	Alioto Antonetta †	153	housewife	43	"
	N	LaSpina Lillian M †	155	"	39	"
	o	LaSpina Paul J	155	printer	46	"
	P	Alioto Ernest	155	manager	46	"
	R	Alioto Frank S	155	pipefitter	24	"
	s	Alioto May A †	155	housewife	42	"
	T	Sindoni Marion †	155	nurse	22	"
	U	Sindoni Mary †	155	housewife	57	"
	V	Sindoni Rose †	155	nurse	24	"
	W	Sindoni Thomas D	155	agent	60	"
	X	Booth Edward F	160	retired	62	"
	Y	Booth Helen B †	160	saleswoman	39	"
	z	Fitzpatrick Katherine L †	161	at home	60	"
1730						
	A	Fitzpatrick Sarah J †	161	"	86	"
	B	Fitzpatrick Theresa A †	161	teacher	61	"
	c	DellaGrotte Anthony	166	toolmaker	23	116 Gladstone
	D	DellaGrotte Mary †	166	housewife	23	116 "
	F	Messina Joseph	166	baker	29	here
	G	Messina Mary †	166	housewife	29	"
	H	Rossi Anthony	167	salesman	28	"
	K	*Rossi Augustine	167	retired	55	"
	L	Rossi Edith †	167	factoryhand	23	"
	M	Rossi Julia †	167	"	29	"
	N	*Rossi Mary †	167	housewife	55	"
	o	Biagiotti Ida †	167	factoryhand	21	92 Gladstone
	P	*Biagiotti Mary †	167	housewife	48	92 "
	R	*Biagiotti Ralph	167	factoryhand	48	92 "

19

Leyden Street — Continued

s	Cardosi Leonetto	167	cook	52	92 Gladstone
T	Celone Grace †	168	factoryhand	36	here
U	Celone Stephen	168	clerk	39	"
V	Carideo Augustino	168	machinist	25	"
W	Carideo Carmela †	168	housewife	43	"
X	Carideo Frank	168	U S N	22	"
Y	Carideo Samuel	168	shoemaker	50	"
Z	Natale Mario	168	woodworker	35	"

1731

A	Natale Mary †	168	housewife	32	"
B	Memmolo Domenic	169	U S A	21	"
C	Memmolo Nellie †	169	housewife	44	"
D	Memmolo Ralph	169	laborer	47	"
E	Fanaznai Anna †	172	factoryhand	30	"
F	*Fanaznai Antonetta †	172	housewife	54	"
G	Fanaznai Dora †	172	factoryhand	26	"
H	Fanaznai Joseph	172	student	21	"
K	*Fanaznai Louis	172	tailor	61	"
L	DeCristoforo Carl	174	salesman	37	"
M	DeCristoforo Charles	174	retired	71	"
N	DeCristoforo Dorothy †	174	housewife	36	"
P	Frassica Maria †	175	"	70	"
R	Frassica Phillipa M †	175	clerk	47	"
O	*Forlani Mary †	175	housewife	44	"
S	Pareschi Alba †	176	saleswoman	24	152 Leyden
T	Pareschi Celso	176	grocer	55	here
U	Pareschi John	176	U S A	26	152 Leyden
V	*Pareschi Mildred †	176	at home	20	152 "
W	Landry Helen †	177	waitress	28	122 Gladstone
X	McDonald Clement	177	machinist	30	122 "
Y	McDonald Estelle †	177	housewife	26	122 "
Z	Marshall Concetta C †	177	"	45	here

1732

A	Marshall Joseph A	177	engineer	45	"
B	*Mazzarino Julia †	177	bookkeeper	20	"
C	Mazzarino Pauline †	177	housewife	52	"
D	Mazzarino Sebastiano	177	factoryhand	53	"
E	Magnifico Eleanor †	178	housewife	30	"
F	Magnifico Jerome W	178	druggist	34	"
G	Sinnatra Carmen	180	salesman	36	"

Leyden Street Continued

	H	Sinnatra Constance †	180	factoryhand	32	here
	K	Sinnatra Josephine †	180	"	35	"
	L	DeGregorio George	180	butcher	33	"
	M	DeGregorio Jennie †	180	housewife	34	"
	N	Pallazola Stephen	180	U S N	23	260 Saratoga
	O	Pallazola Theresa †	180	factoryhand	22	229 Princeton
	P	Flaherty Adele M †	182	operator	24	here
	R	Flaherty Catherine †	182	housewife	56	"
	S	Flaherty Lawrence J	182	U S A	27	"
	T	Flaherty Lorraine T †	182	factoryhand	23	"
	U	Flaherty Mary F †	182	"	22	"
	V	Flaherty Michael J	182	guard	62	"
	W	Gallagher Frances †	183	housewife	21	"
	X	Gallagher Frank	183	U S A	29	61 St Andrew rd
	Y	*Grieco Domenic	183	chauffeur	52	here
	Z	*Grieco Louise— †	183	factoryhand	20	"

1733

	A	Grieco Michael	183	U S N	27	"
	B	Grieco Vito	183	chauffeur	25	"
	C	Sgroi Frances— †	183	housewife	40	"
	D	Sgroi Samuel	183	painter	47	"
	E	*Grieco Constance †	183	factoryhand	20	"
	F	Grieco Joseph	183	U S A	22	"
	G	*Grieco Josephine †	183	housewife	44	"
	H	Grieco Mary — †	183	factoryhand	25	"
	K	*Grieco Michael	183	retired	50	"
	L	Grieco Phyllis— †	183	stitcher	24	"
	M	Terriciano Angelina †	186	housewife	39	"
	N	Terriciano Joseph	186	painter	42	"
	O	DeAngelis Florence †	186	housewife	41	"
	P	DeAngelis Henry C	186	engineer	42	"
	R	*Serignano Luigi	186	retired	82	"
	S	Scotti Esther †	186	saleswoman	44	"
	T	Scotti Marion †	186	clerk	25	"
	T	Salerno Cecelia †	188	housewife	32	"
	U	Salerno John P	188	bartender	33	"
	V	Salerno Peter M	188	waiter	53	"
	W	Salerno Rose †	188	housewife	52	"
	X	*Fennell Annie †	192	at home	65	"
	Y	*Fennell James	192	longshoreman	68	"

21

Leyden Street — Continued

z	Fennell William	192	longshoreman	37	here	
1734						
A	Frazier Arthur	194	fireman	45	"	
B	Frazier Marie †	194	housewife	29	"	
C	Moltedo Henry P	196	lawyer	65	"	
D	Moltedo Kathryn S †	196	housewife	61	"	
E	Biggi Louis	198	shipper	54	"	
F	Biggi Peter	198	operator	56	"	
G	Biggi Theresa †	198	at home	89	"	
H	Conway Norma †	198	clerk	24	"	
K	Conway William F	198	U S A	29	"	
L	Cristoforo Nellie †	198	housewife	49	"	
M	Cristofor Olga †	198	factoryhand	22	"	
N*	Allegra Iola †	200	housewife	38	"	
O	Allegra Stephen	200	machinist	39	"	
P	Maglitta Albert	200	musician	33	"	
R	Maglitta Rose †	200	housewife	31	"	
S*	Maglitta Salvina †	200	at home	72	"	
T	Kelley Mary R †	210	housewife	44	22 Ashley	
U*	Kelley Mary R †	210	saleswoman	20	here	
V	Kelley Ruth A †	210	stenographer	21	22 Ashley	
W	Kelley William F	210	clerk	46	22 "	
X	Cipoletta Anthony	214	retired	27	here	
Y	Cipoletta Josephine †	214	housewife	50	"	
Z	Fraga Betty †	226	"	30	"	
1735						
A	Fraga John	226	factoryhand	39	"	
B	Turner Catherine †	226	housewife	71	"	
C	Turner Frederick	226	retired	87	"	
D	Fraga Josephine B †	226	at home	54	"	
E	Fraga Manuel J	226	policeman	51	"	
F	Fraga Mary †	226	housewife	79	"	
G	McRae Anna †	226	factoryhand	37	"	
H	McRae Dorothy †	226	clerk	24	"	
K	McRae Mary L †	226	housewife	58	"	
L	McRae Mildred †	226	factoryhand	40	"	
M	McRae Walter	226	U S N	26	"	
N	McRae William	226	retired	28	"	
O	Ballerino Ernamo	240	"	33	"	
P	Ballerino Rose †	240	laundress	32	"	
R*	Cardinale Michael	240	retired	68	"	

Leyden Street (Continued)

s	Cardinale Raffaela †	240	housewife	65	here
t	DeAngelico Mary †	240	"	24	"
u*	Merola Domenica †	240	"	49	"
v	Merola Guido	240	tailor	51	"
w	Toscano Carmen	240	"	35	"
x	Toscano Mary †	240	housewife	24	"
y	Giusti Dante	240½	millhand	26	"
z	Giusti Muriel †	240½	housewife	26	"

1736

a	Desimone Constance †	242	"	27	"
b	Desimone Oliver	242	attendant	27	"
c	Zunino Alfred J	242	buyer	50	"
d	Zunino Gertrude †	242	housewife	44	"
e	Zunino Joseph	242	shipfitter	47	"
f	Velona Anna †	242	housewife	30	387 Benningt'n
g	Velona Nicholas	242	welder	27	324 Chelsea
h	Deeran Josephine †	244	housewife	20	106 Morris
k	Deeran Sarkis	244	laborer	31	262 Benningt'n
l	Corbett Dennis P	244	shipfitter	29	3 Orient av
m	Corbett Eleanor E †	244	housewife	27	3 "
n	Bruxelles Agnes †	244	"	56	here
o*	Bruxelles Gregory	244	student	20	"
p	Bruxelles Pasquale	244	cutter	51	"
r	Giella Edward	246	mason	41	"
s	Giella Ida †	246	housewife	34	"
t	Zaggari Jennie †	246	"	44	"
u	Zaggari Mary †	246	stitcher	24	"
v	Zaggari Salvatore	246	printer	26	"
w	Zaggari Vincenza †	246	clerk	21	"
x	Capabianco Josephine †	246	factoryhand	30	"
y*	Capabianco Mary †	246	housewife	60	"
z	Sacco Salvatore	246	factoryhand	35	"

1737

a	Cincotta Grace †	250	housewife	22	"
b	Cincotta Phillip	250	laborer	26	"
c	Erickson Eleanor †	250	housewife	27	"
d	Erickson Henry	250	machinist	29	"
e	Bianco Angelina †	250	housewife	62	"
f	Bianco Bartholomew	250	attendant	42	"
g	Bianco Lawrence	250	chauffeur	44	"
h	Grasso Angelina †	250	factoryhand	30	"

23

Leyden Street—Continued

K	Grasso Clara †	250	clerk	27	here
L	Grasso Mary †	250	factoryhand	28	"
M	Grasso Rosa †	250	housewife	65	"
N	Messina James	256	salesman	42	"
O*	Messina Josephine †	256	housewife	62	"
P	Messina Margaret †	256	saleswoman	32	"
R	Messina Mary †	256	stitcher	32	"
S	Mulone Diega †	256	housewife	39	"
T	Warren Florence †	258	"	49	"
U	Warren John	258	machinist	49	"
V	O'Brien Edward	258	shipfitter	27	"
W	O'Brien Florence †	258	housewife	23	"

Montmorenci Avenue

X	Clark Arthur R	68	milkman	52	here
Y	Clark Myrtle W †	68	housewife	50	"
Z	Taft Harold	68	chauffeur	52	"

1738

A	Taft Marie †	68	housewife	29	"
B	Burnett James	75	operator	24	Gallop's Island
C	Burnett Lorraine †	75	housewife	20	53 Beachview rd
D	Angeluccie Assunto	75	contractor	48	here
E	Angeluccie Genea †	75	saleswoman	20	"
F	Angeluccie Mary †	75	housewife	41	"
H	Rejo Ernest D	91	manager	37	"
K	Rejo Helen F †	91	housewife	37	"
L	Phillips Anthony L	111	operator	53	"
M	Phillips Edna M †	111	housewife	49	"
N	Phillips Richard A	111	U S A	23	"
O	Canellos Peoto †	119	housewife	31	"
P	Canellos Peter	119	salesman	47	"
R	Coronios George	119	shipper	22	"

Orient Avenue

S	LeBlanc Joseph	1	U S N	33	here
T	LeBlanc Margaret †	1	housewife	30	"
U	Quirek Frances †	1	"	69	"
V	Quirek Francis	1	ironworker	41	"
W	Quirek Paul	1	U S A	35	"

Orient Avenue Continued

x	Quirck William J	1	U S N	37	here
y	Greenfield Charles H	1	checker	65	"
z	Greenfield Mary B †	1	housewife	59	"

1739

a	Greenfield William	1	U S A	27	"
b	Johnson Julia †	3	at home	69	"
c	Johnson Lawrence T	3	printer	37	"
d	Johnson Mary K †	3	housewife	36	"
e	Matthews Donald L	3	machinist	42	"
f	Matthews Marie C †	3	housewife	37	"
g	McLoughlin John J	3	retired	67	"
h	McLoughlin Mary A †	3	housewife	60	"
k	Grant Charles	3	U S A	41	"
l	Grant Henry	3	machinist	44	"
m	Whelan Irene M †	5	housewife	34	"
n	Whelan John E	5	clerk	38	"
o	O'Brien Elizabeth †	5	at home	63	"
p	O'Brien James E	5	agent	37	"
r	Sears Margaret †	5	housewife	41	"
s	Sears William	5	chauffeur	43	"
t	Murray George	5	operator	63	"
u	Verry John	5	U S N	36	"
v	Verry Pauline †	5	clerk	32	"
w	Balboni Frances †	7	housewife	31	"
x	Balboni Louis	7	mechanic	37	"
y	Pattee Charlotte A †	7	housewife	31	"
z	Pattee Leon B	7	machinist	32	"

1740

a	Whalen Margaret †	7	housewife	53	"
b	Whalen Patricia H †	7	stenographer	21	"
c	Whalen Rita M †	7	"	23	"
d	Whalen Thomas J	7	fisherman	52	"
e	Whalen Thomas J	7	U S A	24	"
f	*Donatelli Antonetta †	8	housewife	77	"
g	Donatelli Camillo	8	bricklayer	37	"
h	Merullo Attilio	8	tailor	35	"
k	Merullo Mercedes †	8	housewife	30	"
m	Maffei Nicholas	11	U S A	22	"
n	Maffei Rufina †	11	housewife	64	"
o	Maffei Salvatore	11	guard	59	"
p	Cray Eliza A †	11	housewife	78	"

Orient Avenue Continued

R	Cray Evelyn †	11	housewife	29	here
S	Cray Richard	11	retired	76	"
T	Cray William R	11	guard	32	"
U*	Crowell Irene L †	11	companion	33	"
V	Fontes Manuel	11	chauffeur	50	"
W	Fontes Natalie †	11	housewife	47	"
X	Cespa Ida †	12	"	52	"
Y	Cespa Orlando	12	tailor	60	"
Z	Smallcomb Peter	12	clerk	36	"

1741

A	Thompson Agnes †	12	tel operator	35	"
B	Thompson James	12	clerk	28	"
C*	Thompson Margaret †	12	at home	86	"
D*	Walsh Bridget †	12	"	74	"
E	Rasmussen Charlotte †	15	housewife	52	"
F	Rasmussen Robert	15	machinist	57	"
G	Callan Madeline †	19	secretary	40	"
H	Callan Mary †	19	at home	80	"
K	Rowe George A	19	electrician	58	"
L	Rowe George A, jr	19	U S A	27	"
M	Rowe Margaret A †	19	housewife	52	"
N	Rowe Margaret A †	19	inspector	25	"
O	O'Donnell Anastasia D †	21	at home	49	"
P	O'Donnell Edwin F	21	U S N	25	"
R	O'Donnell George W	21	"	27	"
S	Adreani Andrew	24	grocer	35	"
T	Adreani Eleanor †	24	housewife	31	"
U	Trongone Albert	24	U S N	37	"
V*	Trongone Maria †	24	at home	60	"
W	Trongone Olga †	24	secretary	24	"
X	Vozella Adelino	24	retired	50	"
Y	McGinn Charles W	27	U S A	29	"
Z	McGinn Harold J	27	agent	49	"

1742

A	McGinn Rose W †	27	housewife	37	"
B	Marchant Maria †	27	at home	86	"
C	Martell Margaret E †	27	factoryhand	33	"
D	Martell Mary F †	27	at home	56	"
E	Martell Mary P †	27	"	84	"
F	Martell Thomas C	27	U S M C	47	"

Orient Avenue Continued

G	Smith Wilfred L	27	retired	58	here
H	Fiorentino Nicholas	28	baker	22	"
K	Fiorentino Pauline †	28	housewife	21	"
L	Pearson Charles J	28	steamfitter	67	"
M	Pearson Charles W	28	inspector	34	"
N	Pearson Frank W	28	shipper	29	"
O	Pearson Henrietta †	28	housewife	65	"
P	Landry Margaret †	29	"	48	"
R	Landry Walter C	29	fireman	59	"
S	Bernard Charles F	29	engineer	61	"
T	Bernard Marie P †	29	housewife	59	"
U	Landry Marie B †	29	saleswoman	55	"
V	Landry Peter	29	machinist	61	"
W	Polodec Mary S †	29	at home	70	"
X	Merlino Andrew	32	barber	54	"
Y	Merlino Christina †	32	housewife	45	"
Z	Merlino Frank A	32	U S A	20	"
	1743				
A	Merlino Nunzia †	32	stenographer	22	"
B	Piscitelli Lucy †	32	housewife	35	56 Frankfort
C	Piscitelli Salvatore	32	pipefitter	48	56 "
D	Santoro Lena †	32	housewife	49	56 "
E	Santoro Samuel	32	shoemaker	55	56 "
F	McLellan Roland	37	retired	73	here
G	McLellan Sarah †	37	housewife	72	"
H	Dondero Arthur	39	U S A	33	"
K	Dondero Florence †	39	clerk	31	"
L	Boudreau Alice †	39	housewife	29	118 Gladstone
M	Boudreau Annie L †	39	"	65	here
N	Boudreau Elmer	39	shipper	27	118 Gladstone
O	Boudreau Paul J	39	U S A	32	here
P	Boudreau Walter S	39	barber	65	"
R	*Boncorddo Dominica †	40	housewife	54	"
S	*Boncorddo Giuseppe	40	retired	69	"
T	Vadala Ignazio	40	chauffeur	50	"
U	Vadala Rose †	40	housewife	34	"
V	Fuccillo Carmen	40	presser	27	"
W	Fuccillo Sadie †	40	housewife	24	"
X	Abramo Florence M †	41	"	34	"
Y	Abramo John A	41	dyesetter	32	"

Orient Avenue —Continued

	z	Campatelli Gino	41	policeman	54	here
1744						
	A	Campatelli Natalie †	41	clerk	22	"
	B	Campatelli Stella †	41	housewife	47	"
	C	*Gravallese Angelina †	42	at home	65	"
	D	Luongo Elizabeth †	42	housewife	43	"
	E	Luongo John	42	restaurateur	52	"
	F	Mastrangelo Charles	44	physician	48	"
	G	Mastrangelo Mary †	44	housewife	45	"
	H	Barker Regina †	48	"	43	"
	K	Barker William H	48	clerk	50	"
	L	Testa Eugene	49	proprietor	68	"
	M	Fiorentino Caroline †	54	housewife	47	"
	N	Fiorentino Domenic	54	student	27	"
	O	Fiorentino Frank	54	baker	65	"
	P	Fiorentino Maria †	54	student	23	"
	R	Fiorentino Raffaela †	54	teacher	28	"
	S	Staffier Domenic T	56	physician	38	"
	T	Staffier Helen †	56	housewife	38	"
	U	Granata Flora †	57	"	26	"
	V	Granata James, jr	57	salesman	35	"
	W	Pilato Anthony	57	repairman	46	"
	X	*Pilato Grace †	57	clerk	32	"
	Y	Pilato Joseph	57	U S A	29	"
	Z	*Pilato Marion †	57	housekeeper	42	"
1745						
	A	*Pilato Rosario	57	retired	81	"
	B	DiMari Mary †	60	housewife	41	"
	C	DiMari Sebastian	60	salesman	46	"
	D	DiNunno Maria F †	62	housewife	31	90 Orient av
	E	DiNunno Vincent	62	clerk	37	90 "
	F	Pilato Charles	63	repairman	39	here
	G	Pilato Louise †	63	housewife	42	"
	H	Pilato Michael	63	repairman	42	"
	K	Pilato Rose †	63	housewife	37	"
	L	Leone Amelia †	68	"	42	"
	M	Leone Lawrence	68	U S N	20	"
	N	Leone Pasquale	68	storekeeper	52	"
	O	Gaughan Anna †	68	at home	26	351 Chelsea
	P	Manfra Jeremiah	68	longshoreman	52	391 "
	R	Manfra Rose †	68	housewife	48	391 "

Orient Avenue Continued

s	Giannattasio Francis	68	U S A	21	here
t	Giannattasio Louise †	68	clerk	23	"
u	Giannattasio Michael	68	carpenter	53	"
v	Giannattasio Philomena †	68	housewife	47	"
w	Giannattasio Phyllis †	68	saleswoman	26	"
x	Marafino Nicholas	72	barber	51	"
y	*Marafino Rose †	72	housewife	39	"
z	Savasta Joseph	72	clerk	27	"
	1746				
a	Savasta Mafalda †	72	housewife	25	"
b	Fobert Lillian †	75	"	30	259 Prescott
c	Fobert Roy	75	machinist	28	259 "
d	Eldridge Francis W	75	policeman	53	577 Benningt'n
e	Eldridge Paul V	75	U S A	20	577 "
f	Eldridge Sophia †	75	housewife	53	577 "
g	Gleason Harold	75	clerk	43	Vermont
h	Gleason Loretta †	75	housewife	33	577 Benningt'n
k	McLoughlin Charles	75	fireman	58	here
l	Quinlan Sophia †	75	at home	76	311 Meridian
m	DePaulo Gertrude R †	76	housewife	37	here
n	DePaulo John	76	leatherworker	45	"
o	Alessandroni Aldo	76	U S N	27	"
p	Alessandroni Ann †	76	operator	25	"
r	Alessandroni Maria †	76	housewife	54	"
s	Alessandroni Nora †	76	operator	28	"
t	Alessandroni Salvatore	76	shoeworker	55	"
u	Selvitella Henry	80	attorney	46	"
v	Selvitella Lena †	80	housewife	43	"
w	Selvitella George	80	U S A	28	"
x	Selvitella Helen †	80	clerk	35	"
y	Selvitella Margaret †	80	"	21	"
z	Selvitella Mary †	80	"	24	"
	1747				
a	Selvitella Vera †	80	"	37	"
b	Masullo Amelia †	81	housewife	32	"
c	Masullo Anthony V	81	baker	34	"
d	Masullo Benjamin	83	barber	62	"
e	Masullo Catherine †	83	housewife	60	"
f	Masullo Dominic	83	barber	33	"
g	Masullo Frank	83	U S A	29	"
h	Lanza Alphonsus	84	engineer	46	"

Orient Avenue Continued

K	Lanza Anna †	84	stenographer	38	here
L	Lanza Concetta †	84	housewife	70	"
M	Lanza Elvira †	84	"	38	"
N	Lanza Frank	84	engineer	70	"
O	Lanza Theresa †	84	secretary	40	"
P	Merlino Louis	86	restaurateur	62	"
R	Merlino Mary †	86	housewife	59	"
S	Merlino Nunzia R †	86	secretary	25	"
T	Belmonte Concetta †	87	housewife	41	"
U	Belmonte Vincenzo	87	restaurateur	41	"
V	Puleo Frances †	89	housewife	43	"
W	Puleo Samuel	89	clerk	47	"
X	Schuster Barbara †	89	"	24	"
Y	Maida Mary †	90	housewife	52	"
Z	Maida Pasquale	90	clergyman	60	"

1748

A	Maida William A	90	student	21	"
B	Forster Charles D	90	clerk	52	"
C	Reagan Anna E †	90	housewife	65	"
D	Reagan Charles A	90	salesman	65	"
E	Reagan Charles J	90	U S A	23	"
F	Pinardi Charles	90	mechanic	25	"
G	Pinardi Pauline †	90	housewife	25	"
H	Marinelli Augustine S	94	policeman	55	"
K	Marinelli Marguerita †	94	housewife	48	"
L	Quarteroni John	98	carpenter	30	44 St Edward rd
M	Quarteroni Joseph S	98	U S A	28	44 "
N	Quarteroni Margaret †	98	housewife	52	44 "
O	Quarteroni Samuel	98	carpenter	52	44 "
P	Perrier Edna M †	98	housewife	33	here
R	Perrier Ralph J	98	machinist	27	"
S	McNamee Anna †	99	housewife	32	"
T	McNamee James	99	mechanic	35	"
U	Dolan Edward	99	tel worker	45	"
V	Dolan Joseph E	99	U S A	30	"
W	Dolan Thomas F	99	repairman	40	"
X	Gallo Anthony	100	meatcutter	46	"
Y	Gallo Josephine †	100	housewife	33	"
Z	Perrier Ruth E †	112	"	42	"

1749

A	Perrier Wilfred J	112	machinist	40	"

Orient Avenue Continued

B	Girrior Annie †	112	at home	69	here
C	Perrier Alphonse	112	custodian	24	"
D	Perrier Delvinia †	112	housewife	65	"
E	Perrier Evangeline †	112	clerk	29	"
G	Couture Cecile †	150	teacher	22	Rhode Island
H	Daly Beatrice †	150	"	32	"
K	DeAngelis Raffaella †	150	cook	31	here
L	*Donovan Mary †	150	"	48	"
M	*Dorion Belemere †	150	housekeeper	75	"
N	*Gagne Claire †	150	buyer	55	"
O	Hinchey Irene †	150	teacher	23	"
P	Jay Lillian †	150	"	44	"
R	*LaCroix Eva †	150	dressmaker	63	"
S	*LeStang Blanche †	150	nurse	64	"
T	Miller Angela †	150	teacher	30	"
U	Nuzzo Josephine †	150	cook	26	Rhode Island
V	*Parayre Lucie †	150	seamstress	57	here
W	*Paulino Clara †	150	laundress	50	Fall River
X	*Presseau Marie A †	150	at home	69	here
Y	Talbot Alma †	150	teacher	44	"
Z	*Thiriard Lucie †	150	"	59	"

1750

A	Van Reeth Clotilde †	150	"	61	"

Overlook Street

B	Larsen Alfred C	14	clerk	27	here
C	Larsen Anna E †	14	housewife	70	"
D	Larsen Edith M †	14	auditor	37	"
E	Larsen Hans C	14	carpenter	64	"
F	Larsen Harry O	14	U S N	39	"
G	Larsen Louis H	14	chemist	29	"
H	Nielsen Fredricka †	18	clerk	34	"
K	Nielsen Heinrich V	18	contractor	66	"
L	Nielsen Louise †	18	housewife	68	"
M	Nielsen Robert	18	accountant	27	"
N	Cameron Archie	26	ironworker	35	"
O	Cameron Christine †	26	housewife	70	"
S	Lane Henry B	26	salesman	52	24 Marion
P	McIntyre Beatrice N †	26	cashier	43	210 Leyden
R	McIntyre Claire F †	26	student	21	210 "

Sea View Avenue

	Letter	FULL NAME.	Residence	Occupation	Age	Reported Residence
	T	Belmonte Angie †	1-3	housewife	38	here
	U	Belmonte Generosa	1-3	bartender	47	"
	V	Ciriello Alton L	1-3	manager	25	44 St Edward rd
	W	Ciriello Carmen	1-3	barber	54	25 Gladstone
	X	Ciriello Eleanor A—†	1-3	housewife	22	44 St Edward rd
	Y	Ciriello Esther †	1-3	"	53	25 Gladstone
	Z	O'Connor Charles J	5-7	clerk	41	here

1751

	Letter	FULL NAME.	Residence	Occupation	Age	Reported Residence
	A	O'Connor Helen J †	5-7	housewife	40	"
	B	Taddonio Joseph	5-7	watchmaker	54	"
	C	Taddonio Joseph, jr	5-7	U S A	22	"
	D	Taddonio Michael	5-7	machinist	23	"
	E	Taddonio Rose †	5-7	housewife	45	"
	F	Puopolo Esther M †	11	"	43	"
	G	Puopolo Rocco A	11	machinist	45	"
	H	*Wallace Mary †	11	at home	95	"
	K	Drew Johanna †	11	housekeeper	55	"
	L	*Drohen Leo J	11	U S A	40	"
	M	Edwards James W	11	U S N	27	"
	N	Edwards Joseph P	11	"	20	"
	O	Edwards Lawrence J	11	manager	29	"
	P	Cavalieri Frank A	15	laborer	34	"
	R	Cavalieri Dorothy †	15	typist	25	"
	S	Cavalieri Henry R	15	U S N	32	"
	T	Cavalieri Jennie †	15	housewife	67	"
	U	Bennett Beatrice †	15	"	29	"
	V	Bennett Walter A	15	typesetter	34	"
	W	Abate Arthur	19	agent	49	"
	X	Abate Marietta †	19	housewife	45	"
	Y	Abate Norma †	19	student	21	"
	Z	Catrone Emma †	19	housewife	38	"

1752

	Letter	FULL NAME.	Residence	Occupation	Age	Reported Residence
	A	Catrone Michael J	19	salesman	40	"
	B	Berardi Albert	27	U S A	42	"
	C	Berardi Joseph	27	retired	72	"
	D	Conti Anthony	27	carpenter	43	"
	E	Conti Liberta †	27	housewife	37	"
	F	Ciancerlli Anthony	31	shoeworker	36	"
	G	*Ciancerlli Louise †	31	at home	74	"
	H	Ciancerlli Sally †	31	housewife	37	"
	K	*Colla Argia J †	39	"	45	"

Sea View Avenue Continued

	L	Colla Edmund	39	machinist	25	here
	M	Colla Francis J	39	tailor	47	"
	N	DePaoli Jennie †	43	housewife	36	"
	O	DePaoli Ottone	43	agent	38	"
	P	Caruso Anne L †	43	housewife	25	Cambridge
	R	Caruso Carmen A	43	announcer	25	"

Selma Street

	S	Cragin Anna E †	10	housewife	47	here
	T	Cragin Evelyn A †	10	hairdresser	22	"
	U	Cragin Thomas E	10	machinist	50	"

Tower Street

	V	Abate Alfred	30	milkman	51	here
	W	Abate Mary †	30	housewife	47	"

Waldemar Avenue

	X	Boudreau Clifford	15	rigger	36	here
	Y	*Boudreau Diana †	15	housewife	35	"
	Z	Boudreau Vander	15	rigger	43	"
1753						
	A	Boudreau Violet †	15	housewife	32	"
	B	Martell Anne H †	17	"	69	"
	C	Boudreau Harold E	17	boatbuilder	30	"
	D	Martell Louis	17	retired	74	"
	E	Muise Alice †	17	clerk	23	"
	F	Muise Alice B †	17	housewife	44	"
	G	Muise Francis J	17	seaman	44	"
	H	Muise Muriel A †	17	operator	22	"
	K	Favello Louis	20	watchman	35	"
	L	Favello Pauline †	20	housewife	34	"
	M	Driscoll Arthur G	21	U S A	26	"
	N	Driscoll Florence J †	21	tel operator	22	"
	O	Driscoll John J	21	U S N	33	"
	P	Driscoll Margaret T †	21	housewife	62	"
	R	Driscoll Marguerite †	21	tel operator	24	"
	S	Leary Mary A †	21	clerk	35	"
	T	Fleming Ellen G †	23	housewife	70	"

1—17   33

Waldemar Avenue—Continued

U	Fleming George J	23	U S A	29	here
V	Fleming William C	23	carpenter	68	"
W	Fleming William W	23	boilermaker	38	"
X	Cadigan Alice †	32	housewife	51	1072 Bennington
Y	Cadigan William J	32	steamfitter	48	1072 "
Z	Nolan Thomas	32	storekeeper	55	1072 "

1754

A	Roach John	32	U S N	22	1072 "
B	Magrath Frederick J	36	mortician	43	here
C	Magrath Mary E †	36	housewife	40	"
D	Johnson Frank J	37	laborer	69	"
E	Johnson Mary A †	37	housewife	66	"
F	Foy Rita E †	40	clerk	30	"
G	Moore John J	40	U S M C	33	"
H	Moore Mary G †	40	housewife	24	"
K	Murphy Mary M †	40	housekeeper	67	"
L	Olsen Caroline †	40	housewife	45	"
M	Olsen Harold J	40	U S M C	21	"
N	Olsen Harry J	40	fireman	45	"
O	Terry David	44	laborer	39	"
P	Terry Nora †	44	housewife	38	"
R	Balboni Alfred	52	laborer	34	"
S	Balboni Anice †	52	housewife	62	"
T	Balboni Evo	52	laborer	35	"
U	Balboni Jean †	52	housewife	32	"
V	Fagone Delia †	52	"	34	"
W	Fagone Steven	52	florist	34	"
Y	Carusso Anthony	93	farmer	20	"
Z	Carusso Esther †	93	checker	23	"

1755

A	Carusso Pasquale	93	farmer	47	"
B	Carusso Rose †	93	housewife	42	"
C	Vignoli John	116	carpenter	46	"
D	Harris Albert	166	clerk	50	"
E	Harris Winifred †	166	housewife	47	"
F	Gallagher William H	230	boilermaker	43	26 Overlook
G	Gallagher Winifred †	230	housewife	42	26 "
H	King Elizabeth †	230	"	47	here
K	King George T	230	chauffeur	50	"
L	Thibeault Edward P	254	seaman	26	"

Waldemar Avenue Continued

M	Thibeault Frances †	254	housewife	24	here
N	MacCormack Berthira T †	254	"	29	"
O	MacCormack Thomas J	254	welder	26	"

Walley Street

R	Howard Joseph	7	machinist	27	84 Horace
S	Howard Virginia †	7	stenographer	25	here
T	O'Neil Geradine †	7	machinist	22	"
U	O'Neil Mary †	7	housewife	63	"
V	O'Neil Valentine	7	fisherman	69	"
W	McGilvery Marion †	7	nurse	32	"
X	McGilvery Minnie †	7	housewife	56	"
Y	Ciampa Carmella M †	10	"	29	"
Z	Ciampa James G	10	barber	31	"
	1756				
D	*Sincotta Mary †	18	housewife	39	"
E	*Sincotta Vincent	18	baker	48	"

Ward 1-Precinct 13

CITY OF BOSTON

LIST OF RESIDENTS
20 YEARS OF AGE AND OVER

(NON-CITIZENS INDICATED BY ASTERISK)
(FEMALES INDICATED BY DAGGER)

AS OF

JANUARY 1, 1943

JOSEPH F. TIMILTY, *Chairman*
FREDERIC E. DOWLING, *Secretary*
WILLIAM A. MOTLEY, JR.
FRANCIS B. McKINNEY
EVERETT R. PROUT

Listing Board.

CITY OF BOSTON PRINTING DEPARTMENT

1800

Barnes Avenue

	Letter	FULL NAME.	Residence	Occupation.	Age	Reported Residence
	B	Cochrane Edward	6	electrotyper	44	here
	C	Cochrane Elizabeth—†	6	clerk	20	"
	D	Cochrane Josephine—†	6	housewife	45	"
	E	*Pizzani Theresa—†	6	candymaker	68	"
	F	Ford Frances C—†	6	housewife	24	"
	G	Ford Jerome J	6	shipfitter	27	"
	H	Disessa Concetta—†	8	housewife	70	"
	K	Disessa Peter	8	policeman	45	"
	L	Disessa Peter J	8	U S N	22	"
	M	Disessa Theresa—†	8	housewife	41	"
	N	Guarente Nicolena—†	8	at home	67	185 Hanover
	O	Thornton Francis A	8	shipfitter	40	742 Benningt'n
	P	Perrone Frances—†	10	at home	24	here
	R	Perrone Frank	10	retired	60	"
	S	Perrone Julia—†	10	housewife	55	"
	T	Palladino Josephine—†	10	"	26	"
	U	Palladino Rocco	10	electrician	32	"
	V	Crowley Anna A—†	14	housewife	57	"
	W	Crowley David J	14	clerk	60	"
	X	Crowley Marie E—†	14	"	27	"
	Y	McCarthy James J	14	"	60	"
	Z	Stewart Grace E—†	17	housewife	69	"

1801

	Letter	FULL NAME.	Residence	Occupation.	Age	Reported Residence
	A	Stewart John A	17	retired	75	"
	B	Lambert Charles	18	finisher	49	"
	C	Lambert Charles	18	U S A	21	"
	D	Lambert Helen—†	18	housewife	47	"
	E	Gjella Florence—†	18	"	45	"
	F	Gjella Vincent J	18	shipfitter	40	"
	G	Hedrington Alice—†	18	at home	50	"
	H	Hedrington Ellen—†	18	saleswoman	47	"
	K	Curtis John	18	agent	35	"
	L	Curtis Mary—†	18	housewife	35	"
	M	*Cavicchi Adelgiza—†	21	at home	73	"
	N	Cavicchi Edward	21	U S A	33	"
	O	Cavicchi Joseph	21	toolmaker	37	"
	R	Barry Mary—†	22	at home	69	"
	S	Jackson Anne—†	22	housewife	26	"
	T	Jackson John	22	shipfitter	28	"
	U	*Liberatore Caroline—†	22	housewife	66	"

2

Barnes Avenue Continued

	V	Liberatore Lena — †	22	stitcher	30	here
	W	Liberatore Michael	22	U S A	27	"
	X	Liberatore Pasquale	22	retired	69	"
	Y	Correnti Frank	22	shipper	25	224 Hanover
	Z	Correnti Vera — †	22	dressmaker	24	163 Endicott
1802						
	A	Melatesta Joseph	25	restaurateur	65	here
	B	Mangini Frederick J	25	merchant	39	"
	C	Mangini Madeline V — †	25	housewife	39	"
	D	Segal Lea — †	25	"	37	"
	E	Segal Samuel	25	lawyer	43	"
	F	Piscopo Alice L — †	26	housewife	33	"
	G	Piscopo Thomas J	26	lawyer	34	"
	H	Carlson Arnold	26	molder	28	"
	K	Carlson Carl S	26	carpenter	60	"
	L	Carlson Vincent	26	U S A	25	"
	M	Hagan Agnes — †	26	housewife	30	"
	N	Hagan John J	26	fireman	40	"
	O	*Chisholm Andrew	30	mechanic	58	"
	P	*Chisholm Annie — †	30	housewife	52	"
	R	Chisholm Virginia — †	30	operator	25	"
	S	Spinney Anne D — †	30	housewife	33	"
	T	Spinney Leland J	30	clerk	35	"
	U	Tollo Clara — †	30	stitcher	29	"
	V	Tollo Joseph	30	chipper	28	"
	W	Vega Amadeo	30	cutter	24	"
	X	Vega Emily — †	30	housewife	51	"
	Y	Vega Pellegrino	30	retired	55	"
	Z	Vega Rose — †	30	secretary	21	"
1803						
	A	Foley Edward D	34	retired	64	"
	B	Regan Arthur	34	chauffeur	25	"
	C	Bowen Annie E — †	40	housewife	53	"
	D	Bowen John P	40	foreman	54	"
	E	White Josephine — †	40	housewife	45	"
	F	White Nathaniel	40	storekeeper	57	"
	G	Rapolla Angelo	42	machinist	29	365 Sumner
	H	Rapolla Jennie — †	42	housewife	29	249 Webster
	K	Indresano Maria — †	44	"	64	here
	L	Indresano Pasquale	44	foreman	43	"
	M	Indresano Pietro	44	retired	70	"

Barnes Avenue—Continued

N	Indresano Ruggerio	44	U S A	32	here
O	Celata C Joseph	49	U S N	22	"
P	Celata Joseph	49	policeman	47	"
R	Celata Lucy †	49	secretary	28	"
S	Celata Palmina †	49	housewife	46	"
T	Whittington John R	50	retired	71	"
U	McCormick Jessie M—†	50	housewife	62	"
V	McCormick Joseph	50	guard	62	"
W	Sheedy George	50	machinist	44	"
X	Sheedy John	50	painter	39	"
Y	Sheedy Lucy †	50	housewife	34	"
Z	Blackwell Louise †	54	clerk	33	"

1804

A	Blackwell Mary †	54	at home	67	"
B	O'Mara Agnes †	54	boxmaker	66	"
C*	MacCrossan Minnie †	54	housewife	60	"
D*	MacCrossan Thomas	54	retired	62	"
E	McLaughlin Dorothea †	54	housewife	27	"
F	McLaughlin William	54	boilermaker	27	"
G	Mucci John	58	ironworker	35	"
H	Mucci Maria †	58	stitcher	32	"
K	Capone Benjamin W	58	U S N	25	"
L	Capone Romilda †	58	housewife	53	"
M	Capone William D	58	U S N	26	"
N*	Capone Angelina †	58	housewife	49	"
O	Capone Antonio	58	laborer	63	"
P	Saggese Salvatore	58	U S A	29	"
R	Nordby Edith †	62	housewife	47	"
S	Nordby Sigwald	62	pipe coverer	52	"
T	Crocker Ina †	62	housewife	32	"
U*	Dahl Olaf	62	fisherman	43	"
V	Alla Elena †	62	housewife	37	"
W	Alla Joseph V	62	mechanic	46	"
Y	O'Leary Ellen †	66	nurse	22	"
Z	O'Leary Grace †	66	housewife	46	"

1805

A	O'Leary Timothy	66	U S N	56	"
B	Brean Lillian †	66	housewife	24	39 Moore
C	Brean Robert	66	machinist	27	39 "
D	Rezendes Alfred	66	shipfitter	32	here
	Rezendes Bento	66	cabinetmaker	57	"

Barnes Avenue Continued

F	Rezendes Ernest	66	clerk	33	here
G	Rezendes Evelyn †	66	inspector	26	"
H	Rezendes Rita †	66	housewife	53	"
K	Accetta Alice †	69	"	60	"
L	Accetta Manfredi	69	clerk	59	"
M	Muldoon Loretta †	70	housewife	58	"
N	Muldoon William E	70	cutter	60	"
O	Nugent William B	70	social worker	50	"
P	Connolly Susan †	70	at home	69	"
R	McCarthy Elizabeth E †	70	marker	48	"
S	McCarthy Mary E †	70	operator	21	"
T	Supple Mary L †	70	at home	44	Everett
U	McDonald Anthony T	70	fireman	43	here
V	McDonald James E	70	clerk	62	"
W	McDonald Winifred E †	70	operator	49	"
X	Myers Arthur H	70	shipfitter	50	"
Y	Fenocketti Alfred	73	operator	60	"
Z	Fenocketti Alma A †	73	teacher	31	"
1806					
A	Fenocketti Mary †	73	housewife	58	"
B	Croce Concetta †	73	"	24	"
C	Croce Frederick	73	engineer	34	"
D	Lovezzola Michael	73	engraver	50	"
E	Lovezzola Theresa G †	73	housewife	49	"
F	Serra Lillian †	74	"	31	"
G	Serra Thomas	74	printer	31	"
H	Sousa Irene M †	74	housewife	29	"
K	Sousa Manuel J	74	U S C G	44	"
L	Abbott Mary E †	74	cook	32	"
M	O'Connell James J	74	mechanic	53	"
N	O'Connell Margaret A †	74	housewife	50	"
O	Kelly Florence C †	78	"	51	"
P	Kelly John C	78	janitor	53	"
R	Kelly Michael T	78	guard	51	"
S	Fitzpatrick Alice M †	78	housewife	42	"
T	Fitzpatrick Edward J	78	policeman	42	"
U	Mahoney William	78	"	48	"
V	Daly Anna P †	78	housewife	55	"
W	Daly Maurice A	78	fireman	55	"
X	Daly Maurice H	78	U S A	26	"
Y	Daly Mildred P †	78	collector	21	"

Barnes Avenue —Continued

z	Daly Rose A —†	78	teacher	28	here

1807

A	Pierce Ellen E—†	82	housewife	29	"
B	Pierce Francis R	82	guard	36	"
C	Sanders William W	82	laborer	56	"
D	Williams Catherine L —†	82	housewife	76	"
E	Williams William J	82	guard	76	"
F	Mandia Mary—†	82	secretary	36	"
G	Mandia Winifred—†	82	houseworker	56	"
H	Bruce Marie—†	86	clerk	28	"
K	Bruce Robert	86	U S A	28	Somerville
L	Schiendhelm Henry	86	engineer	36	here
M	Schiendhelm Louise—†	86	housewife	39	"
N	Murray Margaret—†	86	clerk	58	"
O	Murray Mary—†	86	housewife	62	"
P	Brown Sophie E—†	86	"	72	"
R	Brown William M	86	retired	68	"
S	Burns Clara J—†	90	clerk	37	"
T	Burns Julia A—†	90	at home	80	"
U	McWilliams Alicia —†	90	operator	24	"
V	McWilliams Anna L—†	90	housewife	45	"
W	Kelley Annie M—†	90	inspector	51	"
X	Lane Catherine E—†	90	housewife	40	"
Y	Lane David E	90	fireman	40	"
Z	Deagan Ruth—†	90	secretary	25	"

1808

A	McEachern Charles	90	fireman	47	"
B	McEachern Jeannette—†	90	housewife	47	"

Bayswater Street

C	Landry Arthur	15	U S C G	48	here
D	Landry Clarence	15	welder	42	"
E	Landry Esther —†	15	housewife	35	"
F	Landry Mary —†	15	"	75	"
G	Basil Lena —†	16	"	69	"
H	Basil Michael A	16	retired	82	"
K	McMorrow Mary —†	16	housewife	48	"
L	McMorrow William P	16	B F D	45	"
M	Preble Dorothy —†	16	packer	24	"
N	August Mary T —†	16	housewife	70	"

6

Bayswater Street   Continued

	o	Bordman Charles A	16	retired	73	here
	p	Bordman Marion †	16	housewife	63	"
	r	Stearns Catherine †	21	"	41	"
	s	Stearns Morris	21	engraver	39	"
	t	Bianco Alexander F	22	retired	73	"
	u	Bianco Jane M †	22	housewife	65	"
	v	O'Connell Caroline A †	22	"	29	"
	w	O'Connell David R	22	draftsman	33	"
	x	Avallone John	23	U S N	22	"
	y	Avallone Mary †	23	housewife	47	"
	z	Avallone Matthew D	23	tailor	55	"
1809						
	a	Cantillo Thomas	23	butcher	25	"
	b	Cantillo Tina †	23	housewife	23	"
	c	Keller Andrew J	25	U S A	34	"
	d	Keller Eileen †	25	houseworker	40	"
	e	Keller John J	25	inspector	48	"
	f	Keller Robert J	25	photographer	45	"
	g	Keller Suzan T †	25	housewife	80	"
	h	Sullivan Beatrice T †	29	"	35	"
	k	Bowen Margaret J †	31	"	56	"
	l	Sullivan Charles	33	clerk	35	"
	m	Sullivan Joseph J	33	foreman	30	"
	n	Sullivan Mary †	33	housewife	66	"
	o	Driscoll Catherine M †	35	saleswoman	26	"
	p	Driscoll Irene †	35	manager	43	"
	r	Driscoll Timothy J	35	longshoreman	48	"
	s	Braff Eva H †	37	housewife	49	"
	t	Braff Max M	37	physician	51	"
	u	Bertelson Anna W †	41	housewife	76	"
	v	Willings Dorothea B †	41	"	38	Maryland
	x	Durante Helen †	45	houseworker	22	here
	y	Meloni Charles	45	physician	43	"
	z	Meloni Mary †	45	housewife	41	"
1810						
	a	Barry Helene R †	49	"	42	"
	b	Barry Thomas E	49	U S A	43	"
	c	McGrail John	49	laborer	41	"
	d	Lund Hilma †	49	operator	60	"
	e	Spadafora Anthony	49	manager	37	"
	f	Spadafora Winifred †	49	housewife	27	"

Bayswater Street — Continued

G	Dwyer Elizabeth G—†	50	housewife	71	here
H	Dwyer John J	50	messenger	71	"
K	McGillicuddy William	50	salesman	57	"
L	Leonard Doris M—†	50	housewife	31	"
M	Pryor Matilda E—†	50	"	51	"
N	Pryor Percy J	50	retired	67	"
O	O'Connell Daniel	53	manager	55	"
P	O'Connell Daniel J	53	U S N	24	"
R	O'Connell James S	53	U S A	21	"
S	O'Connell Lillian S—†	53	housewife	47	"
T	Herman Alta—†	54	"	54	"
U	Herman Henry C	54	retired	66	"
V	Connors Eliza—†	54	houseworker	59	"
W	Leahy Pauline A—†	54	cashier	40	"
X	McGunigle Annie—†	54	housewife	63	"
Y	McGunigle Daniel H	54	attorney	40	"
Z	McGunigle George E	54	"	44	"

1811

A	McGunigle Madeline—†	54	houseworker	34	"
B	McGunigle Mary A—†	54	statistician	42	"
C	Reardon Bernard J	54	manager	39	"
D	Reardon Grace T—†	54	secretary	39	Revere
E	MacEachern Lottie—†	55	housewife	45	here
F	MacEachern Peter	55	janitor	56	"
G	Evans George E	57	mason	52	"
H	Evans Mary F—†	57	housewife	60	"
K	Brosnahan Helen—†	58	operator	28	98 Orient av
L	Brosnahan William J	58	U S N	29	98 "
M	Hicks Alice C—†	58	saleswoman	26	98 "
N	Hicks Charles H	58	U S A	29	98 "
O	Solari Louis M	58	manager	67	98 "
P	Solari Rose H—†	58	housewife	50	98 "
R	Roy Walter J	61	molder	56	here
S	Keating Alice D—†	66	probat'n officer	49	"
T	Keating Gertrude C—†	66	instructor	39	"
U	Keating Katherine I—†	66	stenographer	45	"
V	Weafer Leonard E	70	lawyer	42	"
W	Weafer Margaret P—†	70	housewife	36	"
X	Mullen James H	74	machinist	56	"
Y	Queenan Harold R	74	electrician	36	"
Z	Queenan John P	74	inspector	62	"

8

1812
Bayswater Street Continued

A	Queenan Rosanna E †	74	housewife	61	here
B	Halbich Margaret †	74	"	50	"
C	Tipping Charles	74	U S A	24	"
D	Tipping Margaret †	74	clerk	25	"
E	Grisdale Ada †	74	housewife	75	"
F	Saddler Kate †	74	"	70	57 Brighton av
G	White Howard J	74	barber	70	here

Bennington Street

G	Smith George J	715	policeman	47	here
H	Smith Irene A †	715	housewife	42	"
K	Healy Edward C	715	U S A	25	California
L	Healy Francis P	715	U S N	31	N Hampshire
M	Healy Margaret T †	715	housewife	50	here
N	Healy Peter H	715	supervisor	56	"
O	Healy Ruth N †	715	stenographer	27	"
P	Healy Warren J	715	U S A	23	Louisiana
R	Terry Ethel †	719	clerk	22	here
S	Lewis Frank W	719	engineer	35	"
T	Lewis Margaret H †	719	housewife	37	"
U	Healy Peter H, jr	723	mechanic	30	1105 Saratoga
V	Healy Rose †	723	housewife	26	1105 "
W	Nigro Frank	723	blacksmith	66	here
X	Nigro Mary †	723	housewife	66	"
Y	Daniels Charles H, jr	727	operator	42	"
Z	Daniels Evelyn J †	727	housewife	43	"

1813

B	Trevor Francis J	727	shipper	33	"
A	Trevor William A	727	retired	76	"
C	Daniels Charles H	727	machinist	63	"
D	Daniels Delia †	727	housewife	62	"
E	Riley Lawrence A	727	teller	33	"
F	Riley Marie G †	727	housewife	32	"
G	Gazzara Joseph	731	physician	40	"
H	Gazzara Rita G †	731	housewife	37	"
K	Salerno Joseph	731	tailor	42	"
L	Salerno Mary †	731	housewife	39	"
M	Harkins Helen C †	735	clerk	21	"
N	Harkins Mary E †	735	"	24	"

9

Page.	Letter.	Full Name.	Residence, Jan. 1, 1943.	Occupation.	Supposed Age.	Reported Residence, Jan. 1, 1942. Street and Number.

Bennington Street—Continued

	O	Harkins Mary L—†	735	housewife	47	here
	P	Harkins Patrick W	735	mechanic	58	"
	R	Dellano Dominic	735	shipper	24	Cambridge
	S	Dellano Florence—†	735	housewife	22	"
	T*	Maglieri Theodore	735	retired	79	here
	U	Recchia Anthony	735	assembler	27	"
	V*	Recchia Frank	735	tailor	55	"
	W	Recchia Mary—†	735	housewife	53	"
	X	Winston Bernard W	739	custodian	51	"
	Y	Winston John J	739	fireman	61	"
	Z	McCarthy Annie T—†	739	housewife	52	"
1814						
	A	McCarthy Charles J	739	U S A	25	"
	B	McCarthy Charles J	739	engraver	51	"
	C	McCarthy Edward W	739	U S N	22	"
	D	Bagley Grace E—†	743	housewife	30	"
	E	Bagley William U	743	lawyer	35	"
	F	Decker Joseph	743	policeman	48	284 Bellevue
	G	Brogan James	743	"	32	here
	H	Curran Barbara—†	743	housewife	54	"
	K	Curran Catherine—†	743	clerk	22	"
	L	Curran John	743	U S A	24	Ayer
	M	Curran Mary—†	743	bookkeeper	25	here
	N	Curran Michael	743	U S A	21	"
	O	Curran Patrick	743	laborer	63	"
	P	Curran Sarah—†	743	housewife	48	"
	R	DeFranco Anthony	747	policeman	50	"
	S	DeFranco Matilda—†	747	housewife	47	"
	T*	Calla Adeline—†	747	"	56	"
	U	Calla Guido	747	machinist	26	"
	V	Calla John	747	U S A	24	"
	W	Calla Nicodemo	747	tailor	59	"
	X	Meyer Frederick M	751	electrician	28	"
	Y	Meyer Helen—†	751	teacher	31	"
	Z	McLaughlin Albert J	751	operator	48	"
1815						
	B	McLaughlin Catherine—†	751	housewife	74	"
	A	McLaughlin Paul	751	compositor	33	"
	C	McLaughlin Theresa—†	751	housewife	45	"
	D	Bradley Elizabeth J—†	755	stenographer	40	"
	E	Donovan Florence—†	755	clerk	45	"

Bennington Street Continued

F	Donovan Susan K— †	755	agent	47	here
G	McLaughlin Catherine A	755	at home	62	"
H	Ryan Mary A— †	755	clerk	67	"
K	Wall Agnes T — †	755	housewife	51	"
L	Wall Agnes T—†	755	U S A	27	Hawaii
M	Wall James R	755	B F D	54	here
N	Wall Jane S—†	755	stenographer	21	"
O	Corson Louis	759	mechanic	50	"
P	Corson Louise—†	759	bookkeeper	53	"
R	Brown Annie T—†	759	clerk	64	"
S	Stevens Louise N—†	759	housewife	77	"
T	Sweeney James	759	U S N	20	"
U	Sweeney Lena—†	759	at home	74	"
V	Walker Annie—†	759	"	80	"

1816

K	*Sardina Esther—†	989	dressmaker	36	"
L	*Sardina Humbert	989	U S N	37	"
M	Galiazzo Domenic	989	U S A	25	174 Gove
N	Galiazzo Florence—†	989	housewife	22	174 "
O	Hewitt James H	989	retired	74	here
P	Hewitt Margaret—†	989	housewife	79	"
R	Sparaco Anna—†	989	"	30	"
S	Sparaco Samuel	989	U S N	29	"
T	Nora John F	989	machinist	40	"
U	Silvia Emma—†	989	housewife	45	"

1817

A	Ferrara Dorothy—†	1025	clerk	22	"
B	Ferrara Eleanor—†	1025	hairdresser	24	"
C	Ferrara Elizabeth—†	1025	saleswoman	20	"
D	Ferrara Jeanette—†	1025	housewife	48	"
E	Ferrara Peter	1025	agent	48	"
F	Spadafora Marion — †	1025	housewife	68	"
G	Spadafora Michael	1025	retired	74	"
H	Maniglia Carolina — †	1025	tailor	64	"
K	Maniglia Diego	1025	barber	36	"
L	Maniglia Rose—†	1025	housewife	35	"
M	Morgner Edward A	1027	clerk	58	"
N	Morgner Mary I—†	1027	housewife	58	"
O	Sasso Carl	1027	laborer	20	"
P	Sasso John	1027	painter	66	"
R	Sasso Josephine—†	1027	housewife	57	"

Page	Letter	Full Name	Residence, Jan. 1, 1943.	Occupation.	Supposed Age.	Reported Residence, Jan. 1, 1942. Street and Number.

Bennington Street—Continued

	Letter	Full Name	Res.	Occupation	Age	Residence
	s	Ronca Minnie †	1027	at home	79	here
	t	Carter George H	1027	chauffeur	40	"
	u	Carter Rose †	1027	housewife	38	"
	w	Santiano Louis	1065	U S A	20	28 Porter
	x	Santiano Madeline †	1065	housewife	40	28 "
	y	Santiano Michael	1065	electrician	40	28 "
	z	Powers Gerard A	1067	clerk	20	here

1818

	Letter	Full Name	Res.	Occupation	Age	Residence
	A	Powers Martin J	1067	B F D	49	"
	B	Powers Mary V †	1067	housewife	47	"
	C	Russo Abenia †	1069	"	44	"
	D	Russo Anna †	1069	clerk	24	"
	E	Russo Eleanor †	1069	"	22	"
	F	Russo Pauline †	1069	operator	26	"
	G	Nazzaro Clarence	1071	"	27	12 Ashley
	H	Nazzaro Mary †	1071	housewife	28	12 "
	K	*Smarello Josephine †	1073	"	58	here
	L	Smarello Peter	1073	laborer	62	"
	M	Smarello Philomena †	1073	clerk	31	"
	N	Smarello Theresa †	1073	tailor	22	"
	O	Smarello Jennie †	1075	housewife	35	"
	P	*Smarello Vincent	1075	tailor	35	"
	T	Hendricks Albert	1088	laborer	52	"
	U	Hendricks Florence †	1088	housewife	54	"
	V	Marotta Aurelia E †	1088	"	52	"
	W	Marotta Michael A	1088	bartender	52	"
	X	Indrisano Anthony	1088	guard	45	"
	Y	Indrisano Lena †	1088	housewife	42	"

1819

	Letter	Full Name	Res.	Occupation	Age	Residence
	A	Cosgrove James	1092	retired	72	"
	B	Cosgrove Mary †	1092	housewife	72	"
	C	Cosgrove Mary L †	1092	operator	41	"
	D	Mullen Argentina V †	1092	housewife	59	"
	E	Mullen William P	1092	retired	65	"
	F	Casale Gertrude †	1092	housewife	42	"
	G	Casale Herbert	1092	architect	43	"
	H	Walsh Edna †	1092	secretary	31	"
	K	Celona Cosmo	1096	polisher	59	"
	L	Celona Josephine †	1096	housewife	54	"
	M	Celona Geraldine †	1096	"	32	"
	N	Celona Joseph	1096	teacher	34	"

12

Bennington Street (Continued)

		Full Name	Res.	Occupation	Age	Reported
o		Celona Florence †	1096	housewife	36	here
p		Celona Frank	1096	teacher	36	"
r	*	Arena Anthony	1098	retired	79	"
s		Giacoppo Anna †	1098	housewife	48	"
t		Giacoppo Joseph	1098	finisher	55	"
u		Mullaney Alice †	1098	operator	45	"
v		Mullaney Bernard J	1098	ironworker	36	"
w		Mullaney James B	1098	retired	49	"
x		Mullaney Louise †	1098	clerk	49	"
y		Mullaney Mary F— †	1098	housewife	75	"
z	*	Mazzeo Catherine †	1098	"	58	"

1820

		Full Name	Res.	Occupation	Age	Reported
A		Mazzeo Dominic	1098	laborer	60	"
B		Mazzeo Dominic, jr	1098	U S A	28	"
c		Mazzeo Mary— †	1098	at home	25	"
D		Mazzeo Nicholas	1098	U S A	32	"
E		Mazzeo Sarah— †	1098	dressmaker	23	"
F	*	Fasano Carmella— †	1100	housewife	37	"
G		Fasano Nickolas	1100	shoecutter	48	"
H		Fasano Anna— †	1100	housewife	34	"
K		Fasano Patsy	1100	laborer	43	"
L		Campanelle Anna †	1100	housewife	33	"
M	*	Campanelle John	1100	salesman	37	"
N		Iannetti Victor	1100	U S A	24	"
o		Gozzi Joseph	1102	blacksmith	45	"
P		Gozzi Rose— †	1102	housewife	62	"
R		Ferrara Anthony	1102	bartender	38	"
s		Ferrara Olga — †	1102	housewife	38	"
T		Belgiorno Albert J	1102	salesman	29	"
U		Belgiorno Florence †	1102	housewife	27	"
V		Cosimo Biagio	1106	manager	57	"
W		Cosimo Jennie †	1106	housewife	10	"
X		Mini Alice — †	1106½	"	29	"
Y		Mini William S	1106½	bookkeeper	31	"
z		Cunningham Catherine †	1112	housewife	70	"
¹z		Cunningham Catherine †	1112	stenographer	34	"

1821

		Full Name	Res.	Occupation	Age	Reported
A	*	Tyrrell Josephine †	1114	at home	76	"
B		Tyrrell Lillian T †	1114	housewife	60	"
c		Pitman Lucy E †	1114	"	65	23 Breed
D		Pitman Mary E †	1114	auditor	27	23 "

15

Page.	Letter.	FULL NAME.	Residence, Jan. 1, 1943.	Occupation.	Supposed Age.	Reported Residence, Jan. 1, 1942. Street and Number.

Bennington Street—Continued

	E	Pitman William A	1114	guard	61	23 Breed
	F	Cowhig Charles C	1114	policeman	45	here
	G	Cowhig Margaret M—†	1114	housewife	43	"
	H	Cowhig Margaret M †	1114	artist	20	"
	K	Graham Bertha—†	1118	housewife	37	"
	L	Graham Raymond D	1118	manager	38	"
	M	Jensen Edward	1118	U S A	35	"
	N	Miller Annie C—†	1118	housewife	65	"
	O	Miller Charles N	1118	retired	67	"
	P	Chaison Augustus	1124	guard	44	"
	R	Chaison Augustus, jr	1124	U S M C	21	"
	S	Chaison Robert F	1124	diemaker	20	"
	T	Chaison Ruth N—†	1124	housewife	42	"
	U	Wallace John	1130	engraver	47	"
	W	Caputo Gaetana—†	1183	housewife	50	"
	X	Caputo Michael	1183	assembler	26	"
	Y	Caputo Paul	1183	blacksmith	53	"
	Z	Caputo Vincent	1183	chauffeur	27	"
1822						
	A	Dinarello Mafalda—†	1183	housewife	22	244 Leyden
	B	Dinarello Victor	1183	machinist	25	244 "
	C	Antonelli Edith—†	1183	inspector	36	Somerville
	D	Kendall Irene—†	1183	machinist	40	"
	E*	Castagnola Rubina—†	1185	at home	85	here
	F	Lombardi Madelina—†	1185	housewife	60	"
	G	Lombardi Peter	1185	guard	65	"
	H	Lombardi William G	1185	machinist	24	"
	K	Mennella Florence—†	1185	"	21	"
	L	Mennella Margaret—†	1185	housewife	37	"
	M	Mennella Randolph	1185	operator	49	"
	N	Femino James	1185	laborer	21	"
	O	Femino Jennie—†	1185	stitcher	29	"
	P	Femino Mary—†	1185	operator	32	"
	R*	Femino Minnie—†	1185	housewife	57	"
	S	Femino Pasquale	1185	carpenter	22	"
	T*	Femino Paul	1185	baker	57	"
	U	Campatelli Joseph	1189	metalworker	41	"
	V	Campatelli Margaret—†	1189	housewife	39	"
	W	Ferrara Ruth L—†	1189	"	33	"
	X	Ferrara Tony	1189	custodian	33	"
	Z	Gill Cliff	1193	U S A	40	"

Page	Letter	FULL NAME	Residence, Jan. 1, 1943	Occupation	Supposed Age	Reported Residence, Jan. 1, 1942. Street and Number.

1823
Bennington Street Continued

	A	Gill Rita †	1193	clerk	23	here
	B	*Lotti Eugenia †	1193	housewife	49	"
	C	Lotti John	1193	chef	49	"
	E	Prochello Michael	1201	barber	27	"
	F	Prochello Victoria †	1201	housewife	26	"
	G	Brown James	1201	steamfitter	74	"
	H	Brown Lida †	1201	housewife	58	"
	K	Ragin Mary W †	1201	at home	68	"
	L	McCormick Harold	1201	electrician	29	"
	M	McCormick Mary L †	1201	housewife	30	"
	N	Camarda Antoinette †	1203	milliner	22	"
	O	Camarda Jasper	1203	tailor	26	"
	P	Camarda Louise †	1203	at home	42	"
	R	Camarda Salvatore	1203	U S A	20	"
	S	*Venza Anna †	1203	housewife	41	"
	T	Venza Anthony L	1203	laborer	22	"
	U	Venza Jennie †	1203	packer	24	"
	V	Venza Peter	1203	salesman	49	"
	W	Venza Sebastian	1203	U S A	23	"
	X	Lanzilli Eno †	1205	stenographer	23	"
	Y	Lanzilli Joseph	1205	tailor	61	"
	Z	Lanzilli Theresa †	1205	housewife	58	"

1824

	B	Cavaleri Angelina †	1209	"	23	Somerville
	A	Cavaleri Lawrence	1209	machinist	25	"
	C	Trischitta Bernardina †	1209	housewife	54	here
	D	Trischitta Constance †	1209	hairdresser	29	"
	E	Trischitta Rosario	1209	carpenter	60	"
	F	Trischitta Veolanda †	1209	clerk	25	"
	G	Trischitta Virginia †	1209	"	24	"
	H	Spaziani Patricia †	1211	housewife	29	"
	K	Spaziani Peter	1211	barber	39	"
	L	*Lazzari Bittiani †	1211	housewife	49	"
	M	Lazzari Salvatore	1211	tailor	58	"
	O	Contarino Anthony	1215	chauffeur	37	"
	P	*Contarino Frances †	1215	housewife	68	"
	R	*Contarino Joseph	1215	retired	80	"
	S	Contarino Mary †	1215	stitcher	34	"
	T	Rosa Charles	1215	shipper	18	"
	U	Rosa Joseph	1215	U S A	20	"

15

Bennington Street— Continued

v	Girone Catherine—†	1219	housewife	42	here
w	Girone John	1219	U S A	21	"
x	Girone Nicholas	1219	carpenter	63	"
y	Lauricella Anthony	1219	salesman	54	"
z	Lauricella Sarah †	1219	housewife	50	"
¹z	D'Addario Albert	1223	U S A	22	40 Breed

1825

a	D'Addario Gerald	1223	"	21	here
b	D'Addario Gilda—†	1223	milliner	25	40 Breed
c	D'Addario Ida—†	1223	inspector	23	40 "
d*	D'Addario Leuza—†	1223	housewife	53	40 "
e	D'Addario Mario	1223	U S A	29	40 "
f	D'Addario Pasquale	1223	clerk	27	40 "
g	Sirignano Frank	1223	laborer	43	here
h	Buldini Armando	1229	U S A	28	"
k*	Buldini Ralph	1229	butcher	55	"
l*	Buldini Venusta †	1229	housewife	53	"
m	Fussell Vera E †	1229	"	30	"
n	Fussell William R	1229	machinist	32	"
o	Kimble Rena †	1229	housewife	31	"

Blackinton Street

r	Ratto Ernest	1	painter	46	here
s	Ratto Sarah †	1	housewife	39	"
t	Wyke Elizabeth †	3	at home	63	"
u	Wyke Ernest	3	chef	45	"
v	Wyke Jesse	3	machinist	56	"
w	O'Brien Eileen M †	5	at home	30	"
x	O'Brien John F	5	printer	46	"
y	O'Brien Kathleen A †	5	inspector	39	"
z*	O'Brien Margaret M †	5	at home	74	"

1826

a	O'Brien Mary A †	5	bookkeeper	41	"
b	O'Brien Maurice T	5	U S N	37	"
c	Lagamasino John	7	machinist	52	"
d	Lagamasino Lillian E †	7	librarian	26	"
e	Lagamasino Merle C †	7	teacher	24	"
f	Lagamasino Mildred B †	7	housewife	55	"
g	Ratto Frank L	7	retired	50	"
h	Powell Clarence A	9	shipfitter	27	"

Blackinton Street Continued

k	Powell Marie B †	9	housewife	29	here
l	Cianci Aida †	9	"	40	"
m	Cianci Henry	9	optician	40	"
n	Casale Agnes †	11	organist	45	17 Breed
o	Casale Annie †	11	housewife	67	17 "
p	Levezzo Rose †	11	bowmaker	60	here
r	MacPherson Donald W	11	manager	44	"
s	MacPherson Eugenia †	11	housewife	43	"

Leyden Street

y	Dondero Albert	215	operator	39	here
z	Dondero Charles	215	chauffeur	50	"
	1827					
a	Dondero Frank	215	operator	53	"
b	Dondero Theresa †	215	housewife	51	"
c	Favello Anthony	215	clerk	65	"
d	Favello Nellie †	215	housewife	63	"
e	Canavan Margaret A †	215	"	56	"
f	Disario Caroline E †	215	"	56	"
g	Disario Paul C	215	inspector	59	"
h	Disario Paul C, jr	215	U S N	22	"
k	Elwell Henry T	215	U S A	26	"
l	Elwell Martha G †	215	housewife	26	"
m	Dondero Evelyn D †	215	"	40	"
n	Dondero William	215	chauffeur	44	"
o	Solari Mary F †	215	at home	68	"
p	DeVal Floyd	219	clerk	32	Everett
r	Dresser Charles H	219	engineer	38	here
s	O'Blenes Doris †	219	housekeeper	28	"
t	McMillan Mary †	223	clerk	25	"
v	Courtois Lucille †	225	housewife	32	"
w	Courtois Oscar F	225	buffer	33	"
x	Console Anna †	225	housewife	49	"
y	Console Antonio	225	barber	50	"
z	Sergi Benjamin A	225	U S A	28	"
	1828					
a	Cross James	231	laborer	26	"
b	Denaro Beatrice †	231	operator	24	"
c	Denaro Mildred †	231	"	29	"
d	Marino Flora †	231	housekeeper	48	"

1 18   17

Leyden Street — Continued

E	Ness Jennie N — †	235	housewife	57	here
F	Ness Margaret — †	235	typist	23	"
G	Ness Peter H	235	machinist	53	"
H	Olsen Nels	235	laborer	50	"
K	Parker Anton	235	laborer	48	"
L	Rovetti Fiorivanti	239	carpenter	48	"
M	Rovetti Louise — †	239	housewife	46	"
N	Zermani Andrew	239	carpenter	31	"
O	Zermani Lola — †	239	housewife	21	"
P	Beaton Grace — †	241	W A V E	20	"
R	Beaton Helen — †	241	housewife	53	"
S	Beaton Hugh F	241	storekeeper	62	"
T	Ponti Guy	249	chef	64	1130 Bennington
U	Ivers Angelina — †	249	storekeeper	42	here
V	Lamborghini Allesandro	249	operator	63	"
W	*Lamborghini Alvira — †	249	housewife	56	"

Saint Andrew Road

Z	Sullivan Mary E — †	2	housewife	59	here
	1829					
A	Sullivan William J	2	U S A	39	"
B	Kelly John C	2	undertaker	50	"
C	Kelly Rose V — †	2	housewife	52	"
D	Corrigan John L	6	foreman	54	"
E	Corrigan Nora F — †	6	housewife	53	"
F	Corrigan Ruth F — †	6	bookkeeper	27	"
G	Shaughnessy Albert L	8	teacher	49	"
H	Shaughnessy Grace M — †	8	housewife	31	"
K	DeDeyn Jules	10	laborer	44	"
L	DeDeyn Julia — †	10	housewife	50	"
M	Sofrine Edward	10	operator	37	"
N	Sofrine Eleanor — †	10	housewife	29	"
O	Sofrine Manuel	10	retired	79	"
P	Hart Mary A — †	14	housewife	47	"
R	Hart William J	14	policeman	51	"
S	Rollins Josephine — †	16	supervisor	34	"
T	Rollins Thomas E	16	U S A	36	137 Brooks
U	Ryan Lawrence J	16	"	31	here
V	Ryan Mary A — †	16	at home	69	"
W	Adams John O	18	retired	79	"

18

Saint Andrew Road Continued

x	Adams Rose †	18	housewife	69	here
y	Gabrino Anthony	18	retired	73	"
z	Hurley Henry	21	U S A	40	Arlington

1830

A	Hurley Marguerite G †	21	at home	36	"
B	Roche Eileen D †	21	housewife	28	37 Beacon
C	Roche Robert	21	U S N	27	37 "
D	Wellings Albert A	21	"	35	here
E	Wellings August J	21	"	47	"
F	Wellings Gladys D †	21	teacher	30	"
G	Wellings John A	21	retired	72	"
H	Wellings Joseph H	21	U S N	42	"
K	Wellings Timothy F	21	"	45	Hawaii
L	Guarino Frances T—†	24	housewife	36	25 Gladstone
M	Guarino John	24	architect	38	25 "
O	Parrell Catherine L—†	25	housewife	50	here
P	Parrell Richard T	25	retired	58	"
N	Fraser Gertrude S †	25	housekeeper	50	"
R	Powe Thomas J	25	retired	76	"
T	Blue Dorothea A—†	26	librarian	39	"
U	Blue Irene A—†	26	at home	68	"
V	Rego August	29	assembler	39	"
W	Rego Marie—†	29	housewife	39	"
X	Scoppettuolo Albert	29	U S A	31	"
Y	Scoppettuolo Anthony	29	shipper	70	"
Z	Scoppettuolo Anthony, jr	29	U S A	28	"

1831

A	Scoppettuolo Carmella †	29	housewife	70	"
B	Scoppettuolo Lena—†	29	packer	36	"
C	McInnes Archibald	30	salesman	65	"
D	McInnes Ellen E—†	30	stenographer	58	"
E	McInnes Evelyn E †	30	"	35	"
F	McInnes Kathryn E †	30	clerk	27	"
G	Dawley Anna F †	31	operator	44	"
H	Dawley Anna S †	31	housewife	79	"
K	Dawley William J	31	inspector	46	"
L	Kelly Christopher	31	retired	81	"
M	Sullivan Alice D †	32	clerk	22	"
N	Sullivan Arthur M	32	attorney	57	"
O	Sullivan Helen J—†	32	housewife	58	"
P	Carcioffo Edward P	33	salesman	32	Arlington

Saint Andrew Road—Continued

R	Carcioffo John J	33	U S N	31	Arlington
S	Mangini Edmund	33	bartender	32	here
T	Mangini Madeline F — †	33	housewife	33	"
U	Brown Frank P	34	retired	74	"
V	Brown Henry H	34	"	76	"
W	Lootz Ada M — †	34	at home	66	"
X	Lawrence Helen — †	37	secretary	34	"
Y	Lawrence Herbert S	37	laborer	64	"
Z	Lawrence John H	37	pipefitter	36	"

1832

A	Lawrence Sarah S — †	37	secretary	40	"
B	Ford Clarence P	38	lawyer	30	"
C	Ford Helen W — †	38	housewife	27	"
D	Carey Edward L	38	retired	56	"
E	Carey Margaret A — †	38	clerk	51	"
F	Jonasson Sophia — †	39	at home	81	"
G	Maguire James E	41	lawyer	70	"
H	Maguire Katherine R — †	41	housewife	68	"
K	Maguire Richard	41	U S A	28	Georgia
L	Millerick George E	44	chauffeur	44	here
M	Millerick Isabelle — †	44	housewife	39	"
N	Butler Bridie — †	44	"	53	"
O	Butler Edward F	44	plumber	30	"
P	Butler Helen M — †	44	student	20	"
R	Butler William T	44	shipfitter	28	"
S	McCallum Nellie — †	44	clerk	62	53 Waldemar av

Saint Edward Road

T	McCarthy James J	32	bookkeeper	23	here
U	McCarthy Margaret N — †	32	housewife	54	"
V	McCarthy Margaret N †	32	secretary	21	"
W	Mullen Anthony	40	machinist	44	"
X	Wilson Ellen †	40	at home	53	"
Y	Wilson George L	40	U S A	26	Falmouth
Z	Wilson George W	40	printer	53	here

1833

A	Wilson John	40	laborer	22	"
B	Wilson Leo J	40	U S A	20	"
C	Wilson Mary A †	40	housewife	53	"
D	Del Gaizo Guy	40	salesman	33	Newton

Saint Edward Road Continued

E	Del Gaizo Mary—†	40	housewife	32	Newton
F	Lavezzo Frances B—†	40	welder	23	here
G	Lavezzo Mary F—†	40	housewife	42	"
H	Lavezzo Sylvester S	40	bartender	57	"
K	DeRosa Lena—†	44	housewife	29	"
L	DeRosa Vito	44	agent	40	"
M	DeMatteo Albert	44	U S A	22	"
N	DeMatteo Donato	44	operator	52	"
O	DeMatteo Ida—†	44	housewife	45	"
P	Lagana Joseph A	44	carpenter	29	39 Moore
R	Lagana Mary—†	44	housewife	29	39 "

1834 Saratoga Street

G	Giuliotti Adolph J	1042	policeman	44	21 Gladstone
H	Giuliotti Mary V—†	1042	housewife	39	21 "
K	Boyd Avery L	1042	guard	74	here
L	Boyd James A	1042	machinist	48	"
M	McDonald Edward F	1042	U S A	22	"
N	McDonald Elizabeth O—†1042	housewife	44	"
O	McDonald Henry S	1042	B F D	44	"
P	Murphy James J	1042	bartender	52	"
R	Murphy John W	1042	U S A	44	"
T	Capone Margaret—†	1044	housewife	30	"
U	Capone Richard	1044	tailor	34	"
V	Rocciolo Dahlia—†	1044	stenographer	24	"
W	Rocciolo Elvira—†	1044	housewife	47	"
X	Rocciolo John	1044	U S A	22	"
Y	Rocciolo Joseph	1044	retired	79	"
Z	Rocciolo Joseph	1044	draftsman	23	"

1835

A	Rocciolo Pasquale	1044	musician	50	"
B	Rocciolo Sophie—†	1044	at home	76	"
D	Watchmaker Abraham	1045A	storekeeper	63	"
E	Watchmaker Lillian E—†	1045A	housewife	59	"
F	Watchmaker Sadie B—†	1045A	optical worker	25	"
G	Halloran Bridget—†	1046	housewife	39	"
H	Halloran Patrick	1046	manager	40	"
K	Cacchiotti Louise—†	1046	housewife	43	"
L	Cacchiotti Orazio	1046	cutter	51	"
M	Cacchiotti Rose—†	1046	typist	21	"

Page	Letter	Full Name.	Residence, Jan. 1, 1943.	Occupation.	Supposed Age.	Reported Residence, Jan. 1, 1942. Street and Number.

N	McIsaac Anna I—†	1047	clerk	42	here
O	McIsaac Frank A	1047	repairman	44	"
P	Muldoon James A	1047	splicer	52	"
R	Muldoon Katherine I—†	1047	nurse	48	"
S	Zielniger Charles J	1047	U S A	39	"
T	Zielniger Christine M—†	1047	operator	36	"
U	Zielniger Isabella M—†	1047	at home	64	"
V	Barone Palmina—†	1048	housewife	47	"
W	Barone Vito	1048	storekeeper	52	"
X	*Cutillo Annette —†	1048	at home	33	37 Gladstone
Y	*Cutillo Celia —†	1048	"	69	37 "
Z	Cutillo John	1048	shoeworker	47	37 "

1836

A	*Cutillo Joseph	1048	retired	69	37 "
B	Cutillo Richard	1048	U S N	25	37 "
D	*D'Amelio Carmela—† rear	1050	at home	71	here
E	D'Amelio Mary—† "	1050	bookkeeper	34	"
F	McClements Eva—†	1051	at home	58	"
G	Porter Madeline—†	1051	clerk	33	"
H	Shute Francis	1051	mechanic	28	"
K	Shute Louise—†	1051	operator	21	"
L	Shute Manuel J	1051	chauffeur	64	"
M	Shute Paul	1051	U S N	24	"
N	Forgeron Lula—†	1051	optical worker	46	"
O	Forgeron Thelma —†	1051	W A V E	21	"
P	Forgeron Theodore	1051	operator	46	"
R	Hicks Grace—†	1051	at home	27	"
S	Love Margaret F—†	1051	spinner	48	"
T	Marshall Anna M—†	1051	housewife	46	"
U	Marshall John J	1051	U S N	21	"
V	Marshall Joseph J	1051	B F D	56	"
W	Marshall Mildred G †	1051	mechanic	23	"
X	Keefe Annie E—†	1052	at home	54	"
Y	Keefe Elizabeth G—†	1052	housewife	59	"
Z	Keefe Thomas P	1052	clerk	56	"

1837

A	Dahnke Caroline—†	1052	at home	74	"
B	Dahnke Christina F—†	1052	B F D	51	"
C	Dahnke Frederick C	1052	machinist	48	"
D	Haritos Bertha—†	1052	housewife	32	"
E	Haritos Peter J	1052	policeman	49	"

Saratoga Street Continued

F	Morrison Isabelle C †	1053	operator	35	here	
G	Morrison John J	1053	pressman	36	"	
H	Domenico Josephine †	1053	housewife	47	59 Maverick sq	
K	Domenico Thomas D	1053	cleaner	50	59 "	
L	Hanglin Joseph E	1053	U S A	39	186 Sydney	
M	Hanglin Marion †	1053	housewife	38	186 "	
N	Teed Frederick B	1055	sexton	58	here	
O	Teed Frederick J	1055	machinist	24	"	
P	Teed Mabel E †	1055	housewife	56	"	
R	Anderson Pauline R †	1055	"	35	"	
S	Anderson Ralph I	1055	U S C G	45	"	
T	Hansen Alfred B	1055	retired	69	Revere	
U	Dorgan Charlotte †	1055	housewife	64	here	
V	Dorgan Margaret †	1055	optical worker	33	"	
W	Dorgan Michael	1055	retired	70	"	
X	McGeney Edward	1055	U S A	32	"	
Y	McGeney John	1055	laborer	28	"	
Z	McGeney John F	1055	printer	57	"	

1838

A	Buckingham Evelyn †	1057	operator	22	"	
B	Buckingham Florence H †	1057	clerk	42	"	
C	Buckingham Gertrude †	1057	at home	62	"	
D	Buckingham William R	1057	U S N	29	"	
E	Boudreau Caroline J †	1057	at home	24	"	
F	Boudreau Flora G †	1057	housewife	46	"	
G	Boudreau Francis R	1057	seaman	52	"	
H	Boudreau Thomas G	1057	U S A	20	"	
K	Boudreau Vivian F †	1057	teacher	22	"	
L	Georgalos Evangelos	1057	engineer	63	"	
M	Georgalos James E	1057	"	23	"	
N	Georgalos Maria †	1057	housewife	50	"	
O	Georgalos Thomas E	1057	tester	25	"	
P	Jeffers Helen †	1059	at home	34	"	
R	Jeffers Jasper	1059	foreman	41	"	
S	Jeffers Jennie †	1059	packer	36	"	
T	Jeffers Robert T	1059	clerk	38	"	
U	McGee Frank M	1059	retired	81	"	
V	Nilson Ethel B †	1059	housewife	43	"	
W	Nilson Leslie H	1059	decorator	50	"	
X	Stewart David	1059	U S A	29	"	
Y	Venedam Alice †	1059	housewife	53	"	

Saratoga Street Continued

z	Venedam Charles W	1059	carpenter	52	here

1839

A	Venedam James	1059	U S A	21	"
B	Venedam John	1059	"	23	"
C	Cianci Edwin	1060	electrician	37	"
D	Cianci Rachel †	1060	at home	70	"
E	DiMuro Anthony	1060	storekeeper	56	"
F	DiMuro Bernard	1060	U S A	26	"
G	DiMuro Jennie †	1060	housewife	52	"
H	DiMuro Jerome	1060	clerk	24	"
K	Rosenthal Abraham	1060	grocer	47	"
L	Rosenthal Sadie †	1060	clerk	44	"
M	Cianci Josephine †	1060	housewife	42	"
N	Cianci Louis	1060	clerk	48	"
O	Kirwan Arthur P	1061	policeman	43	"
P	Kirwan Rose †	1061	housewife	33	"
R	McFarlan Joseph	1061	shipper	45	"
S	Miller Leila †	1061	lawyer	43	"
T	Miller Susan †	1061	clerk	23	"
U	Miller Walter	1061	machinist	52	"
V	Miller Winifred †	1061	housewife	51	"
W	Polsonetti Pauline †	1061	at home	38	"
X	Puzzanghera Grocefissa †	1061	housewife	53	"
Y	Puzzanghera James	1061	presser	33	"
Z	Puzzanghera Joseph	1061	mason	62	"

1840

A	Puzzanghera Joseph, jr	1061	U S A	25	"
B	Puzzanghera Mary †	1061	housewife	24	"
C	Puzzanghera Salvatore	1061	stitcher	31	"
D	Graceffa Argentine †	1062	housewife	39	"
E	Graceffa John R	1062	painter	32	"
F	Santo Doris †	1062	housewife	34	"
G	Santo Giulio	1062	linotyper	37	"
H	Cardillo Angelo	1062	driller	42	"
K	Cardillo Irene †	1062	housewife	38	"
L	Conley Gertrude †	1065	clerk	50	"
M	Conley Marguerita †	1065	"	45	"
N	Abramo Angelo	1065	retired	76	"
O*	Abramo Lena †	1065	housewife	67	"
P	Grady Joseph J	1066	transitman	63	"
R	Lombardi Peter F. jr	1066	freighthandler	27	"

21

Saratoga Street Continued

s	Lombardi Ruth E †	1066	housewife	27	here
t	Larkin Evelyn †	1068	"	28	"
u	Larkin Joseph D	1068	agent	31	"
v	Biggio Harry	1069	retired	52	"
w	Fiamingo James F	1069	"	65	"
x	Fiamingo Leila M—†	1069	housewife	57	"
y	Mullane Mary T—†	1071	"	48	"
z	Mullane Patrick J	1071	attorney	60	"

1841

a	Murray Anne J—†	1071	operator	40	"
b	Murray Martin A	1071	teacher	43	"
c	Craviotto Prospero	1072	retired	81	"
d	Craviotto Teresa—†	1072	housewife	83	"
e	DiMarchi Mae—†	1072	clerk	48	"
f	Ardina Emma M—†	1072	housewife	54	"
g	Ardina Joseph	1072	steamfitter	64	"
h	Hurley Edward J	1072	manager	67	"
k	Sampson George J	1072	U S A	20	"
l	Sampson John T	1072	U S C G	27	"
m	Sampson John W	1072	collector	56	"
n	Sampson Margaret—†	1072	housewife	34	"
o	Cornetta Benedetto	1073	guard	55	72 Gladstone
p	Crovo John	1073	laborer	46	here
r	Kerrigan James J	1073	boilermaker	53	"
s	Kerrigan John J	1073	"	55	"
t	Kerrigan Margaret †	1073	housewife	46	"
u	Maguire Annie †	1073	housekeeper	75	"
v	Matthews Florence J †	1075	teacher	43	"
w	Riley Arthur	1075	chef	38	"
x	Bimber Adeline †	1075	housewife	50	"
y	Bimber Angelina †	1075	stitcher	27	"
z	Bimber Arthur J	1075	U S A	32	"

1842

a	Bimber George	1075	machinist	63	"
b	Bimber Hilda H †	1075	clerk	20	"
c	Bimber Mary †	1075	at home	29	"
d	Bimber Ottavio	1075	merchant	65	"
f	Sacco Alfred	1078	barber	63	"
g	Sacco Annie †	1078	housewife	62	"
h	Sacco Jennie †	1078	clerk	41	"
k	Sacco Mario A	1078	U S A	29	"

Saratoga Street—Continued

I	Anderson Dena C—†	1078	at home	56	Winthrop
M	Anderson Edith R—†	1078	clerk	27	"
N	Schwartz Lawrence F	1078	operator	27	here
O	Schwartz Thelma M—†	1078	housewife	25	"
R	Simeon Ethel—†	1084	"	33	Revere
S	Simeon Robert	1084	U S A	29	"
T	Belli Gene	1084	diemaker	27	42 Reed
U	Belli Irene—†	1084	housewife	25	Arlington
V	Vivenzio Nicola	1084	tailor	56	here
W	Vivenzio Theresa—†	1084	housewife	54	"
X	Conway Frank B rear	1084	retired	48	108 Faywood av
Y	Shafer Edward "	1084	U S A	37	108 "
Z	Shafer Henry W "	1084	U S N	42	108 "

1843

A	Shafer Ruth—† "	1084	inspector	44	108 "
C	Austin Richard	1085	retired	72	here
D	Bishop Edward L	1085	dentist	42	"
E	Riley Mary F—†	1085	at home	50	"
F	Riley Rose E—†	1085	instructor	60	"
G	Riley William J	1085	dentist	66	"
H	Bucola Francesco G	1088	U S A	26	"
K	*Bucola Maria—†	1088	at home	64	"
L	Bucola Sebastiano	1088	laborer	23	"
M	Genoesa Charles	1088	barber	53	"
N	Genoesa Maria—†	1088	housewife	41	"
O	White Anna—†	1088	"	33	"
P	White Charles E	1088	electrician	30	"

Swan Avenue

S	*Cambria Frank	26	retired	69	here

Thurston Street

T	Connor Mildred—†	2	housewife	28	186 Bayswater
U	Guilfoyle Mary—†	2	operator	30	here
V	Roddy Gertrude—†	2	stenographer	34	"
W	Roddy Helen M—†	2	operator	36	"
X	Roddy Nora—†	2	housewife	64	"
Y	Olpin Bessie J—†	3	clerk	59	"
Z	Scott Elizabeth—†	3	housewife	52	"

1844
Thurston Street Continued

A	Scott James M	3	carpenter	58	here
B	Donnelly Anna T †	3	secretary	35	"
C	Donnelly John F	3	inspector	45	"
D	Anderson Lewis	4	millwright	52	"
E	Anderson Rose †	4	housewife	49	"
F	Silva Guilhermina F †	4	housekeeper	75	"
G	Hollingsworth Daniel J	5	retired	68	"
H	Hollingsworth Mary C †	5	operator	64	"
K	Hollingsworth Sadie M †	5	saleswoman	60	"
L	Sweeney Julia †	5	"	64	"
M	Sweeney Warren	5	U S A	34	"
N	Callahan Bernard G	5	"	36	"
O	Callahan James D	5	"	38	"
P	Callahan James J	5	B F D	68	"
R	Callahan Leo B	5	U S A	25	"
S	Callahan Margaret L †	5	housewife	64	"
T	Callahan Margaret L †	5	at home	30	"
U	Callahan Rita T †	5	operator	27	"
V	Currie Mary †	5	housewife	34	121 Mercer
W	Enos Catherine †	6	"	37	here
X	Enos Edmund T	6	policeman	46	"
Y	Banker Charles G	7	retired	82	"
Z	Banker Charles W	7	"	45	"

1845

A	Benker Frederick W	7	U S A	44	"
B	Benker Jacob	7	retired	72	"
C	Benker William A	7	U S A	42	"
D	Riley Edna E †	7	housewife	32	"
E	Riley Edward J	7	draftsman	32	"
F	Mahoney George	8	adjuster	50	"
G	Mahoney George, jr	8	U S C G	23	"
H	Mahoney Katherine †	8	housewife	48	"
K	Sullivan Thomas	8	investigator	48	"
L	McGunigle Anna M †	8A	clerk	32	"
M	McGunigle John J	8A	U S A	33	54 Bayswater
N	O'Connor Bridget †	8A	housekeeper	76	here
O	O'Connor Daniel P	8A	laborer	50	"
P	Sullivan Robert	8A	salesman	39	"
R	Vieixa Andrew M, jr	8A	barber	48	67 Neptune rd
S	Nolan Mary L †	10	housewife	68	here

Thurston Street   Continued

T	Nolan William S	10	merchant	69	here	
U	Flood Edward J	10A	salesman	65	"	
V	Flood Margaret C — †	10A	housewife	64	"	
W	Cullinane James F	11	foreman	33	"	
X	Cullinane Rita M — †	11	housewife	27	"	
Y	Dunn Helen M — †	11	housekeeper	55	"	
Z	Sacco Annie — †	11A	housewife	62	"	

1846

A	Sacco Henry	11A	operator	26	"	
B	Sacco Louise — †	11A	hairdresser	24	"	
C	Sacco Sylvia — †	11A	saleswoman	20	"	
D	Lazzaro Antonio	11A	machinist	43	"	
E	Lazzaro Mary T — †	11A	housewife	33	"	
F	Mahoney Ellen G — †	12	housekeeper	54	"	
G	Russell Annie M — †	12	housewife	58	"	
H	Russell George A	12	machinist	58	"	
K	Crowley Agnes T — †	12	housewife	64	"	
L	Crowley James T	12	retired	68	"	
M	Cantillo Lucy — †	14	housewife	32	"	
N	Cantillo Maurice	14	clerk	32	"	
O	Cantillo Alfonso	14	storekeeper	56	"	
P	Cantillo Henrietta — †	14	housewife	52	"	
R	Rocco Fiorinda — †	15	"	74	"	
S	Rocco Josephine — †	15	"	43	"	
T	Rocco Louis	15	salesman	48	"	
U	Rocco Michael	15	"	46	"	
V	Kincaid Elsie M — †	16	secretary	37	"	
W	Kincaid Mary S — †	16	housewife	66	"	
X	Kincaid Sterling J	16	upholsterer	39	"	
Y	Murray Kathryn — †	18	housewife	35	"	
Z	Sullivan Mary — †	18	"	59	"	

1847

A	Calhoun George	18	retired	78	"	
B	Calhoun Mary — †	18	housewife	75	"	
C	Graziano Elvira — †	19	"	65	"	
D	Graziano Ida — †	19	clerk	32	"	
E	Graziano Marie C — †	19	"	38	"	
F	Downing Byron O	20	"	62	"	
G	Downing Hiram A	20	guard	64	"	
H	Downing Melissa S — †	20	housewife	54	"	
K	Smith Justina S — †	20	"	78	"	

Thurston Street Continued

L	Smith Willard M	20	retired	82	here
M	Devlin Louise †	21	nurse	36	"
N	O'Rourke Helen F †	21	operator	45	"
O	O'Rourke Irene M †	21	buffer	40	"
P	O'Rourke Mary A †	21	housewife	68	"
R	O'Rourke Thomas L	21	U S C G	38	"
S	Donovan Ellen C †	22	housewife	41	"
T	Donovan Arthur J	22	laborer	43	"
U	Morrison John P	22	constructor	75	"
V	Morrison Julia F †	22	teacher	36	"
W	Morrison Mary E †	22	operator	45	"
X	Tigges Catherine †	25	housewife	44	"
Y	Tigges Walter J	25	machinist	46	"
Z	Alosa Dina †	26	housewife	40	"

1848

A	Alosa Umberto	26	manager	42		"
B	Rossi Angelo	26	tailor	52		"
C	Rossi Gaetano	26	boilermaker	22		"
D	*Rossi Hilda †	26	housewife	49		"
E	Giordano Annette †	26	"	33	73	Charles
F	Giordano Mario	26	chauffeur	33	73	"

Ward 1–Precinct 19

CITY OF BOSTON

LIST OF RESIDENTS
20 YEARS OF AGE AND OVER

(NON-CITIZENS INDICATED BY ASTERISK)
(FEMALES INDICATED BY DAGGER)

AS OF

JANUARY 1, 1943

JOSEPH F. TIMILTY, *Chairman*
FREDERIC E. DOWLING, *Secretary*
WILLIAM A. MOTLEY, JR.
FRANCIS B. McKINNEY
EVERETT R. PROUT

Listing Board.

CITY OF BOSTON PRINTING DEPARTMENT

Page.	Letter.	FULL NAME.	Residence. Jan. 1. 1943.	Occupation.	Supposed Age.	Reported Residence Jan. 1. 1942. Street and Number.

1900

Annavoy Street

A	Cerullo Christie	10	pharmacist	32	here
B	Cerullo Lillian †	10	housewife	30	"
C	Ruggieri Emilia †	10	"	56	"
D	Ruggieri Luigi	10	finisher	57	"
E	Bellusci Josephine †	20	housewife	51	"
F	Bellusci Michael C	20	broker	60	"
G	Montgomery Edward	26	B F D	56	"
H	Montgomery Helen †	26	housewife	52	"
K	Whetsel Leone †	26	"	25	Ohio
L	Whetsel Oslo	26	U S N	26	Iceland

Barnes Avenue

M	MacDonald Clementine B †	95	secretary	58	here
N	MacDonald Kathryn F †	95	operator	54	"
O	MacDonald Mary A †	95	at home	65	"
P	Perrier Alice †	95	housewife	61	"
R	Perrier Eugene	95	laborer	62	"
S	Riley Irene †	95	housewife	28	"
T	Riley William L	95	laborer	30	"
U	Jannini Alice †	99	housewife	37	"
V	Jannini Christopher	99	cutter	38	"
W	Abate Angelo	99	shoeworker	56	"
X	Abate Frank	99	U S A	32	"
Y	Abate Gloria †	99	stenographer	21	"
Z	Abate Jeannette †	99	secretary	31	"

1901

A	Abate Laura †	99	housewife	50	"
B	Mazzeo Grace †	102	"	26	21 Ashley
C	Mazzeo Phillip	102	hairdresser	34	21 "
D	D'Allesandro Louis	102	repairman	34	here
E	D'Allesandro Marion †	102	housewife	30	"
F	Fenlon Mary E †	103	"	74	"
G	Fenlon Warren F	103	attorney	44	"
H	Golden Catherine †	103	at home	65	"
K	Campbell Armina †	103	housewife	75	"
L	Campbell John L	103	retired	79	"
M	McDermott Armina †	103	housewife	41	"
N	McDermott John J	103	policeman	42	"
O	Collins Mary E †	107	matron	58	"

2

Barnes Avenue Continued

P	Hickey Catherine F †	107	housewife	59	here
R	Hickey Edward I	107	collector	25	"
S	Hickey Frances †	107	housewife	35	"
T	Hickey Mary E †	107	operator	36	"
V	Bonugli Anne †	110	housewife	36	"
W	Bonugli John	110	operator	47	"
X	Carbone Elizabeth †	110	clerk	37	"
Y	McCormack James	110	teacher	30	"
Z	McCormack Virginia †	110	housewife	24	"

1902

A	Ahern Helen †	111	saleswoman	51	"
B	Ahern Margaret †	111	housewife	39	"
C	Ahern Nora †	111	saleswoman	53	"
D	Lentini Guy	111	teacher	34	"
E	Lentini Rose †	111	housewife	30	"
F	Callanan Pauline †	115	"	37	"
G	Callanan William	115	U S A	38	"
H	White John J	115	carpenter	67	"
K	White John J, jr	115	plumber	21	"
L	White Josephine A †	115	secretary	23	"
M	White Mary E †	115	housewife	61	"
N	White Mary R †	115	secretary	32	"
O	Lehman Anton	118	clerk	35	"
P	Lehman Arthur B	118	printer	52	"
R	Lehman Dorothy †	118	operator	29	"
S	Lehman Grace †	118	at home	28	"
T	Lehman Lillian A †	118	housewife	51	"
U	Hart Mary †	118	cook	58	"
V	Lane Alice †	118	dressmaker	57	"
W	Lane Catherine †	118	operator	41	"
X	Lane Catherine †	118	housewife	31	"
Y	Lane Helen †	118	operator	46	"
Z	Lane James	118	welder	37	"

1903

A	Lane John	118	U S A	39	"
B	Lane Mary †	118	housewife	58	"
C	Crawford Mary †	126	at home	75	"
D	Ryan Helen †	126	housewife	40	"
E	Ryan James	126	chauffeur	43	"
F	Gallagher Ruth †	126	stenographer	24	"
G	Higgins Lillian †	126	operator	46	"

3

Page.	Letter.	FULL NAME.	Residence, Jan. 1, 1943.	Occupation.	Supposed Age.	Reported Residence, Jan. 1, 1942. Street and Number.

Barnes Avenue—Continued

	H	Nolan Margaret †	126	at home	51	here
	K	Shannon Edward	126	welder	42	"
	L	Shannon Elizabeth †	126	housewife	49	"
	M	Shannon George A	126	welder	37	"
	N	Shannon William F	126	U S N	40	"

Bayswater Street

	O	Kiley Grace †	80	housewife	36	here
	P	Kiley Henry	80	clerk	38	"
	R	Ahearn Bridget †	82	at home	72	"
	S	Recomendes Annie †	82	housewife	68	"
	T	O'Neil Nellie †	84	at home	70	"
	U	Gill James R	86	dealer	39	"
	V	McNamee Anna E †	86	housewife	36	"
	W	McNamee Charles	86	salesman	32	"
	X	Engren Theresa E †	88	housewife	50	"
	Y	Engren Walter F	88	engineer	46	"
	Z	Mullen James	88	retired	84	"

1904

	A	Mullen John J	88	proprietor	46	"
	B	Mullen Marion K †	88	stenographer	42	"
	C	Merritt Arthur R	94	guard	36	"
	D	Merritt Muriel †	94	housewife	30	"
	E	Viglione Anna M †	94	"	42	"
	F	Viglione Patrick	94	manager	41	"
	G	Moschella Anthony	94	U S N	20	"
	H	Moschella Catherine A †	94	housewife	43	"
	K	Moschella Michael	94	meatcutter	54	"
	L	Moschella Samuel	94	student	21	"
	M	Campbell Agnes †	98	housewife	29	"
	N	Campbell Frank J	98	electrician	32	"
	O	DiNucci Americo	98	U S N	38	"
	P	DiNucci Anna †	98	housewife	68	"
	R	DiNucci Anthony	98	U S N	36	"
	S	DiNucci Rose †	98	clerk	40	"
	T	DiNucci Victoria †	98	saleswoman	34	"
	U	Cazziano Evelyn S †	100	housewife	45	70 St Andrew rd
	V	Cazziano Generoso	100	storekeeper	47	70 "
	W	Cazziano Grace E †	100	clerk	21	70 "
	X	Lavezzo Rose †	100	housewife	85	Stoneham

Bayswater Street Continued

Y	Hedrington James	102	motorman	45	here	
Z	Oakes Charles G	102	"	45	"	
1905						
A	Oakes Henry J	102	retired	81	"	
B	Oakes John L	102	U S A	38	"	
C	Oakes Mary A—†	102	housewife	69	"	
D	Oakes Mary E—†	102	bookkeeper	39	"	
E	Nutile Edna V—†	104	housewife	46	"	
F	Nutile Thomas	104	salesman	59	"	
G	Chiccarelli Fortunato	106	U S A	21	"	
H	Chiccarelli Jennie—†	106	housewife	43	"	
K	Chiccarelli Joseph B	106	clerk	51	"	
L	Donohue Cornelius J	108	plumber	36	"	
M	Donohue Frances M—†	108	housewife	36	"	
N	Crowley George S	110	foreman	52	1123 Saratoga	
O	Crowley Helen E—†	110	housewife	45	1123 "	
P	Surdzinski Anna—†	110	cleaner	45	here	
R	Mogan Ethel D—†	112	housewife	52	"	
S	Mogan William H	112	realtor	55	"	
T	Rossetta Angela—†	112	housewife	30	"	
U	Rossetta Anthony	112	chauffeur	31	"	
V	Alexander William J	114	clerk	54	"	
W	Donohue Cornelius J	114	plumber	70	"	
X	Donohue Harriet N—†	114	housewife	65	"	
Y	Howard Marie—†	114	"	34	"	
Z	Howard William	114	policeman	35	"	
1906						
A	Walters Rose M—†	114	clerk	54	"	
B	Brown Aimee F—†	116	teacher	33	"	
C	Brown Francis T	116	retired	72	"	
D	Brown Margaret—†	116	housewife	60	"	
E	DeSimone Adeline—†	120	"	43	"	
F	DeSimone Lena—†	120	clerk	21	"	
G	DeSimone Michael	120	chauffeur	45	"	
H	*DeSisto Generoso	120	retired	83	39 Salutation	
K	Lane John A	120	teacher	50	here	
L	Lane Mabel J—†	120	clerk	40	"	
M	Pellegrini Helen—†	122	housewife	44	"	
N	Pellegrini Joseph E	122	manager	46	"	
O	Cavaliere Anna—†	124	clerk	20	"	
P	Cavaliere Carmela—†	124	housewife	24	"	

5

Bayswater Street—Continued

	R	Cavaliere Elizabeth—†	124	housewife	47	here
	S	Cavaliere Joseph	124	guard	47	"
	T	Cavaliere Mary—†	124	clerk	22	"
	U	Norton Evelyn—†	126	housewife	39	"
	V	Norton Walter	126	laborer	42	"
	W	Norton Walter	126	"	20	"
	X	Digou Agnes—†	140	housewife	62	"
	Y	Digou Freeman T	140	manager	65	"
	Z	Digou Mary C—†	140	teacher	28	"

1907

	A	Phelan Helen A—†	140	housewife	44	"
	B	Phelan William M	140	B F D	56	"
	C	Whynot George A	144	machinist	61	"
	D	Whynot Lucinda M—†	144	housewife	60	"
	E	Silva Anthony F	144	manager	56	"
	F	Silva Emily C—†	144	housewife	55	"
	G	Brown Hazel R—†	146	stenographer	25	"
	H	Brown James S	146	electrician	62	"
	K	Burns Claire M—†	146	secretary	28	"
	L	Burns Edward P	146	watchman	70	"
	M	Burns Margaret A—†	146	housewife	65	"
	N	Clarke Estelle L—†	146	social worker	45	"
	O	Ciampa Elizabeth—†	148	housewife	55	"
	P	Ciampa Joseph	148	U S A	31	"
	R	Ciampa Lillian—†	148	stenographer	22	"
	S	Ciampa Rose—†	148	clerk	20	"
	T	Boynton Ruth M—†	150	artist	27	"
	U	Boynton Willard H	150	physician	28	"
	V	Watt John G	150	salesman	50	"
	W	Watt Mary L—†	150	housewife	50	"
	X	Montgomery Annie—†	150	"	79	"
	Y	Montgomery Hugh J	150	artist	53	"
	Z	Montgomery Rose E—†	150	housewife	52	"

1908

	A	Montgomery Claire J—†	156	"	45	"
	B	Montgomery Eugene R	156	jeweler	49	"
	C	Chalmers Hazen A	156	policeman	46	"
	D	Chalmers Julia C—†	156	housewife	45	"
	E	Dolan Francis	160	inspector	43	"
	F	Dolan Margaret M—†	160	housewife	41	"
	G	O'Brion Katherine M—†	160	"	73	"

Bayswater Street (Continued)

H	Piazza Anna †	160	housewife	29	here
K	Piazza Lawrence	160	merchant	29	"
L	Rosa Albert V	164	attorney	34	"
M	Rosa Catherine †	164	clerk	31	"
N	Rosa Helen †	164	housewife	36	"
O	Mattola Jennie †	166	"	60	"
P	Mattola Nelson	166	machinist	50	"
R	Butler Helen M †	168	housewife	69	25 St Andrew rd
S	Stenzel Margaret A †	168	nurse	54	25 "
T	Evans Agnes †	170	housewife	37	here
U	Evans John	170	machinist	54	"
V	*Fantasia Amelia †	172	housewife	64	"
W	Fantasia Clement	172	laborer	67	"
X	*Cerulli Domenic	174	retired	65	"
Y	Cerulli Fred	174	manager	38	"
Z	*Cerulli Mary †	174	housewife	54	"

1909

A	Cerulli Rose †	174	"	35	"
C	Lowther Anne V †	174A	operator	36	"
D	Lowther Cecelia E †	174A	housewife	67	"
E	Lowther Frances V †	174A	supervisor	46	"
F	Lowther Grace V †	174A	operator	32	"
G	Lowther Margaret I †	174A	housekeeper	41	"
H	Lafferty Matthew L	186	mechanic	50	"
K	Landry Jeffrey E	186	salesman	55	"
L	Landry May E †	186	housewife	52	"
M	McLaughlin Frances M †	186	"	54	"
N	McLaughlin Frances K †	186	teacher	22	"
P	Mealey Leo	188	clerk	44	"
R	Mealey Mary J †	188	housewife	71	"
S	Platt John	188	clerk	40	"
T	Platt Marion †	188	housewife	39	"
U	Harkins Celia †	188	"	50	"
V	Harkins Charles J	188	manager	28	"
W	Harkins John P	188	U S N	27	"
X	Harkins Mary E †	188	operator	32	"
Y	Harkins William J	188	secretary	24	"
Z	Hall Fritz S	190	painter	46	"

1910

A	Hall Marion †	190	housewife	40	"
B	Harrigan Julia †	190	"	76	"

7

Benner Street

	D	Fraser Joseph	rear 8	roofer	55	here
	E	Bassett Elmer	" 8	machinist	47	"
	F	Bassett Evelyn †	" 8	housewife	35	"

Lillian Street

	G	Keleher Dennis J	1	probat'n officer	66	here
	H	Keleher Katherine W †	1	housewife	65	"
	K	Keleher Mary M †	1	clerk	27	"
	L	Rinehart Antoinette †	14	housewife	28	Medfield
	M	Reinhart Harold	14	engineer	30	"
	N	Zagarella Gemma †	14	housewife	45	here
	O	Zagarella Joseph	14	U S A	24	"
	P	Zagarella Peter	14	busboy	21	"
	R	Zagarella Salvatore	14	barber	47	"

Nancia Street

	S	Heggem Dagney F †	2	housewife	44	here
	T	Heggem Lars J	2	clergyman	54	"
	U	Nordby Alma E †	2	at home	75	"
	V	Greco Louis	9	U S A	45	"
	W	Romano Anna †	9	housewife	40	"
	X	Romano Phillip	9	tailor	44	"
	Y	Bradley Joseph H	10	policeman	46	"
	Z	Bradley Madeline M †	10	housewife	41	"

1911

	A	Potito Domenic D	14	physician	33	"
	B	Potito Leonora †	14	housewife	26	"

Saint Andrew Road

	D	Chiarini Elisa †	50	hairdresser	31	here
	E	Chiarini Joseph	50	musician	54	"
	F	Chiarini Josephine †	50	housewife	53	"
	G	Ciampa Lillian †	50	"	46	"
	H	Marsolini Robert A	50	U S M C	25	"
	K	Massa Ida †	50	waitress	41	"
	L	Massa Rose †	50	bookkeeper	38	"
	M	Capomaccio Joseph	51	tailor	29	49 Brook av
	N	Capomaccio Laura †	51	housewife	30	49 "

Saint Andrew Road   Continued

O	Penta Ida †	51	at home	28	33 Brook av
P	Penta Maria †	51	housewife	67	49 "
R	Penta Theresa †	51	operator	35	49 "
S	Lyons James	51	"	45	here
T	Lyons Joseph	51	machinist	41	"
U	Penta Vera †	51	clerk	39	"
V	Miller Joseph	51	laborer	35	"
W	Curran Theresa A †	53	housewife	41	"
X	Curran William C	53	salesman	44	"
Y	Winston James J	53	supervisor	57	"
Z	Winston John E	53	statistician	51	"

1912

A	Winston Katherine B †	53	housewife	44	"
B	Winston Mary F †	53	"	46	"
C	Watts Gertrude H †	55	"	58	"
D	Anderson Christine †	55	secretary	36	"
E	Anderson Josephine †	55	clerk	38	"
F	Regan Donald A	55	U S N	27	"
G	Regan Herbert G	55	"	28	"
H	Regan Louise G †	55	housewife	54	"
K	Regan Miriam L †	55	teacher	22	"
L	Ryan Agnes M †	56	housewife	41	"
M	Ryan Thomas B	56	electrician	42	"
N	Aronson Harry	57	clerk	36	"
O	Aronson Margaret †	57	housewife	33	"
P	Corrigan Anna K †	57	secretary	35	"
R	Corrigan Catherine F †	57	housewife	67	"
S	Crowley Margaret R †	59	"	52	"
T	Hart Helen S †	59	"	36	"
U	Hart Peter J	59	printer	38	"
V	Sullivan Jane A †	59	nurse	44	"
W	Sullivan Susie A †	59	at home	75	"
X	McLeavey Anna E †	60	housewife	62	"
Y	McLeavey Patrick F	60	retired	73	"
Z	Plunkett Bernard	60	"	77	"

1913

A	Reardon Katherine M †	60	at home	67	83 St Andrew rd
B	Ingersoll Charles	61	clerk	30	here
C	Ingersoll Claire †	61	housewife	28	"
D	Gill Mary E †	61	"	70	"
E	Gill Richard F	61	watchman	76	"

9

Saint Andrew Road—Continued

	F	Gill Richard M	61	U S A	23	here
	G	Cirfone Alice †	63	saleswoman	40	"
	H	Cirfone Louis	63	tailor	44	"
	K	Musto Albert S	63	manager	35	"
	L	Musto Mary A †	63	housewife	34	"
	M	*Yirrell Mary M †	63	at home	67	10 Old Morton
	N	Murphy Agnes †	63	forewoman	26	here
	O	Murphy Cornelius	63	salesman	30	"
	P	Murphy Ella †	63	housewife	30	"
	R	Francis Adelaide †	64	at home	71	"
	S	Lamb Ethel B †	64	housewife	47	"
	T	Lamb Frank T	64	policeman	48	"
	U	Lamb Trevor E	64	inspector	23	"
	V	Roome Mortimer	64	retired	77	"
	W	Haley Arthur	65	executive	28	"
	X	Haley Susan G †	65	housewife	55	"
	Y	McGovern Margaret A †	65	inspector	50	"
	Z	Gavagan Catherine †	66	operator	29	"

1914

	A	Gavagan Ethel †	66	"	35	1118 Saratoga
	B	Gavagan Helen †	66	housewife	40	1118 "
	C	Gavagan Walter	66	clerk	42	1118 "
	D	Carey Alice M †	66	housewife	24	here
	E	Carey Edward M	66	machinist	33	"
	F	Colbert Alice †	66	at home	88	1118 Saratoga
	G	Colbert John	66	manager	50	1118 "
	H	Colbert Nellie †	66	artist	60	here
	K	McGuigan Ann †	68	clerk	22	"
	L	McGuigan Anna †	68	teacher	52	"
	M	McGuigan Bernard	68	U S A	26	"
	N	McGuigan Mary †	68	clerk	26	"
	O	Matrone Irene †	68	stenographer	22	"
	P	Matrone Josephine †	68	housewife	49	"
	R	Strong Anne A †	68	at home	66	"
	S	Strong Ellen L †	68	"	68	"
	T	Strong William H	68	dentist	53	"
	U	Hoey Edward A	69	paymaster	55	"
	V	Hoey John W	69	B F D	54	"
	W	Hoey Mary L †	69	housewife	50	"
	X	McDonald Dorothy †	69	social worker	31	"
	Y	McDonald Margaret †	69	at home	51	"

Saint Andrew Road Continued

z	Leary Helen M †	69	housewife	55	here
1915						
A	Leary Matthew M	69	probat'n officer	65	"
B	Caggiano Arthur	70	U S C G	34	"
C	Caggiano Catherine †	70	at home	36	"
D	Caggiano Florence †	70	candyworker	32	"
E	Caggiano Grace †	70	housewife	67	"
F	Caggiano Joseph	70	barber	73	"
G	Caggiano Mundo	70	B F D	38	"
H	Schoenfeld Lena †	70	secretary	40	"
K	Cadillo Anthony	70	storekeeper	42	Revere
L	Cadillo Rose †	70	housewife	40	"
M	Cataldo Chiarina †	72	at home	73	here
N	Cataldo Pasquale	72	retired	82	"
O	Zizza Alfred	72	packer	40	"
P	Zizza Ermalinda †	72	housewife	37	"
R	DiFronzo Michael	72	storekeeper	62	"
S*	DiFronzo Philomena †	72	housewife	64	"
T	Bellusci Louise †	72	"	26	"
U	Bellusci Nicholas	72	laborer	31	"
V	Duffy Mary M †	73	housewife	38	"
W	Duffy Michael H	73	U S N	43	"
X	Callahan Jean M †	73	student	20	"
Y	Callahan John J	73	U S A	52	"
Z	Callahan Rose M †	73	housewife	51	"
1916						
A	Dolan Anna L †	73	at home	55	"
B	McCarthy Mary F †	73	"	65	"
C	Carangelo Louise †	74	teacher	38	"
D	Miraldi Gerald	74	attorney	41	"
E	Miraldi Olive †	74	housewife	39	"
F	Cohan Alice A †	75	"	64	"
G	Cohan Edward J	75	U S A	24	"
H	Cohan William M	75	foreman	64	"
K*	Cerullo Annie †	75	housewife	67	"
L	Cerullo Anthony	75	U S A	30	"
M	Cerullo Salvatore	75	retired	65	"
N	Pellegrino Adeline †	76	housewife	33	"
O	Pellegrino Vincent	76	clerk	34	"
P	Femino Bruno	77	barber	53	33 Gladstone
R	Femino Jennie †	77	operator	27	33 "

11

Saint Andrew Road—Continued

s	Femino John	77	machinist	26	33 Gladstone
t	Femino Paul	77	U S A	24	here
u	Femino Ralph	77	chauffeur	39	33 Gladstone
v	Femino Rose—†	77	tailor	48	33 "
w	Femino Salvatore	77	U S A	22	33 "
x	Maresco Helen—†	77	operator	30	33 "
y	*Calamoneri Domenica—†	77	at home	77	33
z	Indresano Emelio	77	chipper	29	here

1917

A	Indresano Mildred—†	77	housewife	29	"
B	*Nuccio Peter	77	retired	75	33 Gladstone
c	Elmore Joseph F	78	inspector	54	here
D	Elmore Margaret J—†	78	at home	82	"
E	Elmore Mary G—†	78	clerk	48	"
F	McAdams Alfred J	78	machinist	52	"
G	McAdams Eleanor—†	78	housewife	52	"
H	Callahan Mary A—†	80	at home	69	"
K	Holden Catherine T—†	80	"	79	"
L	Murphy John D	80	yardmaster	65	"
M	Murphy Margaret L—†	80	housewife	52	"
N	Kelly Emmett J	81	assessor	42	51 St Andrew rd
O	Kelly Theresa C—†	81	housewife	37	51 "
P	Lagamasino Margaret A—†	81	clerk	42	51 "
R	Cunningham Mary E—†	81	at home	72	here
S	Drowney Agnes C—†	81	attendant	60	"
T	Shaw Henry F	81	broker	52	"
U	Shaw Henry F, jr	81	mechanic	20	"
V	Shaw Marie A—†	81	housewife	48	"
W	Shaw Marie A—†	81	secretary	28	"
X	McLaughlin Constance M—†	82	inspector	24	"
Y	Nagle John E	82	tollman	64	"
Z	Nagle Rebecca—†	82	housewife	54	"

1918

A	Mauceri Helen—†	82	"	28	"
B	Mauceri Joseph	82	shipper	36	"
C	McNeil Catherine M—†	82	at home	74	"
D	Stout Lena G—†	82	housewife	53	"
E	Stout Walter A	82	pharmacist	56	"
F	Reardon Catherine—†	83	housewife	28	"
G	Reardon John	83	teller	33	"
H	Labedessa Joseph	85	watchman	58	"

12

Saint Andrew Road Continued

K	Labedessa Lucia †	85	housewife	55	here	
L	Love Lena †	85	typist	42	"	
M	Arnone Adele †	86	housewife	31	"	
N	Arnone Angela †	86	"	55	"	
O	Arnone Nicholas	86	foreman	57	"	
P	Arnone Phillip	86	auditor	34	"	
R	Martins Anna M †	86	housewife	50	"	
S	Martins John H	86	salesman	69	"	
T	Dunn Ann †	87	housewife	32	"	
U	Dunn Joseph A	87	contractor	38	"	
V	DeSimone Joseph	89	manager	50	"	
W	DeSimone Joseph, jr	89	U S A	21	"	
X	DeSimone Lena †	89	stenographer	24	"	
Y	DeSimone Lucas	89	U S A	20	"	
Z	DeSimone Margaret †	89	housewife	48	"	

1919

A	Collyer Albert	90	laborer	42	"	
B	Stoner Beverly †	90	secretary	20	"	
C	Stoner Elizabeth E †	90	housewife	52	"	
D	Stoner George H	90	instructor	55	"	
E	Stoner George H, jr	90	architect	25	"	
F	Gorman Charles W	90	storekeeper	63	"	
G	Gorman Nellie R †	90	housewife	60	"	
H	Pendergast Catherine †	90	"	67	"	
K	Pendergast Lillian †	90	finisher	42	"	
L	McBride Alvina †	91—93	clerk	38	"	
M	McBride Daniel	91—93	"	47	"	
N	McBride Margaret J †	91—93	at home	46	"	
O	Smith Francis X	91—93	letter carrier	48	"	
P	Smith Mary A †	91—93	shoeworker	44	"	
R	Smith Sarah E †	91—93	housewife	45	"	
S	Whaland Helen E †	92	"	42	"	
T	Whaland Phillip P	92	policeman	53	"	
U	Schlosberg Freda †	94	housewife	27	"	
V	Schlosberg Harold	94	U S A	21	"	
W	Schlosberg Leon	94	pharmacist	27	"	
X	Schlosberg Louis	94	salesman	57	"	
Y	Schlosberg Sadie †	94	housewife	52	"	
Z	Crowley James	96	chauffeur	30	104 Bayswater	

1920

A	Crowley Sally †	96	housewife	29	104 "	

13

Saint Andrew Road — Continued

B	Greer Herbert A	98	U S A	27	here
C	Greer Margaret—†	98	housewife	54	"
D	Greer Nicholas J	98	letter carrier	63	"
E	Kinnaly Ellen T—†	100	at home	65	311 Emerson
F	Kinnaly George	100	manager	39	here
G	Kinnaly Theresa—†	100	housewife	34	"
H	Petrillo Henry	101	tailor	39	"
K	Petrillo Mary—†	101	housewife	41	"
N	Selvitella Joseph	103	waiter	45	"
O	Selvitella Mathilda—†	103	housewife	38	"
L	Selvitella Adeline—†	103	"	35	"
M	Selvitella James	103	manager	43	"
P	Corrado John	104	physician	34	"
R	Corrado Maria—†	104	housewife	31	"
S	D'Amore Marie—†	105	waitress	30	"
T	*Stasio Anna—†	105	housewife	71	"
U	Stasio Helen—†	105	dressmaker	35	"
V	Olsen Margaret—†	106	housewife	50	"
W	Olsen Olaf	106	printer	54	"
X	Monahan John B	107	clerk	31	1114 Saratoga
Y	Monahan Nora T—†	107	housewife	31	114 "
Z	*Vallie Adele—†	108	at home	72	here

1921

A	Valli Blanche M—†	108	housewife	36	"
B	Valli George E	108	dairyman	40	"
C	Calafato Eva—†	109	housewife	30	"
D	Calafato Thomas	109	machinist	34	"
E	Capuana Betty—†	110	housewife	35	"
F	Capuana John	110	bartender	36	"
G	D'Ambrosio Adamo	111	seaman	41	"
H	D'Ambrosio John	111	musician	36	"
K	D'Ambrosio Josephine—†	111	housewife	30	"
L	D'Ambrosio Marie—†	111	"	71	"
M	Aylward Alice L—†	112	student	21	1117 Saratoga
N	Aylward Alice R—†	112	housewife	45	1117 "
O	Aylward Richard F	112	B F D	49	1117 "
P	Hanagan John P	112	"	52	1117 "
R	Abruzese Louis	113	manager	58	here
S	Abruzese Pasquale	113	U S A	24	"
T	Abruzese Suzan—†	113	houseworker	26	"
U	Greene Patrick J	114	buyer	30	"

14

Saint Andrew Road Continued

	v	Greene Rita A †	114	housewife	27	here
	w	Abruzese Assunta †	115	"	42	"
	x	Abruzese Carl	115	manager	51	"
	y	Abruzese Theresa †	115	housewife	46	"
	z	Carresi Gemma †	121	"	40	"

1922

	A	Carresi Leo	121	salesman	40	"
	B	Ciccarelli Michael	121	manager	50	"
	C	Ciccarelli Rachel †	121	housewife	40	"
	D	Blinn Ellen L †	123	nurse	26	"
	F	Blinn Frederick W	123	U S A	21	"
	E	Blinn Katherine L—†	123	housewife	51	"
	G	Blinn William C	123	machinist	56	"
	H	Overlan Francis P	123	fishcutter	43	"
	K	Overlan Leo H	123	bookbinder	45	"
	L	Cianciulli Charles	123	welder	46	31 Sea View av
	M	Cianciulli Mary—†	123	housewife	28	185 Marion
	N	DiChristoforo Carmelina †	125	"	36	here
	O	DiChristoforo Emilio	125	printer	41	"
	P	Irwin Cecelia—†	127	housewife	31	"
	R	Irwin Francis W	127	clerk	37	"
	S	Brennan Mary F—†	127	housewife	62	"
	T	Shanahan James A	127	clerk	56	"
	U	Shanahan James A, jr	127	U S A	26	"
	V	Shanahan Mae—†	127	housewife	48	"
	W	Donovan Daniel J	137	longshoreman	49	"
	X	Donovan John J	137	U S C G	26	"
	Y	Donovan Julia A †	137	housewife	49	"
	Z	Donovan William F	137	U S A	22	"

1923

	A	Ricciardelli John	140	pipefitter	32	68 Brooks
	B	Ricciardelli Rose †	140	housewife	31	68 "
	E	Kenefick Matthew J	140	clerk	55	here
	F	Kenefick Violet M—†	140	housewife	53	"
	C	McFarland Mildred M—†	140	"	30	"
	D	McFarland Vincent J	140	packer	30	"
	G	Bartlett Catherine M †	142	housewife	50	"
	H	Bartlett John	142	custodian	52	"
	K	Bartlett John T	142	U S A	26	"
	L	Bartlett Robert J	142	"	21	"
	M	Sacco Elizabeth †	142	housewife	45	"

15

Page.	Letter.	Full Name.	Residence, Jan. 1, 1943.	Occupation.	Supposed Age.	Reported Residence, Jan. 1, 1942. Street and Number.

Saint Andrew Road Continued

	N	Sacco Frank	142	policeman	47	here
	O	Harris Charles	144	clerk	26	"
	P	Harris James	144	millhand	52	"
	R	Harris Margaret †	144	housewife	52	"
	S	Blangio Albert J	144	U S N	32	"
	T	Blangio Albert R	144	manager	57	"
	U	Blangio Anna †	144	housewife	50	"
	V	Blangio Charles	144	U S A	29	"
	W	Blangio Dorothy †	144	clerk	22	"
	X	Blangio John	144	U S A	31	"
	Y	Blangio Lillian †	144	clerk	24	"
	Z	Blangio Michael J	144	"	30	"

1924

	A	Smith Alice M †	146	housewife	45	"
	B	Smith William A	146	manager	45	"
	C	DeStefano Eleanor †	146	housewife	42	"
	D	DeStefano George	146	machinist	43	"
	E	Bacciola Elisa †	147	buyer	49	"
	F	Bacciola Emma †	147	clerk	44	"
	G	Bacciola Giacomo	147	retired	79	"
	H	Bacciola Nella †	147	teacher	41	"
	K	Bacciola Theodore	147	engineer	35	"
	L	Litchman Joseph	148	proprietor	30	"
	M	Litchman Rose E †	148	housewife	30	"
	N	Rapa Anita †	148	"	38	"
	O	Rapa Fiore	148	manager	43	"
	P	Wynters Elmer F	150	U S A	34	"
	R	Wynters Henry A	150	chauffeur	35	"
	S	Wynters Sylvester J	150	"	63	"
	T	Cancian Emma †	150	housewife	44	"
	U	Cancian Ottario	150	contractor	44	"
	V	Dahlgren Eric	150	U S N	34	"
	W	Barnard Warren E	152	U S A	24	"
	X	Montgomery Cyril	152	policeman	46	"
	Y	Montgomery Florence †	152	housewife	32	"
	Z	Lombardozzi Angelina †	152	stitcher	32	230 Saratoga

1925

	A	Lombardozzi Mary †	152	candyworker	42	230 "
	B	Vestute Domenica †	152	housewife	45	here
	C	*Vestute Joseph	152	proprietor	50	"
	D	Kincaid Grace †	154	housewife	49	"

16

Saint Andrew Road Continued

E	Kincaid Paul	154	foreman	50	here	
F	D'Amico Arline †	154	manager	35	119 Cottage	
G	D'Amico Visconte	154	bricklayer	42	119 "	

Saint Edward Road

K	Cecero Mary—†	35	housewife	34	here	
L	Cecero Nicholas	35	draftsman	34	"	
M	Lagana Anthony	35	electrician	22	"	
N	Lagana Concetta †	35	housewife	50	"	
O	Lagana Placido	35	barber	55	"	
P	Battaglia Frederick	35	"	33	"	
R	Battaglia Lena †	35	housewife	31	"	
S	*Guarino Louise—†	35	"	63	"	
T	Guarino Raffaele	35	laborer	65	"	
U	DelBianco Florindo E	36	milkman	40	"	
V	DelBianco Margaret—†	36	housewife	37	"	
W	Albanno Fred	37	mechanic	32	84 Havre	
X	Albanno Mary—†	37	housewife	26	84 "	
Y	Minichiello Anthony	37	mechanic	25	here	
Z	Minichiello Antonio	37	U S A	29	"	

1926

A	Minichiello Felice	37	retired	73	"	
B	Minichiello Philomena—†	37	clerk	27	"	
C	Albanno Antonette—†	37	at home	60	"	
D	Albanno Felix	37	engineer	35	"	
E	Albanno Mary E—†	37	housewife	29	"	
F	Mauceri Achille	39	retired	70	"	
G	Mauceri Constance—†	39	clerk	28	"	
H	Mauceri Corradina †	39	housewife	69	"	
K	DiLorenzo Anna—†	39	"	26	"	
L	DiLorenzo Carmen	39	shipfitter	28	"	
M	DiLorenzo Rose †	39	clerk	23	"	
N	DiLorenzo Stella †	39	stitcher	29	"	
O	DiLorenzo Theresa—†	39	housewife	52	"	
P	Bongiovanni Amelia—†	39	"	45	"	
R	Bongiovanni Anthony	39	shoemaker	50	"	
S	Bongiovanni Domenic D	39	mechanic	26	"	
T	Bongiovanni Katherine	†39	dressmaker	23	"	
U	Anderson Elin M—†	41	clerk	38	"	
V	Anderson Sarah L †	41	housewife	59	"	

Saint Edward Road—Continued

	X	Sullivan Benjamin	41	shipfitter	38	here
	W	Sullivan Theresa—†	41	housewife	29	"
	Y	Allavesen George A	41	laborer	48	"
	Z	Allavesen George D	41	"	23	"
1927						
	A	Allavesen Louise—†	41	housewife	46	"
	B	Joyce William A	41	painter	52	"
	C	Mitchell Louis J	41	foreman	46	"
	D	Thompson Helen M—†	41	operator	29	"
	E	Sacco Albert	43	B F D	34	"
	F	Sacco Helen—†	43	housewife	27	"
	G	Babine Benjamin J	43	cook	50	"
	H	Babine Ella—†	43	housewife	43	"
	K	Savio Amelia—†	43	stenographer	21	"
	L	Savio Claire—†	43	bookkeeper	28	"
	M	Savio Domenica—†	43	housewife	52	"
	N	Savio Domenica—†	43	bookkeeper	26	"
	O	Savio George A	43	U S A	20	"
	P	Savio Joseph	43	waiter	58	"
	R	Bombaci Carmella—†	45	stenographer	26	"
	S	Bombaci Elvira—†	45	housewife	46	"
	T	Bombaci Leo	45	carpenter	53	"
	U	Bombaci Peter	45	"	22	"
	V	Lagana John L	45	U S N	27	87 Gordon
	W	Lagana Stella—†	45	housewife	27	87 "
	X	Boyce Charles H	45	installer	25	here
	Y	Boyce Nora—†	45	tel operator	29	"
	Z	Mortimer Margaret I—†	45	"	21	Somerville

1928   Saratoga Street

	A	Boudreau Catherine G—†	1093	at home	75	here
	B	Boudreau Elizabeth B—†	1093	librarian	39	"
	C	Boudreau Mary F—†	1093	musician	52	"
	D	McDonald Edward A	1093	U S M C	23	"
	E	McDonald Mary—†	1093	housewife	53	"
	F	McDonald Thomas E	1093	U S A	22	"
	G	McDonald Thomas F	1093	foreman	53	"
	H	McDonald Walter F	1093	U S A	30	"
	K	Peers Arthur	1093	chauffeur	54	"
	M	Seix Marion F—†	1095	bookkeeper	53	"
	N	McHugh Edward J	1095	contractor	48	"

18

Saratoga Street Continued

		FULL NAME				
o	McHugh Marguerite	†	1095	housewife	46	here
p	Powell William L		1095	cook	55	New York
r	Blais George A		1096	storekeeper	38	here
s	Legare Rose	†	1096	housekeeper	35	Groton
t	Adams Edward W		1096	U S A	38	here
u	Bradley Edna G	†	1096	housewife	39	"
v	Walker Dorothy	†	1097	tel operator	28	"
w	Walker Lillian	†	1097	clerk	26	"
x	Walker Michael		1097	"	24	"
y	Geggis Catherine	†	1097	housewife	39	"
z	Geggis Ellen	†	1097	at home	83	"

1929

		FULL NAME				
a	Geggis James		1097	salesman	46	"
b	Geggis John		1097	sorter	58	"
c	Rego Charles		1098	clerk	50	"
d	Rego Frances	†	1098	housewife	50	"
e	Rego Mary	†	1098	stenographer	26	"
f	Karasik Betty S	†	1098	attorney	35	"
g	Karasik Nathan M		1098	retired	65	"
h	Baldassaro Elizabeth	†	1101	housewife	33	"
k	Baldassaro Louis		1101	plumber	36	"
l	Latorre Frank		1101	realtor	48	"
m	Latorre Maria	†	1101	housewife	42	"
n*	Latorre Philippa	†	1101	at home	76	87 Falcon
o	Doyle Mary	†	1102	housekeeper	75	here
p	Gomes Arthur		1102	pressman	49	"
r	Gomes Arthur E		1102	U S A	22	"
s	Gomes Madeline	†	1102	housewife	43	"
t	Busalacchi Andrew		1105	U S A	22	"
u	Busalacchi Antonio		1105	merchant	59	"
v	Busalacchi Guilia	†	1105	stenographer	25	"
w	Busalacchi Helen	†	1105	dressmaker	27	"
x	Busalacchi Josephine	†	1105	housewife	64	"
y*	Huey Annie E	†	1105	at home	27	44 W Eagle
z	Huey Forrest W		1105	seaman	64	44 "

1930

		FULL NAME				
a	Cappuccio Antonio		1106	cementworker	66	here
b	Cappuccio Louis		1106	U S A	29	"
c*	Cappuccio Lucy	†	1106	housewife	66	"
d	Morelli Allessandro		1106	student	22	"
e	Morelli Angelina	†	1106	housewife	40	"
f	Morelli John		1106	bartender	46	"

19

Saratoga Street—Continued

	G	Ross Leo F	1109	retired	57	here
	H	Ross Mary E—†	1109	housewife	59	"
	K	Ross Mary M—†	1109	teacher	33	"
	L	Baldassaro Enrico	1109	U S N	20	"
	M	Baldassaro Frank	1109	U S A	26	"
	N	*Baldassaro Maria—†	1109	housewife	64	"
	O	Baldassaro Pasquale	1109	realtor	65	"
	P	Fernald Agnes M—†	1110	housewife	59	"
	R	Fernald Robert A	1110	dispatcher	59	"
	S	Gibbons Daniel J	1110	custodian	50	"
	T	Gibbons Elizabeth F—†	1110	housewife	48	"
	U	Zimmerman Margaret H—†	1110	clerk	21	"
	V	Musto Armand	1111	machinist	29	"
	W	Musto Linda—†	1111	housewife	28	"
	X	Billings Anna M—†	1111	"	44	"
	Y	Billings Kenneth U	1111	chauffeur	45	"
	Z	Leahy Catherine—†	1111	tel operator	42	"
1931						
	A	Leahy Hugh F	1111	tollman	50	"
	B	Leahy Mary E—†	1111	tel operator	38	"
	C	Leahy Sarah—†	1111	housewife	45	"
	E	Hazelton James E	1114	engineer	52	"
	F	Hazelton James E, jr	1114	machinist	21	"
	D	Hazelton Mary M—†	1114	housewife	49	"
	G	Monahan Dennis G	1114	retired	70	"
	H	Monahan Francis L	1114	shipfitter	28	"
	K	Monahan Helen—†	1114	tel operator	23	"
	L	Monahan Nellie F—†	1114	housewife	66	"
	M	Cairns James C	1115	printer	53	"
	N	Cairns Louise M—†	1115	at home	23	"
	O	Cairns Theresa L—†	1115	housewife	55	"
	P	Nelson Gardner N	1115	storekeeper	54	"
	R	Nelson Howard G	1115	machinist	20	"
	S	Nelson Norma A—†	1115	housewife	49	"
	T	Leary Arthur D	1116	clerk	24	"
	U	Leary Sarah A—†	1116	housewife	62	"
	V	Lynch Edward M	1116	B F D	45	14 Lillian
	W	Arthur Joseph L	1116	merchant	47	here
	X	Arthur Lawrence	1116	clerk	42	"
	Y	Arthur Thomas	1116	U S A	45	"
	Z	Arthur Veronica—†	1116	housewife	47	"

1932
Saratoga Street Continued

A	McGinn Charles E	1116	salesman	26	here	
B	McGinn Josephine M—†	1116	housewife	26	"	
C	Flynn Anna M—†	1117	clerk	33	"	
D	Flynn Annie B—†	1117	housewife	63	"	
E	Flynn Edna M—†	1117	at home	32	"	
F	Flynn Robert J	1117	U S A	26	"	
G	Flynn Thomas J	1117	B F D	31	"	
H	Flynn Walter F	1117	laborer	29		
K	Russo Angelo M	1117	packer	38	290 E Ninth	
L	Russo Nancy E—†	1117	housewife	32	290 "	
M	Silipigni Grace—†	1117	"	63	1136 Saratoga	
N	Silipigni Lawrence	1117	barber	65	1136 "	
O	Silipigni Mary—†	1117	operator	34	1136 "	
P	Cleary Edward	1118	fisherman	46	Canada	
R*	Cleary Margaret—†	1118	housewife	44	"	
S	Kelleher Jeremiah	1118	driller	60	77 St Andrew rd	
T	Kelleher John V	1118	laborer	62	77 "	
U	Kelleher Mary M—†	1118	housewife	50	77 "	
V	Kelleher William P	1118	drawtender	56	77 "	
W	Callanan Edward V	1119	U S A	22	here	
X	Callanan James J	1119	retired	72	"	
Y	Callanan Mary A—†	1119	housewife	65	"	
Z	Sampson Margaret—†	1119	"	45	"	

1933

A	Sampson Nicholas	1119	fisherman	46	"	
B	Jackson Edward	1120	U S A	32	"	
C	Jackson Mary—†	1120	housewife	30	"	
D	Bartlett Francis	1120	blacksmith	66	"	
E	Bartlett Mary K—†	1120	housewife	60	"	
F	Walsh John P	1121	retired	73	"	
G	Walsh John P, jr	1121	"	33	"	
H	McCauley Frank T	1121	maint'n'ceman	48	"	
K	McCauley Gerald	1121	U S A	42	"	
L	McCauley Mary B—†	1121	nurse	56	"	
M	McCauley Ruth—†	1121	at home	53	"	
N	Sherry Frank	1122	drawtender	50	"	
O	Corbett Mary D—†	1122	bookkeeper	23	"	
P	Donohue Daniel J	1122	motorman	55	"	
R	Donohue Mary A—†	1122	housewife	55	"	
S	DeMartino Frances—†	1123	saleswoman	31	148 Bayswater	

Saratoga Street—Continued

	T	DeMartino Guisto	1123	U S N	30	148 Bayswater
	U	DeMartino Rose—†	1123	housewife	56	148 "
	V	Susi Anna—†	1123	packer	22	here
	W	Susi Frances—†	1123	housewife	45	"
	X	Susi Frank	1123	candymaker	49	"
	Y	Susi Rose—†	1123	secretary	24	"
	Z	Barresi Joseph	1124	shoemaker	46	28 Chelsea
1934						
	A	*Barresi Nicholas	1124	U S A	21	here
	B	*Barresi Sarah—†	1124	housewife	45	28 Chelsea
	C	Drohan Genevieve A—†	1124	"	40	56 Byron
	D	Drohan John F	1124	agent	41	56 "
	E	Cashman Richard J	1125	foreman	67	here
	F	Cashman Susan A—†	1125	housewife	54	"
	G	McCarthy Edward L	1125	drawtender	61	"
	H	McCarthy Gerald D	1125	calker	23	"
	K	McCarthy John F	1125	U S N	30	"
	L	McCarthy Josephine B—†	1125	housewife	57	"
	M	Lenzi Lillian—†	1126	"	40	"
	N	Lenzi Thomas V	1126	assembler	39	"
	O	DeVita Mary—†	1126	housewife	45	"
	P	DeVita Michael	1126	printer	47	"
	R	Donatelli Alfred	1127	shoeworker	42	"
	S	Donatelli Immacolata—†	1127	housewife	33	"
	T	Greco Anthony F	1127	sorter	41	"
	U	Greco Lucy—†	1127	housewife	37	"
	V	Canney Evelyn—†	1127	bookkeeper	34	"
	W	Canney John	1127	accountant	38	"
	X	Giuffre Carmello	1128	operator	41	"
	Y	Giuffre Josephine—†	1128	housewife	39	"
	Z	Barry Annie J—†	1128	"	55	"
1935						
	A	Barry Joseph H	1128	B F D	64	"
	B	Vesce Francis	1129	salesman	27	"
	C	Vesce Josephine—†	1129	housewife	26	"
	D	McDonald Beatrice—†	1129	clerk	44	"
	E	Vesce Joseph	1129	liquors	53	"
	F	Vesce Norma—†	1129	operator	24	"
	G	DeSimone Americo	1130	realtor	40	31 Faywood av
	H	DeSimone Edith—†	1130	fitter	39	31 "
	K	Cogliani Nicholas	1130	laborer	59	here

Saratoga Street Continued

Letter	FULL NAME.	Residence	Occupation	Age	Reported Residence
L	Cogliani Vincenza †	1130	housewife	56	here
M	Kaddaras George	1130	U S A	30	Lynn
N	Kaddaras Mary †	1130	housewife	32	here
O	Hazelton Anna †	1132	"	32	"
P	Hazelton Charles R	1132	stevedore	31	"
R	Cogliano Antonetta †	1132	housewife	43	"
S	Cogliano Joseph	1132	chauffeur	45	"
U	O'Brien Edmund	1141	attorney	27	Winthrop
V	O'Brien Margaret †	1141	housewife	24	"
W	Smiddy Margaret †	1141	"	44	here
X	Smiddy Mary R †	1141	saleswoman	21	"
Y	Smiddy William P	1141	stevedore	49	"

1936

Letter	FULL NAME.	Residence	Occupation	Age	Reported Residence
A	Fenlon Ruth C †	1143	housewife	40	"
B	Fenlon William	1143	electrician	45	"
C	Fenlon William F	1143	salesman	23	"
D	Sullivan Stephen C	1143	clerk	50	"
E	Rosetti Dorothy †	1145	saleswoman	21	"
F	Rosetti Frank	1145	pressman	43	"
G	Rosetti Joseph E	1145	U S M C	21	"
H	Giannotti Alica †	1147	housewife	35	"
K	*Giannotti Antonia †	1147	"	61	"
L	*Giannotti Egidio	1147	cook	67	"
M	Giannotti Egidio A	1147	policeman	34	"
N	Crane Joseph A	1149	supervisor	45	101 St Andrew rd
O	Crane Mary E †	1149	housewife	42	109 "
P	Casassa Emma †	1151	"	50	here
R	Casassa Stephen D	1151	dealer	63	"
S	DeBeneditto Evelyn †	1151	housewife	25	"
T	DeBeneditto John	1151	chauffeur	38	1187 Saratoga
U	*DeBeneditto Pasquale	1151	retired	72	1187 "
V	*Spruegel Edith †	1179	housewife	34	Winthrop
W	Spruegel Walter S	1179	attorney	37	"
X	Meaney Catherine †	1179	housewife	36	here
Y	Meaney Joseph	1179	mechanic	37	"
Z	Hutchinson Stacia †	1181	housewife	38	1124 Saratoga

1937

Letter	FULL NAME.	Residence	Occupation	Age	Reported Residence
A	Hutchinson William C	1181	shipper	39	1124 "
B	Famolare Anthony	1181	hairdresser	37	here
C	Famolare Mary †	1181	shoeworker	34	"
D	Jones Louis	1181	U S N	62	"

23

Page.	Letter.	FULL NAME.	Residence, Jan. 1, 1943.	Occupation.	Supposed Age.	Reported Residence, Jan. 1, 1942. Street and Number.

Saratoga Street—Continued

	E	Gallagher Nora—†	1187	housekeeper	65	66 Barnes av
	F	Green Charles	1187	clerk	29	66 "
	G	Hill Charles	1187	optical worker	30	66 "
	H	Hill Mary—†	1187	stenographer	30	66 "
	K	Pasillo Anna—†	1187	housewife	46	here
	L	Pasillo John R	1187	U S A	22	"
	M	Pasillo Joseph M	1187	waiter	60	"
	N	*Ciamma Ida—†	1189	housewife	50	"
	O	Ciamma Renato	1189	shipfitter	21	"
	P	Ciamma Thomas	1189	U S A	24	"
	R	Pagliarulo Caroline—†	1191	housewife	38	"
	S	Pagliarulo Emil	1191	student	20	"
	T	Pagliarulo Joseph	1191	salesman	41	"
	U	DeMild Leonard	1193	machinist	40	"
	V	DeMild Thelma—†	1193	housewife	37	"
	W	Meoli Antionette—†	1195	"	37	"
	X	Meoli Gaetano	1195	laundryworker	47	"
	Y	Repucci Anna—†	1197	housewife	37	Winthrop
	Z	Repucci Anthony	1197	builder	39	"
1938						
	A	Caggiano Jean C—†	1199	housewife	41	here
	B	Caggiano Michael	1199	mortician	42	"
	C	Sacco Edward M	1201	mechanic	26	"
	D	Sacco Frank J	1201	bartender	28	"
	E	Sacco Joseph	1201	shipper	52	"
	F	Sacco Mary A—†	1201	housewife	47	"

Shawsheen Road

	H	Driscoll Florence J	30	B F D	59	here
	K	Shaw Christine W—†	30	housewife	46	"
	L	Shaw Frank P	30	merchant	46	"

Teragram Street

	M	Kirby John F	25	compositor	33	here
	N	Kirby Louise—†	25	housewife	33	"
	O	Beringer Catherine B—†	25	"	54	"
	P	Beringer Catherine E—†	25	operator	22	"
	R	Beringer Jacob	25	B F D	56	"
	S	Beringer Mary—†	25	operator	26	"

24

Teragram Street Continued

T	Tiano Domenic	26	architect	40	here
U	Tiano Helen †	26	housewife	30	"
V	Arone Joseph	26	machinist	27	"
W	Arone Victoria †	26	housewife	25	"
X	Centracchio Anthony	30	attorney	36	"
Y	Centracchio Lillian †	30	housewife	30	"
Z	Cicco Mary—†	30	"	39	"

1939

A	Cicco Michael	30	plumber	44	"

Ward 1–Precinct 20

CITY OF BOSTON

LIST OF RESIDENTS
20 YEARS OF AGE AND OVER

(NON-CITIZENS INDICATED BY ASTERISK)
(FEMALES INDICATED BY DAGGER)

AS OF

JANUARY 1, 1943

JOSEPH F. TIMILTY, *Chairman*
FREDERIC E. DOWLING, *Secretary*
WILLIAM A. MOTLEY, JR.
FRANCIS B. McKINNEY
EVERETT R. PROUT

Listing Board.

CITY OF BOSTON PRINTING DEPARTMENT

Page.	Letter	FULL NAME.	Residence, Jan. 1, 1943	Occupation.	Supposed Age	Reported Residence, Jan. 1, 1942. Street and Number.

2000

Castle Court

	B	Pepe Giuseppe	3	blacksmith	45	here
	C	*Pepe Lena—†	3	housewife	38	"
	D	*Pepe Patricia—†	3	at home	69	"
	E	Hrono James	3	rigger	45	"
	F	Hrono Mary—†	3	housewife	30	"
	G	Severo Flora †	5	clerk	28	400 Walk Hill
	H	Severo Jerry	5	U S C G	20	here
	K	*Severo Rose—†	5	housewife	58	"
	L	Severo Samuel	5	retired	64	"
	M	Severo Samuel	5	clerk	23	"

Cottage Street

	O	*Lambiase Nancy—†	115	housewife	40	here
	P	Lambiase Salvatore	115	baker	45	"
	R	Freda Elizabeth—†	115	sausagemaker	23	"
	S	Freda Rocco	115	"	49	"
	T	Freda Susie—†	115	housewife	43	"
	U	DiDonato Mary—†	117		30	"
	V	DiDonato Rocco	117	laborer	31	"
	W	Grasso Lucy—†	117	shoeworker	21	"
	X	Grasso Margaret—†	117	housewife	44	"
	Y	Grasso Michael	117	shoeworker	47	"

2001

	A	*DiDonato John	117	retired	75	"
	B	Bernabei Anna †	117	housewife	35	"
	C	Bernabei Antonio	117	operator	35	"
	F	Pascone Ferrara	119	chauffeur	32	"
	G	Pascone Rose †	119	housewife	30	"
	H	Siccone Carmella †	119	"	45	"
	K	Siccone Nicola †	119	laborer	51	"
	L	*Mazzetti Benedice †	119	housewife	46	5 North sq
	M	*Mazzetti Carmello	119	laborer	51	5 "
	N	*Zampanti Madalena †	119	housekeeper	58	here
	O	Santoro Angelina †	119	housewife	22	68 Lubec
	P	Santoro Benedino	119	laborer	27	68 "
	R	Troiani Albert	119	U S A	23	here
	S	*Troiani Mary †	119	housewife	48	"
	T	Troiani Pasquale	119	laborer	53	"
	U	*Paolini Mary †	121	at home	68	"

Cottage Street Continued

v	DePaolo Antonetta †	121	housewife	27	here
w	DePaolo Pasquale	121	bartender	31	"
x	Barry Dorothy †	121	clerk	20	"
y	Prisco Mary †	121	at home	75	"
z	*Valerio Mary †	121	housewife	36	"

2002

A	Valerio Peter	121	laborer	40	"
B	*Pellegritti Angelo	121	retired	71	"
c	Pellegritti Angelo	121	laborer	22	"
D	*Pellegritti Josephine †	121	housewife	65	"
E	*Grasso Lorenzo	121	laborer	61	"
F	*Grasso Victoria †	121	housewife	58	"
G	Marotta Carnelia †	123	"	39	"
H	Marotta John	123	shoeworker	41	"
K	Boschetti Anthony	123	cabinetmaker	40	"
L	*Boschetti Emilia †	123	housewife	41	"
M	Liberatore Olive †	123	"	28	"
N	Liberatore Pompeo	123	molder	32	"
O	Giangregorio Antonio	123	laborer	48	"
P	Giangregorio Jennie †	123	housewife	38	"
R	Palumbo Emily †	125	operator	22	"
s	*Palumbo John	125	laborer	60	"
T	Palumbo Leonard	125	student	25	"
U	*Palumbo Rose †	125	housewife	57	"
v	Martino Domenic	125	laborer	65	"
w	Martino Mario	125	tailor	23	"
x	Martino Rafaela †	125	housewife	60	"
y	LoConte Angelina †	125	candymaker	23	"
z	*LoConte Carmella †	125	housewife	46	"

2003

A	LoConte Carmine	125	shoeworker	58	"
B	LoConte Maria †	125	"	20	"
c	Pellegritti Maria †	125	housewife	40	"
D	Pellegritti Peter	125	shoeworker	41	"
E	Giglio Benjamin	125	laborer	30	"
F	Giglio Helen †	125	housewife	26	"
H	Nazzaro Angelina †	127	rubberworker	20	"
K	Nazzaro Catherine †	127	candyworker	21	"
L	Nazzaro Jennie †	127	"	26	"
M	Nazzaro Mary †	127	housewife	56	"
N	Nazzaro Phyllis †	127	rubberworker	30	"

3

Cottage Street—Continued

O	Nazzaro Vincent	127	U S A	23	here	
P	Nazzaro Assunta—†	127	housewife	50	"	
R	Nazzaro Frank	127	brakeman	22	"	
S	Nazzaro Gilda—†	127	at home	20	"	
T	Valletta Rose—†	129	housekeeper	42	"	
U	Salamoni Frank	129	laborer	23	"	
V	Salamoni Vincenza—†	129	housewife	21	"	
W	Saporito Joseph	129	laborer	22	"	
X	Saporito Josephine—†	129	housewife	21	"	
Y	Tremontozzi Assunta—†	129	"	22	"	
Z	Tremontozzi Daniel	129	laborer	25	"	

2004

A	Lessa Antonetta—†	129	housewife	50	"	
B	Lessa Domenic	129	laborer	21	"	
C	Lessa Helen—†	129	clerk	22	"	
D	Lessa Olga—†	129	"	24	"	
E	Checo Fredrick	131	laborer	49	"	
F	Checo Mary—†	131	housewife	42	"	
G	Scopa Frank	131	laborer	45	"	
H	Pisano Jennie—†	131	housewife	23	"	
K	Pisano Louis	131	shipfitter	24	"	
L	Beatrice Assunta—†	131	housewife	24	141 Cottage	
M	Beatrice Pasquale	131	bartender	28	141 "	
N	Scopa Elizabeth C—†	131	housewife	64	here	
O	Scopa Ralph	131	chauffeur	50	"	
P	Stagliola Antonette—†	131	housewife	31	"	
R	Stagliola Domenic	131	pressman	34	"	
S	Inglese Grace—†	133	housewife	43	"	
T	Inglese Joseph	133	chauffeur	49	"	
U	Inglese Luciano	133	U S A	21	"	
V	*Inglese Mary G—†	133	housekeeper	87	"	
W	Cantofanti Samuel	133	contractor	55	"	
X	Giardina Joseph	133	machinist	33	"	
Y	Giardina Raffaela—†	133	housewife	31	"	
Z	Sacco Evelyn—†	133	candyworker	21	"	

2005

A	*Sacco Jennie—†	133	housewife	59	"	
B	Sacco Pasquale	133	laborer	37	"	
C	Sasso Joseph	135	shoeworker	43	"	
D	*Sasso Mary G—†	135	housekeeper	67	"	
E	Sasso Theresa—†	135	housewife	41	"	

Cottage Street Continued

F	Beatrice Filomena †	135	housewife	50	here
G	Beatrice Helen—†	135	rubberworker	21	"
H	Beatrice Marcellio	135	laborer	57	"
K	Derocco Louise—†	135	packer	39	"
L	Costanza Mary—†	135	housekeeper	40	"
M	Magnanti Malcolm	135	musician	29	"
N	Magnanti Vincent	135	retired	68	"
O*	DiPietro Maria—†	137	housekeeper	76	"
P	Giangregorio Josephine—†	137	housewife	60	"
R	Giangregorio Louis	137	laborer	65	"
S	Mazzone Assunta—†	137	housekeeper	44	"
T	Mucci Antonetta—†	137	clerk	26	"
U*	Mucci Lucy—†	137	housekeeper	55	"
V	Ferrullo John J	137	shipfitter	36	"
W	Ferrullo Mildred G—†	137	housewife	33	"
X	Giangregorio Attilio	137	laborer	25	"
Y	Giangregorio Mary—†	137	housewife	23	"
Z	Cirame Joseph	139	machinist	44	"
2006					
A	Cirame Mary—†	139	housewife	39	"
B	Fiandaco Domenic	139	laborer	55	"
C*	Fiandaco Pasqualina—†	139	housewife	55	"
D*	Cirame Carmella †	139	housekeeper	68	"
E	Rubino Josephine—†	139	housewife	40	"
F	Rubino Louis	139	machinist	50	"
G	Luiso Carmella—†	139	housewife	24	"
H	Luiso Ralph	139	laborer	28	"
K	Giodarni Anthony	139	boxmaker	24	188 Paris
L	Giodarni Antonette—†	139	housewife	20	188 "
M	Gricci Angelo	141	shipfitter	37	here
N	Gricci Mary—†	141	housewife	34	"
O	Spataro Joseph	141	laborer	64	58 Cottage
P	Spataro Stella—†	141	housewife	62	58 "
R	Perdichizzi Frank	141	laborer	33	here
S	Perdichizzi Josephine—†	141	housewife	28	"
T	Trunfio Edith—†	141	"	25	"
U	Trunfio Ralph	141	electrician	26	"
V	Lanavaro Joseph	141	chipper	25	"
W	Lanavaro Rita—†	141	housewife	24	"
X*	Giangregorio Carmella †	143	"	48	"
Y*	Giangregorio Lorenzo	143	laborer	64	"

5

Page	Letter	Full Name.	Residence, Jan. 1, 1943	Occupation.	Supposed Age.	Reported Residence, Jan. 1, 1942, Street and Number.

Cottage Street—Continued

	Letter	Full Name.	Res.	Occupation.	Age	Reported Residence
	z	Giangregorio Sabina —†	143	stitcher	22	here
2007						
	A*	Santella Mary—†	143	housekeeper	62	"
	B	DeLucca Anthony	143	pipefitter	32	"
	c	DeLucca Grace—†	143	housewife	30	"
	D	Sacco Anthony	143	U S A	27	60 Frankfort
	E	Sacco Olga—†	143	housewife	20	60 "
	F	Coviello Bernardino	143	painter	46	here
	G	Coviello Matilda—†	143	housewife	45	"
	H	Colarusso Anthony	145	laborer	63	"
	K	Colarusso Elizabeth—†	145	housewife	56	"
	L	Colarusso Angelina—†	145	"	56	"
	M	Colarusso Domenic	145	laborer	28	"
	N	Colarusso Felix	145	"	58	"
	O	Colarusso Theresa—†	145	at home	21	"
	P	Molinaro Anna—†	145	candyworker	30	"
	R	Molinaro Blanche—†	145	"	24	"
	s	Molinaro Pasqualina—†	145	housewife	59	"
	T	Molinaro Raffaela—†	145	candyworker	21	"
	U	Molinaro Tomaso	145	laborer	63	"
	V	Molinaro Yolanda—†	145	at home	28	"
	W	Polsonetti Emilio	147	U S A	20	"
	X*	Polsonetti Joseph	147	laborer	56	"
	Y*	Polsonetti Michelena—†	147	housewife	40	"
	z	Palumbo Angelo	147	laborer	29	Woburn
2008						
	A	Palumbo Mary—†	147	housewife	28	"
	B	Mollinaro Edith †	147	"	37	here
	c	Mollinaro Peter	147	blacksmith	39	"
	D	Grasso Antonetta †	147	housewife	25	"
	E	Grasso Michael	147	laborer	25	"
	F	Bavaro Domenic	147	"	31	"
	G	Bavaro Virginia †	147	housewife	30	"
	H	Coviello Antonio	149	welder	38	"
	K	Coviello Ida—†	149	housewife	32	"
	L	Guarino Christina †	149	"	26	"
	M	Guarino Fred	149	laborer	27	"
	N	DiGenova Phyllis—†	149	housekeeper	40	"
	O	Coviello Alexander	149	machinist	26	"
	P	Coviello Lillian †	149	housewife	24	"
	R*	Coviello Rosa —†	149	"	70	"

6

Cottage Street Continued

s	*Coviello Sabatino	149	retired	70	here
u	Sciarrillo Antonio	151	storekeeper	42	"
v	Sciarrillo Gabriele—†	151	housewife	46	"
w	Sciarrillo Josephine—†	151	"	26	"
x	Sciarrillo Philip	151	clerk	22	"
y	Sciarrillo Theresa—†	151	hairdresser	22	"
z	Evangelista Margaret—†	151	housewife	28	"

2009

A	Evangelista Nicholas	151	laborer	35	"
B	Soldano Anna—†	151	housewife	37	217 Webster
C	Soldano Francesco	151	laborer	38	217 "
D	Marciello Giovina—†	151	housewife	52	here
E	Marciello Joseph	151	laborer	49	"
F	Cammarata John	151	"	26	"
G	Cammarata Mary—†	151	housewife	26	"
H	Catanzariti Clara—†	152	"	30	"
K	Catanzariti Onofrio	152	laborer	35	"
L	*Luongo Assunta—†	152	housewife	60	164 Cottage
M	Luongo Jiacomo	152	laborer	65	164 "
N	Uva Antoinette—†	152	clerk	20	here
O	*Uva Nancy—†	152	housewife	46	"
P	Uva Rocco	152	storekeeper	52	"
R	Uva Stanley	152	shipper	25	"
s	*Benedetto Eleanor—†	152	housewife	42	"
T	Benedetto Thomas	152	tailor	52	"
U	Iannaccone Eugenio	152	laborer	51	"
v	*Iannaccone Josephina—†	152	housewife	50	"
w	*Salerno Vincenza—†	153	housekeeper	89	"
x	*Umana Antonetta—†	153	"	53	"
z	Schettino Frank	154	laborer	45	"

2010

A	Schettino Susie—†	154	housewife	39	"
B	Tramonte Lena—†	154	"	28	"
C	Tramonte Oreste	154	cutter	45	"
D	*Mercurio Angelina—†	154	housewife	43	"
E	Mercurio Domenic	154	guard	43	"
F	Fusco Joseph	154	grinder	20	"
G	Fusco Martha—†	154	at home	54	"
H	*D'Alto Louise—†	154	housewife	59	"
K	D'Alto Pasquale	154	retired	63	"
L	Vernarelli Alfred	154	chauffeur	30	"

7

Cottage Street — Continued

	M	*Vernarelli Grace —†	154	housewife	28	here
	N	Ruggiero Anthony	154	shoeworker	40	"
	O	Ruggiero Eva—†	154	housewife	38	"
	P	DeMarco Antonette —†	155	"	26	"
	R	DeMarco Vincent	155	shipper	29	"
	S	Peppino Frances—†	155	shoeworker	34	"
	T	*Peppino Mary— †	155	housekeeper	59	"
	U	Peppino Sadie—†	155	shoeworker	36	"
	V	Guzzardi Daniel	155	shoemaker	49	"
	W	Guzzardi Gina— †	155	housewife	40	"
	X	Guzzardi Joseph	155	U S M C	21	"
	Y	*Vinciguerra Odella—†	155	housewife	55	"
	Z	*Vinciguerra Ralph	155	shoemaker	56	"

2011

	A	Vinciguerra Ralph, jr	155	laborer	22	"
	B	Vinciguerra Theresa—†	155	shoeworker	21	"
	C	Caporale Carmella—†	155	housewife	38	"
	D	Caporale Peter	155	shoeworker	39	"
	E	DeFuria Grace —†	155	housewife	38	"
	F	DeFuria Nicola	155	laborer	48	"
	G	*DeMaio Leonarda— †	156	at home	67	"
	H	LaCorte John	156	U S A	22	"
	K	*LaCorte Lucy—†	156	housewife	45	"
	L	LaCorte Michael	156	presser	55	"
	M	LaCorte Michelina †	156	stitcher	21	"
	N	Memmolo John	156	electrician	28	"
	O	Memmolo Raffaela †	156	housewife	22	"
	P	Albaro Josephine —†	156	"	32	"
	R	Tramonte Ernest	156	laborer	52	"
	S	Tramonte Rose †	156	housewife	42	"
	T	Gatto Anthony	156	inspector	64	"
	U	Gatto James	156	retired	67	"
	V	Gatto Natale	156	U S A	31	"
	W	Gatto Natalie — †	156	housekeeper	32	"
	X	Gatto Rose —†	156	shoeworker	35	"
	Y	Gatto Carmen	156	machinist	29	"
	Z	Gatto Mildred—†	156	housewife	28	"

2012

	A	Cioto Anthony	157	U S N	22	"
	B	*Cioto Frank	157	laborer	61	"
	C	Cioto Gilda †	157	clerk	29	"

Cottage Street Continued

D	Cioto Lucy †	157	shoeworker	21	here
E	*Cioto Marion †	157	housewife	55	"
F	Annese Catello	157	oiler	64	"
G	Annese Rose †	157	housewife	64	"
H	Cioto Lucy †	157	"	24	"
K	Cioto Mario	157	chauffeur	25	"
L	Spazziani Sista †	157	housewife	65	"
M	Silva Domenic	157	laborer	46	"
N	Silva Rose †	157	housewife	43	"
O	*Capuana Ida †	158	"	52	"
P	*Capuana Joseph	158	storekeeper	56	"
R	Capuana Josephine †	158	dressmaker	28	"
T	Leone Carmine	158	tailor	53	38 Chandler
U	Leone Julio	158	"	20	38 "
V	Leone Maria †	158	housewife	53	38 "
W	Frederico Herman	158	laborer	26	273 Maverick
X	Frederico Pearl †	158	housewife	21	273 "
Y	Beatrice Alexander	158	laborer	26	here
Z	Beatrice Maria †	158	housewife	27	"

2013

A	Castagnozzi John	158	mechanic	20	here
B	*Castagnozzi Maria †	158	housewife	49	"
C	Castagnozzi Sebastino	158	laborer	54	"
D	Ferrantino Benjamin	158	chauffeur	34	"
E	Ferrantino Frances †	158	housewife	28	"
F	Piscioneri Dominic	158	storekeeper	39	"
G	*Piscioneri Jennie †	158	housewife	32	"
H	DelGreco Giovanne	159	foreman	37	"
K	DelGreco Mary †	159	housewife	32	"
L	*DelGreco Nicholas	159	laborer	63	"
M	Costantino Antonio	159	freighthandler	48	"
N	*Cocca Mary †	159	housewife	37	"
O	Mucci Alfred	159	bricklayer	39	"
P	*Mucci Gemma †	159	housewife	32	"
R	Girolamo Frank	159	laborer	46	"
S	*Girolamo Phyllis †	159	housewife	36	"
T	Ciullo James	159	laborer	47	"
U	Ciullo Philomena †	159	housewife	40	"
V	Fitzgerald Antoinette †	159	"	34	"
W	Fitzgerald Lawrence R	159	machinist	33	"
X	*Recchia Alfonse	159	laborer	54	"

9

Page	Letter	Full Name.	Residence, Jan. 1, 1943.	Occupation.	Supposed Age.	Reported Residence, Jan. 1, 1942. Street and Number.

Cottage Street—Continued

	Y	Recchia Antonetta—†	159	housewife	46	here
	Z	Villano Alfred	160	U S A	24	"
2014						
	A*	Villano Antonetta—†	160	housewife	50	"
	B*	Villano Joseph	160	laborer	50	"
	C	Villano Rose—†	160	at home	21	"
	D	Villano Sophie—†	160	dressmaker	22	"
	E	Genualdo Ciro	160	presser	28	188 Benningt'n
	F	Genualdo Gaetana—†	160	housewife	28	188 "
	G	Aiello Alveria—†	160	"	49	here
	H	Aiello Joseph	160	tailor	55	"
	K	Aiello Joseph P	160	U S A	22	"
	L	Dempola John	160	tailor	40	"
	M*	Dempola Rita—†	160	housewife	35	"
	N*	Angelo Josephine—†	160	"	80	"
	O*	Franchina Antonio	160	laborer	54	"
	P*	Franchina Virginia—†	160	housewife	44	"
	S	Giggi Esther—†	160	at home	33	"
	T	Giggi Lucy—†	160	candymaker	36	"
	U	Giggi Michael	160	retired	70	"
	V	D'Avolio Angelina—†	161	housewife	39	"
	W	D'Avolio Domenic	161	carpenter	42	"
	X	DiStaula Louis	161	laborer	30	"
	Y	DiStaula Margaret—†	161	housewife	30	"
	Z	Paolini Amedeo	161	laborer	54	"
2015						
	A	Paolini Desolina—†	161	housewife	58	"
	B	Cioto Domenic	161	forger	27	125 Trenton
	C	Cioto Sabina—†	161	housewife	28	125 "
	D	Capecci Antonio	161	U S A	21	here
	E	Capecci Frank	161	lithographer	23	"
	F	Capecci Nicola	161	laborer	53	"
	G*	Capecci Nina—†	161	housewife	43	"
	H	D'Amico Reginald	161	shipfitter	31	"
	K	D'Amico Rose—†	161	housewife	32	"
	L	Dizio Armando	161	metalworker	23	"
	M	Dizio Croce	161	laborer	57	"
	N*	Dizio Marianna—†	161	housewife	51	"
	O	Lanna Michael	162	shoemaker	43	"
	P	Tedeschi Concetta—†	162	housewife	26	"
	R	Tedeschi Gerard	162	agent	26	"

Cottage Street Continued

	Full Name	Res.	Occupation	Age	Reported
s	*Nobilio Vincenza †	162	housewife	72	here
t	Sulprizio Bernard	162	laborer	73	"
u	*Sulprizio Theresa †	162	housewife	65	"
v	Laicona Guy	162	barber	24	"
w	Laicona Mary †	162	housewife	24	"
x	Sulprizio Bernard	162	U S C G	21	"
y	Sulprizio Carmella †	162	housewife	49	"
z	Sulprizio Joseph	162	laborer	58	"

2016

	Full Name	Res.	Occupation	Age	Reported
a	Sulprizio Laura †	162	stitcher	22	"
b	Abbondanza Gaetano	162	laborer	38	"
c	Abbondanza Virginia †	162	housewife	28	"
d	Scannelli Edith †	162	"	32	"
e	Scannelli Robert	162	chauffeur	31	"
f	Dionisi Josephine †	163	housewife	24	"
g	Dionisi Philip	163	chauffeur	24	"
h	LaCorte John B	163	"	40	"
k	LaCorte Leona †	163	housewife	35	"
l	LaCorte Jennie †	163	"	29	"
m	LaCorte Vincent	163	laborer	43	"
n	LaCorte Gaetano	163	"	53	"
o	*LaCorte Italia †	163	housewife	45	"
p	LaCorte John	163	electrician	31	"
r	LaCorte Mary †	163	housewife	31	"
s	LaCorte Angelina †	163	"	54	"
t	LaCorte Felice	163	retired	59	"
u	LaCorte Patrick	163	electrician	25	"
v	Camiolo Anthony	164	salesman	50	"
w	Camiolo Antonetta †	164	dressmaker	21	"
x	*Camiolo Concetta †	164	housewife	45	"
y	Camiolo Nunzio	164	U S A	26	"
z	D'Agresto Antonetta †	164	clerk	28	"

2017

	Full Name	Res.	Occupation	Age	Reported
a	D'Agresto Carmella †	164	at home	21	"
b	D'Agresto James	164	U S A	26	"
c	*D'Agresto Mary †	164	housewife	55	"
e	Morrelli Luigi	164	laborer	46	"
f	*Morrelli Philomena †	164	housewife	41	"
g	*Meoli Ernest	164	laborer	46	"
h	*Meoli Mary †	164	housewife	37	"
l	DeRosa Angelo	164	rigger	29	"

11

Cottage Street —Continued

M	DeRosa Theresa — †	164	housewife	24	here
N *Rossetti Josephine — †	165	"	51	"
O	Rossetti Rocco	165	shoeworker	54	"
P	Monica Angelo	165	laborer	53	"
R	Monica Samuel	165	U S A	23	"
S	Maiona Anthony	165	cook	50	"
T	Maiona Catherine †	165	housewife	42	"
U	Palmerini Guerino	165	laborer	61	"
V	Palmerini Pasqualina †	165	clerk	20	"
W *Palmerini Santa — †	165	housewife	59	"
Y	Porazzo Michael A	165	diecutter	29	"
Z	Porazzo Olga — †	165	housewife	25	"

2018

A	Morretti Joseph	166	laborer	52	"
B *Peppi Gaetano	166	"	77	"
C *Peppi Josephine — †	166	housewife	70	"
D *Pisano Rose — †	166	"	38	131 Orleans
E	Guerra James	166	laborer	32	here
F	Guerra Jane — †	166	housewife	33	"
G	Porcaro Anthony	166	shipper	23	64 Bremen
H	Porcaro Mary — †	166	housewife	20	415 Frankfort
K	Navarro Celia — †	166	"	24	here
L	Navarro Michael	166	chauffeur	28	"
N *Cammarata Albert	166	laborer	47	"
O	Cammarata Josephine †	166	housewife	42	"
P *Mucci Anthony	167	painter	29	"
R	Mucci Lena †	167	housewife	28	"
S	Moriello Augustine	167	laborer	31	"
T	Moriello Carmella †	167	garmentworker	22	"
U	Moriello Concetta †	167	at home	59	"
V	Moriello Flora †	167	"	25	"
W	Bolognese Lucy †	167	housewife	32	"
X	Bolognese Ottavio	167	laborer	40	"
Y *DeProfio Moria †	167	housewife	74	"
Z	DeProfio Sabatino	167	retired	74	"

2019

A	Memmolo Ida †	167	clerk	21	"
B	Memmolo Luigi	167	laborer	52	"
C	Memmolo Mary †	167	housewife	47	"
D *D'Amico Adelina — †	167	at home	74	"

Cottage Street — Continued

E	D'Amico Edward	167	student	21	here
F	D'Amico George	167	laborer	27	"
G	DiFranza Frances †	167	housewife	38	"
H	DiFranza Paul	167	laborer	45	"
L	Fasciano Joseph	168	storekeeper	62	"
M	*Fasciano Josephine †	168	housewife	49	"
N	Palmerini Luigi	168	laborer	31	"
O	Palmerini Mary †	168	housewife	32	"
P	Cerase Carmelo C	168	U S N	31	"
R	Cerase Pauline †	168	housewife	31	"
S	Caliste Joseph	168	laborer	63	"
T	Angelo Mary †	168	housewife	49	"
U	Angelo Matteo	168	painter	56	"
V	Inchiesca Raymond J	168	machinist	23	2 Everett ct
W	*Zaffino Antonetta †	168	housewife	37	here
X	*Zaffino Gennaro	168	shoemaker	48	"
Y	*DeBole Pasquale	169	buffer	29	"
Z	DeBole Salvina †	169	housewife	27	"
	2020				
A	*Salini Vincenza †	169	"	62	"
B	*Salini Vincenzo	169	retired	69	"
C	Gasparini Dante	169	mechanic	27	"
D	Gasparini Rina †	169	housewife	26	"
E	Gasparini Victor	169	U S A	20	"
F	D'Alessandro Michael	169	laborer	42	"
G	D'Alessandro Sarah †	169	housewife	38	"
H	*Giorgione Carmella †	169	"	44	"
K	Giorgione Rafaele	169	laborer	40	"
L	*Salini Americo	169	baker	31	"
M	Salini Palmina †	169	housewife	29	"
O	*Presterone Joseph	170	candymaker	39	42 Cottage
P	*Presterone Rita †	170	housewife	32	42 "
R	*Paolini Anna †	170	"	17	here
S	Paolini Umberto	170	laborer	52	"
T	Patuzzi Ludivico	170	"	26	"
U	Patuzzi Mary †	170	housewife	24	"
V	Durbano Angelina †	170	"	29	"
W	*Durbano Giacomo	170	laborer	32	"
X	Paolini Donato	170	U S A	22	"
Y	*Paolini Elizabeth †	170	housewife	19	"

Cottage Street—Continued

	z	*Paolini Vincent	170	laborer	49	here
2021						
	A	DiGiovanni Domenic	170	U S A	24	"
	B	DiGiovanni Dora—†	170	dressmaker	28	"
	C	*DiGiovanni Galerana—†	170	housewife	53	"
	D	DiGiovanni Joseph	170	storekeeper	52	"
	E	DiGiovanni Nicholas	170	U S A	26	"
	F	DiGiovanni Philomena—†	170	at home	22	"
	G	DeLuca Sophie—†	171	housewife	25	"
	H	DeLuca Vito	171	repairman	27	172 Cottage
	K	Meneguzzi Enrico	171	U S A	23	here
	L	Meneguzzi Louise—†	171	operator	26	"
	M	*Meneguzzi Regina—†	171	at home	64	"
	N	Ferrara Mary—†	171	housewife	47	"
	O	Ferrara Rose—†	171	packer	22	"
	P	*Ferrara Theodore	171	storekeeper	50	"
	R	Carbone Ceriaco	171	retired	76	"
	S	Carbone Ceriaco, jr	171	chauffeur	30	"
	T	Carbone Rose—†	171	housewife	29	"
	U	Iacoviello Carmella—†	171	"	40	"
	V	Iacoviello Vito	171	engineer	50	"
	W	Grasso Angelo	171	laborer	62	"
	X	*Grasso Jennie—†	171	housewife	60	"
	Y	Grasso Nicholas	171	U S A	21	"
	Z	DiSciscio Sarah—†	172	housewife	22	160 Bremen
2022						
	A	DeSciscio Theodore	172	U S A	24	here
	B	DeSciscio Antonetta—†	172	packer	21	"
	C	DeSciscio Antonio	172	laborer	55	"
	D	DeSciscio Lucy—†	172	housewife	45	"
	E	*Cieri Alveria—†	172	"	49	"
	F	Cieri Frank	172	laborer	55	"
	G	Cieri Pasqualina—†	172	clerk	26	"
	H	Cieri Philomena—†	172	packer	28	"
	K	DiPietro Elvira—†	172	housewife	24	358 Harris'n av
	L	DiPietro Louis	172	carpenter	26	358 "
	M	Odoardi Antonetta—†	172	at home	23	here
	N	Odoardi Florence—†	172	clerk	20	"
	O	Odoardi Vincent	172	laborer	44	"
	P	Genaro James	172	mechanic	53	"
	R	Genaro Vincenza—†	172	housewife	46	"

14

Cottage Street Continued

s	Lima Lena †	172	housewife	28	Chelsea
t	Lima Manuel	172	cook	32	"
u	Carmosino John	173	shipper	22	44 Princeton
v	Carmosino Louise †	173	housewife	21	179 "
w	Iannillo Antonio	173	retired	60	here
x	Iannillo Antonio, jr	173	U S A	20	"
y	Iannillo Ada †	173	at home	25	"
z	Iannillo Maria †	173	housewife	60	"

2023

A	Gulla Josephine †	173	"	24	"
B	Gulla William	173	polisher	29	"
C	*Carbone Carmella †	173	housewife	22	144 Chelsea
D	Carbone Ralph	173	rigger	28	144 "
E	Agostinelli Arthur	173	machinist	20	here
F	*Agostinelli Lucia †	173	housewife	50	"
G	*Agostinelli Renaldo	173	laborer	54	"
H	*Mai Anna †	173	at home	48	"
K	Mai Louise †	173	packer	24	"
L	DiGianvittorio Josephine †	174	"	23	"
M	DiGianvittorio Nora †	174	"	21	"
N	DiGianvittorio Ralph	174	carpenter	52	"
O	*Patezzi Amelia †	174	housewife	64	"
P	Nappi Eva †	174	"	24	Revere
R	Nappi Isadore	174	salesman	27	"
S	Sofia Elizabeth †	174	housewife	26	here
T	Sofia Ernest	174	laborer	27	"
U	*Forcellese Bice †	174	housewife	43	"
V	Forcellese Norma †	174	dressmaker	20	"
W	*Forcellese Peter	174	tailor	45	"
X	Forcellese Tito	174	U S A	21	"
Y	D'Amico Antonio	174	bricklayer	21	"
Z	D'Amico Sabastino	174	"	52	"

2024

A	O'Keefe John	174	B F D	34	"
B	O'Keefe Mary †	174	housewife	26	"
C	*Recchia Alfred	174	laborer	53	"
D	Recchia Peter	174	"	20	"
E	*Recchia Tobia †	174	housewife	43	"
F	Papa Mary †	175	"	28	"
G	Papa Patrick	175	diemaker	30	"
H	Mucci Albert	175	operator	33	"

15

Cottage Street Continued

K	*Mucci Mary †	175	housewife	66	here
L	*Mucci Pasquale	175	retired	68	"
M	*Mucci Anna †	175	housewife	40	"
N	Mucci Frank	175	candymaker	42	"
O	Chaput Edmund	175	laborer	27	"
P	Chaput Louise †	175	housewife	24	"
R	DiNardo Anna †	175	finisher	22	"
S	DiNardo Flaviano	175	laborer	54	"
T	*DiNardo Joseph	175	"	28	"
U	*DiNardo Pasqua †	175	housewife	52	"
V	Grasso Liziario	175	laborer	50	"
W	Grasso Marsilio	175	U S A	23	"
X	*Grasso Rosina †	175	housewife	54	"
Y	Grasso Rosina †	175	clerk	25	"
Z	Cieri Alfonso	177	laborer	55	"

2025

A	*Cieri Palmina †	177	housewife	52	"
B	Rulli Antonio	177	laborer	52	"
C	*Rulli Domenica †	177	housewife	45	"
D	Rulli Viola †	177	packer	21	"
E	Carbone Carmen	177	toolmaker	38	171 Cottage
F	Carbone Caroline †	177	housewife	37	171 "
G	Costa Albert	177	laborer	25	here
H	Costa Josephine †	177	housewife	27	"
K	Sinibaldi Angelina †	177	"	61	"
L	Sinibaldi Frank	177	laborer	63	"
M	Sinibaldi Nicholas	177	U S C G	30	"
N	Sinibaldi Raymond	177	U S A	21	"
O	Catania Jennie †	177	housewife	36	166 Gove
P	Catania Joseph	177	machinist	40	166 "
R	Marmiane Emilio	179	mechanic	34	here
S	Marmiane Ida †	179	housewife	31	"
T	DeBenedetto Adeline †	179	"	50	"
U	DeBenedetto John	179	retired	52	"
V	Placido Emilio	179	storekeeper	52	"
W	Flammini Ernesto	179	laborer	47	"
X	*Flammini Florenda †	179	housewife	45	"
Y	Carpone Joseph	179	laborer	54	"
Z	*Carpone Paulina †	179	housewife	53	"

2026

A	Flammini Nancy †	179	"	21	"

46

Cottage Street (Continued)

B	Flammini Nicholas	179	chauffeur	23	here
C	Cordone Angelina †	179	housewife	46	"
D	Cordone Lorato	179	janitor	46	"
F	Battaglia Carmen	181	laborer	64	"
G	Battaglia Mary †	181	housewife	60	12 Eaton
H	DiNocco Anna †	181	"	25	here
K	DiNocco Erminio	181	salesman	31	"
L	Nappi Anna—†	181	clerk	26	"
M	Nappi John	181	retired	66	"
N	*Nappi Julia †	181	housewife	60	"
O	Fiorillo Cosimo	181	U S C G	20	"
P	Fiorillo Giuseppe	181	laborer	55	"
R	Fiorillo Louise—†	181	housewife	45	"
S	Fiorillo Michael	181	U S A	22	"
T	Iannetti Raymond	181	mechanic	26	"
U	Marotta Anthony	181	upholsterer	27	"
V	Marotta Cologero	181	laborer	54	"
W	*Marotta Lucia †	181	housewife	44	"
X	Sarro Carmen	181	U S A	23	"
Y	Sarro Frances †	181	housewife	22	"

2027

A	*Costa Mary †	182	"	50	98 Chelsea
B	*Gaglini Maria †	182	"	63	here
C	Mucci Camillo	182	shipfitter	42	"
D	Mucci Laura †	182	housewife	32	"
E	DeBenedetto Angelo	182	U S A	21	"
F	DeBenedetto Enrico	182	laborer	46	"
G	*DeBenedetto Laura †	182	housewife	42	"
H	DeBenedetto Theresa †	182	packer	20	"
K	Scaderto Angelina †	182	housewife	43	"
L	Scaderto Joseph	182	candymaker	50	"
M	Scaderto Joseph C	182	U S A	25	"
N	*Puccino Carmella †	182	housewife	46	"
O	Puccino Carmen	182	U S A	21	"
P	*Puccino Marindo	182	laborer	57	"
R	*Grande Concetta †	182	housewife	48	"
S	Grande Flavia †	182	packer	21	"
T	Grande Stephen	182	bricklayer	50	"
U	Ciambriello Angie †	182	packer	23	"
V	*Ciambriello Frances †	182	housewife	45	"
W	*Ciambriello Frank	182	mechanic	62	"

1—20

17

Cottage Street—Continued

y	Napolitano Andrew	184	laborer	23	here
z*	Napolitano Assunta—†	184	housewife	53	"

2028

A	Napolitano Bridget—†	184	packer	25	"
B*	Napolitano Girard	184	laborer	48	"
C	Taranti Anthony	184	"	28	45 Chelsea
D	Taranti Josephine—†	184	housewife	21	45 "
E*	Giambartolomei Elvira—†	184	"	42	here
F	Giambartolomei John	184	laborer	52	"
G	Cianciarulo Joseph	184	carpenter	24	"
H	Cianciarulo Mary—†	184	housewife	24	"
¹H	Spagnoli Ivo	184	U S A	21	"
K*	Spagnoli Louis	184	laborer	46	"
L	Spagnoli Louis	184	"	20	"
M	Naso Doris—†	184	housewife	23	"
N	Naso Joseph	184	mechanic	26	"
O	Guarino Peter	186	laborer	23	"
P	Guarino Rose—†	186	housewife	65	"
R	Barbaro Eugene	186	laborer	32	"
S	Barbaro Sarafina—†	186	housewife	26	"
T	Palombi Roseto	186	shipfitter	58	New York
U	Pepi Pasquale	186	mechanic	30	here
V	Pepi Pauline—†	186	housewife	31	"
W*	Fiantaca Grace—†	186	"	56	"
X	Fiantaca Joseph	186	student	22	"
Y*	Fiantaca Philip	186	laborer	56	"
Z	Fiantaca Philip	186	musician	27	"

2029

A	Fiantaca Salvatore	186	U S A	24	"
B	DiGiampaolo Concetta—†	186	housewife	51	"
C	DiGiampaolo Domenic	186	U S A	23	"
D	DiGiampaolo Eda—†	186	lawyer	24	"
E	DiGiampaolo Luigi	186	laborer	56	"
F	DiGiampaolo Romanina—†	186	clerk	21	"
G	Iritano Anna—†	186	housewife	36	"
H*	Iritano Antonio	186	shoemaker	48	"
K	Iritano Joseph	186	laborer	48	"
L	Ventura Virginia—†	186	housewife	34	"
M	Ciulla Jennie—†	186	clerk	24	"
N	Ciulla Joseph	186	laborer	52	"
O	Ciulla Lena—†	186	housewife	44	"

18

Cottage Street Continued

P	Ciulla Stephen	186	U S A	22	here
R	Palumbo John	188	machinist	45	"
S	Palumbo Mary †	188	housewife	38	"
U	Capuano Louis	188	shoemaker	42	135 Chelsea
V	Capuano Lena †	188	housewife	38	135 "
X	Natulucci Lucy †	188	housekeeper	61	here
Y	Natulucci Mary †	188	stitcher	23	"

2030

A	Albano Anthony	188	checker	26	"
B*	Albano Carmen	188	laborer	53	"
C	Albano James	188	U S A	23	"
D	Beatrice Clementina †	188	stitcher	23	"
E	Beatrice Eleanor †	188	at home	21	"
F	Beatrice Louis	188	mechanic	21	"
G	Beatrice Maria †	188	presser	27	"
H	Beatrice Pasquale	188	laborer	58	"
M	Forlizzi Antonetta †	190	at home	26	194 Cottage
N	Forlizzi Pasquale	190	laborer	54	194 "
O	Leone Archille	190	"	46	here
P*	Leone Philomena †	190	housewife	38	"
R	Giangregorio Anthony	190	U S A	20	"
S*	Giangregorio Caroline †	190	housewife	52	"
T	Giangregorio Felicia †	190	at home	24	"
U*	Giangregorio Pasquale	190	laborer	55	"
V	Giangregorio Ralph	190	U S C G	22	"
W*	Amato Mary †	190	housewife	43	"
X	Amato Pasquale	190	laborer	53	"
Y	Leone Amelio	190	"	40	"
Z	Leone Peter	190	"	38	"

2031

A	Serrecchia Anthony	190	"	42	166 Bremen
B	Pistone Frank	190	"	52	here
C	Pistone Frank	190	U S A	21	"
D	DiNocco Louis	190	carpenter	25	"
E	DiNocco Margaret †	190	housewife	23	"
F*	Albanese Ciriaco	192	laborer	68	196 Benningt'n
G	Lugiano Augustino	192	ironworker	46	here
K*	Margaroni Maria †	192	housewife	50	"
L	Margaroni Pasquale	192	U S A	25	"
M	Margaroni Paul	192	laborer	55	"
N	Bolognese Dominic	192	"	52	"

Cottage Street Continued

o	Bolognese James	192	U S A	22	here
p	*Bolognese Lettie †	192	housewife	42	"
r	Bolognese Mary †	192	at home	21	"
s	*Fulco Carmella †	192	housewife	46	"
t	Fulco Charles	192	laborer	47	"
u	*Leone Anna †	192	housewife	44	"
v	Leone Salvatore	192	laborer	42	"
w	DiNocco Antonio	192	"	64	"
x	DiNocco Antonio	192	U S A	22	"
y	DiNocco Benjamin	192	laborer	26	"
z	Danna James	192	"	27	"

2032

a	*Danna Joseph	192	"	59	"
b	*Danna Josephine †	192	housewife	48	"
c	*Cianzi Natala †	194	"	47	"
d	Cianzi Pauline †	194	stitcher	27	"
e	Cianzi Sebastino	194	laborer	57	"
f	DeDomenico Antonio	194	"	43	"
g	DeDomenico Dominic	194	U S A	21	"
h	*DeDomenico Liberato †	194	housewife	44	"
l	Galante Michael	194	brazier	28	"
m	Galante Nellie †	194	housewife	21	"
n	Vespa Angelo	194	laborer	46	"
o	Vespa Eva †	194	housewife	29	"

Everett Street

r	DeFilippo Anthony	124	chauffeur	25	here
s	DeFilippo Carmella †	124	housewife	23	"
s	*Pagliarulo Rafaela †	124	"	62	"
t	Pagliarulo Vito	124	laborer	60	"
u	Buono Carlo	126	welder	27	"
v	*Buono Concetta †	126	housewife	62	"
w	Buono Elena †	126	"	26	"
x	D'Andrea Pauline †	126	packer	41	"
y	*Sileno Antonio	128	retired	69	"
z	*Sileno Maria †	128	housewife	65	"

2033

a	*Catalano Frances †	128	"	53	"
b	Catalano Joseph	128	laborer	63	"
c	Catalano Josephine †	128	stitcher	22	"

Everett Street Continued

D	Martini Assunta †	128	housewife	27	here
E	Martini Gerardo	128	brazier	30	"
G	Maglio Frank	134	machinist	31	"
H	Maglio Julia †	134	operator	32	"
K	Sereti John	134	shipworker	45	"
L	Sereti Mary †	134	housewife	41	"
M	Leon John	134	laborer	43	"
N	Leon Mary †	134	housewife	38	"
O	Melito James V	136	chauffeur	46	"
P	Melito Phyllis †	136	housewife	35	"
R	LaPorta Mafalda †	136	stitcher	21	"
S	*LaPorta Stella †	136	housewife	46	"
T	*LaPorta Vincent	136	laborer	47	"
U	*Mancusi John	136	retired	77	"
V	*Farulla Helen †	140	housewife	40	"
W	*LaIacona Frances †	140	"	61	"
X	LaIacona Frank	140	U S A	28	"
Y	*LaIacona Salvatore	140	retired	65	"
Z	DiGloria Florence †	140	housewife	39	"

2034

A	DiGloria Samuel	140	laborer	47	"
B	Salamone Joseph	142	"	46	185 Everett
C	*Salamone Maria †	142	at home	89	185 "
D	Luongo Nicholas	142	laborer	45	here
E	*Luongo Rafaela †	142	housewife	45	"
F	Buonopana Florence †	142	operator	22	"
G	Buonopana Michael	142	laborer	48	"
H	Buonopana Priscilla †	142	housewife	48	"
K	Coscia Antoinetta †	144	"	43	"
L	Coscia Frances †	144	at home	20	"
M	Coscia Helen †	144	clerk	22	"
N	Coscia Louise †	144	stitcher	25	"
O	Coscia William	144	carpenter	49	"
P	*Famularo Achille	144	laborer	57	"
R	Famularo Elizabeth †	144	housewife	53	"
S	Butera Jean †	144	"	42	"
T	*Mangone Pearl †	146	"	35	"
U	Mangone Thomas	146	operator	36	"
V	Consalvi Emilio	146	shoeworker	34	"
W	Consalvi Rose †	146	housewife	28	"
X	Albanese Lucy †	146	at home	22	"

21

Everett Street — Continued

	Y	Albanese Raymond	146	U S A	26	here
	Z	Petruccelli Frances †	146	housewife	48	"
2035						
	A	Calvino Caroline †	146	"	26	"
	B	Calvino James	146	electrician	30	"
	C	Drago Frank	148	painter	57	"
	D	Murray Nellie J †	148	housekeeper	49	"
	E	*Briganti Esther †	148	housewife	54	"
	F	Briganti John	148	laborer	21	"
	G	Briganti Samuel	148	"	61	"
	H	Maranna Alexander	148	foreman	26	"
	K	Maranna Amelia †	148	housewife	54	"
	L	Maranna Edward	148	U S A	24	"
	M	Maranna William	148	tinsmith	61	"
	N	*Rauseo Antonio	150	storekeeper	54	"
	O	*Rauseo Catherine †	150	housewife	55	"
	P	Rauseo Christine †	150	at home	22	"
	R	Rauseo John	150	U S A	20	"
	S	Rauseo Joseph	150	"	25	"
	T	Rauseo Anna †	150	housewife	27	"
	U	Rauseo Michael	150	U S N	27	"
	W	Sgobbo Antonio	153	laborer	48	"
	X	*Sgobbo Leonarda †	153	housewife	40	"
	Y	Sgobbo Ralph	153	U S A	21	"
	Z	Salamone Benedetto	153	laborer	29	"
2036						
	A	Salamone Elvira †	153	housewife	23	"
	B	Varone Fred	153	painter	26	142 Webster
	C	Varone Janina †	153	housewife	23	142 "
	E	Rauseo Anna †	155	"	30	here
	F	Rauseo Rocco	155	chauffeur	30	"
	G	Salamone Josephine †	155	housewife	29	"
	H	Salamone Peter	155	shoeworker	30	"
	K	Zeoli Alfred	155	U S A	22	"
	L	*Zeoli Clara †	155	housewife	48	"
	M	*Zeoli Domenic	155	tailor	58	"
	N	Lewis Edith †	156	housewife	33	"
	O	Lewis John G	156	clerk	35	"
	P	*Vitale Filomena †	156	housewife	41	"
	R	Vitale Modestino	156	U S N	21	"
	S	Vitale Paul	156	shoemaker	41	"

Everett Street Continued

U	*Capidilupo Mary —†	158	housewife	66	here	
V	Capidilupo Theresa —†	158	stitcher	24	"	
W	Cerbone Amelia —†	159	hairdresser	30	"	
X	Cerbone Frank	159	U S A	21	"	
Y	*Cerbone Josephine —†	159	housewife	59	"	
Z	Cerbone Mary —†	159	stitcher	23	"	

2037

A	*Cerbone Peter	159	laborer	64	"	
B	*Frusciante Angelina —†	160	housewife	52	"	
C	Frusciante Anthony	160	retired	58	"	
D	Frusciante Joseph	160	U S N	24	"	
E	Frusciante Ralph	160	U S A	26	"	
F	Guarino Carmella —†	160	housewife	21	"	
G	Guarino Carmen	160	U S A	25	"	
H	Turco John B	160	cleaner	46	"	
K	*Pierro Annamaria —†	160	at home	60	"	
L	Pierro Anthony A	160	compositor	27	"	
M	Pierro Jennie— †	160	housewife	26	Everett	
N	Folino Anna—†	164	"	24	here	
O	Folino Joseph	164	painter	26	"	
P	Vitale Anthony	164	U S A	20	171 Everett	
R	*Vitale Antoinetta —†	164	housewife	42	171 "	
S	Vitale Michael	164	shoemaker	21	171 "	
T	Vitale Rocco	164	tailor	44	171 "	
U	Caforio Bridget —†	165	at home	67	here	
W	Caforio Laura —†	165	secretary	23	"	
X	*Salamone Josephine—†	165	at home	53	"	
Y	Salamone Josephine —†	165	stitcher	22	"	
Z	Penta George	165	shipfitter	35	"	

2038

A	Penta Viola— †	165	housewife	33	"	
C	Festa John	166	U S A	21	"	
D	*Festa Josephine —†	166	housewife	58	"	
E	Festa Landi	166	plumber	22	"	
F	Festa Louis	166	laborer	28	"	
G	*Derrico Carmella —†	166	housewife	48	"	
H	Derrico Dominic	166	U S A	22	"	
K	Derrico Michael	166	laborer	30	"	
N	Sarro Angelina —†	170	at home	74	"	
O	Sarro Carmino	170	retired	74	"	
S	Correale Carmen	172	rigger	47	"	

23

Everett Street — Continued

T	Correale Mary—†	172	housewife	34	here
V	Richardson William V	176	welder	21	"
W	*Clarizzio Antoinette—†	176	stitcher	42	"
X	Ravagno Alice—†	176	housewife	33	"
Y	Ravagno Salvatore	176	toolmaker	37	"
Z	Stella Rose—†	176	housewife	35	"

2039

A	Shuntz Angie—†	177	"	28	"
B	*Shuntz Eva—†	177	at home	70	"
C	Shuntz Helene—†	177	operator	23	"
D	Shuntz John	177	seaman	31	"
E	Shuntz William	177	"	28	"
F	O'Connell Hilary J	177	U S C G	42	"
G	O'Connell Mary—†	177	housewife	39	"
H	Quigley Maurice	177	fisherman	47	"
K	O'Connell Annie—†	177	at home	79	"

Gove Street

S	D'Amico Jean C—†	142	at home	39	here
U	*Ricciardi Maria—†	142	"	75	"
V	St George Louise—†	142	housewife	22	378 Sumner
W	St George Patrick	142	seaman	25	378 "
X	*Puorro Antonette—†	142	housewife	50	here
Y	Puorro Emilio	142	machinist	23	"
Z	Puorro Gaetano	142	U S A	20	"

2040

A	Puorro Julia—†	142	stitcher	26	"
B	Puorro Natalie—†	142	"	28	"
C	Cappucci Carmella—†	142	clerk	32	"
D	*Cappucci Carrolla—†	142	at home	62	"
E	Cappucci Virginia—†	142	clerk	33	"
G	*Liberatore Linda—†	142	housewife	57	"
H	Liberatore Marguerite—†	142	clerk	25	"
K	Liberatore Mario	142	U S A	20	"
L	Liberatore Rocco	142	blacksmith	57	"
M	Liberatore Umberto	142	machinist	24	"
N	Porfido Margaret—†	146	housewife	38	"
O	Pasone Carmella—†	146	stitcher	27	"
P	Pasone Eustachio	146	carpenter	62	"
R	Pasone Olga—†	146	clerk	21	"

24

Gove Street Continued

s	Pasone Theresa — †	146	housewife	62	here
t	Pasone Vito	146	chauffeur	34	"
u	Petrillo Colombia — †	146	housewife	37	"
v	Petrillo Henry	146	janitor	35	"
w	Corsano Annie — †	146	housewife	60	"
x	Corsano Nicholas D	146	engineer	38	"
y	DelFraino Antonio	146	laborer	38	134 Gove
z	DelFraino Margaret — †	146	housewife	32	134 "

2041

a	DiLaura Carmela — †	146	shoeworker	21	here
b	Scrima Raymond	146	"	45	"
c	Lopilato Anthony	164	mechanic	24	"
d	Lopilato Margaret — †	164	housewife	22	"
e	Lopilato Catherine — †	164	"	64	"
f	Lopilato Michael	164	retired	72	"
g	DeFilippo Grace — †	164	housewife	28	"
h	DeFilippo Joseph	164	clerk	30	"
k	Musiello Mary — †	164	shoeworker	30	"
l	Laezza John	164	laborer	41	"
m	*Laezza Victoria — †	164	housewife	40	"
o	*Tedescucci Lucia — †	164	"	53	"
p	Zarlingo Carmen	164	laborer	48	"
r	Gambole Bertha — †	164	stitcher	39	"
s	Scalfani Frances — †	164	housewife	25	"
t	Scalfani Frani	164	cutter	29	"
u	LoVecchio Albert	165	U S A	22	"
v	*LoVecchio Angelina — †	165	housewife	61	"
w	*LoVecchio Anthony	165	laborer	66	"
x	LoVecchio Augustine	165	mechanic	23	"
y	LoVecchio Frank	165	"	20	"
z	LoVecchio Joseph	165	machinist	25	"

2042

a	LoVecchio Mildred — †	165	clerk	30	"
b	LoVecchio Sarah — †	165	"	27	"
c	Puccillo Carmen	165	laborer	37	"
d	Puccillo Maria — †	165	housewife	28	"
e	Pepicelli Antonette — †	165	"	36	"
f	Pepicelli Antonio D	165	shipwright	38	"
g	Lunetta Eva — †	165	housewife	31	"
h	Lunetta Stephen	165	diestamper	38	"
k	DiFonzo Berardo	165	laborer	44	"

Gove Street — Continued

L	*DiFonzo Marie — †	165	laborer	44	here	
M	Lochiatto Jennie — †	165	"	21	"	
N	Lochiatto Peter	165	inspector	23	"	
O	Naples Domenic	165	mechanic	39	"	
P	Naples Mary — †	165	housewife	34	"	
R	DiBello Flora — †	165	"	23	"	
S	DiBello George	165	laborer	25	"	
T	Iannaccone Achille	166	"	27	"	
U	Iannaccone Charles	166	"	58	"	
V	Iannaccone Louis	166	barber	29	"	
X	Iannaccone Mary J †	166	housewife	53	"	
W	Iannaccone Michael	166	shipper	22	"	
Y	*Dannoffo Mary — †	166	housewife	44	"	
Z	Masiello Pelligrino	166	driller	46	"	

2043

A	*Masiello Philomena — †	166	housewife	42	"	
B	Troiani Anna — †	166	"	68	32 Cottage	
C	Troiani Serafino	166	retired	72	32 "	
D	Masiello Rose — †	166	housewife	35	here	
E	Masiello Tiberio	166	laborer	43	"	
F	*Mazzone Catherine — †	166	housewife	35	Chelsea	
G	Molinaro Albert	166	machinist	31	here	
H	Molinaro Elvira — †	166	housewife	26	"	
K	DeRosa Arthur	168	U S A	26	"	
L	DeRosa Christopher	168	U S N	31	"	
M	Romano Anna — †	168	candymaker	49	"	
N	Romano Frank	168	shoeworker	60	"	
O	Romano Louis	168	U S A	20	"	
P	Salini Adriana — †	168	housewife	25	65 Lubec	
R	Salini Leo	168	machinist	26	65 "	
S	DiGiomittorio Adeline — †	168	dressmaker	64	here	
T	*DiGiomittorio Concetta †	168	housewife	45	"	
U	*DiGiomittorio Giovanni	168	shoemaker	47	"	
V	DeMarco Anthony	168	candymaker	39	"	
W	DeMarco Eleanor †	168	housewife	30	"	
X	*Selvitella Anthony	168	pedler	65	"	
Y	*Selvitella Pasqualina †	168	housewife	68	"	
Z	Savino Giovanni	168	blacksmith	49	"	

2044

A	*Savino Regina †	168	housewife	48	"	
B	DeLucia Alfred	168	retired	55	"	

Gove Street — Continued

c	DeLucia Anthony	168	mechanic	21	here
D*	DeLucia Paulino—†	168	housewife	52	"
E	Kootz Herbert	174	florist	32	112 Webster
F	Kootz Rose—†	174	housewife	32	112 "
G	Giglio Frances—†	174	"	49	here
H	Giglio Joseph	174	laborer	53	"
K	Giglio Pauline—†	174	clerk	27	"
L	Giglio Peter	174	U S N	20	"
M	Giglio Rose—†	174	dressmaker	24	"
N*	Antonioli Eleanor—†	174	housewife	43	"
O*	Antonioli Mary A—†	174	at home	72	"
P	Sinibaldi Armand	174	U S C G	21	"
R	Sinibaldi Joseph	174	laborer	60	"
S*	Sinibaldi Maria—†	174	housewife	59	"
T	Melchionda Edward	176	welder	30	273 Sumner
U*	Melchionda Josephine—†	176	housewife	38	287 "
V	Barrasso Angelina—†	176	packer	27	here
W	Lanza Angelo	176	laborer	40	"
X	Lanza Palmina—†	176	housewife	34	"
Y*	Florio Celia—†	176	"	75	"
Z*	Florio Frank	176	retired	72	"
	2045				
A	DiLorenzo Edward	176	tailor	68	"
B*	DiLorenzo Giuseppina—†	176	housewife	66	"
C	DiLorenzo Joseph	176	U S N	21	"
D*	Citrano Julia—†	176	housewife	42	"
E	Citrano Tito	176	laborer	49	"
F	Petrocelli Agnes—†	176	housewife	33	17 Oneida

Hooten Court

G	Semminelli Josephine—†	1	housekeeper	50	here
H	Fabiano Angelina—†	1	housewife	31	"
K	Fabiano Nicholas	1	chauffeur	37	"
M	Pace Frank	2	cabinetmaker	24	"
N	Pace Pantaleone	2	laborer	48	"
O	DiAmato Angelina—†	2	housewife	27	"
P	DiAmato Ralph	2	chauffeur	26	"
R	Ciampa Angelo R	3	assembler	24	"
S*	Ciampa Carolina—†	3	housekeeper	52	"
T	Rozzi Antonio	5	laborer	49	"

Hooten Court—Continued

U	Rozzi Carmela—†	5	factoryhand	21	here
V	Rozzi Elizabeth—†	5	"	24	"
W	Rozzi Theresa—†	5	housewife	49	"
X	Pero Catherine—†	6	at home	65	"
Y	Pero Charles	6	foreman	55	"
Z	Pero James	6	chauffeur	50	"

2046

A	Salamone Biagio	6	factoryhand	25	"
B	*Salamone Josephine—†	6	housewife	58	"
C	Salamone Liborio	6	U S A	23	"
D	Salamone Venedetto	6	barber	27	"
E	Donavan James	8	longshoreman	66	"
F	Donavan Nora—†	8	housewife	71	"
G	Laracy Harold	8	U S A	30	"
H	Laracy Herbert	8	"	24	"
K	Laracy James	8	fisherman	38	"
L	Laracy Margaret—†	8	factoryhand	28	"
M	Driscoll John H	11	longshoreman	45	"
O	Soldano Antonio	12	laborer	43	"
P	Soldano Edith—†	12	housewife	37	"

Lamson Street

R	DeFeo Ralph	19	cutter	30	here
S	DeFeo Vincenza †	19	housewife	28	"
T	*Cacchiotti Antonetta †	19	"	42	"
U	Cacchiotti Constanzio	19	machinist	21	"
V	Cacchiotti Frank	19	laborer	50	"
W	Bevere Josephine †	19	housewife	23	"
X	Bevere Nicholas	19	baker	28	"
Y	*DiFranza Filomena †	21	housewife	50	"
Z	DiFranza Marie †	21	instructor	22	"

2047

A	Clark Lottie G †	21	clerk	38	"
B	Clark Margaret †	21	housewife	56	"
C	Clark Margaret L †	21	clerk	23	"
D	Fagone Angelina †	21	housewife	27	"
E	Fagone Michael	21	shipfitter	29	"
F	Mingolelli Josephine † rear 21		housewife	51	"
G	Mingolelli Lena † " 21		saleswoman	29	"
H	Mingolelli Michael " 21		U S M C	22	"

28

Lamson Street Continued

	K	Mingolelli Pasquale	rear 21	laborer	54	here
	L	Mingolelli Raffaela †	" 21	bookkeeper	20	"
	M	Bartolo Catherine †	35	housewife	21	"
	N	Bartolo Leonard	35	mechanic	22	"
	O	Mirabello Anthony	35	U S A	30	"
	P	Mirabello Frank	35	machinist	55	"
	R	Mirabello Rose †	35	housewife	50	"
	S	Mirabello Ralph	35	guard	26	"
	T	Mirabello Theresa †	35	housewife	27	"
	U	*Surette Emeline †	36	"	47	"
	V	Surette John	36	U S A	23	"
	W	*Surette Martin	36	carpenter	52	"
	X	Ruggiero Gaetano	36	laborer	51	"
	Y	Ruggiero Rose †	36	clerk	24	"
	Z	Bandanza Chiarina †	38	housewife	35	"

2048

	A	Bandanza Joseph	38	operator	40	"
	B	Morelli Natalina †	38	housewife	28	"
	C	Puorro Gerardo	39	storekeeper	49	"
	D	Puorro Mildred †	39	housewife	38	"
	E	Guarracino Alfred	39	electrician	21	"
	F	*Guarracino Bambina †	39	housewife	56	"
	G	Leone Alfred F	39	electrician	29	"
	H	Leone Jeane †	39	stitcher	24	"
	K	DeStefano John	39	repairman	34	483 Summer
	L	DeStefano Olympia †	39	housewife	34	483 "
	M	Benson Margaret †	41	operator	42	here
	N	Cahill Archie	41	pipefitter	45	"
	O	Trainor Alice †	41	housewife	33	"
	P	Trainor John	41	longshoreman	35	"
	R	Callanan Nora E †	43	at home	60	"
	S	Nelson Mary T †	43	"	49	"
	T	Mirabello Laura †	45	housewife	26	35 Lamson
	U	Mirabello William	45	laborer	29	35 "
	V	Papsadoro Mary †	45	inspector	20	Maine
	W	Parziale Emilio	45	laborer	45	here
	X	*Parziale Violanda †	45	housewife	43	"
	Y	*Parziali Allesandro	47	U S A	41	"
	Z	Parziali Franco	47	laborer	33	"

2049

	A	Parziali James	47	U S A	26	"

Lamson Street — Continued

B	*Parziali Joseph	47	retired	60	here	
C	Parziali Joseph, jr	47	U S A	23	"	
D	Parziali Julia — †	47	housekeeper	21	"	
E	*Parziali Susie — †	47	housewife	63	"	
F	*Cieri Marie — †	47	"	55	"	
G	D'Argenio Faustino	47	shipper	28	"	
H	D'Argenio Susie — †	47	stitcher	29	"	

Lubec Street

K	Corsano Vincenzo	55	retired	73	here	
L	Stella Charles, jr	55	electrician	42	"	
M	Stella Charles W	55	U S A	20	"	
N	Stella Ruth — †	55	housewife	41	"	
O	Stella Sadie — †	55	librarian	22	"	
P	Corsano Dora — †	55	housewife	31	146 Gove	
R	Corsano Edmund	55	engineer	35	146 "	
S	Caldarelli Armando	57	machinist	23	here	
T	Zompanti Catherine †	57	at home	20	"	
U	Zompanti James	57	laborer	53	"	
V	Zompanti Tina †	57	housewife	42	"	
W	Dizio Angelo	57	metalworker	27	"	
X	Dizio Anna †	57	housewife	25	"	
Y	Bellafonti Nicholas	57	seaman	54	"	
Z	Indelirato Carmella †	57	housewife	54	"	

2050

A	Indelirato Joseph	57	U S A	24	"	
B	Indelirato Vincenzo	57	retired	67	"	
C	Dattolli Mary †	57	housewife	35	"	
D	Dattolli Michael	57	shoeworker	43	"	
E	Serime Generoso	57	U S A	22	"	
F	*Serime Mary †	57	housewife	49	"	
G	Serime Pasquale	57	shoeworker	52	"	
H	*Giampietro Amelia J †	59	at home	49	"	
K	Rossetti Joseph	59	chauffeur	33	"	
L	Rossetti Nancy †	59	housewife	33	"	
M	Mustone Andrew	59	chauffeur	30	191 Border	
N	Mustone Marie †	59	housewife	25	191 "	
O	Carangelo Domenic G	59	laborer	29	here	
P	Carangelo Marie L †	59	housewife	28	"	
R	Giardina Mary †	59	"	30	60 Lubec	

Lubec Street Continued

	s	Giardina Salvatore	59	operator	29	60 Lubec
	T	DiFranza Armando	59	U S A	21	here
	U	DiFranza Assunta †	59	housewife	52	"
	V	DiFranza Carmella †	59	at home	30	"
	W	DiFranza Leonardo	59	shoecutter	54	"
	X	DiFranza Mary †	59	clerk	29	"
	Y	*Zichittella John	61	painter	50	"
	Z	Zichittella Martin	61	U S A	23	"
2051						
	A	*Zichittella Mary †	61	housewife	50	"
	B	Caruso Josephine †	61	"	21	"
	C	Caruso Nicholas	61	U S A	23	"
	D	Serino Armandio	61	carpenter	48	"
	E	Serino Joseph	61	laborer	24	"
	F	Serino Ralph	61	U S A	22	"
	G	*Serino Theresa †	61	housewife	46	"
	H	D'Angelico Alfred	61	carpenter	25	"
	K	D'Angelico Anita †	61	housewife	27	"
	L	Severino Jennie †	61	packer	24	Waltham
	M	Severino Nicholas	61	U S A	23	170 Gove
	N	Marcantonia Carmen	61	laborer	52	here
	O	Marcantonia Jean †	61	clerk	21	"
	P	Marcantonia Margaret †	61	housewife	50	"
	R	Leto Gandolfo	63	carpenter	39	"
	S	Leto Jennie †	63	housewife	29	"
	T	Rizzo Joseph	63	laborer	62	"
	U	*Rizzo Josephine †	63	housewife	66	"
	V	*Trasolini Luigi	63	plumber	53	"
	W	Ciambriello Domenic	63	clerk	26	"
	X	Ciambriello Theresa †	63	housewife	26	"
	Y	Luongo George	63	finisher	40	166 Cottage
	Z	Luongo Jennie †	63	housewife	33	166 "
2052						
	A	Mussetts Mary †	63	dressmaker	43	here
	B	Scanziello Angelo	63	laborer	38	"
	C	*Scanziello Louise †	63	housewife	35	"
	D	*Manucci Samuel	65	retired	67	24 Shelby
	E	*Rizzo Elizabeth †	65	at home	42	24 "
	F	Pardo Dena †	65	housewife	25	here
	G	Pardo Lawrence	65	shipper	24	"
	H	Pardo Joseph	65	retired	65	"

Lubec Street Continued

	K	Pardo Mary †	65	housewife	54	here
	L	Pardo Nora †	65	shoeworker	22	"
	M	Annese Carlo	69	packer	31	73 Lubec
	N	Annese Edith †	69	housewife	25	73 "
	O	Doria Edith †	69	"	26	here
	P	Doria Frank	69	painter	35	"
	R	*Giordano Angelina †	69	at home	64	"
	S	Giordano Antonetta †	69	stitcher	30	"
	T	Giordano Caroline †	69	at home	36	"
	U	Giordano Edith †	69	stitcher	22	"
	V	Giordano Eleanor †	69	at home	28	"
	W	Giordano Emma †	69	"	26	"
	X	Giordano Jennie †	69	folder	38	"
	Y	Giordano Sue †	69	"	33	"
	Z	Marinelli Amelia †	69	housewife	36	"
2053						
	A	Marinelli Joseph	69	mechanic	36	"
	B	*Nocillo Josephine †	69	at home	64	"
	C	Nocillo Vincent	69	foreman	33	"
	D	Mercurio Antonetta †	71	housewife	25	"
	E	Mercurio William	71	supervisor	29	"
	F	DeGregorio Alfonso	71	laborer	59	35 Chelsea
	G	DeDomenica Dominic	71	"	52	here
	H	DeDomenica Louise †	71	stitcher	48	"
	K	Brocaccini Joseph	71	laborer	42	"
	L	*Brocaccini Mary †	71	housewife	35	"
	M	DeLibero Alexander	71	mason	39	"
	N	*DeLibero Rose †	71	housewife	42	"
	O	Serra Anthony	71	laborer	24	"
	P	Serra Joseph	71	"	49	"
	R	Serra Mary †	71	stitcher	22	"
	S	*Serra Rose †	71	housewife	48	"
	T	Arimento Matteo	73	retired	62	"
	U	Domenico Grace †	73	packer	35	"
	V	Domenico Joseph	73	laborer	38	"
	W	Marrazzo Domenic	73	agent	20	"
	X	*Marrazzo Margaret †	73	at home	37	"
	Y	Nazzaro Ciro	73	carpenter	47	"
	Z	Nazzaro Phyllis †	73	stitcher	20	"
2054						
	A	*Nazzaro Raffaela †	73	housewife	49	"

Lubec Street Continued

B	D'Amico Antonetta †	73	at home	52	here
C	D'Amico Josephine †	73	stitcher	24	"
D	Cibene Anthony	73	shipfitter	25	"
E	Cibene Rose †	73	housewife	24	"
F	*Parrelli Anna †	73	"	47	"
G	Parrelli Modestino	73	laborer	57	"
H	Siciliono Gregorio	73	tinsmith	59	193 Maverick
K	Siciliono Raffaela †	73	housewife	55	193 "
L	Siciliono Salvatore	73	U S A	32	193 "
M	*Danna Grace †	75	at home	53	here
N	Danna Salvatore	75	U S A	23	"
O	Danna Sebastian	75	welder	29	"
P	Danna Anna †	75	clerk	32	"
R	Danna Josephine †	75	operator	21	"
S	Collarusso Elvira †	75	housewife	46	"
T	Collarusso Pellergrino	75	laborer	52	"
U	Micciche Helen †	75	housewife	25	"
V	Micciche Michael	75	laborer	27	"
W	Fuccillo Anthony	75	"	29	"
X	Fuccillo Esther †	75	stitcher	25	"
Y	*Fuccillo Michael	75	laborer	63	"
Z	*Fuccillo Nuncia †	75	housewife	54	"

2055

A	Polito Bartolo	75	laborer	50	"
B	Polito Grace †	75	housewife	47	"
C	Guffonte Cecelia †	75	"	36	"
D	Guffonte Luigi	75	operator	40	"
F	*Rosetti Mary †	77	housewife	54	"
G	Rosetti Michael	77	retired	66	"
H	Straccia Joseph	77	laborer	39	"
K	Straccia Palmi †	77	housewife	37	"
L	Vigliotta Angela †	77	saleswoman	23	"
M	Vigliotta Antonio	77	laborer	50	"
N	Vigliotta Joseph	77	U S A	21	"
O	*Vigliotta Maria †	77	housewife	47	"
P	Vigliotta Natalie †	77	stitcher	20	"
R	Memmelo Louise †	77	clerk	20	"
S	Memmelo Marchino	77	laborer	53	"
T	*Memmelo Michelina †	77	housewife	57	"
U	*Paradiso Anna †	77	at home	79	"
V	Paulicella Grace †	77	housewife	31	"

Page	Letter	FULL NAME	Residence, Jan. 1, 1943	Occupation.	Supposed Age	Reported Residence, Jan. 1, 1942. Street and Number.

Lubec Street Continued

	w	Paulicella Michael	77	laborer	32	here
	x	*DeFlumeri Mary †	77	housewife	38	"
	y	*DeFlumeri Vincent	77	laborer	53	"
	z	Caldarelli Clara †	77	at home	30	"

2056

	a	Caldarelli Faustino	77	laborer	57	"
	b	*Caldarelli Lorraine †	77	housewife	58	"
	c	Caldarelli Natale	77	machinist	28	"
	d	*DiFilippo Angelo	77	laborer	47	"
	e	DiFilippo Antonetta †	77	housewife	50	"
	f	DiFilippo Leonora †	77	clerk	21	"
	g	DiFilippo Louise †	77	laundress	23	"
	h	*Diotalevi Allesandro	79	laborer	56	"
	k	*Diotalevi Emilia †	79	housewife	50	"
	l	Ditomasso Joseph	79	chauffeur	35	"
	m	Ditomasso Rose †	79	housewife	35	"
	n	Arcadipane Andrew	79	laborer	47	"
	o	Arcadipane Grace †	79	housewife	45	"
	p	*Lomuscio Donatella †	79	"	42	"
	r	Lomuscio Joseph	79	laborer	50	"
	s	Galante Jeannette †	79	clerk	24	"
	t	Galante Joseph	79	candymaker	44	"
	u	Galante Lena †	79	housewife	43	"
	v	DiFlumeri John	79	mason	38	"
	w	DiFlumeri Rose †	79	housewife	35	"
	x	*Grifone Pasquale	79	retired	67	"
	y	Porcella Lena †	79	housewife	28	"
	z	Porcella Peter	79	laborer	30	"

2057

	a	Tuttavillia Dora †	79	housewife	39	"
	b	Tuttavillia Michael	79	laborer	52	"
	c	Tuttavillia Vincenza †	79	clerk	20	"
	d	Nazzaro Raffaela †	81	packer	45	"
	e	Dramoni Mary †	81	at home	34	"
	f	Caso Louis	81	painter	44	"
	g	Caso Tessie †	81	housewife	36	"
	h	Castaldo Christina †	81	"	38	"
	k	Castaldo Ralph	81	laborer	42	"
	l	Caso Concordia †	81	at home	80	"
	m	Caso Frank	81	laborer	41	"
	n	Dieso Donato	81	"	59	"

34

Lubec Street—Continued

o	Dieso George	81	U S A	22	here
p	Dieso James	81	"	24	"
R*	Dieso Marie †	81	housewife	49	"
s	Bernabei Domenic	81	laborer	62	"
T*	Bernabei Josephine †	81	housewife	52	"
u	Bernabei Loretta †	81	stitcher	22	"
v	Pelosi Agostino	81	student	20	"
W*	Pelosi Anna †	81	housewife	42	"
x	Pelosi Michael	81	shoemaker	46	
y	Trodoslavich Francis	83	laborer	24	4 Liverpool
z	Trodoslavich Margaret †	83	housewife	27	69 Lubec

2058

B*	Gallo Generosa †	83	"	58	here
c	Gallo John	83	laborer	60	"
D	Gallo Patrick	83	electrician	21	"
E	Montanino Carmen	83	U S A	24	"
F	Montanino Joseph	83	shoeworker	32	"
G	Montanino Michael	83	laborer	61	"
H	Montanino Sadie †	83	waitress	28	"
K	Montanino Sue †	83	at home	22	"
L	Casciolo Emilia †	83	housewife	37	"
M	Casciolo Joseph	83	repairman	41	"
N	Pellecchia Albert	83	laborer	22	"
o*	Pellecchia Josephine †	83	at home	59	"
P	Pellecchia Minnie †	83	clerk	23	"
R	Pellecchia Peter	83	laborer	27	"
s	Colannino Frank	85	U S A	24	"
T*	Colannino Raffaella †	85	housewife	58	"
u	Colannino Rosario	85	laborer	60	"
v	Colannino Joseph	85	operator	25	"
w	Colannino Rose †	85	housewife	23	"
x	Sullo Antonio	85	laborer	58	"
y	Sullo Connie †	85	clerk	21	"
z	Sullo Joseph	85	U S A	20	"

2059

A*	Sullo Mary †	85	housewife	49	"
B	Sullo Nicholas	85	U S A	23	"
c	Ministari Charles	85	laborer	24	"
D	Ministari Tina †	85	housewife	22	"
E	DeFratis Louis	85	laborer	32	"
F	DeFratis Phyllis †	85	saleswoman	34	"

Maverick Street

L	Santarpio Concetta †	244	housewife	28	here
M	Santarpio Joseph	244	proprietor	32	"
N	Schifino John	244	laborer	25	14 Chelsea
O	Schifino Lena †	244	candyworker	31	14 "
P	Schifino Nicolina †	244	at home	65	14 "
R	Schifino Santa †	244	candyworker	35	14 "
S	Bisciotte Mary †	246	at home	68	here
T	Rizzo Alfred C	246	machinist	27	"
U	Rizzo Rose †	246	housewife	26	"
V	Messina Cecelia †	246	"	24	"
W	Messina Edward	246	proprietor	52	"
X	Messina Edward, jr	246	U S A	27	"
Y	Messina Frances †	246	housewife	45	"
Z	Bevilaqua Alfred	246	U S N	21	"
	2060				
A	*Bevilaqua Ralph	246	shoeworker	56	"
B	*Bevilaqua Victoria †	246	housewife	52	"
C	Campagna Armond	248	metalworker	30	"
D	Campagna Josephine †	248	housewife	30	"
E	Scopa Amorosa †	248	"	36	320 Sumner
F	Scopa John	248	driller	55	320 "
G	*Castaldo Michael	248	laborer	53	here
H	Castaldo Pasquale	248	U S A	25	"
K	*Castaldo Rose †	248	housewife	50	"
L	Castaldo Theresa †	248	stitcher	21	"
M	Zuccaro Anna †	250	at home	20	"
N	Zuccaro Anthony	250	draftsman	23	"
O	Zuccaro Erestina †	250	housewife	60	"
P	Griffin Catherine †	250	typist	37	"
R	Walsh Mary †	250	housewife	74	"
S	Miraglia Albert	250	engineer	32	"
T	Miraglia Lena †	250	housewife	31	"
U	Paolini Orsola †	252	"	60	"
V	Paolini Donato	252	laborer	61	"
W	Paolini Pasquale	252	carpenter	39	"
X	Paolini Phyllis †	252	housewife	31	"
Y	Picillo Carmella †	252	"	27	"
Z	Picillo Michael	252	freighthandler	27	"
	2061				
	Cake Lucy †	252	shoeworker	38	"
	Giulio Baldasaro	252	laborer	51	"

36

Maverick Street — Continued

c*Grillo Caroline †	252	housewife	63	here
D	D'Agostino Mildred †	254	"	31	"
E	D'Agostino Salvatore	254	electrician	34	"
F	Mastascusa Attilio	254	tailor	32	"
G	Mastascusa Clementine †	254	housewife	67	"
H*DiFranza Letitia †	254	"	50	"
K	DiFranza Mario	254	U S N	22	"
L	DiFranza Michael	254	shoeworker	54	"
M	Germano Charles C	260	machinist	30	"
N	Germano Josephine †	260	housewife	27	"
P	Liberti Angelo	260	physician	52	"
R*Liberti Vincenzo	260	teacher	56	"
S	DiNardo Domenic	262	ironworker	50	"
T	DiNardo Laura †	262	stitcher	23	"
U	DiNardo Livia †	262	candyworker	21	"
V	DiNardo Maria †	262	housewife	46	"
W	Marmorale Mary †	262	"	32	"
X	Marmorale William	262	chauffeur	33	"
Y*Ficcaglia Antonetta †	262	housewife	50	"
Z	Ficcaglia Ugo	262	operator	23	"

2062

A	Ficcaglia Vincent	262	shipper	28	"
B	Rossetti Benjamin	262	chauffeur	29	"
C	Rossetti Mary †	262	housewife	26	"
D*Pollastone Mary †	264	"	37	"
E	Pollastone Pietro	264	ropemaker	44	"
F	DiBello Catherine †	264	housewife	53	"
G	DiBello Edward	264	U S A	25	"
H	DiBello Michael	264	tailor	56	"
K	Gifun Gerard	264	clerk	37	"
L*Stella Carmella †	264	housewife	61	"
M	Stella Generoso	264	bricklayer	61	"
N	Stella Helen †	264	tailor	28	"
O	Stella Marion †	264	clerk	20	"
P	Stella Pasquale	264	U S N	23	"
R	Gulla Flora †	266	housewife	27	"
S	Gulla William	266	barber	31	"
T	DiNush Joseph	266	foreman	38	"
U	DiNush Mary †	266	housewife	37	"
V	Tarzia Domenic	266	laborer	56	"
W*Tarzia Palma †	266	housewife	65	"

	FULL NAME	Residence, Jan. 1, 1943.	Occupation.	Supposed Age	Reported Residence, Jan. 1, 1942. Street and Number.

Maverick Street Continued

	FULL NAME	Res.	Occupation	Age	Reported
x	Tarzia William	266	U S A	26	here
y	Cataldo Rose †	268	housewife	28	"
z	Cataldo Victor	268	clerk	30	"

2063
A	Cataldo Generoso	268	laborer	66	"
B	Cataldo John	268	seaman	36	"
C	Cataldo Lucy †	268	housewife	65	"
D	Recchia Adeline †	268	"	35	"
E	Recchia Vincent	268	tailor	43	"
F	Sullivan Elizabeth A †	270	housewife	57	"
G	Sullivan Thomas A	270	inspector	64	"
H	*Hovde Nils	270	retired	75	"
K	*Hovde Olivia A †	270	housewife	66	"
L	O'Keefe Anna †	270	printer	60	"
M	O'Keefe Margaret †	270	"	48	"
N	Giordano Frank	276	plumber	49	"
O	Giordano Josephine †	276	housewife	43	"
P	Giordano Madeline †	276	stitcher	21	"
R	Sammartino Anthony	276	shipfitter	30	"
S	Sammartino Maria †	276	housewife	72	"
T	Innio Joseph	276	painter	44	"
U	Innio Phyllis †	276	housewife	31	"
V	Ventola Domenic	276	U S A	32	"
W	Festa Sylvia †	278	boxmaker	28	"
X	Grillo Frank	278	teacher	42	"
Y	Grillo Gerardo	278	retired	73	"
Z	Grillo Josephine †	278	housewife	61	"

2064
A	Drago Mary †	278	"	35	"
B	Drago Robert	278	tailor	39	"
C	Grillo Americo	278	barber	38	"
D	Grillo Linda †	278	housewife	37	"
E	Intonti Americo	280	laborer	29	"
F	Intonti Jennie †	280	housewife	29	"
G	Maddalena Gilda †	280	"	31	"
H	Maddalena Lucy †	280	stenographer	28	244 Maverick
K	Maddalena Theodore E	280	machinist	33	here
L	Intonti Albert	280	U S N	25	"
M	Intonti Angelina †	280	at home	32	"
N	Intonti Ciriaco	280	laborer	61	"
O	Coviello Carmella †	280	housewife	62	"

38

Maverick Street Continued

P	Coviello Domenic	282	U S A	23	here
R	Coviello Nicola	282	foreman	62	"
S	Vitale Antonetta C †	282	operator	23	"
T	Vital Gemma †	282	housewife	54	"
U	Vitale Joseph	282	barber	55	"
V	Vitale Josephine †	282	stitcher	22	"
W	Vitale Maria F—†	282	"	25	"
X	Vitale Marion †	282	shoeworker	20	"
Y	*Schittino Nellie †	282	housewife	52	"
Z	Schittino Vincent	282	shoeworker	21	"

2065

A	Capezza Alice—†	284	housewife	27	"
B	Capezza Anthony	284	carpenter	28	"
C	Nybert Audrey E †	284	student	20	"
D	Nybert Mabel F—†	284	housewife	46	"
E	Nybert Swen	284	machinist	51	"
F	Assenza Benjamin	284	mechanic	34	"
G	Assenza Phyllis †	284	housewife	34	"
K	Palmieri Enrico	286	shoeworker	33	"
L	Palmieri Lena—†	286	housewife	32	"
M	Palmieri Antonetta †	286	"	35	"
N	Palmieri Frank	286	barber	45	"
O	*Palmieri Joseph	286	retired	82	"
P	DelPo Antonio	286	glazier	52	"
R	*DelPo Caroline †	286	housewife	47	"
S	DelPo Michael	286	marbleworker	48	"
U	Griffin Mary A †	296	housewife	53	"
V	Griffin Patrick J	296	blacksmith	54	"
W	Marruzzi Angelina †	296	housewife	41	"
X	Marruzzi Michael	296	proprietor	41	"
Y	*DiSilvio Carmillo	296	retired	63	"
Z	DiSilvio Domenic	296	clerk	35	"

2066

A	DiSilvio Frank	296	laborer	20	"
B	DiSilvio Joseph	296	U S A	23	"
C	DiSilvio Nina— †	296	at home	33	"
D	Porzio Assunta †	297	housewife	25	"
E	Porzio Louis	297	laborer	27	"
F	Porzio Antonetta †	297	stitcher	20	"
G	Porzio Henrietta—†	297	housewife	50	"
H	Porzio John	297	barber	54	"

Maverick Street Continued

K	Porzio Joseph	297	clerk	24	here
L	Palmieri Luigi	297	shoeworker	42	"
M	Palmieri Rose †	297	housewife	38	"
N	Fasano Carl	298	furrier	30	"
O	Fasano Eleanor †	298	housewife	30	"
P	Fera Caroline †	298	operator	27	"
R*	Fera Frank	298	retired	68	"
S	Fera John	298	machinist	32	"
T*	Fera Mary †	298	housewife	63	"
U	Fiandaca Adeline †	298	"	32	"
V	Fiandaca Pasquale	298	tailor	32	"
W	DeLuca Henry	299	U S A	22	"
X	DeLuca Jennie †	299	housewife	55	"
Y	DeLuca Salvatore	299	U S A	27	"
Z	LaRossa John	299	carpenter	30	"

2067

A	LaRossa Theresa †	299	housewife	26	"
B	Rivoire Concetta †	299	"	56	"
C	Rivoire Lamy	299	printer	58	"
D	Russo Albert	300	U S A	20	"
E	Russo Giuseppe	300	salesman	64	"
F	Russo Susie †	300	housewife	58	"
G	Shubert David	300	welder	27	193 Trenton
H	Shubert Josephine †	300	housewife	29	193 "
K	D'Agostino Irene †	300	at home	23	here
L	D'Agostino Joseph	300	pressman	50	"
M	D'Agostino Josephine †	300	stitcher	21	"
N*	D'Agostino Maria †	300	housewife	65	"
O	Woodford Anna †	301	"	30	"
P	Woodford William	301	chauffeur	31	"
R	Rowan James P	301	U S N	20	"
S	Rowan Mary J †	301	at home	45	"
T	Lombardi Ralph	301	chemist	35	"
U	Lombardi Rose †	301	housewife	31	"
V	Marasca Ferdinand	302	mechanic	37	"
W	Marasca Lucy †	302	housewife	32	"
X*	Marasca Alfred	302	tailor	67	"
Y	Marasca Edith †	302	stitcher	25	"
Z*	Marasca Jennie †	302	housewife	66	"

2068

A	Marasca Joseph	302	diestamper	37	"

Maverick Street Continued

B	Masasca Vincent	302	diestamper	29	here
C	Rapino Phyllis †	302	housewife	27	"
D	Rapino Vincent	302	undertaker	30	"
E	Hale Madeline †	303	operator	26	"
F	Hale Mary †	303	nurse	54	"
G	McCarthy James J	303	longshoreman	38	"
H	McCarthy Johanna †	303	housewife	63	"
K	McCarthy Mary G †	303	saleswoman	27	"
L	Jansen Hilda S †	303	housewife	72	"
M	Mattson Eric	303	foreman	46	"
N	Murdoca Eleanor †	304	housewife	27	"
O	Murdoca Peter	304	electrician	32	"
P	Vigliotta Domenico	304	clerk	27	"
R	Vigliotta Eva †	304	housewife	25	"
S	Murdoca Elizabeth †	304	stitcher	21	"
T	Murdoca Jennie †	304	rubberworker	28	"
U	Murdoca Joseph	304	U S A	26	"
V*	Murdoca Maria †	304	housewife	60	"
W*	Murdoca Vincenzo	304	laborer	66	"
Y	Savino Helen †	306	packer	31	"
Z	Savino Patrick	306	U S A	38	"

2069

A	Savino Yolanda †	306	housewife	29	"
B	Manuele Mario	306	U S A	25	"
C*	Manuele Mary †	306	housewife	59	"
D	Manuele Yolanda †	306	operator	24	"
E	Doyle Margaret †	307	housewife	35	"
F	Doyle Thomas V	307	timekeeper	37	"
G	Nelson Bridget A †	307	at home	72	"
H	Gambale Michelina †	315	housewife	34	"
K	Gambale Nicola	315	laborer	54	"
L	LaRaia Catherine †	315	stitcher	21	"
M*	LaRaia Frances †	315	housewife	54	"
N	LaRaia Vincenzo	315	U S A	24	"
O*	Polcari Caroline †	315	housewife	42	"
P	Polcari Pasquale	315	barber	46	"
R	DiMaro Henry	317	machinist	31	4 Jeffries
S	DiMaro Susie †	317	housewife	22	4 "
T	Wardell Mary †	317	"	30	2 "
U	Wardell Sterling	317	U S A	32	2 "
V	Alberto Giovanna †	319	housewife	41	here

I 20

Maverick Street — Continued

	W	Alberto Matteo	319	laborer	52	here
	X	*Nicolossi Carmello	319	candyworker	64	"
	Y	DeDomenic Joseph	321	U S N	21	"
	Z	DeDomenic Concetta †	321	housewife	47	"

2070

	A	DeDomenico Frank	321	machinist	52	"
	B	D'Agostino Rose †	321	housewife	27	"
	C	D'Agostino Sabatino	321	pressman	26	"
	D	Valardo Antonio	323	bricklayer	55	"
	E	Valardo Gaetano	323	U S A	24	"
	F	Valardo Jennie †	323	stitcher	25	"
	G	*Valardo Mary †	323	housewife	54	"
	H	Valardo Salvatore	323	U S A	23	"

Porter Street

	L	*DeAngelis Carmella †	191	at home	64	here
	M	DeAngelis Helen †	191	clerk	27	"
	N	Indelicato Alfonso	191	longshoreman	32	"
	O	Indelicato Angelina †	191	candymaker	32	"
	P	Arinello Michael	191	operator	31	"
	R	Arinello Philomena †	191	housewife	31	"
	S	Antonelli Elizabeth †	191	"	37	"
	T	*Antonelli James	191	laborer	41	"
	U	Pisani Joseph	191	U S N	23	"
	V	Pisani Virginia †	191	at home	57	"
	W	Magaletta Roberta †	191	housewife	26	"
	X	Magaletta Vito	191	operator	33	"
	Y	Stafferi Donardo	191	laborer	20	"
	Z	Stafferi Philomena †	191	at home	53	"

2071   ## Sumner Street

	A	Curran Bridget †	442	at home	70	here
	B	Santos Hilda †	442	factoryhand	22	"
	C	Santos John	442	steamfitter	32	"
	D	Santos Josephine †	442	housewife	51	"
	E	Jenkins Charles J	442	boilermaker	60	"
	F	Jenkins Elizabeth F †	442	bookkeeper	56	"
	G	Jenkins John S	442	laborer	48	"
	H	Jenkins Mary †	442	housewife	50	"

Page.	Letter.	FULL NAME.	Residence, Jan. 1, 1943.	Occupation.	Supposed Age.	Reported Residence Jan. 1, 1942. Street and Number.

Sumner Street Continued

	K	Welch Charles S	444	clerk	49	here
	L	Welch John F	444	foreman	47	"
	M	Burns Julia F †	444	tel operator	21	"
	N	Burns Mary †	444	attendant	21	"
	O	Hearn Annie †	444	housewife	64	"
	P	Hearn William H	444	secretary	47	"

Venice Street

	S	Vederico Annie †	1	housewife	60	here
	T	Vederico Helen †	1	shoeworker	24	"
	U	Vederico George	1	laborer	29	"
	V	Vederico Theresa †	1	housewife	28	"
	W	Tentindo Louisa †	1	"	23	"
	X	Tentindo Salvatore	1	laborer	25	"
	Y	Miller Alfred	2	machinist	60	"

Ward 1–Precinct 21

CITY OF BOSTON

LIST OF RESIDENTS
20 YEARS OF AGE AND OVER

(NON-CITIZENS INDICATED BY ASTERISK)
(FEMALES INDICATED BY DAGGER)

AS OF

JANUARY 1, 1943

JOSEPH F. TIMILTY, *Chairman*
FREDERIC E. DOWLING, *Secretary*
WILLIAM A. MOTLEY, JR.
FRANCIS B. McKINNEY
EVERETT R. PROUT

Listing Board.

CITY OF BOSTON PRINTING DEPARTMENT

2100

Bremen Street

A*	Amoroso Michael	100	laborer	51	3 Porter
B*	Prisco Stanley	100	finisher	44	here
C	Langone Anthony	102	printer	30	"
D	Langone Winifred—†	102	housewife	26	"
E	Pilcher Emma—†	102	"	21	"
F	Pilcher Stephen	102	laborer	22	"
G	Ferrara Antonette—†	102	housewife	43	"
H	Ferrara Louis	102	mechanic	45	"
K	Ray Evelyn †	104	housewife	27	"
L	Ray Salvatore	104	welder	27	"
M	Cogliano Dominic	104	U S A	24	"
N	Cogliano Frank	104	"	21	"
O	Cogliano Gerardo	104	retired	66	"
P	Cogliano Rita—†	104	housewife	54	"
R*	Jasonna Antonette—†	104	"	65	"
S	Jasonna Attillio	104	bartender	35	"
T	Jasonna Salvatore	104	laborer	68	"
U	Ricupero Arthur	106	salesman	21	"
V	Ricupero Humbert	106	shipper	22	"
W*	Ricupero Lena—†	106	housewife	60	"
X	Ricupero Angelo	106	agent	39	"
Y	Ricupero Barbara—†	106	housewife	39	"
Z	Ruggiero Blanche—†	106	"	23	"

2101

A	Ruggiero Louis	106	laborer	27	"
B	Sepe Carmella †	108	at home	75	"
C*	Maratea Elizabeth †	108	housewife	49	"
D*	Maratea Giacomo	108	laborer	51	"
E	Maratea Susan †	108	candymaker	24	"
F	Maratea Vincent	108	jeweler	27	"
G	Avone Angelina †	108	housewife	51	"
H	Avone Lawrence	108	pressman	53	"
K	Avone Louise †	108	clerk	23	"
	Tavella Frank	110	mechanic	21	148 Bremen
	Nigro Donato	110	candymaker	48	here
	Nigro Mary †	110	housekeeper	50	"
	Mesh Alice †	112	housewife	37	"
	Mesh Louis	112	instructor	39	"
	Chiesa Anastasia †	112	housewife	65	"
	Chiesa Anthony	112	retired	70	"

2

Page.	Letter.	Full Name.	Residence, Jan. 1, 1943	Occupation.	Supposed Age.	Reported Residence, Jan. 1, 1942. Street and Number.

Bremen Street Continued

	u	Chicariello John	112	mechanic	28	here
	v	DeMarco Angelina M †	112	housewife	40	"
	w	DeMarco Nicholas D	112	tailor	41	"
	x	Federico Angelina †	114	housewife	27	"
	y	Federico Joseph	114	U S M C	25	"
	z	Braccia Alfred	114	pressman	32	"

2102

	A	Braccia Josephine †	114	housewife	28	"
	B	*Grillo Angelina †	114	"	56	"
	c	*Grillo Francisco	114	laborer	59	"
	D	Capozzi Pauline †	116	housewife	21	"
	E	Capozzi Tiberio	116	laborer	22	"
	F	Inotti Nicolo	116	retired	73	"
	G	*Inotti Pasqualina †	116	housewife	70	"
	H	Capozzi Alphonse	116	shoeworker	47	"
	K	Capozzi Rose †	116	housewife	45	"
	L	*Cicatelli Joseph	118	operator	62	"
	M	*Cicatelli Rose †	118	housewife	52	"
	N	Cicatelli Louise †	118	clerk	26	"
	O	*Cicatelli Rosario	118	operator	65	"
	P	Bozza Anna †	118	housewife	38	"
	R	Bozza Samuel	118	laborer	38	"
	S	Mamiero Alice †	120	housewife	33	"
	T	Mamiero Fred	120	painter	36	"
	U	Mamiero Frank	120	retired	72	"
	V	Mamiero Marion †	120	housewife	39	"
	W	Mamiero Phillip	120	retired	41	"
	X	Cammarato Baldassare	122	"	71	"
	Y	Cammarato Josephine †	122	housewife	63	"
	z	*Belletti Charles	122	retired	60	"

2103

	A	*Bellitti Crocefissa †	122	housewife	47	"
	B	Bellitti Frank	122	laborer	22	"
	c	Bellitti Gaspar	122	U S N	20	"
	D	Bellitti John	122	U S A	26	"
	E	Lamattina Josephine †	122	housewife	36	"
	F	Lamattina Louis	122	retired	42	"
	G	Lamattina Salvatore	122	welder	21	"
	H	Reggione Antonetta †	124	housewife	42	"
	K	DelGrosso Pasqualina †	124	"	39	"
	L	DelGrosso Pasquale	124	chauffeur	44	"

3

Bremen Street—Continued

M	Accardi Mary—†	124	stitcher	21	66 Chelsea
N	Siciliano Carmela—†	124	"	44	66 "
O	Siciliano Rocco	124	laborer	55	66 "
P	Patti Catherine—†	126	housewife	29	here
R	Patti Joseph	126	barber	30	"
S	DeMarco Angela—†	126	housewife	24	"
T	DeMarco Pasquale	126	fishcutter	27	"
U	*Paolatta Adeline—†	126	housewife	52	"
V	Paolatta Albert	126	printer	22	"
W	Paolatta Antonio	126	laborer	53	"
X	Paolatta Arthur	126	U S A	21	"
Y	Paolatta Mildred—†	126	stitcher	24	"
Z	DiPasquale Angelo	128	tailor	30	"

2104

A	DiPasquale Rosalie—†	128	housewife	31	"
B	DeBlasio Catherine—†	128	"	46	"
C	DeBlasio Louis	128	U S A	23	"
D	DeBlasio Michael	128	polisher	46	"
E	DeBlasio Michael, jr	128	machinist	20	"
F	DeBlasio Samuel	128	U S A	24	"
G	Limoli Josephine—†	128	stitcher	20	116 Bremen
H	Limoli Vincent	128	U S M C	21	65 Salem
K	Tunnera Angelo	130	laborer	35	here
L	Tunnera Jennie—†	130	housewife	34	"
M	DePaulo Anna—†	130	"	32	"
N	DePaulo Louis	130	presser	35	"
O	*DePaulo Theresa—†	130	stitcher	57	"
P	Puopolo Helen—†	130	operator	24	"
R	Puopolo Joseph	130	laborer	57	"
S	*Puopolo Marie—†	130	housewife	57	"
T	Leone Dominic	132	U S A	22	"
U	*Leone Emilia—†	132	housewife	60	"
V	Leone John	132	U S A	23	"
W	*Leone Philip	132	rubberworker	59	"
X	*Scimone James	132	musician	33	"
Y	Scimone Mary—†	132	housewife	33	"
Z	Cecere Antonio	132	retired	59	"

2105

A	*Cecere Elizabeth—†	132	housewife	63	"
B	Cecere Florence—†	132	seamstress	27	"
C	DeMarco Theresa—†	136	housewife	54	"

4

Page.	Letter.	FULL NAME.	Residence, Jan. 1, 1943.	Occupation.	Supposed Age.	Reported Residence, Jan. 1, 1942. Street and Number.

Bremen Street—Continued

D	*Giansiracusa Colegara—†	136	stitcher	51	here
E	Giansiracusa Paolo	136	mason	59	"
F	Giansiracusa Frank	136	machinist	32	"
G	Giansiracusa Mary—†	136	housewife	32	"
H	*Petrelli Rosie—†	138	"	50	"
K	Petrelli Sabino	138	operator	50	"
L	Malta Lawrence	140	floorlayer	32	"
M	Malta Mary—†	140	housewife	36	"
N	Nocito Pauline—†	140	"	32	"
O	Nocito Vincent	140	longshoreman	29	"
P	Collucci Ralph	140	foreman	39	"
R	Collucci Theresa—†	140	housewife	39	"
S	Spelladora John	140	U S A	40	"
T	Testa Costantino	142	tinsmith	61	"
U	Testa Gabriel	142	mechanic	35	"
V	Testa Palmina—†	142	hairdresser	24	"
W	DiPesa Josephine—†	144	housewife	21	96 Chelsea
X	DiPesa Ralph	144	mechanic	27	96 "
Y	Farro Carmella—†	144	stitcher	25	96 "
Z	Barrasso Anthony	144	U S A	23	here
2106					
A	Barrassi Grace—†	144	stitcher	21	"
B	*DeStefano Theresa—†	144	housewife	44	"
C	Palermo Carmella—†	144	"	31	"
D	Palermo Ignazio E	144	tinsmith	29	"
E	*Constantino Angelina—†	146	housewife	55	"
F	Constantino Mary—†	146	operator	28	"
G	Barker Frank	146	freighthandler	28	"
H	Barker Mary—†	146	housewife	25	"
K	Pagliarulo Louis	146	U S N	36	"
L	Pagliarulo Pauline—†	146	housewife	32	"
N	*Maratorana Antonetta—†	148	"	53	"
O	*Maratorana Joseph	148	storekeeper	55	"
P	Dellaia Antonio	148	laborer	53	"
R	*Dellaia Josephine—†	148	housewife	44	"
S	Vetrano Dominic	150	shoeworker	35	"
T	Vetrano Frances—†	150	housewife	34	"
U	Cheffro Rose—†	150	"	32	"
V	Cheffro Sylvester	150	shipfitter	32	"
W	Bellone Antonio	150	baker	30	"
X	Bellone Virginia—†	150	housewife	28	"

5

		Full Name.	Residence, Jan. 1, 1943.	Occupation.	Suppssed Age.	Reported Residence, Jan. 1, 1942. Street and Number.

Bremen Street—Continued

	Full Name.	Residence	Occupation.	Age	Reported Residence
y	*Rossi Armando	152	chef	37	here
z	Rossi Carmelinda—†	152	housewife	34	"
	2107				
a	*Carralbis Antonette—†	152	"	46	"
b	Carralbis Carmen	152	laborer	46	"
c	Storella Alfonso	152	shipfitter	46	"
d	Storella Thomasina—†	152	housewife	40	"
e	Filadoro Louis	154	operator	35	"
f	Filadoro Rose—†	154	housewife	34	"
g	Volta Eleanor—†	154	operator	21	"
h	*Volta Theresa—†	154	housewife	65	"
k	Albanese Josephine—†	156	"	29	"
l	Albanese Louis	156	guard	30	"
m	LaValle Alfred	156	laborer	51	103 Orleans
n	*LaValle Concettina—†	156	housewife	57	103 "
o	Testa Emma—†	156	"	30	here
p	Testa Guy	156	shipfitter	29	"
r	Martino Anna—†	158	housewife	46	"
s	Minichiello Rocco	158	laborer	59	"
t	Stella Anna—†	158	housewife	32	"
u	Stella Joseph	158	steamfitter	37	"
v	Scarpa Frank	158	wrestler	27	"
w	Scarpa Helen—†	158	housewife	24	"
x	Lanetta Martina—†	160	"	30	"
y	Lanetta Stephen	160	machinist	35	"
z	*Barone Sarah—†	160	housekeeper	62	"
	2108				
a	Rizzari Nicholas	160	laborer	48	"
b	*Rizzari Nora—†	160	housewife	42	"
c	*Brunaccini Placido	160	retired	74	"
d	*Morosino Frank	160	"	55	"
e	*DiOrio Anna—†	162	housewife	71	"
f	*DiOrio Antonio	162	retired	77	"
g	Niscosia Angelo	162	"	75	"
h	*Niscosia Jennie—†	162	housewife	60	"
k	Corti Giovanni	162	retired	76	"
	D'Amico Angelina—†	174	housewife	33	"
	Bonchiaro Angelo	174	U S C G	23	"
	Bonchiaro Lena—†	174	packer	27	"
	Bonchiaro Philip	174	laborer	59	"
	Bonchiaro Rose—†	174	housewife	59	"

6

Bremen Street Continued

T	*Frederico Esther †	174	housewife	35	here	
U	Frederico Joseph	174	painter	34	"	
W	*Nutaro Concetta †	190	housekeeper	59	"	
X	Nutaro James	190	printer	21	"	
Y	Meneguzzi Louis	190	shipfitter	36	"	
Z	Meneguzzi Marion †	190	operator	34	"	

2109

B	Napolitano Jennie †	192	housewife	27	75 Lubec	
C	Napolitano Ralph	192	laborer	27	75 "	
D	Amato Mary †	192	housewife	37	New Jersey	
E	Amato William	192	tilesetter	40	"	
F	Ristino Anna †	192	housewife	28	here	
G	Ristino Arthur	192	inspector	28	"	
H	*Cianciarulo Gabriella †	194	housewife	52	"	
K	Cianciarulo Joseph	194	presser	55	"	
L	Cianciarulo Margaret †	194	seamstress	22	"	
M	Cianciarulo Mary †	194	stitcher	28	"	
N	Ciacia Elizabeth †	194	seamstress	26	"	
O	Ciacia Joseph	194	presser	29	"	
P	Fucillo Anthony C	194	U S A	22	"	
R	Fucillo Helen †	194	clerk	21	"	
S	Fucillo Henry M	194	chauffeur	48	"	
T	Fucillo Nancy †	194	housewife	45	"	
U	McDonald Bernard F	196	janitor	31	108 Chelsea	
V	McDonald Celeste †	196	housewife	33	108 "	
W	Margarone Benedict	196	student	20	here	
X	Margarone Henrietta †	196	packer	22	"	
Y	Margarone Mary †	196	housewife	46	"	
Z	Margarone Peter	196	candypacker	47	"	

2110

A	Pascucci Anthony H	196	operator	33	"	
B	Pascucci Matilda †	196	housewife	27	"	
C	Mahoney Donald	198	laborer	24	Somerville	
D	Mahoney Phyllis †	198	housewife	24	"	
E	Gandolfo Frank	198	U S A	27	here	
F	Gandolfo Lena †	198	presser	28	"	
G	Giannasoli Andrew	198	foreman	52	"	
H	Giannasoli Henry	198	U S A	20	"	
K	*Giannasoli Lucy †	198	housewife	50	"	
L	Zambuto Anthony	200	ropemaker	26	"	
M	Zambuto Mary †	200	housewife	25	"	

7

Page	Letter	FULL NAME.	Residence, Jan. 1, 1943	Occupation.	Supposed Age.	Reported Residence, Jan. 1, 1942. Street and Number.

Bremen Street—Continued

	N	LaCava Angelo	200	repairman	26	here
	O	LaCava Victoria †	200	housewife	27	"
	P	LaCava Dominic	200	operator	47	"
	R	LaCava John	200	U S A	22	"
	S	*LaCava Maria †	200	housewife	49	"
	T	LaCava Thomas	200	U S A	20	"
	U	*Faraci Catina †	202	housewife	73	"
	V	Ferro John	202	pressman	30	"
	W	Ferro Mary †	202	stitcher	26	"
	X	Chiango Joseph	202	operator	32	"
	Y	Chiango Rose †	202	housewife	33	"

2111

	A	*Cassara Marie †	204	"	66	157 Chelsea
	B	Cassara Thomas	204	retired	74	157 "
	C	Campochiaro Charles	204	merchant	31	here
	D	*Campochiaro Crosifissa †	204	housewife	58	"
	E	*Campochiaro Joseph	204	retired	61	"
	F	Cannarozzo Joseph	204	laborer	49	"
	G	*Cannarozzo Vincenza †	204	housewife	32	"
	H	Fulginiti Delia †	206	"	27	"
	K	Fulginiti Joseph	206	chauffeur	29	"
	L	Anistasio Salvatore	206	retired	66	"
	M	*Anistasio Vincenza †	206	housewife	62	"
	N	Testa Pauline †	208	stitcher	64	"
	O	Matera Anthony	208	tailor	60	"
	P	Matera Beatrice †	208	housewife	65	"
	R	Matera Americo	208	U S A	25	"
	S	Matera Ann †	208	clerk	22	"
	T	*Alba Agnes †	210	housewife	31	"
	U	Alba James	210	tinsmith	37	"
	V	Magnasco James	210	operator	25	"
	W	Magnasco Lucy †	210	housewife	22	"
	X	Palermo Annie †	210	"	52	"
	Y	Palermo John	210	laborer	57	"
		Palermo Pauline †	210	hairdresser	22	"

2112

		Palermo Vincenza †	210	stitcher	24	"
		Calvaro Angelina †	212	operator	22	"
		Calvaro Antoinetta †	212	housewife	55	"
		Calvaro Thomas	212	laborer	48	"
		DeMarco Antoinette †	212	housewife	44	"

Bremen Street Continued

F	*DeMarino John	212	laborer	52	here
G	*DeMarino Michael	212	"	49	"
H	Ortolano Bernardo	212	U S A	21	"
K	*Ortolano Peter	212	operator	47	"
L	Lasofsky Anthony	214	chauffeur	32	"
M	*Lasofsky Malvina †	214	housewife	56	171 Trenton
N	*Lasofsky Michael	214	laborer	62	171 "
O	DeVito Frank	214	mechanic	29	Revere
P	DeVito Natalie †	214	housewife	30	"
R	Zambella Anna †	214	"	21	here
S	Zambella Robert	214	machinist	23	"
T	Spitaleri Anna †	216	housewife	23	154 Princeton
U	Spitaleri Michael	216	chauffeur	24	154 "
V	Sacco Elaine †	216	housewife	25	here
W	*Sacco Gene	216	carpenter	31	"
X	*Miniscalco Emilia †	216	housewife	53	"
Y	Miniscalco Frank	216	U S A	20	"
Z	Miniscalco Joseph	216	carpenter	58	"

2113

A	Cifuni Angelo	218	fishcutter	27	"
B	Cifuni Lucy †	218	housewife	21	"
C	*Lauria Concetta †	218	housekeeper	74	"
D	Lauria Joseph	218	laborer	31	"
E	Lauria Louise †	218	housewife	26	"
F	Lauria Peter	218	foreman	37	"
G	Messina Concetta †	218	housewife	23	Chelsea
H	Messina Nicholas	218	laborer	25	"
K	Lunetta Grace †	220	housewife	20	255 Marion
L	Lunetta Salvatore	220	repairman	25	17 Cottage
M	Puras Anastasia †	220	housewife	52	here
N	*Puras Bernard	220	candymaker	60	"
O	Puras Josephine †	220	packer	24	"
P	Campagna Edith †	220	"	37	"
R	Campagna Napoleon	220	painter	40	"

Chelsea Street

T	Sorendino Joseph	55	machinist	28	here
U	Sorendino Lucy †	55	housewife	24	"
V	Maragioglio Baldassaro	55	storekeeper	45	"
W	Maragioglio Josephine †	55	housewife	39	"

Chelsea Street—Continued

	Full Name	Res.	Occupation	Age	Reported Residence
x	Albano Grace †	57	housewife	24	92 Bremen
y	Albano Robert	57	mechanic	25	92 "
z	Brosca Anthony	57	laborer	48	here
	2114				
a	*Brosca Maria †	57	housewife	46	"
b	Patti Andrew	57	metalworker	46	101 Orleans
c	*Patti Grace †	57	housewife	42	here
d	Macaluso Rosario	59	carpenter	57	"
e	Russo Charles	59	waiter	34	"
f	Russo Mary †	59	housewife	32	"
g	DiLorenzo Frank	59	longshoreman	35	"
h	DiLorenzo Phyllis †	59	housewife	24	"
k	Macaluso Joseph	59	boilermaker	39	"
l	*Macaluso Salvatore	59	retired	85	"
m	*Macaluso Tina †	59	housewife	81	"
n	Nigro Anthony	61	millworker	22	"
o	Nigro Josephine †	61	housewife	20	"
p	Tassinari Elizabeth †	61	"	59	"
r	Tassinari Mary †	61	stenographer	34	"
s	*Marrone Marion †	61	housewife	53	"
t	Marrone Paul	61	factoryhand	27	"
u	Boitana Loretta †	63	housewife	47	"
v	Boitana Robert	63	storekeeper	47	"
w	Giuffreda Anna †	63	factoryhand	27	"
x	*Giuffreda Antoinetta †	63	housewife	61	"
y	*Giuffreda Mario	63	retired	70	"
z	Theall Delia †	63	at home	72	"
	2115				
a	Teri Anthony	63	laborer	45	"
b	*Teri Mary †	63	housewife	38	"
c	Petrillo Concetta †	65	"	56	"
d	Petrillo Gaetano	65	barber	38	"
e	Petrillo Grace †	65	stitcher	26	"
f	Petrillo Palmerino	65	retired	68	"
g	Petrillo Palmerino	65	U S A	27	"
h	Marco Marion †	65	housewife	65	"
k	Marco Petro A	65	retired	66	"
l	Lorenzo Carolina †	65	factoryhand	34	"
m	Lorenzo Pasquale	65	"	66	"
n	Lanza Rosina †	65	operator	33	"
o	Lanza Tomasino †	65	housewife	59	"

10

Page.	Letter.	Full Name.	Residence, Jan. 1, 1943.	Occupation.	Supposed Age.	Reported Residence, Jan. 1, 1942. Street and Number.

Chelsea Street Continued

	P	LoConti Gertrude H—†	67	housewife	25	here
	R	LoConti Joseph O	67	machinist	29	"
	S	Ianuzzi John	67	laborer	46	"
	T*	Ianuzzi Mary—†	67	housewife	35	"
	U	Erichiello Donato	67	laborer	56	"
	V	Erichiello Filomena—†	67	housewife	37	"
	Y	Maiullo Alvira—†	69	"	35	75 Cottage
	Z*	Maiullo Michael	69	barber	44	75 "
2116						
	A	Mustone Crescenzio	69	laborer	44	here
	B*	Sorendino Carmela—†	69	housewife	60	"
	C	Sorendino Leonardo	69	laborer	60	"
	D	Sorendino Pasquale	69	"	24	"
	E*	Tarzia Mary—†	69	housewife	43	"
	F	Tarzia Pasquale	69	laborer	43	"
	G	Mandarino Frank	71	operator	42	"
	H	Mandarino Susie—†	71	housewife	32	"
	K*	Accomando Lucy—†	71	"	44	"
	L*	DeGeorge Raphio	71	laborer	69	"
	M*	Mustone Marie—†	71	housewife	59	"
	N	Mustone Vincenzo	71	laborer	63	"
	P*	Todaro Lucy—†	73	housewife	30	"
	R	Todaro Phillip	73	millworker	38	"
	S	Lucca Louise—†	73	housewife	28	"
	T*	Lucca Samuel	73	timekeeper	28	"
	U*	Simone Anna—†	73	housewife	30	"
	V	Simone Louis	73	laborer	31	"
	W	Iorio Frances—†	75	housewife	43	"
	X	Iorio Luciano	75	barber	52	"
	Y*	Guerra Catherine—†	75	housewife	70	"
	Z	Guerra Mary—†	75	stitcher	24	"
2117						
	A	Guerra Salvatore	75	U S A	27	"
	B	Guerra Theresa—†	75	stitcher	30	"
	C	Mazzotta Antonio	75	metalworker	52	"
	D*	Mazzotta Catherine—†	75	housewife	47	"
	E	Mazzotta Domenick	75	leatherworker	28	"
	F	Mazzotta Mary—†	75	stitcher	22	"
	G	Mazzotta Stephen	75	U S A	27	"
	K*	D'Addona Raffaelo	79	chef	60	"
	L	Lingovardi Luigi	79	baker	60	188 Benningt'n

11

Chelsea Street—Continued

	FULL NAME.	Res.	Occupation.	Age.	Reported Residence
M	Macrina Annie—†	79	housewife	31	142 Gove
N	Macrina Anthony	79	optical worker	35	142 "
O	Ariello Leonard	81	plumber	35	here
P	Ariello Sadie—†	81	housewife	33	"
R	*Ariello Michael	81	retired	64	"
S	Giordani Maria—†	81	stitcher	28	"
T	Gullo Pantilone	83	laborer	49	"
U	*Gullo Rose—†	83	housewife	43	"
V	*Gioia Andrew	83	painter	62	"
W	Gioia Carmella—†	83	factoryhand	30	"
X	Gioia Eugenia—†	83	cigarmaker	25	"
Y	Gioia James	83	painter	22	"
Z	Gioia Joseph	83	"	26	"

2118

A	*Gioia Mary—†	83	housewife	54	"
B	Zito Angelo	83	chauffeur	49	"
C	Zito Carmella—†	83	housewife	49	"
D	Zito Joseph	83	U S M C	20	"
E	Zito Marie—†	83	at home	23	"
F	Zito Paul	83	chauffeur	26	"
G	Brignolo Cyril	85	electrician	40	78 Chelsea
H	*Brignolo Mary—†	85	housewife	31	78 "
K	Marotta Anna—†	85	"	33	196 Paris
L	Marotta Louis	85	laborer	37	196 "
M	DeStefano Alvira—†	85	housewife	21	130 Bremen
N	DeStefano Vincent	85	inspector	22	144 "
O	Guidaro Leo	85	U S A	24	15 Neptune rd
P	Guidaro Lucy—†	85	housewife	22	130 Bremen
R	Christoforo Assunta—†	87	at home	67	here
S	Pesaturo Margaret—†	87	housewife	40	"
T	Pesaturo Salvatore	87	U S A	20	"
	Pesaturo Vincenzo	87	laborer	48	"
	Cabecino Celeste—†	87	tel operator	22	"
W	Cabecino Constantina—†	87	housewife	46	"
	Cabecino Frank	87	barber	52	"
	Cabecino Frank, jr	87	repairman	20	"
	DePietro Joseph	87	chipper	43	"

2119

	DePietro Margaret—†	87	housewife	35	"
	Terrace Jennie—†	89	"	60	"
	Terrace Vincenzo	89	millworker	60	"

12

Chelsea Street — Continued

D	Ferrara Arthur	89	electrician	31	here
E	Ferrara Anna — †	89	housewife	31	"
F	*Farro Andrew	89	retired	62	"
G	*Farro Rose — †	89	housewife	58	"
H	*Fringuelli Nicholas	91	retired	59	"
K	Cassiraro Baldassaro	91	laborer	52	"
L	Cassiraro Mary — †	91	housewife	44	"
M	*Cravotta Joseph	91	laborer	46	"
N	*Cravotta Rosaria — †	91	housewife	46	"
O	Cravotta Salvatore	91	machinist	22	"
P	*Belengeiro Thomas	rear 91	retired	79	"
R	Grieco Carmella — †	" 91	housewife	34	"
S	Grieco Ercole	" 91	laborer	43	"
U	Bua Frank	95	fishcutter	28	"
V	Bua Lena — †	95	housewife	26	"
W	*Gaudino Anna — †	95	"	48	"
X	*Gaudino Nicholas	95	laborer	59	"
Y	Gaudino Rose — †	95	shoeworker	28	"
Z	Gaudino Steve	95	U S A	22	"

2120

A	Rubino Joseph	95	laborer	49	"
B	Rubino Josephine — †	95	housewife	37	"
D	Smith Benjamin	97	storekeeper	62	"
E	Smith Euncie — †	97	stenographer	21	"
F	Smith Evelyn — †	97	"	23	"
G	Smith Florence — †	97	artist	34	"
H	Arnesano Anthony	97	barber	49	"
K	Arnesano Filomena — †	97	housewife	48	"
L	Arnesano Louis	97	accountant	24	"
N	Cohen Jacob	99	storekeeper	46	"
O	Cohen Jennie — †	99	housewife	48	"
P	Ferrara Domenic	99	laborer	61	"
R	Ferrara Joseph	99	U S A	33	"
S	*Ferrara Josephine — †	99	housewife	63	"
T	Ferrara Salvatore	99	laborer	25	"
U	Ciulla Lucy — †	101	housewife	23	"
V	Ciulla Michael	101	machinist	27	"
W	Spinazzola Christopher	101	operator	20	"
X	Spinazzola Lucy — †	101	stitcher	24	"
Y	*Spinazzola Mary — †	101	housewife	54	"
Z	Conti Frank	101	laborer	24	131 Cottage

2121
Chelsea Street—Continued

	Letter	FULL NAME.	Residence	Occupation	Age	Reported Residence
	A	Conti Theresa †	101	housewife	52	131 Cottage
	B	*Monteleone Emanuel	103	storekeeper	49	here
	C	*Monteleone Mary †	103	housewife	32	"
	D	Orlando Crucia †	103	dressmaker	27	"
	E	*Orlando Maria †	103	housewife	50	"
	F	Orlando Pasquale	103	foreman	23	"
	G	Orlando Peter	103	factoryhand	29	"
	H	Orlando Rose †	103	dressmaker	20	"
	K	*Orlando Simone	103	laborer	58	"
	L	Principe Elvira †	103	dressmaker	21	"
	M	Principe Joseph	103	painter	23	"
	O	Stiebel Benny	105	sexton	61	Lynn
	P	Stiebel Regina †	105	housewife	55	"
	R	Trocano James	107	shoeworker	37	here
	S	Trocano Virginia †	107	housewife	38	"
	T	Gilormini Constantino	107	machinist	48	"
	U	Gilormini Raffaella †	107	housewife	44	"
	V	*Smaldone Mary †	107	"	65	"
	W	Smaldone Rosario	107	carpenter	26	"
	X	Grasso Adeline †	109	housewife	52	"
	Y	*Grasso Patsy	109	foundryman	63	"
	Z	Grasso Vincenzo	109	pedler	47	"

2122

	Letter	FULL NAME.	Residence	Occupation	Age	Reported Residence
	A	Bonura Angelo	109	shoemaker	57	"
	B	Bonura Rose †	109	housewife	44	"
	C	Spataro Jennie †	109	"	33	"
	D	Spataro Philip	109	barber	42	"
	F	Hagstrom Charles	113	seaman	20	"
	G	Hagstrom Oliver	113	boilermaker	47	"
	H	Hagstrom Robert	113	U S A	21	"
	K	Suarez Antoinetta †	113	housewife	36	"
	L	Suarez Joseph	113	machinist	38	"
	M	Wardell James	113	guard	23	"
	N	Lamattina Mary †	113	housewife	37	"
	O	Lamattina Salvatore	113	mattressmaker	49	"
	S	Parziale Filomena †	123	housewife	48	"
	?	Parziale Mary †	123	student	21	"
	?	Mascialli Nichola	123	bookkeeper	65	"
	?	Rosse Dominick	123	chauffeur	55	"
	W	Cardozo Nicola	123	retired	66	"

14

Chelsea Street Continued

x	*Costanza Lena †	123	housewife	43	here
y	Costanza Placido	123	roofer	43	"

2123

A	Infantino Joseph	125	factoryhand	39	"
B	Infantino Mary †	125	housewife	42	"
c	Rosa Theresa †	125	"	68	"
D	Frandaca Charles	125	tailor	24	"
E	Frandaca Gilda †	125	housewife	21	"
G	Natali Gaetano	127	retired	59	"
H	*Pagliuco Lucia †	127	housewife	56	"
K	Pagliuco Simone	127	waiter	65	"
L	Capalupo Maria C †	127	at home	30	"
M	Paglici Maria †	127	stitcher	22	"
x	*Meloni Joseph	129	laborer	75	"
P	LaRosa Benedicto	129	mechanic	20	152 Chelsea
R	*LaRosa Lena †	129	housewife	55	152 "
s	LaRosa Rosario	129	laborer	68	152 "
U	Albizer Albert	131	U S N	20	here
V	Albizer Ignatius	131	laborer	47	"
W	Albizer Theresa †	131	housewife	54	"
X	Cassara Joseph	131	chipper	28	"
Y	Cassara Sarah †	131	housewife	27	"
z	*Aronson Anna †	131	"	68	"

2124

A	*Aranson Zelman	131	laborer	71	"
B	Giannusa Benedetto	133	guard	28	"
c	Giannusa Cecelia †	133	housewife	27	"
D	*DeChristoforo Antonetta †	133	"	54	"
E	DeChristoforo Mary †	133	packer	27	"
F	DeChristoforo Nunzio	133	laborer	58	"
G	Palia Louis	133	"	58	"
H	Martello Antonetta †	133	housewife	30	"
K	*Martello Lazzaro	133	laborer	69	"
L	*Martello Maria †	133	housewife	62	"
M	Martello Michael	133	laborer	30	"
N	Jordan John	135	"	83	173 Chelsea
o	Jordan Mabel H †	135	at home	41	173 "
P	*Yudelman Hannah †	135	housewife	88	here
R	*Yudelman Morris	135	storekeeper	83	"
s	DiFranzio Otino	135	laborer	42	133 Chelsea
T	DiFranzio Theresa †	135	housewife	48	133 "

15

Page.	Letter.	FULL NAME.	Residence. Jan. 1, 1943.	Occupation.	Supposed Age.	Reported Residence, Jan. 1, 1942. Street and Number.

Chelsea Street—Continued

C	Giacobelli Joseph	135	musician	28	133 Chelsea
X	Botte Frank	137	laborer	54	here
W	Botte Josephine—†	137	stitcher	28	"
X	Botte Michael	137	U S N	30	"
Y	Botte Rachael—†	137	housewife	54	"
Z	Botte Ernest	137	laborer	25	"

2125

A	Botte Frank	137	U S A	20	"
B	Botte Matilda—†	137	stitcher	27	"
C	Botte Pearl—†	137	clerk	23	"
D	Botte Salvatore	137	"	22	"
F	Francis Joseph B	139	U S A	22	321 Lexington
G	Francis Phyllis—†	139	housewife	21	here
H	Lalli Anna—†	139	"	45	"
K	Lalli Constantino	139	laborer	54	"
L	DeFusco Albert	139	chauffeur	36	"
M	DeFusco Margaret—†	139	housewife	34	"
N	DiCristoforo Antonio	139	candymaker	36	"
O*	DiCristoforo Lucy—†	139	housewife	38	"
P	Guttel Herbert	141	mechanic	20	"
R	Guttel John	141	U S A	25	"
S*	Guttel Lena—†	141	housewife	48	"
T*	Guttel Louis	141	fitter	53	"
U*	Franko Salvania—†	141	housewife	54	99 London
V	Franko Vincent	141	laborer	53	99 "
W	Mari Arthur	141	mechanic	23	here
X	Mari Frank	141	shipper	50	"
Y	Mari Gloria—†	141	clerk	20	"
Z	Mari Lillian—†	141	housewife	50	"

2126

A*	Maragarone Agrippina—†	143	"	55	194 Bremen
B	Gniggi Helen—†	143	stitcher	22	here
C	Gniggi Joseph	143	laborer	61	"
D	Gniggi Julia—†	143	packer	20	"
E*	Gniggi Louise—†	143	housewife	50	"
F	DeSouza Aderito	143	laborer	43	"
G	DeSouza Mary—†	143	housewife	49	"
H	DeSouza Mary—†	143	spinner	21	"
K	Ciampa Angelo	145	chauffeur	22	Saugus
L	Spolsino Frank	145	barber	53	here
M*	Spolsino Philomena—†	145	housewife	49	"

16

Chelsea Street Continued

X	Lavine Edith †	145	housewife	70	here	
O	*Potcheokoff Jennie †	145	"	72	"	
P	Potcheokoff Joseph H	145	chauffeur	66	"	
R	Stassano Anthony	147	laborer	50	"	
S	Stassano Dorothy †	147	packer	20	"	
T	Stassano Joseph	147	laborer	30	"	
U	Stassano Michael	147	U S A	25	"	
V	Stassano Nicholas	147	laborer	23	"	
W	Stassano Nora †	147	housewife	33	"	
X	Stassano Vito	147	plumber	35	"	
Y	DeGregorio Carmella †	147	housewife	34	136 Havre	
Z	DeGregorio Joseph	147	laborer	35	136 "	

2127

A	Ciaburri Joseph	149	"	49	here	
B	Ciaburri Teresa †	149	housewife	37	"	
C	Esposito Loretta †	149	"	40	"	
D	*Esposito Salvatore	149	storekeeper	50	"	
E	Galeota Vito J	149	U S N	20	"	
F	Brattaniti Gertrude †	149	housewife	50	"	
G	Brattaniti Joseph	149	laborer	50	"	
H	Caruso Angelo	151	"	63	"	
K	Caruso Frances †	151	packer	22	"	
L	*Caruso Margaret †	151	housewife	55	"	
M	Caruso Teniro	151	laborer	30	"	
N	*Cacceviallo Esther †	151	housewife	54	"	
O	*Cacceviallo Michael	151	laborer	67	"	
P	Cacceviallo Michael	151	U S A	21	"	
R	Cacceviallo Susan †	151	packer	23	"	
S	Cacceviallo Theresa †	151	"	24	"	
T	Silvestri Albert	151	brazier	21	"	
U	Silvestri Anthony	151	laborer	67	"	
V	*Silvestri Mary †	151	housewife	63	"	
W	Cipriano Amando	153	U S A	25	"	
X	Cipriano Annette †	153	factoryhand	23	"	
Y	*Cipriano Michelina †	153	housewife	47	"	
Z	*Cipriano Nicholas	153	laborer	55	"	

2128

A	Cipriano Phillip	153	clerk	27	"	
B	Cipriano Sylvia †	153	at home	21	"	
C	Durante Emily †	155	housewife	32	"	
D	Durante Pasquale	155	mechanic	29	"	

1—21

17

Chelsea Street — Continued

E	*DeStasi Frances — †	155	housewife	33	38 Frankfort
F	DeStasi Luca	155	laborer	45	38 "
G	Durante Angie †	155	factoryhand	20	here
H	Durante Marco	155	laborer	49	"
K	*Durante Theresa — †	155	housewife	45	"
L	Bossi Dominic	157	U S A	23	"
M	Bossi Frank	157	laborer	57	154 Chelsea
N	*Bossi Maria A †	157	housewife	57	154 "
O	*Indingaro Caroline — †	157	"	70	here
P	Indingaro James	157	U S A	37	"
R	Indingaro Prisco	157	guard	43	"
S	DiGiuleo Anthony	157	U S A	27	"
T	*DiGiuleo Michael	157	laborer	60	"
U	DiGiuleo Michael	157	"	20	"
V	*DiGiuleo Rosaria — †	157	housewife	50	"
W	DiGiuleo Yolanda †	157	operator	25	"
X	*Weinberg Abraham	159	salesman	44	"
Y	*Weinberg Katie †	159	housewife	41	"
Z	*Kaplan Ethel †	159	"	51	"

2129

A	*Kaplan Max	159	chauffeur	60	"
B	Clayman Freda †	159	at home	22	"
C	Clayman Harry	159	laborer	73	"
D	*Clayman Jennie — †	159	housewife	52	"
E	Privitera Charles	161	laborer	58	"
F	*Privitera Josephine †	161	housewife	53	"
G	Privitera Santo	161	laborer	20	"
H	*Arkan David	161	"	66	"
K	*Mendel Minnie †	161	housewife	55	"
L	Pitari Catherine †	161	"	57	"
M	Pitari Gabriel	161	retired	66	"
N	Pitari Nicolas G	161	shipfitter	24	"
O	Boncore Angelo	163	laborer	82	"
P	Boncore Catherine †	163	housewife	71	"
R	Boncore Joseph	163	tailor	29	"
S	Mancuso Joseph	163	laborer	50	"
T	Mancuso Phyllis †	163	housewife	35	"
U	Boncore Guy	163	tailor	32	"
V	Boncore Josephine †	163	housewife	31	"
W	Pitari Catherine †	163	"	52	"
X	Pitari Gabriel	163	laborer	60	"

18

Chelsea Street (Continued)

	Y	Pitari Nicholas	163	mechanic	23	here
		2130				
	A	Manuel Eva †	165	housewife	32	"
	B	Manuel Frank	165	druggist	35	"
	C*	Gambardello Carmella †	165	housewife	49	"
	D	Gambardello Mary †	165	factoryhand	21	"
	E	Gambardello William	165	chef	53	"
	F*	Giachetti Joseph	165	laborer	41	"
	H	Yorks Abraham	167	plumber	61	"
	K	Yorks Rose †	167	housewife	61	"
	M	Anzalone Anthony	169	electrician	27	"
	N	Anzalone Benedetta †	169	housewife	45	"
	O	Anzalone Carmela †	169	"	23	"
	P	Cammarata Antonetta †	169	"	31	"
	R	Cammarata Charles	169	baker	33	"
	T	Previte Antonio	171	laborer	51	"
	U	Previte Dominic	171	shipfitter	24	"
	V	Previte Peter	171	U S A	20	"
	W	Previte Sarah †	171	housewife	48	"
	X	Emma Charles	171	candymaker	50	"
	Y*	Emma Lucy †	171	housewife	39	"
	Z*	Viola Mary †	171	"	66	"
		2131				
	B	Maze George L	173	pipefitter	37	401 Meridian
	C	Maze Thelma E †	173	housewife	34	401 "
	F	Cannella Alphonsus	175	laborer	66	here
	G*	Cannella Antonetta †	175	housewife	57	"
	H	Cannella Salvatore	175	laborer	20	"
	K*	Faraci Phyllis †	175	housewife	53	242 Paris
	L	Faraci Stella †	175	at home	21	242 "
	M	Tracia Anthony	175	pipefitter	32	here
	N	Tracia Camella †	175	housewife	26	"
	O*	Lee Tom	177	laundryman	60	"
	P*	Eremka Catherine †	177	housewife	60	"
	R	Eremka John	177	laborer	60	"
	S	Vozzella Raffaele	177	"	45	"
	T*	Marquad Matilda †	177	housewife	36	"
	U*	Marquad Michael	177	shoemaker	40	"
	W	Rece Lillian †	179	stenographer	32	"
	X	Wood Frederick	179	waiter	46	"
	Y	Wood Margaret †	179	housewife	79	"

19

Chelsea Street—Continued

z	*Eruzione Concetta— †	179	housewife	55	here	
2132						
A	Eruzione Eugene	179	U S A	22	"	
B	*Eruzione Michael	179	laborer	58	"	
C	Eruzione Phyllis— †	179	packer	26	"	
D	Eruzione Vincent	179	U S A	24	"	
E	Flynn John J	181	laborer	37	"	
F	O'Connell Clara †	181	at home	49	"	
G	*Cohen Bessie †	181	housewife	63	"	
H	Cohen Celia †	181	"	34	"	
K	Cohen Jacob	181	printer	39	"	
L	Mangone Anna— †	181	housewife	35	190 Paris	
M	Mangone Michael	181	laborer	37	190 "	
P	Ginensky Jacob H	183	storekeeper	57	278 E Eagle	
R	Ginensky Lena— †	183	housewife	57	278 "	
S	Kaplan Nellie— †	183	"	58	278 "	
T	Lamoly Catherine— †	185	"	29	here	
V	Lamoly Joseph	185	painter	28	"	
W	DiGregorio Felice— †	185	housewife	49	"	
X	*DiGregorio Frank	185	laborer	67	"	
2133						
A	Cardinale Carmine	187	"	50	"	
B	Cardinale Catherine— †	187	at home	20	"	
C	Cardinale Philomena— †	187	housewife	51	"	
D	*Cipriano Frances— †	189	"	79	"	
E	Cipriano Salvatore	189	laborer	82	"	
F	*Tripodi Joseph	189	"	76	"	
G	*Tripodi Theresa †	189	housewife	54	"	
H	*Silva Manuel	189	laborer	59	"	
K	*Silva Mary †	189	housewife	56	"	
L	LaGrasse Elizabeth †	191	"	42	225 London	
M	Hafey Albert	191	laborer	22	149 Marion	
N	Hafey Joseph	191	U S A	29	here	
O	Hafey Mabel †	191	housewife	49	149 Marion	
P	Hafey Paul	191	U S A	24	here	
R	Hafey Virginia †	191	packer	21	149 Marion	
T	*Bellitti Catherine †	193	housewife	43	7 Chelsea pl	
U	*Bellitti Joseph	193	laborer	58	7 "	
V	Bellitti Mario	193	"	27	7 "	
W	Powers Josephine †	193	housewife	24	7 "	
X	Antileano Julia †	193	factoryhand	25	69 Chelsea	

Chelsea Street Continued

y	*Autilitano Peter	193	laborer	60	69 Chelsea
z	*Autilitano Vincenza †	193	housewife	54	69 "
2134					
A	Cohen Isidore A	195	storekeeper	55	here
B	Cohen Tillie †	195	housewife	54	"

Cottage Street

C	Atavilla John	114	blueprints	30	here
D	Atavilla Olympia †	114	housewife	54	"
E	Atavilla Ralph	114	barber	59	"
F	Rizzutti Pasquale	114	U S A	22	"
G	Somma John	114	"	28	"
H	*Somma Ralph	114	laborer	59	"
K	*Somma Rose †	114	housewife	59	"
L	Fondini Angelo	114	casing maker	27	"
M	Fondini Concetta †	114	housewife	25	"
N	*Rizzutti Domenic	114	chauffeur	29	"
O	Rizzutti Sarah †	114	housewife	30	"
P	Gulla Mary †	114	"	31	"
R	Gulla William	114	blacksmith	31	"
S	Milano Antonio	114	machinist	26	"
T	Milano Calogero	114	retired	64	"
U	Milano Mary †	114	housewife	64	"

Frankfort Street

Y	Guglielmo Mary †	12	housewife	33	150 Bremen
Z	Guglielmo Pasquale	12	U S A	38	150 "
2135					
A	Venezia Armando	12	laborer	20	here
B	Venezia Margaret †	12	housewife	58	81 Cottage
C	Venezia Michael A	12	retired	68	81 "
D	*Stellato Elena †	14	housewife	40	here
E	*D'Amico Betty †	14	"	39	"
F	*D'Amico Gaetano	14	laborer	41	"
G	Narda Anna †	15	housewife	65	"
H	Narda Francisco	15	retired	70	"
K	Bartoli Edith †	15	housewife	27	"
L	Bartoli Joseph G	15	pedler	29	"
M	Brunetta Antonetta †	15	dressmaker	21	"

21

Frankfort Street—Continued

N	Brunetta Antonia †	15	housewife	58	here
O*	Brunetta Antonio	15	laborer	58	"
P	Brunetta B William	15	U S A	24	"
R	Giacchetti Jennie †	15	housekeeper	35	"
S	Mosca Alfred	15	longshoreman	25	"
T	Mosca Josephine †	15	housewife	22	"
U	Gioiosa Antonio	16	laborer	57	"
V	Gioiosa Daniel	16	"	31	"
W*	Gioiosa Mary †	16	housewife	55	"
X	Mitriano Jennie †	16	"	24	"
Y	Mitriano Joseph	16	U S A	26	"
Z	Sergi Gaetano	16	salesman	27	"

2136

A	Sergi Patricia †	16	housewife	27	"
B	Prisco Alfonso	16	chauffeur	57	"
C	Liberatore Louis	16	shipwright	25	"
D	Liberatore Mary †	16	saleswoman	26	"
E*	Liberatore Restituta †	16	housewife	54	"
F	Albo Christoforo	16	tailor	65	"
G	Durante John	17	inspector	26	"
H	Durante Mary †	17	housewife	24	"
K	Durante Eugene	17	laborer	54	"
L	Durante Theresa †	17	housewife	59	"
M	Prieno George	17	U S A	24	"
N	Prieno Nancy †	17	housewife	22	"
O	Tomaro Michael	17	laborer	64	"
P	Martarocca Cecil	17	"	32	"
R	Martarocca Elvira †	17	housewife	25	"
S	Cieri Domenic	18	laborer	34	"
T	Cieri Theresa †	18	housewife	24	"
U	Braccia Joseph	18	janitor	35	30 Boston
V	Braccia Valentina †	18	housewife	30	30 "
W	Milano Catherine †	18	"	45	here
X	Milano Philip	18	carpenter	47	"
Y	Carr Emile	19	tailor	82	"
Z	Carr Martha †	19	clerk	46	"

2137

A	Carr Martha †	19	"	46	"
B	DePasi Amilia †	19	housewife	27	"
C	DePasi Frank	19	machinist	32	"
D	DeFilmore Ambrose	19	U S A	21	"

22

Frankfort Street Continued

E	DeFlumere Anna †	19	housewife	44	here
F	DeFlumere Anthony	19	lineman	49	"
G	DeFlumere Louise †	19	operator	22	"
H	Leone David	20	U S A	22	"
K	Leone Yolanda †	20	housewife	21	"
M	Stergois James	20	machinist	41	"
N	Stergois Rose †	20	housewife	33	"
O	D'Amico Madalena †	20	"	44	"
P	D'Amico Vincenza	20	confectioner	52	"
R	LoColzo Antonio	20	laborer	50	"
S*	LoColzo Carmella †	20	housewife	40	"
T	Capo Anthony	20	laborer	33	"
U	Capo Louise †	20	housewife	29	"
V*	Marini Anna †	24	housekeeper	79	"
W	Giustina Margaret †	24	housewife	34	"
X	Giustina Victor	24	laborer	36	"
Y	Fatalo Anthony	24	"	28	"
Z	Fatalo Sarah †	24	housewife	24	"

2138

A	Giambrone Anthony	24	shoeworker	31	"
B	Giambrone Jennie †	24	housewife	29	"
C	Gioditta Adeline †	24	"	32	"
D	Gioditta Frank	24	shoeworker	32	"
E	Magliano Rose †	24	"	34	"
F	Mattaroccia Vito	24	laborer	24	"
G	Parisi Joseph	26	metalworker	30	"
H	Parisi Rocco	26	"	28	"
K	Sollitto Margaret †	26	housewife	58	"
L	Carnivalle Anthony	26	chauffeur	30	"
M	Carnivalle Irene †	26	housewife	32	"
N	Ziccone Frances †	26	"	57	"
O	Ziccone John B	26	retired	71	"
P*	Lacorazza Anna †	26	housewife	67	214 Bremen
R	Lacorazza Filomena †	26	assembler	29	214 "
S*	Lacorazza Frank	26	repairman	62	214 "
T	Maglione Frank	26	painter	33	12 Henry
U	Maglione Josephine †	26	housewife	34	12 "
W*	DeBerto Concetta †	32	clerk	34	here
X*	DeBerto Erminia †	32	housekeeper	60	"
Y	Vaccari Columbia †	32	packer	37	214 Bremen
Z	Vaccari Lena †	32	assembler	34	214 "

23

2139
Frankfort Street—Continued

A White Francis	32	inspector	28	here
B White Gilda †	32	housewife	27	"
C Ferzani Anna †	32	"	66	"
D Ferzani Joseph	32	tailor	67	"
E *Meluzzo Marina †	32	housekeeper	33	"
F *Fiore Josephine †	34	housewife	50	"
G *Fiore Vincenzo	34	laborer	56	"
H *Rainone Andrea	34	retired	74	"
K Velardo Clementina †	34	housewife	42	"
L Velardo Domenic	34	laborer	45	"
M *D'Alessandro Angelina †	34	housekeeper	55	"
N D'Alessandro Ricco	34	laborer	30	"
O Venezia Marguerita †	34	housewife	21	"
P Venezia Ralph	34	chauffeur	22	"
R *Cimino Antonetta †	36	housewife	67	"
S *Cimino Simione	36	laborer	59	"
T Muscato Angelo	36	"	35	59 Lubec
U Muscato Rose †	36	housewife	30	59 "
V *Ciullo Angelina †	36	"	56	here
W Ciullo Genaro	36	retired	72	"
X Ciullo George	36	U S A	28	"
Y Ciullo Ralph	36	laborer	22	"
Z Gueli Helen †	36	housewife	23	"

2140

A Gueli Joseph	36	operator	25	"
B Sestito Buonaventure	36	laborer	48	"
C Sestito Mary †	36	housewife	52	"
D Ciofli Anthony	36	painter	25	"
E Ciofli Mary †	36	housewife	23	"
F Filipone Antonio	38	laborer	61	"
G Filipone Benjamin	38	student	21	"
H Filipone Theresa †	38	housewife	44	"
K Rosette Mary A †	38	laundress	55	"
L Silvestra Joseph	38	laborer	45	"
M Silvestra Louisa †	38	housewife	42	"
N Buonanno Anne †	38	"	62	"
O Buonanno Nicolo	38	laborer	65	"
P Oliva Gilda †	38	housewife	20	"
R Oliva Samuel	38	U S A	20	"
S Casetto Lena †	38	housewife	23	"

24

Frankfort Street Continued

T	Casetta Vincent	38	U S A	29	here	
U	Colangelo Alfred	40	"	24	"	
V	*Colangelo Carmella †	40	housewife	41	"	
W	Colangelo Leonard	40	blacksmith	50	"	
X	Colangelo Mary †	40	candyworker	21	"	
Y	Colangelo Nicholas	40	laborer	25	"	
Z	*Dundonato Mary †	40	housekeeper	68	"	

2141

B	Schettino Dorothy †	40	housewife	28	"	
C	Schettino Nicolo	40	laborer	31	"	
D	*Sturniolo Mary †	40	housekeeper	65	"	
E	Catina Carmella †	42	housewife	36	"	
F	Catina Cresenzo	42	laborer	47	"	
G	*LaTerzia Theresa †	42	housekeeper	69	"	
H	*D'Amico Anna R †	42	"	56	"	
K	D'Amico Gennaro	42	laborer	24	"	
L	DiGiacomandrea Carmine	42	"	44	"	
M	DiGiacomandrea Elvira †	42	housewife	33	"	
N	Lavagno Maria †	42	"	58	"	
O	Lavagno Michael	42	laborer	62	"	
P	Piro Vincent	42	"	31	"	
R	Cafarelli Mary †	44	housewife	31	"	
S	Cafarelli Romeo	44	electrician	34	"	
T	Ranieri Alfred	44	U S A	20	"	
U	Ranieri Concetta †	44	housewife	52	"	
V	Ranieri Gina †	44	boxmaker	24	"	
W	Ranieri Tito	44	laborer	57	"	
X	Olivolo Jerry G	44	painter	25	Revere	
Y	Olivolo Lucretia †	44	housewife	22	"	
Z	Ranieri Helen F †	44	"	26	here	

2142

A	Ranieri Oscar	44	machinist	29	"	
B	Zinna Joseph	44	rigger	32	"	
C	Zinna Theresa †	44	housewife	24	"	
D	Barry Helena †	48	teacher	42	"	
E	Corcoran Margaret M †	48	"	51	"	
F	Cunningham Martha †	48	"	35	"	
G	*Driscoll Julia A †	48	housekeeper	39	"	
H	Duffy Bridget †	48	teacher	47	"	
K	*Dunning Mary †	48	"	26	"	
L	Harrington Kathleen †	48	"	36	"	

Frankfort Street—Continued

M	*Murray Margaret—†	48	teacher	32	here
N	O'Donohue Nora—†	48	"	47	"
O	Paone Albina—†	48	"	43	"
P	*Ryan Mary J—†	48	"	21	"
R	Yennock Molly—†	48	"	49	"
T	Consalvo Dora—†	56	housewife	30	"
U	Consalvo Victor	56	laborer	35	"
V	Luongo Carmella—†	56	housekeeper	44	"
W	D'Amboris Severio	56	retired	79	"
X	Zerolla Mary—†	56	housewife	39	"
Y	Zerolla Michael	56	laborer	41	"

2143

A	Salvato Amadeo	56	"	55	"
B	Salvato Josephine—†	56	housewife	48	"
C	Salvato Marie—†	56	at home	21	"
D	Palombi Marion—†	56	housewife	24	"
E	Palombi Paul	56	musician	28	"
F	*Francese Maria—†	58	housekeeper	60	"
G	Cardinale Joseph	58	laborer	32	"
H	Cardinale Mary—†	58	housewife	28	"
K	Russo Antonio	58	laborer	39	"
L	Russo Julia—†	58	housewife	33	"
M	*Russo Maria—†	58	housekeeper	70	"
N	*Pasqualina Marie—†	58	"	58	"
P	DiLorenzo Edward	60	clerk	31	176 Gove
R	DiLorenzo Kathleen—†	60	housewife	22	176 "
S	Avola Alexander	60	shoeworker	29	here
T	Avola Edith—†	60	housewife	29	"
U	Leto Rose—†	60	"	23	"
W	Leto Vincent	60	laborer	25	"
X	*Tedesco Filomena—†	60	housewife	60	"
Y	Tedesco Joseph	60	laborer	65	"
Z	Jannuzzi Mary—†	62	housewife	32	"

2144

A	Jannuzzi Veto	62	bottler	35	"
B	Ciardini Biagi	62	laborer	63	"
C	Raia Camile—†	62	housewife	26	"
D	Raia Matthew	62	laborer	25	"
E	Porcella Constanza—†	62	housewife	48	"
F	Porcella Vincent	62	laborer	50	"

26

Page.	Letter.	FULL NAME.	Residence, Jan. 1, 1943.	Occupation.	Supposed Age.	Reported Residence, Jan. 1, 1942. Street and Number.

Frankfort Street Continued

G	Simole Joseph	62	operator	24	here
H	Simole Mary—†	62	housewife	23	"
K	Vellani Anita †	62	stitcher	22	"
L	Vellani Maria—†	62	housekeeper	42	"
M	Alterio Elisa—†	63	housewife	60	"
N	Alterio Lucy—†	63	operator	24	"
O	Alterio Pasquale	63	baker	55	"
P	Ciampa Mary—†	63	housewife	34	"
R	Ciampa Ralph	63	painter	43	"
S	Ceruolo Angelina—†	63	housewife	28	"
T	Ceruolo Louis	63	assembler	25	"
U	Grillo Anna—†	63	housewife	30	"
V	Grillo John	63	laborer	42	"
W	Zirrelli Paul	63	"	65	"
X	Zirrelli Rafaela—†	63	housewife	46	"
Y	Ruggiero James C	64	salesman	43	"
Z	Ruggiero Josephine—†	64	housewife	39	"
	2145				
A	Jorda Herrico	64	welder	58	"
B	Jorda Rose—†	64	housewife	57	"
C	*Grifone Filomena—†	64	"	39	"
D	Grifone Michael	64	repairman	43	"
E	Famiglietti Antonio	64	laborer	26	49 Everett
F	Famiglietti Joseph	64	retired	52	49 "
G	*Famiglietti Mary—†	64	housewife	54	49 "
H	Cafazzo Antonio	64	laborer	50	here
K	Cafazzo Maria—†	64	housewife	44	"
L	Aulino Salvatore	65	finisher	36	"
M	*Aulino Theresa—†	65	housekeeper	60	"
N	Aulino Theresa †	65	housewife	33	"
O	Fiore Madeline—†	65	"	26	"
P	Fiore Salvatore	65	packer	24	"
R	*Schettino Antonio	65	rubberworker	55	"
S	*Schettino Vincenzo—†	65	housewife	50	"
T	Bartolo Anna †	65	"	40	"
U	Bartolo Joseph	65	laborer	43	"
V	Bartolo Marie—†	65	stenographer	20	"
W	Gangi John	65	cabinetmaker	49	"
X	Gangi Phyllis—†	65	housewife	39	"
Y	*Barrese Erminia—†	66	"	61	"

		Residence, Jan. 1, 1943.		Occupation.		Supposed Age.	Reported Residence, Jan. 1, 1942.
	Full Name.						Street and Number.

Frankfort Street—Continued

z	Minichiello Pasquale	66	laborer	53	here	
	2146					
a	Minichiello Rosina—†	66	housewife	53	"	
b	*Ricatti Lucy—†	66	"	67	"	
c	Ricatti Vincenza—†	66	candyworker	29	"	
d	*Dichio Antonetta—†	68	housewife	45	"	
e	Dichio Lucy—†	66	candyworker	23	"	
f	Dichio Pasquale	66	U S A	20	"	
g	*Pelosi Raffaela—†	66	housewife	48	"	
h	Pelosi Raffaele	66	laborer	55	"	
k	*LoConte Angelina—†	66	housewife	36	"	
l	LoConte Federico	66	pressman	36	"	
m	LoConte Raffaele	66	laborer	45	"	
n	Ventri Adeline—†	67	housewife	31	"	
o	*Ventri Crescenzo	67	blindmaker	43	"	
p	Visconte Rose—†	67	housewife	22	92 Marginal	
r	Visconte Veto	67	laborer	30	92 "	
s	Crisafulli Justin	67	U S A	24	here	
t	Crisafulli Thelma—†	67	housewife	22	"	
u	Sereneo Cornelia—†	67	"	21	"	
v	Sereneo Thomas, jr	67	U S N	24	"	
w	*Amore Asunta—†	67	housewife	59	"	
x	*Amore Mateo	67	laborer	59	"	
y	Ruggiero Rose—†	67	housewife	23	"	
z	Ruggiero Salvatore	67	longshoreman	29	"	
	2147					
a	*Annese Emilia—†	68	housewife	35	"	
b	Annese Joseph	68	laborer	34	"	
c	Matta Carmella—†	68	housewife	57	"	
d	Matta Nicholas	68	U S A	27	"	
e	Matta Sabino	68	laborer	58	"	
f	DiChiara Josephine—†	68	housewife	37	"	
g	DiChiara Thomas	68	laborer	39	"	
h	Bucci Albert	68	U S A	20	"	
k	Bucci Antonio	68	shipper	55	"	
l	Bucci Arualdo	68	boilermaker	24	"	
m	Bucci Frank	68	"	21	"	
n	Bucci Maria—†	68	housewife	56	"	
o	Cappelizzo Augustino	68	laborer	44	"	
p	Cappelizzo Raffaela—†	68	housewife	46	"	
r	Monterichi Madeline—†	68	at home	56	"	

28

Page.	Letter	Full Name.	Residence, Jan. 1, 1943.	Occupation.	Supposed Age.	Reported Residence, Jan. 1, 1942. Street and Number.

Frankfort Street Continued

s	Putignano Domenic	69	tailor	58	here
t	*Putignano Lucy—†	69	housewife	48	"
u	*Trunfio Jean—†	69	"	22	"
v	Trunfio Vincent	69	electrician	23	372 Sumner
w	Bucci Delia—†	69	stitcher	40	here
x	Bucci Ovidio	69	cabinetmaker	44	"
y	Rizza Jennie—†	69	housewife	28	"
z	Rizza Joseph	69	laborer	35	"
	2148				
a	Straccia Ferdinando	69	retired	67	"
b	Tamborino Asunta—†	69	housewife	26	"
c	Tamborino Gino	69	laborer	27	"
d	*Faretra Felica—†	70	housewife	54	"
e	Faretra Nicola	70	retired	68	"
f	Leandro Giuseppe	70	laborer	51	"
g	*Leandro Immacolata—†	70	housewife	38	"
h	Leandro Sabina—†	70	clerk	20	"
k	Annese Antonetta—†	70	housewife	38	"
l	Annese Antonio	70	laborer	48	"
m	Schena Antonio	70	"	50	"
n	*Schena Rose—†	70	housewife	47	"
o	Gasbarro Arthur	70	U S A	22	"
p	Gasbarro Domenico	70	finisher	55	"
r	Gasbarro Eleanor—†	70	stenographer	20	"
s	Gasbarro Rubina—†	70	housewife	50	"
t	Petrillo Domenic	70	rubberworker	24	"
u	Petrillo Frank	70	laborer	58	"
v	Petrillo Louise—†	70	secretary	20	"
w	*Petrillo Rose—†	70	housewife	57	"
x	Mootrey Angelina—†	71	"	33	"
y	Mootrey James	71	presser	36	"
z	Simonelli Angelo	71	guard	63	"
	2149				
a	Simonelli Louise—†	71	operator	21	"
b	Simonelli Rafaela—†	71	housewife	56	"
c	*Casa Francesca—†	72	at home	56	"
d	Clericuzio Luigi	72	laborer	57	"
e	*Terrino Clementina—†	72	at home	79	"
f	*Terrino Vincenzo	72	retired	73	"
g	Amendola Alfred	72	operator	26	156 Webster
h	Amendola Elvira—†	72	housewife	28	156 "

29

Frankfort Street—Continued

K	Dellacroce Amelia—†	72	housewife	48	here	
L	Dellacroce Jerry	72	shoeworker	51	"	
M	Celone Leila—†	72	housewife	22	"	
N	Celone Stephen	72	machinist	28	"	
O	Napolitano Antonetta—†	72	housewife	46	58 Frankfort	
P	Napolitano Francesco	72	bricklayer	46	58 "	
R	Ruggiero Frances—†	74	housewife	63	here	
S	Ruggiero Genaro	74	U S A	38	"	
T	Ruggiero John	74	laundryman	23	"	
U	Ruggiero Frederick	74	shipper	36	"	
V	Ruggiero Helen—†	74	housewife	28	"	
W	Ruggiero Lucy—†	74	packer	28	"	
X	*Datoli Bella—†	74	housewife	42	"	
Y	Datoli Giovanni	74	operator	42	"	
Z	Ruggiero Carmen	74	laundryman	33	"	

2150

A	Ruggiero Josephine—†	74	housewife	31	"	
B	Aloisi Mary—†	74	"	34	"	
C	Aloisi Salvatore	74	storekeeper	44	"	
D	Catena Michael	76	retired	67	"	
E	Piscitelli Angela—†	76	housewife	28	"	
F	Piscitelli Michael	76	laborer	36	"	
G	Colarusso Edward J	76	machinist	27	"	
H	Colarusso Marie L—†	76	housewife	23	"	
K	Matta Adeline—†	76	"	47	"	
L	Matta Alfonse	76	coremaker	49	"	
M	Matta Carmen	76	U S A	22	"	
N	Gaeta Mario	76	cutter	25	291 Sumner	
O	Gaeta Rose—†	76	housewife	20	222 E Eagle	
P	DiGianni Antonio M	76	carpenter	46	here	
R	DiGianni Nancy C—†	76	student	22	"	
S	DiGianni Rosalie—†	76	housewife	47	"	
T	Stella Anna—†	78	"	33	"	
U	Stella Gaetano	78	laborer	44	"	
V	Cafano Cosimo	78	U S A	27	"	
W	Cafano Mary—†	78	housewife	45	"	
X	Cafano Peter	78	machinist	21	"	
Y	Basilesco Potenza	78	tailor	45	"	
Z	Pantuosco Palma—†	78	housewife	69	"	

2151

A	Pantuosco Pio	78	retired	72	"	

30

Frankfort Street Continued

B	Landano Mary †	78	housewife	31	here
C	Landano Michael	78	machinist	30	"
D	Scialabba Anthony	78	engineer	31	"
E	Scialabba Joseph	78	clerk	26	"
F	Scialabba Josephine †	78	housewife	25	"
G	Faiella Lucy †	78	"	21	"
H	Polsonetti Gus	80	operator	24	"
K	Polsonetti Rita †	80	housewife	24	"
L	Nigro Filomena †	80	"	28	"
M	Nigro Frank	80	shoeworker	36	"
N	Murano Antonio	80	laborer	62	"
O*	Murano Assunta †	80	housewife	59	"
P	Murano Biago	80	storekeeper	21	"
R	Murano Raymond	80	U S C G	26	"
S	Farinola Edith †	80	stitcher	21	"
T	Farinola Giovannina †	80	housewife	49	"
U	Farinola Salvatore	80	laborer	59	"
V	Lucibello Andrew	80	baker	40	"
W	Lucibello Filomena †	80	housewife	36	"
X*	Caiazza Antonio	80	cutter	58	"
Y*	Caiazza Maria †	80	housewife	50	"
Z	Caiazza Thomas J	80	U S A	30	"

2152   Gould's Court

A	Lespasio Dominic	5	welder	25	here
B	Lespasio Margaret C †	5	stitcher	27	"
C	Lespasio Mary †	5	packer	20	"
D*	Lespasio Ralph	5	roofer	69	43 Haynes
E	Lespasio Thomas S	5	U S A	22	here
F	Thornton Alice †	6	housewife	54	"
G	Thornton Ruth B †	6	clerk	23	"
H	Thornton Thomas H	6	boilermaker	67	"

Gove Street

K	D'Amico Theresa †	60	housewife	20	199 Lexington
N*	Catalfamo Carmella †	62	"	55	37 Decatur
O	Catalfamo Phillip	62	laborer	62	37 "
P	Filippone Joseph	62	"	26	here
R	Grosso Mercurio	62	U S A	23	"

		Full Name.	Residence, Jan. 1, 1943.	Occupation.	Supposed Age.	Reported Residence, Jan. 1, 1942. Street and Number.

Gove Street — Continued

		Full Name.	Res.	Occupation.	Age	Reported Residence
s	*	Grosso Susan †	62	housewife	60	here
t		Bisignani Richard	62	lawyer	32	"
u	*	Bisignani Rosalia †	62	housekeeper	70	"
v	*	Lalicata Paul	64	laborer	58	"
w	*	Lalicata Rosalia †	64	housewife	49	"
x		Ferragamo Angelo	64	carpenter	32	198 Havre
y		Ferragamo Jean †	64	housewife	24	198 "
z		Famiglietti Josephine †	64	"	27	here
		2153				
a		Famiglietti Michael	64	blacksmith	32	"
b		DeFazio Antonio	66	longshoreman	68	"
c		DeFazio Peter	66	laborer	26	"
d	*	DelMuto Frank	66	carpenter	48	"
e	*	DelMuto Philomena †	66	housewife	46	"
f		Ligiero Marie †	66	"	27	"
g		Ligiero Orlando	66	machinist	31	"
h		Borrelli Henry	128	clergyman	31	"
k		Cervone Gerard	128	cook	60	"
l		Checchia Dominic	128	clergyman	39	"
m	*	DeFabio Ferdinand	128	"	39	"
n		Nix Christopher	128	teacher	50	"
o	*	Nuti Joseph	128	"	65	"
p	*	Pechillo Guido	128	clergyman	65	New York
r		Simoni Romano	128	"	63	here
s		Triconi Eleanor †	132	clerk	32	"
t		Triconi Jennie †	132	housewife	48	"
u		Triconi Josephine †	132	at home	30	"
v		Triconi Peter	132	barber	58	"
w		Triconi Sarah †	132	clerk	20	"
x		Muldoon Helen †	132	housewife	29	133 Cottage
y		Muldoon Joseph	132	longshoreman	28	133 "
z		Ferraro Angelo	132	rigger	28	here
		2154				
a		Ferraro Helen †	132	housewife	27	"
b		Gioroso Anthony	132	laborer	26	"
c		Gioroso Julia †	132	housewife	25	"
d		Maniglio Leo	132	barber	41	"
e		Maniglio Rose †	132	housewife	29	"
f		Dittile Gerald	134	retired	78	"
g		Dittile Rose †	134	housewife	83	"
h		Dennocrini Gaspara †	134	"	62	21 Decatur

32

Gove Street Continued

K	Demortimi Joseph	134	laborer	62	21 Decatur
L	*Piacenzia Frank	134	"	53	here
M	*Piacenzia Mamie †	134	housewife	48	"
N	*Solazzo Angelina †	134	"	49	"
O	Solazzo Concetta †	134	clerk	23	"
P	Solazzo Frank	134	"	25	"
R	Armata Anna †	134	"	24	"
S	Armata Antonette †	134	"	22	"
T	Armata Frank	134	laborer	58	"
U	*Armata Maria †	134	housewife	60	"
V	Mosco Agatha †	134	"	26	29 Lexington
W	Mosco Supreme	134	carpenter	28	29 "

Lubec Street

X	*DelloRusso Angelina †	58	housewife	48	here
Y	DelloRusso Gaetano	58	storekeeper	51	"
Z	Intraversato Joseph	58	retired	65	134 Meridian
2155					
A	*Intraversati Maria †	58	housewife	61	134 "
B	Intraversati Savino	58	laborer	38	134 "
C	*DeLisi Adeline †	58	housewife	48	here
D	DeLisi Nicholas	58	U S A	21	"
E	DeLisi Philip	58	laborer	50	"
F	Errico Edith †	58	packer	29	"
G	*Errico Mary †	58	at home	71	"
H	Colarusso Helen †	58	housewife	32	"
K	Colarusso John	58	laborer	36	"
L	Aceto James	58	"	34	20 Frankfort
M	Aceto Josephine †	58	housewife	26	20 "
N	*Dattoli Grace †	58	"	38	here
O	Dattoli Vincent	58	barber	40	"
P	*Cardinale Florence †	60	housewife	78	39 Border
R	*Cardinale Michael	60	retired	70	39 "
S	Lazzara Carmella †	60	housewife	59	here
T	Lazzara Joseph	60	laborer	67	"
U	Lazzara Salvatore	60	machinist	24	"
V	Badamo Antonio	60	laborer	43	"
W	*Badamo Josephine †	60	housewife	39	"
X	DiOrio Domenica †	60	"	23	Everett
Y	DiOrio Joseph A	60	welder	24	"

Lubec Street — Continued

z	*Muse Anthony	60	laborer	59	here

2156

A	*Muse Susan †	60	housewife	60	"
B	Giunta Ida †	60	stitcher	42	"
C	Giunta Philip	60	candymaker	49	"
E	*Dellaria Concetta †	62	housewife	52	"
F	Dellaria Jennie †	62	candyworker	26	"
G	Dellaria Vito J	62	laborer	64	"
H	Dellaria Vito J, jr	62	U S A	20	"
K	*Gambino Anna †	62	at home	65	"
L	Gambino Catherine †	62	candyworker	32	"
M	LaRosa Benedetto	62	shoemaker	54	"
N	LaRosa Salvatore	62	U S A	25	"
O	LaRosa Santa †	62	dressmaker	26	"
P	Terrazzano Frank	62	contractor	43	"
R	Terrazzano Grace †	62	housewife	28	"
S	Martin Joseph	62	laborer	52	"
T	*Minerva Caroline †	64	housewife	45	"
U	*Minerva Nunzio	64	laborer	53	"
V	Minerva Angelina †	64	stitcher	20	"
W	Minerva Joseph	64	U S A	24	"
X	Minerva Nicholas	64	"	22	"
Y	Morrotta Angie †	64	housewife	23	85 London
Z	Morrotta Gus	64	machinist	23	85 "

2157

A	Barrese Jerry	64	laborer	32	here
B	Barrese Marie †	64	housewife	27	"
C	*Cibene Ann †	64	"	50	"
D	Cibene Silvino	64	finisher	53	"
E	DeGregorio Clementina	† 64	housewife	44	"
F	DeGregorio Vincent	64	laborer	48	"
G	Spiltieri Marie †	64	operator	21	"
H	Spiltieri Nicholas	64	U S M C	21	95 Paris

Marion Street

K	Silva Mary †	247	housewife	64	here
L	Tassone Grace †	247	"	33	"
M	Tassone Ventura	247	welder	49	"
N	*Papasodoro Catherine †	247	housewife	63	"
O	*Papasodoro Joseph	247	laborer	64	"

34

Marion Street Continued

P	Papasodoro Lucy †	247	packer	21	here
R	Marmand Francis	249	U S A	22	"
S	Marmand Maria A †	249	housewife	42	"
T	Landry James E	249	fishcutter	30	"
U	Landry Mary †	249	housewife	30	"
V	Carnabuci Caroline †	249	packer	31	"
W	Carnabuci Jennie †	249	candymaker	33	"
X	*Carnabuci Peter	249	tailor	55	"
Y	Capobianco Raffaella †	251	housewife	25	"
Z	Capobianco Ralph	251	U S N	26	"
	2158				
A	Manna Donaline †	251	housewife	25	"
B	Manna Joseph	251	laborer	32	"
C	*Scheppici Concetta †	251	housewife	64	"
D	*Scheppici Stellario	251	laborer	56	"
E	*Interbartolo Rose †	251	housewife	55	"
F	Interbartolo Salvatore	251	instructor	25	"
G	Interbartolo Tony	251	clerk	20	"
H	*Monte Calvo Angelina †	253	housewife	63	"
K	Monte Calvo George	253	U S M C	20	"
L	Monte Calvo Josephine †	253	candymaker	23	"
M	*Monte Calvo Nicholas	253	laborer	71	"
N	Simili Angelina †	253	housewife	42	258 Marion
O	Simili Frank	253	laborer	51	here
P	Simili Mary †	253	packer	20	"
R	Monte Calvo Angela †	253	housewife	40	"
S	Monte Calvo Mancano	253	laborer	43	"
T	Colagiovanni Donato	255	shoemaker	51	"
U	Colagiovanni Louise †	255	housewife	47	"
V	Parente Antonetta †	255	"	25	"
W	Parente Saverio	255	agent	30	"
X	Lunetta Grace †	255	packer	20	"
Y	Lunetta Joseph	255	laborer	70	"
Z	*Lunetta Rose †	255	housewife	50	"
	2159				
A	Lunetta Tony G	255	laborer	23	"

Maverick Street

E	DiTroia Bruno	172	mechanic	40	26 Frankfort
F	*DiTroia Pia †	172	housewife	32	26 "

35

		FULL NAME.	Residence, Jan. 1, 1943.	Occupation.	Supposed Age.	Reported Residence, Jan. 1, 1942. Street and Number.

Maverick Street—Continued

		FULL NAME.	Residence, Jan. 1, 1943.	Occupation.	Supposed Age.	Reported Residence, Jan. 1, 1942. Street and Number.
G		Guarino Henry	172	U S A	21	here
H		Guarino Louis	172	carpenter	47	"
K	*	Guarino Rose—†	172	housewife	42	"
L		Lambiasi Enrico	174	operator	44	305 Sumner
M	*	Veillella Theresa—†	174	housewife	57	here
N	*	Veillella Thomas	174	tailor	60	"
O	*	Bertuccio Concetta—†	174	housewife	58	"
P		Bertuccio Rose—†	174	rubberworker	23	"
R		Bertuccio Salvatore	174	laborer	21	"
T		Cadelo Catherine—†	178	housewife	68	"
U		Cadelo John	178	agent	59	"
V		Falardo Carmen	178	machinist	42	"
W	*	Falardo Mary—†	178	housewife	39	"
X	*	Villella Filomena—†	178	at home	62	"
Z	*	Gulla Antonio	180	laborer	48	115 Everett
		2160				
A		Galla Mary—†	180	stitcher	21	115 "
B	*	Galla Vincenza—†	180	housewife	45	115 "
C		Rizzo Joseph	180	chauffeur	29	here
D		Rizzo Rose—†	180	housewife	28	"
E		Poto James V	186	machinist	43	"
F		Poto Mary—†	186	housewife	38	"
H		Dinuccio Alfonse	186	shoeworker	39	"
K		Dinuccio Eleanor—†	186	housewife	32	"
L		DeSimone Pasquilena †	186	sorter	38	117 Orleans
N	*	Cadello Antonette—†	188	housewife	47	59 Lubec
O		Cadello Salvatore	188	laborer	55	59 "
P		Ferrante Gaetano	188	U S A	20	here
R		Ferrante Jennie—†	188	cigarmaker	23	"
S	*	Ferrante Josephine—†	188	housewife	55	"
T	*	Ferrante Sabastiano	188	retired	68	"
U		Gusto Joseph	188	U S A	32	"
V		Ierardi Carmella †	190	housewife	51	"
W		Ierardi Domenic	190	engineer	32	"
X		Ierardi Joseph	190	U S N	34	"
Y		Rinaldi Anthony	190	riveter	42	"
Z		Rinaldi Bridget †	190	saleswoman	24	"
		2161				
A		Rinaldi Florence †	190	housewife	43	"
B		Rinaldi Lucy †	190	factoryhand	26	"
C		Rinaldi Antonetta—†	190	housewife	44	"

Maverick Street—Continued

D	Rinaldi Bridget — †	190	bookkeeper	20	here
E	Rinaldi Dominick A	190	custodian	53	"
F	Rinaldi Rocco M	190	accountant	22	"
H	*Spano Carmela — †	192	housewife	27	"
K	Spano John	192	shoeworker	32	"
L	Turco Antonio	192	millhand	41	"
M	Turco Elvena — †	192	housewife	47	"
N	Turco Phyllis — †	192	stitcher	20	"
O	Costa Anthony	194	printer	31	"
P	Costa Mildred — †	194	housewife	33	"
R	D'Addario Matteo	194	machinist	33	"
S	D'Addario Rose — †	194	housewife	32	"
T	Argenzio Angela — †	194	"	38	"
U	Argenzio Louis	194	painter	45	"
V	Renda Assunta † rear	194	housewife	42	"
W	Renda Joseph "	194	shoeworker	55	"
X	*Melchionda Carmella — †	196	housewife	54	273 Summer
Y	Melchionda Florence — †	196	shoeworker	23	273 "
Z	*Melchionda Ralph	196	laborer	61	273 "

2162

A	Luongo Alfred	196	presser	21	164 Cottage
B	*Luongo Amelia — †	196	housewife	50	164 "
C	Luongo Antonetta — †	196	dressmaker	25	164 "
D	Luongo Carmella — †	196	"	23	164 "
E	Luongo Marino	196	retired	54	164 "
F	Sardellitti Jennie †	196	housewife	54	here
G	Sardellitti Joseph	196	U S A	25	"
H	Sardellitti Louise — †	196	at home	34	"
K	Sardellitti Ralph	196	electrician	24	"
L	Bettano Anthony	198	bartender	39	"
M	Bettano Helen — †	198	housewife	40	"
N	*Naglieri Jennie †	198	"	48	"
O	Naglieri Joseph	198	clerk	23	"
P	Naglieri Michael	198	laborer	22	"
R	Naglieri Sabina †	198	stitcher	21	"
S	Picarello Anthony	198	storekeeper	29	"
T	*Picarello Mary †	198	housewife	57	"
U	Parillo Domenic	200	shoeworker	39	"
V	Parillo Jennie †	200	housewife	39	"
W	*Tarallo Mary †	200	"	39	"
X	Tarallo Romano	200	storekeeper	19	"

Page	Letter	Full Name.	Residence, Jan. 1, 1943.	Occupation.	Supposed Age.	Reported Residence, Jan. 1, 1942. Street and Number.

1263

Maverick Street—Continued

A	DiPietro Concezio	204	mortician	58	here
B	DiPietro Raffaele	204	U S A	25	"
C	DiPietro Rose—†	204	housewife	56	"
D	DiPietro Silvio	204	teacher	28	"
E	Marini Anna—†	204	at home	80	"
G	*Nalolletta Raffaele	206	retired	70	"
H	Bonfiglio Laura—†	206	stitcher	23	"
K	Bonfiglio Santo	206	chipper	59	"
L	Bonfiglio Vincenza—†	206	housewife	57	"
M	Kelly Lena—†	206	"	21	"
N	Kelly William J	206	U S A	22	Revere
O	*Cino Anna—†	206	at home	64	333 Maverick
P	Cino William	206	brusher	20	333 "
R	Diorio Anthony	206	chauffeur	24	333 "
S	Diorio Josephine—†	206	housewife	32	333 "
T	D'Agostino Angelo	208	repairman	61	here
U	D'Agostino Anthony	208	machinist	29	"
V	D'Agistono Edith—†	208	at home	27	"
W	D'Agostino Gloria—†	208	"	20	"
X	*D'Agostino Josephine—†	208		86	"
Y	D'Agostino Louise—†	208	dressmaker	36	"
Z	D'Agostino Nancy—†	208	housewife	54	"

2164

A	Pellechia Jean—†	208	"	35	"
B	Pellechia Joseph	208	laborer	37	"
C	Ravagno Louise—†	208	housewife	26	"
D	Ravagno Santo J	208	U S A	27	"
F	Romano Anthony	208	laborer	33	"
G	Romano Margaret—†	208	housewife	33	"
H	Lawford Fred	210	salesman	51	"
K	Lawford Lillian M—†	210	physician	53	"
L	Vinacci Fred	210	retired	68	"
M	Vinacci Helen—†	210	stitcher	33	"
O	Selvitella Lucy—†	210	housewife	27	158 Gove
P	Selvitella Michael	210	machinist	46	158 "
R	Nocito Antonio	210	laborer	25	here
S	Nocito Rita—†	210	housewife	20	"
T	Cerulli Nina—†	212	"	40	"
U	Cerulli Victor	212	cutter	62	"
V	*Conti Giovanina—†	212	at home	66	"

38

Maverick Street — Continued

w		Conti Giuseppe	212	repairman	62	here
x		*Turco Antoinetta †	212	housewife	47	"
y		Turco John	212	laborer	48	"
z		*Petrone Celestina †	212	housewife	58	"
		2165				
a		*Petrone Luigi	212	candyworker	59	"
b		*Fenochio Anna †	212	housewife	46	"
c		Fenochio Frank	212	laborer	60	"
d		Fenochio Guido	212	U S A	20	"
e		Caton Frances †	226	housewife	40	"
f		Caton Joseph	226	inkmaker	41	"
g		Campiglia Catherine †	226	milliner	45	"
h		DeStasio Louis	226	laborer	39	"
k		DeStasio Pauline †	226	housewife	34	"
l		DeMayo Charles	228	retired	58	"
m		DeMayo Charles A, jr	228	operator	24	"
n		DeMayo Elizabeth †	228	housewife	52	"
o		DeMayo George	228	U S A	26	"
p		McGaffigan Cassie †	228	saleswoman	32	"
r		DeMayo Edward M	228	manager	29	"
s		DeMayo Mildred †	228	housewife	23	"
t		DiDonato Ralph	230	painter	26	"
u		DiDonato Theresa †	230	housewife	25	"
v		Costa Albert	230	mechanic	22	"
w		Costa Andrew	230	draftsman	24	"
x		Costa Jennie †	230	mechanic	27	"
y		Costa Joseph	230	carpenter	36	"
z		*Costa Rose †	230	housewife	63	"
		2166				
a		Fuccillo Catherine †	230	"	32	Everett
b		LaRaia Frances †	230	"	50	here
c		Leonardi Angelina †	230	"	56	"
d		Leonardi Eugene	230	printer	20	"
e		Leonardi Mary †	230	stitcher	24	"
f		Leonardi Nicholas	230	laborer	65	"
k		Pinto Antonio T	236	manufacturer	37	"
l		Pinto James F	236	U S A	22	"
m		*Pinto Rose †	236	housewife	70	"
n		*Minao Carmella †	236	"	60	177 Maverick
o		*Minao Eugene	236	salesman	56	177 "
p		*Minao Luigi	236	barber	64	177 "

39

Maverick Street — Continued

R	Minao Olga †	236	typist	27	177 Maverick
S	Pignato Marguerite †	236	housewife	25	here
T	Pignato Vincent	236	laborer	25	"
U*	Venerelli John	236	"	65	"
V	Costanza Catherine †	238	housewife	43	"
W	Costanza Pasquale	238	physician	43	"
X	Costanza Linda †	238	forewoman	31	"
Y	Costanza Mary †	238	housewife	65	"
Z	Costanza Pasquale A	238	retired	81	"

2167

A	Giordano Henry	238	operator	42	"
B	Giordano Rose †	238	housewife	35	"

McKay Place

C*	Pasto Alba B †	2	at home	47	here
D	Pasto Elizabeth B †	2	typist	20	"
E	Pasto Salvatore J	2	U S N	22	"
F*	Pilegi Catherine †	2	at home	83	"
G	Magaletta Francisco	2	operator	52	"
H	Magaletta Josephine †	2	housewife	46	"
K	Magaletta Michael	2	clerk	25	"
L	Prestanza Philomena †	2	at home	88	"
M	Terraglia Alfonso	2	laborer	58	"
N	DeFlorio Blanche †	2	housewife	41	"
O	DeFlorio Joseph J	2	laborer	47	"
P	Ferrullo Emilia †	2	at home	80	"
R	Messina Eleanor S †	9	saleswoman	42	"
S	Kinnealy Anna †	9	housewife	35	"
T	Kinnealy James F	9	inspector	37	"
U	Galasso Florence L †	9	housewife	33	"
V	Galasso Joseph	9	metalworker	34	"
W	Zicconi Grace †	9	housewife	28	"
X	Zicconi James	9	toolworker	32	"
Y	Cerro Julio	9	retired	77	"

2168

Orleans Street

	Roco Filippo	101	laborer	55	here
	Roco Francesca †	101	housewife	22	"
	Roco Frank	101	laborer	25	"

Orleans Street — Continued

E	*Falange Joseph	101	clerk	63	here
F	*Falange Maria †	101	housewife	62	"
H	*DiVincinzo Diana †	102	"	54	133 Orleans
K	DiVincinzo Filippo	102	U S C G	21	here
L	DiVincinzo Tomasso	102	laborer	54	133 Orleans
M	Almeida Anthony	102	"	42	here
N	Almeida Mary †	102	housewife	37	"
O	McFarland Margaret †	102	laundryworker	27	"
R	Poto Filomena †	103	operator	20	"
S	Poto George	103	painter	39	"
T	Poto Yolanda †	103	housewife	38	"
U	Santoro Madeline †	103	"	48	"
V	Santoro Madeline †	103	clerk	21	"
W	Santoro Nicholas	103	laborer	50	"
Y	Messer Joseph A	104	retired	72	"
Z	*Pina Carlotta †	104	at home	50	"

2169

A	Pina Jennie †	104	rubberworker	26	"
B	*Roddy Joseph	104	millworker	49	101 Orleans
D	Holland Abbie †	106	at home	64	107 Everett
E	*Callace Mary †	106	"	62	5 Wilbur ct
F	Bracci Amodeo	106	U S A	22	here
G	*Bracci Filomena †	106	housewife	55	"
H	*Bracci Michele	106	laundryworker	64	"
K	Constantine Joseph	107	mechanic	24	"
L	Constantine Rose †	107	housewife	20	"
M	*DiBenedetto Mary †	107	at home	62	"
P	Barbarcane Gaetano	107	U S A	21	"
R	*Barbarcane Sabino	107	laborer	51	"
S	DeNaro Joseph	107	electrician	39	"
T	*DeNaro Rose †	107	housewife	29	"
U	Indelicato John	107	operator	23	"
V	Indelicato Louise †	107	housewife	21	"
X	Amoroso Louise †	107	"	36	"
Y	Amoroso Rosario	107	painter	46	"
Z	DeMattia Nove	107	welder	37	"

2170

A	DiMattia Rose †	107	housewife	31	"
B	Montalto John	107	mechanic	29	"
C	Montalto Josephine †	107	housewife	23	"
E	Santilli Anthony	108A	U S A	26	Everett

H

Orleans Street — Continued

F	Santilli Marion †	108A	housewife	21	Everett
G	Lespasio Michael	108A	laborer	24	here
H	Lespasio Nicolena †	108A	housewife	29	"
K	Terranagra Frank	108A	laborer	29	"
L	Terranagra Sylvia †	108A	housewife	28	"
M	Mascato Thomas	108A	laborer	36	"
N	Mellilo Mary †	108A	housewife	24	589 Saratoga
O	Mellilo William	108A	U S N	26	589 "
P	Casaburi Antonio	109	inspector	31	here
R	Casaburi Florence †	109	housewife	29	"
S*	Casaburi Addolorata †	109	"	58	"
T	Casaburi Nicolo	109	laborer	59	"
U	Cottone Ignazio	109	laundryworker	50	"
V*	Cottone Margaret †	109	housewife	45	"
W	Commorado Anthony	111	barber	28	"
X	Commorado Margaret †	111	housewife	27	"
Y	Cerullo Anthony	111	plasterer	62	"
Z	Cerullo John	111	printer	35	"

2171

A	Crullo Josephine †	111	at home	29	"
B	Crullo Maria †	111	housewife	59	"
C	Crullo Ella †	111	"	25	"
D	Crullo Pasquale	111	welder	23	"
E	Monica Josephine †	113	housewife	38	"
F	Monica Sabino F	113	chauffeur	39	"
G	Rindoni Santo	113	laborer	37	"
H	Rindoni Vincenza †	113	housewife	31	"
K	Sallese Carmela †	113	"	30	"
L	Sallese Pasquale	113	marketman	34	"
M	Siracusa Antonette †	115	housewife	22	"
N	Siracusa John	115	U S M C	21	"
O	Siracusa Louis	115	laborer	23	"
P	Tripoli Antonina †	115	dressmaker	44	"
R	Tripoli Francesco	115	storekeeper	56	"
S	Tripoli Mary A †	115	stenographer	25	"
T	Tripoli Mildred †	115	hairdresser	23	"
U*	Maggio Vita †	115	at home	68	"
V	Tripoli Frank C	115	clerk	21	"
W*	Tripoli Salvatore	115	candyworker	54	"
X	Romano Paul	115	U S N	20	"
Y*	Romano Santa †	115	at home	44	"

Page.	Letter	FULL NAME.	Residence, Jan. 1, 1943.	Occupation.	Supposed Age	Reported Residence, Jan. 1, 1942. Street and Number.

Orleans Street Continued

	z	Durante Elizabeth †	115	housewife	38	here
2172						
	A	Durante Joseph	115	shoeworker	48	"
	B	Durante Salvatore	115	U S A	20	"
	C*	Georgione Carmela †	115	at home	59	"
	D	Sotera Salvatore	115	electrician	42	"
	E	Sotera Vita †	115	housewife	34	"
	F	Georgione Marguerita †	115	packer	27	116 Webster
	G	Georgione Mario	115	inspector	25	here
	H	Georgione Vincenzo	115	U S A	28	"
	K	Maggio Anthony	115	meatcutter	32	"
	L	Maggio Grace †	115	housewife	28	"
	M	Mancuso Frank	117	retired	73	"
	N*	Mancuso Grace †	117	housewife	57	"
	O	Melito Jennie †	117	rubberworker	21	"
	P*	Marotta Guiseppe	117	laborer	56	"
	R	Marotta Libario	117	electrician	28	"
	S*	Marotta Rosalie †	117	housewife	46	"
	T	Marotta Rose †	117	at home	20	"
	U	Marotta Salvatore J	117	U S A	26	"
	V	Capone Agnes †	117	housewife	30	"
	W	Capone Alfred	117	attendant	53	"
	X	Costanza John	117	laborer	59	"
	Y	Costanza Rose †	117	packer	21	"
	Z*	Costanza Vincenza †	117	housewife	60	"
2173						
	A*	Cornacchio Palmira †	117	"	52	206 Maverick
	B	Cornacchio Peter	117	U S A	20	206 "
	C	Cornacchio Tullio	117	laborer	49	206 "
	D*	Lunetta Francesca †	117	housewife	60	here
	E	Lunetta Joseph	117	U S A	23	"
	F	Lunetta Salvatore	117	carpenter	63	"
	G	Celata Alfonso	117	calker	39	"
	H	Celata Annetta †	117	housewife	40	"
	K*	DeLuca Joseph	117	retired	82	"
	L	Plunder Donato	117	U S A	20	"
	M	Plunder Gerard	117	retired	62	"
	N	Plunder Mary †	117	milliner	25	"
	O*	Plunder Pasqualina †	117	housewife	65	"
	P	Plunder Robert	117	painter	26	"
	S	Presutti Mario	118	tailor	55	"

43

Orleans Street — Continued

v	D'Allesandro Antonio	118	laborer	40	here
v	D'Allesandro Carmela—†	118	housewife	38	"
v	DeRosa Frank	119	engineer	23	"
w*	Spinazola Mary †	119	at home	50	"
x	Pepi Filomena—†	119	housewife	26	"
y	Pepi Lawrence	119	laborer	26	"
z	DeSimone Charles	125	manufacturer	37	Medford
	2174				
A	Magnasco Giovanni	129	blacksmith	68	here
B	Magnasco Josephine—†	129	operator	32	"
C	Magnasco Mary—†	129	packer	26	"
D	Magnasco Nicolo	129	U S A	34	"
E	Magnasco Rosa—†	129	housewife	57	"
F	Magnasco Vittorio	129	shipper	23	"
G	Giunta Angelo	129	bartender	22	79 Webster
H	Giunta Pasqualina †	129	housewife	21	79 "
K*	Magnasco Fiornida †	129	"	55	here
L	Magnasco Georgia †	129	leatherworker	23	"
M	Magnasco Jennie †	129	packer	25	"
N	Magnasco Rosildo	129	shoeworker	62	"
O	Gallo James	129	laborer	35	"
P	Gallo Marguerite †	129	inspector	29	"
R	Chiulli Maria †	129	housewife	45	"
S	Chiulli Sabatino	129	laborer	42	"
T*	Recchia Helen †	130	housewife	44	32 Orleans
U	Recchia Louis	130	foreman	52	32 "
V	Recchia Mario	130	U S A	23	32 "
W	Recchia Mary †	130	dressmaker	22	32 "
X	Giglio Carmela †	130	housewife	57	3 Everett ct
Y	Giglio Charles	130	U S A	23	3 "
Z	Giglio Francesco	130	laborer	69	3 "
	2175				
	Giglio Pasquale	130	"	26	3 "
	Puzzo Maria †	131	packer	48	here
	Puzzo Michael	131	laborer	50	"
	Siciliano Joseph	131	U S A	30	Cambridge
	Siciliano Josephine †	131	housewife	30	"
	D'Agostino Angelina †	131	"	46	here
	D'Agostino Gaetano	131	laborer	52	"
	(name) per	131	retired	59	"
	(name) evieve †	131	stitcher	23	"

44

Orleans Street — Continued

	N	Armata John	131	rubberworker	26	here
	O	Armata Victor	131	U S A	28	"
	P*	Armata Vincenzina †	131	housewife	59	"
	R	Giardina Angelo	131	inspector	27	"
	S*	Giardina Frances †	131	housewife	28	"
	T*	Zona Angelina †	132	"	46	"
	U	Zona Filippo	132	barber	51	"
	V	Zona Frank	132	U S A	25	"
	W	Zona Concetta †	132	hairdresser	20	"
	X	Zona Jennie †	132	"	23	"
	Y*	Leone Mary †	132	stitcher	54	"
	Z	Leone Romolo	132	factoryhand	52	"

2176

	A	Edwards Mary †	133	cleaner	27	"
	B*	Rose Manuel	133	seaman	22	"
	D	Lunetta Nicola J	133	carpenter	27	117 Orleans
	E	Petracca Josephine †	133	at home	58	112 Havre
	F	Petracca Josephine †	133	leatherworker	24	112 "
	G	Correale Esther †	133	housewife	30	here
	H	Correale James	133	laborer	34	"
	K	Casaletto Amanda †	133	at home	24	4 Paris ct
	L	Martinole Aida †	135	housewife	62	here
	M	Martinole Emelio	135	U S A	37	"
	N	Martinole Guiseppe	135	blacksmith	67	"
	O	Martinole Maria †	135	leatherworker	26	"
	P	Marando Pasquale	135	laborer	48	"
	R	Marcone Frank	135	"	20	"
	S	Marcone Nicolena †	135	housewife	22	"
	T	Cardinale Florence †	135	"	30	"
	U	Cardinale Michael	135	painter	34	"
	V	Messina Carmela †	135	housewife	32	"
	W	Messina Vincent	135	rubberworker	41	"
	X	Cozzo Eleanor †	137	boxmaker	24	"
	Y	Cozzo Jennie †	137	stitcher	39	"
	Z*	Cozzo John	137	bricklayer	72	"

2177

	A*	Cozzo Lena †	137	housewife	64	"
	B	Bonfiglio Carl	137	electrician	34	"
	C	Bonfiglio Minnie †	137	housewife	27	"
	D	Mazzone Nicholas	137	shipfitter	26	"
	E	Mazzone Rose †	137	housewife	26	"

Orleans Street — Continued

F	Lanzo Concetta †	137	housewife	29	here
G	Lanzo Joseph J	137	foundryman	33	"
H	Speziale Angelo	137	laborer	57	"
K	Speziale Grace †	137	housewife	46	"
L	Speziale Pasquale	137	U S A	20	"
M	Casaletto Michael	140	laborer	36	37 Decatur
N	Chambers James A	140	U S C G	20	Texas

Percival Place

O*	Danato Peter	1	retired	75	here
P*	Pettinicchio Luigi	1	laborer	59	"
R*	Tango Angelina †	1	at home	65	"
S	Abruzzese Generoso	1	machinist	29	"
T	Vertuccio Domenic	2	marbleworker	60	"
U	Ciulla Philip	2	laborer	53	87 Paris
V*	Mercantante Concetta †	2	nurse	53	here
W	Colacusso Frank A	2	carpenter	34	"
X	Colacusso Mary S †	2	housewife	34	"
Z*	Lespasio Louisa †	3	"	75	"
	2178				
A	Lespasio Vito	3	retired	75	"
B	Ciardi Valentino	3	laborer	41	"

Porter Street

D	Venuti Frances †	119	housewife	33	here
E	Venuti Frank	119	carpenter	36	"
F	DeAmelio Carmela †	119	candymaker	54	"
G	DeAmelio Gerardo	119	welder	20	"
H	DeAmelio Michael	119	retired	65	"
K	D'India Agatha †	130	at home	54	"
L	D'India Victor	130	U S A	23	"
M	Nuccio Rose †	134	housewife	27	154 Chambers
N	Nuccio Salvatore	134	welder	27	154 "
O	Arnesani Frances †	136	housewife	37	here
P	Arnesani Joseph	136	barber	43	"
R	Stiti Joseph	136	shoeworker	59	"
S*	Stiti Maria †	136	housewife	58	"
T	Stiti Silvio	136	machinist	26	"
U	Capozzi Crescenzo	138	sealer	20	"

Porter Street Continued

V		Capozzi Margaret †	138	packer	23	here
W		Capozzi Michelina †	138	"	27	"
X	*	Capozzi Nicoletta †	138	at home	54	"
Y		DeMarco Filippa †	138	stitcher	21	"
Z		DeMarco Louis	138	U S A	21	"

2179

A		Nigro Concetta †	138	at home	30	"
B	*	Nigro Michelina †	138	housewife	52	"
C		Nigro Rosario	138	farmer	56	"
D	*	Mannke Josephine †	140	housewife	36	56 Cliff
E		Mannke Robert J	140	machinist	38	56 "
F		Cetrullo Elizabeth †	142	housewife	43	here
G		Cetrullo Frank	142	retired	52	"
H		Pastore Maria †	142	operator	27	"
K	*	Pastore Pasqualina †	142	housewife	54	"
L		Pastore Vincenzo	142	bootblack	56	"

Rockingham Court

N		D'Andrea Carmen	2	laborer	45	here
O	*	D'Andrea Mary †	2	housewife	33	"
P		Matarazzo Amato	2	laborer	65	99 Everett

Ward 1 Precinct 22

CITY OF BOSTON

LIST OF RESIDENTS
20 YEARS OF AGE AND OVER

(NON-CITIZENS INDICATED BY ASTERISK)
(FEMALES INDICATED BY DAGGER)

AS OF

JANUARY 1, 1943

JOSEPH F. TIMILTY, *Chairman*
FREDERIC E. DOWLING, *Secretary*
WILLIAM A. MOTLEY, Jr.
FRANCIS B. McKINNEY
EVERETT R. PROUT
Listing Board.

CITY OF BOSTON PRINTING DEPARTMENT

2200

Antrim Street

A	Colleary James W	2	laborer	46	here
B	Colleary Jessie —†	2	beautician	40	"
C	Pennell Amelia —†	2	at home	48	"
D	Pennell Augustine	2	retired	84	"
E	Pennell Orelia —†	2	at home	76	"
F	Taylor Sadie —†	2	"	37	"
H	Cagliardi Joseph	5	machinist	26	"
K	Cagliardi Mary —†	5	housewife	25	"
L	*Cagliardi George	5	retired	75	"
M	Cagliardi Maria —†	5	housewife	46	"
N	Cagliardi Salvatore	5	laborer	51	"
O	Scopa Mary —†	5	housewife	27	"
P	Scopa Roland	5	chipper	35	"
R	Halpin Gertrude —†	7	housewife	37	"
S	Halpin Thomas P	7	U S N	46	"
T	McGeney Theresa A —†	7	inspector	24	"
U	Martarano Anthony	7	U S A	25	"
V	Martarano Elizabeth —†	7	housewife	58	"
W	Martarano Jean —†	7	stitcher	22	"
X	Martarano Julia —†	7	saleswoman	29	"
Y	Martarano Michael	7	retired	72	"
Z	Martarano Sylvia —†	7	candyworker	27	"

2201

A	Maglio Domenic	7	pipefitter	45	"
B	Maglio Ida —†	7	housewife	39	"
C	O'Shea Annie —†	8	"	59	"
D	O'Shea Irene —†	8	clerk	32	"
E	O'Shea James C	8	watchman	60	"
F	Caprio Agnes —†	8	housewife	38	"
G	Caprio Charles	8	shipfitter	43	"
H	Donohue David	8	U S N	42	"
K	Sheehan James	8	seaman	27	"
L	Weber Barbara —†	8	housewife	46	"
M	Weber Carl	8	machinist	58	"
N	Zimmerman Agnes E —†	9	clerk	26	"
O	Zimmerman Frank K	9	policeman	30	"
P	Graham John J	9	bridgetender	52	"
R	Graham Theresa A —†	9	housewife	52	"
S	Landrigan Michael	9	painter	62	"
T	O'Brien Edith —†	9	housewife	27	"
U	O'Brien Thomas A	9	electrician	31	"

2

Antrim Street Continued

	v	Celona Frank —†	10	finisher	51	here
	w	*Celona Ratzia	10	machinist	20	"
	x	*Celona Sarah—†	10	housewife	53	"
	y	Catapano Anna —†	10	"	42	"
	z	Catapano Frank	10	tailor	45	"
2202						
	a	Celona Frank, jr	10	teacher	30	"
	b	Celona Rose—†	10	housewife	29	"
	c	Calicchio Albert	11	carpenter	52	"
	d	Calicchio Diana —†	11	clerk	25	"
	e	*Calicchio Lucy—†	11	housewife	52	"
	f	DiPesa Alexander	11	U S A	26	Nahant
	g	DiPesa John	11	seaman	23	here
	h	DiPesa Michael	11	U S A	25	Nahant
	k	DiPesa Patrick	11	metalworker	49	here
	l	DiPesa Phoebe —†	11	housewife	46	"
	m	Silveria Maria—†	11	at home	80	"
	n	Powers Arthur	12	clerk	42	"
	o	Powers Dorothy—†	12	"	35	"
	p	Ford Arthur S	12	salesman	45	"
	r	Ford Lillian M —†	12	housewife	41	"
	s	McCarthy Margaret —†	12	at home	80	"
	t	*Palandro Caesar	12	retired	54	"
	u	Palandro Domenic	12	machinist	25	"
	v	Palandro Esther —†	12	waitress	28	"
	w	*Palandro Martha —†	12	housewife	53	"
	x	Palandro Rose —†	12	at home	23	"
	y	Palandro Ruth —†	12	clerk	21	"
	z	DiLorenzo Jerry	14	presser	28	25 Gladstone
2203						
	a	DiLorenzo Mary —†	14	housewife	30	25 "
	b	Errobino Assunta —†	14	operator	20	209 London
	c	Errobino Mary—†	14	housewife	42	209 "
	d	Errobino Michael	14	U S A	22	209 "
	e	Errobino Pasquale	14	laborer	46	209 "
	f	Blasi Arthur	14	shoemaker	52	here
	g	Blasi Nerina —†	14	housewife	51	"

Ashley Street

	h	DeLauri Emilia —†	12	housewife	50	here
	k	DeLauri Peter	12	U S N	21	"

3

Page	Letter	FULL NAME.	Residence, Jan. 1, 1943.	Occupation.	Supposed Age.	Reported Residence, Jan. 1, 1942. Street and Number.

Ashley Street—Continued

	L	Malloy Harry	12	retired	67	102 Regent
	M	Malloy Mary C —†	12	at home	42	102 "
	N	Santarpio Edward H	18	custodian	39	here
	O	Santarpio Theresa —†	18	housewife	37	"
	P	Pucillo Anthony	18	barber	44	"
	R	Pucillo Bettina —†	18	housewife	41	"
	S	Palladino Antonio	18	shipwright	35	"
	T	Palladino Jennie —†	18	stitcher	26	"
	U	*Palladino Joseph	18	retired	66	"
	V	Palladino Josephine —†	18	stenographer	21	"
	W	Palladino Nunzio	18	shipwright	34	"
	X	Staffier Anthony	22	clerk	35	"
	Y	Staffier Jennie —†	22	housewife	35	"
	Z	Blasi Louis	22	retired	55	"

2204

	A	DiLorenzo Alda —†	22	waitress	26	"
	B	DiLorenzo Thomas	22	tailor	56	"
	C	O'Brion Cornelius	22	shipper	55	269 Princeton
	D	O'Brion John J	22	U S A	28	269 "
	E	O'Brion Margaret —†	22	housewife	51	269 "
	F	*O'Brion Ruth —†	22	"	20	269 "
	G	O'Brion Thomas L	22	U S A	22	Maryland
	H	O'Brion William	22	"	24	269 Princeton
	K	Capone John	26	chauffeur	27	here
	L	Fineberg Adele —†	26	housewife	28	"
	M	Fineberg Morton	26	chauffeur	28	"
	N	LoConte Fortunata —†	26	housewife	50	"
	O	*LoConte Joseph	26	salesman	49	"
	P	Spagnolo Annabile	26	shoeworker	42	"
	R	Spagnolo Elizabeth —†	26	factoryhand	40	"
	S	Mandra Joseph	32	bartender	55	"
	T	Mandra Mary —†	32	housewife	45	"
	U	*Smith Frances —†	32	clerk	20	"
	V	Smith Ralph	32	U S A	21	Worcester
	W	*Mosarra Anna —†	32	at home	64	here
	X	*Scalata Angelina —†	32	housewife	37	"
	Y	Scalata Joseph	32	barber	45	"
	Z	DiLorenzo Louis	32	laborer	24	"

2205

	A	*DiLorenzo Mary —†	32	housewife	64	"
	B	Zitano Mary —†	32	"	37	"

4

Ashley Street—Continued

c	Zitano Peter	32	laborer	40	here
d	Boncorddo Joseph	36	welder	29	Revere
e	Boncorddo Marie—†	36	housewife	29	"
f	LoConte Concetta—†	36	"	38	here
g	LoConte Frank	36	salesman	46	"
h	Gauthier Charles H	36	U S N	20	40 Russell
k	Gauthier Mabel A—†	36	saleswoman	39	40 "
l	Trevor Helen F—†	36	housewife	41	here
m	Trevor Joseph H	36	U S A	43	"
n	Trevor Lawrence J	36	mechanic	47	"
o	Franzese Jennie—†	36	factoryhand	35	"
p	Franzese William	36	salesman	40	"
r	Capillo Anna—†	40	housewife	36	"
s	Capillo Rosario	40	chauffeur	36	"
t	Capillo Assunta—†	40	instructor	24	"
u	Capillo Carl	40	accountant	33	"
v	Capillo Pauline—†	40	housewife	59	"
w	Vigue Rinaldo	40	beautician	27	46 Melrose
x	Burton Charles F	40	engineer	56	here
y	*Burton Lawrence J	40	U S N	20	"
z	Burton Margaret E—†	40	housewife	49	"
	2206				
a	Noonan Margaret—†	40	at home	81	"
b	Gaglini George	44	cutter	36	"
c	Gaglini Jean—†	44	housewife	33	"
d	Staflier Angelo	44	tailor	43	"
e	Staflier Olympia—†	44	housewife	35	"
f	Vozzella Angelo	44	U S A	24	"
g	*Vozzella Antonetta—†	44	housewife	48	"
h	Vozzella Charles	44	blacksmith	51	"
k	*Statuti John	49	retired	73	"
l	*Statuti Louise—†	49	housewife	65	"
m	Maffei Eleanor—†	49	"	30	"
n	Maffei Vincent	49	lawyer	30	"
o	Siragusa James J	52	physician	46	"
p	Siragusa K Paula—†	52	housewife	43	"
r	Sweeney Mary—†	52	"	65	"
s	DiGiovanni John	70	salesman	36	"
t	DiGiovanni Rose—†	70	packer	31	"
u	DiMare Esther—†	70	at home	33	"
v	DiMare Santo	70	candymaker	33	"

5

Ashley Street Continued

w	Battles Elizabeth M—†	87	teacher	42	here
x	Bonner Mabel T—†	87	"	56	"
y	Connolly Helen T—†	87	"	23	"
z	Finn Mary E—†	87	"	23	"

2207

a	Hughes Frances A—†	87	"	27	"
b	Kelleher Mary E—†	87	"	40	"
c	Lyons Claire A—†	87	"	35	"
d	McMurrer Mary R—†	87	"	46	"
e	Nagle Julia C—†	87	"	51	Lynn
f	Ryan Mary J—†	87	"	27	here
g	Ursula Barbara B—†	87	domestic	24	"
h	Donahue Ethel N—†	91	housewife	38	"
k	Donahue Thomas A	91	tel worker	40	"
l	Miller Joseph	91	printer	42	"
m	Miller Mary—†	91	tel operator	43	"
n	Damiano Anna C—†	91	teacher	25	"
o	Damiano Mary—†	91	housewife	48	"
p	Damiano Patrick J	91	U S A	23	"
r	Damiano Peter	91	shoeworker	51	"
s	Connell Kenneth	135	laborer	22	"
t	Connell Louis	135	chauffeur	57	"
u	Connell Rose—†	135	housewife	56	"
v	Bertuccelli Jessie—†	135	tailor	33	"
w	Bertuccelli Placido	135	retired	67	"
x	Bertuccelli Virginia—†	135	housewife	64	"

Bennington Street

y	Rich Ardina—†	728	at home	62	here
z	Rich Eleanor—†	728	dressmaker	35	"

2208

a	Sablone Alfred	728	U S A	22	"
b	Sablone Alice—†	728	stitcher	26	"
c	Sablone Angelina—†	728	housewife	52	"
d	Sablone Antonio	728	salesman	50	"
e	Sablone Frank	728	laborer	24	"
f	Balduzzi Mario	728	attendant	46	"
g	Balduzzi Natalie—†	728	housewife	43	"
h	Balduzzi Rachel—†	728	at home	68	"
k	Anzalone Maria—†	732	housewife	67	"

6

Bennington Street Continued

M	Anzalone Phillip	732	millhand	72	here
N	Green Josephine—†	732	stitcher	27	"
O*	Anzalone Filippa—†	732	housewife	48	"
P	Anzalone Joseph	732	U S N	20	"
R	Anzalone Placido	732	proprietor	55	"
S	Anzalone Charles	732	U S A	22	"
T	Anzalone Frank	732	storekeeper	57	"
U	Anzalone Joseph	732	painter	24	"
V	Anzalone Josephine—†	732	at home	27	"
W	Feeley Edward J	734	B F D	47	"
X	Feeley Edward J, jr	734	U S A	27	"
Y	Feeley Lorraine—†	734	clerk	24	"
Z	Feeley Mary F—†	734	housewife	47	"

2209

A	Hollander Edna—†	734	clerk	20	"
B	Hollander Gertrude—†	734	inspector	22	"
C	Hollander Helen—†	734	at home	53	"
D	Hollander Helen T—†	734	"	29	"
E	Cadigan James T	734	laborer	48	"
F	Cadigan John L	734	chauffeur	38	"
G	Cadigan Katherine—†	734	at home	69	"
H	Brady Austin	736	U S A	21	"
K	Brady John	736	mechanic	23	"
L	Brady Mary—†	736	at home	45	"
M	Doyle Gladys—†	736	housewife	35	"
N	Doyle Walter	736	foundryman	34	"
O	Celantano Bruno	736	draftsman	22	"
P	Celantano James	736	meatcutter	47	"
R	Celantano Josephine—†	736	housewife	43	"
S	Celantano Orlando	736	clerk	24	"
T	Kingsbury Alice V—†	738	housewife	68	"
U	Kingsbury Emily C—†	738	at home	64	"
V	Kingsbury Herbert	738	operator	65	"
W	Doyle Catherine—†	738	at home	68	"
X	Doyle Cecile V—†	738	operator	43	"
Y	Doyle Edward F	738	B F D	49	"
Z	Doyle Eleanor D—†	738	clerk	37	"

2210

A	Sullivan Alyse C—†	738	tel operator	40	"
B	Stewart John J	738	U S N	31	"
C	Stewart John P	738	engineer	61	"

7

Bennington Street—Continued

D	Stewart Mary †	738	housewife	61	here
E	Terry Mary L †	738	"	22	719 Benningt'n
F	Terry William J	738	U S N	26	719 "
H	Delaney Catherine G †	740	housewife	45	here
K	Delaney Thomas M	740	shipper	45	"
L	Curran Edith C †	740	housewife	40	"
M	Curran Patrick J	740	electrician	32	"
N	Thornton Annie I †	742	housewife	47	"
O	Thornton William	742	machinist	44	"
P	Uliano Helen I †	742	housewife	22	"
R	Uliano Joseph	742	machinist	21	687 Benningt'n
S	Cieri Thomas	742	tailor	27	Winthrop
T	Cieri Virginia †	742	housewife	27	"
U	DeFronzo Alfonso	742	pharmacist	35	"
V	DeFronzo Rose †	742	housewife	35	"
W	*Cook Catherine †	742	"	36	here
X	Cook Cecil	742	shipper	39	"
Y	Cook Elizabeth †	744	at home	71	"
Z	Cook James J	744	U S A	35	"

2211

A	McAteer Margaret F †	744	housewife	39	"
B	McAteer Thomas	744	rubberworker	39	"
C	Clogston Abbie L †	744	housewife	68	"
D	Clogston Frank A	744	draftsman	65	"
E	*Monahan Bridget †	744	at home	79	"
F	Monahan John J	744	shipfitter	43	"
G	Monahan Richard	744	U S A	44	"
H	Merola Augustine	746	shoeworker	31	"
K	Merola Clara †	746	housewife	27	"
L	Beale Benjamin T	746	retired	79	"
M	Beale Benjamin T, jr	746	clerk	44	"
N	Beale Ellen G †	746	housewife	70	"
O	Beale Gertrude E †	746	clerk	42	"
P	Beale John P	746	shipfitter	41	"
R	Hines Beatrice M †	746	tel operator	35	47 Neptune rd
S	Sears Albert F	746	foreman	44	here
T	Musto Fortuna †	746	housewife	62	"
U	Musto Joseph	746	machinist	63	"
X	Arena Salvatore	960	salesman	34	"
Y	Arena Teresa †	960	housewife	33	"
Z	Merola Ascanio	960	shoeworker	57	"

s

2212

Bennington Street Continued

A	Merola Carina †	960	lithographer	25	here
B	Merola Elvira †	960	housewife	53	"
C	Impeduglia Dora †	960	"	25	"
D	Impeduglia Salvatore	960	ropemaker	26	"
E	Dacey Concetta †	962	packer	32	"
F	Dacey Timothy	962	repairman	34	"
G	DiAnni John	962	boxmaker	56	"
H	DiAnni Mary †	962	housewife	34	"
K	Albanese Josephine †	962	"	39	"
L	Albanese Sabino	962	shoeworker	42	"
M	Polsonetti Agostino E	964	electrician	32	"
N	Polsonetti Ethel R †	964	housewife	31	"
O*	Polsonetti Crucifissa †	964	tailor	35	"
P	Polsonetti Innocenzo	964	"	42	"
R	Polsonetti Luigi	964	"	56	"
S*	Polsonetti Olympia †	964	housewife	57	"
T	Burke Catherine †	966	candyworker	48	"
U	Burke George F	966	carpenter	56	"
V	Perkins Celia †	966	housewife	34	"
W	Perkins William H	966	contractor	36	"
X	Farrey Catherine †	966	at home	76	"
Y	Farrey John	966	retired	77	"
Z	Napier Helen †	966	housewife	52	"

2213

A	Napier Stephen	966	inspector	56	"
B	DiFiore Filomena †	968	housewife	51	"
C	DiFiore Frank	968	barber	53	"
D	Fleming Eleanor †	968	housewife	25	29 Wordsworth
E	Fleming John R	968	U S A	30	29 "
F	Ciccolo James	968	barber	72	here
G	Ciccolo Joseph	968	musician	34	"
H	Ciccolo Providenza †	968	manager	32	"
K	Ciccolo Santa †	968	housewife	67	"
L	Ciccolo Sophia †	968	"	29	"
M	Famulari Anthony	968	optician	31	"
N	Famulari Mary †	968	housewife	36	"
O	Arena Esther †	970	operator	20	"
P	Arena Gaetano	970	laborer	55	"
R	Arena John	970	shipper	25	"
S	Arena Josephine †	970	operator	22	"

9

Bennington Street—Continued

F	Arena Paulina—†	970	stitcher	26	here
G	*Arena Providenza—†	970	housewife	47	"
V	*Giordano Peter	970	laborer	66	"
W	Bergamasco Angelo	970	student	23	82 Leyden
X	Bergamasco Mary—†	970	housewife	45	82 "
Y	DeFrancesco Frank	970	barber	54	here
Z	*DeFrancesco Grace—†	970	housewife	51	"

2214

A	*DeMarco Josephine—†	972	"	34	"
B	DeMarco Sabino	972	bartender	37	"
C	Borso Brigida †	972	tailor	47	"
D	Borso Frederick	972	"	49	"
E	Picardi Aurelio A	972	electrician	38	"
F	Picardi Jennie—†	972	housewife	35	"
H	Indelicato George	976	B F D	35	94 Havre
K	Indelicato Olympia—†	976	housewife	34	94 "
L	Fraser Doris †	976	"	22	here
M	Fraser Reed	976	U S A	22	Ohio
N	Lafferty Florence—†	976	secretary	25	here
O	Pescatelli Mabel—†	976	at home	44	"
P	Berretta Theresa—†	976	"	76	"
R	DiLorenzo Louise †	976	"	50	"
W	Harrington John H	1004	retired	65	"
X	Harrington Mary E—†	1004	housewife	63	"
Y	Stewart Ellen S †	1004	at home	72	Revere
Z	Belange Pauline †	1004	clerk	30	77 Byron

2215

A	Belange Peter P	1004	caretaker	48	77 "
D	Goulston Louis	1008	dentist	43	here
E	Sacco Rose L †	1008	housewife	24	"
F	Sacco Vincent J	1008	chauffeur	46	"
	Gundersen Mary †	1008	cook	60	"
H	Rossi Basilio	1008	janitor	53	"
K	DePalma Mary †	1008	stitcher	28	"
L	DePalma Nancy †	1008	at home	56	"
M	Caledonia George	1008	painter	29	"
N	Caledonia Gilda †	1008	housewife	31	"
O	Capillo Domenic	1008	U S A	29	"
P	Capillo Orietta †	1008	stitcher	27	"
R	DiPipio Concetta †	1008	at home	55	"
S	Coscia Anthony	1008	checker	24	Medford

Bennington Street Continued

T	Coscia Ethel †	1008	housewife	25	Medford
U	Cimmino Carmela †	1008	dressmaker	63	37 Lonsdale
V	Cimmino Rose—†	1008	marker	28	37 "
W	Coronella Joseph	1008	letter carrier	38	1 Allen
Y	Russo Anthony	1008	laborer	62	here

2216

D	McCarthy Florence A—†	1022	housewife	39	81 Homer
E	McCarthy John R	1022	custodian	51	81 Horace
F	Lotti Frank	1022	clerk	52	here
G	*Lotti Nellie—†	1022	housewife	52	"
L	Hicks Mary—†	1024	housekeeper	50	"
M	Iannelli Elaine—†	1024	at home	22	89 Morris
N	Kelley Frederick	1024	B F D	29	Gardner
O	Willis Ira E	1024	operator	54	Revere
P	Coleman John	1024	chauffeur	44	here
R	Delaney Henry	1024	laborer	53	172 Princeton
S	Foster Agnes—†	1024	housewife	49	here
T	Foster Joseph	1024	chauffeur	50	"
U	McIntire William	1024	manager	28	Medford
V	Quartarone John	1024	proprietor	53	here
W	Thompson Walter	1024	policeman	60	"

2217

B	Moschella Michael	1046	guard	32	"
C	Moschella Teresa—†	1046	housewife	32	"
D	Moschella Valentino	1046	U S A	31	"
E	DiAlfonso Cornelia—†	1048	clerk	23	"
F	DiAlfonso Louise—†	1048	photographer	25	"
G	*DiAlfonso Teresa †	1048	tailor	46	"
H	*Greici Assunta †	1050	"	35	"
K	*Grieci Christina †	1050	housewife	62	"
L	*Grieco Pasquale	1050	retired	70	"
M	Fagan Daniel	1052	laborer	66	"
N	Fagan Daniel	1052	U S A	25	"
O	Fagan Douglas	1052	U S N	24	"
P	Fagan Ellen—†	1052	housewife	65	"
R	Kerrigan Patrick	1052	retired	70	"
S	Gunn Elizabeth—†	1052	operator	22	"
T	Gunn Joseph F	1052	U S A	26	"
U	Gunn Margaret—†	1052	operator	24	"
V	Gunn Mary A—†	1052	at home	54	"
W	Gunn Mary B—†	1052	operator	30	"

11

Page	Letter	Full Name.	Residence, Jan. 1, 1942.	Occupation.	Supposed Age.	Reported Residence, Jan. 1, 1942. Street and Number.

Bennington Street— Continued

	Letter	Full Name.	Residence	Occupation	Age	Reported Residence
	x	Gallagher Catherine—†	1052	housewife	56	here
	y	Gallagher George	1052	clerk	57	"
	z	Gallagher William	1052	"	25	"
2218						
	a	Casanova Alfred	1054	welder	35	198 Orient av
	b	Casanova Antonette †	1054	stitcher	24	198 "
	c	DeAngelis Domenic	1054	U S N	25	here
	d	DeAngelis Florence †	1054	housewife	42	"
	e*	DeAngelis Leonard P	1054	operator	44	"
	f	Ballerini Adele †	1054	stitcher	22	"
	g	Ballerini Dante	1054	U S A	23	"
	h	Ballerini Edmund	1054	U S N	29	"
	k	Ballerini Felice	1054	retired	65	"
	l	Ballerini Gaetano	1054	U S A	34	"
	m	Ballerini Lena—†	1054	stitcher	35	"
	n	Ferrante Aida †	1054	"	40	"
	o	Ferrante John	1054	tailor	45	"
	p	Damigella Santina A †	1056	housewife	24	"
	r	Damigella Thomas M	1056	machinist	24	"
	s	Addressi Alice †	1056	clerk	28	"
	t	Addressi Frank	1056	machinist	28	"
	u*	Addressi Nicoletto †	1056	housewife	57	"
	v	Addressi Pauline †	1056	operator	27	"
	w	Hesenius Annie F †	1056	at home	55	"
	x	Hesenius Helen M †	1056	cashier	32	"
	y	Hesenius Robert J	1056	chauffeur	23	"
	z	Petrone Frances †	1058	housewife	25	"
2219						
	a	Petrone Frank	1058	salesman	30	"
	b	Tosney Frances G †	1058	clerk	21	"
	c	Tosney John J	1058	letter carrier	62	"
	d	Tosney Mary A †	1058	housewife	59	"
	e	Tosney Mary E †	1058	clerk	21	"
	f	Tosney Rita M †	1058	operator	26	"
	g	Tosney Christopher J	1058	teacher	32	"
	h	Tosney Harriet †	1058	housewife	33	"
	k	Mantica Domenic	1062	chauffeur	49	"
	l	Mantica Mary †	1062	clerk	21	"
	m	Mantica Sarah —†	1062	housewife	49	"
	n	Lord Irene †	1062	"	27	"
	o	Lord Michael	1062	sign painter	28	"

Bennington Street Continued

P	*Campanilla Bartolo	1062	laborer	62	here
R	*Campanilla Jennie †	1062	housewife	62	"
S	Campanilla John	1062	U S A	21	"
T	Vadala Diego	1062	B F D	50	"
U	Famolare Carolina †	1064	housewife	65	"
V	Famolare Domenic	1064	retired	67	"
W	Famolare John	1064	barber	45	"
X	Famolare Paolo	1064	U S A	38	"
Y	Cappa Joseph	1064	U S C G	23	"
Z	*Cappa Josephine †	1064	housewife	46	"

2220

A	Cappa Maria †	1064	dressmaker	21	"
B	*Cappa Pasquale	1064	plasterer	53	"
C	Fasolino Elvira †	1064	housewife	48	"
D	Fasolino Michael	1064	clerk	62	"
E	Fronduto Louis	1066	U S A	22	964 Benningt'n
F	Fronduto Louise †	1066	housewife	23	964 "
G	*Polsonetti Filomena †	1066	tailor	52	964 "
H	Ciarfella Diego	1066	coppersmith	42	here
K	Ciarfella Mary †	1066	housewife	41	"
L	Polsonetti Agostino	1066	U S A	20	"
M	*Polsonetti Antonio	1066	tailor	46	"
N	Bruno Angelina †	1070	housewife	48	"
O	Bruno Frank	1070	painter	52	"
P	Johnson Mary †	1072	housewife	23	108 Pearl
R	Johnson Paul	1072	shipfitter	29	108 "
S	Cuneo Emma M †	1072	housewife	59	here
T	Cuneo John B	1072	retired	68	"
U	Cuneo John J	1072	U S N	28	"
V	Cuneo Mable L †	1072	assembler	39	"

2221   Boardman Street

A	Cataldo Carmela †	7	typist	23	here
B	*Cataldo Charles	7	plasterer	56	"
C	Cataldo Charles, jr	7	U S A	21	"
D	Cataldo Elizabeth †	7	mechanic	25	"
E	*Cataldo Theresa †	7	housewife	52	"
F	Baldassaro Bernard	7	pipefitter	35	"
G	Baldassaro Esther †	7	housewife	33	"
H	Gleason Walter	7	U S N	40	"

13

Boardman Street—Continued

	K	Palazzo Margaret—†	7	stitcher	30	here
	L	Bernardi Henry	9	chauffeur	54	Revere
	M	Campbell Benjamin	9	inspector	32	here
	N	Campbell Mary—†	9	housewife	27	"
	O	*Iapicca Isabella—†	9	stitcher	52	"
	P	Iapicca Michael	9	barber	47	"
	R	DiLorenzo Carmen	9	U S A	29	"
	S	*DiLorenzo Gaetano	9	barber	57	"
	T	*DiLorenzo Madeline—†	9	housewife	52	"
	U	DiLorenzo Rose—†	9	laundress	21	"
	V	Grieco Joseph L	11	carpenter	24	"
	W	Grieco Marie—†	11	housewife	24	"
	X	Croce Helen—†	11	saleswoman	35	"
	Y	Croce Matilda—†	11	houseworker	58	"
	Z	Spagnola Elizabeth—†	11	stitcher	38	"

2222

	A	Spagnola Vincent	11	shoeworker	45	"
	B	Famulari Domenic	11	retired	74	"
	C	*Famulari Rhoda—†	11	housewife	61	"
	D	Guardabassio John	15	clerk	34	"
	E	Guardabassio Mary—†	15	stitcher	28	"
	F	Bagarozza Camille—†	15	housewife	39	"
	G	Bagarozza Nunzio J	15	proprietor	39	"
	H	Fisher Minnie—†	15	housewife	43	"
	K	Fisher Vincent	15	coppersmith	52	"
	L	Lopez John A	16	laborer	39	"
	M	Lopez Mildred—†	16	housewife	39	"
	N	Sacco George M	16	U S A	29	"
	O	Sacco John M	16	"	30	"
	P	Anderson Arthur T	19	electrician	32	"
	R	Anderson Margaret—†	19	housewife	29	"
	S	Bonanno Carmela—†	19	"	28	"
	T	Bonanno Joseph	19	chauffeur	35	"
	U	Maiellano Alphonse	19	attorney	29	"
	V	Maiellano Diana—†	19	housewife	34	"
	W	Morse Andrew	23	longshoreman	40	"
	X	Morse Eva—†	23	housewife	41	"
	Y	Patti Mary—†	23	"	31	"
	Z	Patti Salvatore	23	machinist	42	"

2223

	A	Raffo George	23	retired	40	"

14

Page.	Letter.	FULL NAME.	Residence, Jan. 1, 1943.	Occupation.	Supposed Age.	Reported Residence, Jan. 1, 1942. Street and Number.

Boardman Street—Continued

	B	*Raffo Mary †	23	housewife	60	here
	C	Raffo Edward	23	machinist	21	"
	D	Raffo John	23	U S A	44	"
	F	Vecchio Emily †	29	housewife	32	"
	G	Vecchio Vito	29	salesman	33	"
	H	Caprini Pasquale	31	welder	32	"
	K	Caprini Rose †	31	housewife	28	"
	L	Dante Ida M †	31	"	26	"
	M	Reynolds Eleanor †	33	"	43	"
	N	Cerullo Antonio	33	laborer	53	"
	O	Cerullo Carmen	33	factoryhand	23	"
	P	*Cerullo Mary †	33	housewife	48	"
	R	Cerullo Ottavio	33	machinist	21	"
	S	Vecchio Domenic	33	clerk	34	"
	T	Vecchio Margaret †	33	housewife	36	"
	U	*Sparaco Concetta †	35	"	59	"
	V	Sparaco Emilio	35	operator	32	"
	W	Hanna Marie †	35	housewife	28	"
	X	Borrelli Eleanor †	41	"	28	"
	Y	Borrelli Vincent	41	machinist	31	"
	Z	DeSimone Anna †	41	housewife	52	"

2224

	A	DeSimone Vincent	41	laborer	52	"
	B	LaVita Leonora †	41	machinist	25	"
	C	Cotter Frederick J	47	clerk	28	219 Lexington
	D	Cotter Mary C †	47	housewife	24	219 "
	E	Cucchiarella Giacomo	49	laborer	72	here
	F	Perricotti Charles	49	"	32	"
	G	Perricotti Edith †	49	housewife	30	"
	H	Frongillo Adeline †	53	"	32	"
	K	Frongillo John	53	B F D	33	"
	L	Martinello Frank	53	laborer	48	"
	M	*Martinello Josephine †	53	housewife	44	"
	N	Collarusso Palmina †	53	seamstress	27	"
	O	*DeFeo Domenic	53	retired	60	"
	P	Martinello Augustine	53	U S A	22	"
	R	*Martinello Rose †	53	seamstress	20	"
	U	McGilvery Alfreda †	111	housewife	23	"
	V	McGilvery Paul	111	machinist	24	"
	W	Ness John H	111	electrician	28	235 Leyden
	X	Ness Thelma L †	111	housewife	26	28 Trenton

15

Boardman Street—Continued

y	Kelleher Charles P	111	tester	24	Cambridge
z	Kelleher Marion—†	111	housewife	21	15 Boardman
	2225				
A	*Vecchio Joseph	162	retired	74	here
B	*Vecchio Maria †	162	housewife	64	"

Breed Street

L	McDonald Edward	7	chauffeur	40	here
M	McDonald Jeanette—†	7	housewife	35	"
N	*Cavagnaro Mary—†	7	at home	65	"
O	Cavagnaro Robert	7	U S N	43	"
P	Garvey Anna—†	7	spinner	32	"
R	Bernardi Isadore	7	laborer	37	"
S	Bernardi Mary—†	7	housewife	34	"
T	Pungenti Domenic	9	painter	37	"
U	*Pungenti Marie—†	9	housewife	35	"
V	Benincuora Arcangela †	9	clerk	20	"
W	Benincuora Nicola	9	barber	58	"
X	Celia Carmella †	9	housewife	31	"
Y	Celia Joseph	9	electrician	37	"
Z	Carresi John	10	merchant	42	"
	2226				
A	Carresi Rose †	10	housewife	41	"
B	Lucozzi Domenic E	10	realtor	54	"
C	Lucozzi Teresa P †	10	housewife	58	"
D	Dong Bow Hay	15	laundryman	62	Brookline
M	DeSimone Joseph	17	retired	63	here
N	DeSimone Josephine †	17	cashier	32	"
O	DeSimone Leanora †	17	housewife	57	"
P	DeSimone Rose †	17	clerk	22	"
R	Sirianni John	17	salesman	33	20 Breed
S	Sirianni Rose †	17	housewife	26	20 "
	Giuffre Joseph	17	fish dealer	43	here
	Giuffre Josephine †	17	housewife	40	"
	London Anna †	17	at home	64	"
W	Vitale Gaetano	20	U S A	25	"
X	Vitale Nicola	20	retired	72	"
	Vitale Rose †	20	housewife	60	"
	Vatalaro Anthony	20	laborer	44	63 Leyden

2227

Breed Street Continued

A	Vatalaro Marie †	20	housewife	32	63 Leyden
B	Corso Maria †	20	"	26	here
C	Corso Nazareth	20	U S A	24	"
D	Patti Antonio	20	retired	67	"
E	Patti Joseph	20	U S A	24	"
F	Patti Josephine †	20	housewife	65	"
G	Patti Sebastiano	20	clerk	27	"
K	Kelly Josephine D †	23	housewife	44	43 Montmorenci av
L	Kelly William J	23	B F D	46	43 "
M	Kelly William J, jr	23	U S A	21	43 "
N	Malatesta Isadore	23	manager	31	here
O	Mangini Albert	23	"	35	"
P*	Mangini Angela †	23	at home	66	"
R	Porcello Fiore	23	shoeworker	46	"
S	Porcello Florence †	23	housewife	52	"
T	Porcello Gennaro	23	shoeworker	54	"
U	O'Brien Alma F †	23	housewife	33	"
V	O'Brien Francis P	23	machinist	29	"
W	Culkeen Elizabeth L †	25	housewife	52	"
X	Culkeen John J	25	realtor	57	"
Y	Culkeen John L	25	U S A	24	"
Z	Moltedo Aurelia †	25	at home	50	"

2228

A	Moltedo Henry	25	maint'n'ceman	41	"
B	Moltedo Mildred B †	25	manager	54	"
C	Moltedo Virginia †	25	at home	75	"
D	Reidt Mary L †	25	housewife	43	1084 Saratoga
E	Reidt William	25	clerk	50	1084 "
F	Buckley Edmund	26	clergyman	31	here
G	Cronin Francis	26	"	70	"
H	Norton Richard	26	"	37	52 Walk Hill
K	Talbot Celanine †	26	housekeeper	64	here
L	DeRose Concetta †	40	housewife	46	"
M	DeRose Domenic	40	plasterer	51	"
N*	Zucco Grace †	40	housewife	36	"
O	Zucco Peter	40	baker	40	"
P*	Filipponi Emily †	40	housewife	39	126 Leyden
R	Filipponi Pasquale	40	rubberworker	51	126 "
S	Santarpio Frank	42	salesman	25	8 Barnes av
T	Santarpio Marion †	42	housewife	21	8 "

1—22

17

Breed Street—Continued

	U	Fiorillo Anna—†	42	clerk	30	here
	V	Fiorillo Josephine—†	42	candymaker	42	"
	W	Fischer Joseph	42	policeman	44	"
	X	Fischer Mary C—†	42	housewife	38	"
	Y	Saggese Assunta—†	42	at home	78	"
2229						
	A	DiCenzo Annette—†	46	examiner	22	"
	B	DiCenzo Arthur	46	U S N	33	"
	C	DiCenzo Giuseppe	46	retired	63	"
	D	DiCenzo Michelina—†	46	housewife	56	"
	E	DiCenzo Yola—†	46	clerk	25	"
	F*	Meoli Antonette—†	46	housewife	37	"
	G	Meoli Felix	46	U S A	20	"
	H	Meoli Marino	46	candymaker	48	"
	K	Tuberosa Lena—†	46	housewife	31	"
	L	Tuberosa Michael	46	U S C G	34	"
	O	Maio Helen—†	82	housewife	43	"
	P	Maio Joseph	82	electrician	43	"
	R	Wood Alice—†	82	housewife	33	"
	S	Wood Waymon W	82	superintendent	41	"
	T*	Berando Angela—†	82	at home	58	"
	U	Berando Ann—†	82	clerk	29	"
	V	Berando Catherine—†	82	saleswoman	32	"
	W	Berando Julius	82	inspector	61	"

2230   Ford Street

	A	Lento Ida—†	4	housewife	35	here
	B*	Lento Pasquale	4	laborer	69	"
	C	Lento Samuel	4	machinist	41	"
	D	Pepe Lena—†	4	clerk	28	100S Bennington
	E	Diminico Crescenzio	4	laborer	55	here
	F	Diminico Vincenza—†	4	housewife	55	"
	G	Margareci Antonio	6	laborer	52	"
	H	Margareci Josephine—†	6	floorwoman	23	"
	K	Margareci Lillian—†	6	housewife	47	"
	L	Margareci Mary—†	6	domestic	21	"
	M	Famolare Joseph	6	chauffeur	23	33 Breed
	N	Famolare Mildred—†	6	housewife	21	33 "
	O	Terillo Joseph	6	chauffeur	29	here
	P	Terillo Mary—†	6	housewife	24	"

Ford Street Continued

R	Bartello Leo	7	machinist	41	here	
S	*Bartello Maria †	7	housewife	64	"	
T	Picciotto Luigi	7	retired	72	"	
U	Sullivan Emma L †	7	housewife	45	"	
W	Caresse Salvatore	7	laborer	42	"	
X	Lombardi Sebastian	8	manager	30	"	
Y	Lombardi Yolande †	8	housewife	27	"	
Z	Famolare Constance †	8	"	28	"	

2231

A	Famolare Salvatore	8	chauffeur	29	"	
B	Famolare Angelina †	8	housewife	46	"	
C	Famolare Charles	8	U S N	23	"	
D	Famolare John	8	U S A	20	"	
E	Famolare Phillip	8	chauffeur	47	"	
F	*Sarro Emanuela †	11	housewife	63	"	
G	Sarra Peter	11	gardener	63	"	
H	Abramo Cremerdina †	11	tailor	31	222 Gladstone	
K	*Abramo Salvatore E	11	cabinetmaker	36	222 "	
L	Pepe Darte	21	machinist	22	1008 Bennington	
M	Pepe Nellie †	21	housewife	49	1008 "	
N	Pepe Pasquale	21	U S A	24	1008 "	
O	Martucci John	21	laborer	61	here	
P	Martucci Mary †	21	machinist	24	"	
R	Martucci Vincent	21	U S A	23	"	
S	Martucci William	21	"	27	"	
T	*Cataldo Clorinda †	21	housewife	42	"	
U	Cataldo Louis	21	candymaker	47	"	
V	Cataldo Phyllis †	21	laborer	20	"	

Gladstone Street

W	DeCristoforo Angelina †	136	housewife	29	here	
X	DeCristoforo Raymond	136	salesman	32	"	
Y	Mannetta Mary †	136	bookkeeper	24	"	
Z	*Marino Genevieve †	140	housewife	56	"	

2232

A	Marino Joseph	140	draftsman	35	"	
B	Marino Philip	140	retired	58	"	
C	Tacelli Susan †	153	housewife	40	"	
D	Tacelli Vincent	153	shoeworker	18	"	
E	Zito Emily †	153	housewife	50	"	

19

Page	Letter	FULL NAME.	Residence, Jan. 1, 1943.	Occupation.	Supposed Age.	Reported Residence, Jan. 1, 1942. Street and Number.

Gladstone Street Continued

Letter	FULL NAME.	Residence	Occupation	Age	Reported Residence
F	Zito Marguerite †	153	hairdresser	21	here
G	Zito Vincent	153	contractor	53	"
H	*Motta Concetta †	165	housewife	56	"
K	Motta Domenic	165	laborer	22	"
L	*Motta Mary †	165	stitcher	37	"
M	Motta Salvatore	165	U S A	30	"
N	*Motta Sebastiano	165	fisherman	65	"
O	Bramante Sebastiano	165	manager	48	"
P	Bellavia Carmella †	175	housewife	28	"
R	Bellavia Charles	175	upholsterer	29	"
S	Zani Adeline †	175	housewife	47	"
T	Zani Caroline †	175	clerk	27	"
U	Zani John	175	contractor	49	"
V	Zani Joseph	175	U S A	25	"
W	Missucco Rita †	176	housewife	36	"
X	Missucco Robert	176	chauffeur	38	"
Y	Missucco Ernest	176	"	33	"
Z	Missucco Helen †	176	housewife	32	"

2233

Letter	FULL NAME.	Residence	Occupation	Age	Reported Residence
A	Foley Eleanor †	176	clerk	28	N Hampshire
B	Foley Francis	176	U S A	30	"
C	Meehan Edward J	176	pipefitter	59	here
D	Meehan Elizabeth †	176	housewife	59	"
E	Pochini Albert	176	bartender	30	"
F	Pochini Alma †	176	housewife	28	"
G	Beatrice Joseph	183	student	22	"
H	Beatrice Margaret †	183	housewife	42	"
K	Beatrice Mary †	183	clerk	25	"
L	Beatrice Peter	183	manager	45	"
M	DeRocco Caroline †	184	housewife	38	"
N	DeRocco Domenic	184	candymaker	42	"
O	Douglas Dorothea A †	184	clerk	33	"
P	Douglas Frances †	184	housewife	63	"
R	Douglas James A	184	inspector	64	"
S	Douglas John	184	U S N	21	"
T	Belli Nicholas	184	engineer	30	"
U	Belli Rose †	184	housewife	31	"
V	Lombardo Beatrice †	185	"	32	"
W	Lombardo Marghertino	185	shoeworker	41	"
X	Mastrolio Alfred	185	longshoreman	30	"
Y	Mastrolio Liberato	185	salesman	60	"
Z	Mastrolio Rose †	185	housewife	58	"

Page.	Letter.	FULL NAME.	Residence, Jan. 1, 1943.	Occupation.	Supposed Age.	Reported Residence, Jan. 1, 1942. Street and Number.

Gladstone Street — Continued

A	Mastrolio William	185	U S N	28	here
B	Benvissuto Mary E — †	185	housewife	53	"
C	Benvissuto Paul	185	bricklayer	65	"
D	Maggioli Agnes — †	187	housewife	40	"
E	Maggioli Doris — †	187	clerk	20	"
F*	Maggioli Leo	187	chauffeur	43	"
G	Marabella Anthony	189	mechanic	29	Chelsea
H	Marabella Nora — †	189	housewife	27	"
K	Staffier Angelo	189	tailor	57	here
L	Staffier Louis	189	shipper	33	"
M	Staffier Mary — †	189	clerk	20	"
N	Staffier Phyllis — †	189	at home	27	"
O	Staffier Rocco	189	U S A	23	"
P	Barbanti Anthony	191	chauffeur	28	"
R	Barbanti Joseph	191	laundryman	40	"
S*	Barbanti Rose — †	191	housewife	37	"
T	Sykes Angelina — †	191	"	38	"
U	Sykes Walter F, jr	191	clerk	40	"
V	Bianchi Carlo	192	painter	63	"
W	Bianchi Rosa — †	192	housewife	63	"
X	Bianchi Stefano	192	U S A	23	"
Y	Cella Joseph	192	machinist	30	"
Z	Ciullo Michael	192	shipfitter	31	"

A	Ciullo Phyllis — †	192	housewife	28	"
B	Abramo Joseph	195	millhand	40	"
C	Abramo Mary — †	195	housewife	34	"
D	Ferri Alfred	195	U S A	21	"
E*	Ferri Fortunato	195	salesman	53	"
F	Ferri Lillian — †	195	clerk	23	"
G*	Ferri Marcella — †	195	housewife	50	"
H	Gardella Lawrence	196	U S N	41	"
K	Solari Andrew	196	chauffeur	43	"
L	Solari Mary R — †	196	housewife	43	"
M*	Uguccioni Attilio	196	laborer	50	"
N*	Uguccioni Marcella — †	196	housewife	47	"
O	Morris Catherine R — †	196	"	45	"
P*	Morris Mary — †	196	at home	73	Medford
R	Morris Stanley E	196	U S A	23	here
S	Morris William C	196	pharmacist	42	"
T	DiCenzo Dena — †	199	housewife	33	"

Gladstone Street — Continued

c	DiCenzo William	199	electrician	35	here
v	Battaini Ambrose	199	mechanic	30	"
w*	Battaini Theresa †	199	housekeeper	59	"
x	Colombo Joseph	199	tilesetter	52	"
y	Lazzari Adeline †	203	housewife	45	68 Orient av
z	Lazzari Augustus	203	U S N	22	68 "

2236

a	Lazzari Stephen	203	tailor	46	68 "
b	Lazzari Yola †	203	clerk	21	68 "
c*	Cappanella Blanche †	203	housewife	42	here
d	Cappanella Domenic	203	carpenter	52	"
e	Cappanella Ralph	203	U S N	24	"
f	Crovo Herman	204	laborer	38	"
g	Crovo Mary †	204	housewife	34	"
h	Bottini Elena †	204	"	43	"
k	Bottini Sebastian	204	carpenter	47	"
l	Miller Edwin S	204	wireman	58	"
m	Miller Mary L †	204	housewife	58	"
n	Marino Alphonso	207	retired	49	"
o	Marino Antonette †	207	housewife	48	"
p	Marino Peter	207	clerk	21	"
r	Solari Edmund J	207	laundryman	35	"
s	Solari Nellie †	207	housewife	30	"
t	Watson John A	208	electrician	44	"
u	Watson Martha S †	208	at home	76	"
v	Petrillo Anthony J	211	baker	34	"
w*	Petrillo Concetta †	211	housewife	29	"
x	Nasta Alphonso	211	shoemaker	42	"
y	Nasta Josephine †	211	housewife	32	"
z*	Nasta Rose †	211	"	46	"

2237

a*	Nasta Salvatore	211	laborer	49	"
b	Maglio Anthony	215	machinist	26	1066 Bennington
c	Maglio Elena †	215	housewife	30	1066 "
d	Sacco Charles S	215	mechanic	43	here
e	Sacco Louise †	215	housewife	38	"
f	Zagarella Josephine †	219	at home	74	"
g	Zagarella Mary †	219	housewife	46	"
h	Zagarella Peter	219	machinist	51	"
k	Venezrano Emma †	223	housewife	42	"
l	Venezrano Salvatore	223	mechanic	45	"

Leyden Street

M	Pugliese Jennie †	10	housewife	30	here
N	*Pugliese Vincent	10	baker	33	"
O	Vecchio Concettina †	10	housewife	22	"
P	Vecchio William	10	clerk	24	"
R	Buldini Daniel	14	engineer	30	"
S	Buldini Florence †	14	housewife	29	"
U	Ricci Ann †	15	"	34	"
V	Ricci Silvio	15	mechanic	37	"
X	*Bernardi Angeline †	29	housewife	61	"
Y	Bernardi Clara †	29	"	29	"
Z	*Bernardi Dino	29	chef	61	"

2238

A	Bernardi Louis	29	U S N	33	"
B	*Donati Maria †	29	cook	65	"
C	Martini Angelina †	29	at home	32	"
D	Avolio Anthony	29	U S A	23	"
E	Avolio Gene	29	U S N	20	"
F	*Avolio Margaret †	29	housewife	55	"
G	Avolio Mary †	29	operator	20	"
H	Salotti Mary †	29	housewife	47	"
K	Salotti Paul	29	laborer	51	"
L	Bonugli Arlene †	33	clerk	28	"
M	Bonugli Domenic	33	storekeeper	54	"
N	Bonugli Jessie †	33	housewife	54	"
O	Pedone Anna †	35	"	29	"
P	Pedone Samuel	35	chauffeur	28	"
R	Evans Jennie †	35	housewife	50	"
S	Evans Grover G	35	metalsmith	39	"
T	Simonini Casimiro	35	butcher	54	"
U	Simonini Esola †	35	housewife	42	"
V	Simonini George	35	U S A	22	"
W	Simonini Joseph	35	factoryhand	20	"
X	Sacco Brisco	35	watchman	54	"
Y	Sacco Jerome	35	U S A	25	"
Z	Sacco Mary A †	35	housewife	52	"

2239

A	Sacco Rose †	35	millhand	22	"
B	DeMarchi Anna †	35	housewife	51	"
C	DeMarchi Frank	35	mechanic	58	"
E	DeLeo Anthony	47	metalworker	25	75 Allerton
F	DeLeo Mary †	47	housewife	25	here

Leyden Street — Continued

	G	Pasqua Margaret †	47	housewife	35	here
	H	Pasqua Phillip	47	clerk	40	"
	K	Salani Eva I †	49	"	58	"
	L	Forti Rose †	53	housewife	21	Cambridge
	M	Forti Vincent P	53	shipper	27	"
	N	Lucca Jennie †	55	housewife	37	here
	O	Lucca Rocco	55	laborer	43	"
	P	Catroni Dana	57	waiter	43	"
	R	*Catroni Victoria †	57	dressmaker	44	"
	S	Capillo Antonette †	59	stitcher	45	40 Faywood av
	T	*Sarro Anthony	59	laborer	49	here
	U	Sarro Joseph	59	U S A	20	"
	V	Anson Sophie †	60	factoryhand	21	New York
	W	DeLeo Achille	60	machinist	29	here
	X	*DeLeo Anna †	60	housewife	29	"
	Y	Bacigalupo Joseph	60	U S A	23	"
	Z	Bacigalupo Louis	60	"	28	"
2240						
	A	Bacigalupo Louise †	60	bookkeeper	27	"
	B	Bacigalupo Mary †	60	hairdresser	55	"
	C	Bacigalupo Walter	60	retired	58	"
	D	Bacigalupo Walter, jr	60	boilermaker	30	"
	E	Barboza Mary †	60	housewife	20	17 Gladstone
	F	Barboza Stanley	60	chauffeur	29	17 "
	G	Serra Natale	61	U S A	26	26 Leyden
	H	Serra Rose †	61	housewife	24	26 "
	K	Colantuone Jennie †	61	"	58	here
	L	Colantuone Paul	61	millhand	61	"
	M	Brady Lena †	61	housewife	28	"
	N	Brady Robert	61	chauffeur	30	"
	O	Rauseo Frank	63	"	29	"
	P	Rauseo Mary †	63	housewife	24	"
	S	Rossi Andrew	65	chauffeur	29	"
	T	Rossi Doris †	65	housewife	25	"
	U	Amoroso Evelyn †	67	"	28	"
	V	Amoroso Peter	67	manager	30	"
	W	Palumbo Eugene	67	machinist	26	"
	X	Palumbo Sarah †	67	housewife	23	"
	Y	Christopher John	68	factoryhand	51	"
	Z	Christopher Domenic	68	shipfitter	38	"

2241
Leyden Street—Continued

A	Christopher Jeremiah	68	shoeworker	60	here
B	Christopher Mary †	68	housewife	34	"
C	Christopher Mary R †	68	shoeworker	26	"
D	*Christopher Rose †	68	housewife	86	"
E	Femia Joseph	70	laborer	48	"
F	Femia Mary J †	70	inspector	24	"
G	Femia Victoria †	70	housewife	43	"
K	Massa Amelia †	71	"	75	"
L	Massa Amelia F †	71	candyworker	48	"
M	Massa Andrew L	71	U S A	40	"
N	Massa Charles A	71	"	43	"
O	Lemos Anna †	71	candyworker	40	"
P	Lemos Joseph	71	factoryhand	54	"
R	Lemos Lawrence	71	engraver	35	"
S	Lemos Lucinda †	71	candyworker	38	"
T	DeStefano Frank	71	metalworker	52	"
U	DeStefano Josephine †	71	housewife	47	"
V	Femia Charles	72	coppersmith	23	"
W	Femia Nicholas	72	"	26	"
X	Testa Albert	72	"	26	"
Y	Testa Benita †	72	housewife	26	"
Z	*Casenza Salvatore	72	retired	81	"

2242

A	Delaney James	74	carpenter	45	"
B	Delaney Robert	74	U S N	21	"
C	Delaney Virginia †	74	housewife	42	"
D	Delaney Virginia †	74	packer	20	"
F	Lagamosino Anthony	78	laborer	50	"
G	*Lagamosino Victoria †	78	housewife	73	"
H	Lagamosino Laurence	78	machinist	23	"
K	Lagamosino Louis	78	carpenter	55	"
L	Lagamosino Mary †	78	housewife	55	"
M	Daloia Carmen	79	pipefitter	35	"
N	Daloia Nellie †	79	housewife	28	"
O	Mattera Elizabeth †	79	"	26	"
P	Mattera Mario	79	machinist	26	"
R	Mattera Umberto	79	"	24	"
S	Dappollonio Hugh	79	manufacturer	22	"
T	Dappollonio Rose †	79	housewife	49	"

25

Leyden Street Continued

c	Rossi Anello	80	butcher	33	here
v	Rossi Linda †	80	housewife	22	"
w	*Gelona Domenica †	80	"	54	"
x	Sardini Angela †	80	"	26	32 Ashley
y	Sardini Stephen	80	laborer	29	32 "
z	Chillami Concetta †	82	housewife	63	139 Trenton

2243

a	Chillami Grace †	82	shipper	27	139 "
b	DiCicco Albert	82	welder	31	here
c	DiCicco Caroline †	82	housewife	29	"
d	DiCicco James	82	retired	82	"
e	DiCicco Catherine †	82	housewife	29	"
f	DiCicco John	82	pipefitter	35	"
g	Rossi Anna †	83	stitcher	22	"
h	Rossi Mary †	83	"	20	"
k	*Rossi Natalina †	83	housewife	53	"
l	*Rossi Ottavio	83	butcher	54	"
m	*Rossi Adele †	83	housewife	62	"
n	Rossi Alfred	83	factoryhand	27	"
o	*Rossi Andrew	83	butcher	54	"
p	*Zozzi Nicola	83	meat packer	58	"
r	*Zozzi Lena †	83	housewife	52	"
s	Caradonna Mary †	87	"	36	"
t	Caradonna Peter	87	supervisor	39	"
u	*Puzo Frank	87	retired	69	"
v	Puzo Lena †	87	candymaker	34	"
w	*Puzo Mary †	87	housewife	69	"
x	Puzo Teresa †	87	typist	25	"
y	Mayo Emma †	87	clerk	33	"
z	Mayo Frank	87	jeweler	35	"

2244

a	Sherwin Francis	88	U S N	28	474 Sumner
b	Sherwin Tina †	88	housewife	34	821 Saratoga
c	Saisi Ella †	88	"	33	here
d	Saisi Orlando	88	manager	36	"
e	Morganti Egidio	88	meat packer	21	"
f	Morganti Georgia †	88	housewife	55	"
g	Morganti Raffaelo	88	laborer	57	"
h	Morganti Vincenzina †	88	at home	31	"
k	Carley Mary A †	91	housewife	54	"
l	Murphy Caroline †	91	"	51	"

26

Leyden Street Continued

M	Murphy James H	91	inspector	56	here
N	Murphy Robert H	91	U S A	31	Pennsylvania
O	Murphy Adeline R †	91	stenographer	24	here
P	Murphy Lawrence F	91	U S N	22	"
R	Guarino Freolino	96	rigger	38	"
S	Guarino Mary †	96	housewife	33	"
T	*Gaetani Francesco	96	barber	44	"
U	Gaetani Margaret—†	96	embroiderer	39	"
V	Cassasa Alfred	100	chauffeur	27	"
W	Cassasa Rita—†	100	housewife	24	"
X	Massucco Domenic	100	retired	68	"
Y	Massucco Susan †	100	housewife	61	"
Z	Pochini Michael	100	waiter	65	"
2245						
A	Mazzarella Albert	101	clerk	25	"
B	Mazzarella Ernest	101	U S N	27	"
C	Mazzarella Filomena †	101	housewife	64	"
D	Mazzarella Leonard	101	U S A	39	"
E	Mazzarella Mary—†	101	candymaker	31	"
F	Marotta Anthony	101	woodworker	38	"
G	Marotta Lena †	101	housewife	38	"
H	Mazzarella Margaret †	101	"	31	"
K	Mazzarella Orlando	101	mechanic	36	"
L	Saurino Anthony	101	expressman	33	959 Saratoga
M	Saurino Margaret †	101	housewife	29	959 "
N	Cipoletta Palmina—†	103	"	29	here
O	Cipoletta William G	103	U S N	30	"
P	Pignat John	103	tileworker	45	"
R	*Sozio Angelo	105	retired	66	"
S	Sozio Anthony	105	U S N	26	"
T	Sozio Guy	105	U S A	32	"
U	*Sozio Josephine †	105	housewife	60	"
V	Sozio Patsy	105	chauffeur	34	"
W	Rosatto Alfred	115	attendant	20	"
X	Rosatto Frank	115	machinist	25	"
Y	Rosatto John	115	operator	26	"
Z	Church Agnes R †	115	secretary	33	"
2246						
A	Church Mary B †	115	saleswoman	57	"
B	Fatta Graziadio	125	clergyman	67	"
C	Stoma Louis	125	"	61	"

Leyden Street—Continued

D	Maestri Edmund	126	U S A	30	here
E	Maestri Louis	126	pressman	66	"
F	Maestri Max	126	machinist	38	"
G	Maestri Rosa †	126	operator	27	"
H	Maestri Salvatore	126	U S A	35	"
K	*Maestri Vita †	126	housewife	64	"
L	*Scaramazenio Mary †	126	"	50	"
M	*Scaramazenio Phillip	126	tailor	52	"
N	Colantuone Joseph A	128	chauffeur	35	"
O	Colantuone Rose M †	128	housewife	33	"
P	Nonni Carmela †	129	"	48	"
R	LaRosa Esther †	129	"	30	"
S	LaRosa John	129	laborer	35	"
T	DiMarco Antonio	131	operator	45	"
U	DiMarco Lutezia †	131	housewife	43	"
V	Yebba Carmella †	131	at home	50	"
W	Garrone Charles	131	machinist	26	"
X	Garrone Pasquale	131	chef	60	"
Y	*Garrone Victoria †	131	housewife	47	"
Z	Gaeta Anna †	131	"	27	"
	2247				
A	Gaeta Giro	131	maint'n'ceman	31	"
B	Curti Edward G	135	painter	29	"
C	Curti Marie C †	135	housewife	27	"
D	Curti Constantino	135	painter	63	"
E	Curti Marion †	135	housewife	25	"
F	Curti Victor	135	printer	26	"
G	Colantuoni Alfred	136	laborer	47	"
H	Colantuoni Frank	136	U S A	20	"
K	Colantuoni Jennie †	136	housewife	44	"
L	Colantuoni Pasquale	136	metalworker	22	"
M	Meole Anna †	136	housewife	37	"
N	Meole Jerry	136	bricklayer	51	"
O	Caliani Anthony	136	U S A	24	"
P	Caliani Ellen †	136	housewife	54	"
R	Caliani Walter	136	bartender	50	"
S	Covalucci Rose †	137	housewife	32	"
T	Covalucci Vito	137	rigger	32	"
U	Allegra Joseph	137	barber	42	"
V	Allegra Josephine †	137	housewife	38	"

Page.	Letter.	FULL NAME.	Residence, Jan. 1, 1943.	Occupation.	Supposed Age.	Reported Residence, Jan. 1, 1942. Street and Number.

Leyden Street Continued

	w	Bray George F	137	assembler	43	here
	x	Bray Mary †	137	housewife	38	"
	z	DeTroia Mary †	139	"	40	"
2248						
	A	DeTroia Peter	139	superintendent	42	185 Maverick
	B	Sullivan Emily †	140	housewife	35	here
	C	Sullivan James J	140	painter	35	"
	D	Ciampa Bella †	140	housewife	32	"
	E	Ciampa Frank A	140	laborer	34	"
	F	Sorace Domenic	142	guard	28	"
	G	Sorace Olive †	142	housewife	27	"

Montmorenci Avenue

	K	Dinarello Aphrodite †	2	milliner	21	here
	L	Dinarello Joseph	2	salesman	46	"
	M	Dinarello Mary †	2	housewife	40	"
	N	Maggio Mario	2	salesman	45	"
	O	Lamborghini Dorothy †	4	housewife	32	"
	P	Lamborghini Frank	4	salesman	32	"
	R	Palladino Alonsine †	8	housewife	29	"
	S	Palladino Anthony	8	salesman	33	"
	T	Foster Lawrence B	12	"	43	"
	U	Foster Martha K †	12	at home	81	"
	V	Paterson Julia O †	16	housewife	37	"
	W	Paterson Thomas A	16	manager	43	"
	X	Bonner Catherine †	24	housewife	76	"
	Y	Bonner William N	24	superintendent	53	8 Irvington
	Z	Rawson Anna N †	32	housewife	56	here
2249						
	A	Rawson Thomas R	32	electrician	60	"
	B	McCarthy Mary †	43	housewife	41	40 W Eagle
	C	McCarthy William F	43	foreman	38	40 "
	E	Bradley Barbara †	63	clerk	22	here
	F	Bradley Carlton	63	U S A	24	"
	G	Bradley Hugh	63	salesman	47	"
	H	Bradley John	63	U S A	25	"
	K	Bradley Mildred †	63	housewife	47	"
	L	Peterson Anna †	63	retired	75	"

Page	Letter	Full Name	Residence, Jan. 1, 1943	Occupation	Supposed Age	Reported Residence, Jan. 1, 1942. Street and Number.

Orient Avenue

	M	Domatelli Jennie — †	162	housewife	43	here
	N	Domatelli Joseph	162	cobbler	47	"
	O	Domatelli Assunta — †	164	housewife	47	"
	P	Domatelli August	164	tailor	46	"
	R	Lanza Angelina — †	166	housewife	52	"
	S	Lanza Concetta — †	166	at home	31	"
	T	Lanza Frank	166	U S A	26	"
	U	Lanza Louis	166	engineer	53	"
	V	Venezia Philomena — †	166	at home	29	"
	W	Gagliardi Daniel	169	operator	21	"
	X	Gagliardi Josephine — †	169	housewife	23	"
	Y	*Viscione Anna — †	169	"	50	"
	Z	Viscione Ralph	169	candymaker	55	"

2250

	A	Watson Mary G — †	170	housewife	66	"
	B	Watson Rudolph F	170	clerk	66	"
	C	Paterson Charles E	176	treasurer	73	"
	D	Paterson Dorothy L — †	176	housewife	59	"
	E	DeStefano Anthony	190	contractor	43	"
	F	DeStefano Cathrine — †	190	housewife	43	"
	G	DeStefano Ralph A	190	engineer	20	"
	H	Carroll Helen T — †	191	at home	34	Malden
	K	MacLeod Alexander	191	fireman	35	here
	L	MacLeod Rosalie — †	191	housewife	33	"
	M	Walsh Ella W — †	191	"	67	"
	N	Walsh Peter S	191	laborer	67	"
	O	Sonego Elmira — †	198	housewife	36	"
	P	Sonego Sante	198	marbleworker	39	"
	R	Tarquinio Mary — †	198	housewife	39	"
	S	Tarquinio Sabatino	198	pipefitter	43	"
	T	Ruggiero Guy	205	contractor	48	"
	U	Ruggiero Kathrine — †	205	housewife	39	"
	V	Pelligrini Ernest	208	sculptor	53	"
	W	Pinardi Mary — †	208	housekeeper	56	"
	X	Carbone Dora — †	216	broker	30	"
	Y	Carbone Judith — †	216	housewife	59	"
	Z	Carbone Olga — †	216	bookkeeper	30	"

2251

	A	Carbone Paul A	216	U S A	24	"
	B	Carbone Vito	216	superintendent	59	"
	C	Anderso Augusti — †	232	cook	56	47 Ocean

Orient Avenue Continued

	D	Palladeno Louise †	232	housewife	36	here
	E	Palladeno Rocci	232	horse trainer	36	"
	F	McNeill Beatrice W †	236	housewife	52	"
	G	McNeill Charles W	236	expediter	57	"
	H	McNeill Hazel W †	236	nurse	29	Rhode Island
	K	McNeill William H	236	U S A	26	here
	L	Murphy Doris E †	236	W A A C	26	Rhode Island
	M	Federico Angelina †	240	housewife	44	here
	N	Federico Jeanette †	240	at home	21	"
	O	Federico Paul	240	welder	23	"
	P	Federico Paul	240	"	52	"
	R	Bumpus Sarah A †	244	housewife	37	"
	S	Bumpus Warren E	244	teacher	42	"
	T	Hochmuth Eva A †	248	housewife	49	"
	U	Hochmuth Francis W	248	U S A	27	"
	V	Hochmuth William W	248	superintendent	54	"
	W	Stone Betty L †	251	housewife	36	"
	X	Stone Julius	251	lawyer	41	"
	Y	Tobia Elvira †	252	housewife	32	"
	Z	Tobia Fredrico	252	salesman	39	"

2252

	A	Umana Guy	255	baker	33	"
	B	Umana Yolanda †	255	housewife	33	"

Saratoga Street

	C	Jackson Gaynell M †	865	housewife	68	here
	D	McClusky Charles F	865	U S N	43	"
	E	Ramsell Harry E	865	operator	57	"
	F	*Santangelo Anna †	869	housewife	52	"
	G	*Santangelo Joseph	869	laborer	54	"
	H	Santangelo Michael	869	U S A	23	"
	K	Santangelo Santa †	869	packer	20	"
	L	Santangelo Thomas	869	mechanic	24	"
	M	Sacco George	871	U S N	21	"
	N	Sacco John	871	mechanic	28	"
	O	*Sacco Louise †	871	housewife	52	"
	P	*Sacco Sabato	871	laborer	53	"
	R	Martiniello Carlo	871	mechanic	43	53 Leyden
	S	Martiniello Lucy †	871	housewife	34	53 "
	T	Durante Armando	873	laborer	33	here

Page.	Letter.	FULL NAME.	Residence, Jan. 1, 1943.	Occupation.	Supposed Age.	Reported Residence, Jan. 1, 1942. Street and Number.

Saratoga Street—Continued

c	*Durante Virginio	873	storekeeper	58	here
v	Durante Irene M †	873	housewife	36	"
w	Durante Vincent	873	mechanic	40	"
x	Oliver Ferdinand	875	"	39	"
y	Oliver Mary J †	875	housewife	70	"
z	McDonald John	875	laborer	47	"

2253

a	McDonald Margaret †	875	housewife	42	"
b	Buldini Antonetta †	877	"	25	"
c	Buldini Guido	877	mechanic	29	"
d	Conigliano Antonio	877	laborer	54	"
e	Conigliano Concetta †	877	housewife	51	"
f	Conigliano Joseph	877	U S A	22	"
g	Farmer John J	879	mechanic	24	Somerville
h	Farmer Mary †	879	housewife	53	"
k	Mastromarino Catoline †	879A	"	47	here
l	Mastromarino Donato	879A	laborer	52	"
m	Mastromarino Edith †	879A	packer	26	"
n	Mastromarino Mary †	879A	"	29	"
o	Mastromarino Michael	879A	U S A	26	"
p	Joy Edward	897	laborer	20	"
r	Joy John	897	U S A	30	"
s	Joy Margaret †	897	packer	24	"
t	Joy Mary †	897	operator	28	"
u	Joy Sarah †	897	housewife	59	"
v	Joy Walter	897	mechanic	27	"
w	Joy Winifred †	897	packer	23	"
x	Caruso Anthony	898	farmer	30	"
y	Caruso Celia †	898	nurse	28	"

2254

a	Caruso Domenic	898	farmer	21	"
b	Caruso Gloria †	898	hairdresser	20	"
c	Caruso Pasquale	898	U S A	25	"
d	Caruso Ralph	898	"	23	"
e	Ricciardella Anthony	898	"	31	64 Brooks
f	Ricciardella Mary †	898	housewife	29	64 "
g	Strete Maria †	901	"	56	here
h	Crosley Anna C †	901	forewoman	48	"
k	Crosley Catherine F †	901	clerk	49	"
l	Crosley Martin J	901	chauffeur	40	"
m	Crosley Mary I †	901	clerk	36	"

Saratoga Street Continued

N	Crosley Rose A †	901	housewife	77	here
O	Barker Edward	901	U S A	22	"
P	Barker Harry L	901	chauffeur	54	"
R	Barker Margaret †	901	housewife	51	"
S	Barker Margaret †	901	clerk	20	"
T	Gylling Selma †	903	housewife	65	"
U	LaChance Edward E	903	laborer	57	"
V	Williams Albert L	903	"	42	"
W	Thornton George J	903	mechanic	43	"
X	Thornton Mary M †	903	housewife	42	"
Y	Pellegrino Frank	903	janitor	55	"
Z	Pellegrino Nicholas	903	mechanic	22	"
	2255				
A	Pellegrino Philomena †	903	housewife	49	"
B	Faulkner Grace V †	905	"	33	"
C	Faulkner Joseph R	905	clerk	43	"
D	Duffy Catherine †	905	housewife	75	"
E	Duffy John J	905	U S A	43	"
F	Duffy Thomas	905	laborer	75	"
G	Faulkner George	905	mechanic	70	"
H	Faulkner Mary M †	905	stenographer	36	"
K	Interbartolo Louise †	907	housewife	38	"
L	Interbartolo Rosario	907	storekeeper	39	"
M	Iarussi Frances †	907	clerk	21	"
N	Iarussi Mary †	907	housewife	42	"
O	*Lizzi Louise †	907	"	93	"
P	Celino Edward	907	welder	21	"
R	Celino James	907	"	28	"
S	Celino Lucy †	907	housewife	51	"
T	Celino Pasquale	907	barber	62	"
U	Swanson Eric P	911	mechanic	45	"
V	Swanson Gretta †	911	housewife	45	"
W	Arrigo Marie †	911	"	47	"
X	Arrigo Phillip	911	musician	46	"
Y	Larsen Lawrence	911	U S N	26	Winthrop
Z	Larsen Lena †	911	housewife	22	"
	2256				
A	Cosato Anthony	911	U S N	22	here
B	Cosato John	911	laborer	25	"
C	*Cosato Mary †	911	housewife	46	"
D	Cosato Rudolph	911	U S N	20	"

Saratoga Street — Continued

E	Cosato Virginia —†	911	tailor	53	here	
F	Fresco Joseph	951	chauffeur	24	126 Thornton	
G	Fresco Muriel—†	951	housewife	24	126 "	
H	Maggiore Agrippino—†	951	"	67	here	
K	Maggiore Imprimo	951	laborer	80	"	
L	Maggiore Louise —†	951	packer	25	"	
M	Covalucci Alberta —†	951	housewife	33	406 Sumner	
N	Covalucci Mario	951	bricklayer	35	406 "	
O	Sacco Henry E	953	chipper	29	here	
P	Sacco Mary G —†	953	housewife	29	"	
R	Corrado Frank	953	shoemaker	50	"	
S	Corrado Phyllis—†	953	housewife	45	"	
T	Scaromozzino Angelo	953	tailor	32	"	
U	Scaromozzino Celia—†	953	housewife	32	"	
V	McKinnon John	955	salesman	28	Somerville	
W	McKinnon Rose—†	955	housewife	23	"	
X	Crucioli Domenic	955	laborer	49	here	
Y	*Crucioli Pasqualina—†	955	housewife	39	"	
Z	Guinta Joseph	955	barber	48	"	

2257

A	*Guinta Margaret —†	955	housewife	47	"	
B	Margareci Placido	955	candymaker	49	"	
C	Tannozzini Ido	957	painter	56	"	
D	Tannozzini Joseph	957	draftsman	25	"	
E	Tannozzini Louie	957	U S A	21	"	
F	Tannozzini Mabel —†	957	housewife	46	"	
G	Pennacchini Francis M	957	barber	58	"	
H	Pennacchini Rose —†	957	housewife	50	"	
L	Iannetti Mary —†	957	"	49	"	
M	Iannetti Raymond	957	laborer	28	189 Cottage	
N	Iannetti Ugo	957	U S A	21	here	
O	Iannetti Vincent	957	barber	60	"	
P	Guanera Joseph	958	mechanic	30	"	
R	Guanera Mary —†	958	housewife	29	"	
S	Caizzi Mildred —†	958	"	25	"	
T	Caizzi Thomas	958	chauffeur	29	"	
U	Jefferson Ernest	958	salesman	30	"	
V	Jefferson Madeline—†	958	housewife	34	"	
W	Parrelli Catherine —†	958	"	42	"	
X	Parrelli Ernest	958	shoemaker	38	"	

34

Saratoga Street — Continued

		FULL NAME	Residence	Occupation	Age	Reported Residence
Y		Campanaro Anna †	959	dressmaker	32	here
Z		Campanaro Florence †	959	"	27	"
	2258					
A		Campanaro Gabriel	959	U S A	44	"
B	*	Campanaro Pasqualine †	959	housewife	66	"
C		Anzalone Mary J †	959	"	30	"
D		Anzalone Thomas	959	mechanic	42	"
E		Micciche Anna †	959	housewife	31	104 Paris
F		Micciche Santi	959	shoemaker	42	104 "
G		Guarino Carlo	960	laborer	49	21 Ford
H		Guarino Lucia †	960	housewife	50	21 "
K		Donovan Helene †	960	clerk	33	Winthrop
L		Sovio Mario	961	shoemaker	34	here
M		Sovio Mary †	961	housewife	28	"
N		Leccese George	961	mechanic	28	"
O		Leccese Josephine †	961	housewife	27	"
P		Arena Concetta †	961	"	30	"
R	*	Pino Mary †	961	"	51	"
S	*	Pino Orazio	961	butcher	56	"
T		Richards Edwin S	962	machinist	58	9 Boardman
U		Richards Florence †	962	housewife	50	9 "
Y		Iannaccone Louise †	963	"	29	here
Z		Iannaccone Pellegrino	963	mechanic	29	"
	2259					
A	*	Siragusa Celia †	963	housewife	46	"
B		Siragusa Frank	963	weaver	57	"
C		Panaro Concenzio	963	tailor	60	"
D		Panaro Edith †	963	dressmaker	26	"
E		Panaro Nino	963	U S A	22	"
F		Panaro Olga †	963	dressmaker	28	"
G		Panaro Olivia †	963	housewife	65	"
H		Leighton Anna †	965	"	36	"
K		Leighton John	965	laborer	50	"
L		Leighton Joseph	965	U S A	20	"
M		Sgroi Joseph	965	storekeeper	40	"
N	*	Sgroi Josephine †	965	housewife	68	"
O		Mazzapica Alveria †	965	packer	22	"
P	*	Mazzapica Anna †	965	housewife	45	"
R		Mazzapica Charles	965	barber	50	"
S		Mazzapica Peter	965	U S A	23	"
T	*	Florentino Michael	967	baker	58	"

35

Saratoga Street — Continued

U	Sacco Blanche —†	967	clerk	22	here
V	Sacco Carmella —†	967	"	29	"
W	Sacco John	967	retired	56	"
X	Sacco Raffaella —†	967	housewife	49	"
Y	Camelliere Mildred —†	967	"	27	Chelsea
Z	Camelliere Victor	967	chauffeur	27	"

2260

A	McGeney Alfred J	968	retired	69	here
B	McGeney Mary —†	968	housewife	65	"
C	Fooks Abraham	968	storekeeper	55	"
D	*Fooks Agusta —†	968	housewife	49	"
E	Fooks Mildred —†	968	saleswoman	22	"
F	*Stangie Frank	968	laborer	54	"
G	*Strangie Josephine —†	968	housewife	42	"
H	Strangie Pasquale	968	laborer	20	"
M	Hines Agnes A —†	971	housewife	48	242 Meridian
N	Hines Leo F	971	U S A	28	242 "
O	Hines Robert F	971	U S N	52	242 "
T	Vesce Anthony D	974	treasurer	50	here
U	Vesce Clara —†	974	housewife	44	"
V	Vesce Frank	974	retired	85	Winthrop
W	Cianci Delphia —†	974	housewife	40	here
X	Cianci William	974	musician	41	"
Y	Maniglia Alphonse	974	barber	30	"
Z	Maniglia Diega —†	974	housewife	26	"

2261

A	*DeStefano Josephine —†	974	"	69	"
B	DeStefano Lillian —†	974	clerk	35	"
C	DeStefano Munzia —†	974	"	34	"
D	Whitman Grace —†	974	operator	37	"
E	Berry Carmela —†	974	housewife	32	"
F	Berry Lawrence	974	chauffeur	36	"
G	Paci Joseph C	974	mechanic	29	"
H	Paci Julia —†	974	housewife	29	"
R	Cavagnaro Rose —†	980	domestic	63	"
S	Nautta Pietro	980	barber	53	"
T	DePino Grace —†	980	housewife	67	"
U	DePino Leo	980	mechanic	30	"
V	DePino Mary —†	980	stitcher	25	"
W	DePino Nicholas	980	clerk	33	"
X	DePino Sarah —†	980	housewife	29	"

Saratoga Street—Continued

z	Famolare Celia—†	984	housewife	32	here
2262						
A	Famolare Manuel	984	shipper	35	"
B	DeNatila Etta—†	984	housewife	40	"
c	DeNatila Frank	984	barber	44	"
D	*Casallo Frank	984	laborer	64	"
E	*DeAngelis Josephine—†	984	housewife	73	"
F	DeAngelis Robert	984	mechanic	29	"
G	*DeAngelis Sabino	984	laborer	84	"
K	Capillo Charles B	986	inspector	55	"
L	Capillo Esther—†	986	at home	31	"
M	Capillo Ethel—†	986	housewife	53	"
N	Cantillo Florence—†	986	"	25	"
O	Cantillo James	986	salesman	27	"

Tower Street

P	Cotter Mary—†	20	housewife	48	here
R	Cotter William J	20	porter	48	"

Trident Street

S	Roskilly Colin	16	retired	65	here
T	Roskilly Josiah	16	metalworker	60	"

Whitby Street

U	Famolare Charles	9	contractor	41	here
V	Famolare Joseph	9	retired	70	"
W	Famolare Josephine—†	9	housewife	67	"
X	Famolare Steve	9	U S A	35	"
Y	Famolare Domenic	9	milkman	40	"
z	*Famolare Elena †	9	housewife	41	"
2263						
A	DeMella Angelina—†	9	"	49	"
B	DeMella Domenic	9	tailor	53	"
c	DeMella Josephine—†	9	dressmaker	20	"
D	DeMella Louise J—†	9	clerk	28	"
E	DeMella Nicholas J	9	U S A	23	N Carolina
F	Giuffre Anna T—†	10	housewife	30	here
G	Giuffre John A	10	painter	37	"

Whitby Street—Continued

H	DeFrancesco Andrew	10	U S A	25	Maryland
K	DeFrancesco Angelina—†	10	housewife	48	here
L	DeFrancesco Frank	10	salesman	23	"
M	DeFrancesco John	10	finisher	53	"
N	DeFrancisco Rose—†	10	at home	28	"
O	Covino Josephine †	10	dressmaker	23	"
P	Covino Sarah †	10	housewife	47	"
R	Schipellite Jennie †	12	"	32	"
S	Schipellite Vincent	12	clerk	35	"
T	Bartolo Lena †	12	housewife	46	"
U	Bartolo Louis E	12	barber	46	"
V	Luongo Helen †	12	tailor	24	"
W	Famolare Angelina—†	12	housewife	65	"
X	Famolare John	12	retired	63	"
Y	Famolare Louis	12	laborer	33	"
Z	Bonugli Mary †	16	housekeeper	48	"
2264					
A	Bonugli Rose †	16	at home	84	"
B	Ratto Emma †	16	housewife	44	"
C	Ratto Joseph	16	clerk	48	"
D	Ratto Mildred †	16	stenographer	21	"
E	Luti Annie †	16	housewife	55	"
F	Luti Charles	16	metalworker	34	"
G	Luti Christina †	16	"	35	"
H	Carideo Carmine	21	retired	68	"
K	Carideo Carolina †	21	housewife	58	"
L	Fortunate Ella †	21	laborer	37	"
M	Strollo Lillian †	21	clerk	28	"
N	Carideo Irene †	21	housewife	40	"
O	Carideo Patrick	21	bookkeeper	43	"

Ward 1—Precinct 23

CITY OF BOSTON

LIST OF RESIDENTS
20 YEARS OF AGE AND OVER

(NON-CITIZENS INDICATED BY ASTERISK)
(FEMALES INDICATED BY DAGGER)

AS OF

JANUARY 1, 1943

JOSEPH F. TIMILTY, *Chairman*
FREDERIC E. DOWLING, *Secretary*
WILLIAM A. MOTLEY, Jr.
FRANCIS B. McKINNEY
EVERETT R. PROUT
Listing Board.

CITY OF BOSTON PRINTING DEPARTMENT

2300

Cheever Court

F	*Cacavello Philomena—†	8	housewife	59	here
G	Cacavello Philomena—†	8	factoryhand	21	"
H	*Cacavello Vincenzo	8	laborer	65	"
K	Ruggiero Dora †	9	housewife	69	"
L	Ruggiero Francesco	9	repairman	25	"
M	Ruggiero Joseph	9	retired	70	"
N	DeStefano Josephine —†	10	housekeeper	58	"
O	Brissette James	10	molder	27	35 Charles
P	Brissette Mary †	10	operator	24	35 "
R	Georgio Assunta †	10	factoryhand	21	here
S	Georgio Mary—†	10	housekeeper	60	"
T	*Paci Angelina—†	10	housewife	47	"
U	Paci Fillipo	10	mechanic	21	"
V	Paci Joseph	10	operator	22	"
W	Paci Vincenzo	10	laborer	54	"
X	Pirello Cirro	11	clerk	22	"
Y	Pirello Charles	11	laborer	55	"
Z	Pirello Josephine †	11	housewife	46	"

2301

A	Pirello Mary †	11	factoryhand	21	"
B	Pirello Phillip	11	U S A	24	"
C	Indelicato Charles	12	clerk	30	"
D	Indelicato Rose †	12	housewife	31	"
E	Castalano Mary—†	12	housekeeper	29	"
F	Indelicato Catherine †	12	factoryhand	26	"
G	Indelicato Mary †	12	"	27	"
H	Indelicato Michael	12	"	63	"
K	Indelicato Serafina †	12	housewife	57	"
L	Castalano Carmela †	12	"	37	"
M	Castalano Joseph	12	mechanic	40	"

Cottage Street

	Ciarlone Charles	57	retired	70	here
O	Ciarlone Mary †	57	housewife	68	"
P	*Marino Charles	57	barber	49	"
R	Marino Concetta †	57	saleswoman	20	"
S	Marino Grace †	57	stitcher	21	"
T	Marino Rose †	57	housewife	44	"
V	Bonacosta Annette †	59	"	27	"

Page.	Letter.	FULL NAME.	Residence, Jan. 1, 1913.	Occupation.	Supposed Age.	Reported Residence, Jan. 1, 1912. Street and Number.

Cottage Street Continued

	W	Bonacosta Fred	59	laborer	28	here
	X	Simonelli Carmen	59	U S A	34	"
	Y	Simonelli Evelyn †	59	at home	30	"
	Z	Simonelli Marion †	59	housewife	65	"
2302						
	A	Simonelli Mary †	59	at home	32	"
	B	Simonelli Rubina †	59	hairdresser	26	"
	C	Simonelli Samuel	59	barber	61	"
	D	Simonelli Theodore	59	clerk	43	"
	F	DeMasellis Louis	61	tailor	43	"
	G*	DeMasellis Rose †	61	housewife	41	"
	H	DeMasellis Vincent	61	U S A	20	"
	K	Selvitella Carmen	61	storekeeper	40	"
	L*	Selvitella Grace †	61	housewife	50	"
	N	Guida Genaro	67	calker	32	"
	O	Guida Vincenza †	67	housewife	25	"
	P	DeNisco John	67	butcher	50	"
	R	DeNisco Natalie †	67	housewife	37	"
	S	Cogliandro Michael	68	U S A	24	"
	T	Cogliandro Paola M †	68	housewife	48	"
	U	Cogliandro Saverio	68	storekeeper	56	"
	W	Turilli Fannie †	69	housewife	26	"
	X	Turilli Serafino	69	chauffeur	27	"
	Y	Gambardella Carmella †	69	stitcher	24	"
	Z	Gambardella Gaetano	69	storekeeper	58	"
2303						
	A	Gambardella Lucy †	69	housewife	59	"
	B	Wardell Joseph	69	guard	32	"
	C	Wardell Josephine †	69	housewife	28	"
	D	Briatico Antonio	70	laborer	19	"
	E	Briatico Barbara †	70	operator	24	"
	F	Briatico Carmella †	70	housewife	43	"
	G	Capparello Angelo	70	machinist	26	Barre
	K*	Pacella Nicholas	72	retired	59	170 Everett
	L*	Nucci Joseph	72	salesman	58	here
	M*	Nucci Maria †	72	housewife	47	"
	N*	Cresta Elizabeth †	73	"	27	5 Cottage
	O	Cresta Gerardo	73	laborer	28	5 "
	P	Rozzi Genevieve †	73	housewife	24	2 Hooten ct
	R	Rozzi Vincenzo	73	laborer	26	2 "
	V	Morello Carmen	75	candyworker	23	72 Cottage

3

Cottage Street — Continued

w	Morello Mary †	75	housewife	20	72 Cottage
x	*Angelo Anna †	75	"	43	here
y	Angelo Leonardo	75	laborer	54	"
z	Nacosia Antonina †	75	housewife	29	73 Cottage

2304

A	Nacosia Louis	75	electrician	38	73 "
C	*Ravallesa Louise †	76	at home	61	here
D	*Ravallesa Michael	76	storekeeper	65	"
E	*Corrado Lucy †	76	housewife	43	"
F	Corrado Ralph	76	carpenter	47	"
H	*Cerpentino Antonio	77	retired	71	"
K	Tiso Annie †	77	housewife	24	315 Summer
L	Tiso Pasquale	77	laborer	26	315 "
M	Mercurio Charles	77	boilermaker	41	here
O	Brencola Anthony	78	presser	30	"
P	Brencola Theresa †	78	housewife	27	"
R	Galuna James	78	welder	42	"
S	Galuna Jeanette †	78	housewife	27	"
U	Smith Concetta †	79	"	22	37 Haynes
V	Smith Lawrence	79	welder	27	37 "
W	*Tromba Christina †	79	housewife	56	here
X	Tromba Pasquale	79	laborer	60	"
Y	Tromba Salvatore	79	welder	20	"
Z	Tromba Severio	79	machinist	25	"

2305

A	Abramo Anita †	79	housewife	38	"
B	Abramo Domenic	79	fisherman	45	"
D	Picardo Aurelio	80	storekeeper	53	102 Cottage
E	Picardo Lucia †	80	housewife	43	102 "
F	Picardo Rudolph	80	U S A	20	102 "
G	Vigliotte Pasquale	80	shoeworker	44	here
H	Vigliotte Rose †	80	housewife	40	"
L	Velleux Arthur A	81	mechanic	47	Maine
M	Velleux Laura †	81	housewife	28	"
	Lania Giuseppe	81	laborer	67	here
O	Lania Mary †	81	housewife	66	"
	Mercurio John	87	electrician	33	"
	Mercurio Rose †	87	housewife	31	"
U	Inzirillo Constance †	87	operator	33	"
V	Inzirillo Mary †	87	housewife	60	"
W	Inzirillo Sebastiano	87	retired	72	"

Page.	Letter.	FULL NAME.	Residence, Jan. 1, 1913.	Occupation.	Supposed Age.	Reported Residence, Jan. 1, 1912. Street and Number.

Cottage Street Continued

y	Vazza Americo	88	embalmer	38	here
z	Vazza Clara †	88	housewife	30	"

2306

A	*Vazza Emanuela †	88	"	76	"
B	Cancian Charles J	88	collector	39	"
C	Cancian Edith †	88	housewife	32	"
D	Raffaele Angelo	88	machinist	33	"
E	Raffaele Jennie †	88	housewife	31	"
G	Ciampa Angelo	89	laborer	63	"
H	*Ciampa Antonetta †	89	housewife	60	"
K	Inzirillo Antonio	89	laborer	53	"
L	Inzirillo Josephine †	89	housewife	41	"
N	*Rose Dominga †	90	"	63	Revere
O	*Rose Manuel	90	retired	73	"
P	Silva Antonio	90	seaman	62	372 North
R	Manzone Samuel	90	foreman	31	here
S	Manzone Sarah †	90	housewife	28	"
T	Pastore John	90	barber	54	"
U	Pastore Maria †	90	housewife	50	"
W	Kingston Rosalina †	91	"	20	64 Everett
X	Kingston Thomas	91	laborer	26	64 "
Y	Micciche Lena †	91	housewife	21	222 E Eagle
Z	Micciche Paul	91	cutter	22	77 London

2307

B	Scalafani Antonio	92	laborer	31	183 Maverick
C	Scalafani Stella †	92	housewife	27	183 "
D	Evangelista Carmen	92	shoeworker	28	here
E	Evangelista Rose †	92	housewife	22	"
F	Pastore Charles	92	engineer	22	"
G	Pastore Lucy †	92	housewife	25	"
K	Quarantello Angelo	93	foundryman	39	"
L	Quarantello Sarah †	93	housewife	32	"
M	Annese Antonio	93	foundryman	37	"
N	*Annese Elsie †	93	housewife	34	"
O	Spinelli Benjamin	94	storekeeper	27	"
P	Spinelli Maria †	94	housewife	26	"
R	*Spinelli Giovanina †	94	"	69	"
T	DiLongo Alfred	95	U S A	22	New York
U	DiLongo Maria †	95	housewife	26	here
V	Marano Francesca †	95	stitcher	25	"
W	Marano John	95	laborer	65	"

5

Page	Letter	Full Name.	Residence, Jan. 1, 1943.	Occupation.	Supposed Age.	Reported Residence, Jan. 1, 1942. Street and Number.

Cottage Street Continued

	Letter	Full Name.	Residence	Occupation.	Age.	Reported Residence
	x	*Marano Regela †	95	housewife	56	here
	y	Capobianco Joseph	95	bricklayer	47	"
	z	Capobianco Mary †	95	housewife	41	"
2308						
	c	Viarella Joseph	96	fisherman	34	"
	d	Viarella Vita †	96	housewife	28	"
	e	Angella Giochina †	96	"	46	"
	f	Angella Joseph	96	laborer	58	"
	h	Mazzola Christina †	97	leatherworker	26	"
	k	*Mazzola Frank	97	retired	66	"
	l	*Mazzola Jennie †	97	housewife	56	"
	m	Mazzola Lawrence	97	U S A	28	"
	n	Mazzola Victoria †	97	leatherworker	24	"
	o	Zueli Antonio	97	storekeeper	46	"
	p	Zueli Mario	97	U S A	20	"
	r	Zueli Michael	97	welder	24	"
	s	Zueli Vincenza †	97	housewife	49	"
	v	DiGregorio Anthony	98	salesman	34	"
	w	DiGregorio Jennie †	98	housewife	33	"
	x	*Silvitella Carmen	98	retired	75	"
	y	*Silvitella Maria †	98	housewife	73	"
	z	Butera Vincent	98	laborer	23	5 Cheever ct
2309						
	B	*Chioccola Anna †	99	housewife	45	here
	c	Chioccola Domenic	99	barber	46	"
	D	Chioccola Michael	99	laborer	21	"
	E	Chioccola Rose †	99	leatherworker	20	"
	k	Pergola Michael	101	operator	22	"
	l	Pergola Vincenza †	101	housewife	21	"
	m	Guercio Angela †	101	at home	39	"
	n	*Guercio Calozera †	101	housewife	77	"
	o	Guercio Ida †	101	candyworker	37	"
	r	Guercio Marie †	101	designer	35	"
		Modugno Carmella †	102	housewife	34	"
		Modugno Carmen	102	laborer	42	"
		Cinelli Domenic	102	machinist	55	549 Summer
		Pullio Joseph	103	laborer	24	here
		Pullio Nunziata †	103	housewife	22	"
		Bibbo Caroline †	103	"	33	"
2310						
		Bibbo Domenic	103	repairman	47	"

6

Page.	Letter.	FULL NAME.	Residence, Jan. 1, 1943	Occupation.	Supposed Age.	Reported Residence, Jan. 1, 1942. Street and Number.

Emmet Place

	B	*Bisciotti Peter	1	teamster	62	here
	C	Gallo Alfonso	1	laborer	38	"
	D	Evangelista Giuseppe	1	"	38	"
	E	Nostro Domenic	2	retired	74	"
	F	*Bomba Vincenzo	2	laborer	63	"
	G	*Maraio Giuseppe	2	"	48	"
	H	*Maraio Mary — †	2	housewife	42	"
	K	Falcucci Marion †	3	"	38	"
	L	*Falcucci Pasquale	3	retired	78	"
	M	*Falcucci Rocco	3	chauffeur	40	"

Everett Street

	N	Capone Giuseppe	4	laborer	48	here
	O	*Capone Mary — †	4	housewife	41	"
	P	Capone Mary — †	4	florist	22	"
	R	Porazzo Anna — †	4	housewife	33	"
	S	Porazzo Nicholas	4	laborer	35	"
	W	Amabile John	8	carpenter	34	"
	X	Amabile Josephine — †	8	housewife	32	"
	Y	DeSimone Concetta — †	8	"	25	"
	Z	DeSimone Fiore	8	candymaker	31	"

2311

	A	Scaramella Dora C — †	8	housewife	37	"
	B	Scaramella John	8	clerk	49	"
	D	*Maurice Rose — †	11	candyworker	39	37 Decatur
	E	Frongello Anna — †	11	housewife	45	here
	F	Frongello Gaetano	11	carpenter	49	"
	G	Frongello Julia — †	11	clerk	20	"
	K	Picillo Achille	13	laborer	56	"
	L	Picillo Henry	13	dairyman	29	"
	M	Vitagliano Catherine — †	13	housewife	33	"
	N	Vitagliano Mariano	13	laborer	37	"
	O	Barrasso Adeline †	15	operator	28	"
	P	Barrasso Caroline — †	15	housewife	56	"
	R	Barrasso Crescenzio	15	laundryworker	62	"
	S	Barrasso Emilio	15	U S A	30	"
	T	Barrasso Ernest	15	"	26	"
	U	*Marmiani Rose — †	17	at home	59	"
	V	Stone Laura L — †	17	housewife	39	"
	W	Vitale Helen — †	18	"	24	Chelsea
	X	Vitale Vincent	18	packer	26	"

7

Everett Street Continued

y	Vicay Elizabeth †	18	housewife	26	217 Webster
z	Vicay Richard	18	packer	28	217 "

2312

A	Giansiracusa Nelson	19	dyesetter	29	here
B	Giansiracusa Violet †	19	housewife	28	"
C*	Todesco Antonetta †	19	at home	43	"
D	Todesco Pasquale	19	laborer	20	"
H	Brogna Amelia †	21	housewife	27	"
K	Brogna Joseph	21	pipefitter	29	"
L	Ventresca Charles	21	retired	60	"
M	Ventresca Mary †	21	clerk	20	"
N	Ciampa Carmella †	21	housewife	27	"
O	Ciampa Joseph	21	welder	28	"
R	DeMarco Philip	23	shipper	52	"
S	DeMarco Rose †	23	housewife	41	"
T	Riggi Giulio	23	chauffeur	29	190 Cottage
U	Riggi Margaret †	23	housewife	26	190 "
V	DeRose Anthony	25	foreman	42	here
W	DeRose Josephine †	25	housewife	37	"
X*	DiZio Anna †	25	"	37	"
Y	DiZio Warren	25	tailor	46	"
Z	Abbati Angela †	27	at home	39	"

2313

A*	Giunta Candolfo	27	retired	71	"
B*	Giunta Lena †	27	housewife	68	"
C	Bincucci Albert	28	U S A	21	211 Maverick
D	Bincucci David	28	fireman	23	211 "
E*	Bincucci Domenica †	28	housewife	56	211 "
F	Pardi Nicholas	28	laborer	55	211 "
G	DiZio Conrad	29	U S A	21	here
H*	DiZio Evelina †	29	housewife	51	"
K	DiZio Frances †	29	at home	22	"
L	DiZio Vincenzo	29	laborer	55	"
M	Palmerini Mary †	31	operator	21	"
N	Testa Antonio	31	laborer	54	"
O	Testa Maria †	31	housewife	46	"
P	Brunick William	33	U S A	28	19½ Centre
R	Marciano Gaetano	33	pedler	56	here
S	Raso Anthony	33	U S A	21	"
T	Raso Filomena †	33	housewife	46	"
U	Raso Rocco	33	laborer	46	"

8

Everett Street Continued

v	Fratelli Aldolfo	35	ropemaker	49	here
w	Terrazano Concetta †	37	housewife	39	"
x	Terrazano Pasquale	37	welder	43	"
y	Sardella Angelo	39	retired	73	"
z	*Sardella Concetta †	39	housewife	69	"
	2314				
A	Camplese Olga †	39	stitcher	22	"
B	*Camplese Theresa †	39	at home	51	"
C	*Guarino Carmen	39	laborer	57	"
D	Baptista Carmela †	42	housewife	35	"
E	Giusto Frank	42	laborer	46	"
F	Giusto John	42	U S A	21	"
G	Giusto Pasquale	42	"	23	"
H	*Giusto Theresa †	42	housewife	46	"
K	Baptista Mario	42	shoeworker	30	"
L	*Baptista Samuel	42	retired	67	"
M	*Baptista Theresa †	42	housewife	64	"
N	Morrissey John	44	painter	28	"
O	Morrissey Rose †	44	housewife	32	"
P	Barrett Mary †	44	at home	50	"
R	Larkin Delia †	44	"	70	"
S	Larkin Helen R †	44	housewife	27	"
T	Larkin John P	44	electrician	33	"
U	DiPietro Anna †	45	at home	58	"
V	DiPietro Helen †	45	packer	36	"
W	DiPietro Josephine †	45	"	35	"
X	DiPietro Margaret †	45	at home	32	"
Y	DiPietro Alfred	45	laborer	24	"
Z	DiPietro Anthony	45	steelworker	26	"
	2315				
A	DiPietro Lawrence	45	U S A	22	"
B	DiPietro William	45	U S N	28	"
C	Pisano Gaspare	45	baker	60	"
D	Pisano Mary †	45	housewife	50	"
E	Tango Hugo V	46	operator	40	"
F	Tango Mildred †	46	housewife	33	"
G	*Bandanza Santo	46	retired	68	"
H	Capozzi Mario	46	electrician	31	"
K	Capozzi Mary †	46	housewife	32	"
L	*Fruscione Matteo	46	painter	58	"
M	*Fruscione Nancy †	46	housewife	50	"

9

Everett Street — Continued

	N	*Narro John	46	laborer	58	here
	O	DiPietro Ethel †	48	housewife	48	"
	P	DiPietro Michael	48	pipefitter	46	"
	R	Matarazzo Anthony	48	cashier	21	"
	S	Matarazzo Isabella †	48	housewife	62	"
	T	Matarazzo Minnie †	48	stitcher	25	"
	U	Matarazzo Pellegrino	48	laborer	65	"
	V	Matarazzo Victoria †	48	stitcher	24	"
	W	Annese Cecelia †	48	housewife	28	256 Webster
	X	Annese Joseph	48	metalworker	31	256 "
	Y	Marmiane Alexander	49	chauffeur	27	171 Cottage
	Z	Marmiane Helen †	49	housewife	24	171 "

2316

	A	Morello James	49	U S N	35	here
	B	Morello Peter	49	retired	90	"
	C	Morello John	49	coppersmith	40	"
	D	Morello Susie †	49	housewife	38	"
	E	Trevisani Anibale	50	tileworker	59	"
	F	Trevisani Guido	50	U S A	21	"
	G	*Trevisani Maria †	50	housewife	56	"
	H	Ferrara Maria E †	50	"	51	"
	K	Ferrara Nicola P	50	laborer	62	"
	L	Caccamesi Marie †	50	stitcher	23	"
	M	*Caccamesi Theresa †	50	housewife	53	"
	N	DiPietro Joseph	51	tailor	34	"
	O	DiPietro Mollie †	51	packer	28	"
	P	Bertalino Albert	51	U S A	25	"
	R	*Bertalino Andrew	51	fisherman	59	"
	S	Bertalino Angelo	51	fishcutter	20	"
	T	*Bertalino Vita †	51	housewife	55	"
	U	Masselli Frank	51	fishcutter	28	"
	V	Cardarelli Felicia †	51	housewife	48	"
	W	Cardarelli Nicola	51	laborer	50	"
	X	Ficarra Joseph	52	factoryhand	29	"
	Y	Ficarra Rosa †	52	at home	24	"
	Z	Ficarra Vincenzo	52	laborer	68	"

2317

	A	Vanelli Albert	52	"	31	282 Summer
	B	Vanelli Anna †	52	housewife	32	282 "
	C	Dalelio Josephine †	52	"	27	here
	D	Spano Clementina †	54	"	60	"

Page.	Letter.	Full Name.	Residence, Jan. 1, 1943.	Occupation.	Supposed Age.	Reported Residence, Jan. 1, 1942. Street and Number.

Everett Street Continued

	E	Spano Pasquale	54	stonecutter	64	here
	F	D'Alessandro Americo	54	operator	33	"
	G	D'Alessandro Eva — †	54	"	30	"
	H	Leone Antonetta †	54	housewife	31	"
	K	Leone Raffaele	54	laborer	44	"
	L	Bua Anthony	56	welder	22	"
	M	*Bua Michela — †	56	housewife	58	"
	N	Collorone Mary — †	56	"	35	"
	O	Collorone Michael	56	laborer	36	"
	P	Lombardo Giacomo	56	fisherman	28	157 Endicott
	R	Lombardo Leonarda — †	56	housewife	22	157 "
	S	Sansone Andrea	58	retired	70	Chelsea
	T	Sansone Joseph	58	U S A	24	N Carolina
	U	*Sansone Sylvia †	58	housewife	66	Chelsea
	V	*Simpson Arthur	58	clerk	45	here
	W	Simpson Lillian — †	58	housewife	28	"
	X	Palazzuolo Anthony	58	laborer	49	"
	Y	Palazzuolo Constantina — †	58	housewife	52	"
	Z	Palazzuolo Lillian — †	58	stitcher	21	"

2318

	A	*Mastrola Alphonso	60	bartender	47	"
	B	*Mastrola Lena — †	60	housewife	47	"
	C	Mastrola Amelio	60	U S A	25	N Carolina
	D	Mastrola Anna — †	60	housewife	23	here
	E	Imparato Phillip	60	retired	64	"
	F	Principato Joseph	60	clerk	36	"
	G	Principato Mary — †	60	housewife	32	"
	H	Pinabell Anthony	62	factoryhand	22	"
	K	Pinabell Virginia — †	62	housewife	21	"
	L	Beatrice Antonio	62	laborer	36	"
	M	*Beatrice Martin	62	retired	75	"
	N	Beatrice Michael	62	painter	26	"
	O	*Beatrice Philomena †	62	housewife	61	"
	P	Verde Angelina — †	62	"	30	"
	R	Verde Frank	62	factoryhand	32	"
	S	Santilli Frank	64	chauffeur	25	32 Frankfort
	T	Santilli Jennie †	64	housewife	25	32 "
	U	Cinicola Anthony	64	machinist	29	here
	V	Cinicola Joseph	64	U S A	22	"
	W	*Cinicola Ralph	64	retired	71	"
	X	Cinicola Rosina †	64	stitcher	26	"

11

Everett Street—Continued

Y	Cinicola Susan †	64	housekeeper	25	here
Z	Deloprato Luigi	64	laborer	53	"
2319					
A	Deloprato Michael	64	seaman	27	"
B*	Deloprato Michelina †	64	housewife	53	"
C	Scorziello Anna †	72	"	36	77 Cottage
D	Scorziello Nicolo M	72	molder	39	77 "
E*	Fanara Anna †	72	storekeeper	57	here
F	Fanara James V	72	seaman	26	"
H*	Fiore Carmen C	74	printer	29	"
K	Fiore Rose †	74	housewife	27	"
L	DeNisco Henrietta †	74	"	67	"
M	DeNisco Joseph	74	retired	67	"
N	DeNisco Olga †	74	factoryhand	21	"
O	Ciampa Antonio	74	laborer	59	"
P*	Ciampa Rosaria †	74	housewife	48	"
R	Simonelli Carmen	75	barber	29	"
S	Simonelli Catherine †	75	housewife	25	"
T	Polecari Angelina †	75	"	45	"
U	Polecari Joseph	75	manager	47	"
V	Santilli Ida †	75	housewife	35	"
W	Santilli Salvatore	75	chauffeur	34	"
X	Simonelli John	75	barber	62	"
Y	Romani Adeline †	76	factoryhand	28	"
Z*	Romani Ermenegildo	76	machinist	65	"
2320					
A	Romani Jennie †	76	housekeeper	23	"
B	Pantalone Anthony	76	laborer	41	"
C	Pantalone Elizabeth †	76	factoryhand	35	"
D	Ferrara Amelia †	76	"	23	"
E	Ferrara Ida †	76	"	21	"
F*	Ferrara Theresa †	76	housewife	48	"
H	Giacobelli Charles	78	longshoreman	42	"
K*	Giacobelli Mary †	78	housewife	32	"
L	Sorrentino Frances †	78	"	34	548 Benningt'n
M	Sorrentino Frank	78	shipper	34	548 "
O	DellaRusso Catherine †	80	housewife	39	here
P	DellaRusso Harry	80	freighthandler	48	"
R	DellaRusso Josephine †	80	factoryhand	20	"
S*	Sersante Concetta †	80	housewife	67	"
T*	Sersante Gervasio	80	retired	73	"

Everett Street Continued

v	*Sersante Giuseppe	80	laborer	33	here
x	Guarino Joseph	83	steamfitter	40	"
y	Guarino Turina—†	83	housewife	33	"
z	*DiMichael Angelina—†	83	"	36	"
	2321				
a	DiMichael Christopher	83	baker	37	"
b	Zuffante Mary †	83	housewife	36	"
c	Zuffante Salvatore	83	salesman	37	"
e	McVey Elizabeth—†	85	housewife	28	"
f	McVey Gerald	85	laborer	32	"
g	Bagaroza Alberta—†	85	housewife	30	"
h	Bagaroza Joseph	85	letter carrier	35	"
k	Guazzerotti Assunta †	85	housewife	37	"
l	*Guazzerotti Genaro	85	metalworker	40	"
m	*Villani Mary—†	87	at home	55	"
n	Spano Ralph	87	mechanic	36	"
o	Spano Rose †	87	housewife	30	"
p	Perriello Caroline—†	87	"	38	"
r	Perriello Felix	87	painter	38	"
s	Marroni Alfred	88	storekeeper	23	"
t	Marroni Algeri	88	U S A	25	"
u	Marroni Amos	88	U S N	33	"
v	Marroni Elisa—†	88	housewife	55	"
w	Marroni Primo	88	laborer	60	"
x	Guaetta Mary †	89	housewife	23	90 Everett
y	Guaetta Peter	89	clerk	26	90 "
z	*Morcucci Margaret—†	89	housewife	48	here
	2322				
a	Morcucci Michael	89	butcher	40	"
b	Stoia Marion †	89	housewife	25	40 Frankfort
c	Stoia Pasquale	89	laborer	26	40 "
d	Lipizzi Frank	90	baker	23	here
e	Lipizzi Helen †	90	housewife	24	"
f	Guerra Amelia †	90	factoryhand	26	"
g	*Guerra Catherine—†	90	housewife	51	"
h	*Guerra James	90	cook	54	"
k	Accomando Angelina †	91	housewife	27	"
l	Accomando Louis	91	machinist	32	"
m	*DeDonato Antonetta †	91	housewife	42	"
n	DeDonato Florenzo	91	shoemaker	48	"
o	DeDonato John	91	U S N	21	"

Everett Street — Continued

p*	Petricca Carmelina †	91	housewife	36	here
R	Petricca Domenic	91	carpenter	39	"
s	Giardina Fannie †	92	housewife	23	"
T	Giardina Guy	92	laborer	23	"
U*	DiGiulio Susan †	92	housewife	41	"
V	DiGiulio Vincent	92	laborer	46	"
w*	Pace Lucy †	92	housewife	37	275 Sumner
X	Pace Phillip	92	laborer	45	275 "
Y*	Arciero Mary †	93	housewife	38	here
Z	Arciero Michael	93	shoeworker	39	"

2323

A	Polino Antonette †	93	housewife	40	"
B	Polino John	93	machinist	47	"
C	Sinicola Anthony	93	retired	70	"
D	Polino Angelo J	93	U S A	21	183 Chelsea
E	Polino Louise †	93	housewife	21	183 "
F	Mazzuchelli John	94	engineer	48	N Hampshire
H*	Tiso Antonetta †	94	housewife	51	here
K*	Tiso Domenick	94	factoryhand	53	"
L	Tiso Jennie †	94	laundress	23	"
M	Tiso Michael	94	seaman	26	"
N*	DeGloria Gianina †	94	housewife	48	"
O	DeGloria Phillip	94	laborer	50	"
P*	Faccaro Carmella †	94	stenographer	20	"
R*	Faccaro Rocco	94	retired	57	"
S*	Faccaro Victoria †	94	housewife	55	"
T	Costa Angelina †	94	"	46	155 Chelsea
U	Costa Joseph	94	welder	21	155 "
V	Costa Salvatore	94	retired	51	155 "
W	Carsto James	94	operator	46	8 Winthrop
X	Carsto Mary †	94	housewife	37	New York

2324

A	Martone Joseph	96	laborer	49	164 Everett
B	Martone Mary †	96	housewife	40	164 "
C	Piazza Charles	96	retired	66	10 Cottage
D	Piazza Leo	96	U S A	23	10 "
E	Piazza Stephen	96	"	22	10 "
F	Santangelo Bambina †	96	housewife	46	here
G	Santangelo Michael	96	laborer	57	"
H	Santangelo Phillip	96	"	24	"
K	Santangelo Salvatore	96	U S A	22	"

Everett Street Continued

L	*Amari Cruce †	96	stitcher	39	here
M	Amari Peter	96	laborer	49	"
N	Piro Mary †	96	stitcher	43	Lawrence
P	*Bertolino Louis	97	laborer	54	here
R	*Bertolino Ramonda †	97	housewife	48	"
S	Marcucci Americo	97	electrician	24	99 Everett
T	Marcucci Angela †	97	housewife	24	99 "
U	Bertolino Christopher	97	baker	31	here
V	Bertolino Theresa †	97	housewife	28	"
W	Gilardi Adeline—†	98	"	30	510 Summer
X	Gilardi Frank	98	laborer	30	510 "
Y	Serino Joseph	98	U S A	22	here
Z	Serino Pasquale A	98	carpenter	46	"

2325

A	Serino Victoria—†	98	housewife	43	"
B	*Crescenzi Angelina †	98	"	40	"
C	Crescenzi Carmen	98	packer	45	"
D	Crescenzi Mathew	98	welder	20	"
E	*Amaru Elvira †	99	housewife	40	168 Cottage
F	Amaru Salvatore	99	laborer	45	168 "
G	*Lombardi Anne—†	99	housewife	33	here
H	Lombardi Humbert	99	laborer	33	"
K	Connolly John	99	clerk	28	249 Maverick
L	Connolly Lucy—†	99	housewife	28	249 "
M	Mercurio Alice †	100	"	23	Somerville
N	Mercurio George	100	boilermaker	29	"
O	Andracchio Frank	100	butcher	35	here
P	Andracchio Mary †	100	housewife	31	"
R	Rigano Letterio	100	carpenter	45	"
S	Rigano Margaret †	100	housewife	40	"
T	*Bellofatto Concetta †	102	"	43	70 Chelsea
U	Bellofatto Louis	102	tailor	49	70 "
V	Dausilio Salvatore	102	janitor	63	here
W	Iannarono Alfred	102	shoeworker	61	325 Sumner
X	Melchione Anthony	102	laborer	32	here
Y	Melchione Marie †	102	housewife	32	"
Z	Vonimano Augustus	102	butcher	56	151 Maverick

2326

A	Mercurio Louis	103	storekeeper	76	here
B	*Mercurio Nicolina †	103	housewife	72	"
C	Vaccaro Anna †	103	"	42	"

15

Everett Street—Continued

D	Vaccaro Filippo	103	laborer	52	here	
E	*Gucciardi Concetta †	103	housewife	39	"	
F	Gucciardi Settimio	103	plasterer	55	"	
G	DeLuca Mary †	105	housewife	30	"	
H	DeLuca Michael	105	laborer	38	"	
K	Musto Louis	105	repairman	28	"	
L	Musto Sophie †	105	housewife	27	"	
M	Musto Angelo	105	tailor	59	"	
N	Musto Julia †	105	housewife	58	"	
O	Trapasso Antoinette †	106	"	52	"	
P	Trapasso Rose †	106	clerk	20	"	
R	Trapasso Salvatore	106	engineer	56	"	
S	*Colandrillo Julia †	106	at home	86	"	
T	Analoro Mary †	106	"	20	115 Trenton	
U	Bottaro Frank	106	machinist	51	here	
V	Bottaro Josephine †	106	electrician	22	"	
W	Bottaro Theresa †	106	housewife	43	"	
X	*Argenio Carmella †	107	"	43	"	
Y	Argenio Joseph	107	carpenter	53	"	
Z	Garadozzi Freda †	107	tailor	23	"	

2327

A	Sacco Alexander	107	shipper	26	"	
B	Sacco Margaret †	107	housewife	27	"	
C	Giasullo Anthony	110	mechanic	40	"	
D	Giasullo Josephine †	110	housewife	38	"	
E	*Melito Maria †	110	at home	60	"	
F	Tozzi Amato	110	welder	23	461 Sumner	
G	Tozzi Anthony	110	laborer	25	238 Everett	
H	*Tozzi Ursula †	110	at home	60	461 Sumner	
K	D'Amelio Flamino	110	laborer	43	here	
L	D'Amelio Florinda	110	"	34	"	
M	D'Amelio Ida †	110	housewife	42	"	
N	D'Amelio Mary †	110	stitcher	20	"	
O	Dionisi Amedeo	111	baker	46	"	
P	Dionisi Marie †	111	housewife	44	"	
R	Dionisi Vincenza †	111	at home	21	"	
S	*Salini Julius	111	baker	36	"	
T	Salini Phyllis †	111	housewife	26	"	
U	Perna Helen †	114	"	32	"	
W	Perna Raymond	114	shoecutter	38	"	
X	Angelo Catherine †	114	clerk	21	"	

Everett Street Continued

	Full Name	Residence	Occupation	Age	Reputed Residence
Y	Angelo Joseph	114	tilesetter	47	here
Z	Angelo Josephine †	114	housewife	37	"
	2328				
A	D'Italia Angelo	114	presser	52	"
B	D'Italia Pauline †	114	housewife	43	"
C*	Guerra Frank	115	shipper	47	"
D	Guerra Josephine †	115	housewife	26	"
E	Capoccia Antonio	115	laborer	23	"
F	Capoccia Eleanor †	115	at home	52	"
G	Capoccia Yolanda †	115	clerk	21	"
H	Cipriani Giovanni	115	retired	73	"
K*	Sasso Angelo	115	laborer	54	"
L*	Sasso Josephine †	115	housewife	49	"
M	Sasso Louis	115	chauffeur	24	"
N	Sasso Mary †	115	clerk	22	"
O*	Luongo Genaro	rear 115	retired	76	"
P*	DeCora Carmen	" 115	"	78	"
R*	Rinaldi Domenic	" 115	laborer	47	"
S*	D'Ambola Giacinto	" 115	"	68	"
V	Maggiore Carmen	116	baker	33	"
W	Maggiore Victoria †	116	housewife	28	"
X	Guarino Jennie †	116	at home	30	"
Y	Guarino Joseph	116	cabinetmaker	63	"
Z	DiGiorgio Carmella †	116	tailor	34	"
	2329				
A	DiGiorgio John	116	"	63	"
B	DiGiorgio John A	116	student	22	"
C*	DiGiorgio Lucy †	116	housewife	54	"
D	DiGiorgio Marie †	116	tailor	32	"
E	Digan Bernard	120	electrician	30	319 Border
F	Digan Catherine †	120	housewife	30	319 "
G	Collins Catherine †	120	domestic	62	here
H	Collins Catherine †	120	clerk	29	"
K	Collins Margaret †	120	"	25	"
L	Dionne Ethel †	120	at home	33	"
M	Grant James	120	laborer	41	"
N*	Grant Mary †	120	at home	73	"
O	Penta Frances †	122	housewife	32	"
P	Penta Salvatore	122	guard	38	"
R	Vitale Felix	122	barber	42	"
S*	Vitale Jennie †	122	housewife	36	"

1 23   17

Everett Street—Continued

I	Mastrangelo Amelia—†	122	housewife	28	here
U	Mastrangelo Severio	122	chauffeur	30	"
X	Constantino Theresa—†	131	housewife	22	"
V	D'Amato Henry	131	mechanic	35	"
W	D'Amato Maria—†	131	at home	63	"
X	D'Amato Theresa—†	131	housewife	29	"
Z	Calvino Charles	131	U S N	21	"

2330

A*	Calvino Gaetano	131	plater	58	"
B*	Calvino Lucia—†	131	housewife	48	"
C	Bruno Carmella—†	131	"	48	"
D	Bruno Giuseppe	131	janitor	58	"
E	Bruno Philip	131	machinist	20	"
F	Morelli Claire—†	133	clerk	24	"
G	Morelli John	133	"	22	"
H	Morelli Ralph	133	laborer	30	"
K	Morelli Virginia—†	133	storekeeper	64	"
M	Parziale Sabino	137	welder	25	370 Sumner
N	Amico Joseph	137	"	28	75 Cottage
O	Amico Yolanda—†	137	housewife	21	75 "
S*	Melloni Anthony	141	laborer	58	Quincy
T*	Melloni Josephine—†	141	housewife	41	"
U*	Olivien Celia—†	141	at home	50	here
V*	Maglio Michael	143	laborer	39	"
W*	Maglio Rose—†	143	housewife	33	"
X	Olivolo Alfonso	143	laborer	56	"
Y	Puopolo Michael	143	"	58	"
Z	Puopolo Milly—†	143	clerk	26	"

2331

A	Puopolo Raffaele	143	laborer	62	"
B	Puopolo Rose—†	143	housewife	49	"
C*	Razzo Sabatino	143	laborer	76	"
D	Delillo Carmen	145	retired	68	"
E*	Montesanti Domenic	147	repairman	60	"
F	Montesanti Domenic	147	U S A	22	"
G	Montesanti Mary—†	147	housewife	53	"
H	Montesanti Rose—†	147	laundryworker	29	"

Lamson Court

M	Cummings James	3	longshoreman	46	here
N	Cummings Richard	3	"	40	"

Lamson Court Continued

s	Johnson Charles	5	laborer	64	here
t	Johnson Sophia †	5	housewife	55	"
u	Iaconelli Biagio	7	plumber	55	"
v	Iaconelli Carmella †	7	housewife	56	"
w	Rossi Carlo	9	laborer	39	"
x	Rossi Philomena †	9	housewife	36	"
y	DelGaudio Carmella †	10	factoryhand	50	"
z	DelGaudio Giuseppe	10	laborer	54	"

2332

a	Volppi Leonard	10	retired	70	"
b	Martella Joseph	10	factoryhand	24	Lincoln
c	Ruggiero Helen †	10	housewife	27	here
d	Ruggiero Michael	10	laborer	25	"
e	Stack Helen †	10	housewife	32	195 Webster
f	Stack Lawrence	10	shipfitter	31	195 "
g	Hall Margaret †	11	housewife	41	here
h	Hall Thomas	11	longshoreman	45	"
k	Daniels Millie †	12	housekeeper	60	"
l	Nickerson Chester	12	U S A	21	"
m	Nickerson Helen †	12	factoryhand	22	259 Everett
n	Thibault Clarence	12	U S A	40	here
o	Manganiello Raffaele	15	laborer	54	"
p	Marcantonio Andrew	17	machinist	27	Cambridge
r	Marcantonio Gaetano	17	laborer	59	"
s	Marcantonio Guy	17	machinist	25	"
t	Marcantonio Josephine †	17	factoryhand	28	"
u	Marcantonio Vincenza †	17	housewife	56	"
v	Marcantonio Yolanda †	17	factoryhand	22	"

Lamson Street

w	Beatrice Frank	16	shipfitter	21	651 Benningt'n
x	Beatrice Lena †	16	housewife	20	651 "
y	Pezzella Angelina †	16	housekeeper	30	498 Sumner
z	Sicciardi Mary †	16	housewife	65	here

2333

a	Sicciardi Vincenzo	16	carpenter	63	"
e	Pellegrini Francis J	26	seaman	22	"
f	Pellegrini Mary R †	26	housekeeper	88	"
g	Pellegrini Margaret M †	26	housewife	41	"
h	Pellegrini Thomas S	26	guard	44	"
k	Pellegrini William T	26	U S A	21	"

19

					Reported Residence, Jan. 1, 1942.
Place.	Letter.	FULL NAME.	Residence, Jan. 1, 1943.	Occupation.	Supposed Age.	Street and Number.

Lowland Place

	L	Mario Filomena †	1	housewife	29	here
	M	Mario Louis	1	salesman	34	"

Maverick Street

	o*	Durante Stella †	169	housewife	78	here
	p	Iocca Pasquale	169	locksmith	52	"
	R	Morelli Fred	169	mechanic	37	"
	s	Morelli Rose †	169	housewife	34	"
	T*	Trocano Joseph	169	retired	78	"
	U	Trocano Joseph	169	metalworker	31	"
	V*	Trocano Mary †	169	housewife	76	"
	W*	Sica Bruno	171	mattressmaker	55	"
	X*	Sica Leonard	171	laborer	53	"
	Y*	Addonizio Gaetano	171	retired	61	"
	Z*	Addonizio Josephine †	171	housewife	54	"
		2334				
	A	Addonizio Mary †	171	houseworker	20	"
	B	Amato Dominic	171	shoemaker	48	"
	C	Amato Mary †	171	housewife	48	"
	D	Aiello Frank	173	U S A	33	"
	E*	Aiello John	173	janitor	44	"
	F	Aiello Joseph	173	mechanic	35	"
	G	DeAngelus Joseph	173	chauffeur	40	"
	H	DeAngelus Sadie †	173	housewife	39	"
	K	Spano Angela †	173	"	26	273 Sumner
	L	Spano Frank	173	painter	29	here
	N*	DeAngelus Antonetta †	175	housewife	66	"
	o	Forte Natale	175	mechanic	36	194 Maverick
	P	Forte Rose †	175	housewife	37	194 "
	R*	DeAngelus Angelina †	175	"	37	here
	s	DeAngelus Frank	175	clerk	38	"
		Fortinallis Helen †	177	housewife	24	"
		Orolo Christine †	177	"	29	"
		Orolo Joseph	177	manager	31	"
		Galli Ralph	183	"	43	Chelmsford
		2335				
		Cuccillo Carmella †	183	housewife	72	here
		Sangi Nellie †	183	"	41	176 Gove
		Jordo Jennie †	183	"	49	here
		Mantzos Marie †	185	"	50	"

20

Maverick Street (Continued)

f	Blundo Gasper	185	retired	63	here
g	*Blundo Vincenza †	185	housewife	60	"
h	Digianvittorio Domenic	185	U S A	21	12 Gove
k	*Digianvittorio Egidio	185	laborer	58	12 "
l	*Digianvittorio Lena †	185	housewife	55	12 "
n	*Cataldo Carmella †	187	"	41	here
o	Cataldo Modestino	187	teamster	41	"
p	Testa Americo J	187	candymaker	34	"
r	Testa Palmira †	187	housewife	33	"
t	Troisi Joseph	191	retired	70	73 Cottage
v	*Troisi Mary †	191	housewife	67	73 "
w	LaRosa Emma †	191	"	37	here
x	LaRosa Giacomo	191	baker	44	"
y	DiCicco Irene †	191	housewife	45	"
z	DiCicco John	191	clerk	45	"

2336

a	Bettano John	191	mechanic	36	"
b	Bettano Katherine †	191	housewife	35	"
*c	Brunetti Angelo	191	retired	66	"
d	Gosdalic John	191	laborer	51	"
e	*DeSimone Louis	193	painter	49	62 Barnes av
f	DeSimone Mary †	193	housewife	36	24 Dennis
g	Maglio Angelo	193	candymaker	50	here
h	*Maglio Concetta †	193	housewife	48	"
k	Guglielmi Angelo	193	clerk	32	"
l	Guglielmi Catherine †	193	housekeeper	56	"
m	Guglielmi Louis	193	U S N	28	"
n	Guglielmi Mario	193	machinist	25	"
o	Guglielmi Yolanda †	193	factoryhand	24	"
p	Luti Anna †	195	housewife	35	"
r	Luti Attilio	195	meatcutter	42	"
s	Testa Mary †	195	housewife	62	"
t	Testa Vincent	195	candymaker	62	"
u	Testa Anthony J	195	bartender	37	"
v	Testa Nancy †	195	housewife	36	"
x	Guisto Josephine †	211	"	23	40 Cottage
y	Guisto Pasquale	211	U S A	23	42 Everett
z	Imbriano Louis	211	manager	29	here

2337

a	Imbriano Viola †	211	housewife	29	"
b	Baptista Angie †	211	"	31	"

21

Page Letter	FULL NAME.	Residence, Jan. 1, 1943.	Occupation.	Supposed Age.	Reported Residence, Jan. 1, 1942. Street and Number.

Maverick Street—Continued

c	Baptista William	211	shoeworker	33	here
d	Amante Fortunato	213	retired	76	"
e	Watts Irene V—†	213	stitcher	58	"
f	Romano Anthony	213	student	21	"
g	Romano Carmella—†	213	stenographer	21	"
h *Romano Mary—†	213	housewife	62	"
k	Romano Pasquale	213	seaman	23	"
l	Romano Ralph	213	U S A	25	"
m	Romano Rose—†	213	clerk	27	"
n	Salvo Lorenzo	213	U S A	29	"
o *Salvo Rosaria—†	213	housewife	47	"
p	Salvo Vita †	213	clerk	26	"
r	Siracusa Nicolas	215	mechanic	34	"
s	Siracusa Theresa—†	215	housewife	33	"
t	DiSimone Fred	215	machinist	24	"
u	DiSimone Jennie—†	215	houseworker	28	"
v *DiSimone Mary †	215	housewife	54	"
w	DiSimone Peter	215	attendant	54	"
x	DiSimone Rocco	215	"	22	"
y	Bagmera Anthony	215	rigger	55	"
z	Bagmera Helen †	215	presser	28	"

2338

a	Bagmera Lena †	215	housewife	52	"
b	Bagmera Mary—†	215	packer	20	"
c	Caruso Rose †	217	"	21	211 Maverick
d	Fioretti Michael	217	painter	39	here
e	Fioretti Nellie †	217	housewife	30	"
f *Mercurio Elizabeth—†	217	"	55	"
g *Mercurio Joseph	217	laborer	58	"
h	Mercurio Salvatore	217	U S A	20	"
k	Conti Carl	217	boilermaker	52	"
l	Conti Peter	217	U S A	26	"
m *Conti Rose †	217	housewife	46	"
n	Denietolis Anthony	219	shipfitter	38	"
o	Denietolis Mary †	219	housewife	34	"
p	Denietolis Edith †	219	"	28	"
r	Denietolis Emilio	219	machinist	32	"
s	Denietolis Vincent	219	retired	76	"
t	DeMinico Rose †	219	housewife	26	"
u *Ramuno Antonetta †	219	"	54	"
v	Ramuno Florence—†	219	stitcher	20	"

22

Maverick Street Continued

w	*Ramuno Joseph	219	welder	54	here
x	Ramuno Josephine—†	219	stitcher	23	"
y	Cericola Joseph	223	waiter	29	"
z	Cericola Stella—†	223	housewife	29	"

2339

a	DePersis Guido	223	U S A	25	Winthrop
b	DePersis Theresa—†	223	housewife	20	here
c	*Giello Frances—†	223	"	58	"
d	Giello Nicolas	223	cooper	59	"
e	Constanza Jennie—†	223	housewife	49	"
f	Constanza Louis	223	molder	50	"
g	Battaglia Louis	225	agent	37	"
h	Battaglia Marie—†	225	housewife	37	"
k	Gravallese Anthony	225	salesman	38	"
l	Gravallese Josephine—†	225	housewife	39	"
m	Dente Albert	225	U S M C	22	"
n	Dente Alessio	225	woolhandler	60	"
o	Dente Concetta—†	225	housewife	58	"
p	Pirone Domenick	227	U S M C	20	"
r	*Pirone Josephine—†	227	housewife	48	"
s	*Pirone Pasquale	227	shoeworker	51	"
t	Cianfrocia Gustavo	227	tailor	46	"
u	Cianfrocia Josephina—†	227	housewife	45	"
v	*Pirone Filomena—†	227	"	39	"
w	Pirone Genaro	227	shoeworker	47	"
x	Repoli Abina—†	229	housewife	40	173 Maverick
y	Repoli Sylvia—†	229	stitcher	21	173 "
z	Maddalone Carmella—†	229	housewife	27	here

2340

a	Maddalone Frank N	229	laborer	29	"
b	Maddalone Rose—†	229	housewife	65	"
c	Delprete Antonietta †	229	"	30	"
d	Delprete Genaro	229	laborer	32	"
f	Brenna Phyllis †	231	manager	45	"
e	*D'Angelo Antonio	231	"	57	"
g	Sabia Anthony	231	clerk	37	"
h	Sabia Dora †	231	housewife	34	"
k	Sabia Joseph	231	manager	65	"
l	Sabia Mary—†	231	waitress	37	"
m	Sabia Peter	231	manager	44	"
n	Sabia Theodora—†	231	housewife	65	"

Maverick Street Continued

		Full Name	Res.	Occupation	Age	Reported
o		Collarone Gaetano	233	U S A	25	here
p	*	Collarone Josephine †	233	housewife	56	"
R		Collarone Richard	233	laborer	65	"
s		Collarone Salvatore	233	shoeworker	26	"
T		Gioiosa Charles J	237	plumber	43	"
w	*	Coletto Benjamin	241	retired	65	"
x		Maher Mary †	241	houseworker	33	"
y		Sabia Marion †	241	dentist	35	"
z		Sabia Michael	241	attendant	45	"
		2341				
A		Pulicari Josephine †	247	housewife	21	"
B		Pulicari Mario	247	laborer	25	"
c		Camuso Amelia †	247	housewife	27	"
D		DeMinico Robert	247	designer	68	"
E		DeBellis Ann †	247	shoeworker	20	"
F		DeBellis Benedetto	247	laborer	52	"
G		DeBellis Louise †	247	housewife	42	"
H		DeBellis Rose †	247	stitcher	22	"
K	*	Leone Dominick	249	laborer	59	"
L		Leone Lillian †	249	rubberworker	20	"
M		Leone Lucy †	249	packer	27	"
N		Leone Nicolas	249	U S A	25	"
o	*	Leone Victoria †	249	housewife	51	"
R		Ricco Eugene	249	chauffeur	30	"
s		Ricco Matilda †	249	housewife	30	"
T		Peter Manuel	249	U S N	20	"
U		Palange Joseph	249	retired	67	"
V		Palange Michelina †	249	housewife	64	"
w		Orlando Liborio	249	U S A	30	"
x		Orlando Olga †	249	housewife	23	"
y		Anzalone Josephine †	249	"	49	"
z		Anzalone Pasquale	249	musician	61	"
		2342				
		Masiello Carmen	249	baggageman	45	"
		Masiello Magdaline †	249	housewife	39	"
		Hamel Alphee	249	laborer	35	"
		Hamel Antonette †	249	housewife	30	"
		DiMario John A	249	laborer	53	"
		DiMario Joseph	249	mechanic	26	"
		DiMario Pasqualina A †	249	housewife	55	"
K		Rosso Angelo	249	laborer	38	"

24

Maverick Street Continued

L	*Ziagella Antonio	249	repairman	40	here	
M	Martinola Beatrice †	249	housewife	24	14 Orleans	
N	Martinola Octavius	249	mechanic	26	14 "	
O	DiPerri Joseph	249	laborer	48	21 Battery	
P	DiPerri Rosaria †	249	housewife	45	21 "	
R	DiPerri Victoria †	249	clerk	23	21 "	
W	*Stella Alphonse	273	retired	62	here	
X	Stella Arman †	273	housewife	41	"	
Y	Ventre Antonia †	273	retired	80	"	
Z	Capanegro Genardo	273	laborer	52	"	

2343

A	Lepore Albert	273	U S A	24	"	
B	Lepore Anthony	273	laborer	28	"	
C	*Lepore Joseph	273	retired	56	"	
D	Lepore Mary †	273	housewife	33	"	
E	Paolini Edith †	273	"	38	6 Everett pl	
F	Calderone Anthony	273	laborer	46	here	
G	Calderone Mary †	273	housewife	39	"	
H	Calderone Phyllis †	273	clerk	24	"	

Noble Court

K	Naumann Henry	4	laborer	44	here	
L	Naumann Mary †	4	housewife	44	"	
M	Gifford Fred	6	longshoreman	48	"	
N	Gifford Margaret †	6	factoryhand	24	"	
O	Gifford Theresa †	6	housewife	43	"	
P	Politano Elizabeth †	7	superintendent	24	"	
R	Politano Evelyn †	7	cutter	22	"	
S	Politano Josephine †	7	housekeeper	65	"	
T	Politano Stella †	7	stitcher	24	"	
V	Seto Joseph	9	U S N	31	"	
W	Seto Josephine †	9	housekeeper	54	"	
X	Seto Josephine †	9	advertising	24	"	
Y	Seto Lucy †	9	dressmaker	36	"	
Z	Seto Salvatore	9	toolmaker	28	"	

2344

A	Loracy Clarence	10	painter	24	"	
B	Loracy Ethel †	10	clerk	22	"	
C	Loracy Mary †	10	housekeeper	48	"	

Orleans Street

F	*Cencini Gaspar	80	plasterer	56	here
F	Minichiello Josephine—†	80	housewife	26	"
G	Minichiello Zachary	80	machinist	33	"
H	*Murano Immaculata—†	80	housewife	54	"
K	Murano Salvatore	80	operator	21	"
L	Trocchio Gilda †	80	factoryhand	33	"
M	Trocchio Lydia—†	80	"	35	"
N	Trocchio Nicholas	80	tailor	64	"
O	*Bonasoro Josephine—†	80	housewife	48	"
P	Bonasoro Vincent	80	plasterer	59	"
R	Bonasoro Vito	80	U S A	24	"
S	Cammarata Mary—†	80	housewife	27	"
T	Cammarata Michael	80	shoeworker	25	"
U	*LaGrasta Jennie—†	80	housewife	49	174 Cottage
V	LaGrasta Sabino	80	laborer	50	174 "
W	Trippi Giacomo	80	"	52	here
X	Trippi Josephine †	80	housewife	49	"
Y	Trippi Rose †	80	clerk	24	"
Z	Trippi Virginia—†	80	"	20	"
	2345				
A	Mechetti Egisto	80	driller	30	"
B	Mechetti Sarah—†	80	housewife	29	"
C	Tosiello Angelina—†	80	"	40	"
D	Tosiello Joseph	80	laborer	40	"
E	*Tosiello Rosario—†	80	housekeeper	63	"
F	Gulla Anthony, jr	80	U S A	27	"
G	Gulla Antonio	80	blacksmith	58	"
H	Gulla Lucrizia—†	80	housewife	47	"
K	Gulla Rose—†	80	shoeworker	25	"
L	Emmett Mary †	83	housewife	44	"
M	Emmett Oliver	83	ironworker	48	"
N	Zarba Christopher	83	student	20	"
O	Zarba Elvira †	83	housewife	42	"
P	Zarba Joseph	83	carpenter	46	"
R	Coveney Ellen F †	83	clerk	59	"
S	Ring Lillian †	83	teacher	43	"
T	Ring Margaret †	83	stenographer	46	"
U	Mosca Anthony	85	U S N	21	"
V	*Mosca Leonard	85	fisherman	57	"
W	Mosca Mary—†	85	housekeeper	21	"
X	*Carbone Mary—†	85	housewife	63	"
Y	Carbone Nicholas	85	U S A	25	"

Orleans Street Continued

z	Burnash Andrew	85	laborer	42	here	
2346						
A	Burnash Camille—†	85	clerk	43	"	
B*	Candella Jeanette—†	87	operator	31	"	
C*	Candella Luigi	87	retired	73	"	
D	Grant William	87	laborer	49	"	
E	Lomba Concetta—†	87	housewife	29	210 E Eagle	
F	Lomba Marcelina—†	87	painter	38	210 "	
G	Graham Mary C—†	89	housewife	22	here	
H	Graham Robert	89	letter carrier	21	"	
K*	Contrada Adelina—†	89	housewife	42	"	
L	Contrada Josephine—†	89	stitcher	21	"	
M	Contrada Pasquale	89	welder	48	"	
N*	Azzellino Filomena—†	89	housewife	56	"	
O*	Azzellino Joseph	89	laborer	56	"	
P*	Azzellino Luciano—†	89	clerk	57	"	
S*	Grandolfi Angelina—†	93	housewife	47	"	
T	Grandolfi Antonio	93	storekeeper	48	"	
U	Grandolfi Gloria—†	93	operator	21	"	
V	Grandolfi Grace—†	93	factoryhand	25	"	
W	Blandini Emma—†	93	housewife	23	5 Seaver	
X	Blandini Rocco	93	welder	25	5 "	

Seaver Street

Y	Ciavola John	3	diecutter	27	here	
z	Ciavola Vincenza—†	3	housewife	27	"	
2347						
A	Masala Antonetta—†	3	"	39	"	
B	Masala John	3	laborer	17	"	
C	Mini Anthony	3	electrician	25	"	
D	Mini Jeanne †	3	housewife	22	"	
E	Napier Charles J	5	baker	32	"	
F	Napier Elvira †	5	housewife	30	"	
G	Zichittella Mildred †	5	"	39	"	
H	Zichittella Vincent	5	painter	42	"	
K	McGown Peter	5	janitor	62	"	
L	Porrazzo Anna F †	5A	housewife	27	"	
M	Porrazzo Joseph	5A	diecutter	31	"	
N	Mattei Euninia †	5A	housewife	42	"	
O	Mattei Eugene	5A	mechanic	22	"	
P	Mattei Mario	5A	"	49	"	

27

Sumner Place

		Full Name		Occupation		
s		Faretra Ann †	3	housewife	26	here
t		Faretra Thomas P	3	machinist	29	"
u		DeBole Leo	3	storekeeper	54	"
v		DeBole Leo, jr	3	U S A	26	"
w		DeBole Mary †	3	housewife	53	"
x		Campocharrio Fannie †	3	"	26	"
y		Campocharrio Guy	3	metalworker	29	"
z		Petrucelli Anthony	3	storekeeper	26	"
		2348				
A		Petrucelli Rose †	3	housewife	26	"
B		Langone Frank	3	printer	27	"
C		Langone Mary †	3	housewife	27	"
D		DeBole Joseph	3	pipefitter	28	"
E		DeBole Josephine †	3	housewife	28	"
F		Faiello Arcangelo	5	laborer	67	"
G		Faiello Christina †	5	housewife	62	"
H		Faiello Florence †	5	factoryhand	21	"
K		Faiello Orlando	5	steamfitter	35	"
L		Faiello Pasquale	5	factoryhand	29	"
M		Ryan Mary †	6	housewife	74	"
N		Ryan Thomas	6	longshoreman	63	"
O		DiGiulio Antonio	6	laborer	39	"
P		Hagstrom Martha †	6	housekeeper	40	"
R		Zirpolo Anthony	6	chauffeur	42	"
S		Zirpolo Sophie †	6	housekeeper	39	"
T		Massa Carolina †	6	"	80	"
U		Massa Marciano	6	longshoreman	54	"
V		Giore John	7	"	38	"
W		Giore Margaret †	7	housewife	25	"
X		Falzone Louis	7	carpenter	45	227 Everett
Y		Falzone Mary †	7	housewife	36	227 "
Z		DeRocco Domenic	7	laborer	52	here
		2349				
		DeRocco Ida †	7	housewife	36	"
		Broccella Alice †	8	"	53	"
		Broccella Angelina †	8	stitcher	25	"
		Broccella John	8	U S M C	24	"
		Broccella Mario	8	U S A	22	"
		Broccella Rosario	8	laborer	50	"
		Broccella Anna †	8	housewife	43	"
		Broccella Sabatino	8	laborer	42	"

Sumner Place Continued

L	Silvestio Ernest	s	millwright	53	here
M	Silvestio Mary †	s	housewife	51	"
N	Thornton Josephine †	9	secretary	37	"
O	Thornton Mary †	9	housekeeper	45	"
R	Reed Josephine †	9	teacher	37	"

Sumner Street

W	Ferrullo Gloria †	254	housewife	21	259 Border
X	Ferrullo Pasquale	254	chauffeur	21	256 Sumner
Y	Hogan Anna †	254	housekeeper	73	here
Z	Hogan Christopher	254	retired	70	"
2350					
B	Ferrullo Fortuna †	256	housewife	47	"
C	Ferrullo Joseph	256	laborer	48	"
D	Sepriano Nina †	256	housewife	40	"
E	Sepriano Pasquale	256	laborer	21	"
F	Sepriano Pietro A	256	clerk	45	"
G	Sepriano Rose †	256	stitcher	20	"
K	Alberti Germano	264	laborer	35	"
L	Alberti Mary †	264	housewife	32	"
M	Falzone Lucy †	264	"	21	"
N	*Lombardi Concetta †	264	"	53	"
O	*Lombardi Joseph	264	woolhandler	56	"
T	Culkeen Edward	268	chauffeur	42	"
U	Culkeen Mary †	268	housewife	29	"
V	*Cutrone Jennie †	268	"	54	"
W	Cutrone Joseph	268	machinist	56	"
X	*DeDonato Filippina †	270	housewife	47	349 Sumner
Y	Stellabotta Daniel	270	clerk	20	here
Z	*Stellabotta Lucy †	270	housekeeper	46	"
2351					
A	Stellabotta Mary †	270	clerk	22	"
B	Lupoli Gelsimina †	270	housewife	27	"
C	Lupoli Salvatore	270	brazier	24	"
E	*Martucci Carmella †	272	housewife	50	"
F	Martucci Joseph	272	buyer	57	"
G	Martucci Rose †	272	stitcher	21	"
H	Chiaramonte Camello	272	laborer	30	"
K	Chiaramonte Mary †	272	housewife	30	"
L	*Cipriano Rose †	272	housekeeper	67	"

Sumner Street—Continued

M	Armendi Anthony	274	joiner	29	here
N	Armendi Hilda—†	274	housewife	27	"
O	Nuzzo Americo	274	chauffeur	45	"
P	Nuzzo Marie—†	274	clerk	21	"
R	Nuzzo Virginia—†	274	housewife	39	"
S	Pittore Josephine—†	274	"	28	"
T	Pittore Sebastian	274	operator	30	"
U	Pignato Josephine—†	276	housewife	35	"
V	Pignato Michael	276	laborer	44	"
W	Grazziano Antonio	276	technician	30	"
X	Grazziano Mary—†	276	housewife	28	"
Y	Ciccarelli Bessie—†	276	"	44	"
Z	Ciccarelli Philip	276	tailor	51	"
	2352				
A	Cantalupo Alessio	278	laborer	32	"
B	Cantalupo Jennie—†	278	housewife	25	"
C	Cantalupo Anthony	278	U S A	22	"
D	Cantalupo Dante	278	laborer	21	"
E*	Cantalupo Josephine†	278	housewife	59	"
F	Cantalupo Lillian—†	278	dressmaker	27	"
G*	Cantalupo Louis	278	retired	62	"
H	Naumann Delia—†	278	housewife	38	"
K	Naumann Frederick	278	inspector	37	"
M	Cervizzi Bernard	282	grocer	62	"
N	Cervizzi Domenic	282	U S A	29	"
O	Cervizzi Maria—†	282	housewife	54	"
P	Cervizzi Marie C—†	282	stenographer	20	"
R	Cervizzi Vincent	282	U S N	27	"
S	Pallidino Louis	282	tinsmith	37	"
T	Pallidino Mary—†	282	housewife	31	"
U	Mastrolio Liberato	284	U S A	23	"
V	Mastrolio Matilda—†	284	clerk	20	"
W	Mastrolio Nicholas	284	laborer	50	"
X	Santilli Mary—†	284	housewife	32	"
Y	Santilli Victor	284	chauffeur	36	"
	2353				
A	DeFlumere Amelia—†	286	housewife	41	"
B	DeFlumere Joseph	286	laborer	43	"
C	Arricale Anthony	286	shoemaker	36	"
D	Arricale Louise—†	286	housewife	33	"
E	Porrazzo Louise—†	286	dressmaker	20	"

30

Sumner Street Continued

F	Porrazzo Luigi	286	laborer	53	here
G	Porrazzo Mary †	286	housewife	51	"
H	Porrazzo Pasquale	286	laborer	21	"
K	Sardella Joseph	288	stitcher	43	"
L	Sardella Mamie †	288	housewife	38	"
M	Regardo Joseph	288	retired	75	"
N	Mastrangelo Frank	288	"	67	"
O	*Mastrangelo Josephine †	288	housewife	61	"
P	Mastrangelo Maria †	288	clerk	25	"
R	Mastrangelo Michael	288	laborer	23	"
S	Ripa Anthony S	290	physician	31	Idaho
T	Ripa Veronica A †	290	housewife	31	here
U	*Maquina Filomena †	292	"	55	here
V	*Maquina Joseph	292	black-smith	64	"
W	*Farrella Chiriacchini †	292	housekeeper	57	"
X	Guirino Antonette †	292	housewife	36	"
Y	Guirino Michael	292	laborer	37	"

2354

A	Scadutto John	294	guard	49	"
B	Scadutto Joseph	294	U S A	21	"
C	Scadutto Lena †	294	housewife	41	"
D	Scadutto Mary †	294	operator	20	"
E	Rubano Barbato	300	laborer	58	"
F	Rubano Josephine †	300	housewife	58	"
G	*Mercuri Carmella †	300	"	36	"
H	Mercuri George	300	tailor	43	"
K	Rubano Frank A	300	electrician	36	"
L	Rubano Helen †	300	housewife	32	"
M	Buttaro Anthony	302	laborer	25	"
N	Buttaro Joseph	302	"	60	"
O	*Buttaro Lena †	302	housewife	50	"
P	Salerno Joseph	302	salesman	34	"
R	Salerno Olga †	302	housewife	32	"
S	Dascoli Antonio	302	shipworker	35	"
T	Dascoli Palma †	302	housewife	32	"
U	*Marando Joseph	304	barber	51	"
V	*Marando Mary †	304	housewife	62	"
W	Perroni Frances †	306	dressmaker	48	"
X	Perroni John	306	shoemaker	59	"
Y	*Luongo Addolorata †	306	housekeeper	80	"
Z	Rollo Nettie †	306	housewife	38	"

	Letter	FULL NAME.	Residence, Jan. 1, 1943	Occupation.	Supposed Age.	Reported Residence, Jan. 1, 1942. Street and Number.

2355

Sumner Street—Continued

A	Rallo Vito	306	laborer	42	here
B	Dalto Ellen †	308	housewife	23	"
C	Dalto Michael	308	laborer	25	"
D	Tentindo Ernest	308	printer	21	"
E	Tentindo Nunzio	308	carpenter	51	"
F*	Tentindo Theresa †	308	housewife	45	"
G	Hock Dorothy B †	312	clerk	21	"
H	Hock Emma C †	312	typist	29	"
K	Hock Margaret M †	312	housewife	58	"
L	Hock William H	312	watchman	58	"
M	Casey Dennis J	312	clerk	65	"
N	Day Sidney F	314	tel worker	60	"
O	Quinn Eleanor M †	314	clerk	24	"
P	Quinn Mary G †	314	housewife	53	"
R	Quinn William J	314	freighthandler	49	"
S	Quinn William R	314	U S A	26	"
T	Lynch Michael	314	shipper	28	"
U	Lynch Ruth †	314	housewife	27	"
V	Falanga Andrew	318	shoeworker	36	"
W	Falanga Mary †	318	housewife	34	"
X	Caprio Adeline †	318	"	46	"
Y	Caprio John	318	rigger	48	"
Z	Caprio Louis	318	U S N	21	"

2356

A	Giglio Carmen †	318	housewife	28	"
B	Giglio James	318	laborer	30	"
D*	Brogna Anthony	320	"	60	"
E	Molay Filippina †	320	housewife	36	"
F	Molay Rudolph	320	laborer	38	"
H	Graco Edith †	324	clerk	25	"
K	Graco Flaminio	324	storekeeper	63	"
L	Graco Frances †	324	housewife	58	"
N	Soldani Grace †	328	"	60	"
O	Soldani Josephine †	328	clerk	38	"
P	Soldani Louis	328	laborer	41	"
R	Soldani Michael	328	retired	62	"
S	Soldani Vincenza †	328	housewife	41	"
T	Turilli Frances †	334	"	22	"
V	Turilli Raymond	334	laborer	27	5 Wilbur ct
W	Rossa Joseph	334	shipfitter	28	Medford

32

Page.	Letter.	FULL NAME.	Residence, Jan. 1, 1943.	Occupation.	Supposed Age.	Reported Residence Jan. 1, 1942. Street and Number.

Sumner Street Continued

	X	Bova Olga †	334	housewife	29	Medford
	Z	Acone Iris †	336	operator	20	here
2357						
	A	Acone Mary †	336	housewife	45	"
	B	Acone Robert	336	U S A	22	"
	C	Dabeni Anthony	336	retired	62	"
	D	Dabeni Josephine †	336	operator	23	"
	E	Dabeni Lucy †	336	"	29	"
	F	Dabeni Martha †	336	housewife	58	"
	G	Dabeni Vincent	336	fishcutter	32	"
	H	Scozzelli Anna F †	344	clerk	22	"
	K	Scozzelli Louis	344	butcher	56	"
	L	Scozzelli Mary A †	344	housewife	58	"
	M	Capone John A	346	shipwright	25	"
	N	Capone Mary C †	346	housewife	24	205 Saratoga
	O	Capone Eda †	346	"	49	here
	P	Capone Joseph	346	U S N	22	"
	R	Capone Josephine E †	346	operator	27	"
	S	Capone Pasquale	346	storekeeper	55	"
	T	Capone Rita †	346	operator	20	"
	W	Cuozzo Concetta C †	348	housewife	23	"
	X	Cuozzo Italo	348	machinist	26	"
	Y	Elba Carmen	248	laborer	20	"
	Z	Elba Julia †	348	clerk	23	"
2358						
	A	Elba Mary †	348	housewife	49	"
	B	Elba Nicholas	348	contractor	52	"
	C	Capone Julia †	348	housewife	39	"
	D	Cuozzo Antonio	350	laborer	55	"
	E	Cuozzo Gino	350	U S A	35	"
	F	Cuozzo Mario	350	laborer	22	"
	G	Picardi Filomena †	350	housewife	30	"
	H	Picardi Louis	350	cleanser	29	"
	K	Picardi Amato	350	laborer	55	"
	L	Picardi Antonio	350	U S A	20	"
	M	Picardi Carlo	350	"	22	"
	N	Picardi Sofia †	350	housewife	53	"
	O	Keohane Fannie †	351	"	28	"
	P	Keohane Joseph	351	painter	27	"
	R	Marmud Florence †	351	at home	75	"
	S	O'Dea Margaret †	351	"	78	"

1 23   33

Sumner Street—Continued

T	Aiken Catherine—†	351	housewife	50	here
U	Aiken Edna—†	351	operator	23	"
V	Aiken Edward	351	shipper	30	"
W	Aiken George	351	painter	52	"
X	Aiken Mary—†	351	saleswoman	28	"
Y	Incagnola Mary—†	352	housewife	24	"
Z	Incagnola Nunzio	352	shoeworker	26	"

2359

A	*Magliano Josephine—†	352	housewife	53	"
B	Magliano Pasquale	352	laborer	62	"
C	Scrima Adella—†	352	housewife	26	"
D	Scrima John	352	tailor	27	"
E	Rotondo Angelo	353	clerk	42	"
F	Rotondo Mary—†	353	housewife	38	"
G	Cuozzo Adela—†	353	hairdresser	26	"
H	*Cuozzo Antonette—†	353	housewife	56	"
K	Cuozzo Antonio	353	laborer	64	"
L	Cuozzo Carlo	353	U S C G	31	"
M	Cuozzo John	353	U S A	33	"
N	Cuozzo Louis	353	electrician	34	"
O	Manzoni Leonard	354	retired	69	"
P	*Manzoni Vincenza—†	354	housewife	61	"
R	Iarocci Antonetta M—†	354	inspector	21	"
S	*Iarocci Carmella—†	354	housewife	68	"
T	Iarocci Michael	354	laborer	68	"
U	Sciaraffa John	356	cook	31	"
V	Sciaraffa Josephine—†	356	housewife	29	"
W	Talieri Anthony	356	checker	34	"
X	Talieri Jennie—†	356	housewife	35	"
Y	Johnson Anna—†	357	at home	24	"
Z	*Johnson Beda—†	357	"	65	"

2360

A	Johnson Elizabeth—†	357	clerk	31	"
B	Marino Christine—†	357	at home	35	"
C	Altri Ida—†	357	housewife	33	"
D	Altri Joseph	357	shipfitter	29	Winthrop
E	Lynch Edward	357	longshoreman	45	here
F	Mazzarella Constance—†	358	housewife	32	222 Everett
G	Mazzarella Frank	358	shoeworker	35	222 "
H	Ventullo Gaetano	358	pipefitter	22	here
K	Ventullo Mary—†	358	housewife	23	"

34

Sumner Street Continued

L	Contilli Dora †	361	housewife	28	here	
M	Contilli Frank	361	electrician	28	"	
N	O'Connell Ellen †	361	at home	79	"	
O	O'Connell John J	361	shipfitter	45	"	
P*	Locatelli Alexandria †	361	housewife	69	"	
R	Locatelli Frank	361	retired	71	"	
S	Locatelli Victor	361	U S A	24	"	
T	Colarusso Eleanor †	362	stitcher	24	"	
U*	Colarusso Joseph	362	laborer	64	"	
V	Colarusso Patrick	362	U S A	29	"	
W	Constantine Elizabeth †	363	housewife	37	"	
X	Constantine William	363	longshoreman	37	"	
Y	Galvin John G	363	laborer	42	"	
Z	Galvin Julia †	363	housewife	36	"	

2361

A	Goglia Frank	363	retired	79	"	
B*	Goglia Louise †	363	housewife	64	"	
C	Locatelli Elizabeth †	363	"	25	"	
D	Locatelli Frank, jr	363	inspector	28	"	
H	Clifford Marie A †	365	housewife	24	"	
K	Clifford Theodore	365	mechanic	28	"	
L	Rapolla Daniel	365	U S A	20	"	
M	Rapolla Domenic	365	barber	52	"	
N	Rapolla Mary †	365	housewife	51	"	
O	Rapolla Ralph	365	clerk	27	"	
P	Rapolla Theresa †	365	"	25	"	
R	Ferranti Angelina †1st r 365		housewife	38	"	
S	Ferranti Ralph	1st r 365	mechanic	44	"	
T	Gioioso Domenic	1st r 365	laborer	53	"	
U	Gioioso Mary †	1st r 365	housewife	50	"	
V*	Arpino Antonio	2d r 365	plumber	55	270 Sumner	
W	Arpino Concetta †	2d r 365	stitcher	24	270 "	
X*	Arpino Lucy †	2d r 365	housewife	18	270 "	
Y*	DeFlumeri Elizabeth †	2d r 365	"	52	here	
Z	DeFlumeri Jerry	2d r 365	laborer	52	"	

2362

A	DeFlumeri William	2d r 365	rubberworker	23	"	
B	Frazier Mary †	3d r 365	at home	45	"	
C	Goglia John	3d r 365	mechanic	30	363 Sumner	
D	Goglia Rita †	3d r 365	housewife	24	here	
E	Petrillo Alexandro	3d r 365	finisher	46	284 Sumner	

Page	Letter	FULL NAME.	Residence, Jan. 1, 1943.	Occupation.	Supposed Age.	Reported Residence, Jan. 1, 1942. Street and Number.

Sumner Street — Continued

F	Petrillo Antonette—† 3d r	365	housewife	36	284 Sumner
H	Constantino Nicholas	367	machinist	34	here
K	Constantino Ruth—†	367	housewife	25	"
L	Martinello Alexandro	367	laborer	62	"
M	Martinello Anna —†	367	at home	34	"
N	Martinello Michael	367	U S A	32	"
O*	Martinello Vincenza—†	367	housewife	58	"
P	DeMarco Albert	367	laborer	38	"
R	DeMarco Sylvia— †	367	housewife	33	"
S	Venezia Anthony	368	laborer	36	"
T	Rumley Joseph	368	lineman	41	"
U	Rumley Rose †	368	housewife	40	"
V	Wist Joseph	368	U S A	22	"
W*	Caprio Catherine—†	368	housewife	22	"
X	Caprio Frank	368	mechanic	28	"
Y	DiFranzo Josephine—†	368	housewife	33	"
Z	DiFranzo William	368	salesman	35	"

2363

A	Aceto Anna — †	368	housewife	26	"
B	Aceto Louis	368	tailor	30	"
C	Grella Alfred	368	machinist	30	"
D	Grella Armando	368	electrician	33	"
E	Grella Esther †	368	stitcher	28	"
F	Grella Margaret—†	368	clerk	21	"
G	Grella Ralph	368	U S N	24	"
H*	DiNapoli Enrico	368	salesman	73	"
K	Marotta Louis	368	laborer	32	"
L	Kirby Robert	368	foreman	25	19 Haynes
M	Spinos Agnes— †	368	inspector	43	5 Wash'n
N	Piro John	368	clerk	43	here
O	Piro Josephine —†	368	housewife	40	"
S	Hunt Mary †	370	at home	52	"
T	Hunt Vere	370	mechanic	44	"
U	Colangelo Michael	371	dredger	26	"
V	Colangelo Virginia †	371	housewife	21	"
W*	Lupoli Dominic	371	baker	63	"
X*	Lupoli Nicholas	371	"	24	"
Y	Lupoli Ralph	371	"	21	"
Z	Lupoli Samuel	371	"	22	"

2364

A	Lupoli Theresa †	371	housewife	53	"

Sumner Street Continued

B	Landolfi Dewey	371	mechanic	36	here
c*	Landolfi Lucy — †	371	housewife	35	"
D	Ferullo Julia — †	371	"	35	"
E	Repucci Henry	371	pipefitter	46	"
F	Repucci Mary J — †	371	housewife	47	"
G	LoScinto Mary — †	371	"	24	"
H	LoScinto Thomas	371	chauffeur	28	"
K	Buccieri Ann — †	371	housewife	26	100 Cottage
L	Buccieri Charles	371	shipfitter	35	100 "
M	Trumpro Lena — †	372	at home	50	here
N	Trumpro Pasquale	372	barber	53	"
O	Pingitore Antonio	372	shoemaker	50	"
P*	Pingitore Mary — †	372	housewife	45	"
R	DeFilippo Florence — †	372	"	35	"
S	DeFilippo Vincent	372	clerk	37	"
U*	Scifo Josephine — †	376	housewife	32	"
V	Giglio Antonio	376	mechanic	50	"
W	Giglio Pompelia — †	376	housewife	45	"
X	Zirpolo Angelo	rear 376	mechanic	56	"
Y	Zirpolo Elizabeth — †	" 376	housewife	47	"
Z	Zirpolo Ralph	" 376	U S A	21	"
	2365				
A	Zirpolo Thomasina — †	" 376	housewife	21	389 Sumner
B	Scopa Dominic	" 376	laborer	32	here
C	Scopa Louise — †	" 376	housewife	32	"
D*	Santoro Adeline — †	" 376	"	65	"
E	Santoro Joseph	" 376	longshoreman	35	"
F	Tamburrion Edith — †	" 376	housewife	29	"
G	Tamburrion John	" 376	rigger	30	"
H	Para Andrew	" 376	engineer	46	"
K	Para Louis	" 376	oiler	50	"
L*	Paraboschi Caroline — †	" 376	housewife	72	"
M*	Paraboschi Gaetano	" 376	retired	85	"
N	Jones Ruth L — †	378	housewife	42	11 Everett
O	Jones Thomas R	378	longshoreman	47	11 "
P	Marino Angelina — †	378	housewife	32	here
R	Marino Salvatore	378	fisherman	34	"
T	Blackburn Ella — †	380	housekeeper	65	"
U	Catanese Joseph	381	operator	25	"
V	Catanese Lena — †	381	housewife	24	"
W	DiRienzo Antonio	381	laborer	44	"

Sumner Street—Continued

x	*DiRienzo Concetta—†	381	housewife	41	here
y	Bruno Anna—†	381	"	23	"
z	Bruno Joseph	381	U S A	22	"

2366

A	Bruno Mary—†	381	housewife	25	"
B	Bruno Vincent	381	laborer	25	"
c	O'Neil Annie—†	382	laundress	74	"
D	O'Neil Grace—†	382	"	65	"
E	*Walsh Jessie—†	382	housewife	62	"
F	*Walsh Richard	382	longshoreman	63	"
G	Walsh Richard, jr	382	"	27	"
K	Colangelo Carmella—†	387	housewife	48	"
L	Colangelo Joseph	387	splicer	47	"
M	*Buono Fortuna—†	387	housewife	50	"
N	Buono Michael	387	U S A	21	"
O	Buono Nicola	387	oiler	47	"
P	Buono Peter	387	seaman	23	"
R	Buono Phyllis—†	387	clerk	24	"
S	DiCicco John	389	laborer	44	"
T	DiCicco Margaret—†	389	housewife	42	"
U	Little Delia—†	391	"	60	"
V	Little Phillip	391	laborer	22	"
W	Little Valentine	391	"	62	"
Y	*Santilli Anthony	406	retired	65	"
Z	Santilli Ralph	406	U S A	21	"

2367

A	*Santilli Julia—†	406	housewife	53	"
B	Santilli Phillip	406	U S A	24	"
C	Spagnolo Domenic	406	laborer	21	45 Chelsea
D	Spagnolo Esther—†	406	housewife	21	45 "
E	Casey Charles	408	fireman	37	122 Gladstone
F	Casey Helen B—†	408	housewife	58	here
G	Casey Jeremiah	408	engineer	62	"
H	Casey Marie L—†	408	housewife	33	122 Gladstone
K	Collotta George	410	U S A	22	here
L	Collotta Samuel	410	mechanic	25	"
M	Collotta Albert	410	U S A	20	"
O	Collotta Orazio	410	painter	30	"
N	Collotta Tillie—†	410	housewife	26	"
P	Grasso Phyllis—†	412	"	29	"
R	Grasso Sylvio	412	salesman	29	"

38

Sumner Street Continued

s	Grasso Alfred	412	clerk	31	here
t	Grasso Americo	412	pedler	40	"
u	Grasso Armando	412	clerk	27	"
v	*Grasso Concetta †	412	at home	65	"
w	Bolino Antonio	412	chauffeur	37	"
x	Bolino Elvira †	412	housewife	36	"
y	Cassetina Alfred	414	clerk	33	"
z	Cassetina Rose †	414	housewife	28	"
	2368				
a	Johns Edward	414	painter	42	"
b	Johns Theresa †	414	housewife	40	"
c	Bibo Anthony	414	U S A	22	"
d	Bibo Gabriel	414	retired	66	"
e	Bibo John	414	"	64	"
f	Leonard Arthur	414	welder	30	"
g	Leonard Dora †	414	housewife	24	"
h	Ahern Bridget †	418	at home	82	"
k	Ahern Daniel	418	U S A	42	"
l	Ahern Joseph B	418	salesman	40	"
m	Ahern Nora C †	418	at home	58	"
n	Ahern Theresa †	418	clerk	44	"
o	Nee Anna †	420	housewife	55	"
p	Nee Thomas	420	carpenter	55	"
r	Brophy Caroline †	420	clerk	41	"
s	Brophy Mary †	420	"	42	"
t	Kelley John	420	retired	75	"
u	Cassley Arthur	422	"	74	"
v	Gillespie Frederick J	422	electrician	54	"
w	Griffin Clara †	422	at home	55	"
x	Griffin Clara G †	422	typist	22	"

Webster Avenue

y	Faretio Edward	1½	laborer	47	here
z	Costello James	1½	longshoreman	31	"
	2369				
a	Costello Mafalda †	1½	housewife	26	"
b	Scardetta Anthony	1½	laborer	30	"
c	Scardetta Helen †	1½	housewife	29	"
d	*Batiste Felicia †	3	"	35	"
e	Batiste Sabatino	3	laborer	37	"

Page	Letter	FULL NAME.	Residence, Jan. 1, 1943	Occupation.	Supposed Age.	Reported Residence, Jan. 1, 1942. Street and Number.

Webster Avenue—Continued

F	DiTomaso Nicola	3	laborer	45	here
G	DiTomaso Sylvia †	3	housewife	45	"
K	*Perito Paul	5	retired	80	"
L	Lopilato Elizabeth †	5	housewife	31	"
M	Lopilato Saverio	5	manager	38	"
N	Spirito Antonio D	7	laborer	67	"
O	Spirito Mary †	7	factoryhand	25	"
P	*Spirito Rubina †	7	housewife	68	"
R	Perry Eileen †	7	"	29	"
S	Perry Joaquin	7	electrician	36	"
T	Ferullo Lucy †	9	housewife	52	"
U	Ferullo William	9	laborer	54	"
V	Ferullo William, jr	9	factoryhand	21	"
W	Contestabile Attilio	11	machinist	28	"
X	Contestabile Margaret †	11	housewife	27	"
Y	Misiano Dominic	11	laborer	23	"
Z	Misiano Helen †	11	housewife	22	"
2370					
A	Collins Antonette †	15	"	34	"
B	Collins James	15	foundryman	34	"
C	Colarusso Joseph	15	retired	75	"

Webster Street

D	Gigliello Alfred	146	engineer	28	97 Addison
E	Gigliello Gervasio	146	storekeeper	30	here
F	Gigliello Victoria †	146	housewife	32	"
G	Filippone Frances †	146	factoryhand	55	141 Webster
H	Filippone Henry C	146	U S C G	55	141 "
K	St John Mary †	146	housewife	25	here
L	Goddard Albert	146	factoryhand	47	"
M	Goddard Jennie †	146	housewife	39	"
O	Balzotti Cesare	148	carpenter	47	"
P	Balzotti Elizabeth †	148	housewife	37	"
R	Caristo Catherine †	148	nurse	23	Brookline
S	Belzotti Arthur	148	U S A	26	here
T	Belzotti Domenick	148	factoryhand	30	"
U	*Belzotti Mary †	148	housewife	68	"
V	Belzotti Michael	148	U S A	23	"
W	*Belzotti Paul	148	laborer	68	"
X	*Spinazola Jennie †	148	housewife	46	"

Webster Street Continued

Y	Spinazola Joseph	148	laborer	46	here
Z	Spinazola Louise †	148	factoryhand	25	"
2371					
A	Spinazola Mary †	148	"	21	"
B	*Barbato Anthony	150	presser	42	"
C	Barbato Louise †	150	housewife	35	"
D	Gigliello Catherine †	150	"	49	"
E	Gigliello Gerald	150	U S N	52	"
F	*Scifo Florence †	150	housewife	70	"
G	Scifo Joseph	150	factoryhand	40	"
H	Scifo Mary †	150	housewife	36	"
K	*Contestabile Antonio	150	gardener	65	"
L	Contestabile Peter	150	milkman	31	"
M	Yachetti Louis	150	barber	31	"
N	Yachetti Mildred †	150	housewife	30	"
O	Salamanca Annie †	154	stitcher	22	"
P	Salamanca Manuel	154	U S A	27	"
R	*Salamanca Mary †	154	housewife	42	"
S	Salamanca Peter	154	shipwright	26	"
T	Abate Alfred	154	shoemaker	25	"
U	Abate Alvino	154	U S N	24	"
V	*Abate Amadeo	154	shoemaker	57	"
W	Abate Jennie †	154	clerk	22	"
X	*Abate Mary †	154	housewife	50	"
Y	Occhipinti Adeline †	154	clerk	20	"
Z	Occhipinti Anthony	154	rigger	53	"
2372					
A	Occhipinti Mary †	154	housewife	44	"
C	Agnew Margaret M †	156	at home	55	"
D	DiAngelis Carmen A	158	machinist	22	34 Morris
E	DiAneglis Jennie †	158	housewife	24	34 "
F	St John Edith †	158	factoryhand	22	here
G	*St John Edward	158	longshoreman	56	"
H	St John Edwin L	158	U S A	26	"
K	*St John Mary †	158	housewife	58	"
L	Hanson Angela †	160	"	26	"
M	Hanson James F	160	longshoreman	29	"
N	Pesella Angelo	160	clerk	34	"
O	Pesella Assunta †	160	housewife	57	"
P	Pesella Charles J	160	U S A	38	"
R	Pesella Joseph	160	"	32	"

Page	Letter	FULL NAME.	Residence, Jan. 1, 1943.	Occupation.	Supposed Age.	Reported Residence, Jan. 1, 1942. Street and Number.

Webster Street— Continued

s	Pesella Pasquale	160	engineer	66	here
t	Pesella Rose—†	160	at home	30	"
u	Pesella Helen—†	160	"	29	106 Byron
v	Nigro Anna—†	162	housewife	35	here
w	Nigro Domenick A	162	chauffeur	38	"
x	Brennan Francis	162	U S N	42	"
y	Brennan Sarah—†	162	teacher	48	"
z	Brennan William	162	seaman	52	"
	2373				
A	Cacici Arthur	166	barber	58	"
B	*Cacici Concetta—†	166	housewife	50	"
C	*Modica Angelina—†	166	"	37	291 Sumner
D	Modica Gioacchino	166	retired	38	291 "
E	Scire Louis	166	electrician	33	New York
F	Scire Pauline—†	166	housewife	33	"
G	Maragioglio Anthony	168	mechanic	41	here
H	Maragioglio Eleanor—†	168	housewife	35	"
K	Rossi Francis	168	machinist	34	346 Sumner
L	*Rossi Louise—†	168	housewife	29	346 "
M	Martinello Anna—†	172	"	52	here
N	Martinello Jennie—†	172	at home	28	"
O	Belgiorno Florence—†	172	housewife	31	"
P	Belgiorno John	172	manager	34	"
R	Delligato Jerry	174	policeman	34	"
S	Delligato Marie—†	174	housewife	28	"
T	Pepe Antonio	174	retired	71	"
U	Pepe Louise—†	174	housewife	31	"
V	Pepe Ralph	174	boxmaker	35	"
W	*Scherma Catherine—†	176	housewife	45	"
X	*Scherma Ciro	176	barber	48	"
Y	Scherma Joseph	176	U S A	20	"
Z	DeModena John	176	musician	56	"
	2374				
A	DeModena Silvio	176	electrician	26	"
B	Cutrone Theresa—†	176	housewife	71	"
C	Santangelo Guy	178	storekeeper	46	"
D	Santangelo Nicholas	178	U S A	21	"
E	Santangelo Rosaria—†	178	housewife	45	"
F	Vsseglio Edward	178	meatcutter	35	"
G	Vsseglio Mary—†	178	housewife	32	"
H	Schifino Angelina—†	178	"	60	"

Page.	Letter.	FULL NAME.	Residence. Jan. 1, 1943.	Occupation.	Supposed Age.	Reported Residence, Jan. 1, 1942. Street and Number.

Webster Street Continued

K	Schifino Antonetta—†	178	stitcher	21	here
L	Schifino Irene—†	178	"	29	"
M	*Schifino Michael	178	packer	63	"
N	Schifino Mildred—†	178	factoryhand	27	"
O	Pizzi Benjamin	182	laborer	27	"
P	Pizzi Phyllis—†	182	housewife	22	"
R	Knowles Bridget †	182	"	81	"
S	Knowles Mary—†	182	factoryhand	38	"
T	Knowles Thomas	182	retired	42	"
U	Hayes Rose—†	182	typist	25	151 Meridian
V	Roan John F	182	U S N	27	151 "
W	Roan Rose—†	182	housewife	55	151 "
X	Shoemaker Clementine—†	184	"	28	here
Y	Shoemaker William	184	shipfitter	28	"
Z	Ciccia Arthur	184	cutter	22	809 Saratoga

2375

A	Ciccia Rose—†	184	housewife	22	265 Webster
B	*Guardabascio Incoronata—†	184	"	47	here
C	Guardabascio Nicola	184	tailor	49	"
D	Giangregario John	186	laborer	56	"
E	*Giangregario Susan—†	186	housewife	44	"
F	Parente Fannie—†	186	"	35	410 Sumner
G	Parente Frederick C	186	agent	40	410 "
H	Cirone Guerino	186	pipefitter	44	here
K	Cirone Settinnia †	186	housewife	37	"
M	Arcone Benjamin	188	laborer	50	"
N	McIsaac Hilary	188	longshoreman	48	"
O	McIsaac Sylvester J	188	"	51	"
P	Ambrose Crescenzio	188	laborer	48	"
R	Ambrose John	188	engineer	51	"
S	*Ambrose Pauline †	188	housewife	52	"
T	Iorio Jennie—†	188	factoryhand	30	"
U	Iorio John	188	barber	38	"

Ward 1–Precinct 24

CITY OF BOSTON

LIST OF RESIDENTS
20 YEARS OF AGE AND OVER

(NON-CITIZENS INDICATED BY ASTERISK)
(FEMALES INDICATED BY DAGGER)

AS OF

JANUARY 1, 1943

JOSEPH F. TIMILTY, *Chairman*
FREDERIC E. DOWLING, *Secretary*
WILLIAM A. MOTLEY, JR.
FRANCIS B. McKINNEY
EVERETT R. PROUT

Listing Board.

CITY OF BOSTON PRINTING DEPARTMENT

2400

Appian Place

A	*Ingala Carmella— †	1	housewife	47	here
B	Ingala Nicholas	1	U S A	20	"
C	*Ingala Salvatore	1	laborer	53	"
D	Serina Josephine— †	2	housewife	38	210 Benningt'n
E	*Nocilla Calogero	2	retired	80	here
F	*Nocilla Paula— †	2	housewife	69	"
H	DiSalvo Giovino	3	shoeworker	61	"
K	DiSalvo Mary— †	3	forewoman	29	"
L	*DiSalvo Rose— †	3	housewife	48	"
M	Green Francis V	4	rigger	26	"
N	Green Maria— †	4	housewife	28	"
O	Martella Guiseppe	4	longshoreman	65	"
P	*Martella Liboria— †	4	housewife	62	"

Bennington Street

S	Campbell Alice— †	84C	housewife	68	here
T	Campbell Edward A	84C	longshoreman	62	"
X	Murley Alice D— †	89	teacher	46	"
Y	Murley Margaret A— †	89	housekeeper	60	"
Z	Gorman Alice M— †	90	housewife	55	"

2401

A	Gorman Margaret— †	90	clerk	30	"
B	Keough Patrick	90	meatcutter	40	"
C	*Belliveau Joseph R	90	welder	37	"
D	Belliveau Louise— †	90	housewife	54	"
E	*Theophiles Bessie— †	90	"	58	"
F	Theophiles Georgia— †	90	stitcher	27	"
G	Theophiles James	90	watchman	60	"
H	Theophiles Mary— †	90	operator	20	"
K	Theophiles Speros	90	U S A	23	"
L	Hegner Albert P	91	clerk	29	"
M	Hegner Andrew	91	retired	85	"
N	Hegner Edward L	91	machinist	30	"
O	Hegner Francis L	91	engineer	34	"
P	Hegner Mary E— †	91	housewife	66	"
R	Hegner Paul J	91	clerk	23	"
S	Freitas Augustine	92	longshoreman	46	"
T	*Freitas Mary— †	92	housewife	50	"

2

Bennington Street Continued

u	McGrane Stella †	92	housewife	22	179 Putnam
v	McGrane Thomas	92	electrician	22	179 "
w*	Alves Joseph	92	retired	72	here
x	Jorge Henrietta F †	92	housewife	50	"
y	Jorge Joaquin J	92	U S A	21	"
z	Cicciarello Angelina †	94	housewife	43	"

2402

A	Cicciarello Frances †	94	leatherworker	21	"
B	Cicciarello Frank	94	laborer	45	"
c	Campana Anthony	94	machinist	21	"
D*	Campana Louise †	94	housewife	50	"
E	Campana Phillip	94	laborer	50	"
F	Campana Thomas	94	U S A	25	"
G	Porfido Concetta †	94	housewife	34	"
H	Porfido Eugene	94	butcher	39	"
K	Rizzo Fred	95	bartender	40	"
L	Pomponi Mary †	95	housewife	38	"
M	Pomponi Vincent	95	tailor	44	"
N	Leddy Julia †	96	housekeeper	69	"
O	Leddy Mary †	96	"	39	"
P	Moran Mary †	96	housewife	68	"
R	Moran Michael	96	retired	67	"
s	Smith Catherine †	96	housekeeper	70	"
T*	Mirra Carmela †	97	housewife	74	"
U	Mirra Martino S	97	stitcher	44	"
V	Perez Anthony	99	fireman	52	"
W	Perez Anthony, jr	99	U S A	20	"
X	Perez Armonia †	99	stenographer	24	"
Y*	Perez Aurora †	99	housekeeper	63	Cuba
Z*	Perez Concha †	99	housewife	43	here

2403

A	Perez Frank	99	carpenter	33	"
B	Perez Rose †	99	teacher	25	"
c	Quinn Dorcas †	100	housekeeper	85	"
D*	Rubin Max	100	glazier	63	"
E	Rubin Phillip	100	U S A	24	"
F*	Rubin Rose †	100	housewife	63	"
G*	Marino Marion †	100	"	27	"
H	Marino Patrick	100	engraver	35	"
K*	Lopes Manuel	101	millhand	18	13 Winthrop
L	Tolentino Antonio	101	"	33	5 Appian pl

3

Page	Letter	FULL NAME.	Residence, Jan. 1, 1943	Occupation.	Supposed Age.	Reported Residence, Jan. 1, 1942. Street and Number.

Bennington Street — Continued

M	Tolentino Louise †	101	housewife	28	5 Appian pl
N	Carrozza Annie †	103	operator	20	here
O	Carrozza Anthony	103	"	26	"
P	Carrozza John	103	U S N	21	"
R	Carrozza Sarah †	103	housekeeper	23	"
S	Carrozza Vincent	103	letter carrier	29	"
T	DiMarino Mary †	104	housewife	30	"
U	DiMarino Vincent	104	foreman	29	"
V	Rizzo Joseph	104	U S A	22	"
W	*Rizzo Mary †	104	housewife	51	"
X	*Rizzo Richard	104	tailor	51	"
Y	Cardone Anna †	104	packer	29	"
Z	Cardone Anthony	104	U S A	26	"
	2404				
A	Cardone John	104	brazier	23	"
B	Cardone Michael	104	operator	20	"
C	Cardone Pasquale	104	laborer	53	"
D	*Cardone Themasina †	104	housewife	53	"
E	Irwin Lillian †	105	"	23	"
F	Irwin Thomas	105	laborer	26	"
G	McNamara Edna †	105	housewife	28	"
H	McNamara John	105	shipfitter	27	"
K	Murphy Lena †	105	laundryworker	46	"
L	Forziati Aida †	107	housewife	57	"
M	Forziati Alfonso	107	chemist	32	"
N	Forziati Francesco	107	tailor	59	"
O	Gracie Julius	108	rigger	59	"
P	Gracie Mary †	108	housewife	55	"
R	Marino Americo	108	laborer	37	"
S	Marino Emma †	108	presser	33	"
T	Marino Mary †	108	housekeeper	35	"
U	Marino Mildred †	108	stitcher	36	"
V	*Marino Rose †	108	housekeeper	75	"
W	Marino Virginia †	108	clerk	32	"
X	Faretra Arthur	108	barber	42	"
Y	Faretra Sarah †	108	housewife	40	"
Z	Miccichi John	109	chauffeur	26	"
	2405				
A	Miccichi Josephine †	109	housewife	25	"
B	Cipriano Mary †	109	clerk	37	"
C	*DiAngelis Joseph	109	shoeworker	61	"

Bennington Street Continued

D	DiAngelis Josephine —†	109	forewoman	24	here
E	DiAngelis Mary †	109	housewife	48	"
F	Lombardi Anthony	110	laborer	28	51 Saratoga
G	Lombardi Dorothy †	110	housewife	26	51 "
H	Marino Emilio	110	tailor	42	here
K	Marino Emma †	110	"	37	"
L	Rauseo Olga—†	110	clerk	24	174 Cottage
M	Rauseo Vincenzo	110	laborer	24	118 Webster
N	DiOrio Adam	111	U S A	29	here
O	DiOrio John	111	clerk	26	"
P	DiOrio Mary—†	111	housewife	45	"
R	DiOrio Thomas	111	printer	51	"
S	Russo John	113	"	35	"
T	Russo Mary C—†	113	housewife	35	"
U	Constant Thomas B	114	retired	79	"
V	Lavoie Della—†	114	housekeeper	65	"
W	Buttiglieri Katina—†	114	housewife	26	"
X	Buttiglieri Louis	114	salesman	26	"
Y	Gravallese Alfred E	115	U S N	22	"
Z	Gravallese Catherine—†	115	operator	20	"
	2406				
A	*Gravallese Linda —†	115	housewife	52	"
B	Lamb Nina M—†	116	"	59	"
C	Lamb William	116	boilermaker	62	"
D	Dobbins Aloysius	116	rigger	28	115 Eutaw
E	Dobbins Margaret †	116	housewife	26	115 "
F	Russell Catherine V—†	116	"	56	here
G	Russell Florence †	116	operator	23	"
H	Russell Joseph L	116	clerk	54	"
K	McNeil Elizabeth —†	117	housekeeper	64	"
L	Messina Mario	118	tailor	27	43 Gove
M	Messina Sarah —†	118	housewife	26	here
N	Barrett James M	118	U S A	21	"
O	Barrett John J	118	foreman	57	"
P	Barrett Margaret —†	118	housewife	56	"
R	Barrett Mary A †	118	operator	26	" .
S	Barrett William J	118	U S C G	21	"
T	Perrone Clement	118	"	25	"
U	Perrone Grace —†	118	housewife	24	"
W	Biancordi Elisabeth —†	119	"	43	13 Porter
X	Coelho Ruth —†	119	housekeeper	42	here

Bennington Street—Continued

Y	Stewart James	119	retired	84	here

2407

A	DiGregorio Pasquale	120	painter	34	141 Paris
B	DiGregorio Rose †	120	housewife	32	here
C*	Marottoli Mary †	120	"	44	48 Marion
D*	Marottoli Oreste	120	tinsmith	44	48 "
E	Miccichi Joseph	120	laborer	59	here
F	Miccichi Mary †	120	seamstress	23	"
G	Miccichi Peter	120	U S A	21	"
H*	Miccichi Vincenza †	120	housewife	58	"
K	Degulio Helen †	121	"	21	62 Brooks
L	Degulio Michael	121	U S A	27	74 Prince
M	DiStasio Albert	121	"	27	62 Brooks
N	DiStasio Arthur	121	rigger	22	62 "
O	DiStasio Frank	121	bartender	52	62 "
P	DiStasio Mary †	121	housewife	52	62 "
R*	Marciello Mary †	123	"	36	37 Decatur
S	Marciello Phillip	123	machinist	39	37 "
T	Gobez Ronald	124	anglesmith	28	here
U	Gobez Sarafina †	124	housewife	32	"
V	Pullo Annie †	124	"	64	"
W	Pullo Benedict	124	retired	68	"
X	Pullo Francis	124	shipfitter	29	"
Y	Cappucci Joseph	125	inspector	43	"
Z	Cappucci Lucia †	125	candymaker	42	"

2408

A	Cappucci Luigi	125	oiler	28	"
C	Mazzariello Joseph	128	storekeeper	55	"
D*	Mazzariello Mary †	128	housewife	55	"
F	Manfredoni Ella †	136	operator	22	83 Brooks
G	Mastrangelo Fannie †	136	housewife	30	83 "
H	Mastrangelo Rocco	136	laborer	30	83 "
L	Chafetz Dora †	138	housewife	60	here
M	Chafetz Harry	138	tailor	61	"
N	Sheehan Gertrude M †	138	operator	23	"
O	Sheehan Mary E †	138	housewife	58	"
P	Sheehan William G	138	U S A	29	"
R	St George Alice †	140	housewife	42	"
S	St George Joseph J	140	longshoreman	57	"
T	Powell Elizabeth †	140	housewife	50	"
U	Powell Frank T	140	laborer	21	"

Page.	Letter	FULL NAME.	Residence, Jan. 1, 1943	Occupation.	Supposed Age.	Reported Residence, Jan. 1, 1942. Street and Number.

Brooks Street

	v	Sen James	52	engineer	27	here
	w*	Sen John	52	retired	65	"
	x	Sen Mary †	52	teacher	26	"
	y	LeBlanc Agnes †	52	housewife	33	"
	z	LeBlanc Louis	52	fishcutter	32	"
		2409				
	a	Giarle Loretta †	54	housewife	27	"
	b	Giarle Louis	54	serviceman	27	"
	c	DiOrio Angelo	54	U S A	25	"
	d	DiOrio Joseph	54	shipfitter	47	"
	e	DiOrio Joseph	54	U S A	20	"
	f	DiOrio Minnie †	54	housewife	45	"
	g	DiOrio Rose †	54	stitcher	22	"
	h	Ebba Gennaro	54	shipfitter	46	"
	k*	Ebba Philomena †	54	housewife	35	"
	l	Ebba Ralph	54	U S A	22	"
	o	Cross Daisy †	62	housewife	42	163 Benningt'n
	p	Leeman Frederick	62	shipfitter	49	163 "
	r	Lachiana Louis	62	laborer	22	here
	s*	Lachiana Maria †	62	housewife	51	"
	t	Lachiana Pietro	62	laborer	51	"
	u	Ricciardello Antonetta †	64	housewife	28	68 Brooks
	v	Ricciardello Philip	64	checker	27	68 "
	w	Ricciardello Grace †	64	clerk	24	here
	x	Ricciardello Louise †	64	teacher	21	"
	y	Ricciardello Luigi	64	pipefitter	57	"
	z	Ricciardello Michelina †	64	housewife	53	"
		2410				
	a	Scalli Anna †	68	"	23	149 Benningt'n
	b	Scalli John	68	mechanic	25	6 E Eagle
	c	Meaney Alice †	68	housewife	21	here
	d	Meaney Margaret †	68	clerk	21	"
	e	Meaney Thomas	68	laborer	58	"
	f	Bonura Joseph	68	shoeworker	45	44 Morris
	g	Bonura Madelina †	68	housewife	32	44 "
	h	D'Agostino Antonio	76	baker	64	63 Webster
	k*	D'Agostino Pasqualina †	76	housewife	63	63 "
	l	Masiello Josephine †	76	"	40	44 Falcon
	m	Masiello Sabatino	76	bartender	45	44 "
	n	DeFeo Irene †	78	housewife	32	here
	o	DeFeo Joseph	78	blacksmith	31	"

7

Brooks Street — Continued

	p	Bennett Margaret—†	78	housekeeper	73	here
	r	Nesbitt George A	78	laborer	68	221 Benningt'n
	s	Nesbitt George P	78	U S M C	20	221 "
	t	Nesbitt Georgina —†	78	housewife	58	221 "
	u	Wise Margaret —†	80	housekeeper	52	here
	v	*Zaccaria Esther —†	80	housewife	42	"
	w	*Zaccaria Salvatore	80	laborer	52	"
	x	Francis Antoinette —†	80	housewife	26	"
	y	Francis Joseph	80	U S N	29	"
	z	Donners Elizabeth †	82	housekeeper	79	"

2411

	a	Garisto Theresa †	82	housewife	41	"
	b	Murray Alice—†	82	"	24	"
	c	Murray William	82	chauffeur	26	"
	e	Capezzuto John	84	U S A	26	"
	f	Capezzuto Joseph	84	laborer	21	"
	g	Capezzuto Louise—†	84	housewife	45	"
	h	Capezzuto Nicholas	84	U S A	23	"
	k	Simonelli Dominic	84	tailor	48	"
	l	*Simonelli Jennie —†	84	housewife	44	"
	m	Heres Rose—†	86	"	33	"
	n	Heres William	86	seaman	33	"
	o	Mastrangelo Margaret †	86	housewife	45	"
	p	Mastrangelo Michael	86	laborer	46	"
	r	Marciana Michael	86	"	30	"
	s	Marciana Sophie —†	86	housewife	28	"
	t	Soe Joe	88	laundryman	55	14 Tyler
	u	Martella Frank	88	sand blaster	28	here
	v	Martella Mary —†	88	housewife	26	"
	w	Guiliano Angelo	88	metalworker	23	"
	x	Guiliano Rosaria —†	88	housewife	21	"

2412 Chelsea Street

	a	Antonucci Carmella †	122	stitcher	28	here
	b	Frizzi Gaetano	122	painter	53	"
	c	*Frizzi Jennie †	122	housewife	53	"
	d	Frizzi Victoria †	122	stitcher	21	"
	e	Zagorsky Isaac	124	glazier	62	"
	g	Zagorsky Rebecca—†	124	housewife	62	"
	h	Sicuranza Angelo	124	clerk	33	"

8

Chelsea Street Continued

K	Sicuranza Mildred—†	124	housewife	32	here
L	*Ingala Philippa—†	126	at home	70	"
M	LaSala Carmella—†	126	housewife	41	"
N	LaSala Louis	126	barber	44	"
O	DeSimone Nicholas	126	operator	34	Revere
P	Morico Emilio	126	janitor	36	"
R	Morico Louise—†	126	operator	32	"
T	Poto Antoinette—†	128	housewife	27	138 Porter
U	Poto Vito	128	clerk	29	138 "
V	Lopez Mary—†	128	at home	38	here
W	Mattivello Albert	128	pedler	24	"
X	Mattivello Eleanor—†	128	housewife	31	"
Y	DeMarco Carmen	130	laborer	66	"
X	*DeMarco Rose—†	130	housewife	66	"

2413

A	Mattivello Elvira—†	130	"	26	"
B	Mattivello Joseph	130	machinist	36	"
C	Mattivello Martin	130	shipwright	27	"
D	Mattivello Rose G—†	130	dressmaker	26	"
E	Belmonte Carmen	132	machinist	31	"
F	Belmonte Patricia—†	132	housewife	31	"
G	*Mattivello Petrina—†	132	"	59	"
H	Mattivello Russell	132	dealer	38	"
K	Mattivello Salvatore	132	machinist	63	"
L	Mattivelo Edna—†	132	housewife	30	"
M	Mattivello Salvatore, jr	132	shipfitter	29	"
O	*Drago Charles	134	retired	65	"
P	Drago Charles	134	tailor	25	"
R	Drago Joseph	134	"	23	"
S	*Drago Josephine—†	134	housewife	56	"
T	*Cavallaro Angela—†	134	"	57	185 London
U	Cavallaro Charles	134	laborer	62	185 "
V	Cavallaro Josephine—†	134	operator	21	185 "
X	*Abbisso Crocifissa—†	136	stitcher	50	here
Y	Abbisso Salvatore	136	retired	57	"
Z	Milano Josephine—†	136	stitcher	27	"

2414

A	Milano Pasquale	136	painter	30	"
B	Mattarazzo Antoinetta †	138	operator	31	"
C	Mattarazzo Augustino	138	chauffeur	33	"
D	*Mattarazzo Marguerite †	138	housewife	45	"

9

Chelsea Street—Continued

E	*Mattarazzo Rafaelo	138	retired	47	here
F	*Petrola Palmina †	138	housewife	43	"
G	Petrola Umberto	138	laborer	55	"
H	*Lipizzi Grace †	138	housewife	49	"
K	*Lipizzi Michael	138	laborer	48	"
L	Gallucci Phyllis †	140	housewife	28	"
M	Gallucci Victor	140	shipwright	28	"
N	Bongivanni Josephine †	140	stitcher	22	"
O	*Bongivanni Mario	140	laborer	60	"
P	*Bongivanni Rosaria †	140	housewife	49	"
R	Bongivanni Vincenza †	140	stitcher	21	"
S	Cardinale Joseph	140	baker	55	"
T	*Cardinale Josephine †	140	housewife	53	"
U	Matarazzo Angelo	142	welder	29	"
V	Matarazzo Anna †	142	housewife	30	"
W	Matarazzo Joseph	142	laborer	32	"
X	Matarazzo Maria †	142	housewife	56	"
Y	Matarazzo Mary †	142	candymaker	30	"
Z	Matarazzo Massimino	142	laborer	57	"

2415

A	Marino Marion †	142	stitcher	21	"
B	*Marino Mary †	142	housewife	46	"
C	*Marino Nicholas	142	pedler	51	"
D	Marino Theresa †	142	stitcher	25	"
E	Angelo Louis F	144	U S N	29	345 Maverick
F	Angelo Mary P †	144	clerk	28	345 "
G	Martori Maria †	144	housewife	45	here
H	Martori Vincenzo	144	presser	57	"
K	Pasciscia Antonio	144	inspector	25	"
M	Pasciscia Joseph	144	laborer	48	"
L	*Pasciscia Josephine †	144	housewife	48	"
O	Giannetti Anthony	152	florist	30	"
P	Giannetti Florence †	152	housewife	27	"
R	Giannetti Frank	152	laborer	65	"
S	*Giannetti Joanna †	152	housewife	60	"
T	Giannetti Margaret †	152	stitcher	22	"
U	Giullo Joseph	152	welder	23	"
V	Giullo Vincenza †	152	housewife	23	"
X	Nappi John	154	laborer	57	"
Y	*Nappi Lena †	154	housewife	57	"
Z	Nappi Mary †	154	operator	24	"

2416

Chelsea Street Continued

A	*Oliva Alphonse	154	laborer	50	here
B	*Oliva Carmella—†	154	housewife	55	"
C	DeFronzo Anna—†	154	"	35	119 Cottage
D	DeFronzo Severio	154	clerk	33	119 "
F	*Manganello Concetta—†	156	housewife	43	here
G	Manganello Genaco	156	gardener	53	"
H	Vozella John	156	machinist	53	"
K	Vozella Josephine—†	156	housewife	49	"
L	Vozella Theresa—†	156	stitcher	21	"
M	*Cresta James	158	laundryman	63	"
N	Cresta Jennie—†	158	stitcher	20	"
O	*Cresta Mary—†	158	housewife	51	"
P	Lamattino Felipa—†	158	"	73	1 Savage ct
R	Lamattino Salvatore	158	retired	77	1 "
S	*Pompeo Angelo	158	laborer	50	here
T	*Pompeo Anna—†	158	housewife	42	"
V	Gardina Joseph	162	laborer	45	28 Chelsea
W	Scopa Carmen	164	molder	45	here
X	Scopa Laura—†	164	housewife	48	"
Y	White Annie B—†	164	at home	44	"
Z	Scopa John	164	cutter	45	"

2417

A	Scopa Lucy—†	164	housewife	39	"
B	*Pagliarulo Maria—†	164	"	54	"
C	Pagliarulo Paul	164	laborer	55	"
D	*Falzarano Angelo	164A	butcher	34	"
E	Falzarano Julia—†	164A	housewife	32	"
F	Lucca Leo	164A	cabinetmaker	39	"
G	Lucca Louise—†	164A	housewife	39	"
H	Scopa Elizabeth—†	164A	"	41	"
K	Scopa Frances—†	164A	stitcher	21	"
L	Scopa Ralph	164A	mechanic	42	"
M	*Sbriglio Concetta—†	166	housewife	52	126 Havre
N	*Sbriglio Paolo	166	laborer	61	126 "
O	*Caggiano Amelia—†	166	housewife	50	here
P	Caggiano Angelo	166	chauffeur	50	"
R	Caggiano Fred	166	U S A	20	"
S	Dampolo Joseph	166	cutter	37	"
T	Dampolo Mary—†	166	housewife	34	"
U	Ricci Concetta—†	166A	"	26	"

11

Page	Letter	FULL NAME.	Residence, Jan. 1, 1943.	Occupation.	Supposed Age.	Reported Residence, Jan. 1, 1942. Street and Number.

Chelsea Street—Continued

	v	Ricci Leonard	166A	rigger	29	here
	w	*Russo Theresa —†	166A	housewife	43	"
	x	Gaeta Albert	166A	milkman	28	11 Paris
	y	Gaeta Concetta —†	166A	housewife	23	11 "
	z	DiStefano Angelo	168	storekeeper	52	here
2418						
	a	DiStefano Charles	168	U S A	24	"
	b	*DiStefano Mary —†	168	housewife	39	"
	c	Alberelli Arturo	168	tailor	63	"
	d	*Alberelli Jennie —†	168	at home	57	"
	e	Celata Bernard	168	electrician	42	"
	f	Celata Josephine —†	168	housewife	36	"
	g	Iarrobino Florence —†	168	stitcher	26	"
	h	Iarrobino Frank	168	U S A	24	"
	k	Iarrobino James	168	tailor	56	"
	l	*Iarrobino Lorenza —†	168	housewife	48	"
	m	Iarrobino Louis	168	U S A	22	"
	n	Iarrobino Rudolph	168	butcher	20	"
	r	Gargiulo Florence —†	170	housewife	36	"
	p	*Gargiulo Giro	170	cabinetmaker	54	"
	s	Spolsino Anthony	170	U S A	21	"
	t	Spolsino Jennie †	170	housewife	45	"
	u	Spolsino Michael	170	laborer	49	"
	v	Buonopane Generoso	170	mechanic	48	166A Chelsea
	w	Buonopane Margaret —†	170	housewife	36	166A "
	x	Sponpinato Antoinetta †	174	tailor	29	here
	y	Sponpinato Joseph	174	painter	34	"
	z	Riccio Anna †	174	stitcher	23	"
2419						
	a	Riccio John	174	shipfitter	20	"
	b	*Riccio Marianna †	174	housewife	49	"
	c	Riccio Otto	174	operator	59	"
	d	Barresi Angelo	174	laborer	55	"
	e	Barresi Antoinetta †	174	candyworker	21	"
	f	Barresi Frank	174	U S A	26	"
	g	Barresi George	174	"	25	"
	h	Barresi Helen †	174	candyworker	22	"
	k	Barresi Joseph	174	bartender	31	"
	l	*Barresi Josephine †	174	housewife	53	"
	m	*Cataldo Carlo	176	storekeeper	53	"
	n	Cataldo Louisa †	176	housewife	40	"
	o	Cataldo Margaret †	176	"	45	"

Chelsea Street Continued

Letter	FULL NAME	Residence	Occupation	Age	Reported Residence
P	Rapino Rose †	176	metalworker	20	here
R	Geraci Benedetto	176	U S A	21	"
S	Geraci Calogero	176	carpenter	52	"
T	Geraci Catherine †	176	clerk	26	"
U	Geraci Colombia †	176	housewife	52	"
V	Geraci Josephine †	176	stitcher	22	"
W	Geraci Vincent	176	machinist	20	"
X	DiFronzo Joseph	180	tailor	66	"
Y	DiFronzo Sarah †	180	housewife	65	"
Z	Bruno Alfonso	180	millhand	31	"
2420					
A	*Bruno Gabriel	180	chauffeur	52	"
B	*Bruno Mary— †	180	laundryworker	52	"
C	Addario Josephine †	180	housewife	31	342 Chelsea
D	Addario Santino	180	printer	33	342 "
E	DiStefano Charles	182	machinist	29	here
F	DiStefano Mary— †	182	housewife	27	"
G	Petitto Rocco	182	cutter	49	"
H	*Petitto Sadie— †	182	housewife	44	"
K	Lorino Anthony	182	barber	34	"
L	Lorino Josephine— †	182	stitcher	35	"
M	Arimento Ada †	184	housewife	23	"
N	Arimento Daniel	184	pharmacist	26	"
O	Paterno Angelo	184	shipworker	41	"
P	Paterno Anna †	184	housewife	33	"
R	Mari Domenic	184	carpenter	63	"
S	Mari Eugenia †	184	housewife	59	"
T	Pechner Benjamin	186	U S A	29	"
U	Pechner Isaac	186	retired	61	"
V	Pechner Jasper	186	photographer	28	"
W	Pechner Leo	186	U S A	26	"
X	Pechner Sarah †	186	housewife	54	"
Y	Guerriero Christopher	186	shipwright	52	"
Z	Guerriero Florence †	186	housewife	43	"
2421					
A	Burke Grace †	186	"	42	"
B	Burke John L	186	U S A	21	"
C	Burke John P	186	shipper	43	"
D	Stasio Mary †	186	at home	70	"
F	*Santarpio Incoronata †	188A	housewife	63	"
G	*Agri Angelina †	188A	"	30	"
H	Agri Lucio	188A	tailor	33	"

Davis Court

K	Sylvestre Gertrude †	1	housewife	30	here
L	Sylvestre Samuel	1	brazier	33	"
M	Faretra Concetta †	1	housewife	57	"
N	Faretra Louis	1	U S N	24	"
O	Sylvestre Thomas	1	steelworker	26	"
P	Sylvestre Virginia †	1	at home	28	"
R	Sylvestre Walter	1	U S N	21	"
S	Tropea Caroline †	3	housewife	24	"
T	Tropea Salvatore J	3	chauffeur	29	"
U	Guerreri Lucy †	3	clerk	22	"
V	Guerreri Philip	3	millhand	59	"
W	Guerreri Susie †	3	housewife	48	"

Havre Street

X	*Sardina Carmella †	174	housewife	60	here
Y	Sardina Gerard	174	laborer	38	"
Z	*Sardina Joseph	174	"	64	"
	2422				
A	Dunn James	174	boilermaker	29	"
B	Dunn Rose †	174	housewife	27	"
D	Nickerson Clara †	175	"	73	"
E	Tramonte Albert	175	laborer	50	"
F	Tramonte Nellie †	175	housewife	47	"
G	Tramonte Olympia †	175	packer	24	"
H	Tramonte William	175	U S A	22	"
K	*DiCino Antonio	175	laborer	63	"
L	DiCino Margaret †	175	housewife	43	"
M	Stokes Eva M †	176	"	39	"
N	Stokes George J	176	clerk	40	"
O	Stokes John C	176	U S N	37	"
P	Columbo Angelina †	176	housewife	24	"
R	Columbo Mario	176	laborer	29	"
S	Miano Paul	178	clerk	24	8 Chelsea
T	*Spadoni Josephine †	178	housewife	44	8 "
U	D'Apolito Pasquale	178	mechanic	31	here
V	D'Apolito Rocco	178	retired	55	"
W	*D'Apolito Rose †	178	housewife	52	"
X	Crescenzi Adam	178	laborer	51	"
Y	Crescenzi Angelina M †	178	housewife	46	"
Z	Crescenzi Ethel †	178	at home	24	"

11

2423

Havre Street Continued

A	Crescenzi Louis	178	shipfitter	20	here
B	Bertulli Louise †	179	packer	32	"
C	Bertulli Patrick	179	U S A	28	"
D	*Bertulli Ursula N †	179	housewife	59	"
E	Bertulli Angela †	179	packer	26	"
F	Bertulli Enso	179	U S A	21	"
G	Bertulli William	179	grinder	24	"
H	*Crisafulli Philomena †	179	housewife	59	"
K	Crisafulli Rose †	179	packer	20	"
L	*Donatelli Cecelia †	181	housewife	65	"
M	Donatelli Gaetano	181	laborer	66	"
N	Donatelli Maria †	181	packer	32	"
O	Ferranti Elizabeth †	181	housewife	30	"
P	Keane Agnes—†	183	"	39	"
R	Keane Catherine—†	183	operator	22	"
S	Keane Edward R	183	plumber	51	"
T	Keane John W	183	U S N	21	"
U	Deluple Florence †	183	housewife	37	"
V	Deluple John	183	fishcutter	42	"
W	Gleason Catherine †	183	housewife	37	"
X	Gleason George	183	U S A	42	"
Y	Falzone Elsie †	184	housewife	33	"
Z	*Falzone James	184	buyer	36	"

2424

A	Falzone Enrico	184	U S A	25	"
B	*Falzone Louis	184	laborer	72	"
C	Reale Antonio	184	storekeeper	38	"
D	*Reale Theresa †	184	housewife	28	"
E	Tasha Anthony F	185	chauffeur	51	"
F	Tasha Arthur	185	U S C G	20	"
G	Tasha Dorothy †	185	packer	24	"
H	Tasha Grace †	185	housewife	42	"
K	*Pandolfo Angela †	185	"	45	"
L	Pandolfo Martin	185	laborer	54	"
M	Pandolfo Rosario D	185	U S N	20	"
N	Pandolfo Sarah †	185	packer	22	"
O	*Ciarcia Anna †	185	housewife	42	"
P	Ciarcia Michael	185	laborer	52	"
R	*Dulcetta Assunta †	186	housewife	52	"
S	*Dulcetta Joseph	186	millhand	56	"

15

Havre Street — Continued

F	Dulcetta Joseph	186	U S A	24	here
G	Dulcetta Ralph	186	U S N	21	"
V*	Sciortino Angelina †	187	housewife	50	"
W	Sciortino Joseph	187	laborer	50	"
X	Sciortino Rosaria †	187	packer	23	"
Y	Vella Alphonso	187	tailor	37	"
Z	Vella Rose †	187	housewife	30	"
2425					
A*	Leonardi John	187	laborer	79	"
B	Leonardi Rose †	187	housewife	57	"
C	Dellaria Jack	189	laborer	74	153 Princeton
D*	Dellaria Rose †	189	housewife	64	153 "
E	Dellaria Vito	189	laborer	41	153 "
F	Palagreco Michelina †	189	at home	36	here
G*	Palagreco Phillipa †	189	housewife	71	"
H	Palagreco Charles	189	chauffeur	41	"
K	Palagreco Josephine †	189	housewife	35	"
L	Annese Carmen	194	laborer	51	"
M	Caporella Angelina †	194	operator	22	"
N	Covino James	194	chauffeur	49	"
O*	Covino Mary †	194	housewife	60	"
P*	Mazzarella Frank	195	shoemaker	42	"
R*	Mazzarella Mary †	195	housewife	54	"
S	Pirrmattei Agnes †	195	"	29	196 Paris
T	Pirrmattei Dominic	195	clerk	30	196 "
U*	Balcom Susan †	195	housewife	43	here
V	Balcom Thomas	195	retired	76	"
W	Bennett Peter	195	carpenter	54	10 Winthrop
Y	Flannagan Gladys †	196	housekeeper	44	here
Z	Nealon Catherine †	196	at home	71	"
2426					
A	Pomodoro Frank	197	laborer	57	"
B	Pomodoro Josephine †	197	housewife	48	"
C	DeSalvo Maria †	197	"	40	"
D	DeSalvo Michael	197	storekeeper	42	"
E	DeSalvo Paul	197	U S A	21	"
F	Amato Frank	197	carpenter	35	"
G	Amato Mary †	197	housewife	28	"
H	DeStefano Josephine †	198	"	20	164 Marion
K	DeStefano Salvatore	198	U S A	21	168 Chelsea
L	Landuzzi Firmino	198	tilesetter	40	here

16

Havre Street Continued

M	*Lenduzzi Mary †	198	housewife	34	here
N	*Roberts Clara †	198	"	58	"
O	Roberts Frank	198	U S A	22	"
P	Roberts Joseph	198	factoryhand	20	"
R	Roberts Luigi	198	laborer	59	"
S	*Falzarano Dominic	199	"	62	"
T	*Falzarano Frances †	199	housewife	61	"
U	Falzarano Gabriel	199	laborer	32	"
V	Falzarano Henry	199	"	25	"
W	Corsi Angelo	201	"	55	"
X	Cuozzo Angelina †	201	stenographer	21	"
Y	*Cuozzo Rose †	201	housewife	50	"
Z	*Cuozzo Valentino	201	laborer	55	"

2427

A	Cuozzo Viola †	201	saleswoman	20	"
B	*Danpolo Mary †	201	housewife	36	"
C	Bruno Aniello	201	laborer	49	122 Havre
D	Bruno Frank	201	U S A	21	122 "
E	Bruno Helen †	201	housewife	38	122 "
F	*Quarantiello Celia †	202	"	48	here
G	Incrovato Frank	202	shipfitter	29	"
H	Incrovato Mary †	202	housewife	26	"
K	Falzarano Angelina †	202	"	36	"
L	Falzarano Vincent	202	chauffeur	41	"
M	Falzarano Columbia †	206	housewife	25	4 Brooks
N	Falzarano Louis	206	rigger	27	4 "
O	*Arinella Anna †	206	housewife	52	here
P	*Arinella James	206	longshoreman	60	"
R	Arinella John	206	U S A	24	"
S	Arinella Louis	206	"	20	"
T	Arinella Mary †	206	hairdresser	26	"
U	Arinella Mildred †	206	factoryhand	32	"
V	Guerra Antonio	206	leatherworker	32	"
W	Guerra Grace †	206	housewife	31	"
X	Giangrande Anthony	207	U S A	23	"
Y	Giangrande John	207	laborer	50	"
Z	Giangrande Mary †	207	housewife	41	"

2428

A	Mustone Mary †	208	"	48	"
B	Mustone Saverio	208	laborer	56	"
C	*Capuzzi Christos	208	retired	84	"

1—24   17

Havre Street—Continued

D	Mustone Etta—†	208	clerk	20	here
E	Mustone Eugene	208	chauffeur	22	"
F	*Rizzuto Frances—†	208	forewoman	38	191 London
G	Saggese Ferdinand	209	laborer	60	Chelsea
H	Gioioso Phyllis—†	209	housewife	26	here
K	Gioioso Vincent	209	clerk	30	"
L	*Greco Catherine †	209	housewife	60	"
M	*Dell Russo John	rear 209	laborer	50	"
N	Palagreco Joseph	" 209	carpenter	29	"
O	Palagreco Rose †	" 209	housewife	23	"
R	Russo Angelo	210	candymaker	50	"
S	Russo Frances †	210	housewife	44	"
T	Peluso Joseph	211	blacksmith	47	"
U	Peluso Mary †	211	housewife	41	"
V	Juliano Joseph	213	laborer	42	"
W	Juliano Lena †	213	housewife	38	"
X	Alessi Edward	213	mechanic	74	"
Y	Alessi Eufemia †	213	housewife	72	"
Z	Cullen Margaret M †	214	"	61	308 Paris

2429

A	Timmons Richard L	214	U S A	30	308 "
B	Lippert Elizabeth †	214	housewife	51	here
C	Lippert Rudolph A	214	repairman	60	"
D	Casiello Antonio	215	laborer	61	"
E	*Casiello Filomena †	215	housewife	63	"
F	Casiello John	215	U S A	25	"
G	Dittmer Ellen †	215	housewife	21	276 Paris
H	Dittmer Myron	215	U S N	27	276 "
K	Lacorazza Elvira †	215	housewife	30	here
L	Lacorazza Joseph	215	mechanic	31	"
M	Coliano Florence †	215	housewife	29	"
N	Coliano John	215	U S A	30	Medford
O	Rossetti Jennie †	215	housewife	50	here
P	Rossetti Nora †	215	packer	30	"
R	*Bennett Minnie †	216	housewife	55	"
S	Goodwin Clifford	216	fisherman	59	"
T	Trainor Dorothy A †	216	housewife	32	"
U	Trainor Owen J	216	longshoreman	33	"
V	Tait Joseph J	216	"	41	"
W	Tait Margaret T †	216	stenographer	35	"
X	Provinzano Helen †	rear 216	housewife	52	"

18

Havre Street Continued

Y		Provinzano Salvatore	rear 216	mason	53	here
Z	*	Corcio Michael	217	laborer	39	"

2430

A	*	Quartrone Frank	217	barber	55	"
B	*	Quartrone Jennie †	217	housewife	56	"
C		Quartrone Mary †	217	packer	24	"
D		Dello Russo Lucy †	217	housewife	29	"
E		Dello Russo Orlando	217	printer	40	"
F		Dello Russo Amedeo	217	laborer	36	"
G		Dello Russo Amerina †	217	packer	22	"
H	*	Dello Russo Carlo	217	barber	66	"
K		Dello Russo Edith †	217	factoryhand	20	"
L		Dello Russo Matilda †	217	packer	34	"
M	*	Dello Russo Raffaella †	217	housewife	65	"
N		Dello Russo Romeo	217	U S A	27	"
O		Saurino John	218	chauffeur	28	"
P		Saurino Marion †	218	housewife	26	"
R	*	Crescenzo Biagio	218	factoryhand	46	"
S	*	Crescenzo Rose †	218	housewife	36	"
T		Maenza Joseph	218	factoryhand	21	"
U		Maenza Rose †	218	housewife	53	"
W		Quigley Helen †	220	"	36	"
X		Quigley William	220	meat packer	40	"
Y	*	Mayo Lucy †	220	housewife	55	"
Z		Merullo Enrico	rear 220	laborer	36	Newton

2431

A		Merullo Mary †	" 220	housewife	28	"
B	*	DiVicentis Anna †	" 220	"	74	here
C		Nigro Nicholas	" 220	laborer	50	"
D	*	Cerulli Clara †	" 220	tailor	50	"
E		Pinkshaw Anna †	" 220	millhand	36	"
F		Feno Virginia †	" 220	at home	63	"
G		DiSario Ellen †	221	housewife	26	"
H		DiSario Frederick	221	clerk	27	"
K	*	Durante Cecelia †	221	housewife	59	"
L	*	Durante Pasquale	221	laborer	54	"
M		Durante Peter	221	U S N	21	"
N		Colotti Carmen	221	mechanic	28	"
O		Colotti Frances †	221	housewife	24	"
P		Arena Josephine †	223	"	60	"
R	*	Rotundo Joseph	223	laborer	55	2 Liverpool av

Havre Street   Continued

s	*Teza Giacomina †	223	housewife	51	here	
r	Teza Sebastian	223	laborer	58	"	
v	Dioguardi Clara †	226	factoryhand	29	"	
w	Dioguardi Ida †	226	stitcher	30	"	
x	Dioguardi Louis	226	U S A	25	"	
y	*Dioguardi Marie †	226	housewife	70	"	
z	Dioguardi Nicholas	226	carpenter	38	"	

2432

a	Fucillo Eleanor †	227	packer	20	"	
b	Fucillo Marto	227	plumber	45	"	
c	Fucillo Ruth †	227	housewife	45	"	
d	Grace Rita †	227	"	26	"	
e	Rutsky Thomas	228	janitor	43	"	
f	*Terlino Frank	228	mason	59	"	
g	Terlino Margaret †	228	stitcher	26	"	
h	*Terlino Marian †	228	housewife	58	"	
k	*Impeduglia Joseph	228	shoemaker	46	"	
l	*Impeduglia Josephine †	228	housewife	38	"	
m	*Bowen Mary †	229	"	69	"	
n	*Bowen Patrick	229	laborer	66	"	
o	*Hazelwood Annie †	229	housewife	71	"	
p	Hazelwood Charles S	229	mechanic	71	"	
r	*King Catherine †	229	housewife	54	"	
s	King Gustin	229	U S A	22	"	
t	King Thomas	229	watchman	63	"	
u	Sullivan Evelyn †	230	factoryhand	21	"	
v	Sullivan John	230	retired	54	"	
x	Rodrigues Antonio	230	textileworker	41	"	
y	*Rodrigues Mary †	230	housewife	42	"	
z	Maroccio Antonetta †	232	"	36	"	

2433

a	Maroccio Domenic	232	pedler	38	"	
b	Paluso Gabriel	232	foreman	22	"	
c	Paluso Gaetano	232	factoryhand	49	"	
d	Paluso Mary †	232	housewife	41	"	
e	Fusco Carmella †	232	"	53	"	
f	Fusco Constance †	232	factoryhand	20	"	
g	Fusco Joseph	232	"	58	"	
h	Fusco Vincent	232	U S A	29	"	
k	Hennessey John	236	machinist	35	"	
l	Doherty Margaret †	236	housewife	80	"	

Page	Letter	FULL NAME.	Residence, Jan. 1, 1943.	Occupation.	Supposed Age.	Reported Residence, Jan. 1, 1942. Street and Number.

Havre Street Continued

	M	Donovan Catherine— †	236	housewife	70	here
	N	Hennessey Catherine T—†	236	clerk	39	"
	O	Amaroso Anna—†	238	hairdresser	23	"
	P*	Amaroso Catherine—†	238	housewife	46	"
	R	Amaroso Phillip	238	machinist	24	"
	S	Amaroso Salvatore	238	laborer	55	"
	T	Amaroso Salvatore	238	U S A	27	"
	U	Mancuso James	238	"	20	"
	V*	Mancuso Mary—†	238	housewife	43	"
	W*	Fulginiti Frances—†	238	"	40	"
	X	Fulginiti Frank	238	U S A	22	"
	Y*	Fulginiti Joseph	238	plasterer	43	"
	Z	Fulginiti Joseph, jr	238	U S C G	20	"
2434						
	A	Wilson Julia—†	239	housewife	21	118 Trenton
	B	Wilson Samuel	239	chauffeur	25	118 "
	C*	Kelly Delia—†	239	housewife	70	here
	D	Williams Mary E—†	239	"	66	176 N Harvard
	E	Frizzi Angelo	240	fireman	23	here
	F	Frizzi Anthony	240	painter	49	"
	G*	Frizzi Elvira—†	240	housewife	49	"
	H	Frizzi Victoria —†	240	factoryhand	21	"
	K	Kennedy Anna — †	241	housewife	75	"
	L	Melanson Anthony	241	chauffeur	26	"
	M*	Melanson Mary —†	241	housewife	66	"
	N	Boyan Patrick	241	longshoreman	60	"
	O	Sears Mary— †	243	housewife	73	"
	P*	Reardon Lillian — †	243	at home	63	"
	R	Robins Evelyn †	243	housewife	24	"
	S	Robins Roland	243	welder	29	"
	T*	Gozzo Angelina †	244	housewife	48	"
	U	Gozzo Paul	244	laborer	20	"
	V	Gozzo Sebastiano	244	"	58	"
	W	Locardo Anna — †	244	clerk	24	"
	X*	Locardo Mary — †	244	housewife	49	"
	Y	Baker Loa—†	244	laundryworker	21	321 Border
	Z	Gayheart John	244	longshoreman	20	321 "
2435						
	A	Gayheart Mary — †	244	housewife	52	321 "
	C*	Chiminara Mary —† rear	244	at home	56	here
	D	Lennon George F	245	laborer	25	704 Tremont

21

Havre Street—Continued

E	Lennon Louise M —†	245	housewife	22	704 Tremont
F	McPhee Catherine — †	245	"	28	here
G	McPhee Joseph	245	mechanic	36	"
H	Teixeira Barbriano	245	laborer	42	"
K	*Teixeira Mary — †	245	housewife	51	"
L	*Curtis Michael	246	fisherman	42	"
M	*Curtis Violet — †	246	housewife	42	"
N	Milillo Antonio	246	U S A	23	"
O	*Milillo Elvira †	246	housewife	50	"
P	Milillo Guy	246	laborer	26	"
R	Milillo Pasquale	246	U S A	22	"
S	Simone Charles	247	laborer	80	"
T	*Simone Jennie—†	247	housewife	69	"
U	Pitta Manuel	247	U S N	20	"
V	*Pitta Manuel C	247	weaver	48	"
W	Soares Jacinto	247	laborer	49	333 Saratoga
X	Wolfram Jennie—†	247	housewife	25	here
Y	Wolfram Raymond J	247	U S C G	22	"
Z	*Puglisi Antonetta—†	259	housewife	56	"

2436

A	*Puglisi Carmen	259	carpenter	59	"
B	*Puglisi Laura —†	259	housewife	85	"
C	DiLorenzo Frances —†	259	"	36	"
D	DiLorenzo Jerry	259	salesman	37	"
E	Fortunate Joseph	259	laborer	79	
F	Connors Francis N	259	rigger	43	317 Paris
G	*Connors Mary—†	259	housewife	42	317 "
H	Pagana Anthony	261	upholsterer	48	here
K	Pagana Frank	261	U S A	23	"
L	*Pagana Rose †	261	housewife	48	"
M	Zona Elvira †	261	stitcher	27	"
N	Zona Frances †	261	factoryhand	25	"
O	*Zona Grace †	261	housewife	50	"
P	Zona Grace †	261	stitcher	20	"
R	Zona Jennie —†	261	"	29	"
S	Zona Josephine †	261	"	21	"
T	Zona Martin	261	U S A	23	"
U	Zona Michael	261	candymaker	54	"
V	Trainor Dorothy †	261	packer	21	"
W	Trainor James	261	U S N	23	"
X	Trainor Lawrence	261	"	26	"

Havre Street Continued

	Y	Trainor Olive M †	261	housewife	55	here
	Z	Quartarone Mario	262	laborer	38	"
2437						
	A	*Quartarone Minnie †	262	housewife	40	"
	B	*Covino Catherine †	262	"	30	"
	C	Covino Pasquale	262	laborer	39	"
	D	*Capucci Dominick	262	bootblack	49	"
	E	*Capucci Rose †	262	housewife	45	"
	F	Beck Harry	263	electrician	55	"
	G	Beck Ida †	263	housewife	48	"
	H	Beck Leo	263	U S A	24	"
	K	Salamone Louis	263	shoemaker	43	"
	L	Salamone Mary †	263	housewife	33	"
	M	Gannon Dorothy †	263	"	35	"
	N	Gannon Matthew	263	U S N	35	"
	O	Silva Anthony	264	machinist	36	"
	P	Silva Kathleen †	264	housewife	28	"
	R	DiSilvestro Joseph	264	U S N	31	"
	S	DiSilvestro Theresa †	264	housewife	27	"
	T	Sindoni Anthony	264	finisher	42	"
	U	Sindoni Dominica †	264	housewife	36	"
	V	*Guiffrida Frances †	265	"	67	225 Benningt'n
	W	Guiffrida Grace †	265	"	45	225 "
	X	Guiffrida Joseph	265	laborer	47	225 "
	Y	Avola Alexander	265	U S A	21	here
	Z	Avola Anna †	265	housewife	46	"
2438						
	A	Avola John	265	shoemaker	49	"
	B	Avola Salvatore	265	U S A	20	"
	C	*Miraglia Carmella †	265	housewife	37	"
	D	*Miraglia Josephine †	265	"	75	"
	E	*Miraglia Rocco	265	shoemaker	47	"
	F	Panzini Dominick	266	candyworker	34	"
	G	Panzini Filomena †	266	housewife	30	"
	H	*Colotti Celia †	266	"	53	"
	K	Colotti Geraldine †	266	stitcher	24	"
	L	Colotti Michael	266	laborer	58	"
	M	Marotta Liborio	267	U S A	26	159 Marion
	N	Marotta Rose †	267	housewife	25	159 "
	O	Avola Liborio	267	shoemaker	55	here
	P	Avola Rose †	267	housewife	47	"

Page.	Letter	FULL NAME.	Residence, Jan. 1, 1943	Occupation.	Supposed Age.	Reported Residence, Jan. 1, 1942. Street and Number.

Havre Street—Continued

R	Seminatore Florence—†	267	clerk	20	here
S	Seminatore Joseph	267	laborer	51	"
T	Seminatore Mary—†	267	mechanic	21	"
U	Seminatore Susan—†	267	housewife	41	"
V	Cordischi Achille	268	millhand	40	"
W	*Cordischi Angelina—†	268	housewife	30	"
X	DiAngelo Vincent	268	laborer	53	"
Y	D'India Americo	270	painter	31	"
Z	D'India Phyllis—†	270	housewife	20	"

2439

A	*Mastrangelo Antonetta †	270	factoryhand	46	"
B	Mastrangelo Rocco	270	laborer	44	"
C	Cerbone Mary—†	271	housewife	24	"
D	Cerbone Salvatore	271	welder	26	"
E	*Lopezzo Susannah—†	271	housewife	50	"
F	Martinelli Edith—†	271	"	36	"
G	Martinelli James	271	chauffeur	39	"
H	Caulfield John G	272	retired	67	"
K	Caulfield Mary E—†	272	housewife	58	"
L	Caulfield Nellie M—†	272	at home	47	"
M	Griffiths Walter	273	laborer	62	"
N	Murphy Elizabeth M—†	274	housewife	59	"
O	Murphy John H	274	guard	27	"
P	Murphy Richard G	274	U S N	22	"
S	Terriciano Florence—†	275	packer	21	"
R	Terriciano Helen †	275	"	31	"
T	Terriciano Marian—†	275	housewife	28	"
U	Terriciano Salvatore	275	laborer	26	"
V	Russo George	275	chipper	33	"
W	Russo Margaret †	275	housewife	29	"
X	Battista Emilio	rear 275	laborer	49	"
Y	Battista Rose †	" 275	housewife	39	"
Z	Pace Anthony	276	laborer	55	"

2440

A	Pace Rachael †	276	housewife	55	"
B	Blanchette James E	277	U S A	29	"
C	Blanchette Pauline †	277	housewife	28	102 Benningt'n
D	Avila Anna †	277	"	40	here
E	Avila Josephine †	277	dressmaker	26	"
F	Fortes Irene †	277	housewife	20	221 Webster

21

Havre Street Continued

G	Fortes John	277	welder	27	14 O
H	Cambria Joseph	278	U S A	20	here
K	*Cambria Lillian—†	278	housewife	51	"
L	Cambria Pasquale	278	pedler	68	"
M	DeAngelo Nicholas	278	U S A	26	"
N	Gaeta Edwin	279	"	24	"
O	Gaeta Irene—†	279	housewife	21	"
P	*Surette Mary—†	279	"	40	"
R	Stella Angela—†	279	"	42	"
S	Stella Charles	279	barber	51	"
T	Pesce Carmella—†	279	packer	25	"
U	Pesce Ignazio	279	laborer	54	"
V	Pesce Joseph	279	"	27	"
W	*Pesce Josephine—†	279	housewife	50	"
X	Stringi Frank	280	welder	22	176 Gove
Y	Stringi Rosanne—†	280	housewife	20	186 London
Z	Gravallese Charles	280	plumber	34	here

2441

A	Gravallese Rose—†	280	housewife	32	"
B	Mulcahy Loretta—†	281	at home	62	"
C	Shea Mary—†	281	clerk	39	"
D	Shea Morris	281	retired	71	"
E	Carlton Marian A—†	281	manicurist	29	"
F	Carlton Sarah T—†	281	housewife	60	"
G	Carlton William H	281	salesman	57	"
H	Foley William C	283	U S A	21	"
K	Gessner Bernard	283	policeman	40	"
L	Gessner Mary T—†	283	housewife	42	"
M	Teddy Mary—†	283	"	70	"
N	Ferguson William J	283	clerk	63	"
O	Wintersow Catherine F—†	283	at home	45	"
P	Harkins Anna L—†	283	"	44	"
R	Harkins Anna M—†	283	housewife	83	"
S	*Scolletta Angelina—†	289	"	34	"
T	Scolletta Leo	289	laborer	40	"
U	Costello Elizabeth—†	289	housewife	38	285 Havre
V	Costello Valentino	289	carpenter	40	285 "
W	DeSimone Albert	289	U S A	20	here
X	DeSimone Gertrude—†	289	stitcher	22	"
Y	DeSimone Joseph	289	laborer	49	"

25

Page	Letter	Full Name.	Residence, Jan. 1, 1943.	Occupation.	Supposed Age.	Reported Residence, Jan. 1, 1942. Street and Number.

Havre Street — Continued

	Letter	Full Name.	Residence	Occupation.	Age	Reported Residence
	z	DeSimone Lena †	289	housewife	45	here
2442						
	A	Fiumara Charles	291	chauffeur	25	"
	B	Fiumara Jennie †	291	housewife	25	"
	D*	Reale Joseph	291	laborer	70	"
	C*	Reale Maria †	291	housewife	60	"
	E	Caldoralli Albert	291	laborer	24	"
	F	Caldoralli Constance †	291	housewife	23	"
	G	Buccheri Joseph	291	carpenter	38	"
	H*	Buccheri Mary †	291	housewife	35	"
	K	Grafola Carmen	293	engineer	60	"
	L*	Grafola Donata †	293	housewife	58	"
	M*	Grafola Pasquale	293	retired	73	"
	N	Panzini Margaret †	293	housewife	30	207 Saratoga
	O*	Panzini Pasquale	293	retired	67	295 Havre
	P	Panzini Vito	293	metalworker	33	207 Saratoga
	R	Nicosia Angelina †	293	housewife	54	here
	S	DeMarco John	295	machinist	24	"
	T	DeMarco Nellie †	295	housewife	23	"
	U	Viola Ethel †	295	"	26	53 Salem
	V	Viola Frank	295	laborer	30	53 "
	W*	Andriotti Pasquale	295	retired	82	here
	X	Bruno Felice	295	woodworker	67	"
	Y	Bruno Filomena †	295	housewife	55	"
	Z*	Moscaritolo Emma †	297	"	48	"
2443						
	A	Moscaritolo Nicholas J	297	bartender	22	"
	B	Moscaritolo Pasquale B	297	storekeeper	50	"
	D	Muise Frank P	301	retired	71	"
	E*	Muise Genevieve †	301	housewife	71	"
	F	Muise John F	301	cook	26	"
	H*	White David W	301	fisherman	63	"
	G*	White Marguerite †	301	housewife	54	"
	K	Meloni Rose †	305	"	32	"
	L	Meloni Victor	305	printer	32	"
	M*	Rosa Concetta †	305	housewife	62	"
	N*	Rosa Guiseppe	305	retired	65	"
	O	Rosa Roger	305	clerk	21	"
	P*	Chevarie Frederick D	307	blacksmith	54	"
	R*	Chevarie Helen J †	307	housewife	52	"
	S	DeStefano Joseph	307	brazier	23	"

London Court

F	*Farina Bellonia †	1	housekeeper	80	here
U	Spano Adam	2	mason	45	"
V	*Spano Frances †	2	housewife	35	"
W	Poli Joseph	3	welder	20	"
X	Poli Ottavio	3	chef	58	"
Y	Poli Theresa †	3	housewife	56	"
Z	Poli Virginia †	3	packer	22	"

2444

A	Termiella Dena †	3	"	27	"

London Street

C	Petroccione Joseph	165	candymaker	48	here
D	Petroccione Mary †	165	housewife	35	"
E	Vitagliano Philomena †	165	"	35	"
F	Vitagliano William	165	butcher	35	"
G	Tortolano Alfred	171	U S A	34	"
H	Tortolano Anna †	171	dressmaker	38	"
K	Tortolano Celia †	171	at home	24	"
L	Tortolano Elvira †	171	packer	30	"
M	Tortolano Francis W	171	U S A	21	"
N	Tortolano Mary †	171	seamstress	32	"
O	Internicola Nicola	173	laborer	49	"
P	*Internicola Philomena †	173	housewife	40	"
R	Landolfi Anthony	173	U S A	20	"
S	Landolfi Josephine †	173	laundryworker	21	"
T	Landolfi Maria †	173	housewife	48	"
U	Landolfi Vincenzo	173	laborer	49	"
V	White Cecelia †	177	housewife	65	"
W	White Lawrence P	177	carpenter	65	"
X	Mecciche Jennie †	177	housewife	42	"
Y	Mecciche Pasquale	177	barber	50	"
Z	Emma Philip	177	operator	39	"

2445

A	Emma Vincenza †	177	housewife	34	"
B	Palladino Frank	179	candyworker	38	"
C	Palladino Mary †	179	housewife	27	"
E	Rosso Antonio	179	laborer	55	"
F	*Rosso Carmella †	179	packer	43	"
D	D'Apice Elsie †	179	operator	42	"
G	Moscatello Michael	179	laborer	38	"

Page.	Letter.	FULL NAME.	Residence, Jan. 1, 1943.	Occupation.	Supposed Age.	Reported Residence, Jan. 1, 1942. Street and Number.

London Street—Continued

H	Casaletto James	181	pipefitter	26	here
K	Casaletto Lillian — †	181	housewife	23	"
L	Tracia Angelina — †	181	cook	31	"
M	Tracia Louis	181	pipefitter	31	"
N	Casaletto John	181	leatherworker	34	"
O	Casaletto Rose — †	181	housewife	28	"
P	Provanzano Salvatore	183	chauffeur	28	"
R	Provanzano Virginia — †	183	housewife	29	"
T	Gurliaccio Geraldine — †	183	operator	20	"
U	Gurliaccio Joseph	183	U S A	23	"
V	Gurliaccio Josephine — †	183	housewife	46	"
S	Gurliaccio Lazzaro	183	lather	58	"
X	*Cannata Anna — †	185	at home	52	"
Y	Cannata Josephine — †	185	leatherworker	21	"
Z	Schieber Ida — †	185	housewife	25	"

2446

A	Schieber Max	185	U S C G	23	Missouri
B	Cannata Michael	185	operator	32	here
C	Cannata Rose — †	185	housewife	30	"
E	Salomonie Anthony	187	machinist	21	"
F	Salomonie Ignazio	187	U S N	30	"
G	*Salomonie Luigi	187	retired	60	"
H	*Salomonie Stella — †	187	housewife	50	"
K	Lima Elsie — †	187	"	33	"
L	Lima John	187	operator	37	"
M	Johnson Allen	189	freighthandler	27	"
N	Johnson Mollie — †	189	housewife	25	"
O	Stornaiuolo Albert	189	retired	69	"
P	Stornaiuolo Angelina — †	189	shoeworker	21	"
R	*Stornaiuolo Jennie — †	189	housewife	65	"
S	Mendum Adelaide †	189	"	50	"
T	Mendum Benjamin	189	driller	54	"
U	Mendum George	189	U S A	25	"
V	Mendum Lorraine †	189	trimmer	23	"
W	Rizzuto Anthony	191	guard	27	"
X	Rizzuto Emily †	191	rubberworker	23	"
Y	Rizzuto Mary †	191	at home	46	"
Z	*Buttiglieri Carmella †	191	"	64	"

2447

A	Buttiglieri Carmello	191	U S A	28	"
B	Buttiglieri Mary †	191	operator	22	"

28

London Street Continued

c	Buttiglieri Philomena †	191	candyworker	34	here
d	Buttiglieri Sarah †	191	at home	21	"
e	Alu Catina †	191	housewife	37	"
f	Alu Michael	191	pressman	46	"
g	*Peretti Angelina †	193	at home	50	"
h	Tessone Joseph	193	laborer	48	"
k	*Tessone Maria †	193	housewife	44	"
l	*Bernhardt Rose †	193	at home	68	"
m	Superia Jacob	193	retired	73	"
n	Costa Joseph	197	laborer	56	"
o	Costa Nellie †	197	housewife	54	"
p	Montague Laura †	197	matron	53	"
r	Fariole Lawrence	197	clerk	27	"
s	Fariole Margaret †	197	housewife	28	"
t	DiGregorio Joan †	199	"	20	20 Wales
u	Cimino Domenic	199	welder	26	here
v	Cimino Georgianna †	199	housewife	23	"
w	Fasciano Alphonso	199	laborer	46	"
x	*Fasciano Mary †	199	housewife	40	"
y	Stellato Clementina †	203	"	32	265 Havre
z	Stellato Francesco	203	laborer	30	265 "
	2448				
a	Lentine Michael	203	machinist	47	here
b	Lentine Stephen	203	student	22	"
c	*Lentine Theresa †	203	housewife	40	"
d	Emma Lucy †	203	"	34	"
e	Emma Philip	203	rubberworker	39	"
f	Serima Angelina †	205	inspector	24	"
g	Santosuosso Henry	205	electrician	36	"
h	Santosuosso Mary †	205	housewife	27	"
k	*Grimaldi Gloria †	207	"	59	"
l	Grimaldi James	207	laborer	58	"
m	Tropea Margaret F †	207	housewife	23	Woburn
n	Tropea Vincent C	207	coremaker	25	"
o	Marques Joaquin	207	fireman	40	here
p	Rossetti Angelo	209	salesman	29	"
r	Rossetti Evelyn †	209	housewife	30	"
s	Rossetti Josephine †	209	shoeworker	26	"
t	Babcock George	209	seaman	32	"
u	Incerto Genaro	209	electrician	32	"
v	Incerto Nancy †	209	housewife	30	"

29

London Street - Continued

w	Bonillo Casimo	211	retired	74	here	
x	Cooper Joseph	211	chauffeur	26	"	
y	Cooper Sarah †	211	housewife	21	"	
z	Cangeni Lena †	211	at home	61	"	
	2449					
B	Silva Anthony	221	foreman	36	"	
c	Silva Mildred †	221	housewife	35	"	
D*	Adreani Anita †	221	"	55	"	
E	Adreani Jennie †	221	at home	32	"	
F	Adreani Lena †	221	saleswoman	22	"	
G	Adreani Luigi	221	grocer	65	"	
H	LaBlanc Willis	223	manager	57	"	
K	Shaughnessy William P	223	retired	68	"	
L	Surette Howard	223	fisherman	46	"	
M	Surette Lennie †	223	housewife	44	"	
N	Mennella Annie †	223	"	52	"	
o	Mennella Anthony	223	motorman	52	"	
P	Matarazzo Charles E	223	U S A	31	"	
R	Matarazzo Geama †	223	at home	21	"	
s	Matarazzo Joseph	223	U S A	27	"	
T	Matarazzo Mary †	223	housewife	45	"	
U	Matarazzo Michael	223	laborer	47	"	
w	Merchant Charles E	225	leatherworker	31	"	
x	Merchant Lucy A †	225	at home	68	"	
y	Merchant Pauline S †	225	housewife	31	"	
z	O'Neil Albert R	225	bartender	33	"	
	2450					
A	O'Neil Harriet †	225	housewife	32	"	
B	Silvac Emma †	227	at home	58	"	
c	Silvac Louise E †	227	operator	29	"	
D	Caponigro George	227	electrician	28	"	
E	Caponigro Sally †	227	housewife	22	"	
F	Barker Olive †	227	"	24	"	
G	Barker William	227	shipfitter	30	"	
H*	Lizzini Nina †	229	at home	65	"	
K	Murphy Grace †	229	counter girl	36	"	
L	Umbro Rocco	229	packer	21	180 Porter	
M	Umbro Theresa †	229	housewife	20	150 Havre	
N	Viola Anna †	231	"	28	here	
o	Viola Vito	231	laborer	30	"	
P	Ferullo Anthony	231	chauffeur	23	"	

30

London Street Continued

R	Perullo Rose †	231	housewife	21	here	
S	Salvaggio James	231	U S A	21	"	
T	*Salvaggio Josephine †	231	housewife	45	"	
U	Salvaggio Rocco	231	candymaker	54	"	
V	Musto Joseph	233	welder	43	"	
W	Musto Pasqua †	233	housewife	34	"	
X	Ford Harold E	233	shipfitter	56	"	
Y	Ford Mabel E †	233	housewife	47	"	

Marion Street

Z	Newhook Charles	156	laborer	49	here	

2451

A	Newhook Emma R †	156	housewife	52	"	
B	Kraytenberg Ernest B	156	guard	42	"	
C	Kraytenberg Louise M †	156	packer	33	"	
D	Proto Alfonso	158	U S A	22	"	
E	Proto Salvatore	158	laborer	54	"	
F	*Proto Theresa †	158	housewife	52	"	
G	Altri Julia †	158	at home	38	"	
H	Crouse Spurgeon E	162	U S A	25	"	
K	Ivory Eva A †	162	housewife	49	"	
L	Ivory John R	162	longshoreman	56	"	
M	Healy Agnes †	162	clerk	52	"	
N	Healy Mary †	162	at home	53	"	
O	Petersen Louise †	162	"	50	"	
P	Hawes Thomas F	164	retired	63	"	
R	Sterett Frances †	164	waitress	30	"	
T	Fariole Catherine †	166	housewife	51	92 Bennington	
U	Fariole John J	166	laborer	43	92 "	
S	Green Harold	166	U S A	34	Connecticut	
V	*DeVeau Catherine †	166	packer	23	here	
W	*DeVeau Mary †	166	"	48	"	
X	DeVeau William L	166	U S A	20	"	
Y	Hankard James	168	longshoreman	21	"	
Z	Hankard Mary †	168	housewife	43	"	

2452

A	Hankard Thomas F	168	longshoreman	47	"	
B	Hankard Thomas F. jr	168	U S A	22	"	
E	Budnar Bessie †	172	housewife	61	"	
F	Budnar Charles	172	U S A	37	"	

Marion Street—Continued

G	*Budnar Harris	172	shoemaker	70	here	
H	Leone Rosaria †	172	at home	34	"	
K	*Musillo Carmela †	174	"	74	"	
L	Goldberg Nathan	174	tinsmith	55	"	
M	*Levenstein Bella †	174	housewife	58	"	
N	*Levenstein Isaac	174	pedler	65	"	
O	Mangino Caroline †	174	housewife	34	"	
P	*Mangino John	174	candymaker	46	"	
S	Blake Andrew F	176	mechanic	58	81 White	
T	Collyer Mary †	176	at home	76	81 "	
U	*McGowan Catherine †	176	"	68	81 "	
V	Burditt Edward J	176	carpenter	27	here	
W	Burditt Helen M †	176	housewife	23	"	
X	*Venuti Carmela †	176	"	52	"	
Y	Venuti Joseph	176	laborer	56	"	
Z	Venuti Joseph	176	U S A	21	"	

2453

A	Seland George	178	tailor	24	"	
B	*Seland Virginia †	178	at home	63	"	
C	*LaMonica Catina †	178	"	48	479 Hanover	
D	*Siracusa Antonio	178	retired	78	here	
E	Siracusa Carmen	178	laborer	42	"	
F	Siracusa Maria †	178	cook	32	"	
G	*Siracusa Salvatora †	178	housewife	70	"	
H	Mazzeo Angelina †	179	housekeeper	61	"	
K	Mazzeo Angelo A	179	bartender	63	"	
L	*Puleio Anna M †	179	housekeeper	79	"	
M	Puleio Anthony	179	retired	58	"	
N	Puleio Anthony, jr	179	welder	23	"	
O	Puleio Peter	179	U S N	21	"	
P	*Puleio Rosaria †	179	housewife	48	"	
R	*Papandrea Carmela †	180	"	37	"	
S	Papandrea John	180	retired	68	"	
T	*Pecci Filomena †	180	housewife	73	"	
U	*Pecci Francesco	180	retired	76	"	
V	Pecci Arthur	180	U S A	22	"	
W	*Pecci Concetta †	180	housewife	45	"	
X	*Pecci Leopold	180	shoemaker	49	"	
Y	Pecci Mintana †	180	clerk	23	"	
Z	Canno Joseph	181	U S A	23	17 Saratoga	

Page.	Letter.	FULL NAME.	Residence, Jan. 1, 1942.	Occupation	Supposed Age	Reported Residence, Jan. 1, 1942. Street and Number.

2454

Marion Street Continued

A	Ganno Josephine †	181	housewife	22	17 Saratoga
B*	Pinto Grace †	181	at home	52	here
C	Pinto Pasquale	181	welder	23	"
D	D'Avola Angelina †	181	stitcher	25	"
E	D'Avola Filippo	181	laborer	51	"
F	D'Avola Jennie †	181	packer	20	"
G	D'Avola Josephine †	181	operator	22	"
H	D'Avola Stella †	181	packer	45	"
L*	Marconi Anna †	182	housewife	49	"
M*	Marconi Gerardo	182	laundryworker	60	"
N*	Anzalone Annie †	182	housewife	47	"
O	Anzalone John	182	barber	50	"
P	Anzalone John, jr	182	laborer	20	"
R*	Dellorfano Carmella †	183	housewife	47	"
S	Dellorfano Carmen	183	salesman	26	"
T	Dellorfano Michael	183	U S A	21	"
U*	D'Angelo Dominic	183	laborer	60	"
V*	D'Angelo Louise †	183	housewife	58	"
W	Pizzano Mary †	183	"	20	"
X	Pizzano Raymond	183	plumber	23	"
Y	Ione Frank	184	laborer	27	"
Z	Ione Louisa †	184	housewife	22	"

2455

A	Vistola Louis	184	laborer	60	"
B*	Vistola Pasqualena †	184	packer	58	"
C	Ciriello Antonio	184	laborer	56	"
D*	Ciriello Maria †	184	housewife	56	"
E	Dionizio Josephine †	185	"	30	"
F	Dionizio Manuel	185	porter	34	"
G	LaRocco John	185	operator	31	"
H	LaRocco Joseph	185	U S A	29	"
K*	LaRocco Nancy †	185	packer	64	"
L	LaRocco Nora †	185	operator	26	"
M*	Perretti Philomena †	185	housewife	52	"
N	Perretti Ralph	185	fireman	51	"
O*	Foti Samuel	186	finisher	53	126 Havre
P	Gravellese Domenica †	186	housewife	21	here
R	Gravellese Victor	186	plumber	21	"
S	Terraciano Benjamin	186	factoryhand	34	"

Page.	Letter.	FULL NAME.	Residence. Jan. 1, 1943.	Occupation.	Supposed Age.	Reported Residence. Jan. 1, 1942. Street and Number.

Marion Street Continued

	T	Terraciano Theresa †	186	housewife	32	here
	U	LaRocca Anna †	187	"	27	145 Havre
	V	LaRocca Guy	187	laborer	28	145 "
	W	Fiore Angelina †	187	housewife	37	here
	X	Fiore Morris	187	timekeeper	39	"
	Y	Letterello Mary †	188	housewife	27	227 Border
	Z	Letterello Nicolas	188	pipefitter	29	227 "

2456

	A	Carco Constantine	188	machinist	41	here
	B	*Carco Josephine †	188	housewife	43	"
	C	Serino Anna †	188	"	35	260 Maverick
	D	Serino Herbert	188	chauffeur	42	260 "
	G	Forgione Angelina †	191	housewife	28	3 Morris
	H	Forgiene Joseph	191	welder	27	3 "
	K	Finamore Angelina †	191	housekeeper	35	here
	L	Finamore Gaetano	191	barber	38	"
	M	Finamore Margaret †	191	housekeeper	33	"
	N	Finamore Mary †	191	housewife	57	"
	O	Finamore Romeo	191	laborer	32	"
	S	Bavaro Anna †	192	housewife	36	"
	T	Bavaro Peter	192	laborer	39	"
	U	Barrasso Carmela †	192	laundryworker	25	"
	V	Barrasso Emily †	192	packer	23	"
	W	Barrasso Helen †	192	supervisor	22	"
	X	*Barrasso Maria †	192	housewife	58	"
	Y	Barrasso Nicolas	192	chauffeur	52	"
	Z	Barrasso Nicolas, jr	192	U S A	21	"

2457

	A	Sullivan Anna †	193	housewife	24	"
	B	Sullivan Thomas	193	fisherman	30	"
	C	Dangelico Dominic	193	electrician	28	"
	D	Dangelico Rose †	193	housewife	28	"
	E	D'Angelico Carl	193A	barber	55	"
	F	*D'Angelico Emma †	193A	housewife	52	"
	G	Anzalone Emilio	194	laborer	21	"
	H	Pegriato Anna †	194	presser	21	"
	K	Pegriato Domenica †	194	at home	27	196 Marion
	L	*Pegriato Sebastian	194	laborer	55	here
	M	Anzalone Anthony	194	metalworker	22	"
	N	Mazzurrella Angelo J	195	laborer	36	195 Havre
	O	Mazzurrella Yolanda †	195	housewife	27	195 "

Marion Street Continued

Page.	Letter.	Full Name.	Residence. Jan. 1, 1913.	Occupation	Supposed Age.	Reported Residence Jan. 1, 1912. Street and Number.
	p	Lombardi Agostino	195	laborer	21	here
	R	Lombardi Antonio	195	shipwright	52	"
	s*	Lombardi Emma †	195	housewife	46	"
	T	Lombardi Hannah †	195	operator	24	"
	v	Amoroso Angelina †	195	at home	55	"
	v	Amoroso Helen †	195	rubberworker	24	"
	w	Fagan John	196	fisherman	41	"
	x	Forgione Olympia †	196	housewife	23	127 Eutaw
	Y	Forgione Robert	196	laborer	22	127 "
	z*	Gangi Antonia †	196	housewife	60	here
2458						
	A	Gangi Nicola	196	laborer	65	"
	B*	Giglio Antonina †	196	at home	58	21 Unity
	c	Maio Catherine †	197	operator	21	here
	D	Maio Joseph	197	laborer	50	"
	E*	Maio Mary †	197	housewife	42	"
	F	Saetti Albert	197	machinist	63	69 Webster
	G*	Saetti Mary †	197	housewife	47	69 "
	H	Saetti Santa †	197	at home	24	69 "
	L	Puler Lily A †	198	stitcher	22	here
	M	Rocco Eleanor E †	198	candymaker	39	"
	N	LaFrazia Frank	198	laborer	49	"
	o	LaFrazia Josephine †	198	housewife	46	"
	R*	Gianpuso Carmela †	199	"	44	"
	s	Gianpuso Charles	199	laborer	54	"
	T	Gianpuos Giovanni	199	U S A	24	"
	v	Gianpuso Salvatore	199	"	23	"
	v	Ardito Crucifissa †	199	housewife	52	"
	w	Ardito John	199	laborer	52	"
	x	Ardito Vincenza †	199	stitcher	21	"
	Y*	Pungetola Rosina †	199	at home	43	"
2459						
	A	Villani Louise †	200	"	32	"
	B	Cassero Frances †	200A	dressmaker	46	"
	c	Cassero Joseph	200A	laborer	51	"
	D	DiCristoforo Elizabeth †	201	housewife	25	"
	E	DiCristoforo Joseph	201	laborer	32	"
	F	Conte Angelo	201	U S A	26	"
	G	Conte Catherine †	201	stitcher	22	"
	H	Conte Josephine †	201	at home	58	"
	K	Conte Margaret †	201	stitcher	23	"

Marion Street Continued

L	Hawes Edward J	201	U S A	32	here
M	Hawes Francis	201	"	42	"
N	Hawes Margaret †	201	at home	70	"
O	Hawes Marguerite †	201	millhand	21	"
P	Hawes Russell J	201	U S A	31	"
R	*DePari Pauline †	205	housewife	30	"
V	DePari Sebastian	205	laborer	33	"
W	Puzzanghera Mary †	205	stitcher	20	"
X	Rao Frank	205	foreman	31	"
Y	Rao Mary †	205	housewife	28	"
Z	Rao Nunzio	205	manager	67	"

2460

A	Cioffi Guilio	206	U S A	24	"
B	Cioffi John	206	baker	57	"
C	Cioffi Joseph	206	U S A	31	"
D	*Cioffi Theresa †	206	housewife	50	"
E	*Vinziano Catherine †	206	stitcher	37	139 Paris
F	*Vinziano Charles	206	presser	47	139 "
H	*Caccamesi Angelo	207	shoeworker	24	here
K	Caccamesi Giacomo	207	retired	67	"
L	Caccamesi Salvatore	207	U S A	22	"
M	*Caccamesi Salvatrice †	207	housewife	59	"
N	Chiarenza Charles	207	U S A	21	"
O	*Chiarenza Maria †	207	housewife	38	"
P	Chiarenza Vincenzo	207	tailor	46	"
R	Rosenfield Beatrice †	209	typist	20	"
S	Rosenfield Harry	209	laborer	53	"
T	*Rosenfield Sarah †	209	storekeeper	52	"
V	Greco Biagio	213	"	53	"
W	*Boncore Ada †	213	housewife	38	"
X	Boncore Filippo	213	pressman	43	"
Y	Ferullo Joseph	213	welder	44	"
Z	Ferullo Rena C †	213	housewife	33	"

2461

B	Arnone Elizabeth †	219	stitcher	24	"
C	Arnone Josephine †	219	rubberworker	21	"
D	Arnone Peter	219	laborer	45	"
F	Arnone Theresa †	219	housewife	42	"
L	Rossetti George	219	welder	37	"
G	Rossetti Serafina †	219	housewife	28	"
K	*Schratto Antonetta †	221	"	57	"

Marion Street Continued

	Letter	Full Name	Res.	Occupation	Age	Reported Residence
	L	Schraffo Gaetano	221	laborer	58	here
	M	*Soldano Angelina †	221	housewife	48	"
	N	Soldano Frank	221	U S A	20	"
	O	Soldano Gabriel	221	molder	49	"
	P	Soldano Rosina †	221	stitcher	22	"
	R	Natola Antonette † rear	221	housewife	29	"
	S	Natola Frank "	221	candyworker	29	"
	T	*Giardullo Liberato "	221	laborer	73	"
	U	Giardullo Mary † "	221	laundryworker	26	"
	V	Giardullo Rosina † "	221	inspector	20	"
	W	*Giardullo Theresa † "	221	housewife	60	"
	X	Blundo Angelo	223	laborer	48	"
	Y	*Blundo Maria A †	223	housewife	47	"
	Z	Giordano Lillian †	223	"	23	"
2462						
	A	Giordano Vincent	223	operator	24	"
	B	Blundo Angelina †	223	housewife	25	67 Frankfort
	C	Blundo John	223	baker	21	67 "
	D	*Goldenberg Morris	225	storekeeper	67	here
	E	Goldenberg Myer	225	"	37	"
	F	*Goldenberg Rose †	225	clerk	63	"
	G	Finamore Adelina †	225A	housewife	45	"
	H	Finamore Joseph	225A	tailor	48	"
	K	Addario Carmen	225A	chauffeur	27	"
	L	Addario Mary †	225A	housewife	28	"
	M	Rizzo Bertha †	227	"	55	"
	N	Rizzo John	227	U S C G	21	"
	O	Rizzo Mary G †	227	stitcher	28	"
	P	Avilla Antonio	227	retired	73	"
	R	Avilla Rosaria †	227	housewife	62	"
	S	*Figillio Antonio	227	painter	41	"
	T	Figillio Carmela †	227	housewife	32	"
	U	Vaccaro Giovanni	229	carpenter	53	"
	V	Vaccaro Maria †	229	housewife	44	"
	W	Barrasso Laura †	229	"	50	"
	X	Barrasso Pasquale	229	barber	57	"
	Y	*Belgiorno Alberico	229	retired	60	"
	Z	Belgiorno Anna †	229	milliner	30	"
2463						
	A	*Belgiorno Lucia †	229	housewife	58	"
	B	Belgiorno Vincenzo	229	salesman	25	"

Page	Letter	FULL NAME.	Residence Jan. 1, 1943.	Occupation.	Supposed Age.	Reported Residence, Jan. 1, 1942. Street and Number.

Marion Street—Continued

	D*	Feldman Eva—†	237	housewife	46	here
	E	Feldman Hyman	237	collector	25	"
	F*	Feldman Max	237	operator	49	"
	G	Insano Frank	237	laborer	57	"
	H	Insano Maria—†	237	housewife	53	"
	K	Insano Mary—†	237	rubberworker	30	"

Paris Street

	L	Kaplan Rose—†	163	housewife	49	here
	M	Richmond Mamie S—†	163	"	63	"
	N	Drevitch Bessie—†	163	saleswoman	46	"
	O	Drevitch Solomon B	163	agent	48	"
	P*	Hoffman Dora—†	163	housewife	70	"
	R	Hoffman Phillip S	163	salesman	36	"
	T	Insogna Matthew	165	mechanic	25	"
	U	Insogna Rose—†	165	housewife	22	"
	V*	Elibero Edward	165	laborer	59	"
	W*	Elibero Grace—†	165	housewife	67	"
	X	Elibero Phillip	165	U S A	25	"
	Y*	Iarossi Mary—†	165	packer	39	212 Chelsea
	Z	Vecchio Angelina—†	166	housewife	35	here
2464						
	A*	Vecchio Florence—†	166	"	70	"
	B	Vecchio Michael	166	shoemaker	42	"
	D*	Daddario Accurzia—†	166	housewife	58	"
	C	Daddario Anthony	166	laborer	24	"
	E	Daddario Joseph	166	mechanic	22	"
	F	Daddario Luigi	166	laborer	60	"
	G	Marselia John	166	"	53	"
	H	Marselia Louis P	166	mechanic	21	"
	K*	Marselia Mary—†	166	housewife	52	"
	L*	Pascarella Leonda—†	167	"	57	"
	M	Pascarella Louise—†	167	candymaker	29	"
	N	Alfieri Josephine—†	167	housewife	39	"
	O	Alfieri Louis	167	U S N	21	"
	P	Alfieri Thomas	167	pipefitter	20	"
	R	Massie Angie—†	167	housewife	23	"
	S	Massie Philip	167	mechanic	25	"
	T	DeMarco Angelo	168	chauffeur	31	"
	U	DeMarco Mary—†	168	housewife	32	"

Paris Street Continued

v	Cammisa Frank	168	repairman	25	here
w	Cammisa Phyllis †	168	housewife	22	"
x	Raso Palmira—†	168	"	30	"
y	Raso Rosalino—†	168	rigger	32	"
z	Taylor Mary †	169	housewife	59	"

2465

A	Taylor William	169	baggageman	52	"
B	Ferreira Joaquin	169	merchant	72	"
C	Fratus Rose—†	169	at home	69	"
D	Bush Esther—†	169	housewife	35	"
E	Bush Henry J	169	clerk	34	"
F	Mercandante Celia †	170	housewife	35	"
G	Mercandante John	170	welder	35	"
H	Cogliani Angelina †	170	stitcher	23	"
K	*Cogliani Antonetta †	170	housewife	56	"
L	Cogliani Antonio	170	U S N	31	"
M	Cogliani Michael	170	laborer	63	"
N	Cogliani Raffaella †	170	packer	25	"
O	Umbro Antonio	170	salesman	52	"
P	Umbro Elizabeth—†	170	housewife	41	"
S	*Hassed Jennie—†	171	"	58	"
R	*Hassed Wolf	171	retired	60	"
T	Goldberg Henry	171	U S A	31	"
U	*Goldberg Joseph	171	retired	60	"
V	Goldberg Louis	171	U S A	21	"
W	Goldberg Milton	171	welder	23	Rhode Island
X	Goldberg Shirley—†	171	housewife	20	Revere
Y	Goldberg Solomon	171	U S A	28	here
Z	Muse Mary †	172	housewife	33	"

2466

A	*Muse Phillip	172	chauffeur	34	"
B	Mingola Salvatore	172	laborer	48	"
C	*Mingola Stella †	172	housewife	36	"
D	*Framontana Mary †	172	"	48	"
E	Framontana Vincent	172	laborer	49	"
F	DeLeo Giuseppe	173	"	50	"
G	DeLeo Josephine †	173	housewife	40	"
H	*Rindone Josephine †	173	at home	64	108 Havre
K	Rindone Mamie—†	173	clerk	28	108 "
L	*Rindone Michael	173	operator	36	108 "
M	Rindone Salvatore	173	U S A	43	108 "

Page	Letter	FULL NAME	Residence, Jan. 1, 1943	Occupation	Supposed Age	Reported Residence, Jan. 1, 1942. Street and Number.

Paris Street—Continued

	N	Cigna Catherine †	173	housewife	48	here
	O	Cigna Joseph	173	laborer	50	"
	P	Campagna Ernest	174	"	25	"
	R	Campagna Rose †	174	housewife	22	"
	S*	Cocca Assunta †	174	"	46	"
	T*	Cocca Pellegrino	174	laborer	53	"
	U	Arinello Edwin	174	U S A	29	"
	V	Arinello John	174	"	21	"
	W	Arinello Joseph	174	painter	56	"
	X	Arinello Mary †	174	housewife	51	"
	Y	Vella Antonetta †	175	"	23	172 Paris
	Z	Vella Joseph	175	laborer	22	160 Putnam

2467

	C	Pascucci Henry	176	electrician	36	here
	D	Pascucci Josephine †	176	housewife	34	"
	E	Carfagna Henry	176	clerk	24	"
	F*	Carfagna Josephine †	176	housewife	47	"
	G*	Carfagna Richard	176	porter	52	"
	H	Pascucci Antonetta †	176	nurse	29	"
	K	Pascucci Ida †	176	housewife	64	"
	L	Pascucci Phillip	176	retired	67	"
	M	Incrovato Anthony	177	laborer	38	"
	N	Incrovato Mary †	177	housewife	31	"
	O	Paterna Angelina †	177	"	37	175 Paris
	P	Paterna Joseph	177	tailor	46	175 "
	R	Kenney Andrew J	177	retired	87	here
	S	Consalvi Anthony	178	clerk	36	"
	T	Consalvi Millie †	178	housewife	32	"
	U	Greco Frank	178	shoemaker	53	"
	V	Greco Grace †	178	housewife	41	"
	W	Kaplan Pearl †	178	"	42	"
	X	Kaplan Samuel	178	storekeeper	47	"
	Y	Modica Joseph G	179	chauffeur	24	"
	Z	Modica Rose †	179	housewife	22	"

2468

	A	Finamore Arthur	179	pipefitter	35	"
	B	Finamore Mary †	179	housewife	31	"
	C*	Covotto Angelina †	179	"	74	"
	D*	Covotto Michael	179	retired	69	"
	E*	Pastore Francesca †	180	stitcher	43	229 Benningt'n

Paris Street Continued

f	Pastore Mary †	180	stitcher	20	229 Benningt'n	
g	Grimaldi Angelo	180	U S A	25	here	
h	Grimaldi Joseph	180	machinist	53	"	
k*	Grimaldi Mary †	180	housewife	53	"	
l	Grimaldi Reto	180	U S A	26	"	
m	Capobianco John	180	shoeworker	52	"	
n	Capobianco Lucia †	180	housewife	49	"	
o	Capobianco Pasquale	180	U S A	25	"	
p	Akell Anna †	181	housewife	31	"	
r	Akell Harold	181	shipper	30	"	
s	Macchione Ernest	181	U S A	27	"	
t*	Abramo Grace †	181	housewife	46	"	
u	Abramo Louis	181	U S A	23	"	
v*	Abramo Natale	181	storekeeper	53	"	
w	Abramo Salvatore	181	U S A	26	"	
x	Ferullo Anthony	181	welder	23	"	
y	Ferullo John	181	clerk	26	"	
z	Ferullo Joseph	181	retired	59	"	

2469

a	Ferullo Joseph	181	U S A	24	"	
b	Ferullo Mary †	181	stitcher	27	"	
c*	Ferullo Susan †	181	housewife	50	"	
d	Lombardo Antonetta †	182	"	24	"	
e	Lombardo Edward	182	machinist	24	"	
f	Venuti Anthony	182	chairmaker	35	180 Paris	
g	Venuti Celia M †	182	housewife	34	here	
h	Calvagno Anthony	182	operator	37	"	
k	Calvagno Theresa †	182	housewife	30	"	
m	Cunningham John	183	clerk	29	"	
n	Cunningham Mary †	183	at home	60	"	
o	Ginsburg Albert	183	storekeeper	64	"	
p	Ginsburg Flora †	183	housewife	60	"	
r	Ginsburg Ida †	183	bookkeeper	38	"	
s	Buck Mary †	183	housewife	53	"	
t	Buck Michael	183	longshoreman	66	"	
u	DiAngelus Mary †	184	housewife	48	"	
v	DiAngelus Nicolas	184	laborer	50	"	
w	Adamo Gabriel	184	"	70	"	
x	Adamo Mary †	184	housewife	55	"	
y*	Cosco Andrew	184	retired	75	"	

44

Paris Street—Continued

z	Pucci Dominic	184	welder	53	here
2470						
A	Pucci Sarah—†	184	housewife	40	"
B	Cambria Frank	185	laborer	36	"
C*	Cambria Tina—†	185	housewife	37	"
D*	Scarpa Carmella—†	185	"	52	"
E	Scarpa Carmine	185	laborer	56	"
F	Scarpa Antonio	185	chipper	31	"
G	Scarpa Lucy—†	185	housewife	27	"
H	Picarelli Irene—†	186	"	27	"
K*	Picarelli Philip	186	laborer	40	"
L*	Renna Anna—†	186	housewife	33	"
M	Renna Paul	186	laborer	38	"
N	Marro Benjamin	186	trackman	55	"
O*	Marro Rose—†	186	housewife	54	"
R	Albanese Caroline—†	190	"	25	"
S	Albanese Rocco	190	laborer	32	"
T	Petrone Anthony	190	barber	53	"
U*	Petrone Nancy—†	190	housewife	45	"
V	D'Agostino Arthur	190	painter	45	"
W	D'Agostino Mary—†	190	saleswoman	20	"
X*	D'Agostino Olympia—†	190	housewife	53	"
Y	DeLorenzo Concetta—†	190	laundryworker	28	"
Z	DiChiaro Antonio rear	190	welder	39	"
2471						
A*	DiChiaro Lena—† "	190	housewife	57	"
B	Eatarill Elizabeth—† "	190	"	29	"
C	Eatarill Ralph "	190	laborer	29	"
D	DiMinico Angelina—†	192	sorter	21	"
E	DiMinico John	192	clerk	27	"
F	DiMinico Josephine—†	192	"	22	"
G	DiMinico Sabato	192	laborer	60	"
H	Giunta Beatrice—†	192	housewife	42	"
K	Giunta John	192	U S M C	20	"
L	Giunta Salvatore	192	laborer	48	"
M	Salamone Angelina—†	192	housewife	48	"
N	Salamone Benedetto	192	laborer	55	"
O	Salamone Benedetto	192	U S A	22	"
P	Salamone Stella—†	192	clerk	21	"
R*	Campagna Filomena—†	196	housewife	65	"
S	Campagna Joseph	196	stockboy	22	"

42

Paris Street — Continued

T	Campagna Robert	196	oiler	20	here
U	Fabrizio Antonio	196	laborer	55	"
V	Fabrizio Thomasina †	196	janitor	30	"
W	Vietro Michael	196	laborer	52	130 Saratoga
X	DeCristoforo Amelio	196	metalworker	36	here
Y	DeCristoforo Emma †	196	housewife	35	182 Paris

2472

A	Daddieco Patrick H	196	longshoreman	39	here
A	Daddieco Santa †	196	housewife	28	"
B	*Bontanza Ciriaco	196	retired	68	"
C	*Bontanza Phyllis †	196	housewife	66	"
D	*Guardino Mary †	196	"	69	"
E	DeLeo Achilles	196	shoeworker	56	"
F	*DeLeo Julia †	196	housewife	51	"
G	Dagnino Frank P	196	chauffeur	37	"
H	Dagnino Margaret M †	196	housewife	40	"
K	Mazzaferri Mary †	196	"	24	"
L	Mazzaferri Rocco	196	U S A	25	"
N	DeRosa Rose †	196	housewife	32	"
O	Risti Ernest	196	laborer	48	116 Webster
P	Risti Jennie †	196	housewife	47	116 "
R	Ferrera Alice †	202	"	21	here
S	Ferrera Natale	202	shipfitter	23	"
T	Recuppero Henry	202	plumber	37	106 Bremen
U	Recuppero Marie †	202	housewife	22	196 Paris
V	Recuppero Alphonse	202	pipefitter	26	here
W	Recuppero Elizabeth †	202	housewife	24	"
X	Cheverie Agnes †	206	"	73	"
Y	Cheverie William	206	fisherman	71	"
Z	Longo Joseph	206	salesman	46	"

2473

A	Longo Mamie †	206	housewife	44	"
B	Lippert Henry	206	meatcutter	24	"
C	Lippert Louise †	206	housewife	33	"
D	Luongo Camino	207	chauffeur	31	"
E	Luongo Emily †	207	housewife	24	175 Paris
F	Luongo Anthony	207	U S A	27	here
G	*Luongo Filomena †	207	housewife	60	"
H	Luongo Pasquale	207	laborer	63	"
K	DeSena Mary †	207	housewife	32	"
L	DeSena Thomas P	207	meatcutter	39	"

Paris Street—Continued

	FULL NAME.	Residence	Occupation	Age	Reported
M	Spina Anthony	209	baker	28	here
N	Spina Eleanor †	209	housewife	27	"
O	Dallelio Fiore	209	laborer	58	"
P	Dallelio Fiore	209	electrician	26	"
R*	Dallelio Grace †	209	housewife	58	"
S	Dallelio John	209	metalworker	27	"
T	Dallelio Mary †	209	dressmaker	21	"
U*	Alessandro Alfredo	209	ironworker	58	"
V*	Alessandro Elvira †	209	housewife	54	"
W	Fowler Edward	210	machinist	55	"
X	Fowler Ella— †	210	housewife	50	"
Y	Hansen Marion †	210	candymaker	34	"
Z	Ryan Daniel J	210	janitor	67	"
	2474				
A	Ryan Daniel, jr	210	laborer	30	"
B	Ryan Mary A †	210	housewife	65	"
C	Murray Anna †	210	"	32	"
D	Murray Henry	210	laborer	33	"
E	Zarrella Marie †	216	housewife	38	"
F	Sugarman Bernard	216	machinist	25	"
G	Sugarman Israel	216	junk dealer	55	"
H*	Sugarman Rose †	216	housewife	52	"
K	Armeato Carmen	216	welder	27	"
L	Spolsino Alfred	216	U S A	21	"
M*	Spolsino Filomena †	216	housewife	52	"
N	Spolsino Martino	216	wool sorter	60	"
O	Cahill Anna T †	217	housewife	71	"
P	Cahill Frederick C	217	U S A	35	"
R	Cahill Regina E †	217	waitress	28	"
S	Cahill Robert W	217	shipworker	32	"
T	Johnson Peter J	217	retired	64	"
U	D'Argenio Americo	218	operator	27	"
V	D'Argenio Antonette †	218	housewife	25	"
W*	Cecere Carmella †	218	"	55	"
X	Cecere Hilda †	218	stitcher	20	"
Y	Cecere Louis	218	compositor	28	"
Z*	Cecere Paul	218	retired	61	"
	2475				
A	Venute Jennie †	218	housewife	28	"
B	Venute Salvatore	218	shipfitter	30	"
D	Trepodi Anthony	220	machinist	48	"

44

Paris Street Continued

E	Trepodi Mary †	220	housewife	36	here
F	Spalvero Albert	220	laborer	47	"
G	Spalvero Grace †	220	housewife	34	"
H	Gerace Angelina †	220	"	26	"
K	Gerace Anthony	220	pipefitter	30	"
L	Indingaro Helen †	221	housewife	26	"
M	Indingaro Leo	221	clerk	26	"
N	Indingaro Michael	221	bootblack	53	"
O	Cozzi Abbie †	222	housewife	23	"
P	Cozzi Patrick	222	painter	25	"
R	DeLorenzo Rose †	222	housewife	30	"
S	DeLorenzo Vincent	222	painter	29	"
T	Paone Alexander	222	jeweler	45	"
U	Paone Elia †	222	housewife	44	"
V	Paone Grace †	222	clerk	20	"
W	Paone Mary †	222	"	21	"
X	Paone Paul	222	U S A	22	"
Y	Cascia Angelo	223	laborer	57	"
Z	*Cascia Crocefissa †	223	housewife	52	"

2476

A	Tontodonato Albert	223	meter reader	27	"
B	Tontodonato Mary †	223	housewife	29	"
C	Abate Charles	223	U S N	20	"
D	*Abate Jennie †	223	housewife	46	"
E	Abate Joseph	223	pressman	59	"
F	Abate Paul	223	operator	21	"
G	Sciarappo Angelo	224	welder	42	"
H	Sciarappo Carmella †	224	housewife	41	"
K	Ryan Lawrence J	224	clerk	26	Revere
L	Ryan Susan †	224	housewife	26	"
M	Caccamesi Carmella †	224	"	26	201 Havre
N	Caccamesi Peter	224	shoemaker	31	201 "
O	Martorane Joseph	225	operator	27	here
P	Martorano Sylvia †	225	housewife	27	"
R	Alferi Anna †	225	"	38	"
S	Alferi Gaetano	225	checker	50	"
T	Cinelli Salvatore	225	laborer	22	"
U	D'Ortona Mary †	225	housewife	31	"
V	D'Ortona Nicholas	225	shipfitter	33	"
W	LoVerme Charles	226	rubberworker	52	50 London
X	LoVerme Lucy †	226	housewife	41	50 "

Paris Street—Continued

Y	DeBlasi Anthony	226	manager	54	79 Marion
Z	DeBlasi Mary †	226	housewife	49	here
2477					
A	Marasca Elda †	226	"	32	"
C	Antonuccio John	236	operator	25	"
D	Antonuccio Peter	236	machinist	53	"
E	Antonuccio Sarah †	236	housewife	41	"
F	Antonuccio John	236	U S A	35	"
G	Sgro Anthony	236	machinist	27	"
H	Sgro Lena †	236	houseworker	36	"
K*	Sgro Marie †	236	housewife	46	"
L	Sgro Natale	236	machinist	54	"
M	Ballerini Domenic	240	operator	16	"
N	Ballerini Filomena †	240	housewife	34	"
O*	Duarte John C	242	seaman	30	"
P*	Duarte Mary †	242	housewife	46	"
S	Grasso Mary †	242	"	27	"
T	Grasso Victor	242	merchant	31	"
U	Guarente Francis A	244	painter	32	"
V	Guarente Josephine †	244	housewife	28	"
W*	Silva Rose †	244	"	64	Revere
X	Brass Helen †	244	stenographer	22	here
Y	Brass Martin	244	student	23	"
Z	Brass Myer	244	salesman	65	"
2478					
A	Brass Sarah †	244	housewife	53	"
B	LaGrassa Peter	244	mechanic	26	"
C	LaGrassa Virginia †	244	housewife	27	"
D	Vernacchio Frank	252	millhand	35	"
E	Vernacchio Lucy †	252	housewife	25	"
F	DiTroya Joseph	252	agent	31	"
G	DiTroya Theresa †	252	housewife	31	"
H	DeFeo Arthur	252	draftsman	25	"
K	DeFeo Lena †	252	stenographer	23	"
L	Forgione Alphonso	254	shoeworker	57	"
M	Forgione Delia †	254	housewife	48	"
N	Forgione George	254	U S N	24	"
O	Forgione Vincent	254	U S A	20	"
P	Leddy Mildred E †	256	housewife	40	"
R	Brangeforte Philip	256	machinist	42	"
S	Brangeforte Phyllis †	256	housewife	31	"

Page	Letter	FULL NAME.	Residence, Jan. 1, 1943	Occupation.	Supposed Age.	Reported Residence, Jan. 1, 1942. Street and Number.

Paris Street Continued

	T	Palermo Antonio	256	U S A	32	262 Paris
	U	Palermo Paul	256	laborer	53	262 "
	V*	Palermo Rose — †	256	housewife	52	262 "
	W	Kenney Francis	rear 256	U S A	21	here
	X	Kenney Harold	" 256		22	"
	Y	Kenney Harry	" 256	pipefitter	43	"
	Z	Kenney Theresa — †	" 256	housewife	41	"

2479

	A	Blase Emilio J	258	welder	24	"
	B	Blase Frances J — †	258	housewife	25	"
	C	Prudente Anthony	258	longshoreman	38	"
	D	Prudente Rose — †	258	housewife	39	"
	E	Caverretta Mary — †	258	"	48	"
	F	Caverretta Vincent	258	storekeeper	50	"
	G	Francis Ellen — †	260	housewife	28	"
	H	Francis George A	260	gaugemaker	27	"
	K	Carr Blanche — †	260	printer	30	"
	L	Francis Anthony G	260	woodworker	52	"
	M	Francis Mary E — †	260	housewife	51	"
	N	Gill Dennis A	260	printer	47	"
	O	Littlewood Mary †	260	housewife	78	"
	P	Nappi Americo	262	welder	32	"
	R	Nappi Mary — †	262	housewife	32	"
	S	DeLiscio Margaret †	262	candymaker	34	"
	T	Zollo Florence †	262	housewife	39	"
	U	Zollo James	262	laborer	39	"
	V*	Mastromarino Margaret — †	262	housewife	45	"
	W	Schepici Andrew	264	laborer	24	"
	X	Schepici Anna †	264	housewife	20	"
	Y	Longo Joseph	264	shipper	32	"
	Z	Longo Theresa F †	264	housewife	31	"

2480

	A	Prusco Mary †	264	"	80	"
	B	Nappi Alfonse	264	chauffeur	39	"
	C	Nappi Dora — †	264	housewife	36	"
	D	Mongello Angelo	266	welder	33	261 Paris
	E	Mongello Concetta †	266	housewife	54	261 "
	F	Chase Eleanora — †	266	"	23	here
	G	Chase George W	266	machinist	26	"
	H	Amico Josephine †	266	housewife	35	"
	K	Amico Michael	266	laborer	36	"

47

Paris Street Continued

L	Ferno Anthony	268	U S M C	21	here
M	Ferno Louis R	268	garageman	45	"
N	Ferno Millie †	268	housewife	43	"
O	DiGregorio Angela †	268	"	25	221 Marion
P	DiGregorio Armando	268	electrician	25	221 "
R	Delaney Louise T †	268	housewife	42	here
T	Barbaro Angelo	276	laborer	34	"
U	Barbaro Jennie †	276	housewife	31	"
V	Masoli Alfredo	276	U S A	20	"
W	Masoli Anthony	276	clerk	22	"
X	Masoli Joseph	276	laborer	50	"
Y*	Masoli Mary †	276	housewife	43	"
Z	Alfano Alphonse	276	tailor	54	"

2481

A	Alfano Domenic	276	welder	22	"
B	Alfano Louis	276	machinist	20	"
C*	Alfano Rose †	276	housewife	40	"

Porter Street

E	Stellato Frances †	40	nurse	23	here
F	Stellato Pasquale	40	shoeworker	42	"
G*	Stellato Pasqualina †	40	at home	60	"
K*	Amarto Concentina †	42	housewife	47	"
L*	Amarto Frank	42	laborer	50	"
N	Petrillo Anthony	42	tailor	29	133 Endicott
O	Petrillo Antonetta †	42	housewife	25	133 "
W*	Petrillo Frederico	42	retired	59	133 "
R*	Ciriello Linda †	46	housewife	49	here
S	Ciriello Nicholas	46	U S A	28	"
T*	Ciriello Peter A	46	foreman	53	"
U	Ciriello Vito	46	shipper	26	"
V	Recca Angelo	46	U S A	27	"
W	Recca John	46	clerk	23	"
X	Recca Joseph	46	laborer	59	"
Y	Recca Mary †	46	housewife	52	"

2482

A	LoConte Matteo	48	laborer	24	"
B	LoConte Tomasina †	48	housewife	21	"
C	Zamballo Frank	48	butcher	53	"
D	Zamballo Lucia †	48	housewife	43	"

18

Porter Street — Continued

Page	Letter	FULL NAME.	Residence, Jan. 1, 1943.	Occupation.	Supposed Age.	Reported Residence, Jan. 1, 1942. Street and Number.
	E	Attardo Anthony	52	storekeeper	29	here
	F	Attardo Carmella †	52	housewife	23	"
	G	Martarana Gaetano	52	laborer	25	169 Havre
	H	Martarana Lucy †	52	housewife	21	169 "
	L	Napolitano Florence †	60	at home	27	here
	M	Gatti Almo	60	laborer	45	"
	N	*Gatti Lena †	60	housewife	42	"
	R	Arinella Anna †	72	"	32	"
	S	Arinella Carmen	72	shoeworker	36	"
	U	Guidara Concetta †	72	housewife	27	"
	V	Guidara William	72	painter	34	"
	W	D'Meo Anthony	72	laborer	43	"
	X	D'Meo Margaret †	72	housewife	34	"
	Y	Baudanza Joseph	72	laborer	40	"
	Z	*Baudanza Maria †	72	housewife	65	"
		2483				
	A	*Baudanza Rose †	72	stitcher	42	"
	B	*Baudanza Walter	72	retired	72	"
	C	Rao Fannie †	72	housewife	27	"
	D	Rao Samuel	72	laborer	31	"
	F	Lipani Jennie †	76	housewife	22	"
	G	Lipani Sam	76	electrician	28	"
	H	Coco Anthony	76	mechanic	24	"
	K	*Coco Carmella †	76	housewife	46	"
	L	Coco Carmello	76	student	21	"
	M	Coco Charles	76	mechanic	22	"
	N	*Coco Mario	76	retired	53	"
	O	Coco Orazio	76	U S A	20	"
	P	Arena Nellie †	80	housewife	41	254 Everett
	R	*Noto Nancy †	80	"	60	188 Cottage
	S	*Noto Salvatore	80	factoryhand	59	188 "
	U	*Lancia Angelina †	82	housewife	64	here
	V	Lancia Anthony	82	U S A	25	"
	W	Lancia Domenick	82	carpenter	61	"
	X	Pieri Noe	82	pedler	51	"
	Y	*Bonaffine Giuseppe	84	retired	85	"
	Z	*Bonaffine Josie †	84	at home	59	"
		2484				
	A	Bonaffine Mary †	84	stitcher	21	"
	B	*DeLuca Salvatore	84	floorlayer	56	7 Henry
	C	*DeLuca Santa †	84	housewife	46	7 "

Porter Street—Continued

F	Rossi Evelyn †	86	housewife	25	here
G	Rossi Michael	86	laborer	35	"
I	DiLuigi Domenick	88	pipefitter	20	"
M*	DiLuigi Joseph	88	pedler	59	"
N*	DiLuigi Maria †	88	housewife	50	"
O	Zarrella Ciriaco	90	retired	76	"
P	Zarrella Conziglia †	90	housewife	67	"
R	Zarrella George	90	machinist	24	"
S	Zarrella Ida †	90	housewife	23	"
W*	Valanzola Josephine †	94	at home	73	"
X*	LoBue Josephine †	94	housewife	45	"
Y	LoBue Josephine †	94	stenographer	22	"
Z	LoBue Luigi	94	storekeeper	47	"

2485

A	LoBue Vincent	94	USA	25	"
C*	Cardarella Joseph	96	laborer	61	"
D*	Cardarella Lucy †	96	housewife	57	"
E*	Moscone Anna †	96	"	37	"
F*	Moscone Frederick	96	bricklayer	42	"
G	Moscone John	96	factoryhand	20	"
K*	Costo Joseph	110	retired	51	"
L*	Costo Rosaria †	110	housewife	42	"
M	DeFratos Adeline †	110	"	51	"
N	DeFratos Charles	110	retired	63	"
P	Odierno Kathryn †	112	housewife	24	"
R	Odierno Louis	112	operator	32	"
S	Odierno Assunta †	112	housewife	53	"
T	Odierno Elsie M †	112	factoryhand	30	"
U*	Squitieri Luigi	112	"	28	"

2486   Saratoga Street

A	Gehm Gertrude †	101	housewife	51	here
B	Gehm John	101	laborer	45	"
C	Cowan Emma E †	101	housewife	58	"
D	Cowan Lyman W	101	engineer	57	"
E	DeChristoforo Amedeo	103	laborer	62	"
F	DeChristoforo Frederick	103	chauffeur	21	"
G	DeChristoforo Mary †	103	housewife	53	"
H	Smith Anna F †	103	"	65	"
K	Smith Lewis B	103	salesman	65	"

Saratoga Street Continued

L	Gardner Helena E †	105	at home	67	here
M	Gardner Joseph E	105	U S A	24	"
N	Gardner William B	105	fishcutter	35	"
O	Moore Lillian J †	107	at home	62	"
P	Nagle Annie E †	107	"	53	"
R	*Gillberg Axel B	109	asbestos worker	67	"
S	*Henriksen Charles	109	pipecoverer	69	"
T	Paulson Hansine †	109	at home	84	"
U	Currier Mary †	111	"	82	"
V	DeSouza John	111	retired	29	111 Meridian
W	Morse Edna G †	111	housekeeper	63	here
X	Verkosky Michael J	111	porter	27	363 Meridian
Y	Malfy Anna †	113	housewife	30	here
Z	Malfy Rocco	113	inspector	30	"

2487

A	*Camponaro Florence †	113	at home	72	"
B	Scarparto Leo	113	laborer	48	"
C	Scarparto Rocco	113	"	45	"
E	D'Addieco Josephine †	117	at home	58	"
F	D'Addieco Louis	117	guard	32	"
G	D'Addieco Mary †	117	housewife	32	"
H	D'Addieco Ruth †	117	operator	20	"
K	MacDonald Abigail †	119	at home	62	"
L	MacDonald Catherine †	119	housewife	72	"
M	MacDonald James	119	carpenter	79	"
N	*MacDonald James G	119	inspector	48	"
O	MacDonald William	119	retired	78	"
P	Small Ada †	121	housewife	35	"
R	Trask Ada †	121	at home	69	"
T	Carter Charles	125	upholsterer	30	"
U	Carter Sylvia †	125	stenographer	22	"
V	Cucugliata Charles	125	shipsmith	58	"
W	Cucugliata Eleanor †	125	operator	25	"
X	Cucugliata Grace †	125	housewife	53	"
Y	Cucugliata Marie †	125	clerk	28	"
Z	Ciandella Joseph	127	carpenter	41	"

2488

A	Ciandella Pierina †	127	housewife	36	"
B	Pompeo Domenica †	127	"	46	"
C	Pompeo John	127	mason	52	"
D	Christopher Marian †	129	clerk	22	New York

51

Pare.	Letter.	FULL NAME.	Residence, Jan. 1, 1943.	Occupation.	Supposed Age.	Reported Residence, Jan. 1, 1942. Street and Number.

Saratoga Street—Continued

	E	Crowley Annie—†	129	housekeeper	46	here
	F	Crowley Michael	129	shipworker	60	"
	G	Maggnossen Oscar	129	carpenter	60	"
	H	Shakerian Thomas	129	manager	50	"
	K	Young Frederick	129	rigger	25	384 Lowell
	L	Andolina Angelo	131	retired	75	here
	M	Andolina Charles	131	clerk	45	"
	N	Andolina Josephine—†	131	"	48	"
	O	Andolina Mary—†	131	"	31	"
	P	Andolina Rose—†	131	housewife	76	"
	R	Brown Catherine—†	133	domestic	45	273 Paris
	S	Terravecchia Anna—†	133	housewife	34	here
	T	Terravecchia John	133	sugar refiner	37	"
	U	O'Halloran Marian—†	135	housewife	26	"
	V	O'Halloran Michael J	135	motorman	27	"
	W	Pardo Angelo	135	guard	52	"
	X	Pardo Emma G—†	135	housewife	45	"
	Y	Salvaggio Eleanor—†	137	bookkeeper	30	"
	Z*	Salvaggio Paul	137	agent	47	"
2489						
	A*	Salvaggio Salvatrice—†	137	at home	80	"
	B	Argentina Minnie—†	137	secretary	28	"
	C	Bates Amy L—†	139	housekeeper	75	"
	D	Bates David S	139	retired	73	"
	E	Price John	139	"	63	"
	F	Swenson Constance—†	141	stenographer	33	"
	G	Pope George H	141	U S A	25	"
	H	Pope Mary E—†	141	at home	62	"
	K	Pope Thomas F	141	engineer	28	"
	L	Lazzora Filippa—†	143	at home	63	"
	M	Gangi Grace—†	143	dressmaker	30	"
	N	Gangi Rose—†	143	housewife	58	"
	O	Gangi Salvatore	143	retired	67	"
	P	Gangi Salvatore	143	upholsterer	38	"
	R*	Vecchio Carmen—†	145	housewife	43	"
	S	Vecchio Celeste—†	145	inspector	20	"
	T	Vecchio Michele	145	storekeeper	55	"
	U	Vecchio Rose—†	145	housewife	22	172 Cottage
	V	Vecchio Victor	145	welder	22	here
	W	Daly Walter	147	machinist	26	"
	X	Davis Patrick	147	fisherman	38	"

52

Saratoga Street Continued

Y	*Kalland Anna—†	147	at home	70	here
Z	Murphy Mary—†	147	"	57	"
2490					
A	Zers Peter	147	retired	72	62 W Newton
B	*Cannata Jennie—†	149	housewife	47	here
C	Cannata John	149	candymaker	53	"
D	Cannata Vincenza—†	149	clerk	22	"
E	*Cembrone Vita—†	149	at home	75	"
F	*Vanella Anna—†	149	housewife	42	"
G	Vanella Benjamin	149	salesman	47	"
H	Stoico Albert	149	machinist	22	"
K	*Stoico Libera—†	149	housewife	51	"
L	Stoico Nicholas	149	laborer	53	"
M	Munn Edna—†	151	housewife	29	"
N	Munn William	151	fitter	38	"
O	McNeely Donald	151	U S A	20	"
P	McNeely Madeline—†	151	at home	39	"
R	Vitale Giuseppe	151	laborer	50	"
S	*Vitale Nicolina—†	151	housewife	43	"
T	Corbett Adeline—†	153	"	22	"
U	Corbett Florence—†	153	"	51	"
V	Corbett James H	153	boilermaker	51	"
W	Corbett Joseph	153	shipfitter	23	"
X	Consilvio Benjamin	153	retired	69	"
Y	*Consilvio Concetta—†	153	housewife	63	"
Z	Consilvio Enrico P	153	laborer	33	"
2491					
A	Consilvio Felix	153	U S A	30	"
B	Consilvio Frank	153	"	32	"
C	Consilvio James V	153	clerk	44	"
D	Consilvio John	153	student	21	"
E	Cataruzzolo Angelina—†	153	housewife	47	"
F	Cataruzzolo Anna—†	153	driller	23	"
G	Cataruzzolo Felix	153	presser	53	"
H	Cataruzzolo Florence—†	153	"	26	"
K	Brizzi Catherine—†	155	stitcher	21	"
L	Brizzi Joseph	155	fisherman	45	"
M	Brizzi Josephine—†	155	housewife	37	"
N	Flamingo Amelia—†	155	"	42	"
O	Flamingo Leonard	155	molder	46	"
P	Flamingo Rocco	155	U S A	20	"

Saratoga Street—Continued

R	Minichiello Nunziata †	155	housewife	42	here
S	Minichiello Ralph	155	U S C G	20	"
T	Minichiello Salvatore	155	candymaker	43	"
U	Mori Catherine †	157	housewife	31	"
V	Mori Joseph P	157	laborer	32	"
W	Fasciano Alfonso	157	"	23	"
X	Fasciano Beatrice †	157	at home	33	"
Y	*Fasciano Jennie †	157	housewife	54	"
Z	Fasciano John	157	laborer	62	"

2492

A	Patti Anthony, jr	159	bookkeeper	31	"
B	Patti Yolanda †	159	housewife	22	"
C	Candella Alfonso	159	laborer	34	"
D	Candella Mary †	159	housewife	33	"
E	*Savoia Vittorio	159	retired	74	"
F	DiNocco Frances †	161	housewife	27	"
G	DiNocco Romeo	161	laborer	33	"
H	Bognanno Angelo	161	chauffeur	24	"
K	Bognanno Mary †	161	housewife	24	"
L	Messina Dora †	161	"	38	"
M	Messina Joseph	161	clerk	36	"
N	*D'Amelio James	163	janitor	55	"
O	*D'Amelio Rose †	163	housewife	50	"
P	D'Amelio Angelo	163	seaman	21	"
R	D'Amelio Jeanette †	163	presser	23	"
S	*Cerbone Mary †	163	housewife	49	"
T	*Cerbone Michael	163	millhand	59	"
W	LaCascia Catherine †	165	housewife	37	"
X	LaCascia Frank	165	baker	41	"
Y	Fingerman Irving	165	storekeeper	39	"
V	Fingerman Rose †	165	housewife	38	"

Savage Court

Z	Coia Pietro	1	shoeworker	55	here

2493

A	Divona Rocco	2	laborer	44	"
B	Sevramento Caralino	2	millhand	50	"
B	Gulli Michael	2	retired	74	"
C	Gulli Paul	2	metalworker	38	"
E	*Giampietra Louis	3	carpenter	51	"

Page	Letter	Full Name	Residence, Jan. 1, 1943	Occupation	Supposed Age	Reported Residence, Jan. 1, 1942. Street and Number.

Savage Court Continued

	F	Cooper Benjamin	3	orderly	21	181 Chelsea
	G	Cooper Israel	3	seaman	33	181 "
	H	Cooper Jacob	3	laborer	55	181 "

Sharon Court

	L	Dwyer Frederick	1	laborer	47	157 Western av
	M	Dwyer Mary †	1	housewife	43	157 "
	N	Dwyer James	1	retired	82	157 "
	O	Hiscock Richard	2	"	72	here
	P	DiNublia Josephine †	3	at home	25	"
	R	Falzarano Frank	3	printer	20	"
	S	Falzarano Lawrence	3	plumber	28	"
	T	Falzarano Ralph	3	U S A	33	"
	U	*Falzarano Sabatina †	3	millhand	63	"

Washington Avenue

	V	Barisano Annie †	1	housewife	32	here
	W	Barisano Salvatore	1	laborer	40	"
	Y	Milano Louise †	1	housewife	32	"
2494						
	A	*Funicella Anna †	2	"	35	"
	B	Funicella Nunzio	2	painter	39	"
	C	Pires Albert	2	welder	44	"
	D	Pires Marie †	2	housewife	32	"
	E	Martucci Josephine †	3	"	39	195 Marion
	F	Ferullo Alfonse	3	agent	24	here
	G	Ferullo Dorothy †	3	housewife	26	"
	H	Ferullo Edith †	3	"	26	"
	K	Ferullo Samuel	3	shipfitter	28	"